ISBN 978-0-428-95997-5
PIBN 10450524

THE

ASIATIC JOURNAL

AND

MONTHLY REGISTER

FOR

BRITISH AND FOREIGN INDIA, CHINA,

AND

AUSTRALASIA.

———

VOL. XX.—NEW SERIES.

—

MAY—AUGUST, 1836.

═══════

LONDON:

Wm. H. ALLEN AND CO.,

LEADENHALL STREET.

———

· 1836.

PRINTED BY J. L. COX AND SONS, 75, GREAT QUEEN STREET,
LINCOLN'S-INN FIELDS.

CONTENTS OF VOL. XX.

PART I.

CONTENTS.

PART II.

ASIATIC INTELLIGENCE.

REGISTER.

THE

ASIATIC JOURNAL

FOR

MAY, 1836.

CONTENTS.

Asiatic Intelligence.

CONTENTS—(continued).

THE

ASIATIC JOURNAL

FOR

JUNE, 1836.

CONTENTS.

CONTENTS—(continued).

NOTICE.

Several communications and reviews intended for insertion this month, as well as all our Critical Notices and Literary Intelligence, are unavoidably deferred. Amongst the first is a communication from Paris, which will appear next month.

The article on the Military Law of India should have been sent earlier.

Erratum.

The binder is directed to cancel the Title-page of vol. xix. (marked xviii.) appended to the last number.

THE

ASIATIC JOURNAL

FOR

JULY, 1836.

CONTENTS.

Asiatic Intelligence.

CONTENTS —(continued).

NOTICES.

We have several Reviews of Books (including La Borde's and Capt. Back's), omitted for want of room. We shall endeavour to bring up the arrear next month.

The " Memoir of Capt. Horsburgh" next month.

THE

ASIATIC JOURNAL

FOR

AUGUST 1836.

CONTENTS.

CONTENTS—(*continued*).

THE

ASIATIC JOURNAL

MAY—AUGUST,
1836.

SKETCHES OF THE LATER HISTORY OF BRITISH INDIA.

No. II.—The Appointment of a Governor-general in 1806.

THE mode of administering the government of India is one altogether without precedent and without parallel. The consent of two independent bodies is, in ordinary cases, required to give validity to the instructions which are to guide the local rulers: a system having no claim to novelty or originality in regard to the exercise of the legislative power, but never applied to the executive except in the single instance of India. In legislation, if one of two bodies, having an equal voice, reject a measure which has the sanction of the other, the only result is, that the state of things remains precisely as it was before. There is no probability of a suspension of the functions of the government; the old law continues to be administered instead of the new, and, if any inconvenience be felt, it can only be one which previously existed, and which the new enactment was intended to remedy. But it is obvious that the subjection of the executive functions to a two-fold authority may produce consequences very different. The obstinate resistance of one to the views of the other might be the cause of incalculable mischief and confusion. In the course of the half-century during which India has been thus governed, collision has, indeed, very rarely taken place; it has been generally averted by discretion and mutual forbearance. Still, it has sometimes arisen, and one remarkable occasion occurred in the year 1806, when the Whigs, having formed a coalition with the party of which Lord Grenville was the head, returned to office after a long exclusion from it: an exclusion originating, in the first instance, in the plan which they had proposed and endeavoured to carry through Parliament for the administration of the affairs of India, and which was so unfortunately formed as to excite at once the jealousy of the Crown and the aversion of the people.

The Marquess Cornwallis had a second time proceeded to India as Governor-general, at a very advanced age, and his government met an early termination by his death. Intelligence of this event became known in England almost simultaneously with the accession of the new ministers to office. It was deemed expedient to make immediate provision for the exercise of the full powers of the Governor-general, and Sir George Barlow, at that time possessing the full confidence of the Court of Directors, was appointed Governor-general, with the entire approbation of the new President of the Board of Control. That functionary, indeed, stated that the appointment must be regarded as temporary; but he added, that no immediate change was in contemplation. After such an announcement, it must have been concluded that the new Governor-general would be permitted to enjoy his appointment for a period of some moderate duration; and few speculators upon political probabilities would have assigned to Sir George Barlow's tenure of office a shorter existence than that of a few months. No one, at least, could have expected that the acquiescence of his Majesty's Ministers was to expire in ten days, and that, at the end of that period, a communication would be made of their desire that the appointment which they had so recently sanctioned should be superseded, and another Governor-general named; yet such was the fact. The person selected for this high office by the servants of the Crown was the Earl of Lauderdale; but it being found that the claims of this nobleman were very unfavourably regarded by the Court, the proposal was withdrawn, not however without an intimation that it would be revived at a future period. The first correspondence on the subject took place in March. In May (a change in the Chairs having occurred in the interval), the subject was again brought forward by Ministers; but without success. The Court of Directors refused to revoke the appointment of Sir George Barlow, and, of course, unless their resolution could be changed or their authority overcome, the case of the nominee of Ministers was hopeless. But the Cabinet was not prepared to yield. The death of Mr. Pitt had shattered the administration, of which he was the head, into fragments, which no one appeared to have either the capacity or the confidence to reunite. The coadjutors of that statesman had, in the language of Mr. Tierney, "stultified themselves" by the tender of their resignations on the death of their leader. The new Ministers, in consequence, felt strong in the weakness of their opponents. It was at that period almost universally held to be impossible to form any other administration than that which, under Lord Grenville, swayed the councils of the state; and though a very few months dissipated this illusion, and demonstrated the extreme weakness of the coalition government, which in fact had no hold on the affections of either the sovereign or the people, the Ministry of 1806, up to the period when, in the language of Sheridan, it ran its head against the wall of its own building, claimed possession of "all the talents" of the country, and on this ground placed opposition at defiance. Flushed with confidence in their own strength, the Ministers were not inclined to be very delicate as to the means by which they accomplished their object; and, finding their recommendation without weight, they resolved to call into exercise an extraordinary power vested in the Crown by the Act of 1784, but which had never been exerted. That Act enabled his Majesty, by an instrument under his sign manual, to vacate any appointment in British India without the consent of the Court. The right was unquestionable—so is the right to withhold the assent of the Crown from Bills which have passed both Houses of Parliament—and the exercise of the latter prerogative was almost as much to be expected as that of the former, after it had been allowed for so many years to sleep. But, unprecedented and invidious as its exercise was, Ministers did not shrink from advising it; and the commission by which Sir George Barlow had been appointed Governor-general was vacated by the royal authority.

So remarkable an exercise of prerogative did not, of course, pass without notice. On the 8th of July, the subject was brought before the Upper House of Parliament by Lord Melville. After adverting to the principal facts connected with the transaction, his lordship called the attention of the House to the Act of 1784, by which the power of recall was given to the Crown ; and contended that the clause in question, if construed so as to warrant the proceedings of his Majesty's Ministers, with regard to Sir George Barlow, would be altogether at variance with the spirit and intent of the Act of which it formed part. He stated that, at the period when that Act was passed, the whole country was convulsed with conflicting opinions on the best mode of governing India, and that the two principal plans were embodied in two bills, which were known by the names of the leaders of the two parties by whom they were respectively introduced, one being called Mr. Fox's bill, the other, Mr. Pitt's. It must, he said, be recollected, that these two bills were universally understood to be framed in accordance with the different views of the two parties in the great struggle upon the question, whether the patronage of India should be vested in the hands of the Crown or of the Company. The bill of Mr. Pitt, which passed into a law, disclaimed the patronage on the part of the Crown, and was based on the assumption that it might be more beneficially exercised by the Company; and it could not be supposed that the Legislature intended that the bill should convey a power inconsistent with the spirit in which it was framed and passed :—it could not be supposed that it intended to enable His Majesty's Ministers, at any future time, by exercising *at pleasure* the power of recall, to appropriate to themselves the patronage of India. The design of the clause was obvious. It was intended as a check upon the Court of Directors, in the event of their being led by partiality to make an improper appointment : it also enabled government to interfere in differences between the Court of Directors and the Court of Proprietors,— a case not merely hypothetical, a remarkable instance having occurred not long before the passing of the Act, where the Court of Proprietors refused to acquiesce in the recall of Mr. Hastings, when proposed by the Court of Directors. He urged that the power thus entrusted to the Crown would be grossly abused if applied to any other purposes than those contemplated by the law—if exercised merely with a view to enforce the appointment of a particular individual whom his Majesty's Ministers wished to see Governor-general. This was the first instance in which the power had been exercised, and those who advised its exercise, were bound to shew good cause for it. Lord Melville pronounced a high panegyric upon the character and public services of Sir Geo. Barlow, and animadverted with great severity upon the conduct of the Ministers, which, he said, if the result of mere caprice, was highly blameable, but, if originating in an intention to seize the patronage of India, was a direct violation of the spirit and meaning of an Act of Parliament. After dwelling upon the inconveniences likely to arise to the public service, from the extraordinary course pursued by Ministers, Lord Melville concluded, by moving for certain papers connected with the removal of Sir George Barlow, and with the financial affairs of the Company.

The exercise of the royal prerogative was defended by the premier, Lord Grenville, who contended that the law must be taken in its plain meaning, not according to any fanciful interpretation, and that the Act of 1784 clearly gave a power of recall. That power had been objected to, at the time of passing the Act, on one of the grounds now taken by Lord Melville, namely, that it might virtually give to Ministers the patronage of India ; but it was answered then, as it might be answered now, that because the Crown had the power of negativing an Act of Parliament, it could not be said that it had the power of directing the legislature ; and, by parity of reasoning, it could not reasonably be contended that, because a particular appointment in India was reversed, the whole of the appointments must fall under the control of his Majesty's Ministers. He admitted, however, that if it could be shewn that the power had been exercised merely for the purpose of procuring the appointment of a particular person it would be a violation of the law ; but he called upon Lord Melville to recollect, that from the passing of the Act in 1784 to 1801, there had not been a single governor appointed who had not been recommended by that nobleman himself : and as the same system had prevailed from 1801 downward, there did not appear much to justify the surprise expressed on this occasion. His lordship then reminded the House, that Sir George Barlow had been appointed to succeed the Marquess Wellesley, and had almost immediately been superseded in favour of the Marquess Cornwallis. In connection with the latter appointment, Lord Grenville passed a censure upon the late administration, for a neglect which had placed their successors in some difficulty. Possessed of every other qualification for the high office to which he was called, the Marquess Cornwallis wanted youth and health. It was generally supposed, in London, that he would be unable to bear the voyage, and that if he arrived in India he would survive only a short time : yet his Majesty's late advisers made no provision for an event which must have been expected, and from their criminal neglect, his Majesty's present Ministers were called upon, within twenty-four hours of their acceptance of office, to provide for the government of India, in consequence of the communication of the death of the Marquess Cornwallis. In this emergency, they recommended the Court of Directors to appoint Sir George Barlow ; but they never regarded this appointment as being any thing more than temporary. For these reasons, and on the grounds of the inconvenience which would result from acceding to the motion, he opposed the production of the correspondence.

Several other peers took part in the discussion, and among them Lord

Hawkesbury, who, as a member of the late government, denied that it was necessary to take more than ordinary precaution against the decease of the Marquess Cornwallis. Considering the advanced age of the Marquess he had never known a man more likely to live; and such was the opinion of his friends who had last seen him at Portsmouth. The arguments used by the other speakers were little more than repetitions of those brought forward by Lords Melville and Grenville; and, on the question being put, both motions were lost without a division.

Three days afterwards, the subject underwent some discussion in the House of Commons. In a committee of the whole House on the India Budget, Mr. Johnstone, after taking a review of the conduct of Sir George Barlow, and passing on it a high eulogy, condemned the conduct of Ministers in nullifying their original appointment. He said, he had heard that Sir George Barlow was recalled because he did not possess the confidence of Ministers; but he believed that two noble lords, under whose administrations the British interests in India had flourished in an extraordinary degree, —he meant Lord Macartney and Lord Cornwallis (the latter as Governor-general and the former as the head of one of the other presidencies),—he believed that those noble persons possessed little of the confidence of those who, during the period of their respective administrations, held the reins of government in England. Lord Castlereagh joined in reprehension of the conduct of Ministers, and stated that he was able to furnish a testimony to the merits of Sir George Barlow, which was not generally known. It was the express wish of Lord Cornwallis before he went to India, that when he should have completed the object of his mission, Sir George Barlow should be appointed to succeed him in the government. The Chancellor of the Exchequer, Lord Henry Petty, defended the course taken by Ministers; and Mr. Francis, who disclaimed offering an opinion of his own, alleged that, on former occasions, Sir George Barlow had incurred the displeasure of the Court of Directors, who now supported him. Sir Arthur Wellesley defended the conduct of Sir George Barlow throughout the negociations for peace, as did also Mr. Grant on the 15th July, when the committee sat again. Mr. Paul justified the removal; he maintained that, to secure the respect of the native courts, the Governor-general should be a man of high rank; and that, though Sir George Barlow was an excellent revenue officer, he had none of the qualities necessary for a Governor-general.

The ministerial speakers in the House of Commons seem rather to have evaded discussion; either because no specific motion was made on the subject, or from a conviction that the course which they had advised was an unpopular one. In fact, the country, even at that early period of the existence of the coalition ministry, regarded it with so little confidence, that the cabinet must have been conscious that they had no reputation to sport with, and that, upon any questionable matter, silence, if it could be maintained, was their wisest policy. But, though possessing little strength in the country, the ministry had one advantage, which probably most cabinets value more than popular favour—they had majorities in Parliament, and these enabled them to submit with great philosophy to charges which it might have been troublesome to answer.   The knowledge that the Ministers had the means of triumphing in the division, though they might be van-quished in the argument, probably withheld those members of the House of Commons who especially represented East-Indian interests, from the steps which might have been expected from them.   The novelty of their situation might also have some effect in diminishing the vigour of their efforts.   The Company had enjoyed the countenance and protection of the Ministers, to whom they regarded themselves as mainly indebted for the preservation of their chartered rights, during a period of twenty-two years, with the excep-tion of the short administration of Lord Sidmouth; and the policy of his administration differed, indeed, little from that of Mr. Pitt, whom he had succeeded.   Accustomed for so long a time to act in concert with the Minis-ters of the Crown, those Directors who had seats in Parliament seem to have felt as though there would be something indecorous in any very decided pub-lic opposition, even when the enemies of the privileges of the Company had obtained the reins of power.   This feeling, combined with a conviction of the hopelessness of struggling in a place where the victory was already ad-judged, will account for the feebleness of the efforts made within the walls of Parliament to justify the conduct of the Court of Directors in opposition to that of the Ministers of the Crown.   But, though apparently declining any public appeal against the dictation to which it was sought to subject them, they steadily persevered in resisting it; and it being ultimately found im-possible to overcome the objections of the Court of Directors to the Earl of Lauderdale, that nobleman withdrew his claim to the office of Governor General; the Court consented to nominate the President of the Board of Control, Lord Minto, and thus the differences between the Court of Di-rectors and his Majesty's Government were terminated.

The dispute opens a variety of questions, all of them possessing a cer-tain degree of interest.   The first that naturally occurs relates to the cha-racter of the person who for ten days enjoyed the full sunshine of ministerial favour; at the end of which time, with a fickleness unusual even in courts, it was deemed expedient to relieve him from the greatness which had been so suddenly thrust upon him, and to provide, at his expense, for some ad-herent of the ruling party.   The merits of Sir George Barlow, as an intel-ligent, able, and zealous servant of the Company, seem not to have been questioned.   He was certainly not removed by the Ministers of the day because he was unfit for the station to which they had appointed him, but because, when they found leisure to survey the circle of their noble friends, they met with many to whom a splendid provision in the East was an object of desire, and one of these they determined to foist upon the Court of Di-rectors.   In the desire to grasp at patronage, the fitness or unfitness of the person to be appointed was evidently regarded as of little importance, and the fitness or unfitness of the person to be removed as of no importance at all.—If, separate from all party considerations, we enquire whether Sir

George Barlow was altogether fitted for the high office of Governor-general, the answer must depend upon the standard of qualification which is set up.   If the office demand a mind of the highest order, enlarged by extensive information, and cultivated by assiduous study, the claims of Sir George Barlow are at once negatived; but if it be fair to found the standard upon the average amount of ability, knowledge, and good sense possessed by the occupants of the office, the advocates of Sir George Barlow need not shrink from the test.   It is beyond all doubt, that he was at least as well qualified as some who preceded, and as some others who have followed him. His precise views on the great questions of Indian policy it is not very easy to gather: it has often been urged against him, that after warmly co-operating in the promotion of the policy of the Marquess Wellesley, he entered with apparently equal cordiality into the widely different views of the Marquess Cornwallis; and, indeed, the vindication of his consistency is the hardest task which his friends have to encounter.   The best apology that can be offered for changes which cannot be denied, is to suppose that at both periods he regarded himself as acting only ministerially—as merely fulfilling the designs of others, whom he felt it his duty to obey.   During the time that he exercised the functions of Governor-general, he appears to have adhered very strictly to what he believed to be the wishes of the home authorities; and had the period of his rule been extended, he would, in all probability, have persevered in the same course.   Excluding then the question of ability, the fitness of Sir George Barlow for the exercise of the supreme authority in India will be differently determined, according to the view taken of the precise duties of a Governor-general.   Those who think that there is little room for the exercise of discretion, and that a rigid obedience should be yielded to the positive instructions and implied wishes of the controlling powers, may regard the conduct of Sir George Barlow with entire approbation.   Those, on the contrary, who think that the peculiar advantages of local observation enjoyed by our Indian functionaries justify them in the use of a large discretion in the discharge of their duties, will very materially qualify their approval.

But the merits or demerits of Sir George Barlow appear, in fact, to have had little influence upon the decision of the cabinet of 1806, and they certainly had none upon the voices of those majorities which that cabinet was able to command in the two houses of parliament.   India was in a state of peace, which was in no immediate danger of being disturbed; and if Sir George Barlow wanted that commanding character of intellect called for by extraordinary times, he was at least equal to the comparatively tranquil state of things which there was reason to anticipate.   But it was the ministerial will that he should be removed—it was therefore necessary to devise some pretext to justify the removal.   That it was made merely for the pleasure of indulging in a despotic act of power—that it was intended to annoy the government of the Company, and to exalt at their expense the ministers of the Crown—that its object was to force on India a protegé of the party who, in the political lottery, had just drawn the great

prize,—none of these reasons could be avowed. Other motives, consequently, were put forward more decent though less real. One of them was
no less absurd in itself, than it was insulting to the entire service of India,
civil and military. It was asserted to be necessary, in order to support the character of the British nation at the native courts, that the Governor-general should be a man of high rank in this country. This
assertion was made by some who ought to have known better, and who
must have known better. Among the Mahomedans, hereditary rank does not
exist, unless the respect which has been sometimes yielded to the family of
the Prophet may be regarded as forming an exception. All rank is
merely official. Those distinctions which, in the Western World, have
operated so powerfully, and which, in our own country, are so highly
esteemed, are utterly valueless in the eyes of the Mahomedan, and a governor in whose veins circulated " all the blood of all the Howards,"
would not, on that account, receive one iota of respect. But, in truth, if
the feeling of the followers of the Prophet of Mecca were different—if they
were disposed to yield to birth and rank, all the homage accorded to them
by a *preux chevalier* of the age of Louis the Fourteenth, what degree of
knowledge is an Indian potentate likely to possess of Lodge's Peerage, or
of that very interesting volume, common though it be, familiarly known as
the Red Book? What knows he of Sir Egerton Bridges, or Sir Francis Pal-
grave, or Sir Harris Nicolas, and all their multiform researches into the
history of the British aristocracy? But though of all these things he is as ignorant as is an English labourer of the constitution and government of China;
though a Mahomedan has no sympathy with our notions of nobility, and
neither Mahomedan nor Hindoo can have any skill in coronets, the authority
and influence resulting from high office are perfectly intelligible to all; and
the immense power of a Governor-general, by whomsoever wielded, cannot
fail to be respected in a country where, from time immemorial, the people
of all gradations have ever been the supple slaves of power. If the minister of the day could succeed in appointing his cook Governor-general of
India, the appointment might and would give disgust to the European population—and as the studies of the new functionary had lain in a widely different line, it is probable that he might shew but an indifferent acquaintance with the science of government—but the native population and the
native governments, with whom he would have to maintain the accustomed
relations, would receive no shock. When invested with the pomp, and
state, and power of his office, their feelings towards him would be just
the same as if he could trace his pedigree to Charlemagne. Actual power
and actual wealth they can understand; but their imaginations are too cold
as well as too coarse to have any reverence for those ideal sources of distinction which among a more refined and imaginative people are of such
high value. The opponents of Sir George Barlow must have been hardly
pushed for an argument, when they stumbled upon one so untenable as this.

But what must be thought of the policy or the equity of a rule, which
should utterly and peremptorily exclude the regular servants of the Company

from all chance of arriving at the highest reward which the Company has
to bestow? What must be thought of the wisdom which should place
under a ban of prohibition the highest intellect and most extensive knowledge if found in the service of the Company, that intellect too having been
exercised, and that knowledge matured, in the very place and underthe very
circumstances most likely to fit the possessor for the very office to which he
is forbidden to aspire? What an outrage would it be to the feelings of
those whose lives have been devoted to the promotion of the welfare of
India and the protection of the country, if they were to be told that under no
circumstances should they be permitted to attain the highest place in the
government! that the veriest idler that walks St. James's-street shall be
preferred before them, because they do not possess a recommendation
which, in India, is perfectly useless: It is true, that the admission of the
servants of the Company to the competition for the prize may be regarded
as a very small boon.   Even if it were always bestowed upon one of them,
the number who could attain it would be small, and as such an arrangement
is neither to be expected nor desired, the chance of any individual servant
must be trifling indeed.   But this affects not the question.   The advantage given by admission may be little, but the insult conveyed by exclusion
is great ; and slender as must be the hope which any one can cherish of
gaining this bright object of ambitious desire, who shall say that it will be
ineffective?   In every profession, the great prizes can fall to the lot of
only a very small number of those who engage in it—few clergymen can
hope to attain the primacy, and few lawyers the custody of the great seal
—but it would justly be regarded as a great discouragement to rising
talent, as a withering blight upon honest ambition, as a gross affront to
merit of humble origin, if a rule existed which restricted the attainment
of those high stations exclusively to men of rank.   It is held to be at
once highly creditable to our country, and beneficial to its interests, that
the highest offices both in church and the state may be attained independently of any claims derived from rank—that they are open to the competition of all who can shew the necessary qualifications.   Why should that
which is so beneficial in England be so injurious in India? No one has
ever proposed to exclude the aristocracy of Great Britain from the field—
they may and ought to be fairly admitted to it.   For the purpose of binding
India more closely to the British government, it may be desirable that the
representative of the crown in India should generally be chosen from the
nobility of the protecting country.   Among other good effects, this may
have the effect of attracting some small degree of attention to interests
which have been almost systematically neglected by British statesmen and
legislators.   But an occasional deviation from the established practice in
favour of pre-eminent talents and acquirements in a servant of the Company, would be likely to operate most beneficially both on the service and on
the interests of India.   No set of Ministers have indeed ever avowed that
they acted upon the principle of excluding servants of the Company from any
but a provisional enjoyment of the highest post both in point of honour and

emolument; but without avowing it, they have generally made it pretty clear that such was the fact, and these days of boasted liberality, so far from having brought any relaxation in this respect, have actually rendered the indulgence of ambition on the part of the Company's servants more hopeless than ever.

Another ground taken by the Ministers of 1806 and their advocates, was somewhat more plausible,—the alleged necessity for the Governor-general of India possessing the confidence of the advisers of the Crown; but even this plea cannot be admitted without considerable qualifications. That confidence which results from the character of the individual holding this high office for talent, integrity, discretion, and devotedness to the duties of his station, cannot, indeed, be dispensed with; but the confidence depending upon conformity of political opinion is, under the circumstances, unnecessary, and has, in practice, been almost constantly disregarded. To the instances which were adduced at the time of the discussion, the experience of the last thirty years has made several additions. Lord Minto, the choice of the Whig administration of 1806, was permitted to retain his office without any objection during the successive Tory administrations of the Duke of Portland, Mr. Perceval, and the Earl of Liverpool. The Marquess of Hastings was actually recommended to office by the political party of which he had all his life been the steady opponent; and the appointment of Lord William Bentinck, made under an administration composed of his own personal and political friends, was sanctioned by a subsequent one with which he had no connection. We may perhaps regard the liberality displayed in one of these instances as matter of regret, but they all tend to shew that the government of India has not been invariably looked upon merely as a splendid provision for some influential friend of the reigning minister. That it ought not to be so viewed will be at once admitted by all but those who have an interest in defending the opposite opinion. Removed altogether from the influence of most of the questions which here divide men into factions, can there be any valid reason why India and its government should be involved in the vortex of European politics? The inconveniences of such a course are obvious; and they are so great, that a single glance at them will be sufficient to shew, that if the happiness of India, or its retention by this country, be worth a thought, we must have the forbearance to exempt her from the influence of our own party disputes. If it be necessary, in any one instance, that the Governor-general of India should be a member of that political party which happens at a given time to direct the counsels of the state, it must be necessary in every other instance. If one party may demand this, it must be conceded to all parties. That which arrogates to itself the title of liberal, cannot, it is presumed, claim an exclusive right to the privilege of nominating its own friends to the government of India. Grant the principle, then, that there must be a perfect sympathy of feeling between the governors of India and the cabinet at home, and it follows, that the Governor-general, like the Lord Lieutenant of Ireland, must be changed with every change of adminstration. Let this principle be once recognized and acted upon to its full extent, and all hope of effecting improvement in the vast and important empire subjected to our rule, will be at an end.   But, in truth, on this point we need give ourselves little concern, for we should soon be relieved from the trouble of governing India; nor could such an event be regretted by any friend to justice, seeing how grossly we had betrayed a sacred trust, by prostituting it to the purposes of party.   Our position in India, though on the whole a subject of pride and congratulation, is not such as to permit us to despise ordinary precautions.   Not only have we active and insidious enemies around, but even within our own territories; and with a government veering about with every change in the political atmosphere, what would the chance for the continuance of our dominion be worth?   All hope of a vigorous government,—of such a government as India demands, and must possess, or she is lost,—would be at an end.   Hesitation and uncertainty would characterize all the proceedings of those who would still be called the governors of India, though they would be only the puppets of political gamblers at home.   Without the means of being informed of what was passing in the protecting country until some months after the occurrence of the events which would determine the destinies of India as well as of England, no rational opinion could be formed of the probable stability of the existing state of things.   In this uncertainty, a Governor-general, unless, like some that we have seen, he happened to be of a remarkably active temperament, would most probably do nothing but pocket his magnificent income, and on the receipt of every instalment bless his stars for his good luck.   Or if, impelled by that restless spirit, which leads some men into perpetual action without end or object, he should endeavour to carry out his own opinions or those of his party into actual practice, he would have the satisfaction of knowing, that whatever he might do, his successor would amuse himself by undoing.   How soon that successor might arrive, it would be utterly impossible to guess.   At the moment when a governor-general was debarking at Calcutta, the instrument of his recall might be signed, and on its way to put an end to his authority.   Nay, before he reached his destination—while on his voyage, luxuriating in the splendid visions in which, it may be presumed, outgoing Governors-general indulge, his successor might be on the sea in full chase of him, with a *supersedeas* in his pocket.   Let us look back only nine years to the rapid succession of the administrations of Lord Liverpool, Mr. Canning, Lord Goderich, and the Duke of Wellington—let us look back only one year, and find Lord Melbourne suddenly displaced in favour of Sir Robert Peel, and he, after a very brief possession of office, giving way to Lord Melbourne again. Let us suppose a case in connection with these latter changes, and it happens that the supposition will not be a very extravagant exaggeration of the facts. Let us suppose that, a short time before the decease of Lord Melbourne's administration, a Governor-general had been appointed, and had sailed for India, just on the eve of the noble lord's journey to Brighton.   Sir Robert Peel takes the helm of state, and recommends another governor-general, a

of course he would have done, had it been the established practice to change that functionary with each change of the ministry at home. In such a state of things no time would be lost, and the Conservative Governor-general would be posted off with the least possible delay. The new administration are beaten in the House of Commons, and resign. Lord Melbourne returns to office, and his first act is to procure the recal of the Governor-general, who may perhaps be at Madeira, and the restoration of his own nominee, who, if he has been fortunate, may be just receiving his first impressions of the City of Palaces—but the Conservative arrives, and the Whig departs in ill-humour with himself and every body else. If by great good fortune he should encounter the vessel which bears his reprieve, he may turn back if he think it worth while, though, if he be a man of sense, he most likely will not; but the most probable chance is that the old Governor and his new commission will cross each other, and that the former will arrive in England, either to be bandied back again or sullenly to decline the proffered honour. Would not this be a delectable method of governing a great empire ? How stable must be our sway, under such a system ! how conducive to the happiness of the people of India ! how well calculated to uphold the honour of the British nation ! But such rapid changes are not of constant occurrence. A ministry in ordinary circumstances may be expected to endure more than two or three months. Perhaps it may—but the political barometer at the present period does not promise any very settled weather. But let it be conceded that a ministry may generally calculate upon a longer duration than was enjoyed by those of Lord Goderich and Sir Robert Peel—let us allow an average of three years, and if we look at the administrations of the last century, with the exception of that of Mr. Pitt, this will not be found an unfair allowance—then every three years there will not only be a change of the man, but, it must be presumed, a corresponding change of measures. We must not suppose that British statesmen are actuated by factious or selfish motives—we must give them the credit of seeking the appointment of their own friends, solely for the sake of extending the influence of their own opinions. What then must be the effect upon India of a rapid succession of rulers, selected under the influence of every varying shade of party opinion? What but an unsteady and vacillating policy,—a series of experiments, immature and ill-executed, succeeding each other like a phantasmagoria, and leaving as few traces behind them. India is not in a condition to be suffered to remain stationary, but still less is she in a condition to be made the subject of indiscreet experiment. To accelerate her career of improvement is at once our interest and our duty ; but our plans of improvement must be well devised and steadily pursued, or they will end in our expulsion, and the surrender of the people of India to a long and dreary night of barbarism and misrule. If Englishmen should ever learn to feel justly the value of our Indian possessions—and they have never yet felt it— they will become sensible that they form too precious a deposit to be tampered with, or to be thrown heedlessly into the scramble of party.

But the evils of eternal change would not be confined to the entail upon India of a weak and wavering policy, injurious to the people governed and dishonourable to those who govern them—the general character of the individuals who would fill the office of Governor-general would be lower than it has hitherto been. High-minded men would hesitate to accept an appointment which, with all its splendour, is attended with many inconveniences and privations, if the tenure were understood to depend upon a point so utterly beyond calculation, as the continuance in office of a particular party. And who would occupy the place which has hitherto been filled by those who, whatever their pretensions in other respects, were at least gentlemen, and men of honour? For the most part, persons of desperate fortunes, who would speculate on the enjoyment of the salary of the Governor-general for a few months—men without talent, character, or property, obsequiously waiting, hat in hand, upon the party to which they might happen to be attached, for any casual donation which it might have to bestow, and ready for an eleemosynary fee to run on any errand, although it should carry them half across the globe. Now and then, the monotony might be relieved by the despatch of some political quack—some legislative nostrum-monger, panting for an opportunity of trying the effects of his grand state panacea, and delighted to find in India a field where he might freely practise without any fear of the fate that awaits the vendors of Morison's pills. If any man of better class could be prevailed upon to accept the office, it would not be until he had secured a snug pension or comfortable sinecure to fall back upon in case of need.

These evils are not, indeed, likely to result from the occasional supercession of an Indian functionary by the Ministers of the Crown, for an insufficient reason or for no reason at all; but they are consequences resulting from carrying out to its full extent the principle that the Governor-general of India must possess the full confidence of the existing ministry. Unless, therefore, any one set of ministers can convert their Cabinet appointments into patent situations, or unless the professors of liberal politics—for they alone have hitherto acted upon the principle—can shew that the privilege of removing a Governor-general who is displeasing to the ministry, ought to be exercised by no party but their own, those consequences must ensue or the principle must be given up. It is certainly not that upon which the laws regulating the Government of India have been framed. The legislature which, amid so many changes, has steadily adhered to the principle of vesting the patronage of India in the Company, evidently intended to disconnect that country as much as possible from the turmoil of party contentions at home. The minister, therefore, who grasps at the patronage of India, though he may not violate the letter of the law, evidently outrages its spirit. He seeks to acquire that which the Legislature has determined he ought not to possess.

The Act of 1784 undoubtedly gives to the Crown the power of recall, without imposing any conditions upon its exercise. It would, indeed, be extraordinary if such a power had been withheld; but it is quite clear that it was not intended to be used as an instrument for enabling the King's

Ministers to force into the government of India any particular individual.
The patronage of India was probably vested in the East-India Company,
partly from the consideration that the local and peculiar information which
they possessed, would enable them to estimate the wants of the country
more accurately, and to provide for them more judiciously, than a ministry
whose attention was distracted by a variety of subjects; partly because the
Court of Directors being comparatively a permanent body, the delicate
connection between India and Great Britain would, while the government
was in their hands, be in a great measure secured from the shocks which it
would be liable to encounter in the fierce struggles of political party; and
partly from a reluctance to increase the influence of the Crown. If these
reasons have any validity, the Directors should be permitted to exercise the
power delegated to them by the Legislature, as freely and independently as
possible; subject to no control but such as is absolutely necessary to the
safety of the state. It was certainly not intended to give to the ministry
the right of nomination to official station in India, and the power of governing that country in the name of the Court of Directors, who were merely to
register the decisions of the Cabinet. Extraordinary powers should be reserved for extraordinary occasions, and it seems quite impossible for any
impartial person to consider the difference of opinion between the Court of
Directors and his Majesty's Ministers in 1806, as one of those extraordinary
occasions in contemplation of which the power was granted, and the actual
rise of which alone can justify its exercise. The causes which led to the capricious course pursued by the Ministers of the Crown, prove the inconvenience
of interfering with Indian patronage beyond their duty; and that their duty
is simply to protect the interests of the two countries from the injury that
might result from the occupation of office by an improper person. When
the change of ministry was in progress, the vacancy occasioned by the death
of the Marquess Cornwallis was not expected, and the new servants of the
Crown were not prepared to recommend any one in his place. A few days
were sufficient to remove this impediment, and it would have evinced more
respect to the Court of Directors, and more regard to the feelings of Sir
George Barlow, as well as more consistency and dignity in their own conduct, had the ministers determined to suspend proceeding for those few
days, instead of hastily ratifying an appointment almost immediately to be
revoked. When they had decided upon the person whose pretensions to the
office they intended to support, they communicated their wishes to the
Directors, who were naturally surprised by a communication so unlooked-
for. They were unwilling to participate in the levity displayed by Ministers
with regard to Sir George Barlow, whom they moreover regarded as the
fittest person to conclude those negotiations on which he had successfully
entered; and they had insuperable objections to the nobleman recommended
as his successor. Into the nature of those objections it is, perhaps, useless
at this distance of time to inquire; but there were undoubtedly some circumstances in the early political career of the Earl of Lauderdale, that
might lead prudent men to hesitate as to the propriety of selecting him to

wield the mighty and, in indiscreet hands, the dangerous power of Governor-general of India.   Whether, however, the objections of the directors were well or ill-founded, the ministry had no right to judge; and when they perceived the little probability which existed of overcoming them, both duty and policy should have forbidden them to persevere.   By calling into exercise, for the first time, the prerogative of the Crown, and revoking the appointment of Sir George Barlow, not because he was unfit to retain it, but solely to make way for their own nominee, they shewed an extraordinary disregard to the rights of the Court of Directors, as well as to the welfare of India, and a highly reprehensible desire of engrossing the patronage of the most valuable appointments there.   Had the directors been actuated by similar motives, the government of India would have been placed in abeyance, and a contest must have resulted, as little calculated to advance the dignity of the contending parties, as to promote the interests of the two divisions of the empire.   But the Court of Directors, though firm, were not factious; they steadily resisted the appointment of the Earl of Lauderdale, but they did not retaliate upon ministers, by naming for the office a person disagreeable to the Cabinet and hostile to its policy.   When a nobleman was recommended in whose appointment they could conscientiously acquiesce, no remains of ill-feeling prompted them to keep alive differences between two bodies which the best interests of the state require to agree, and they cheerfully consented to appoint Lord Minto as the successor to Sir George Barlow.   It would be well if their example were more generally followed by the Ministers of the Crown, if party connection were less regarded, and personal qualification somewhat more.   India is not like Ireland, essentially mixed up with party opinion and feelings; she has no natural connexion with them, and to drag her into conflicts which do not and cannot concern her, is doing gross wrong, and frustrating to a great extent the intention of the Legislature, in bestowing the patronage on a body of men who, for the most part, are not likely to be actuated by party motives.   India should be governed with a strict regard to her own benefit, as well as to that of England, and should not be unnaturally converted into a stage for the gladiatorial combats of political partizans.

But the supersession of Sir George Barlow does not remain a solitary instance of the interference of the Cabinet to appropriate the patronage of India.   A more recent attempt of the like nature has attracted no inconsiderable portion of attention, and it is a remarkable fact, that it has been made by the same party.   The appointment of Lord Heytesbury was made by the Court of Directors, certainly not on party principles. They anticipated, no doubt, that it would be approved by Sir Robert Peel's cabinet; for it would have been both foolish and factious to name a person for an office subject to the approbation of the advisers of the Crown, when there was reason to expect that such approbation would be withheld. The concurrence of the Court in the appointment of Lord Heytesbury, it is believed, was unanimous; and the Crown, by its official organ, approved of their choice.   It is worthy of notice also, that though party spirit at that time ran unusually high, the attempts to impugn the propriety of the appointment were few and feeble ; but, according to the old proverb, "new lords" introduce "new laws." The solemn ratification of the Crown had been affixed to the appointment of Lord Heytesbury. But the King's new advisers determined that he should revoke the approval which he had so recently bestowed. Every one knows, that in ascribing this and similar acts to the Crown we are using a mere fiction, and that in fact what is called the pleasure of the King is but the pleasure of his ministers, who hold their places nominally by his will, but virtually by that of Parliament. Still, there is something indecent in thus casting upon the Sovereign a levity, of which he is perfectly innocent; in making him a stalking-horse for ministerial ambition and intrigue. The cases of Sir George Barlow and Lord Heytesbury are not perfectly similar in their circumstances. In the former, it was understood that the appointment was only for a limited term. Lord Heytesbury was intended to be permanent. With regard to Sir George Barlow, the ministry turned round upon themselves. In revoking the appointment of Lord Heytesbury, they adopted a mode not the most fair or courteous, of aiming a blow at their opponents. Sir George Barlow was in India at the time of his appointment—Lord Heytesbury had not quitted England after receiving his. But this circumstance surely could not be allowed any effect. Lord Heytesbury was fit to be Governor-general, or he was unfit. If unfit, he ought to have been displaced notwithstanding he might have been actually exercising his functions in Calcutta; if fit, he ought not to have been superseded because he happened to be still sojourning in England. If it be justifiable to prevent a governor from proceeding whom it would not be justifiable to recall from India, the government of that country must altogether depend upon the chapter of accidents. The most important events, indeed, have often been thus brought about; but here is the administration of a great empire deliberately placed at the mercy of accidents—among others, of the wind and the weather, of all things the most variable and uncertain.

It would, most surely, not be decent to avow this as a cabinet principle ; it far surpasses in enormity the conduct of the worthy judge, who, after hearing the causes brought before him, decided them by the casting of the dice, for the interests involved are much greater, and the possible mischief much more serious. Of the comparative merits of Lord Heytesbury and Lord Auckland no comparison can be made. What the latter will do as Governor-general of India, we know not yet; what the former would have done, we never can know. But in taking leave of a subject, little creditable to the character of British politics, two remarks may be made. First, that the champions of liberality have been, at every period, far less tolerant of political differences than those whom they brand as its enemies ; and secondly, that in the supersession of Lord Heytesbury the champions of economy wantonly sacrificed a sum of five thousand pounds, which, according to law, had been awarded to that nobleman as his outfit ; the same expenditure being again necessary in order to set Lord Auckland afloat for India.

E.

MISSIONARY VOYAGE TO THE NORTH-EAST COAST
OF CHINA.

The London Missionary Society, having determined to make an effort to
diffuse a knowledge of Christianity and of the Scriptures on the coast of China,
employed on this expedition the Rev. W. H. Medhurst, who has devoted the
last eighteen years of his life to the Chinese mission in Batavia and other
places in the Indian Archipelago, and acquired a knowledge of several dialects
of the Chinese language. This gentleman accordingly arrived at Canton in
June last, but could meet with no vessel suited to his purpose till August,
when he engaged the American brig *Huron* for three months. The vessel was
of the burthen of 211 tons, manned with twelve men, and armed with two
guns and some swivels. A few bags of rice were taken on board, to be sold or
not; but the cargo consisted of 20,000 volumes of books on theological subjects, including some copies of the Scriptures. Mr. Medhurst took with him
an American (a missionary, we believe,) named Stevens, who has furnished to
the *Chinese Repository* a copy of his journal of this voyage, of which the
following is a *resumé*:—

The vessel sailed from the Cum-sing-moon on the 26th August, and, in
about a fortnight after getting out of the Lema passage, rounded the eastern
point of Shan-tung promontory, situated in lat. 37° 25′ N., long. 122° 45′ E.,
and anchored in the excellent harbour of Wei-hae-wei, in lat. 37° 50′ N., long.
122° 12′ E., which was the place proposed for commencing their work. Not a
sail was seen, nor any movement, but that of sending off from the island of
Lew-kung-taou (which shelters the harbour on the north and north-east)
several loaded boats towards the town of Wei-hae. In order to remove all
apprehensions which might be excited at the appearance of a foreign ship, the
missionaries landed at a village on the island. Most of the people fled from the
beach, but a few of the oldest or boldest remained, who, when they heard Mr.
Medhurst address them in their own language, invited him and his companion
into a house, as the rain was falling heavily. When told the object of the
visit, they accepted, cautiously, one or two copies of the books, alleging that
few of the poor people could read. The house, like the others, was built of
granite, and covered with thatch-work; it had neither floor nor seats, except
the bed, beneath which was the fire-place! It was soon filled with people,
who were in no wise uncivil.

In the afternoon of the next day (September 12th), a boat came alongside
the brig, with three naval officers and a train of followers, who inquired of Mr.
Medhurst his name, country, and object. He informed them he had come to
distribute books teaching the religion of Jesus, to communicate oral instruction respecting Christianity, and to give medicines to the sick. They inquired
for the books, and took away a plentiful supply, stating that the superior
officer of Wei-hae would have come off to pay his respects, but for the incle-
ment weather.

On the ensuing day, the weather being fine, the party prepared for another
visit ashore. They put a number of books and the medicine-chest into the
boat, and proceeded westward to a distant village, which they supposed to be
Wei-hae. They gave books on board the junks they passed, and landed amidst
a crowd of people, amongst whom they began immediately distributing books.
An officer, who had hailed them when in the boat, now endeavoured to prevent their advancing, first by entreaties, then by taking Mr. Medhurst by the

arms. They, however, pressed on till they came to the village, where the chief officer (who had gone to visit the brig), having landed from his junk, received them. He wore a blue button, and was a *tsan-tseang*, or sub-colonel. One of his lieutenants, who was the chief speaker, assuming a stern countenance and angry manner, asked whence they came and their business. Mr. Medhurst replied, that he was an Englishman come to do good by distributing books and medicines. The officer then desired them to go on board a junk, that they might confer on the subject. Mr. M. insisted upon first taking a walk in the town. The officers, thereupon, placed themselves before the party, stating that the laws of the celestial empire forbade foreigners from setting foot in it. Mr. Medhurst observed that these laws could refer only to enemies, not to him and his companions who came only to do good; and he proposed that they should discuss the matter in some house over a cup of tea. The chief officer (contrary to the advice of the lieutenant) proposed entering a temple hard by, whither the whole assemblage proceeded. Upon reaching the temple, Mr. Medhurst and his companion, " finding none to hinder them, determined not to stop at present, but went forward, over hill and dale, till they reached a high summit, which commanded an extensive view of the country and of the Gulf of Chîb-le." They returned to the temple, where the officers were awaiting them. It was a neat building, dedicated to the Queen of Heaven. The officers received the party standing, and offered Mr. M. the highest place. Tea was brought in, and the object of the visitors was again stated, and accompanied by a short exposition of the principal doctrines of the Gospel. The officers appear to have acted with urbanity; they said they were well assured of their visitors' friendly intentions, but their orders left them no discretion to permit their intercourse with the people; that they saw no other objection to the distribution of the books, which they had read, and which, though they differed in some respects from their own classics, yet contained many good things. They offered supplies of provisions, but these were declined. Mr. Medhurst declared that they did not come to trade, which, he knew, was confined to Canton; and that, " if the government is really so absurd as to design to prevent good men from speaking to their fellow-men, and doing them any offices of kindness and good-will in their power, we felt it to be our duty, notwithstanding any such prohibitions, to obey God rather than man." After some complimentary expressions in answer, the conference broke up.

The crowd had now greatly increased, and, on reaching the beach, the party determined to distribute some books amongst the people. A basket-full was accordingly brought out of the boat, but an officer ordered it back again. As soon as it was opened, however, the crowd rushed suddenly forward, and, in spite of the police, seized the books.

In the afternoon of the same day, they landed, with a fresh supply of books, on the island of Lew-kung-taou, where they met with no impediment. They then crossed the bay again, re-landed on the main, and entered a village, passing from house to house, giving books and conversing familiarly with the inhabitants. The females were shy and withdrew. In other places they were ordered in-doors or into the fields.

The villages in Shan-tung are marked by clumps of trees. Many of the hills were cultivated, and nearly all were covered with a green sward. The villages are situated in the temperate and fertile vallies between the hills of this most hilly country. The houses never stand alone, but are built in clusters of from 25 to 500.

Encouraged by the favourable disposition of the people, the missionaries

resolved to visit the south side of the harbour, where they could discern numerous villages, and to coast it round to the western side. They landed on a
small eminence, mounted as usual with a watch-tower, attended by one sailor
to carry the books, and proceeded directly towards the nearest village. At a
public threshing-floor at the entrance, they were met by a large number of
persons, with the school-master at their head, to whom they announced their
errand, proceeding to distribute books, which were readily received. As they
proceeded over the hills to other villages, the peasantry, who were diligently
employed in cultivation, greeted them with cheerful words, and directed them
on their way. Their stock of books was soon exhausted, and they sent down
to the boat for more. In these two days, the number of books distributed was
1,000 volumes of 100 pages each. In some places they were received suspi-
ciously; at others the applicants were clamorous, and too eager to wait for the
regular distribution. "Sometimes," says the Journal, "we found them more
ravenous for books, and sometimes also afraid to take any at all; but this is
nearly a fair sample of the way in which we were ever treated by the people,
when free from the influence of the officers of government." In one of the
villages, it is remarked, the urgency of the people for the books did not arise
from a just value for them, inasmuch as the choice was determined by the
colour of the cover!

During their absence, two junks, with a large party of soldiers, visited the
brig; but, learning from a card, which Mr. Medhurst had left on board, that
he had gone on shore, the officers, who acted in a very friendly way, contented
themselves with examining every thing in the vessel, and taking away some
books.

On the 15th they weighed anchor, and after two days came into the spacious
bay of Ke-shan-so, about forty-seven miles west of Wei-hae. This bay is
formed on the north-west by the high and bold cape of Zeu-oo-taou, and by the
Kung-kung-taou group of islands on the north-east, extending also several
miles southward into the main land. It derives its name from the village of
the same name, which stands on the west side, and which is a place of considerable business, being an open port, where many junks touch on their way
to the north. The chart of the harbour by Ross is well executed, except that
the eastern sand-bank, as laid down by him, does not extend sufficiently far
from the island. This bank was found to be very bold, having seven fathoms
at a few yards' distance, and a safe channel between it and the island from
which it appears to put off. The whole coast of the extensive bay appeared
dotted with villages of white-walled houses in clusters of trees; whilst the
skirts of the town of Ke-shan-so appeared at the bottom of another bay further
to the west.

In attempting to make a tour of the villages, as in other parts, they were
opposed by the people, who gladly received the books, but refused to admit
the missionaries into their villages. One man said it was against the law for
foreigners to enter their country; another man, an elder of one of the villages, impressed his fellow-villagers with the belief that the foreigners had
come to take possession of the country, and few ventured to receive any
books. Upon this, the party determined to push on to Ke-shan-so. Taking
to their boat, they passed a white tower, where a few men were on the look-
out, and landed amidst a crowd, who, on hearing the object of the visit, and
seeing the books, were so rude and outrageous, that they overturned the
sailor who carried them, and bore off the volumes by violence. The magistrates interfered, and, in great wrath at the tumult, were proceeding to basti-

nado those who had been engaged in it; two or three poor fellows had been
seized by the queue, preparatory to the infliction, when Mr. Medhurst came
up and entreated, in a courteous manner, that they might be pardoned. The
officer coldly desired Mr. M. to mind his own business; the latter replied that
it was his business to interfere, as he had been the innocent occasion of the
tumult, and he should consider the punishment of these men a premeditated
insult offered to him. The officers, at length, promised to release the men
when he departed; but, upon Mr. Medhurst assuming a bolder tone, and saying he would not stir till he saw the men released, the officers yielded in an
instant, and became more civil. These concessions, which are commonly
imputed to fear, are more probably the effect of courtesy.

Next day they landed on the west side of the bay, and passed through all
the villages in that quarter, being "every-where treated with suspicion, yet not
with distinct unfriendliness." At the entrance of one village, two elders
addressed them: "we have seen your books," said they, "and neither desire
nor approve of them; in the instructions of our sage we have sufficient, and
they are far superior to any foreign doctrines you can bring; we do not want
your books: there is the road—go." On their return to the boats this day,
they observed, for the first time, a war-junk, which came from the westward
round Cape Zeu-oo-taou.

The next day, whilst the missionaries were on shore, visiting the villages
which lined the bay (where the books were received "neither too eagerly nor
too indifferently,") the brig was visited by several officers, with a large train,
who conducted themselves with politeness, and left a card, importing that they
had come to pay their respects to the "supercargo," and inviting him to meet
the general of the district at Ke-shan-so, the ensuing day, "that he may
suitably arrange matters." Accordingly, on the 21st September, the missionaries complied with this invitation. On landing, it was easy to see, by the
crowds and the bustle, that it was no common day. An attempt was made to
keep them waiting in the rain, on the pretext that some officers had not
arrived; but, on Mr. Medhurst's objecting to this incivility towards guests,
they were conducted to the custom-house, where two state-chairs were placed
for them. During the long time they were detained here, waiting the arrival of
the great general, Mr. Medhurst, observing some Füh-këen people amongst
the immense crowd of curious spectators, addressed them in their own language, which pleased them as much as it displeased the officers, who did not
understand it. Several hours elapsed before the audience was duly arranged,
during part of which time, the missionaries were allowed to walk about the
town. The discussions about the ceremonies were brief. When they were
told that it was the custom to "knock head" on coming into the presence of
such exalted personages, Mr. Medhurst cut the matter short by saying that
they reserved prostrations for the Superior Being alone, and that they should
pay respect in their national mode, as was customary to persons of rank. They
were then conducted to the hall of audience, preceded by heralds and horsemen, and introduced by two fine-looking officers. We now quote the Journal:

"No one entered with us, but the paved way to the temple was lined with
twenty-five unarmed soldiers on each side, drawn up in the form of a semi-
circle. These were beyond all comparison the finest soldiers I have ever seen
in China; of a size fit for grenadiers, and, for a wonder, clad in clean uniform.
Behind the altar, and in front of the gods, sat two officers, preserving, as we
approached, the most immoveable rigidity of limb, and muscle, and eye, looking neither to the right nor left. When we came to the threshold, in front of

them, we took off our hats and saluted them with a respectful bow. They returned it in succession, by slowly raising their united hands to a level with their chin, and slightly inclining the head. One of the attendants, of whom there were six or eight on each side, then motioned us to take seats arranged lower on the left hand. The inferior officer held the right seat; he was the *che-foo* of Tang-chow-foo, and wore a blue crystal button. His attendants were well-dressed. The officer who was seated on the left hand was named Chow, and a *tsung-chin*, or military general; he wore a red button of the highest rank, and was adorned with a peacock's feather, and a string of court-beads. His attendants never spoke to him but with bended knee. The *che-foo* was the chief speaker, and a lawyer-like examiner. His inquiries were directed entirely to Mr. M., and, as usual, regarded his country and object in coming hither. But he proceeded much further, and extended his questions to many other topics, making minute and judicious inquiries. His enunciation was rapid and guttural, and had not only the peculiarities of the Shan-tung dialect, but partook also of the court dialect. Hence it was sometimes exceedingly difficult to catch his meaning, while one of his attendants, who also spoke the court dialect, was perfectly and easily understood. I give the following notes of this interview in the words of Mr. Medhurst: ' He asked who this Jesus was, and what was the meaning of the word *Christ*, which he found in our books; which gave me an opportunity to explain the Gospel of our Saviour. Here the general interposed, with his gruff voice: " How! do you come to China to exhort people to be good ? Did we suppose there were no good people in China ?" " No doubt," I replied, " they are good to some extent, but they are not all so; and they are all ignorant of the salvation of Jesus." " We have Confucius," said the *che-foo*, " and his doctrines, which have sufficed for so many ages; why need we any further sage ?" " Confucius," I replied, " taught, indeed, moral and social duties, but he revealed nothing respecting divine and eternal things, and did nothing for the salvation of the human race; wherefore it was by no means superfluous to have another teacher and a Saviour, such as was proposed to them." " In your opinion it may be good, but in ours it is evil, and these doctrines tend only to corrupt the people, and their dissemination therefore cannot be permitted. We neither want nor will we have your books, and you ought not to go from place to place distributing them, contrary to law." " What law, if you please ?" I replied. " I have read the laws of the present dynasty, but do not recollect any against distributing good books." " That against the dissemination of corrupt doctrines." Here they spoke so rapidly, and so close upon each other, as to leave me no chance to thrust in a word, unless by violent interruption. When I thought of doing so, at last, " listen," said the attendants, " to the words of the great men ;" so that, when I perceived they would have all the conversation to themselves, I was not sorry to let the topic be changed. The *che-foo* then asked whether the vessel was mine, what was the price of chartering her, whether the money was my own, or furnished by government. I informed him that the money was raised by a society of private Christians at home; that the same society was sending the Gospel not only to China, but to many other parts of the world, according to the command of the Saviour. They then asked where the books were made, and where I had learned the language. I answered, that many of them were made, under my own inspection, at Batavia, where I had picked up the language among the Chinese emigrants. He then inquired the numbers of these emigrants, and from what provinces they came, and whether they all became Roman Catholics in foreign lands. I replied, that they generally retained their religion, but that I knew little of the Roman Catholics, as we had no connection whatever. Here the old general interrupted the conversation, and gave me his *ultimatum :* " he would advise me to return to my own country as soon as possible, and tell those that sent me, it was all labour in vain, and money thrown away, to attempt to introduce books into China, for none except a few vagrants on the coast either would or could receive them ; that the orders from court were to treat foreigners with kindness and liberality, whenever they came, but by no means to allow them to stay and propagate their opinions. Accordingly, they had provided for us a liberal present, with which they hoped we would be content to depart, but by no means to touch at any other part of the coast, lest we might not be so well treated, and disagreeable consequences should ensue; that, as they had treated us politely, in return we ought to treat them with politeness by touching at no place in Shan-tung, all of which was under his jurisdiction." I thanked him for their liberality, but, perceiving they meant to assume the air of benefactors, told them I could not think of receiving anything without making some return. This they said could never be allowed.

" Among other inquiries they asked of what country Mr. Stevens was, and when I told them from New England, the *che-foo* again struck off with a whole new series of interrogatories. " What," said he, " is there a New as well as an Old England?" " Yes, as also a new and an old world." I then related the discovery of America by Columbus, and the colonizing a part of it by the subjects of England. " Under what government is this new country, and who is the king?" This gave me an opportunity to astonish them by declaring that the country had no king, but two great elective assemblies, and a president, all chosen by the people, whose wishes were consulted in every thing that regarded government ; that, after four years, the president is re-elected, or another is chosen in his place, and he returns to private life again. They asked what became of the old president, and whether, on going out of office, he did not use his power to excite rebellion, and create a party in his favour. At all this news they could scarcely cease wondering. They inquired how I, an Old Englander, could so readily agree with Mr. Stevens, a New Englander; which gave occasion to describe the points of similarity between the two nations, as well as our own coincidence of views and feelings. Besides these and other topics, the *che-foo* described the reception or rather rejection of Lord Amherst's embassy, in order to show the small value attached to foreign intercourse by the emperor. He also alluded to and inquired after Messrs. Lindsay, Gutzlaff, and Gordon, and seemed well acquainted with all those expeditions, so far as the Chinese account could make him informed. It was now dark, while yet the conference was scarce closed. The same style of ceremony was observed on retiring as on entering, and we departed on friendly but not cordial terms."

The party now deliberated upon their ulterior proceedings,—whether to proceed further to the west, or to return round the promontory of Shan-tung. Several considerations induced them to adopt the latter course, amongst which were the danger of exposure to a north-east gale, and the certainty that their further operations in the neighbourhood must be much impeded, if not prevented, by the interference of the government They, therefore, relinquished their first intention of going to Tang-chow-foo, and returned to Wei-hae. On the 23d, they ran round the cape, and coasted the eastern side of the province a short distance from land. Several capacious bays were observed, whose distant shores were sprinkled with numerous villages. There are several instances in which the coast is inaccurately-laid down in the charts. They landed at Tsing-hae-wei, a walled place of some consideration. The town, as well as the defences, is, however, going to decay. This is the case all along the coast of Shan-tung. "Everywhere there are look-out towers, on the hills, fallen to ruins; forts dismantled, or nearly so; and long lines of mud fortifications inclosing many acres of land, some of which are now turned to cultivated fields without a building within the walls, and others still inclose a small hamlet, the miserable remnant of a fortress, where perhaps the enemies of their country were once withstood." Here they distributed books, and commenced an excursion into the interior, but were annoyed by an attendant officer on horseback, who warned the people against holding intercourse with them. By taking to the boat, and sailing around into a deep bay, farther inland, they escaped pursuit, and enjoyed the whole day among the villagers. Though they were cautious and reserved, yet they were ever friendly; but they did not receive many books. Having never seen foreigners before, some of them being quite ignorant of the name of England, they knew not what to make of being presented with books by such strange-looking men. As in all other places, the people appeared to be very industriously engaged, some in ploughing, others in reaping, some carrying out manure, and others bringing home produce; numbers were collected on the threshing-floors, winnowing, sifting and packing wheat, rice, millet, pease, and in drying maize or Indian corn. Sometimes they scarcely turned aside from their work to gaze at the strangers. Their teams for ploughing exhibited ludicrous combinations. Sometimes a cow and an ass, or a cow, an ox, and an ass, or a cow and two asses, or four asses, were yoked abreast. The women had all small feet, and throughout Shan-tung were of a pale and sallow aspect, much unlike the healthy and robust look of the men. They were not always shy, but were generally ill-clad and ugly, labouring in the fields apparently little less than the men. But, on several occasions, young ladies were seen clothed in gay silks and satins, riding on asses, sitting astride on the top of a bag that almost covered up the donkey on which they rode; the ass was always led by the hand of a man.

The two following days were spent at anchor and in beating twenty miles to the westward along the coast towards Hae-yang heen. The 29th was spent on shore among the villages. There was nothing to remark except an increasing fear manifest among the people of having intercourse with and receiving books from them. One or two policemen in disguise were observed following them, and alarming the people by words and signs, so that they often refused books. In one or two villages they received none at all. The next day they sailed westward, about fifteen miles, and came to anchor in a fine land-locked harbour, in four fathoms, which they supposed must lead to the town, and the appearance of a fort on a hill confirmed this opinion. In the afternoon, therefore, leaving the vessel, they stood into a shoal bay which runs up far into the land. Here was no town, however, but several large villages, where they left books to a small extent, and experienced some opposition. In one of the best-looking villages, a crowd as usual gathered, when a well-dressed young man came up, and began to interfere with a loud voice. Mr. M. asked him if he would receive a book. " No," cried he, " I cannot read." " Well, if you cannot read, I cannot help you, but others can read; if you are so ignorant or foolish, it is not right that others should suffer for your doltishness." The people enjoyed his confusion, and received books the more readily. Mr. M. was now invited into a school-house, where their young opponent was only a pupil. They wished to know how many ships were on the coast, as they had heard of a very large one on the north side, with 200 men on board. The party proceeded through several villages, but found no town, and learned that Hae-yang-heën was still thirty miles distant.

" On returning to the boat, we found her high and dry, the water having left nearly all the bay. While waiting for the return of the tide, we visited the fort. It is of brick, fifty feet square, but quite dismantled, without soldier, or gun, or door, or any article of furniture whatever, and its naked walls are fast crumbling to ruins. Descending to the sea, we examined the rocks at the base of the hill. Never have I seen so manifest marks of a violent convulsion of nature as are here exhibited. The original strata are broken up and turned at all angles, contorted into all shapes, and the fissures filled with a dark species of rock, apparently basalt, which some mighty effort seems to have protruded from beneath in a liquid state, and opened a tortuous passage through the superincumbent mass of primitive stone. After leaving the hill and descending to the boat, we observed an officer riding fiercely towards us, and were informed by an old Chinese who was with us, that it was the commander of the fort and his garrison coming forward to meet us. He rode a small but not ill-looking horse, led by a servant, and followed by one soldier, and another straggler, which composed the whole garrison! He alighted, and entered into earnest conversation, expatiating on the insecurity of the harbour on account of the strong southerly wind, that raised the waves which sometimes dashed terribly on the naked shore, and the sandy bottom which would not hold the anchor. The latter half of the information we already knew to be totally false, having well ascertained that the ground was soft mud, and the anchorage very eligible; and, while it afforded shelter, allowed also a passage to sea either westward or southward, and perhaps eastward.

" This was the last of our excursions on the inhospitable shores of Shan-tung: inhospitable, as previous accounts had led us to expect, and in which we were but partially disappointed. The inhabitants of the villages were indeed suspicious and reserved, but cannot be accused of hostility or treachery towards us. Many times have we been surrounded by large crowds of them, ourselves but two in number, totally unarmed and far beyond the sight of our vessel. Thus in security have we passed from village to village, giving a friendly salute to those whom we met, or saw at their labours, from whom in return we usually received a friendly salutation. They are indeed far different in their manners towards foreigners from the ready cordiality of their more southern and more roguish countrymen. This province is the native place of their revered sage, Confucius; and the people of all classes speak the pure court-dialect, the poorest beggar there excelling in elegance of pronunciation the scholar of the south. The number of readers appeared to be much less than I had anticipated; not one female have we seen who could read, and a small proportion of the poor countrymen in the villages could read a page intelligibly: but, in cities and wealthier places, the proportion of readers may be greater. The towns, and even the villages, which are noted on the old maps, we found as delineated, unchanged except by decay, and unimproved in any respect. Few of the comforts of life can be found among them; their houses consisted in general of substantial granite, and thatch-roofs, but neither table, nor chair, nor floor, nor any article of furniture could be seen in the houses of the poorer classes. Every man, however, had his pipe; and tea of some kind was found in most of the families. But the miserable, squalid, and sallow aspect of all the females excited in our minds an indelible feeling of compassion for their helpless lot."

Having spent about three weeks on the coast of Shan-tung, they put to sea on the 1st October, intending to visit Shang-hae. The southern coast of Shan-tung is no ways different from the northern, both presenting a constant succession of hill and dale. " We found no place of importance on this side, though, had we proceeded some ninety miles further westward, we should have seen Keaou-chow, which is described as a chief commercial city in this province. The coast to the southward for several degrees is quite unknown to foreigners, and in order to avoid the uncertain limits of the sands off the great Yellow River and the Yang-tsze-keäng, we kept eastward at the distance of 100 miles from land."

On the morning of the 8th, standing over to the north, they ran up a channel, in a N.E. storm, and came into the mouth of the Woo-sung river, and at noon anchored between two forts. " They immediately gave us a salute, though, such was the dilapidated state of that on the western bank, that I thought every discharge must shake the crazy walls quite down. This fort had been undermined by the heavy rains of the sixth moon, and nearly half of it had fallen to the ground. The waters of the river, and indeed of the whole channel, were very turbid, quite as much so as those of the Mississippi, but of a yellower hue. They tinged the copper of our vessel so that all the dashing of the waves against it till our return to Lintin did not wholly remove the colour. A tumbler of the water soon deposited a sediment of soft yellow mud, the twelfth of an inch in depth." The Journal gives the following account of their visit here :—

" The contrast between the province we had just left, and the level and rich fields of Keäng-soo, was most striking. Trees and foliage here were abundant, and the soil seemed to be profuse of her gifts. But, owing to the extremely unfavourable weather during our stay, and to other events beyond our control, we saw comparatively little of this celebrated emporium of native commerce. Owing to the violence of the storm, no vessels were seen passing out or in, and the river about a mile above us was filled with a numerous fleet waiting for fair weather to go to sea. The tides were strong, and the rise and fall two fathoms. In the afternoon, we determined to land, notwithstanding the inclemency of the weather, in order to enjoy the advantage of some intercourse with the people, before the news of our arrival should awaken any opposition. A number of people awaited our landing at the town of Woosung, among whom were the magistrates of the place, who invited us into a house. But our chief object being intercourse with the people, we delayed to accept the invitation till Mr. M. had established a good understanding with the crowd, by means of some Füh-këen men, who are ever ready to welcome strangers, as well as by giving some books. We afterwards met the officers in a temple, where the usual questions were proposed and answered, and no opposition or dislike expressed. Finding the streets of this naturally dirty town rendered altogether impassable by the rain, we prepared to return. The crowd had now become great at the boat, and so eager to obtain books, that there was much pulling and thrusting about each other, which violation of propriety excited the wrath of the officers, so that they seized two noisy fellows by the queue, and were about to lay the bamboo on them. Mr. M. observed it, and bidding the officer look him in the face, requested the release of the prisoners. The officer replied that such rudeness was quite unpardonable towards us, who had come so far to do them good, but that, out of respect to Mr. M.'s face, they should be released. They were so, and the poor fellows ran away gladly, and the people were none the less pleased with us.

Next morning, though the storm continued unabated, we set out in the long-boat with five men, without an officer, to ascend the river to Shang-hae. Scarce a boat was moving upon the river, and none from the many junks appeared to observe us, so that we had a clear river and none to oppose our passage. The Woo-sung is a noble stream, maintaining a very uniform breadth of half a mile or more, and a depth from eight to three fathoms. Both shores are a dead level, under high cultivation, and very populous. The city was estimated to be between fifteen and twenty miles from the mouth of the river; a strong wind and tide brought us to it in three hours. A forest of innumerable masts both told us of our near approach to the city and of its commercial importance. The native shipping of Canton, in the height of the season, never amounts to half of that which was now lying at Shang-hae. Discovering the temple of the Queen of Heaven, where Messrs. Lindsay and Gutzlaff had been entertained, we stopped in front of it, welcomed by smiling crowds on shore and in the junks and boats. As usual, Mr. M., immediately on stepping ashore, began to give books, but, before a moment had passed, the noise of officers approaching was heard, and their attendants clearing the way right and left with heavy bamboo cudgels, with which they belaboured the people unmercifully. The officers greeted us civilly, and invited us into the temple. Passing through immense crowds, assembled as well to witness the theatrical performances, then acting, as to see the strangers, we entered a retired apartment, and took seats with several officers, having with us a sailor and a bag of books. After a short conversation, tea and cakes were served up, and they requested to see the books, to which they helped themselves profusely, but requested us to delay giving them to the people till the rain was past. Perceiving their intention, while Mr. M. was detaining the officers in the hall in conversation, I proceeded to the boat, attended by several policemen and inferior officers. Breaking open a box of books, I stood in the boat and attempted to hand them out singly to the multitude that lined the shore. By moving from place to place, this measure partially succeeded, till the whole box was finished. The petty officers then, with upraised hands, implored me not to distribute the other box; but seeing, as I did, such crowds assembled that not one in fifty could have got a book, and that no other opportunity could be had, I was obliged to be inexorable, and commenced the last box. But such a press was there upon the boat, that at length I found it impossible to do better than to scatter them indiscriminately over their heads, letting them fall into their upraised hands, till a thousand volumes were given among the thousands of Shang-hae. In the bustle unavoidably occasioned by the simultaneous moving of such a mass of human beings, the officers' clubs were sometimes seen playing above their heads, and again officers and cudgels were borne down together.

" Mr. M. meanwhile remained in the temple. The officers spoke of Messrs. Gutzlaff and Lindsay, and inquired where they now were. Hearing a great noise outside, he understood it was caused by the arrival of the *che-heen*, and several officers came to conduct Mr. M. into his presence. ' I found him,' said Mr. M., ' seated in an adjoining apartment, with a string of officers standing by his side, and, after salutation, took a seat in front of him. " Rise up, rise up," cried all the attendant officers, and the disconcerted *che-heen* beckoned me to stand near him. I then asked whether it was not allowed me to sit during this conference, and, being informed that I could not, immediately rose and left the room. Several officers followed, and tried various arguments for half an hour to persuade me to return and be examined by the *che-heen*.

But, knowing that other private foreigners had, in this very city, met with officers of higher rank than the *che-héen*, without submitting to stand in their presence, I refused to comply, and they ceased importuning when they found I could neither be driven nor persuaded.' After waiting an hour, that officer retired without granting an audience. The remaining officers then grew more familiar, and agreed to procure the provisions of which we gave them a list. After these proceedings, we attempted to enter the city, but, so resolute was the opposition of the military officers and lictors, that it seemed impossible to advance without resort to actual force. Yet, when the attempt was relinquished, we soon had occasion to regret having made it, or that it had not been persevered in; for the officers were none the more civil after this yielding on our part. A hasty dinner was now served up, when we prepared to return to the brig, contrary to our first intention, finding no disposition in our hosts to be cordial and friendly. But, at the wharf, an occurrence took place, which clearly evinced the true feelings of the officers towards us and our object. On the steps, before our eyes, was placed a basket half-filled with loose straw, and covered with fragments of a few torn books. Seeing that some disrespect was designed, Mr. M. ordered our boat to be cleared of the various articles of provisions with which as presents they were cramming her full; while this was doing, one of the policemen took a torch and applied it to the straw. Perceiving that, whatever was the design of this strange and unprecedented movement, they meant to offer public disrespect to our books, I thought we could do no less than treat the emperor's presents in the same way; and accordingly took up some and threw them into the blazing basket, both putting out the fire, and disconcerting the officers; when they repeated the attempt again, it was defeated in the same way, till the poor policeman drew back in alarm. But the characteristic readiness of the Chinese to make a good retreat was never better exemplified than in this case, when Mr. M. remonstrated with the chief officer. ' Sir,' said he, ' these are books that were torn in the tumult, and to prevent their being trodden upon—for we consider it a sin to tread on written paper — I ordered them to be burned.' But, unfortunately, Mr. M. recollected having just heard the same officer give orders to tear some books for this very purpose, though at the time Mr. M. did not fully comprehend the order, till the event explained it. In this manner we left the city, and after five hours' rowing and sailing, and vainly asking for lodgings on board of two junks, we arrived at the *Huron* near ten o'clock at night."

The two following days, while the storm continued, were spent in visiting the junks in the river, which amounted to hundreds. Books were eagerly taken. They called again at Woo-sung, where all the necessary purchases were made, and by permission of the officers, though there was pasted up an order, forbidding all dealings with the barbarians. They also visited both forts, entering the barracks of the soldiers, and left some books in their hands, which were gratefully received. In these excursions, the attendant soldiers or police occasioned much annoyance. The long guns remain still lying on the platforms by the forts, as when Lindsay visited them, but none of these were fired in giving salutes. Though the number of tents for soldiers increased on shore, yet no war-boats appeared till the 10th, when a junk came over from Tsung-ming, bearing an admiral's flag, and followed by twenty-five sail of vessels of war, of all sizes. The military on shore were drawn out to the number of 300 or 400 to salute. Each junk as she passed the brig to the windward luffed and fired a salute or two. The soldiers were armed with long spears, or swords, or short ones and a shield, or with matchlocks, or with nothing.

The next morning, an officer with a crystal button came on board the brig, deputed, as he said, by the general, to pay his respects. Tsaou (which was the name of the officer) declared that he had seen the books, and thought them very good. But he gently hinted that Mr. Lindsay had presented him with a spy-glass and a piece of broadcloth. But all such hints were lost on his hearers.

On the 12th, in order to escape notice, they started before daylight, in the longboat, for the island of Tsung-ming, twelve miles distant; but a strong west wind and ebb tide drove them back, past the brig, down to the main land, two miles eastward of the Woo-sung river, where they pleasantly spent half a day among the numerous hamlets. Every person was friendly, and all desired to receive a book. The fields appeared rich, having large crops of rice and cotton ripening on them. The females were much less timid and more handsome than those of Shan-tung. One or more coffins were generally found near each house, either awaiting the time for the living to die, or containing the remains of their deceased kindred. After the flesh is quite wasted away, the bones are deposited in urns, which are arranged in rows. The language spoken here was an impure court dialect, but sufficiently intelligible to Mr. Medhurst, whose facility in conversation was so great as well as diversified, that, while the people of Shan-tung, who spoke the pure national language, claimed him as one of themselves, the inhabitants of Füh-këen insisted that he was their countryman. In almost all places, inquiries were made for opium, and their broadcloth garments attracted attention; but only in this port was any offer made to trade: here the people of the junks were especially desirous of it. When the weather became settled, and these traders began to put out to sea, many of them, in dropping down close by the boat, inquired what point of the compass they should steer; and all alike urged them to remove to a place outside of the port, where they would meet them, and take all their cargo, of whatever description. But immediately on arriving at the brig, they set sail for Kin-tang, on the 12th of October.

They reached the harbour at the N.W. end of Kin-tang, lat. 30° N., long. 122° E., on the 15th, and were visited next morning by the captains of several war-boats anchored near the brig, who offered no obstruction to their intercourse with the people. One of the most delightful days during the voyage was passed on the island of Kin-tang; this was owing to entire freedom from restraint, the universal friendliness and politeness of the people, and to the beauty of this romantic island itself. Some of its highest peaks commanded a view of Ningpo (Takeä) river and the town of Chin-hae, as well as of numerous islands in the Chusan group.

Foreseeing much annoyance in going to Ningpo, they did not attempt it, but made sail on the next morning for the island of Poo-to, one of the eastern Chusan group. All the day, a fleet of vessels of war pursued the brig, joined by others from Kin-tang and the Great Chusan, till the number amounted to eleven. At evening, they anchored near. The missionaries stopped one day and visited the town, and several other villages on the Great Chusan, where the people were ready to receive books. Next morning, October 19th, with the wind N.N.W., they passed safely through a difficult passage, of only three and a-quarter fathoms at half-tide, between the south-east point of Chusan and a rock lying distant a quarter of a mile, and came to anchor half a-mile distant from the southwest shore of Poo-to. The imperial fleet still followed, but offered no opposition whatever. The missionaries spent the day in travelling over the rocky hills and shaded vales of Poo-to. Multitudes of temples, priests, grottoes, and inscriptions were found as they appeared to Mr. Gutz-laff three years ago. The priests themselves, as well as many others, received the books with readiness, but without rudeness. Several of the poorer priests were labouring in the fields with their servants. The vallies are not highly cultivated, and the hills are quite untouched, except to erect among the rocks some Buddhist temple.

" On returning to the brig, we found the commodore of the Chinese fleet, and one of his captains, who had long been waiting our return to pay their respects. The superior officer was a *yew-keih*, and wore a blue button; he was a smooth-faced good natured man, who spoke little and did nothing. His inferior wore a crystal button, was very lively, friendly, and talkative. In reply to our inquiry, Why they followed us ? they said it was their design to show us the way through these difficult passages, only they had the misfortune to be always astern of us ! They accepted an invitation to dine with us, and, as their hearts grew more at ease, did not hesitate to lament the impolitic res-trictions of their government, which prevented an extension of commerce that would be beneficial to both countries. When they said these things, and expressed themselves satisfied now that our object was good and in no respect evil, it was impossible not to feel unusual pleasure in the company of such Chinese officers, whose good sense or whose complacency led them to utter views so congenial to our own."

Next morning (October 20th), they stood to the eastward, till carried be-yond the numerous islands and rocks about Poo-to ; bore away for Fŭh-kĕen, and on the 23d ran in for shelter under the largest of the Nan-jeih (Lam-yet) islands, in Hing-hwa-foo, on which they landed and distributed books. On the 27th, they again made sail, and keeping well out from the shore in passing Tseuen-chow (Chin-chew) and Heä-mun (Amoy), on the 29th, anchored in the fine harbour of Tung-shan (Tang-soä). The brig lay in such a position that she could not be seen from the city of Tung-shan, and till they landed on the beach before the suburbs, no one suspected their approach. But five minutes sufficed to bring together as many hundreds of smiling people ; and half an hour sufficed to distribute some hundred volumes. One more excursion to the eastern shore, next day, took away the last book. The city of Tung-shan is of no inconsiderable size, if we include its suburbs, which are vastly larger than the city itself. An extensive wall and towers inclose a large area on the top of a rocky hill, but it is not apparently half-filled with dwellings. Several merchant junks were at anchor on the north side of the city, and in less than twenty-four hours some war-junks came in from Nan-gaou (Namoa).

Next day, they sailed out through the western entrance to the harbour, and keeping outside of Nan-gaou, arrived at Lintin on the 31st of October, after an absence of two months and five days.

This voyage appears to have given great displeasure to the court, which has issued an edict* forbidding foreign ships from running into the waters of every province, and distributing books " with the intention of madly exciting doubt and disturbance."

* See the Edict, last vol. Asiat. Intell. p. 287.

CHINESE ACCOUNT OF CEYLON.

IN the *Wăn-hëen-t'hung-kaou*, or Literary Encyclopædia, of Ma-twan-lin, a Chinese author who flourished in the thirteenth century, is an account of *Sze-tsze-kwŏ*, 'Kingdom of the Sons of Lions,' or Ceylon, for a translation of which we are indebted to an able sinologist of Paris.

Our correspondent remarks, that the name of *Sze-tsze*,' Sons of Lions,' is a translation of the Sanscrit and Pali name of the Island of Ceylon, सिंहल *Sinhala*, 'Abode of Lions,' or सिंहलाद्वीप *Sinhaládwípa*, 'Island of Lions,' whence the various subsequent alterations have been formed; as Σιελιδίβα of Cosmas Indicopleustes; *Serandives*, 'inhabitants of Ceylon,' of Ammianus Marcellinus; سراندیب, *Serándíb*, of the Arabian writers. The Chinese term is, however, more likely to have been translated from सिंहबाहु *Sinhabáhú*, 'descendants of lions.'

"The kingdom of the Sons of Lions was known from the time of the eastern Tsins (A.D. 317-420); it is not far from Tëen-choo (India), and is situated in the midst of the western sea. Its extent, from north to south, is about 2,000 *le*. It produces a vast number of rare and precious articles, which yield great profit to its inhabitants. There is no difference there between winter and summer; the five kinds of grain are sowed without the necessity of consulting prescribed or limited seasons.

" This kingdom was not in former times inhabited by human beings; it was occupied only by demons and genii (spirits in general); dragons or large serpents also made it their abode.* The merchants of other kingdoms carried on a barter with them without seeing their forms: it was only rare, valuable, and brilliant articles (such as pearls, diamonds, &c.), that they could give in return for the goods they received. The people of the other kingdoms heard of the luxuries of this land; hence they resolved to attack it. Some broke off all intercourse with the island, and, joining in the plans of the great kingdoms, they were able to expel thence the spirits or genii and the lions: it was from this it obtained the name of Island of Lions.

" The manners and customs (of this kingdom) were the same as those of the Po-lo-man (or Brahmans). The inhabitants did not obey the laws of Füh (Buddha): it was in the years *e-he* of Gan-te (A.D. 397—418) that ambassadors came, for the first time, to offer a statue of Füh, in Yu-stone, 4½ feet high, and painted of five different colours. Its shape was hardly rough-hewn, and did not approach the performance of an artist. It was placed during the Tsin and Sung dynasties in the hall of the magistrates of the Kang-wa.

" In the 5th year *yuen-kea* of Wăn-te of the Sungs (A.D. 428), the king of this island, named Cho-cho Mo-ho-nan,† sent an ambassador to offer tribute. The first year *ta-tung* of Woo-te, of the Leang dynasty (A D. 535), later kings named Kea-yïh, and Kea-lo-ho-le-yïh, sent ambassadors to offer tribute. The third year *tsung-chung* of the Tangs (A.D. 670), an ambassador from the same kingdom brought tribute. At the beginning of the year *tëen-paou* (A.D. 742), She-lo-shoo-kea sent for the second time an ambassador with tribute, consisting of strings of large and fine pearls, valuable gold necklaces, elephants'-teeth, and fine white wool.

* This is exactly conformable to the mythological traditions of the island, which represent that it was formerly tenanted by demons.

† This, there can be no doubt, was raja Manam, or Manam-raja, who reigned in Ceylon from A.D. 422 to 437, according to the *Rájdvali*, or History of the Kings of Ceylon. This coincidence in the chronology of two distinct nations is a fact which tends to establish the authenticity of Oriental history.

MR. RICH'S "RESIDENCE IN KOORDISTAN."*

To very few individuals in modern times is the science of Oriental Ar-
chæology so much indebted as to the late Mr. Rich. Placed in a very
favourable position for prosecuting antiquarian investigations, and for making
collections of remains of past ages which are rapidly disappearing, he permitted neither expense nor the dread of fatigue to check his exertions : his
magnificent collection of manuscripts, coins, gems, arrow-head inscriptions,
and other antiquities, which now graces the British Museum (and which the
nation obtained for a sum little more than the actual outlay upon the manuscripts alone),† attests the judgment and success with which these exertions
were applied.

In the correspondence contained in the highly interesting life of Sir James
Mackintosh, lately published by his son, are detailed some parts of the
early history of Mr. Rich, and the circumstances under which he became
acquainted with Sir James, whose daughter he married. This lady, now
the widow of Mr. Rich, and his editor, has prefixed to the present work a
short biographical "Notice" of him, written by a friend, which presents
a more complete outline, and from whence we shall extract the principal
facts. A curiosity to know the private history of those who have been
eminent for virtue or for talent is one of the pardonable and even amiable
weaknesses of the world.

Mr. Rich was born in the year 1787, near Dijon, in Burgundy, and
was carried, while an infant, to Bristol, where he was brought up under
the eye of his parents. He very early evinced an extraordinary capacity,
and a remarkable aptitude for acquiring languages. He applied himself to
Arabic at nine years of age, at fourteen he attacked Chinese, and at fifteen,
he had made "no mean progress" in several Oriental tongues, including
Hebrew, Syriac, Persian, and Turkish : and all this with "little or no
assistance." About this time, as he was taking a walk on Kingsdown,
near Bristol, he met a Turk, and being desirous of trying his own pronunciation of the language, addressed him. He had not only the satisfaction
of finding himself understood, but, learning from the Turk that he was a
distressed merchant, who had been shipwrecked, he enjoyed the higher gratification of contributing to his relief. By one of those extraordinary accidents, which are considered the most improbable features of novels and
romances, about three years after, when Mr. Rich was threading the Greek
archipelago, on his voyage from Malta to Constantinople, he fell in with
and went on board a Turkish merchantman, on the deck of which was a
Turk richly dressed, who proved to be the identical person whom he had
relieved at Bristol.

The extraordinary talents and acquisitions of Mr. Rich occasioned him

* Narrative of a Residence in Koordistan, and on the site of Ancient Nineveh ; with a Journal of
a Voyage down the Tigris to Bagdad, and an Account of a Visit to Shirauz and Persepolis. By the
late CLAUDIUS JAMES RICH, Esq., the Hon. E. I. C. Resident at Bagdad. Edited by His Widow.
Two Vols. London, 1836. Duncan.

† Professor Lee stated to the Committee of the House of Commons that the MSS. (Arabic, Persic,
Turkish, and Syriac) were the best he had seen collected by any one man.

to be noticed by Mr. (now Dr.) Marshman, Dr. Ryland, Mr. Fox, Robert Hall, and other men of letters at Bristol. His Oriental studies were not prosecuted at the expense of general improvement, nor even of manly exercises and accomplishments. His bias was, however, in favour of the former, and this circumstance pointed out the East as the fittest scene for his career. " Let me but get to India," he said; "leave the rest to me." Accordingly, in 1803, he obtained a cadetcy in the Company's service; but, on arriving in London, Mr. (now Sir Charles) Wilkins, having his attention called to the young man's prodigious acquirements in the Oriental tongues, and which he found, upon trial, to exceed his anticipations, brought the subject before the Directors, and Mr. Parry presented him with a writership, and in order that he might perfect himself in the Arabic and Turkish, he was attached as secretary to Mr. Lock, who was proceeding to Egypt as consul-general. The vessel in which he sailed was accidentally burnt in the Bay of Rosas, and he was enabled, through this circumstance, to make a residence of some length in Italy. Mr. Lock having died before he entered upon his mission, Mr. Rich was allowed by the Court of Directors to travel to India by a route indicated by Mr. Wilkins, with a view to his improvement. He proceeded to Malta, Constantinople, and Smyrna; from thence to Egypt, and through Palestine and Syria to the Persian Gulf, visiting Damascus, whilst the great body of pilgrims was there, and even entering the grand mosque in the disguise of a Mamaluke. From Aleppo he proceeded by Bagdad to Bussora, and reached Bombay in September 1807. In these travels over the greater part of Turkish Asia, " with the eye and pencil of an artist, and with the address and courage of a traveller amongst barbarians," he seems to have made his way not more by his mastery of the languages than by his captivating manners, which conciliated even the fiercest Musulmans. Mr. Robert Hall described him as a young man " of most engaging person and address;" and Sir James Mackintosh, when he arrived at Bombay, found his wonderful Oriental attainments the least part of his merit. " With the strongest recommendations of appearance and manners, he joined every elegant accomplishment and every manly exercise; and, combined with them, spirit, pleasantry, and feeling."

In January 1808, he married Miss Mackintosh, and soon after set out for Bagdad, where he had been appointed the first British resident in the Pashalik. In this office he continued to uphold the British interests with spirit and judgment, establishing a high character by his generosity as well as by his perfect knowledge of the native character. During the revolutions which afflicted the country, he afforded an asylum to the suffering party, which a sense of his justice and good faith exempted from violation. With the exception of a visit to Europe in 1813, occasioned by ill-health (upon which occasion Mrs. Rich accompanied him from Bagdad to Constantinople *on horseback*), he spent the rest of his life on or about the scene of his duties. In 1821, he had been appointed to an office of importance at Bombay, but, owing to a violent attack on the residency, which Mr. Rich repelled by force of arms, he was detained, and whilst waiting the orders of the British government, he made a tour to Shirauz, where the cholera-morbus suddenly appeared for the first time. Mr. Rich, though he appears to have had considerable apprehensions of this disease, courageously stayed in the city (which had been deserted by the prince-governor and the local authorities), quieting the alarm of the inhabitants and administering medicines to the sick, to which charitable office he probably fell a victim. In his last letter to Mrs. Rich (who had been compelled by ill-health to take a voyage to Bombay), he says: " the cholera has been here and has passed away, *El-humd-u-lilla* (' thanks be to God!'). I was unwilling to take my pen in my hand during its continuance, as I would not disguise any-thing, bad or good, that happens, from you; and I was loth to mention the cholera while it lasted. Thank God! it is all over." This letter is dated the 2d October 1821 ; on the 4th he was seized with cholera, and on the 5th he expired.

The Memoirs on Babylon were the only writings published by Mr. Rich, except a few communications to the *Mines de l'Orient.* He has left a considerable number of manuscripts, besides the work before us.

The journey to Koordistan, a country till then almost unknown in Europe, was undertaken in April 1820, partly to survey this new country, partly to escape the intense heat of a Bagdad summer (when the therm. is 110° at night), amongst the mountains of the Koords, with some of whose chiefs Mr. Rich was acquainted, and from whom he had received pressing invitations to visit them. Mr. Rich travelled in some state, with his lady in a *takt-rewan,* and a large retinue, including some of the servants of the residency and its guard of twenty-five sepoys. The pasha furnished fir-máns and recommendations.

North of the Hamreen hills, a sandstone chain, which runs N.W. and S.E., Mr. Rich examined a high mound, which the natives call the Mount of Prayer, and found it full of fragments of urns and bones, like those found at Seleucia and Babylon. At Kifri, some twenty or thirty miles far-ther to the north, he dug into some ruins, and laid open a small room, with plaster ornaments, one of which was of a Grecian character. This ap-pears to be the site of some Sassanian city. Coins and sepulchral urns are met with. At another place, called Eski Kifri, a little to the south-west, are other ruins, with an artificial mount like the Mujelibe of Baby-lon, 960 feet long, in which fragments of pottery and bones were found, as well as Arsacian and Sassanian coins. The ruins are of considerable extent.

Descending the hills, they entered the plain of the Beiats, occupied by a Turcoman tribe from Khorasan, who consider themselves independent. At Toozkhoormattee, they came upon the naphtha pit, which yields about two gallons of the oil a-day ; it is skimmed off the surface of the water.

As they approached the high country of Koordistan, Mr. and Mrs. Rich, as well as the invalids of the party, seemed to inhale a new existence. Descending into a valley near Leilan, a scene presented itself, which called forth an exclamation of rapture from the whole party from its contrast

with the "hideous desert" of Bagdad. "By the brook, which turned a
a little mill, was a small assemblage of cottages, completely embosomed
in a wood of poplars, willows, fig, plum, and rose-trees, the latter all in
full bloom; this grove was tenanted by nightingales, who joined their mellow voices to the murmuring of the rill." Amongst the vegetable products
of this happy valley, was "a briar-rose of England," the wild perfume of
which was infinitely more delightful to the Europeans of the party than all
the odours of the East.

The Koordish mountains presented the aspect of a natural fortification.
The line immediately before the party, extending from N. to S.E. was a
narrow precipitous bare ridge, called the Bazian mountains. To the north
of the pass of Derbent-i-Bazian, they make a turn to the west, and form
the Khalkhalan mountains. To the south of the pass, the ridge continues
in a straight line south and a little east, where is another pass called Der-
bent-i-Basterra, beyond which the ridge assumes the name of Karadagh:
here is the third road into Koordistan from the plains, which has been
deemed almost impassable by an army. The villages are all situated in
hollows, by the sides of the little streams. All cultivation is watered solely
by the rains, there being no artificial irrigation.

The party entered Koordistan by the pass of Derbent-i-Bazian, which
is formed by a mere ridge, or wall, which advances as it were to close the
valley, and slopes down very gradually, leaving but a small opening. The
valley soon became open and winding, having the Bazian hills on each side.
The strata inclined towards the west; the hills were calcareous. Artificial
mounds and Sassanian ruins abounded: these mounts, Mr. Rich was of
opinion, are probably royal stations, marking the progress of an army,
"perhaps of that of Xerxes or Darius Hystaspes."

On emerging from the hills, the route to Sulimania, the residence of the
pasha, diverged from north to east. That part of Koordistan inclosed between the Bazian and Karadagh ranges, on the west, and the Goodroon
range, on the east, appeared to be subdivided into valleys running nearly
S.E. and N.W., all of which terminate and have a common issue at the pass
of Derbent. These valleys are formed of small subordinate ranges of hills,
dependent upon, though not extending the whole course of, the greater ranges
before-mentioned.

On Mr. Rich's arrival at Sulimania, he was received by Mahmood
Pasha with great distinction. He conferred, indeed, an unlooked-for
honour, by paying Mr. Rich the first visit, before his entrance into the city.

The sight was a gay and barbaric one. He alone was on horseback; and,
being a very small man, was almost hid by the crowd of tall Koords, habited
in every colour of the rainbow, but chiefly in pink, yellow, and scarlet, which
hues especially made up the tassels and fringes which covered their heads.
The march was silent, and yet their tread was heard from afar. When my
guard saluted, the Pasha immediately returned them the compliment, by laying
his hand on his breast with considerable dignity. I sent my tchaoushes to
meet him, and advanced myself beyond the door of the tent to receive him.
As soon as he saw me, he alighted from his horse, his tchaoushes shouting
out; and shaking hands with me with both his hands, we came into the tent,

and sat down together on a shawl, which I had prepared for the occasion. It was with difficulty, and only after some time, that I could persuade him to adopt the easier mode of sitting and crossing his legs: he wished to persist in the more respectful and difficult attitude of kneeling, resting on his heels. He welcomed me again and again to Koordistan, assured me that the country was mine, and many other such eastern compliments.

The younger and more dashing brother of the pasha, Osman Beg, came to conduct him into the town, accompanied by all the members of the council on horseback, and an immense party of Koords on foot, The crowd assembled to witness the procession was very numerous; but the utmost order prevailed. His reception was very honourable. The house, however, prepared for the party,—the dwelling of one of the chief officers of the palace,—was a dismal place, ruinous and filthy. The description of this abode is given in a very graphic manner in Mrs. Rich's Journal, which forms a number in the appendix, and fills up very agreeably the occasional blanks in that of Mr. Rich:

But all my curiosity about the capital, the country, and its inhabitants, was converted into disgust at them all, on beholding the place destined for my residence. It required considerable courage to venture in through the mass of ruins it presented from the outer court; however, at last, I made a desperate effort, and rushed in, followed by Mr. Bellino and the little Italian doctor, the former very judiciously endeavouring to puff the dust off, the other holding up his hands and shrugging up his shoulders most theatrically. But I must try, if possible, to describe it.

The building is composed of bricks baked in the sun, with a facing inside of mud and chopped straw. The roof, which is of mud, and flat, is supported on bamboos by large beams, laid crossways, that have no other painting or colouring than that produced by the smoke of the winter-fires; which, to judge by the colour of the ceilings of all the rooms, must be pretty considerable; and perhaps the smoke is encouraged by the Koords on the same principle as old Eleanor's, the Irish peasant in Ennui, because *it kept her warm!* The building is raised on a platform about three feet from the ground, upon which are disposed all the different apartments, there being no upper story. The entry is by a portico, in which the natives sleep during summer. On the right is a small room, and in front a long, dark, dismal-looking gallery, with mud floor and walls, and in which was a very damp unwholesome smell. Here the delicate Koords pass the heat of the summer-days, as being a cool retreat, though I should prefer being subjected to the burning heat of our Bagdad deserts.

On the left is a passage, with another door, into the court—a large room, with three windows looking into the garden, and the same number towards the gallery. It had once been whitewashed, but was now in such a state that a plain mud wall would have been infinitely preferable.

The passage is terminated by another similar room, within which are two smaller ones. Returning from these into the passage, and on the left hand, were one or two doors leading, I believe, into some kind of rooms, but I had not courage to explore them. Much rather would I have entered with Emily into the east turret.

The ordinary houses of Sulimania are mere mud hovels; they are perfectly exposed, but the people do not seem to regard this. Amongst the *agrémens* of this city are fleas, which are peculiarly formidable here, sand-flies, a tormenting pest, scorpions, numerous, large, and venomous, centipedes, and large venomous snakes.

The favourite recreations of the Koords include wrestling, partridge-fighting, and dog-fighting. Mahmood Masraf, the pasha's prime-minister, a keen sportsman, gratified his master's guest with a sight of his game birds :

After a round of coffee and pipes had passed, the approach of the army, as the old gentleman called it, was announced by a prodigious cackling and crowing of the partridges, which was audible for a great distance off; and soon a party of stout Koords appeared, bearing on their shoulders thirty-two cages, each containing a cock-partridge. The collective and incessant cackling or crowing of this party caused a strange noise, something like the ticking of a thousand immense watches: they were not silent an instant, except when fighting. A number of lads of the fancy followed, all eagerness for the sight; and more would have rushed in, if, to spare the clubbing and cudgelling, by which alone they could be kept back, I had not ordered the doors to be closed. One of the assistants now opened the door of a cage, and let out a bird, who whirled himself up in the air as if in defiance, and then strutted about, waiting for his adversary. Another partridge being let loose, they fell to. The sight was amusing and by no means cruel. It was highly entertaining to see the little birds strut about on tiptoe, in defiance, jump up, bite at each other, play about to seize a favourable opening, and avoid letting their adversary take hold on a bad place. I observed the great feat was to get hold of the nape of the neck. When a partridge succeeded in seizing his adversary in this manner, he would hold him like a bull-dog, and sometimes lead him two or three times round the ring. Sometimes a bird would be frightened and run away out of the ring. The battle was then fairly lost ; and the bird so beaten will not feel disposed for fighting for two or three months afterwards. Every bird had its own name; and their wings were not clipped. They were so tame as to allow themselves to be handled without resistance ; and when a match was over, the birds would return to their cages almost of their own accord. Their great feat is to seize the adversary by the nape of the neck, hold him fast, like a bull-dog, and then fly up with him and overturn him on the ground; and the skill exhibited in the attempting and evading this manœuvre constitutes the interest of the sport. One bird being foiled several times in his attack, in a paroxysm of rage, seized himself fast by the wing, and was with difficulty brought to let go his hold : thus realising what has been thought preposterous in Harpagon.

The Koords are the only Orientals who sit up late at night, and rise late in the morning. Their fashionable life approximates pretty much to our own :

Few gentlemen in Sulimania go to bed till two or three o'clock, or show themselves abroad till nine or ten in the forenoon. Their chief visiting-time is at night. When it grows dark, they begin going about to each other's houses, where they amuse themselves with conversation, smoking, and music. They will pay two or three visits of this kind in the course of a night. About an hour before sunset also, a kind of club or assembly is held before the house of the Masraf, in an open place in the town, called the Meidan. Friends meet and chat on various subjects ; arms or horses are displayed ; and sometimes matches are made of wrestling, partridge or dog-fights. The Koords appear to me to be a remarkably cheerful social people, with no kind of pride or ceremony among them; and they are neither envious of one another, nor have I ever heard a Koord speak an ill-natured word of another, however different they may be in party or interest.

There is a broad distinction between the tribes of Koordistan and the peasant Koords; the latter are a totally distinct race, distinguishable by countenance as well as speech, and are never soldiers, whilst the tribes-men, rarely, if ever, cultivate the soil. Clanship exists in as much rigour as in Rajpootana. The clannish Koords call themselves *Sípah,* or military Koords; the peasants are called *Royahs.* The condition of the peasantry throughout this country appears wretched, " resembling that of a negro slave in the West-Indies." A tribesman confessed to Mr. Rich that the clans conceived the peasants were created merely for their use. The pasha appreciated a delicate compliment to his clannish pride paid by Mr. Rich, who dated the *degradation* of his family from the period when they be-came pashas!

The want of a permanent, stable government is much felt in Koordistan. One of the principal chiefs observed that the country was in a wretched state between the Turks and the Persians; the one insulted and oppressed them; the others teased them for money. Another said, " The want of security in our possessions is the sole ruin of the country. While we tribes-men are not sure of holding our estates, we never will addict ourselves to agriculture; and, until we do, the country can never prosper. Why should I, for instance, throw a *tagar* of seed into the ground, when I am not sure that my master will hold his government, and I my estate, until the season of harvest? Instead of doing this, I allow the peasants to cultivate my estate as they may find it convenient; and I take from them my due, which is the *zakat,* or tenth of the whole, and as much more as I can squeeze out of them by any means, and on any pretext."

The pasha, Mahmood, was an amiable man, serious, unassuming, mild, and religious, without fanaticism or insensibility; but his character was unsuited to those he had to govern: " a worse man," as Mr. Rich observed, " would make a better prince." His wife (his only wife), according to Mrs. Rich's report, was equally amiable. " They were much attached to each other, and were depressed at the loss of many of their children by the small-pox." One little boy remained at Sulimania, and at Mrs. Rich's visit, Adela Khanum seemed almost afraid to speak of him: " her eyes filled with tears, as she most tenderly looked at him, and added, ' he is not mine but God's; his will be done!' " This child was carried off, before they left Sulimania, by the small-pox, a disease which makes dreadful havock in Koor-distan. An attempt of Mr. Rich to introduce vaccination failed through the ignorance and unskilfulness of the person who undertook it. Conjugal and parental affection is a trait of this people: " all the Koords love their wives and children."

The condition of the women is far better in Koordistan than in Turkey or Persia; they are treated as equals by their husbands, and there is something approaching to domestic comfort. The women are not secluded; and the lower classes go about even without a veil. Yet "no women can conduct themselves with more propriety than the Koordish ladies, and their morality far exceeds that of the Turkish females." Compulsory marriages are not uncommon amongst the princes. The dance is the great passion of the Koordish females: "on occasion of a wedding, they will volunteer their services, when not invited, and even bring small presents to the bride for permission to exhibit in the dance. On such occasions, they always perform in public without any veil, however great the crowd of men may be."

The dress of the ladies in Koordistan consists in the usual Turkish large trowsers and loose shift, over which they buckle a belt, with two very large gold or silver clasps. The gown is next put on. It is cut like a man's, and is buttoned at the throat, but is left flowing open from the neck downwards, displaying the shift and girdle. It is of striped or variegated silk, chintz, or Guzerat or Constantinople gold stuff, according to the season or wealth of the wearer. Next comes the benish, or cloak, of satin generally, made like the gown, but with tighter sleeves, which do not reach down to the elbows. This, in winter, is replaced by a libada, which is a garment of the same form, but quilted with cotton. In the winter they also wear the tcharokhia, but made of a species of Tartan silk. This tcharokhia is a kind of cloak, or mantle, without sleeves, fastened over the breast, and hanging down behind to the calves of the legs. It is not reckoned full dress, and is replaced on gala days by the benish, which has been borrowed from the Turks or Persians, and is therefore more esteemed than the tcharokhia, which appears to belong peculiarly to Koordistan. They do not use pelisses, but supply the place in very cold weather by an additional gown or two. Of their head-dress, it is rather difficult to give an adequate description. It is formed of silk handkerchiefs, or rather, I may say, shawls, of every colour of the rainbow, artificially pinned together in front, so as to form a sort of mitre, about two feet in height. The ends of the shawls hang down behind as low as the ancles. Those who can afford it, ornament the front of their mitres with rows of broad gold lace; from each of which depends a row of little gold leaf-like ornaments. From each side of the turban hangs a string of coral; and under the turban is worn a large muslin shawl, which in front is furled up, and brought into a coil over the breast; behind, it hangs down the back. But this, I am informed, is only worn by married ladies. Much hair is not shown on the forehead; but a zilf, or lock, depends from each side of the head. The poorer female inhabitants of towns imitate the ladies in the fashion of their habiliments. The peasants in the country merely wear a shift and trowsers of coarse blue calico, the former buckled about the waist with a strap. The tcharokhia is of darker blue stuff, with several white stripes at the bottom, and is knotted by the ends over the breast. The head-dress is a small cap.

The ladies' head-dress is prodigiously heavy, and gives them great pain in learning to wear it. It frequently rubs off a good deal of the hair from the top of the head. What will appear scarcely credible is, that they actually sleep in it. They have small pillows on purpose to support it. They have very few jewels among them. Their ornaments chiefly consist of gold and coral. Ordinary persons have them of small silver coins, little pieces of metal, and glass beads.

The Koords are, in general, much more eager after information, much more diffident of themselves, and much easier to instruct, than the Turks, or even the Persians. Islamism, however, is a formidable obstacle to mental improvement. " Mahomet has made every thing—science, art, history, manners,—matters of religion, and placed a bar against all improvement, or new notions in any of them." The Koords, like all uncivilised people, are greatly given to music of a melancholy cast.

" I have in no place," says Mr. Rich, " seen so many fine hale old people of both sexes as in Koordistan; and, notwithstanding the apparent disadvantages of the climate, the Koords are in general a very stout healthy-looking people." The climate is severe. In winter, the cold is intense, snow lying on the ground sometimes from six weeks to two months; in summer, the easterly wind is hot and relaxing, and the *sherki*, or siroooo, is distressing. The town of Sulimania is situated in a hollow; the hills are steep and bare, and reflect the sun's rays. Mr. Rich mentions a curious fact, which he ascertained by a long course of observations: " at dawn, it is generally quite calm. As the sun rises above the hills, a slight air comes on from the point of sunrise. This follows the sun to the meridian, at noon there being generally a breeze, or at least a strong puff or two from the south. When the sun passes the meridian, the wind comes round to the west. The mornings are generally disagreeable, and the afternoons extremely pleasant, with a fine westerly breeze. I have observed this always to be the case when the *sherki* did not prevail. The hottest time of the day is from noon until 3 p.m."

The usual increase of grain in Koordistan is about five to ten to one of seed; wheat and barley are sown alternately in the same ground, the land not being allowed to lie fallow, except in the hilly country. The other products are cotton (of the annual kind), tobacco, rice, Indian corn, and other pulse. No hemp or flax is grown in Koordistan.

The mountaineers of Koordistan appear to be peculiar races. On the Sinna hills, the people are described as in the last state of barbarism, living in forests and fastnesses, cultivating nothing, and subsisting on acorns and wild fruit. The Jaf tribe, who likewise inhabit the highest of these mountains, on the frontier of the Sinna territory, are nomades, living in tents. They are a fine-looking, brave people, but esteemed uncivilized and barbarous even by the Koords. They form a body of cavalry 2,000 in number, and can turn out 4,000 musketeers. Their chief has uncontrolled power of life and death. Mr. Rich fell in with a party of these Koords:

Their tents and baggage were neatly packed on bullocks and cows. The use of these animals as beasts of burden seems peculiar to the Koordish nation. I remember observing the same custom among the Rishwan Koords, in Asia Minor, of whom, by the bye, the Jafs somewhat reminded me. The men and women travelled on foot, and a fine stout-looking people they were. The women were clothed in a blue chemise and trowsers, and wore on their heads a small cap, their hair seeming to curl about their faces. They wore the tcharokhia, which is a cloak of blue and white checked calico thrown over their shoulders. In its form it resembles the plaid of the Highlanders of Scotland. It is an indispensable part of every Koordish woman's dress: the higher class wear it of yellow and red silk. The Jaf men wore a dress belted round their middles, light drawers, with the worsted shoe, which is a comfortable covering for the feet, and a conical felt cap on their heads. All were armed with a sabre and light target; some added a pistol, and the horsemen always carried a lance. We saw one lady who appeared to be a person of some distinction. She was mounted on a mare, whose bridle and trappings were curiously ornamented with shells and beads, and her saddle was covered with a carpet decorated with tassels. A couple of animals carried her baggage, on which a servant rode, and a well-armed horseman attended her. None of the women had the slightest pretensions to a veil, nor had they even a handkerchief round the lower part of the face, like the Arab women.

Of the tribes, Mr. Rich has given the following particulars :

The people of Khoshnav and Rewendiz are to the last degree savage and stupid. They have no sort of scruple about killing a man, but would not miss a prayer for the world, though they have been known to fight in the mosque. Many years ago, there was a quarrel between two districts about a dog, in which seventy men were killed on the spot, of whom thirty fell in a mosque, after they had joined together in public worship. They still fight at intervals about this same quarrel ; and no encounter takes place without the slaughter of some men. There is a Khoshnav chief now alive, whose name I forget : a fly once settled on his eye, and teased him ; he drove it off ; the insect returned two or three times ; and, at last, the Koord getting into a fury, struck himself in the eye with his khanjar or dagger, blinded himself of one eye, and was very nearly killed.

In the tribes which form the Bulbass nation, every man, even of the meanest rank, has a voice in public affairs. You may be settling business with Bulbass chiefs, and have come to an agreement with them, when, on a sudden, some common fellow will start up and say, " I do not agree to it !" and this is enough to spoil the whole affair in a moment. When Abdurrahman Pasha had finished a war in which he had been engaged with the Bulbassis, a treaty was concluded ; and it was agreed that Kako Hassan, or brother Hassan, the Bulbass chief, should visit Sulimania, Selim Bey, the pasha's brother, remaining as hostage among the Bulbassis. When Kako Hassan was setting out, on a sudden, a common fellow laid his hand on his dagger, and said very coolly, " If the Bebbehs get hold of Kako Hassan, they will certainly kill him, and then they will boast of having shed the blood of a Bulbass chief ; it is better for me to kill him myself here." All attempts to make him hear reason were in vain. Selim Bey, therefore, mounted his horse, and resolved on returning to his own home, and having nothing to say to Kako Hassan. When he had rid a little way, the savage suddenly changed his mind, and hallooed after the Bey, desiring him to come back. " Take Kako Hassan," said he, " and go with him yourself ; we don't want a hostage ; if you are men, you will behave properly to him." All the Bulbassis agreed to this arrangement ; and the Bey and Kako Hassan departed together."

Before the party quitted Koordistan, they visited the Vali, or chief, of Sinna (a mountainous district), whose character offers a strong contrast to that of the pasha of Sulimania. He was a brutal tyrant, whose daily recreation was tearing out the eyes of his officers and servants who displeased him. Yet he was a perfect master of Persian politeness, elegance, and policy ; " his manners so insinuating, and his tact so perfect, that he can gain whomsoever he pleases."

Mr. Rich has given, from report, a curious description of the Chaldean Christian tribes, mentioned by Gibbon, in the Koordish province of Hakkari, between Amadia and Van, who are represented as " ferocious, vindictive, capricious, and irritable." The province is high, steep, and covered with forests. In person, these Christians are stout and tall. Their huts are built of logs ; they are unacquainted with wheat or barley, and subsist upon rice, walnuts, and honey. They wear hats resembling the European, made of rice-straw. They are independent and live in a perfectly barbarous state. They are followers of Nestorius, and are the only Christians in the East who have successfully resisted the Mahomedans.

They took leave of Sulimania, and of their kind and hospitable host, the pasha, after a stay of nearly six months. The remarks, with which Mr. Rich closed the record of his residence there, speak much in favour of the people :

I quit Koordistan with unfeigned regret. I, most unexpectedly, found in it the best people that I have ever met with in the East. I have formed friend-ships, and been uniformly treated with a degree of sincerity, kindness, and unbounded hospitality, which I fear I must not again look for in the course of my weary pilgrimage ; and the remembrance of which will last as long as life itself endures.

On his return, Mr. Rich took a different route, for the purpose of re-visiting (for the fourth time) Mousul and the supposed ruins of Nineveh. Here ends his journal ; the description of the ruins, and the rest of the nar-rative, are detailed in memoranda.

The village, or little town, of Nebbi Yunus, consisting of about 300 houses, is built on an artificial mount, which is part of the ancient city, and the antiquity of which is well ascertained by the remains (bricks, and pieces of gypsum covered with cuneiform characters) found on digging deep. One inscription which Mr. Rich met with seems to occupy its original position, about two feet below the surface of the mound, the height of which, in the highest part, is about fifty feet above the level of the plain. The foun-dations of the mosque which covers the pretended tomb of Jonah (which has displaced a Christian monastery) seem to consist of vaulted passages, probably part of the ancient city. The area of Nineveh is about a mile and a-half to two miles broad, and four miles long. There are the remains of walls, and of a ditch. The *sherki*, or east wind, from which the pro-phet Jonah[*] suffered so grievously, is described by Mr. Rich as " hot, stormy, and singularly relaxing and dispiriting." The شرقي is evidently the same as the سموم, *samŭm*, which is identified with the שׁחת.

The relics of the " exceeding great city," as it is termed in the sacred narrative, were again carefully surveyed by Mr. Rich ; and we are informed that the results of this and former surveys will be published in a fuller shape in a future work.

Many of the bricks and cylinders in his collection were found in the mount at this place, as well as the curious little stone chair. Some years ago, an immense *bas-relief*, in stone, representing men and animals, was dug up, but destroyed in a few days. There is a custom amongst the pea-

---

[*] " And it came to pass, when the sun did arise, that God prepared a vehement East wind ; and the sun beat upon the head of Jonah, that he fainted, and wished himself to die."—*Jonah*, iv. 8.

santry here, which seems a relic of superstition far anterior to the date of
Islamism.   Once a-year, they assemble, and sacrifice a sheep at a spring or
well, called *Damlamajeh*, with music and other festivities.   The spring,
which Mr. Rich called Thisbe's well (having erroneously supposed the
"*busta Nini*" of Ovid to be here, instead of Babylon), issues out of a
concretion of pebbles, and is covered by a dome, built with large fragments
of stone from the ruins of the city, and having a pedestal or capital of a
column on each side the door-way.   He notices the equality of age of all
the vestiges.   " Whether they belonged to Nineveh or some other city, is
another question, and one not so easily determined, but that they are all of
the same age and character does not admit of a doubt.   The vestiges or
traces of building within the area are, with the exception of Nebbi Yunus
and Koyunjuk, extremely slight; and I am now confirmed in the opinion I
formed in viewing the ruins many years ago, that the inclosure formed only
a part of a great city, probably either the citadel or royal precincts, or perhaps both, as the practice of fortifying the residence of the sovereign is of
very ancient origin."   A mode of building, is still practised hereabouts
like that adopted in some of the remains of Nineveh.   Pebbles, lime,
and red earth or clay are mixed together, and in a short time the concrete
becomes (especially after exposure to water) like a solid rock.

He made an excursion to the Syrian monasteries in the mountains north-
east of Nineveh.   That of Mar Mattei is constructed like a fortress on the
abrupt face of the mountain.   It is said to have been founded A.D. 334, by
one of the companions of St. George, who fled from the persecution of Dio-
cletian.   Here Mr. Rich met with inscriptions and MSS. in *Stranghelo*, or
the ancient Syriac character, some of the latter (including part of a Bible)
he procured, and thereby rescued from total decay.   The native Yezids,
in the district, appear to have some barbarous remains of Christianity
amongst them.   They admit both baptism and circumcision; but believe
likewise in the metempsychosis.

We must hurry over the remainder of the work.   Mr. Rich and his party
descended the Tigris on a *kellek*, or raft composed of inflated goat-skins,
a conveyance used in remote antiquity, and described by classical writers,
and arrived at Bushire, whence Mrs. Rich departed for Bombay, and Mr.
Rich, being compelled, by an event already noticed, to remain for some
time in the Gulf, made an excursion to Shirauz, where he died.   The letters
written from thence to Mrs. Rich complete the volume.

The novelty of the ground travelled over, the talents and facilities of the
describer, and the minute accuracy with which the traits of character, local
scenery, and geographical facts, are detailed, render this a work of much
value, and make us eager for the rest of Mr. Rich's memoranda.

ANGLO-INDIAN SOCIETY IN FORMER DAYS.

No. II.

In the endeavour to make ourselves acquainted with the circumstances and situation of the early English traders to the East-Indies, we are, in many transactions, of which a record has been preserved, occurring between rival parties, obliged to be content with *ex-parte* statements. Many of the cases, it must however be confessed, are made out very strongly, and when these are slightly noticed, or faintly contradicted by the advocates on the other side, we may reasonably infer that they are not very far from the truth. Amongst the existing documents, relative to the competition between the old East-India Company, and a set of adventurers who encroached upon their privileges, under the sanction of letters-patent from the king, few are more interesting, and it may be said, amusing, than those which bear the name of " Mr. Courten's tragedy," " Mr. Courten's Catastrophe and Adieu to India," and one or two others on the same subject. This gentleman was the son of Sir William Courten, who, through the interest possessed by Sir Endymion Porter at court, contrived to procure a license to trade to the East-Indies. Sir William had amassed a fortune in the employment of the chartered company, and it was, no doubt, a heavy grievance to the enterprizing individuals comprising it, to see their own servants becoming their rivals, and obtaining by the most unjustifiable arts a commerce which they had held to be exclusively their own. In order to give a colour to their usurpation, Sir William Courten, Captain Weddall, and others, who were well acquainted with the European settlements in India, alleged that the Company had forfeited the privileges secured to them by their charter, by neglecting to comply with its provisions. They represented the unguarded state of the factories, which they were bound to fortify, in order to render them places of protection for the resort of British subjects trading to India, and by other misrepresentations obtained the not unwilling ear of a government beginning to be distressed for supplies. Letters and licenses were granted, to the no small consternation of the Company, who saw at once the danger to which their interests were exposed by the intrusion of persons so well acquainted with all their affairs, and so apparently determined to turn this knowledge to their own advantage. There can be no doubt that these licenses were instances of bad faith on the part of the monarch who was so easily induced to listen to the representations of persons interested in the perversion of the truth. The Company had already many difficulties to contend against, from the opposition of the Portuguese and the Dutch; and it was still more galling to find their remaining resources weakened by the intrusion of their own countrymen, who, reckless of all consequences, pursued their private projects without the slightest consideration for the welfare of others. Some idea of their grief and dismay may be formed from the following paragraph, transcribed from a letter from the governor and the court of committee in London to the president and council of Surat. " Wee could wish that wee could vindicate the reputation of our nation in those partes, and do ourselves ryghte for the losse and dammage of our estate in those partes have sustayned, but of all of these we must beare the burthen, and with patience set still, untill we find these frowning tymes more auspicious to our affaires." Other portions of the correspondence, it may be presumed, breathed a less subdued spirit, meekness under provocation not being characteristic of the times.

The president of Surat, unaware of the circumstances which had taken place at home, was surprized by the appearance of several ships, chartered by a new company, and demanding, in the King's name, that he should afford them every assistance they might require. Permission to burn, sink and destroy, would have been much more gladly received; for the authorities at Surat and other places were only beginning to feel themselves able to cope with some prospect of success with traders from Holland and Portugal, and here were new rivals in the field who, headed by a man of considerable talent and enterprize, succeeded in establishing agencies at Goa, where he, Captain Weddall, was well known, Acheen, Carwar, Rajapore, and other places. Hostilities of the most deadly nature immediately sprang up between the contending parties, one of whom, animated by the expectation of success, made the boldest and most strenuous attempts to gain a permanent footing in India, while the other, who saw its trade decline, and the prospect of aggrandizement, so fondly cherished, melt away under the influence which these interlopers obtained in the East, lost no opportunity of endeavouring to cut off their resources, and to ruin their credit. The conduct of both parties appears to be equally indefensible and unjustifiable; each, however, lays claim to superior virtue, and while the old Company are stigmatized in the printed papers of their adversaries as the most cruel, merciless, and inexorable tyrants upon earth, the new adventurers are stated to have set out with, and acted upon, very different principles. They are represented as behaving with the utmost magnanimity and generosity to the people belonging to the ships and factories of their adversaries, whenever they had an opportunity of serving them, " relieving their ships with provisions, their factors with monies, and redeeming sundry times their men with large summes from the miserablest Malabar captivity that ever was heard of." " Some of these unfortunates " continues our author, " lying ten or twelve months together in most sad distresse, conceiving the Turkish slavery a paradise to their doleful captivity, and to aggravate their misery, those that suffered most were taken (not in the Company's service, as we learn by their own relation, but employed by their presidents and others in private trade) from port to port, being therein (to use their own language) the Company's competitors, and, to serve their afflictions to the height, the then president of Surat, by whom they were principally employed, would neither relieve them himselfe, nor appoint any other, nor afford them their own wages and debts due from the said Company for their ransom and subsistence. No, not so much as any, the least comfort in word or writing, as by their own most grievous, woful, and patheticall expressions to Mr. Courten's factors may more largely appear." The Company's partizans, of course, tell a different story, as will be shewn in the sequel. Meanwhile, Sir William Courten died, leaving his son to do battle as best he might with his opponents, both at home and abroad. It happened that the factories belonging to both parties were frequently in want of money, and upon many occasions it appears that neither were very particular respecting the means by which they obtained it. A ship belonging to Mr. Courten, named the *Little William*, was wrecked off Cape Bona Esperanza, as it was then called, but, by the great industry of the people on board, two brass guns, about £5,000 in Barbary gold, and seventeen men belonging to the crew, were saved. These people escaped in the long-boat of the ship, and established themselves upon the island of St. Lawrence, or Madagascar, as it is now styled, where they subsisted in the most orderly manner for nearly nine months, expecting to be relieved by a ship belonging to their employer, who, they doubted not, would

hear of their disaster. In May 1644, the year following that of their misfortune, the ship *Endeavour*, commanded by Robert Bowen, belonging to the
old Company, sailed into St. Augustine's bay. This personage did not, it is
said, at first evince any desire to assist his countrymen ; but, upon learning
from some of the crew of the wrecked vessel that the gold had been saved, he
became more interested in their situation. Coming on shore a second time,
after the receipt of this intelligence, he paid a visit to the master of the *Little
William*, one Thomas Cox, who, with Thomas Hill, the purser, had maintained the little colony in a manner highly creditable to both. Unbending from
the haughtiness of the reserve shewn on his first arrival, Bowen offered to give
a passage to the officers and crew of the wrecked vessel to the island of
Joanna, or to some one of his employers' factories upon the coast, assuring
Cox that he could easily procure bills of exchange for the gold, or a safe
conveyance by land to some of the settlements belonging to Mr. Courten.
Cox hesitated, at first, inquiring whether he might not expect to be taken off
the island by one of the vessels of his employers, who, he felt assured, would
make earnest endeavours to afford him relief. Bowen, however, assured him
he had no chance of getting away by any ship belonging to Mr. Courten ; for,
though several were ready for sea, they were detained by order of the parliament, and that, moreover, Mr. Courten himself was upon the very verge of
bankruptcy. This intelligence was, as may be guessed, pure fiction, fabricated
to suit a very dishonest purpose, a vessel, the *Loyalty*, belonging to Mr.
Courten, being known to be upon her voyage, and arriving at Madagascar two
months after the departure of the *Endeavour*. Cox, deceived by these representations, agreed at length to accept the apparently disinterested offer of his
new acquaintance, choosing to proceed to Joanna, as the nearest port ; but,
after he had been a few days at sea, he was induced to relinquish this purpose,
in consequence of an assurance on the part of Bowen, that the climate was
so exceedingly unhealthy as to prove certain death to every European who
attempted to brave it. He was told that no Englishman ever survived a single
night passed on shore, and that it would be madness to expose himself and his
crew to the dangers of so fatal an atmosphere. Cox, being a stranger, and
his company equally ignorant of the true state of the country, were easily
imposed upon, and it was agreed that they should go on to Madrasspatam,
whence they were promised a safe conveyance to one of their own factories,
with every accommodation for the voyage. Shortly after this arrangement,
Bowen desired to see the gold, in order to satisfy himself respecting the
quantity, requiring also to peruse the invoice and the bill of lading ; declaring
at the same time that he would not be answerable for the security of the property unless his demand should be complied with. The gold was accordingly
produced, together with the papers, which Bowen caused to be copied, he
then weighed the bullion, and sealing it up in canvas bags, deposited it in one
of the ship's chests, under his own custody. No sooner had he secured possession of this treasure, than a change of conduct became manifest towards
the people of the *Little William*. Bowen brought out his commission upon
deck, and with all the bluster and importance so commonly assumed by the
petty despots of the sea, began to read it aloud, in the hearing of the crews
of both ships. In this document, the word " interloper," was frequently introduced,—an ominous expression in the existing state of affairs,—and when this
pompous recitation of the power, authority, &c., delegated to the traders of
the regular company, had been triumphantly delivered, Cox was required to
shew his commission. The poor man complied, but the papers with which

he had been furnished, proving only to be orders and instructions by virtue of letters-patent, the captain of the *Endeavour* took upon himself to say that, if he had met the *Little William* at sea, he possessed authority sufficient to justify him in capturing the vessel, and making prisoners of the crew. The parties arrived in safety at Madrasspatam, and were accommodated in the fort. Cox took the earliest opportunity of stating the circumstances of the case to Mr. Day, the Company's agent, demanding the property embarked on board the *Endeavour*, either in its original state, or in bills of exchange, and requesting also that, in compliance with the promises given by Capt. Bowen, facilities should be granted for the conveyance of the people and the guns to one of the factories established by Mr. Courten. Day, at first, attempted to procrastinate, stating that the country was up in arms, and that there could be no safe despatch of men or goods, on account of the hostility of the natives; but, being hardly pressed, he scorned further evasion, and declared at once his determination to keep the bullion. The unfortunate master of the wrecked vessel was told, in round terms, that, if he persisted in his demand, he should be expelled the fort, and must take the consequences, for, though no threats of violence would be held out, it was impossible to say what might follow, since the Company's agents were bound by their employers not to succour or assist the people belonging to Mr. Courten, if they were in the greatest need, even with a piece of bread. Moreover, the captain of the *Endeavour* now said openly, that he had determined not to leave St. Augustine's bay without the gold, and if he could not have got it by fair means, he had resolved to use force, " Whereby," continues the narrator, " I conceive that we might have continued upon the island for all of them, if there had been no gold." Cox and Hill protested very warmly against this unjust detention of treasure destined for a very different purpose; both endeavoured to recover the property by expostulation; and, believing it to be impossible that Bowen and Day could persist in so flagrant an outrage, engaged a junk for the conveyance of the gold and guns to Acheen. They also endeavoured, at the same time, to prevail upon an Englishman, not in the Company's service, who was established at the factory, either to convey himself, or cause a letter to be conveyed, by land to Goa and other settlements on the coast, to acquaint the agents of Mr. Courten of their situation. This man, it appears, entertained so strong an apprehension of incurring the resentment of Day, who is represented to have had both the power and inclination to work the ruin of those who thwarted his views, that he could not be induced to interfere. It may appear strange that Europeans, not deficient in intellect and energy, and who were in some sort at least permitted to be at large, should have absolutely been unable to devise any other means of communicating with their friends upon the coast; but, it must be remembered, that they were perfect strangers, ignorant of the country and the language, and sharply looked after, if not closely confined, by the authorities of the place. Natives seldom trouble themselves about the affairs of people with whom they are unacquainted; they have little of the meddling curiosity which prompts people to interference in the concerns of others, and though, in many instances, they have nobly exposed themselves to the danger of punishment and even death, by their humanity to prisoners entrusted to their charge, it requires no small degree of distress and suffering to arouse them to active exertion, where they have no particular acquaintance with the parties.

Left entirely to their own resources, Cox and Hill tried every art of persuasion and remonstrance in vain. " Could not," observes Mr. Day, in the name of himself and his colleagues, " the said Cox, Hill, and company, be contented to have their own lives for a prey, being now in our power, for have we not told you that, if we could not have had it (the gold) by faire means, we would have had it by foule means, or by force; and will you still be so importunate and impudent to demand that which you shall never have, were it as much more? Wherefore, take warning, and let us hear no more of demanding, least we give it you with a witnesse, *viz.* thrust you out of our fort, and so, peradventure, you may be knocked on the head, or have your throats cut, for it would be no hard matter to overtake you, and then take what follows, for have we not told you sufficient to inform you that we have power and commission from our imployers in England to have taken your ship as well as your gold, wheresoever met at sea, and not to assist you with a piece of bread to save you from perishing either by sea or land? therefore, take warning and resolve upon some other way." After this rebuff, Cox and Hill, who felt that they had incurred a very heavy responsibility, became anxious to procure some acknowledgment, in order that they might at least be exonerated in the eyes of their employers. It was necessary, however, to be very modest in their demand, and, after considerable altercation, and a refusal on the part of Day to agree to pay interest, the following compromise was agreed to. Cox and Hill were induced to prefer a request to the president and council of Madrasspatam, to take charge of the gold and guns delivered by them to Bowen on board the ship *Endeavour*, " and which," says the document, " having safely arrived at your hands, that you would please to continue your protection, and referre the satisfaction thereof unto your honourable imployers and the worshipful William Courten, Esq., because we know not how to secure it from our own men, nor to dispose to any of the factories of William Courten, Esq., whose servants here transcribe themselves."

To this humble solicitation, framed of course by the authorities of Madrasspatam, Day and his colleagues condescended to reply in the following terms : " Your request we confesse to be now somewhat rationall ; therefore, shall continue the gold in our custody ; and we promise, in our next advices to Europe, to acknowledge our possession thereof to our honourable imployers." Cox and Hill felt deeply mortified by this unsatisfactory result ; the more so, as they had hitherto been so successful in their exertions for the preservation of the treasure, which, notwithstanding the unjust imputation they had been compelled to cast upon the crew of the *Little William*, had hitherto been kept inviolate. A residence of nine months in so difficult and dangerous a situation was quite sufficient to try the conduct of both officers and men, and it was a little hard to be obliged to affect to distrust persons who merited the highest eulogiums at their hands.

It appeared that the supply of gold, thus surreptitiously obtained, came very opportunely for the relief of the necessities of the factory, which was reported to be much in want of a replenishment of the kind; indeed, the exchequer was said to be so low, as to constrain the merchants to part with their gold chains and silver buttons, in order to convert them into ready cash. Under these circumstances, the gold belonging to Mr. Courten, which consisted of " ducats, knobs, and barres," went into the mint, and was speedily converted into pagodas, and employed for the use of the settlement. Having gained his end, Day, it is said, thought it prudent to quit the scene of a transfer which, to say the best of it, was of a very dubious nature; he proceeded, in the first instance, to Bantam, and thence to England, taking Cox and Hill with him. The remainder of the crew of the *Little William*, all of whom were entirely ignorant of India, none ever having visited the coast before, were, according to the report of Mr. Courten's agents, so dispersed over different parts of the world by the contrivances of the people at Madrasspatam, that many years elapsed before any of them could be found to furnish a correct account of a transaction, which, notwithstanding all the arts employed to keep it concealed, got rumoured abroad. The partizans of the Company gave a different version of the story which shall be subjoined; but, meanwhile, it may be said, that their account of the transaction is far too slight and general to satisfy those who have perused the evidence on the other side. Cox died on his passage to England, and, after his decease, means were found to prevent Hill from making communications which would have embarrassed the Company, by embroiling them still more deeply with Mr. Courten. He was not heard of during a period of seventeen years; at length, however, being recognized, he was called upon to give his testimony respecting the seizure of the gold and guns, and, though at first unwilling to comply, on account, it is said, of the depressed state of Mr. Courten's fortune, he was compelled by an order from the House of Lords to make a statement by affidavit before the Court of Chancery, of every particular in which he had borne a part.

Long before this circumstance happened, the conduct of Day and Bowen had got noised throughout the European settlements of India ; and the agents of Mr. Courten, being made acquainted with the fact of their having possessed themselves of the gold and guns, left no means untried to recover their value. The ship *Loyalty* arrived at Madagascar two months after the departure of the people of the *Little William*. The captain of this vessel discovered the arti fices which had been employed to induce Cox to accept the offer of a passage on board the ship belonging to the rival company, for he immediately made sail to Persia in pursuit of the *Endeavour*, which was supposed to have steered her course in that direction. The *Loyalty* was " fitted for close fight," and, had the two ships met, in all probability a severe action would have ensued. Meanwhile, the agents of Mr. Courten at Goa, and other places, were not idle; upon learning the fate of the treasure. saved from the *Little William*, they wrote to the agents of the old Company established at Surat in the following terms :

" Gentlemen : To you that are employed at Surrat for the honourable East-India Company, as formerly at Madrasspatam, we are constrained to direct these lines, giving you thereby to understand of our extreame sufferings by reason of some discourteous dealing, by some of yours in the same imploy-ment (especially at Madrasspatam as aforesaid); the passage was knowne to you long agoe (as we are credibly informed), and since to us by accident. It is concerning Mr. Thomas Coxe, late commander of the *Little William*, Thos. Hill, &c. and the cargo about 5,000*l*. sterling, belonging to William Courten, esqr., our worthy imployer, consigned to us or other his factories or factors here in India, &c. We have already endeavoured what we could, and ad-dressed our severall expresses to your foresaid port of Madrasspatam, with much expence and losse of time, and we feare of life, to a young gentleman not yet heard of, employed by us nearly upon the same occasion. Wherefore, we entreat that which we hope that you, in reason and equity, cannot deny, *viz.* our owne monies ; we and none else in these parts having just power to dispose of the same. We intended likewise to send to Bantam, to the Com-pany's president and councell there ; but, understanding by Dutch report at the bar of Goa, that they were gone and removed both thence and from Macassar, but when and whether they related not; wherefore, conceiving no other course at present so proper as to make our addresses unto you, well hoping that the justnesse of our request, or demand (terme it how you please), will so far prevaile as, that we may receive full and speedy satisfaction in the premises without farther delay and trouble. In confidence, therefore, of your respect to your own reputation, honour of your imployment, and the remembrance of those small courtesies (as we conceive them) formerly received from us, you will not add further dammage to what we have, for want of the premises, already sustained." No reply to this epistle being vouchsafed, a second was indited in the same strain, super-scribed as before: " Mr. Francis Britain, our first and last to you, bearing date Dec. 26th, 1644, we hope is safely come to your hands (though hitherto no answer received), whose contents to us appear so just they can receive no deniall, and delay where able is *summa injuria.* If the case had been contrary, we should have thought ourselves accursed with respect to divinity as Christians, to have denied or neglected such a small courtesie in humanity, whether to Jewes, Turkes, or Infidels. Assuredly, you know the passage, (we favour you in the terme), and the person that compleated the same, Mr. Francis Day. It was contrived in England, we understand, and effected at Madrasspatam. The injury being so palpable makes our expressions the more patheticall, and the rather because we find it accompanied, in all parts and places, with aspersions, detractions, and damageable defamations, which with us works this good effect, *viz.* a diligent inquiry into the actions of ourselves and of our imployers, and can find no ground at all for any of these discourtesies, that imputation of Cob and Eyres before authority being fully cleared and fairly vindicated, after sundry yeares search, though a few minutes were, before the same authority, found too much on the contrary part. By touching upon this string you may plainly perceive our ignorance deserves information, as well as our desires or demands present satisfaction, to prevent further and future proceedings. A foundation laid in blood may as well expect prosperity, as a trade maintained or managed by violence or iniquity. We are not yet so happy to have the knowledge of our errours, wherein justly to accuse ourselves towards you or your imployers, in this query, what evill have we done if lawful living be allowed? Therefore, in all obedience and humility to all just and equal orders and lawes, proceeding from authority, we rest in hope you will recollect your actions, and satisfy our just desires, that brotherly love may begin where wanting, and begun, continue. In expectation whereof, we rest your loving friends, Jo. F.—Jo. D."

These indignant, dolorous, but somewhat rambling remonstrances were of no avail, and Mr. Courten, "poor distressed gentleman," as he is styled by the historiographer of these events, obtained no sort of redress. The allusion to Cob and Eyres, in the preceding letter, relates to a transaction which took place in the outset of Mr. Courten's expedition; these persons were accused of seizing two junks belonging to the natives of Surat, of plundering them of their property, and torturing their crews: an act of piracy which exposed the European inhabitants of the factory to great suffering and danger. The president and counsel were imprisoned, and the goods of the Company confiscated, to recompense the losses of the owners of the captured vessels. At least, this account of the affair is given in the annals of the East-India Company, which indeed characterizes the whole of the followers of Mr. Courten as Buccaneers of the most lawless description. As a set-off, however, we have the printed papers of Mr. John Darrell, a factor in the service of Mr. Courten at Goa, from whose rather voluminous publications the subject of the present article has been chiefly taken. This person appears to have been a very zealous, diligent, and able servant, gifted with some talent, although not quite so clear and concise in the narratives which he has handed down, respecting the wrongs sustained by his patron, as might be wished. The reader, desirous to unravel the tangled web of his story, is obliged to gather information from a mass of affidavits, representations, and protests, huddled together in a very unsatisfactory manner, in three different pamphlets, which have for their object, firstly, the exposition of the scandalous conduct of those who desired to monopolize the whole of the trade of the East-Indies to themselves; secondly, the crying wrongs heaped upon Mr. Courten in particular; and, thirdly, to point out the great advantage which would accrue from our commerce with India, if it were properly managed. Mr. Darrell characterizes the East-India trade as " vast, spacious, necessary, and of extraordinary high concernment to enrich and advance kingdomes and commonwealths; being the trade of trades, the magazine of merchandizes, the honour of nations, and the glory of the world." With singular truth and modesty, he styles his own production " a breefe, uncouth, and unpollished discourse," a critical opinion in which all his readers must concur; but, although it requires some slight degree of skill, and no small exertion of patience, to reduce the materials, with which he has furnished us, to order, the light which he throws upon the conduct of the rival adventurers to India renders the time bestowed upon their unravelment not ill-spent.

The second letter despatched to Surat obtained no more attention than the first; a protest was then framed and forwarded to the same authorities, in which, in addition to the circumstances already related, respecting the seizure of the gold and guns, complaints were made of the great prejudice which the affairs of Mr. Courten sustained on account of the violence and aggression committed by the ships belonging to the old Company, upon the natives in whose territories his factories were established. It is necessary to observe that the annals of the Company make no mention whatever of the charge preferred in this document against the conduct of the legitimate traders, not taking the slightest notice of the outrage upon the ships of Mamula Croe, while a great deal is said concerning the piracies of Cob and Eyres, who belonged to the opposite faction. The opening passages of this protest, one of the most curious and valuable documents contained in the three pamphlets, run thus :—" Know all men by these presents, that whereas William Courten, Esq., and other adventurers, by vertue of his Majesty's letters, under his royal signature and privy signet, bearing date the 20th day of December 1635; as also his letters-patent, under the great seale of England, bearing date the first day of June 1637, was thereby licensed to trade to sundry parts of East-India, and elsewhere, as by the said letters-patent more at large appeareth; and thereby also injoined with the East-India Company, then trading into some of those parts or places of East-India, or elsewhere, aforesaid, equally to observe the ordinances, conditions, and limitations therein specified, which he, the said William Courten, Esq., and adventurers, and his or their agents, factors, and servants, on their partes, have hitherto kept and observed. And whereas the now East-India adventurers, their governors, deputies and other their committees in England, as also their presidents, agents, factors, commanders, or servants to East-India, or parts adjacent aforesaid, have by their misdoings there committed divers and sundry outrages, and actions tending greatly to the dishonour of God, and inevitable danger and damage to their brethren, especially the said William Courten, Esq., and other his partners and adventurers, viz. (*inter alias*) the said Company's ships, the *Sea Horse,*

Robert Tindal, commander, and Thomas Britain, merchant, also their ship called the *Hinde*, William Broadbenth, commander, and William Thurston, merchant, with others belonging to the said East-India adventurers, violently taking and surprising, in the month of May 1643, sundry and some very rich vessel or vessels, neare or upon the coast of Mallabar as aforesaid, belonging to Mamula Croe, king of that country, and other great men and merchants there inhabiting; destroying and drowning their men without mercy, thereby indamaging and preventing the said William Courten, Esq., and adventurers in East-India aforesaid, and all other, his or their factors, in their accustomed ports or places of trade, scituate in or neare the government and jurisdiction of Mamula Croe aforesaid; thereby also mightily incensing and exasperating sundry kings, princes, and governors, not only to molest and imprison, but also to kill, burne, and destroy all and every, the servants, houses and ships, whether by sea or by land, belonging to the said William Courten, Esq., and other adventurers, and to threaten revenge, and utterly to raze their fortifications down to the ground, especially at Carwar, compelling us thereby to fortifie the same for the safeguard of our lives, and desist from our lawful course of commerce (being in continuall danger), and to stand upon our guard, consuming much of our imployer's estate in raising fortifications and procuring other necessaries for our present security and subsistance, without any profit or hope of advantage; also the said East-India new adventurers, their ships actors, and servants, contrary to the contents of the foresaid letters and patents, frequenting, sundry years by-past and still, the ports and places of trade properly belonging to the said William Courten, Esq, as Rajapore, Acheen, and others, to his and their exceeding prejudice, and damage of the whole imployment, &c." Next comes a recapitulation of the fraud and violence by which Bowen and Day obtained possession of the cargo of the *Little William*, and an exposition of the arts by which the ship's company saved from the wreck were " deterred and kept, transported and conveyed, so as not personally to appear or even to be able to make it known that they were living;" although, when at Madrasspatam, they were not above twenty days' journey from the factories belonging to Mr. Courten." The protest ends by denouncing the governor and committees of the old India Company in England, and their agents or factors abroad, as the authors of the ruin of the fortunes of Mr. Courten, and with a demand of indemnification for the losses he had sustained.

After framing and despatching this protest, Darrell, whose indefatigable exertions in behalf of his employer seems never to have flagged, proceeded to England, in order to make an attempt to procure redress for the grievances of which he complained. Being unsuccessful, he returned to India, where he found, as he had too great reason to expect, the affairs of Mr. Courten in a very " wofull, sad, distracted, and languishing condition." The letters and protests despatched southward to Madrasspatam had been sent back " null and void of all hopes of receipt or satisfaction," those addressed to the president of Surat sharing the same fate. The ship *Loyally* returned, after an unsuccessful cruise in pursuit of the *Endeavour*, and no tidings of either Hill, Cox, or any of the crew of the *Little William*, being obtainable, Darrell and his friends were left to conjecture their fate, and to lament over the impossibility of bringing the adverse party to justice. After such repeated disasters, the affairs of the new company became desperate, and totally incapable of restoration; therefore, the unfortunate Mr. Courten and his " vertuous honourable and distressed lady," as she is styled by the recorder of these lamentable events, having sustained losses which were computed to amount to fifty thousand pounds, were obliged to retire upon the wreck of their property.

" This short narrative," observes our author, " is wholly lamentable, almost incredible to consider (in the serious apprehension of some), that such grave, rich, civill, religious seeming, wise men, should be so very cruell and unreasonable, or rather so exceedingly injurious and unnaturall. to their brethren and friends in particular, and to this nation or land of their nativity in general." Mr. Darrell does not appear to take the not unjust indignation into the account, which the old Company must have felt at seeing themselves overreached at home, and their rights invaded abroad by people whose interests were diametrically opposed to their own, and with whom it was impossible to act in concert. Without entering into minute particulars, the partizans of the Company deny, in general terms, the allegations brought against them, and with respect to the history of the *Little William*, take upon themselves to praise the conduct observed by Bowen and Day, in the affair of the gold and guns. They say that this vessel having foundered upon the African coast, the presidency of Surat *purchased* the remains of the wreck, and granted bills of exchange on the court at home for the value, giving the surviving crew a passage to Madras, where they were taken into the Company's service to recruit the garrison. This latter piece of information accounts satisfactorily enough for the manner in which the persons, who could have corroborated the evidence of Hill, were disposed of, but is not calculated to convince those who have seen the affidavit which he made before the court of Chancery, seventeen years afterwards, that any thing like a fair bargain had been made for the valuable property which they are accused of appropriating to themselves. Speaking of the apparently benevolent conduct shewn to the crew of the *Little William*,—who, by the way, formed a desirable addition to the garrison of Madras,—the author of the annals observes, " this act, however humane, had not the effect of lessening the opposition of Courten's agents." It would have been strange had it not, as we have seen, exasperated them more highly, since they would much rather have learned the account of the final destination of the crew and cargo of their own ship, from their own people, than have been left to collect the particulars from hearsay. Darrell, exaggerating in all probability the extent of the mischief, imputes the downfall of Mr. Courten to the loss of this five thousand pounds in gold. We are told that, when the affairs of the new company became so much depressed, that it appeared to be impossible they could carry on their rivalry much longer, a new danger, of which they were the cause, threatened their adversaries, for, as their credit declined, apprehensions were entertained that they would seize upon the vessels and cargoes belonging to the native powers, as a resource at hand for the relief of their immediate necessities. Reprisals from the natives were, therefore, to be dreaded, and as the regular company had reason to believe that they would be made responsible for all the damage sustained, they were obliged to circumscribe their investments in order to leave sufficient coin in the treasury to meet any sudden demand. Other sources of vexation occurred, the formation of a settlement at Madagascar had been a favourite project with the early traders to India, and Mr. Courten had so far succeeded as to establish a factory at St. Augustine's bay; he and his associates did not, however, possess the means of maintaining themselves there, and being reduced to great pecuniary difficulties, they are accused of having resorted to the desperate expedient of coining counterfeit pagodas and rials, at that place,—" a plan which," remarks our author, " had it only exposed themselves, might have had a good effect on the Company's trade; but the natives, being unable to distinguish between them and the Company, considered the proceeding a stain on the English character as merchants."

FINANCES OF CEYLON.

TO THE EDITOR.

SIR :—IN the *Westminster Review* for January last, in an article headed "Colonial Expenditure," is the following tirade:—

Ceylon affords a local revenue of £475,563; but this is not enough for its administration, and England, as before-mentioned, is called upon for an additional sum of no less than £113,340; so that the whole expenditure amounts to the enormous sum of £588,903. There is no country that could be governed more economically than Ceylon, did the disposition to economize exist. There is no internal or external enemy to apprehend; for the timid population has been unresisting for fifteen years; the island is sea-girt, and has no neighbourhood that is not British. It has been shown that its administration is twice as expensive as that of the East-India Company, without being one-half so respectable. Let Ceylon by all means be annexed to the territories of the East-India Company; whereby England will be relieved from a sum exceeding one hundred thousand pounds per annum, and the oppressed natives, at the same time, unburthened of taxation to the extent of some two hundred thousand pounds per annum, while their agricultural and commercial industry will have some chance given to them of rising to a level with those of their Indian neighbours. There is no pretext, except the love of extravagant expenditure and jobbing, for making Ceylon a government distinct and independent from that of our other East-Indian possessions. The soil, the climate, the national products, and the people, with their manners, institutions, religion, and language, make it only one of the many provinces of the great Indian empire. An offset, in the way of deputy, of the Governor-general of Bengal, under the protection of a moderate detachment of the Indian army, would administer its affairs economically; and, in truth, they were so administered during the first seven years of British possession.

This statement is full of errors. In the first place, our expenditure for 1834 (the last returns received in this country) was only £317,500, including island allowance to his Majesty's troops. In 1835, the expenditure will, it is expected, have been less, and the local government may reckon upon having a surplus revenue of some amount.

With respect to the insinuation conveyed in the paragraph I have just quoted, *viz.*, "that the administration of Ceylon is twice as expensive as that of the East-India Company," it is too ridiculous to deserve any comment, and only shows the writer to be entirely ignorant of the subject he treats upon. As to the remainder of the charge, "that the administration" (public officers) "is not one-half as respectable as that of the Company," if the writer of the article will take the trouble of making inquiries at the proper quarter, he will ascertain that the public officers of Ceylon will yield to none in talents, gentlemanly feeling, and general efficiency. If he had ever read the evidence of practical men, taken before the Committee of the House of Commons upon East-India affairs, a year or two ago, he would find that it is stated that the cultivator in Ceylon was far better off than his neighbour on the continent of India. Ceylon may well be considered the key of India, the "*point d'appui*," in the event of our ever being driven from the continent. It is now passing through an ordeal which requires the best exertions of an enlightened and energetic governor, such as the present one, Sir R. Wilmot Horton. Monopoly has disappeared; a legislative council, composed of official and non-official members, both European and native, has superseded the *close* council of former years;* European colonization is spreading; Ceylon coffee, in consequence of the equalization of the duty with that imposed on West-India, will at once come into the London market, and compete with the produce of those colonies.

In short, I am not too sanguine in prophesying that this "bright gem of the Indian Ocean" will become, in a few years, the most valuable dependency of the British crown.

Your obedient servant,
P.

* A meeting was held at Colombo, on the 8th of September last, of natives (Singhalese), being the first of the kind that had ever taken place, for the purpose of thanking his Majesty and his representative for the new council.

SONNET FROM HAFIZ.

رو بر رهش نهادم و بر من گذر نکرد
صد لطف چشم داشتم و یک نظر نکرد
سیل سرشک من زدلش کین بدر نبرد
در سنگ خارہ قطرہء باران اثر نکرد
ماهی و مرغ دوش نخفت از فغان من
وآن شوخ دیدہ بین که سر از خواب بر نکرد
میخواستم که میرمش اندر قدم چو شمع
او خود گذر بما چو نسیم سحر نکرد
یا رب تو آن جوان دلآور نگاہ دار
کز تیر آہ کوشہ نشینان حذر نکرد

I watched her coming—but she passed not by:
I thought to win her smile—she did not deign
To cast one glance from that love-kindling eye:
I strove, with floods of tears, but strove in vain,
To chase indifference from her heart;—the rain
Would scoop the flinty rock ere this might be!—
The listening birds, to hear me thus complain,
All night were wakeful;—on her pillow she
Unbroken slumber took—unfeelingly.
Then sought I, at her feet, but my last breath
To breathe, and, dying, end my misery:
She came not near me, reckless of my death!—
Heaven shield her from the darts she heedeth not—
Expiring lovers' sighs—from many a lone cell shot!

BRITISH RELATIONS WITH CHINA.*

WE are extremely unwilling to surfeit our readers with this topic,—a topic not very inviting to those whose interests are not directly involved therein,—especially since the question, which lies in a nutshell, has been pretty well exhausted by us already; but we see so many symptoms of a design to carry a certain object by a kind of *coup d'état*, that we are resolved nothing shall be wanting on our part to open the eyes of the British public to the dangers, into which, a party, for its own immediate objects, is endeavouring to hurry it. The misfortune is that, in almost all questions of policy, where the interests of the nation are not directly and palpably at issue, the bulk of the community remains passive, and is easily lifted by levers skilfully applied by a fraction of it. Moreover, highly as we think of the moral character of the English, compared with that of other people, we yet entertain some grains of doubt whether, if a Themistocles were to propose a political project, "than which nothing could be more advantageous and nothing more unjust," British virtue would prove as staunch as the Athenian.

During the present month, two pamphlets have appeared on this question, one of them by Sir George Staunton; and it is highly gratifying to us to find it taken up and treated so satisfactorily by one who, considering his familiarity with the language, literature, laws, institutions, and character of the Chinese, his long residence at Canton, and habits of intercourse with the authorities there, his liberal views and principles, and his entire freedom from interest or bias, is entitled to be regarded as the highest individual authority.

I very reluctantly take up the pen (says this gentleman) for the purpose of entering into the field of controversy; but, feeling, from early associations, and much subsequent intercourse, diplomatic as well as commercial, with the people of China, a deep interest in the preservation of our peaceful relations with them; and entertaining, also, an anxious wish that the great change, that has been effected in our system of trade with that country, may be rendered productive of the utmost possible advantage to the general commercial and manufacturing interests of the British empire, I have conceived it to be my duty to submit to the public, in this shape, my deliberate opinion upon what I conceive to be the mischievous and dangerous tendency of some of the doctrines at present afloat on this important subject.

Sir George clearly understands the tendency of these doctrines (and which, in fact, is avowed) to be the bringing about a war with China. We have failed in our endeavours to *force* our *friendship* upon the Chinese, and have suffered by that failure " some disparagement of our national character;" the failure of national measures of hostile aggression would, he considers, " be infinitely more fatal, and in part, at least, irreparable: it would not only prove a death-blow to our Chinese commerce, but greatly

* Remarks on the British Relations with China, and the Proposed Plans for improving them. By Sir GEORGE THOMAS STAUNTON, Bart. London, 1836. Lloyd. Simpkin and Marshall.

The Present Position and Prospects of the British Trade with China; together with an Outline of some leading Occurrences in its Past History. By JAMES MATHESON, Esq. of the firm of Jardine, Matheson, and Co., of Canton. London, 1836. Smith, Elder, and Co.

weaken, if not absolutely annihilate, that *moral* influence, with which our hitherto honourable and successful career has invested our name and character throughout the East; and without which, no *physical* force we could employ would prevent our vast Indian empire from falling to pieces with a rapidity far greater even than that, signal as it was, with which it has been acquired."

The main object of Sir George is to counteract the strange and dangerous doctrines set forth in Mr. Lindsay's pamphlet, which we noticed last month; and he expresses his deep regret that the direct aim of that gentleman should be " to recommend to his Majesty's Government to involve this country in immediate and extensive hostilities with China; and that he has thus given the respectable sanction of his name to the wild and desperate project of attempting, and that without any new ground or provocation, ' to coerce by a direct armed interference the Chinese empire, with its countless millions of inhabitants.' "

The " infatuation," which could make an individual, who is returning to China as a merchant, and desirous of " insuring peace and tranquillity," and " establishing confidence in commercial affairs," dream of blockading a thousand miles of coast, " annihilating all vestiges of a naval force" there, with a line-of-battle ship, two frigates, and six corvettes ; of " capturing thousands of native merchant vessels," starving millions of the population of the maritime provinces, and reducing the merchants to beggary, as the means of *conciliating* the people,—is well exposed by Sir George Staunton.

According to Mr. Lindsay's own shewing, the prospects of the enterprize are considered by Sir George as "not very encouraging." He next inquires into the nature of that "intolerable pressure,"—that " overwhelming necessity,"—which is "to compel us to have recourse to these hostile operations against a friendly power, with which, for upwards of a hundred years, we have carried on a most beneficial commercial intercourse." The six topics of grievance are enumerated in our notice of the pamphlet; and with respect to "opprobrious epithets," Sir George remarks that " it must be obvious, that these must be wholly unworthy of notice, as a matter of formal complaint, except so far as they may be introduced into official documents; and I think," he adds, "I shall be able to show, hereafter, that the most prominent instances of offensive language imputed to such documents, are to be ascribed either to a very highly-coloured or absolutely false translation." As to the rest (excepting that which relates to the law of homicide, a matter involving peculiar considerations), he observes, that "to denominate these ' grievances,' which would justify the employment of an ' armed interference ' for their redress, appears to me an utter perversion of language, and to be wholly inconsistent with any interpretation of the law of nations, with which I am acquainted."

With respect to the affair of Lord Napier,—the conduct of the Chinese towards whom, Mr. Lindsay thinks, affords " perhaps, the strongest grounds for resentment which they have ever given,"—Sir George Staunton shows that this " strongest ground" is, in fact, " no ground at all ; but that, on the contrary, we were, in a national point of view, totally and entirely in the wrong in all our proceedings upon that occasion." And we shall cite this part of the pamphlet fully, because it confirms the accuracy of the views we took of that unfortunate affair, as soon as it was known in this country.

What are the simple facts of the case? It is perfectly notorious to all persons connected with the China Trade, and Lord Napier could not be ignorant of the fact, as he had persons of the greatest local experience and information joined with him in his commission, that no foreigners of any description have ever been permitted by the Chinese government to establish themselves at Canton except in strictly a commercial character; and that, moreover, no person, even if habitually resident at Canton in such commercial character, was permitted to visit that city from Macao, without previously obtaining a certain license or passport. It does not signify that these regulations were often disregarded, and the infractions connived at by the Chinese authorities, in cases of little moment, and which did not necessarily come, in any way, under the cognizance of the government. This, however, was notoriously the *law;* and, in a case of so much publicity and importance as the arrival of a public officer, claiming important rights and privileges, connivance at any infraction was obviously impossible. I fearlessly ask, then, what right or pretext had Lord Napier to signalize his first appearance in China by a violation of the known and acknowledged regulations of the country? There were, no doubt, ample public grounds to justify our government in appointing a superintendent of trade to reside in that official character at Canton; and, if the motives of the appointment had been previously submitted to the proper authorities, in due form, and their sanction requested (as would have undoubtedly been done in the event of sending a superintendent of trade, or consul, for the first time, to any port of Europe), either the point would have been gained, or at least a plausible pretext for complaint established. But not only was this previous sanction not applied for, but Lord Napier did not even bring with him any kind of official document from his own government, addressed to the authorities of China, for the purpose of in any manner authenticating and explaining the nature of his appointment. The Chinese authorities had absolutely no voucher from him but his own *ipse dixit,*—the *ipse dixit* of an individual, whose first act within the Chinese territories was a violation of its laws! Mr. Lindsay admits that "Lord Napier may have acted in some respects injudiciously;" but the fact is, that a far greater share of the blame appears to lie with his lordship's instructions, than with himself. He seems to have been simply instructed to proceed direct to Canton, and to assume at once his official character there, without the least anticipation of difficulty or discussion, just in the same way as a successor would have been appointed to any vacant consulship in Europe.

Sir George considers this a point of some importance, as the "hinge upon which the whole question turns in a national point of view;" and he cites, with superfluous caution, we think, a passage from the *Lex Mercatoria* of Beawes, who lays it down that "those potentates, with whom we have no commercial treaties, stipulating the appointment of a consul," and there is no other office more analogous to that of *superintendent of trade,* " may not only refuse the person, but the commission itself, without violation of the peace and amity subsisting between the powers so refusing and this country; for the law of nations does not include this appointment." Sir George adds:

The Chinese authorities acted upon this occasion as I apprehend those of any other nation would have done, under similar circumstances. They ordered him away to Macao; directing him to apply for permission to come up to Canton from thence in the usual way. The Chinese would certainly have been, what we are too apt to consider them to be, the most contemptible nation upon earth, if they had permitted such a violation of their laws, not only to pass with impunity, but to reap all the fruits of a victory! Lord Napier resists—declares he will not quit Canton, except at the point of the bayonet—and orders, or at least invites, the captains of two of his Majesty's frigates to bring their ships up the river, in order to give him assistance and protection;—another illegal act, which was only accomplished by forcing the Chinese batteries, and by a smart engagement with them, in the course of which several individuals on both sides were killed or wounded. All this was done without any actual need of either their assistance or their protection. Lord Napier was perfectly safe—his person was not threatened—he had only to go away, and return from whence he came. The object, therefore, neither was nor could have been any other than that of aiding him in his resistance to the orders of the government.

Let us for a moment make the case our own: let us suppose a couple of French frigates forcing their way up the Thames, and battering down Tilbury fort, in order to aid and assist the French ambassador in his negociations in Portland-place; and we may then form some notion of what the feelings of the Chinese are likely to have been at the storming of the forts of the Bocca Tigris! Or let us suppose a British consul landing at some French port, where no consul had ever been allowed, without even a passport; and then, after having been ordered away by the constituted authorities, setting them at defiance, and declaring he would not stir but at the point of the bayonet. Would not his speedy removal to a comfortable asylum in the public prison be the inevitable result?

Nevertheless, even now, no personal violence was offered to Lord Napier. After matters had come to such a crisis, that he was himself convinced of the necessity of a surrender, the whole amount of the outrage of which he had to complain, under circumstances, I must contend, of very great provocation, was his detention in the Chinese boat, in which he had consented to embark, (as a sort of hostage apparently) until certain information was received that the men-of-war had retired from the river. This act would have been justly characterized, had it occurred under ordinary circumstances, as an insult. Mr. Lindsay calls it "treacherous," and no doubt it was so, as far as the intention of detaining Lord Napier as a hostage had not been previously avowed; but it could hardly be called a "violation of the solemn assurances of a safe conduct." This detention very probably so far aggravated his sufferings from previous illness and anxiety of mind at an unhealthy season, that, as Mr. Lindsay observes, it may "be justly considered to have hastened, if not caused, his death."

No man can entertain a higher personal respect for the memory of Lord Napier than I do, or more deeply deplore the melancholy and unhappy result of his mission; but, when viewing the question exclusively in a political light, and with reference only to the political measures it ought to suggest to us, we must not suffer ourselves to be carried away by personal feeling, or misled by the high colouring of facts which those feelings would naturally lead to, especially at the moment. I do not find that any of the annoyances, to which he was actually subjected, were such as would have been considered by any individual in health worthy of serious notice, or such as he would have himself considered, had he happily recovered, matter for a formal complaint.

I think I have pretty well established that the case of Lord Napier is not a tenable position in argument against the Chinese; and that, considering how easily our claims for reparation might be met, by far stronger claims for reparation on their side, for forts dismantled, and troops killed in their defence, besides sundry smaller violations of their laws and territory, it will be our wisest course, even if on other accounts involved in negociations with the Chinese, to suffer this portion of the history of our transactions with them to remain in oblivion.

Sir George Staunton concurs in Mr. Lindsay's proposal (with some modification in detail), to withdraw his Majesty's commissioners, and to send out " a person of no pretensions " as agent for the customs; but Sir George is also of opinion that a third embassy to China, on a judicious plan and in very skilful hands, with the co-operation of the British commercial community at Canton, might succeed: and this opinion we have always entertained and expressed.

Sir George has touched upon the much-talked-of epithet of " barbarian," said to be applied offensively to Europeans, and which constitutes one of Mr. Lindsay's " grievances;" and he pronounces it " not a correct translation." Here again, as the opinion of this profound Chinese scholar coincides with that which we have all along declared, we cite the passage:

With respect to the term *E*, which has been translated ' Barbarian,' I am far from undertaking to say that it is the most honourable one that might have been employed to denote foreigners; and I shall consider it a symptom of the existence of a better feeling towards us in China, whenever it shall be abandoned, and a more honourable one substituted for it. I only contend that it is wrong to give it a directly vituperative sense; and that, as the practice of thus giving the most offensive sense to such words, naturally tends to widen the breach between us and the Chinese, I think the sooner it is abandoned the better. Mr. Lindsay complains that the Quarterly Reviewer has misrepresented him; but he only quoted his own words when he says that he had admitted that " some distinguished Chinese scholars have hesitated in their opinion, whether the term could be justly objected to by us." Among these distinguished Chinese scholars must be reckoned the late Dr. Morrison himself, though the reviewer erroneously concedes the weight of his opinion to be in the opposite scale; for the word *E* is thus explained in his dictionary:— " Foreigners in the East;—foreigners generally; the character *E* being formed of *ta*, ' great,' and *kong*, ' a bow,' in allusion to the *great bows* used by foreigners in the East. *E-jin*, ' a foreigner:' *E-chuen*, ' a foreign ship.' "—Vol. i. p. 131. Various other meanings follow; but not one which justifies, in the smallest degree, the interpretation of " barbarous," or " barbarian." In defence of the latter interpretation of the word *E*, Mr. Lindsay says he could quote numerous passages from Confucius. Now, although the Chinese are certainly not a very *changeable* race, yet to undertake to justify a translation of a word in modern usage by the sense in which it is supposed to have been employed by an author who flourished more than 2,000 years ago, is placing rather too great confidence in Chinese immutability. But what, after all, does Confucius say, according to Mr. Lindsay?—that the term *E* " denotes those *out of the pale of the Chinese empire*, and is used *almost* always in a derogatory sense." I might, therefore, contend, even on the authority of Confucius, that "foreigner" is the preferable word. "Barbarian" is *never* used by us in the sense of "out of the pale of the empire;" and not *almost always*, but *always*, in a derogatory sense.

I cannot omit here also. to protest against the nonsensical phrase " barbarian eye." The Chinese word, here translated 'eye,' is thus explained in Dr. Morrison's dictionary :—" *Moo* or *muh*, 'the eye;' that which directs—the head or principal person." Now it is quite obvious that, when this epithet was applied to Lord Napier, the *third*, and not the *first*, of these senses was intended ; and that, therefore, in point of fact, his title of " foreign superintendent" was very fairly translated. It is very difficult, therefore, to discover any adequate reason for employing the phrase "barbarian eye," which has been so much ridiculed and animadverted upon, except that of exaggerating the offensive and ungracious character of the document in which it appeared. I will not, however, impute to the translator any such intention, but merely observe, that this plan of translating, as it were, in "caricature," may be very harmless, as long as it is confined to cases in which it merely excites a laugh at Chinese ignorance or absurdity ; but when it has the effect of producing or increasing ill-blood between our merchants and the authorities of the country, and inflaming their minds with indignation at imagined insults, which nothing but the sword and the bayonet can expiate, it cannot be too severely reprobated. It is unfortunately but too true that the Chinese have often recourse to offensive and insulting phraseology in speaking of foreigners ; and I am no advocate for dissembling the fact when it really occurs : but the phrase " barbarian eye" appears to me as false to the letter, as it is to the spirit of the original.

Under the sanction of these remarks, we venture to express our astonishment that the execrable style in which Chinese documents are translated should have been tolerated so long. The Chinese-English jargon, which is employed to give an appearance, we suppose, of literal rendering, if it could be appreciated by the scholars of China, would justify their application of the term *E* thereto, in its most offensive sense. Why should Chinese official papers be differently rendered from those of European states ? In our Journal for March 1835,* the reader will find a version in decent English of Governor Loo's celebrated edict respecting Lord Napier, in which the language alone is changed, not a single new idea being interpolated; and he will be surprised at the sense and dignity which that state-paper discovers.†

We had intended to devote a few pages to the examination of Mr. Matheson's work, which is a far more respectable production than Mr. Lindsay's ; he is tolerably successful in scraping together proofs on *one side* of

* Vol. xvi., p. 150.

† The *Chinese Repository*, a work which would not lessen its usefulness or its respectability (considering that it is edited by a missionary and publ'shed under the auspices of a missionary society), if it abstained from controversial politics altogether, has sneered at this version, though without denying its accuracy. The conductor of that work may, perhaps, thank us for informing him that we never suffer topics to be treated editorially by persons who have any interest therein : this information may save him from the sin of uncharitable insinuation in future.

the question. Whilst we were engaged in its perusal, however, we received the subjoined letter from a correspondent, who, though anonymous, proves himself thoroughly conversant with the subject: in his hands, therefore, we leave Mr. Matheson.

Sir :—Mr Matheson, a gentleman long connected with the trade with the Chinese, as a private merchant, has lately published a book under the title of "Present Position and Prospects of the British Trade with China." He commences by giving the following description of the foreign policy of the Chinese, which, with one exception, is, no doubt, substantially correct :

" They permit to Europeans no intercourse but of a commercial character, and that only of the *scantiest* and most ungracious description—restricted to the veriest outposts and confines of the empire. Foreign trade receives no support from the Government; it is barely tolerated; for it is always at variance with that jealous policy which draws a line of perpetual demarkation between China and the rest of the world "—p. 2. The permission which we enjoy to trade with the Chinese may be *ungracious*, but it certainly cannot be termed *scanty ;* since it appears from Mr. Matheson's own appendix, that the value of the British imports to China, in the last year in which the accounts were made up, exceeded *twenty millions of dollars*, and that the exports fell little short of that amount. He states also, very truly (p. 32), that this trade "supplies an article of indispensable use to our population, and an almost indispensable source of revenue to our government, involving the fortunes, and even livelihood, of hundreds of thousands of persons." So valuable is this trade to us, that Mr. Matheson describes the abrupt suspension of it, for a month or two, as absolutely *ruinous.*—p. 6.

Mr. Matheson complains (p. 45) that this trade is " bowed down with the most grievous and increasing exactions;" and there can be no doubt that it is subjected to many very unpleasant and objectionable exactions: but, even under all these disadvantages, it is extremely beneficial and valuable to England; and, as the Chinese cannot be ignorant of this fact, it is not very surprising that they should sometimes reply to our complaints in the manner thus stated by Mr. Matheson :—" If they (the English) dislike the restraints imposed by the orders of government, and consider their own private affairs to be disadvantageous, they may entirely withdraw from the trade, and not trouble themselves to come from a great distance, through many countries of different languages."—p. 12.

In the same spirit, the Chinese appear to have replied very plausibly to a complaint which had been made respecting certain "insulting proclamations suspended against the Company's hong." They said, " It has been stuck up against the Company's hong for *more than thirty years ;*" why did they (the English) not " early indulge their anger," and " cease to come ?"—p. 20.

I am certainly somewhat surprised to find it distinctly and unequivocally admitted, by so avowed an opponent of the Company as Mr Matheson, that the *real* cause why our grievances in China, which we had previously found it convenient to tolerate for centuries (p. 50), had become all at once *insupportable*, is no other than *the abolition of the East-India Company's monopoly !* He observes, " That our intercourse with China has continued in a comparatively prosperous condition, under the management of the East-India Company, is to be attributed solely to the judgment and firmness *occasionally* displayed by the resident representatives of the Company."—p. 24. Again he says, " When these interruptions (collisions and stoppages of trade) occurred during the East-India Company's monopoly, their united influence and capital enabled them sometimes to make a stand against the Chinese, and to sustain the heavy commercial losses attendant on the struggle. Widely different, however, would be the case under present circumstances : when the free-traders, pursuing each his separate and disunited view, and having no common head recognised by the Chinese, must fall a sacrifice, in detail, to their well-combined machinations."—p. 55. And, lastly, " Having seen fit recently to alter altogether our system of commercial intercourse with China,—a measure which must be presumed to have been thoroughly and wisely considered before it was adopted,—we shall become the laughing-stock of the world, if the direct effect of our elaborate legislation be, either to shut us out altogether from China, or place our intercourse upon an infinitely more precarious, oppressive, and ignominious footing than ever : as will infallibly be the result, if we be not now fully alive to the nature of our claims upon China, and prepared to assert them with resolution and vigour."—p. 51.

The scheme, by which the pernicious consequences, which it is thus declared would *infallibly result* from the abolition of the monopoly, are to be *averted*, and our legislation in that respect is to be *saved* from becoming the *laughing-stock of the world*, appears to be the following one :

" It is submitted that his Majesty's Government would act wisely in adopting the suggestions of the present Canton merchants, who—humbly pray, that an ambassador be directed to proceed to a convenient station on the eastern coast of China, as near to the capital of the country as might be found expedient, in one of his Majesty's ships of the line, attended by a sufficient maritime force, which,—they are of opinion need not consist of more than two frigates, and three or four armed vessels of light draft, together with a steam-vessel, all fully manned—and that he might be thus placed in a position to demand the reparations and concessions above suggested."—p. 74.

These had been thus described : " we desire him (the emperor of China) to drop for ever the arrogant and offensive language so long adopted by himself and his ministers, in speaking of the King of Great Britain and his subjects ; to give reparation for the fatal insults offered to Lord Napier, and to the national honour, in firing at her flag ; as well as remuneration for the losses we sustained by the detention of our ships during the stoppage of our trade on that occasion ; to extend to our fellow-subjects at Canton the full protection of the Chinese laws ; to forbid the longer infliction by the local authorities of the intolerable indignities and impositions under which our traders have so long suffered, and to accede to commercial arrangements that may be reasonable and mutually beneficial. This is the short sum of all that it is desired our government should demand from that of China."—p. 71.

It is difficult to restrain a smile at the propositions which this *little armament* is to enforce ; the concession of which, it is easy to shew, nothing but the most abject submission of the vast empire of China to the terror of our arms, and the reduction of its emperor to much the same position as that which the Great Mogul at present has the honour of holding under our protection at Delhi, could possibly be expected to extort from them. For, however reasonable *some* of the propositions may be, is there any nation in the world, having the smallest shadow of independence left, that would submit to them in the aggregate? Take one of the propositions, by way of an example. We force a passage between their forts, up one of their principal rivers ; and, upon being resisted, we nearly demolish their forts, killing several of the garrison who defended them; and, after this violent and most inexcusable aggression, instead of coming forward with any explanation or apology, we have the unblushing effrontery to call upon the poor defeated Chinese to make reparation for having presumed to resist us, and for having fired on our national flag !

As to desiring the emperor of China to drop for ever his arrogant and offensive language; we might almost as well call upon the poor emperor to drop the Chinese language altogether, and to speak and write in future in English ! for the spirit of *supreme and universal dominion*, however absurd it may be, is so incorporated in all their state phraseology, that I doubt whether even a single word of it could be retained, that might not be construed into an offence. Arrogant, however, as the emperor of China's language may be, he never went quite the length of calling himself "king of England," as our sovereign for centuries called himself "king of France;" and yet France, high-spirited as she is, tolerated this insult, and never went to war with us, in order to compel us to renounce the title !

It is mentioned, p. 78, "that the whole expense of the immense preparations recently made by the local government to oppose the expected advance towards Canton, of his Majesty's frigates, after they had passed the Bogue, has been extorted from the hong merchants." This seems hard; but it must be remembered that these hong merchants enjoy, by favour of the state, the exclusive profits of the trade; and that it is, therefore, not quite so unreasonable to make them bear the burthens arising out of it, such as the armament in question might be fairly considered. We act precisely upon the same principle in this country, when we call upon the East-India Company to defray, in certain cases, a portion of the charge of his Majesty's navy.

Much is said by Mr. Matheson about the English ladies not being allowed to visit Canton. "The laws of nature are outraged—for their wives are separated from their husbands and compelled to reside eighty miles off, at Macao— an insult perfectly gratuitous."—p. 49. "Is it not revolting to common sense and common humanity, to think that the mere appearance of an English lady at Canton, should have led to the most alarming and protracted misunderstandings?"—p. 66. This seems very hard and very absurd; but when we reflect a little, and recollect that the Chinese know very well, that we commenced at Calcutta, as well as at Canton, with nothing but a *factory*, but ended in the former case by the conquest of the whole country, it is not quite so unnatural in the Chinese to act upon the principle of *obsta principiis*, and accordingly to insist that our *factories* should be limited to their *original purposes*, and not allowed to be made *domiciles for our wives and families*.

Mr. Matheson has inserted, p. 109, a translation of a singular imperial edict, on the subject of the failure of Lord Napier's mission; in which the emperor expresses a suspicion that the conduct of "Lord Napier, and others, disobeying the national laws, and bringing forces into the inner river," might be "owing to the numerous extortions of the Canton native merchants." It is, in fact, a part of the refined and artful policy of the Chinese system of government, to impute, in *every case of disturbance*, a share of the blame to its own officers and people. The power that foreigners derive from this circumstance, if *at any time* implicating the local authorities, to a certain degree, with their superiors, has sometimes been wielded by the servants of the Company with great advantage; but it obviously must be exercised with moderation and discretion; and under the guidance of that intimate knowledge of the character and feelings of this singular people, which nothing but mature experience can supply.

London, April 15th, 1836.   I am, &c.   SINENSIS.

THE FAY AND THE PERI.

The Peri.

Beautiful spirit, come with me
Over the blue enchanted sea:
Morn and evening thou can'st play
In my garden, where the breeze
Warbles through the golden trees;
No shadow falls upon the day:
There thy mother's arms await
Her cherish'd infant at the gate.

Of Peris I the loveliest far—
My sisters near the morning-star,
In ever-youthful bloom abide;
But pale their lustre by my side—
A silken turban wreathes my head,
Rubies on my arms are spread,
While sailing slowly through the sky,
By the up-looker's dazzled eye,
Are seen my wings of purple hue,
Glittering with Elysian dew.

Whiter than a far-off sail
My form of beauty glows,
Fair as on a summer night
Dawns the Sleep-Star's balmy light;
And fragrant as the early rose
That scents the green Arabian vale,
Soothing the pilgrim as he goes.

The Fay.

Beautiful Infant (said the Fay)
In the region of the Sun
I dwell, where in a rich array
The clouds encircle the king of day,
His radiant journey done.

My wings are golden of glorious sheen,
As oft on amorous poet's strain,
Glimmer at night, when meadows green
Sparkle with the perfumed rain,
While the Sun goes and comes again.
And clear my hand, as stream that flows;
And sweet my breath, as airs of May;
And o'er my ivory shoulders stray
Locks of sunshine;—music creeps
From my odorous lips of rose.

Follow! follow! I have caves
Of pearl beneath the azure waves,
And tents all woven pleasantly
In verdant glades of Faery.
Come, beloved child, with me,

And I will bear thee to the bowers
Where clouds are painted o'er like flowers,
And pour into thy charmed ear
Songs a mortal cannot hear;
Harmonies so sweet and ripe,
As no inspired Shepherd's pipe
Ere breathed into Arcadian glen,
Far from the busy haunts of men.

The Peri.

My home is afar in the bright Orient,
Where the Sun, like a king, in his purple tent,
Reigneth for ever in gorgeous pride—
So wafting the prince of a rich countrèe
 To the soft flute's melody,
A golden vessel is seen to glide,
Kindling the water by its side.

Vast cities are mine of power and delight,
Lahore with its flowers, Golconda, Cashmere;
And Ispahan, dear to the pilgrim's sight;
And Bagdad, whose towers to heaven uprear;
 Halep that pours on the startled ear,
From its busy marts the gathering roar,
As of ocean beating at night on the shore.

Mysore is a queen on her stately throne,
Thy white domes, Medina, gleam on the eye,—
Thy radiant kiosks with their arrowy spires,
Shooting afar their golden fires
 Into the flashing sky,—
Like a forest of spears that startle the gaze
Of the enemy with the vivid blaze.

Come then, beautiful child, with me,
Come to the bowers of Araby,
To the land of the date and the purple vine,
Where Pleasure her rosy wreaths doth twine,
 And Gladness shall be always thine;
Singing at night beside thy bed,
Scattering flowers under thy head.

Beneath a verdant tent of leaves,
Arching the flowery carpet o'er,
Thou shalt hear the pipe on summer-eves
Its lay of rustic music pour—
 While, upon the grassy floor,
Light footsteps, in the hour of calm,
Darken the shadow of the palm.

The Fay.

Come to the radiant homes of the Blest,
Where meadow, and fountain, in light are drest,
And the bowers of verdure never decay,
And the glow of the summer dies not away.

Come where the autumn-winds never can sweep,
And the streams of the forest sing thee to sleep,
Like a fond sister charming the eyes of a brother;
Or a little one lulled on the breast of its mother.

Beautiful, beautiful! hasten to me!
Coloured with purple thy wings shall be;
Flowers that fade not thy forehead shall twine,
Over thee, sunlight, that sets not, shall shine.

The infant listened to the strain,
Now here, now there, its thoughts were driven—
But the Fay and the Peri waited in vain—
The child hath flown to Heaven.

EGYPTIAN HIEROGLYPHICS.

M. CHAMPOLLION'S GRAMMAIRE EGYPTIENNE.

THE extension which the late M. Champollion gave to the discoveries of Dr.
Young in Egyptian cryptography, created a vivid curiosity to learn the exact
principles of his system of interpretation, which he never expounded in his
life-time, but which he was supposed to have developed in his grammar, which
is now publishing as a posthumous work. We happened to have been amongst
the few who doubted from the beginning the truth of M. Champollion's theory,
and the authenticity of the interpretations he professed to give of hieroglyphical texts. The chief grounds of our distrust were, first, the apparent impossibility of testing their accuracy, owing to our ignorance of the intermediate
language into which the signs, symbolic or phonetic, were translated; and,
secondly, from the suspicious shyness of M. Champollion of trying his theory
by such imperfect tests as were accessible. The objections to the system are
detailed in an article in a preceding volume,* which was written by the late
M. Klaproth, and more fully in a work by that profound linguist, entitled
Examen Critique des Travaux de feu M. Champollion, sur les Hiéroglyphes.

The *Grammaire Egyptienne* has been recently subjected to an acute and
skilful criticism by Dr. Dujardin, of Paris, who has devoted much time and
attention to the subject of hieroglyphics, and is an excellent Coptic scholar,
in some consecutive numbers of a Paris scientific paper.† Two of these papers
are anonymous; but, from internal evidence, we shall probably not err in ascribing them all to his pen.

In his first article, he expresses himself as follows:

" The publication of M. Champollion's *Grammaire Egyptienne* has thrown
me into a strange perplexity. I fancied that I was preparing myself advantageously for penetrating this sanctuary, by replenishing my memory with the
contents of Coptic books, and of the grammars and dictionaries which are to
be met with in our libraries. I had some reason for indulging this notion, though,
unhappily, it has proved completely fallacious. M. Etienne Quatremère had
informed me, in his researches into the literature of Egypt, that, according to
the opinions of most scholars, the Coptic version of the Scriptures existed in
the second century of the Christian era; it would, therefore, follow that this
version would supply us with the language spoken in Egypt at the period of

---

* Vol. vi. p. 273.   † *L'Echo du Monde Savant*, for March 3, 10, 17, and 24.

the Antonines; and the researches of M. Latronne demonstrated to me, very
satisfactorily, that Egyptian monuments were erected at that date, and decorated with hieroglyphical legends, like those on the most ancient monuments.
' The Egyptians,' he observes, ' repaired the temples of their gods, completed
or decorated them, and even built new ones, at least down to the end of the
second century of our era; and these works were executed in a style of architecture and sculpture very like the antecedent style; so much so, that the
difference was perceptible only by the experienced eye of an artist.' In fact,
it results, beyond all doubt, from the inscriptions restored by this able archæo-
logist, that the great temple of Denderah was decorated under Tiberius, and
that of Esneh, under Claudius; and that all the sculptures of the pronaos, as
well as the zodiac, of the little temple of Esneh, must have been traced in the
early part of the second century of our era.

" When M. Champollion, after reading on the monuments referred to the
names of different Roman emperors, such as Tiberius, Claudius, Adrian, and
Antoninus, declared that, applying the same method of reading to the texts in
which these names were contained, he had succeeded in reading at least three-
fourths of each inscription, I was naturally led to think that the result of
these readings could be nothing else than phrases belonging to the Egyptian
tongue of the early ages of the Christian era, contained in the Coptic version
the Bible. If I fell into an error, it is undoubtedly an excusable one, and
others have erred with me; for example, M. Peyron and Mr. Tattam. The
former, in the arrangement of his dictionary, has sacrificed the customary, and
most convenient order, with the only view of rendering his work more adapted
to facilitate the reading of hieroglyphical legends. Mr. Tattam, without abandoning the ordinary alphabetical arrangement, has indicated at the commencement of each letter the different homophonous characters which correspond to
it in the system of M. Champollion. These two gentlemen must, therefore,
have been deceived as well as I; for it is incongruous to suppose that they
knew at the time of what little utility their labours would prove towards the
reading of hieroglyphical legends according to the principles of the new
method.

" I will not insist upon the ill success which has attended my attempts to
apply this method; because it will be said, with reason, that the inexpertness
of the student proves nothing against its principles; but I may state that I
have endeavoured to compare the results obtained by the master with this
Coptic language with which I had stored my head. Most assuredly, after
M. Champollion affirmed that, in the hieroglyphical texts, may be found most
of the words of the Egyptian language transcribed in phonetic signs, and
differing from those very words written in Greek letters, in Coptic texts, only
in the absence or position of certain vowels,—after hearing this, I was far from
looking for the misadventure I have experienced. True it is, I have, in the first
place, met with a table containing a number of words, all of them, or nearly
all, Coptic, placed in correspondence with isolated groupes, which, by means
of the new method, may be read in the same manner. In the next place, other
tables of the same kind, in which the phonetic name is followed by the form of
the object expressed, or by some peculiar sign, which the author calls *deter-
minative*. If to these lists of indications had been added the inscriptions
from whence the groupes were taken, and proof that, in those inscriptions,
the groupes in question have the sense attributed to them by M. Champollion's
reading, such tables might prove something. M. Champollion has signs for all
the Coptic articulations; it would, therefore, be by no means difficult to draw

up a complete Coptic dictionary by means of his alphabet. The only result to be drawn from these tables is, that when we choose to take the trouble, we may substitute for the Coptic letters signs which have, or to which are attributed, the same value. I do not mean to assert that the groupes adduced by M. Champollion have been made up for the purpose of the new method; but what is requisite to be shewn is, that they have the sense which M. Champollion's method of lecture ascribes to them in the places where they occur. Another consequence seems to me, however, likely also to result from the tables, which is, that the author regards the words of our Coptic dictionaries as necessarily to be read in the hieroglyphical inscriptions; but there is not a single one of the phrases employed as examples in the work, which does not show that such an inference would prove an egregious mistake. M. Champollion tells us that the language read by his method is *antique* Egyptian. This *antique* Egyptian is read on the monuments of the Pharaohs, or those of the Ptolemys, in the Rosetta inscription, and on the monuments of the Roman era. Hieroglyphics were read in *antique* Egyptian at the very period when the Coptic which now remains was spoken. Moreover, in order not to deprive himself of the only possible demonstration of his new method, M. Champollion is careful to notice, that between the *antique* Egyptian and the Coptic, which were spoken simultaneously, there is no *essential* difference. He, therefore, assumes the Coptic language as the term of comparison; and this is the way he establishes his system:—

" ' My alphabet, resulting from the reading of proper names, is equally applicable to all hieroglyphical texts, which are three parts or less phonetic; in short, to cite only terms most frequently employed, 'God' is *noute* in the language of the second century of our era; well! my method gives *nter*; 'king' is *pourro, perro;* my method gives *souten* or *hik;* 'father' is *iôt;* my method gives *tfe, etf, tye:* and here occurs a circumstance which is peculiar to the antique Egyptian, namely, that *y* is never preceded by a consonant in Coptic words. 'Son' is *schere, schire;* my method gives *se,* or *si;* 'old' is *phello;* my method gives *oéri;* 'soul' is *pahe;* my method gives *pbai;* 'discourse' is *pschage;* my method gives *got* or *gt;* 'to be veracious' is *geme;* my method gives *metaue;* here again is a peculiarity in the antique Egyptian, which is that, in a compound word, the verb is placed after its case, which never occurs in Coptic words. I might here go on to cite a multitude of other resemblances of a like nature. You see, then, that my method of lecture is admirable; and if you observe a few differences between the words read by my method and those in the Egyptian language of the second century, there is nothing *essential* in these variations.'

" Here I must pause a little, to take breath; for one cannot assent to such a kind of demonstration at once, and with perfect ease. If such a mode of reasoning is allowed, I must frankly confess, that it might be demonstrated that there is no *essential* difference between black and white.

" As I have already observed, that not one of the examples adduced by M. Champollion sanctions the belief that he had intended to read the hieroglyphical legends by means of the Egyptian language of the second century of our era, I am bound in conscience to make one or two quotations, which are taken at random. The phrase 'and to other gods of this temple,' on the pronaos of the temple of Esneh, decorated under the Emperor Claudius, reads in antique Egyptian, *hr chet nter nerpe pen;* in the Egyptian language of the second century, it reads: *men enkenoute empeierpe pai.* Observe, that the word 'erpe,' common to the two, is not read according to the phonetic method, but taken from a Coptic dictionary and placed under a mute symbol. Another example is from the same temple of Esneh: '*psi mai oéri tfe nnentr*,' which, read by the new method, signifies, in antique Egyptian, ' the beloved son, the eldest of the father of the gods ;' in the Egyptian language of the second century this could be expressed no otherwise than by *pschere emmerit pscherpemmise entepeiôt ennenoute*. Lastly, not to cite from one end of the book to the other, the skilful inventor of the new method read on the palace of Kurnah, at Thebes, this phrase: *get ennentr enpsensi*, which signifies, he says, in antique Egyptian, ' discourse made by the gods to their son,' which cannot be expressed in Coptic in any other way than this: *pschage ennenoute ha pouschere*.

" Whoever has opened a Coptic book will ask himself what this new, this really new language can be, in which are mixed and confounded together words borrowed indifferently from the Thebaic, the Memphitic, and the Bashmuric dialects. For my own part, after incurring great expense and great loss of time, and turning over all that remains in the Coptic tongue, I now run my head against the *antique* Egyptian, which, verily, is new indeed !"

In a subsequent article, to which M. Dujardin has appended his name, he examines the *Grammaire* with rigour, and with some pleasantry, but without unnecessary asperity ; and we may remark that the complaint made by one of M. Champollion's admirers, in the *Echo*, of the " more than vivacious attacks upon an *illustration* that does honour to France," is neither reasonable in itself nor complimentary to the author of the Egyptian grammar. " We can readily conceive," says M. Dujardin, " that our correspondent (the writer of the preceding letter) must have been sadly disappointed when he sought the key of the new method in the grammars of Tuki, Valperga and Scholtz, in the grammar and dictionary of Mr. Tattam, as well as in the dictionaries of Lacroze and M. Peyron. But, my dear Sir, the books you unfortunately opened are the most determined adversaries,—the most cruel enemies,—of the work of our illustrious antiquary. You will have pretty work, indeed, in comparing Coptic words with those of antique Egyptian, Coptic phrases with phrases of the sacred language. What does this prove ? That the difference between the two tongues is great,—vast if you please,—I must admit; but that is all. You will have to conclude that the antique Egyptian must have been spoken at the same time as that of the Coptic books, and that the latter has nothing to do with the new method. M. Champollion, being unable to find all at once a complete glossary of the sacred tongue, termed the antique Egyptian, and being unwilling to leave the translation of the examples he cited, incomplete, was obliged to borrow a little from the Coptic language, to employ it as an auxiliary, when the texts, becoming symbolical, no longer allowed of his method of lecture : but he made those loans with so affected a *negligence*, and so manifest a disdain of the simplest rules of this tongue, that one cannot suspect any secret design. M. Champollion knew the Coptic ; he knew it perfectly, there can be no doubt; but he seems to say, at every line of his book : you perceive that the Coptic language is here but a kind of out-work ; it is but a mere redundancy in the edifice I have raised; if I make any use of it at all, it is in order not to shock those who are still prejudiced in favour of the Coptic tongue : but you see in what manner I employ it.

" Throughout M. Champollion's book, in fact, you will constantly find the plural indeterminate article of the Memphitic dialect, *han*, associated with the plural of the Thebaic dialect, and followed or preceded by a noun of number, which Coptic syntax does not admit any more than ours. In every page will be found, under a symbol which appears to express the idea of *totality*, the word *nib* preferred, I know not why, to *nim* of the Thebaic dialect, and to *niben* of the Memphitic, and clapped to a substantive which precedes a simple or possessive article, and it will also be found employed absolutely, whereas the Coptic admits of neither. The words *go*, 'head,' *rat*, 'foot,' *ro*, 'mouth,' never appear but with simple or possessive articles : *petro*, 'thy mouth ;' *netrat*, 'thy feet ;' *ensengo*, 'their heads ;' whereas, in Coptic books, the same words admit of terminations only ; such as *rof*, 'his mouth ;' *gos*, 'his head ;' *ratou*, 'their feet.' I may add that the possessive articles *pet, net, ensen*, are altogether foreign to the Coptic language, and belong only to the antique Egyptian."

Dr. Dujardin then points out instances of words distorted from their true meaning ; of arbitrary changes of gender and even of parts of speech (adjectives being used as verbs), of false compounds, &c.

In another article, he considers the assertion of M. Etienne Quatremère, that the reading of the Pharaonic inscriptions is fortified by irresistible evidence of the following fact,—that the modern Coptic language was that of the ancient subjects of Sesostris.

" This assertion," observes M. Dujardin, " is far from being demonstrated. M. Champollion has endeavoured to apply his method of lecture to the hieroglyphical legends ; but what has been the fruit of his essays ? Numerous monuments, bearing hieroglyphical inscriptions, are scattered throughout the valley of the Nile ; some were covered with their sculptures in the early ages of Christianity ; others are of a date two thousand years anterior to the Roman domination ; the rest occupy the vast interval between these two limits. The whole of these inscriptions, to whatever epoch they belong, have, down to the present day, eluded every attempt at interpretation. What resource have we for deciphering them ? The learned concur in thinking that the Coptic, as we now possess it, was the language spoken in Egypt in the early times of Christianity. If we discard the hypothesis of a sacred language, employed by the sacerdotal caste at the same time that the rest of the people used a vulgar tongue, it is in the rules of the Coptic, and in its vocabularies, that we must necessarily find our starting point, and establish our *point d'appui*, in an attempt to decypher the hieroglyphical legends. Taking into account the differences which possibly exist between the lapidary style and that of books, we must, in the first place, make our new experiments on the most recent monuments,—the temples of Esneh for example,—and if the results shall but so slightly differ from the Coptic as to justify our ascribing the difference to the ellipses of the lapidary style, the method employed will receive a primary demonstration. Passing, in the next place, to monuments of a date a little more remote,—the Rosetta inscription, for example, which carries us back to the Greek domination,—if we obtain results a little further removed from the modern Coptic, without, however, exceeding certain limits, the method will have successfully sustained a second test. In fact, the Egyptian language may very well have undergone, in the interval of several generations, some modifications ; but the difference must not overpass certain limits, otherwise the syntax and the dictionaries of the Coptic will become useless, and we shall be unable to proceed a step further. With respect to the Rosetta inscription, we have a means of verification in the Greek translation placed below the hieroglyphics, which is wanting in the first demonstration. Ascending gradually, step by step, towards the most ancient monuments, by a succession of slight modifications, we may arrive at the interpretation of the inscriptions of the era of Sesostris, and be able to translate with certainty an Egyptian language differing perceptibly from the Coptic, yet not so much as to neutralize its syntax and dictionaries, whereby we should lose the only thread which can guide us.

" The course I have here traced is, in my opinion, the only rational one: such a method, which will reveal to us, from age to age, some slight modifications to be introduced into the grammar and dictionaries of the Coptic language, will be readily admitted. Can it be said that this is M. Champollion's method? Let us see.

" But, before I proceed, I am bound to notice an objection that may be offered; namely, that, as only a third part of the *Grammaire Egyptienne* has yet appeared, but a small portion of the principles of the new method can be disclosed, and how is it possible to form a judgment of a system the exposition of which is incomplete? But the first part of the grammar contains a vast number of examples translated by the author in conformity with his system of principles; these examples are taken from monuments of all ages, as well those of the early ages of Christianity as of the remotest epochs; the relations which may subsist between these translations and the Coptic language of the Scriptures cannot be affected by the publication of the second and third parts, and these relations alone I have proposed to examine.

" I know not whether M. Champollion has proceeded according to chronological order; but I perceive that his readings of the most recent inscriptions differ from the Coptic, *which was in use at the period when they were made,* quite as much as those of the more ancient inscriptions; and this difference is so striking, that, if we reject the Coptic characters, *which alone give the phrases cited an Egyptian aspect,* it would be, I do not say very difficult, but absolutely impossible, to discern the most distant affinity between them and the modern Coptic. The instances are so numerous, that I need adduce no more than those noticed in a former article.

" M. Champollion has, therefore, failed in his attempts to make out the only practicable demonstration, namely, that which the Coptic language ought to furnish. He has fallen into a complete illusion as to the result of his essays, and, persuaded of the certainty of his method, he has forgotten that it must be capable of being demonstrated by practical application, and that, instead of modifying dictionaries by means of his new principles, those principles ought themselves to be firmly established upon our dictionaries.

" Moreover, was the author of the *Grammaire Egyptienne* properly qualified to judge as to the point where the differences between the Egyptian language of the second century and that of preceding ages ought to stop? Of this we may be permitted to doubt when we find (as I have before shewn) that, when he set about translating texts mostly symbolical, with the aid of the Coptic, he paid very little regard to the simplest rules of its syntax. M. Champollion was under a delusion if he thought it needless to study carefully the Coptic, because he did not expect to find it on monuments such as we have it now; since, in the first place, there are inscriptions existing of the second century, and consequently of a period when the Egyptian language we now possess was actually spoken; and secondly, because this language is the only foundation upon which we can safely rest in our endeavours to decypher the inscriptions. What, then, is the result of the whole? Why, that M. Champollion *has completely failed, and that he erroneously persuaded himself that he had arrived at the solution of a problem which yet remains to be resolved.*"

MAY-DAY WITH THE MUSES.

O nursed at happy distance from the cares
Of a too anxious world, mild pastoral muse;
That, to the sparkling crown Urania wears,
And to her sister Clio's laurel wreath,
Preferr'd a garland culled from purple heath,
Or blooming thicket moist with morning dews;
And was it granted to the simple ear
Of thy contented Votary
Such melody to hear?
Him rather suits it, side by side with thee,
Wrapped in a fit of pleasing indolence,
While thy tried lute hangs on the hawthorn tree,
To lie and listen, till o'er-drowsied sense
Sinks, hardly conscious of the influence,
To the soft murmur of the vagrant bee.

Wordsworth's " Vernal Ode."

Once more, once more, beloved May,
I see the beauty of thy feet
Gilding the eastern hills afar,
The summer's Morning Star;
And many a gladdening silver horn,
Unto the opening eyes of morn,
Breathes its welcome clear and sweet,—
While o'er the breezy upland lawn
Glimmers the purple dawn.

Faintly in the dewy grass,
As with lingering step I pass,
'Mid the odorous light and dark
Rustles now the waking lark;
Soon on twinkling wings to rise
Into the gardens of the skies,
With heart-felt pleasure, all day long,
Cheering its pilgrimage of song.

I cannot choose but sit and gaze
Upon thy features, gentle May!
While all the joys of other days
Begin to brighten in thy rays,
That melt the cloud of tears away.
For many a dark and wintry day
My heart hath sigh'd for thee;
While, like a bird upon a tree,
Leafless, barren, drearily,
Waving in the autumn wind—
Hope in silence sat and pined.

But lo! thou comest, and the gloom
Kindles with thy face of bloom;
Winter now is over-past,
Peace and sunshine come at last!
And thoughts,—sweet birds that build their nest
In the poet's vernal breast,
After raging storm and rain,
Begin to trill their notes again.
Then blessings on thee, cheerful May,
Thus I hail thee with my lay!

Miscellanies, Original and Select.

PROCEEDINGS OF SOCIETIES.

Royal Asiatic Society.—At the Meeting on the 16th April, Sir George Staunton, Bart., in the chair, various presents were laid before the Meeting. Professor Horace Hayman Wilson read an Analysis of the *Bráhma Purána*, with introductory Remarks on the Pauranic writings.

Mr. Wilson stated, that, according to the definition of a *Purána* by Sanscrit writers, the collections under that name treated of the creation and renovation of the universe; the divisions of time; the institutes of law and religion; the genealogies of the patriarchal families; and the dynasties of kings. They, therefore, offered a prospect of our penetrating the obscurity in which the Hindu social system had so long been enveloped. They comprised eighteen distinct works, besides several of a similar class called *Upa*, or minor *Puránas*. The former were exceedingly voluminous, comprehending about 400,000 *slokas*, or 16,000,000 lines—a quantity which no single European scholar could expect to peruse with care, even if his whole time were devoted to the task. Besides the obstacles to their examination arising from their extent, a still greater impediment presented itself in scarcely any of them being furnished with a table of contents, or index, and in their not conforming to any given arrangement; so that, to know what any one contained, it was necessary to read the whole of it. The immensity of the labour seemed to have deterred Sanscrit students from the publication or translation of even one or two of the principal *Puránas*, and to the present day not one of them has been made accessible to the English public.

The unsatisfactory nature of the process adopted by Sir William Jones, in examining the *Puránas*, namely, by employing Pundits to make extracts from them, was obvious; because the Pundits themselves were but imperfectly acquainted with the *Puránas*, seldom reading more than one or two of them, the *Bhagavat* and the *Vishnu*, and because it was impossible to know how the passages extracted were modified or illustrated by what preceded or followed them. Besides, not to describe what was wanted, left the Pundit at a loss what to supply; and to indicate a desire to find any particular information, was to tempt him to supply it, even if he fabricated it for the purpose. Colonel Wilford, it is well known, was imposed upon in this way. Extracts from the *Puránas* were, however, as yet the only sources on which any reliance whatever could be placed for accurate accounts of the notions of the Hindus. A full and correct view of the mythology and religion of India could only be expected when the *Puránas* had been carefully examined, and their character and chronology, as far as possible, ascertained. In order to effect the latter object he (Professor Wilson) commenced, several years ago, a careful investigation of these writings. He employed several able pundits to make a copious index of the contents of each *Purána*, verifying its correctness by collation with the text; and, when he thought it likely that any article of the Index would afford useful information, he either translated it himself, or had it done by some young natives of Bengal, who could write English intelligibly. In this manner he had collected materials for a tolerably correct estimate of the value of each of the *Puránas*, with one or two exceptions; and had been able, without any very disproportionate labour, to effect an analysis of them, of which three or four specimens had been published, and of which it was his present purpose to offer an example to the meeting.

The learned Professor then read his Analysis of the *Bráhmá Puróna*, or *Puróna* of Bráhmá, belonging to the *Sákti* class, in which the worship of *Sákti*, the personified female principle, is inculcated. In this analysis much curious information was disclosed relative to the Hindu account of the origin, existence, and destruction of the universe, as it was revealed by Bráhma to the patriarchs—the manifestation of the system of the universe, as described in Menu—the divisions of the earth, the regions under the earth, and the different hells—the spheres above the earth—the size and distances of the planets and constellations—the influence of the sun and moon in producing rain and fertility—places to which pilgrimage should be performed—the worship of the sun in various forms in the country of Orissa—the birth and actions of Krishna —ceremonial and moral observances—on the merit of worshipping Vishnu—on the duration and influence of the four *Yugas*, or ages—the degeneracy of mankind in the last or *Kali* age—and the periodical destruction of the world— means of obtaining emancipation from destruction—sketch of the *Sánkhya* system of philosophy—description of the practices of the *Yogí*, as suppression of breathing, and particular postures, intended to withdraw the senses from all external objects—description of the *Sátwika*, or perfect man, attained by these means, and his becoming identified with Krishna, &c. &c.

According to Hindu authorities, the *Bráhma Puróna* is considered the earliest of the Pauránic writings, at least in the estimation of the Pauránic writers themselves. Professor Wilson thinks, however, it has no pretensions to be considered as the earliest of the *Puránas*, or indeed as a *Puróna* at all; for although the first few chapters may have belonged to an ancient and genuine composition, the greater part of the work belongs to the class of *Máhátmyas*, or legendary and local descriptions of the greatness or holiness of particular temples or individual divinities.

The thanks of the Society were returned to Professor Wilson for his interesting communication.

The Chairman announced that the thirteenth Anniversary Meeting of the Society would take place on the 7th of May, at one o'clock.

Bombay Branch of the Royal Asiatic Society.—The annual meeting of the Bombay Branch of the Royal Asiatic Society was held on the 30th November.

The Rev. Mr. Wilson presented a translation of the general *Siroze* of the Parsees; in doing which he observed, that there were in the third volume of Anquetil du Perron's translations of the *Zand-Avasta*, versions of two small liturgical works of the Parsees, entitled by him the lesser *Siroze*, and the greater *Siroze*. There is another *Siroze*, however, possessed by the Parsees, which he does not translate. It treats of the qualities of the thirty days of the month, as auspicious or inauspicious. Though its intimations are absurd in the highest degree, it exercises great influence over the whole body of Zoroastrians. It is, indeed, so much regarded by them, that there is scarcely a family without a copy, and there are few individuals who have not its precepts written on the tablet of their hearts. On this account, as well as because of the brief information which it gives respecting the Amsh'spands and Izads, to whom the days of the month are sacred, it is not unworthy of the attention of Europeans. It exists in the Persian language; but there are several Gujarathe versions, which are generally used. The translation which he gives is very literal, and is formed from a collation of these versions, and a comparison with the original. He has added a few explanatory notes.

The secretary then read the following report of the Committee of Management:

" The committee is happy in being able to report that the funds of the Society still continue to exhibit a very prosperous appearance; the receipts during the year having amounted to Rs. 11,435.

" It is to be observed, that, during the last year, the Society has been subjected to several extraordinary charges. Of the very extensive order for books voted at the last anniversary meeting, to the amount of about £900, above £500-worth have already been received—the charges for which are included in the debt above alluded to; and amongst other heavy and extraordinary expenses, may be enumerated the donations of Rs. 600 granted to the family of the late librarian, as also the outlay of Rs. 774 in the erection of new book-cases, rendered necessary by our losing the lecturing room of the Elphinstone college; to which may be added the heavy charge for bookbinding in the last year, amounting to Rs. 661, which the tattered condition of several old and valuable works—many of them in manuscript and hitherto unbound—rendered unavoidable.

" The estimated charges for the year 1836 amount to Rs. 21,404, while the estimated receipts are calculated at Rs. 20,724, leaving a balance against the society at the end of the year 1836 of Rs. 680.

" The committee lately learned with the deepest regret that the expected departure from Bombay of Col. Vans Kennedy has rendered it necessary for him to tender his resignation as president of the Society. They cannot advert to this circumstance without expressing their deep sense of the great debt of gratitude which the institution owes to him, on the one hand, for his eminent talents, profound erudition, and indefatigable research, evinced in his various communications to the Society, and other publications, which have elevated him to the highest rank amongst orientalists; and, on the other, for the zeal and ability with which, for a long period, he has discharged the duties of the office which he vacates. They rejoice in the assurance which he has given, that it is his intention to prosecute the objects of the Society, and to do all that is in his power to promote its interests. They recommend that he may be elected honorary president of the Society, in token of the high respect with which he is regarded."

This report was approved by the meeting, and Col. Kennedy was accordingly elected honorary president of the Society—a distinction, by the bye, originally conferred on the founder of the institution, Sir James Mackintosh, and which, since his death, has remained in a state of abeyance.

It was then proposed by Mr. Wedderburn, and seconded by Mr. Farish, and unanimously resolved, that the Rev. Mr. Wilson be requested to accept the office of president in succession to Col. Kennedy.

Mr. Wilson upon this returned his best thanks for the honour which had been conferred upon him by the Society. It was an honour, he observed, which he could sincerely say was alike unexpected and unsought for by him. Nothing could have induced him to accept of it, but the consideration that it would increase his influence among the natives, and enable him, through them, to prosecute with greater facilities the interesting objects which the Society has in view, and to advance which, he was most solicitous.

VARIETIES.

*Assam.—The Tribes near Sudiya.—*The first tribe we mentioned in our survey of the country beyond Upper Assam was that of the Mootuks or Maomareeas, who inhabit the country on the south bank of the Brumhapootra, from the mouth of the Debooroo to a point nearly opposite the town of Sudiya. Their number is said to be about sixty thousand. They profess to be Hindoos, and worshippers of Vishnoo exclusively; but they hold their religion so loosely, and are so negligent or ignorant, both of its tenets and observances, that the people of Hindoostan, who have visited the country, will scarcely acknowledge them as Hindoos. They were formerly subject to Assam, but threw off their allegiance between fifty and sixty years ago, and established a sort of democracy, as some of their neighbours have likewise done. They have a chief, however, styled the *Bur-seenaputhee,* or commander-in-chief, as we should interpret it, who draws an inconsiderable revenue from presents on occasion of settling disputes, taxation upon new settlers, and labour contributed by the people. The tribe were much dreaded by the Assamese as a warlike people, and they suffered greatly from their predatory incursions. Many of them who had been reduced to slavery by the Maomareeas, were restored to liberty when the British Government took possession of the country. At present, the Bur-seenaputhee and his people are in perfect submission to the British authority. The internal administration, however, is left almost entirely in the hands of the Bur-seenaputhee; but, in order to introduce a sense of the value of human life, they have been required to give information of every case of murder, or of any capital offence, to the political agent, Captain White, or his assistant, by whom it is fully investigated and decided. It was also a part of Mr. Scott's policy, in setting the relations of the British Government with this and some others of the rude tribes, to require them to furnish a military contingent for the protection of the state, to whom muskets and accoutrements were allowed by the Supreme Government. But this part of his system has not answered well; for it has put superior arms into the hands of a wild people addicted to plunder, who can easily find opportunities of abusing them in a country so little open to inspection and control. It seems desirable, therefore, that such contingents should be dispensed with, and the defence of the country be intrusted to the regular troops. The country of the Bur-seenaputhee resembles the rest of Assam. At present it is lying waste, and over-run with grass and forest; but it has every advantage for agricultural prosperity. The inhabitants occupy but a very small tract on the banks of the Debooroo, and profit but little by their natural advantages. We must look to the continuance of external and internal peace, and the progress of colonization, as the means of bringing their country to the state of productiveness for which it is fitted. No revenue or tribute, we believe, is derived by the Supreme Government from this tribe; although, in proportion as the benefits of the protection and pacification bestowed by it become apparent, and the resources of the country increase, it will be nothing more than equitable that they should contribute towards the expenses of the state. We have seen a notice of the Moamareeas as a distinct people from the Mootuks, but inhabiting a different section of the same country, and being equally under the authority of the Bur-seenaputhee, and holding the same relations with the British Government; but whether this view be correct, or the two names are properly applied to the same people, we cannot tell.

The next tribe we mentioned was that of the Meerees; who thinly inhabit the country on the north bank of the Brumhapootra, below the junction with it of the Dihong. This tribe seem to be but an off-shoot from others of the same name, who live in the mountains to the north intermingled with the Abors; and the cause of their settling where they are now, is said to have been the oppressive assumptions of the Abors, who held them to be little better than their slaves, and reduced them to the lowest kind of servitude. Their number is small, but increasing. They acknowledge the authority of a chief or gaum; and they are recognized and protected by the British authorities in the same manner as the other tribes. They are in a very rude state, and have no sort of affinity with the inhabitants of Assam proper. Their customs are much the same as those of the Abors.

The appellation of Abors is given to a number of small tribes of one origin, and the same language and customs, who are not however united by a common government. They occupy the mountains immediately to the north and north-west of the plain of Sudiya. The term *Abor*, as Lieut. Wilcox observes, is that which the Assamese have applied to them, and is not used by the people themselves. Its signification is ' independent ;' and, as might be supposed, it is given to tribes who have not been brought into subjection. The name by which they designate themselves is *Padam*. They are in a very barbarous state ; but their disposition appears to be frank and friendly ; and they have an un-doubted claim to the title of independence, for they are not only unsubdued by a foreign power, but very jealous of their liberties at home. Each tribe appears to have a democratic government of its own, called the *raj*—the *res publica*—and all its proceedings are ordered by the voice of the people met in open council. Nevertheless, they have their chiefs, whose business it is to carry the will of the raj into execution. Lieut. Wilcox remarks, that the Abors are not particular in their diet, but eat the flesh of the elephant, rhinoceros, hog, buffalo, kid, and deer, as well as fowls and duck ; but they express an abhorrence of feeders on beef. The wild animals they make their prey by shooting them with poisoned arrows ; for they do not find that the poison ren-ders the flesh unwholesome by its operation. It is obtained from the moun-tains still more distant than their own, which are occupied by the Bor-Abors and Meeshmees, to the north-east. It is a root, which is brought to Sadiya for sale in baskets containing twenty roots each ; and for five such baskets, a string of beads is given, worth about two annas. When the root is freed from its fibrous coat, it is pounded very fine ; and the powder being worked up with a mucilaginous vegetable juice, is brought to a jelly or paste, which is smeared over the points of the arrows. Its power is certainly great. We have seen it stated, that an animal wounded with one of the poisoned arrows will fall before it can advance a hundred yards ; but Lieut. Wilcox appears to ascribe a less rapid effect to it. The Abors are very partial to spirituous liquors, and have a fermented liquor of their own. Their dress is sufficiently slight ; and of its use for decency's sake they appear perfectly careless. They have a sort of dhoolee, made of the bark of the uddal tree, which they tie about their loins, or use as a mat to sit on, or for a pillow at night. They sometimes wear basket or cane caps ; and they have nearly all " some article of woollen dress, varying from a rudely-made blanket-waistcoat to a comfortable and to-lerably well-shaped cloak." Of the religion of the Abors we have heard nothing, except that they pay some sort of worship to a mountain deity.

The Bor Abors appear to be merely a superior tribe of the same scattered family. They live in the higher ranges of mountains more distant from Assam ; and are both more powerful, and in a somewhat higher state of civilization, than the Abors generally. The prefix *Bor*, or rather we imagine *Burhu*, with the guttural *rh*, is the well-known adjective ' great ;' and in this sense is applied by the Assamese to the most eminent branch of all the rude tribes in their neighbourhood ; and thus we have Bor-Nagas and Bor-Kangtees, as well as

Bor-Abors. We have seen a list of as many as fourteen different chiefs of the Abors, with the particular localities of some of them specified; but it would not interest our readers. The population is considerable.

The Meeshmees appear to be a different race mingled with the Bor-Abors, and rather looked down upon by them. Over the whole, the Sudiya Khava Gohein appears to have so much influence as to be able to give a sort of safe conduct through their territories to pilgrims to the Lama country, whose route lies that way from Sudiya. The journey from Sudiya to Rohemah, the first important town of the Lama country, is said to occupy twenty days. For eight days the traveller is traversing the country of the Meeshmees and Abors; and on the sixteenth day he reaches Bahlow, the frontier post of the Lama country. Rohemah is reported to be a very fine large city, with brick houses three stories high, and having judges, collectors, soldiers, and all the apparatus of a civilized government. The Abors and Meeshmees do not appear to keep up any trade or intercourse with the Lama country themselves; but indirectly they receive cloth, and copper pots, and other articles from it. The articles which they bring to market themselves are chiefly musk and ivory; which we shall have to notice afterwards, when speaking of Sudiya as a general mart for the trade of the surrounding countries.—*Friend of India.*

CRITICAL NOTICES.

The Despatches, Minutes, and Correspondence, of the Marquess Wellesley, K. G., during his Administration in India. Edited by Mr. MONTGOMERY MARTIN. Vol. I. London, 1836. Murray.

THE valuable state-papers (for they may be so termed without impropriety) contained in this work and the "Despatches of the Duke of Wellington," recently published, will not only afford precious materials for the future historian, but supply a highly interesting body of information to statesmen, the military and general reader. They afford complete and authentic delineations of some of the most important crises of the politics of the last half-century, and, as far as relates to India, their worth is almost inappreciable. The present work will contribute to rectify many erroneous notions in respect to the policy of Lord Wellesley, and the public is much indebted to Mr. Martin for having suggested its publication.

This volume commences with the Governor-General's correspondence from the Cape of Good Hope (while on his voyage to India), and terminates with the fall of Seringapatam: thus embracing the origin and conclusion of the war in Mysore.

Conversations at Cambridge. London, 1836. Parker.

THIS will be found a delightful little collection of fragmental sketches, bearing the marks of reading, taste, and original reflection. "Its chief object" the author tells us, "is to inculcate the necessity of purifying the intellectual faculties, by elevating them above the sordid pursuits of the world; and to impress upon the youthful mind, in particular, the inestimable value of learning, when *Christianized* by devotion and humility of temper, and sought after and beloved for itself alone." Let not, however, those who are in search of literary amusement only shrink from the perusal of this volume; they will find in it reflections upon our old classical writers, upon living and late departed ones, and upon topics of general interest. A few of the poetical pieces first saw the light in our Journal.

The Principles of Descriptive and Physiological Botany. By the Rev. J. S. HENSLOW, M.A., F.L.S. &c., Professor of Botany in the University of Cambridge. Being Vol. LXXV. of Dr. Lardner's *Cabinet Cyclopædia.* London, 1836. Longman and Co. Taylor.

THIS work forms a very valuable companion to the admirable treatises of Sir John Herschell and Mr. Swainson, in the department of the *Cabinet Cyclopædia* as pro printed to Natural History. The name and reputation of Professor Henslow, suffice to afford a sure guarantee of the character of the work, which is professedly adapted (an additional recommendation to those for whom the *Cyclopædia* is principally intended) to the general reader more than for the scientific adept. It is, nevertheless, a work of a superior kind, well-digested, comprehending all the remote parts of the philosophy of the Vegetable Kingdom, and is illustrated by an abundance of excellent cuts.

The treatise is divided into two parts, " Descriptive Botany" and " Physiological Botany." The subdivisions of the former are Organography and Glossology, Taxonomy and Phytography. The latter division consists of the following heads :—Vital Properties and Stimulants,—Functions of Nutrition and Reproduction,—and Epirrheology, Botanical Geography, and Fossil Botany. This syllabus will give the reader the best idea of the contents of the volume which our space allows.

The Fellow-Commoner. In three Vols. London, 1836. Churton.

A NOVEL, which is an expansion of a narrative contained in a series of papers published in the *Court Magazine,* under the title of " Remarkable Escapes of a predestinated Rogue." The hero is the offspring of an Irish thief, who was executed for burglary, and sees the light in a cellar of St. Giles' ; his career is a series of remarkable escapes, terminating in fortune and conversion to virtue ! We are no admirers of pictures of life in its lowest state of degradation.

Coins of the Romans, relating to Britain, described and illustrated by JOHN YOUNGE AKERMAN, F.S.A. London, 1836. E. Wilson, jun.

A little work, which, whilst it contains much new information to the student of numismatics, is not without interest to the careful reader of ancient British history.

England in 1835; being a Series of Letters written to Friends in Germany, during a Residence in London and Excursions into the Provinces. By FREDERICK VON RAUMUR. Translated from the German, by SARAH AUSTIN and H. E. LLOYD. Three Vols. London, 1836. Murray.

HERR von Raumur's work is of a class which is exactly suited to the generality of English readers ; we are curious beyond all other people to see draughts of our national character, manners, and institutions, as well as of our remarkable personages, by a foreigner. If vanity is an ingredient in this feeling, rational and commendable curiosity enters largely into it ; if the describer is faithful, and sets down the conclusions of his own judgment, he not only gives us new views of ourselves, but very frequently discovers deformities which escape our own notice.

Amongst a great deal of what is (to us) common-place, and some things which are erroneous, Raumur's book, as a whole, gives a candid, judicious, and amusing picture of England and the English : we are not surprised that it should be so popular.

Mrs. Austin (who has translated the chief part of the work with her usual ability) has acknowledged that she has suppressed those passages of the original which express unfavourable opinions of Mr. Bentham, for which she has assigned no better reason than that *she* believes them to have been founded on an entire misapprehension of his character and sentiments. Mrs. Austin's conclusion may *possibly* be true: but, nevertheless, we must very decidedly protest against this act, which is virtually condemned by Mrs. Austin herself, in the very next page of her Preface, where she justly remarks that " it is the peculiar and invaluable privilege of a translator, as such, to have no opinions." We could point out passages in the work, referring to persons as well as things, which would bear expurgation far better than those which Mrs. Austin has most unjustifiably excluded.

History of the Reformation. By the Rev. HENRY STEBBING, M.A., &c. Vol. I. Being Vol. LXXVII. of Dr. Lardner's *Cabinet Cyclopædia.* London, 1836. Longman and Co. Taylor.

MR. STEBBING has followed up his History of the Christian Church, with a History of the Reformation, to which he gives a fuller development than Mr. Blunt. These able expositions of Ecclesiastical history will prove of great utility in correcting errors and imparting facts, and thereby tend, we should hope, to mitigate the rancour with which the Church (and, covertly, religion itself) is assailed.

Mr. Stebbing is careful in his digest of facts; his style is clear, though it is not sufficiently concise, and wants animation.

A Tour round Ireland, through the Sea-Coast Countries, in the Autumn of 1835. By JOHN BARROW, Esq. London, 1836. Murray.

IT is a strange thing, that Englishmen generally take up a book of travels in Ireland,—an integral part of the Empire—with the same feelings as if it were the description of a foreign country. It may be doubted whether English travellers and tourists are not better acquainted with France and Italy than with the unfortunate island, of which Mr. Barrow has given so amusing an account.

Mr. Barrow's tour, performed in the autumn of 1835, embraced the maritime counties of Ireland from Belfast northward, round the west, south, and east coast to Dublin. His description of the *richness* and the *poverty* of the country, of the political and sectarian evils which afflict it, of the wretched hovels in which most of the peasantry huddle together, are true to the letter. Speaking of Mayo, he says, with too much truth, " There is no other country on the face of the earth where such extreme misery prevails as in Ireland ; the negro slave, if only from interested motives, is well taken care of; even the American Indian, the Esquimaux, the Hottentot. live and die in luxury, compared with this description of Irish peasantry." He gives, in the text and the Appendix, a very interesting account of the mission on the isle of Achill, in this county, under the successful management of a Mr. Nangle, " another Luther in boldness, but not in violence of temper."

Stanfield's Coast Scenery. Part VIII.

The subjects of this part are Ramsgate, Roque de Guet, Guernsey, Brading Harbour, Isle of Wight, and St. Michael's Mount, Normandy. This work keeps up its high character.

LITERARY INTELLIGENCE.

Mrs. Davids has completed a French translation of the excellent Turkish Grammar by her lamented and highly-gifted son, Arthur Lumley Davids. The King of the French has followed in the steps of the present enlightened Sultan of the Osmanlis, in graciously permitting the French edition to be dedicated to him.

Report on the Commerce of the Ports of New Russia, Wallachia, and Moldavia. made to the Russian Government in 1835, in pursuance of an investigation undertaken by order of Count Woronzow. ; by Julius de Hagemeester; translated from the original, published at Odessa by J. J. Heibner. is in the press.

The following Works are preparing for Press :

The Life and Letters of the late Robert Morrison, D.D. and F.R.S., with an Appendix, comprising the language, history, religion, and government of China ; by John Thomas, some time fellow-student with Dr. Morrison.

The LYRE of David ; or Analysis of the Psalms in Hebrew, critical and practical, with a Hebrew and Chaldee Grammar ; by Victorinus Bythner. Translated by the Rev. Thomas Dee, A.B.

Rajah Kali Krishna Badahur, of Calcutta, has published a lithographic representation of an orrery, with a description in Bengalee, which he has circulated extensively among his countrymen.

Mr. Cowley, of Calcutta, has printed a Lithograpic Picture of the Trial of the Nuwaub Shums ood deen Khan: its dimensions 24 inches by 18, and the number of figures introduced into it 109; the principal of which are the portraits of the Nuwaub, Unnia Meo, A. Colvin and T. T. Metcalfe, Esqrs , and the other European and Native Gentlemen connected with, and spectators of the trial.

Dr. William Barrett Marshall, of New Zealand, has announced " a Personal Narrative of two Visits to New Zealand, A.D. 1834, comprising notices of the Church Mission Settlement in the northern island, and a detailed account of the measures resorted to for the rescue of several British subjects who had been shipwrecked at Cape Egmont, and were afterwards detained in slavery among the native tribes." Dr. Marshall was also engaged in preparing for the press a work on " Norfolk Island and Secondary Punishments," in which he proposes to detail the success of the mode and general management of the prisoners in Van Diemen's Land.

MEMOIRS OF LORD CLIVE.*

FIRST ARTICLE.

It is strange that such tardy justice should have been rendered to the memory and merits of the great Lord Clive, to whom the British nation is probably indebted for its vast possessions in the East. The delay of an authentic biography of this much-injured nobleman for sixty years has been not only unjust to him, but to the nation:—to the latter, because it has a direct interest in vindicating its benefactors from obloquy, and has, therefore, a qualified right to whatever biographical records they leave behind; to the individual himself, because his memory has been, in the meantime, obnoxious to the suspicions which malevolence has laboured to fix upon his fame, and which vague eulogy is least calculated to remove. The brilliant exploits of Clive, and the splendid reward they yielded him, as well as the straightforwardness of his character, would have created enemies under the most favourable circumstances; but, at the close of his career, he aspired to a triumph infinitely more arduous, though far less glorious, than any he had achieved over the armies he had routed in the field; he grappled with the hydra of corruption, and experienced a worse than the common fate; for it can scarcely be said of him:

Comperit invidiam supremo fine domari.

It is difficult to say whether the acrimonious censure of the "philosophical" historian of India, or the elaborate panegyric in the *Biog. Britan.*,† has done most wrong to the character of Clive; both have, though in opposite ways, countenanced the ignominy with which malice sought to load it, and which the last act of his life has been supposed to sanction. In justification of the delay, it may be alleged that, during the generation contemporary with Lord Clive, obstinate prejudices might have obstructed his perfect vindication; and we are certainly very favourably disposed towards this apology, by the consideration that a better biographer of Clive could scarcely have been found than the late Sir John Malcolm—an individual whose fame as a statesman and a soldier is likewise inseparably associated with the history of British India—whose whole professional life may be said to be a training for the office; who could accurately appreciate his political policy, criticise, as *an Indian commander*, his military operations upon the spot, and collect testimonies to his character whilst they were fresh in the recollection of persons by whom he was best known.

Apart from the consideration of its consequences, the narrative of Lord Clive's career in India is one of the brightest pages in the modern history of that country. He found British interests, sunk to the lowest depth short of annihilation; in a short period, he raised them to the pinnacle of prosperity; and so plain was the alliance between cause and effect, that their depression was exactly co-eval with his retirement. The heroism and intuitive military skill which Clive suddenly developed, the facility with which he neutralized

* The Life of Robert Lord Clive, collected from the Family Papers communicated by the Earl of Powis: By Sir John Malcolm, G.C.B. F.R.S., &c. Three vols. London, 1836. Murray.
† This memoir, which has been attributed to Dr. Kippis, was written by Henry Beaufoy, Esq., M.P.

the disadvantage of opposing numbers, the remarkable instances of good-fortune (as it is termed), which created a kind of *prestige* in his favour, though sufficiently striking in themselves, are too common to exalt him above the level of mere leaders of soldiers, and are subordinate to that command-ing genius, which raised Clive, by universal consent, to the direction of affairs; which enabled him to seize with happy audacity the exact moment, when the safety of our commercial interests demanded the shield of a political character; and which taught him to choose those measures, means, and implements, which were best adapted to effectuate his object.

The subject of this work, therefore, calls for a larger examination than can be given to it in the space ordinarily allotted to reviews of books. The plan we propose to adopt, is to devote the present article to the biography of Clive, properly so called, and, in succeeding articles, treat of the policy he pursued, and endeavour to clear his fame from the slanders which disap-pointment and enmity originated, and which unintentional error and precipi-tancy have contributed to prolong.

Clive was a member of an ancient Shropshire family, which had for a long period possessed the small estate of Styche, near Market-Drayton; and at this seat of his ancestors, Robert Clive was born on the 29th September, 1725. His father, Mr. Richard Clive, was of the profession of the law; his mother was the daughter of Mr. Nathaniel Gaskill, of Manchester. One of her sisters married Mr. Bayley, of Hope Hall, Manchester; the other, Lord Sempill. Robert Clive, the eldest of six sons, from the age of three, was trained and educated for several years in the family of his uncle Bayley. A letter from this gentleman, dated in 1732, when the future hero was only seven, gives a lively picture of his embryo qualities. " I hope," he says, " I have made a little farther conquest over Bob, and that he regards me, in some degree, as well as his aunt Bayley. He has just had a suit of new clothes, and promises by his reformation to deserve them. I am satisfied that his fighting (to which he is out of measure addicted) gives his temper a fierceness and imperiousness, that he flies out upon every trifling occasion : for this reason, I do what I can to suppress the hero, that I may help for-ward the more valuable qualities of meekness, benevolence, and patience."

That his father should have " formed high hopes of his son while a child," founded on his display of courage and sagacity, was no very sure indication of his future greatness; but the prediction of Dr. Eaton, to whose school, at Lostocke, in Cheshire, he was sent when very young, and who said of him, " that, if his scholar lived to be a man, and opportunity enabled him to exert his talents, few names would be greater than his," was entitled to more weight.

After passing through a school at Market-Drayton, he was sent to that of Merchant-Taylors, in London, and afterwards to a private academy at Hemel Hempstead, where he remained till the age of eighteen, when he was appointed a writer in the civil service of the East-India Company. These changes of the place and system of tuition denote his intractable dispo-sition, and his feat of ascending to the top of Market-Drayton church-steeple, and bestriding the stone spout, and more especially his organizing a little band in that town, which levied contributions on the shop-keepers, on pain of broken windows, attest his characteristics. His biographer states, that " wherever he went, he had the reputation of being a most unlucky boy;" that " he did not probably carry from school any great stock of acquired knowledge;" that " he was impatient of control," and that " his application, in which, however, he was not deficient, was not directed to his books." These ebullitions of qualities which were to form the future commander appear to have had no other ill-effect than to check the extravagant hopes of his friends; the leisure he enjoyed on his first arrival in India gave him an opportunity to revive and improve his knowledge, and to complete that self-education, which, as Sir John Malcolm truly observes, " after all, is of all educations the most important." His idleness and impatience of temper never subdued the charities of the heart: he was an affectionate son and brother, and appears to have always been imbued with religious feelings. Like many other eminent men, he seems to have owed much to his mother, a woman of exemplary character and great talents.

Clive reached Madras in 1744. His letters to his family, on his arrival in the country, are preserved; but they contain nothing remarkable, except his commendation of the public servants, as " a set of very prudent and industrious people," and an indication of that melancholy which occasionally attended him through life. The anecdotes related of him during the two or three first years of his Indian life, shew what his biographer terms a waywardness and reserve, and an " impracticable firmness." He is said to have hazarded, on more than one occasion, the loss of the service, by acts of wildness; and a story is told, which he never contradicted, that he made, at this early period, an attempt upon his own life. " A companion, coming into his room in Writers' Buildings, was requested to take up a pistol and fire it out of the window: he did so. Clive, who was sitting in a very gloomy mood, sprang up, and exclaimed: ' Well, I am reserved for something! That pistol I have twice snapped at my own head."

Reserving for the present a survey of the state of India, at the period of Clive's arrival there, we shall merely remark, that war was declared between France and England in 1744, and that, in 1746, Madras was taken by the French Admiral La Bourdonnais, when Clive became a prisoner, and gave his parole. The conditions of the surrender were violated by Dupleix, and Clive, thereby released from his parole, escaped to Fort St. David. Here he fought a duel, in which his determined character was manifested. He had charged an officer with playing unfairly at cards; the latter called him out; Clive missed his antagonist, who stepped up to him, and, putting a pistol to his head, insisted upon his recanting his assertion respecting foul play. " Fire," replied Clive, coolly, " I said you cheated; I say so still."

The temperament of Clive was too ardent and restless for the dull routine of a commercial life, even if the excitement of war had been wanting. The rupture between France and England seems to have inspired both their companies in India with a spirit not very congenial to the mercantile character; they prepared to prosecute hostilities on a grand scale. The young writer applied for and obtained, in 1747, a commission in the army, and became at once distinguished for his gallantry and activity. Both Lawrence and Orme state that, at this time, divisions and discontent had crept into our army in India, which, says the latter, " made it necessary to remove several of them, at a time when there were very few to succeed to their posts." Mr. Mill, who speaks (without authority) of the turbulence and insubordination of Clive, at this period, as preventing him from acquiring the benevolence of his superiors, observes, that his daring intrepidity, in courting posts of danger, recommended him to Major Lawrence, who " perceived, along with his rashness, a coolness and presence of mind, with a readiness of resource in the midst of danger." The quality here termed *rashness* was, perhaps, that which most recommended him to his discerning commander. The narrative of Major Lawrence* abounds in testimony to the military skill and judgment developed by the young officer, in a profession to which accident had directed his attention, and for which he had had no previous education.

The failure of an expedition, under Capt. Cope, against Devecotta, led to another attempt under Major Lawrence, with whom Clive went with a lieutenant's commission; and the gallantry and talent he displayed in storming the embankment before the breach, which mainly caused the capture of the place, and an alliance with Tanjore, established his military name.

The affairs of the Carnatic were becoming more and more unfavourable to the English, and the authorities of Madras were unauthorized to depart from the observance of strict neutrality in respect to the native states. Lawrence had proceeded to England, and the French were left almost to play the game of conquest undisturbed, under the artful policy of Dupleix.

Clive had returned to his civil duties, and was, moreover, lingering under the effects of a nervous fever. A British battalion, which had been already discomfited, was surrounded at Trichinopoly, and there were so few English officers of any experience at the presidency, that the governor was obliged to send a member of council in charge of some recruits and stores thither. Clive accompanied this party, and narrowly escaped capture. Another reinforcement was sent under Clive, who was promoted to a captaincy; upon his return, he suggested, as a mode of relieving Trichinopoly, that an attack should be made on Arcot, the capital of the French nawab, Chunda Sahib. The suggestion was adopted, and he was nominated to conduct the enterprize—the event of which crowned the fame of the young soldier, and is recorded in imperishable colours in the history of Orme. The force at Trichinopoly did not exceed 600 men; the French had 900, and the troops of Chunda Sahib outnumbered the English nawab's ten to one. The detachment under Clive consisted of 200 Europeans and 300 sepoys; and of the eight officers, six had never been in action, and four of these were young writers. The details of this operation, which amply redeem the military

* In Cambridge's *War in India.*

character of Clive from the imputation of rashness, which Mr. Mill ascribes
to it, are too long to cite; let it suffice to say, that he obtained possession of
Arcot,* which was not defended, and sustained a siege in his turn, wherein
he defeated a very superior force.   Mr. Orme bears the following testimony to this first exploit of the young commander, whose age was 25 :—

Thus ended this siege, maintained fifty days, under every disadvantage of
situation and force, by a handful of men, in their first campaign, with a spirit
worthy of the most veteran troops: and conducted by their young commander with indefatigable activity, unshaken constancy, and undaunted courage : and, notwithstanding he had at this time neither read books, nor conversed with men capable of giving him much instruction in the military art,
all the resources which he employed in the defence of Arcot, where such as
are dictated by the best masters in the science of war.

Sir John Malcolm adds: " I have it in my power, from authority I cannot doubt, to add to the account of this celebrated siege an anecdote, singularly illustrative of the native troops of India.   When provisions became so
scarce that there was a fear that famine might compel them to surrender, the
sepoys proposed to Clive to limit them to the water in which the rice was
boiled. ' It is,' they said, ' sufficient for our support: the Europeans
require the grain.' "

The confidence which his little army, of 200 Europeans and 700 sepoys,
acquired, justified him in attacking, with a small party of Mahrattas, a
French force of 300 Europeans, 2,000 horse, and 2,500 sepoys, which,
after a well-contested action, he routed.   These and other minor successes
raised the reputation of the English ; but at the close of the campaign, when
Clive withdrew to the presidency, Chunda Sahib's forces, under his son, Raja
Sahib, began to regain courage.   This personage, with an army of 400
Europeans and 4,500 native troops, laid siege to the territories of Mahomed
Ali, the *protegé* of the English.   Clive marched against him with 380
Europeans and 1,300 sepoys, and engaged these superior numbers at Covers-
pak.   The result was a splendid victory: fifty Frenchmen and 300 sepoys
were killed, and the rest of the army fled, except sixty Europeans, who
(with nine cannon) were taken.   The victory was won principally by the
remarkable skill and promptitude of Clive, who had come upon the enemy
unawares; and it destroyed the French force in this quarter, and " restored
or rather founded the reputation of the British arms in India."   The whole
of the Carnatic might now have been conquered for Mahomed Ali,
but for the state of affairs in Trichinopoly, on which account Clive was
recalled.

The relief of Trichinopoly was undertaken by Clive, but, before he
marched, Major Lawrence arrived from England, and he joyfully placed
himself under this veteran, for whom he seems to have cherished an affectionate regard.   In the succeeding operations, Lawrence, by the advice of

* Major Lawrence says of the affair at Arcot: " The expedition was attended with uncommon
success, which some people were pleased to term fortunate and lucky ; but, in my opinion, from the
knowledge I have of the gentleman, he deserved and might expect, from his conduct, every thing as it
fell out."

Clive, risked the consequences of dividing his force ; and the result of their plans was the capture and death of Chunda Sahib and the surrender of the French troops. Sir John Malcolm justly eulogizes the powers of combination, self-possession, and intrepidity, which Clive exhibited in the operations against Seringham and Pondicherry, in 1752.

He had been despatched from Trichinopoly with 400 Europeans and 4,700 native troops, to intercept the intercourse between the two places, in consequence of an error committed by M. Law, which the penetrating eye of Clive saw and took advantage of. The plan proposed by Clive and adopted by Lawrence was a bold one ; " for it implied," in the words of Mr. Gleig, " the necessity, not under any circumstances to be hastily incurred, of throwing the army in the face of an enemy scarce inferior to itself, astride upon two rivers." It, however, fully succeeded. At Semi-averam, he had nearly experienced one of those singular surprises, which were common in Indian warfare, proceeding from a chain of wrong information : a French party had nearly gained possession of the fort, when the presence of mind and dexterity of Clive extricated him, though at some risk : one of the party fired his musket at him, as he was leaning on two serjeants (being wounded), through whose bodies the ball went, missing his own, which, as the men were shorter than he, was bent behind, so as to be out of the line of the shot.

The surrender of Law and the assassination of Chunda Sahib did not establish the authority of Mahomed Ali. The Mysoreans and the Mahrattas were dissatisfied, and the intrigues of Dupleix, who had now obtained from the soubahdar of the Deccan the nawabship of the Carnatic, were more successful against the English interests than the arms of his countrymen· Clive, though his health was much impaired, was again called to the field ; but the government had no army to give him, but 200 recruits from England, the refuse of the London gaols, and 500 raw sepoys. With such an army, which he had to teach even courage, he took the forts of Covelong and Chingleput, the latter a place of considerable strength ; shewing, as his biographer remarks, that, " where real military talent exists in the leader, there is no description of troops with which he may not command success." His shattered health now compelled Captain Clive to return to England.

Just before he embarked at Madras, in 1753, he married Miss Margaret Maskelyne, sister of Dr. Nevil Maskelyne, astronomer royal, a lady of beauty and accomplishments, who survived him many years.

The fame of his military achievements had preceded him. The Court of Directors received him with distinction, and his father and mother with delight. " Your brave conduct," says this excellent lady, in a letter to her son, " and the success which Providence has blessed you with, is the talk and wonder of the public, the great joy and satisfaction of your friends ; but more particularly so to me." He began to form connexions in this country which might have led him into another career of public life ; but in less than two years the state of affairs in India rendered his presence necessary there, and he was appointed governor of Fort St. David, with a provisional commission to succeed to Madras. A plan was concerted in England of attacking Salabut Jung, the soubahdar of the Deccan, and expelling the French from India, which was found impracticable to attempt. To obviate the disputes about military precedence, he received a commission of lieutenant-colonel in the British army.

He proceeded to Madras by way of Bombay, where he commanded the land-force in an expedition against the pirate Angria, whose strong-hold (Gheria) was captured.

By a singular coincidence, Clive took charge of Fort St. David on the very day, namely, 20th June 1756, on which the nawab of Bengal, the execrable Suraj-u-Dowlah, took Calcutta. Upon receipt of this intelligence at Madras, a despatch was sent to require the presence of Colonel Clive, who received the command of an expedition for the recovery of Calcutta and the re-establishment of the Company's almost ruined affairs in Bengal. In his letter to the Court on this occasion, he intimates his expectation, that the expedition will not end with the taking Calcutta, and that the Company's affairs in those parts will be settled on a more lasting footing than before.

The strength of the expedition was seriously diminished by the unseasonable pretensions of Colonel Aldercron, commanding a king's regiment at Madras, who, irritated at the preference shown to Clive, refused to permit the king's troops or artillery to join the expedition. It consisted of a fine body of 900 Europeans, and 1,500 excellent sepoys. It arrived in the Hooghly in December.

It is superfluous to relate an event so well known as the history of the taking of Calcutta by Suraj-u-Dowlah, and the melancholy tale of the Black Hole. Calcutta was retaken, and in his letters Clive complains of the mortification he experienced from Admiral Watson and the officers of the navy: "they are such," he says, "that nothing but the good of the service could induce me to submit to them." The Company's troops were refused admittance into the fort, till the admiral had appointed by his authority Colonel Clive, who had claimed the command as senior officer on shore, to be governor, when the fort was delivered up to the Company's representatives in the king's name. His independent powers, he says, gave umbrage to the gentlemen of Calcutta, whose motives he arraigns without much reserve. "His sentiments upon this occasion," observes his biographer, speaking of Clive's private letter to Mr. Pigot, the governor of Madras, "are stated with that severity and careless boldness, which made him so many enemies, but which nevertheless continued, through life, to mark all his communications on points, where he considered that private feelings and interests had interfered with the performance of public duties." He speaks of those individuals as jealous of his authority, callous to any feeling but their losses, "bad subjects and rotten at heart." These difficulties threw more impediments in the way of Clive's operations than the power of the enemy; but they were overcome by firmness. The call of the weak and disunited Select Committee of Bengal to surrender his power, he met with a point-blank refusal.

The first conflict with the enemy was in an attack upon the fort of Budge-Budge, on the left bank of the Hooghly, about ten miles below Calcutta. On this occasion he was surprised, and has been severely censured by Mr. Gleig for "the absence of common vigilance," in not planting pickets or sentries, an omission mentioned by Orme. It now appears, from the correspondence, that Clive was ill; that he committed the preparations for advance on Budge-Budge to Major Kilpatrick, an officer of high reputation; and Clive states that this march was "much against his inclination."

After reducing the fort of Hooghly, and strengthening Calcutta with fresh works, Clive, who hoped to bring matters to a speedy settlement, and whose letters breathe an ardent desire to return to Madras—there being so little prospect of wealth or aggrandizement in Bengal, that he lost in the expedition £2,500,—was plunged into new measures by the arrival of the Nawab, with a large army. Clive persevered for some time in endeavouring to effect an amicable settlement, but soon determined, seeing the treacherous temper of his antagonist, to bring matters to a crisis. A deputation from Clive to the Nawab, requesting him, if his intentions were friendly, to withdraw, met with a haughty refusal, upon which he marched out and attacked the Nawab, who retired, and soon after made overtures for peace. Clive was convinced that his object was only to amuse him, to cover his retreat and gain time: "till he is well thrashed," he remarked to the admiral, "don't, sir, flatter yourself he will be inclined to peace." Apprehensive, however, that the Nawab might be driven to despair, and hurried into an alliance with the French, he consented to treaties, one by which the Nawab restored all the English possessions and property, and another, by which the English were to regard the Nawab's enemies as their own. Clive justified this step in a letter to Mr. Payne, the Chairman of the Court, wherein he clearly shews that his own interest and military reputation were adverse to a cessation of hostilities; but that the interests of the Company and of the nation required peace. He adverts to the jealousies he had encountered, and to the "bankrupt condition" of the gentlemen of Calcutta; he distrusts the fidelity of the Nawab, and therefore urges the necessity of keeping up a respectable force in the province.

It was deemed expedient to dislodge the French force at Chandernagore; the fall of the place is attributed principally to the fleet under Admiral Watson. The depression of the French power, and the success of the English, alarmed the Nawab, and Clive, who appears to have made arrangements for returning to Madras, saw the necessity of keeping down the intrigues of this treacherous man by the presence of a large force and by a commanding influence at Moorshedabad. "The President of the Committee at Calcutta was unequal to the duties now performed by Clive; nor was there any one officer in Bengal upon whom these could devolve with the slightest hope of preserving, much less of improving, the advantages that had been obtained." Even prior to this time, the discernment of Clive foresaw the critical posture of affairs; "if you attack Chandernagore," he says to the Committee at Calcutta, "you cannot stop there; you must go further. Having established yourself by force, and not by the consent of the Nabob, he by force will endeavour to drive you out again."

Clive was aware, at this time, that a conspiracy against the Nawab was organizing at his Court, to which Mr. Watts, the British resident, and Omichund, his native agent (whose history is connected with a very important transaction of Clive's life), were privy; and he was naturally anxious to wait the result of this revolution. In a private letter to Mr. Pigot, he observes: "it is a most disagreeable circumstance, to find that the troubles are likely to commence again: but the opinion here is universal, that there can be neither peace nor trade without a change of government."

When Chandernagore was taken, Clive saw that the snake was "scotched, not killed;" that it was plain, from the steps taken by Dupleix, the French must be "rooted out of India." This appears, his biographer states, from all his letters, public and private. It was his confirmed opinion, "that the English and their European rivals could not have co-existence, as political powers, in India; and both had gone too far to be able to recede." The plan of Dupleix, executed by Bussy, of establishing a paramount power and influence in the Deccan, had in a great measure succeded, and Godeheu, though he at first acted upon opposite maxims, soon adopted those of his predecessor. The policy of the French must, therefore, have been, by the help of the native powers, to expel their European rivals, and Clive looked for a powerful attack upon Calcutta. His sense of the danger was so strong, that in a letter to Mr. Orme, his agent at Madras, he requests him to remit his money to England, as "the times were dangerous." The state of public affairs, therefore, affords a very natural, if not imperative reason for Clive's stay in Bengal; though Mr. Mill, who resolves every difficulty by reference to his ambition and sordidness, observes: "the time had now arrived when, according to his instructions, Clive ought no longer to have deferred his return to Madras;" as if the public interests, not those of individuals, ought not to have been his rule of conduct; "on the other side, Clive beheld an opening for exploits, both splendid and profitable, in Bengal; overlooked all other considerations; violated his instructions; and remained."

That Suraj-u-Dowlah had been strongly importuned by the French to enter into their plans, is shewn by the author of the *Seer Mutakhareen,* who states, that M. Law revealed to the Nawab the dissatisfaction of his principal officers, and their connexion with the English; but that the conspirators enforced upon him the impolicy of quarrelling with the victorious English, on account of the vanquished and fugitive French. It is idle to speculate upon the motives which operated upon the mind of a weak, cruel, voluptuous prince, like Suraj-u-Dowlah; especially in a dilemma, where men of firmer and more generous character would have vacillated. We know that he hated the English, and was in communication with the French;

that he was chagrined at the fate of Chandernagore, and alarmed at the success of Sabut Jung* (the name he gave to Clive, and by which he is to this day known amongst the natives of India); and these are considerations sufficient to explain the conduct of both parties, in recommencing hostilities. That conduct at this critical moment was as different as their characters. The Nawab, careless (for, according to the native historian, he was not ignorant) of the disaffection of his officers, with three-fourths of his own army his enemies, and on the very edge of a precipice, acted as if he could direct the course of political events with as much ease as the transactions of his haram.

Although the conspiracy against the Nawab amongst his subjects was spreading too wide for concealment, combining all classes and all interests, who were actuated by a general sentiment of disgust and detestation against their ruler, the committee of Calcutta did not accede to the urgent invitations of the conspirators to join or countenance the confederacy, without great hesitation. "It was the genius of Clive," Sir John Malcolm remarks, "which guided their councils, and pointed out the road by which he was to lead them to safety and honour, through a labyrinth of such apparently inextricable windings, that even his experience and courage were at times startled by its intricacies."

Mr. Orme has detailed these complicated transactions with great minuteness, but without the advantage of the lights which Clive's entire correspondence throws upon them; and it appears to us that no moral imputation whatever rests upon Clive, who seems to have steered his way through the shoals with admirable dexterity, though he was not merely left alone to the resources of his own mind, "but was embarrassed by the conduct of those who should have aided him." Admiral Watson (to whom, it should be observed, he communicated all his measures) declined, though requested by Clive, to give his opinion as to the measures to be pursued; observing, that the fleet could be of no use, every thing being done that they are capable of undertaking: "you, gentlemen of the committee," he added, "will, therefore, best judge what steps will now be necessary for the Company's interest." To some captious and frivolous objections of the committee, Clive replied with a straightforwardness, which is entirely inconsistent with the selfish motives attributed to him by Mr. Mill. He justifies, in a temperate manner, the measures objected to; adding, however, "you may be assured, as I will never make use of the power vested in me to the injury of the Honourable Company's affairs, that I will be as far from suffering you to take away any part of it. I say thus much to prevent any further disagreeable intimations, which can tend to no good end."

The train of the conspirators, and the hostile demonstrations of the English, impelled the Nawab to assemble his whole force, with which he advanced to Plassey, the place appointed by Clive as a rendezvous where Meer Jaffier, the Nawab's commander-in-chief, and one of the

* ' Daring in War.'

conspirators, was to desert his master. Clive's force consisted of 650 European infantry, 100 topases, 100 Malabar Portuguese, 150 artillery, including fifty seamen furnished by Admiral Watson, 2100 sepoys, eight six-pounders, and a howitzer. The Nawab's force consisted of 50,000 infantry, 18,000 well-mounted cavalry, with 50 pieces of cannon.

The position of Clive has been described, by a military critic, to be " as perilous as the general of a small army ever occupied;" and his circumstances were still more critical, for he was not sure of the defection of Meer Jaffier. He felt it, therefore, politic to call a council of officers, to whom he proposed the following question : " Whether, in our present situation, and on our own bottom, it would be prudent to attack the Nabob ; or whether we should wait till joined by some country power ?"* Nine officers (*including Clive*) voted in the negative, against an immediate attack ; seven, including the name of " Eyre Coote," for giving battle to the Nawab. " Clive," says his biographer, " though he had voted with the majority, appears, almost immediately afterwards, to have satisfied himself that there was no other road to safety and honour but by moving forward ; and, without consulting any individual, much less the council of war he had so unwisely assembled, on the very evening of the day on which the council had been held, changing his purpose, he determined to march against the enemy, and accordingly gave orders for his army to cross the river the following morning." But it seems evident that there was no change of opinion on the part of Clive ; he had (contrary to practice) given his own opinion first, with a view, probably, to encourage the other officers to be sincere, or to take as little of the responsibility of such a step as he could help : and this conclusion appears to be confirmed by the testimony of Major Coote, in his evidence before the House of Commons, who stated, that " after the council of war, Lord Clive spoke to me first, unasked, of the army marching." Clive afterwards said, that " this was the only council of war he had ever held; and that, if he had abided by that council, it would have been the ruin of the Company."

It is almost superfluous to detail the particulars of a conflict so well known as the battle of Plassey. It was little more than a cannonade and rout ; when Jaffier fulfilled his stipulations, the Nawab fled, with 2,000 attendants ; the fate of a kingdom (in fact), with a population of thirty millions of people, was decided, with no more loss than seventy-two men killed and wounded on the side of the victors. A simple narrative of the battle is given by Clive in a letter to the Secret Committee of the Court of Directors, dated the 26th July 1757, the battle being fought on the 23d June; and this it may be worth while to insert.

" About this time some of his principal officers made overtures to us for dethroning him (the Nawab). At the head of these was Meer Jaffier, then Bukhshee to the army, a man as generally esteemed as the other was detested. As we had reason to believe this disaffection pretty general, we soon entered into engagements with Meer Jaffier to put the crown on his head. All neces-

---

* The query, list of officers and original proceedings of this council are transcribed by Sir John Malcolm from the Clive MSS.

sary preparations being completed with the utmost secrecy, the army, consisting of about one thousand Europeans, and two thousand sepoys, with eight pieces of cannon, marched from Chandernagore on the 13th, and arrived on the 18th at Cutwa Fort, which was taken without opposition. The 22d, in the evening, we crossed the river, and landing on the island, marched straight for Plassey Grove, where we arrived by one in the morning. At day-break we discovered the Nabob's army moving towards us, consisting, as we since found, of about fifteen thousand horse, and thirty-five thousand foot, with upwards of forty pieces of cannon. They approached apace, and by six began to attack with a number of heavy cannon, supported by the whole army, and continued to play on us very briskly for several hours, during which our situation was of the utmost service to us, being lodged in a large grove, with good mud banks. To succeed in an attempt on their cannon was next to impossible, as they were planted in a manner round us, and at considerable distances from each other. We therefore remained quiet in our post, in expectation of a successful attack upon their camp at night. About noon the enemy drew off their artillery, and retired to their camp, being the same which Roy Dullub had left but a few days before, and which he had fortified with a good ditch and breast-work. We immediately sent a detachment, accompanied with two field-pieces to take possession of a tank with high banks, which was advanced about three hundred yards above our grove, and from whence the enemy had considerably annoyed us with some cannon managed by Frenchmen. This motion brought them out a second time; but on finding them make no great effort to dislodge us, we proceeded to take possession of one or two more eminences lying very near an angle of their camp, from whence, and an adjacent eminence in their possession, they kept a smart fire of musketry upon us. They made several attempts to bring out their cannon, but our advanced field-pieces played so warmly and so well upon them, that they were always drove back. Their horse exposing themselves a good deal on this occasion, many of them were killed, and among the rest four or five officers of the first distinction, by which the whole army being visibly dispirited and thrown into some confusion, we were encouraged to storm both the eminence and the angle of their camp, which were carried at the same instant, with little or no loss; though the latter was defended (exclusively of blacks) by forty French and two pieces of cannon; and the former by a large body of blacks, both foot and horse. On this, a general rout ensued, and we pursued the enemy six miles, passing upwards of forty pieces of cannon they had abandoned, with an infinite number of hackaries*, and carriages filled with baggage of all kinds. Suraj-u-Dowlah escaped on a camel, and reaching Moorshedabad early next morning, despatched away what jewels and treasure he conveniently could, and he himself followed at midnight, with only two or three attendants.

" It is computed there are killed of the enemy about five hundred. Our loss amounted to only twenty-two killed, and fifty wounded, and those chiefly blacks. During the warmest part of the action we observed a large body of troops hovering on our right, which proved to be our friends; but as they never discovered themselves by any signal whatsoever, we frequently fired on them to make them keep their distance. When the battle was over, they sent a congratulatory message, and encamped in our neighbourhood that night. The next morning Meer Jaffier paid me a visit, and expressed much gratitude at the service done him, assuring me, in the most solemn manner, that he would

* A species of cart drawn by a couple of bullocks.

faithfully perform his engagement to the English. He then proceeded to the city, which he reached some hours before Suraj-u-Dowlah left it."

The site of this battle has almost disappeared, owing to the encroachments of the river: even the "grove" has vanished.

The results of this victory were of the most important character.

DAVID SHEA, Esq., of the EAST-INDIA COLLEGE.

In our obituary this month, it is our melancholy duty to record the death of a gentleman, whose loss will be felt no less by the Oriental literary world, to which he was a valuable benefactor, than by the circle of his friends and colleagues, to whom he was peculiarly endeared by amenity of manners, benevolence of heart, and the unfailing resources of a richly stored mind, ever ready to contribute to the cheerfulness of social intercourse.

In the present age, facilities for acquiring the most extensive knowledge of the languages and literature of the East, are multiplied to such an extent, and rendered so easily attainable, as to hold out the strongest allurements to all who may feel the slightest inclination to pursue these studies: but, in the instance of the lamented subject of this brief memoir, the case was widely different. His zeal had to contend against difficulties insuperable to a mind less ardently devoted to the attainment of knowledge. Far from the countries in which the languages are spoken; compelled to acquire his information by laborious mental application alone; the means of reference few and meagre; and even of these not many, by his peculiar circumstances, within his reach, he yet, amidst the incessant distractions of laborious and uncongenial employment, acquired a knowledge, to the extent and accuracy of which the works he has left behind bear full and unquestionable testimony.

Mr. Shea's translations of the History of the Kájárs, the family of the reigning monarch of Persia, and of a portion of Mirkhond's History of Persia, are already before the public. A more important work, and for which his wide range of information peculiarly qualified him, would shortly have been completed, had his valuable life been spared. The *Dabistán*, a book of considerable authority in the East, giving an account of the various religious and philosophical sects that have appeared in the world, is not unknown in Europe; but the abstruseness of the subjects treated, and the obscurity of the style, are such as hitherto to have deterred the most hardy oriental scholars from undergoing the labour of translation. We trust the friends of this estimable individual will not allow the result of his valuable exertions to be lost to the world.

THE MASCARENHAS.*

THIS work must, we presume, be classed among the historical novels. The period selected by the author, through which to weave the rather intricate tissue of her story, is the lengthened reign of Aurungzebe,—the commencement of the rise of the Mahratta, and the decline of the Mahomedan power; and she has woven it with no small share of talent and ingenuity. The leading characters are historical, and well sustained. Episodes, in which intrigue and love bear, among fictitious personages, necessarily an important part, are adroitly intermingled, and the catastrophe is developed with corresponding effect—exhibiting throughout a knowledge of local costume, and a command of the flowery dialect of Orientals; and breathing, moreover, a spirit of charity creditable to a Christian philosopher.

As a specimen, we will give a passage illustrative of the character of a well-known personage :—

Aurungzebe himself, at thirteen, had fought in the Deccan; and his great ancestor Tamerlane, at an earlier age, had commenced his career of pillage and of conquest. Suspicious of his other sons—one of whom was now suffering the penalty of rebellion—he looked on the timid, unaspiring character of Akbar as a security for future obedience. To slay or to be slain, the sceptre or the shroud, were the unavoidable alternatives assigned in the book of destiny to the rival candidates for a succession not determined by established regulations. Aurungzebe had not scrupled to avail himself of the license such provident reasoning affords. The murder of his brothers, Dara and Morad, the imprisonment of his father, and the persecution and consequent destruction of Suja and his family, testified to the inflexibility of his utilitarian philosophy. He was not insatiate of blood. Had he been born the undisputed heir to sovereignty, he might have merited the surname of " beneficent ;" but, in his indefeasible code of self-advancement, he was careless of human life, as was the prophet whose ferocious creed he had adopted : esteeming his duty to himself his first and greatest law, to be fulfilled no matter with what violation of the social compact. The corollary deduced from the downfal of his family and his own exaltation, was *not* that he was the most guilty, but that he was the most discerning. Had either of his brothers possessed his sagacity, his crimes would have been *theirs*, their fortunes *his*. Providence, by gifting him with superior intelligence, had manifested its will that he should govern. And was the sceptre which he had snatched from the lion to be struck from his hand by the gazelle ? was the fly to torment the limb that had crushed the alligator ? A thoughtless and impatient villain would have speedily extinguished this ephemeron; but the pervading eye of the cold-blooded calculator saw more convenience in delay.

The following picture of the mode of travel of an eastern court, is graphic :—

This letter found Aurungzebe, with all his court, preparing to depart for Kashmere. The day and hour propitious to the movement of so vast a multitude had been arranged by the astrologers. Delhi was active to its very dust.

---

* The Mascarenhas; a Legend of the Portuguese in India. By the Author of " Prediction." Three Volumes, 1836. Smith, Elder, and Co.

Its population seemed increased threefold; for marble domes, and granite halls
and cane-thatched huts, had all discharged their inmates, to swell or to survey
the royal train. This pageant, in the martial aspect of its outline, encom-
passed by light and heavy ordnance, by musketeers and bowmen, preceded by
bands of horns and kettle-drums, and closed by horsemen clad in quilted mail,
resembled a besieging force, destined to attack some mighty strong-hold, rather
than a gay procession to the 'Vale of Roses.' Its nucleus, however, presented something more in keeping with a monarch's pilgrimage—gilt palankeens,
with fine-spun curtains and pictured veils ; towers canopied with gold brocade,
cars with azure awnings, tabernacles studded with gems, litters hung with
gauze and net-work. These sumptuous vehicles, stored with the luxuries indispensable to Oriental indolence, were variously disposed:—some swaying to
the elephant's drowsy nod ; others suspended between hardy camels; others
pressing the shoulders of swift-footed bearers—while eunuchs, black and white,
lacqueys and pages, sumpter slaves and sumpter horses, tent-pitchers, porters,
and straggling pioneers, fan, parasol, and mace attendants, hemmed in and hid
from curious or profane regard the sacred coverts destined to convey the
breathing wonders of the monarch's harem. All was in readiness, even to the
sutler's unwieldly and important retinue. The ladies had already rambled
from their clustered haunts to the capacious tents erected to enclose them,
while entering their gilded cages ; and waited, fretfully impatient, for the
appointed signal. Along the splendid host the banners only moved, for man
and beast seemed equally observant.

Suddenly a crier from the great Minar proclaimed, "The pilgrimage to Kashmere is postponed." Silence for a second reigned—and then a hurly-burly.
The ladies chattered in the tent, shrilling forth their indignation. The din
might have been stunning in more ordinary cases ; but now their pretty wail
was, in proportion to the outer hubbub, as is the squeaking of the jews-harp
to the roar of clarions. The Omrahs, indeed, whose solemn dignity disdained
to be astonished, filed off with grave indifference : but their vexed subordinates, afraid of giving open vent to sullenness, evinced their disappointment
by covert acts of irritation. The mahout goaded his sagacious quadruped
until the huge creature roared indignant, and whirled the cow-tails dangling at
his ears full in the face of his tormentor. The chûbdars, to keep silence,*
pinched the pages ; the pages slyly struck their silver wands against the naked
skins of the wide-scampering fan-bearers ; the fan-buffs, well applied, blinded
the running-footmen; and these, in turn, attacked a file of red-capped bar-
bers, who fell upon the link-boys ; porters, sutlers, pioneers, each passed
unto his neighbour the cuff he had received. Nay, it is chronicled that blows
were bandied by more distinguished personages ; for the court calendar relates,
that the Princess Roshunara, in her spleen, applied the slipper to the cheek
of her handmaid, who, to exhaust her menial rancour, turned upon the royal
Nubian, Sharoc, and coolly boxed his ears.

Those who have felt the delicious climate of Western India, in a mild
rainy season, above the Ghauts, and witnessed the beaming exuberance of
nature immediately after, will recognize, in this eloquent passage, a correct
delineation of their sensations :

From all his mountain strongholds, Ranagurgh had been selected by the

---

* *Chúbdár* means, not a 'silence-keeper,' as early travellers supposed, but a mace or baton-bearer.
The *chûb*, or *choob*, is usually of silver, of unequal length, from two to five or six feet, and of various
shapes.—REV.

Raja Seraji for his fixed abode, the residence of his court, and depositary of his wealth. This cloud-enveloped region of cliff and ravine, abyss and cataract, dark pass and trackless jungle, ramparted with naked rocks painfully reflecting the hot sunbeam, was soon reclaimed into the grand, the picturesque and wildly beautiful. Many a broad fissure strewed a vale or bushy dell, which even the dwellers in a Tempe might have seemed a paradise. In India, vege-.tation laughs at the puny barriers which in less teemful climates limit her luxuriance. Now, revelling in primitive sublimity, she rears the teak, the palm, the tamarind, and all the giant natives of eternal forests—now, mirthful as a frolic child, she scatters here and there the flowers committed to her· guardianship, which, falling on a generous mould, render for each solitary germ a thousand fragrant blossoms. The very nullahs, which the stormy months convert to channels for the blustering torrent, become, in the genial interval between the rains and drought, receptacles for quick-ripening seed; yielding the listless cultivator an easy crop. The sun, whose scorching ray in later months calcines the rock, in this delicious season sends forth a tempered heat, ripens the fruit, and merely warms the stream which bubbles over sands that his fiery beam had brightened into gold. A few weeks change the river-bed into the melon-garden; rice waves where cataracts had swept; roses and jasmines spring from the changeful soil; shrubs hide the swamp, and the blue petals of the lotus peep through the murky pool.

Nor will the following be deemed a less correct and animated description of phenomena, no-where seen in such sublimity as about the ghauts in Western India:—

At the sentry's outcry, the soldier, who stood above upon the beetling ledge, looked towards the spot the man had designated. A heavy stroke boomed from the fortress far into the distance. The sun had burst forth—the mass of fog was broken—fragments of the vapour sailed majestically up the sides of the ravines; and, rarifying as they ascend, floated over the glowing firmament, like draperies of etherial net-work. The grand panorama of mountain-scenery became gradually developed. Crag and pinnacle, precipice and slope, as touched by prismatic rays, or veiled by hovering mist, now started forth, now vanished. All, for a while, looked flitting and unstable: rock, glen, and ghaut, alternately illumined and obscured, resembled the mockery of some phantom pageant. As the dense volume which hid the plain around the hill-fort parted and re-closed, tents, flags, spear-points, and canvas-walls peeped forward and retreated. At times, a whole encampment seemed borne on a sea of cloud—at times, engulphed: now magnified behind a thin blue mist, now buried in a mass of vapour. At length, the illusory haze, yielding to the sun's increasing force, soared into the heavens, leaving each feature of the landscape distinct and well defined. A canvas city has sprung up during the night.

. Some useful notes are conveniently postfixed to each volume.

THE JUWAUB CLUB.

DOUBTS concerning the existence of the *Juwaub Club* have been entertained by persons well-acquainted with the nature and structure of Anglo-Indian society, perhaps in consequence of the secresy observed by those who have the misfortune to belong to it. Although, however, the rules and regulations established by this unhappy confraternity of bachelors have not transpired, it is well known that a single *juwaub* entitles a member to admission. The term "*juwaub*" being Hindustani, and exclusively Indian, it may be necessary to explain it. Literally, it implies simply 'an answer,' but a wider signification has been given to it by the European community, who have made it equivalent to 'refusal;' and it is used in both senses by the natives, who, in dismissal from service, are said to have had their *juwaub*. In like manner, when a Christian gentleman makes a proposal of marriage to a young lady, and is rejected, he is *juwaubed*, and qualified for a club instituted, according to common report, in order that disappointed lovers may be sure of consolation and sympathy from others who have suffered a similar fate. The presidents and vice-presidents are selected from those who have been many times *juwaubed*. These offices are often to be filled up, their untiring perseverance occasioning the secession of a member, who, after having sustained repeated *juwaubs*, is accepted at last, and in his new character of Benedict, triumphs over those who, overpowered by one or two rebuffs, dare not venture to try their fortune again. The publicity given in India to all affairs of the kind proves, however, a very serious obstacle to ultimate success. Young ladies are very apt to look shy upon those who have been placed in so awkward a position, and it is not often that the melancholy fact can be concealed. The narrowness of the circle makes all the lookers-on acquainted with the game played before them; they perceive the first beginnings of the "soft impeachment," in the language of Mrs. Malaprop; and they are seldom left in ignorance of the result. Should the young lady herself observe the delicacy and consideration which a discarded lover has some right to expect, her friends are not always equally scrupulous, and the *innamorato* himself, in many cases, becomes the herald of his own defeat, by proclaiming his sorrows or his wrongs aloud. In some instances, the sting is rendered more poignant by the manner in which it is conveyed; a slight laconic answer inflicts a severe mortification; but the grand affront, in the estimation of a society, the male portion of which are great sticklers for etiquette, is a *juwaub* indited upon China paper. This is esteemed an inferior article of stationery in India, being obtainable at a low price in the bazaars; it is thin, with a watery edge, which will not bear the ink; and one side only being hot pressed, the other is rough and unsightly, and in fact scarcely capable of being written upon. The reader may judge of the depth of the annoyance occasioned by this "unkindest cut of all" by the following dialogue, which may be relied upon as the genuine effusion of a Corydon suffering in all the freshness of a newly-inflicted wound:—

"Do not mention her name to me, Alfred; speak of her no more; false, perfidious, ungrateful girl!" "Now be tranquil, my dear fellow; regard the matter philosophically; she is a mere girl, undeserving such an ebullition of feeling; indeed, the difference in your age renders the affair scarcely a subject for regret; you may consider it a fortunate escape." "No, Alfred, no; I might have viewed the circumstance in the light in which you have placed it; I might even have made it a subject of congratulation; but consider the insult

I have received; the heartless creature has positively rejected me upon China paper !"

In behalf of the fair delinquent, it may be urged that offers of marriage are so often made in India upon such slight encouragement, that the aspirant scarcely merits the tenderness which, in more touching cases, ought to be accorded to an unfortunate admirer; one who loves "not wisely, but too well." It is only from those in the same predicament with themselves that the *juwaubed* youth of India can obtain the slightest commiseration; men who have either never wooed, or have wooed and won, are not sufficiently generous to regard their less fortunate or less discreet brethren with the sentiment which their melancholy situation is calculated to inspire in every feeling breast. On the contrary, they are certain to manifest a higher degree of respect and admiration for the imperious beauty, or unprincipled coquette, who has trifled with the affections of some half-dozen suitors, or who is supposed to be so difficult, that few have a chance of pleasing.

Should any circumstance, however adventitious, prevent a young lady from receiving an offer during the first year of her residence in India, she will sink very low in the estimation of the bachelorhood of the presidency; notwithstanding any superiority of beauty or other personal attractions she may possess, she is like an actress who fails to make a decided hit upon her first appearance, and who, therefore, in spite of qualifications which may afterwards appear, is seldom or never honoured with the approbation of a "discerning public." As it has been before observed, it is only those young ladies who are unwilling to lose any opportunity of securing an establishment, who can be easily prevailed upon to accept a man who has had the reputation of being refused, especially if such a circumstance should have occurred more than once; and even after consent has been obtained, the fair one has deemed the fact, lately coming to her knowledge, that her suitor has belonged, or has been entitled to belong, to the *juwaub* club, quite sufficient to justify her in breaking off the match.

Notwithstanding the doubts expressed upon the subject by a writer in a late number of the *British and Foreign Review*, it is quite certain that there are many male residents in India, gifted with more enterprize than discretion, who, feeling a great anxiety to change their condition, do not hesitate to propose, almost *instanter*, to every unmarried lady who comes in their way. These gentlemen are the inditers of letters which meet spinsters on the road; and who, upon the strength of the most common-place civility, will build up hopes which are, nine times out of ten, destined to vanish into thin air. There is a homely distich, familiar to rustic life in England, which, if reversed, will apply to the persevering of the other sex in India :—

> No goose that swims so grey, but, soon or late,
> Shall find some honest gander for its mate.

Accordingly, after repeated denials, when the luckless wight has obtained the most undesirable celebrity for his ill-success with the fair, he finds some one in the happy mood, and bears off the prize in triumph. In the majority of these instances, neither party is very particular; scandal may have been busy with the lady, who is but too happy to get somebody to give her his name; or she may have been so long neglected as to be glad of any relief from her despair. These unions, as it may be expected, do not usually turn out well; the determination to be married, at all events and at all risks, not proving the firmest basis for connubial happiness; but occasionally, when mere caprice or some fortuitous circumstance has been the cause of disappointment, those who have been set down as permanent members of the *juwaub* club, meet with some congenial spirit, and are rewarded for all the mortifications of their early life. It sometimes happens, that the ill-luck attendant upon the Anglo-Indian matrimonial speculator pursues the party to Europe, and, finding some obstacle wheresover he may present himself as a suitor, he returns to India still unblessed; but these, it must be confessed, are rare cases, and even where not a single hope has remained to cheer the disconsolate lover, a ray of sunshine has suddenly beamed upon him, giving promise of perpetual brightness.

It chanced that a gentleman who had attained to considerable rank and fortune, and a respectable age, had not in India succeeded in prevailing upon any lady to unite herself to him in the bonds of matrimony. He proceeded to England, where he fell in love with a celebrated beauty; one, however, who, it was said, had, in the pursuit of universal admiration, neglected to secure an establishment, which, being portionless, was a very essential object to her. These considerations, or the persecutions of her friends, induced her to accept an offer which appeared to be more eligible than any she had received during several preceding years. Her consent brought rapturous emotions to a bosom long unaccustomed to such guests, and every thing was speedily and satisfactorily settled respecting a marriage which was to take place a fortnight or three weeks before the departure of the vessel selected to take the bride and bridegroom out to India. A commodious cabin was engaged, and a splendid outfit purchased by the *futur*, which, carefully inclosed in tin and wood, was put on board the vessel. Alas, for the mutability of human affairs! A few days before the one appointed for the celebration of the nuptials, the lady fell seriously ill; a physician of eminence was sent for; she did not grow better under his hands, and he, being a man of great discernment, soon discovered that the malady was mental, not bodily. Gifted with equal good sense and benevolent feeling, he won her confidence by his kindness, and representing in a forcible manner the necessity of revealing the secret cause of her complaint, he prevailed upon her at length to confess that it was the horror she entertained at the idea of fulfilling an engagement in which her inclination had no part, which had caused her distress of mind and consequent illness. The physician immediately recommended that this melancholy truth should be made known to the party whom it most deeply concerned, offering to be himself the medium of communication. The fair invalid, who had expected to find every body armed with arguments to shew the necessity of her keeping her plighted word, was delighted by the prospect of emancipation held out by her kind adviser, and gladly availed herself of his proposed mediation in the affair. Who can paint the consternation of the unfortunate lover at a disclosure, which dashed the cup of bliss from his hand, just as it was about to reach his lips? His condition was most pitiable; and the doctor, finding all attempts at consolation unavailing, recommended change of scene, and more particularly a visit to Cheltenham, it being the gay season at that place of fashionable resort. There was nothing better to be done; London had become odious, and, distracted by the mortifying thought, that he should be compelled to carry the *trousseau* out to India without the bride whom it was intended to adorn, our poor friend reached the place of his destination. He possessed military rank, he was known to be rich, and young ladies, bent upon matrimonial projects, thought little of a voyage to India on the shortest notice. Smiles were showered upon the lately discomfited bachelor, and he began to think that his evil fortune might be retrieved. He had engaged and paid for the passage of two persons to Calcutta, and it would be any thing but agreeable to go out *solus*, thus exposing himself to the secret derision of his companions, who could not be ignorant of the contents of certain bandboxes, or of the party for whom so much accommodation had been provided. Under these circumstances, he seized an auspicious moment, and, before he had been three days in Cheltenham, was again affianced to a willing fair, who had no objection to step at once into the cabin and the outfit which another had scorned. The marriage took place as soon as it was possible, and the happy couple embarked a few days afterwards, to spend their honey-moon on board ship. There is no reason to believe that this union, strangely as it had been brought about, was not productive of lasting happiness to both parties.

A few years ago, when female society was not so extensive as it now is in India, and when beauty was so scarce a commodity, that the possessor might torment her adorers as much as she pleased, there were not wanting those who displayed an inclination to put the patience and endurance of their lovers to the severest trials. A case in point is recorded at Benares, which will serve to shew the extreme length to which a vain, self-willed, capricious woman will venture to go, when spoiled by adulation and secure of conquest. A young lady, celebrated for her beauty, attracted the attention of a civilian, who was not supremely gifted with personal advantages, and who was entirely unskilled in the ways of womankind. To counterbalance these deficiencies, he had large allowances, an excellent disposition, and a high character for zeal and ability in the department of the service to which he belonged. He was, in short, an *eligible*, and, having obtained the approbation of the lady's friends, the lady herself consented to become his wife. He was stationed at the distance of a day's journey from the abode of his betrothed, and the duties of his office obliged him to be at his post during the period of his engagement. He employed the interval in new furnishing his house, and in procuring from Calcutta the most elegant and expensive articles to be found there, taking care to make the young lady acquainted with all his plans, and to ensure her approbation of what he was about to do. At length, the day appointed for the wedding was at hand, and he hastened down to Benares to receive the reward of all his pains. There was no church at that time at the station, and the ceremony was to be performed in the drawing-room of the mansion in which the bride-elect resided. It was tastefully fitted up for the occasion, and when the company had assembled, and the clergyman, a pious gentleman of very retired habits, had arrived, the young lady made her appearance. The moment, however, that all was ready, she, in the most bewitching manner, entreated her lover to postpone the nuptials until the arrival of some looking-glasses, to which she had taken a fancy, from Calcutta, alleging, in excuse for her wish for the delay, that she was determined to prove whether he really felt the attachment to her which he had professed. The poor man was astounded at being so unexpectedly called upon to evince his affection by such a test; but, after some hesitation, overpowered by the blandishments and persuasions of his fair enslaver, he complied, returning bootless home, to await the despatch of the looking-glasses. They came in due course of time, the same party assembled, and the clergyman again opened his book. The lady had prepared herself for another scene, and a second time assailed her lover with a request for delay, upon some frivolous pretext; but it was not now quite so easy to prevail; the betrothed, in spite of his inadequate knowledge of the sex, began to suspect that she had changed her mind, and that there was some deeper reason for the demur than the one she chose to give. At length, he insisted that the marriage should proceed or be broken off altogether, and the perfidious fair chose the latter alternative. On both these occasions, the clergyman had looked on in silence and utter amazement; what, therefore, was his farther astonishment, to hear from the lips of the lady herself, when pressed by her friends to reveal the true cause of her capricious conduct, that she had been suddenly struck with a passion for him, at the moment in which he was about to perform the ceremony which would make her the bride of another, and that she had, in consequence, hastily framed an excuse to delay a marriage which had become hateful to her. This explanation put the civilian immediately to the rout; he took leave, while the man for whom he had been rejected, maugre the gravity of his disposition, the sobriety of his habits, and the horror he had entertained of the vanity, folly, and insolence of a thorough-bred coquette, was so touched and taken by the declaration in his favour, that he became in turn a suitor, and ventured upon marriage with this flighty, and not very highly principled, damsel.

In these good old times, a young lady would sometimes receive two or three offers in the course of a day, and if, even after the first had been accepted, the second or third should appear preferable, she would not hesitate in the trifling matter of changing her mind, and discarding the betrothed for the last comer. Modern days have presented similar instances, though they are becoming more rare. Flushed with delight after the receipt of an elegant-looking billet, filled with sweet words purporting consent, the lover has hastened to the residence of his charmer, and found a rival there, whose successful pleading dooms him to the willow. One belle in particular was celebrated for the multitude of her engagements, but she took care not to play the game too long, and fixed at last upon a cavalry officer, though it was very dubious whether he had really obtained any preference, in a heart given wholly up to vanity.

The male coquette is a scarcer animal in India than in England, but specimens of the genus are to be found, and doubtless the number would be greater were it not for the active vigilance exercised by parents and guardians, who, upon the earliest symptoms of an intention to enact the part of dangler only, make very pertinent inquiries respecting the intentions. Sometimes, the whole affair is marred by a too early interference, as the following transcript from the pen of one of the Bengallee bachelors, whom the author deemed it necessary to consult, in order to give a correct idea of the whole arcana of Indian courtships, will sufficiently shew:

" The beautiful Louisa was the admired of the station; at every public ball or private party, the most flattering competition was evinced to obtain her hand for the first quadrille, that being the distinction most coveted by the aspiring youth of the place: so desirous were they to secure this enviable privilege, that visits were frequently paid a week beforehand, for the purpose, and happy was the man who led her forth in triumph to the set. Dear creature, she bore her honours meekly, all who approached her being enchanted with the sweetness of her manners, and the obliging kindness of her disposition; in fact, she was the prototype of her, of whom Pope has said:

> To all she smiles extends,
> Oft she rejects, but never once offends.

No cutting, withering monosyllable ever fell from her lips. No disdain of those who sued humbly; in fact, she did not give herself airs, a necessary precaution to secure popularity in India; for, though downright ill-treatment is frequently endured, the senior bachelors especially (by senior, old is not implied) are extremely sensitive upon points of etiquette, and are not to be affronted with impunity. Amongst the number of gay butterflies fluttering round this lovely flower, was one every-way calculated to make an impression upon a susceptible heart. He was handsome, accomplished, rode to admiration a Barbary courier of the purest breed, and moreover wore a blue jacket (*i. e.* he was a cavalry officer). No wonder that the sweetest smile was bestowed upon this favoured youth, or that the same soft emotion warmed the heart of both. Visits, which had before been casual, now became frequent; each felt a sudden passion for the food of love,—music; and the *innamorato* ransacked every public and private depositary for the loan or purchase of sentimental airs,—duets, of course. In the delightful task of accompaniment, time flew on its lightest wings, and frequently eleven o'clock, which is regarded as a late hour in India, arrived, ere they could imagine that the cantonment gong had tolled the hour of nine. Three weeks sped away in this manner, the lady of the house looking on all the while, and thinking it time that something definitive should be said. Now it must be presumed that a gay handsome young man, who is accustomed to be well-received every-where, requires a longer period to make up his mind to the serious consideration of matrimony, than one who is more diffident of his own powers, and who eagerly takes advantage of a little encouragement. Unhappily, the matron, to whose care Louisa had been consigned, did not apprehend this nice point. The young officer's visits were paid every day, and frequently twice a day, the test by which the strength of a passion is tried,—a lesser degree of assiduity being construed into lukewarmness and indifference;—and, therefore, it was considered necessary to make him "speak out." Accordingly, one morning, the visitor missed Louisa from her accustomed seat, and found himself *tête-à-tête* with her too officious friend. The battery was opened with praises of the young lady, in which the gentleman cordially joined; hints were then given that a serious impression had been made by attentions well calculated to inspire the tender passion. A little alarmed, the guest affected to treat these insinuations as mere *badinage*, and provoked, by the carelessness of his manner, out of the small remains of her discretion, the mistress of the house told her astonished auditor, that it was a most unjustifiable thing to trifle with the affections of an inexperienced heart, and that he ought at least to give the friends of this young lady an assurance of the nature of his intention. The answer of a high-spirited young man may be anticipated; he had *no* intentions; had never given the subject the slightest consideration; felt himself as free as air, and was sorry that his meaning had been so much misconstrued. Patience and temper were now utterly exhausted on the part of the matron. In no measured terms, she commanded him to leave the house, and to take away at the same time an immense quantity of music books, with which one of the chairs had been piled. Bowing, he did as he was bid, and, not without some anger and considerable confusion, collected his property under his arm,—a heavy, and somewhat slippery burthen. In the endeavour to raise the *chik*, or curtain of fine network, hung across the doorways, to keep out insects and admit air, down fell all the books, an unlucky twist of the body, at the moment, causing them to spread themselves in various directions all over the room. Unwilling to call in servants to be witnesses of the scene, he picked them up again, the lady looking daggers at him all the time, and, at length, getting clear of the apartment, flung the parcel into his buggy and drove home, making both horse and syce feel the effects of his irritation. The unlucky issue of this flirtation prevented other offers during the young lady's residence at the place in which it occurred; but, going upon a visit to a distant station, she became again the admired of all admirers, and made a better match, though with a less dashing suitor."

Other instances, of a still more heinous nature, have occurred in India, to shew that even where there are so few ladies to distract the attention of a plighted heart, the proverbial inconstancy of man will find occasions for its display. A marriage broken off upon the part of the gentleman, seldom fails to have a very injurious tendency upon the character of the deserted fair, who, by a world prone to ill-natured surmises, is supposed to have given some cause for the change of sentiment. A story is still told in the circles of Madras, which proves that, in one instance at least, the society of India acted more generously towards the ill-used party than that of her native country.

An affection had sprung up between two young persons acquainted with each other from childhood, which received the approbation of their mutual friends: the youth of the parties, however,—the lady being only fifteen, and the gentleman three years her senior,—rendered it advisable that the marriage should not take place until both had reached a more mature age. The failure of some expectations obliged the lover to accept a cadetship, and, with the full consent of his relations, he went out to India under an engagement to send for his betrothed as soon as circumstances would admit of his taking upon him the expense of maintaining a wife. The youth continued true to his first attachment during a considerable period, and the receipt of the lady's portrait, which was forwarded to him just as she had attained the full bloom of womanhood, shewed that the promise she had given of beauty had been more than fulfilled. At length, feeling himself to be in a condition to support an increased establishment, he wrote to the lady, requesting her to come out to him, and she, never having thought of any one else, obeyed the mandate as soon as it was possible for her to embark upon her voyage. Some delay had taken place in consequence of the death of her father, and the gentleman at first grew impatient, then angry, and, finally, meeting with somebody who struck his fancy, transferred his affections to a new object. While in the height and frenzy of this passion, news reached him that his first love was upon her way to India, and he was obliged to make arrangements for her reception at the house of a female acquaintance, and to proceed himself to Madras to give her the meeting. She arrived, delighting all who beheld her with the beauty of her person, the elegance of her manners, and the accomplishments of her mind. Captain S—— was considered to have gained a prize, and she, in the fond expectation of the warmest welcome which love could give, awaited an interview which was to lead to a union of the most indissoluble nature. The gentleman made his appearance, but the coldness and constraint of his manner shewed that all was not right. He either averted his eyes, or raised them in displeasure at an object formed to attract and captivate, and refusing an invitation to dinner upon the plea of an engagement, quitted the house, leaving the fair stranger in dismay at conduct so cruel and so unaccountable. Adding insult to injury, the inconstant took every opportunity which offered to utter slighting and disparaging remarks to one who had anticipated the most affectionate treatment. At length, the change in his sentiments was so glaringly displayed, that she felt obliged to inquire the cause and to come to a final explanation. He then acquainted her with the truth, taking no pains to spare her feelings in the recital, and offering some provision if she chose to remain in India. Indignant at a conclusion so different from that which she had a right to expect; and disgusted by the conduct of the man who had induced her to quit kind friends and a home for a long and dangerous voyage, in the *full* confidence that

she was seeking the arms of a protector, she declared her intention of returning to England; nor could she be dissuaded from a measure resolved upon in
the bitterness of a wounded spirit, though several families of the highest distinction entreated her to make their houses her home, and though the gentlemen of the presidency shewed an earnest desire to induce her to give herself
away in marriage. Too deeply distressed in mind to think of the latter alternative, she sought her native shore, where, but for some unfortunate circumstance, she might have found peace. Her mother had died during her absence,
and imagining that she was provided for, left her so small a proportion of her
own very limited property, as to oblige her to be in a great degree dependent
upon an aunt. The treatment which she experienced under the roof of this
relative surprized and alarmed her; upon some pretext or other, she was sent
away whenever any visitors came to the house, and at length, when a party
were to assemble, was told that she must not make her appearance, as her
returning unmarried from India had given the world reason to suppose that
her own misconduct had caused the non-fulfillment of her engagement, and
the apparent disinclination of other gentlemen to form an alliance with her.
She had never contemplated such a view of the case, and, conscious of innocence, immediately made up her mind to go back to Madras, and oblige her
faithless lover to vindicate the fame which he had so deeply injured. The
spirit which had prompted her to leave the country which had been the scene of
disappointment and insult, supported her through her new determination; she
proceeded without delay to London, where she found the captain who had
taken her out, and brought her home again, upon the eve of sailing. He
instantly offered her a free passage, and other friends coming forward to assist
her with pecuniary means, she embarked for the second time, and pursued
her voyage. Her beauty remained unimpaired by the trials she had encountered, and her manners and disposition having lost nothing of their attraction,
she won the heart of a fellow-passenger, a colonel in the army, who was re-
pairing on military duty to Ceylon. She would not, however, consent to enter
into an engagement with him until she should have procured a written testimonial from the pen of her first lover, that she had given him no cause for
the imputation which had been cast upon her, either through his own report
of the affair at home, or the uncharitable suppositions of the world. No argument could induce her to forego this resolution; and, notwithstanding the
colonel's unwillingness to submit to what he considered to be unnecessary
delay, she went on to Madras. Captain S —— was up the country at the time,
but letters were immediately despatched to him, demanding the contradiction
of the scandal; meanwhile, the residents of Madras came forward in the
handsomest manner with assurances of respect and regard, and in due course
of post the document arrived, which she had travelled so far to obtain. She
had now to all appearance surmounted the evils of her destiny; the purity of
her fame was established, and an impassioned lover waited to receive her
hand. The colonel had commissioned the captain of the ship to make several
expensive purchases for his bride at Madras; these had all been embarked for
Ceylon, but the lady for whom they were intended did not live to accompany
them. The excitement, which had so wonderfully enabled her to brave every
difficulty, having ceased, she sunk rapidly, and had scarcely received the con-
gratulations of her friends upon the triumph of her innocence, before the pul-
sations of a too-deeply agitated heart stopped, and life ebbed away. This
melancholy event occasioned the deepest regret to all the society of the presidency, and is still remembered by many with almost undiminished sorrow.

The danger attendant upon a protracted engagement, to terminate in the voyage of the lady to join her intended husband, has been exemplified, though by a less shocking catastrophe, in Bengal. The contracting parties were from the green hills of Scotland, that land which has sent out so many of its cadets to make the most of the rupee-trees of the East; and many years elapsed before the careful North Briton deemed it prudent to take upon himself the charges of an increased establishment. Meanwhile, no man could be more constant; he treasured up the image of the beloved girl in his heart, and found nothing comparable to it around him. In process of time, he became a captain, afterwards a major, and at length a lieut.-colonel. Promotion, however, had not been rapid, and the colonel had passed the middle age of life before he had attained the rank which had been the object of his ambition. Accustomed to the gradual change which increasing years had made in his person, he forgot that time would not stand still with the lady, and expected to see the same individual with whom he had parted so long ago. She came at his long-expected summons, bringing with her a niece, the counterpart of what she once had been. The colonel hastened on board the ship, which contained the object of all his hopes, and recognized in an instant the blooming girl who had lived so faithfully in his memory. " Oh, my own Maggie !" he exclaimed, clasping her to his heart; " this moment repays me for all my anxieties." " Hoot ! hoot mon !" exclaimed a withered personage beside him ; " she's no your Maggie; I'm your Maggie, and gude enough in all conscience for sic a grizzled auld parchment-faced fellow as yoursel." It was too true, and, notwithstanding a difference of opinion upon the subject, the colonel was obliged to keep his faith with his first love; the lady had not waited so long and travelled so far to be disappointed, and, in spite of no small degree of reluctance on the part of the bridegroom, the nuptials were celebrated.

It is said that younger ladies have manifested equal determination to secure a partner for life; and the bachelors delight in telling a story of one who, being seated in a palankeen, which did not keep pace with her wishes, on her way to the church, called out to the bearers, " *Juldee juldee jhow, hum shadee ko jate !*" " Quick, make haste, I am going to be married !" Such an admonition, of course, induced the poor fellows to push on with all their might, and, panting and groaning, they deposited their fair burthen at the church-door. Another anecdote is also related, which bears out the assertion that courtships in India are frequently the most summary affairs in the world. A gentleman, having seen a young lady at a ball, where, not being a dancer, he had no chance of approaching her, called the next morning at the house of the relatives with whom she was staying. He remained so long that he was asked to take tiffen, and, repeating the visit on the following day, he obtained an invitation to dinner; a third call sealed his fate, and, determined to make a bold effort, he proposed to the fair one by letter. The billet was concise, though certainly to the purpose, and, despatching it by a *claishee* (tent-pitcher) in his service, awaited the answer in feverish impatience. He was an inhabitant of a large house in the cantonments called Subaltern Hall, in consequence of the number of young officers who chummed together in it, and though the apartments were extensive and lofty, they could not contain him in the perturbed state of his mind : notwithstanding the hot winds were blowing at a fearful rate, he repaired to a long range of out-houses, where he paced up and down for an hour or more, until at length the *claishee* made his appearance at the gate of the compound. A pretty little three-cornered note was placed in his hands, containing an assurance from the lady, that she considered herself fortunate in having met with a person possessing such a congenial mind; that she thought there could be no doubt of their mutual happiness, and concluded by signing herself "your affectionate Kate." The ecstasy, with which this message was perused, passes description, and therefore must be imagined: let it suffice, that the marriage took place as soon as the license could be procured from Calcutta.

Match-making, it might be supposed, would, where both parties are so willing, be an act of supererogation in India; but the contrary is the fact, many of the chaperons of the East taking especial delight in the management of such affairs. It is said that numbers of deluded gentlemen get upon the lists of the *juwaub* club, in consequence of lending too favourable an ear to the representations of married ladies, who worm themselves into their confidence, and, by affording a false hope, induce them to propose, an act of precipitancy which in many cases ends in rejection. To sensitive minds, such a catastrophe proves a severe infliction; they betake themselves at once to the club, and never can be induced to tempt their fate again; while others, as we have had occasion to remark, little daunted, continue to try their fortune, and, as habit reconciles us to every thing, learn to think nothing of being *juwaubed.*

THE SHOOTING STARS.

Berger! tu dis que notre étoile
Règle nos jours, et brille aux cieux.
Oui, mon enfant! mais de son voile
La nuit la derobe à nos yeux.
Berger! sur cet azure tranquille
De lire on te croit le secret;
Quelle est cette étoile qui file,
Qui file, file; et disparaît?

Beranger.

" Shepherd! thou say'st that our star doth keep
    Bright vigil o'er us in the skies."
" Yes, my child, but the curtain deep
    Of darkness hides it from our eyes."
" Shepherd! upon this placid heaven,
    The secret thou canst read, they say;
What glittering star is that which shoots,
    Which shoots, and dies away?"

" My son! a mighty lord expires,
    His star of glory falls;
But now the shout of a hundred lyres
    Uprose from his rejoicing halls.
Happy he, for still he slumbers,
    Silent as the minstrel's lay."—
" But look—another star that shoots,
    That shoots, and dies away!"

" A gentle lady, pure and bright !
 How precious to the soul thou art !
Thrice happy girl—this very night
 Hope danceth in thy lover's heart ;
The wreath about thy head is bound,
 Already gleams the long array."—
" But see, another star that shoots,
 That shoots, and dies away !"

" My child ! it is the vanishing star
 Of a mighty Prince's son ;
His cradle of purple shone afar,
 But his little race is run—
The flatterer's poisonous milk of praise
 His breast shall not betray."—
" But, lo ! another star that shoots,
 That shoots, and dies away !"

" My son ! what a gloomy flame !
 The star of a Favourite dies,
Who knew not Pity's gentle name,
 Laughed at the sorrow in our eyes ;
The parasite hath cast aside
 His portrait to decay."—
" But look again—another star,
 That shoots, and dies away !"

" Alas, my child ! we well may weep,
 A Father from the land hath past ;
A Father's eyes are closed in sleep,
 His liberal hand is shut at last ;
This very evening to his door
 Widow and orphan took their way."—
" But see, another star once more,
 That shoots, and dies away !"

" A monarch passeth from the earth—
 But go, my son, and guard thy breast,
That ever clearly in thy heart
 May shine the Star of Rest ;
Lest, burning idly, at thy death
 Haply the passers-by may say—
' 'Tis but a vanishing star that shoots,
 That shoots, and dies away !' "

ANCIENT INSCRIPTIONS IN GUJERÁT.

Mr. Wathen, Persian secretary to the Bombay Government, has communicated to the Asiatic Society of Bengal* the contents of some inscriptions on copper-plates found in the peninsula of Gujerát, in an ancient character, unknown to the learned on that side of India, but which, by the help of the keys published in the Society's Journal, he has been able to decypher and exhibit in the modern Devanagari character. They turn out to be both grants of lands to priests; one about 1,500 years old, the other some hundred years subsequent. They are curious, inasmuch as they contain some names and dates which coincide with and confirm certain historical facts. The character, Mr. Wathen thinks, is evidently derived from the more ancient one which is found in the caves of Kaneri, Carli, and Verula (Ellora), and resembles that of the cave-inscription decyphered by Sir C. Wilkins, in the *As. Res*, vol. i. "One original character, being that found in the caves, appears to have first existed throughout the western parts of India, that is, in the Dakhan, Konkan, Gujerát, and perhaps more generally. It seems to have undergone gradual changes, until, about two centuries subsequent to the æras of Vicra'maditya and Saliva'-hana, an alphabet nearly similar, or identical with that at present noticed, would appear to have been introduced." Analogies have been perceived between the ancient Indian character and those of Tibet, Java, and Siam.†

In the first inscription, as well as in the second, the origin of this dynasty is traced to Bhatarca Senápati, who is said to have established his power by signal bravery and prowess: his capital, named Valabhipura,‡ is also expressly mentioned in the first grant; both the founder of this sovereignty, and two first successors, did not take the title of 'king,' but *Senápati*, or 'general,' whence it may be inferred, that they were under a paramount sovereign, by whom the province of Gujerát was committed to their charge; and it is stated in the description of the fourth prince of this family, that he was raised to the royal dignity by "the great monarch, the sole sovereign of the entire world," meaning India. The third in succession to him, named Sridhara Sena, would appear to have thrown off all dependence on this paramount sovereign of Ujayana or Kanouj; for, by the date of the first inscription, the Valabhi Samvat, or æra, would appear to have been instituted in his reign, its date being Samvat nine: this circumstance induced the belief, at first, that the æra referred to was that of Vicramáditya, until, on referring to the first volume of Tod's *Rájast'han*, the existence of a Surya-vansa dynasty in Gujerát, whose capital was Valabhipura, and title 'Bhatarca,' and also of a Samvat, or æra, peculiar to those kings, as proved by Jaina legends, and inscriptions found at Somnáth, Pattan, &c., shewed that these grants must belong to those princes and their æra alone.

Colonel Tod established, from the materials already mentioned, the particulars of which may be seen on reference to his work,§ the following historical data:—

"1. The emigration of a prince named Keneksen, of the Surya-vansa, or race of the sun, from Koshala‖ dèsha, and his establishing himself in Gujerát about A.D. 144.

* The communication appears in the Journal of the Society.

† We are glad to find, from Mr Prinsep's note on this paper, that there is some reason to expect a comprehensive palæographical table of characters, which will prove of great utility.

‡ In Pracrit, it is written with a *b*, "Balabhi."

§ See the chapter entitled "Annals of Mewár." ‖ The present Oude.

" 2. The institution of an æra, called the *Valabhi Samvat,* by his successors, who became the independent kings of Gujerát : the first year of which æra was the 375th of Vicramáditya, or A.D. 319.

" 3. The invasion of the kingdom of the Valabhi princes by a barbarian force, the destruction of their capital Valabhipura, in A.D. 524, and the removal of the seat of government to the north-eastern part of Gujerát, most probably at first to Sidhapura, about A.D. 554.

" The inscriptions confirm, in a singular manner, these several epochs. The first inscription is dated 9th Valabhi Samvat, corresponding with 384 of Vicramáditya, and A.D. 328.

" Now, allowing twenty years for the average reign of the six princes of the first inscription, this will give 129 years for the interval between Sridhara Sena, in whose reign this æra may be supposed to have commenced, and Bhatarca Senápati, the founder of the dynasty, which will place him as having lived in A.D. 190, or within forty-six years of the time specified by Tod, as that of Keneksèn's establishment in Gujerát. That Bhatarca was a family title, and not the real name of this chief, is shewn by its being alone used in the seals affixed to both the inscriptions.

" From the second inscription, we have a long line of princes, the last of whom, Siláditya Musalli, would appear, from an allusion therein, to have removed the capital to Sidhapura.

" Taking the number of kings, whose names are given subsequent to Sridhara Sena, the founder of the Valabhi æra, at twelve, and the length of their reigns at an average of twenty years each, this calculation will shew a term of about 240 or more years to have elapsed from this time, to that of Siláditya Musalli of Sidhapura, or A.D. 559, about thirty-five years after the sack of Valabhipura by the barbarians.

" On referring to the list of kings, another of the name of Siláditya, it will be seen, just preceded the prince who made the grant contained in the second inscription, whose reign will thus approximate to A.D. 524, stated in the Jaina legends to be the date when the capital was surprised by a foreign army. From the same source, also, we find the name of the prince, who then reigned, to have been Siláditya, as above.

" These coincidences are curious, and tend to confirm the authenticity of those fragments of early Hindu history, which Tod has so carefully collected.

" The Jaina historical legends all mention the kings of this dynasty, and their æra, the Valabhi Samvat; the capital, from its geographical position, would appear to have been the Byzantium of Ptolemy ; its kings were of the dynasty called by foreigners the Balhára, which may have been a corruption of the title Bhatarca,* or derived from the adjoining district of Bhala, and Rai or prince; the absurd manner in which Hindu names were, and still are, corrupted by the Arabs and other foreigners, may easily account for the difficulty of reconciling real names with their corruptions.

" It is a singular circumstance connected with the destruction of Valabhipura, that it would appear to have been conquered by a Mblechha, or Bactro-Indian army, which, it may be presumed, came from a Bactrian kingdom then existing, in which were probably comprised the present Múltán, Sindh, Cachha, and perhaps many other provinces ; whether this state became subsequently divided into several petty principalities, one of which held the southern part of Sindh and Cachha, is a query which remains to be solved ; the southern part of Sindh, however, has been known, from the most ancient times, by the

---

* *Bhatarca* literally means ' cherishing sun ;' it is a royal title.

appellation of Lar, which would be in Sanscrit Larica : now the kingdom of Larike is mentioned expressly by Ptolemy, but is made to comprise the coast of Gujerát, which might have been conquered by it ; the strongest fact in support of this theory is, that many Bactro-Indian coins, with the head of the prince, evidently of inferior Greek workmanship, something similar to those found at the Manikyála Tope, &c., have been found in great numbers in Cachha, and in parts of Sauráshtra.*

" It may be here mentioned, that it is from this very family of Valabhipura, that the legends of the present ránas of Udayapur (Oodipoor) deduce their descent.

" After reigning some years in the north of Gujerát, the power of the dynasty was destroyed, its kingdom dismembered, and the city of Anhalwara Pattan became the capital, under the succeeding dynasties of the Chawura and Chalukia (*vulgo* Solanki) races.

" Both of these grants convey fields to brahmans as religious gifts. The lands granted in the second inscription are stated to be situated in Sauráshtra, and the donees are said to have come from Girinagara (Júnagur or Girnal), and to have settled at Sidhapura.

" Two facts, proving the great antiquity of these grants, are,—first, the measure of land being square paces ; and the other, the existence of the worship of the sun : one of the princes is named as being of that sect.

" In the course of antiquarian researches in India, we cannot but remark the very opposite course pursued by the Jainas and the Brahmans, in regard to the preservation of historical legends ; the Brahmans are accused by the Jainas of having destroyed, wherever they gained the supremacy, all the historical books in existence, which related facts anterior to the Musalman conquest ; and we certainly do not find in the Dakhan, and other countries which have been long under their exclusive influence, anything whatever prior to that period ; whereas, on the contrary, the Jainas have treasured up in their libraries every historical legend and fragment that could be preserved by them.

" May it not be inferred, that the Brahmans, sensible of the great changes introduced by themselves, to serve their own avaricious purposes, in the Hindu worship, at the æra of the Musalman conquest, neglected the preservation of the historical works which then existed ; for as no king of their own faith remained, and their nobles and learned men must have lost their power and influence, no one was left who took any interest in their preservation ; and it appears probable, that, at such period, the *Puránas* were altered, and the novel practices now existing introduced, to enable these wily priests still to extort from the superstition of the people what they had formerly enjoyed by the pious munificence of their own kings.

" The Jainas, indeed, assert, that the *Puránas* are mere historical works ; that Parasuráma, Rámachandra, Krishna, &c. were merely great kings, who reigned in Oude and other places, and have not the slightest pretensions to divinity.

" It may tend to confirm this theory, when we consider, that all the great reformers of the Hindu religion, whose doctrines and whose expositions of that faith are now followed, flourished about the same period, when India was thrown into confusion by the invasions of those ferocious and fanatical barbarians, the Arabs, the Turks,† and Afghans, or from 500 to 800 years back ; Sankara A'chárya, Valabha A'chárya, and Ramanuja A'chárya, are all supposed to have lived between those periods.

* Sauráshtra, or the region of the worshippers of the sun, comprised the whole of the peninsula at present called Kathiawar.   † By Turks, I mean natives of Central Asia.

" The great Hindu sovereignties falling to pieces, it became impossible to perform sacrifices requiring such prodigious expenditure,* the kings of foreign faith no longer ruling by the shástras, no check existed to the intermixture of castes: hence the Warna Sankara; the Kshetriyas overcame, and, fleeing from their foes, emigrated into various parts, laid down the warlike profession, and engaged in civil and commercial pursuits: hence the present Kshetri, the Prabhi, the Bhatti, &c., once warriors, now scribes and merchants; the Brahmans then, to raise themselves, and degrade the other castes, invented the fable of the destruction of the whole Kshetriya tribe by Parasuráma—a thing in itself incredible; but which story enabled them to substitute the *Puránas* for the *Vedas*, in conducting the sacred offices, as connected with those classes.

"Further, if we inquire into the origin of many of the present most popular incarnations, as worshipped in Western India, we shall no doubt trace them to the æra when the *Puránas* were interpolated and converted from mere historical legends into books of scripture. A new impetus was thus given to superstition by the discovery of these supposed miraculous emanations of Siva, Vishnu, and Ganesa, in the shape of Khundeh Rao,† Wittoba, and the Chinchwara Ganapati.

" That great changes were introduced, about the period of the Musalman invasion, into the practices of the Hindu religion, and that many, as they now exist, are far different to what they were previous to that æra, are facts which will become better known and ascertained, as the ancient history of the country becomes more cleared from the obscurity in which it is at present involved."

List of Kings of the Valabhi or Balhára Dynasty, as found in the Two Inscriptions.

A.D. 144 or 190	1. Senápati	Bhatarca.	
	2.	Dhara Sena.	
	3. Mahárája	Drona Sinha.	
	4.	Dhruva Sena, I.	
	5.	Dharapattah.	
	6.	Griha Sena.	
A D. 300	7.‡	Srídhara Sena, I.§	
	8.	Siladitya, I.	
	9.	Charagriha, I.	
	10.	Srídhara Sena, II.	
	11.	Dhruva Sena, II.	
	12.	Srídhara Sena, II.	
	13.	Siladitya, II.	

At this part of the copper-plate the writing is so obliterated, that the names of two or three princes cannot be made out.

	16. Mahárája	Charagriha, II.
A.D. 524	17.	Siladitya, III.
A.D. 559	18.	Siladitya Musalli, IV.

The first two princes have the title "Senápati" alone. All those subsequent to No. 3, " Mahárája." The whole had the title of " Srí Bhatarca," and the device on their banner was the " Nandi," or sacred bull of Siva, as appears from the seals attached to both inscriptions.

* Such as Asvamedha, &c.: notwithstanding the assertions of the brahmans that these sacrifices of the horse, &c. have been abolished in this Kali-yuga, we find instances of their performances recorded in inscriptions of 800 years and later date.

† These are all peculiar to the Mahratta country, their temples being at Jejury, Pundarpur, and Chinchwar.

‡ These seven are from the first inscription, the following from the second inscription.

§ A.D. 319. In his reign, the Valabhi æra is supposed to have commenced.

ON FISH FALLING IN RAIN.

TO THE EDITOR.

Sir :—It is no very unfrequent thing to find in the *Asiatic Journal*, as well as in papers connected with the East, accounts of fish having *fallen from the clouds*, in rain; and the subject is well calculated to excite curiosity and speculation, in order to explain so strange a phenomenon. I believe that, with many scientific men in Europe, the fact has been doubted or altogether disbelieved, in the same manner as the accounts of *meteorites*, or stones from the sky, were once looked upon as mere fables of the ignorant and superstitious. As in this latter case, however, the fact has been long since proved, beyond a doubt, although the *cause* yet remains (and may long remain) a matter of speculation; so, also, in the former, I am inclined to think that the subject is no longer a matter of question; and that it only requires an accumulation of well-authenticated facts, and of attentive observations, to account for what, at first sight, seems startling and almost incredible.

I have, for several years, been occasionally in the habit of making inquiries as to this fact, from men who have been long in India; and, although I have never been so fortunate as to meet with any individual who could speak to it, from direct *personal* knowledge, as having had *ocular* demonstration of its occurrence; yet I have rarely met with any one who had not heard of it ; and, in some few cases, I have even attained all but ocular proof of the point in question. In the idea that there can be no method more likely to elicit fresh evidence, on this curious question, than by addressing your numerous Indian readers, through the medium of your Journal, I take the liberty of placing the following reflexions on the subject at your disposal.

In the *Asiatic Journal* for July 1834 (p 176), we are told that "The *Journal of the Asiatic Society* contains a body of evidence, which seems to leave no doubt of the fact, of the falling of fish, from the sky, during rains. Nine natives of respectability have deposed to their *seeing* a large number of fish fall, and picking them up;" and the writer adds, "I was as incredulous as my neighbours, until I once found a small fish, *which had apparently been alive when it fell*, in the brass funnel of my pluviometer at Benares, which stood on an isolated stone pillar, raised five feet above the ground, in my garden."

I have not been able to peruse the evidence above alluded to, in the *Journal of the Asiatic Society;* but if the fact stated by the above writer is to be depended on (and we have no reason to doubt it), the fact of fish *sometimes* falling in rain, in India, may be looked upon as fully established.

The following account was sent me by a friend, as being lately cut from a newspaper; but not having the exact date I am unable to refer to it :—" A correspondent of the *Asiatic Journal*, at Bengal, gives the following particulars of a fall of fish, which happened on the 17th of May last, in the neighbourhood of Allahabad. ' The zemindars of the village have furnished the following particulars, which are confirmed by other accounts. About noon, the wind being from the west, and a few distant clouds visible ; *a blast of high wind*, accompanied with *much dust*, which changed the atmosphere to a reddish hue, came on. *The blast appeared to extend in breadth* 400 *yards*.' (It may here be observed, that this description gives much the idea of a passing whirlwind) ; 'choppers were carried off, and trees blown down. When the storm had passed over, they found the ground, south of the village, to the extent of two bigahs, strewed with fish, in number not less than 3,000 or

4,000. The fish were all of the *Chalwa* species (*clopea cultrata*, Shakespear's Dictionary), *a span or less* in length, and from one and-a-half to half a seer in weight. When found, they were all *dead* and *dry*. *Chalwa fish are found in the tanks and rivers in the neighbourhood.* The nearest tank, in which there is water, is about half-a-mile south of the village;' (the wind is said to have been *from the west ;*) 'the Jumna runs about three miles *south* of the village; the Ganges fourteen miles N. by E. The fish were not eaten; it is said that, in the pan, *they turned into blood.*' "

It is such impossibilities as we find mentioned at the conclusion of the above otherwise clear account, that cast a shade of *doubt* upon such statements, when coming perhaps from uninformed natives, and unsupported by the evidence of intelligent Europeans. But, with this exception, the above account seems to bear the appearance of truth. We find, however, no mention made of *rain*. On the contrary, it is stated that there were but a few distant clouds; and the blast appears to have been heavily charged with *dust,* from which we cannot wonder that the fish that fell were both *dead* and *dry.*

" On June 15th, 1834 (or 5), was read before the Linnæan Society an extract of a letter from Mrs. Smith, dated Moradabad, July 20th, 1829, addressed to a friend in Somersetshire, giving an account of a number of fish that had fallen in a shower at that place. That lady states that many were observed by her from the windows of her house, *springing about upon the grass,* immediately after the *storm.* The letter was accompanied by a drawing of one of the fish, taken from life at the moment, which represents a small species of *cyprinus,* two inches and a-quarter long, green above, silvery white below, with a broad lateral line, bright red."

It is to be regretted that the above interesting statement does not mention whether the fish (which, from there being only one drawing, we are to presume were all of one kind) were common to the neighbouring waters.

I have lately had a good deal of conversation on this subject with a gentleman who has spent many years in India, and who speaks of having often heard this matter discussed among Europeans, and various opinions broached, both as to the reality of the fact, and its cause. It has frequently been remarked in parts of the country far from rivers, where tanks are constructed at great expense, hollowed and embanked *on the solid ground,* and only supplied with water *from the clouds,* that fish are not long in appearing where no such fish have been liberated by man. In the ditches and puddles of the country, which are for months together quite parched and dry, and only filled after heavy rains, little fish are also frequently observed. This gentleman states, that, although he never actually *saw fish fall* in rain, yet he has frequently remarked fish in situations, immediately after heavy rains, where he thinks they could not possibly have been, except by falling *with the rain.* He more particularly mentioned two instances, which struck him forcibly; one in which he saw fish in pools of water *on the high road,* while travelling from Barrackpore to Calcutta; the other in an excavation at the side of a road, and close to a village, which hole was usually quite dry, and which was a common receptacle for rubbish. He does not speak with certainty as to the *kinds* of fish seen on these occasions, but says that they were a small flattish fish (somewhat resembling the Sardinia), about an inch and-a-half long; and either the *chilwah* (or *chalwah,* as it is called in the former account), or a fish much resembling it. This is a kind commonly known in India as a delicacy, being served on skewers made for the purpose.

We certainly cannot wonder that new tanks are speedily furnished with fish, if even the temporary puddles on the roads are sometimes supplied with them. Nor can we well doubt, under such circumstances, that they really do fall, as is generally supposed, in rain from the clouds. But we must not hence suppose that this is an *every-day* occurrence; on the contrary, it is so rare that even the natives seem to regard it as extraordinary. One of the ideas which are broached in opposition to that of their falling with rains is, that in the ditches or ponds which are dry during the hot months, these little fish may possibly have the power of burying themselves deep in the mud, and of again issuing out on the fall of rain, as earth-worms are known to sink themselves six or seven feet down, to avoid the severity of our winter frosts. Another idea is, that the ground may be impregnated with spawn, which is quickly matured in a tropical climate. Both of these ideas seem far-fetched and improbable, nor will either of them account for fish being found *on dry land* after rain.

Supposing it then admitted, that fish actually fall *from the sky* in rain, the next and greatest question is as to *how they got there?* If it be true, as the evidence seems to prove, that such fish either are often *alive* when they fall, or soon *recover* in the puddles, tanks, or ditches into which they are speedily drained; we have proof to demonstration *that they could not have been long out of their native element.* Few will argue that the *clouds* form an element in which either the weight of the fish, however small, could be sustained, or their lives preserved for any length of time, even supposing them by whatever means to be so suspended in mid-air. None but ill-informed persons can now suppose, as was once done, that the clouds are composed of water in the same fluent state as when they discharge moisture in rain. Many travellers, myself amongst the number, have risen *into the clouds,* passed for a considerable distance *through them,* at the expense of such dampness as any other *fog* occasions, and have at length, in Alpine regions, reached *far above them,* a pure and sunny region, from whence they appeared like a vast sea of wool or cotton, with the mountain-tops protruding and resembling islands in this woolly ocean. Clouds are mere vapours, composed it is true of water, but so divided as to have the nature rather of *ærial* than of *aqueous* fluidity. They only fall in *rain* when condensed by cold into drops, which thus become too heavy to resist the common laws of gravity, and are, therefore, impelled towards the earth with a force proportioned to their size. Now, in passing through clouds in a state of vapour, however dense, were we to throw up into the air such little fish as are now the subject in question, they, being much heavier than many united drops of rain, could not fail to be subject to the same laws of gravity, and would instantly fall to the ground. In like manner seems to fall to the ground by its own weight, the idea that fish could remain suspended in clouds in the state we commonly see them, and be discharged in *common* rain. Therefore, even supposing the powers of evaporation (by which alone they could be elevated *under common circumstances*) to be sufficiently great in the tropics to suck up fish in vapours from fens or tanks, we are forbidden by the laws of gravity to suppose that such vapours, under the form of clouds, are capable of sustaining them. But I cannot admit that fish of an inch or two in length can be raised into the air by any powers of evaporation, even under a tropical sun. It is far from impossible (it may be even probable), that animalcules of many minute sorts may be so sucked up and kept in life in the minute subdivisions of evaporized water; and that the well-known fact may thus be accounted for, of pure distilled water being soon furnished with these minute beings, if isolated and freely exposed to the atmospheric air. I have frequently considered this as a possible cause of *mal-aria* in fenny regions, under a hot sun. But such fish as are now in question cannot possibly be accounted for in this manner. If they are not raised, therefore, in the common and tranquil state of nature, we must necessarily look for a solution of the difficulty to some more *occasional* and more powerful mechanism.

The only explanation that occurs to me as probable is, that they are sucked up, together with considerable bodies of water, from rivers or tanks, by the vortex of such whirlwinds as commonly occasion *water-spouts*, both at sea and on land; that they are thus sustained against the opposing laws of gravity, by so violent an action; are forced to accompany the sweeping tempest, and are at length scattered on the surface of the earth, at perhaps no very great distance from their native waters. On suggesting this idea to the gentleman already alluded to, he immediately stated, as in some degree supporting it, that whirlwinds are extremely common in India, and so powerful as to raise prodigious columns of dust into the air, which are driven along to a great distance. We have all seen examples, on a small scale, of such whirlwinds even in England. They always occur in very hot weather and generally in calm days; and I remember on one occasion, in the midst of the most perfect tranquillity, and in a very sheltered garden in the south of Scotland, seeing a quantity of clothes, which had been spread to dry on a smooth bowling-green, suddenly thrown into the utmost confusion, and some of the articles carried up into the air so high, as to be nearly lost to view. They were watched by myself and others for upwards of half-an-hour, and were found, next day, at a distance of three miles. The instance already mentioned, as having occurred near Allahabad, seems to have been accompanied by a tempest of this description, but on a scale more proportioned to the greater heat of that climate. It is true that *rain* is not mentioned in that account, but it may not have been wanting, nevertheless, although perhaps expended before the fish reached the ground. The account of Mrs. Smith, of the *living* fish which she saw fall on the grass at Moradabad, in July 1829, is also highly corroborative of this idea in certain points. The shower is there called a *storm*, bespeaking great severity; and the fish having been seen living when they fell on the grass, plainly proves that they could not have been long out of some neighbouring tank or river. In one thing all accounts seem to agree, viz. as to the fish being *invariably small*, and as we know that prodigious shoals of such small fish frequently swim near the surface of waters, especially to enjoy the warmth of the sun, we can have less difficulty in subscribing to the *possibility* of numbers of them being sucked up, if a violent whirlwind or water-spout should chance to pass over them.

I can, at present, conceive no other mode by which to account for such bodies (*especially if in life*) falling from the sky. I do not offer it, however, as more than an idea, and requiring the corroboration of acute observers of the atmospheric phenomena in India. It may perhaps further tend to an explanation of this point, if I suggest the following heads of inquiry, for the guidance of such as may have it in their power to examine into the subject:—

1st. To remark particularly the species of the fish that fall; whether they are all *of one kind*, and especially if they are such as are common in the waters of the surrounding country; for it must be kept in mind, that, as clouds, in their common state, are often driven to vast distances from the countries in which they may have been drawn up in vapour, we have no right to expect in their discharges of rain such fish as are common where that rain chances to fall, if the fish are raised into the air by *common* evaporation.

2d. To observe whether they are *alive* or *dead*, and, if dead, whether they appear to have been so for some time. In a hot climate they would soon become putrid; and we know, besides, that a thundery atmosphere quickly taints fish or meat. If they are *alive*, or if they soon recover on falling into water; and if, combined with this, they prove to be the common fish of the district, it may be considered as certain that they have not been many *minutes* out of their native waters; and also that these waters cannot be at any very great distance. Should they prove to be of a kind well known in the country, it would also be of great importance to ascertain the length of time this species retained life after being caught with a net; and also whether they could be recovered after a certain time, when apparently dead. By their *greater* or *less* tenaciousness of life, we may be in some degree guided as to the *time* occupied by their flight, and the distance from whence they may have been brought.

3d. To observe the nature and degree of force of the rain or tempest, in which they may fall, whether always *violent* and accompanied with wind; and also, whether, in the direction from whence it comes, there be any tank or river from which the fish might have been sucked up together with water. This is of material importance with a view to the theory which I have ventured to propose; for no one, who has seen the phenomena of water-spouts at sea, can doubt that such small fish as happen to be near the surface at the point of contact would be drawn up into the vortex together with the water.

These are the chief points which I would suggest as worthy of observation, and I cannot but think that with the combined attention of so many observers of nature as are now to be found in India, the obscurity in which this curious fact has hitherto been shrouded may speedily be cleared away; and should these observations chance to meet the eye of any one who has studied the subject in the East, it will be satisfactory either to have my suggestion strengthened by his testimony, or entirely set aside by a clear statement of opposing facts.*

I am, Sir,
Your obedient humble Servant,
GEO. FAIRHOLME.

April 13*th*, 1836.

Postscript.—I have, since writing the above, had an opportunity through the kindness of Mr. Yarrell, F.L.S., the author of a beautiful work on fish, now in the course of publication, of seeing a copy of the letter above alluded to from Mrs. Smith. She was the wife of the resident judge at Moradabad. The drawing of the *Cyprinus*, which she made from the life, in 1829, represents a kind very common in the Indian waters. This is known from the published description of the fish of the Ganges. It appears that this lady speaks of two occasions on which she had witnessed the fall of fish. She thus writes from Silhet, July 30, 1826:—" Have you not heard of its raining *fish* in India? I can assure you that our men went out and picked them up during a tremendous storm. I saw them myself from the window leaping about on the grass, while the men were picking them up. Is it possible that the violence of the rain may force them out of the river? or may they not be drawn up by the

* I have been informed by respectable persons from the spot, that fish had, on one occasion, a few years ago, fallen near Dunkeld in Perthshire during a heavy shower. The late Dr. Forbes, the medical man of the district of Dunavoid, near Logierait, is said to have picked up, immediately after the shower, one or more little fish, said to be *par* (a kind common in that country), and about two inches long. This was on an elevated spot, distant from any lake or river. I have not been able to satisfy myself fully of the correctness of this *hearsay* evidence, but I know no reason whatever to doubt it, as the parties are all respectable and intelligent. I think I have somewhere read of similar falls of fish occurring in the New World, and of their being found alive in tanks on the tops of the houses.

ascending foam or vapour, and fall down in rain? but that many were springing about on the grass is most certain. They are small; the largest I saw was about the size of a small gudgeon." From this letter it appears that Mrs. Smith speaks of "*the river*" and of the fish having probably belonged to it, as she endeavours to account for their having been forced out of it during the storm, which is also called "*tremendous*," and, therefore, such as we may imagine as the cause or effect of water-spouts.

The fish, of one of which a drawing was sent, seem to have fallen at Moradabad July 29th, 1829. I have also seen the following notice which appeared in a newspaper :—" On the 9th of March 1830, the inhabitants of the island of Ula, in Argylshire, after a day of very hard rain, were surprised to find numbers of *small herrings* strewed over the fields, perfectly fresh, and some of them exhibiting *signs of life*."

In the British Museum, I find a bottle containing two small herrings about four inches long, with the following notice attached: " Found in an arable field in Rosshire, April 21st, 1828. Presented by Thos. Allan, Esq." (The late banker in Edinburgh and an eminent mineralogist and collector).

In Hasted's History of Kent, vol. v. p. 2. (8vo. edit.), it is stated that, " About Easter 1666, in the parish of Stansted, which is a considerable distance from the sea or any branch of it, and a place where there are no fishponds and rather a scarcity of water, a pasture-field was scattered all over with *small fish*, in quantity about a bushel, supposed to have been *rained down from a cloud*, there having been at the time a great tempest of *thunder, rain, and wind*. The fish were about the size of a man's little finger. Some were like small whitings; others like sprats, and some smaller like smelts. Several of these fish were shewn publicly at Maidstone and Dartford."

In conclusion, I may mention that a few small fish have been sent to me by a friend, as having fallen in rain, but without mention either of date or place. They have been for many years in the possession of my friend, in Scotland. Mr. Gray, of the British Museum, immediately recognised them as an Indian species of the *Periopthalmus*. They are less than an inch in length, and are remarkable for a sucker below the opening of the gills. It is probable that they were sent or brought to England by some one who had been in India.

Mr. Yarrell remarks, that the fry of fish are generally observed near the surface, as they are incapable of sustaining the great pressure of deep water; and we have thus a greater probability of the above instances having occurred by the agency of violent hurricanes or water-spouts.

THE EASTERN BEAUTY BATHING.

> Chaque fois que la nacelle,
>   Qui chancelle,
> Passe à fleur d'eau dans son vol,
> On voit sur l'eau qui s'agite,
>   Sortir vite
> Son beau pied et son beau col.
>
> *Victor Hugo.*

Zillah, full of indolent pleasure,
    Stoopeth now, with marble brow,
Over the calm and crystal water ;
Never hath a lovelier daughter,
With richer eyes, or sweeter mouth,
From sunny east, or scented south,
    Rejoiced in more voluptuous leisure !

Now with snowy foot she parteth
   The waters blue of emerald hue,
Now in the rippling stream you see
Her bosom and neck of ivory;
Now, like a wreath of lilies bright,
Her radiant arm of cloudless white,
Through the gilded water darteth.

Let us hide,—within an hour,
   From her watery bower,
With glowing cheek and flashing eye,
The Beautiful will hasten by;
No gossamer veil, no shadowy vest—
Her white arms crossed upon her breast.

A star gleams through the waves of pearl—
   It is, it is the lovely girl;
The silver dew from every curl
Drops like a sparkling April rain,
Making her cheeks of bloom look brighter;
But hark! the rustling leaves affright her—
The star is gone again.

Listen to the voice that sighs,
   Like music from the skies—
" If I were a mighty queen,
How soon upon the flow'ry green
A yellow marble bath for me
Should shine through the boughs of the orange-tree!

And I would have a silken tent,
   Purple as the element,
Like a vast flower spreading round
Its golden shadow on the ground;
And idly should my limbs recline,
(While warbling rills of water ran—
Making melody divine—)
Upon the perfumed ottoman.

Then might I at the sultry hour,
   Within my garden bower,
Amid the balmy water play
All the pleasant summer day;
Nor every moment fear to see,
Through the thick foliage of the tree,
Two bold eyes turned that way."

Thus the Beauty spoke, while she
   Ever most voluptuously
Upon the amorous bosom lies
Of the water, nor takes heed
How morning o'er the fragrant mead
Opens now her glittering eyes.

INDIVIDUALLY, perhaps, no one building in the City of Palaces, with the single exception of Government House, possesses any particular claims to the admiration of those who are well acquainted with the principles of architecture, and who have a taste for its beauties. It is as a whole that Calcutta must be viewed, since, in detail, numerous blemishes may be dis٭ covered, affording abundant materials for the exercise of the hypercriticism which so many persons affect, and furnishing subject for regret to the more judicious, though perchance somewhat fastidious, spectator. Bishop Heber passes the Town Hall with a single remark, that it has no merit beyond its size ; but, however faulty, it can scarcely be denied that it adds a grand feature to the noble range of buildings which stretch along the esplanade towards the river. The interior is spacious, and the range of apartments appropriated to public assemblages well adapted for the purpose for which they are intended. The central and principal saloon has the usual fault of apartments of the same description in India, that of being too long for its width, a blemish which is rendered more conspicuous by the orchestra having been erected at the extreme end : an injudicious selection, as the music is in consequence almost inaudible at the bottom of the room, when there is a crowded assembly to assist in deadening the sound. The ball-room is divided, according to the Anglo-Indian fashion, by rows of pillars, marking off a sort of aisle on either side ; it is approached through a handsome ante-chamber, and leads into some noble apartments, where card-tables may be placed or refreshments laid out. The entrance-hall and the staircase are wide and well-proportioned, and the ornaments in good taste. Altogether, especially when illuminated at night, with the floods of brilliant light, which all Indians, both anglo and native, delight to pour upon the scene, the *coup d'œil* is very striking, and it would be difficult to find any other building erected for the same purpose at all approaching in splendour to the public rooms of Calcutta.

The Town Hall was built by a Colonel Garstin, an officer who speculated very largely in brick and mortar, and to whom the seat of government is indebted for a great number of those princely residencies, which have justly entitled it to be styled the City of Palaces. Garstin-buildings, in the neighbourhood of the Town Hall, commemorates the name of one of the most enterprizing amid those who so materially assisted in reclaiming the bog and jungle, which at no very distant period stretched over the most fashionable quarter of Calcutta. It would be an interesting employment to trace the progress of the city from the period in which the village, whence it derived its name, *Calicata*, was selected as the principal settlement of the British Government in Bengal ; but should there be such a work in existence, we have no guide-book or picture of Calcutta at hand, and must be content with a very limited antiquarian research. Originally, we are told that, at the time Calcutta was taken by Suraja-ud-Dowlah, there were about seventy houses in the town belonging to the English ; these increased a-pace, but, for some considerable period, the Loll Bazar, Cossitollah, and Council House-street, were considered to be the most fashionable parts of the city ; and, until a comparatively late era, the site of Government House presented an even worse appearance than that of the marshy wastes which still incroach upon the limits of Chowringee. The progress of improvement has levelled the huts and drained the marshes, which so closely environed the habitations of the European residents, and it is now necessary to travel into the suburbs before we can form a very correct idea of the state of affairs, when the forest and the swamp occupied the ground now glittering with buildings which have given to Calcutta a proud pre-eminence amongst the cities of modern times.

Some doubts existed respecting the stability of the Town Hall at the period of its erection ; a rumour went abroad that it was unsafe, and the supposed danger to be incurred prevented many persons from patronizing it as a place of public resort. Whether it was strengthened by additional pillars, or the report was discovered to be groundless, the writer has no present means of ascertaining ; but, whatever might have been the cause, the panic has subsided, and at all times and seasons the rooms are crowded, whenever any thing very attractive is held forth in the shape of a ball or public meeting. Although there is no scarcity of wood, bricks, or mortar, in Calcutta, building is very expensive ; and the climate, in occasioning premature decay to materials, which in other countries would last for a considerable period, adds greatly to estimates involving the necessity of constant repair. Bricks form a small item in the account, as they are very abundant and exceedingly cheap in Calcutta. In the absence of stone and gravel, in the alluvial soil which pervades the greater portion of Bengal, they are used whole, broken, and pounded, in the construction of the roads, which, being of a deep red, have a very peculiar appearance. Two or three layers of whole bricks are given to the centre of these roads, lessening as they approach the sides ; rubbish, broken bricks, and coarse sand are then added, and the surface is covered with the pounded brick, the whole becoming firm, compact, and very durable, lasting, it is said, longer than those made in England with gravel, flint, and limestone. However, it must be allowed that the burthens brought upon them are not nearly so heavy, the native *hackery* being a light vehicle compared to our waggons, and carrying of course very inferior weights to those permitted by Act of Parliament at home. The lime employed in Calcutta is imported from a considerable distance, and is chiefly brought down from the Morungs, whence it is shipped in large boats, either slaked, or in its quick state. As it has to travel a considerable distance, never less than three hundred miles, it does not always reach Calcutta in great perfection, and is sometimes sold at a very high price. The lime thus obtained is very inferior to that which comes from the coast of Coromandel, and the borders of Malabar, which is made from shells, and is nearly, if not quite, equal to that made in Italy, and in some parts of India, from broken marble, taking as fine a polish, and furnishing decorations equally ornamental. At Rajmhal, there is a manufacture of *serais,* or water-bottles, from the refuse marble, made into lime, which is curious and beautiful; but at Agra, where the material is more abundant, the interiors of many houses are decorated with a variety of ornaments moulded from the marble *chunam,* which is so much in request.

Engineer officers are usually the best architects in India, and some of them have succeeded in manufacturing bricks of a very superior kind; one employed a very ingenious method to render a house, which he was building for himself, more than commonly durable; he constructed the whole of the walls of *cutcha,* with mud bricks, dried in the sun, cementing the whole with mud : the places for the doors and windows were carefully arched, and the interior being formed into a brick kiln, the fire was lighted, and while bricks for future buildings were in progress, the whole of the walls became a solid mass of impenetrable substance, into which neither insect nor reptile could penetrate. Where any public works are going on, this example might be followed with advantage, the manufacture of bricks in this manner not being more expensive, while it secures a residence impervious to the elements and to the numerous intruders which often prove very disagreeable companions. Formerly, the materials were either cheaper, or less expense was spared in the buildings of Calcutta, the old fort being perfectly ball-proof after a lapse of forty years, and a similar degree of solidity having been found in the old terraces still remaining in Calcutta, which have retained their position, acting as roofs to the godowns, or warehouses, below, after the decay or removal of the beams intended originally for their support. Much of the wood, which is attainable for the purpose of building in Calcutta, is rendered almost useless by the facility with which it is penetrated by white ants. These insects do not object to timber abounding in turpentine, and some other powerful scents; but they have so great an aversion to the *mutty ke tale,* earth oil, as the petroleum imported from Pegu and Ava is called, that a few drops will suffice to preserve a beam from destruction. Teak wood possesses some property which is repellent to the white ant, for several years at least after it is cut, but it is too expensive to be brought into general use; and the saul-tree, which is cheaper, but which boasts no such antidote, furnishes the greater portion of the timber employed in the buildings of Calcutta: even this, however, though a saving when compared to teak, is still high-priced, and, in addition to the roofs which must be constructed of solid masonry, renders the cost of building very great. While an excellent bungalow may be erected from about 5,000 to 8,000 rupees, a residence fitted for the accommodation of the same establishment, at Calcutta, would cost 50,000 or 70,000 rupees.

The Town Hall has been built according to the newest and most approved fashion in Calcutta, with a basement-floor equalling in elegance the upper parts of the erection; there is, therefore, nothing unsightly to be seen at the entrance, and the whole, bating perhaps some architectural blemishes, is worthy of the city to which it assuredly forms an embellishment. Public meetings of every sort and kind are convened at the Town Hall, and many have been the stormy discussions which its saloons have witnessed; latterly, the walls have rung with the grievances of a portion of the Christian population, whose alleged rights and aspiring claims appear to be of very difficult adjustment. It cannot be denied that the Indo-Britons, or Eurasians, as they call themselves, are placed in a very unfortunate position, and it seems almost next to impossible to devise any remedy, so long as native prejudices are so strongly opposed to their admission to places of public trust. The treatment they receive from Europeans boasting a purer descent, affords little or no just grounds for complaint; for there can be no doubt that their exclusion from the court-parties, and government-employments, arises solely from the hostile feelings of the proud Hindoo and the intolerant Mohamedan, both determined not to endure any species of control from persons sprung from the lower, or less virtuous, portion of their own community. The whole system of caste must give way, before the native mind can be disabused upon the subject of human rights, and it will take a long time before the doctrine of equality can be established amongst a people accustomed to look upon the circumstance of ignoble birth as fatal to every hope of rising in the scale of created beings. These considerations have been either wholly overlooked or entirely disregarded by the Eurasians, who usually leave native opinion entirely out of the question, when flourishing about their wrongs, in strains worthy of king Cambyses himself. But these are not the only mal-contents whose declamations echo through the saloons of the Town Hall; whatsoever may be the object of the meeting, whether to inquire into the affairs of insolvent houses of agency, to pass a vote of thanks to a public functionary, or to propose a ball in honour of some individual or individuals of note, there may always be expected considerable opposition from a party who make a point to interfere whether they have any right or not. The harangues of the morning, however, may be considered dispassionate and sober, compared to those which take place after a public dinner; some of the most inflated of these speeches, through the zeal of reporters, get printed in the daily papers, and often give rise to long and tiresome controversies between the cavillers on the one side, and the partizans on the other, which, like the majority of such discussions, are usually carried on without temper, taste, or discretion.

During many years, the Town Hall was the scene of great festivity, throughout the cold season; the principal inhabitants entered into a subscription for a series of balls upon a very grand scale, and, so long as the pay and allowances of the civil and military residents of the presidency remained untouched, these were supported with great spirit and *éclat*. Latterly, many adverse circumstances have arisen, which have had the effect of interrupting, and occasionally of entirely preventing, the gay doings at the Town Hall. As the society of Calcutta increased, it divided into different grades, and questions arose concerning the eligibility of certain parties to admission. Some, who possessed an undoubted title, on account of their attendance at Government House, were not considered to do sufficient honour to the assembly, and names appearing at the head of the list of the subscription, which it was thought would have been better placed at the fag-end, gave offence to high and fastidious folk, who declined the insertion of their patronymics below those of persons of inferior note. The reduction of pecuniary means rendered the expense of subscription a serious objection; many could not afford the sum required, and the late bankruptcies put a stop to every thing of the kind for the time. During one season, there was a revolt of the bachelors; the community of " The Buildings," that depôt of incipient judges, collectors, and members of the *corps diplomatique*, refused to subscribe to the whole series, on the plea of the expectation en-tertained by the greater number, that their appointment to distant places would prevent them from being present. The renters of the Town Hall protested against the innovation of an old established rule, which went far to deprive them of the profits they had calculated upon, and, neither party feeling inclined to come to terms, the balls were given up, to the great hor-ror and consternation of the ladies, who began to entertain well-grounded fears that the reign of beauty was drawing to an end. Fortunately for them, it pleased the liberal party in Calcutta to celebrate the intelligence brought from Paris of the glorious "Three Days," with a ball and supper; a mode of commemorating the event, which, notwithstanding the compliment paid to the ladies, was open to many objections, and was considered to be par-ticularly unfeeling to the sufferers on both sides upon such an occasion. Many, however, were glad of any excuse for a ball, more especially as the company were invited to come in fancy costume, and though, in con-sequence of a difference of opinion respecting the politics of the day, seve-ral families declined to appear, the rooms were very tolerably filled with a brilliant assembly. Yet, notwithstanding the muster of beauty and fashion, and the gay dresses sported on the occasion, those who had known Calcutta in its better times could not help remarking the lamentable falling-off in the spectacle. With the exception of a few tri-coloured banners, the rooms had no decorations beyond the usual fixtures, nor were the groupes so splen-did as they had been in days of yore, when all the characters, from the most picturesque and popular of the Waverley Novels, made their appearance together. Of these, Quintin Durward, the Talisman, and the Betrothed, will long be remembered for the correctness of the details, and the splendour of the materials of which the dresses were composed. The Welch prince wore the gold armlet upon his head, enriched with precious stones, and the correspondent armlet mentioned in the tale, constructed of gems and gold, not unworthy of the sovereign of the marches; and the cost of many of the other dresses amounted to five, six, and seven hundred pounds. In fact, the mania for splendid array upon these occasions had become almost ruinous ; and it was found that the best-filled purses were unequal to support the expense. A reaction, the result of necessity, had now taken place, and the ball in honour of the last revolution in France was chiefly remarkable for the profusion of blue, red, and white ribbons, worn in compliment to the Citizen King. Many of the ladies, however, had the good taste to decline appearing in the party colours, choosing French costumes, out of courtesy to the numerous guests belonging to that nation, who had been invited. The residents of the French settlement of Chandernagore, near Calcutta, had not usually attended the balls at the presidency; but, upon this occasion, they mustered in considerable numbers, appearing to be highly gratified by an entertainment so well suited to the national character.

The supper-rooms of the Town Hall are upon the ground-floor, and correspond in size and splendour with the apartments above; the entertainments given are under the superintendance of Messrs. Gunter and Hooper, names,—especially the first,—which give promises of superior elegance not always fulfilled. Some late advices from Calcutta afforded reason to hope that a reform had been effected in a department in which it was so much required, and we were led to believe that something, at least, in the shape of improvement had been manifested at the supper-tables of the presidency balls; however, it has been shewn by the last arrivals of Calcutta newspapers, that such, unfortunately, is not the case: and it will appear from the following extract, that the taste of the commentators upon the public amusements of the City of Palaces is about as refined as that of the purveyors of the banquets set before them; the article is headed " Presidency Gaieties," and is couched in the following terms:—

The Réunions.—These assemblies for the present season commenced on Monday evening, and were on the whole very well attended, notwithstanding that no temptation had been held out in the shape of Vaudevilles, Italian vocalists, or Punch. Sir Henry Fane and family, who appear very well disposed to patronize all sorts of rational gaiety, remained until a late hour; and the rest of the guests continued enjoying themselves until the stewards intimated that it was time to go to bed. Amongst the company were several enchanting pocket Venuses, who have been recently imported, and the usual supply of destructive youths with smooth chins, and killing ship-captains of all hues and singular gaits. The music was unspeakably bad, and the waltzes and quadrilles precisely the same hackneyed compositions as have been played since the time of the Lord Hastings, whose monument stands in Tank Square. Gunter and Hooper provided the refection, which, as usual, was swept away with *avidity*, though Carème, Beauvilliers, and Ude would have shuddered at the ordinary character of some of the *comestibles*. We did not see one single temple of sugar-candy, nor a solitary *panier de miel glacé à la Mont St. Bernard.*

Such is the style in which the entertainments and guests of the Mahratta ditchers,—as the Anglo-Indian inhabitants of Calcutta are sometimes elegantly termed,—are held up to the public eye in the columns of the newspapers. It need scarcely be said that the disgust occasioned by similar effusions, frequently has the effect of causing a temporary cessation of festivities, which seldom are so fortunate as to give general satisfaction in a society affecting to be so difficult to please as that of Calcutta. The Vaudevilles and the Italian vocalists, which, coupled with Punch, are mentioned so contemptuously, were amongst the most agreeable portions of the evening's entertainment at the first establishment of the Calcutta reunions. All the amateur and professional talent of the presidency was called into action, and the result was such as to merit the gratitude of those who could enjoy an escape from the eternal first set of Paine's quadrilles, and the miserable attempts to get up a waltz. In order to give due effect to the dramatic part of the entertainment, which consisted of proverbs, acted charades, and scenes from popular Italian operas, a very beautiful stage was erected at the end of the long ball-room. A portion of the front, parted off by a moveable pannelling of painted canvas, decorated with appropriate devices, formed the orchestra, and assuredly in no private assembly could there be found a more effective set of performers than those who congregated on these occasions. The profession always lent their aid; the amateurs were not to be exceeded in talent and enthusiasm for their art by any who delight the societies of the capital of Europe; and those who felt pleasure in doing justice to merit, were delighted and surprised by the versatility of the genius which rendered the most profound scholars in Sanscrit, and the most scien-tific philosophers, equally at home, when assisting at some of the finest com-positions of Beethoven, Mozart, and Rossini. The curtain, which, when drawn aside, disclosed one of the prettiest stages ever erected, was of pale blue velvet, studded with silver stars, descending from a very rich pro-scenium, beautifully painted. The scenery, entirely the work of amateurs, was exquisite, extraordinary effects being produced in the narrow limits to which the artists were restricted. One view, in particular, of a garden overlooking the bay of Naples, employed in a selection from *Il Turco in Italia*, was of surpassing excellence. The skilful management of the per-spective, and the judicious disposal of the lights, affording an idea of distance which made the illusion almost magical; real foliage was in some instances introduced to heighten the effect, and with great advantage, the air coming through the open windows gently agitating the feathery boughs and branches of living trees waving over some romantic building. Four or five different scenes, all admirably executed, were frequently exhibited in one night; a charade requiring three, and a portion of an opera a fourth.

The charades performed at Calcutta differed from those exhibited in London, in the circumstance of their not being the extemporaneous effusions of the actor, but written before-hand, and learned by rote, like any other dramatic piece. Probably, this was necessary, in consequence of the splendid manner in which they were got up, as any failure in the midst of so much serious preparation would have been doubly felt. Where the scene is merely a drawing-room, and the actors content with table-covers, house-made aprons, and fire-screens, for the drapery and properties, a little ready wit is alone necessary to keep up the spirit of the affair; but the case is widely different upon a regular stage, with scenery, dresses, and decora-tions of the most faultless nature. In order to give the tragedians an oppor-tunity for the full display of their powers, the title of a play or character of Shakespeare was usually selected for the puzzle, and there, as in the case of *Rich*, and *Hard*, which enabled the most distinguished hero of the buskin to enact the last dying scene of the crooked-backed usurper, were some-times a little strained for the purpose. In this ingenious trifle, the produc-tion of one of the contributors to the *Bengal Annual*, the late Mr. Can-

ning's celebrated colloquy between the patriot and the knife-grinder, was
introduced with very happy effect; the latter being most admirably personified by a gentleman who boasts a more felicitous union of accomplishments
than has been found since the days of the Admirable Crichton.　Another
very amusing performance gave, in its two comic scenes, the compound
word *Hamlet:* the first turned entirely upon the horror of pork, of every
description, exhibited by a fine lady, who discards a lover on account
of his partaking of the abhorred food, in the shape of ham, at supper, and
gets entangled with an adventurer at Ramsgate, the son of an eminent
pork-butcher in the borough, who, having a noble ambition, passes himself off for a man of fashion, until discovered by his enraged parent.　The
second scene introduced the audience to the lodgings of an old Indian,
lately returned to Europe, in Regent Street; the landlord, disgusted with
the habits of his inmate, and the multitude of cockroaches and native servants which he has brought with him, endeavours to get him out by placing
a placard at his drawing-room window, intimating that the apartments are
" to let," which of course has the effect of bringing all sorts of intruders
upon the testy old gentleman.　Amid these, a radical M.P. makes speeches
about the condition of the people of, and the conduct of the Europeans in,
India, which were of course calculated to keep a Calcutta audience in a roar
of laughter.　But, perhaps, the most entertaining portion of the whole, was
the unconscious manner in which a hookah-burdar performed a part in the
scene.　This man, who would have thought his dignity, nay even his respectability, compromised, by engaging in an exhibition considered so degrading in India, that none save outcasts can be found to personate any
fictitious character, excepting in dramas of a religious nature, made no
objection to his usual post behind his master's chair, although that chair
happened to be placed upon the stage.　In his ignorance of the English
language, he was perfectly unaware that the tirades of the radical M.P.
were addressed to himself, and that he stood before the audience an imper-
sonation of the wrongs of the " muslined millions " enslaved by the tyrants
of the West.　There was no difficulty in procuring his entrances and exits
when they were essential to the business of the stage; and, absorbed in the
performance of his own peculiar duties, he never dreamed that the *gist* of
the whole scene would have failed had he taken the alarm, and retreated
before his time.　It must be admitted, that a great part of the audience
manifested equal obtuseness, and, while enjoying the broader portions of
the humour, were too much accustomed to the attendance of native servants
upon all occasions, to enter into the comicality of the situation of the
hookah-burdar, in his " first appearance upon any stage."

Since the period of which we write (1831), a company of English and
Italian performers have settled themselves in Calcutta, and, from private
accounts as well as newspaper report, it appears that some of the most
popular compositions of the modern German and Italian schools have been
got up very creditably.　Previously, however, to the arrival of this *corps
dramatique*, with the exception of an occasional concert given by Masoni,

or some other resident musical *artiste*, the Mahratta ditchers were entirely indebted to amateurs for an entertainment, without which, people in an advanced state of refinement can scarcely exist. Many of the *attachés* of the vice-regal court would have followed the example of the celebrated French cook, who quitted the service of the Marquess of Wellesley, when Lord Lieutenant in Ireland, because, " in dat dam Dublin, there vas no opera," could they have felt as equally secure of a situation elsewhere. Gratitude, however, is not the virtue of the society of Calcutta, and, so far from entertaining any sentiment of the kind towards the parties who so amiably volunteered their talents for the general amusement, their appearance in public provoked considerable censure. In many respects, the fashionable circles of Calcutta resemble those of a large watering-place in England; but it must be confessed, that they are even still more fastidious and intolerant towards all who depart in the slightest degree from the beaten track, and the endeavour of a few liberal and spirited individuals to establish a greater degree of ease and freedom, usually meets with very determined opposition. The strictures upon the scenes, selected from operas, in which some ladies were induced to make their appearance on the stage, in order to support by their presence one who executed the music allotted to the heroine, in a manner which enchanted all who possessed ears and souls, were confined to private society; but the charades fared worse. It unfortunately happened that, in illustrating the name of Shakespeare's celebrated Jew, the latter syllable suggested to the author the idea of a station or lock-up house, and one of the disorderly personages introduced was a sort of Moll Flaggon, represented by a gentleman who, without outraging propriety, might give some offence to the overstrained delicacy of a part of the audience. A gentleman, whose " ears polite " were shocked by the slang phrases used upon this occasion, wrote a letter, which was published in the newspapers, denouncing the performance as unfit for representation before ladies; a defendant, of course, started up on the other side, and those who had hitherto catered for the public amusement, disgusted by the failure of their attempts to please, and the severity of the reprehension which a slight error in judgment had drawn upon them, felt disinclined to try their fortune again. At the ensuing Reunion, there was no charade, and the *programme* of the entertainment presented a very different appearance from those of former meetings, and, in consequence of the omission of the gayest portion of the entertainment, the whole affair went off, as it might have been expected, in the flattest manner possible. Few, if any, of the persons who were either subscribers or guests, took into consideration the arduous nature of the efforts made for their amusement by the gentlemen who had the management of the affair. The Reunions had been established in the hottest weather, in order to afford some diversity to a season which in general is characterized in Calcutta by the most profound dullness. The painting, the scenery, and the getting-up of the performance, to say nothing of the misery of being clad in costumes which, however appropriate to the characters assumed, were not adapted to a thermometer of at least eighty degrees,

were exertions which did not induce the assembly to look over any defect, or
to make any allowance for the difficulties to be contended against. Happily,
the committee, though discouraged, were not entirely disheartened; they
rallied again, and consoled themselves by a good-humoured reproof conveyed to their assailants, in their next dramatic performance. In the absence of another charade, the interlude of Sylvester Daggerwood, altered
to suit the occasion, was introduced, and, after some well-directed remarks
upon the difficulty of pleasing that many-headed monster, the Town, an
attack was made upon the ultra-refinement of the objectors to the last representation, in a new version of the celebrated bill of the performance for the
benefit of Mr., Mrs., Misses, and the Master Daggerwoods, at the Dun-
stable Theatre. It was stated that the last act of Don Giovanni would be
given, "the devils and all other improper characters being left out by particular desire." After this evening, the course of the Reunions ran more
smoothly to the end; they were interrupted, or rather not resumed, in consequence of the failures, which threw for a time so deep a gloom over the
society of Calcutta; and their re-establishment does not, to judge from the
comments in the newspapers, appear to give that general satisfaction which
the projectors and supporters so strongly merit. The concerts, dramatic
scenes, &c., were diversified by quadrilles, the ball-room being large
enough to admit of sufficient space to accommodate the dancers, notwithstanding the portion occupied by the theatre, and the chairs and benches
placed in front of it for the audience. All these were moveable, but it
was only necessary to take away a few at the end nearest to the place
appropriated to dancing. It being intended to divest these Reunions of all
form and ceremony, the gentlemen were invited to come in white jackets,
and the ladies in demi or morning dress. The former, too glad to escape
from the trammels which etiquette usually imposed, obeyed the injunction to
the letter; but the ladies took a wider latitude, and, either on account of
convenience, or upon the score of superior becomingness, arrayed themselves according to their own fancy: some appeared in silks, satins, and
gauzes, and others in coloured muslins, or some equally simple manufacture. They who chose to walk in silk attire, gave great offence to the gentlemen connected with the press, and the "preposterous dresses of many of
the ladies" were strongly censured in the diurnal, and hebdomadal, and
tri-weekly oracles, although they did not exceed in splendour what might
have been worn with great propriety at any dinner-party at home. Not
content with full liberty to indulge habits which too often degenerate into
slovenliness, these male dictators desired to circumscribe the privileges,
which women have been wont to exercise time out of mind, to curtail their
furbelows, and abbreviate their flounces. Many were frightened into the
required dowdiness; but others, less inclined to submit to such unheard-
of tyranny, continued to flirt their ribbons and gauzes in the faces of the
malcontents, who, of course, were well-known to the assembly at large.

The Reunions were attended by several of the native gentlemen, and
Hindoos, Mahomedans, and Armenians were to be seen amid the gay

throng; the dresses of the two former produced a very striking effect, and, in particular, the diamonds worn by Dwarknauth Tagore gleamed like meteors while reflecting the lights around.

Although the hypocritical spirit of an Anglo-Indian community renders any attempt to establish a novel method of beguiling time exceedingly difficult, a stranger, who has had some acquaintance with the state of society in other places, cannot fail to be struck with the abundance and versatility of the talent which is to be found amongst the civil and military servants of the Company resident at Calcutta. It is impossible to say whether the places of those who have returned to Europe, or quitted the presidency for other parts of India, have been adequately filled up, but those who still remain are quite sufficient to keep up the ancient reputation. Of this number, the most distinguished is a gentleman who, either in the character of actor, author, or musician, never fails to give delight; he possesses the happy faculty of investing the dryest subject with comic interest, and by his gaiety and good humour in the discussion of disputed points, no less than by the solidity of his arguments, enlists every unprejudiced reader in his favour. It happened that, in his capacity of covenanted salt-officer, he felt called upon to defend the salt monopoly from the attacks made upon it in some pamphlets which found their way to Calcutta. Several unadvised individuals having taken the matter up on the other side, this intellectual gladiator engaged the whole at once, and convulsed every station throughout the presidency with laughter by the witty illustrations of his arguments. He confuted his adversaries in every shape and way, introducing sometimes a dramatic scene, in which the Molunghees, or salt-gatherers, figured as the principal characters, and, at others, quotations from the *Molunghead,* a threatened epic, in forty cantos. Every body, with the exception perhaps of the worsted parties, regretted when the controversy was at an end; and the republication of all the articles, with explanatory notes, could scarcely fail to excite as much attention in England as the correspondence of the celebrated Major Downing, reprinted from the New York papers. Mr. Parker's contributions to the *Bengal Annual* have not failed to attract the notice of the London press, but they deserve to be much more generally and extensively known; and, could he spare the time from his numerous avocations, there is no one who could furnish the reading world with more amusing and accurate portraitures of native and Anglo-Indian society.

EXPEDITION TO THE TEA-DISTRICT OF FÜH-KËEN.

THE following Journal of an attempted ascent of the Min river, to visit the tea plantations of the Fŭk-këen province of China, by G. J. Gordon, Esq., secretary to the Calcutta " Tea-Committee," is abridged from the *Journal* of the Asiatic Society of Bengal, for October last :—

May 6th, 1835.—Anchored in the Min river, a short way below a narrow passage, guarded on each side by a fort, and hence named by Europeans the Bogue, as resembling the entrance to the inner river of Canton. We determined on trying the western branch of the Min, as laid down in Du Halde's map of the province of Füh-këen. We took with us one copy of a petition, for permission to import rice, on the same footing of exemption from charges as is granted at Canton, and grounded upon the unusual drought of the regular season for planting rice. Another duplicate we left with Capt. McKay, of the *Governor Findlay*, to be presented by him to any mandarin who might come on board to urge the departure of the vessel from the river. As the subject of the petition would require reference to Pekin, we calculated, that sufficient time would thus be gained to enable us to accomplish our object. The copy in our own possession would be resorted to only in case of our being intercepted. Capt. McKay was requested to be in no hurry about presenting his copy, but to let all persons understand that he had come with such a petition.

May 7th.—At 1 A.M. we left the ship, with a fair wind and flood-tide. We were fourteen persons in all; namely, Mr. Gutzlaff, Mr. Stevens, and myself, the gunner of the *Findlay*, a native of Trieste, a tindal, eight lascars of various nations, Bengal, Goa, Muscat, Macao, and Malayan Islands, and my Portuguese servant, a native of Bombay. Having studied such charts of the river as we possessed, we resolved on turning to the left as soon as we came to the entrance of a river called in them the Chang : its position corresponding with that of the re-junction of the right branch of the Min, as laid down in the Jesuits' map. Mr. Stevens kept the look-out at the head of the boat, and the gunner steered, while the tindal sounded. The night was fortunately clear, and by four o'clock we struck off into the western river. This soon widened into a very broad channel, which a little further on seemed to branch into two. That to the left-hand appeared full of shoals, and low sedgy islands, and we accordingly followed that to the right, which appeared still broad and clear. It was on our right, besides, that we had to look for the main stream of the Min. We had not proceeded far before the expanded sheet of water we were proceeding by gradually diminished in width, sending off several small branches in various directions, until at last it dwindled away into a narrow nullah, over which there was a stone bridge. Relying on the strength with which the tide flowed up this creek, as proof that it must lead into some other channel, we struck our masts, and passed the bridge, going on, till we saw reason to believe the reports of the villagers, that there was really no passage into the Min by that course. We accordingly came to, that our people might cook, intending to retrace our way with the assistance of the ebb. Unfortunately, however, the depth decreased so rapidly, that, before we had proceeded far, we were fairly brought up, and obliged to wait for the return of the flood. Mr. Stevens and Mr. Gutzlaff went a-shore to reconnoitre, and satisfied themselves that the branch we had avoided in the morning was the proper one to be pursued ; in which opinion they were confirmed by the villagers. We were unable to get a pilot. To all inquiries as to our destination, we replied that we wished to go to Min-tsing, the next hĕen town above Fŭh-chow. We bought a few supplies, but had a copper basin stolen while we were aground.

At daylight of the 8th, we found ourselves surrounded by sandbanks in all directions, without any visible channel by which we might advance when the tide should rise. One man agreed to pilot us into the Min for five dollars, and then left us. A second agreed for two, taking one dollar in advance, and after accompanying us a short way, made off. At half past nine A.M. Mr. Gutzlaff landed, with the view of engaging some one to show us the way, when all at once a kwan-foo, with a gilt knob, said he would be happy to be of any use to us ; and, as the wind was contrary, would, assist by towing us with his own boat. Mr. Gutzlaff accepted his offer. The man appeared to be of the rank of a subaltern officer ; such a proffer, coming from such a quarter, was of a very ambiguous character. He was probably sent to watch our motions, and took this method of defeating our object. We had, however, no alternative ; our attempts to engage a pilot had failed, and we had found from experience, that without some guide we could not advance. Besides, we could cast off from our professed friend as soon as we should see grounds for alarm. In fact, he led us back towards the mouth of the Chang river, and when he came close to a small hill-fort, which we had observed the preceding morning, went ashore. We cast off immediately, and went into the Fŭh-chow branch, where, after running up a little way, we anchored for the night. A cold drizzling rain made our situation not very comfortable, and what was more, we found ourselves, about two in the morning, in danger of canting over into deep water, from the fall of the tide, leaving the boat's keel deeply fixed in the mud of a sloping bank.

May 9th.—The tide favouring us at 7 A.M., we got under weigh, followed by a government-boat ; and, with a rattling breeze, soon reached Fŭh-chow-foo. When near the bridge, we anchored, and struck our masts, and then shot through one of the openings with great ease. There were about a score of soldiers drawn up in arms at the bridge, and after we had passed through, four boats with soldiers put off after us. Mr. Gutzlaff told the people on board, that if they came alongside when we came to anchor, we would communicate with them. They continued to follow us at a little distance. Soon afterwards, we came in sight of a second bridge, when we feared we should have been obliged to dismast ; on approaching it, however, we perceived that the road-way, connecting the piers, had fallen in at two places, through both of which, boats under sail were able to pass. We selected what appeared to be the widest, and got safely through ; but Mr. Stevens observed, that the stones which had fallen in, were but a trifle below the surface, and narrowed the passage so as to leave very little to spare beyond the width of our boat. We were now so far a-head of the war-boats, that a fisherman ventured alongside to sell us fish. At ½ past 11 A.M. we came to anchor, that the people might refresh themselves ; and, the tide having turned against us, we remained at anchor till four in the evening. The war-boats, in the mean time, came up, and a civil inquiry was brought from one of them as to what nation we belonged, whither we were bound, and with what object. Mr. Gutzlaff, in reply, stated, that we wished to ascend the river, to see tea-plants growing, to talk with tea-merchants, and to ramble amongst the hills. No objection was made, but that the river was rapid and dangerous. When we weighed, however, these war-boats weighed also, and after we had come to at night, they came up and took their station near us. We weighed early on the morning of the 10th, the drizzling rain still continuing, and the thermometer at 57° ; but

having no boats in sight, to serve for our guidance, we thought it better to
come to anchor again, and let the people have breakfast: as we weighed, the
war-boats weighed, and when we again anchored, they too came to an anchor.
Before we set out the second time, two other war-boats came up, which made,
at first, as if they intended to run foul of us, but showed no other marks of
opposition, and we pushed on. I now reminded my friends of my uniform
declaration, that I would not attempt to force my way if any actual resistance
was offered, and that I even questioned the expediency of proceeding at all, if
we were to be continually under the eyes of the government officers. However, as we greatly outsailed them, and might possibly wear out their vigilance,
we resolved to persevere. As we advanced, we found that none of the boats
going up the river would answer our questions, the people sometimes clapping
their hands on their mouths, or answering, that they durst not give us any
information. After having got a long way a-head of the war-boats, however,
we found the people communicative and friendly. We were told of several
rapids on the Min river, which could not be passed without a very strong
wind, and of other places where the current was not only violent, but the
stream too shallow to float our boat. We had, in fact, already reached a
place where the stream, swollen by the hill-torrents that conveyed the rain
which had fallen during the last thirty hours, was so rapid, that with a light
breeze and our oars, we were unable to make any way against it, and were
obliged to come to an anchor accordingly.

The war-boats, by dint of pulling and tracking, surmounted the obstacle,
and did not come to till they were about a mile or upwards a-head of us. We
found the people very kind and friendly; but they were soon checked by the
appearance of a kwan-foo, who came to us in a little sampan, with some loose
papers in his hand. He addressed himself to me, but I answered with truth
and nonchalance, that I did not understand him: Mr. Gutzlaff, who stood by,
recommended that little notice should be taken of him; that all communications with the mandarins should be avoided, if possible; and that the papers
which he offered, not being in the form of a letter, or otherwise in an official
shape, should not be received. The officer then asked some of the people
who were on shore near our boat, whether they knew if any of us could speak
Chinese. Pointing to Mr. Gutzlaff, they said he knew a few words, enough to
enable him to ask for fowls, eggs, and ducks, which he wanted to buy; and
that he spoke about nothing else. One of them was saying something about
his distribution of books; but the kwan-foo was at that moment laughing
heartily at the odd appearance of one of our men, and the remark about the
books, which was immediately checked by one of the by-standers, passed unnoticed. He still persevered, rather vociferously, in requiring us to receive
his papers; when he was motioned to be off. Our gunner gave the boat a
hearty shove with his foot, which decided the movement of the envoy. After
it was dark, the people of the village brought us bambús for pulling, with other
supplies. The lull of the wind continuing during the night, we distinctly heard
much beating of gongs, firing of arms, and cheering, in the quarter where the
war-boats lay; but at day-break of the 11th, we thought we saw them under
weigh in advance. A rather suspicious-looking man came to the shore, with a
paper, which he wished to deliver. We showed no inclination to receive it, and
in attempting to throw it into the boat, tied to a piece of stick, it fell into the
water, and was lost. Soon after, a simple-looking peasant-boy showed another
piece of paper, which, from its rude appearance, I thought not likely to have
come from the authorities, and therefore received and handed it to Mr. Gutz-

laff. It was an intimation, that multitudes of officers, with an army of 9,000 men, were drawn up close by, and that there were many tens of thousands of soldiers further on. This was the first decided threat we had of resistance, and it was so grossly exaggerated, that we attached no other importance to it, than that it intimated decided objection to our further advance. We had already fully resolved on not having recourse to force, unless it became necessary to resort to it, in order to extricate ourselves, if an attempt were made not merely to drive us back, but to seize our persons; and we now proposed to use every exertion to get as far as possible a-head of the war-boats, engage chairs for our conveyance by some inland route, and send back the boat under the charge of the gunner.

The day being for the first time clear, we were engaged all the morning in baling out and washing the boat, and in cleaning our weapons, much rusted by the wet weather we had hitherto experienced. A breeze springing up a little after 11 o'clock, we hastened to avail ourselves of it, and all our arms were stowed away as speedily as possible.

We had gone on some way, ploughing the stream in beautiful style, when all at once shot began to fall about us. We deliberated for a moment what was to be done. We believed that retreat would not save us from further firing, as long as we were within its reach, if we would take the practice of the troops at the Bogue as an example of the general rule of the Chinese in such cases; and if we could get out of the reach of their shot by running a-head, we might have time for negociating. On turning a point, however, the wind failed us, and, our enemies pursuing us, the firing became more hot and dangerous than ever. My next idea was to run the boat ashore, and attack the Chinese; but the river was very narrow, and on the opposite bank they had erected a mud breast-work, from which they could fire on us with their small cannon, with full effect; and it would be exceedingly difficult to get at our assailants, on account of the steepness of the bank where they now stood. After receiving a good peppering, we put about; but, as I anticipated, they continued to fire upon us; and my servant, with one of the lascars, was wounded, though both slightly, and all of the party had narrow escapes from death. The strength of the current soon carried us beyond their fire, and we were in a fair way of reaching Füh-chow before day-break of the 12th, when we unfortunately missed our way, some time after the top of high-water, at two o'clock A.M. At day-break, we found ourselves on high ground, sixty yards from the nearest point of the river. We had nothing for it, therefore, but to wait the return of the tide. Numbers of men, women, and children came about us, to sell geese, fowls, and fish. Some amongst the crowd we recognized as having been amongst those we had seen while attempting the western branch of the river. They noticed the marks of the balls that had passed through the gunwale, or stuck in the sides of the boat; but this did not seem to make any difference in the friendliness of their demeanour. While we were at breakfast, two boats came up filled with soldiers, who were immediately landed, and one party marched towards our boat, while another was drawn up as a reserve. The officer, who commanded the advance, with several of his men, scrambled into the boat. They were desired by Mr. Gutzlaff to retire; but not complying, our people were desired to turn them out, which they did accordingly. I collared their officer, and was on the point of tripping up his heels, when he threw himself down, and Mr. Gutzlaff begging me to leave him to him, I desisted from further violence, though the loud and insolent manner of the man made forbearance not very agreeable. Mr. Gutzlaff then commenced rating the fellow in such animated language, that he became

apparently thunderstruck, having no apology to offer for the rudeness and violence with which he came to execute his commission, which he said was merely
to inquire who we were, and what we wanted, and to desire us to be off. Mr.
Gutzlaff informed him that we came to present a petition to the viceroy, but
not having met with an accredited officer, its delivery had been postponed; that
we had taken an excursion on the river, in order to see the tea-plant; that we
had proceeded openly, and avowed our intention without being told; that so
innocent an object could never draw on us treatment such as no civilized government would offer to innocent strangers. He then harangued, with great energy
and effect, on the base, treacherous, cowardly, and barbarous conduct we had
experienced on the preceding day, and on our own forbearance in not returning
the fire; showing him, that we had plenty of arms, which we had taken for our
defence against robbers, and assuring him, that we were not afraid to risk our
lives against numbers; but had not come with the intention of making war on
the government of the country, and would therefore wait to see whether that
government would afford us redress by punishing those villains who had thus,
without any provocation, attempted to take our lives, before having recourse
to other means. If justice should be withheld by the provincial government,
the case might go before the emperor, and, if punishment were not then
inflicted on the guilty, the affair was not likely to end there. Mr. Gutzlaff's
eloquence, with the display of our fire-arms, left the kwan-foo without a word
to say for himself, or for his country. He acknowledged that we had been
shamefully treated; but that he was not of the party, and could not be implicated in their guilt, and promised that we should experience nothing but
civility from himself. He received our petition, which he handed to one of his
people to take to his boat, and ordered off the rest of his men. He agreed to
assist us in getting off from the field where we lay, and to tow us on our way
as far as Mingan—a tower and fort, a short way below the place, where the
western branch rejoins the Füh-chow river. We asked him if there was no
way of going down without passing under the bridge of Füh-chow. He said
there was; and that he would probably take us by that route. We got afloat
about 11 A.M., and two or three hours afterwards, recognized our position to
be that which we had abandoned in despair four days before. Had we remained
where we lay on the 8th till the flood had made, it would have carried us into
the main river, and we should have had one or two days' start of the war-
boats, or perhaps entirely escaped their observation. The kwan-foo continued
on board, except when relieved by an inferior officer from the towing-boat, intending, as we presume, that we should appear to be his prisoners. In the
afternoon the wind became very strong, and the fleet ran in towards a large
village, where they proposed anchoring for the day. Finding, however, that
the bottom was stony, and that there was already too little water for our boat,
we refused to remain, and were preparing to set sail, when the officer, who
had brought us on, earnestly requested to be taken into our boat again. We
received him on board, and were again taken in tow, the other war-boats
accompanying. At dusk, they wished to take us to another large village; but
we pointed out a more sheltered spot, and they took us there accordingly.
The officers still remaining on board, Mr. Gutzlaff was requested to desire
them to withdraw, which they did; and, as they had been uniformly civil since
morning, I sent each of them a pair of blue printed cotton handkerchiefs. It
was settled that we should again get under weigh with the morning's ebb, and
that, after reaching Mingan, we should pursue our way to the ship, without
further attendance. At 10 o'clock P.M., I was surprised by a letter from Capt.

M'Kay, of that day's date; he stated that he had been importuned in the most abject manner to recall us, as orders had been issued to drive us out; which could not be carried into effect. He concluded that we must by that time have got so far on our way, that, before we could be overtaken, we must have accomplished our object. At one A.M. of the 13th, we got under weigh, towed as before; but escorted by a numerous fleet of war-junks, one of which carried three lanterns, and the others one each, on their poops ; as all these vessels had to make short tacks in a narrow channel, the sight was rather fine; and, when we reached Mingan, a number of rockets were discharged, which had a very grand effect. We had not permitted any Chinese officer to come on board our boat when we started; but, contrary to stipulation, they now again insisted on coming; while we showed a determined resolution to resist: on consulting their commander, they were directed to let us go freely. We lost our way, however, in the darkness of the night, and were assisted by a war-boat, in the morning, in recovering it. As we approached the right channel, we found several war-junks stationed as a guard. Three or four of them accompanied us for some time, but gradually dropped off. The towing-junk, too, took occasion to make us over to a large open boat, from which we soon afterwards cast off. On passing the forts at the Bogue, we were honoured with a salute of three guns from each, as well as from some war-junks above, and others below, the forts. At two P.M., we got on board the *Findlay*. In pursuance of our declared intention, I prepared a petition to the viceroy, praying for inquiry into the conduct of our assailants on the 11th, and the infliction of adequate punishment upon them, for their unjustifiable attempt on our lives. Mr. Gutzlaff was good enough to put my petition into Chinese form, and have it ready for delivery next morning, in expectation that, as had been the practice hitherto, some officer of rank might come on board. None having arrived, however, I resolved to go on board the admiral's junk, and deliver my petition there, explaining its object to that officer. Mr. Gutzlaff and Mr. Stevens accompanied me; we found in the cabin two messengers from the viceroy, both of them assistant-magistrates, wearing colourless crystal knobs; two vice-admirals ; Tsung-ping-knan, one of them, the naval commander-in-chief of this station ; one colonel of the army, Yen-keih; and one pa-tseang, or subaltern. Having handed to them the petition, one of the messengers wanted to open it; but, on being requested to deliver it to the viceroy, began to inquire what were its contents. Before coming to that subject, Mr. Gutzlaff adverted generally to our character as foreign merchants, and our wish to import rice. The Chinese assured us, that it was from no unwillingness on their parts that we were not allowed to trade, but that they were obliged to act under the prohibitory orders of the emperor. As to the importation of rice, the pa-tseang at first affected to misunderstand us, as if our application were for permission to export rice to our own country from Füh-këen. One of the messengers told us, that the viceroy would give us no answer, when Mr. Gutzlaff quoted some instances of official replies from head-quarters, that made him waive this objection.

Having shewn them the impracticability of efficiently excluding foreign trade from so long a line of coast, Mr. Gutzlaff urged very strongly the expediency of rendering legitimate what was now conducted with all the defiance of the laws, and other evils attendant on a smuggling trade already so apparent in Canton. Both messengers assented very readily to the soundness of the advice, adding arguments of their own in a very conciliatory strain, and regretting much that it was against the imperial orders. Mr. Gutzlaff dwelt particularly on the facility which Füh-chow possessed for the tea-trade; this they fully admitted; but again, the emperor having confined the trade to Canton, there was really no remedy; and it was quite in vain attempting to open the trade at this port. Mr. Gutzlaff then adverted to the murderous attack upon us on the 11th ; of this they at first alleged total ignorance, and then ascribed the attack to the treachery of the common natives. Mr. Gutzlaff, however, told them, that it was their officers and soldiers, who acted, to the best of their ability, the part of treacherous and cowardly murderers; while the poor peasantry had always conducted themselves towards us with the greatest kindness; that we were now come with a petition, calling for redress by the punishment of those assassins, the granting of which was the only means of preventing retaliation ; the lives of peaceful people having been brought into the most imminent danger, which violence justified violence in return, even if we were to take a life for each of our lives that had been so endangered. Here all concurred in reprobating such conduct as we had experienced, and in assuring us, that we should meet with no such molestation from them, trying to put as good a construction as possible on the past. Mr. Gutzlaff repeatedly requested them to allow the people to bring us provisions; but to this they turned a deaf ear. As we rose up to come away, the messenger of the viceroy, to whom I had handed the petition, wished to return it; but I refused to receive it back. He said he could report what we had said; but durst not deliver the petition. Mr. Gutzlaff, however, succeeded in getting him to promise its delivery, by reminding him, that he had been sent hither on our account, and that it would be strange if, after all, we should be obliged to carry our remonstrance ourselves to Füh-chow. This hint had the desired effect. On the afternoon of the 15th, a polite note was sent to the admiral's junk, requesting a supply of provisions to be procured for us, as the people were prohibited from bringing any thing to the ship. The boat brought back a remnant of a shoulder of pork, a dried cuttle-fish, and four pieces of sugar-cane; these were immediately returned. Mr. Gutzlaff was good enough to go on board by another boat, accompanied by Capt. McKay and Mr. Stevens, to require an explanation of this piece of rudeness; and to inform them, that if in two days I got no answer to my petition for redress, the consequences would not be imputable to me, but to their government. They at first denied that any thing had been sent; but finding this would not do, they alleged, that the pork and fish were intended for the boatmen, and the sugar-cane for the little lad that steered the boat. No indication of such appropriation was made when the things were put into the boat, so that the excuse was evidently an after-thought. Finding that another admiral, who had arrived in the forenoon, was of the party, Mr. Gutzlaff again expatiated on the atrocity with which we had been treated. No attempt at defending it was offered. The messenger of the viceroy said, that the petition had been sent, but he was unable to say how soon we might expect an answer. At this second meeting, Mr. Gutzlaff pointed out the freedom with which Chinese subjects were allowed to follow any honest avocation they chose at our settlements, and claimed, on the principles of reciprocity, the accordance of similar privileges in return.

On the 16th, Mr. Gutzlaff, having found some passages of Chinese law particularly applicable to our assailants, went in the evening to point them out to the mandarins, and, for their further consideration, copied them out in their presence, and left the extracts with them. Applications for provisions, and promises to supply them, were renewed. On the 17th, a boat arrived from Füh-chow, at eight A.M., and was received by the junks with a salute. A little after, a boat came alongside, and made off again with all expedition, after leaving an open note, stating that the orders of the viceroy had arrived, and that we ought to go on board the admiral to receive them. Mr. Gutzlaff wrote in reply, that the person who was charged with the communication of the order was in duty bound to deliver it, and that we expected he would bring it accordingly. This was sent by the ship's boat, which soon after returned with a note, stating that, since we were afraid to go on board the admiral's junk, they had made out a copy of the order, not choosing to send the original by the young man whom we had sent in charge of the boat. The half hour that our boat was detained was entirely occupied in framing and copying this note. The paper, which they pretended to have copied in that time, was a roll nearly six feet in length, which could not have been written, in the fair style which it exhibited, by the most expert penman, in less than a couple of hours. We afterwards compared it with the original, and found that it was written in the same hand, and was in every respect, except in the sealing, a fac-simile of the original. Our second petition accompanied this copy. The intention was, no doubt, to cheat us out of the original—an object of some value in the eyes of the Chinese diplomatists, who are always anxious to withhold authenticated papers, for fear of furnishing documents that may some day be brought forward in evidence against themselves—a use to which no unsealed documents can be applied, according to Chinese law and practice. The possession of this copy enabled us to prepare a final communication to the viceroy, and in order to secure the delivery into our hands of the original, the ship was dropt up with the flood abreast of the junk fleet, and her broadside brought to bear upon them. There were nineteen vessels in all on the spot; but all the smaller ones immediately got under weigh, and passed within the forts. When we went on board the admiral of the station, we learned that the orders of the viceroy were addressed to the admiral of Hae-tan. who was on board another junk. He and the envoys from Fŭh-chow were sent for; but it was some time before they made their appearance. Our host, in the mean time, appearing very uneasy and dispirited, we asked what was meant by saying that we were afraid of going on board his ship. Some of us had been there on each day since our return. It was obvious, that fear of retaliation had prevented him from renewing his visits since we came back ; but if we thought it right to retaliate it, we should not have imitated the treacherous and cowardly conduct of his countrymen, but openly brought our ship to fight the whole of theirs, and he must be perfectly aware, that, as she then lay, she could sink his whole fleet, and destroy every one on board. But this was not our object. The government had implicated itself in the business by inventing such a string of notorious falsehoods in defence of the conduct of its officers, and we should leave it to our government to obtain for us the redress which theirs refused to our simple and respectful application. The original letter of the viceroy and his colleagues having been at last produced, and taken possession of by me, I returned the copy sent in the morning. We were promised our supply of provisions as soon as we got under weigh. The final reply to the viceroy, along with my second petition, under a fresh cover, were now placed in the hands of the principal envoy, who pressed me hard to receive them back, and even followed me out, as if he intended to throw them after me into the boat. Judging, apparently, that this would be of no avail, he kept them till evening, and then sent a small fishing-boat with them to the ship. The fisherman, however, being warned off, carried them back, and we saw no more of them. On the 18th and 19th, we gradually dropped down to the outer bay. No provisions were ever sent us.

MR. WILSON'S NOTES ON CTESIAS.*

WE are, perhaps, too prone to condemn to indiscriminate neglect those early writers who have left written descriptions of contemporary nations, on account of the manifest inaccuracies with which their works abound. It is essential, however, in estimating the worth of evidence of any kind, that we should keep in view the broad distinction between accidental and wilful misrepresentation. Even where the credulity of the narrator exceeds the bounds of ordinary caution, there is a wide interval between him and the deliberate artificer of falsehoods. The skill and learning of the best-informed critic are foiled or misled in the latter case; in the former, they have been eminently successful in reducing the exuberant narrative to the sober standard of truth. We cannot mention a more decisive example than the result produced by the learning, acuteness, and industry of Mr. Marsden, upon an author who was long regarded as the very pattern of liars,—Marco Polo. In the infancy of science, when, consequently, the *unknown* teemed with the *wonderful*, not only were the minds of mankind ready to adopt for realities the phantoms of fear or the reveries of fancy, when related by others, but, in visiting countries foreign to their own, even their senses, not being under the restraint of a correct understanding, acted the traitor's part, and, especially when a native of Europe travelled in the gorgeous East, taught them to give Nature credit for boundless fecundity, and a power of generating

> —— all monstrous, all forbidden things,
> Gorgons, and Hydras, and Chimæras dire.

It is but charitable to suppose that the Christian travellers in Eastern countries, in the fifteenth century, who tell of nations with one leg,—of others with one arm, of gigantic and dwarfish races,—of children growing as vegetables,—and other particulars still more miraculous,—were deluded rather than deluders; and it would be doubly uncharitable to deny the same plea to heathen writers, whose creeds rendered them easier dupes to deception.

It is, therefore, by no means a sacrifice of time, when a writer so well-prepared for the task as Professor Wilson, endeavours to redeem an ancient describer of India from the reproach of being a mere fabulist, as Ctesias was considered by Aristotle, Plutarch, and others, as he is pronounced by Dr. Vincent, and as he certainly must appear, upon a superficial reading, to an ordinary critic. There seems to be no reason for discrediting him when he declares that he wrote nothing but what he had seen or heard; for what he saw, as Mr. Wilson remarks, amounts to very little, and to nothing extraordinary.

Ctesias was a native of Cnidos; he entered the service of Cyrus, whom he attended on his expedition, and was taken prisoner in the battle wherein Cyrus fell. Artaxerxes Mnemon having been wounded, Ctesias was employed to dress his wounds, and gave so much satisfaction in that office,

* Notes on the Indica of Ctesias. By H. H. WILSON, M.A., F.R.S., of Exeter College [Oxford], Boden Professor of Sanscrit. Read to the Ashmolean Society, February 5, 1836. Oxford.

that the king took him into his service, and he resided for some years at the Persian court (B.C. 460), in the character of chief physician, adding thereto the functions, open or secret, of agent to the Greeks.   He is said to have written a history of Persia in twenty-three books, and a history of India, extracts of which (all that is extant of the writer, except casual passages in classical authors) have been preserved by Photius, Patriarch of Constantinople in the ninth century.

Mr. Wilson very naturally expresses surprise that such absurdities as this writer has recorded of India could have originated so near that country, and that a man of the talents of Ctesias, " imbued with a spirit of intelligent curiosity," could have been a party to their dissemination.   We should, for the same reason, be inclined to think lightly of his intelligence, and to regard his authority as altogether valueless, on the ground of egregious want of judgment, but that it would be necessary, by the same rule, to discredit not only the whole of the Mahomedan travellers, who have chronicled for truths as many fables as Ctesias, but even the Father of History himself.   In fact, these wonderful tales appear to have been the most attractive parts of the ancient narratives; and it is curious to remark, as a corroboration of this conclusion, that, in the epitome made from the larger works of Arabian travellers, the *facts* are mostly excluded, as destitute of interest, whilst all the *wonders* are studiously retained.

The Notes before us are systematized by an arrangement of the fragments of Ctesias under two heads; the first embracing all that is left of his remarks on the country and people of India; the other comprehending his descriptions of its natural products, animal, vegetable, and mineral.   We shall merely select a few examples from the former.

Some of the most marvellous narrations of Ctesias relate to races of people by whom he says India is inhabited; yet even in them there appears to be a slight tincture of truth, or at least some foundation for the strange details that are given.

" The people," he says, " are black by nature, not by the action of the sun.   A few amongst them are very fair (λευκοτάτοι):" and he mentions having seen two women and five men of such a complexion.   There are Albinos in every part of India, the whole of whose skin is, as Dr. Ainslie[*] describes it, like that of a dead European who has not been much exposed to the sun. And Dubois[†] observes, that it is no uncommon thing to meet with a class of individuals much whiter than Europeans : they have light hair and weak eyes, but can see well in the dark.   It might have been to some such objects that Ctesias refers; but, if that was not the case, it is very possible that he might have met with Indians, whom, as contrasted with the swarthy complexion of the Persians, and of the Greeks themselves, he might have considered fair. Many of the people of the west and north of India, and of Turkestan, are not darker than the nations of the south of Europe, with a warmth of tint and a ruddiness of complexion that is not always found amongst the latter.

Of the manners and customs of the Indians, their justice, loyalty, and contempt of death, we have only the titles of the chapters.   Devotedness to their employers and contempt of death are still their characteristics; and som

---

[*] Materia Medica of Hindostan. Madras, p. 300.
[†] Description of the People of India, by the Abbé Dubois, p. 199.

remarkable instances of both have very lately occurred. The kings of the Indians, according to him, are not allowed to be intoxicated.* And drinking is one of the vices which Manu enjoins a king most carefully to shun : " With extreme care let him shun eighteen vices ; ten proceeding from love of pleasure, eight springing from wrath, and all ending in misery. Drinking, dicing, women, and hunting, let a king consider as the four most pernicious of those vices which love of pleasure occasions."†

" None of the Indians," he says, " ever suffer head-ache or tooth-ache, or maladies of the eyes, or have pimples about the mouth. They live to the age of 120 or 130, and some even to 200."

The simple diet of the people of India preserves them very generally from affection connected with disorders of the stomach ; and they are remarkable for good teeth. Diseases of the eyes, however, are far from uncommon, and the duration of life is greatly exaggerated. Longevity, however, in the natives of the north-western provinces, is not rare; and the standard authorities of the Hindus regard a century as the natural boundary of human life ; after which, voluntary death is not only excusable, but becoming : as it is said of king Sudraka, " Having attained the age of one hundred years and ten days, he entered the fire."‡ The prayer to be addressed by its parent to a newly-born infant also says, " Thou art born of my body, my child, to live for a hundred years."§

We next come to races of a different description, but who, amidst the cloud of fable which invests them, are very probably of Indian origin, either through the medium of fact or fiction.

The author then gives a very particular description of " a black people of pigmies," in Central India, who served the king of the other Indians as archers; and Mr. Wilson remarks, that " the belief that a people of Lilliputians existed, appears to have been very general amongst the ancients, and was very widely disseminated before the times of Ctesias." This certainly acquits him of fraud, but not of imbecile credulity; and were not the ancient Persians a grave people, we should be tempted to suspect, from some of the details recorded of these pigmies, that the wits of Artaxerxes' court had made themselves merry at the expense of the Greek physician. Perhaps, however, he did not well understand the Persic, and may have mistaken an account of a Hindu mythological legend, respecting the pigmy tenants of the *Kalpa druma*, for reality. It must be acknowledged that there is some justice in Mr. Wilson's observation, that the wild hill-tribes of the Vindhya range, the Bhils, Goands, and Kholes, black and short, diminutive races, who are skilful archers, might suggest the idea of the " black pigmies of middle India."

Mr. Wilson is very successful in palliating one enormity of his author, who speaks of men with tails existing in an island in the ocean.

A remarkable illustration of the insular satyrs of our author is of modern occurrence. It is not a century since that a lieutenant of a Swedish vessel asserted of the people of the Nicobar islands, that they had tails like cats, which they moved in the same manner. Linnæus vouched for the narrator's

* Apud Athenæum, lib. x.   † Manu, vii. v. 45—50. Sir Wm. Jones's translation.
‡ Hindu Theatre, i. 15.   § Bagbhatta Uttara Tantra.

honesty, and Lord Monboddo* exulted in his evidence as decisive of the question. The mystery is thus solved by Mr. Fontana, who, describing the people of the Nicobars, observes of their dress : " A long narrow cloth, made of the bark of a tree, round their waist, *with one extremity hanging down behind*, is all their dress.†" Lieutenant Keoping saw the people only from the ship; and the blunder was pardonable in a person impressed probably by the previous assertions of Careri and Struys, Marco Polo and Ptolemy,‡ with a belief that men with tails had a real existence.

The dog-headed people, Kalystrii, or Kunokephali,—" who are said to inhabit the mountains that extend to the Indus, to the number of 120,000, and who have the heads of dogs, with large teeth and sharp claws, and their only language is a sort of bark,"—are ascribed by Mr. Wilson to a verbal blunder.

Kalystrii is given as the native name, meaning in the Indian language, according to Ctesias, κυνοκιφαλοι; and the question is, how far he or his informant have accurately written or explained the word. Some distinguished scholars and Orientalists, as Reland in his Miscellaneous Dissertations,§ and Tychsen in the Appendix to the second volume of Heeren's Historical Researches,‖ have expressed an opinion, that all the foreign words which occur in Ctesias are not Indian, but Persian. That one or two are Persian may be admitted; but there is no reason to question the Indian origin of several of them: and the attempts of the writers in question to assign a Persian etymology to the greater number have been exceedingly unfortunate. The word

kalystrii is an instance. Reland would derive it from *kalleh shikari,* كله شكارى which, he says, means " caput caninum, unde contracte Kaliskaroi scripsit Ctesias, et per incuriam librariorum Kalustrioi." But even if his gratuitous correction of the reading were admissible, his etymology is not; for *kalleh* means rather the crown of the head, than the head; and *shikari* means hunter, hunting, any thing belonging to the chase, not a dog in particular. Tychsen proposes either *kelek-sir,* كلك سر ' wolf-headed;' or *kalus,* كالوس ' foolish,' ' stupid;' in the superlative form *kalusterin,* كالوسترين ' very foolish;' converting *dog-head* into *block-head.* He is avowedly dissatisfied with either of these conjectures, and they are by no means satisfactory. The ingenuity of Col. Vans Kennedy¶ has supplied a much more probable origin in the Sanscrit *kála-vastri,* easily convertible into *kalustri,* as *v* and *u* are' interchangable letters. The sense of the compound, it is true, is not " having the head of a dog," but " having black raiment;" and this would be fatal to the identification, if the interpretation of Ctesias were to be relied upon. There is, however, in favour of the affinity, an argument of more weight, that Col. Vans Kennedy has not adverted to it, and by which, therefore, he was not previously biassed in proposing the Sanscrit compound. This is the existence of a people inhabiting a mountainous district in the direction to which Ctesias refers, who have been known certainly for five centuries by the term in question. These are the people denominated by Mohammedan writers, and by the people surrounding them, the Siah-posh Kafirs, ' the black-vestured infidels.' At the end of the fourteenth** century, they provoked the wrath of Tamerlane, on his way

---

* Origin of Language, part. I. b. ii. c. 3; and Ancient Metaphysics, iii. 250.
† Asiatic Researches, iii. 151.   ‡ Buffon, Hist. Natur. de l'Homme, vol. v. p. 45.
§ Dissert. de veteri lingua Indica, I. 309.   ‖ Historical Researches by Heeren, ii. 376.
¶ Calcutta Quarterly Magazine and Review, June 1827, p. 218.   ** Rozet al Sefa.

to invade Hindustan, and were thence brought to the knowledge of the Persian historians. They are described as a brave though barbarous people, speaking a language peculiar to themselves, and occupying narrow valleys, amidst lofty and almost inaccessible mountains. Although unable to contend with the overwhelming power of the Tartar monarch, they were not reduced without difficulty and loss. At a later period, the Siah-posh were said by Baber and Abul-fazl to be the descendants of the Macedonians; but the inquiries of Mr. Elphinstone,* when on his embassy to Cabul, induced him to disbelieve the tradition. Lieut. Burnes also denies this descent of the Kafirs,† although he thinks the pretensions of the chiefs of Badakshan and the valley of the Oxus, which were first noticed by Marco Polo, better founded. Of the black-vested Kafirs, he remarks, that they appear to be a most barbarous people, eaters of bears and monkeys, fighting with arrows, and scalping their enemies, circumstances quite in harmony with the character given by Ctesias of the Kalystrii. They are fairer than most Asiatics; and a Kafir boy of ten years of age, whom Lieut. Burnes met with, differed in complexion, hair, and features from other Asiatics, and had eyes of a bluish colour, affording some authority for the white-complexioned children mentioned by Ctesias, those of a people who Pliny asserts were called by him *Pandoræ,* a genuine Sanscrit word, *pandura* meaning pale or fair. Lieut. Burnes supposes the Siah-posh to have been the aborigines of the plains, who fled to the mountains from the advance of the Mohammedans. From information obtained by Messrs. Moorcroft and Trebeck, when in Little Tibet, it appears that the Siah-posh Kafirs are nothing more than a tribe of the people called by the Hindu geographers, both in past times and in the present day, Dáradas or Durds, दरद and who have borne that appellation from time immemorial, being the Daradræ of Ptolemy, situated at the sources of the Indus; and the Dardai of Megasthenes, as quoted by Strabo,‡ who inhabited the country of the gold-making ants. Now the sense of *Dárada* is tearer, render, from *dri,* ' to tear to pieces;' and this name, which is no doubt as old as Ctesias, may have contributed to form the canine teeth and talons of the people so called: whilst their other appellation, *Kálavastri,* indicating the usage which they still observe, and whence they are called by their neighbours *Siah-posh,* ' black-vested,' that of wearing black goat-skins, furnished the denomination *Kalystrii,* although the purport of it was inaccurately explained.

It is worthy of remark, as affording an apology for the Greek author, in addition to those furnished by Mr. Wilson, that the existence of a race of dog-men was credited by the Mongols and the Chinese. In the narrative of a journey performed by the Armenian king, Hethum, to Mangoo Khan, in the years 1254 and 1255, recorded by the Armenian historian Kirakos Kandtsaketsi,§ it is said that king Hethum, on his return, related many strange and wonderful things which he had heard amongst the " barbarous nations ;" amongst which was this—that, beyond the Khatayans, there was a country where the men were like great dogs, covered with hair. A Chinese Encyclopædia, entitled *San-tsae-thoo-hwuy,* contains an account of the *Keukwŏ* or ' Kingdom of Dogs,' which coincides in several particulars with the story told to and by Ctesias. It states that the men have the body of a

---

* Embassy to Cabul. Account of Kaferistan, 617.   † Travels to Bokhara, ii. 210.

‡ B. xv.   § *Asiatic Journal,* x. 137.

dog; their head is covered with long hair; they go without clothing, live in caves, and their language is like the barking of dogs.

These specimens of Mr. Wilson's erudite and ingenious speculation, will shew the curious and learned reader the entertainment he may expect to find in this apology for the Greek author.

———

ODE ON THE ROYAL ACCESSION.

BY THE LATE SHAH OF PERSIA.

Throne of Iskendar—of Dara—rejoice!
  A new Iskendar now,
Binding the royal circlet on his brow,
Recalls the gorgeous light of vanished hours:
Bright as the Sun; as Suleiman sublime;
Beneath his rule, Earth smiles as Minu's bowers;
  Justice and mercy waken at his voice;
His spirit is a sea of boundlessness;
Nations with pride his sceptred sway confess;
  Whilst, in glad triumph, Universal Earth
Smiles on the cradle that received his birth.
  His throne aspires above th' etherial reign,
And Fortune o'er his destiny presides;
The mightier than the mighty wheel that guides
    Celestial spheres;
Through wide Immensity's outstretched domain,
Still urging on with Youth's impetuous tides,
  While Youth itself bows with the weight of years.
For him, the vernal grape its flush bestows;
For him, in banquets sweet the cane-juice flows:
For him, the thorny briar puts forth the rose;
For him, in lavish mines, the sparkling metal glows:
  Oh king! whose aid the pride of Genius boasts;
Whose regions wide as yon blue vault extend;
  Whose legions, countless as celestial hosts;
Lo! to thy threshold Heaven itself shall bend,
And, with each favouring Power, thine every wish attend!

Poetic visions ever wake thy thought;
  Arabia's lore, or Persia's softer lay,
Sparkling in musk along thy gilded scroll:
  Themes of Zelman,* and Saadi,* and Zoheir;*
Till Mani's self, with spell sublimer fraught,
  Spurns his own Englioun's† wonder-pictured sway;
And Ghereir's* fire, and Akhtal's* ravished soul,
  Resign the lute—entrancing, but to hear!

Upon thy brow sits Majesty enshrined:
Who shall escape thy vengeance in it's hour?
  Thy face bespeaks the inly-conscious mind;
  Thy hand o'er nations scatters fortune's dower.

* Names of Poets.
† *Englioun, Evangelion,* or Gospel of the famous painter, Mani, embellished (or expressed) by his pictures, the beauty of which are held proof of their divinity.

The first, the ray night's starry radiance throws ;
   The next, fierce flame of all-consuming dread ;
Warm as the third, the grape's rich nectar flows ;
   The last, as amber-gleams, unceasing spread.
Thee her sole aim Creation erst designed :
Thy life, the birth Love granted to mankind :
Thy being fixed by Nature's earliest laws—
By Him,—the First, Sole, Universal Cause !

See from the dust thy portal yields
   Sweet perfume for the ringlets given,
Of dwellers in celestial fields,
   The youths and maids of heaven :
See, at the gifts thy bounty makes,
   Each vest's inwrought embroidery,
The very firmament forsakes
   Its azure robes of rivalry.

Turn'st thou to conquest o'er thy foes ?
    Earth trembling owns thy tread of might—
The bravest fear—the foremost those
   To shun thine arm by headlong flight.
Thus, as the Sun his orb displays,
The planets sicken in his blaze—
Lost in his light ;—outworn, and pale,
They seek the western deep, and plunge beneath its veil.
What can escape thine eye ?—Thy judgment clear,
   Intelligent with light, the heart pervades ;
The Sun, when thus Messiah's rays appear,
   But hastens to the Christian's western shades.

Oh, blest with empire's every gem !
   When he, thy loved, thy monarch-sire,
Too soon in life condemned to feel
The bounded course of fortune's wheel ;
   Lost victim to her ire !
Borne by that blind, resistless sway,
From Bardah's walls to fatal Rey,
Exchanged his royal couch of rest
For brighter couches of the Blest :
Ah, day, that durst to spoil condemn
Dara's proud throne and diadem !
When he, the chief, whose daring crime
   From Fate won one propitious hour :—
Omnipotent, controlling power !
   That spared his treason, for a time :—
When he, the accursed, presumed to soil
   With robber-hand the lordly prey ;
While, scattered in the impious toil,
The glittering heaps and jewelled spoil
   In dust, like starry sparklings, lay :—
Wealth of a thousand regal caves,
Enriching thus a thousand slaves !
How swift the dreadful tidings ran,
   The messengers of wrath and fear !
Far, far, to farthest Farsistan,
   To win thy wondering ear.

Thou heardst:—thy valiant bands around
In rage received the mournful sound,
   And burst their headlong way:
Beneath their feet the dusty waves
Heaved Moonwards, high as Ocean raves;
Soon to extend their thousand graves
   To vengeance-boding Rey:
There, deep th'embattled lines were gored;
There, fast th'ensanguined torrent poured;
There, Fortune bowed before thy sword,
And late thy ravished crown restored;
   Oh, Hatem of thy day!
Thou new Iskandar!—new Daras enchaining—
Thou Suleiman!—thy sovereign ring regaining—
Mount empires, thou!—Heaven and thine arm sustains:
This slays thy foes; and that, thy right maintains.
Oh king! no thought unkingly swayed thy mind;
   No baser impulse lowered thy soul sublime;
Thy nation's wealth no grasping imposts grind;
   Thy pardoned rival dies not for his crime:
Thus as thy justice, mercy, goodness, spread,
Even thus shall mightiest Heaven with blessings crown thy head.

   Yet, Victor of the foughten field!
Awake thy heart to thoughts of gentlest joy—
Such as unclouded days of peace employ;
   Such bliss as Beauty loves, with lingering charms, to yield.
On the Fairest of the Fair
Fix thine eye, and fix thy care:
Golden cups of ruby wine
Steep thy sense in love divine;
Lulled in fondest raptures mute,
Breathings of the lyre and flute!

   But, not in love and wine drown all thy soul:
Oh, prince! while Pity wooes thy milder sway,
Know, in thy heart, there are, whom stern control
   Of frowning Doom, from Hope compels to stray;
Be thou the Mourners' friend: the wandering Dervise stay.

In those days of baleful war,
   When the spear's sharp-pointed gleam
Menaced every tranquil star,
   Gilding Heaven with golden beam;
Timid earth, with trembling throes,
   Shook beneath the coursers' feet;
While her moving sands arose,
   Wave on wave, as Oceans meet.
Dusty clouds, spread o'er the flying,
   Wrapped them in funereal veil;
And the blood-streams of the dying,
   Crimson sheets, o'erlaid the dale,
Crime ever waits on Rage and foul Disorder,
   The fierce, the fatal foe of human kind:
With ruthless dagger, still intent on murder,
   Piercing the bravest breasts that fame would find.

See the flamy sabres flashing ;
  Mark Giboons* of slaughter there ;
Or the fiery war-horse, dashing
  Dusty whirlwinds into air !
Weeping Hope would urge the flying :
  " Shew me :" still she loudly cries ;†
But, his sword and arrows flying,
  Death, in sullen wrath, denies.
Affliction's wonted course tends from the skies ;
But, born of war, towards Heaven afflictions rise :
The drum's wild jar ; the fife, and trumpet's cry,
Wake, in its sacred bosom, agony !

Prince—for noblest virtues crowned !
Prince—for generous deeds renowned !
Fire and air, and land and deep,
Dread thy sabre's circling sweep :
See thy lance's point entail
Tears of blood from eyes of mail !
Mejnoun's thus of old were streaming,
Pierced by Leila's glances gleaming.

The war-shout, when triumph exults o'er the dying,
  Rings grief through blue Heaven, looking down on the doom :
Whilst sad o'er the scene our first parents are sighing,
  And deem their whole race consigned to the tomb.
Oh, conquering king ! 'mid the ranks of thy foemen,
  Attending thy sword, ever Victory flies ;
And Saturn, dismayed by the death-dealing omen,
  Retires in alarm to the steeps of the skies.
How shall past ages emulate thy praise,
  Since Rustam yields his arms, by Thee outshone?
Or how shall this accord the admiring lays,
  That mark the Poet grateful for his own ?
Even from the hour when first my forehead, bending,
  Submissive, touched the threshold of Thy state,
My lofty soul, with planets freely blending,
Yon northern pole and starry pair transcending,
  . Enjoys the pride thy gifts could elevate—
But vain imagination's weak pretence
  To reach the theme ;
For gratitude, how faint is eloquence !
  For majesty, how dim bewildered sense !
Though favoured by its fostering influence
  Brighter than mightiest bards, these verses beam.
Racked with a thousand pains, my anxious mind
  Hath vainly sought thy praises to declare,
But now, too late th'ambitious task resigned,
  I bow mine humbled spirit low in prayer.
King of exalted state, and boundless sway !
  Oh ! may thy glories spread, thy power endure—
Wide, as the seven-fold climes that earth o'er-lay—
Long, as the seven-fold planets hold their way
  Through azure ether, infinite and pure !
As the nine-circling heavens this globe surround,
  So with revolving bliss be all thy fortunes crowned !

                                       B. E. P.

* The Oxus river.   † An allusion to the *Koran*, not very intelligibly introduced in the original.

SKETCHES OF THE LATER HISTORY OF BRITISH INDIA.

No. III.—CAPTURE OF BOURBON AND MAURITIUS.

DURING the wars which followed the French Revolution, the injuries sustained by our commerce, from the enemy's settlements in the Indian seas, were severely felt. The principal seats of annoyance were the Mascarenha Isles, comprising the Isle of Bourbon, or Mascarenha, properly so called; Mauritius, or the Isle of France; the small island of Rodriguez, and another of inferior note. Such a group, lying on the very highway of the commerce between India and England, could not be left in the hands of an active and insidious foe with impunity, and the actual results fully realized all that might have been anticipated. From the Mauritius especially, French cruizers issued, in vast numbers, to prowl over the Indian seas, and the consequent loss was immense. It has been said that, previously to the fall of this island, the insurance offices of Bengal alone were losers to the amount of three millions sterling from captures. The amount may be exaggerated, but there can be no doubt of its having been very great. That such a course of things should have been allowed to proceed so long unchecked, argues little either for the wisdom or the activity of the British Government: but its toleration was in perfect harmony with the indifference usually manifested on such occasions. A persuasion had indeed long prevailed, that the Mauritius could not be successfully assailed by a hostile force, and this persuasion the French naturally used their best endeavours to encourage. A plausible error, once established, is hard to be shaken, and the currency of a belief that the island was impregnable, combined with the imperturbable apathy with which British statesmen have generally regarded the interests of our Indian possessions, must account for the supineness which so long left a valuable branch of commerce at the mercy of the enemy. The enormous extent of the evil at length roused the British cabinet to some exertions. Admiral Bertie, who commanded on the Cape of Good Hope station, was ordered to enforce a rigorous blockade. The service was entrusted to Captain Rowley; and, to assist the contemplated operations, Lieut. Col. Keating was, in 1809, despatched from India, with a small force, to occupy the Island of Rodriguez, about 100 miles distant from the Mauritius. On his arrival, he found only two families on the island, and of course took possession of it without difficulty. After some time spent in acquiring a perfect knowledge of the coast, Commodore Rowley resolved to make an attack upon the town of St. Paul's, the chief port of the Isle of Bourbon, and for this purpose requested the co-operation of Colonel Keating. A detachment was forthwith embarked from Rodriguez to join Commodore Rowley off Port Louis, the capital of the Mauritius.

On the evening of the 19th of September, the force destined for the attack stood for the Isle of Bourbon, and, on the following morning, disembarked to the southward of Pont de Gallotte, seven miles from St. Paul's. The landing was effected with great dexterity, and the troops immediately commenced a forced march, in order, if possible, to cross the causeways extending over the lake or pond of St. Paul's, before the enemy discovered their debarkation. In this they succeeded; and they had the further good fortune of passing the strongest position of the enemy before the French had time to form in sufficient force. By seven o'clock, the assail- ants were in possession of the first two batteries, Lambousiere and la Cen- tiere, and the guns were forthwith turned against the enemy's shipping, whose well-directed fire of grape, from within pistol-shot of the shore, had greatly annoyed the British force. A detachment, consisting of the second column, under Captain Inbeck, was now despatched to take possession of the third battery, La Neuve, which the enemy had abandoned; but, on its way, it fell in with the main force of the enemy, strongly posted within stone walls, with eight six-pounders on its flanks. They were charged in gallant style, but without driving them from their position. Captain Harvey, with the third column, then moved to support Captain Inbeck, and succeeded in taking two of the enemy's guns. The action now became warm and general. The French were re-inforced from the hills, and from the ships in the harbour—the British by the advance of the reserve, which had pre- viously covered the batteries. The guns of the first and second batteries were spiked, and the third was occupied by seamen under the command of Captain Willoughby, who soon opened its fire upon the shipping. The enemy now gave way, the fourth and fifth batteries were won without resis- tance, and at half-past eight the town of St. Paul's was in the possession of the British. Till this period, the naval force had been compelled to remain inactive, as they could not venture to attack the enemy's ships, lest they should annoy the British troops who were within range. They now stood in, Capt. Pym taking the lead, and opened their fire upon the enemy's ships, all of which cut their cables, and drifted on shore. The seamen, however, succeeded in heaving them off without material injury.

The force by which this brilliant exploit was achieved was inconsiderable. The detachment embarked from Rodriguez consisted of only 368 officers and men. It was strengthened by 100 seamen and 136 marines from the blockading squadron; thus making a total of 604. The victory was gained with the comparatively trifling loss of 15 killed, 58 wounded, and 3 missing.

The success which attended this attempt seems to have paralized the enemy. General des Brusles, the commander of the island, marched from the capital, St. Denis, to repel the invaders, and on the evening of the 22d appeared with considerable force on the hills above St. Paul's; but either from overrating the numbers of the British, or from some other cause, at which it were vain to guess, he retreated, and terminated his career by shooting himself. He left behind him a paper, which sufficiently illustrates the state of his feelings, though it but imperfectly accounts for his despair of success. It was to this effect: " I will not be a traitor to my country. I will not, in consequence of what I foresee from the hatred and ambition of some individuals who are attached to a revolutionary sect, sacrifice the inhabitants in the useless defence of an open colony. Death awaits me on the scaffold. I prefer giving it myself; and I recommend my wife and children to Providence, and to those who can feel for them." Judging from the temper with which Buonaparte was accustomed to regard unsuccessful commanders, the apprehensions of General des Brusles cannot be considered unreasonable. It is gratifying to know that his wishes, with regard to his family, were not disappointed; they found in the British commander those humane and generous feelings which their deceased protector had invoked on their behalf. The widow of the general having expressed a wish to go to her own family at the Mauritius, Commodore Rowley immediately appointed a vessel, with a cartel flag, to convey her thither, with her children, servants, and effects.

The career of the British force had been highly brilliant, and, in addition to its actual achievements, it had obviously inspired a degree of terror altogether disproportioned to its extent; but it was quite unequal to undertake the conquest of the island; and this result formed no part of the plan of those who projected the attack. In the destruction of the batteries and the capture of the shipping in the harbour, a part of which were prizes which had been recently taken by the enemy, all that was sought for was attained. As much public property as could he carried away was embarked, the remainder was destroyed, and the island for awhile abandoned; the squadron resuming its usual occupation, and Colonel Keating with his troops returning to Rodriguez.

In the following year, preparations were made for a serious attempt to annihilate the French power in the Indian seas; an attempt encouraged by the success of a desultory but brilliant exploit achieved by Captain Willoughby, who, at the head of about a hundred of the crew of the *Nereide,* which he commanded, landed at Jacolet in the Mauritius. The landing was effected under the fire of two batteries, and, as the assailants formed on the beach, they became exposed to a heavy discharge of musketry; but in ten minutes the first battery was in their possession, and having spiked the guns, they marched to the guard-house, which was protected by ten field pieces, some regular troops, and a strong detachment of artillery. They were charged by Captain Willoughby and his little band, and immediately gave way, abandoning their guns and their commanding officer, who was made prisoner in the act of spiking them. The British then pushed on to the second and stronger battery, to gain which they had to pass the river Le Gulet, swollen and greatly increased in rapidity by heavy rains. The difficulty of crossing the river having been conquered, the battery was immediately carried, and the commander taken. Here, as before, the guns were spiked, and the party were about to return to their ship, when the troops, which had fled from the first battery again appeared, strongly reinforced by militia and irregulars. Capt. Willoughby advanced towards them, and on his coming within musket-shot, they opened their fire. Suspecting that they would again have recourse to flight, the British commander made an oblique movement, with the intention of getting into their rear, but the moment this was discovered by the militia, they fled, followed by

the regulars, with a celerity that defied pursuit.   Finally, Captain Willoughby burnt the signal-house and flag-staff, and, carrying with him some
field pieces and stores, re-embarked with all his men except one, who was
killed.

The organized system of operations against the French islands was not
acted upon until later in the year.   The first step was to renew the attempt
against the Isle of Bourbon, with sufficient strength to take and retain possession of that colony.   For this purpose, the force at Rodriguez, under
command of Colonel Keating, was augmented from the three presidencies
to the number of 3,650 rank and file, of whom above one-half were Europeans.   Colonel Keating had been long occupied in training his troops at
Rodriguez to the service to which they were destined, accustoming them to
a country intersected with ravines and precipices, like that in which they
were about to act.   The transports, which conveyed the reinforcements,
arrived off Rodriguez on the 20th of June; but the unfavourable state of
the weather detained the expedition from proceeding until the 3d of July.
Before it sailed, Colonel Keating communicated to the commanders of brigades the information he had acquired as to the enemy's strength and position,
and his own determination as to the mode of operations.   This, in his own
words, was "to strike the first blow at the heart of the enemy," to gain
possession of the capital, and let further proceedings be guided by circumstances: Every thing during the night, or before daylight, was to be carried
by the bayonet, Colonel Keating judiciously concluding that the French
island force, trained in a system of firing from behind walls and houses,
and from the opposite side of impassable ravines, would never be brought
to stand against English bayonets.

On the 6th, the whole of the expedition came to a rendezvous about fifty
miles to the windward of the Isle of Bourbon, when part of the troops were
removed from the transports on board his Majesty's squadron, consisting of
the *Boadicea*, the *Sirius*, the *Iphigenia*, the *Magicienne*, and the *Nereide*, under the command of Commodore Rowley, which immediately
stood for the different points of debarkation.   On the afternoon of the 7th,
most of the ships had arrived at their destined stations off the island, and
preparations were made for landing the troops.   This was effected to some
extent.   Captain Pym landed the whole of the troops on board his frigate,
the *Sirius*, at Grande Chaloupe, a part of the beach, about six miles to
the westward of St. Denis, the capital of the island; and Lieut. Watling,
of that frigate, with his men, took possession of a neighbouring height,
thereby preventing re-inforcements being sent to St. Denis from the neighbouring town of St. Paul's.   The other point of descent was the River de
Pluies, about three miles to the eastward of St. Denis.   The beach on
that side of the island is composed of large shingles, steep, and difficult of
access, and the wind, which is very uncertain in these latitudes, suddenly
and violently increasing, the surf rose to an unexpected height.   Captain
Willoughby, ever the first at the post of danger, pushed off with a party of
seamen and a detachment of troops, in the *Estafette*, prize schooner.   A

few boats followed, and the men were landed with the loss of only four; but the schooner and several of the boats were dashed to pieces in the surf. Another small body of troops effected a landing somewhat more to the right, under Lieut. Col. Macleod. A small transport was placed upon the beach to act as a breakwater, in the hope that the men might be enabled to land over her stern or under her lee; this was ably performed by Lieut. Lloyd, of the *Boadicea,* but the violence of the weather, and the natural difficulties of the situation, frustrated the success of the attempt, and it was found impossible to land any more troops that evening. Those who had succeeded in landing had lost a considerable part of their arms, and all their ammunition was damaged.

It now became an object of importance to communicate with the detachment on shore, but all hope of doing so seemed cut off by the circumstances which had suspended the landing of the troops. In this emergency, the desired means of communication were furnished by that unconquerable spirit which our countrymen have so often displayed under circumstances which almost justify despair. Lieutenant Foulstone, of the 69th regiment, volunteered to swim to shore;—his offer was accepted; he made the attempt, and succeeded, by diving under the surf, from whence he was dragged by a boat-hook. By the gallantry of this high-spirited officer, orders were conveyed to Colonel Macleod, the senior officer of the detachment on shore, to take possession of St. Marie for the night. That officer immediately marched with his slender force, and carred the fort at the point of the bayonet.

The impracticability of disembarking any more troops to the windward during the existing state of the weather being apparent, it was resolved to despatch the remainder to Grande Chaloupe,* where the landing was successfully effected.

In the mean-time, the brigade under Lieut. Col. Fraser, which had previously landed at Grande Chaloupe, had pushed forward a party, the commanding officer leading the way, to dislodge a body of riflemen, who occupied the heights and kept up a harassing fire. This was soon accomplished, and the brigade moved rapidly over the mountains towards St. Denis. They halted there during the night, they began to descend at four o'clock on the following morning, having in the interval been joined by sepoys, pioneers, and artillery. They found the enemy drawn up on the plain, in two columns, each with a field piece at its head, supported by some heavy cannon on the redoubt. A severe fire of ordnance and musketry was opened upon the British force, who, however, advanced in admirable order. On reaching the plain, orders were given to charge. The French remained steadily at their guns until the British grenadiers came in contact with them,

* St. Pierre, who visited this spot in 1770, says, "We descended and came to the Grande Chaloupe. It is a frightful valley, formed by two mountains that are very steep. We walked part of the way, which the rain had rendered dangerous, and at the bottom we found ourselves between the two mountains in the strangest solitude I had ever seen; we were, in a manner, between two walls, the heavens only hanging over our heads: we crossed the rivulet, and came at length to the shore opposite the Chaloupe. At the bottom of this abyss there reigns an eternal calm, however the winds blow or the mountains."

when, finding that the thunder of their ordnance was to be met with the silent but deadly thrust of the bayonet, they retired and attempted to form behind the parapet of the redoubt. From this they were speedily driven by the weapon they so much dreaded; the British colours were hoisted on the top of the redoubt, two guns which had been spiked were rendered service-able and turned against the enemy, and the batteries to the west of the river St. Denis were stormed and demolished. Thus the main force of the island was totally defeated by a body of troops not amounting to six hundred men. The commandant, Colonel St. Susanne, escaped with difficulty, and the second in command was wounded and made prisoner.

About two o'clock in the afternoon, a brigade under Lieutenant-colonel Drummond, which had been landed that morning at Grande Chaloupe, ar-rived in sight of St. Denis, after a severe march over the mountains, har-rassed by the enemy's chasseurs, who hung upon their flanks. As they ap-proached, they were exposed to a heavy fire of cannon, grape, shells, and musketry from the town, without a possibility of either returning or avoiding it. Colonel Fraser, however, kept up a brisk fire upon the town from the redoubt. About four o'clock, he was joined by Lieut. Col. Drummond's bri-gade, and Colonel Keating, who had landed at noon with the rest of the troops, appeared on the heights. Preparations were now made for a simul-taneous attack upon the place, when, at the very moment of advance, a flag of truce arrived to treat for the surrender of the island, Colonel Fraser having refused to negociate on any other terms. The articles of capitula-tion stipulated for the immediate evacuation of all the military posts and the surrender of all public stores; the troops of the line and *Garde Nationale* to march out with the honours of war; the former to surrender as prisoners, the officers being allowed to retain their swords and military decorations, and embarked, as well as the troops, either for England or the Cape, with the exception of the commandant, St. Susanne, who was to be allowed to depart either to France or the Mauritius on his parole of honour. To these a provision of an unusual kind was added,—that funeral honours should be paid to the French officers who had fallen, according to their respective rank. The laws, customs, and religion of the inhabitants, as well as their private property, were to be respected.

The ordnance found at St. Paul's and St. Denis amounted to 145 pieces of heavy artillery. The loss sustained in making the conquest was slight; eighteen killed, seventy-nine wounded, and four drowned in landing. That of the enemy was never precisely ascertained, but it was very considerable.

The capture of the island of Bourbon was principally desired as a preli-minary to that of the still more important settlement of the Mauritius; and in anticipation of our attempts upon that island, Mr. Farquhar, the English governor of the Isle of Bourbon, published an address to the inhabitants of the Mauritius, the distribution of which he found means of effecting from the little island of Passe, which had been taken possession of by a party from his Majesty's cruisers. This acquisition was made in a very brilliant man-ner. Five boats from the *Sirius* and the *Iphigenia* proceeded on the night of the 13th August to the landing-place on the north-west side of the island, which was defended by a *chevaux-de-frise* and two howitzers. To gain this spot, it was necessary to pass a battery of several guns, and, fortunately, the attempt was favoured by a heavy cloud suddenly obscuring the moon, which had previously been shining with great brightness. Before, however, the boats reached the landing-place, the enemy discovered and commenced firing upon them; two men were killed and several wounded, but, nothing daunted, the assailants advanced and landed. Lieut. Norman, in attempting to scale the works, was shot through the heart by a sentinel overhead: he was immediately shot by one of the seamen, who, headed by Lieut. Watling, speedily ascended the walls. A brief but warm encounter followed, in which the British had seven men killed and eighteen wounded; but they succeeded in obtaining possession of the walls. Lieut. Watling then proceeded to attack the batteries on the south-east side, where he was met by Lieut. Chads, who had landed at another point and stormed and carried the works there, without the loss of a man. The two parties being united, the French commandant offered no further resistance, but surrendered at discretion. The island was entrusted to the charge of Capt. Willoughby, who availed himself of its proximity to the Mauritius to pay visits to the coasts of the latter island. His first attack was upon Pont du Diable, which was stormed and carried; the French commander and three of his men killed, and three gunners made prisoners; the guns were spiked, the carriages burnt, and the magazine blown up; after which, Capt. Willoughby moved on to Grand Port, a distance of twelve miles. He remained on the island until sunset, and a strong party of the enemy, which attacked him, were put to the rout with the loss of six men. On another occasion, he destroyed the signal-house and staff at Grand Riviere, blew up the remaining works at Pont du Diable, and retired without molestation.

The British arms had hitherto been eminently successful, but the flattering hopes which their success had called forth, now sustained a severe check by a series of disasters, which for a time gave the enemy the dominion of the Indian seas. Among other prizes they succeeded in capturing the *Windham* and *Ceylon*, East-Indiamen. These ships, with another Company's ship, the *Astell*, were sailing for Madras, when they were attacked by a French squadron under Commodore Duperne. The Indiamen maintained a very gallant and hard-fought contest with a very superior force for several hours; when the *Windham* and the *Ceylon*, having sustained serious loss in killed and wounded, and much injury in their hull, masts, and rigging, were compelled to strike. The *Astell*, after taking its share in the unequal struggle, effected its escape under cover of the darkness of the night. The French account of this transaction was marked with that bad faith, which has too often characterized the official statements of our neighbours, and which was almost universal during the reign of Buonaparte. It asserted that the *Astell* had struck her colours previously to her escape,—an accusation which the captain and his officers publicly refuted.

The success of the enemy was not restrained to encounters with merchant

ships.   The French squadron, with the two Indiamen their prizes, ran for
Port Sud-Est, in the Mauritius, at the entrance of which lay the isle of
Passe, which the English had occupied and garrisoned.   Four British
frigates were also cruizing off the station, and in the attempt to make the
port, the *Windham* East-Indiaman was turned and re-captured by the
Sirius, Captain Pym.   Having despatched his prize to Bourbon, that
officer formed the design of attacking the French squadron in the harbour;
but, not being sufficiently aware of the difficulties of the navigation, the
attempt terminated in defeat and serious loss.   Three of the ships took the
ground, and the fourth was prevented from closing with the enemy.   These
unfortunate occurrences enabled the foe to open all their guns upon a single
vessel, the *Nereid*, commanded by Captain Willoughby.   The fortitude
and courage displayed by this officer and his crew were beyond all praise,
and probably have never been surpassed.   Deprived of all efficient assistance
from the other frigates, the *Nereid* singly maintained the contest for the
almost incredible space of ten hours.   Captain Willoughby lost an eye, and
was otherwise dreadfully injured in the head.   A boat was sent from the
Sirius to bring him off, but he declared that he would neither abandon his
men, nor strike the British flag while there was a single man on board able
to support it.   He kept his word—he fought the ship till every man of her
whole crew, consisting of two hundred and eighty, was either killed or
wounded; and when the enemy took possession of their dearly-purchased
prize, they found only a miserable wreck, peopled with the maimed, the
dying, and the dead.   Of the remaining vessels, two, the *Sirius* and *Magicienne*, were so situated, that their abandonment became necessary, and
after setting fire to them, their respective crews were landed on the isle of
Passe; the fourth, the *Iphigenia*, was with some difficulty warped up to
that anchorage, the enemy making no attempt to prevent her.   In this
situation she lay without the power of removing from it, while the state of
the little garrison at the isle became every day more forlorn; their stock,
both of provisions and water, was low, and they had no prospect of receiving succour.   To complete their distress, they were blockaded by a French
force; and as their means of subsistence were almost at an end, and escape
was impossible, they were compelled to surrender.

No one object of this unfortunate attempt was achieved; its disastrous
issue was complete: all the vessels engaged in it were either destroyed, or
fell into the hands of the enemy.   But though, as it subsequently appeared,
the undertaking was ill-judged, the conduct of those engaged in it was such
as to enable their countrymen to call up the recollection, even of discom-
fiture, without a blush.   Heroism like that displayed by Captain Willoughby
and his intrepid comrades, sheds over defeat the lustre of victory.   Amid
scenes of blood and suffering, far surpassing the ordinary horrors of warfare,
they were insensible to every thing but their own duty and their country's
honour.   Never was duty more devotedly performed, never was honour
more completely sustained.

The record of disaster, though drawing to a close, is not yet entirely com-plate. The *African* frigate was taken by the enemy, after a severe action, in which her commander fell; and another frigate, the *Ceylon*, shared the same fate. This vessel, having on board General Abercrombie, appointed by the Governor-general to take the command of the troops destined for the reduction of the Mauritius, fell in with some French cruizers off the island of Bourbon. An action ensued, which was gallantly maintained for five hours, when the *Ceylon*, being dismasted and rendered ungovernable by this and other causes, was compelled to yield to adverse fortune and overwhelming force. It is said that the French commander observed, that he should have the honour of introducing General Abercrombie to the governor of the Isle of France sooner than he had expected. But this honour he was not destined to enjoy. In a few hours, the *Ceylon* was retaken by the English, when the General, thanking M. Hamlen for his kind intention, said he felt extremely happy in being able to return the compliment, by introducing him to Commodore Rowley.

The necessity of wresting the Mauritius from the enemy now became more than ever apparent, and preparations for the attempt were carried on with renewed vigour. On the 14th of October, Commodore Rowley sailed with a gallant squadron from the harbour of St. Paul's, to resume the blockade of the Mauritius, taking with him Major-general Abercrombie, to reconnoitre the situation of the French colony, and concert the necessary measures for its reduction. He arrived off Port Louis on the 19th, where he found the whole of the enemy's naval force at anchor in the port, two only of the ships in a state of apparent readiness for sea. Having left a sufficient force to watch the enemy's movements and blockade the port, he proceeded to Rodriguez, where the different divisions destined for the attack on the Mauritius were appointed to assemble. He found that the troops from Bombay had already reached their destination. They were soon followed by those from Madras; but the non-arrival of the divisions from Bengal and the Cape at the expected time was a source of great disappointment and anxiety, as the stormy season was approaching, and in the event of unfavourable weather, the danger to the fleet would be extreme. He, therefore, suggested to the General, the propriety of standing out to sea with the troops already assembled, and cruizing to the windward of the French island to await the junction of one or both of the divisions so anxiously looked for. To this suggestion the General assented, and the 22d November was fixed for the departure of the fleet from Rodriguez. Every thing was in readiness on the previous evening, when the welcome intelligence was received that the Bengal division was seen in the offing. That not a moment might be lost, it was resolved that the convoys just arrived should be supplied with the requisite provisions from the beach and shipping, and, without dropping anchor, be ordered to accompany the fleet then getting under weigh; and soon after, the fleet, consisting of nearly seventy sail, stood from the anchorage of Rodriguez to the selected point of debarkation.

The coasts of the Mauritius are beset by dangerous reefs, and the island has only two good harbours. That called Port Sud-Est, which was principally used by the Dutch, is the more capacious, and being on the windward side of the island, it is the easier of entrance, as well as the more healthy; but the wind almost perpetually blowing in, the difficulty of ships getting out counterbalances the facility with which they can enter. For this reason, Port Nord-Ouest was preferred by the French when the Mauritius came into their possession, and there, during the administration of Mahé de la Bourdonnais, who was governor from 1734 to 1766, the only town in the island was erected, in a narrow valley at the head of the harbour. This henceforward was the seat of government, and the port and town were denominated Port Louis.

The Portugueze, by whom the island was discovered, do not appear ever to have taken possession of it. It was first occupied by the Dutch, in the seventeenth century, who gave it the name of Mauritius, in honour of Prince Maurice of Nassau. These indefatigable traders are said to have been driven out of the island by the swarms of rats, with which it was infested, and it is certain that they abandoned it about the year 1710. Whether the French had less dread of the disagreeable quadrupeds which had conquered their predecessors, or possessed better means of contending with them, is not recorded; but they took possession of the island after it was forsaken by the Dutch, and always attached great importance to it. Raynal dwells enthusiastically upon its political and commercial advantages, and especially on its value as the means of annoying the commerce of Great Britain.* The statesmen of that country had participated in this feeling, and much labour had been employed to place Port Louis in a posture of defence. They seem, however, to have relied too implicitly upon the reef which surrounds the island, and to have concluded too hastily, that the town would only be attacked by sea. To guard against such an attack, works of considerable strength were constructed. As the approach of the English was not unexpected, additional means of defence were resorted to, and the fortifications on the sea-side placed in such a state, as to render an attack an act of extreme temerity. But the governor seems to have relied entirely upon his sea-works, and in a great degree to have neglected the means of defence on the land side.

The advantages of superior knowledge of the coast were now manifest. The French had supposed that the reefs which surround the island rendered it impregnable, and that the depth of water without the reef rendered it impossible for a fleet of transports to find anchorage. These impressions

* This writer, after adverting to certain plans for securing the resources of the Mauritius, exclaims, " Then this island will be what it should, the bulwark of all the settlements which France possesses, or may one day acquire, in the Indies; the centre of all military operations, offensive or defensive, which her interest will oblige her to undertake or to sustain in those distant regions. It is situated in the African seas, just at the entrance of the Indian ocean. Though raised as high as arid or burning coasts, it is temperate and wholesome. As it lies a little out of the common track, its expeditions can be carried on with greater secrecy. Those who wish it was nearer to our continent do not consider, that if it were so, it would be impossible to pass in so short a time from its road to the gulphs, in the most distant of those regions, which is an invaluable advantage to a nation that has no sea-port in India. Great Britain sees, with a jealous eye, her rivals possessed of a settlement where the ruin of her property in Asia may be prepared. At the breaking out of a war, her utmost efforts will certainly be exerted against a colony which threatens her richest treasures. What a misfortune for France, should she suffer herself basely to be deprived of it !"

were not unknown to the British commanders; but, instead of supinely acquiescing in the popular belief, they took measures for ascertaining its accuracy. Every part of the leeward side was examined, and sounded with the most minute and scrupulous attention. This service was performed by Captain Paterson, of his Majesty's ship *Hesper,* and Lieutenant Street, commanding the government armed ship *Emma.* The soundings were taken in the night, to avoid observation, and it was by these means discovered, that a fleet might safely anchor in a narrow strait, between an islet called the Gunner's Coin and the main land, and that there were also openings in the reef here, through which several boats might enter abreast. The only objection to this place of debarkation was its distance from Port Louis; but this was not to be placed in competition with its manifold advantages.

On the morning of the 29th, the English fleet came to anchor in the strait. Two brigs, which drew but little water, anchored on the reef, within a hundred yards of the beach, to cover the landing; the conduct of which was entrusted to Captain Philip Beaver, of the *Nisus* frigate. Soon after one o'clock, the debarkation commenced, and in three hours, ten thousand men, with their guns, stores, ammunition, and three days' provisions, were landed, without the slightest loss, or even a single accident. The enemy appear to have been astonished by the boldness and novelty of the attempt. On the first appearance of the British fleet, they abandoned a fort called Malastrie, the only fortified place in the vicinity. The landing having been thus happily effected, no time was lost in following up the success which had attended it. The troops were instantly put in motion, to prevent the enemy from gaining possession of a thick wood which lay on the road, and using the means which it afforded of harassing the flanks of the invading army. On reaching it, the advanced guard fell in with a picquet of the retreating corps, which, after a feeble attempt to dispute the passage, was driven from its position. This was the only opposition encountered till the columns reached the more open country. About midnight, they halted, and before day-break resumed their march. It was the intention of General Abercrombie not to halt again till he was before Port Louis, but the march of the preceding day, though short, had been so extremely harassing, that his intention could not be persevered in. The men were greatly exhausted by their previous exertions, their way having lain for four miles among thick brushwood, through which the artillery and stores had to be dragged, with a degree of labour almost intolerable. The inconvenience arising from the heat of the weather was increased by a deficiency of water. Several men and two officers had sunk under their exertions, and were left dead on the march. It was fortunate that these harassing circumstances were not aggravated by any operations of the enemy; but the condition of the troops rendered it obviously imprudent to attempt to reach Port Louis without rest. About noon, therefore, a position was taken up at Moulin-à-Poudre, on a gentle elevation, a wood stretching along its front, and extending with some intervals to Port Louis, five miles distant. In the afternoon, the French General de Caen, with a party of cavalry and riflemen, approached the British lines to reconnoitre, and surprised a small picquet. They were driven back and pursued by some light companies.   A few men were killed, and the general himself received a contusion from a ball.

Before daylight, on the following day, a brigade, under the command of Lieut.-col. Macleod, was detached to attack some batteries, the possession of which was necessary to enable the troops to draw their supplies from the fleet. Some of the batteries had already yielded to our seamen; the remainder were evacuated as the troops approached. At five o'clock, the main body of the troops was put in motion.   It shortly afterwards encountered a corps of the enemy, who, with several field-pieces, had taken up a strong position, very favourable for making an attack on the head of the column.   The march of the British troops lay along a narrow road, with a thick wood on each flank. On meeting the enemy, the European flank battalion, which composed the advanced guard, formed with as much regularity as the bad and broken ground would admit, and charged the enemy with such spirit, as compelled them to retire with the loss of their guns, and many killed and wounded; but this advantage was obtained by the fall of Colonel Campbell and Major O'Keefe, two officers of distinguished ability.   There was a signal-post on a hill, called the Vivebot, from whence every movement of the enemy could be discerned. The French being driven from their position, a corps ascended this eminence, removed the enemy's flag, and hoisted the British ensign in its place; which was then, for the first time, planted in the Mauritius.

The weather still continued oppressive, and the troops were greatly exhausted.   These circumstances, combined with the lateness of the day, rendered desirable a suspension of active operations until the morning, when a general attack was determined upon. During the night, a mistake occurred, which was productive of unfortunate results.   A party of marines arrived to join the British force; they were dressed, as customary in India, in white and blue, and in the darkness were unhappily mistaken for French soldiers. An alarm was given, several corps stood to their arms, some gave fire, and the consequence was that many were wounded, and a few killed.   But misapprehension was not confined to the British: the enemy were likewise disturbed by a false alarm, during which, it has been said, the National Guards betrayed such a degree of irresolution, as had considerable effect in determining the events of the following day.

On the approach of morning, preparations were made for the intended attack; but they were interrupted by the arrival of a flag of truce from General de Caen, offering to capitulate upon conditions.   Three of the conditions were, that the troops and seamen should be sent to France; that the four frigates and two corvettes in the harbour should be retained by the French; and that inventories should be taken of all the articles belonging to the French emperor, and such articles restored to him at the conclusion of peace.   General de Caen did not then foresee that this last article, had it been complied with, would produce no benefit to the individual in whose favour it was framed; it was not then anticipated that peace never would be made with the French emperor, nor that he was to end his days on an island in the Southern Ocean immeasurably inferior in every respect to that, for the surrender of which, General de Caen was negociating; that even over that narrow and barren rook he should hold no sovereignty, but should sojourn there a prisoner to the power from whose victorious forces such insolent terms were now demanded. The articles which stipulated for the retention of the shipping, and the property of the French emperor, were. rejected; that which claimed for the enemy's troops and seamen immunity from the ordinary fate of the vanquished, was assented to;—a fact which could not fail to create surprise in all acquainted with the relative situations of the invading and defending forces; while it was equally calculated to excite regret, not unmixed with indignation, in all who valued the honour of the British arms. That such a condition should have been demanded was nothing remarkable; it was but a fresh instance of that insolent pride, which, in modern times, had invariably marked the conduct and demeanour of the "great nation," and which, under Napoleon and his captains, attained its climax; but that British officers should have been found to yield to the demand, is one of those rare instances in the military history of his country, which call up on the cheek of an Englishman the hue of shame. There was not the slightest reason for the indulgence thus unreasonably asked, and thus unreasonably conceded. We were in a condition to dictate our own terms. We had reduced the enemy to an offer of surrender, with only a part of the army destined to the undertaking; and, during the progress of the negocia- tion, the Cape squadron arrived with the remaining force, amounting to two thousand men. To the British army, without this addition, the French could have offered no effectual resistance; thus reinforced, all pretext for hesitation was removed; the duty of the British general was clear, and his compliance with a demand quite unusual, and almost unprecedented, cannot be regarded otherwise than as a surrender of a portion of national honour, and consequently of national interest, for the loss of the one involves that of the other. At this time, it was more important than at any previous period, that no portion of either should be sacrificed. The French were masters of the entire Continent, and England stood alone in arms against the people who had enslaved all Europe. The superiority of the French over other nations in the arts of war had been loudly proclaimed by themselves, and implicitly admitted by almost all the world; and to this universal belief in the omnipotence of French tactics, and immutability of French fortune, much of their success is to be attributed. It was, therefore, of immeasurable importance to break the charm which hung over these alleged invincibles, and to exhibit them as ordinary men. To beat them, and then, as if alarmed at what we had done—as if glad to be rid of their presence upon any terms—to give them safe-conduct to their own shores, was to confirm the prejudice from which such fearful consequences had flowed—to sign and seal a certificate of our own weakness and the enemy's strength, and to send him forth, bearing, under the hand of the British commanders, a testi- monial of the homage of England to the great idol before whom all Europe bowed. The pretence for such acts of discreditable submission is always that of humanity—a desire to curtail the horrors of war; but here the hope of offering successful resistance to the invaders was beyond the reach of

even the sanguine mind of a French general; and there is no reason for
believing that, had the British commanders been stedfast in rejecting the
obnoxious article, the negociation would have come to an end, or even that
its progress would have been greatly impeded.   But, if it had—if the insane
confidence of the French commander in the good star of his country had led
him to protract the surrender of the island, and if hostile operations had, in
consequence, been renewed, on his head would have rested the guilt of the
additional bloodshed.   The British general would only have discharged his
duty, in refusing to assent to terms unsanctioned by the usages of war.
With the enemy prostrate and powerless at his feet, there was but one safe
and honourable course, and, in departing from it, he committed an error,
which, judged upon military and national principles, must be pronounced
unpardonable.   His own feelings, doubtless, prompted him to treat a vanquished enemy humanely and generously, and the honour of his country
demanded this; but those estimable feelings were indulged to an undue
extent, when he forgot the distinction between a victorious and a beaten
army, and suffered the one to usurp the privileges of the other.   Conven-
tions were in fashion about the time of the capture of the Mauritius, and
this may in some degree account for the course taken there, though it cannot
excuse it.   Such temporizing expedients cannot be too severely reprobated;
they are, in truth, no more beneficial to the general interests of humanity,
than they are creditable to the nation which submits to them.   War is a
fertile source of evil and misery, but no rational man expects to see the
necessity for it banished from the world.   While the nature of man remains
unchanged, war will occasionally be inevitable; and, if it must arise, to pursue it with vigour and decision is the most effectual way to shorten its duration, and thus to diminish the mischief of which it is the cause.   To cripple
the resources of an enemy, is to lead him to desire peace—to restore to him
the men we have vanquished, to be again employed in active hostility against
those whose weakness has released them, is but to feed the flames of war,
and to assist in perpetuating their ravages.

The prize was gained at comparatively small cost.   Our loss amounted to
only twenty-nine killed, ninety-nine wounded, and forty-five missing.   The
conquest placed in our possession a large quantity of ordnance and shipping
—some of the latter of great value, the island having long been the depôt
for the prizes made by the French privateers in the Indian seas.   At home,
the island was justly regarded as a most valuable acquisition, but the terms
upon which it was obtained excited general disgust, and became the subject
both of private and public reprobation.

The Mauritius is still ours, but the Island of Bourbon was, at the peace
of 1814, restored to the French.   This has been the usual course of
events—what we have gained by arms, we have lost by diplomacy; our
soldiers and seamen having poured out their blood in the purchase of conquests, to be calmly yielded up by the liberality or the incompetence of our
statesmen.   The island of Bourbon is, from its position, of less importance
than the Mauritius, but the possession of both is necessary to the security of
our Eastern possessions and commerce, and, by surrendering one, we have

compromised our power of retaining the other. In the event of war, it will be a question, whether the French shall recover the Mauritius, or the English the isle of Bourbon. The dominion of the Indian seas we ought never to have surrendered; it is an essential appendage to our commercial greatness, and to the safety of our Asiatic empire. Never was a more mistaken policy, than to settle a probable enemy upon the road to our most valuable possessions, and in the immediate neighbourhood of the colony which is the key to them.

𝔐𝔦𝔰𝔠𝔢𝔩𝔩𝔞𝔫𝔦𝔢𝔰, 𝔒𝔯𝔦𝔤𝔦𝔫𝔞𝔩 𝔞𝔫𝔡 𝔖𝔢𝔩𝔢𝔠𝔱.

PROCEEDINGS OF SOCIETIES.

Royal Asiatic Society, 7th of May.—The thirteenth anniversary meeting was held this day; the Right Hon. C. W. Williams Wynn, M.P., the President of the Society, in the chair.

The secretary read the Annual Report of the Council. From this document, it appeared that the Council had been under the necessity of selling out a portion of the Society's stock in the Three per cents.; and that the greatest attention to economy would be necessary to enable the Society's income to meet the demands upon it. A larger number of new members had been elected last year than ordinary, but the losses had been greater than usual.

The Report contained brief memoirs of several of the members, of whom death had recently deprived the Society; among whom were Lieut. Colonel James Tod, the well-known author of the *Annals of Rajast'han;* Major David Price, author of an excellent work on Mahommedan history; and Colonel Broughton, formerly secretary to the Society. Among other topics, the Report alluded to the withdrawal, by the Bengal Government, of the patronage and support it had previously extended to the publication of standard oriental works, under the auspices of the Committee of Public Instruction in Calcutta; and stated that a deputation had waited on the Chairman and Deputy-Chairman of the East-India Company, and afterwards on the President of the Board of Control, to intercede for a reversal of this measure. From the reception the deputation had met with, and from the attention which had been paid to its representations, the Council were of opinion the best results might be anticipated by the friends of Oriental literature. A deputation from the Society had also waited upon the Chancellor of the Exchequer, to urge the claims of the Society for public accommodation; and the Council had grounds for hoping that these claims would be acceded, to whenever the rooms in Somerset House or in any other public building that could be made available for the purposes of the Society, became vacant. The Report then adverted to the operations of the Oriental Translation Fund; and specified the valuable works which that institution had published since the last anniversary. After referring to a proposition that would be submitted to the meeting, relative to the formation of a separate section of the Society, to investigate matters connected with agriculture and commerce, in relation to the East, the Report concluded by expressing the acknowledgements which were due from the Society to the Hon. the Court of Directors of the East-India Company, for its continued liberality towards the Society; and by calling upon the members for renewed exertions to increase the welfare and prosperity of the institution.

The auditors' report on the financial affairs of the Society was then read. The thanks of the meeting were voted to the auditors; and their report, together with that of the Council, was received, and ordered to be printed in the Journal of the society.

Sir Alexander Johnston, Chairman of the Committee of Correspondence of the Society, in an able speech, gave to the meeting a full detail of the various subjects connected with the East that had engaged the attention of the Committee during the preceding year; and particularly referred to the suggestion which had been made to it relative to the formation of a Committee of Trade and Agriculture. Thanks were unanimously returned to Sir Alexander for his valuable statement; which he was requested to reduce to writing, in order that it might be published in the Society's Journal.

The secretary then read the minutes of a committee appointed to report to the Council, on the practicability and expediency of carrying into effect the recommendation of the Committee of Correspondence for the formation of a Committee of Trade and Agriculture, in relation to the East; and which had been ordered by the Council to be submitted to the consideration of the Society at its anniversary. This report fully concurred in the expediency of adopting the proposed plan; but as that would involve the necessity of an additional expenditure on the part of the Society, which the state of its funds would not admit of, the committee was compelled to recommend that, unless an appeal to the liberality of the members proved successful, the scheme should at least be postponed. [After the meeting, several gentlemen put down their names as annual subscribers to the proposed committee.]

William Stanley Clarke, Esq., rose to move a vote of thanks to the Council for their valuable services during the past year. Allusion had been made in the report to the circumstance that the chairman, for the time being, of the Hon. the Directors of the East-India Company, had been requested to accept the office of Vice-Patron of the Society. As he was the humble individual who had been the first to receive that honour, he could not allow the opportunity to pass without returning his thanks for the distinction.

Seconded by Colonel Strover, and carried unanimously.

The Right Honourable the President rose, and said that it was his duty to submit to the meeting such observations as occurred to him on the annual proceedings of the Society. He, in common with every member present, experienced a lively pleasure in witnessing the continual progress of the Society towards the accomplishment of the great objects for which it was instituted. In the increased attendance of members, it was impossible not to perceive an increased interest in the proceedings of the Society. Its sphere of usefulness was widely extended; and it might be expected to become still more so. He felt particular gratification in congratulating the meeting on the proposal which had been laid before the Society for establishing a Committee of Agriculture and Trade in relation to the East. That suggestion had come from individuals of such eminence, and who were so intimately acquainted with the capabilities of India, that it was doubtful whether the measure did not acquire as much importance from the movers, as from its own intrinsic worth. The manner in which the natives of India were now considered in this country was another source of gratification. Truer ideas were now formed of their capacity, disposition, and acquirements; and he needed scarcely to remind the meeting that to obtain such accurate ideas was the chief object of the Society. The plan just alluded to would be the means of introducing into India the useful discoveries of Europe in arts and sciences; but, in the encouragement lately given by Government to a more extended intercourse with the East, would be found the true efficient for those ends; because, after all, whatever the Society might do to forward the objects in question, the results would still be inferior to those arising from individual enterprise directed to individual interest. He thought he did not assert too much when he termed this the commencement of a new era. As the proposal relative to trade and agriculture must, if carried into effect, produce increased means of acquiring information on the capacity of the different nations of the vast empire of India, he hoped it would meet with encouragement, not only from the Society, but from those engaged in commercial intercourse with the East. In leaving this subject, which had called for congratulation, he must refer to another which did not present an equally pleasing aspect. He meant the discontinuing of printing standard oriental works, under the patronage of the Indian Government. Most of the gentlemen present had doubtless seen the able remarks of the Sanscrit professor at Oxford, Mr. Wilson, on this subject, and he perfectly agreed with the professor. He agreed also in the views of the Bengal Government, for spreading the English language among the natives; but he felt convinced that that object could only be attained by promoting the cultivation of the native languages. Nothing was more likely to produce a feeling of repugnance to such a plan than to withdraw the encouragement already given to the cultivation of the native literature. He was not sanguine as to the introduction of the English language into the East; but any attempt to force the natives to adopt it would, he felt sure, be unsuccessful. When he considered how warmly the people of India were attached to their own learning and literature, it was not probable, that, out of compliment to their rulers, they would adopt, all at once, another language. A striking example of the truth of this observation might be found in the case of his own country, Wales. Though Wales had been united to England in the closest and most faithful intercourse for 600 years, the native language was still retained,—in union with that of England,—but still retained. Nothing would militate more against the free introduction of English into Wales than a *fiat* to discourage Welch. Poland was another instance of what he alleged. Among the severities which had been practised towards Poland, nothing had generated greater acrimony and ill-will among the people than the order for the disuse of the Polish language; for, in being compelled to use the language of their conquerors, they were perpetually reminded of their degradation and slavery. He considered, therefore, that the attempt to suppress the native languages in India could not be deemed a wise one. The gentlemen who had been associated with him in the duty, had waited on the President of the Board of Control, and on the Chairman and Deputy-Chairman of the Hon. the Court of Directors of the East-India Company, to represent the sentiments of the Society on this subject; and, from the manner in which the representations of the deputation had, in both instances, been received, he hoped the efforts of the Society would be attended with a good effect. In conclusion, he congratulated the meeting on the full attendance; and trusted that every one would promote the interests of the Society, by exerting himself among his friends to procure new members. It must be obvious that the funds of the Society, although in a less unfavourable state than they were last year, were still inadequate for all the objects of the Society; and no question came before the Council on which they were not cramped in their deliberations by the inability of the funds to meet any additional expense.

Sir George Staunton, in rising to propose a vote of thanks to the Right

Hon. President, did not think it necessary to expatiate on his merits and services; they were well known to all. He could not, however, deny himself the gratification of pointing out two instances of them, which had occurred that season. The first was, when, at the head of the deputation, he waited on the Chancellor of the Exchequer to lay before him the claims of the Society to some public building, in which accommodation could be afforded for the museum and library of the Society; and the other, when he waited, as had already been stated, on the President of the Board of Control, and the Chairman and Deputy-Chairman of the East-India Company, to state the evils which must arise, in a moral point of view, to the natives of India, if the intention of discontinuing all encouragement to the cultivation of the native languages was persisted in. He could not say what the result of that statement might be, but the able manner in which the President brought it forward, evidently had great effect on the eminent persons addressed. He considered, therefore, that the President had acquired fresh claims to the Society's gratitude. As some of the members might think that, in consequence of the invitation that the Council had held out of additional subscription, the Society was in a declining state, he wished to express his opinion, that the Society was perfectly equal to carry into effect its objects, so far as the abstract questions of literature were concerned. The reason of a wish to augment the funds was not that the resources of the Society had diminished, but that its prospects and aims had enlarged. Should the application which has been made to enable the Society to carry out these enlarged views fail, still the Society would continue in action. It would still publish in its Transactions the valuable papers it collected; and the Committee of Correspondence, under the care of its Right Hon. Chairman, would not, he was sure, relax in its operations. He felt convinced that the Society contained within itself no seeds of decay; though it certainly might not occupy so high a station as it would if possessed of additional funds. Sir George concluded by proposing a vote of thanks to the President, which was carried unanimously.

Mr. W. Stanley Clarke requested permission to make an observation, as the deputation which had waited on the Chairman of the Court of Directors had been spoken of. In reference to that subject, he could venture to state, that the Court of Directors were extremely anxious for the intelligence and moral improvement of the natives of India; and would be well pleased to promote those objects in every way.

Sir Alexander Johnston proposed the thanks of the meeting should be given to Maulavi Mohammed Ismáel Khán, the King of Oude's astronomer, for the favour of his attendance that day: carried unanimously.

Sir Gore Ouseley communicated this to the Maulaví, who returned thanks in Hindustani, Sir Gore acting as interpreter. The Maulavi concluded his expression of thanks to the Society with a quotation from a Persian classic, signifying that, were every hair on his head a tongue, they would not suffice to speak his gratitude.

The thanks of the meeting were afterwards voted, respectively, to the Director, Vice-Presidents, Treasurer, Secretary, and Librarian of the Society. Eight new members of council were elected; all the officers were re-elected; and the meeting concluded. In the evening, a large party of the members and their friends dined together at the Thatched House Tavern.

SIR CHARLES WILKINS,

K.H. ; D.C.L. ; F.R.S. ; &c., &c.

Our last month's obituary announced the death of that eminent Oriental scholar, Sir Charles Wilkins; and we have collected a few particulars of his history and labours from authentic sources.

Mr. Wilkins was born in 1750, in the county of Somerset; and, in the year 1770, he proceeded to Bengal, as a writer in the East-India Company's civil service. On his arrival, he was placed in the Secretary's office, and two years after, he was sent up to Malda, to assist in superintending the Company's factories at that station.

At this early period of our sway in India, the internal administration of affairs in Bengal had not taken that consistent form which it has since assumed; and, consequently, the knowledge of the native languages, so essential to the due administration of justice to the natives, was, with a very few distinguished exceptions, generally neglected by our countrymen. Mr. Wilkins felt at once the necessity and value of the acquisition; and, im-pelled by predilections arising from the consciousness of a superior aptitude for the acquisition of languages, he commenced the study of Bengáli and Persian : these were soon mastered by his extraordinary diligence and capacity. Encouraged by the success of his first efforts, he aimed at a still higher object,—one which was then deemed beyond the reach of Europeans, requiring a life especially devoted from infancy to its study, and which had been preserved by its sacred guardians, not merely from foreigners, but from all but the privileged castes of their own race :—the sacred Sanskrit, with its antique structure and mysterious literature and science, became the object of his invincible perseverance. From the preface to Mr. Wilkins' Sanskrit grammar, as well as from the assertion contained in Mr. Hastings' letter, it might be supposed that the honour of being the first among Europeans who acquired a knowledge of the Sanskrit language, belongs to Mr. Halhed; but, though the example of this most accomplished scholar was the cause of Mr. Wilkins' turning his attention to the language, Mr. Halhed does not appear to have obtained more than a *glimpse* of this primæval tongue. Mr. Halhed's fame as an oriental scholar rests upon his translation of the code of Gentoo laws and his Bengáli grammar.

The prejudices of the brahmins had been removed and their confidence won, by the kindness and conciliatory manners of our countrymen, and particularly the governor-general, Warren Hastings, towards them, and the other natives with whom we were brought into intercourse by the success of our arms and the extension of our mercantile pursuits. The exertions of Mr. Wilkins were crowned with complete success; and the Indian public, in a few years, heard with surprise and admiration that he had not merely acquired the language, but had read some of its finest works, and was preparing translations of those which appeared to possess the highest interest. To understand the full value of this astonishing effort, it must be borne in mind that there were then no dictionaries and grammars prepared after the European manner; and that the first adventurer on this literary ocean might be considered a sort of Columbus, venturing to explore unknown regions. Even the celebrated baptist missionary, Dr. Wm. Carey, who commenced his studies nearly thirty years later, declared that, after all that had been done by Mr. Wilkins and Sir William Jones, he was two years learning merely the system of *sandhi*, or junction of the letters of the language, from his *pandits;* and another Orientalist, much more distinguished than even Dr. Carey, has made a nearly similar acknowledgment: a proof of the extraordinary difficulties which were surmounted by Mr. Wilkins.

The governor-general being anxious to see something like a faithful version from the Sanskrit (for the few translations made into Persian had conformed so servilely to Persian idioms and notions, that they gave anything but a faithful idea of the original), Mr. Wilkins sent him down to Calcutta his translation of the *Bhágavad Gítá*, or dialogue between the incarnate god Krishna and his favourite pupil Arjun, which is one of the many episodes of the *Mahábhárata*, the great national epic poem of the Hindus, which contains a hundred thousand couplets. The effect which this first production of Mr. Wilkins' labours had upon Warren Hastings, may be appreciated from the opinion which, at a recent period, though the glare of novelty was past, a most competent judge, the late Mr. Charles Butler, has expressed, who pronounced it to be "executed in that admirable style of severe simplicity, which a consummate taste can only reach." Warren Hastings was so captivated with this exquisite specimen of ancient Indian theology and metaphysics, as well as with the translation, that he sent the work home to the Court of Directors, and wrote, expressly, to request that they would cause it to be made known to Europe, through the press. This wish was fulfilled to the utmost extent by that body; it was printed in 1785, at their expense, and they distributed numerous copies, with their usual munificence; and the letter of Mr. Hastings, which is itself a triumphant proof of the elevation and refinement of his mind, and the benevolent feelings of his heart, was prefixed to the work, together with a short and appropriate advertisement from the Court of ·Directors. Indeed, of Mr. Hastings' letter it may be said, that, if no other memorial remained of his existence, posterity would pronounce from it, that he was both a wise and a good man.

The effect which this little work, of only 156 pages, including notes, produced upon the literary public in England and throughout Europe, was electrical. All hailed its appearance as the dawn of that brilliant light, which has subsequently shone with so much lustre in the productions of Sir William Jones, Mr. Colebrooke, Professor Wilson, &c., and which has dispelled the darkness in which the pedantry of Greek and Hebrew scholars had involved the etymology of the languages of Europe and Asia.

The science of etymology has now been placed, by a knowledge of Sanskrit, upon a basis which nothing can shake ; and the subsequent researches of Bopp, a man as excellent as he is erudite, has thrown such light on the comparison of languages, that this important branch of knowledge is as superior to what it was, as the labours of the chemist and the astronomer are to those of the almost forgotten absurdities of the alchymist and the astrologer.

Sir William Jones, on his arrival in Bengal, in the year 1783, where he had been appointed judge, felt his ardour rekindle for Oriental studies, which he had previously relinquished for many years, in order to devote himself exclusively to his profession (as he announced in his elegant grammar of the Persian language); and, besides founding the Asiatic Society of Calcutta, he was impelled, by the enthusiasm which Mr. Wilkins' success had excited, notwithstanding the laborious duties of his judicial station, to obtain some insight into the sacred literature of the brahmins. He, therefore, applied to him for assistance and advice, and both were liberally granted. Mr. Wilkins, soon after, shewed Sir William Jones his translation of the first four of the twelve books of the Institutes of Menu. Sir William was so delighted with the work, that he requested Mr. Wilkins not to proceed with it, but as its objects were so much connected with his own legal pursuits, that he would allow him to make an entire translation of such an extraordinary relic of ancient civilization and wisdom. This request was generously complied with; and the use of what he had himself prepared in the way of translation, as well as the honour of publishing that primæval legislator, was conceded to his distinguished friend. Sir William Jones' version is too well known to require any notice here.

It is proper to mention a fact that will shew the extraordinary resources and fertility of Mr. Wilkins' talents. His friend, the celebrated Nathaniel Brassey Halhed, of the Bengal Civil Service, had just completed his elegant grammar of the Bengáli language, but there were no Bengáli types with which to print it. In this juncture, Warren Hastings, who was anxious that the Company's servants should have every facility for the study of the native languages, himself solicited Mr. Wilkins to prepare a fount of Bengáli types, as he was aware that he had, by way of amusement, made some very successful experiments in that way. He did so; and the work was brought out in the year 1778, though Mr. Wilkins was "obliged to charge himself with all the various occupations of the metallurgist, the engraver, the founder, and the printer." The attempt to prepare a fount of Bengáli types in London had, previously, "egregiously failed:" we quote Mr. Halhed's words. There is, however, one point to which his friend Mr. Halhed has only faintly alluded, which deserves to be specially recorded, as a proof of Mr. Wilkins' great ingenuity. A *fac-simile* of a Bengáli letter was engraved by him, and added to the work, as a specimen of the cursive style of the writing employed in Bengal. The *Nágari* copies, too, which Mr. Wilkins added to his own beautiful Sanskrit grammar, at a subsequent period, are more correct and elegant than can be obtained in India from professed writing-masters. Mr. Wilkins was afterwards induced to prepare a Persian fount of types, which was continued to be used, up to a very late period, for printing the Company's Regulations, notwithstanding all the improvements that more enlarged experience might have been expected to introduce into this branch of the art.

The health of Mr. Wilkins being somewhat impaired by a residence of sixteen years in a tropical climate, he was obliged to return to his native country in 1786, after leading a life of singular exertion, as a most active Company's servant, as well as a scholar of unexampled perseverance. Here, of course, he became acquainted with all who were eminent in literature and science, by whom he was held in the highest estimation. Warren Hastings, who was his warm patron while he remained in India, continued ever after his attached friend; and the death of that great and injured man alone put a period to their friendship. Among the eminent individuals with whom he became intimate on his return to this country, may be mentioned Sir Joseph Banks, Major Rennel, the great geographer, the Hon. Mr. Cavendish, and Mr. Marsden. A firm and mutual regard bound them all together in the strongest ties of friendship. Four of these excellent men are now no more; Mr. Marsden—*antiquâ homo virtute ac fide*—alone remains to remember and deplore the friends whose presence once gladdened, and whose playful converse enlivened, the hours of literary ease and social conviviality. His acquaintance with Mr. Wilkins commenced in 1787, which was the year after the return of the latter to this country, and arose out of the congenial nature of their literary pursuits. Mr. Wilkins' offer to afford his valuable assistance to Mr. Marsden, in decyphering the inscriptions on his Cufic coins, was the occasion of this distinguished scholar becoming a very frequent visitor at his house, which of course gave him the opportunity of being very intimately acquainted with his family; and when Mr. Marsden retired from his situation as Secretary to the Admiralty, he became the son-in-law of his old and esteemed friend, by marrying his eldest daughter. There is still another distinguished name, which cannot be omitted even in this brief record. The late Mr. Samuel Davis, one of the ablest men that ever went to India (afterwards a member of the Court of Directors of the East-India Company), by whose science and wonderful penetration, the Hindu system of astronomy was laid open to Europe, was one of Mr. Wilkins' warmest and most attached friends.

Shortly after Mr. Wilkins' return, while residing at Bath, he published his translation of the *Hitopadésa*, or Fables of Pilpay, from the Sanskrit language. A cotemporary review of this performance designates it as " a curious work, that may be consulted as a useful common-place book of Oriental ethics, or a storehouse of their best apophthegms, illustrated with apposite fables."

In the year 1800, the East-India Company resolved to have a librarian for the invaluable collection of MSS. of which they had become possessed by the capture of Seringapatam, and from various other sources; and they accordingly, at the suggestion of one of their own members (the late most amiable Mr. Edward Parry, brother-in-law to Lord Bexley), appointed Mr. Wilkins to the office. This situation he retained to the day of his death.

The Company founded their college* at Haileybury in 1805; and they made him their visitor in the Oriental department. He continued, from the time of his appointment till the end of last year inclusive, without a single exception, to examine, twice a year, the whole of the students in the various Oriental languages taught at that establishment, as well as at their Military Seminary, Addiscombe: a singular proof of vigorous health, as well as perfect possession of faculties at such an advanced age. The wants of the college urged him to prepare and publish his excellent Sanskrit Grammar,† which is remarkable for its clearness and simplicity; and, from the same motive, he edited, in 1806, the first volume of a new edition of Richardson's Persian and Arabic Dictionary, which he enlarged with many thousand words. The second volume did not appear till 1810, as he had to recast the whole of its contents. His last work was the roots of the Sanskrit language, which he published in 1815. There are also several papers by him in the *Asiatic Researches* of Calcutta. That which contains an ancient inscription decyphered by him, though no *pandit* could read it, is ample evidence of his extraordinary perseverance and sagacity. There is also a translation by him from the Sanskrit of the episode of " *Dushmanta* and *Sakoontalá*," in Dalrymple's *Oriental Repertory;* and he likewise published a small portion of his MS. translation of the *Mahóbhárata* in the *Annals of Oriental Literature.* There are, no doubt, other small contributions of his to the periodical literature of the day; and his assistance was always willingly and liberally afforded to those who required the aid of his great resources. His last effort in the way of literature was a translation of a large antique seal, with a Sanskrit inscription, in an ancient and obscure form of *Nágari*, which he had decyphered many years ago, when it was brought home after the close of the last Mahratta war, in which it was taken among the booty of one of the Mahratta camps. This will, in all probability, appear in the Journal of the Royal Asiatic Society.

As a proof of the general estimation in which he was held, it should be mentioned that he was not only a Fellow of the Royal Society, but that the Institute of France, so careful and discriminating in its selections, made him a foreign associate. Oxford conferred on him the honorary degree of Doctor in Civil Law, the 26th June 1805, and he had diplomas from other bodies at home and abroad. Sir Charles was also a member of *the* club which was established by Dr. Johnson, &c., and immortalized by Goldsmith. In 1825, the Royal Society of Literature presented Mr. Wilkins with the royal medal, bearing the following inscription: " CAROLO WILKINS LITERATURÆ SANSCRITÆ PRINCIPI." His present Majesty, too, about three

---

* The College system began in 1805 at Hertford Castle, where the professors and students remained till Haileybury College was completed in Midsummer 1809. The foundation stone of the College was not laid till the 12th May 1806.

† Mr. Wilkins began to print a grammar of the Sanskrit language in the year 1796, while residing in Kent; but his house being totally consumed by fire, in which he appears to have had his printing-press, the few pages he had printed-off were destroyed; and, in all probability, if it had not been for the motive supplied to his exertions by the demands of the Company's College, we should never have had the benefit of his labours on this subject. In the preface to his grammar, he places this event one year too early.

years ago, when bestowing distinctions upon those who were most eminent in literature and science, at the suggestion of the Earl of Munster and the Right Hon. C. W. Williams-Wynn, President of the Royal Asiatic Society, conferred on him the honor of knighthood, accompanying that act of favour with the Guelphic order.

A cold, accompanied by influenza, brought his valuable and active life to a termination; otherwise, from the vigour of a constitution, that had never been injured by any of those excesses which generally lay the foundation of disease and premature decay, he might have survived for some years longer.

Sound common sense was the characteristic of Sir C. Wilkins' understanding; and he never gave way to those flights of fancy, which tend to mislead men from the sober results of the judgment,—a quality which he possessed in an eminent degree. He was playful and agreeable in those moments when he unbent from business; and his sallies were at once lively and happily expressed. His friends were always sure of a kind reception; and his hospitality was suited to his position in life, and the numerous claims of friendship. To the many applications, often of the most inconsiderate nature, to which his official station rendered him peculiarly liable, he shewed every attention that was consistent with the conscientious discharge of his duties.

It has seldom fallen to the lot of any individual to have enjoyed so many advantages. Uniform health, with the exception of the temporary derangement of the system which brought him from India, high reputation, easy circumstances, an affectionate family, and a large circle of attached friends, may be said to have made his life a round of rational and social enjoyment.

Sir Charles was twice married. By his first wife, he has left two daughters, and by Lady Wilkins, who died only a few months before him, he has also left a daughter. He had no son.

Eminently has this venerable scholar fulfilled the injunction of the Arabian poet, who has said, so happily and feelingly—

> " Be a tale worthy of remembrance;
> For truly the life of man is but a tale."

A large body of attached friends paid the last tribute of respect to his memory by attending his remains to the grave.

We may observe, that a very accurate and faithful likeness of Sir Charles Wilkins has recently been published.

ACCOUNT OF ISKARDOH.

THE following particulars are extracted from notes taken by Capt. C. M. Wade, political agent at Ludiána, relative to the territory and government of Iskárdoh (in Little Tibet), from information given by Charágh Ali, an agent deputed to him by Ahmed Shah, the *gelpo*, or ruler of that country, and which were read before the Asiatic Society of Bengal in November last:[*]

Iskárdoh is a mountainous country, divided into valleys of various extent. It is situated towards the point where the Belat Ták and Mus Ták mountains converge and separate the lofty ledges of Tibet, from the plains and valleys of Turkistan : among the natives it is generally known by the name of Beldestán.

The tradition is, that Alexander the Great came here on an expedition towards Khatá or Scythia (modern China), and that the Koteli Musták, or the Musták mountains, which lie between Yárqand and Khatá, being at that time impassable, on account of the depth and severity of the snow, the Macedonian halted on the present site of the capital, until a road could be cleared for his passage; when, leaving every part of his superfluous baggage, together with the sick, old, and infirm of his troops, behind, in a fort which he erected while there, he advanced against Khatá. These relics of the army founded a city, which they named Iskandariá or Alexandria, now pronounced Iskárdoh.

In length, the territory of Iskárdoh is estimated to be a journey of eleven days, and its average breadth about nine days' journey. On the east, it is bounded by Ladákh, which is a journey of eleven days from the capital ; and on the west, by Gilget, a journey of nine days. Yárqand bounds it on the north, at a distance of twelve days' journey, and Kashmír, on the south, a journey of nine days.

No correct estimate can be formed of the population of the country. It is said to amount to three lakhs of families, which in all probability greatly exceeds the actual number. The people are divided into several different tribes, but they are generally known by the name of Baldi. Among them there is a tribe called Kerah, the members of which are enjoined by their religious laws to follow four ordinances, *viz.* first, to destroy their female infants ; second, not to tell falsehoods; third, not to desert their party in the day of battle; fourth, not to slander any one. The natives are described to be of a phlegmatic disposition, like other Tibetan tribes.[†] They are a stout, well-made race of people, with ruddy complexions and good features; but have little hair on their body, and scarcely any beard. It is said, they are deficient in enterprise, and of a treacherous and designing disposition. Barley, wheat, and flesh, are the chief articles of food ; rice is not generally used. All those who can afford it are in the habit of drinking tea at their breakfast, and in the course of the day it is usual with them, as with their neighbours of Ladákh, to greet their visitors with a cup of tea. The use of this luxury is becoming more general than it was, though it bears a high price. There is little variation in the dress of the people from their neighbours of Ladákh. The wealthy classes generally wear qábas (a kind of coat, with skirted margin all round), and caps, &c.; while the dress of the peasantry consists of jamahs (another kind of coat, formerly much used in India); it resembles the vest worn by the Indian dancing-girls, and is made of pattú, which is manufactured both of a coarse and fine

* Journ. As. Soc. of Bengal, for November.

' † Asiatic physiologists maintain the opinion, that the temperament of man is affected by the nature. of the animal or vegetable production on which he feeds; and the phlegmatic character of the inhabitants of little Tibet is accordingly ascribed to barley, millet, and fruits, being their chief articles of food.

quality, from goat's wool. They wear caps of the same stuff. Cotton is not produced here. It is imported from Yárqand to Kashmír, but very few people shew a desire to wear cotton clothes. Their houses are mostly made of layers of stones and wood, with flat roofs, and are two or three stories high, with far projecting roofs, somewhat similar to those on the southern face of the Himálaya range.

The common religion of the people is Muhammedan, of the Shia sect, and the followers of the Imám Jáfar; but towards Gilget, there is a race of people which does not seem to possess any well-defined religious system: some of them are idolators, and worship trees; while others, like the Hindus, do not eat the flesh of kine, and yet profess to be Muhammedans. Tibetan is the common language of the country, but the people have no books in it. They are beyond the influence of the Lámas, and receive their education, which is exclusively confined to the chiefs and priesthood, in Persian. They have no system of coinage in the shape of rupees, pice, or kourís. The only means of exchange known among them is in small pieces of unwrought gold, which is found in the country both in mines and in the beds of rivers.

The government of Iskárdoh is absolute, but the ruler, Ahmad Sháh, who claims his descent from Joseph, the prophet of the Israelites, is mild and benevolent; his title is *Ergh mayúm*, signifying ' the Lord of the mountains;' but among his people he is called *Gelpo*, or 'king,' and his tributaries and petty chiefs, *Ju*. He usually resides in the fort of Iskárdoh. It is asserted, that the dynasty of the present ruler has been in uninterrupted possession of the country for the last fourteen generations. He does not owe allegiance to any foreign state, being subject to none in tribute or service; but the Sikhs have attempted to extend their conquests beyond Kashmír in that direction, which has tended to excite his alarm and jealousy. There is no standing army; the troops of Ahmad Sháh consist of his vassals. They are landed proprietors, who receive no regular pay, but are exempted from taxation in requital of military service. Whenever an exigency occurs to render the collection of a force necessary, the ruler calls out the peasantry of the country, and forms them into a sort of militia. He provides them with arms and ammunition, so long as they may be kept embodied; and when the occasion for their services is over, they are disarmed and dismissed. The revenue of the state is collected in kind in the following form:—one kharwár of wheat, one of barley, and one of mustard or millet, are levied from each landholder. Some of the zemindars pay their rents in one kharwár of ghí each, instead of the other three articles. A kharwár is about forty seers in weight.

About a year and a-half ago, a report was received of the Russians having taken Kapchaq, and arrived at Ilah, which is a great entrepôt of commerce. Between Ilah and the Russian frontier post is an extensive lake, on the border of which the Russians are stated to have established a fort, and to have built a town in its vicinity. Not wishing to be involved in hostilities with the Russians, the Chinese are said to have paid them a large sum of money to purchase peace. The chief of Ladákh has informed the Emperor of China, that the English are constructing a road to Kaughri, which is situated near Ispitti. On the receipt of which intelligence, the emperor sent a Zandu, or personal inquiry, to Arzeng, to watch the state of affairs in that quarter; and ordered, at the same time, his garrison of Rodokh, which is twelve stages from Ladákh, to be reinforced by a large force.

" CINNAMON AND PEARLS."

THE descriptions given in the Arabian Night's Entertainments, of the island of Serendib, the name allotted in that delightful work to our splendid possession in the bay of Bengal, Ceylon, have created a very strong interest in the minds of all who have surrendered themselves to the pleasure of the perusal, towards a place associated with every thing that is gorgeous in wealth, and splendid in scenery. The arena of the most striking adventures of Sinbad the sailor, even when divested of the romance of the Arab legends, possesses so many claims to admiration, that it is scarcely possible for any poetically feeling person to regard it otherwise than as a scene of enchantment. The idea of its cinnamon-gardens, and fishery for pearls, is highly exciting to a vivid imagination, and though, upon a closer examination, the charms, with which these have been invested by florid writers, may fade away, other productions less celebrated arrest the attention and captivate the senses, while the general aspect of the place is such as to realize our notions of eastern, fairy, or rather peri-land.

During a very long period after the settlement of a European colony in Ceylon, very little information could be obtained respecting the state of the interior, and scarcely any thing could be done for the improvement of the natives, in consequence of the hostility of the government of Candy: but the rapid progress which has been made, in the last few years, give the strongest hope that in a comparatively short time the obstacles which still impede the exertions of those who constitute the directing power, will be overcome. The whole island is now under British control, and, though the Government have still to struggle with difficulties, arising from native indolence and ignorance on the one hand, and want of capital on the other, it has already effected so much with slender means, that there can be no doubt of the ultimate result under more prosperous circumstances. While, however, so much has been achieved, so much still in progress, and there is such strong hope of the success of an enlightened and liberal policy, the authorities at Ceylon have to endure the mortification of being misrepresented in England in works which the talent employed in their construction has rendered deservedly popular. It is half amusing, and half annoying, both provoking and ludicrous, to peruse in the place where the scene is laid, the narratives and descriptions of persons who gather all the information they possess from the writings of others, and take what happens to suit their purpose, without inquiry whether it be true or false, or whether the whole of the circumstances have not changed since the period of publication. The mistakes of a writer of considerable celebrity, who talked of sailing down the Ganges in a *bungalow*, and who described the scenery of Bengal in terms more appropriate to the Himalaya, were only reprehensible upon the score of taste, since no injurious impression concerning the acts of government was intended to be made upon the public mind. The information extant at that period, 1809 or 1810, was also exceedingly scanty, and difficult of access; but there is no such excuse for the errors into which Miss Martineau has fallen in her tale entitled " Cinnamon and Pearls." Having been favoured with a perusal of a series of letters originally published in the *Ceylon Gazette*, containing a refutation of the numerous misrepresentations contained in a story which has been extensively perused, and much admired in England, it appears to be only an act of justice to the maligned parties to put the reader in possession of the real state of the case. The publication of these letters upon the spot, adds considerably to their authority, since no one in their senses would attempt to expose the fallacies of a writer of eminence by statements at variance with facts known to the whole of the community, to whom the vindication is addressed. In the opening part of the work, in which the reviewer shews that Miss Martineau is almost wholly unacquainted with the subject upon which she has employed her pen; he observes: "It is very well to smile at such absurdities, but, unfortunately, for *one* person who will ever read their contradiction, nine hundred and ninety-nine will *read* and *believe* Miss Martineau, and many may act upon that belief." It seems, therefore, to have been a fortunate accident which has opened a wider circulation, through the medium of the *Asiatic Journal*, to a document calculated to interest those who have regarded our Eastern colonies with a friendly feeling.

Miss Martineau dwells, it is well known, at great length upon the miserable condition of the Cingalese peasantry, a condition which she entirely imputes to the government monopolies of Cinnamon and Pearls. Not having space for the whole of the remarks made by our author upon the extraordinary representations which it has pleased the fair political economist to promulgate in support of her proposition, we must be content with a few extracts, and, passing over at present the first letter, commence with No. II. The writer observes: "The story of 'Cinnamon and Pearls' opens with a description of a night adventure of a Ceylonese peasant, Rayo, and his betrothed Marana. They are described as being too poor to marry, 'not having money enough to build a house, and provide new clothing.' This is plausible enough, but I should strongly suspect that no single case could be cited in this island, by its oldest inhabitant, where a couple were prevented from marrying by the want of such a house and such clothing as are usually possessed by persons in the situation of life in which these parties are supposed to be. As a remedy of this evil of poverty, a little innocent poaching suggests itself, and they secretly repair to the chank beds, 'which the Ceylon government guard,' under a cruel system of monopoly. This expedition is undertaken upon a raft of the simplest construction. Rayo, who is qualifying himself as a pearl-diver, reaches the chank bed in safety, and raises from their resting-place some of these prohibited shells. 'The raft,' says Miss Martineau, 'might have appeared to the government guard-boat, even to close observation, to be no more than a piece of drifting wood, but for the gleams sent forth from the PRECIOUS STONES with which Marana's silver hair-pins were set.' I will venture to appeal to all Ceylon readers, whether anything can be more completely out of keeping than to describe a Ceylonese woman, who wears silver hair-pins ornamented with precious stones, as desirous of obtaining chanks as a *personal* ornament, which she could at any time purchase for a comparative trifle. In fact, such an ornament as Marana's hair-pin is described to have been, would have purchased half a-dozen houses, and the most ample assortment of bridal attire, male and female. The episode of the chank beds is only the prelude to the more important subject of the pearl-fishery. Miss Martineau advances the opinion, that ' if the Government would *give away* its pearl banks to those who now fish those banks for the scantiest wages which will support life, government would soon gain more in a year from the pearls of Ceylon, than it has hitherto gained by any five fisheries.' What a pity it is that clever young ladies will write upon subjects with which they are *utterly unacquainted*."

Our author then goes on to shew that there are three propositions contained in the quoted paragraph, which only require examination to be confuted. He denies that the pearl-divers, and those persons engaged in the fishery, are compelled to the employment for the scantiest wages, proving the contrary by the statement of the rate of remuneration, and the circumstance of the numerous volunteers from the continent of India, who, attracted by the gains to be obtained, flock to the scene of action, in order to secure a participation in them. He then proceeds to refute the assertion that the prosperity of the island would be secured by the fishery being surrendered to the hands of the peasants, and concludes by the following interesting account of the gem which is the object of it:—" The pearl oyster of Ceylon is considered to arrive at perfection in its seventh year; if taken *before* that period, it is only imperfectly developed; if taken *after* that period, it is found to have decayed: the oyster dies—the shell opens—the fleshy part, in which the pearl is embedded, wastes away, and the pearls disappear, either having been washed into the sand, or perished by decay. The art of fishing for Ceylon pearls consists, therefore, in keeping up the most rigid inspection of the pearl banks, so that each bank may be fished *precisely* at the period of its perfection, each bank being available for about twenty days in seven years. If, under an adherence to this necessary condition, the banks were sufficiently numerous and productive to supply a large fishery every year, we should have large annual fisheries; but, as that is not the case, in some years the fishery is small, in others there is no fishery at all, not omitted from a spirit of monopoly, but from the plainest principles of common sense, there being no pearl oysters to fish which had arrived at perfection. It is also to be remembered that it is only in the calm, which commences generally about the 5th of March, and which lasts from thirty to thirty-five days at the utmost, when the sea is clear and free from currents, that the operation of fishing can be *successfully* carried on in the *deep waters*, where the banks of Ceylon pearls are found. But, in fact, there is no *monopoly* of the pearl-fishery, in the ordinary sense of the word 'monopoly.' The pearls are sold by the Ceylon government to the BEST BIDDERS, and their price is measured by the price of pearls in other markets of the world, which are derived from *other* sources of production, Ceylon having no natural monopoly of them." Here follows a quotation from Miss Martineau's tale, which it is not necessary to insert, since her illustrations of the theories of her school, regarding political economy, are so widely circulated, that the great majority of the readers of the *Asiatic Journal* will be able to refer to the work. She argues upon the erroneous supposition that the store of pearls is boundless, which it is not, being circumscribed by the natural causes enumerated above. She next imagines that freedom of fishing would, with its influx of wealth, produce an immediate, or at least rapid, change in the character and habits of the Cingalese, and that they would of their own accord commence those public works, which are so essential to the continued prosperity of the island. This assumption betrays a lamentable ignorance of the Asiatic character. Commenting upon this part of the subject, our author observes: " If the Ceylon peasantry were permitted to fish when they chose, and how they chose, the pearl banks, would the colony necessarily become more rich and prosperous under this hypothetical system, than under the actual one? In discussing this query, let me first inquire, for *whose benefit* is the sum employed which is now raised under the present system? Unless the government be both weak and wicked, it is employed *for the benefit of the inhabitants of Ceylon.* The true question therefore, is, would Ceylon be more improved, enriched, and advanced, by those sums which the natives would themselves receive for pearls, were their fishery as open as the fishery of turbot in the channel, or by the sums received under what is called, and miscalled, the ' monopoly system,' and applied by government for the improvement of the island? Ceylon never can be as flourishing a country as she ought to be, as long as there are no *debouches* for her productions; in other words, until she has roads which will admit of the transport of commodities from the interior; and, above all, as long as the absence of the means of irrigation devotes so large a portion of her area to unnecessary sterility."

Now, we may humbly ask, are the natives sufficiently acquainted with the nature of their true interests to volunteer these works, or have we not too much reason to suppose that, satisfied with the means of procuring food and freedom from toil, they would sit down contented at the very threshold of the undertaking, not deeming it necessary to advance a step farther in pursuit of advantages, of which they have never formed a distinct notion? Sound lessons in political economy have been imparted to the Ceylonese, long before Miss Martineau thought of writing her romance of "Cinnamon and Pearls," as the following extracts from a journal kept in 1786,* will sufficiently testify: " I asked the wannia how it could possibly happen that, in a province where there were so many rivers, there could ever be a want of water, and why it was impracticable to construct a dam to remedy that deficiency? I saw I was not understood, and therefore ordered a hollow tree to be brought, and practically shewed them how easily my project might be accomplished. They then persisted in saying that the scheme might have answered well at a time in which Kotzair was well populated, but that works of that magnitude could not be executed now that the population had so sensibly diminished by the abandonment of the inhabitants, and the prevalence of dysentery and small-pox; that persons now only cultivated as much as was required for their own annual consumption. I explained to the wannia and many of the people that were present, that this was the very means by which the increase of population was prevented; that if, for example, every landholder cultivated more than was necessary for his own support, he might then send the excess of his crop to Trincomalee, and receive the value of it in exchange, which was now done by the coast people (coast of Madras) and other strangers, who thus impoverished the country by carrying money away from it, which never came back, as we had no produce to offer them in return." In another place, our author inculcated the same doctrine, in the following manner: " I then repeated my exhortations respecting the improvements of agriculture, and in answer to the remark of the Moor men, that, being merchants or fishermen, they cultivated no paddy lands; I told them that their condition as merchants was in itself valuable to society, but must end in the ruin of the inhabitants, and finally in their own, if the province they inhabited produced no commodity to export in exchange for that which was imported, and that, if they hoped eventually to become possessed of property, the value of their exports must exceed that of their imports; that, in order to obtain this object, if really their occupations prevented their applying themselves to agriculture, they should clear the high lands, and plant coco-nut, areca, teak, and bread-fruit trees, &c.; that, if each of them would at once plant fifty coco-nut trees, and add ten more annually, the first fifty would in five years yield produce, and that this would soon become a profitable concern, as all the inhabitants would

* The author of the journal quoted above was Jacques Fabrice Van Sanden, governor of Trincoma-lee, in the year 1786. His work has been translated from the Dutch MS. records, and gives evidence of a tolerant spirit and a benevolent desire to improve the condition of the natives, for which his nation have not been celebrated in their colonial policy. The translation was published in Colombo in 1834, and forms a very interesting document, to which we hope to return in some future page of the *Asiatic Journal*.

in ten years become possessed of fruit-bearing trees, for oil, rope, and home-consumption; that it was true the other trees would require more time before they yielded profit, but that the expense of planting was so trifling in comparison with the advantage to be derived from them, that it was worthy the experiment. I added that I myself had shortly before planted coco-nut trees which had already shot up, and that it was only necessary to pay them a little attention to obtain, as I had done, considerable profit."

Observing at another place quantities of potter's earth, he recommended to the persons engaged in brick and tile-making, for the use of government, the employment of buffaloes, instead of lazy Malabars, in treading it down; but it is difficult to find a stimulating power, where the climate does not compel the people to labour for comforts, and where the actual necessaries of life are easy of attainment. Those persons who possess a few, or even one coco-nut tree, will sit down quietly beneath its shade, eating its fruit and drinking its juice, and employing the oil, leaves, and fibres, solely as the means of their own daily support, not cultivating more than is necessary for themselves, and indifferent to other productions of the earth, while it continues to yield sufficient for the maintenance of life. Too many instances of this nature occur before the eyes of those who have opportunities of studying the native character, for any doubt to remain upon the subject: improvement must, in the first instance, be the act of the government, and the process is too expensive to be carried on without a commensurate revenue. Our author, disappointed by the non-productiveness of some plantations of coco-nut and areca trees, was told that, although they grew luxuriantly, they yielded no fruit: a circumstance which was attributed to the quality of the ground. "The people," he continues, "shewed me several in this state, to prove the truth of their words. I at once explained to them the reason of this. I assured them that the ground was fully as good here as elsewhere, perhaps even better; but that wild trees, which they themselves owned were hardly good as fuel, drew the best saps from the earth, and deprived the fruit-trees of its nutritious aid; that the coco-nut trees were full grown, because in that respect they needed no more nourishment than jungle trees; but in order to bear fruit they required the sap which was now diffused among trees of no value. I besought them to clear away the useless bushes, which encumbered the fruit-trees, and to reduce them to ashes, which would serve as manure, and they would soon perceive that, even if they planted no other trees, those which were already on the ground would flourish luxuriantly."

When there is not an equal degree of ignorance and laziness to contend against, other obstacles arise, owing to the extreme dislike which Asiatics entertain to adopt any thing new. When our traveller offered to the inhabitants of a village from whom he augured good, in consequence of the appearance of the paddy fields, six young coco-nut trees, and stated the advantage that would be derived from their cultivation, they hesitated about accepting the gift, saying, "Why should we do all this, our grandfathers and fathers never did so?" The same reply met him when inquiring why the children were not taught to read. The parents had not learned, and the children might equally do without it. In some places, our author found fruit-trees, which had been planted in former years, neglected and rotting. Such a state of things forced upon him the conviction, "that nothing excepting a long time, excess of patience and perseverance in principles well laid down, could effect the changes necessary for the advancement of civilization."

The efforts of the government were retarded from the causes already stated;

but although it has done much towards creating a spirit of industry, and a desire to benefit by an exchange of product, no one, we believe, who has had late opportunities of studying the habits and modes of thinking of the great mass of the people of Ceylon, would be of opinion that free fishing for pearls would effect the desired end. We fear that the pearls would be exhausted long before the people had acquired sufficient knowledge to make the best use of their riches. We have no desire to enter into the defence of monopolies, or to combat the opinions of the advocates of free-trade. Restrictions may be very injurious to people who either have learned, or may be easily taught to learn, that their own particular and individual interests, are bound up with those of the public at large; but when the multitude not only object to benefit their immediate descendants, but are indifferent to their personal comforts, they can scarcely be left at liberty to act according to their own devices, with any hope of a good result. It would have been more fair towards the colony of Ceylon, and certainly more advantageous to herself and to the public, if Miss Martineau had, in inculcating the principles illustrated in her story of "Cinnamon and Pearls," laid her scene in some region of Utopia, when she could have had every thing her own way, without outraging truth. The practice of political economy appears in the abstract not to be more difficult than a game of chess to an experienced player, in which every move can be calculated upon, and the results considered; but unless we have the proper number of pawns and checks upon the board, our science will only avail to divine some expedient by which their absence may be remedied, and at any rate we must begin at the beginning. This, however, Miss Martineau and many of her predecessors disdain to do; they are too apt to take a great many things for granted which have no existence; to believe that they have all the castles, knights, bishops, and pawns, at command, and to advocate means totally inadequate to the end. As an historical account of Ceylon, Miss Martineau's narrative is worse than worthless. She talks of the cruelty of sending out labourers " half naked" to their toil, while the real hardship, with the thermometer above eighty degrees, would be to force them to encumber themselves with clothing. She is in perfect ignorance of the fact of the encouragement given to the cultivation of European vegetables, which are to be found in every bazaar in abundance, and excellent in quality, a most agreeable addition to the peas, onions, cabbages, and potatoes, being the holcol, which has been brought from the Cape, and which thrives admirably. It is to be hoped that, in a new edition of "Cinnamon and Pearls," the following passage will be altered to suit the real state of the case: " If any one in Ceylon has a fancy for potatoes and onions, he must get them from Bombay. If his ambition extends to peas and cabbages, he must wait till they are brought from England !"

Miss Martineau is exceedingly expert in making a giant, but her method of slaying him when made is the finest in the world. She in the first place assumes that the peasants of Ceylon are prohibited from selling ghee to the Arabs,—of which people, by the way, not more than twenty customers are to be found in the island,—and then goes on to say that, were a free commerce permitted, as herds of buffaloes were seen feeding amidst the rank vegetation of the hills, " many a peasant would have gone among them morning and evening, with his bottle of hide over his shoulder." It may be very easy for a person to talk of milking wild buffaloes, while quietly seated in an English drawing-room, or looking on at the dairy-maid's task with the kine at home; but it is quite another thing to encounter the horns and hoofs of animals unaccustomed to the process, and there needs no government edict to prevent the experiment, which could be only made at the risk of life and limb. It is scarcely necessary to say, however, that the protection does not exist, and that, to employ the Ceylonese commentator's words, "Arabs, camels, and all, if they were in the island," and willing and able to purchase it, might solace themselves with ghee, to the exportation of which there is no more impediment than can be experienced in England in exporting broad-cloth. "It may be very well," continues our author, "in avowed works of fiction, such as Robinson Crusoe, Philip Quarles, or Peter Wilkins, to describe a race or caste of people, according to the fancy of the author; but strict adherence to accurate statement is an imperative duty, when the parties treated of have a real existence."

Miss Martineau describes the languid manner in which the cinnamon-peelers perform their task, and descants at length upon their inadequate remuneration, and the dreadful state of destitution consequent upon the low rate of their wages; as a set-off, we subjoin at length the following refutation:—"A cinnamon-peeler may be estimated to deliver in averagely about five pounds weight of cinnamon per day; for the first and second sorts, he receives the same rate of remuneration, being, according to the free-labour prices of 1832-3, four-pence a pound in the preserved gardens, and five-pence three-farthings if the cinnamon is collected in private property, abandoned gardens, or the jungle, and they receive three half-pence for the third sort. This discrepancy of rate arises, as is known to all practical persons, from the greater facility of peeling a branch of larger diameter, on account of the more easy separation of the bark. In one of my former letters, I have mentioned that six-pence per day is the general and ample rate of labourers' pay. From the above statement it is apparent that a cinnamon-peeler's average rate of hire is *at least* one shilling and three-pence per day, being 150 per cent. above the ordinary rate of wages. To state, therefore, that labourers so *amply paid* are so wretched as to be exposed to the dreadful disease of Elephantiasis, in consequence of the inevitable poverty of their diet, is to deal in romance and not in reason. Upon the same principle of calculation, a pearl-diver, who receives three pounds sixteen-shillings in the course of eight days, does in fact receive 152 days' wages at six-pence per day; or, taking the estimate on another principle, he receives on fishing-days twenty-two times the daily wages received by the common labourers, which affords him an ample fund for the contingencies incidental to his quitting his country and returning to it. To proceed with the narrative. The captain of the peelers complains that, although the bark might be preserved from spoliation, it was very difficult to prevent persons from "entering to pluck *the fruit* which was so precious to the people." This is the first time that I ever heard this fruit considered as precious, and cannot imagine from whence Miss Martineau derived her information. Alice (a young lady who figures in the work under review), who must have had a miraculous acuteness of smell, is charmed with the "rich scent" arising from the rolls of the bark.[*] "Though the hands of the workmen moved languidly, like the hands of other workmen who do not labour for themselves, though the process of peeling was clumsy, and the waste of material excessive, yet such quantities of bark fell from innumerable boughs and twigs that Alice could not imagine what was

---

[*] The spicy gales of Ceylon have been much lauded by writers, and are supposed to proceed from the Cinnamon gardens, it even being said that the perfume is wafted out to sea many miles from the island. The cinnamon-tree itself does not emit any odour to the breeze, it being necessary to pull off a leaf or a twig before the senses can be regaled by the scent. There is, however, a very fragrant flower to be found growing in the cinnamon-garden, which has the property of exhaling its perfume; but it does not belong to the tree, although casual observers may attribute the odour proceeding from it to the far-famed spice, which is so grateful when broken in the hand.

to be done with it all." Now here there are as many mistakes of fact, as lines. The hands of the peelers, stimulated as they are by adequate wages, are not languid, for the *free* labourer peeled in 1832, at the *very same rate* which the *compelled* labourer peeled for in 1828, 1829, 1830 and 1831. Instead of " the process of peeling being clumsy," it is remarkably dexterous, and might be said scarcely to admit of improvement ; and as for not labouring for themselves, they were as much employed for their own benefit as the journeyman tailor is, when he is stitching the suit which is to be worn by the customer of his master. Miss Martineau describes the packing of Cinnamon in the Government-gardens, and talks of " kneeling groupes with each a *chest* in the centre, a heap of black pepper lying beside it, to strew between the layers of cinnamon, and pots of resin wherewith to stop the seams and crevices of the chests." Is it possible for narrative to be more inaccurate? Cinnamon never is packed in the gardens, but is carried in bundles to the sorting store, and there sorted, and ultimately *embaled* for exportation. " In the eye of philosophy, there may be but little difference between one mode of preparation and another, but as a statistical datum, in a work of political economy, it is objectionable in the extreme "

Miss Martineau accuses the Government, in more than one place in her work, of burning the cinnamon which a favourable season has produced in too great abundance; an assertion which is utterly untrue, the surplus being warehoused to provide a supply upon any future emergence; the effect upon the market between cinnamon thus withheld and cinnamon burned, may be the same ; but in the endeavour to increase the odium of the monopoly, the consequences arising from the lessened value of testimony not in strict accordance to fact, are disregarded. Miss Martineau has evidently borrowed many of her notions regarding Ceylon from Mr. McCulloch, who, for reasons best known to himself, has, in his Dictionary of Commerce, chosen to make statements respecting the Cinnamon and Pearl monopolies of Ceylon at complete variance with the facts of the case. We cannot in our limited space enter into the statistical details which the Columbo journals afford, and which prove incontrovertibly that the head of the school, to which Miss Martineau belongs, has been misled himself by wrong information, or that he has deemed it expedient to support his theory by a perversion of the truth. Nothing save the most entire ignorance upon the subject, in the absence of any unworthy motive could occasion the supposition that " native energies " are weighed down by vexatious restraints ; the real wants of Ceylon are concentrated capital to be applied to elementary public improvements, such as roads, bridges, the opening of canals, the widening of rivers, and which will stimulate the labours of the inhabitants, and afford the means of transport to the commodities produced. It is from the extraordinary advantages of the soil and climate, which are both so favourable to the growth of the richest productions of the earth, rather than to the "industrious energies " of the inhabitants, that we may expect to derive all the benefit arising from prosperous commerce ; and nothing seems to be more desirable than the exposition of the actual state of affairs in the colony, since the errors and misstatements which have been printed and reprinted, until they have almost come to be undisputed authority, have done, and still must continue to do, much towards the prevention of the investments of large sums in a commerce which capitalists now regard with natural distrust.

Miss Martineau tells us, and with truth, that Ceylon possesses the most valuable woods: the " jack-wood, rivalling the finest mahogany, ebony, satin-wood, calamander, growing like thorns in the thicket, yet *the natural proprie-tors of this wealth*, to which the world looked with longing eyes, were half-fed and not clothed, while their English fellow-subjects, located in a far less favour-able habitation, were taxed to afford them such meagre support as they had." Our critic, in noticing this passage, inquires whether Miss Martineau ever asked herself what was the reason that the " world," with its "longing eyes," did not get possession of these valuable woods. " Does she," he continues, " suppose that there is no difference between a tree standing in the midst of an unpenetrated jungle, and a squared log, lying on the beach of a harbour for transport ? From the total absence of roads, as well as of water-carriage, in many parts of the island, the expense of bringing down these woods from the primæval forest, where they are doomed to flourish and to fade, would be so enormous as to yield no profit for the trouble of conveying them. In many places, they could only be conveyed on bullocks or on men's shoulders, and, as an available ingredient of wealth, they are about as useless as the gold in Robinson Crusoe's island. If Miss Martineau is under the *delusion* of sup-posing that the natives themselves can, and will voluntarily, make these roads, canals, &c., and that there is either knowledge, combination, or capital among them to effect such a purpose, she is egregiously mistaken. Nothing can effect such improvements but *revenue*, in other words, concentrated capital judicious-ly applied. Miss Martineau would not permit the cinnamon and pearls of Ceylon to be sold by the government for the benefit of the natives, and trans-muted into roads, and canals, and railroads ; so that produce, which is now hermetically sealed by natural impediments, might find a vent, and gladden the world with its longing eyes. She insists that, if the natives were allowed to sell their own cinnamon, and their own pearls, all these improvements would rapidly succeed. In the true solution of these antagonist propositions are involved the deepest interests of colonial policy." That the natives would make the best use of the advantages afforded to them by the abandonment of the system of monopoly, may be justly doubted ; but of the anxiety on the part of the government to effect every desirable object, there is ample proof. Having had an opportunity of consulting the journal of Mr. Brookes, master-attendant of Trincomalee, during the period employed by him in exploring and surveying the Mahavillagana in 1833, we are enabled to present the readers of the *Asiatic Journal* with an extract, which will shew that the authorities at Ceylon are not inattentive to the true interests of the people, or unwilling to engage in objects of public utility : " The only export from Trincomalie is timber, chiefly consisting of halmaniel ebony, and satin-wood, well known for their valuable qualities. They at present form a small return for the great quantity of grain and cloth imported. Satin and ebony grow in all the jungle about Trincomalie, especially upon the sea-coast. Halmaniel is chiefly procured in the interior, on the banks of the Ma-havillaganga, cut during the dry season, but remains in the forest for many months before it is rafted down. Should the wood-cutters, who are generally inhabitants of Trincomalie, have returned to their homes, and neglected to take advantage of the full rise, they lose the opportunity of getting the rafts down. Circumstances of this nature often occur ; when the timber must remain another year, to the loss and detriment of the timber-merchant. In the mean time, it becomes deteriorated from rot, and is liable to be stolen or washed away by a sudden overflow of the banks. An instance of this oc-curred in January last, when 375 logs of timber were lost in the Virgel. I am also aware that timber has been detained in the jungle by neglect till it became so decayed as to fetch only one-sixth of its original value. If, therefore, the river were opened, timber would be no sooner cut than floated down, and the merchant be enabled to exercise an efficient superintendance over his property. At present, being obliged to advance wages to the wood-cutters, he is completely at their mercy, and instances are not unfrequent of timber which has been felled for one person being sold to another.

" As another proof of the necessity of removing these impediments (setting aside advantages that must eventually accrue to government), I would remark that timber in the forests is cut into logs about eighteen-feet long, and twelve inches square, although the trees are capable of furnishing logs of a much larger size. Timber thus reduced in size must also be so in value. It is particularly worthy of notice, that the timber now brought down the Mahavillaganga, is of a kind that will float, whilst ebony, satin, callamander, and ironwood, abundance of which are to be found growing on the banks and in the Tambankadewa and Vedah country, being too heavy to float, are altogether neglected. If the river were opened, boats, canoes, and rafts, would be able to convey these woods to a market, and I have not the slightest doubt, that the advantages to be derived from such an undertaking would soon repay the expenses." Whether the precise suggestions proposed by Mr. Brooke were adopted, we have no immediate means of ascertaining. We only know that the government is actively employed in opening such channels of communication, whether by land or by water, as appears to it to be most advantageous to the interests of the community. That encouragement, rather than prohibition in the cultivation of the natural products of the land, is afforded, notwithstanding the monstrous monopoly of cinnamon, can be proved beyond all doubt, and, in support of this assertion, we appeal to a document which no one can dispute. Miss Martineau attributes the diseases, consequent on the poor way of living of the peasantry of Ceylon, to the want of seasoning to their food; adding, that monkeys may gather pepper and cardamums, but the people must go without. " If," she continues, " they were allowed to grow as much pepper as they pleased, and sell it to any part of the world where it is wished for, they would have a great deal of money wherewith to buy things which the government could sell much more profitably than pepper." A certain portion of pepper was required for the packing of cinnamon, which was until lately procured from the Malabar coast. The absence of this spice in the markets of the island, where it was known that the finest quality could be produced, induced the government to publish the following notice, with a view of encouraging its cultivation :—

" Government Advertisement. Pepper. His Excellency the Governor, being desirous to afford every encouragement to the cultivators of this article of colonial produce, has authorized the export and import warehouse-keepers in Colombo, and the collector of Galle, to receive on account of Government, until further orders, such quantities of pepper as may be tendered of a sufficiently good quality, being *bonâ-fide* the produce of this island, and immediate payment to be made to the party or parties delivering the same, at the rate of nine shillings per parra, and in proportion for a less quantity. Notice of this circumstance is therefore given to the inhabitants cultivating pepper, in order that they may avail themselves of the opportunity of disposing of their produce accordingly. By his Excellency's command. Signed. John Rodney, Chief Sec. to Govt. Colombo, 17th Nov. 1827."

In the first year, the number of parras offered for sale was forty-six, and this in five years afterwards, 1831, amounted to 6,955. It having now become evident that the cultivation was rapidly increasing, the quantity tendered having exceeded the wants of the government, it was considered expedient to lower the price offered, which, although below that at which contracts had been previously procured, was productive of a loss of almost twenty-four per cent. on the sale in England, and was, therefore, in the nature of a bounty; great caution was, however, necessary in effecting this object, as a sudden diminution would have been productive of much disappointment to the grower, and would, in consequence, have checked the rapidly increasing cultivation. A notice was, therefore, published in 1831, stating that the price would be reduced to eight shillings per parra from the 1st of Jan. 1832, and it is intended that this reduction should gradually continue, until the trade may be left to itself.

Instead, therefore, of annihilating the trade of Ceylon, the government is thus progressively opening a new source of wealth, which, but for its interference, might have remained closed for ever. It need scarcely be mentioned, that all the restrictions respecting the private cultivation of cinnamon have ceased, although it is still subject to an export duty of three shillings per pound. This latter fact, however, Miss Martineau does not seem to be acquainted with, for, in dilating on the advantages of the new system, she says that a cultivator may take his cinnamon on board any ship of any nation, and sell it for what he can get. There can be nothing more gratifying to a benevolent mind than to see the advantages attendant upon commerce extending themselves to the poorest classes of the people; but, while rejoicing in the prospect before us, we question whether the new system could have been introduced with the same expectation of a successful result, at an earlier period, and our sense of justice is offended by aspersions, which even the old Dutch government did not merit. Miss Martineau chooses to suppose that the natives were prevented from digging for the precious stones which Ceylon produces—from enriching themselves by the sale of ivory and of tortoise-shell, which she says " may be had for the trouble of polishing." No impediments ever existed to the search after gems; a premium of three shillings per tail was offered by government, the head being too bulky for transfer, to any *native* killed by a native, the injuries committed upon private property by those animals rendering the authorities desirous to destroy them; and so little tortoise-shell is found upon the island, that the material for the combs worn by the natives is chiefly imported from the Maldives. Yet, the apparent authority with which these and many other similar statements are advanced, can scarcely fail to carry conviction of their truth to those who have no means of obtaining better information.

SKETCHES OF THE LATER HISTORY OF BRITISH INDIA.

No. IV.—Conquest of the Dutch Settlements.

The attention of Lord Minto was directed, with laudable perseverance, to the reduction of the power of the enemy in the East. He understood the value of our Indian possessions, and he felt the necessity of securing them. The subjection of the Republic of the United Provinces to the dominion of France, had placed the colonial possessions of the Dutch in the hands of England's most inveterate foe. Among the most important of these were the Molucca Islands, and the settlements in Java. The British Cabinet suggested the blockading of those islands; the more vigorous policy of Lord Minto planned and directed their conquest. They were, in succession, attacked with the same spirit that was displayed in the movements against the French Islands, and the expeditions were followed by the same results.

The first attack was on the Island of Amboyna, a place which has attained an infamous celebrity, from the atrocities of which it was once the scene. The island had been taken by the British during the first war with revolutionary France, but was restored at the peace of Amiens; since that period, it was understood that the means of defence had been greatly augmented, and that several additional works had been raised at considerable labour and cost. The principal fortress had, however, the radical defect of being overlooked and commanded by eminences of superior height. The naval part of the expedition designed for the reduction of Amboyna, consisted of the *Dover* Capt. Tucker, the *Cornwallis* Capt. Montague, and a sloop commanded by Capt. Spencer: the chief command was intrusted to the first-named officer. The military force, composed of a part of the Company's Madras European Regiment, and a small body of artillery, was placed under the command of Capt. Court.

On the morning of the 16th February 1810, the plan of attack was arranged by the commanders, and, on the afternoon of that day, the expedition was in motion. By a series of very skilful and well-executed manœuvres, the attack was kept concealed from the enemy till it was too late to offer any successful resistance to the landing of the British force. When the vessels got under weigh, they stood across the bay, as if intending to work out to sea; but, by a dexterous management of the sails, they were kept drifting towards the landing-place: the boats in the meantime were all out, with the men in them, but were kept on that side of the ships which was out of the enemy's sight. On approaching within a short distance of the shore, the ships, according to signal, bore up together; and, when within about a cable's length of the landing-place, the boats were all slipped at the same moment: the ships immediately opened their fire upon the batteries, and the party in the boats proceeded to land without opposition. The entire force of the British did not much exceed four hundred men. It was immediately on its landing formed into two divisions; the first, under Capt. Phillips, proceeded to attack one of the batteries, which, though defended

with obstinate bravery, was finally carried, and three of the guns brought
to bear upon the enemy in his retreat.

With the other division of the British force, Capt. Court had advanced
to dislodge the enemy from the principal fort. It being inexpedient to
make the attack in front, it was necessary to take a circuitous and most
fatiguing line of march. Vast steeps had to be ascended and descended
successively, for five hours, and it was frequently necessary for the men to
use their hands to assist their progress, and to trust for safety to the hold
which they were able to gain upon the slight and thinly scattered shrubs.
These difficulties being surmounted, the British reached an eminence which
commanded the enemy's position. The perseverance which had been displayed seems to have struck the garrison with panic, for they immediately
spiked their guns and retreated. On the following day, the island was
surrendered to the British force, the number of which has already been
mentioned. That of the enemy amounted to above thirteen hundred men,
and was supported by two hundred and thirty pieces of ordnance. The
surrender of Amboyna was followed by that of the subordinate islands,
five in number.

Another brilliant exploit was the capture of Banda Neira, the principal
of the spice islands: this took place in August of the same year. The
service was performed by Capt. Cole, who had been despatched from India
with the *Caroline, Piedmontaise,* and *Baracouta,* to the relief of the
division off Amboyna. Captain Cole had requested from Admiral Davy
permission to attack some of the enemy's settlements, which lay in his way,
and it was granted; but not without a cautionary intimation of the disproportionate strength of Banda Neira to the means at his disposal. Not dismayed by this warning, Capt. Cole departed on his course, and, having obtained from the government of Penang twenty artillery-men, two field-pieces,
and some scaling-ladders, he proceeded into the Java sea, against the south-
east monsoon. During the passage, which occupied six weeks, the ship's
company were daily exercised in the use of the pike, sword, and small arms,
and in mounting the scaling-ladders placed against the masts, as a preparatory exercise for any attempt at escalade. On the evening of the 8th of
August, the Banda islands became visible, and preparations were made for
an attack. It was intended to run the ships into the harbour before daylight
in the morning, but, about ten o'clock, they were suddenly fired upon from
the island of Rosigen; an occurrence perfectly unexpected, as the British
commander was not aware that the island was fortified. The attempt to
take Banda Neira by surprize was thus, for the time, frustrated; but, on
the following night, it was renewed with signal courage and good fortune.

The party destined for the service was about 390 strong, but those actually
engaged did not exceed 200. While the ships were standing towards the
land, the men rested with their arms by their sides. At eleven o'clock, they
were ordered into their boats, and directed to rendezvous close under the lee of
the point of Great Banda. The night, however, was dark and stormy, and,
at three o'clock, only a few boats had reached the place appointed, the rest

having been driven to leeward. As the success of the attack depended upon its taking place under cover of darkness, Capt. Cole determined not to wait for the arrival of the remainder of the boats, but to make the attempt without delay. They, accordingly, pulled for the shore, but, within a short distance of it the boats grounded on a coral reef, and, after labouring through a dark and stormy night, the men had to wade up to their waists in water. The landing was effected close to a battery of ten guns. This was immediately attacked and carried by the pikemen, the officer and his guard being made prisoners without the firing of a single shot, although the enemy were at their guns, with matches lighted. Though success had crowned their daring, the situation of the British force was now most critical. Daylight was approaching, and the bugles of the enemy were spreading alarm throughout the island. A rapid movement was made towards Fort Belgica, and in twenty-minutes the scaling-ladders were placed against the walls. So silent was the march of the British, that the garrison were not aware of their approach till they were within a hundred yards of them. The outworks were speedily carried, and the ladders hauled up, under a sharp fire from the garrison; but they were found too short for the escalade of the inner walls. A rush was then made for the gateway, which, at the instant, was opened to admit the colonel-commandant and three other officers, who lived in houses at the foot of the hill. The enemy fired a few guns, and kept up a discharge of musketry for about ten or fifteen minutes; they then fled in all directions. A few were killed, and among them the colonel-commandant, who refused to receive quarter, and fell in the gateway, sword in hand; some threw themselves from the walls, but the greater part escaped. A flag of truce was forthwith despatched to Fort Nassa, demanding its surrender; it was answered by the verbal submission of the governor; but the Dutch colours continuing hoisted, Capt. Cole despatched a second flag, announcing his determination to lay the place in ashes if they were not immediately struck. This threat, aided by a well-placed shot from Fort Belgica, produced the desired effect, and the handful of Englishmen, who had been engaged in this gallant enterprize, were undisputed masters of the island, with its two forts and various batteries, mounting nearly 120 pieces of cannon, and which had been defended by 700 disciplined troops besides the militia.

The only possessions now remaining to the enemy, in the East, were Batavia, in the island of Java, and its dependencies. An extraordinary value had been placed upon these settlements by the Dutch, who used to call Java the most precious jewel in the diadem of the Company, and Batavia the Queen of the East. Unfortunately, like many other Eastern potentates, Batavia was regardless of the lives of her subjects; for though, soon after its foundation, this settlement had been pronounced as healthy as any part of the Indies, experience had shewn that it was, beyond all places in the world, destructive to the lives of Europeans. This circumstance was regarded by the Dutch as an advantage, the terror of the climate affording, as they supposed, a sufficient defence against any hostile attempt. But such a defence was no longer relied on when its sovereignty was transferred from the Dutch to the French. The skill which the latter so eminently possessed in the art of war was called into operation at Batavia, and a considerable body of French troops, officers, and engineers, sent out for its defence.

The reduction of the Dutch settlements was first suggested to Lord Minto by Mr. Raffles, and his lordship was induced, by the information brought to his notice, to determine on the attempt upon his own responsibility. This was previous to the capture of the French islands. In the meantime, the Governor-general received from home a qualified approval of his meditated operations against Batavia. The views of the home authorities, however, extended no further than to the expulsion of the Dutch, the destruction of their fortifications, and the distribution of their arms and stores; after which it was proposed that we should evacuate the island, resigning possession to the natives. Such a termination of the expedition would have been singularly ill-judged and mischievous. There is not, perhaps, a more dissolute place in the world than Batavia, nor one which contains a larger proportion of the elements of crime and disorder. The Malays are sufficiently notorious for perfidy and cruelty. The Chinese, forming another large proportion of the population, less ferocious and blood-thirsty, are generally distinguished by dishonesty and want of principle, and could scarcely be expected to have forgotten the atrocious murder of so many of their countrymen by the Dutch, in 1740. The number of slaves, too, was enormous; many of them having been reduced to captivity by violence and fraud, and almost all treated with great cruelty. These, maddened by their wrongs and sufferings, would eagerly have embraced any opportunity that might have offered for revenge. To withdraw from such a population the European control, by which they had been so long coerced, without substituting in its place any other, would have been to abandon the colony to all the horrors of insurrection and massacre; to invite in another quarter of the world, a repetition of the scenes which had been acted at St. Domingo, or, if possible, something still more frightful and appalling. Lord Minto, therefore, declined acting upon these instructions, and determined, in the event of success, upon establishing such a government as should be sufficient for the preservation of public order.

The preparations for the reduction of this last relic of the colonial dominion of the Hollanders, were upon a scale commensurate with the object to be attained. The armament sailed from Malacca, and the Governor-general himself accompanied it. It had been objected, that so much time had been consumed in preparation, that the favourable season for its departure had been suffered to pass, and that it would have to contend against the adverse monsoon. This danger was obviated by the route chosen for the expedition. On leaving the straits of Singapore, it stood across to the western coast of Borneo; then, under the shelter of the land, and with the assistance of the land-wind, made good its course to Sambdar, and from thence striking across to Java, made the coast of Point Indremergan. The merit of ascertaining the practicability of this passage was attributable to Capt. Greigh. On the 4th of August 1811, the expedition arrived in the

Batavia roads.   The army, which was under the command of Sir Samuel Auchmuty, was divided into four brigades, one forming the advance, two the line, and one the reserve.   Nominally, the force employed on this expedition consisted of 5,344 Europeans and 5,777 Native troops, making a total of 11,960 ; but of these about 1,200 were left sick at Malacca, and about 1,500 more became so at Java.

The place of landing was a spot similar, in some respects, to that selected for the purpose at Mauritius; the natural obstacles which it presented having been considered sufficient to deter an invading army.   In consequence of this belief, it was left unguarded, and the debarkation of the troops took place without resistance.   The different corps had ground allotted to them, as they landed, on which to form, and as soon as the principal part of each battalion was on shore, it proceeded to the position which it was to occupy. The advanced posts were pushed on, and the troops were formed in two lines, one fronting Batavia, and the other Corsellis.   In the course of the night, a patrol of the enemy's cavalry, accompanied by an aid-de-camp of General Janssens, galloped into the advanced posts on the Batavia road, where they received the fire of two six-pounders, and that of a picquet of infantry, and retired with the loss of an officer, and two or three men.

On the following day, the horse-artillery and cavalry were landed, and the position of the army was advanced towards Batavia.   On the 6th, the roads to the city, and the country all along the coast, were reconnoitered. From some symptoms manifested in Batavia, the General judged it to be the intent of the enemy to evacuate the city.   On the 7th, the infantry attached to the advance pushed forward, the only serious impediment to their progress arising from the destruction of the bridge over the river Aujol.   A bridge of boats was constructed, by which a passage was effected late at night ; but, as the troops could only pass over in single file, considerable delay took place.   On the following day, the burghers of Batavia surrendered the city without opposition, the garrison having retreated to Weelsbudin.   Though the enemy had declined an engagement, he had made ample preparations for what may be called passive resistance.   The houses were deserted, the bridges broken down, and the conduits which supplied the city with water destroyed.   The public store-houses had been burned, and considerable efforts had been made to destroy every species of public property. Happily, some public granaries were preserved, and provisions were abundant.

Only a small part of the British force entered the town, in the first instance.   Their arrival afforded a timely check upon the system of depredation and destruction which the Malays had commenced, and they succeeded in rescuing several large stores of colonial goods from plunder.

Many circumstances combined to excite in the minds of the British authorities a suspicion that the enemy meditated an attack, and this was confirmed by the report of Capt. Roberts, aid-de-camp to Lord Minto, who had been despatched with a summons to General Janssens to surrender the island.   He was conducted blindfolded through the lines, but, as he passed along, he heard a considerable movement of men, horses, and artillery-carriages. The answer which he brought back was in the style of gasconade which characterized the military school of revolutionary France. It was to the effect, that the commander-in-chief was a French general, and would defend his charge to the last extremity. Soon after the receipt of the French commander's answer, the troops were silently called out, and ordered to lie on their arms in the great square in front of the town-house. They had scarcely reached it, when the head of the enemy's column appeared, and opened a fire of musketry. Colonel Gillespie sallied out, at the head of a party, from a gateway on the west side of the city, with the intention of charging the assailants in flank. The firing immediately ceased, and no more was seen or heard of the enemy during the night. It appears that they had calculated upon the British force in the city being less numerous than it really was, and they had also relied on the expectation of disabling our men by means not recognized among the ordinary instruments of warfare. A large quantity of deleterious spirit was stored up in the town, and this, the Chinese, in compliance, it was understood, with instructions from the enemy, pressed upon our soldiers instead of water, which was extremely scarce—a proclamation having been issued by the French general, forbidding any family to possess more than one jar of water for their own use. By the judicious and decisive measures of Colonel Gillespie, their designs were frustrated, and the British force was preserved from surprise and destruction. Early on the morning of the 10th, the troops, together with the inhabitants, had a narrow escape. A Malay was discovered, with a firebrand in his hand, in the act of setting light to some wooden magazines, containing a considerable quantity of gunpowder. He was taken, and, on the following day, in a spirit of summary justice, hanged. These were not the only acts of similar character which occurred. The commanding officer's quarters were kept by a Frenchman, and, as an honourable mode of serving his country, this man poisoned the coffee prepared for the breakfast of Colonel Gillespie and his staff: the atrocious attempt was unsuccessful, the effects of the poison having manifested themselves before sufficient of the adulterated beverage had been taken to produce the intended effect. In the hurry of the moment, it is to be lamented, that the author of this abominable act escaped.

On the 10th, Colonel Gillespie advanced with his corps towards the enemy's cantonment at Weellerneeder, supported by two brigades of infantry. They found the cantonment abandoned, but the enemy was in force at a short distance beyond. Their position was strongly defended by an *abbatis*, occupied by three thousand of their best troops and four guns, horse artillery. It was promptly attacked by Colonel Gillespie; and after an obstinate resistance, carried at the point of the bayonet, the enemy's force driven to the shelter of their batteries, and their guns taken.

But, though vanquished, the enemy were not entirely subdued. They were greatly superior in numbers to the invading force, and they entrenched themselves in a strong position, between a large river and an artificial watercourse, neither of which was fordable. Their position was further defended by a deep trench strongly palisadoed, seven redoubts, and many batteries. The fort of Corsellis was in the centre, and the whole of the works were defended by a numerous and well-organized artillery. The season was far advanced, and the heat violent; and these reasons, combined with the insufficient number of the British troops, determined the general to decline attempting the reduction of the position by regular approaches, and to endeavour to carry the works by assault. Some batteries were erected with a view of disabling the principal redoubts, and a heavy fire was kept up for two days with great effect; and, though answered by a far more numerous artillery, it succeeded in silencing the nearer batteries of the enemy, and considerably disturbing their entire position.

At dawn of day, on the 26th, the assault was made. It was proposed to surprise one of the redoubts constructed by the enemy beyond the Salken, to endeavour to cross the bridge over that stream with the fugitives, and then to assault the redoubts within the lines. The enemy was under arms and prepared for the combat, and General Janssens, the commander-in-chief, was in the advanced redoubt when the attack commenced.

Colonel Gillespie, after a long *detour* through a close and intricate country, came on their advance, which he routed almost instantly, and with extraordinary rapidity proceeded, under a heavy fire of grape and musketry, to the advanced redoubt, of which he was soon in possession. He then, in accordance with the proposed plan, passed the bridge, and, after an obstinate resistance, carried with the bayonet a second redoubt. The operations of other columns were directed with equal success against different parts of the works; but the explosion, either by accident or design, of the magazine of one of the redoubts, destroyed a number of brave officers and men, who were crowded on its ramparts, which the enemy had just abandoned. The park of artillery was attacked and carried in a masterly manner, and a body of cavalry, which had formed to defend it, speedily put to flight. A strong body of the enemy, which had taken their position in the lines in front of Fort Corsellis, were attacked and driven from them, and the fort taken. The enemy was now completely put to flight; a vigorous pursuit followed, and the whole of the army was either killed, taken, or dispersed. So close was the combat, that in the course of the day almost every officer was engaged hand to hand. Colonel Gillespie in person took prisoners two generals and a colonel, and another colonel fell by his hand. General Janssens, the commander-in-chief, succeeded with some difficulty in reaching Buitzenzorg, a distance of thirty miles, with a few cavalry, the sole remains of an army of ten thousand men.

The loss on the part of the British was severe, that of the enemy still more so. About a thousand bodies were buried in the works, many perished in the river, and many in the flight. Nearly five thousand were made prisoners, among whom were three general officers, thirty-four field officers, seventy captains, and one hundred and fifty subalterns. In the British army, about one hundred and fifty men, European and Native, were killed or missing, and upwards of seven hundred wounded.

The conquest of the island might now be considered as achieved, but as General Janssens shewed no intention of giving up the contest, Sir Samuel

Achmuty prepared to push his success with vigour. Captain Bean was despatched with a detachment to Cheribon, and, on arriving there, proceeded in the exercise of his duty with great spirit, by summoning the French commander to surrender, allowing him five minutes for decision. The terms he proposed were, that the garrison should be prisoners of war, all public property surrendered, but all private property respected. Immediately after the flag of truce had been despatched, Captain Bean stood in with the frigates towards the fort. The result was, that the terms were submitted to, the French colours hauled down, the marines landed, and placed in possession of the fort. At this moment, the French general, Jamelle, and two other officers, one of them an aid-de-camp of the commander-in-chief, arrived with tidings that detachments to succour Cheribon were on their way, and that three hundred infantry and two hundred and fifty cavalry might be hourly expected. But it was too late—the officers were made prisoners, and Captain Bean, who had not waited for the ship which had the troops on board, landed one hundred and fifty seamen to garrison the fort, leaving the marines to act offensively in the field if requisite. The prisoners, being all natives, except one or two officers, were dismissed to their homes, with an intimation that if afterwards found acting against the British they would be hanged. It was said, that this caution did not appear at all to diminish their gratitude for their deliverance.

The marines were then marched to Cavang Sambig, thirty-five miles inland, where nine waggon-loads of silver and copper money, with stores to a great amount, were deposited. Seven hundred prisoners, including a very large proportion of officers, were taken, without the loss of a single man killed or wounded during these operations.

Sir S. Achmuty having proceeded to Samarang, and being joined there by Admiral Stopford and a few of the troop-ships, called upon General Janssens to surrender the island on terms of capitulation. This was refused, and the French general succeeded in making such a show of strength, as led Sir Samuel Achmuty to conclude that it was not advisable to assault the fort until further reinforced. Some fishermen, however, having reported that Janssens was withdrawing his troops into the interior, and had fortified a position a few miles on the road towards Kirta Sterer, Sir Samuel Achmuty, on the 12th, prepared to attack the town, when it was immediately surrendered. Janssens had retired to the position which he had chosen, where he was completing batteries and entrenchments, and where he had succeeded, with the assistance of the native princes, in drawing together a large force. The British commander, having waited in vain two days for reinforcements, determined upon hazarding an attack, which be entrusted to Colonel Gibbs. In the course of the night, one ship arrived, which enabled the European garrison from the fort to join the field force, which was further strengthened by a company of sepoys. But with these additions it only amounted to about eleven hundred infantry, was totally deficient in cavalry, and almost without artillery.

At two in the morning, on the 16th, the troops marched from Samarang; and, after advancing about six miles, discovered the enemy's force. They were attacked without delay, their flank soon turned, and they took to flight in the utmost disorder. But the British force was too much fatigued to pursue them, and in the night General Janssens made an offer of capitulation. 'The negotiations were conducted on the part of Sir Samuel Achmuty with much firmness, and ended in the surrender of the island, as well as that of the French general, with all that remained of his army, as prisoners of war.'

The naval operations were conducted with equal success. Captain Harris and Captain Pellew succeeded in reducing the French fortress in the island of Madura, and detaching the sultan from the interests of the enemy. This service was performed with extraordinary brilliancy. Leaving their ships at anchor under the isle of Pondrik, these officers landed about two miles from fort Samarap, and forming their men into columns of sixty bayonets and thirty pikemen each, flanked by two or three pieces of artillery, and with a body of marines for their reserve, they marched with such perfect silence towards the fort, that, though the boats had been seen standing in for shore, they were not discovered till they were through the outer gate. In ten minutes, the fort was carried by storm, and several hundred Madura pikemen were made prisoners. At day-break, the natives began to assemble in great numbers, when Captain Harris called on the governor to surrender in ten minutes. In reply, he was required to evacuate the fort within three hours, on peril of having it stormed.

The governor commanded three thousand muskets, sixty artillery-men, and about fifteen hundred armed with pike and pistol, and he had four field-pieces planted on a bridge, commanding a straight road of a quarter of a mile in length, along which the British must pass before they could reach the bridge. Captain Harris, however, determined to attack them. Leaving about fifty men in the fort, he led a body of ninety to turn the left flank of the enemy, and to make a diversion in favour of Captain Pellew's party, which was to advance as soon as this column should fire the first gun. This bold attempt was entirely successful. Some sharp firing took place while the British columns were advancing, but as soon as they were near enough to charge, the contest was at an end. The governor was made prisoner, and the colours and guns taken. Friendship always follows success : the sultan of Madura forthwith joined the conquerors, and offered four thousand men to assist in attacking Sourabaya. But this aid was not needed, in consequence of the surrender of the whole island. The appointment of lieutenant-governor was conferred by Lord Minto upon Mr. Raffles, who had preceded the expedition for the purpose of collecting information, and to whose judicious advice its success may in a great degree be attributed.

The fall of Batavia was followed by an event so remarkable as to deserve notice.

The sultan of Palambang, a petty chief in the south-eastern part of Sumatra, no sooner received intelligence of the success of the British arms, than he conceived the atrocious resolution of destroying the Dutch Resident, and every male person belonging to the factory at Palambang, not excepting even children, and of razing the fort to the ground. This horrible scheme he executed, in spite of the remonstrances of some Malay agents of the British Government, who represented that the destruction of the fort would be an act of hostility against those to whom the Dutch establishments had been transferred by right of conquest. The number of persons thus wantonly massacred was nearly a hundred, thirty of whom were European-born.

The motives which led to this barbarous policy were probably twofold. The Dutch are regarded throughout the Malay states with inveterate hatred, and the feeling is not altogether without cause. The sultan perhaps rejoiced in an opportunity of taking signal revenge upon a people, towards whom the feeling of hostility was universal and long cherished. He might further think that the circumstances which had occurred presented a favourable opportunity for dissolving all connections with European powers. The entire proceeding appears to have been marked by that sinister policy unfortunately so common among the chieftains of the East. The Malay agents alleged that, in the first instance, the sultan compelled them to sign a false report of the transactions, and afterwards, with a view of preventing a disclosure of the real facts, endeavoured to add them to the number of his victims.

Previously to these facts becoming known to the government of Java, a mission had been despatched for the purpose of taking charge of the factory at Palambang, and of making arrangements for the preservation to the British of a monopoly of tin, produced in the island of Baneim, but on terms far more advantageous to the sultan than those existing under the Dutch government. The mission was received in the most contemptuous manner; the claims of the English to succeed to the rights and privileges of the Dutch were denied, and the sultan even ventured to assert, that he had completed his hostile proceedings against the Dutch before the conquest of Java had been achieved. The real character of those proceedings he did not avow; but represented them to be confined to the destruction of the fort and expulsion of the garrison. This mission, therefore, returned without accomplishing its object. Its arrival was soon followed by that of an embassy from the sultan, who repeated the statements of their master; but by this time the truth was known, and vigorous measures were determined on, to assert the rights of the British Government, and punish the faithlessness and cruelties of the sultan.

For this purpose, a force, consisting of nearly a thousand men, was put in motion, under the command of Colonel Gillespie; it sailed from Balasore on the 20th March 1812, but its progress was considerably retarded by contrary winds and currents. On the 3d of April the fleet reached Hawk's Island, and continued a week at anchor. Tents were pitched on shore, and a number of artificers employed in the completion of the boats intended for the passage of the Palambang river, in constructing platforms for the field pieces, and providing shelter for the troops from the oppressive heat of the day, and the noxious air of the night. On the 10th, the fleet got under weigh, and came to anchor on the 15th, opposite the west channel of the

Palambang river.   On the arrival of the British force, the sultan attempted to negotiate, transmitting messages to the commander filled with expressions of the most profound respect, and the warmest attachment to the English nation; but his treacherous character was too well known to allow of any one being deceived by such professions.   Colonel Gillespie refused to treat except with the sultan in person at Palambang.   The expedition accordingly advanced and took possession of the works at Borang; on learning which, the sultan fled, leaving the fort, palace, and city in a state of inconceivable disorder.   He had previously removed his treasures and his women into the interior.

After the occupation of the works at Borang, the troops had been re-embarked : but, on learning the state of the capital, Colonel Gillespie determined to push on with the light boats, and endeavour to stop the scenes of confusion and carnage which were taking place there.   The city, which stretched along the banks of the river for upwards of seven miles, presented to the view of the British an awful scene of murder and pillage. . The most dreadful shrieks and yells were heard in all directions, and conflagrations appeared in various places.   An eye-witness declares, that "romance never described any thing half so hideous, nor has the invention of the imagination ever given representations equally appalling."   Amid these horrors, Colonel Gillespie stepped on shore, accompanied by only seven grenadiers, and proceeded into the city, surrounded by the glittering weapons of ferocious Arabs and treacherous Malays.   One of the latter nation pressed through the crowd, approached the colonel, and was walking by his side, when a large double-edged knife was silently put into his hands by one of his countrymen.   He received the instrument, and was in the act of concealing it in his long loose sleeve, when a sudden flash of lightning discovered it. The man was instantly disarmed, and his murderous design thus frustrated : but amid the confusion that prevailed at the moment, he found means to mix in the crowd and escape.

On approaching the palace, the horrors of the spectacle were aggravated. The apartments had been ransacked ; the pavements and floors were flowing with blood ; the flames were rapidly consuming all that plunder had spared, and while they were pursuing their devastating career, the crackling of the bamboos is said to have resembled the discharge of musquetry.   At intervals, the roofs of the various buildings fell with tremendous crash, and notwithstanding the torrents of rain, the fire continued to spread, and threatened even that part of the palace where the British forces were compelled to take up their temporary abode.   This force consisted only of a few grenadiers and seamen, and they were surrounded on all sides by hordes of assassins.   The best means of defence were adopted by the little band ; at midnight, they were joined by a small reinforcement under Major French, and in the morning by another under Colonel M'Leod : resistance was now no longer thought of, and the resolution of Colonel Gillespie had thus, without the loss of a man, placed in the possession of the British, the city, fort, and batteries, defended by two hundred and forty-two pieces of cannon.

Notwithstanding the subjugation of the Dutch and French power, parts of Java remained in a disturbed state; the sultan of Djoejyocarta,. one of the most turbulent and intriguing of the native princes, manifested a hostile disposition to the British Government; in consequence of which, Mr. Raffles, the Lieut.-Governor, proceeded in person to his court, in December 1811, with the hope of definitively fixing by treaty the relations between the two governments. His visit was attended with some danger, and it seems not easy to acquit the Lieut.-Governor of the charge of rashness in undertaking it. His escort consisted only of a small part of the 14th regiment, a troop of the 22d Light Dragoons, and the ordinary garrison of Bengal sepoys in the fort and at the Residency-house. The sultan received Mr. Raffles surrounded by several thousands of his armed followers, whose deportment was marked by extraordinary violence. Creesses were unsheathed, and it was plain that those who brandished them, only waited for the command to put all the English to the sword. The command did not issue, and the Lieut.-Governor and his retinue retired in safety ; but they certainly had as much reason to congratulate themselves on their good fortune, as the stork when he withdrew his head in safety from the throat of the wolf. Negociations with native princes, especially until they are considerably tamed, should be carried on at the head of a commanding military force.

A treaty was concluded, by which the sovereignty of the British over the island of Java was acknowledged by the Sultan, and the English East-India Company were confirmed in all the privileges, advantages, and prerogatives which had been possessed by the Dutch and French Governments. To the Company also were transferred the sole regulation of the duties, and the collection of tribute within the dominions of the Sultan, and the general administration of justice in all cases where the British interests were concerned.

This treaty was concluded before the expedition against Palambang. The occupation of the troops, which had been despatched thither, seemed to afford the Sultan of Djoejyocarta a favourable opportunity of breaking the treaty into which he had so recently entered, and this, in the true spirit of native policy, he eagerly embraced. By his agency, a confederacy was formed of all the native courts, the object of which was to expel all European settlers of every country, and to sweep from the island every vestige of European power. As soon as the design became apparent, preparations were made for resisting it by such means as were at the disposal of government, and in the emergency Colonel Gillespie opportunely arrived from Palambang. The Lieut.-Governor and the Commander of the Forces immediately proceeded to Djoejyocarta with such military force as could be collected, and hostilities were precipitated by Colonel Gillespie, arriving with a reconnoitering party, unexpectedly falling in with a large body of the Sultan's horse. As offensive measures had not been determined on, Colonel Gillespie refrained from attacking them, and endeavoured, through Mr. Crawford the resident, to prevail upon them to return to the palace. They for a while refused, and some stones were thrown at the English party. This outrage was not repelled, and at length the Sultan's troops consented to retire, but taking advantage of the growing darkness, they threw stones at our men, and a serjeant and four dragoons were wounded. This attack was followed by several others, and our dragoons were ultimately obliged to cut their way out sword in hand.

On the following day, an attempt was made to negociate, but without success, and it was clear that nothing was left but an appeal to force. The residence of the sultan was about three miles in circumference, surrounded by a broad ditch with drawbridges, a strong high rampart, with bastions, and defended by nearly one hundred pieces of cannon. In the interior were numerous squares and court-yards, enclosed with high walls, and all defensible. The principal entrance or square, in front, had a double row of cannon facing the gate, and was flanked with newly erected batteries, right and left. Seventeen thousand regular troops manned the works, and an armed population of more than a hundred thousand surrounded the palace for miles, and occupied the walls and fastnesses along the sides of the various roads. The Dutch had erected a fort close to the palace, and this was now occupied by the British. Their force was small, not exceeding 600 firelocks; but what was wanting in number was made up by intrepidity. They forthwith commenced cannonading the palace; this was immediately returned, and in the evening the sultan sent a message demanding an unconditional surrender. In the course of the night, Major Dalton, who with a party of the Bengal light infantry, occupied part of the Dutch town between the fort and the palace, was attacked four times in succession, but on every occasion repulsed the enemy with great steadiness. Various skirmishing took place between parties of the enemy and others of our dragoons, in which the latter displayed remarkable gallantry. The day after, a detachment under Colonel McLeod, whose arrival had been anxiously expected, reached head-quarters, but their long march and exposure to a burning sun rendered some repose necessary. In the evening Colonel Gillespie ordered all the troops, both cavalry and infantry, into the fort, and this measure fully persuaded the sultan that he had struck the British commander with terror.

He was mistaken. No symptom of concession having been evinced by the enemy, Colonel Gillespie had determined on an assault. Two hours before day, the leaders of columns received their orders, and instantly proceeded to execute them. The assault was made by escalade, and was completely successful. The British force quickly occupied the ramparts, and turned the guns of the enemy upon themselves. The word was " Death or Victory," and no other thought seems to have occupied the minds of those engaged. The sultan was taken in his strong-hold. He was subsequently deposed, and the hereditary prince raised to the throne. The other confederated princes readily acceded to the terms proposed to them. The conquest of Java was thus complete, and the British power was paramount throughout the island.

The general peace restored Java to its former possessors, and it may, therefore, be deemed a task of little utility to record the circumstances by which it became a temporary appendage of the British crown. But it is not an unimportant matter that Englishmen should bear in mind what their fellow-countrymen have achieved, although diplomatists may compliment away the possessions which have been so dearly earned. The magnanimity of Great Britain in restoring Java has been much praised. She has too frequently been magnanimous to her own cost, and her sacrifices have never been paid by anything but praise. Java unquestionably ought to have been retained. One great power must predominate in the East, and it is not for us to raise a question what power that should be. The acquisition of territory by any other European nation ought especially to be guarded against, as far as we possess the means. We ought not, indeed, to wage a war of ambition or aggression—we ought not to draw the sword for the sake of conquest; but when hostile operations become justifiable, as they undoubtedly were at the period of our conquests in the Indian seas, we ought not to throw away their results. We should have the firmness to insist upon retaining what we have had the courage to win. Java was important, not only in itself, but also from its proximity to other islands, over which the British authority ought at fitting opportunities to have been extended; but England has always been afraid of her own good fortune in the East.

The transfer of Java was to be lamented, perhaps, even more on account of the inhabitants than on our own. The Dutch Government had never been strong, and it has, on many occasions, had recourse to the usual expedients of conscious weakness—oppression and cruelty. Under the dominion and influence of the English, various beneficial changes were introduced, and the country was in a progressive state of improvement. This was checked by its surrender to the Dutch, and since that event there has been no lack of discontent and disturbance.

The establishment of the British power in the East, without an European rival, was the crowning act of Lord Minto's administration, and it was one of which he had reason to be proud. Having completed the usual period of residence, he resigned his office and proceeded to England. But he was not destined to enjoy that period of repose to which men look, as the termination and reward of public services—his death having taken place within a few weeks after his arrival in this country.

The administration of Lord Minto was distinguished by great moderation, but it was marked also with very considerable ability. The line of policy pressed upon him from home was that of peace, and he laboured assiduously to preserve it. But he was not insensible to the peculiarities of our situation in India, surrounded by those who regarded us as hostile intruders; he was conscious that a pacific policy might be carried too far for national interest, no less than national honour, and his views on subjects which, soon after his retirement, became of vital importance, were probably not very dissimilar to those of his successor. He was fully conscious of the inapplicability to our situation in India, of that timid and indecisive policy which was fashionable in England, and the expression of his opinions was not without effect in the most influential quarters. His mistakes and failures may fairly be attributable less to himself than to public opinion in England, which overawed and controlled him. The outrages of the Pindarries, the encroachments of the Ghoorkas, and the insolence of the Burmese, attracted his attention; but he waited for encouragement from home to determine him to grapple with them. This was the most exceptionable part of his policy, and it must be attributed to constitutional caution. The most brilliant, as well as valuable, acts of his government, were the well-planned and successful expeditions against the enemy's possessions in the East. He here showed that he understood his country's interests, and he acted upon his convictions with vigour and decision. Upon the whole, though a few of those who have occupied the same high station with himself have left behind them a reputation more brilliant and dazzling, that of Lord Minto rests on a basis of substantial service, and he well deserves to be held in remembrance as one of the eminent statesmen of India.

THE GYPSIES.

TO THE EDITOR.

Sir: I believe the only remaining difficulty, with respect to the theory of Hindostan being the father-land of the Gypsies, is the claim which they appear to have, by the assumption of this name, to a connection with Egypt; a circumstance which Grellmann seems to admit, without attempting to account for; and which Sir Wm. Jones, if I mistake not, would explain by the hypothesis, that they were carried to Abyssinia by the maritime Arabs, and thence migrated into Europe through Egypt. In looking through the *Asiatic Researches*, lately, I observe, however, that tribes of this strange people are still found,—and, as both tradition and history agree, have for centuries existed,—in the different countries lying in the *direct overland route* from Bohemia (the place of their first appearance in Europe) to Hindostan, which, added to the difficulty presented by their journeying to Egypt, as well as that of accounting for their pursuing so unusual a track, and the circumstance that there are few if any Coptic or Egyptian words to be found in their language, renders the fact of their having passed through that country liable to doubt.

I, therefore, suggest, that the name which they were first known by, and from which their present appellation of *Gypsies* is derived, namely, the people of " *Lesser Egypt*," is an European corruption of some Hindoostanee or Oriental word or words, by which they designated themselves on their first arrival in Europe,—and perhaps may to this day,—and having no reference whatever to Egypt.

I have quoted both Grellmann and Sir W. Jones from memory; but I believe I am correct in my quotation.

I am, sir, your obedient servant,

T. ELLIS INMAN.

11, *Commercial Rooms, Mincing Lane,*
    May 12, 1836.

THE CYMBALEER AND HIS BRIDE.

A Ballad.

Monseigneur le duc de Bretagne,
A, pour les combats meurtriers,
Convoqué de Kante à Mortagne,
Dans la plaine, et sur la campagne,
L'arrière-ban de ses guerriers.　　　*Victor Hugo.*

———

He comes from the wars in Aquitain—
He comes—my Cymbaleer;
But look upon his flashing crest,
The polished mail upon his breast—
A gallant knight, you'd say, was here.

Now the dying sunlight burns,
The Duke in victor-pride returns,
Triumphs on his path await—
Hasten to the eastern gate,
Hasten, sisters—they appear—
The Duke and my Cymbaleer.

See the tide of warriors flow;
First march the pikemen, proud and slow;
And next a hundred barons bold,
In radiant vests of silk and gold;
While the glad trumpets pour aloud
Their thunder o'er the crowd.

And see, in vests of shining mail,
The Templars riding into sight,
Before the fury of whose might,
The Paynim heart grew pale;
Then comes a wild and daring clan,
The iron archers of Lausanne.

Hasten, sisters, come and see,
Glancing spear and sword;
And, list! the war-horse laughs aloud,
Whilst o'er his flaming eyes are bow'd
The red plumes of his Lord.

The Duke is coming; his banner red
Floats in splendour o'er his head;
I see the blaze of a thousand spears,
I hear the thunder of their tread—
Sisters! here are the Cymbaleers!

She spoke, and through each glittering rank,
Her eye with anxious terror ran,
Every shadowing plume to scan, —
But pallid now, and all aghast,
Amid the wondering crowd she sank—
The Cymbaleers were past!

THE INDIAN ARMY.

A copy of a letter, by an officer of the Indian army, who has had much experience in the office of judge advocate (whose name we are not authorized to mention), recently addressed to the Chairs of the Court of Directors, touching the state of the military law in the Indian army, and the present position of the European portion of it, consequent upon the removal of corporal punishment from the native portion, has fallen into our hands; and, as the subject is well treated, and as the letter has been (we hear) very favourably received by those military authorities to whom it has been privately communicated, we think an analysis of it may be of considerable interest to our military readers.

The first point touched upon by the writer is the confused and diversified state of the military law of the three presidencies, and of the systems under which it is administered,—"superintended by three judge-advocates-general, neither of them of the legal profession, acting independently of each other, and under separate chief authorities." The writer recommends that the military law of British India should be not only revised, but consolidated, and rendered uniform in practice throughout the three presidencies, under a single advocate-general, a member of the legal profession, and in immediate communication with the supreme authority. The soundness of this suggestion is, to us, apparent, not only from the argument derived from analogy with the British army at home, but from the obvious inconveniences which must arise, and which (notoriously) have arisen, from the conflict of co-ordinate and (comparatively speaking) incompetent authorities; or, as Lord Wm. Bentinck observed, in his minute of 16th February 1835, from "the caprice of individuals." The placing of the native armies of the three presidencies under one code, assimilated more to the King's Articles of War, was recommended by the committee assembled at Madras to report upon the question of corporal punishment.

Evidence of the imperfect state of military law in India, and of its practice, as well as of the general dissatisfaction excited amongst the Indian army, owing to their being under the control of rules and liabilities which have been long ago modified in the Mutiny Act, as regards the Royal Army, may be collected from the public journals in India. For instance, the last-framed Articles of War for his Majesty's army enact :—

" That any officer or soldier who shall give, send, convey, or promote, a challenge to any other officer to fight a duel ;—or shall upbraid another for refusing a challenge; or, if commanding a guard, shall knowingly and willingly suffer any person to go forth to fight a duel, *shall*, if an *officer*, on conviction, be *liable* to be *cashiered*, or suffer such other punishment, according to the nature and degree of the offence, as by the judgment of a *general* court-martial may be awarded, &c.

But, in the old Articles of War, by which the army of India is still governed, this offence is more severely treated, by limiting the punishment to cashiering *only*. " This difference," observes the writer, " places the officers of the Indian army under a great disadvantage compared with those of the royal army serving with them; and it has fallen within my observation to see an officer of the former, when on trial for sending a challenge, put in his King's commission, and desire to be judged by the more recent and mild enactment for the government of his Majesty's forces. The attention of supreme authorities has been consequently called to this striking discrepancy by courts-martial, who have been constrained, under the existing law, to award the severer sentence, contrary to their estimate of the offence."

Again :—If an officer in his Majesty's army, serving in either presidency, be tried by court-martial and sentenced to dismissal, the power of reviewing the proceedings, and of confirming the sentence or otherwise, is vested in the Commander-in-chief *of all India.* But if an officer of the Indian army be similarly sentenced, the power is given, by the existing Articles of War for that army, to the subordinate *local* commanders-in-chief. " In this essential point also," he remarks, " officers of the Indian army feel themselves placed under an additional disadvantage ; for the proceedings on their trials are thus submitted to the review and report of *local* judge-advocates-general, to whose opinion their cases are submitted *in the first instance,* and at whose recommendation the trials are commonly instituted, founded upon charges prepared by *themselves,* on the *ex-parte* evidence furnished by the accusers. And further, the judgment of the court, accompanied by the report made under circumstances so prejudicial to the party tried, receives its final confirmation or disapproval from the *very* general officer by whom the trial is ordered, who thus exercises an arbitrary, irresponsible power, equally opposed to the spirit of law and justice, and liable to glaring abuse in such far distant possessions."

The writer is of opinion that the evils obviously attending this system would be corrected, and that general satisfaction would take the place of an opposite feeling amongst the officers of each presidency, if the power of deciding upon the proceedings of all courts-martial on commissioned officers were confined to the Governor-general, aided by a professional judge-advocate-general.

The operation of the discrepancy between the two systems upon the non-commissioned officers and privates of the two armies is forcibly pointed out. Whilst in the King's army there are the following grades of courts, namely, general, district (or garrison), detachment, and regimental courts-martial,—and whilst the Articles of War classify offences and prescribe specific punishments for each and every degree of offenders in the royal army,—the non-commissioned officers and privates of the Indian army continue subject to the two courts of extreme powers,—the general and regimental courts-martial, with the imperfect classification of crimes and ill-regulated punishments contained in the Mutiny Act and Articles of War of 1823 : so that the Indian army has been deprived of the benefits which the improvements in Sir Robert Peel's Act have worked in the *morale* of the royal army.

" To manifest, in a most striking manner, the ill-effects of these varied laws for the same body, or even for different bodies serving together, and the unequal discipline produced by them in the native armies of the several presidencies, it will suffice to refer to the remarkable difference in the number of corporal punishments awarded, and of lashes actually inflicted, upon men of the native cavalry and infantry of the three armies, for the five years from 1829 to 1833 :—

		Cavalry Regts.	Infantry Regts.
Average number of lashes *awarded* per regiment, for the five years from 1829 to 1833	In Bengal ...	1,054	1,521
	Madras ...	2,984	5,187
	Bombay...	12,601	8,104
Average number of lashes *inflicted* per regiment, for the five years from 1829 to 1833	In Bengal ...	209	516
	Madras ...	1,852	3,588
	Bombay...	7,657	5,415
Average number of discharges per regiment, for the five years from 1829 to 1833	In Bengal ...	43	96
	Madras ...	64	84
	Bombay...	93	109

At the period to which this extraordinary statement refers, the strength of the regiments at each presidency was equal; and although *some* variation in number of crimes and in severity of punishments may be ascribed to the facilities existing in Bengal for filling the ranks with men of superior caste, the *very great* difference is attributed to the three armies being unprovided with an *uniform military code,* of one established system of *adequate rewards,* and of recruiting, paying, and pensioning; and to their not being concentrated under *one supreme authority.*

The writer observes: "I apprehend that, among those who have had an opportunity of observing the state and practice of military law in the Madras presidency of late years, there are very few who will not concur with me in ascribing to two or three particular sources a large proportion of the evil referred to, *viz.*—to the before-mentioned uninteresting nature of the duties in a period of prolonged peace and inactivity,—the diminished powers which, in corps, garrisons, and even divisions, are now allowed to commanding officers in controlling their troops,—and the increased disposition at head-quarters too rigidly to review and comment on the proceedings of *minor* courts-martial, and to augment the duties of the judge-advocate-general's department, by referring to trial by *general* courts, matters which might otherwise be more promptly disposed of. Formerly, and also during the most recent hostilities, while commanding officers exercised greater power in advancing the meritorious, they did not hesitate also to administer punishment more summarily and arbitrarily than is now allowable; subject, as they have thus been made, to the very scrutinizing and jealous observation of head-quarter authorities, in the absence of loftier claims on *their* powers of direction and control. Hence it has followed that commanding officers, rather than risk censure by exercising their power of effectually checking offenders in the commencement of a vicious career, or endure having their judicial conduct so minutely supervised and remarked upon by divisional deputies-judge-advocate, have become indifferent to that progress in crime, on the part of such characters, which must subject them to the jurisdiction of the higher tribunal, and expose them to the degradation of more public and severe punishment. And these are the causes, combined with the variations and imperfections of the existing very old military law of India, the anomalies of which have been greatly increased by the existence of three distinct judge-advocates-general, neither of them of legal education, which have in public opinion tended principally to produce the increased frequency of our general courts-martial, and the severity of the punishments awarded."

The writer of the letter adverts to the "dark gloom" which has for some time pervaded the army of India, resulting from extensive reductions, consequent extreme slowness of promotion, general diminution of the number of superior commands and staff places, and reduced allowances; and to the dissatisfaction among the royal troops serving in India through the abolition of corporal punishment in the native army only, whereby "their feelings, mental and physical, have been brought into extremely invidious collision with the native soldiery." Upon this delicate question, the writer speaks with commendable caution, and distrust of his own judgment. From the experience of eleven years in India, and from the results obtained from the observations of others, the writer is induced to dissent from the conclusion of those high authorities, the Duke of Wellington and Lord William Bentinck, who are of opinion that the European troops in India now feel, and will continue to feel indifference about the matter. The writer apprehends " a very different and serious result in so peculiar an empire of military opinion." He adds: " I may state that, having closely observed the combined duties and conduct of the European and native soldiery, in garrison, in field cantonments, and in warfare, I consider that there *now* exists an intimacy between the two classes, which quickly communicates and explains to the one whatever occurs affecting the other;" and he expresses his belief, that " if the degrading *distinction* be maintained, occurrences of more marked danger to our Eastern supremacy must naturally be expected."

In the existing dilemma, the writer suggests that the home authorities should avail themselves of the opportunity to extend to the Indian army, so far as applicable, all the amendments which have been contained in the Mutiny Acts and Articles of War for the King's forces, passed yearly since 1823 (the date of the latest act and articles for the Company's service); bring the whole army of India, so far as can be, under one code and system, rendering every portion thereof amenable to the same description of courts, and liable to punishments similar both in nature and degree,—and repeat this assimilation of military government *annually*, by inserting at the conclusion of the act passed for the royal army, a clause somewhat to the following effect :—

And be it enacted, that wherever the provisions of this Act apply to officers, non-commissioned officers, soldiers, and others of his Majesty's army serving in the possessions and territories of the East India Company, or, under the orders of their government, in other countries in the East, the same shall, so far as applicable, apply to the officers, non-commissioned officers, soldiers, and others, European and native, of the army of the said Company:—and that wherever the provisions of this Act do not so provide for matters affecting the necessary good order and government of the troops, European and native, of the said Company, it shall and may be lawful for the supreme legislative council of India, to enact such laws as shall be best adapted to provide for the same: power being reserved to the said Company, to frame rules and articles for the better government of the officers, non-commissioned officers, soldiers, and others in their service, in conformity with the provisions of this Act ; and to the supreme legislative council of India to add thereto, from time to time, agreeably to such additional enactments as the nature and formation of the armies of the said Company may render advisable.

To this system of assimilation, which squares with the policy now pursued in other departments of the Indian government, we imagine there can be no objection, and it will be a graceful and gracious mode of extricating the government from embarrassment.

We may embrace this occasion, especially since a new governor and new commander-in-chief are on their departure for one of the presidencies, to make (without meaning any invidious insinuation) the following suggestions:

It would be well for a commander-in-chief to take no reports or communications against individuals into his consideration, without first calling on the individuals to submit what they may have to say against them; and never to send any matter, affecting commissioned officers especially, to trial, without first submitting it to the investigation of an impartial court of enquiry of three officers at least: as in civil law no criminal matter is carried into court until a grand jury has first found a true bill. Farther; that no officer should be placed in arrest without having, *at the time*, a copy of the accusation or charge whereon he was so proceeded against;—that no one should be placed in arrest until as near as possible to the assembly of the court for his trial;—and that, if the commander-in-chief should deem it necessary to disapprove of, and find fault with, the proceedings of courts-martial, he should do so—*not in public general orders*, by which amendment is not, and much irritation is produced;

but by temperate letters addressed *from himself to the President of the Court*, to be read by the President to the Court previous to its dissolution. By such course, much of the angry feeling now existing throughout the army on courts-martial matters would be allayed, and these assemblies might be brought to their proper character; and well would the army appreciate the change. It would be well, moreover, if courts-martial could be brought to a closer affinity with "courts of honour;" at all events, if they could be purged of that species of legal quibbling, special pleading, and sophistry, which is creeping into them, and totally changing their character in India.

LOVE AND TIME.

A voyager passant sa vie,
　Certain viellard, nommé le Temps,
Près d'un fleuve arrive et s'ecrie :
　Prenez pitié de mes vieux ans.　　　*Count de Ségur.*

THE summer sun was setting fast,
　When, lo ! an aged Pilgrim came
Unto a pleasant river's banks,—
　TIME was the traveller's name.
" Hasten, hasten—while I speak,
　The sands within the glass are flying,
Come and ferry me across "—
　Thus the traveller kept crying.

On the other side, a youthful band
　Unto the pilgrim listen'd :
And many a foot ran o'er the sand,
　And many an eye of beauty glisten'd ;
While merry LOVE began to loosen
　His bark with a joyful chime ;
" He sinketh oft," sigh'd a wiser voice,
　" Who sails in a boat with TIME."

Now LOVE upon the stream is rowing,
　And soon to TIME he draweth nigh,
And TIME leaps in, and they are going,
　Unmindful of the wind or sky ;
His light oars through the waters flash,
　And still the burden of his song :
" See, shepherd-maids, how pleasantly
　LOVE sails with TIME along."

But fainting LOVE grew weary soon,
　(Alas ! he had done so before !)
Then TIME unto the mirthful tune
　Began to ply the oar.
" Alas ! poor child, how weak thou art !
　How soon thy powers decay !
How soon toil chills thy bounding heart !
　HOW SOON WITH TIME LOVE DIES AWAY !"

MEMOIRS OF LORD CLIVE.

SECOND ARTICLE.

THE fruits of the victory at Plassey, were, as we have already observed, of the most important character. Meer Jaffier found himself in peaceable possession (shortly after secured by the assassination of Suraj-u-Dowlah) of the palace, treasures, and authority of his master; but he refused, Clive states, to seat himself on the musnud, till placed upon it it by him: thus acknowledging, in the most public manner, his obligations to the English. The terms of a treaty were agreed upon, which stipulated, on the part of the new Nawab, a confirmation of all the grants and privileges in the treaty of the late Nawab; an alliance, offensive and defensive, against all enemies; the expulsion of the French; the payment of a crore of rupees (a million sterling) to the Company, to cover losses and expenses of the campaign, besides seventy-seven lacs to the sufferers at the loss of Calcutta; the entire property of all lands within, and for 600 yards without, the Mahratta Ditch, to be vested in the Company, as well as the zemindary of the country to the south of Calcutta as far as Calpee, &c. To defray this demand of 177 lacs, there were but 150 lacs in the treasury; and it was arranged that half the demand should be paid down in money and valuables, and the other half in three annual instalments. Mr. Mill has painted, in the warm colours of his fancy, the disappointment of the English at the scantiness of the Bengal treasury; he supposes that Clive and his party, " accustomed to a fond and literal belief of oriental exaggeration on the subject of Indian riches, with great difficulty were brought to admit so hateful a truth."

This, however, was not the only tax which Meer Jaffier had to pay for his elevation to the throne. A donation of fifty lacs was made to the army and navy, besides a gift* to each of the members of the Secret Committee and of Council; and, in addition to these sums, he was induced, " by gratitude and feeling, as well as by usage," to make liberal presents to those who had been the immediate instruments of placing him on the throne: Clive's share of the latter was stated by himself at £160,000.

Viewing these gifts with our present jealous and prudent notions in regard to pecuniary transactions between native princes and officers of the government, we should necessarily pronounce a severe condemnation upon the conduct of the recipients; but, at that period, gifts were not only received openly, but without the slightest impression that there was any culpability attached thereto. Between the act of a modern resident at a native court, who barters his power and patronage for a secret bribe, and that of a servant of the Company who, without violating any law or precept, openly received a present from a native prince, for no breach of duty or confidence, there is not the slighest analogy. This distinction is not always borne in mind.

But there is an incident in this affair, which has been distorted by Mr. Mill into a charge against Lord Clive of the blackest kind; we refer to

* To Clive £28,000—to each member of the Committee £24,000.

the treatment of the merchant Omichund, to whom we have already alluded. The details of this incident have been dissected in so full and skilful a manner by an able coadjutor of ours (now no more), in some strictures upon Mr. Mill's history,* and who has demonstrated the injustice of the charge against Clive, that we might, on the present occasion, pass it by ; but that a notice of the career of Clive would be thereby imperfect.

Omichund was established at the court of the Nawab Suraj-u-Dowlah, as a native agent.　He was a man of the most insatiable avarice, and being in the possession of immense wealth, had great influence at Moorshedabad. When the intrigues were maturing against Suraj-u-Dowlah, Omichund became of necessity privy to it; and his avarice was the only anchorage-ground by which he could be fixed in his fidelity to the party opposed to the Nawab.　Both Meer Jaffier and Mr. Watts, the British resident, had doubts of Omichund ; the success or failure of this enterprize was considered by this sordid individual as secondary to the promotion of his present interest, and he was prepared to take any course that would be subservient to his avarice.　Omichund had been a loser at Calcutta, and he contrived, at the time he was in concert with the conspirators, to extract from the Nawab, on the ground of his feigned attachment to him, four lacs of rupees, the estimated amount of his losses.　When the intrigues were ripe, and all was prepared for action, Omichund came to Mr. Watts, and threatened instant discovery of the plot †, unless he should receive thirty lacs of rupees (£300,000), as for reimbursement of losses, and reward of services.　Under the dread of discovery, Watts, in great alarm, soothed Omichund with promises, while he conveyed intelligence to Clive.　It was obvious that there was no alternative between submitting to the exorbitant terms of this man, whom no honest ties could bind ; or of deceiving him into a belief that he should receive the full amount of his extravagant and dishonest demands.　No man would think it a violation of moral duty to preserve his own life from a highwayman, by signing an obligation to pay whatever sum he required, and to refuse payment when the danger is over.　Clive viewed Omichund (the extent of whose villainy he was long unwilling to believe), from the position he had taken, as a public enemy, and considered every artifice that could deceive him to be not only desirable, but just and proper.

" I have your last letter," he observes to Mr. Watts, in his communication on this subject, " including the articles of agreement.　I must confess the tenor of them surprised me much.　I immediately repaired to Calcutta ; and, at a committee held, both the admirals and gentlemen agree that Omichund is the greatest villain upon earth ; and that now he appears in the strongest light, what he was always suspected to be, a villain in grain.　However, to counterplot this scoundrel, and at the same time to give him no room to suspect our intentions, enclosed you will receive two forms of agreement; the one real, to be strictly kept by us ; the other fictitious.　In short, this affair

* See *As. Journ.* O. S., Vol. xxvii. p. 535.
† " Secure to me, under a sealed treaty, thirty lacs of rupees, or I will this night inform the Nabob of your plot for his dethronement, and have you all put to death," was the direct emphatic meaning, if not the exact words, of his speech to Mr. Watts.

concluded, Omichund will be treated as he deserves. This you will acquaint Meer Jaffier with."

Two treaties were accordingly framed; one real, the other fictitious. In the former there was no mention of Omichund; the latter had an article which expressly stipulated that he should receive twenty lacs of rupees; and Mr. Watts was desired to inform him, that "thirty lacs" was not inserted, as it might give rise to suspicion; but that a commission of five per cent. should be given to him upon all sums received from the nabob, which would fully amount to the other ten lacs.

When the real treaty was disclosed to Omichund, after the danger was over, the effect may be readily conceived: he was (Mr. Orme states) overwhelmed by it. "He fainted on the spot, was carried home, evinced symptoms of a disturbed reason, and subsequently went upon a pilgrimage to a holy Hindu shrine, near Maulda, whence he returned in a state of idiotism, from which he never recovered."

This transaction,—which, though, tried by the rigid rules of an austere morality, it may not be wholly defensible, is justifiable as a political expedient, dictated by stern necessity,—is described by Mr. Mill in the blackest colours, as the essence of treachery—Omichund's treachery being suppressed, and even his exorbitant avarice palliated or mitigated by a comparison between him and men "whose minds were in such a state, that the great demands of Omichund did literally appear a crime."

The battle of Plassey, and the subversion of the power of Suraj-u-Dowlah, afforded scope for the development of that political sagacity which formed the most striking and elevated quality of Clive's mind. He had long foreseen (as we have already observed) that a period must arrive when the Company would be constrained to assume a political character, and become, as he expresses it, "nabobs in fact, if not in name." That critical period had now arrived; the foundation of our Indian empire was now laid, and the goodly superstructure is attributable to the foresight, the skill, and the prudence of Clive.

From the period of the capture of Chandernagore, (says Sir John Malcolm), till Meer Jaffier was established upon the throne, Clive was unaided in the great and difficult task he had undertaken. He rested solely upon his own judgment, which in almost all cases was in opposition to that of the persons with whom he was associated.

Admiral Watson, though he had withdrawn himself from any participation in the enterprize, stated honestly and decidedly his doubts of its success. The Select Committee of Calcutta threw off all responsibility. Thus unaided and alone, Clive had to counteract treachery, to stimulate timidity into action, and when the period arrived, openly and boldly to confront danger. He was, throughout this arduous labour, supported by the conviction, that the end he sought was indispensable to the interests, and indeed to the safety, of the government he served, and that the means he employed were the only ones by which it would be accomplished. With this conviction, he proceeded towards his object with a caution and firmness that have seldom been equalled, and never surpassed.

His success was great beyond all expectation; but it has been erroneously attributed to the battle of Plassey. It was not the result of that action, but of the whole series of his measures, and of the operation of well-laid plans carried into execution by the same wise and firm mind by which they had been formed.

One of the difficulties which Clive had to contend with, at this juncture, arose from disputes in the army as to the division of the prize-money, the military officers being disinclined to allow the navy to share. The conduct of Clive was, as usual, prompt and straightforward; his letter to the officers exhibits the openness and decision of his character; it produced an immediate acknowledgment of error on their part, which was followed by a return to friendly feelings on the part of Clive.

Before we enter upon the subsequent parts of his career, it may be well to exhibit the sentiments of Sir John Malcolm upon the military character of this extraordinary personage, which has been somewhat damaged by the strictures of mere professional critics.

It has already been shown (he observes), that throughout this eventful period, the military operations of Clive were subordinate to his political negociations. But, independent of this fact, which placed his conduct as a military officer beyond the common rules of judgment, I confess that I have little faith in the correctness of that general criticism, which refers exclusively to the numbers and quality of the troops engaged, and to the ground upon which the conflict was decided. Even in Europe, where the character of the troops is known, and their fidelity to their banners undoubted, it is much oftener the genius of the commander, exercised during the changing moments of a battle, than the best preconcerted plan, which decides the combat. The mere tactician rests entirely on his plans; if they fail, he is lost: but the eye of an able leader penetrates the mind of his own army and that of the enemy, and by exciting valour to extraordinary efforts, or pressing upon faltering opponents, he snatches a victory, which is the more glorious from having been gained contrary to all calculations of art. In India, success in war depends far less upon plans and evolutions, than on a correct knowledge of the nature of the enemy's force. The character and composition of the incongruous materials, of which eastern armies are formed, have already been explained. From some part of this body the most resolute resistance may be expected, from their attachment to their chief. Others, probably from being lukewarm in the cause, and discontented with their leader, require only a pretext to fly. No corps places confidence in, or expects support from, that which is next to it. The consequence is, that the mere suspicion of treachery, or any misfortune or misconduct in the prince under whom these bands are for the moment united, dissolves the whole. These facts will account for the frequent defeat of large armies in India by a few disciplined and united men. Yet the armies thus discomfited contain thousands of the same tribes and nations, of whom a few hundreds (when attached to their chiefs and loyal to the cause for which they fought) have been found to resist, with the aid of very slight defences, all the efforts of a large and highly disciplined European force.

One of the grounds upon which Clive's conduct has been arraigned is, the wealth which he acquired by the revolution which placed Meer Jaffier on the throne; and, undoubtedly, if that wealth was obtained in a dishonest or even an equivocal manner, it would leave a stain upon his character which his services, splendid as they were, could not efface. But we have already said enough upon this head to exculpate him from a charge which sprung, in the first instance, from envy, and his present biographer has fully cleared him from any imputation upon this score. He observes :

His acceptance of this reward (as it was termed) of his labours and success, was open and avowed ; and though subsequently made the subject of a charge against him, we do not find that at the time any one arraigned, either the amount of the donation, or the principle of receiving it. The fact is, that at that epoch of our Indian-government, the public officers of the Company had very limited salaries : their perquisites and advantages, when employed on civil, military, or political stations, appear to have been such as had been enjoyed by native functionaries, performing the duties to which they, in times of conquest and revolution, had succeeded. These, on ordinary occasions, were derived from a per-centage on particular branches of revenue, privileges of trade, or presents from inferiors, and were always considerable ; but when such events occurred as negociating a peace, or replacing a monarch upon a throne, the money, gifts, and territorial grants to the chief instruments of such changes, were limited only by the moderation of one party and the ability of the other.

It is evident that Clive did not imagine that he violated any duty or engagements in accepting these presents. He made no secret of them, or of their amount, either in his own official or private letters. In writing to Mr. Payne,* he says, speaking of these presents: " I never made the least secret of this affair, but always thought the world ought to be acquainted with the Nabob's generosity. If I had been disposed to grow rich by receiving presents from any other hands but those of the Nabob, surely no one had ever the like opportunity ; but there is not that man living, among the daily temptations which offered, who can accuse me of receiving any thing of value but from the Nabob himself." But what is more to the point, the Court of Directors themselves, in their letter to the Secret Committee of Bengal,† fully recognized the usage of receiving presents by public servants, and added, " we do not intend, by this, to break in upon any sums of money which have been given by the Nabob to particular persons, by way of free gift or in reward of their services."

Sir John Malcolm has related a remarkable anecdote on this head. A gentleman of high respectability, who had filled an official station in India, stated to the present Lord Powis, that, it being known that he was on personal grounds discontented with his father, he was summoned, in 1773, as a witness before the Parliamentary committee appointed to investigate the charges against Lord Clive, and he added, that when Governor Johnstone, in the committee, observed, that it had been proved that his Lordship had received upwards of £100,000 after the battle of Plassey, Lord Clive calmly replied, that he had received a much larger sum ; " but," said he, " when I recollect entering the Nabob's treasury at Moorshedabad, with heaps of gold and silver to the right and left, and these crowned with jewels (striking his hand violently on his head), by God, at this moment, do I stand astonished at my own moderation !"

It is no imputation upon the judgment of Clive that Meer Jaffier was

* 25th December, 1757.   † 8th March, 1758.

soon found to be deficient as a ruler. Accident had placed him foremost in the avenue to the throne, and English influence was not yet sufficiently strong to regulate, at it does at present, the affairs of native durbars. Meer Jaffier, however, had one redeeming quality; he was grateful to the man through whose instrumentality he had been placed on the musnud.

Clive's departure for Calcutta was the signal for dissention at the court of the Nawab; and the vizier of Oude, Suja-u-Dowlah, threatened his frontier. Mr. Scrafton urged Clive to return to Moorshedabad, as the Nawab had evaded compliance with several of the most important articles of the treaty, and his presence, with or without an army, appeared the only means of averting ruin. Clive's answer was brief and decisive : " I shall march," said he, " with the whole army."

He accordingly joined the Nawab, and conferred with him on the state of his affairs. His letter to the Select Committee of the Court of Directors gives a very clear account of the condition of the prince's government, and of the measures adopted for its settlement. Clive remarks that " the Nabob is a prince of little capacity, and devoid of the talent of gaining the love and confidence of his principal officers; that his mismanagement threw the country into confusion, and, but for our own known attachment to him, he would have been hurled from the throne." He states his determination to procure assignments on the revenues for the payment of the money still due by treaty, which would render the Company less dependent upon the prince and his ministers. Clive had a more difficult part to perform in adjusting the disputes between the Nawab and his subordinates, especially Ramnarrain, the ruler of Patna, a Hindu of rank, and who was universally loved and respected. His negociations, however, were successful, and before he quitted Patna, he secured the monopoly of the saltpetre of that province for the Company.

It is not easy, with our present associations and prejudices, duly to appreciate the difficulty of Clive's task in exercising this controlling power over the Nawab. " This was the first instance in Bengal of the power of a proud Mahommedan sovereign being overshadowed by that of a body of merchants, who, before this great change, had never appeared at the court of his predecessors but as humble supplicants, endeavouring to obtain commercial privileges. Many of the nobles and generals by whom the Nabob was surrounded had been, a year or two before, courted by bribes and flattery to protect the persons, or to promote the trade, of the very English agents on whose pleasure or policy their fortune and character now depended. To add to the strong and rankling feeling which such a change must have excited, the Mahommedan prince and his chiefs found themselves deserted by the wary and pliant Hindus, who, possessing greater foresight, and expecting security and advancement from the change of masters, were ready, on the first alarm of danger to their life or property, to seek the protection of the English."

There was an accident in the construction of the English authority in India, which, though complimentary to Clive, was a source of danger. The natives, struck by his commanding talents, ascribed every thing to him; " they considered him as the exclusive author of the success which had attended the English arms; and with his life many expected it to terminate. The existence of such sentiments gave probability to the reports of plots said to have been formed, both at Moorshedabad and at Patna, for his assassination; and he was warned of them by persons who deemed their information authentic."

On Clive's return to Calcutta, a mortification awaited him. The Court of Directors had received his letter, expressing his hope that in a few days he should take his passage for Madras, and accordingly they made an arrangement for the government of Bengal, in which Clive was excluded. The new council, however, with a promptitude which did as much credit to their zeal as to the talents of Colonel Clive, made a tender of the presidentship to him. "Your being named," they say, "as head of the General Committee (in the letter of the 3d of August last), established at that time for conducting the Company's affairs in Bengal, your eminent services, abilities, and merit, together with your superior weight and influence with the present soubah and his officers, are matters which have great force with us on this occasion; and all concur in pointing at you, at the present, as best able to render our honourable employers necessary service at this juncture, till they shall make their further pleasure known by the appointment of a president for their affairs here."

This disinterested tender, by persons of all parties, some of them not friendly to Clive, is a high tribute to the character of the latter. Mr. Mill, however, observes, that it evinced " disregard and contempt for the judgment and authority of their superiors," but which it does not appear that the Directors ever felt or resented.

Clive was much hurt at this apparent mark of distrust: but he ought to have recollected (as well as Mr. Mill), that the Directors supposed he had returned to Madras; and they were, besides, totally ignorant of the events which had so entirely altered the state of affairs in Bengal. The scheme of government, which the court adopted and ordered,—that of nominating a council of ten, the four senior members of which were to preside in rotation, each for four months,—is characterized by Sir John Malcolm as an " extraordinary expedient, which was no doubt the crude offspring of faction and distrust." But he seems to have overlooked the important fact we have just mentioned, and the consideration that the alternate presidency of the senior members, for a short period, had been the previous course, the Company's affairs being then merely of a mercantile character, and conducted upon mercantile principles. As soon as the home authorities were aware of the real state of the facts,[*] and before they knew of the resolution of the Bengal council, they immediately[†] appointed Clive sole president and governor of Fort William. A letter from Mr. Payne, the chairman of the Court, written before the news had reached them,[‡] clearly shews that the Court had no distrust of Clive, and were fully alive to the value of the services he had performed previous to the battle of Plassey. Mr. Payne

---

* In February, 1758.
† 8th March, 1758.   ‡ 11th November, 1757.

states, that he had urged upon Mr. Pitt the propriety of giving Clive higher military rank, and that it had been intended by the Duke of Newcastle to confer upon him some mark of the royal favour; but as this was unaccompanied by a suggestion of a similar honour to Admiral Watson, it was deemed prudent by the Court to discourage it.   Mr. Payne concludes thus: " Be assured, sir, I shall always be as ready to propose as to concur in any measure, that may be hereafter thought of, to do you honour or pleasure; and that it is a great one to me to reflect, that your attention to the service you are engaged in, by exposing your person on so many different occasions, may and has been attended not only with the honour and laurels that adorn the brow of a conqueror, but with some more solid fruits of your labour; which may in some degree compensate for the toils that precede victory and success.'

The ticklish state of affairs in Bengal and in the Deccan made Clive anxious, before his departure for Europe, to place them on a better footing. He succeeded in inducing the Nawab to pay him a visit at Calcutta, which he thought would make a useful impression upon both friends and enemies. Colonel Forde was in the Deccan, with a fine detachment, and Warren Hastings was selected to succeed Mr. Scrafton as resident at the court of Moorshedabad.   Nothing (as we have before remarked) affords a more decided test of the elevated character of Clive than the discernment displayed in the selection of fit persons to carry his plans into effect.   Warren Hastings was not more than twenty-five when he was appointed to this arduous and responsible situation, rendered still more difficult by the task imposed upon him of upholding the authority of Roy Dullub, the minister, in opposition to that prince's secret dislike of him.

In February 1760, Clive quitted India.

We have been constrained, in reviewing this important period of the history of Clive and of British India, to extend our observations to a greater length than we expected.   It has been our object to show, that the foundation of our territorial power in India originated from the foresight and prudence of Clive; that this scheme was not an accident, surprising him unexpectedly, or happening in spite of his endeavour to avoid it, but the result of a deliberate design to convert the Company into lords paramount of India, it being really an event compounded of both, discerned by the master-mind of Clive whilst in embryo, and brought to maturity by his skill neither sooner nor later than it ought to have been; that his character in the delicate transactions in which he was employed, notwithstanding temptations of no ordinary kind, stands free from imputation, and that his employers are not chargeable with conduct towards Clive, which would either justify suspicions against his integrity, or imply the blackest ingratitude on their part.

CHINESE ACCOUNT OF INDIA.*

Tĕen-choo (or India) was known in the time of the latter Hans; the country was then called the Kingdom of *Shin-too.*†

Note of the Chinese Editor.

Chang-kĕen, when first sent (B.C. 126) into Ta-hea (or Bactriana), saw stems of bamboos, as in the Shoo country (modern province of Sze-chuen). He inquired how they obtained these bamboos; some men of Ta-hea replied: "Our merchants procure them in the markets of the kingdom of Shin-too, which is Tĕen-choo. Some call this kingdom Mo-kea-to;‡ others name it Po-lo-mun (country of the brahmans); it is situated to the south of the Tsung-ling§ (or Blue Mountains), distant some thousands of *le* to the south-east of the Yuĕ-che‖ (Massagetæ, or Indo-Scythians).

This country is about 30,000 square *le*¶ in extent; it is divided internally into five Indias; the first is termed Middle or Central India; the second Eastern India; the third Southern India; the fourth Western India; and the fifth Northern India. Each of these divisions of the territory contains several thousands of *le*; and fortified cities, surrounded with walls, and towns of the second order, are placed a few hundred *le* apart.

Southern India is bounded by the Great Sea (the Gulf of Bengal); Northern India is situated opposite to the Snowy Mountains;** on the four sides, there are mountains sloping to the south, and a valley which crosses them forms the gate (or entrance) of the kingdom. Eastern India is bounded on the east by the Great Sea, as well as by Foo-nan (Pegu) and Lin-e (Siam), which are separated only by a little sea. Western India adjoins Ke-pin (Cophenes) and Po-sze (Persia);†† Central India is situated in the middle of the four other divisions of India.

All these kingdoms had kings in the time of the Han dynasty. There is besides the kingdom of Yuen-too, which is distant from Chang-gan‡‡ 9,800 *le*; it is 2,800 *le* from the residence of the Governor-general of the Chinese provinces in Central Asia.§§ To the south it adjoins the Blue Mountains; to the north its frontiers are contiguous to those of the Woo-sun.

Yăn-sze-koo has stated that Yuen-too is no other than Shin-too; and Shin-too is Tĕen-choo; there is no difference but in the pronunciation more or less strong.

From the kingdom called Kaou-foo¶¶ of the Yuĕ-che, going to the west and

* Translated from the *Wăn-hĕen-t'hung-kaou*, or 'Deep Researches into Ancient Monuments;' by Ma-twan-lin; book 338, fol. 14.

† In Sanscrit सिन्धु , *Sindhi*, Hindustan.

‡ मगध *Magadha.*

§ A chain of mountains to the north of Cashmere, which separates Eastern Turkestan, or Little Bucharia, from Great Bucharia.

¶ M. Rémusat has given a translation of Ma-twan-lin's account of the Yuĕ-che in his *Nouv. Mélanges Asiat.*, t. i. p. 220.

¶ According to Dr. Kelly (*Orient. Metrol.*, p. 64), 200 *le* are equal to one degree of the meridian = 69·166 E. miles; whence 30,000 *le* will give about 10,375 English miles.

** *Seuĕ-shan*, an exact translation of the Sanscrit हिमालय *Himálaya*, ' abode of snow,' or rather हिमालगिरि *Himálagiri*, ' mountain whereon the snow rests.' This division of India must include the modern Cashmere, the description of which, by Masúdi, the Arabian historian, coincides in a striking manner with that of the Chinese author: "The kingdom of Cashmere," he says, " which forms part of India, is surrounded with very high mountains; it contains a prodigious number of towns and villages; it can be entered only by a single pass, which is closed by a gate."

†† See for an account of these countries by Ma-twan-lin, the translation by M. Rémusat, *Nouv. Mél. Asiat.*, t. i. p. 205 and 248.

‡‡ Capital of the Hans, situated in Shen-se; now Se-gan-foo.

§§ This position of the kingdom of Yuen-too affords reason to think that it may be the same as that of Shin-too. It is only in the transcription of the Sanscrit word *Sindhi*, the name of the Indus and of the countries bathed by that river, that there is a slight difference. The proximity of the Woo-sun, however, suggests that Yuen-too must comprehend the country in which modern Badakshan is situated.

¶¶ The following account of this kingdom is given by Ma-twan-lin elsewhere (b. 338, f. 27): " The kingdom of Kaou-foo was known in the time of the Hans. It is situated to the south-east of the great Yuĕ-

south, as far as the Western Sea (the Indian Ocean); to the east, as far as Pan-ke; all these countries form the territory of Shin-too. It has a number of fortified towns, in about a hundred, commandants reside. There are also different kingdoms; ten of them have kings. There is, however, little difference between them, and the whole have the collective denomination of Shin-too.

Note of the Chinese Editor.

The narrative of Foo-nan states: "The kingdom of She-wei (Kapila) belongs to that of Kea-she* in India, which some call the kingdom of Pho-lo-nae, and others the kingdom of Sze (or) She-pho-lo-na-sze.

Choo-fa-wei, in his *Fŭh-kwŏ-ke* (Memoir on the kingdoms of Fŭh, or Buddha), states that the kingdom of Pho-lo-nae (or Benares) is situated 1,480 *le* south of the kingdom of Kea-wei-lo-wei (or Kapila). In the account of the kingdom of Ching-le by She-fă, it is said : " Few oxen are killed in this kingdom ; the sheep of the country are black ; their horns, which are slender and apart, may be four feet long ; one is killed about every ten days, but if any of these sheep happen to die of disease, the inhabitants use the blood of bullocks. These animals live a long time ; the people of this country likewise are very long-lived. Their kings commonly reign a hundred years, and the bullocks live as long as the men. This kingdom is a dependency of India.

The royal residence overlooks the river Hăng or Găng (Ganges)† which some call Kea-pĭh-le. Here is situated the mountain Ling-tseaou ; called in the language of the Hoo-yu country, Ke-too-keu : it is a green rock, the head (or summit) of which resembles that of the bird *tseaou.*

Note of the Chinese Editor.

Choo-fă-wei says, in his *Fŭh-kwŏ ke*, that this mountain is situated to the south of Mo-kĕĕ-te,‡ which is also a kingdom dependent on India.

At the period§ when all these kingdoms belonged to the Yŭĕ-che, the latter

---

Yŭĕ-che (Massagetæ). It is likewise a considerable state. Their manners resemble those of the inhabitants of India, and they are gentle and humane. They carry on much commerce. India, Cophenes, and the country of the Asæ, are three kingdoms which are *conquered by force and lost by weakness.*" The latter expressions are borrowed from the *Taou-tĭh-king* of Laou-tsze.

• वाशी *Kăsi* or *Kăshĭ*, ' splendid,' epithet of the sacred city of Benares, called वरणसी *Varanasi* or वरणासी *Varanăsĭ.* The latter denomination is represented as closely as is permitted by the monosyllabic language of the Chinese (which wants the articulation *ra*) by *Pho-lo-nae :* the Sanscrit व *v* having so often the sound of ब *b*, that they are not distinguished from each other in Bengáli writing : *Sze* (or) *She-pho-lo-na-sze* is also a faithful transcript of श्रीवरणासी *Srĭ Varanăsĭ*, ' the holy, the fortunate Benares.'

† In Sanscrit गङ्ग *Gangá ;* this river, in sacred writings, bears also the name of कपिल *Kapila*, and more commonly कपिलधारा *Kapiladhărá.*

‡ मगध *Magadha*, the southern portion of the modern Bahar.

§ This important epoch in the history of India may be fixed with precision by means of Chinese historians ; and it is not one of the least advantages derivable from the study of the writers of this nation. Ma-twan-lin, in his account of the Great Yŭĕ-che, or Indo-Scythians (book 338, fol. 2), states that the Chinese general Chang-kĕen was sent as an ambassador to the Yŭĕ-che by the emperor Woo-to (B.C. 126), and that, about 100 years after, a prince of this nation, who possessed one of the five governments of the country of the Dahæ, subjected the Getæ in Cophenes, and that Tĕen-choo, or India, was again subjugated by the Yŭĕ-che. This other conquest of India by the Scythians must be placed, therefore, about the year B.C. 26. Ma-twan-lin adds, that these Yŭĕ-che, having become rich and powerful (by these conquests), remained in this state till the time of the latter Hans, who began to reign A.D. 222. It results from hence that the Scythians (or Yŭĕ-che) must have been masters of Western India from about B.C. 96 till A.D. 222, that is, for a space of 948 years. The first invasion of India by the Yŭĕ-che, or Scythians, must have taken place before the reign of Vicramáditya, whose celebrated era, which begins fifty-six years before ours, originated from the complete defeat of the Scythian armies by this Indian prince; an event which deserved to be thus immortalized. See *Indian Algebra* by Mr. Colebrooke (Preface, p. 43), and Lassen, *De Pentapotamid Indiæ Commentatio*, p. 56. The first of these learned Indianists,

put their kings to death and substituted military chiefs. They enjoined all their people to practise the doctrine of Fŭh-too (Buddha); not to kill living creatures; to abstain from wine; and to conform entirely to the manners and customs of the inhabitants of the country, which is low and damp, and the temperature very hot. This kingdom is traversed by large rivers; the people fight upon elephants; they are of a feeble constitution compared with the Yuĕ-che.

The emperor Woo-te, of the Hans (B.C. 142 to 87), sent an expedition of about ten persons, by the west and south, in search of Shin-too. All information having been refused to the persons composing this expedition, they could not reach the country.* Under Ho-te (A.D. 89 to 106), several ambassadors from that country came to offer tribute.† The western countries (subjected to the Chinese) then revolted, and separated from the empire.

In the second of the years *Yan-he* of Hwan-te (A.D. 159) strangers often came by the way of Jĭh-nan ('south of the sun;' Tonquin and Cochin China), to offer presents.

A tradition of this time relates that the emperor Ming-te (A D. 58 to 76), having dreamed that he saw a man of gold, very large, whose head and neck shone with prodigious brightness, interrogated his ministers on the subject. One of them told him that, in the western region (*se-fang*), was a spirit (*shin*), whose name was Fŭh; that his statue was six feet high, and his colour that of gold. The emperor, upon this, despatched ambassadors to India to learn the laws and doctrine of Fŭh, and to bring to China his portrait painted, as well as some of his statues. The king of Tsoo (a petty feudatory kingdom of China), named Ying, was the first who believed in this false doctrine (of Fŭh); hence it was that other persons in the Middle Empire adopted it.

Thereupon, Hwan-te (A.D. 147 to 167) imbibed a great partiality for the *shin* (spirits or genii); he sacrificed repeatedly to Fŭh-too and to Laou-tsze. The people of China gradually adopted (this new religion): its followers augmented greatly.

In the time of the How and Tsin dynasties (A.D. 222 to 280), no new relation took place between India and China; it was not till the period of the Woo dynasty, that the king of Foo-nan, named Fan-chăn, sent one of his relations, named Soo-wĭh, as ambassador to India. On quitting Foo-nan, the embassy returned by the mouth of the Taou-keaou-le,‡ continuing its route by sea in the great bay (or Gulf of Martaban), in a north-westerly direction; it then entered the bay (of Bengal), which they crossed, and coasted the frontiers of several kingdoms. In about a year, it was able to reach the mouth of the river of India, and ascended the river 7,000 *le*, when it arrived at its destination. The king of India, astonished at the sight of the strangers, exclaimed: "the sea-coast is very far off; how could these men get here?" He commanded that

dismists, from whom we are sure of deriving information, whenever we are engaged in the investigation of a great philological, scientific, and philosophical question respecting India, cites an ancient scholiast on Varáha Mihira, who thus explains the word "sakas" employed by this astronomer to denote the Samvat era: "epoch when the barbarian kings named *Sakas* (the *Sacæ*) were defeated by Vicramáditya."

* This same emperor gained some trifling particulars respecting Shin-too, or India, by his general Chang-kĕen, whom he had sent to the Yuĕ-che, which are preserved by the historian Sse-ma-tsĕen, in his *Sse-ke* (book 123, fols. 6 and 7), where it is stated that Shin-too is situated to the east of Ta-hea, the capital of which was the city of Lan-she.

† At this period, China was still considered as the paramount state of all the half-civilized nations inhabiting Central Asia. It is not, therefore, surprising, that the chiefs of India subject to the Yuĕ-che, or Scythians, should have thought of sending ambassadors to China, in search of means of delivering their country from barbarians, by the aid of the Chinese armies, which could oblige their revolted subjects to return to their duty. Thus we may easily explain facts apparently so improbable.

‡ The Irrawaddy, in the Burman empire.

the ambassadors should be shown the interior of the kingdom, and with this view, he appointed as guides to attend him, two strangers of the same race as the Chinese,* and he supplied Soo-wĭh (the ambassador) with provisions for his journey and presents for Fan-chăn, king of Foo-nan, consisting of Scythian horses, and four pieces of valuable woollen stuffs.†

During this time, the Woo dynasty‡ despatched an officer of the second rank, named Kang-tae, as ambassador to Foo-nan, where he saw foreign guides of the same nation as the Chinese. To all the questions he put to them, concerning the manners and customs of the people of India, they answered him as follows: " The doctrine of Fŭh is that which is in vogue in this kingdom. The population is very numerous; the soil rich and fertile. The king who rules here has the title of Maou-lun ;§ the suburbs of the fortified city in which he resided are watered by rivulets, which flow on all sides, and fill the deep ditches surrounding the city. Below it flows the great river (the Ganges). All the palaces are covered with sculptured inscriptions, and other ornaments in relief. A winding street forms a market, a *le* in length. The dwelling-houses have several stories.‖ Bells and drums are their instruments of music, and the dress of the people is adorned with fragrant flowers. They travel by land and by water; their commercial transactions are considerable, in jewels and other valuable articles of luxury, and every thing which the heart can desire is procurable here. On every side, to the right and to the left, you behold only agreeable and seductive objects; the houses are overshadowed by foliage, and cooled by the motion of waters of all kinds. There are sixteen great kingdoms which are remote from India; some distant 2,000 *le* ; others 3,000. All these kingdoms honour and respect India, which they regard as placed between heaven and earth."

The fifth of the years *yuen-kea* of Wăn-te, of the Sungs (A.D. 428), the king of the kingdom of Kea-pĭh-le (Kapila) in India, named Yuĕ-gae ('beloved of the moon'¶), sent an ambassador to him to present him with letters of submission (*peaou*), and to offer diamonds, valuable rings, bracelets, as well as other ornaments of worked gold, and two parrots, one red and the other white.

The second of the years *tae-she* of Ming-te (A.D. 466), an ambassador came to offer tribute. This ambassador had the rank of lieutenant-general of the army.

Note of the Chinese Editor.

The eighteenth of the years *yuen-kea* (A.D. 441), the king of the kingdom of Soo-mo-le sent an ambassador to offer the products of his country. The second of the years *heaou-kŭen*, of the emperor Heaou-woo (A.D. 455), the king of the kingdom of

---

* Literally: "in consequence, as attendants or guides (he had given to him) two men, foreigners, of the same species as the Sung." By *Sung-jin*, 'men of Sung,' Ma-twan-lin designates the Chinese, who were so called in his time; he wrote under the Sung dynasty, in the latter part of the thirteenth century. The sense which 陳 *chin* has received is that which it bears in the phraseology of the *Lo-ke*, cited by the dictionary of Kang-he, in explaining this character.

† 四疋 *Sze-pei.*

‡ One of the three dynasties which reigned simultaneously over three divisions of the Chinese empire : it subsisted from A.D. 222 to 280.

§ This title must be the Chinese transcription of महारण *Mahdrana* ; there can be no doubt in respect to the first syllable, *maha* (in composition) 'great ;' but the Sanscrit word reprented by *hen* (or *run*, *ran*) is less certain. At all events, this must be a king of India whose reign corresponded with this date, between A.D. 222 and 280.

‖ This is the case at Benares, where many of the houses have seven or eight stories ; and the numerous temples and public edifices are covered with sculptures and bas reliefs.

¶ In Sanscrit, *Chandrakánta*, ' well-beloved of the moon,' a name also given to a precious stone; or rather it would be *Chandrananda*, ' joy or delight of the moon,' cited in the fifth table of the *Ayeen Akbery*, in the history of Cashmere.

Kin-to-le*. sent a superior officer to offer gold coin and precious vases. On the first of the years *yuen-wei*, of Fei-te (A.D. 473), the kingdom of Pho-le (?) sent an ambassador to offer tribute. All these kingdoms practised the doctrine of Fŭb.

In the beginning of the years *tëen-këen* of the dynasty Leang (A.D. 502), the king of India, named Keu-to, sent his great officer, named Choo-lo-ta, to present letters of submission, and to offer vases of crystal, perfumes of all sorts, precious talismans, and other articles of this kind.

This kingdom (India) is traversed by great rivers.† The spring or source, Sin-taou,‡ issues from mount Kwăn-lun;§ its waters then divide into five streams, and form what are termed the affluents of the Ganges (*ming Găng shwuy*). Their waters are sweet and beautiful, and at the bottom of their bed they deposit a real salt, the colour of which is as white as that of the essence of the water (*shwuy tsing*).

In the time of Seuen-woo, of the dynasty of the latter Wei (A.D. 500 to 516), South India sent an ambassador to offer as presents some horses of a fine breed. This ambassador stated that the kingdom produced lions, leopards, panthers, camels, rhinoceroses, and elephants; that there was a species of pearl there, called *ho-tse*, similar to talc (*yun-moo*), the colour of which was yellowish red (*tse*, 'reddish blue'); if it is divided, it disperses like the wings of the cricket; if it is heaped up, on the other hand, it becomes compact, like threads of silk strongly woven. There were diamonds resembling amethysts (*tse-shih-ying*). When purified a hundred times in the fire, without melting, this diamond is used to cut jasper (*yu* stone). There were also tortoiseshell (*tae-mei*), gold (*kin*), copper (*tung*), iron (*tëĕ*), lead (*yuen*), tin (*seih*), fine muslins embroidered with gold and silver;‖ there are also a variety of odoriferous plants, *yŭh-kin*, sugar-canes, and all kinds of products; honey-bread (or solid honey¶), pepper, ginger, and black salt.

On the west, India carries on a considerable commerce by sea with Tatsin (the Roman empire), the An-se (or Asæ, Syrians); some of the Indians come as far as Foo-nan and Keaou-che (Tonquin) to traffic in coral necklaces and pearls of inferior quality (or which only resemble pearls—*san-kan*). These merchants are accustomed to dispense with books of accounts (in their commer-

---

* The *Gandari* of Herodotus and Strabo ? In Sanscrit गन्धरि *Gandhari*, or गन्धर *Gandhara.*

† " *Kuŏ lin ta keang,*" literally, ' the kingdom overlooks great rivers.'

‡ These curious details, the exactitude of which may excite surprise, prove that the Chinese historians were better informed than might be expected of facts and circumstances concerning Central and Western Asia. We are indebted to Mr. Colebrooke for the means of ascertaining the accuracy of the Chinese writer. In fact, the Chinese words *Sin-taou* are but the transcription of the Sanscrit word सीता *Sítá*, the name of one of the sources of the Ganges. In a memoir on the sources of this river, this illustrious and profound Indian scholar cites the following passage from the astronomer Bháskara Achárya: " The holy stream which escapes from the foot of Vishnu, descends from the abode of Vishnu on Mount Meru (the Kwăn-lun), whence it divides into four currents, and passing through the air, it reaches the lakes on the summit of the mountains which sustain them. Under the name of *Sítá*, this river joins the Bhadráswa; as the *Alakanandá*, it enters Bharatavarsha (Hindostan); as the *Chackshu*, it proceeds to Ketumala, and as the *Bhadra*, it goes to the Kuru of the'north."—*Siddhánta-Sirómani; Bhavana-Kosha*, 37 and 38.

§ Mount Meru. " The Hindus say that the Ganges falls from heaven upon its summit, and thence descends in four currents; the southern branch is the Ganges of India; the northern branch, which flows into Turkey, is the Bhadrasámá; the eastern branch is the Sítá, and the western is the Chakshu, or Oxus."—Watson, Sanscrit Dict., 2d edit., art. *Meru*. The name *Meru* is the Μηρος of the Greeks.

‖ These are, no doubt, the fine brocades, embroidered with gold and silver, for which Benares is still so celebrated, which continue to constitute an extensive article of commerce throughout India, and which European industry, however successful its efforts to imitate the products of the East, has not yet been able to rival.

¶ *Shih-meih,* ' stone-honey.'

cial transactions). Teeth (elephants' or rhinoceros'?) and shells form their articles of exchange. They have men very skilful in magical arts.* The greatest mark of respect which a wife can show towards her husband is to kiss his feet and embrace his knees: this is the most energetic and persuasive demonstration of the interior sentiments. In their houses, they have young girls who dance and sing with much skill.† Their king and his ministers (*ta-chin*, ministers about the sovereign) have a vast number of silk dresses and fine woollen fabrics. He dresses his hair on the top of his head‡ (like the Chinese women), and the rest of the hair he cuts, to make it short. Married men also cut their hair, and pierce their ears, to hang valuable rings in them. The general practice is to walk on foot. The colour of their dress is mostly white. The Indians are timid in battle; their weapons are the bow and arrows, and shield; they have also (like the Chinese) flying or winged ladders ;§ and, according as the ground will permit, they follow the rules of the *wooden oxen* and *rolling horses*.‖ They have a written character and a literature, and they are well versed in astronomy or the science of the heavens, in that of numbers, and in astrology. All the men study the instructive books denominated *Seth-than*, written on the leaves of the tree *pei-to*, intended to preserve a record of things.¶

Yang-te, of the Suy dynasty (A.D. 605 to 616), wishing to know the western countries (Se-yu), sent Pei-too to endeavour to determine the boundaries of the kingdoms of Se-fan (ancient Tibet). This envoy traversed many countries, but did not penetrate to India, believing that the emperor had some animosity against the king of this country, whose family was of the race of Ke-le-he, or Cha-le :** at this period, there were no troubles, no revolts in his kingdom.

The grain sowed in the marshy soils ripens four times a year.†† The barley, which grows the highest, exceeds the height of a camel. The women wear ornaments of gold and silver on their head, and necklaces of pearls. The dead are burnt, and the ashes of their bodies are collected and deposited in a place set apart; or they throw them into a waste spot, and sometimes cast

† These are, no doubt, the nautch-girls.

‡ To form the जटा *jatá*. See the laws of Menu, book ii. v. 219, &c.

§ *Fe-ts*; this is a scaling-ladder, of which a representation may be seen in the *Art Militaire Chinois*, figs. 48 and 49.

‖ *Mûh-meaou*, and *low-ma*. These are machines of war, of which we know not the form.

¶ The following is the Chinese text of this important passage :—

The two Chinese characters 悉 曇 *seth-than* are a transcription of the Sanscrit word सिद्धान *Siddhánta*, which signifies 'established truth,' 'demonstrable conclusion,' and which forms the titles of many scientific books, as the *Súrya-Siddhánta*, a celebrated treatise on astronomy; the *Brahma Sidd-hánta*; the *Siddhánta Kaumudí*, &c. The leaves of trees, 貝 多 *pei-to*, are the *olas*, on which most of the Sanscrit MSS. are written, especially those in Telinga characters which come from Southern India. *Pei-to* may be the transcription of पीत *pita*, 'yellow,' or पीतक *pitaka*, the Sanscrit name of the aloe, the leaves of which are well adapted to the purpose indicated by the Chinese author, especially for writing traced with a style.

** That is, the royal and military caste of Kshatriyas; क्षत्रिपतातिं *Kshattriya játi.*

†† *Tsou*, 'grain that is planted amongst water; the paddy of the southern regions.'—*Morrison's Dict.*

them into a river: in this manner, funeral ceremonies with cakes of flesh of birds, wild animals, fish and tortoises, are dispensed with.

Those who excite revolts and foment rebellions are punished with death; slight crimes are expiated by money. A person who has no filial duty (or fails in duty towards his parents), suffers mutilation of hands, feet, nose, ears, and is exiled beyond the frontiers. There is a written character and a literature (in this country); the study of astronomical sciences has made great progress there; there are astronomical books in the *Fan* (or Sanscrit) language; leaves of the *pei-to* are used to preserve a record of things.*

There is a spot in this kingdom, where are said to be, and where are pointed out, ancient vestiges of the foot of Fŭh (or Buddha); in their creed, the followers of this religion affirm that these vestiges of Buddha really exist. They relate that, by carefully reciting certain prayers, they may acquire the shape of dragons, and rise into the clouds.

In the years *woo tih,* of the Tang dynasty (A.D. 618 to 627), there were great troubles in the kingdom. The king, She-lo-ye-to,† made war and fought battles such as had never been seen before. The elephants were not unsaddled in their rapid marches; the soldiers quitted not their shields, because this king had formed the project of uniting the four Indias under his rule. All the provinces which faced the north submitted to him.

At this same period of the Tang dynasty, a zealous follower of Fŭh-too (Buddha), surnamed Heuen-chwang, arrived in this kingdom (of India.) She-lo-ye-to caused him to enter his presence, and said to him: "Your country has produced holy (great) men. The king of Tsin,‡ who has routed the armies of his enemies, ought to be well satisfied; he may be compared to me; tell me what sort of man he is?" Heuen-chwang replied by vaunting the exploits of Tae-tsung, who had put down revolt and reduced the four nations of barbarians to submission to him. The Indian prince, full of fire and energy, was highly satisfied with this recital, and observed: "I will send (an embassy) to the court of the emperor of the East."

In fact, in the 15th of the years *ching-kwan* (A.D. 642), ambassadors from the king of the country called Mo-kea-to (Magadha) came to offer books to the emperor (Tae-tsung), who directed that an officer of cavalry of inferior rank, named Leang-hwae-king, should go at a prescribed time to assure the (king of India) of the peace and harmony which subsisted between them. She-lo-ye-to, surprised, inquired of the men of the kingdom (Indians), saying: "From the time of antiquity to the present day, have ambassadors from Mo-ho-chin-tan§ come into our kingdom?" They all replied: "None have hitherto come;

---

* This is a repetition of what has been before said; but, as the object of Ma-twan-lin was to combine all the ancient documents and all the authorities known to him, which could tend to establish a fact, we only see in this a fresh proof of the exactness of the various Chinese accounts. Some of the Sanscrit astronomical treatises were translated into Chinese under the Tang dynasty.

† This proper name might be intended to represent the Sanscrit श्रीरहित *Sri-rahita.* It remains to be seen whether a king of this name reigned in India at this period.

‡ Tsin is the name of the dynasty which reigned over China from B.C. 249 to 202, during which the Chinese power caused it to be known for the first time in Central and Western Asia, its conquests being extended to the Caspian Sea and Bengal, in the reign of Tsin-she-hwang-te, the celebrated Burner of the Books. The name of this dynasty has formed that of *China,* in Sanscrit चीन *China,* which occurs in the Laws of Menu, book x. sl. 44, and therefore at a date anterior to the third century before our era, which may be easily explained in referring the name of *China* to the period of the foundation of the kingdom of Tsin in the western province of Shen-se, about B.C. 1000.

§ In Sanscrit, *Mahá-China,* 'great China;' in the modern dialects of India, *Mahá-Chinestan,* 'the country of great China.'

what is termed the Kingdom of the Middle, is Mo-ho-chin-tan." Whereupon, the king, going to meet the ambassador, bent his knee in token of obedience and respect (*mŏ-pae*) to receive the letter (*chaou-shoo*) of the emperor of China, which he placed on the top of his head. Ambassadors (from the king of Magadha) came again,'and directly, to the court. An imperial order directed an assistant of the department of war, named Le, to take cognizance of the letter of submission (brought by the Indian ambassadors), and to make a report upon it. The ministers reconducted the ambassadors without the city, and it was ordered that in the capital perfume should be burnt as they went along.

She-lo-ye-to, surrounded by his ministers, received, with his face turned to the east, the imperial document (*chaou-shoo*); he again sent a present of pearls of fire (*ho-choo*), *yŭh-kin* plants, and the tree *poo-te.**

The 22d year, of the same period (*i.e.* A.D. 648), the emperor of China sent a superior officer, named Wang-heuen-tse, as ambassador into this kingdom (of Magadha), in order that the principles of humanity and justice, which had been diffused in that country, should have a protector and representative there. But before his arrival, She-lo-ye-to was dead; the people of the kingdom had revolted, and the minister (of the deceased king), named Na-foo-te-o-lo-na-shun, had taken his place. He sent troops to oppose the entry of Heuen-tse (the Chinese ambassador); under these circumstances, the latter took with him some tens of cavalry, and attacked the troops (of the usurper), but could not vanquish them, and his little force was exterminated; and the result was, that the tribute received (by the Chinese ambassadors) in the different kingdoms (he had visited) was taken. Heuen-tse retired alone, with all expedition, to the western frontiers of Too-fan (Tibet); and he ordered (*keaou-chaou*) the neighbouring kingdoms to furnish him with troops.† Too-fan sent him 1,000 armed men; Nёё-po-lo‡ furnished 7,000 cavalry. Heuen-tse, after organizing his force, advanced to give battle as far as the city of Too-poo-ho-lo,§ which he took by assault in three days. He caused 3,000 persons to be beheaded, and 10,000 were drowned in the river. O-lo-na-shun escaped into the kingdom of Wei. He there rallied his dispersed troops and returned to the charge. The (Chinese) general made him prisoner, with 1,000 men, whom he beheaded. The remainder of the people retired with the king's wives to the banks of the river Kan-to-wei.|| The humanity of the Chinese general (*sze-jin*)¶ attacked them, and created a great disorder amongst this population. He likewise captured the concubines and children of the king, as well as other prisoners,

---

* The words *poo-te* are probably the transcription of the name of a tree in Sanscrit, perhaps the *vata*, a sacred tree employed in religious ceremonies, and of which mention is often made in Sanscrit poetry. What confirms this conjecture is the following passage in Kang-he's dictionary, under the character *poo* : " *poo-te* is the name of a tree which grows in the kingdom of Mo-kea-to (Magadha)." The same dictionary adds, that in the books of Fŭh, it is said, " Poo-te-sa-to (Bodhisattva) signifies the essence of what is manifest, declared; by abbreviation, we say ' Poo-sa.' " The term *Bodhisattva*, in Sanscrit, signifies literally, ' truth of intelligence:' it is the name given to certain Buddhist patriarchs, who have raised themselves to the state of divine sanctification.

† This authoritative demand, if it be not introduced here, as the facts, indeed, show, to gratify Chinese vanity, would denote that, at this period, Tibet was already dependent upon the Chinese empire as well as several other neighbouring kingdoms.

‡ Nepála, or Nepal: see the account given by Ma-twan-lin (book 335, fol. 14), in the translation by M. Rémusat, *Nouv. Mél. Asiat.*, t. i. p. 193.

§ *Too* (the first character) may be read *cha*, or *tea*. If it be read *cha*, the pronunciation of the epoch in question, *Cha-poo-ho-lo* would be an exact transcription of *Champaren*, a city placed by Abul-Fazil in Bahar, the ancient kingdom of Magadha, and probably the same as *Chapra*, on the Ganges, higher up than Patna; for *Chapra* is but a variation of *Champaran*, as the latter is likewise of *Champaranagora*.

|| This is no doubt the Godáveri, which falls into the Gulf of Bengal, to the eastward of Masulipatam.

¶ The *humanity* is, at the least, a singular expression to be used in these circumstances; yet the text admits of no other sense.

men and women, to the number of 12,000, besides animals of all kinds, amounting to 20,000. He subjected 580 cities and towns, and his power grew so formidable, that the king of the kingdom of eastern India, named She-keaou-mo,* sent him 30,000 oxen and horses to feed and mount his army, as well as bows, sabres, precious collars, and cords of silk. The kingdom of Kea-mŏ-loo† furnished different articles, with a chart of the country,‡ amongst which was a portrait of Laou-tsze.

Heuen-tse took with him O-lo-na-shun, to present him to the emperor (as a vanquished enemy). There had been an imperial order, which prescribed that the ancestors should be informed hereof, in the temple dedicated to them ; and Heuen-tse was elevated, at the court, above the magistrates (*ta-foo*) of all ranks.

In his travels, the Chinese ambassador had encountered a doctor named Na-lo-urh-po-so-mei,§ who told him that he was 200 years old, and possessed the recipe of immortality. The emperor‖ (having learned this intelligence) imme-diately quitted the hall of audience, in order to despatch an envoy in search of the philosophical stone (*tan*). He directed the president of the ministry of war to furnish the envoy with all the necessary instructions and provisions to enable him to prosecute his journey. This envoy traversed " the world " on horseback, to collect supernatural drugs, as well as the most rare and extraor-dinary stones. He travelled over all the kingdoms of the Po-lo-mun (Brah-mans), in the country called the Waters of Pan-cha-fa,¶ which (waters) come from the midst of calcareous rocks (*shih-kew*, ' stone-mortar,' or ' rock '), where are elephants and men of stone to guard them. The waters are of seven different species ; one is hot, another very cold (or frozen, *ling*). Plants and wood may be consumed in it ; gold and steel may be fused in it ; and a person who dips his hand into it will have it entirely burnt off. This water is poured into vases by means of skulls of camels, which turn round. There is also a tree there, called *tsoo-lae-lo*, the leaves of which are like varnish or blacking. It grows upon the top of scarped and desert mountains. Enor-mous serpents guard it ; and those who wander in the neighbourhood cannot approach it. A person who wishes to gather the leaves employs different arrows to strike the branches of the tree ; the leaves then fall. A multitude of birds also take the leaves into their beaks, and carry them a great way : it is necessary, in like manner, to direct arrows against them, to obtain these leaves. There are other curiosities in this country of the same kind.

The drug (of immortality) could not be found or verified by this envoy, who, being recalled, could not proceed further, and returned and died at Chang-gan (the capital).

* Sri-kumára?

† This kingdom must be that of Káma-rúpa, mentioned in the Sanscrit inscription on the column of Allahabad, and which formed the western part of the kingdom of Assam, on the frontiers of Tibet. The syllable *kd* is well represented by *kea*, as *ma* is by *mŏ*, and *rú* by *loo ;* the last syllable *pa* is not transcribed. It is worthy of remark, that it is a general law of transcription from Sanscrit into Chinese, that the short *d* should be represented in the latter by *ŏ*.

‡ This curious circumstance is a ground for thinking (for it is not a mere conjecture), that there exist-ed, and perhaps still exist, in India, native geographical charts and works on geography ; but all these articles must have undergone the fate of the royal archives, where they were carefully preserved and con-cealed from the eager eyes of European conquerors.

§ The first two words of this transcription represent faithfully the Sanscrit word नर *nara*, ' man,'

which enters into the composition of many proper names ; but the Sanscrit value of the other four sylla-bles is more difficult to determine.

‖ Tae-tsung, who reigned from A.D. 626 to 649.

¶ This is a very exact transcription of the Persian word پنجاب *Punjáb*, the ' five waters,' or

' five rivers' (in Sanscrit *Panchananda*), which is the designation given to a large and fertile province of India. The last syllable *fa*, in the Chinese transcription, represents the more faithfully the syllable *áb*, inasmuch as the consonants composing it are two labials very often taken one for the other.

In the time of Kaou-tsung (A.D. 650 to 684), a Loo-kea-ye-to,* of the country of Woo-cha,† in eastern India, came likewise to offer homage at the court of the emperor, giving himself out as a possessor of the recipe of immortality, and as being able to transform himself into lieutenant general of armies.

In the third of the years *këen·fung*‡ (A.D. 667), the Five Indias (or five kingdoms of India) sent ambassadors to the court of the emperor. In the years *kae-yuen* (A.D. 713 to 742), an ambassador from Central India proceeded three times as far as the extremity of southern India, and came only once to offer birds of five colours that could talk.§ He applied for aid against the Ta-she‖ (or Arabs) and the Too-fan (or Tibetans), offering to take the command of the auxiliary troops. The Emperor Heuen-tsung (who reigned from A.D. 713 to 756) conferred upon him the rank of general-in-chief. The Indian ambassadors said to him : " the *Fan* (or Tibetan) barbarians are captivated only by clothes and equipments. Emperor ! I must have a long, silk, embroidered robe, a leathern belt decorated with gold, and a bag in the shape of a fish." All these articles were ordered by the emperor.

Northern India also sent an embassy to the court of the emperor.

At the close of the years *kan·yuen* (about A.D. 756), the bank of the river (*Ho-lung*, the Ganges ?) gave way and disappeared.

The third of the years *kwang-shun*, of the modern Chows (A.D. 953), a Sǎ-mun¶ (priest of Buddha), of western India, with several priests of his religion, representing sixteen different tribes or nations (of India), brought tribute, amongst which were some horses of the country.

[*The conclusion next month.*]

* That is, a लोकायतिक *lôkáyatika*, or follower of the atheistical system of philosophy founded by Chárwáka, entitled *Lôkáyata* (see Mr. Colebrooke's Essays on the Philosophy of the Hindus). The suffix *ka*, which forms collective names in Sanscrit, is represented in Chinese by the character *che*, which serves in like manner to form adjectives and collective names in Chinese.

† A kingdom situated near the mouths of the Ganges.

‡ There is an error here in the text ; the years *këen-fung* were only two, 666 and 667.

§ These were of course parrots.

‖ *Ta-she*, ' great eaters,' is the name by which the Chinese designate the Arabs. This curious passage throws great light on this obscure period of Indian history, and confirms a fact hitherto scarcely noticed, but which has been asserted by two Arabian authors, Almakin and Abulfeda, namely, the invasion of India by the Arabs at the beginning of the eight century. " Mahomed ben Cassim," says the former, in his history of the Sarrasins, " took India ; he obtained possession of the countries adjoining the Sind (Indus), gave battle to Dahar, who was king of them, vanquished him, made him prisoner, and put him to death." The other, in his Musulman Annals, translated by Reiske, says : " Mahomed ben Cassim overrun India as conqueror." But the following is a passage, curious in another respect, concerning the same fact ; it is taken from the History of the Empire of the Khalifs, translated from Tabari (Turkish edition), for a knowledge of which we are indebted to M. Reinaud : " This same year, 87 (A.D. 709) was gloriously terminated by the defeat of 200,000 barbarians, who had entered the country of the Musulmans, commanded by Beghaboon, nephew of the emperor of China. The Musulmans confessed that they owed this important victory to the protection of God."

¶ This Indian title is more frequently written *Sha-mun* (with different characters) ; it is a close transcription of the Sanscrit *Samána*.

NATIVE IRREGULAR HORSE.

In addition to the ten regiments of light cavalry, belonging to the Bengal army, there are four or five corps of what are denominated " irregular or local horse." These form a separate service of their own, and bear, with reference to the regular army, the same affinity as our English yeomanry corps to the standing force in this country ; with this distinction, that in India the local horse are always upon duty. The embodying of these corps did not originate with the British government. On our entering into conflict with the different native powers, we found ourselves upon all occasions opposed by shoals of flying cavalry, which proved more formidable than might have been supposed from their disorderly and disorganized condition. Regardless of method, and observing no discipline, these men with wonderful agility skirted on the flanks and on the rear of their opponents; and, though generally a greater source of annoyance than of actual mischief, yet they at times presented no despicable front, forming a serious impediment to the steady advance of our forces, and at all times harassing the march. This mode of warfare appears to be in accordance with the habits of all the northern race of Indians. In Persia and in Bokhara, we find the foray still the favourite system of military tactics, and in the desert we are told that the Túrcoman when on his saddle knows neither father nor mother. The Indian horses are peculiarly adapted to services of this nature, since those of pure native breed will endure fatigue which would prove destruction to a less hardy race. For a series of days and weeks, they have been known to carry their riders with their *paunch itteehar*, their five appointments, a distance daily of fifty or sixty miles. A horseman in India does not consider himself complete without his five appointments, that is to say, his sword, his matchlock, his shield, his spear, and his saddle. The constant and careful grooming, which Indian horses receive from native owners, enables them to go through a surprising degree of work without being distressed ; the moment that the rider dismounts, whatever may be his own fatigue, he begins to rub down his steed, not in any slovenly inefficient manner, but by a regular process of shampooing, which, though laborious in itself, long custom has rendered easy, and which soothes in an extraordinary manner the wearied limbs of the jaded animal, soon reviving its spirits, and enabling it to eat and sleep in comfort. This duty is performed by the Mahratta women for their husbands, and the horses unaccustomed to a stable thrive as well (or even better) at their picquet, with a scanty allowance of fodder, as those belonging to Europeans, which, though well fed and not so much worked, are left to lazy servants, who content themselves with a very little exertion.

When we acquired permanent dominion in India, we adopted the favourite branch of service amid the Patans and Mahrattas, and raised eight regiments of native irregular horse, each consisting of about six hundred men. The command was given to a captain in the regular service, who held this appointment in addition to his company, and he had two subalterns associated with him, also belonging to the native army, one acting as second in command and the other as adjutant, the medical charge being given to an assistant surgeon of the establishment. There are, therefore, only four Europeans attached to each of these regiments, the internal economy being almost entirely left to the native officers. A consolidated allowance is granted to both officers and men, with which they are expected to find and feed their own horses, and to purchase their appointments. The pay of a common trooper is twenty rupees,

about two pounds a-month; they are dressed in uniform, which however differs
entirely from that worn by European soldiers, or natives in the regular service,
as it resembles the loose flowery robes of the Persians; it is a very becoming
costume, consisting of a long vest, in some regiments yellow, in others red, a
pair of trowsers not inconveniently wide, a shawl for a sash, and a steel casque
or a high-pointed cap. In latter years, the number of these regiments has been
reduced from eight to five, and their total abolition was contemplated amid
the sweeping measures of the late Governor-general. Three were disbanded
as a preliminary step; but the urgent and universal opposition made by the
local officers to the entire reduction of so useful a branch of the service, arrested the progress of destruction, and for once in his life induced the reigning
viceroy to forego his intention and relinquish a favourite project.

The soldiers belonging to the native irregular horse are principally employed
in aid of the civil power, acting as mounted police, in which capacity they go
under the name of *suwars*; they are, however, occasionally called into active
service, and one corps distinguished itself in a very honourable manner
throughout the Burmese campaign. Whenever a regiment of irregular horse
has gone into the field with the army, it becomes entitled to participate in the
benefits of the pension list: an institution which the native soldier regards
with peculiar satisfaction, and which is considered by him to emanate from the
wisest and most salutary acts of the government; he feels that when worn out
with long service and hard duty, there is an asylum left for him wherein
he may spend the remainder of his days in ease and comfort, not thrown, as in
the service of his native princes, like a broken tool away, whenever years and
infirmities shall have prevented him from the performance of regimental duty.
It would be impossible to replace the irregular horse at so reasonable a rate,
by any class of troops, and independent of their services in time of war, they
afford great assistance to the civil power, not only by the speedy apprehension
of those who might easily evade less active pursuers, but in the prevention of
crime. It is well known that many are deterred from committing felonies, by
the certainty that immediate and unerring search would be made after them by
the suwars, who upon all occasions have distinguished themselves by their vigilance and their fidelity to their employers. They have been very instrumental
in the measures taken for the total extirpation of thuggy, and the rapid manner in which they reach the scene of disturbance occurring in distant towns
and villages of a district, renders them exceedingly effective upon an emergence
of the kind. Small detachments, consisting of a native officer and a few men,
do duty at all civil stations, and these are increased whenever their presence
is necessary. Civilians of rank were allowed the attendance of four suwars,
and to the curtailment of this guard of honour, the melancholy fate of Mr.
Frazer has been attributed; he went abroad without a sufficient escort, and
having only one mounted attendant with him, the assassin escaped for the time.
European travellers, whose journey lies through a part of the country not
immediately under the British government, usually ask and obtain the escort
of two or more suwars; their progress then becomes easy, and when encamped
on the skirts of some town or village, there are few more amusing sights than
that afforded by the airs and graces exhibited by these troopers. Their caps
stuck rakishly on one side of their heads, and their weapons displayed, the
younger portion will swagger down the streets and bazaars, evidently on the
look-out for homage and admiration, shewing by their appearance and manner
that they are not persons to be slighted or treated with disrespect. The older
warriors cut a grim figure on the early march, or in the cold season, with

shawls folded turban-wise round their caps, the dark flashing eye and the thick moustache fringing a hawk nose, peeping out beneath the cumbrous envelope; their appearance seldom fails to create a sensation, especially in any remote place, and the travellers thus accompanied are quite certain not to meet any obstruction or incivility upon the road.

As the troopers are oftentimes unable to raise sufficient funds for the purchase of a horse fit for the duty, and the requisite appointments of the service, each, thus circumstanced, enters into an arrangement with his officer, who provides him with a horse and trappings for half his allowance, that is, ten rupees a month. In this manner, the native officers, who are of course the persons applied to, make a good deal of money, farming out their cattle to considerable advantage. Very few horses are to be found in these corps, the greater proportion of the troopers being mounted upon mares. It is not from preference that the men select this gender, or rather that the native officers, who job them out, provide them for the service, since it is notorious that mares are unequal to the performance of the same work that horses can do; but they are cheaper, in the first instance, and they also yield the proprietor a little profit, which he gains by breeding from them. Besides the pony race, India has no fewer than eight distinct kinds of horses, though the better sort are not often to be found in the ranks of local regiments. First, the Arab,

> " Round hoofed, short jointed,
>   Fetlocks shag and long,
> Broad breast, full eyes, small head
>   And nostrils wide;
> High crest, short ears, straight legs,
>   And passing strong;
> Thick mane, thick tail
>   Broad buttock, tender hide."

Secondly, the stud bred; thirdly, the country; fourthly, the northern, or Caubul; fifthly, the Duknee; sixthly, the Kattywar; seventhly, the Toorkee; and eighthly, the Turcoman, and Persian. An Arab is never met with belonging to natives in the irregular horse, the ranks being made up principally from the country breed, with here and there one from the Duknee sort. From the high price which Arabian horses always fetch in India, none but those who are in the receipt of a handsome income can afford to purchase them; and as the native gentlemen of India prefer the breeds of their own country, the market for these beautiful strangers is almost exclusively confined to Europeans. Batches, as they are called in Hindostan, though elsewhere, string is the more accepted term, from one to two hundred in a batch, pass through Hindoostan from Bombay annually, and the arrival of these importations at any European station creates a greater sensation than the births, marriages, and deaths of the whole community during the season. Every vehicle that can trundle, and every tat that has a leg to stand upon, are put into requisition to convey their owners to the inspection. There are few men who do not make pretensions to judgment in horseflesh, and on these occasions the nods, winks, and whisperings of the knowing ones become doubly mysterious to the uninitiated. A due mixture of boldness and caution is necessary to impress the bystander with respect, and to stand high in the estimation of his circle as an authority, forms a matter of such great importance in India, that the person possessing it would disdain to barter so enviable a distinction for all the musty honours the bookworm can boast. It is extremely probable that a great many of the horses that are brought to India as Arabs, are of a very mixed breed and impure pedigree ; others again shew every mark of the highest blood and the most unimpeachable descent, and to separate the false from the true, and pronounce upon the merits of the whole, is the ambition of all who belong to the equestrian order, or, to use the slang phrase most in request throughout our Oriental possessions, who are desirous to be considered "varment." As a general rule, the golden chestnut, and the silver grey, always shew high blood, a specimen of the latter brought up to Agra, in 1830, was valued by its owner at eight thousand rupees (eight hundred pounds), and out of the whole stud or batch, amounting to several hundreds, there was scarcely one which came within reach of the purses of the young men of the station. The highest caste Arab seldom exceeds 14-2 in height. It has been stated, as the opinion of a good judge, that the celebrated horses which have from to time run for the great Welter stakes, on the Calcutta course, such as Esterhazy, Champion, Mandamus, and Godolphin, are not descended from the pure blood of the desert. Some English jockeys have endeavoured to lower the reputation of the Arab, though it is an established fact in India, that those of high family, in stoutness and ability to run on, may compete with any breed; and it is well known that the best blood on the English turf has had an Arab cross. Those of the Nujeedee breed are the most esteemed, and bear the highest price in the market. The valuable qualities of the Arab are fine temper, and great bottom, being capable of enduring more fatigue than any other horse; but he is a sluggish and careless roadster, and very apt to trip in his walk. It is rare to meet with a vicious Arab horse : but when this happens, he is an incarnate fiend, and the toil of breaking him in, far exceeds any pleasure to be gained from the triumph. There are few sights, even to those who are neither judges, nor anxious to become purchasers, more interesting than the encampment of an Arab or other native dealer. The merchant himself is domiciled in one or two small low white tents, handsome of their kind, and ornamented with scarlet bordering; he always chooses some picturesque spot, shaded by trees, and in the vicinity of water, and the horses picketed under the spreading foliage, form, with their attendant grooms, groupes of the most striking description.

The second kind are called stud horses. The government of India, finding that they were dependant upon the countries north of the Punjaub for their supply of horses, felt that in case of a rupture with the powerful ruler of those states, Runjeet Singh, this source would be completely cut off. Moreover, the horses that did reach the frontier were of a very vicious and inferior kind, the maharaja's officers having the first choice. Under these circumstances, it was deemed expedient to establish two or three breeding studs; and, for this purpose, some of the more thorough-bred English horses have been imported. The stud colts are generally well tempered, but they are oftentimes leggy, without carcase, or strength of limb proportioned to their height; this, perhaps, is owing to the circumstance of the horses hitherto chosen for the Indian stud having been selected more from their racing qualities, than for size and symmetry; the horses reared at the stud, however, are shewy animals, sure-footed, and have remarkably fine paces. In accordance with the spirit of economy which has of late prevailed in Bengal, it has been proposed within the last two or three years to abolish the stud department, for what is considered a very efficient reason, namely, because it does not pay. The reader need searcely by this time be informed, that every thing in India is measured by the standard of pounds, shillings, and pence; consequently, the fiat has been passed for the gradual absorption of the studs of the Benares province, with a view to increase the one located at Haupper, in the more northern part of our Indian empire. On the whole, it may be said, that the stud cattle are a very fine breed, but at the same time it must be confessed that there is yet much room for improvement. Probably, in the course of a few years, the Indian authorities will import their horses from Australia, and the supply of the Indian market seems likely to prove a source of wealth to the breeders of New South Wales; at present, however, there is little direct communication from Calcutta to Sydney, persons proceeding thither usually going in the first instance to Penang or Singapore, and waiting for a passage. The comparatively low prices at which the stud horses are now sold, will not as yet admit of sufficient profit to the speculator to induce him to incur the expense of freight; but when an increase of numbers shall produce cheapness, the importation of Australian horses will, no doubt, lead to the entire abolition of the government studs. The advantages which would accrue to India from the establishment of a direct commerce with New South Wales, may be estimated by the fact of the English exporters of corn to the colony, having made a hundred per cent. upon their produce. There would have been nothing to prevent the people in Bengal from sending out the supply, if ships had been constantly bound to and fro; but it is, at present, more easy for the Australians to procure grain from England than from India.

The third kind of steed used in India is the country horse, a breed with which the horse artillery and light cavalry were formerly furnished,and which continues to be the kind usually selected for the use of the troopers belonging to the branch of service under review. The term " country horse " is one of very general import, and comprizes horses of every description not falling within the classes already specified. They are very hardy, and have good action, but are brutes to manage. They think nothing of standing right on end, and dancing a *pas de seul* in this attitude; and without a powerful bit, which is made in Hindostan for the purpose, they are beyond control. Fortunately, the natives are excellent riders, and those on the local horse not being compelled to adopt the slippery leather saddle of Europe, they use that of cloth of their own country, and stick like monkeys upon it. The Caubul, or northern horse, is the fourth kind; he is usually of great size and substance, and is held in high respect by native gentlemen. These horses are often as costly as the Arab, and will fetch from one to two thousand rupees. The fifth description is the Duknee, which, without any exception, ranks next to the Arab; indeed, many Europeans prefer the Duknee horses to the steeds of the desert, since they are very superior roadsters, being safer, and having better paces. They are assuredly a splendid race, boasting great bone and shape, together with good action and temper. They possess as fine muscles as Arabs, with more style of figure, having lighter shoulders. The Indian Government have very properly set about establishing a stud in the south of India, for the purpose of increasing the stock from this valuable race, and there can be little doubt of its answering the most sanguine expectations of those interested in its success. Sometimes these horses find their way into the local corps, and are much prized by the troopers. The sixth, or Kattywar horse, is a very peculiar breed; a light, wiry-looking animal, with a small head, flat, light shoulders, light carcase, small across the loins, and drooping much to the croup. A writer, in the *Bengal Sporting Magazine*, describes these horses as having great powers, but adds, " they are usually hot-tempered, to a degree that is quite surprising, as it is unaccompanied with vice.

They are not usually hardy, or up to much weight." In conjunction with the Kattywar horse, may be mentioned the horses from the kingdom of Cutch; they are light, graceful animals, and can always be recognized, from the great depression in the back, formed by a concavity in the spine. This circumstance gives an unnatural appearance to the animal, and a stranger must be accustomed to them before he can bring himself to believe that the horse can do his work properly, with a back so peculiarly shaped. Toorkee and Turcoman horses, which form the seventh and eighth classes, are different, though usually spoken of as the same. The former is a small, but very powerful animal, generally with an exceedingly rough coat, and the legs covered with long hairs, like the English cart-horse. The latter is a large handsome animal, with a fine crest; in fact, handsome in every respect, but still showing a want of blood. He makes a beautiful parade horse. The Persian horses are splendid animals, and many of them make excellent roadsters, and are much sought after for chargers. Besides all these, there is a highly useful nag, as every subaltern in India will allow, called the Country galloway. This is the beast of all-work. When apprehension and hesitation, as to the propriety of ordering out the valuable Arab, is shown, " Ginger," or " Sampson," or " Nick," or whatever may be the cognomen of the hack, is sure to suffer. Neither weather, neglect, nor exposure, seems to hurt him; and whether on the line of march or in cantonments, this poor beast is sure to be made to do all the hard and dirty work. To give the reader an idea of what these galloways are capable of performing, it is only necessary to state, that one was driven on a stretch from Dinapore to Buxar, a distance of thirty miles, in an *ecka*, a light one-horse carriage, used by the natives of the city of Patna. He is hardy, sure-footed, and to be got cheap. Then, again, there are four kinds of ponies, or tattoos: the Duknee pony, a beautiful little animal; the Burmah pony, regarded as the finest in the world; the hill pony, and the Bazaar, or country tat. Some of these latter are the counterparts of the Shetland pony, while others represent the Highland shelty.

The same strict observance of military etiquette, which is imposed upon the regular Native army, is not required from the soldiers of the Native horse. They are permitted to practice a drill peculiar to themselves, and to forego many of the harassing details which are considered essential to the preservation of discipline in the other corps, and which form the great drawback to the pleasures of a military life. Their expertness in horsemanship is truly astonishing; and however surprising the feats at Astley's may appear, to those who have never been in India, they create a very slight degree of sensation after the evolutions we have seen these men perform. In going through their exercises, they jump off their horses while in full gallop. Another exploit is the picking up a tent-pin at the utmost speed; and a third, the hitting a bottle with a single ball from a matchlock. The bottle is either suspended in the air, or placed upon the ground, and the marksman riding by at the swiftest pace, at the distance of fifteen or twenty yards, drops his bridle-rein at the moment of passing, raises the matchlock, and firing, shivers the bottle into a thousand pieces. The ancient tournament, or a sport extremely like it, is still kept up by the soldiers of these · irregular corps, who measure spears with each other according to the most approved practice of former days, frequently unhorsing their adversaries, and displaying the highest degree of skill and grace in the management of both steed and weapon; but the grand collision is displayed in a manner peculiar to Indian warriors, and which is known under the name of the " Mahratta Charge." The whole corps being drawn up in a line of two deep, the battalion advances at first at an easy rate, but increasing in speed from a canter to a gallop, and when in full career, the files open out, and every horseman, uttering the war cry of the east, a wild and piercing shout, comes on like a storm, waving his sword over his head, and appearing to pursue his headlong course in total recklessness. Suddenly, at the word of command, each horse is arrested in its career; the whole are brought upon their haunches, and, notwithstanding the seeming confusion of the onslaught, every man is in his proper place, and all immediately form into order. This manœuvre, when practised with effect, is very imposing, and has often succeeded in putting large bodies of raw or wavering troops to the rout; but it fails with a steady well-disciplined foe, and can scarcely bear a comparison with the close and determined charge of European cavalry. In the same manner, an expert native horseman will ride straight up to a blank wall at full gallop, and turn off his horse at the moment that both it and the rider are expected to come into collision with the object in front. The old sport of the quintin, or something very similar to it, is in equal favour with the tilt. In trying their skill, the successful aspirant who carries off a tent-pin, buried firmly in the ground, with the point of his spear, while passing at full gallop, is cheered by the acclamations of the whole field; while he who misses the mark, rolls on the ground amid the derision, shouts, and laughter of the spectators. The best spearmen occasionally assume the character of champions, tempting the ambitious to a trial of skill which may win for them the renown they court; emulating the exploits of others, the whole field will engage in a melée, some tilting with the most eager impetuosity, others trailing their lances behind them, and ever and anon, when least expected, becoming the assailants, and overthrowing their pursuers by some dexterous thrust. This practice enables native horsemen to add greatly to the spirit and effect of a cavalcade; they carry on their mimic warfare whenever an opportunity is allowed for it, and, however wild and irregular their movements may appear to be, they are governed by some principle, which enables them to fall quietly into the ranks at a proper time and a proper place.

Though the matchlock is considered to be a clumsy weapon, and is wholly disused by European soldiers, the native Indian, notwithstanding its weight and unwieldiness, makes it a toy in his hands. The peculiar construction of the weapon enables it to throw a ball to a far greater distance than the ordinary musket, the bore being small, and very long; it has been known to wound at the distance of eight hundred yards, while its extreme weight assists in rendering the aim more steady. A native Indian trooper is not less expert with the sword, than with the spear and matchlock; it is with this weapon only that he measures his skill with Europeans, who have long ago relinquished the use of the others. The palm in this branch of science is usually accorded to the native, and perhaps a far greater proportion are adepts than are to be found in the British battalions: but Colonel Skinner, who ought to be an authority in such cases, seems to give the preference to the European. An officer, conversing with him on the subject, understood him to say, "that, although contrary to the general opinion, he considered the British swordsman to be decidedly superior to the native, since the feint, or pretended blow, the latter rarely understands, and therefore lays himself open in that quarter where the attack is in reality meditated." Continuing the discourse, the Colonel mentioned, in illustration of the peculiar merits of both parties, "that he recollected, in Lord Lake's wars, a serjeant of dragoons, who was a capital swordsman, and so fond of fighting that he sought every opportunity of displaying his personal prowess against the enemy. On one occasion, having dashed out of the line to find an antagonist worthy of a trial, he fell in with a Mahratta, mounted upon a splendid Duknee horse, and armed with the *bhella*, or lance. The Mahratta, uttering his war cry, bore down upon the European, spear in rest.   The serjeant turned off the meditated stroke with his sword, and in turn became the assailant ; the Mahratta, however, parried or evaded every blow with infinite address, and the contest was carried on without either party gaining an advantage.   Wearied at length by their ineffectual endea- vours to defeat each other, both drew up, as if by mutual consent, and each looking in the face of his opponent with a countenance expressive of admiration and respect, gazed for a moment, and then, turning their horses' heads round, they galloped back to their respective bodies, the Mahratta raising his head, exclaimed at parting, ' *Thubar Bahadoor*,' which the serjeant returned, with a ' bravo, my fine fellow.' "   These sort of single combats, although contrary to the European notions upon the conduct of national warfare, were not uncommon between our cavalry forces and that of the enemy, more particularly during Lord Lake's campaigns, in which we were engaged with an enemy proud of the celebrity obtained in swordman- ship, and whom it was politic to impress with a respectful opinion of our pro- ficiency in that peculiar mode of warfare.   One British officer distinguished himself very highly in numerous encounters, the battle being either a drawn one, like the last recorded, or terminating fatally on the part of the native adversary.   It is said, but the authority is only that of rumour, that he seldom returned to camp without a human head, the token of his victory, hanging at the saddle-bow.   At length, a party who challenged him, objected to the pistols which were contained in his holsters, as giving him an advantage over an adversary who had no fire-arms at his disposal.   The British officer instantly gave his honour that, although in his possession, he would not use them, and immediately the contest commenced.   The native took the earliest opportu- nity of cutting the bridle reins of his opponent, who in attempting to disable him in a like manner, found that they had been furnished with a steel chain as a guard.   This circumstance he had totally overlooked at the time of the parley respecting the fire-arms, and thus baffled, and finding himself wholly at the mercy of an antagonist bent upon taking his life, he drew out a pistol and shot the schemer dead upon the spot.   It was altogether an unfortunate cir- cumstance—the high notions of honour entertained by some persons, render- ing them of opinion that he should not have fired under any provocation. There can be no doubt that a plot had been laid to entrap him, and the question raised, was, whether, as he had not discovered the advantage taken by the addition of the steel chains, at the time that his own pistols were ob- jected to, he should have used them after having pledged his honour that he would not.

Amongst the advantages enjoyed by the regiments of local horse, is that of being permitted to remain for a longer period at one station than other corps, generally five years, while one regiment of this irregular cavalry appears per- manently fixed at Hansi.   This perhaps is an indulgence granted to an officer who has always ranked very highly in the estimation of the government, retaining his popularity at head-quarters throughout all the changes which have taken place in that department.   Without wishing to draw any invidious com- parisons between his corps and others of the like nature in the service, it may be said, that " Skinner's horse" enjoys a higher degree of celebrity than the rest.   This reputation is chiefly owing to the military talents and popular cha- racter of the commandant, who, in his long and honourable career, has gained the respect and esteem of all ranks and classes of the Indian community. Colonel Skinner is the reputed son of an European officer in the service of some of the native princes, but bears no trace of his paternal descent, being of a darker complexion than the majority of the soldiers of his corps. He has followed the trade of war from his earliest youth, and, notwithstanding the number of years which have passed over his head, still enjoys the reputation of being the best lance in his regiment. He distinguished himself greatly throughout the whole of Lord Lake's campaigns, and in latter years gathered fresh laurels at the storming of Bhurtpore. One of his sons, a fine young man, equally master of the matchlock, the sword, and the spear, is the adjutant of the corps, and in the mimic fights, which form one of the grand displays of the field-days, proves a match for the best lance upon the plain.

The astonishing delight taken by the veteran and his son in these military exercises, no doubt, must have its effect upon the troopers; and the station of the regiment, upon the high road from Delhi, from which it is only a few marches distant, is another advantage, since the corps must be under the immediate eye of every commander-in-chief as he traverses the upper provinces, and thus, if not greatly superior, becomes much more talked of than the others. Colonel Skinner has the reputation of being a very rich man, and he lives in a style of magnificence little short of that displayed by native princes boasting considerable revenues. In addition to the rental of his jaghire, an estate at Belaspore, his extensive dealings in horses, shawls, and indigo, has filled his coffers to overflowing, and he spends in a manner commensurate with his wealth. Besides the factory and a handsome house for his own accommodation, the colonel has built a fort at Belaspore for the protection of his property, a picturesque-looking place, well manned and armed with twenty guns, of no contemptible calibre, but which at present are only used upon occasions of rejoicing, and unless some great change shall take place in the affairs of India, must be restricted to the firing of salutes. He has another residence equally handsome at Hansi, and at both places entertains in a most splendid manner; none need pass these noble mansions without partaking of the hospitality of the owner, and upon the occasion of a visit from a commander-in-chief, or other great person, he entertains the whole camp, feasting all its followers during the period of their halt. Colonel Skinner keeps a troop of nautch-girls, and a band of bards, or *Khelàmuts*, in his service, both of which perform for the amusement of his guests: dancing and music are not, however, confined to native *artistes*, since, whenever a sufficient muster of European ladies can be obtained, there are quadrilles, which always attract the attention of the native soldiers, who, though they may despise the possessors of so degrading an accomplishment, delight at looking on at any performance. Colonel Skinner's munificent disposition has ever prompted him to the kindest actions; amongst many others, he adopted and brought up a little girl, the child of a European, who was cast upon his charity in rather a singular manner. When arrived at a proper age, he gave away this young lady in marriage to his own son. Though the family of her guardians are Christians, and though she was educated in the same persuasion, she had been brought up, with something resembling Musselmanee strictness, behind the *purdah*, and had never been seen by the European community of the place, until the period of her marriage. The ceremony was performed by the clergyman who officiates at Agra, and who went over to Hansi for the purpose. He brought back very interesting accounts of the bride, who was attired in a splendid Hindostanee dress, the upper garment of which alone, being seamed and embroidered with pearls, cost eighteen hundred rupees: her jewels were

magnificent ; and though somewhat confused by the presence of strangers, she
acquitted herself with the grace and courtesy which is always to be acquired
in a zenana.

Occasionally, a few of Skinner's troopers appear in a full coat of chain
mail ; but in general the armour worn by the irregular horse is confined to a
casque of polished steel, surmounted by a spike, and supplied with scales to
fasten under the chin, together with gauntlets or greaves of polished steel ;
these, however, are seldom worn, except upon military duty, the undress being
assumed when employed in the civil service. Their horses are at this time
also divested of many of the trappings, which make so great a show when a
review takes place. Every light-coloured horse belonging to a native has,
when fully caparisoned, its tail dyed with *mhendy*, the dye used by the ladies
to stain the palms of their hands and finger-tops with the hue of the rose : natives are also fond of painting stars and crescents upon the foreheads and
haunches of the animal. The local horse are distinguished for the multitude
and richness of their trappings, the officers especially delighting to display their
wealth and taste : a plume of feathers, tipped with pendants of gold, surmounts
the forehead, the head furniture is richly embossed, and the chest is ornamented
by a series of necklaces, which have a very striking effect : some are formed of
blue beads, others of plates of silver containing amulets, as a preventive
against the evil eye. The most approved precaution, however, against all kinds
of *t'haddoo*, or witchcraft, consists of tigers' claws set in gold or silver, back to
back, and encircling the neck. One or more of these talismans seem to be
considered essential to the security of the party, and, accordingly, few horses
belonging to the native troopers are destitute of so effectual a charm. It may
easily be supposed, that to young and dashing European officers, fond of
athletic exercises, and desirous of emulating the natives in their feats of horsemanship, appointments in the local horse are objects of considerable desire.
Upon joining these regiments, the stiff military uniform of the regular army is
discarded for the more picturesque and convenient native costume. The form
is the same both for officers and troopers, the difference being only in the
quality of the long flowery tunic sitting so closely to the form, that Stultz and
Nugee might take a lesson in their craft from the dirzee who cut it out, is composed of the finest materials, either cloth or cashmere, according to the season.
An embroidered belt, of exquisite workmanship, passes over the shoulder,
and is confined round the waist with a shawl of price, while the steel cap is
adorned with a short plume of black and white feathers, tipped with gold,
which rises above the shining aigrette in front of the helmet. The tunic is
edged with black fur ; the nether garment, partaking more of the pantaloon
than the trowser, is convenient for riding, and a pair of long boots, well furnished with spurs, complete a costume which would produce a striking effect at
a fancy ball in Europe, if worn by a person accustomed to its use. When the
countenance has been well bronzed by long exposure to the sun, the European
in command can scarcely be distinguished from his native associates, and it is
scarcely necessary to say, that many gay young men take a pleasure in identify-
ing themselves with the people with whom they have been called upon to serve.
The troopers of the local horse are chiefly Mohammedans, Pytauns by descent ;
but there are some Rajpoots amongst them, and it is always necessary to produce adequate testimony of respectability of birth before admittance can be
gained in these corps, they being tenacious of their dignity. The European
officers are always splendidly mounted, sometimes upon large English horses,
and at others on Arabs, Persians, or the fine animal from the Dukn.

MURRAY'S CHINA.*

WE have examined the compendium of the History of China, compiled
by Mr. Hugh Murray, with the assistance of several able gentlemen, for that
excellent work, the Edinburgh *Cabinet Library*, and we can venture to
pronounce it the best digest which has yet appeared, adapted to the object
in view, that of giving a popular account of the empire of China. It commences with a general view of the natural features of the country, a brief
sketch of its ancient and modern history, an inquiry into the knowledge of
the country possessed by Europeans in ancient times and in the middle ages;
an account of the discovery of China, of the missions and embassies thither
from Europe; a view of the Chinese language and literature; of its religion,
government, and politics; of its national industry and social state; an historical account of British intercourse with China; and the third volume is
wholly devoted to the interior geography of the country, its commerce, and
navigation; Chinese mathematics and astronomy; the geology, mineralogy,
botany, and zoology of China. These different subjects have been appor-
tioned amongst the several gentlemen who have afforded their aid to the
compiler, and they leave scarcely any topic untouched.

It must be obvious that so comprehensive a history of such an empire as
China, embracing the important matters of inquiry which we have enumerated, compressed into the space of three small volumes, must be but a
mere "abstract and brief chronicle,"—that it must necessarily be superficial, not in a sense disparaging to the writers, but only by comparison with
the extent of the subjects.

Mr. Murray has judiciously proportioned the degree of condensation and
curtailment, generally, to the object of the work, that is, he has abridged
most severely those portions which, however attractive to the historical
student or philosophical inquirer, are least likely to captivate an ordinary
reader. Thus, the early history of the empire, and that of the four first
dynasties (including the splendid reign of She-hwang-te), are dismissed in
thirty pages. Of this we complain not; but the modern history, from the
accession of the Hans to the present period, required a greater development than sixty-seven pages could afford. In fact, the *history* of China
(confining the term, in its ordinarily restricted sense, to a record of political events) is far too meagre to be of any practical use. We may add,
that its accuracy is not to be wholly depended upon, for it appears to be a
mere rapid sketch from Mailla's voluminous translation of the *Tung-këen-
kang-mǔh*, which requires to be compared with other authorities. It moreover exhibits the defect common to all such digests executed by persons
unacquainted with the Chinese language, that of retaining the French
spelling of proper names, which (in the absence of the original characters)

* An Historical and Descriptive Account of China; its Ancient and Modern History, Language,
Literature, Religion, Government, Industry, Manners, and Social State; Intercourse with Europe
from the earliest Ages; Missions and Embassies to the Imperial Court; British and Foreign Commerce;
Directions to Navigators; State of Mathematics and Astronomy; Survey of its Geography, Geology,
Botany, and Zoology. By HUGH MURRAY, Esq., F.R.S.L.; JOHN CRAWFURD, Esq.; PETER
GORDON, Esq.; Captain THOMAS LYNN; WILLIAM WALLACE, Esq., F.R.S.L.; and GILBERT
BURNETT, Esq. With a Map and thirty-six [wood] Engravings. In three vols. Being vols. xviii., xix.,
and xx. of the Edinburgh Cabinet Library. Edinburgh, 1836. Oliver and Boyd.

is perplexing to a reader desirous of an accurate knowledge of persons and events, to a degree beyond what persons ignorant of the peculiar language can conceive.

In treating of the knowledge of the ancients respecting China, Mr. Murray conceives that he has thrown an additional light upon this subject, " by tracing an early maritime route to Canton, and the existence of an ancient trade in tea." His theory respecting the former is built upon a statement of Marinus, the ancient Tyrian geographer (preserved by Ptolemy), who speaks of a navigation from the Gangetic bay to the golden Chersonese, and thence northward and eastward, after a long voyage, to *Cattigara.* Mr. Murray endeavours to show, from the details given by Marinus, that they denote a voyage round eastern India to Canton, which he considers to be identical with Cattigara.* There are, however, many objections fatal to this theory. An obvious one, which Mr. Murray endeavours to combat, is, that it is totally incongruous with Ptolemy's own tables. But a still more fatal objection is, that it assumes Canton to have been a flourishing trading port at the era of Marinus, of Tyre; whereas, at that time, this part of the coast did not form a portion of the Chinese empire, properly so called, and was inhabited by races in a state of barbarism. Even in the time of Woo-te, of the Han dynasty (B.C. 138), the whole country comprising the modern provinces of Chě-keang, Fŭh-kĕen, Kwang-tung, and Kwang-se, is described by Chinese authors as governed by chiefs independent of the emperor, and as covered with forests and infested with wild beasts and serpents.

With regard to the other theory of Mr. Murray, namely, that *tea* was known to the ancients, and that it is no other than the celebrated *malabathrum,* we apprehend that this is also entirely groundless. The basis of it is a passage in the *Periplus* of Arrian, which mentions that a certain people called Sesatæ, with a short body, broad forehead, flat noses, and a wild aspect, came, with their wives and children, to the frontiers of the Sinæ, with large mats full of leaves *resembling the vine,* which they used for lying upon ; that, after spending some time in festivity, they returned home, leaving behind the mats and leaves ; that the Sinæ repaired to the place, took possession of the articles thus left, drew out the stalks and fibres of the leaves, which they doubled up, and formed into a circular shape, and thrust them into reeds : "thus three kinds of *malabathrum* were formed." Mr. Murray concludes from these several facts,—namely, that the article was a product of China(?)—that it was exported to India,—that China *imported* betel (hitherto considered to be the *malabathrum*), and that the latter was used *fresh* and not in a *dried* state,—that the article is " unquestionably *tea.*" Now, in the first place, it is clear, from the manner in which the *malabathrum* is spoken of by classical authors, that it yielded a perfume, not a decoction, which is the ground upon which some have identified it with the *laurus cassia* (the *tejpát* of India); in the next place, the use of the decoction of tea was not known in China itself till a comparatively late

* Cattigara was the extreme south-eastern point of the ancient world, according to Marinus.

period. Chinese authors say that the use of this leaf began in the time of the (second) Tsin dynasty, A.D. 265 to 419; but it did not become common till about A.D. 600, when an emperor of the Suy dynasty was cured of a pain in the head by drinking an infusion of the *ming* or *cha* leaf (tea), prescribed by a Buddhist priest. We may remark, by the way, that Mr. Murray tells us that the name *tea* is a corruption of the Chinese word *tcha*, as he writes it from the French. It must appear strange to an etymologist how such a corruption could have taken place, when both sound and letters are so totally distinct. The fact is, that the character *cha* was formerly pronounced *too*, which the early Malay traders articulated *teeh*, whence our *tea*.

The account of the missions and embassies of Europeans nations to China contains some amusing particulars; and the sketch of the social state of the Chinese is as faithful as the study of European authorities permitted the author to make it. The chapter on navigation, by Captain Lynn, is excellent; and the details of natural history are copious and accurate. The chapter on geography is confessedly very meagre; there are abundant Chinese authorities in this department, but they are locked up in the original tongue. The chapters on the language and literature, and the religion, of China, are very imperfect, not to say erroneous. It would, however, require more space than we can dedicate to the subject to point out the errors and their sources. We are bound to say, that Mr. Murray and his coadjutors have performed respectably a difficult task, which to perform well requires greater facilities, and a more familiar knowledge of some of the topics, than they appear to possess.

Miscellanies, Original and Select.

PROCEEDINGS OF SOCIETIES.

Royal Asiatic Society.—4th June. Sir Alexander Johnston in the chair. Various donations to the museum and library were presented. John Tytler, Esq., of the Bengal medical service, read an analysis and translation, made by him, of certain specimens of a Persian work on mathematics and astronomy, compiled by a Maulavi, named Ghulám Hussain. The Maulavi had been introduced to Mr. Tytler, at Calcutta, in the character of a great mathematician and astronomer; and was then in the service of Mírza Khán Behádur, the Mahárájá of Takaree, in Behar. He informed Mr. Tytler, that he had compiled the work under the patronage of the Mahárájá, who had supplied him with a sum of money to publish it at one of the lithographic presses at Calcutta; and that about one hundred pages had been printed. His object in applying to Mr. Tytler was to solicit him to recommend his work to the Government Education Committee. The Maulavi stated, that it would comprehend about 900 closely-written quarto pages. Its title was " The Bahádur Khánian Collection." Mr. Tytler considered that the author's knowledge of the subjects upon which he had treated was very extensive; and that his work deserved the patronage, not only of the Government of British India, but even of all scientific bodies in this country.

18th of June. Sir Alexander Johnston in the chair. Several presents were laid upon the table. The secretary read a letter from B H. Hodgson, Esq. the East-India Company's political resident in Nepál, addressed to Sir Alex. Johnston, stating, that during the many years of his residence among the mountains of Nepál, he had been gradually accumulating materials to illustrate the animal kingdom of that country, especially its quadrupeds and birds, and that it was his wish to publish his drawings and notes with the patronage of some public body, and the aid of some man of science selected by such body; and with whom he might co-operate in some such manner as Richardson did with Swainson. The drawings for his work, executed by two native artists carefully trained for the purpose, amounted to several hundreds in number; and all those of birds were given in the natural size, and in the style of Gould's. Mr. Hodgson's purpose was "to marry opportunity to skill,"—to effect such a union of local facilities, with the ability to turn them to account, as was at once in the highest degree needful and difficult in regard to the researches into the phenomena of animate beings. [We believe subscription lists for this splendid and highly useful work are open at the Asiatic Societies of London and Calcutta, and at the Zoological Society.]

The secretary also read a letter addressed to the Right Hon. Chairman, by P. B. Lord, Esq., of the Bombay medical service, dated Dec. 1835, containing some observations on the port and town of Cambay (where he had been detained a few days), in Guzerat, and of a branch of industry carried on at that place, namely, the cutting and polishing cornelians. Mr. Lord described the process of this art as being very efficient though simple. The original cornelian stones have a black, flint-like appearance; but by exposing them to the heat of the fire or sun, they assume, some a red, some a white, or any intermediate shade of colour.

Mr. Lord alluded to the fact that, for some years past, the upper part of the gulf of Cambay has been decreasing in depth, and said that this decrease was now going on so rapidly as almost to allow the observer to witness, in the formation of dry land before his eyes, a tangible illustration of Mr. Lyall's beautiful and much-talked-of theory. Vessels formerly discharged their cargoes under the very walls of the town;—at the time Mr. Lord was writing, the nearest vessel in the harbour was at least four miles distant; and was then lying sunk in the mud, without any chance of floating till the return of the spring tide. The cause of this was the immense quantity of slime and mud brought down by the river Mhye, which, after a course of nearly one hundred miles through an entirely alluvial country, discharged its turbid contents a short distance to the east of Cambay. The effect of the diminution in the depth of the harbour has been very prejudicial to the trade of Cambay.

Henry H. Spry, Esq.; Maulavi Muhammad Ismáél Khán; John Curtis, Esq.; and the Rev. John Wilson, were elected members of the Society. No less than thirteen native gentlemen of Bombay were proposed, through Sir Charles Forbes, as candidates for non-resident membership.

The next meeting was announced for the 2d of July.

CRITICAL NOTICES.

Illustrations of the Botany and other Branches of the Natural History of the Himalayan Mountains, &c. By J. FORBES ROYLE, Esq., F.L.S. & G.S., &c. Part. IX. London, 1836. Wm. H. Allen & Co.

THE popularity of Mr. Royle's Illustrations rests, not merely on its merits as a splendid accession to natural history, but upon its more general utility, in connection with economical science. The great lode-star of Mr. Royle is the improvement of the natural resources of India, and it is easy to foresee that, as soon as the attention of Government or of capitalists is properly directed to the capabilities of that country, this work will be invaluable, because it shows *what* experiments may be made in naturalizing foreign products in the soil, and *how* they should be set about. In the present Part, when treating of the *Polygoneæ*, Mr. Royle gives some interesting information respecting the *Rheum*, or Rhubarb genus, and indicates the geographical distribution of the plant. " There can be no rational doubt," he observes, " about the successful cultivation of the true rhubarb, in territories within the British influence, as in Kunawar, or the Bhoteah pergunnahs of Kemaon, and that, with little more labour than placing the roots or seeds in favourable situations, and this in a country where little else can be produced fit for export. It would not be difficult for such active and intelligent officers as Messrs. Traill and Hodgson, in Kemaon or Nepal, to obtain some of the seeds or roots." The success of such an experiment would produce an important revolution in the trade, in a most useful drug.

The Plates in this part are, perhaps, finer than in any preceding one.

A History of Russia. Vol. I. Being Vol. LXXIX. of Lardner's *Cabinet Cyclopædia.* London, 1836. Longman & Co. Taylor.

NOTHING more is required by any but a profound student of history, than a superficial sketch of the early events of a country so little connected with the European or Eastern societies as Russia, which did not take its place amongst civilized nations till modern times. But however moderate the demands of English students, they are not easily satisfied; Count Segur has given a bold and rapid sketch of the history of Russia, but it wants precision and distinctness. The present appears to be an excellent compendium of Russian history.

Narrative of a Journey from Lima to Para, across the Andes and down the Amazon ; undertaken with a view of ascertaining the practicability of a Navigable Communication with the Atlantic, by the Rivers Pachitea, Ucayali, and Amazon. By Lieut. W. SMITH and Mr. F. LOWE, late of H.M.S. *Samarang.* London, 1836. Murray.

THIS expedition, though unsuccessful in its object, though no fault of the conductors, like most of these attempts, was not without its value, since it has enabled Mr. Smyth to describe a part of the country of which we have had hitherto little or no knowledge. The Narrative is full of interest, and is written in an unostentatious style.

Illustration of British Birds. BY H. L. MEYER. Longman and Co.

WE have deferred a notice of this publication until a certain progress has enabled us to appreciate its merits. Thirteen numbers have appeared, in monthly succession, under royal, noble, and highly respectable public patronage; and it is, we understand, the intention of the artist to range through the whole extent of British ornithology ; where practicable, the bird is drawn from living subjects, and of the natural size. The classical and trivial names are given ; and a few brief items of hâbitat, size, weight, nest, egg, &c. We may safely assert that, in point of fidelity of outline, character and colour ; taste, beauty, and cheapness, no work has surpassed, if equalled this. Ornithologists are understood to be satisfied that, in number, beauty, and song, no region of the world is more favoured, as to this most interesting portion of animated nature, than Great Britain. Each number of the work before us contains four or five plates, equal to highly-finished drawings, including six or more birds, with their eggs and nests, occasionally. The accessions of flower, insect, fruit, shrub, landscape, bush, &c. are exceedingly tasteful. We can discover no falling off as the work proceeds. It is well adapted for ladies learning to draw, or desirous of improvement in that elegant accomplishment.

The Works of William Cowper, Esq., comprising his Poems, Correspondence, and Translations; with a Life of the Author. By ROBERT SOUTHEY, Esq., LL.D., P.L., &c. London, 1836. Baldwin & Cradock.

THIS work has now reached the fourth volume, and seems deservedly to draw to itself additional materials as it proceeds. We find that the delay in the publication of this volume, has been occasioned by the unexpected acquisition of the collection of Cowper's letters, which had descended to Mrs. Smith, Mr. Newton's neice, which includes many of Mr. Newton's own letters, and of Mr. and Mrs. Unwin's. There is little doubt that this edition of the works of Cowper will be perfect, and that the biography of the poet, moulded into a delightful form in the hands of so able an artist as Dr. Southey, will leave nothing to desire by those who seek an acquaintance with his peculiar character.

The advertisement to this volume contains an ample authority from the administratrix of Cowper to the publishers, "to publish any of his letters which may come into their possession."

Lives of Eminent British Statesmen. By JOHN FORSTER, Esq., of the Inner Temple. Being Vol. LXXVIII. of Dr. Lardner's *Cabinet Cyclopædia.* London, 1836. Longman and Co. Taylor.

THE lives treated of in this volume are two only, but their biography embraces an eventful period of English history,—Sir John Eliot, and Wentworth Earl of Strafford. The first is new; the sketches that have hitherto appeared are unworthy of the subject, of whom they exhibit but dim glimpses. By the help of the Eliot papers, and a very creditable industry, Mr. Forster has presented us with a full-length portrait of that extraordinary character. It is gratifying to find that he has been able to elucidate the affair of the attack on Mr. Moyle, so much to the advantage of Eliot, whose character has much suffered on that score. Lord Strafford's life is a highly interesting piece of biography. To both, appendices are subjoined; that of Eliot contains an account of his unpublished philosophical treatise (written during his last imprisonment), entitled "The Monarchy of Man," which, though disfigured by the pedantry and affectation of the times, has some noble passages, and throws a great light upon the author's intellectual character, as well as his political principles.

A Home Tour through the Manufacturing Districts of England in the Summer of 1835. By Sir GEORGE HEAD. London, 1836. Murray.

THOSE who have never visited that absolutely " new world," our manufacturing districts in the northern counties, will be surprised at the prodigious mass of novelty, information, and amusement, which this volume contains; and those who have seen the mighty Liverpool, the Cyclopean Leeds, and the mineral wonders of Durham, will find much in Sir George Head's book that is new, either in fact or in description.

A Letter to William Stanley Clarke, Esq. and James Rivett Carnac, Esq., Chairman and Deputy-Chairman of the Court of Directors of the East-India Company. By NATHANIEL SMITH, Esq., B.C.S. London, 1836. Richardson.

THE design of this little pamphlet is to recommend, as improvements of our judicial system in India, the following suggestions :—The abolition of the Persian language; the occasional union of Europeans and natives in the same courts, especially in appeals; an extreme latitude for appeals, accompanied by forms calculated to prevent their accumulation; the study of one vernacular language by Europeans, instead either of Persian or Hindoostanee; and an examination of all officers, European and native, in the Regulations.

Songs of Twilight, translated from the French of Victor Hugo. By GEORGE W. M. REYNOLDS. Paris, 1836.

THE poetry, as well as the prose, of Victor Hugo, contains many striking images, which belong intrinsically to the highest class of poetical composition. We have repeatedly brought before the readers of this Journal specimens of M. Hugo's muse. This is an attempt (for the translator announces it as such) to render into English verse *Les Chants du Crépuscule.*) The version is respectable, but it does not, in our opinion, do complete justice (nor is it easy to do it) to the fiery audacity of the original.

EAST-INDIA COMPANY'S MILITARY SEMINARY, ADDISCOMBE.

THE periodical public examination of the gentlemen cadets at this institution took place on Friday the 10th June, in the presence of the Chairman (Sir James R. Carnac, Bart.), the Deputy Chairman (J. Loch, Esq.), and several members of the Hon. Court of Directors.

Of the visitors who were attracted by the interest of the scene, we may enumerate the following:—

The Rt. Hon. Sir J. C. Hobhouse, Bart. (President of the India Board); Sir C. Cockerell, Bart. (Commissioner of ditto); and R. V. Smith, Esq., M.P. (Secretary to ditto); Sir C. Forbes, Bart.; W. Newnham; J. Fraser; L. Kennedy; D. Colvin; G. Forbes; P. Melvill; E. Thornton; C. Currie, Esqrs.; the Moulvee Mahomed Ismael Khan (Astronomer to the King of Oude); Sir H. Willock; Major Generals Sir S. Whittingham, Sir W. McBean, Sir Geo. Elder, K.C.B., and Millar (Director General, R.A.); Colonels Salmond, Sir Joseph O'Halloran, C.B., C. S. Fagan, C.B., C. Fagan (late Adj. Gen., Bengal), Hardy, Mills, Sir Geo. Cox, Bart., Reeves, Pasley, C.B. (Royal Engineers), Adye (Director Royal Laboratory), and Galloway; Lieutenant Colonels J. E. Jones (R.A.), Hay, and Hall; Majors Dynely (R.A.), Kennedy, Hamilton, and Willock; Captains Cotton and Carnac, R.N., Burnaby (R.A.), Procter (Adjutant, &c. Royal Military College), Hay, Smith (Madras Engineers); Dr. Gregory (Professor of Mathematics, Royal Military Academy); J. Narrien, Esq. (ditto Royal Military College); the Rev. Messrs. Lindsay, Cole, Gleig, &c.

The branches of study in which the cadets underwent an examination were mathematics, Hindustani (including written specimens of the two characters in which the language is expressed), and fortification.

The cadets thus publicly tested were selected as follows, viz.—

For the Engineers: R. Strachey and G. Macleod.

For the Artillery: R. Macpherson, G. H. Clifford, and W. Hay.

For the Infantry: E. Hall, S. J. Batten, G. Malcolm, C. F. Grant, W. F. Blake, J. S. Aked, D. C. Scott, M. J. Turnbull, E. Tower, E. Locker, H. Heyman, C. Wright, G. W. Alexander, G. R. Gleig, E. Forbes, J. Montgomery.

And their proficiency in the relative branches of study, and their general good conduct, were rewarded by the following prizes, presented to them by the Chairman on the part of the Court, agreeably to the award of the public examiner, Sir Alex. Dickson, K.C.B., and the Lieut. Governor, Colonel Stannus, C.B., viz.—

To R. Strachey, 1st mathematical, 1st fortification, 1st civil drawing, 1st Hindustani.

To G. Macleod, 2d mathematical, 2d Hindustani, and for general good conduct, a handsome artillery sword. The Chairman expressed the sincere pleasure he felt in presenting it in the name of the Court of Directors, in token of the high appreciation in which Mr. Macleod's general good conduct had been held during the whole period of his residence at the institution,—conduct as creditable to him as it had been beneficial to the interests of the seminary, which he would then leave with credit not easily to be forgotten. "I have no doubt," added Sir James, "that the early promise you have here given of those qualifications which eminently distinguish the officer and the gentleman, will be amply realized in your future career, and I sincerely wish you every success."

To R. Macpherson, 2d fortification, and 2d good conduct.

To S. J. Batten, military drawing.

To Edward Locker, Latin.

To H. Heyman, French.

To gentlemen cadets of the second class, viz.—

R. B. Smith, mathematical fortification, 3d good conduct, and Hindustani.

W. F. Marriott, military drawing and Latin.

R. C. Buckle, civil drawing.

J. T. Johnstone, French.

And to Mr. A. D. Turnbull, of the 3d class, 4th general good conduct.

In this stage of the proceedings, the Chairman addressed them to the following effect:—

" Gentlemen Cadets,—It is with high gratification that we have listened to this day's examination.

" Knowing the admirable arrangements which are made for promoting the advancement of the cadets in their professional and general studies, knowing also the zeal and talents of the distinguished officers filling the stations of the public examiner and the lieut. governor of this institution, and the persevering exertions of the professors to ensure to you the full benefit derivable from those arrangements, we naturally came here with excited expectations; those expectations are, on the present occasion, gratified to their fullest extent; and I think that I may, with perfect truth, affirm that the friends of the Indian army have ample cause for exultation in the results which we have now witnessed.

" It is a source of further satisfaction, that proceedings in which we must feel a high and honest pride, are attended by the President of the Board of Commissioners for India, who is not more distinguished by his interest in the prosperity of our Indian empire, than for his regard for the welfare of this institution.

"One portion of those who have been distinguished in the proceedings which have brought us here, will immediately be called upon to enter on the active duties of an honourable but arduous profession; and in addition to its ordinary difficulties, they will have to encounter some of a peculiar character. In other armies, the officers and men, though differing in education and position in society, have much to bind them to each other,—a common country, a common language, and a common faith; in the Indian army these ties are wanting, and their place must be supplied by the study and practice, on the part of the European officers, of all the means by which man acquires moral power over his fellows. A knowledge of the vernacular languages of the country is, for this reason, an object of high importance, and a familiarity with those languages, combined with the exercise of those manly and soldier-like virtues which are here inculcated, will enable you to establish that influence over the minds of the native troops, which it is essential you should possess, and in the hour of trial, your country will recognise the value of the education you have received.

"Whenever it has been necessary to repel aggression, the Indian army has produced officers prepared to lead their men to victory; and it is but justice to add, they have found troops not unworthy of following them.

"To secure the affections of the native army (and this I cannot too earnestly impress upon you) will be a primary duty, and while discipline must be maintained, the greatest tenderness should be shown towards their feelings, and an indulgent consideration towards their prejudices. The standard of civilization in India is not that to which we are accustomed here. We are greatly in advance of those subjected to our rule, and looking at the extraordinary course of events by which our vast Eastern empire has been attained, it is not too much to conclude, that we are destined by Providence to diffuse among the people the blessings which we ourselves enjoy, and ultimately to raise the native character to the European standard.

"To you a portion of this sacred trust is committed, and it will call for a large share of labour, of discretion, and of self-command.

"I need not remind you that the first duty of a soldier is subordination, and that an officer must himself set an example of that which he requires from those under his command.

"To those who have not yet completed the allotted period of study, I can only recommend perseverance in the honourable path upon which they have entered. It is now that their professional and moral character is to be formed, and upon their conduct here will mainly depend their future destiny. The life of a soldier upon active duty is one of incessant watchfulness, and the best preparation for it will be found in the early acquisition of habits of strict regularity and temperance. I need not say that the opposite vice is inconsistent alike with the character of soldier and gentleman.

"A very brief period will elapse before we shall be again brought together, and I sincerely trust and believe, that it will be under circumstances as satisfactory as the present. Till then, I can offer you, gentlemen, no better wishes than—that you may improve the advantages you enjoy.

"To those who are about to quit the institution, and whom possibly it may be my fortune never to meet again, I wish a long and honourable career of professional success, and to all of you the fullest measure of personal happiness."

The gentlemen cadets were formed into line in open order to receive the Chairman, &c., with a general salute. The ranks closed, broke into open order, and the column marched round in slow time in review order, afterwards in quick time. On arriving on its own ground, the column wheeled into line, the ranks opened, and performed the manual exercise. The ranks closed, and the gun-squads which had been told off, formed on each flank, faced outwards, and filed to the rear, grounded arms, and fell in at the guns which were stationed on each flank of the line. The line, during the time that the gun-squads were forming, performed the platoon exercise, after which fifteen rounds of ammunition were fired from right to left by the guns. The line then advanced and repeated the general salute, after which the cadets went through the sword exercise.

In the entrance hall and rooms of the mansion were various well-executed plans of fortification, military surveys, and drawings. We may notice the system of Choumara, executed by Gentleman Cadet Strachey in a very handsome manner, a plan of St. Helena, projected from the model; and a civil drawing of a scene near the Devil's Bridge;—by Gentleman Cadet Macleod, a detailed plan of the attacks upon Tarragona;—by Gentleman Cadet Macpherson, a penwork drawing of the siege of Mequinenza;—by Gentleman Cadet Hall, ditto of Seguntum;—by Gentleman Cadet Batten (a prize drawing) in penwork, of the attacks upon Tarrogona;—by Gentleman Cadet Grant, a drawing representing the attacks upon St. Sebastian by the army, in 1813, under the Duke of Wellington.

SKETCHES OF THE LATER HISTORY OF BRITISH INDIA.

No. V.—Renewal of the Company's Charter in 1813.

From a feeble and obscure association of traders, the East-India Company had, in the eighteenth century, become the lords of a large portion of Hindostan, and the dominant power in the field of Indian politics. They had attained this high position under the license of the British Crown; but beyond this, their obligations to their own government were few. It was to the talents and intrepidity of their own servants, that they were indebted for the commanding situation which they held; and the extraordinary ability displayed by men educated upon ordinary principles, and taken from the ordinary walks of life, may be received as evidence, that the native vigour of the English character will manifest itself under any circumstances which afford room for its display.

The Company struggled long, but finally triumphed; and the acquisitions of these " Royal Merchants " became so extensive and important, as to render it necessary, in the opinion of Parliament, to place them under the especial supervision of the Crown. Thus shorn of some portion of its regal state, the Company still retained its commercial privileges with little diminution; but these, together with the right to administer the government of India, were to terminate in the year 1814, and that period was, consequently, looked to with no ordinary anxiety.

The renewal of the bargain between the Crown and the Company, always a subject of great interest and keen contention, was now unusually so, from the progress which the principles of free trade had made in the public mind, and the influence which they possessed in the high quarters, where the matter was ultimately to be decided. Those principles had made their way languidly and slowly; but still they had gained ground. The reputation of having first maintained them is usually bestowed on Adam Smith: they are, however, to be found in earlier writers; and whatever be the degree of estimation in which they are entitled to be held—whether they are to be received as fixed and perfect rules, never to be departed from on any occasion—or whether they are to be admitted in a more guarded form, to be qualified by reference to what a modern political economist has not infelicitously called "disturbing forces," and to the peculiar circumstances of the state to which it is proposed to apply them—the honour of their discovery, be it what it may, does not belong to Adam Smith: they had been enunciated by writers who long preceded him. Nor can this be allowed to detract very greatly from his fame, for the principles themselves lying at the very surface of inquiry, little honour can be gained by their discovery; and the merit of having given a clear and lucid exposition of such opinions, is almost equal to that of having been the first to propound them. Previously to the time when the Scottish professor converted a chair of moral philosophy into one of political economy, the advocates of free trade were few; and among practical men of business, they made scarcely any converts. Statesmen and legislators, even in despotic states, are, to a certain extent, guided by the popular will. In a free country, that will, if consistently and continuously expressed for a long period of years, must ultimately be victorious. In such a country, whatever men possess, they hold by the tenure of the public voice; and they grossly and foolishly betray their own interests, if they neglect the use of any of the means which they command for shewing to the public that their claims to retain what they have acquired are reasonable and right. They should be active and unremitting in rendering themselves this justice; —they should also be early. When the flood of public opinion has been suffered to roll on and gather strength, it will require increased efforts to turn it, if even *any* efforts should be availing. The majority of men decline the trouble of judging for themselves. They follow with their neighbours the prevailing opinions of the day; and those who wish to keep possession of their influence over the public mind, must commence early and proceed vigorously in their exertions to give it the desired direction.

On every occasion, when the East-India Company had sought a renewal of their privileges, their claims had been resisted; but the grounds of resistance were different from those taken in later times. Men will always be anxious to participate in a trade which they believe to be profitable; and they will never be unable to suggest plausible reasons for indulging their wishes. But the principles of which Adam Smith, though not the author, was the great disseminator, furnished new weapons for combating all exclusive privileges of trade, and afforded the means of concealing the interested motives of the opponents, under the guise of science. This new sign of the times ought to have been carefully watched by all who were desirous of retaining such privileges; but such precaution was neglected, and the very slow progress of the free trade doctrines afforded a ready, though an insufficient, excuse for the neglect. While the promulgation of these doctrines was confined to the moral philosophy class at Glasgow, those who were hostile to them, might suppose that there was little cause for alarm. But they ought to have recollected that these opinions were propounded in the heart of a great commercial city, by a man of acknowledged talent; and that no inconsiderable number of young men annually quitted the university imbued with the principles of their teacher. The last fact was especially important—no error can be more fatal, than to disregard what are contemptuously called the opinions of boys. It is true that the real value of such opinions is small—they are the result of circumstances—they are taken up on trust, without any exercise of the judgment, and at a time, indeed, when the judgment is altogether unformed; but they enable us to cast the horoscope of the coming age : from the minds of the youth of the present generation are to be traced the spirit and destiny of the next. In the disregard of this truth, lay a great error; and it was not the only one. The appearance of the book, on which the great advocate of free trade expended his strength, ought to have called forth, from those who opposed him, either a manly defence of their opinions, or a candid renunciation of them. It produced neither. The advocates of regulated trade seemed to shrink from the maintenance of their own principles;

and though what is called the mercantile system, for a while, retained the influence which habit had given it, and was the creed alike of the counting-house and the cabinet, intelligent observers could not fail to see that it was undermined, and that the period was rapidly advancing, when the school of Adam Smith would be predominant, both in the commercial world and in the councils of the nation. One party slept, while the other was at work; and the result was, first the slow, but gradual and steady, advance of opinions, which have now attained such an ascendancy, that few have the hardihood to impugn them. Every new battle, therefore, in behalf of regulated trade, was fought under increased disadvantages; and, at last, there was little left for its advocates but to yield to the " pressure from without," and surrender a portion of what they possessed, as the price of a temporary retention of the remainder. Those interested in maintaining it, had despised public opinion, and they paid the penalty. They preferred relying on the ministers of the day, and those ministers invariably deserted them whenever it suited their purposes.

The terms upon which the government and trade of India were to be continued in the Company, gave rise to inquiry and discussion for several years before the expiration of the old Act. In 1808, some correspondence took place on the subject, between the Board of Control and the Court of Directors; and very early in the following year, it was intimated that his Majesty's Ministers were not prepared to concur in an application to Parliament for a renewal of those restrictions by which the trade with India had been hitherto limited. This intimation was, of course, little agreeable to the Company. A variety of arguments were adduced in opposition to the proposed innovation; and it was alleged, not without an appearance of probability, that "the loss of the Indian monopoly, such as it was left by the Act of 1793, would lead, by no slow process, to the entire subversion of the Company, both in their commercial and political capacity; and of that system which the Legislature had appointed for the government of British India: of which system the Company formed an integral and essential part." During these discussions, a parliamentary committee was engaged in an elaborate investigation of all the great branches of the Company's affairs; and upon the ground that it was desirable that the Reports of the Committee should be submitted to Parliament, before the question of renewal was brought forward, the correspondence on the subject was suspended for a considerable period. At the close of the year 1811, it was resumed. The opening of the trade with India, generally, to British merchants and British ships, was again laid down by Ministers, as the only ground upon which the negociation for continuing to the Company any portion of its powers, could be conducted. The clamour from without seemed to excuse the pertinacity of Ministers; a large proportion of the mercantile and manufacturing world appeared to look upon the East in the light in which it had been represented by the writers of fable, and to regard an introduction to it as a passport to the possession of unmeasured wealth. Though the sober habits of men of business would lead us to a different belief, experience shews that no class of men are more open to the influence of such delu. sions.*

The denunciation of monopoly formed the principal ground of attacking the commercial privileges of the Company; and on this point no defence was offered. Monopolies generally were given up; but some attempts were made to shew that they might be tolerated under certain circumstances, and for definite periods of time; and further, that, as the trade was then carried on, the monopoly of the Company was not a very close one. The principle that all monopolies are injurious, was fortified by allegations of particular evils, supposed to result from that of the East-India Company. Manufac-turers of various articles declared themselves, as well as the country, wronged, by being restrained from pouring an unlimited supply of their various commodities into India; and such restraint being pronounced " humiliating to individuals, and degrading to the national character," there could be no difficulty in arriving at the conclusion, that it was " a national grievance." But one of the most remarkable, not to say one of the most amusing, charges against the monopoly was, that " it cooled the ardour of generous and liberal competition." Self-interest has a wonderful effect upon the mental powers, and enables men to discern generosity and liberality, where those not enlightened by the same means, can perceive nothing but selfishness and baseness, and reckless disregard of right. The generosity

* A petition presented from Sheffield was so remarkably eloquent, that it is impossible to resist the temptation to transcribe part of it. Among other things, the petitioners declared themselves to be " fully persuaded," that " if the trade to the East-Indies were thrown open to all his Majesty's subjects, such new and abundant markets would be discovered and established, as would enable them to set at defiance every effort to injure them by that sworn enemy to their prosperity and the peace of Europe, the present unprincipled ruler of France; and that the petitioners doubt not, if the trade of this United Kingdom were permitted to flow, unimpeded, over those extensive, luxuriant, and opulent regions, though it might, in the outset, like a torrent represt and swoln by obstructions when its sluices were first opened, break forth with uncontrollable impetuosity, deluging, instead of supplying, the district before it; yet that very violence which, at the beginning, might be partially injurious, would, in the issue, prove highly and permanently beneficial; no part being unvisited, the waters of com-merce, that spread over the face of the land, as they subsided, would wear themselves channels, through which they might continue to flow ever afterwards, in regular and fertilizing streams; and that, to the wealthy, enterprizing, honourable, and indefatigable British merchant, conducting in person his own concerns, no obstacle would prove insurmountable, no prejudice invincible, no difficulty dishearten-ing; wants, where he found them, he would supply; where they did not exist, he would create them, by affording the means of gratification."

Such was the glowing picture presented to Parliament by the active imaginations of the good people of Sheffield. At a later period, we might have supposed it to be drawn by the present member for that borough, who, on his first appearance as a candidate there, announced to his supporters, the approach of a universal cry for cutlery, extending from Jaffa to Japan. It is unfortunate for both prophecies, that, like those of Johanna Southcote, they have not been fulfilled. There is, as yet, no large export of razors to Tibet; and though the trade with India has been open for above twenty years, and the " unprincipled ruler of France" occupies a few feet of earth on the road thither, England has, during that time, passed through a period of commercial distress altogether without parallel,—while to India " the waters of commerce" have certainly not operated as " fertilizing streams"—to that country they have been the " waters of Marah"—her manufactures have perished—her agriculture has declined, and her people been subjected to intense suffering. " The wealthy, enterprizing, honourable, and indefatigable British merchant" may have found wants, and where he did not find them, he may have created them, by " affording," or rather by "offering," " the means of gratification;" but something is yet deficient. All men desire to possess " the means of gratification;" but to this end, it is necessary that they should have " the means" of purchasing and paying for them. What has India had to export? Her cotton and silk goods have been driven out of almost every market in the world; her sugar, which, when brought to this country, is necessarily subjected to the disadvantage resulting from a long voyage, and consequent increase of freight, has (lest the producers should grow rich too fast) been saddled with a duty greatly exceeding that levied upon the sugar of other British possessions. It is only during the present session of Parliament, that any relaxation has been made in this respect, and the boon has been ungraciously con-fined to a part of British India—and that the most flourishing part—to the exclusion of the less prospe-rous districts, which more especially call for encouragement and support. Thus do our statesmen legis-late for the good of the people of India

and liberality of commercial competition, gave rise to those sanguinary scenes in the East, in which the Portuguese and Dutch were such distinguished actors.   The generosity and liberality of commercial competition, as manifested in the slave trade, deluged Africa with blood, and covered Europe with guilt.   And the generosity and liberality of commercial competition are now strikingly set forth in the factory system of England, under which the happiness of myriads of human beings, through time and eternity, is sacrificed to the Moloch of manufactures; the wages doled out to the wretched victims during their brief career of life being, in fact, not the reward of labour, but the price of blood.   Such are a few of the triumphs of a *generous* and *liberal* commercial competition; and it must be admitted, that they are fully sufficient to justify the call of the woollen manufacturers, in 1813, for an extension of its principles to the whole world.   Yet it is only fair to add, that the generosity and liberality, which mark commercial competition, are so little observable, that the advocates of unlimited freedom of trade deserved great credit for the discovery.

The Company replied by affirming, that the paramount object of any new arrangement for India ought not to be commercial, but political; and that the commercial monopoly was to be regarded as an instrument in the hands of the Company for the government of India; that the Company's territorial rights could only be enjoyed through the medium of commercial privileges; and that no provision made for securing them could be compatible with the entire opening of the Eastern trade.   These assertions were clearly erroneous; the territorial claims of the Company were quite distinct from their commercial privileges; and there could be nothing to prevent the retention of the one, after the other had been relinquished.   Experience, too, has shewn, that the commercial privileges of the Company are not indispensable to the maintenance of its authority in India.   They were more fortunate in referring to their own exertions to effect the introduction and consumption of European commodities—exertions made through a long series of years, with great perseverance and at extraordinary cost; to their labours in upholding our interests in India, against European rivalship and native jealousy; to the magnificent empire which they had added to the British dominions; and to the great wealth which flowed into this country, in consequence of their spirited and judicious policy.   After enumerating some of these advantages, in one of their official papers, they emphatically and justly added, " Such are the injuries, the grievances, the evils—such the degradation, which the East-India Company have brought on the country."

The debts and embarrassments of the Company afforded a ground of accusation peculiarly calculated to render them unpopular; and of course they were not forgotten.   The answer of the Company was to the effect, that they had never had occasion to apply to Parliament for aid to support their own establishments; but that their applications had been in consequence of levies made by Government, on the score of a right to participate in the territorial revenues; or for the purpose of obtaining reimbursement of immense sums, disbursed for the state in military expeditions—

sums very tardily acknowledged, and not then fully paid; or to enable the
Company to meet the transfer to this country of Indian territorial debt, the
increase of which was not to be attributed to the Company, but to his
Majesty's Government and to Parliament.   There was much in these
statements that deserved consideration; but when either individuals or societies expend their funds for the public benefit, they rarely meet with much
gratitude in return.

Political economy did not furnish the whole of the arguments by which
the privileges of the Company were assailed : the higher science of natural
law was invoked to the same end.   A full and free right to trade with all
countries and people in amity with the British Crown, was asserted to be
" the natural birthright and inheritance of the people of this empire, of
every subject of it, and of every port in it."   What may be " the natural
birth-right and inheritance " of a " port," it would not be very easy to
determine; and if the assertion be taken in the sense in which it was probably meant, it may reasonably be doubted whether a position so wild, merited
any answer at all.   If it did, the Company gave it a very proper one by
observing, that men living in society must submit to the laws of society,
and to restraints upon what is called their natural liberty, when, in the
opinion of the Legislature, the public interest demands it; that the Indian
monopoly was established because it was thought beneficial; that it had
been continued on the same principle; and that its abolition, or further
retention, must be a question purely prudential.   In urging their plea of
natural right, some of the opponents of the Company endeavoured to make
a special case.   Their principle, it was alleged, became strengthened by
its application to countries acquired and maintained by the efforts and
valour of the forces of his Majesty.   The countries, however, with which
they wished to trade, had been, for the most part, acquired and maintained
by the efforts of the Company and the valour of their servants, and altogether under the exclusive powers and privileges which it was now desired to
abrogate.

A plausible, and not altogether an unreasonable, objection to the continuance of the Company's privileges, was founded on the fact, that the
existing system gave advantages to foreigners, which were denied to British
merchants; and that the Americans, especially, had availed themselves of
these advantages to secure the markets of Europe, South America, and
the West-Indies.   From this latter circumstance, also, an inference was
drawn in favour of general freedom of trade.   The Company answered,
that the connexion of the Americans with the Indian seas was formed
under peculiar circumstances, and that their success in the market of Europe
was to be ascribed to the political state of that part of the world.

The necessity for the claimants finding new channels of enterprize; the
misery of the manufacturers, occasioned by their exclusion from the continent of Europe; the certainty of finding a remedy in the unbounded field
which the trade to the East would open to manufacturing and mercantile
industry—these, and similar topics, furnished another class of arguments,

which were pressed with extraordinary pertinacity by those who conceived they had interests hostile to those of the Company. It was answered, with much calmness and moderation, that any great extension of the trade with India must take place very gradually; that consequently the benefits to be derived from it must be very distant; and that, though it might be very easy to send out to India large quantities of goods, it might not be equally easy to obtain returns. Experience has shewn that these opinions were correct. The trade which succeeded the Act of 1813 has been little beneficial to England, while to India it has been positively injurious. The petitioners for an open trade had, however, made up their minds to its advantages; and, further, that they were destined to enjoy them—for it was urged, as a reason for extending the trade to the outports, that at Bristol and Liverpool the docks had been enlarged in anticipation of the concession. This specimen of commercial confidence is, perhaps, without parallel: it calls up the recollection of the married lady named Simpkins, who bought a brass plate with the name of Jones upon it, because, if she should happen to become a widow, and marry a gentleman of that name, it would be so useful.

Such were the principal arguments, by which the advocates of free and of regulated trade respectively supported their opinions. But the question was virtually decided before the discussion commenced. The principles of free trade had made too great progress for Ministers to venture to resist them. The efforts of the Company to retain the China trade were permitted to succeed, but that to India it was determined to throw open.

On the 22d of March 1813, the House of Commons resolved itself into a committee of the whole house, to consider of the affairs of the East-India Company; and the various petitions which had been presented having been ordered to be referred to the committee, Lord Castlereagh proceeded to expound the plan which he had to propose on the part of the Ministers of the Crown. The term for which the Charter was to be renewed was twenty years. The Company were to retain for that term the exclusive trade to China, but the trade with India was to be thrown open on certain conditions. It was to be confined to ships of a certain amount of tonnage; the trade outward was to be open to all the ports of the empire, but the homeward-bound trade to be restricted to certain ports, to be hereafter named. The Company were to be left in full possession of the power of deportation, to enable them to remove from India individuals whose conduct or intentions they might find or suspect to be dangerous: and this power his lordship held to be sufficient to calm any apprehension that might be excited by the facility of commercial intercourse about to be established. It was also proposed to continue to them the command of the native army; as, after mature consideration, Ministers were of opinion that, to separate the command of the army from the civil administration of India, would be to sap the foundations of the Government. Another revised arrangement related to the number of King's troops in India. This had fluctuated with the necessities of the times; but it was proposed, that in future there should always be a stated number of troops, to form, as it were, the garrison of India; and when more became necessary, they should be paid by this country, as it was unjust that the Company should defray the whole expense of a system of defence, which was called for by the general interests of the empire. At every recent renewal of the Charter, the Company had been called upon to sacrifice some portion of their authority to the Ministers of the Crown, and, of course, the present could not be suffered to form an exception. The Crown previously possessed the power of recal; but under the pretence that this was an invidious exercise of prerogative, it was proposed to render the sign ·manual of the Crown necessary to the validity of certain appointments. One of the most important and most beneficial of the contemplated changes applied to the defect of the ecclesiastical establishment. The members of the Church of England in India had hitherto been deprived of those rites of the church, the administration of which appertained exclusively to the episcopal function, including among them the rite of confirmation. To remedy this grievance, it was proposed to appoint one bishop and three archdeacons, to superintend the chaplains of the different settlements. Lord Castlereagh embodied in a series of resolutions the principal points of his speech, and concluded by moving them.

He was followed by Mr. Robert Thornton, the Deputy Chairman of the East-India Company; who, after reminding the Committee that the Company had the sanction of sixteen Acts of Parliament, passed under various sovereigns; that it had existed for 213 years; and that eminent statesmen, of different and adverse parties, had agreed in supporting the monopoly, proceeded to animadvert upon the speech of the Minister. Many of the petitions lying on the table he regarded as undeserving of attention; several of them being from places which could derive no benefit from any possible change in the East-India trade: and he instanced one, from a district in Scotland, which had nothing to export but horned cattle. He expatiated upon the attempt made to mislead the public, and the credulity with which they suffered themselves to be misled. The alleged advantages of America arose, he said, out of a treaty, in which the interests of the East-India Company were too little considered; and surely the Company ought not to be sacrificed on that account. He warned the house to pause before they surrendered experience to theory, and claimed the fullest consideration of the subject before final decision.

Mr. Whitshed Keene suggested that evidence should be heard at the bar of the house; a proposal to which Lord Castlereagh appeared inclined to demur. The proposal, however, found a supporter in Mr. Tierney. That gentleman expressed a wish to have the opinion of competent persons, on the probable effects of an influx of all descriptions of persons to India. He knew the noble lord said he had checks; but then he did not see how that could be called a free trade, in which an inhabitant of Liverpool might be allowed, indeed, to go to India, but when there, was to be subjected to the government of his competitors and rivals, who might send him home, without assigning any reason for so doing.   With regard to the advantages of an open trade, he had not as yet met with any thing beyond mere assertion; and after the blunders committed in South America, he was not disposed to place much reliance upon the opinions of manufacturers.   The question, he said, was now narrowed to this point—having an empire well governed, are we to hazard this empire for an increase of trade?   Was it too much to wish to know where the trade was to come from?   If they instituted such an inquiry, and it should turn out that the probable increase would be very small, it certainly would become a question, whether it was worth while to risk what we possessed for the expectatión of a trifling improvement.   All he wanted was, for the house, before it argued the question, to have something to argue upon.   He was, therefore, for hearing evidence, and the calling for it would involve no sacrifice of time; for what was consumed in evidence, would be saved in speeches.   He wished to have the opinions of such men as Lord Teignmouth, the Marquess Wellesley, and Mr. Hastings.

Mr. Canning supported the resolutions generally, but seemed disposed to go further, and throw open the China trade—if not immediately, at an earlier period than the expiration of the proposed Act.   He deemed it unnecessary to call evidence to support the proposal of free trade.   Mr. Canning at this time represented the great trading town of Liverpool, in which the strongest desire prevailed for the opening of the eastern trade.

Mr. Grant was unfriendly to the contemplated change.   He repeated what had been said by Mr. Thornton, that the argument derived from the opening of the trade to the Americans was of no force, as it was the act of the British Government, and not of the Company.   But he went beyond those who preceded him, by suggesting that the remedy was easy—it was only to shut out the Americans.   He quoted the authority of Lord Cornwallis as hostile to colonization; avowed his dislike to the scheme of Ministers, because it went to throw down the whole fabric of the East-India Company; protested against undue haste; and wished that evidence should be heard on certain points.   Lord Castlereagh, finding the sense of the house strong on this point, ultimately consented to hear evidence.

On the 30th, the committee was resumed, and evidence called.   The first witness was a man rendered eminent by his career in India, and no less so by the long and harassing judicial proceedings which awaited him at home.   It was Warren Hastings, then in the eightieth year of his age.   His examination was of some length, and related to various subjects—the settlement of Europeans, the demand for British commodities, and the propagation of the Christian religion.   To the first he expressed himself strongly opposed: he apprehended great injury and oppression to the natives, and regarded the indiscriminate admission of Europeans as fraught with danger to the peace of the country and the safety of the Company.   This opinion, he averred, he had long maintained, and he expressed himself anxious to vindicate himself from the suspicion of being biassed by his obligations to the Company.   With this view, he stated that, twenty years before, when the privileges of the East-India Company were under discussion, he spontaneously addressed a letter to the Chairman of the Court of Directors, in which he strongly urged the necessity of providing against the irruption of British adventurers in India. A clause having been inserted in the Act, permitting strangers to reside by license, he addressed a second letter to the Chairs, remonstrating against it, as likely to produce greater mischiefs than even the permission of indiscriminate residence ; because the favoured parties would appear to have the sanction of the Company, and would thereby possess an influence which no man would dare to resist ; while a body of adventurers without privilege, would be under the jealous eye of Government, and naturally excite its attention. In a still more recent letter, he had repeated these opinions.

On the question as to the probable demand for British commodities, Mr. Hastings was less decided, but he thought it would be inconsiderable.' It was his opinion, that the trade between India and England, as then regulated, was far more beneficial to both countries than if perfectly free. Being reminded that, in a·review of the state of Bengal, which he had written some years before, he had said, "that although we had been ·so long in possession of the sovereignty of Bengal, yet we had not been able so far to change our ideas with our situation as to quit the contracted views of monopolists," and that in the same work he had insisted upon it, as a fixed and incontrovertible principle, that commerce could only flourish when free and equal ; he professed not to recollect the words alluded to, but to have no doubt of their being correctly quoted ; and added, that he did not come there to defend his own inconsistencies,—that if he had ever expressed such opinions, he then abjured them,—that his present sentiments were widely different,—and that he could not say when he changed them.

On the subject of the propagation of Christianity in India, the opinions delivered by Mr. Hastings were singularly vague and undecided. On the proposed episcopal establishment, he expressed himself with an equal degree of oracular darkness ; and, for the son of a clergyman, he certainly evinced a most philosophic indifference, both to the general interests of Christianity and the welfare of the Protestant Episcopal Church. On the whole, he did little for the elucidation of the various questions before the house, and his answers were distinguished by nothing so much as the pompous and inflated language in which they were conveyed. Looking at the exhibition which he made on this occasion, it is impossible to avoid concluding, either that age had materially impaired a once vigorous mind, or that Warren Hastings was a greatly overrated man.

Lord Teignmouth was the next witness examined. His lordship appeared to apprehend that an unrestrained influx of Europeans into India might be prejudicial ; but thought, that though great numbers might be led by the first opening of the country to rush into commercial speculation, the disappointment, which would follow, would soon mitigate the evil. He conceived there would be little difficulty, in the existing state of the police, in confining strangers within due limits. The consumption of any great quantity of European goods, he regarded as improbable ; the natives, according to his experience, having neither the taste for such articles, nor, for the most part, the means of purchasing them.   He saw no danger in discreet and well-regulated efforts for the introduction of Christianity, and did not believe that the natives entertained any alarm on the subject.

The examination of witnesses was resumed on future days, and several distinguished servants of the Company were examined.   Among them was Sir John Malcolm.   It was his opinion that, of all the powers vested in the local government, none was more essential to its existence in full vigour and force, than that which enabled them to restrain the residence of Europeans.   He expected little increase in the consumption of European commodities among the natives.   Sir Thomas Munro, who was also examined, thought that the habits of the Hindoos were too unchangeable to admit of the hope of a large demand for English goods.   He participated, also, in the apprehension felt by some other witnesses, as to the probable consequences of an unrestrained access of Europeans; but saw no evil in an open trade, if confined to the principal settlements.

After being persevered in for some time, the mode of investigation originally adopted was suddenly abandoned.   Ministers either found, as they alleged, that the time of the house was too much occupied, or the affair was taking a tendency opposed to that which they desired.   On the 13th of April, Lord Castlereagh, after complaining of delay and inconvenience, and referring to a precedent to authorize the course that he was about to recommend, moved for the appointment of a select committee, to examine witnesses, and report the minutes to the house.   Mr. Robert Thornton opposed the motion, on behalf of the Company, as did also Mr. Grant. Mr. Canning, the representative of one of the towns most interested in destroying the Company's privileges, supported it.   It was resisted by Mr. Tierney and Mr. Ponsonby, leading members of the opposition; the former of whom insinuated a charge of unfairness against the Ministry.   On a division, the motion was carried, and the select committee met on the 15th, and continued to sit, notwithstanding the house adjourned for the Easter-holidays.

In the mean time, the question of the renewal of the Charter had been introduced into the Upper House.   On the 30th of March, the Earl of Buckinghamshire announced, that though a different course had formerly been adopted, it had been deemed advisable, in the present instance, that the resolutions, which had been laid before the Commons, should also be presented to their Lordships; and that a committee of the whole house should, with all the documents before it, proceed to the hearing of any evidence which might be offered.   Lord Grenville having suggested a select committee, as more advisable, Lord Liverpool, the Premier, immediately assented; and a motion to that effect having been made, it was carried without a division.   On the 5th, the select committee of the Lords met, and proceeded to hear evidence.   As in the Commons, the first witness called was Warren Hastings.   His answers to the questions put to him were of extraordinary length, but added little or nothing in substance to the evidence which he had given before the Lower House. Some further evidence was heard, and on the 9th, an animated debate took place, on a motion, made by the Marquess Wellesley, for the production of certain papers connected with the inquiry in which the house was engaged. The noble marquess introduced the motion by a very long and elaborate speech, in which he lamented the delay which had taken place with regard to the question— a delay which he viewed as prejudicial, inasmuch as it gave time for the propagation of notions respecting freedom of trade, which his lordship considered wild, and even frantic. He equally condemned the mode in which Ministers had ultimately submitted the question to the Upper House, by throwing on the table a set of resolutions unexplained, unconsidered, undebated, and almost unread. He argued, that to apply abstract principles to the present case, without due regard to its peculiar circumstances, was absurd. The origin and progress of our empire in India was altogether singular. A portion of it had fallen into our hands through the medium of commercial enterprize; it had been completed by the combined operation of commerce and military skill; and his object was to shew the impolicy and danger of legislating upon principles which did not arise out of the nature of the case. This was a complex question, and was not to be determined upon the ordinary principles of political economy. He protested against any attempt to decide it upon the pretence that it was an anomalous state of things, when the same person was merchant and sovereign. If it were an anomaly, still if it worked well in practice, he held that it ought not to be disturbed. The objection, that the Company lost by some branches of their trade, he considered no reason why they should be called upon to surrender it. It did not follow, that they could be deprived of this without sustaining even a greater loss. A merchant's books might show, that his trade in a particular article was attended with loss, and yet it might be possible, that to discontinue this particular branch of trade, might disarrange his entire system of commerce, and bring the whole to ruin. There might be such intermixture and connection in various parts of a large establishment, that to touch one was to expose every part to danger ;—thus it was with the Company. The exclusive trade, under proper modifications, was an important ingredient in their character; and he declared most solemnly, speaking, he might venture to say, with some knowledge of the subject, that, in his opinion, to deprive the Company of the trade to India, would most materially and essentially affect their ability to carry on their political functions. If it were objected, that they conducted their trade in a more expensive manner than private merchants, it behoved their lordships to recollect why they did so. It was their mixed political and commercial character which rendered this necessary and expedient. In determining the question of freedom or restriction, reference must be had to the relative condition of the two countries; their different productions, and general habits and manners. In arguing this part of the question, the noble marquess made an assertion which will now appear most extraordinary. He maintained, that if the trade were thrown completely open, the piece-goods of

India would be imported in such quantities, as seriously to injure our home manufactures;—that the fabrics of India would inundate this country, and meet British goods in the foreign markets. · Within a very few years after this prediction was hazarded, the manufactures of England succeeded in displacing those of India, upon their own soil :—a striking instance of the fallacy of political prophecy, even when delivered by able and sagacious statesmen.

The testimony of the marquess, founded on personal experience, was entitled to far more attention; and he gave it most unequivocally in favour of the East-India Company, as an instrument of government. He supported this testimony, by appealing to their banishment of foreign influence and intrigue,—to the consolidation of institutions and authorities,—to the amelioration of the condition of the natives, and especially to the state of tranquillity in which those countries had been placed—the Deccan, for instance, and the provinces north of the Mysore—which, in all previous times, had been constantly exposed to war and devastation. These were the fruits of the government of the East-India Company, and he anticipated still further improvements. The noble marquess denied that the customs, manners, feelings, and habits of the people of India were so immutable as they had been sometimes represented. He asked what it was that made the difference between the native armies that we employed in India, and those raised by the native powers. It was the fact, that our sepoys had departed from many of their original habits and prejudices, and this was the whole substantial difference between our armies and those of native chieftains. Could it be said, then, that such a people were incapable of improvement? They clearly were not; but, at the same time, change must be gradual and voluntary; not crude, precipitate, and forced.

The restrictions upon the residence of Europeans, the marquess regarded as necessary for the benefit of the natives; but he did not see how those restrictions could be maintained after the establishment of a free trade. A free trade to India, and a virtual prohibition to the trader from residing there, was a contradiction too glaring to be admitted for an instant. Some inferior points of the ministerial plan, such as the extension of the trade to the outports, met his lordship's disapprobation. He reiterated his principal objection, that to divest the Company of its commercial character, would incapacitate it as an efficient organ of government, and concluded by moving for copies of various papers illustrative of the subjects to which his speech had been directed.

Lord Buckinghamshire defended the conduct of Ministers, and quoted some opinions given by the Marquess Wellesley, when governor-general of India, favourable to an extension of private trade. He regarded the apprehension of an excessive importation of India piece-goods as visionary —and here, at least, experience has shewn that Lord Buckinghamshire was right.

The opinions of Lord Grenville were delivered in a very long and elaborate speech. He considered all former arrangements relating to the govern-

ment and commerce of India only as experiments, and not always successful ones; at best only calculated for a limited duration, never permanent,
nor even meant for permanence. He wished not to perpetuate these anomalous and imperfect arrangements, but he believed the time had not
arrived when any final regulation could be safely established. Whatever
was now done, should be temporary; and he objected to the part of the
ministerial plan which proposed that the arrangements now entered into
should be for so long a period as twenty years. He regarded the claims of
the East-India Company as nothing, and argued that the first duty of the
British Parliament was to consult the welfare of the country for which it
was called upon to legislate. Next to this object in importance, was the
interest of our own country, which was deeply implicated in the discussion.
Taking his stand upon these principles, he considered both the plan of the
Marquess Wellesley, for re-investing the Company with all their privileges,
and that of Ministers, for divesting them of a portion, as highly questionable. He was friendly to a free trade; but he could not hope that a competition, in which the whole influence of the government, territory, and
revenue of India would be arrayed against the unprotected enterprize of
individual adventurers, could either deserve the name of free trade, or
ensure its advantages. His lordship reprobated the union of the characters
of merchant and sovereign, which he alleged to be opposed to all authority,
and condemned by all experience. For nearly fifty years, the East-India
Company had exercised dominion in India, and the results of their trade,
in a country whose government they administered, and whose commerce
they monopolized, was a serious loss. If they derived a profit from any
part of their trade, it was that with China, where they enjoyed no sovereignty, but, on the contrary, were banished, like outcasts, to a remote and
narrow corner of the empire, there to reside under a perpetual quarantine.
He would not admit that the improved condition of India was to be attributed to the Company, but claimed the praise for the wisdom and justice of
the public councils of the state. For twenty years after the Company
acquired the dewannee, India was so constantly ill-governed, as to compel
the forcible interposition of Parliament; and good government commenced
only in the year 1784, when the power of controlling the Company was
vested in commissioners appointed by the Crown. It is observable, that
this was the precise period at which Lord Grenville, and the party with
which he then acted, commenced a long official career. His lordship proceeded to say that, he was for transferring the government to the Crown
altogether. He thought that arrangements might easily be made with
regard to the patronage, by which all danger of unduly increasing the
influence of Ministers might be avoided; but he did not state that he had
not thought so in 1784, when he opposed, and succeeded in throwing out,
the far-famed India Bill of the coalition ministry, because it deprived the
Company of the patronage. The plan, of which his lordship was the
advocate went to put up the civil appointments for competition among certain
public schools, and to appropriate the military to the sons of deceased officers.

Lord Grenville, adverting to the China trade, condemned the intention of Ministers to continue the monopoly to the Company. He apprehended, that when the India trade was thrown open, it would be, in fact, impracticable to preserve the Chinese monopoly, as the productions of China would be brought down in country vessels to any of the ports of the Eastern Archipelago that our merchants might choose. Lord Grenville made some observations on minor topics connected with the renewal of the Charter, and the debate was closed by Lord Liverpool, who briefly defended the line taken by Ministers. The motion for papers, not being resisted, was, of course, carried without a division; and it seems, indeed, only to have been made for the purpose of enabling the Peers to deliver their opinions on the principal question. The speech of Lord Grenville was, undoubtedly, the most remarkable that was made. The sweeping doctrines which he avowed were, perhaps, at that time, little to be expected from any member of the House of Peers; but, beyond all men, they were least to be expected from the noble baron who gave them the weight of his authority. Lord Grenville had been long on the political stage, and his conduct, on this occasion, must alike have astonished his friends and his foes. His political course had hitherto been guided by expediency, and not by abstract principle. No one had ever suspected him of being a theorist; and the robe of the philosopher was assumed too late in life, to be worn with either ease or grace. It was an incongruous covering for a man who had become grey in habits of official intrigue, and whose political life and liberal doctrines were bitter satires on each other. Independent of his general character, there were some particular incidents in Lord Grenville's career, which certainly did not lend any weight to his advocacy of the destruction of the East-India Company. He had, as has already been mentioned, been one of the most active and zealous of that party which, with Mr. Pitt at their head, had succeeded, in 1784, in displacing the coalition ministry, solely on the ground of their contemplated violation of the chartered rights of the East-India Company. Some years afterwards, he had, as a cabinet minister, given his consent to an Act which continued to the Company that monopoly and that power which he now professed to regard as so dangerous. It was unfortunate that political philosophy should have deferred her visit to this statesman until a period when both his mind and body were enfeebled by age, and his moral vision clouded by those feelings which must attend a man who, after passing a long life in office, finds himself doomed to linger out his declining years in the cold atmosphere of the opposition benches. It is possible, indeed, that there was another cause for Lord Grenville's altered views. The East-India Company had strenuously and effectually resisted the appointment of a governor-general, recommended by the ministry of which Lord Grenville was the head. It is not easy to determine what influence this might have in effecting his lordship's conversion to the principles of philosophy; but, in endeavouring to account for so extraordinary an event, it is not unreasonable to seek for an extraordinary cause.

In the House of Commons, the select committee continued the examina-

tion of witnesses which had been commenced in the committee of the whole
house. This labour lasted much longer than had been expected; but,
having been at length concluded, the Commons, on the 31st May, once
more resolved themselves into a committee of the whole house, in which
Lord Castlereagh proceeded to submit an amended series of resolutions.
The first, declaring that the privileges should continue for a limited period,
with the exception of such as might be subsequently modified or repealed,
having been moved, Mr. Bruce entered into a long and laboured history of
the Company, from its incorporation by Elizabeth, and condemned any
deviation from the existing system, as replete with danger. He was followed on the same side by a far more brilliant speaker—Mr. Charles
Grant junior, now Lord Glenelg. That gentleman glanced at the speech of
Lord Grenville in the Upper House, and argued, that the improvement,
which was admitted on all hands to have taken place in India, was attributable to the Company. He denied that the year 1784 constituted the
epoch of the commencement of a new order of things. The foundations of
improvement were laid earlier; and it was not until after much had been
done, that the Legislature had interfered. The King's Government had,
indeed, subsequently co-operated with the Company; but it did not follow,
that because certain results were produced by the operation of a complex
system, the same results would follow if one part of the system were
removed. Mr. Grant's opinion of Lord Grenville's plan for the distribution of the patronage of India, was delivered with much freedom. He
viewed it as altogether inefficient; and contended that, if adopted, it would
ultimately be the means of effecting that which it professed to guard against,
by placing the patronage at the disposal of the Ministers of the Crown. He
maintained, that the efficiency of the existing system for the government of
India consisted, in a great degree, in its publicity—every man engaged in
it acted on a conspicuous theatre. He could hardly hope that the rules of
the service would survive the extinction of the Company; and if they did,
their vigour and efficiency might be entirely superseded. He objected,
further, to the suggested plan of patronage, on the ground of its exclusive-
ness; and thought it remarkable, that a plan, professing to proceed upon
hostility to all exclusion, should, in itself, involve a system of exclusion the
most cruel and unjust. To confine the civil services of India to the highest
classes of the public schools, and the military service to the sons of officers
who had fallen in battle, was cutting off the larger portion of the British
community from a wide and honourable field of exertion. Proceeding to
the question of the union of the political and commercial functions, the
objection to it, he said, rested upon the authority of a great master of
political economy, Dr. Smith; but it was curious to observe how the charge
had shifted its ground since it was first made. Dr. Smith objected to the
union, because he thought the interests of the Company, as merchants,
would interfere with their duty as sovereigns; his disciples take precisely
the opposite ground. The merits of the Company, as rulers, are admitted;
but it is alleged that they sacrifice their interests, as merchants, to their

duties as sovereigns.   But, after all, the charge rested upon assumption.
It pronounced the junction of the sovereign and mercantile capacities to
be ruinous: but the only instance upon record of such a junction, is that
of the East-India Company; and it seemed like begging the question to
begin with laying down a theory, and then to reason from this theory, and
pronounce *à priori* upon the only fact in history to which it can be applied.
To argue that such a mixture of functions must upon theory be bad—that the
system of the East-India Company is an example of such a mixture, and
therefore is a pernicious system—such a mode of arguing was assuming the
very point to be ascertained.   " Political science," said Mr. Grant, " depends upon an induction of facts.   In no case, therefore, can it be allowed
to close the series of experiments, and to declare definitively that for the future no practical results whatever shall shake an established doctrine.   Least
of all is this allowable, when the doctrine can by possibility refer only to a
single fact, and when that single fact is at war with the doctrine."

The expectation of a great increase of commerce, flowing from an unrestrained intercourse with India, Mr. Grant considered a delusion—a delusion, however, which the evidence which had been heard ought to be
sufficient to dissipate.   The manufacturers had been duped by misrepresentations which had been industriously circulated among them, in some degree,
he believed, from ignorance, but in some degree also, he feared, from motives
less excusable.   To the happiness of the people of India, Mr. Grant apprehended great danger from the influx of Europeans.   With the solitary
exception of Asia, British adventure had not been favourable to the happiness of the countries visited.   He appealed to our intercourse with the
native tribes of North America, and especially to the effects of free trade
in Africa.   In speaking to this part of the subject, Mr. Grant expressed
himself with great severity respecting those who, having participated largely
in the slave-trade as long as it existed, were now the advocates of free
trade in India.   These remarks were especially directed against Liverpool.
The peroration of Mr. Grant's speech was remarkably bold and striking.
Having announced himself the advocate of the Natives of India, he thus
continued :

" On their behalf, in their name, I venture to intrude myself upon the house.
Through me they give utterance to their prayers. It is not my voice which you
hear, it is the voice of sixty millions of your fellow-creatures, abandoned to
your disposal, and imploring your commiseration.   They conjure you by every
sacred consideration to compassionate their condition; to pay due regard to
their situation and your own ; to remember what contingencies are suspended
on the issue of your vote. They conjure you not to make them the objects of
perilous speculation, nor to barter away their happiness for the sake of some
insignificant local interests.   It is a noble position in which this house is now
placed.   There is something irresistibly imposing in the idea, that, at so vast a
distance, and across a waste of ocean, we are assembled to decide upon the
fate of so many millions of human beings ; that we are to them as another Providence; that our sentence is to stamp the colour of their future years, and
spread over the face of ages to come, either misery or happiness. This is, indeed,
a glorious destiny for this country ; but it is one of overwhelming responsibility.

I trust, that, the question will be decided, not upon party principles, not upon trust, not upon vague theories; but upon sound practical policy, and with a view to the prosperity and preservation of our Indian Empire."

After some remarks on the danger of a system of speculation and experiment, and the impolicy of breaking down ramparts which could never be reconstructed, Mr. Grant concluded with the following sentence :

" In maintaining the system which has been the parent of so many blessings to India, we shall find our recompense in the gratitude of the people ; and if that recompense should be denied us, yet, when we look on the moral cultivation and progressive felicity of those regions, and when we reflect that these are the fruits of our wise and disinterested policy, we shall enjoy a triumph still more glorious and elevated ; a delight infinitely surpassing the golden dreams of commercial profit, or the wildest elysium ever struck out by the ravings of distempered avarice."

Such were the views of free trade, of experimental legislation, and of the interests of India, which were then avowed by Lord Glenelg.

On the 2d June, the matter was again resumed in Committee. The third resolution was in favour of free trade to India, subject to certain regulations. Mr. Rickards spoke at length, in favour of it. Mr. Charles Grant senior followed on the other side. Mr. Tierney delivered a powerful speech in behalf of the Company. He condemned altogether the plan of Ministers, which he declared had neither the support of practice nor theory. He denied that the system of 1793 could be regarded as a mere experiment. Lord Grenville had not so regarded it, but had expressed his determination to maintain a regulated monopoly. But if it were an experiment, it was entitled to be examined as to its success. If the happiness of sixty millions of people were the object, was not that obtained? If the extension of dominion were the object, had not the British dominions been extended beyond the expectation of the most sanguine? It had been said that the Company had not traded advantageously ; but if that had been proved, which it had not, it mattered not if they beneficially carried on the government. There was no reason, therefore, for saying that the experiment had failed, if experiment it were. Some of Mr. Tierney's observations evinced a much better acquaintance with the probable effects of abolishing the privileges of the Company, than was displayed by a speaker on the same side in the Upper House. He had not heard, be said, that the persons who talked so much of the happiness of India had ever proposed to allow its manufactures to be freely imported into this country. The general principle was to be, that England was to force all her manufactures upon India, and not to take a single manufacture of India in return. It was true, they would allow cotton to be brought; but then, having found out that they could weave, by means of machinery, cheaper than the people of India, they would say, leave off weaving—supply us with the raw material, and we will weave for you. This, Mr. Tierney said, might be a very natural principle for merchants and manufacturers to go upon ; but it was rather too much to talk of the *philosophy* of it, or to rank the supporters of it as in a peculiar degree the friends of India. If, instead of calling themselves the friends of India, they had professed themselves its enemies, what more could they do than advise the destruction of all Indian manufactures? It appeared to him that these alterations had been proposed for no other purpose but to appease the clamour of the merchants; and he would defy any man to point out any thing like the good of India as being the object of any of the resolutions.

On the following day, the proceedings in Committee were continued, and the speakers were numerous; but the arguments were for the most part the same that had been previously urged. The House then resumed, and the Chairman reported the resolutions. On the 11th, the resolutions were taken into consideration. On this occasion, Sir John Newport recommended delay, for the purpose of framing a more comprehensive measure of freedom, and he therefore moved that the consideration of the report be postponed to that day three months. This was opposed by Lord Castlereagh. Mr. Whitbread delivered a speech hostile to the Company and friendly to delay: ultimately, the amendment was lost by a majority of above eight to one, and the report was ordered to be again taken into consideration on the 14th. On that day, Mr. Howarth suggested the propriety of making the preamble of the bill declare in whom the sovereignty of India was vested, but declined making any motion. Sir John Newport coincided in the suggestion, and proposed a declaratory resolution, asserting the sovereignty of the Crown, and affirming that the first duty of Parliament in legislating for India was to promote its happiness. The motion was resisted by Ministers, and supported by Mr. William Smith, Mr. Horner, and other members of the opposition; Mr. Tierney differed from his friends, with regard to the first part of the resolution, but expressed himself ready to vote for the other part, which laid down the moral duties of the Indian Government. The amendment was negatived.

The next point of discussion was raised with regard to the term for which the charter of the Company should be renewed. Lord Castlereagh proposed twenty years; Mr. Ponsonby moved as an amendment, that the term should be only ten. Two divisions followed, one on the amendment, and a second on the original resolution, which gave a vast majority in favour of the longer term. Another amendment was proposed, limiting the China monopoly to ten years; on this also a division took place, when it was lost by a majority of seventy-five. On the 16th, the House having again resumed the Committee, Mr. Baring moved an amendment, confining the return of vessels from India to the port of London for a limited period. This motion was warmly opposed by the members for the outports. Mr. Grant, Sir William Curtis, and Mr. Astell supported it. On a division, it shared the fate of former amendments, being lost by a large majority. Another amendment, moved by Sir John Newport, to the effect that, the outports to be hereafter admitted to the privileges of the trade should be determined by Parliament, was negatived without a division. Lord Castlereagh then proposed, that, with respect to places not immediately within the Company's charter, applications should be made for licenses only to the Board of Control, who might consult the Directors if they thought proper. This motion, after some discussion and a division, was carried. An amendment, proposed by Mr. Baring, taking from the Board of Control the power of obliging the Company to grant licenses to persons going to India, was negatived without a division; and after a desultory conversation, the whole of the resolutions were agreed to, except one, asserting the duty of this country to extend to India useful knowledge, and moral and religious improvement, and recommending facilities to be given to persons desirous of going to or remaining in India, for the purpose of accomplishing such objects. This it was determined to postpone, and transmit the other resolutions to the Lords.

On the 18th of June, some conversation took place on the resolutions; and on the 21st, the House of Lords went into Committee on them. They were agreed to almost unanimously; the Earl of Lauderdale alone saying, not content to the first, and stating generally, that he objected to them all, but declined at that time discussing them. On the motion that the report should be received on the following day, the Marquess of Lansdowne moved that it be received that day three months. The amendment gave rise to some debate. Lord Melville supported the views of Ministers. The Earl of Lauderdale made a violent speech on the other side. He condemned the conduct of the Directors in the severest terms, and declared them unfit for the civil and military control of India. He alleged, that to say that the Court of Directors afforded the best form of government for India, was to give the lie to all experience. If the position were just, the British constitution of King, Lords, and Commons, ought to give way to a body of twenty-four Directors—for if twenty-four Directors residing in England formed the best government for India, twenty-four Directors residing in India would be the best government for Great Britain. This position of the noble Lord's it is, perhaps, unnecessary to discuss; but it is remarkable that Lord Lauderdale was, a few years earlier, very desirous of becoming the instrument through which the twenty-four Directors, whom he now denounced, were to exercise the powers of Government. Lord Grenville repeated some of his former arguments as reasons for delay; and two or three of the ministerial peers having spoken on the opposite side, the amendment was lost, on a division, by a majority of thirty-five. The bringing up the report, on the following day, gave rise to scarcely any observation.

On the 22d, an important discussion took place in the Commons, on the resolution which had been postponed. Lord Castlereagh delivered a guarded speech in favour of a regulated toleration of missionary exertions. Sir Henry Montgomery opposed it—declared the religion of the Hindoos pure and unexceptionable—denied both the practicability and the necessity of converting the Hindoos to Christianity; and represented their moral character as much superior to that of the people of this country. He treated the missionaries generally with little respect; and threw out some insinuations against the character and labours of Swartz, who, he said, was a politician as well as a preacher. He was answered by Mr. Wilberforce in a speech of great length and power. Mr. Wilberforce argued for the practicability of the conversion of the Hindoos, from experience. He refuted the aspersions cast upon the character of Swartz, and adverting to the charge that he was a politician, he said:

"I thank the honourable Baronet for reminding me of it. Swartz was a politician, but not a volunteer in that service. He became a politician at the earnest and importunate entreaty of the East-India Government; because, having to negociate with Hyder Ally, they could find no one in whose integrity and veracity that chieftain would confide, but Swartz the missionary. He therefore became a politician and an accredited envoy; because, as a missionary, he had secured to himself the universal confidence both of the Mahometans and the Hindoos."

Mr. Wilberforce proceeded to show the degraded moral state of the people of India, and the necessity and duty of permitting the Christian religion to be freely imparted to them. His speech was throughout able, eloquent, and convincing: it must be hoped, that a large portion of it would in the present day be unnecessary. The resolution was carried.

On the 28th, the House resolved itself into a Committee upon the bill. An extended discussion took place, but little additional light was thrown upon the various questions. The most remarkable speeches were those of Mr. Lushington and Mr. William Smith; the former against the conversion of the Hindoos to Christianity; the latter in its favour. "If," said Mr. Smith, "I did not believe one iota of the divine origin of that religion, yet, as a philosopher, I should admire it for the pure principles of morality which it inculcates; and I should be anxious to introduce it among the Hindoos, for the purpose of driving from the shores of India that cruel and bloody superstition which at present disgraces them." Mr. Tierney repeated his former arguments against the proposed changes. Finally, the report was received, and ordered to be taken into further consideration on the 1st of July. On that day, various amendments were proposed and lost. Among them was one against the clause respecting the propagation of Christianity in India. Mr. Marsh made a violent speech against the missionaries, and was answered by Mr. Wilberforce. On the following day, the Committee was resumed, and some discussion took place, but it proceeded languidly. A motion for an establishment for the Scottish Church in India, was lost. On the 12th, the report was brought up, when Mr. Howarth opposed its reception, in a speech of much power. In the course of it, he said:

"The monopoly of the Company was originally granted them for the public benefit; and it is but fair to ask whether it has produced it. Through all the varied vicissitudes of two centuries, they were, undoubtedly, monopolists: nobody was found to claim a participation with them in the drenchings at Amboyna; they were left in the undisturbed possession of the Black Hole in Calcutta; they had the exclusive privilege of fighting, single-handed, against all the powers of Europe who had got a footing on the peninsula of India. But, now that they have, with a valour almost unexampled, driven every hostile European from the Continent of India; now that they have acquired an extent of territory of nearly 4,000 square miles; brought under the government and controul of this country a population of sixty millions; realized a revenue of sixteen millions; raised an army of 150,000 men; erected fortresses; established factories; swept the Indian seas of every hostile flag, and possessed themselves of a sea-coast of 3,000 miles in extent, with all the facilities of commerce; *now* it is that the *liberality* of the British merchant claims an unqualified participation in a free trade to India; *now*, the wisdom of the Legislature interferes to render inefficient that instrument by which these acquisitions have been allowed; and its equity is *now* about to refuse to secure even the dividends of that capital stock which has been sunk in the public service. *Now*, it is discovered that twenty-four merchants are very unfit persons—not to manage the government—for that, they are admitted to be eminently qualified—but to manage the commerce of their dominions."

There was certainly much truth in this; but it was hardly to be expected that truth and justice should be successful in a contest with selfishness and avarice, fortified, as they now were, by the iron doctrines of political economy.

On the 13th, the bill was read a third time, and passed. In the House of Lords it passed almost *sub silentio,* the Earl of Lauderdale alone opposing it, because it did not go far enough; and *his* hostility evaporated in an angry protest.

Thus was inserted the narrow end of the wedge, which was to shatter the mercantile privileges of the East-India Company. It has since been driven home; and the commercial grandeur of the Company is among the things that have passed away.   E.

DAVID HALLIBURTON, ESQ.

We have this month to record the death of David Halliburton, Esq., a gentleman whose long and honourable career in the Civil Service of the East-India Company calls for, at least, a brief notice.

Mr. Halliburton entered the service on the Madras Establishment in the year 1770, and immediately on his arrival in India, was employed in the Revenue Department. From the moment of his landing, he devoted him-self with extraordinary ardour and perseverance to the acquisition of every species of knowledge connected with the interests of the Company, to whose service he had devoted his time and talents. His exertions were as successful as they were unremitting. He rapidly acquired an extraordinary degree of familiarity with the customs and languages of that part of India in which his lot had been cast; and he found ample opportunities of applying his information beneficially for his employers and the country which they governed. At an early age, he obtained the office of Persian translator, and the ability with which he filled it more than justified the selection.

While thus honourably occupied in the laborious discharge of his duties, and the sedulous cultivation of his mind, he had the happiness of being instrumental in introducing to India two individuals, destined to act a conspicuous part in its history. In 1779, Sir Thomas Munro arrived, to join the Madras army, and in 1781, Sir John Malcolm landed for the same purpose. Mr. Halliburton received both these distinguished officers on their arrival, and was not slow in discerning their talents. The countenance and support of a servant of Mr. Halliburton's character and experience were valuable aids to the personal claims of the two young officers, and they were bestowed with frankness and sincerity.

From 1782 till his retirement from office, Mr. Halliburton was unremittingly employed in revenue affairs, and in 1791 he obtained a seat at the Board. Here his fine talents, extensive knowledge, and laborious industry had an ample field for their display. The period was a remarkable and critical one. Among the duties devolving on the Board, was a new arrangement of the territories of the Carnatic. Mr. Halliburton had also to contend against a hostile administration; but though he encountered an opposition both determined and unscrupulous, he finally triumphed. His conduct throughout this arduous period reflected the highest honour on himself, and afforded the fullest satisfaction to the Court of Directors. In 1795, he retired from the service; on which occasion, the Government of Madras transmitted to the Court of Directors a most gratifying testimonial to his merits and services. The judgment of the Court confirmed that of the local Government. The eulogium was declared well-merited, and the conduct of Mr. Halliburton pronounced worthy of the imitation of the service generally.

From the period of his retirement, Mr. Halliburton resided in England, enjoying in the retrospect of an active and useful career, and in the friendship of a wide circle of intelligent and estimable men, the best reward which virtuous exertion can receive on this side the grave. Though withdrawn from any official connexion with India, he never ceased to take a warm interest in its welfare; and every question bearing upon its prosperity seemed to call forth afresh the energies of his youth.

He died at his seat at Bushy, on the 12th June 1836, in the 86th year of his age.

OPERATIONS IN GUZERAT, IN 1803.

At the time the action described in this paper was fought, few military operations in India, except those on a large scale, ever found their way to the Indian, much less to the British public. It is an attempt to rescue from oblivion one of the many gallant, but nearly forgotten, actions performed by the army in India.

" It was on a fine morning in the month of February, 1803, as I recollect, when our brigade, which consisted of the 75th regiment, part of the 86th, and two native battalions, the 2d battalion, 1st regiment, and a battalion of the 7th, was paraded in marching order at day-break; but there being some demur at head-quarters relative to our movement, we remained rather a long time sitting under trees, wrapped up in our cloaks.

" The officers for the advanced guard, however, were at length summoned; the guard moved off, and we fell in, and followed them; the 75th leading, and the detachment of the 86th in the rear.

" I ought, perhaps, to have premised, that this brigade formed a part of the British force stationed in the province of Guzurat, and was employed, after the siege of Baroda, in a harassing pursuit of a rebellious brother of the Guicowur; also, that our encampment was to the northward of the Mehindri or Mihie River, and not far distant from the town of Dakoor.

" Our march, which we now learned was to attack a large body of Arabs, Sind'his, and Mahrattas, under Kanojee, the above-mentioned brother of the

Guicowar, led through a thickly-wooded or jungly country, intersected by deep ravines, and skirting the high banks of the river Mihie, one of the largest in the western provinces of India.

" We had marched through rugged and dusty roads, about eight or nine miles, when, at the entrance into a deep ravine, leading down to the river (which ravine had a small open space before it, and in the vicinity of which the enemy were encamped), of a sudden, we heard a few straggling shots, and by and by a continued blaze of musketry.

" Our men were, therefore, halted to load, and the fire still continuing in front, we moved on. We had not, however, proceeded far, when a rush from the ravine, like a torrent, bore us back a considerable distance, and we found that the advanced guard, penned up in a deep narrow road, exposed to the fire of the Arab sharpshooters, posted on the steep sides or banks behind trees, and without the power to return it, had suffered so severely in killed and wounded, that they had been obliged to retire.

" A six-pounder also, the artillery-men being mostly killed or wounded, had fallen into the possession of the Arabs.

" In these circumstances, the flank companies of the 2d battalion, 1st regiment, and the detachment of the 86th, were immediately ordered from the rear to the front, and headed by our gallant commanding officer, Colonel H., charged, cheering, down the ravine, and being in some measure covered by the fire of our flanking parties, and two six-pounders, after a sharp conflict, in which the combatants fought hand to hand, drove the Arabs back with great slaughter, re-taking the gun, which they had not had time or space to turn against us. Following up their success, and passing over the bodies of friends and enemies, they soon reached the encampment of our concealed foes, in the midst of the jungle, and took almost every article in it,—tents, camels, and baggage of all descriptions.

" The fugitives in their dismay flew to the river, leaving all behind them, and many were said to have been drowned in crossing; however, they soon after collected together at a town about ten or twelve miles off, and we were obliged to follow, abd beat them again, before they dispersed.

" The booty taken was, I believe, considerable, as camels were sold in our camp next day at twenty and thirty rupees each; and one of the native officers of my company obtained a belt belonging to one of the Arab chiefs, filled with knives and daggers, the whole hilted and covered with pure gold.

" The narrow road down to the river was completely covered with the bodies of the slain.—Europeans, Arabs, and native infantry lying promiscuously; some of them across each other. They were, however, strewed thickest near the gun, which appeared to have been the scene of a most desperate conflict.

" No fault could be attributed to the advanced guard for retiring, in the difficulties in which they were placed; the leading sections being killed and wounded to a man.

" After all was over, we were obliged to remain at this place until the evening, to provide for the carriage of the wounded officers and men; and this being effected, and the dead buried, we returned to our encampment of the morning, worn out, and with heavy hearts; for scarcely any but had to regret the loss of a comrade or a friend.

" I forgot to mention that we had a party of Mahratta Horse with us; but, I believe, they restricted their exertions to sharing very largely in the plunder of the enemy's camp."

AUTOBIOGRAPHY OF A BURMAN.

CAPTAIN McCALLY, of the 44th regt. Madras N.I., has transmitted to the Madras Literary Society and Auxiliary of the Royal Asiatic Society, a translation of the Autobiography of Tsura Moung-Bo, his Burmese teacher, " a man truly characteristic of his nation, and whose name may be found quoted in the Reports of the American Baptist Mission in Ava." He is well-known, he adds, to many who have served in Rangoon, and in our newly acquired province in Tenasserim, on account of the accidents which befel him during a long life, and Capt. M'Cally rightly concludes that these sketches of biography make us more familiarly acquainted than any other means, with the manners and habits of the people, and the peculiarities of their government. We extract this curious autobiography from the *Madras Journal of Literature and Science,** edited by the able secretary of the society :—

I was born at Prome, in the month of Gnayon, the fifth day of the waxing of the moon, on Saturday about sunrise, in the year 1134.† My mother, whose name was Maihla, was a Talain from the Pegue country. My father Moung-Biau, whose ancestors lived in Motzobo, the birth-place of Alompra, was a Burman. He was in the service of Noung-daughee, the eldest son of Alompra, and eventually received the office of *toit-thooghee* or *myothooghee*‡ of Prome from him, after he became king; on which occasion, his Majesty gave him for a wife my mother, who, with her sister, had been taken prisoners in the war against Pegue, carried on by Alompra, and had been presented to Noung-daughee the heir-apparent; in whose palace they remained as *kolouks*§ for two years.

My father was a clever man, and commenced teaching me to read and write as soon as I had attained the age of seven years. I continued my studies under him till I was twelve years of age, when he died, leaving my mother, an elder sister, and myself. He had some property in slaves, cattle, ground, &c.; but government demands, to the amount of 6,000 tickals|| of silver were brought against his estate. The property was sold to meet these demands, and did not prove sufficient. The myowon ordered me to pay my father's debt, and to take upon myself his office. I pleaded inability, in consequence of my youth, and my want of means. He sent me to Ava, to which place I was accompanied by my half-brother, Moung-O. I was there presented to the ministers in the *klotdau,*¶ who offered me the situation left vacant by my father's death. I pleaded inability to fill it. The ministers said, one of my elder relations should do the duty for me during my minority. They represented the circumstance to the king, who agreed that I was too young for the office, and therefore directed that my half-brother, Moung-O, should perform the duty in my name, and that I should always be seated in his lap when he was administering justice in the *Goum.***

I returned to Prome, and lived with my mother, enjoying the fruits of the newly-bestowed office for about one year. At this period, my mother's younger sister, who had been presented to the toit-thooghee of Dalla, and had gone on business to Ava with her husband, was on her way back, when she found her sister at Prome. After a most affectionate meeting, my mother formed the determination of quitting Prome, and retiring to her sister's house. Nothing of this was mentioned to me; but one night I was called away, hurried into a

* April 1835. No. vii.   † A.D. 1773.   ‡ Chief civil officer of a district.
§ Ladies of the palace.   ‖ About 1½ rupee is equal to a tickal of silver.
¶ Principal hall of justice, where the ministers sit in council.   ** Court of justice.

boat with many rowers, and carried with rapidity to Dalla. My mother left all her property behind, except a few ornaments.

I lived in the district of Dalla quietly for about one year, at the expiration of which, an insurrection broke out. In the year 1145, Gna-kontau and Gnasat, who were Talains,* and the *paineens*† of two royal boats, headed the insurgents, attacked and carried Rangoon, and kept possession of it for seven days. My aunt's husband, the toit-thooghee of Dalla, joined the insurgents. The royal army at last made its appearance, defeated the rebels, retook Rangoon, and apprehended a vast number of the insurgents, of whom about 3,000 were executed, and amongst them my uncle. A great many were burnt to death, after the usual Burman custom. A house of bamboo trellis-work, with a floor of the same description, was built, under which a quantity of straw and gun-powder was placed; the criminals were bound hand and foot, and put into this house. Neither age nor sex was spared; it was sufficient to be connected by blood or marriage with a rebel, to be deemed worthy of this cruel death. The guilty and innocent suffered alike. A train was laid to the powder, and on a signal given the whole were blown up.

In this insurrection I was accused of having had my share, from the circumstance of my living with my uncle; but on explaining the manner in which I had been withdrawn from my office at Prome, I was, with great difficulty, excused, with the confiscation, however, of all the property I possessed, which left me in great distress. I repaired to Rangoon with my mother, whilst my aunt was ordered up to Ava.

My half-brother had been ordered down with a division of the royal army against the rebels, and found me out at Dalla. He wished me to return with him to Prome, but my mother resolved not to go, and I staid with her. My half-brother gave me fifty tickals of silver, and a *putzo*‡ for my present necessities, and recommended me to a friend of his in Rangoon, who employed me as a clerk. From the emoluments of this office, I had to support my mother and eldest sister, and continued to exercise it for about one year, when my patron, the *tsarai-daughee*,§ on his being summoned to Ava, recommended me to Moungoin, the myothooghee of Zwaithabon, who lived in Rangoon. My duty under this latter person was that of an agent. I had to attend at the *yuom*, and receive the orders addressed to my master for the levy of money, men, or other supplies. These orders I had to take to the *myotsarai*,‖ an officer under my master, and demand the amount of requisition from him. To give an example of the peculation which is prevalent amongst the Burmese officers of government, I will mention that, were the order for the levy of 100 tickals of silver from the district, the myotsarai would levy from the inhabitants 110; of the additional ten he would keep five to himself, and give the other five to the myothooghee. On my receiving the 100 tickals, I would proceed to the yuom, and offer the first day thirty tickals, as the whole sum I had been able to collect up to that period, promising to pay an equal sum the next day, on which I would take thirty tickals more, and promise to pay twenty the following day. The day after paying the twenty tickals, on being asked for the remainder, I would declare the impossibility of obtaining any more; that much difficulty had been experienced in collecting what I had given in. On this I should be seized, tied by the arms, and exposed in the sun. I would then promise to produce the money the next day, and should be released, but failure produced a similar punishment; at last, if I could stand out for some days this kind of

* A race of people inhabiting Pegue.
† Literally helmsmen, people of some consequence in the royal war-boats.
‡ A man's cloth or dress.   § Royal secretary.   ‖ A district-writer or secretary.

treatment, it would be taken for granted that I could not collect any more, and the sum to be levied would be rated at eighty tickals. The twenty tickals which I had obtained in this way, I would divide with the myothooghee. This is a common practice; no shame is attached to it; I had no salary, and was obliged to pay myself in this way.

I continued in office under the Zwaithabon myothooghee for about one year and a-half, at which period I had amassed a little money; and employing it advantageously in the purchase of paddy, at the rate of five tickals per 100 baskets, I was enabled, when the royal army marched to Martaban, and the price of paddy rose, in consequence, to thirty tickals per 100 baskets,* to realize a handsome profit of about 1,000 tickals of silver.

I was now about seventeen years of age, and being anxious to commence my noviciate in a monastery, I proposed it to my mother, and obtained her consent to my becoming a a *shenpèer*.† I delivered the whole of my gains to my mother for her support, and was received, after the usual ceremony, into the monastery of Kenghee Bouai. Here I studied the following works, *viz.* the four *Peetza-wekkana*,‡ *Kandaka*,‡ *Theekeea*,‡ *Lointsaba*,‡ *Dantsaiba*,‡ *Puraikee*,‡ four *Brama-sozas*,‡ &c., all connected with my rank in the monastery. I afterwards studied *Zat-tsaisoung*.‡ In this monastery I remained about one year, and then proceeded to Prome to pursue my studies. There I entered the monastery of Ruhan Tsaradaughee Gnawen, and continued in it for six months, during which time I read *Thuda-sheet-soung*. The tsaradaughee was very old, and I expressed myself desirous of quitting, for fear of giving him trouble; he kindly insisted on my going to Oonanda, one of his disciples, who lived at Lettat-pyeen, about three *dôings*§ from Prome. On arriving there, I found the village small, the number of *ruhans*,‖ probationers, and other orders of the monastery, numerous, and provisions scarce. I continued my studies in *Thuda-sheet-soung*, but I was so inquisitive, and my zeal for learning caused me to make so many references to the ruhan, that he complained of not being able to attend his other disciples and answer my questions too; under these circumstances, I thought it advisable to proceed elsewhere, in hopes of finding a teacher who had more leisure to attend to my wants. I returned to Prome, where my half-brother Moung-O was still exercising the office of toit-thooghee; he received me kindly, and recommended me to go to Pandonghma Ponghee, who had his monastery in the village of Poghan,· near Prome. With this person I sojourned nearly six months. I found him, how-, ever, a man of very limited acquirements, but with modesty sufficient to tell me that he was incapable of adding to my stock of learning. I represented this circumstance to my half-brother, and afterwards took my departure for Amrapoora, and entered the monastery of Bhagya Tsaradau, a man of learning, and staid there two years. With him I studied *Thuda-sheet-soung*,¶ *Weenee*,¶ *Shengyo*,¶ *Bedeen*,¶ &c. At the end of this period, I renounced the priest's garb, and entered the service of the king's son, the *piemen* or prince of Prome, as a *loo-bioo-dau*, or personal follower. I was appointed to teach the young princess Senbiumai to read and write.

This person had many young ladies as companions, all of whom at the same time received instruction from me. I proceeded to the ladies' apartments in the prince's palace daily at eight o'clock in the morning, and was ushered into

---

* A basket contains from thirty to thirty-two Arcot seers.

† A noviciate. Youths generally enter the monasteries as such for their education, shave their heads, and wear the priest's cloth.

‡ Works on ethics, theology, logic, &c.

§ A dôing is about two English miles.

‖ Ruhan is an order of priesthood.

¶ Works on ethics, theology, &c.

an open verandah, where the princess and her ladies were seated on carpets. Cushions raised somewhat higher than the rest, in compliment to my office of tutor, were placed for me. Here I had a difficult task to perform. The young ladies, who were from eight to fifteen years of age, were full of spirit, careless of the arrangement of their dress, and the postures in which they placed themselves. I was a young man, little more than twenty years of age, and subject to all the temptations which surround that age; but a word said, or a look conveyed to give rise to the slightest suspicion that I had formed an attachment for any one of these young ladies, or that I had taken any liberty with them, would have cost me my head. I was the only male person in their society, and this circumstance seemed to have banished from my fair pupils all restraint. In this manner I was employed for more than a twelvemonth.

The piemen, my master, re-established me in my situation of toit-thooghee of Prome. My half-brother continued to act for me, but I received the principal part of the emoluments. The prince was some months afterwards called to Amrapoora by the king, and I accompanied him.

In the year 1152, I took orders as a ruhan, in the monastery of Moungdoung, the isaradaughee, where I remained for three years. At my solicitation, I was permitted by the isaradaughee to visit my mother at Rangoon. At this time I commenced studying the Talain language, in the different monasteries about Rangoon and Pegue. I was engaged by the Dalla myothooghee to superintend the building of a monastery in his district, and after the completion of it, took orders as a *poggo*.* In this new monastery, I staid one year. I afterwards repaired to a monastery at Syriam, where I remained some months, and then went to Martaban. At the end of about three months' residence at this latter place, I again renounced the priest's garb, and betook myself to secular employment.

There was a friend of mine in Martaban, a tara-thooghee or advocate, with whom I lived. From him I borrowed 200 tickals of silver, and turned merchant. I purchased merchandize of various descriptions, and proceeded to the Thoung-yeen river, which falls into the Salween. Here I met with a isaukai or chief of Kariens, with whom I intended to carry on my speculations, and we accordingly performed the ceremony of *tswaithouk*, or drinking each other's blood. As this is a singular ceremony, I will describe it.

It is a custom amongst certain tribes of Kariens,† in order to assure themselves of the fidelity and fair-dealing of those with whom they are about to transact business, that the contracting parties, in the presence of the assembled villagers, should each prick the forefinger of his right hand with a needle, so as to draw blood. The finger is then held over a small vessel of water, and the drop of blood is allowed to fall into it. If the drop diffuses itself immediately in the water, the faith of the person is impeached; but if it retains its globular form, it is a good omen, and the parties drink the blood thus dropped, each drinking the blood of the other.

After performing this ceremony satisfactorily, I was entertained and fed by the Kariens. I delivered all my merchandize to the isaukai, to dispose of according to his discretion. This investment of merchandize was received as a present, and divided by the chief amongst his followers, who amounted to about 500, and lived all in one house or barrack. I was entertained by them for about twenty days, when I expressed my intention of returning. The isaukai communicated this to his followers, and called on them to return to me,

---

* A high order of priesthood.

† Kariens, a race supposed to be the aborigines of the country, chiefly reside on hills and woody tracts.

as a present, some of the produce of their forests, equal in value to what each had received. Some gave a proportion of elephants' teeth, others bees' wax, &c. The Kariens I allude to were subjects of the Zammai Tsaubwa, and the penalty of visiting them was great. I was therefore obliged to return cautiously at night, to prevent discovery. I dared not enter Martaban with my boat; I concealed it in a creek near the town called Dawaikoun. I went myself to Martaban, and communicated my success to my friend. I found an opportunity soon of disposing of my goods to a Chinese junk which was in the river. I had only taken up goods to the amount of 200 tickals, and my return cargo brought me 1,500 tickals of silver.

In those days, there were numerous large and populous villages in the province of Martaban. The Talains had not yet rebelled. I made an advantageous speculation in paddy. I purchased, early in the season, a large quantity, at seven tickals per 100 baskets, and at the latter end of the season, when it became dearer, I sold it at sixteen tickals per 100 baskets. I went to Yë, where I built a large boat, brought it to Martaban, and lading it with rice and glazed jars, despatched it, with a fleet of six other boats, under charge of my nephew, to Penang, for the purpose of trade. I accompanied the fleet as far as Yë, where I stopped. On our way thither, we encountered violent winds from the east, which obliged us to take shelter in the island of Callagouk. It was on this island that, at the suggestion of Moungshoeyai, a rich person who was with us, we set to work, and dug a well, and planted it round with coco-nut and betel-nut trees. This well is the same which I visited in company with some English officers a short time ago. I had not been there for twenty years, but recognized the spot; few of the trees we planted remained, and the sea had made great advances on the island, so as to threaten a speedy destruction of the well, which at present is in good order, and yields abundance of good water. We staid here three days, and then took our departure for Yë. At Yë I remained, and speculated in the building of boats.

On the return of my boat from Penang to Yë, in the month of Pyatho 1170, the *doinwon's** army had reached Martaban, and he had issued an order, that no boats should leave any of the ports without his permission; accordingly, my boat was detained at Yë until the arrival of the doinwon there, with an army consisting, as was generally supposed, of 30,000 men. I petitioned him for the release of my boat, and offered him a present of fifteen tickals of gold, which he would not receive, but directed me to hold my boat in readiness to convey some of the sick of the army to Tavoy, after which, I was told, I might return. I conveyed forty soldiers in my boat to Tavoy, where, in common with many others, I was obliged to anchor in the harbour at the entrance of the river, where I found several other boats full of soldiers. Seven or eight days after reaching Tavoy, the doinwon arrived there with his army by land. We were then ordered up the river, and the troops we had on board were disembarked. An account of our cargoes was demanded. On giving in mine, the doinwon directed me to land the articles and deliver them up to him, saying he would purchase the whole; this was done to all the other boats, also, which had come from Penang. After going through the formality of taking the account, and the delivery of the articles, the doinwon ordered the crews of all the five boats to be seized, and have the *létoik*, or neck-stock, applied to them, on the plea that they had no right to go to Penang to trade. I never afterwards received any payment for my goods.

We remained in confinement for about one month, when it was ordered, that

* The title of the Burmese general entrusted with the expedition.

we should again be put in our boats, our legs in irons, and be sent to Mergui; this was done, and the soldiers rowed the boats. On arriving there, I obtained my personal liberty by making a present to the officer on board the boat, of a ring, which I had caused to be purchased at Penang for eighty dollars.

The doinwon's *tsikkai*, or lieutenant, was at Mergui. He had been an acquaintance of mine at Amrapoora, and I remained under his protection for about fifteen days, when he directed me to proceed with my boat to Martaban, to make some purchases for him. The tsikkai told me that the doinwon had ordered that some one should be deputed to demand the completion of the levies of troops from Dalla, Rangoon, Pantano, Syriam, and Donabew, and that I must proceed under another officer on that duty. It was now the rainy season, the month of Gnayon. Nine boats started from Mergui; every one of which was wrecked. I never heard of any part of their crews being saved, except six men of my own boat, which was wrecked near the river Guwai, in the neighbourhood of Bapain. The boat struck on a sand, about four o'clock in the morning, and we had just time to seize a few oars and other spars, to enable us to keep afloat. Two others and myself tied an oar and one of the masts of the boat together, and by this means, after floating about all day, reached the shore just before sunset; we were almost exhausted, and did not find any others of our companions till the next morning, when we discovered three more, as we were going along the shore.

We had nothing to eat with us, and had recourse to the fruit of the Neepal palm to allay our hunger. Two of us had saved our putzos, which, being torn up and divided amongst us, afforded just sufficient covering for decency. We spent two days and nights, wandering along the uninhabited and inhospitable coast, constantly annoyed by myriads of musquitoes, which deprived us of all rest. We at length arrived at an encampment of *motzos*, or hunters, by whom we were treated kindly, and fed for three days, after which they took us to the residence of their families in the jungle. Their houses were built on trees; they inhabited the jungle for years without going to any town, or seeing any person out of their own society, and were so desirous to continue this secluded life, that when we took our departure, they made us swear that we would not disclose this place of their abode. They gave us a boat, and information as to the route we were to pursue towards the neighbouring Kariens. We accordingly left them, and after one day's journey reached the Karien village, where there was a monastery, into which we were received, well fed, and clothed. Here we remained about one month, after which I accompanied one of the *ponghees** towards Rangoon; but not daring to enter that town, for fear of being apprehended as a deserter from the doinwon's army, I went to Panlang, and there remained till I thought it safe to return to Rangoon, whither I at length went, and met my mother and sister. My half-brother was a *padazo*† in the service of the myedaimen, or prince of Meeaidai, and informed his master of my arrival. I was summoned to his presence, and having related my story, I was appointed by him to act as *oukpanyai*, or writer, to keep the roster of the night-guard which mounted at the prince's. With the myeidaimen I remained a twelve-month, when I was deputed by him to Amrapoora, with presents to the king and other members of the royal family. On delivering the presents, I saw, amongst others, the piemen, who recognized me, and asked me what had become of me since I left the monastery, and why I did not come to him. His royal highness ordered me to stay at Amrapoora, and said he would write to the myeidaimen about me. I staid with the prince about six months, after which

* Priests.   † A sort of butler or majordomo.

he ordered me to Rangoon, to fill the situation of *atsoo-yai** to his royal highness's men, about 800 in number.

About this time, 1174, his Majesty Moungwoin having consulted certain prophecies in some ancient books, and learning by them that his kingdom was to be overturned by rebellion, did, for the purpose of ensuring the fidelity of his subjects, issue a royal edict, that all the twelve different orders of royal servants, *viz.* elephanteers, cavalry, shieldmen, golden spearsmen, silver spearsmen, musketeers, cultivators of royal land, *kulabin* or corps of foreigners, Feringhee musketeers, *pwaabet-yan*, &c. &c., should send their male children, from five to twelve years of age, to the capital, to be organized in corps. Above 40,000 of these children were collected. They were each marked by tattooing on the shoulders; one shoulder bore the effigy of *kyenthai*, the other of the *To* (particular animals). The preparation for tattooing was said to be an antidote to bruises or blows. These children were called *kyagles* (or young tigers), from the circumstance of the king having been born on a Monday, and the *kya*, or tiger, being the corresponding representation of the planet moon. I was appointed to the charge of 1,500 of these children, of whom none were above the age of twelve. They received from the royal granary, each, one basket of paddy per month; and, every ten days, three small copper coins, to buy other articles of food with. In consequence of the tender age of these children, which rendered it necessary to hire people to beat out the paddy, there did not remain sufficient for their sustenance, and they were reduced to a state of starvation. On a representation to the king, his majesty ordered the supply of paddy to be increased to two baskets each, monthly; and that they should each receive two tickals of Dine silver per month, for their bazaar expenses. This money, however, was not entrusted to me or any body else who might have taken care of it, but it was given to the *akiats*, the lowest rank of officers, commanding parties of ten boys. These akiats were themselves boys, the consequence of which was that, as soon as the money was paid, it was quickly dissipated in trash, and, till the next payment, the boys were obliged to resort to the tanks in the neighbourhood, and procure for food the shell fish with which they abound. This had an injurious effect on their health, and the cholera-morbus attacking them, killed a vast number of them. Many hundreds died daily; and of the 40,000, scarcely half that number survived.

Not liking this state of things, I took an opportunity of absconding clandestinely to Rangoon, but I was pursued and apprehended there, and brought back to Amrapoora, where I was imprisoned for one month. From this state I was released through the intercession of the piemen's son-in-law, who employed me in purchasing paddy for him in the lower provinces. On my return to Ava, I solicited the appointment of *atsee-een* to the meeawaddee and piemen's men at Rangoon, which I obtained; but so many exclusive privileges were attached to the office, and it gave such great offence to the myaidemen, who was myowon of Rangoon, that he used his influence to have it cancelled, in which he succeeded.

Whilst this was taking place, the present king's grandfather, who was on the throne, was taken very ill, and the heir to the throne, the present king, took upon himself a kind of regency. He summoned the piemen, his uncle, and the toungoomen, and their principal officers, to court, by order of the king; but when they arrived, he demanded of them to state their sentiments of loyalty to himself. They all represented that the king was still living, and to him alone they owed allegiance. On this they were confined in prison.

* A sort of muster-master.

When the king died, the present king ascended the throne; and one of his first acts was to have the toungoomen's neck broken, his body put into a large jar, and thrown into the Irrawaddy.

The piemen was also murdered by a secret and different process. The jailor was frequently questioned whether the prince was dead, and he was handsomely fee'd; he took the hint, and, after strangling the unfortunate prince, reported his death in prison, as an ordinary occurrence.

The present king also caused twelve of his uncles to have their necks broken, and murdered many more officers suspected of being unloyal.

I was fortunate in not going to Amrapoora, for, if I had, I should certainly have lost my life along with the others.

About this time, Shukeen-Moung-moo, a relation of the present king's grandfather, was appointed myowon* of Martaban. I went to him with some presents, and he expressed his surprize at seeing me, and congratulated me on having escaped the fate that seemed so unavoidable; told me the "fire was not yet quenched," and advised me to accompany him to Martaban, which I did, and was appointed by him to act for the *myo-ok*,† of Durë, in the island of Belew, during the absence of that officer at court. Thukeen Moung-moo had been sent to Martaban to supersede Moung-tsat, or Thumoin Broo, who had got into disgrace, in consequence of not proceeding to court when ordered to do so, on the death of the king. He was directed to be seized, but he fled to Rangoon, where, eventually, he was apprehended.

At the end of five months, I was relieved from my temporary office of myo-ok of Durë, by the return of the myothooghee, and took up my residence again in Martaban. Shortly after this, an army of about 10,000 men, with the sekkiä-won, as commander-in-chief, and Menghee Oozina, lieutenant-general, commanding the van, arrived at Martaban. The sekkia-won made his headquarters there, whilst Menghee Oozina was despatched with the advanced division, consisting of 3,500 men, to Azimee, up the Atraun river. This took place in the year 1183, about the month of Natdau. A stockade was erected at Azimee, and I employed myself in carrying provisions to the army from Martaban.

The object of this expedition was to seize and secure any of the Siamese who might quit their country, through dread of the cholera-morbus, which was raging amongst them. A very exaggerated account of this dreadful scourge had been carried to the king of Ava from Tavoy; and it was said that the king of Siam had lost two of his queens by the disease, and was so terrified, that he had quitted his palace, and became a wanderer from monastery to monastery.

This force continued as an army of observation till the month of Thudeergyot, and the only affair of arms which took place during its occupation of Azimee, was the attack on Kutoinzoin stockade, the advanced post of the Siamese, by the troops of Menghee Oozina. The garrison fled on the first assault, and after pillaging the place, the Burmese troops retired immediately to their position at Azimee. Menghee Oozina was at this time about sixty-five years of age, a tall thin man, about six feet high, fair complexioned for a Burman — greyhaired and nearly bald, and his countenance flushed by the excessive use of spirituous liquors. He was a great consumer of betel-leaf and nut; and from the great use of these stimulants, the sensitiveness of his palate had become so much injured, that he was obliged to use the most stimulating food procurable. His cooks could not suit his taste sufficiently in the

* Governor of a province.   † Chief of a district.

dishes which they prepared for him, and he took into his head the whim of endeavouring to remedy the defect by dressing his own victuals.

He used to put a most extraordinary quantity of chillies, *gnapee,** and salt into his food, so as to render it quite intolerable to the tastes of others. He was a man of exceedingly cruel disposition. I once saw an instance of it. He had ordered his cook to be flogged with a rattan till he nearly died, because he had lost three *maranthees*† entrusted to his charge, fruit of no value at the time. I had in my possession some very fine fruit of the same description, and whilst the cook was undergoing this cruel flagellation, I presented my fruit to Menghee Oozina, and with great difficulty begged the cook off.

The advance under Oozina returned to Martaban in the month of Thudeen-gyat, and the sekkiawoon, after establishing Oozina as myowon of that place, took his departure for the capital.

On the breaking up of the army, I conveyed some of Yé-won Mounkoing's soldiers in my boat to Rangoon, and continued my mercantile pursuits there, trading up the river Irrawaddy as far as Prome, Myaide, and the neighbourhood.

In the year 1184, an army under command of Tsara-wonghee Moungnai, with Bundoola, as lieutenant-general, marched against Cussay to quell an insurrection there, which object being effected, the army was directed against Assam, in 1185, to quell a rebellion in that country. Tsara-wonghee Moungnai is said to have died on his return towards Ava, from the latter expedition. No levies were drawn from the country below Prome for this army. This same year, Bundoola offering his services to the king to conquer Chittagong, was despatched with an army for that purpose. In the month of Taboung, orders came from Ava to prepare for an attack by the English. Bundoola, when the quarrel took place with the English on the Chittagong frontier, wrote to say that he had information of an armament, consisting of forty-seven sail of vessels, having been fitted out with the intention of making a descent on Rangoon. Great activity prevailed in fitting Rangoon for the attack. Defences were thrown up along the river side. News had reached Rangoon of the success of Bundoola on the Chittagong frontier, and, as it was greatly exaggerated, the Burmese did not expect, before this, that the English would come to Rangoon. The town, however, was surprized on the 14th day of the waxing of the moon, in the month Kutzon, by the appearance of a large fleet sailing up the river. I had been ordered to superintend about 160 men in throwing up a parapet of earth on the eastern side of the town, near a creek, close to which was a whitewashed wooden-house, built for ambassadors, and which has since been burnt.

The gai-tsikkai was the first who arrived with news that a vast number of vessels were at the mouth of the river, supposed to be English, and duly reported the circumstance to the *gai-wons*‡ at Rangoon; they said to him: " Why are you come to alarm the people of Rangoon to no purpose, and without cause ?" and put him immediately in confinement. Tsikkai§ Mounglat was despatched by them on the instant to ascertain if the gai-tsikkai's story was true. Having proceeded down the river, the tsikkai Mounglat slept at the chokey during the night, and the next morning went in one of his boats to the first vessel. He was received on board kindly and fed, and on his departure was commissioned to deliver a packet to the authorities at Rangoon. Tsikkai

---

* A preparation of fish, sometimes extremely offensive to the smell.
† A fruit of the mangoe species.   ‡ Officers of the marine department.
§ Tsikkai, deputy or lieutenant.

Mounglat arrived at Rangoon about sunset, and delivered his packet to the gai-wons, excusing himself from attending, on account of not having had his dinner. The packet was broken open, and by the light of a solitary wax-candle, the four gai-wons, each chose one of the eight papers which the packet contained; Tsikkai Moungno took one, Gnakan Moungbai took another, Tsarai-ghee Moungsboe took a third. I was all this time close to the upper stage of the goum where the officers of government were collected. They commenced reading to themselves the contents of the papers by this solitary light, and every now and then I could observe they shook their heads. At last Gai-won Moung Bo said, "it is not a subject to be kept secret; every body should know it." The gountsarai was called, and the document read aloud. It turned out to be a proclamation from Major Canning. Messrs. Turner, Wade, Sarkis, and Aratoon, besides many other merchants, were sent for, and asked their opinion as to the expected result of the proclamation. They, most of them, said that the vessels were not come with any hostile purpose, but merely to negociate on the subject of Bundoola having committed aggressions on the Chittagong frontier. The gai-wons would not believe this, and had all the *kulas** imprisoned in the goum.

There was an immense crowd round the goum. None of the people would believe that forty or fifty vessels had arrived for the purpose of negociation, and expressed their opinion to that effect loudly. The gai-wons immediately set about to call on the different thooghees and gaons of districts, to furnish their quota of men; tied many of them up, and used threats. I was employed the whole night, with the men, under me throwing up a parapet; the next day, about one o'clock, the ships came up the river, and then commenced the cannonade on the town, at which all the chiefs and their people fled from the place. I also went off to Pusandown, where my house was. There I advised my friends to betake themselves to their boats, and fly up the river, which they did. I remained in my house, to look after my property. I had a quantity of betel-nut, oil, tobacco, gnapee, and fish, neepal eaves, rattan, &c., in value about 2,500 tickals, which I could not convey away. I slept that night in the village; the next morning, an English officer, with some sepoys, came to the village; they were accompanied by a Burman mussulman as interpreter. They asked me who I was, and, telling them I was a merchant, and showing my property, they asked for the women; I said they had fled. The officer told me to go and call them, that they had no reason to be afraid, no harm would be done to them. When the officer went away, I got into a small canoe with my attendants, and started up the river. The alarm was so great amongst the people, there was no possibility of persuading any of them to return, nor did I return myself, but left my property to the mercy of the invaders. About 300 boats, full of the poorer families, had assembled at Kureenzoik, about half a tide's journey up the Moyoit branch of the river. Decoits were in great number, but, by dint of watching, we managed to keep our party pretty clear of them; we stayed at this place about fifteen days. Near it was established the stockade of Yaigoo or Gnoung-woin, and for the building of which our party had to furnish the materials: the stockade was attacked by the English and taken; I went to see it after the troops had returned to Rangoon, and found about 300 bodies, principally those of Setoung people, in it. The English force passed close to our position, but of course they knew not that we were there, or they would have endeavoured to secure our numerous families. We were called on again to rebuild the stockade, but whilst engaged in it, many of

* Foreigners.

the families who were with me fled in their boats daily, and seeing this, I thought it prudent to decamp myself to the village of Kobiat, three doings to the east of Pegue. I had not been there above ten days, when the oukmawon, or officer of decoy-elephants, came with an army of 3,000 men from Tounjoo, on his march to Rangoon. He commenced seizing all the boats he could lay hands on; and I, therefore, concealed myself, with my boats, in the neighbour-ing jungles, or long grass, which was flooded sufficiently to allow our boats, about twenty or thirty in number, to traverse it, and afforded excellent means of concealment. After being certain that the oukmawon had passed with his army, we again returned to the village of Kobiat. We found the place, how-ever, too much in the line of march for the different bodies of troops, passing to and fro, and therefore moved off to the village of Kaloin, about one doing to the east of Kobiat, and remained there during the rest of the rainy season.

" Here our autobiographer," observes Capt. McCally, "does well to keep silence. When the Burmese population had recovered its panic, he was one of the first to enlist on the strongest side, and took office under the British authorities at Rangoon; but the deep-rooted habits of the Burman came so frequently in collision with the British exercise of justice, that he was some-times very unpleasantly situated. He has, for the last eight years, been resi-dent at Moulmein, during which period he once visited Madras; he is con-sidered one of the most erudite of his class, but retains too much of his Burmese character to hope for any employment except in the department of literature."

THE NATIVE LOVER'S SONG.

How can I fail to love thee ?
  The sun, that saw us wed,
Still from his throne above me
  · His warming beams doth shed ;
The stars that wove the chain
  That hath together bound us,
Still in the skies remain,
  And pour their light around us.

How can I fail to love thee,
  Sweet flower of beauty bright?
O ! may the sun above me
  Appear without his light,
And stars lose all their beams,
  When love for thee shall part—
(How drear th' idea seems !)—
  From this devoted heart.

How can I fail to love thee?
  Beneath the stars and sun,
Can I a treacher prove me,
  And where for refuge run?
No—like their light, whose flow
  Ceases or slackens never,
My love for thee shall glow
  Thus in my heart for ever.   KASIPRASAD GHOSH.

ATHENS AND ATTICA.*

THIS volume contains an account of Mr. Wordsworth's residence at Athens and Attica, during 1832 and 1833. We opened it with expectations of pleasure and instruction, which have not been disappointed; the academical reputation of the writer, whose name has long been familiar to every member of the University of Cambridge, was a guarantee for novelty of research, and learning and ingenuity of illustration. His Journey in Greece, of which a portion only is now given to the public, presents nothing in common with the frivolous journals that issue from the press; it is not a "Saunter in Greece," but the result of the investigations of a very acute and enthusiastic scholar. Forsaking the beaten paths of other travellers, along which it would be very difficult for the most skilful to collect anything new or valuable, Mr. Wordsworth has applied himself to the illustration of the poetry, history, and oratory of Greece. In this delightful labour, his early and zealously pursued classical studies afford him important aid, and in this volume he has turned the lamp of his learning upon many a monument of antiquity, before indistinctly visible; and has decyphered, so to speak, many inscriptions, which years had rendered almost illegible; and he has done this with a poetical warmth and earnestness of feeling, not unworthy a relation of the author of the *Excursion*. Everywhere, he beholds the past living in the present: in the Albanian women standing before their cottage-doors, with their braided locks falling over their backs in two streams, he sees a realization of the sculptured deities of Greece,—

Candida dividuâ colla tegente comâ.—OVID.

In passing over the glorious plain of Marathon, which presents a dry and melancholy aspect, cheered only at long intervals by a stunted wild-pear tree, the line of Aristophanes, in the *Vespæ*, where he mentions the victory to have commenced in the evening, affords an interesting illustration:

Αλλ' ομως απιωσαμιθα, ξυν θιοις, προς ισπιρρ.

With the assistance of the Gods, we routed them towards the evening.

The hour of the day, combined with the situation of the plain, Mr. Wordsworth suggests, may have contributed to the success of the Athenians; for then the full brightness of a burning Grecian sun would have shone into the eyes of the Persian soldiers, whose conical tiara gave very inadequate shelter from its rays.† Standing upon the hill of the Areopagus, the full power and expressive eloquence of St. Paul's address to the Athenians is vividly felt. From the position in which he stood, he might well, therefore, and with peculiar propriety, looking down upon the statues

* Athens and Attica. Journal of a Residence there. By the Rev. Christopher Wordsworth, M.A. Fellow of Trinity College, Cambridge, and Head Master of Harrow School. London, 1836. Murray.
† " The plain of Marathon has no hedges and few prominent objects of any kind;—there are some low pines by the sea-shore; and, occasionally, there is a small chapel in ruins, rising out of the plain. There is no house visible except on the inland skirts of the plain; and a few peasants ploughing at a distance, with their slow teams of small oxen, are the only living creatures to be seen. In this level solitary place, the eye is naturally arrested by one object, which raises itself above the surface of the plain, more conspicuously than any thing else. That object is the Tumulus which covers the ashes of those Athenians who fell in the battle of Marathon."

and temples glittering around him, exclaim : "Ye men of Athens, I perceive that in all things ye are too superstitious!" The temple of the Eumenides was below him, the Parthenon of Minerva facing him above; before him rose the bronze colossus of Minerva, threatening with spear and shield from the rock of the Acropolis. In the presence of such objects as these, he declared to the wondering Athenians, that they ought not to think the Godhead "like unto gold, or silver, or stone, graven by art and man's device." At almost every step, he thus finds something to elucidate, and, amongst the most delightful dreams of his journey, must have been those suggested by the Grotto on Mount Hymettus, which, not without reason, he conjectures to be the same dedicated to Pan, the Nymphs, and the Pastoral Apollo, to which Plato in his childhood was carried by his parents, who made an offering for him to the deities of the place. "Here," says the traveller, "Time has exerted no power. The integrity of the Grotto has not been impaired by lapse of years. When left alone in the faint light of this cavern, and while looking on these inscriptions, which declare the former sanctity of the place, and on the basins scooped in the rock, from which the sacred libations were made, and the limpid well in the cave's recess—with no other object about you to disturb the impression which these produce—you might fancy some shepherd of this part of Attica had just left the spot, and that he would return before evening from his neighbouring sheep-fold on Hymettus, with an offering to Pan from his flock, or with the spoils of his mountain-chase, or with the first flowers which at this season of the year have just peeped forth in his rural garden." The classical reader will remember a picturesque description of a similar cave—*nympharum domus* — in the romance of Longus. This is the true and abiding charm of travelling in Greece; while modern cities change continually, Antiquity alone is ever the same; and the tourist, who wends his way along the mule-path from Athens to Laureum, is struck by the deep-worn tracks of the wheels, which, so many centuries ago, groaned beneath the treasure from those celebrated mines; and, while gazing upon the impressions still visible of the round shields once attached to the eastern front of the Parthenon, he will enter more fully than he ever did before into the prayer of their tenderest tragic poet, as it issues from the mouth of the chorus, whose eyes were at the moment directed towards these shields:—

> May my spear idle lie, and spiders spin
> Their webs about it! May I, oh may I, pass
> My hoary age in peace !
> Then let me chaunt my melodies, and crown
> My grey hairs with a chaplet !
> And let me hang a Thracian target high
> Upon the peristyle of dread MINERVA's fane !

Mr. Wordsworth supplies another illustration of Euripides, from the same temple. Agave, in the *Bacchæ*, carrying the head of Pentheus, cries out, in her madness, for Pentheus himself:

> Ος πασσαλιων κρατα τριγλυφοις τοδε
> Λεοντος, ον παριμι θηρασας ιγω.

That on the triglyphs I may plant
Here this grim lion's head, my spoil to-day.

" The marble *lion-head* antefixa," he says, "which still terminate the
northern angles of the western pediments of the Panthenon, show Euripides,
in the delineation of this character, to have kept in view one of the most
natural and pathetic elements of madness—namely, its partial saneness and
sense of propriety,"—that element, which Shakspeare has wrought out with
such inimitable force. The Parthenon, from its elevated position, commanded views of surpassing variety and beauty; the farms and vineyards of
Colonos and Acharnæ, with troops of husbandmen studding the fields, and
processions of triumph gleaming along the shady paths. These scenes have
faded, and nothing is now seen but a solitary Albanian peasant, following
his mule laden with wood, or the glittering grove of olives; marking the
spot where the voice of Plato charmed the disciples of the Academy.

Mr. Wordsworth has very ingeniously shown the influence of the surrounding scenery upon the Grecian theatre: with the splendour of the Parthenon
and Acropolis above them,—the beautiful vale of the Ilyssus beneath, under
a sky of infinite purity and sweetness, and an atmosphere refreshed by a
delightful wind from the sea,—in such a situation, sat the admiring thousands
of Athens, following with eyes and ears the windings of many a romantic
tale; now weeping with Euripides, now ravished by Sophocles; now trembling beneath the thunder of Æschylus, now intoxicated with the rich and
poetic mirth and abandonment of Aristophanes. Hence the exclamation of
an ancient writer, that the city drank oblivion from public spectacles, and
that even the pains of hunger yielded to the voice of the lyre. All the dramatic poets availed themselves of these sources of imagery and metaphor; and
none more frequently than Æschylus. So, too, when Sophocles, in the *Ajax*,
speaks of the κλεινα Σαλαμις, the glorious Salamis, dwelling upon the wave,
he required no scene-painter to illustrate the picture—nature had done it for
him; and the spectator had only to turn his eyes towards the west, and behold the peaks of Salamis piercing the horizon. To the peculiar facilities
afforded by the situation of the theatre, Mr. Wordsworth refers those daring
sallies of Aristophanes, that dwindle into obscurity under the pen of the
modern translator. "How," he asks, "in the confinement of a modern
theatre, could we imagine a Trygæus soaring above the sea, in an ærial
excursion? There his journey would be reduced to a mere mechanical
process of ropes and pullies, and would be baffled by the resistance of the
roof. But, in the Athenian theatre, the sky itself was then visible, whither
he was mounting, and in which he was placed by the simple machinery of
the imagination of the spectators. How, again, in a modern theatre,
could the Birds be imagined to build their ærial city? How could the Clouds
have come sailing on the stage from the height of a neighbouring Parnes?
How, in such a position, could the future minister of Athens survey from
the stage, as he did, the natural map of his own future domains, the
Agora, the harbours, and the Pnyx, and all the tributary islands lying in
a group around him ?"

But there is one more place in Athens, which we would gladly visit before we part with the reader — that place where Demosthenes and Æschines contended for the mastery, and which was trodden in the days of Cicero with enthusiasm equal to our own—we allude to the Pnyx, a name which transports the mind into the brightest period of Grecian intellect, and calls up before us the Thunderer wielding from the block of stone, which formed his rostrum, the passions of that fierce democracy, which was scattered before him in the open field, whose area, comprising more than twelve thousand square yards, was capable of containing all the free citizens of Athens. It was preparatory to these tumultuous meetings, that Demosthenes is said by Quinctilian to have wandered along the shores of Phalerum, teaching himself from the dashing waves of the Ægean, which roared at his feet, to look unawed upon the tempest of the popular assembly.* The Pnyx still presents much of its original appearance, and the remarks we have already applied to the Grecian theatre bear, with still greater power, upon its position. The orator was surrounded with the mightiest and most effective instruments of popular eloquence,—the sky of Attica was above his head, the soil of Attica beneath his feet, the sea of Attica rolling behind him; thus it was that, from the Bema, he appealed to the elements, and shook the hearts of the hearers with his sublime invocation to the Earth and Gods: " Ω Γη και Θεοι !" Lord Chatham's famous allusion to the tapestry, in the House of Lords, was not more touching or appropriate. If he sought to arouse the dignity, to kindle the valour, of his audience, he could point to the Island of Salamis; was the commerce of Athens threatened by a foreign invader? — the Piræus, with its sounds of life and industry, its crowded arsenals, and its thousand sails, answered the summons. Did he seek to inflame their patriotism—to elevate their pride—to flatter their vanity?—the Acropolis, the Parthenon, and the costly treasures of the Agora, were within their view. Thus was this mighty patriot enabled to rein in, or to excite, the humorous fickleness and impetuosity of the Athenian multitude; thus was he enabled to pour forth strains of majestic power, which still retain their life and vigour after the lapse of ages, and from which Oratory, in all countries, has gathered some of its noblest passages. He has had Cicero for a disciple, yet he stands alone; unsurpassed; unequalled. Other giants have arisen; other thunderers have

---

* We cannot refrain from adding, in a Note, the following lively and graphic description: " The scenes described as taking place on this spot, gain much in distinctness from local illustration. Placed where we are now, we may imagine Dicæopolis, in the Aristophanic play of the *Acharnians*, arriving here early in the morning, taking his seat on one of these lime-stone steps, and speculating on the Agora beneath him, where the Logistæ are chasing the stragglers with their vermillion coloured ropes. The Prytanes appear from the Agora; they ascend the slope of the Pnyx; a contest takes place for the first seats covered with planks, and perhaps with cushions, at the base of the stone rostrum, round which are ranged the bowmen of the Scythian police. The citizens, equipped with staff and cloak, are seated on this elevated area of the Pnyx. The lustrations are performed. The herald comes forward to invite the future orator to speak; and questions circulate among the audience, what orator will put on the crown, and who now enjoys the sway of the Bema, of that simple block of stone, the political ομφαλος of Greece; what will be the subject of his harangue, to recommend a war or a new tribute. All which speculations, being made under the open sky, may be, in a moment, terminated by a single drop of rain producing the announcement—

Διοσημια 'στιν και ρανις βεβληκε με·
A portent! and I felt a drop of rain.

Acharn. 171.

terrified the world; but no arm has launched those bolts; no hand has bent that bow.

If our rapidly contrasting space did not forbid the attempt, we might furnish many other illustrations of ancient literature, neither less original nor instructive; but we proceed, in conclusion, to offer one or two sketches of a lighter, and to the general reader, perhaps, of a more attractive character. Xenophon's picture of the interior of an Armenian dwelling was recalled to Mr. Wordsworth's memory by the Albanian cottage, in which he passed an evening, and of which he has given a lively sketch.

Our cottage consists of one room, with a clay-floor and thatched roof. At one end of it, near the middle of the wall, on the ground, a fire is blazing with a fresh supply of wood to welcome our arrival. At one side of the fire, our páplomas (equivalent to the ancient στρώματα) are strewed, which in the day time serve for saddles, and for couches by night. The fire is employed in boiling some rice for our repast. On the other side of it sit two Albanian women, twirling their spindles, and occasionally uttering a few syllables, before they put between their teeth the flax which is to be wound upon the spindle. Another is engaged in kneading some cakes, which are inserted in the wood ashes of the fire, and thus baked. The master of the house stands at the door, with his scarlet skull cap on his head, a belt girding his white cotton tunic, over which he wears a shorter vest of woollen, thick woollen gaiters, and sandals, consisting merely of a sole of untanned leather, tied with leathern thongs over the instep. About him are some children, whose necks glitter with gilded coins strung into a necklace. On the wall of the cottage hangs a loom (ἐργαλεῖον), which has probably not altered its form since the contest of Minerva with Arachne: near it are some bins filled with the acorns of the Balanià oak, which are exported for dyeing. There are also, lying near them, some silk works (κυκυλια), from which the silk (μέταξι) is soon to be unwound, and some husks of the cotton plant bursting with their snow-white contents. As the night comes on, these objects about us are only dimly illuminated by the light of our fire: no other light is provided. Ere long, all the children of the family are laid side by side on one mantle on the floor, at the more distant end of the apartment. The master of the house terminates this domestic series, which consists of ten persons. Sleep soon comes and strings the whole family together, like a row of beads, in one common slumber. Further beyond them, and separated from the family by a low partition, is the place allotted to the irrational members of the household. The fowls come there from the open air to roost on the transverse rafters of the roof; the ox stands there at his manger, and eats his evening meal; and the white faces of the three asses, belonging to the family, are seen peering out of the darkness, and bending nearly over their sleeping master and his children. The time and place, the group and glimmering light, remind one of a more solemn scene — of a Christmas præsepe: such, for instance, as would have come from the vigorous and rustic pencil of Bassano.—p. 34.

The present condition and prospects of Greece cannot be regarded without an anxious interest, and the hope that the Muse and the Grace may yet return to a land, which, from the earliest ages, seems to have been consecrated for their peculiar home. War and internal dissentions have dealt hardly with it; during Mr. Wordsworth's residence, it was almost a wilderness, and he travelled for two days along the road from Athens to Sunium, without meeting five persons; the shepherds, who kept their flocks upon the hills, fled at his approach; and almost the only sound that broke the dreariness of the scene, was the moaning of the wintry wind in the pine-trees. Athens, itself, was in ruins; the streets nearly deserted: the houses unroofed; one church alone existing in which service was performed; and all the inhabited dwellings consisting only of a few new wooden houses, one or two of stronger construction, and the two lines of planked sheds forming the bazaar, of which a description is given in a later part of the volume.

The bazar or market of Athens is a long street, which is now the only one there of any importance. It has no foot-pavement; there is a gutter in the centre, down which, in this wintry weather, the water runs in copious torrents. The houses are generally patched together with planks and plaster. Looking up the street, you command a view of the commodities with which this Athenian market is now supplied. Barrels of black caviar, small pocket looking-glasses in red paste-board cases, onions, tobacco piled up in brown heaps, black olives, figs strung together upon a rush, pipes, with amber mouth-pieces and brown clay bowls, rich stuffs, and silver chased pistols, dirks, belts, and embroidered waistcoats—these are the varied objects which a rapid glance of this street presents to the spectator. The objects which are not to be found here, as well as those which are, ought not to be neglected in this description. Here there are no books, no lamps, no windows, no carriages, no newspapers, no post-office. The letters which arrived here a few days since from Napoli, after having been publicly cried in the streets, if they were not claimed by the parties to whom they were addressed, were committed to the flames. Such is the present state of Athens, as far as its streets speak of its condition. This city is still in the hands of the Turks. All the other continental towns of Greece south of Thermopylæ, are independent of Turkey. Strange it is, that of all the towns of southern Greece, a distinction of this kind should have been reserved for Athens! such, however, is the case. The Muezzin still mounts the scaffold in the bazar here, to call the Mussulman to prayer at the stated hours. A few Turks still doze in the archways of the Acropolis, or recline while smoking their pipes, and leaning with their backs against the rusty cannon which are planted on the battlements of its walls. The Athenian peasant, as he drives his laden mule from Hymettus through the eastern gate of the town, still flings his small bundle of thyme and brushwood from the load which he brings on his mule's back, as a tribute to the Mussulman toll-gatherer, who sits at that entrance of the town; and, a few days ago, the cannon of the Acropolis fired the signal of the conclusion of the Turkish Ramazan—the last which will ever be celebrated in Athens."—p. 247.

It may be interesting to compare this picture with the present state of the city, as detailed in a letter to Mr. Wordsworth, by a gentleman named Bracebridge, in April of the present year. From this communication we learn, that the antiquities of the city are undergoing careful examination, and that the masses originally brought for the erection of the Parthenon, have been found scattered about, together with what is not unappropriately called the "workshop" of the Parthenon. Some blocks even have been discovered which belonged to the old Hecatompedon, besides a number of bronze, pottery, and marble fragments, together with *burnt-wood*, which can be attributed only to an era of distinction, preceding the building of that splendid fabric. But the great discovery, he observes, is the long-lost temple of the Wingless Victory, incorrectly pronounced by Wheler to be of the Doric order, whereas it is a fine specimen of the Ionic, and built of Pentelic marble. Its situation perfectly coincides with the description of Pausanias. Two sarcophagi, of considerable excellence, have been very recently discovered, near the modern mint. The improvement of the city advances slowly. The mint, royal stables, a hospital, and a barrack, are the only important public buildings hitherto erected. The new palace, commenced two months ago by the king of Bavaria, is likely to become an ornament to the place. Large houses are rising, and the price of ground increases with the spirit of speculation; land, in a good situation, has lately been sold at the rate of £1,200 and £1,300 per acre; three large streets, the Adrian, Athena, and Æolus, have been opened. The modern German style, as might be expected, principally prevails; while many of the inferior houses are constructed upon the principle adopted at Constantinople. It is matter of congratulation for the lovers of the picturesque, that the unsightly red bricks of England are not yet introduced. The appearance of the city has also been improved by the removal of the walls of the old town. Athens now measures in its diameter about a mile and a-half, with a population of 15,000. Water is pure and abundant. Of the 300 churches in Athens, almost all are in ruins. There are symptoms of life once more at the Piræus, and the dock-yard at Poros shows signs of activity. It may be hoped that the moral and social amelioration of the people will keep pace with these evidences of animation. The trial by jury is growing into esteem; industry begins to be general, and the establishment of a national bank, by an English company, is calculated to promote agriculture, by supplying capital, the want of which is amongst its chief opponents. From personal inspection, combined with the experience of respectable residents, Mr. Bracebridge is of opinion, that Greece holds out to an intelligent and well-informed Englishman, more decided advantages than Canada or Australia. The capital of the emigrant should not be less than £1,500 or or £2,000, upon which he may look for an immediate return of ten per cent. With such inducements, who would hesitate between the woods of America, and the olive groves of Attica?

GHUZZUL.

(*From the Persian.*)

Won by thy charms, my soul in chains,
    Bowed down by sorrows, pines away:
Thou sayest, " For thee but Death remains;
    Arise, and fly his fatal sway."

Yet, by the brows that arch thine eye,
    That forehead's conquering brows, I swear,
'Twere dearer far for me to die,
    Stretched at thy feet, than yield my Fair.

My light of days is turned to shade,
    Black, as thy ringlets' ebon flow;
And *Khacan*, by those lips betrayed,
    No sweet so sweet as their's can know.

THE PARIAHS AND INFERIOR CASTES OF INDIA.

THE degraded state in which a very large portion of the natives of our Eastern empire are doomed to languish, is little known or understood in Europe. Even a very considerable number of intelligent persons, who have resided many years in British India, are almost wholly ignorant of the actual condition of the outcasts whom they employ in their service; and when this knowledge has been obtained, it is difficult to many to enter into, and sympathise with, the prejudices of the natives upon a subject so revolting to those who have been taught to consider, that, in the eye of the Creator, all men are equal. In order, however, to stand high in the estimation of the respectable classes of natives, it is necessary to be thoroughly acquainted with the situation of the Pariahs, so as to avoid sharing the contamination they have incurred; as it is not by affording our countenance to this degraded class that we can hope to raise them in the scale of created beings; on the contrary, the association, springing either from benevolence or thoughtlessness, on the part of European residents in India, with a race who have been placed by common consent without the pale of society, can only tend, in the existing state of feeling, to weaken our influence. We must try other means; and never perhaps did wrongs cry out more loudly for redress, than those suffered by numerous tribes of unfortunate beings, born to irretrievable infamy, for whom in this world there seems to be no redemption. It is but too certain that these wretched people, apparently accursed by God and man, have, in consequence of the hopeless misery of their lot, contracted many abominable and disgusting habits, which render them objects of contempt and abhorrence, and seem to justify the scorn in which they are held. No more abject slavery was ever imposed upon man, than that to which a portion, said to comprehend a fifth of the whole population of the peninsula of India, have been condemned.

In order to give as clear a notion as circumstances will admit, of the condition of the Pariahs, the writer of this article has consulted a gentleman who has made the subject his study, and has been furnished by him with some original information of a highly interesting nature, which gives a melancholy picture of the state of the Hindoo outcasts, and which shews the difficulties which stand in the way of those who desire to remedy the evils of their lot.

It is supposed by some persons that the word *Pariah* is derived or corrupted from *Puharree* or *Puharriyah*, which signifies a 'hill-man,' or 'mountaineer.' The hill-men throughout India are all Hindoos, and are considered to be, on very reasonable grounds, the aborigines of the soil: they have not, however, adopted the Brahminical tenets, and are untrammelled by the distinctions of caste, entertaining few prejudices, and caring little what they eat or drink; flesh and intoxicating liquors being eagerly sought by those whose circumstances will permit of such indulgences. These men are despised by the natives of the plains, and their contemptuous expressions, when speaking of these eaters of beef, have led Europeans to suppose that all who so defiled themselves were considered *Pariahs*. The phrase *Pariah-yat*, a term which is used to designate degraded caste, is seldom or ever employed by the natives in their conversation with each other; but in speaking to persons little versed in the manners and customs of the country, they are in the habit of applying it to those without the pale of their society, encouraging their auditors to do the same; and hence, in Calcutta especially, and its vicinity, the term *Puharriyah*, contracted into *Pariah*, has been bestowed by Europeans upon all outcasts from the respectable members of the Hindoo persuasion. The early settlers in the Bengal presidency made few or no inquiries concerning the distinctions of caste, which is, indeed, very little understood at this day by the great majority of the British residents in India, the small amount of knowledge which they possess being, in a manner, forced upon them by collisions amongst their servants, who never can be well regulated unless the master be acquainted with the distinctions between them. There are many military men, and a few civilians (although the latter class are usually better instructed in the *dustoor*, or customs of the country), who are utterly ignorant of the nature of the different castes to which the servants in their employ belong; and it is even said of some, that they do not recognize the distinction between the Mahomedan and the Hindoo. Persons of this description will give a *hookum* (or order) for a khidmutghar (a table-attendant) to be entertained, without troubling themselves for a moment about his caste or tenets; he may be a Mugh, a dirty-looking, loathsome animal from the coast of Chittagong, frequently to be met with in Anglo-Indian and Indo-British houses in Calcutta, though rarely, if ever, seen in the Upper Provinces, or a Mater, *i.e.* Pariah. Such an abomination was common in Calcutta in earlier days, when Mussulman attendants refused to place a ham upon their masters' tables; and even at the present era, occasional instances of similar disregard of native opinion are to be found in the city of palaces. Strangers ignorant of the usages of the country, and even when partially informed of the prevailing prejudices, unwilling to submit to any inconvenient restriction, are apt to commit many grievous errors at the outset of their career in India. Many also entertain so contemptuous an opinion of the people with whom they live, that they purposely run counter to all their notions of right and wrong, without considering that they bring themselves into disrepute by such conduct. So long as the engine of caste is kept up and cherished by the natives as part and parcel of the institutions of their country, it is incumbent upon Europeans to respect it, so far as to avoid giving offence by polluting themselves by an association which is regarded in the vilest light. There is a great deal more advantage to be derived from understanding and respecting the proper distinctions of the different classes of menials who enter into our service, as relates to their proper *thakoors* (heads of the doctrines they subscribe to), than Europeans are aware of. It is a subject which tells politically, physically, morally, and socially.

The sepahis, and the natives at large, form their own estimate of the characters of their officers and the Europeans who may be placed among them, generally, from the rank and the proper distribution of the duties to be performed amid the respective castes of those who are entertained beneath the roof of an *Ungrey Bāhādoor* (a high-sounding title, equivalent to our English, ' my lord '); while the higher, and consequently the more respectable, the caste of his servants, the greater is the degree of respect and esteem in which he is held by the sepahis, the natives of all classes around him, and, strange as it may appear, by his own servants themselves: those who have been uplifted from their proper sphere being apt to presume upon it, and to think contemptuously of the person who has so exalted them. The menials employed in families in India, particularly in the Bengal presidency, where the trammels of caste are infinitely stronger, more annoying and oppressive, than in the other two, should consist both of Mahomedans and Hindoos of various ranks, the climate being far too enervating to admit of Europeans being engaged for the duties required, or even Indo-Britons, who would need a servant each to attend upon them. They who are desirous to adopt the orthodox creed of the country, regarding the attendants who are considered the most eligible for the fulfilment of the various duties required of them, should select the following classes of servants, belonging to the under-mentioned sects or religions. A khansaman, or purveyor, should invariably be either an Indo-Portuguese, or a Mahommedan; if the latter (and the former is not commonly found), a Shikh, or a Pathan, for, if not exactly castes, there are great distinctions amongst the followers of the Prophet in India. If a Shikh, he is always entitled, when addressed by his fellow servants, *Shikh-see;* when a Pathan, they hail him with *khan sahib;* and if he should happen (a very rare occurrence) to be a *syud*, or descendant of the Prophet's family, he is complimented by his brethren with the appellation of *meer sahib*, whenever his services are put into requisition. The khansaman, being at the head of the establishment, should always be a respectable person; and, perhaps, next to him, the peculiar place occupied by the cook in society should be taken into consideration; although every one of the servants who have any thing to do with the viands produced at table, ought to be immaculate as regards their condition in life. The cook, or *bawurchee*, as he is termed in India, is a most useful and important personage, and his title of honour, as well as that of the tailor, is *khuleefa jee*. In the primitive states of society, those who prepared the food so necessary to sustain life, and those who manufactured fitting covering for the body, were held in very high estimation, and the respectability of their character is recognized to this day in India. Tailors and cooks, while holding a low place in Europe, are, in Oriental countries, regarded in a very different light, it being no degradation for any individual, of the highest rank, to perform the office of cook for his companions, while to partake of food prepared by a person who is looked upon as an inferior, in consequence of some polluting taint, would be to incur the same loss of respectability. As no high-caste Hindoo will enter a kitchen desecrated by the sacrifice of the animals he holds in veneration, if the cook should not belong to the Moslem persuasion, he must of necessity be an outcast from his own race, and the least fastidious European, acquainted with the habits of these unfortunate people, would shrink from the idea of eating the viands which have passed through their hands.

Before the invasion of the Mahommedans in India, tailors were persons wholly unknown, the garments worn by the aboriginal inhabitants consisting only of one or more lengths of muslin, cotton, cloth, &c., folded round the figure; this kind of drapery is still retained by multitudes of Hindoos, especially in Bengal, and it must be confessed that it is ample, graceful, and becoming. Many, however, have adopted the Mussulmanee vest and trowsers, and, therefore, tailors have sprung up amidst the followers of Brahma, though assuredly they cannot compete with their Moslem rivals. The *abdars*, or butlers; *khidmutgars*, or table-attendants; the *hookah-burdah*, or pipe-bearer; the *mussalchee*, or scullion; and the *moorghee-wallah*, employed to look after the fowls, should also be Mahommedans, as likewise the *bheestee*, or water-carrier, and the *durwan*, who acts as door-keeper; the *surwan*, or camel-driver, should come under the same denomination, and, in order to be most perfectly *sans réproche*, it is necessary to substitute a Mahommedan *furash*, as the sweeper of the floors of the interior apartments, instead of the *mater*, who, in ninety-nine cases out of a hundred, is not kept exclusively for out-door work, but admitted into the interior. The presence of these persons is considered to be so tainting and loathsome by the better classes of natives, that it is supposed to contaminate the very carpets and mats upon which they tread; no Hindoo or Mussulman of the least respectability would entertain thém, and if they were to presume to touch any article belonging to the household of a native prince, they would be subjected to a cruel death. In some European families, *maters* are employed in looking after the poultry-yard, and fattening fowls and ducks; but, though proverbially unclean feeders, these animals are considered to suffer dreadful deterioration when purveyed for by such polluted hands. An instance of the repugnance and horror felt by the superior classes of the people of India towards *maters*, occurred at the recent execution of Nuwaub Shumshoodeen, at Delhi. On ascending the fatal scaffold, the prince cast a look upon the person who was to perform the last dreadful ceremony, and asked if he were a *mater*. These were stated to be the only words the criminal uttered, and it is those alone, who are acquainted with the sentiments of his class, who can imagine the thrill of horror which shook his soul, when he learned that a degraded creature, a being only known to him by name, as pariahs are never allowed to stand, walk, or even to be *seen*, in the presence of the great, not only stood before his eyes, but would in another moment touch a person hitherto held so sacred from all contamination. None but an outcast can in India be found to perform the accursed duty delegated to an executioner, and it is well known that sepahis, whether Brahmins or Mahommedans, when about to suffer death upon the gallows, will often request and obtain permission from the officers present, to adjust the fatal cord themselves, rather than go out of the world polluted by the touch of a *mater*.

In Calcutta, we sometimes see the situation of khansaman filled by a Parsee, or fire-worshipper, to which no objection exists in the eyes of the natives, by whom they are held in great respect, although they have customs which do not render them very agreeable to Europeans. The number who follow this faith, on the Bengal side of India, is, however, so small, that they are not very generally to be met with, and in Bombay, where they are more numerous, they are, in a great degree, inadmissible, especially as personal attendants, on account of one particular feature of their religious observances. They never remove a muslin vest worn next their skin until it actually drops off, bathing without taking it off, and allowing it to dry upon their bodies, where it remains day and night, until it falls piecemeal away. A lady, who had engaged a young boy of this persuasion as a page, observing one day the disagreeable effluvia which proceeded from the filthy rags he persisted in wearing, told her ayah to hold him, while she cut away the offending garment with her scissors. But the young urchin, after many struggles, succeeded in breaking loose, exclaiming at the same time that he should become an outcast from his brotherhood should he permit such an outrage, and assuring his mistress that the laws of his faith required that his under vest should fall of itself away, and not be otherwise removed from the body! Another objection to the employment of Parsee servants, consists in their unwillingness to snuff or blow out a candle, or extinguish the fire. Being worshippers of the element, they are enjoined to abstain from its wilful destruction, and though the simple act of snuffing a candle, does not involve more than a chance of its extinction, they entertain an unwillingness to hazard the risk, and refuse upon that plea.

While upon the subject of Mussulman servants, it is necessary to state that the ayah, or lady's maid, should either be a native Portuguese, or a follower of the faith of Islam, and those females, who are content to allow a *matranee* to perform the duties of the office, are considered, both by the natives and the few Europeans who have made themselves thoroughly acquainted with the state of public opinion, to shew a lamentable absence of propriety and respect for the feelings of delicacy which ought to distinguish their sex. Nothing, it is alleged, can be more degrading than the circumstance, for were the husbands and brethren of these outcasts to wait behind their chairs at table, the disgrace incurred could be scarcely of a deeper dye. In behalf of the European ladies, who may have fallen into this error, it must be said, that in some instances they are perfectly ignorant of the scandal which it creates; and in the second, that Portuguese women are expensive and difficult to procure, while those of the Moslem persuasion who go out to service are usually of the worst description.

In spite of all that has been urged against pariahs of every caste and grade, experience of many will prove that the *matrannees* are at least, in the some instances, reclaimable. While the idle, dirty, and profligate Mussulmanee ayah, will desert the sick chamber, her more humble assistant is in attendance, and if it can be permitted to employ the phrase, *respectable*, to women of this class, those of good conduct will not be less decent in their habits and their manners than a European servant, while there is a much better chance of their keeping themselves aloof from the males of the family, and preserving their fidelity to their husbands, than can be hoped for in a Mussulmanee woman, who, with her veil, usually discards every idea of chastity. She is, besides, so very frequently absent without leave, as to compel her mistress, in some measure, to avail herself of the services of the person in attendance, and it is very difficult for a Christian lady always to be deterred by the fear of an unjust and inhuman opinion, which man in his folly has created and supported, from following those purer dictates, which emanate from a righteous God, who is no respecter of persons. The female servants attached to a European establishment in India are few, compared with the males. In many families, however, the *dhya*, or wet-nurse, is indispensable; native Portuguese women have the preference; but such a person is difficult to find. It is not easy to procure a good substitute, since the Mussulmanee women, who seek service, where they mix and mingle with the male domestics, are seldom, as we have before had occasion to remark, good for any thing. It would be about as fair to judge of the whole female community of England by the degraded classes of their sex, as to form our opinion of that of India by the women who seek service in European families. *Matrannees* are sometimes entertained as wet-nurses, but such a practice is very objectionable, it being gravely asserted by those who are well acquainted with the subject, that all Pariahs whatsoever will eat of carrion, and indeed consider it as one of the duties enjoined by their particular religious tenets, to partake occasionally of the vilest repasts: swallowing both meat and vegetables in a putrescent state, not only without the slightest scruple, but with some degree of zest. It is notorious that the lowest grades of these unhappy outcasts are contented to live upon the filthiest and most abominable food, animals that have died of disease, or any carrion; but Anglo-Indians who have had constant opportunities while travelling of observing the habits and customs of their servants, have, in numerous instances, failed to detect any such abomination on the part of the *mater* caste. An experience of a residence of a few years only in the Bengal presidency does not give the writer of the present paper a right to differ from the authority which she has consulted; she can only say that, to all outward appearance, the *matrannees*, who from to time have engaged in her service, were decent and respectable in their habits; that she has often seen them cooking their meals, and that they never to her knowledge ate any thing that was unwholesome or offensive. The fact of their considering it as part of the observances which their situation compels them to adopt, she does not dispute; merely mentioning her own inability to detect the people, who were often engaged in their cookery in places which she could overlook, in so disgusting an occupation : an excuse for the conduct of others who are still more ignorant than herself of the peculiar habits of the natives of India.

It is a matter of indifference, as far as regards respectability, whether the *chuprassees* should be Mahommedan or Hindoo; the situation is one to which no man, who condescends to take service with an European, can possibly object; and the higher classes of both religions are to be found in it, brahmins even, who are of course the most scrupulous of the community. The faith of the *syces*, or grooms, also is deemed of little consequence, although it is said that, while the Mussulmanee grooms make the best appearance, the Hindoos bestow greater care upon the horse, and take a stronger interest in all that appertains to the stable. The bearer, or valet, is (excepting where the tailor performs a double office) chosen from the followers of Brahma, though there does not appear to be any particular reason for the selection. This class is divided into several sects, all Hindoos, yet following different thakoors. In Calcutta, and throughout Bengal and Orissa, the bearers are Bengallees, or Ooreeahs. The latter, who entertain a very high opinion of their importance, are apt to give themselves great airs. During the administration of Lord Hastings, those who were entertained at Government House, refused to pull the punkahs, but were brought to their senses upon hearing that their places would be supplied by people from the Upper Province. Upon the promulgation of this resolution, the malcontents succumbed, and now condescend to officiate when called upon to fan the company at the vice-regal palace. These men may be easily distinguished from the rest of the bearer fraternity, by having their foreheads and noses marked with a preparation of yellow ochre and sandal wood. The up-country bearers are divided into several castes, of which the *Rewannee* is the best, the others, the *Toorahá*, in particular, being addicted to drinking, and guilty of eating village pork. The *dhobees*, or washermen, form a caste of themselves; the Hindoos who follow this occupation being more esteemed than the few Mohammedans who engage in it. The *kulassees*, or tent-pitchers, should be Hindoos, and people offering themselves for service in this capacity are of various castes, such as *thorees, chumars, doosads*. The two last are considered to be only one remove from pariahs, but preponderate over the others in the ratio of nineteen out of twenty. The cow-keeper and the shepherd belong to two peculiar castes, which seldom follow any other occupation. The *garree-wan*, or charioteer, is usually chosen from the Hindoo community; it is a service that several castes will engage in, such as *gwalas, kulwyas*, &c.; the latter, properly speaking, appertains solely to the makers of sweetmeats, but the two employments are not incompatible. In the careful selection of the people enumerated above for servants, the comfort of an establishment consists, since no respectable man will engage if he find that he is to be confounded with people whom he regards with the utmost scorn and contempt. No high-minded native will smoke with a person whom he considers beneath him, and when Europeans complain of the negligence, laziness, uncleanliness, or insolence of their servants, the annoyance which they experience is in nine cases out of ten occasioned by their being ill-assorted in the first instance. The domestics, thus promiscuously huddled together, despise their master for his ignorance, and take every advantage of it to bring him into contempt. Native gentlemen are shy of visiting at European houses, on account of the danger of contact with

persons whom they could not by any possibility meet with elsewhere, there-·
fore it is necessary, while the prejudice exists in so strong a degree, to abstain
from outraging the opinions of those who cannot understand our feelings or
appreciate the motives which induce us to pursue a contrary course. A native
gentleman, resident at Lucknow, consented to dine with a British officer, when
informed that the cook was a Mohammedan; he asked the question, because he
was aware that Hindoos were sometimes entertained in that capacity, and that
such persons could only be *maters*.

The Madras native army, and that of Bombay also, are, or at least were,
recruited from all castes, and numerous experiments have been made, on the
part of the European authorities, to elevate the condition of those who, by
entering an honourable service, had an opportunity of emerging from their
fearful slavery. They were found to make very good soldiers while restricted
to the ranks, but the experiment did not succeed when they obtained promotion. In most cases, they became drunken and insolent, and though released
from every necessity to continue their old customs, would turn away from
wholesome food literally to prey on garbage. In fact, whatever their military
rank may have been, they knew that the place which they occupied in society was
still the same; that they could not escape from the curse which had fallen
upon them, and that the disgust and abhorrence, which they excited in the
breasts of their countrymen belonging to a higher caste, remained undiminished. As we have before remarked, we must begin the work of reformation
with the superior orders, and teach them to assist in the emancipation of their
less fortunate brethren, since there can be little or no self-respect under the
consciousness of fatal and irredeemable ignominy. The Bengal army has
always been distinguished for the unassailable respectability of its recruits;
the castes and sects, however, to which the sepahis who compose it belong,
are more numerous than people usually suppose. The brahmins take precedence in rank; these are divided into several classes, such as *Kunougeea* brahmins, and *Ajudeea* brahmins, the last-mentioned taking their name from the
province of Oude; and, again, there are brahmins who are recognized by an
additional appellation to the one which they are known by, *persaud, sookul,
ditchit, missur,* &c. Then there are Rajpoots, who are entitled to have the
adjunct *singh* added to their names; and, besides those castes, which are un-
disputable, the following are considered to be of sufficient respectability to
gain admittance: *aheer* and *gwala,* both of which are cow-herds; *lodh,* whose
occupation is husbandry; *koormee,* raisers of and dealers in vegetables; *tamoolee,*
employed solely in the cultivation and sale of the plant which furnishes the
paan leaf, and shepherds belonging to the *gurrehree* caste. The Mohamedans
who engage are chiefly *Shéks* and *Pathans;* these, though numerous, are far
outnumbered by the Hindoos in the infantry regiments, the proportion of the
latter being three out of four in nearly every company. Of these, one-third
are brahmins, the remainder being composed of Rajpoots and the inferior
classes of Hindoos. Some inquiry is necessary even when Mahomedans offer
themselves for recruits, since it is essential that they should be respectable
men, who have never followed any degrading occupation. Upon one occasion,
a fine-looking fellow presented himself as a recruit, who answered boldly to
the questions put to him, that he was a Pathan. Being of the standard height
and age, he was admitted without scruple; but, before the expiration of a
week, an unfortunate incident in his life transpired. It was discovered that he
had at one time earned his "salt" by the calling of a *khasye,* or butcher; and
no sooner was this circumstance ascertained, than it became necessary for him

to take measures to secure himself from outrage. Accordingly, the instant he felt that he was detected, he deserted, concealing his route so effectually, that no tidings of his where-about ever reached the regiment afterwards. Had he remained a day longer, his presence might have occasioned a serious disturbance, and possibly the loss of life, since the brahmins would never have allowed a shedder of blood, particularly that of the sacred cow, to reside amongst them. This worst kind of sacrilege is sure to provoke their enmity, and the most dreadful consequences have followed the commission of any murderous assault upon this cherished animal.

In consequence of the domineering spirit which they have upon all occasions manifested, and the frequent disturbances occasioned by their intolerance, it has been determined that no brahmin shall in future be eligible for the military service. Mohamedans are preferred, as being less difficult to manage, and from this class, and from the Rajpoots, the army will in future be recruited. Every Rajpoot, whatever his other occupation may be, considers himself to be a soldier by profession; he takes both offensive and defensive weapons with him while working in the fields, and is ready at any time to engage in the honourable trade of war. This is not the case with the Hindoos generally; it is only the castes enumerated above who are not strictly military by descent, that will embrace a soldier's life. Those who have been directed by a dispensation which is regarded with the deepest reverence, to follow occupations of a purely peaceful nature, will not for any consideration engage in war. Hence, it would be impossible in India to arouse the whole population to arms; not even when their homes and their healths are at stake, will men, who do not belong to the fighting classes, defend them from the assaults of an invader. They will hire soldiers for their protection, and if these are not to be obtained, either fly or surrender. This will account for the greater difficulty which the Moghuls experienced, when, after the conquest of nearly the whole of Hindoostan, they attempted the subjugation of Rajpootana. Here every town and village turned out its male inhabitants to repel the assailants, and when at length the Moslem victor called himself master of the country, he found the greater part a desert, nearly the whole of the population having fallen in its defence. To the circumstance above mentioned, the ease and rapidity of the conquests achieved in India must, in a great measure, be attributable, since, particularly in Bengal, there are whole districts which would not produce a single person, who could be deemed fitting to take the field. Upon this account, when travelling, however large the retinue of servants may be, no dependence can be placed, in the event of an attack, excepting upon those amongst them who belong to castes which exercise the trade of war. It would not be considered an act of cowardice in the others to remain supine, or to seek their own safety in flight, so strong and entrammelling are the fetters of caste, that it deprives a human being of half the powers which have been given to him. Some of the tribes of bearers are of so peaceable a character, that they will bear insult and even blows without resistance, while others, of a different caste, resent the slightest affront, and have been known to murder those, who, confounding the whole of the fraternity together, have ventured to lay a hand upon them in anger.

While upon the subject of caste, it may not be irrelevant to allude to that of the *goojurs*, a tribe inhabiting our north-west provinces, and who are to be met with in great numbers in the neighbourhood of Delhi. They are a race of cultivators, but chiefly devote themselves to the raising of water-melons during the season, being employed the remainder of the year in the manufacture of ropes. This class approach very closely to the pariahs, not being very nice in their persons, or their habits, or scrupulous with regard to their food, since they will eat rats and mice. There is also a class of itinerants entitled *nuths*, who very closely resemble the gypsies of European countries; they follow the profession of basket and mat-making, and the young girls dance and perform a few mountebank tricks, to attract an audience from whom they may collect a little money. The women are called *nuth-nees*, and some of them are very pretty; their features being well-formed and expressive. They are invariably of a slight make, and their complexions are much darker than those of other natives. The *buhaliyas*, or bird-catchers, form another caste, low in the scale, certainly, although instances are known of their being entertained in European families as bearers, or to look after the poultry. Besides those already enumerated, there are many other castes of different degrees of respectability; *dhars* who tend cattle in the fields; *korees*, who are weavers; *kundoos*, employing themselves as sugar-bakers or refiners, &c. But, enough has been said to shew the great difficulty of recognizing the various grades into which the Hindoo community has divided, and to which they are tied down by a law, to all appearance, at present, immutable. The *maters* have split into two castes, *teera-bhaee*, and *halalkhar ;* for, low and rejected as they are, and almost confounded with the loathsome reptiles whom man avoids and destroys, they are particular concerning the tenets of their faith, following different opinions, which has occasioned this division. It is alleged as a sufficient reason for an objection to reside in any of the hotels in Calcutta, that the *maters* of those establishments have the *entré* to the kitchens and pantries, while it is not quite certain whether they may not officiate as cooks. The very idea of the abominations attendant upon their being permitted to handle the cooking utensils, must produce in every well educated person so strong a feeling of disgust, that it is not surprizing that those who know the horrible defilements which ensue, should shrink from a residence in a place where they are permitted. There is not any kind of filth which these people refuse to handle, it being impossible even to hint at the disgusting habits in which they seem absolutely to take a pride, as being the *dustoor* (custom) of their class; therefore, until they can be entirely regenerated, it is absolutely necessary that they should be kept in their places, and never suffered to pollute the kitchen by their presence. Unfortunately, it is absolutely necessary that one of these people should be kept about a house, since the Mahomedans and the Hindoos of a higher caste refuse to perform offices which are essential to the comfort of a family; many objecting to throw away the water in which another has washed; and not being able to do without them, *maters* and *matrannees* are often more than tolerated. At the European farms, *doosads* are entertained for the purpose of curing the salt provisions, especially the bacon, pork, and hams, since Mussulmanees, the only class of servants who ought to belong to the culinary department, have so great an abhorrence of swine's flesh that few can be induced to touch it. The lower classes of Portuguese might be employed in this service, but they are rarely to be found out of Calcutta.

From the foregoing pages, it will be seen, that nothing can be more necessary, in order to secure the comfort of the establishment, and the respectability of the family in the eyes of the natives, than an acquaintance with the customs of the country, and some degree of deference to public opinion. The best way for a stranger to effect these objects, is to place a man of good character at the head of the domestics, and to make him answerable for the conduct of others: he should be told to allow none to engage that are unfit for their situations, and he should be expected to compel all to perform their proper duties. To the obstinacy of Europeans, in insisting upon the performance of things which are repulsive to persons of particular castes, may be attributed the greater number of failures of domestic comfort. Respectable people will not endure the interference with their prejudices, and though there may be some danger of their giving themselves airs, and pretending to more fastidious scruples than their religion enjoins, those who either comply with requisitions which are forbidden by their caste, or who will allow their inferiors to presume upon a stranger's ignorance, are unfit for any office of trust.

CHINESE TARTARY.

In a memoir on Chinese Tartary and Khoten, by Mr. Wathen, Persian Secretary to the Bombay Government, compiled from information obtained from intelligent natives of that country, are the following statements respecting the opinion entertained by the people of the Chinese Government, and the means by which Europeans can gain access thither:

The Chinese government is represented to be very unpopular, at the present time, throughout these countries. There seems to be nothing in its system calculated to conciliate, or productive of advantages tending to reconcile the people to subjection to foreigners. The feeling of dislike, with which the Chinese are regarded has been latterly much increased, in consequence of their carrying on vast works of fortification, and building walled towns, by the forced labour of the natives. · The Musalman princes, chiefs, &c. are said to occupy, by the natives who had passed through India, nearly the same political position under the Chinese residents, or Umbauns, and stand in the same relation to them, as they supposed the Nawábs, Rájas, &c. of this country do to the residents of the English government, the Chinese interfering little in the direct management of the people, and leaving to the native princes the administration of the government and laws. The revenue, however, is realized entirely by the Chinese, the princes, &c. having large landed assignments.

It is known at *Yárkand*, that India is governed by a nation of Europe (Feringís); and, it is said, that the Chinese entertain a high notion of the power of the English, which they view with feelings of apprehension, connected with an idea, that is prevalent in the country, of its being destined to fall into their hands.

It is said, that provided a person would dress as a native, allow his beard to grow, and accompany pilgrims on their return from Mecca, there would not be much difficulty in penetrating into Chinese Tartary; but that the easiest way would be by way of *Kokan* and *Kashgar*, as large káfilás of merchants pass that way. The person must, however, be able to speak Turkí, as very few of the natives of the country understand Persian; whereas, in the *Kokan* country, in Independent Tartary, the population of whole towns speak nothing else. It would not be difficult for the individual to go even to *Pekin*, in China. All that is requisite is to get a pass from the governor, by paying a few tenkehs to the Chinese officers, giving out that his object is trade. My informants stated, that some years ago, a European made his appearance at *Yárkand*, in a native dress. He was discovered accidentally, and brought before the governor, who threatened him with torture if he did not confess who he was; but assured him that he would be well treated, if he spoke the truth. He admitted that he was a European, and was sent out of the country.*

* Journ. Asiat. Soc. of Bengal, Dec. 1835.

THE CELESTIAL LOVER.

A DREAM OF LATIN ROMANCE.*

CANTO THE FIRST.

———

Dreams of delight, farewell! your charms no more
Shall gild the hour of solitary gloom;
The page remains, but can the page restore
The banish'd hours which fancy taught to bloom?
Ah, no; her smiles no longer can illume
The path my Psyche treads no more for me;
Consigned to dark oblivion's silent tomb,
The visionary scenes no more I see;
Fast from the fading lines the vivid colours flee.

Tighe.

———

O for a melting lip to-night,
Into my charmed lute to pour
The gentle Legend of delight,
That oft along the twilight shore
Of old Romance hath drawn the tear,
And won the heart unto the ear!
Come, sweetest Spenser, on whose eye
Shone purple dreams of Faëry;
On many a Grecian stream doth float
The golden shadow of thy boat,
That bore thee on the Sea of Time,
Into the mild Ionian Clime.
For fairest Una's sake, I pray,†
Come to my lonely bower to-day!
And teach me from thy lyre to sing
Of that sweet Daughter of a king,
Who long in sorrow pined away;
Yet, like the Lady of thy Lay,
Neither in word or deed ill-meriting.
Come too, Thou,‡ whose fond hand twin'd
The verdant boughs of myrtle tree
About the tomb of Rhodope;
For Psyche now the garland bind.
Come, gentle Shakspeare, "Fancy's child,"
Warble again thy "wood-notes wild;"
Every forest-leaf is mute,
Let Juliet's finger wake the lute;

* Few readers require to be reminded of that beautiful episode in the *Golden Ass* of Apuleius, devoted to the loves of Cupid and Psyche. In whatever light we regard it, whether as an allegorical representation of the fall, repentance, and restoration of man: or, only as a picture of the "progress of the soul to perfection, the possession of divine love, and reward of immortality," the Allegory is equally delightful. It has been imitated in almost every language, and has been considered the original spring from whence many sparkling tales of Faëry enchantment have flowed. Every poet has thought it a duty to make an offering at this shrine; and the paintings upon the walls of the Farnese palace indicate to the beholder the charm it exercised over the genius of Raphael. The outline of the story is preserved in the following Poem; but it may not be improper to mention from Mr. Dunlop's brief analysis, in his History of Fiction, that a certain king had three daughters, of whom the youngest and most lovely was named Psyche. Her charms were so wonderful, that her father's subjects began to adore and pay her the homage which should have been reserved for Venus, who commands her son to punish her rival, by inspiring her with a passion for an unworthy object. Cupid, however, falls in love with her himself. Psyche, meanwhile, is exposed on a rock, where she is destined to become the prey of a monster. From this perilous situation she is transported by Zephyr, who carries her to a delightful valley. It is during the period of her exposure that the poem opens.

† Una, in the *Faëry Queen*,—that "Una, with her milk-white lamb," who lives also in the line of Wordsworth. ‡ Milton.

Or that sweet Hebrew Maiden pour
Her liquid music in my ear,
Which when the fainting heart doth hear,
The thirsty spirit longs for more.
Nor unremembered Thou, whose voice
Taught sorrowing Hero to rejoice,
Sending across the stormy sea
Thy wandering Melody.

Nor Thou, O Bard belov'd, whose head*
Upon the Muse's bosom slept,
While silver-footed Cupids crept,
Scattering o'er thy ivory bed
Flowers to soothe each drowsy sense,
In the Castle of Indolence!

Nor Thou, who in the balmy eve,†
Unto the blushing Genevieve,
Did'st breathe thy melting tale;
What time from out the foliage pale
With May-moonlight, the nightingale
Unto the sighing woods did grieve,
Old Man Eloquent! unbind
The wreath thy cunning finger twin'd,
Unloosen now some fragrant leaves
From thy perfumed store of sheaves.
Meet offering to Psyche's bloom—
A rose upon her Poet's tomb,‡
Breathe thy magic through the line;
Make the song, like her, divine.

———

Weep not, gentle girl, nor deem
Thyself, in that drear rocky spot,
Of wakeful aid and care forgot.
Although no star of comfort seem
To cheer thy dark path with its gleam—
Oh, faint not—from yon golden sky
Is looking down one guardian eye,
And one serene Elysian face
Makes sunshine in that lovely place;§
Cythera's son is watching thee!
Even now with silvery harmony,
The heavenly guide descends;
Over the trembling Maid he bends,
And Psyche on the Zephyr's breast
Is wafted to a Bower of Rest!

A rose-leaf floating softly by,
Or glittering plume of butterfly,
Sailing through the summer sky,
Might tell that sweet Elysian motion;
Or Cytherea smoothly gliding
Through the rose-empurpled ocean,
The flow'ry-coloured clouds dividing
Before the harmonious wheels of gold.—
So pleasantly that Maid behold,
Treading the liquid paths of air,

---

* Thomson.   † Coleridge.
‡ Apuleius wrote in prose; but in this case, at least, it was " Prose by a Poet."   § Spenser.

Within the Zephyr's arms reclining :
Not Cleopatra on her bed
By silken veils o'er-shadowed,
With fairer hues of beauty shining !
She hath travell'd far, but now
A purer breeze doth fan her brow—
What dream unto her eyes is given ?
The earth has blossomed into Heaven !
A brighter vision never streamed
On Pindar's eye-lids, when the light
Of heavenly plumage charmed his sight,
While through the green boughs of the trees,
Moved lightly by the singing breeze,
The everlasting Bowers of Rest,
The verdant Islands of the Blest,
Bathed in ambrosial beauty, gleamed !*

A flood of glory ! in amaze
The Maiden looked, while, like a dream†
At noon, beside a pleasant stream,
A glittering Palace rose ; the blaze
Of diamond-domes upon the air,
Kindling the heaven with its rays.
Not half so bright the red-sun glowed,
Or the Arabian evening flowed,
Or woke the moon or midnight star,
On the white palace of Sennamar.‡

* Pindar's description is well known.

† In Milton, we see the " fabric huge," that " rose like an exhalation;" and Bishop Heber, in his *Palestine*, very beautifully describes the building of the temple—
　　　　Like some tall palm, the mystic fabric rose,
　　　　Majestic silence !
I remember to have seen the original of this picture, at least a part of it, pointed out by an eminent Cambridge scholar, in the fifth book of Cowper's *Task*. It occurs in that beautiful account of the Empress Catherine's Palace of Ice ; certainly one of the most delicious passages that ever proceeded from his pen :
　　　　　　No forest fell,
　　When thou would'st build ; no quarry sent its stores
　　T'enrich thy walls ; but thou didst hew the floods,
　　And make thy marble of the glassy wave.
　　In such a palace, Aristæus found
　　Cyrene, when he bore the plaintive tale
　　Of his lost bees to her maternal ear ;
　　In such a palace, poetry might place
　　The armory of winter.
　　*　　　　*　　　　*
　　Silently as a dream the fabric rose ;
　　No sound of hammer or of saw was there.
Heber's introduction of the palm is still more poetical and appropriate.

‡ The palace built by the Arabian king, Noman-Al-Omar; a single stone combined the entire building, and the rich colours of the walls changed continually. The name of the architect was Sennamar. Mr. Southey might have had Apuleius in his memory when he wrote the beautiful description of an enchanted palace, in his romance of *Thalaba*. Zeinab is wandering over the uninhabited wilderness, when she is suddenly aroused from her sorrow by a cry of wonder from young Thalaba. Lifting her eyes, she beholds " high in air a stately palace:"
　　　　　Amid a grove embowr'd
　　　　Stood the prodigious pile,
　　　　Trees of such ancient majesty
　　　　Tower'd not on Yemen's happy hills,
　　　　Nor crowned the stately brow of Lebanon.
　　　　Here studding azure tablatures,
　　　　And rayed with feeble light;
　　　Star-like the ruby and the diamond shone:
　　　　Here on the golden towers
　　　　The yellow moonbeam lay,
　　　Here with white splendor floods the silver wall.

Around the streams of crystal creep,
Murmuring pleasant sounds of sleep,
And clear, as if an angel's face
Had left the shadow of its grace
Upon the watery mirror ; she
With lifted foot stands doubtingly,
While hands invisible unfurl
The cloudless gates of orient pearl,
The ruby flashes from the floor.

The pilgrim wondering looked and gazed,
And still the emerald pillars blazed,
While softly rose a tender strain ;
Not Eve's voice sweeter when she prayed
At moonlight in the cedar shade,—
It died, and came again :

" Welcome, to these heavenly Bowers !
Welcome, to the Land of Flowers !
Enter, beautiful Ladye !
Here yellow autumn cometh not,
But Summer from her fragrant grot,
With floral pomp and minstrelsy,
Leads out the purple Band of Hours !
Enter ! beautiful Ladye—
Enter thy radiant home, and we
Unseen about thy path will glide,
For ever watching by thy side."

She enters now a gorgeous hall,
Where, through the windows rich bedight,
Pours in the softened golden light ;
Dancing upon the crystal wall,
Like sunset on a waterfall.
A festal couch before her spread,
With precious flowers, an odorous heap,
Wooing the heavy eyes asleep—
A silken pillow for her head :
Beside her shone the radiant board,
With urns of snowy crystal stored,
Treasuring the sweet blood of the vine—
The maiden quaffed the magic wine.
And soon the entrancing nectar stole,
Sweeter than music, o'er her soul ;
And joyful thoughts were thronging o'er
Her gladdening heart, when through the door
A heavenly sound came gliding in ;
Its tones so beautiful might win
A savage to adore,
And listen, now,—that voice to suit
Awoke the spirit of a lute,

And in a later part of the poem, a scene of still greater richness is painted, with a luxury of fancy more
than Oriental—

Thalaba stood mute,
And passively received
The mingled joy that flowed on every sense ;
Where'er his eye could reach,
Fair structures, rainbow-hued, arose,
And rich pavilions, through the opening woods,
Gleamed from their waving curtains sunny gold.

From its lips of ivory pouring
Notes sweeter than of early lark,
At summer morn, 'twixt light and dark,
Into the kindling æther soaring—
Entranced upon the hymn she hung ;
But all unseen the minstrel sung ;
Did Zephyr breathe upon the lyre ?
But hark ! a deeper, fuller sound—
No Grecian lover, myrtle-crowned,
Ere listened to a more melodious Choir!*

The carol faded into sleep ;
And from the woods a mellow chime
Welcomed the glimmering even-time ;
The Dove beneath the leafy cover
Coo'd unto the leaves above her :
But in that Bower of Bliss unknown,
When morning's cheerful hours were flown ;
For many a shadow bright and vast,
From cloudless jasper columns cast,
Upon the enchanted Palace lay,
Pouring, as from a Fount of Light,
A living lustre on the night,
More beautiful than day.

The carol faded into sleep—
And Psyche's spirit slumbered too ;
As in the balmy time of dew
The South-wind fans a summer rose,
So doth the shadow of repose
Over her drooping eyelids creep.

So calmly on the golden stream
Of love that gentle Lady floated,
And He, to his meek Bride devoted,
Poured freshest beauty on her dream.
Yet oft beneath that glorious sky
The tear-drop glistened in her eye,
And oft her mourning thoughts would roam
Unto the green haunts of her home ;
And often did she start to see,
Beneath the lonely tamarisk-tree,
Some cherished face, that Memory
Had brought to that enchanted spot :
And old familiar voices talked
Of dear friends to her as she walked :
Into their airy arms she rushes,
And then the flood of anguish gushes,
To find those friends were not !

Suddenly, the darkened room
Kindled with a flush of bloom ;
A tender whisper, like the tune
Of a pastoral reed in June,
Into the odorous chamber came,
Breathing the lovely Maiden's name :

* See an account, in Apuleius, of the splendid feast, and of the unseen musicians.

So oft on Grecian glen hath died
A sweet song, from the water heard,
Whose bosom by the light oar stirred,
Flashed on the shepherd's face of glee,
Who to the oaten pipe applied
His lip of rural minstrelsy.*
And comes thy Lover now to thee,
On those sweet waves of melody?
Yes, He reclineth by her side,—
The Heavenly Lover with his Bride!

" Bring my sisters, dear, to me!"
Thus the weeping Maiden sighed
On her lover's breast, and he
In vain with voice or soft caresses
To sooth her saddening anguish tried;
Still her tender suit she presses—
" Oh, bring my sisters, or I die "—
When could a lover's lip deny?
Already through the Portal bright
The Angel-Zephyr's wings unfold,
And, ere the sunny eyes of Light
Slumber upon the breast of Night,
Again he treads the Courts of Gold,
Her sisters in his bosom bearing;
But they, with burning envy, see
The pomp, the pride, the pageantry,
Not for the tender Maiden caring.
And soon their deadly hatred poured
Sharp sorrow into Psyche's bosom,
Her Heavenly Lover, her Adored,
A dreadful monster, to the sword

* May I give in a note that delicious burst of Mr. Wordsworth?

> In that fair clime, the lonely herdsman stretched
> On the soft grass through half a summer's day
> With music lulled his indolent repose;
> And in some fit of weariness, if he,
> When his own breath was silent, chanced to hear
> A distant strain far sweeter than the sounds
> Which his poor skill could make, his fancy fetched
> Even from the blazing chariot of the sun
> A beardless youth, who touched a golden lute,
> And filled the illumined groves with ravishment.

Among our own poets who have successfully described the sweetness of lovers' voices to the objects of their affection, may be mentioned old Gower, in the sixth book of his *Confessio Amantis;* after comparing the " wordes of his mouth" to the " windes of the South," he adds—

> And if it so befall among
> That she carol upon a song,
> When I it hear, I am so fedd
> That I am fro myself so ledd,
> As though I were in Paradis;
> For certes, as to mine avis,
> When I hear of her voice the steven,
> Methinketh it is a bliss of heaven.

In Beaumont and Fletcher's tragedy of *Philaster,* where Bellario is accounting for her assumption of male apparel, she expresses her admiration and love for Philaster by a touching phrase—

> I did hear you talk,
> *Far above singing.*

The thirsty hand of vengeance giveth!*
Oh, wicked hearts, that thus could seek
To dim the lustre of that cheek,
To blight the purest blossom
That on the Tree of Beauty liveth!

Now the dreadful hour is nigh,
And tears are in the Maiden's eye,
And fear hath blanched her lip of rose;
Yet still with faltering step she goes;
Her sisters soothe with whisper bland:
Now she hath passed the ivory door,
And now she stands the couch before—
A lamp and dagger in her hand.

Why starteth she? oh, wondrous sight!
A radiant vision of delight
Upon the wondering Maiden beamed,
Fairer than poet ever dreamed
Through the enchanted Gardens flying,
Or drinking with enamoured eyes
The fragrant bloom of Paradise:
With cheek upon his white arm lying,
Crowned with many a glittering ray,
There the Elysian Wanderer lay;
Still 'neath his shadowy eye-lids came
Purple darts of amorous flame,
And bright Iris pinions' roseate glow,
The rich hues glancing to and fro,†
Painting each voluptuous feather,
Like sunny mists in summer-weather,
Or dewy-glittering flowers; and, lo!
Beside his pillow hung together
The golden Quiver and the Bow!

* Her husband, who was ever invisible, forbids her attempt to see him; but her sisters being envious of her happiness, endeavour to persuade her that her husband is a serpent, by whom she would be ultimately devoured. Psyche resolves to satisfy herself of the truth by ocular demonstration (Dunlop). The reader may like to see the *Cowleian* spirit in which the hesitation and surprise of Psyche are pourtrayed by Apuleius; the incident of the lamp is in the most exaggerated temper of the Marino school, and must have delighted Donne:

Festinat, differt; audet, trepidat; diffidit, irascitur: et, quod est ultimum, in eodem corpore odit (serpentum) bestiam, diliget maritum. Vespere tamen jam noctem trapente præcipiti festinatione nefarii sceleris instruit apparatum. Nox aderat et Maritus aderat primisque Veneris prælis velitatus altum soporem extenderat. Tunc Psyche et corporis et animi alioquin infirma, fati tamen veritia subministrante, visibus roboratur, et prolata lucerina et arrepta rexum audacia mutavit. Sed cum primum luminis oblatione tori secreta claruerunt, videt omnium ferarum mitissimam dulcissimamque bestiam, ipsum illum Cupidinem formosum Deum formose cubantem; cujus aspectu lucernæ quoque lumen hilaratum increbuit et acuminis sacrilegi novacula prænitebat. Et vero Psyche tanto aspectu deterrita et impos animi, marcido pallore defecta tremensque desidit in imos poplites, et ferrum quærit abscondere, sed in suo pectore. Videt aurei capitis genealem cæsariem ambrosia tremulentem cervices letes genasque purpureas, pererrantes crinium globos decoriter impeditos, alios antependulos, alios retrocendulos: quorum splendore nimio fulgurante jam et ipsam lumen lucernæ vacillabat. Per humeros volatilis Dei plumæ roscidæ miranti flore candicant; et quamvis alis quiescentibus extimæ plumulæ tenellæ ac delicatæ resultantes inquieta lasciviunt.—*Apuleii Fabula de Psyche et Cupidine.*

† The colour of Cupid's wings has been a favourite subject for painting among poets. In a fragment ascribed to Virgil, we find the *diversicoloribus alis*, the various-coloured wings. Euripides applies the same epithet, ποικιλόπτερος, in the *Hippol.* You meet with it often in the Anthology and among the Latin poets. The bards of Italy lavished their richest colours upon the son of Cythera, particularly Tasso, Petrarch, and Marino. Spenser, who loved to dip his pencil in the vivid dyes of the South, has commemorated—

The spotted wings like peacock's train

in the *Shepherd's Calendar*, and in the *Faery Queen*, Book iii. Canto xi, he has drawn a still more brilliant picture—

And

Oh, hapless maid! oh, evil hour,
Thy sisters came unto thy Bower!
She stooped, and (sad the tale to tell)
The warm oil on his pinion fell.
The sleeper started from his bed,
And while his flashing wings he spread :
" Farewell, beautiful," he said,
" Sharper pains thy sisters wait,
Deadlier enmity of fate.
Farewell, farewell ! I punish thee
Only, Beloved, by losing me!"
And while he spoke, his glittering wings
Shook round him in a perfumed shower,
The sweet breath of a garden bower; *
In vain the weeping Maiden clings
About her angry Lord—and hark !
A sound of thunder, and the walls
Of crystal and the jasper Halls
Vanish—in a desert dark
The Mourner wanders on alone !

End of the First Canto.

———

L'ENVOI.

Thus at thy summons have I taken
My sad harp from the willow-tree,
Long by the winds of Autumn shaken,
A strain of older love to waken,
Lady of my heart ! for thee !
Sweetest, dearest, Emily !
Not mine that lovely Legend through
To pour the Fancy's honey-dew ;
And yet that tender tale were meet,
Lady ! thy listening ear to greet ;
LIKE PSYCHE, THOU, IN BLOOM AND YOUTH—
LIKE HER—IMMORTAL IN THY TRUTH!

And at the upper end of that fair rowme,
  There was an altar built of precious stone
  Of passing value and of great renowne,
  On which there stood an image all alone,
  Of massy gold, which by his own light shone;
  And wings it had with sondry colours dight,
  More sondry colours than the proud pavone
Bears in his boasted fan, or Iris bright,
When her discoloured bow she spreads through Heaven bright.

It has been proposed in the last line to read *heaven's light,* to avoid the recurrence of the same twice in two following lines. Upton has pointed out the original of this description in Tasso.

* Collins says beautifully—

          And 'midst his frolic play,
      As if he would the charming air repay,
      Shook thousand odours from his dewy wings.

THE ESTATE OF ALEXANDER AND CO.

TO THE EDITOR.

Sir : At length, after three years have elapsed since the stoppage of Alexander and Co., an expected dividend is announced of three per cent., equal to one-eighth of the simple interest which would have been due for that time. This would not be so bad, if the capital of the creditors was likely to be recovered; but to recover it, or any part of it, they must look not to the estate of Alexander and Co., consisting of an accumulation of old bad debts and compound interest created by the operation of some twenty or thirty years, and due by people, some of whom despatched themselves to the other world a great many years ago, and others, of most of whom all efforts to procure any tidings would be a desperate and perfectly fruitless task. It is true, indeed, that one of them appeared in the Court of Bankruptcy here a year or two ago, when a debt for 2,00,000 rupees was proved against him by the official assignee, arising out of an advance of 20,000 rupees! And this may be taken as a fair specimen of the character and value of the debts due to the estate, and carried on in the books *as assets;* but then there were also some indigo works, &c., belonging to this estate, said to be of great value; and this may have been the case, but they were found unavailable, being mortgaged to the utmost; and the question now is, what was done with all the money extracted to such a degree from the estate as to leave nothing for the *general creditors?*

It is not to the estate, therefore, the creditors must look for their capital, but to the retired partners, who carried away that capital, amounting to millions, and which they had no right to carry away, leaving the house insolvent at every period for the last twenty years or upwards, which is quite evident without exhibiting any examination and *exposé* of their books.

Before proceeding with further remarks, perhaps it might not be amiss to request your attention to the strictures passed by the *Englishman* on the proceedings in the Insolvent Court at Calcutta, where it appears that oaths were sworn that there were *real assets,* belonging to the estate, sufficient to pay the general creditors one-half the amount due to them, in order to procure the protection of that court to the members of the firm. Does the law require that condition, *viz.* payment of one-half, to entitle insolvents to protection? And if it does, how has it happened that they have obtained their discharge through that court without paying even the smallest fraction of what they owed, or showing ultimately any real prospect of paying? The total falsity of the prospect held out in Calcutta of eight annas in the rupee, and here of ten shillings in the pound, as well as subsequent smaller estimates, is now apparent, and it would seem that an additional object in holding out these expectations was to pacify and amuse the general creditors; and as the Insolvent Act, as applied to India, appears, upon many points, to have puzzled the judges there, as you must have remarked, perhaps you might be able to procure the means of throwing some light upon it, for the information of your readers who are interested in these unfortunate proceedings.

An able and interesting sketch, respecting the failures in Calcutta, appeared in the *Times* of the 2d October 1833, and some letters on the 9th October 1833, which led to the following observations by the editor of the *Times:* " It cannot fail to be observed, that several of the most wealthy partners in the Indian houses, and others which have lately been declared insolvent, have retired, taking with them large fortunes out of their respective concerns. It deserves investigation, whether the firms were perfectly solvent at the time of the retire-

ment of those fortunate capitalists; otherwise, they might be made to refund
to the general creditors that capital they had withdrawn." Some letters, conveying hints to the general creditors, as to what they might expect as dividends, &c. were also published in your journals of from January to June, both
inclusive, 1834; and also some valuable observations of your own in that of
June 1834, in the interest of the creditors; yet, lamentably, without the effect
of arousing them from a state of apathy and indifference to their losses—claims
of such immense magnitude, and the duty the creditors owe to their families
and heirs, to make every possible effort for the recovery of their property,
are surely weighty considerations, and deserving of their utmost and best
exertions.

It was recommended, in the letters above referred to, to call a meeting in
London of all the creditors at home of the several houses that have failed in
Calcutta, and to send out a couple of able accountants to draw up statements
from their books; but, as regards the house of Alexander and Co., what occasion is there to refer to their books, when we have the matter in question
already clearly and beyond a doubt demonstrated? *viz.* in the balance-sheet
submitted to the creditors in Calcutta is this item: assets, 4,94,31,215 rupees;
deduct from this as bad and *worth nothing*, 3,18,27,000 rupees! And in that in
London: assets, 4,94,30,000 rupees, of which deduct as bad and *worth nothing*,
2,98,30,000 rupees! which shows that they had been in the habit of carrying
on items in their books as *assets* which accumulated to the amount of about
three crores of rupees, or three millions sterling, and *not worth one straw!*
Consequently, the several retired partners who assigned to themselves capital
as profits, which are thus *demonstrated* to have been *fictitious*, as derived from
balance-sheets made up with *such assets* to their credit, ought to be compelled,
as the editor of the *Times* has pointed out, to refund the enormous quantity of
capital they carried away; and their claims as creditors ought not to be
allowed, not one of them or their successors having embarked any capital in
the house, and there never were *real profits* to divide. The capital of the depositors has disappeared; and though there are creditors in England of this firm
to the amount of nearly half a million sterling, there are, unfortunately for
some of the sufferers, who are incapable, from want of means, to make any
exertion to recover their property, few, or rather no men of business amongst
them. Lord Combermere is at the head of the list, a creditor for about
£50,000, which is a round sum, and worth looking after. The other creditors
are looking up to his lordship, as a man of property, rank, and influence, and
therefore able to adopt proceedings; but who, not being a man of business himself, can have no difficulty in finding a fit person to take up, sift, and prosecute
this matter, which has produced such extensive misery to the old, the invalid,
the widow, and the orphan, whilst those retired partners and mushroom capitalists are living in the rank and splendour of princes, or the first people of the
land, and some of their successors are enabled to have splendid apartments
and carriages for their wives, perhaps through the means of the settlements
said to have been made on them from the depositors' funds in their house, for
certain it is, not one of them had any funds of their own.

Then, another point: how does it happen that the house here appropriates
to itself Lord Hastings's prize-money and the title-deeds of a certain estate,
mentioned in the examinations in the Court of Bankruptcy here, &c. &c.?
Surely, Lord Combermere and other creditors, who have means and are capable
of acting, ought to investigate all these matters, or cause them to be investigated, instead of putting up patiently, and perhaps it may be said shamefully,

with the total loss of their deposits. This exertion is due to themselves as men, and would be an act of kindness and charity towards unfortunate and helpless persons who have lost their all by this, which may be called monstrous failure, not to designate it by more ungracious epithets—a failure brought about in consequence of the undue extraction of the capital thrown into the house by the public.

Your insertion of this letter may have the good effect of awaking the attention of Lord Combermere and the other principal creditors, and will oblige, Mr. Editor, your humble servant and constant reader,

A CREDITOR OF ALEXANDER AND Co.

25th June 1836.

TO THE EDITOR.

Sir : The sufferers by the Calcutta failures are indebted to you for information, from time to time, respecting the proceedings on the matter in the Insolvent Court in Calcutta; but as you have not yet favoured them with any account of what has taken place in the Court of Bankruptcy, perhaps you could procure a copy of the official assignee's account-current of his management of the estate of Alexander and Co. here, showing what he has realized, and also disbursed as expenses, such as the amount of the Solicitor's bills, &c. &c., showing thereby the utility of his and their services, if any, to the general auditors, and really whether the introduction of the matter into the court here was, in any degree, necessary, with a view to their benefit, or merely for the purpose of carrying one of the partners through the court, and procuring for him his discharge at the expense of the estate and the general creditors.

It is understood that another of the partners has made his appearance here lately, and is employing the services of the solicitors to the estate, as they are called, to procure the necessary signatures to his certificate, and to perform all other necessary offices in the law to that end, the expenses of which are to be defrayed out of the funds of the estate, in the hands of the assignees here, and, consequently, out of the pockets of the general creditors. If this impression is unfounded, it will be but justice to correct it, and, as many of the creditors are residing at great distances from London, and have not an opportunity of calling at the Court of Bankruptcy, or on the official assignee for information, it would be an attention to them on your part to procure the information in question, and insert it in your journal, which is read in all parts of the country by all persons who have resided in India.

It may be observed, that Mr. Whitmore, the official assignee, in his circular of the 8th July, 1833, held out to the creditors a prospect of " assets in Europe," belonging to the estate; and there was a Mr. Shore, an old friend of the Alexanders, appointed as creditors' assignee, at their first meeting here, and who may be also applied to for information.

Your insertion of this letter in your first number, with the view to its meeting the eyes of the assignees, in London, may have the effect, in addition to your own exertions, of procuring the necessary information for the creditors and your readers.

Your obedient servant,

18th July. A CREDITOR.

MEMOIRS OF LORD CLIVE.

THIRD ARTICLE.

THE prospect of Clive's departure for England had excited much uneasiness in the minds both of natives and Europeans in authority. The Nawab, Meer Jaffier, though displeased at the superiority and influence of Clive, was personally attached to him, and was apprehensive that his successor might not be able to control the subordinate officers, and the natives who had erept into power under the English, and whose malpractices were a growing evil. All the chief civil servants, Mr. Hastings amongst the number, entreated him to remain some time longer, laying before him the state of the country, and the consequences of a junction between the French and the native powers. But Clive had in view the prospect of doing more service to India at home than abroad. His correspondence discovers this to have been one of his motives for quitting India. " He desired to obtain for the governors of the three presidencies commissions from his Majesty as major-generals, in order that their superior rank might put an end to the pretensions and independent powers of his Majesty's officers, which had been found, on some occasions, seriously to impede and injure the public service." This he mentions in a letter to Mr. Vansittart, 20th August, 1759. He wished, too, to be in Europe before peace was concluded between France and England, " for convinced I am," he says, " the directors are not masters sufficiently of the subject, and will probably conclude a peace in Europe which cannot possibly be abided by in the East-Indies."

The court was at this time distracted by party cabals, which ended in the ascendancy of Mr. Sulivan, between whom and Clive, a bitter animosity afterwards arose. The squabbles in the court provoked public clamour and odium; and this consideration, together with some experience of what he imagined to be a slight, led him to conclude that the machine of Indian government in London was not adequate to the large duties which devolved upon it. Under this impression, he addressed a letter to Mr. Pitt (afterwards Earl of Chatham), then Secretary of State, in which, after giving a succinct account of the state of Bengal, the prospect of the extension of our territories, and the tender made by the court of Delhi of the Dewanny, he proceeds :

" But so large a sovereignty may possibly be an object too extensive for a mercantile company; and it is to be feared they are not of themselves able, without the nation's assistance, to maintain so wide a dominion. I have therefore presumed, sir, to represent this matter to you, and submit it to your consideration, whether the execution of a design, that may hereafter be still carried to greater lengths, be worthy of the Government's taking it into hand. I flatter myself I have made it pretty clear to you, that there will be little or no difficulty in obtaining the absolute possession of these rich kingdoms; and that with the Moghul's own consent, on condition of paying him less than a fifth of the revenues thereof. Now I leave you to judge, whether an income yearly of upwards of two millions sterling, with the possession of three provinces abounding in the most valuable productions of nature and of art, be an object deserving the public attention; and whether it be worth the nation's while to take the proper measures to secure such an acquisition,—an acquisition which, under the management of so able and disinterested a minister, would prove a source of immense wealth to the kingdom, and might in time be appropriated in part as a fund towards diminishing the heavy load of debt under which we at present labour. Add to these advantages the influence we shall thereby acquire over the several European nations engaged in the commerce here, which these could no longer carry on but through our indulgence, and under such limitations as we should think fit to prescribe."

Mr. Walsh, the secretary of Clive, and who delivered this letter to the minister, reported the result of his interview, and which is thus fortunately preserved. Mr. Pitt acknowledged that the affair was " very practicable," but of a " very nice nature;" he mentioned that inquiries had been made whether the Company's conquests and acquisitions belonged to them or to the crown, and that the judges seemed to think to the Company; he said the Company were not proper to have it, nor the crown, for such a revenue would endanger our liberties. Mr. Walsh says, he observed to him that it was necessary for him to determine whether it was an object for the Company or the state; for if the state neglected it, he was persuaded that the Company would, in process of time, be obliged to secure it for their greater quiet and safety, exclusive of gain. " He seemed to weigh that; but as far as I could judge of what passed then, it will be left to the Company to do what they please."

This is a remarkable incident; the expressions of Mr. Pitt, scanty as they were, show his constitutional caution; and the conduct of Clive upon this occasion is open to two constructions, which will be adopted by the adverse critics of his character: the suggestion may have been purely patriotic, or it may have been influenced by the ambition of being viceroy of India.

The despatches which he subsequently received from the court, tended by no means to reconcile him to their authority; on the contrary, they so disgusted him and his colleagues, that they penned a letter to the court, wherein they " expressed their sentiments with a freedom, which, though becoming their high sense of the duty they owed themselves, and to their country, was but little suited to the temper or constitution of their superiors." These are Sir John Malcolm's words. The terms of the letter are, however, far stronger than this description would imply. They tell the court that the diction of their letter is unworthy of them ; that it is the result of private pique and personal attachments, &c. The letter excited the utmost indignation at the India-House, and the four gentlemen, who had joined Clive in his remonstrance, were removed and ordered home : thus depriving the service of some of the ablest officers, at a critical period, to which cause Sir John Malcolm attributes the massacre of Patna. Clive now disregarded all entreaties, and took his departure for England.

Had Clive given way to the influence of individual feelings, like some of those who have suffered fancied wrongs from the Company, he would have exerted his great influence and vast wealth to ruin their affairs. His mind was, however, of not so selfish a cast. He reunited himself to those from whom his honourable exile had temporarily severed him, without evincing any bitterness towards his former employers. He entered Parliament, but sat only for a short time there. The first use he made of his wealth was to place all his family (especially his parents) in comfortable independence. He appropriated a part of his fortune to save the family estate at Styche. On his old friend and commander, Col. Lawrence, he settled an annuity of £500. Sir John Malcolm has recorded a number of amusing anecdotes of Clive at this period of his life.

We collect from his private correspondence, that he retained much of that hilarity of disposition, for which he had been remarkable in youth. He was fond of female society; and many of his letters show that he was by no means indifferent to those aids by which personal appearance is improved. It was the fashion of the period to dress in gayer apparel than we now do; and the European visiter at an Indian Durbar, or Court, always wore a rich dress. We find in a letter to Clive, from his friend Captain Latham, a description of a Durbar suit he was preparing from him, in which he says he has preferred a fine scarlet coat with handsome gold lace, to the common wear of velvet. He has also made up, he writes, a fine brocade waistcoat; and he adds to this intelligence, that "it is his design to line the coat with parchment, that it may not wrinkle!"

In a commission which Clive sent to his friend Mr. Orme, there is an amusing instance of his attention to the most trifling parts of his dress.

"I must now trouble you," he observes, "with a few commissions concerning family affairs. Imprimis, what you can provide must be of the best and finest you can get for love or money; two hundred shirts, the wristbands worked, some of the ruffles worked with a border either in squares or points, and the rest plain; stocks, neckcloths, and handkerchiefs in proportion; three corge of the finest stockings; several pieces of plain and spotted muslin, two yards wide, for aprons; book-muslins; cambrics; a few pieces of the finest dimity; and a complete set of table linen of Fort St. David's diaper made for the purpose."

In the list of packages, which Mr. Richard Clive sent to his son in Bengal, one is a box of wigs! Whether Clive had resorted to this ornament from want of hair, or from deference to the fashion of the period, I know not; but there is an authentic anecdote of his boyhood, which proves how essential a wig was considered to all who were full dressed. Clive had, when very young, been admitted by a relation, who was Captain of the Tower, to be one of the spectators when his Majesty George the Second happened to visit that fortress. Nothing was wanted in the boy's dress to prepare him for the honour of approaching majesty except a wig! To supply this want, one of the old Captain's was put upon his head; and his appearance in this costume was so singular as to attract the notice and smiles of the King, who inquired who he was, and spoke to him in a very kind and gracious manner.

Of his wealth at this time, we have the following account:

The whole of Clive's money, when he returned to India in 1755, appears to have been in that country; for we find, from his correspondence, that he had hardly sufficient uninvested cash in England to pay for his annual supplies. He became anxious, however, after he attained great wealth, to remit it home; but this, owing to various causes, was very difficult. The public treasury was so rich from the successes in Bengal, that, for a period, no bills were drawn upon the Directors; Clive, therefore, had recourse to the Dutch Company, through whom he sent the greater part of his fortune; he also transmitted a considerable sum in diamonds (a common mode at that time), and the rest in private bills; and, latterly, two on the Company.

I have carefully examined his letters to his agents, from the 21st of August, 1755, when he advised them of his first remittance, till January, 1759, when he made one of his last; and the amount of property sent to England during that period is, as nearly as the difference of exchange and the loss on bills enable us to judge, £280,000. Of this I calculate that he received £210,000 on the enthronement of Meer Jaffier; and the remaining £70,000 is made up by part of his former fortune, his prize-money at Gheriah and Chandernagore, the receipts from the high stations he held, and the accumulation of interest upon a considerable part of his property during the last five years of his residence in India.

From what has been stated, we may assume that Clive's fortune, before the jaghire was settled upon him, did not amount to £300,000. It appears from documents before me that, previous to this grant, he had given away, or vested for annuities, a sum not less than £50,000 (more than one-sixth of his fortune), to render comfortable and independent those for whom he cherished affection and gratitude.

Clive was, subsequently to these acts of generosity, enriched by the grant of the jaghire, which he himself estimates at £27,000 per annum. With this addition, we may conclude he had an income of upwards of £40,000; a large amount, but far below what this Indian Crœsus (for such he was deemed) was thought by his countrymen to possess.

In 1762, he was created an Irish peer, instead (as he expected) of being an English one. His liberalities had encroached upon his fortune, large as it was, when he was alarmed by an intimation that the Court of Directors were inclined to question his title to his jaghire, which yielded two-thirds of his income. This intimation seems at first intended to keep Clive in a state of helplessness that would subserve the purpose of Mr. Sulivan, who now regarded him as a dangerous rival. " Sulivan might have attached me to his interest if he had pleased," Clive says, in a letter to Vansittart; " but he could never forgive the Bengal letter; the consequence has been that we have all along behaved to one another like shy cocks, at times outwardly expressing great regard and friendship for each other." Clive was the first to break this hollow truce, and thus two parties were formed, advocating opposite principles of government for India: " Sulivan's were the principles of the head of a commercial company; Clive's those of the founder and sustainer of an empire."

He lessened his influence by his honest opposition to the policy of Lord Bute (whose overtures he rejected), voting with the minority who condemned the peace of 1763. Lord Bute patronized Mr. Sulivan.

The ardour with which Clive embarked in the opposition to the minister and the chairman was characteristic; he employed, in the election of directors, in 1763, no less a sum than £100,000 in what was termed " splitting votes," that is, qualifying persons to vote as proprietors, which was not then absolutely forbidden by the law. The object of his partisans was to place him in the chair of the direction; though he says, in his letter, he had no intention of accepting such a post: " I have neither application, knowledge, nor

time, to undertake so laborious an employ." He calculated, however, upon
having something like a paramount influence at the Court, if successful in
his plans, and had chalked out a scheme of administration, in the political
and military departments: he contemplated the establishment of a large
military force in India.

This was a contest beneath the commanding talents of such a man; it
suited them not; he engaged upon unequal terms with opponents who
could employ covert means and petty stratagems; and Clive was, as he
deserved to be, defeated. Mr. Sulivan and his party were victorious, and
lost no time in making him feel the weight of their resentment.

The first step taken by the directors, after the election of 1763, was to
transmit orders to the Bengal government to stop all further payments on
account of Lord Clive's jaghire, and to furnish them with an account of all
sums paid to him since the date of the grant. Clive maintained that his title
to the jaghire* was founded upon the same authority as the Company's right
to the ceded lands; but he offered to relinquish his life-interest to the Company, after he should have enjoyed it a limited number of years. This offer
would doubtless have been embraced, but for the events related, which
enabled Mr. Sulivan and his supporters (including the minister) to avail
themselves of a powerful implement of annoyance to their antagonist.
Lord Clive filed a bill in Chancery against the Court, whose answer set up
these grounds of defence:—that the Company *might* be called to account
for the money by the "Emperor of Hindostan;" that therefore Clive was
accountable to them, and that if the Nawab had a right to alienate this
part of his revenue (which they denied), as he had been deposed by the
Company's agents, the grant became of no effect. The real ground of
refusal creeps out in a *private* and *confidential* letter of Mr. Sulivan to
Mr. Vansittart, the President of Bengal, which (such was the bitter spirit
of the times) was produced in the Court of Chancery, " that all cordiality
being at an end with Lord Clive, the Court of Directors had stopped payment of his jaghire." The eminent lawyers consulted by the Court of
Directors told them (what they well knew), that they could not question the
grant to Lord Clive, or the want of right and power of the Nawab, without
impeaching their own; and that the question between them and Clive was
precisely the same, and should be determined upon the same principles, as a
question between the owners of lands in England, subject to a rent, and
the grantee or assignee of the rent, where both derived from the same
original grantor.

Events were, however, occurring which brought the question to a speedier
adjudication than a suit in Chancery would have done. The violent animosities which these disputes occasioned in India as well as England, were
suspended by intelligence of the dreadful massacre at Patna. The attention of the proprietors, and of reflecting men of all parties, was turned to

---

* By the treaty with Meer Jaffier, in 1757, certain lands near Calcutta, were ceded to the Company a:
perpetual renters, the Nawab reserving the lordship and quit-rents. The Company paid these quit-
rents till 1759, when the Nawab, in consideration of the services of Lord Clive, assigned to him the
quit-rents for life. This is what is to be understood by "Lord Clive's jaghire." The Company had
paid the rents to Clive for three years.

the state of the public interests in India, the recriminations of the opposing parties having brought to light " a scene of corruption, division, and distraction in their internal rule, which, if not early remedied, threatened to bring complete ruin upon their affairs." All eyes were turned to Clive, and at a very full General Court, he was unanimously solicited to return to India. It was at the same time proposed to the directors instantly to restore his jaghire ; but Lord Clive, who was present, with great prudence, interposed, and desired that that point might be deferred till he had made some proposals to the directors. With the boldness and decision of his character, he declared that he differed so much from Mr. Sulivan (who was his personal and inveterate enemy), and considered that he had evinced so much ignorance of Indian affairs, that he could not act with him; that it was indifferent to him who filled the chair, so that Mr. Sulivan did not. The latter gentleman, seeing that the tide of affairs was on the re-flux, intimated an intention of removing the bar to the employment of Lord Clive, to whose talents he bore testimony ; but he wished to stipulate for the retention of some appointments he had made; the General Court, however, would listen to no such compromise, and when it was proposed to try the event of a ballot, though 300 proprietors were present, nine could not be found to sign the requisition.

Every thing now concurred with the views and wishes of Lord Clive ; his right to his jaghire was confirmed (on his own proposal) for ten years, and after waiting till the election for directors was over, he took his departure for India, where he arrived in May 1765.

The victory he achieved must have been highly soothing to his feelings ; more than that, it gave him the support which he required in his short but important administration.

It laid, however, the foundation of the future troubles of his life ; for those over whom he now triumphed cherished their resentments ; and their ranks were early recruited by numerous malcontents from India, whom Clive's reforms had either deprived of the means of accumulating wealth, or exposed to obloquy.

The Nawab, Meer Jaffier, who had been dethroned and restored, imputed all his misfortunes to the absence of Clive, and eagerly hoped to protract his existence till his expected return. The gratification of his hope was, however, denied; he died in February 1765, only a few months before his arrival.

The elevation of Cossim Ali Khan to the musnud, on the deposition of Meer Jaffier, had been accompanied by large gifts to the governor and council of Bengal and others, amounting to £200,000. Mr. Vansittart received five lacs, or £58,333, *tendered* previous to the treaty, but not *accepted* till afterwards. The contrast between the conduct of Clive and his successor in this respect, is well exhibited by his biographer.

The princely presents which Clive merited and received were the rewards of great services rendered to the parties by whom they were given, and in which his first efforts were prompted by considerations that were decidedly uninfluenced by sordid motives. Add to this, that whatever he undertook prospered, and that all the individuals whom he elevated he preserved, not only from their native enemies, but from the still more galling encroachments and rapacity of the Company's servants. By such acts he won the good opinion of all ranks in India. From the King to the peasant, the name of Clive inspired sentiments of respect and confidence. What a contrast was presented by his successors in power! Money for themselves was, in every engagement, one of the stipulations, and *appeared*, though in some cases it might not have *been*, the leading motive of their measures. All their measures failed: every one connected with them was ruined. The character for good faith, which at Clive's departure stood so high, was lost. No one trusted the word of an Englishman. Many of those who engaged in these scenes were able and virtuous; but there was no leading genius among them. The jealousy and party spirit that pervaded the government at home multiplied checks and cherished insubordination in those abroad; till nothing was heard but accusations and recriminations. The army, both European and native, had fallen into a very insubordinate and mutinous state. The officers evinced this spirit on almost every occasion where they deemed their personal interests affected; and many of the privates deserted to the native powers.

These were some of the evils which Clive had now to combat. In his forcible exposition of the state of affairs in Bengal, submitted to the Court of Directors, previously to his departure, he laid open the radical causes of their depression; the revolution in favour of Cossim Ali; the change in the plan of politics which he (Clive) had prescribed in respect to that court, which had left the Nawab to his own projects, whereas, as Clive remarks, with just discernment, " it is now some time that things have been carried to such lengths abroad, that either the princes of the country must, in a great measure, be dependent on us, or we totally so on them;" the encroachments on the Nawab's rights by the trade carried on by the civil servants, dustucks, &c.

Indeed, if some method be not thought of, and your Council do not heartily co-operate with your Governor to prevent the sudden acquisition of fortunes, which has taken place of late, the Company's affairs must greatly suffer.

Lord Clive found the government, as he states, " in a more distracted state, if possible, than he had reason to expect." He was astonished at the bare-faced corruption of the council; " the anarchy, confusion, bribery, and extortion." They began to oppose him, and to dispute his power; but, he says, " I cut that matter short, by telling them they should not be the judges of that power." A party was, of course, formed against Clive, amongst whom was Mr. John Johnstone, who was afterwards one of the most conspicuous of his persecutors at home. They pleaded the example of Clive for acts which they could not deny; printed minutes were recorded by one party recriminatory on the other; the taking of presents was defended by that jesuitical strain of reasoning with which selfishness is easily satisfied, and it required all the firmness and skill of Clive to counteract the opposition he met with. His correspondence, which is copiously introduced into this part of the work, affords valuable materials for the future historian.

At length, some being suspended and sent home, and severe measures being adopted towards the rest, the refractory spirit of the civil servants was subdued. Peace was concluded with Sujah Dowlah, and the Dewanny was conferred by the emperor on the Company: an arrangement which, though it has been censured, Clive justly considers as "fixing firm the foundation of the British empire in India." He then set on foot a thorough examination into the civil and military offices, and suggested, amongst other changes of system, that there should be a governor-general of India, and that the chief seat of the government should be at Calcutta.

The measures which we have glanced at in this summary way, are, perhaps, of more importance to the welfare of British India and to the fame of Lord Clive, than those early deeds which attach more lustre to his name. By his victories and his policy, he sowed the seeds of British power in the East; by his later acts, he arrested the gangrene of corruption, and gave to the Government that form which the plastic hand of genius can alone impart.

Clive now wished to return home. "I have," he wrote to the court, "a large family, who stand in need of a father's protection; I sacrifice my health and hazard my fortune, with my life, by continuing in this climate. The first great purposes of my appointment are perfectly answered."* The court, however, earnestly requested him to continue another year. "The stability of your lordship's plan," they say, "with respect to our possessions and revenues, the peace of the country, and the effecting a thorough reformation in the excessive abuses and negligence of our servants, require time, care, and ability to accomplish."†

In May, 1766, the reduction of double batta occasioned an alarming combination amongst the European officers of the Bengal army, countenanced by Lieut. Col. Sir Robert Fletcher. Lord Clive proceeded to one of the cantonments (Monghyr), and determined that all should be put to hazard rather than the Government negociate with its own army at the bayonet's point. "To submit to the violent demands of a body of armed men," as Mr. Mill remarks, "was to resign the government." The council supported him in his firm resolution, and the malcontents succumbed. This affair occupies a considerable portion of the narrative before us, and it is, indeed, of commensurate importance.

The fatigue and anxiety which this action caused Lord Clive (for it appears, from his letter-books, that he wrote many letters daily himself, besides giving, personally, the most minute attention to every other branch of public affairs), had a dangerous effect upon his health, and in the end totally incapacitated him from business; though he did not quit India till January 1767.

It may be worth remarking here, that, in April 1766, the widow of Meer Jaffier transmitted to Lord Clive a legacy, which had been left by the Nawab, amounting to five lacs of rupees. Considering that the receipt of a legacy was not forbidden by the covenants, he accepted it; but paid it immediately into the Company's treasury, to form a fund (now called Lord Clive's fund), for the relief of disabled officers and men, and their widows. "To this ambiguous transaction," Mr. Mill observes, "the institution at Poplar owes its foundation:" a pretty striking instance of the inaccuracy of

* Letter, 30th September, 1765.   † Letter, 2nd May, 1766.

this writer, since the Poplar Hospital is an institution totally distinct from Lord Clive's fund, in its origin, objects, and support. It was in existence nearly a century before Lord Clive was born, and its objects are persons in the maritime service.

THE CASE OF CAPTAINS NEWALL, BARROW, AND GLASSPOOLE.

We have seen the memorials and correspondence on the subject of the claims of Captains Newall, Barrow, and Glasspoole to compensation, under the Act of 1833, which are so pertinaciously resisted by the Board of Control.

As the details of the case have appeared in our report of the debates in Courts of Proprietors on this subject, it is only necessary briefly to state, that, under the Company's regulations of 1834,—" that their maritime officers, who had served, or were serving, in ships owned, or chartered by the Company and, had not abandoned the service, should be justly and liberally compensated, in consequence of the interest of such officers being affected by the entire discontinuance of the Company's trade,"—these officers sent in their claims for compensation. They were commanders of Company's regular ships, who, having performed five voyages, were disqualified for continuing in that branch of the service, but were eligible for commands in the freighted branch, which formed an integral part of the Company's mercantile service. They have certificates from managing owners of ships in the freight service, that they would have been presented for commands, if the Company's trade had not been abolished; the Court of Directors have declared that they would have been accepted, had they been so presented; and these gentlemen have made declarations "that they had not, previously to August, 1833, quitted the maritime service of the Company, for the purpose of either retiring from it, or of following any other pursuit; and that if the Company had gone on trading in common with the public, it was their intention to continue to follow the maritime profession in that service." The Finance and Home Committee, in January 1835, considered, that it never could have been intended to grant compensation to commanders who had had the peculiar benefits of five voyages in the Company's service, and that there had been no instance of such a commander having again gone in the command of a ship. The Court of Directors, however, negatived this conclusion, which is evidently the result of misconception, and from which the committee themselves subsequently resiled, and admitted the claims. At a General Court, in December 1835, it was resolved unanimously, that these gentlemen were entitled to the pension of £200 per annum, and this resolution was forwarded to the Board of Control, with something like a special recommendation from the Court of Directors.

The present Board of Control, however, adopting the resolutions of the former board, founded upon the misconception of the Finance Committee, refuse to sanction the resolution, on the ground, that these officers " have not been injured by the cessation of the Company's trade," although it necessarily involves the cessation of a lucrative employment, the title to which they had earned by thirty years' service, without an imputation upon their character as officers and gentlemen ! And this refusal is made by a government, which pledged itself, in the negociations with the Company, " that the assignment of the Company's commercial property must necessarily involve, also, a transfer to the government of all the obligations, whether of a legal kind, or *binding on the ground of equity and liberality*, which may attach to that property."

We never knew an instance of this kind, in which, under the peculiar circumstances, justice was more flagrantly violated.

CHINESE ACCOUNT OF INDIA.*

THE third of the years *kan-tĭh*, of the Sung dynasty (A. D. 966), a Buddhist priest of Tsang-chow, named Taou-yuen, who had returned from the western countries (Se-yu), had brought from thence a portion of the body of Fŭh,† vases of crystal, and Sanscrit writings on leaves of *Pei-to*, to the number of forty, which he presented to the emperor. Taou-yuen returned to the western countries (of Asia) in the years *tĕen-fuh* (A. D. 943 to 944); he was twelve years on his travels, wandering in the Five Zin-too for six years. The Five Zin-too (divisions of India) are the same as Tĕen-choo‡ (India). He brought back an abundance of books, to understand the use of which he exerted all his efforts. The emperor Tae-tsoo (who reigned from A. D. 950 to 953) summoned him into his presence, for the purpose of interrogating him respecting the manners and customs of the nations amongst whom he had travelled; the height of the mountains, and extent of the rivers. He answered all the questions one by one. For four years, a priest of Buddha, he dedicated all his cares to one hundred and fifty-seven persons. On his return to the palace, he said he had been desirous of returning into the western countries in search of the books of Fŭh (or Buddha); that he had found some of them where he had travelled, in the provinces of Kan-sha, Se-soo, and others; that these provinces (*chow*) produced tortoises, herbs, and woods, in great abundance, the export of which yielded the revenue of the kingdom. Moreover, he passed beyond the kingdom of Poo-loo-sha and of Kea-she-me.§ Orders were everywhere given that guides should be provided him on his route.

After the years *kae-paou* (about A. D. 969), a Buddhist priest of India brought some Sanscrit books (or Indian presents‖), and envoys continued to bring them from thence. During the winter of the eighth year, the son of the King of Eastern India, named Jang-kĕĕ-kwang-lo (?) came to court to bring tribute. The king of the kingdom of the Law in India¶ happening to die, his eldest son succeeded him; all the other sons of the deceased king quitted their royal abode, and became priests of Buddha, and returned no more to reside in their native kingdom. One of the sons of this Indian king, named Man-choo-she-le,** came into the Kingdom of the Middle (China) as a Buddhist priest. The Emperor Tae-tsoo ordered that he should be provided with an apartment in the palace of his ministers of state, that he should be well treated whilst he remained in the capital, and that he should have as much money as

---

* Concluded from p. 222.

† *Tŭh-Fŭh-shay-le-yĭh:* the characters *shay-le* are the transcription of the Sanscrit word शरीर *Shárira,* 'body,' or शरीरन् *Sháririn,* 'corporeal.' Dr. Morrison, in his Dictionary (Vol. i. Part i. p. 530), states on an authority unknown to us, but apparently to be relied on: " *Shay-le-ta,* a Pagoda, raised over certain relics or pearly ashes of Buddha; these, it is said, are contained in a gold box; if, on being opened, they exhibit a dingy appearance, it is deemed a bad omen; if a red appearance, a good omen."

‡ Another transcription of the Sanscrit सिन्धु *Sindhu,* the river Indus, whence the European and Arabic name of India.

§ These are the kingdoms of Purusha and Cashmere. See Ma-twau-lin, book 335, fol. 15, and M. Rémusat's translation, *Nouv. Mélanges Asiat.* t. 1. p. 196.

‖ *Che-fan-lao,* 'Presents from Che-fan.' It is not said in the text what was the nature of the articles brought; but it is fair to presume, that they were Buddhist books in Sanscrit, which were subsequently translated into Chinese.

¶ *Tĕen-choo-che-fǎ-kwŏ,* 'the kingdom of the Law of India;' apparently the kingdom of the Law of Buddha, *i. e.* Magadha.

** In Sanscrit मञ्जुश्री *Manjusri,* a term which denotes a Buddhist saint.

he required. The body of Buddhist priests conceived a jealousy against him ; and being unable to repel the false accusations, of which he was the object, he requested permission to return to his native kingdom, which was granted by the emperor, who published a proclamation on the subject. Man-choo-she-le, at first, was much alarmed at their intrigues; but when all the Buddhist priests knew the meaning of the imperial proclamation, they were disconcerted in their projects. The Buddhist priest prolonged his stay for a few months, and then departed. He said that it was his intention to embark on the southern sea (perhaps at Canton), in a merchant vessel, to return to his own country. It is not known where he eventually went.

On the 7th of the years *tae-fing-hing-kwŏ* (' the kingdom in great peace and prosperity'), equivalent to A. D. 983, a Buddhist priest of E-chow, named Kwang-yuen, returned from India; he brought from thence a letter from the king, Moo-se-nang,* to the emperor (of China). The emperor ordered that an Indian Buddhist priest should translate the letter, and acquaint him with the contents of it. The letter was to this effect: " I have lately learned, that in the kingdom of *Che-na*, there existed a king, most illustrious, most holy, most enlightened; whose majesty and person subsist in themselves and by themselves. I blush every moment at my unfortunate position, which hinders me from visiting your Court, in order to pay my respects to you in person. Remote as I am, I can only cherish, with hope, a regard for *Che-na*;† whether you are standing or sitting, in motion or at rest (*i. e.* in all circumstances of life), I invoke ten thousand felicities on your holy person."‡

Kwang-yuen also brought certain rare drugs, diamonds, talismans, amulets, to obtain good fortune, and secure the bearer against danger, as well as holy images of She-kea,§ vestments without sleeves, called *kea-sha*, sometimes worn by the priests of Buddha in the exercise of their functions, and various articles used by the hand in eating, which he desired to be humbly offered to the august emperor of China, " wishing him all kinds of happiness; a long life; that he might always be guided in the ' right way;' and that all his wishes might be fulfilled: in the middle of the ocean of life and of death, most of those who cross it are engulphed."‖ Kwang-yuen then presented to the emperor, in person, a portion (or reliques) of the body of She-kea. He likewise translated and explained the entire contents of the letter, brought by a Buddhist priest, from the same kingdom (India); the expressions and sentiments are the same as in that of Moo-se-nang. The bearer of this document learned that it was from the kingdom of Woo-tēen-nang (or Woo-chin-nang); that this kingdom belonged to Yin-too, of the north; that in twelve days, from the west, you arrive at the kingdom of Khan-to-lo (Candahar); twenty days further to the west, you reach the kingdom of Nang-go-lo-ho-lo; ten days

---

* In Sanscrit, *Mahá-Sinha*, ' Great Lion,' an epithet often given to Indian kings ; or, perhaps, rather the transcription of *Madhu-Sinha*, the name of a king of Bengal, mentioned in the *Ayin Akberi*. We shall make here but one observation respecting the law of transcription of foreign names in Chinese, for the benefit of those who have not studied the language; namely, that the Chinese nasal termination *ang* has the same value as the *anuswara* in Sanscrit, or the labial म *m* at the end of words. It is, therefore, equivalent to the Sanscrit accusative : a termination which has become general in the dialect of the south of India.

† The first of the two characters which express this name (and which is an accurate representation of the Sanscrit चीन *China*) is differently written in two places; both are pronounced *Che*.

‡ This letter has been cited by Dr. Morrison, in his *View* of China, but from a different author; from Ma-wan-lin.

§ Shákiá-muni, patronymic name of Buddha.

‖ This, we believe, to be the exact sense of this Buddhist phraseology.

further to the west, you come to the kingdom of Lau-po; twelve days more to the west, is the kingdom of Go-je-nang; and further to the west, that of Po-sze (Persia); after reaching the Western sea (the Persian gulph), from northern Yin-too, in 120 days' journey, you arrive at the Central Yin-too; from thence to the westward, at the distance of three *ching*,* is the kingdom of Ho-lo-wei; still further to the west, in twelve days' journey, you reach the kingdom of Kea-lo-na-keu-je (Karana?); and in twelve days' journey more to the west, you come to the kingdom of Mo-lo-weï (Malwa; in Sanscrit *Má-lava*); further to the west, twenty days' journey, is the kingdom of Woo-jan-ne (Oujein or, Sanscrit Ujjayaní). In another twenty-five days' journey still to the west, you visit the kingdom of Lo-lo; and forty days' journey further to the west, the kingdom of Soo-lo-too (Surat); in eleven days journey further to the west, you get to the Western sea. This makes in the whole a six moons' journey from Central Yin-too. When at Southern Yin-too, in ninety days' journey to the west, you arrive at the kingdom of Kung kea-na; and in one day further to the west, you come to the sea. From Southern Yin-too, in six months' journey to the south, you reach the South Sea (the sea of China). This was what was related by the Indian envoy.

The eighth year (983), a priest of Buddha, master of the law,† came from India, bringing books. In traversing part of the island of Sumatra,‡ he met with the Buddhist priests Me-mo-lo, Che-le-yoo-poo-to; he charged them (as superior priests?) with a letter, which he wished to transmit to the kingdom of the Middle, with a great number of translated books. The emperor caused them to come to court to gratify his curiosity. The master of the law of Buddha (*fă*) again met with some mendicant Buddhists, wearing vestments without sleeves, and valuable head-dresses in the form of serpents.§ He returned with them on their journey to India. A letter of recommendation (*peaou*) was given him, to enable him to traverse the kingdom of Tibet, with letters of credence, delivered by the emperor, to present to the king of the kingdom of San-fuh-tsi or Sumatra. From this remote country he proceeded to the sovereign (*choo*) of the kingdom of Go-koo-lo, and that of the kingdom of Sze-ma-kïé-máng-ko-lan (the Mongul empire?). He recommended Tan-lo to the king of the Western Heaven,‖ and his son formed the design of sending him, by his means, works on the spirits and genii.

In the years *yung-he* (984 to 988), a Buddhist priest of Weï-chow, named Tsoo-hwan, returning from the western countries of Asia (*Se-yu*), with another Buddhist priest from a distant country, named Mïh-tan-lo, where he had been presented to the King of Northern Yin-too, seated on a throne of diamonds, and named Na-lan-to, brought some books. There was besides a Brahman priest, named Yung-she (' eternal age'), and a Persian infidel (*gae-taou*), named O-le-yan, who came together to the capital. Yung-she said that his native country was called Le. It was ascertained that the family name of the king of this kingdom was Ya-lo-woo-te; that his first name was O-jïh-ne-fo; that he wore a yellow dress, and had on his head a cap of gold, adorned with seven precious gems. When he goes out, he mounts an elephant; he is

* The European Chinese dictionaries do not give the value of this itinerary measure. In the Dictionary of Kang-he, it is stated to be a measure of distance, but no equivalent is stated.
† *Sang-fă;* In Sanscrit, *Sangha* and *Dharma* (the priest, or religious meeting), and the law.
‡ *San-fŭh-tsi.*
§ " Valuable head-dresses (or caps), in the form of serpents, " are, doubtless, the shawls which the modern Mahomedans, as well as the Hindus, wrap round their heads.
‖ *Tsan-tan-lo-se-ticn-wang.*

preceded by couriers, with musical instruments on their shoulders; the crowd
rush into the temple of Fŭh, where he distributes gifts to the poor, and succour
to those who need it. His concubine was named Mo-ho-ne; she wore a red
dress, adorned with gold filagree work. She goes out but once a year, and
distributes gifts freely. People flock to attend the king and his concubine,
and raise shouts of joy as they pass. There are four ministers to administer
all the affairs of the kingdom, who are irremovable. The five kinds of grain
and the six kinds of edible fruit, are the same as the Chinese. They use
copper money for purposes of commerce. They have a literature and books,
which are long and are rolled up as in China, except that the leaves are not
pierced and attached one to another.

From their kingdom, six months' journey to the East, you arrive at the
kingdom of the Ta-she (Arabs); in two moons more, you get to Se-chow
(the Western Isle); in three moons more, you arrive at Hea-chow (the Isle of
Summer). O-le-yan says, that the king of his native country was entitled
hĭh-yĭh (Black-dress); that his family name was Chang, and his first name Le-
moo; that he wore silk dresses, embroidered and painted in different colours;
that he wore each only two or three days, resuming them once. The kingdom
has nine ministers, irremoveable, who direct state affairs. Commerce is
carried on by barter, no money being used.

From this kingdom, six months' journey to the East, you arrive at the
country of the Brahmans.*

The second of the years *che-taou* (996), some Buddhist priests from India,
who arrived in ships as far as the mouth of the river (*che-gan*), bringing to the
emperor a brass bell and a copper bell, a statue of Fŭh, and some *Fan*
(Indian) books, written upon leaves of the *pei-to* tree, the language of which
is not understood.

The third and ninth of the year *tëen-shing* (1025 to 1031), some Buddhist
priests of Western Yin-too, lovers of wisdom, knowledge, sincerity, and other
virtues of this kind,† brought *Fan* books‡ as presents, revered as canonical.
The emperor gave to each a piece of yellow stuff, to wrap round the body, in
the form of a band.

The second moon of the fifth year, some *Sang-fŏ*, to the number of five,
denominated 'fortunate' and 'happy,' and by other epithets of the same
nature, brought presents of Fan books. The emperor gave them pieces of
yellow stuff to make trailing robes for them.

The third of the years *king-yew* (1036), nine Buddhist priests, called 'the
virtuous,' 'the exalted,' &c., brought as tribute, Fan books and bones of Fŭh,
with teeth, copper, and statues of Poo-sa (Boddhisatwas): the emperor gave
them caps and bands.

* Here ends the first narrative of the *Yuen-keen-luy-han.*

† These are translations of Sanscrit Bauddha epithets.   ‡ *Fan-shoo-king,* ' classical Indian books.

MR. MORDAUNT RICKETTS.

Sir : As you have thought proper to insert in your Journal for this month certain remarks made upon my case in a Calcutta newspaper, in February last, I now call upon you, as an act of justice, to give equal publicity to an appeal recently made by me to the Court of Directors, on the unjustifiable severity of their extra-judicial proceedings against me. You will perceive from the reply of the Court, that they have not attempted either to deny the facts, or to answer the arguments advanced in that appeal. They shrink still, as they have done from the first, from entering upon any matter which would lead to an exposure, and consequent examination of the principles on which they have acted ; and I, therefore, see nothing to prevent my submitting the grounds of my complaint to the judgment of the public, as I now do in self-justification.

I am Sir, your obedient humble servant,

MORDAUNT RICKETTS.

Lake House, Cheltenham, 15th July, 1836.

To the Honourable the Court of Directors of the East-India Company.

Gentlemen : On my application for the payment of my annuity from the Bengal Civil Service Annuity Fund, in May 1835, I was informed that it was for the present withheld. On making a similar application on the 2d inst., the answer which I received was, " We have no annuity for Mr. Ricketts." In the former instance, the Honourable Court appears to have stopped my pension *in transitu,* in anticipation of the future operation which their influence, or, at least which the influence of the resolution they had passed purporting to dismiss me from the service, would have upon the managers of the fund in India, in inducing them to discontinue their payments to me upon the construction of the 13th Regulation of the Bengal Civil Service Annuity Fund. In the latter instance, the Court may possibly have a substantial declaration, or an expressed determination of the managers to act upon.

If, however, the managers have in truth, come to any decision on the subject, they could only have done so on the presumption that the vote of dismissal passed by the Court against me was valid, and applicable to my case. And as the influence of the Honourable Court is most powerful with their civil servants, (from which body the managers are selected,) and as there can be no doubt that any alteration the Court might make in their views of my case, would effect a corresponding alteration in the decision regarding my annuity, I trust that previous to my adopting the legal measures I contemplate against the managers, there can be no impropriety in my once more addressing the Court on the subject of the *peculiarity* of the circumstances under which they have thought fit to exercise against me the strongest powers of a governing body. There can be no doubt that if the Court were to intimate an opinion that my pension would be restored to me, the opinion would be adopted. I am entitled, therefore, to consider not only the declaration of my guilt, and the resolution for my dismissal, but also the stoppage of my pension, as the act of the Court ; and I associate the latter with the two former, inasmuch as it proceeds from the communications they must have made to the managers of the fund ; and as it was the contemplated result of the measures which they shaped against me.

As the matter stands then, the Court has pronounced a sentence so explicit against my character, and have directed a blow so vindictive against my property, as could only be justified by the previous establishment of unequivocal guilt upon unexceptionable evidence.

It is not, however, to defend my character that I now address your Honourable Court. The nature of the correspondence I had with them last year, and their refusal to give me an opportunity of entering into the merits of the matters of which, as they then informed me, I had been accused before them, imposed on me the necessity of resorting to the public press, in order to exhibit a full refutation of every one of these charges in detail. And the unanimous assurances of my friends have satisfied me that my character needs no further vindication. Upon this head, therefore, I am at ease.

But I have yet a demand upon the justice of the Court. I make it with all respect. They have passed a resolution dismissing me from their service; and connecting this resolution with the 13th Regulation of the Bengal Civil Annuity Fund, they withhold from me that share of its proceeds in which I have, by purchase, acquired a vested interest: and I call upon the Court to give their consideration to the reasons which I have to offer, why they should in justice revise their proceedings in both these matters. It were more becoming the position of both parties that I should owe the restoration of my property to their sense of justice, than that I should be driven to appeal to the British laws, or the British legislature for redress.

Should the Honourable Court, on a review of the real nature of their proceedings against me, see reason to believe that they have violated any great principle of justice, it cannot be derogatory either to their dignity or their integrity to retrace their steps. A call of this nature is daily made upon our Courts of Law, and implies neither presumption in the applicant, nor any imputation on the judges. I proceed then, with the strongest hope, to lay before the Court, the grounds on which I plead for a reversal of their judgment. And first as to the resolution of dismissal.

The Court, I apprehend, will not silence me *in limine* by the assertion of any power inherent in them, of dismissing their servants at the mere avowal of their will; for when they notified to me my dismissal, they assigned a cause for their act, arising out of certain allegations which were made to them regarding my conduct at Lucknow: and indeed there are certain laws of their own, by which they themselves are restrained, which regulate the mode in which charges brought against their civil servants are to be dealt with. These laws forbid the Court to proceed to the extreme act of pronouncing a judicial and penal sentence, like that pronounced against me, until some criminating facts have been established upon evidence, until some case of guilt has been absolutely brought home to the party suspected, *according to the precise mode of proceeding which they enact.*

On this principle the Court must be understood to assume, by the very resolution which they have passed against me, that some case of guilt has been proved upon me, by proceedings conducted according to the provisions of these laws, which were expressly framed by the Company, to prevent accusation from being mistaken for proof, and suspicion from furnishing the same ground of action as crime.

But I now entreat the Court to enquire which of their regulations, which regard the conduct of an investigation of charges brought against their civil servants, has been observed in my case; or rather, which of them has not been violated. No solemn commission was issued by the Governor General for the purposes of the inquiry. No two commissioners were appointed to conduct it. No call was made on me, through my agents or friends, to answer the complaint after the *evidence had been produced. No report declaratory of my guilt* was made by the party who conducted the investigation. No further report expressive of an approval of such investigation was appended to it by the Governor General. And yet, according to Regulations 8 and 10, of 1806; 17 of 1813; 11 of 1814; 8 of 1817, all these are preliminaries indispensable to the pro-nunciation of any sentence by the Court, excepting that of acquittal. I am not now arguing the question of my guilt or innocence, but I humbly submit to the Court, that as a governing body, sitting judicially, they are bound to consider such an investigation, as my case has alone undergone, as an informal, incomplete, extra-judicial and *exparte* proceeding, which cannot be acted upon by them, but in defiance of their own laws.

The Court cannot say that, by such an irregular investigation, I have been tried, or even if that were a trial, they cannot say that a verdict of guilty has been pronounced against me by those who tried me; and I therefore, upon the failure even of the moral and judicial grounds upon which they profess to have founded their resolution for my dismissal, respectfully, but firmly, call upon them to rescind it.

I feel justified in making this call upon the Honourable Court, (not upon the question of my innocence; which, as ,I have said, I abstain from now discussing, because it could not now be entertained in a manner satisfactory to any party,) but, upon the fact of the Court having had no sound foundation for their resolution, even had the resolution itself been applicable to the circumstances in which I stood, when it was passed. But, in the next place, I further call on the Court fairly to ask themselves, as men of honour, whether the attempt to consider me still in their service, in 1834, be consistent with the simple integrity in which justice should be administered; and whether it be not at best a dangerous abandonment of fundamental principles in order to accomplish a particular object. There was nothing in my position at the moment to contradistinguish my case from those of the rest of the retired servants. I had taken every step, without one exception, which had been by invariable custom received by the Court as an actual resignation of the service. No one retired servant had taken any further step towards the announcement of his retirement, than those which I myself had taken. Whatever then was my position in respect to the Company, was also the position of all who had acted like me. And again, I call upon the Honourable Court to ask themselves whether they ever for one moment considered *all the other* civilians on the retired list, and all the other annuitants on the Civil Fund, as actually in their service, and consequently amenable to their authority, on the 30th June, 1834. the date of my dismissal. Surely, they cannot say that they were consciously maintaining a secret hold over all the retired servants, of which these latter were dangerously ignorant. But if they did not consider them in their service, with what uprightness can they persevere in an assertion, with respect to my case, which they abandon with respect to all others similarly circumstanced?

The inapplicability of this vote of dismission will be still more apparent if the Court will advert to the constitution of the Bengal Civil Annuity Fund, and to their own connection with it. The Court have fully recognized the whole body of the regulations, which are laid down for the management of this fund; many of which were insisted on by themselves, and all formally approved by them. So that without entering on the question, whether by such approval they are or may not have become by law, the compulsory administrators of these regulations, I may safely assert that their integrity and good faith stand pledged to the general tenor, as well as to the particular provisions of them.

Now the whole tenor, as well of the constitution of the fund as of the regulations for its management, draws the distinction, which common sense requires, between a subscriber and an annuitant. A subscriber cannot be treated as an annuitant, nor an annuitant as a subscriber:—no one can retain the two capacities at the same time. He who *is* a subscriber, cannot have become an annuitant, and he who is an annuitant must have ceased to be a subscriber.

By 15th regulation, an absolute voidance of the service is indispensably necessary before a subscriber can be entitled to his annuity, and by the 11th regulation, a certain payment is required when the annuity is claimed by a subscriber, not by way of continuance of his annual subscriptions, but as a final adjustment of his subscription accounts " on his quitting the service." The Court themselves caused the 27th regulation to be inserted, which provides that the annuities of the retired servants in England shall be paid through the Company's Treasurer in London, on an order of the Directors; and to prevent any mistake as to the cases in which these payments shall be made, the Court further required, by the 32nd regulation, that notice should be officially and formally given to the Court of Directors, by the managers of the fund in India, of the claim made to the annuity by each individual subscriber on his retirement from the service; and of the fact of his having paid his final adjustment money according to a scale assigned.

Upon these considerations, and upon the further one, that no form of resignation, or of the acceptance of such resignation, is not only not laid down, but not even in the remotest manner alluded to in any of the Company's laws, or in any of the Civil Annuity Fund regulations; it becomes evident that the claim made in India to the retiring annuity, and notified officially to the Court of Directors in England, is considered by all parties as tantamount to a tender of resignation ; and that the actual payment of the annuity, by an order of the same Court, implies without question that such tender has been accepted by them.

If this were not so, every payment hitherto made to an annuitant by the treasury of the Company in Leadenhall-street, has been, and continues to be, a gross and fraudulent violation of the regulations, which make a previous voidance of the service necessary on his part, and deceives him as to his actual position with the Company. For, I call on the Court to declare not merely whether their actual practice has ever conveyed any other, but whether it has not always, under the circumstances mentioned, conveyed the identical interpretation of that regulation which is here contended for. Have they ever, I ask, since the establishment of the fund, received any other tender of resignation than the application for the annuity, coupled with the official notification of the same to themselves? Have they ever signified their acceptance of a resignation in any other way than by the payment of the annuity? Have they ever intimated to the service the necessity of any other, or ever suggested the possibility of a doubt on the subject?

I humbly conceive that I have now established two distinct grounds on which the resolution, which the Court passed for my dismission, should be rescinded. First, that, contrary to their own recorded principles, it was founded on a case of suspicion only, and did not result from an investigation *conducted according to the provisions and restrictions of their own laws;* so that inasmuch as I was never properly and duly tried, I was not obnoxious to a penal sentence. Secondly, that such a resolution was inapplicable to the relation in which I stood to them at the time, inasmuch as whatever quibble of law might under other circumstances be started in their favour, their own integrity and good faith was in the present case pledged to consider all annuitants as no longer in their service.

So much for the moral and judicial grounds on which the resolution · itself stands. I now proceed in the second place to consider it in connection with the 13th regulation, as leading to the stoppage of my pension ; with a view to which result, the resolution was evidently passed, as is sufficiently proved by the fact, that the Court stopped my annuity before any communication could have been received from the managers of the fund in India.

In order to shew the Court that the 13th regulation, which is made to bear upon me, is utterly inapplicable to my case, I have only to advert to the actual position in which I stood in regard to the fund at the time the resolution was passed. I had paid up my adjustment money, *which finished my dealings with the fund as a subscriber.* I had been entered on the manager's books in India as an annuitant ; as an annuitant I had been received at the India House, and so entered on the official list, published by authority ; and as an annuitant for four successive years, I have been paid by an order of the Court.

But what are the terms of the regulation of the fund which is quoted against me? " Any subscriber,who may be dismissed from the Honourable Company's service, shall forfeit all right to benefit by the institution, &c." Now, I call upon the Court to shew explicitly how this regulation applies to me? I call upon them to shew how and when I was ever in the position of a *dismissed subscriber.* The Court can no more apply to the annuitant this regulation, which, in its terms, is limited to the *subscriber,* than they can, under another regulation similarly limited, demand of the former the *annual contribution* which is due only from the latter.

The sum of the matter is this : I have a vested interest in a certain fund, because it was formed partly by my own annual contributions, and because I furnished these contributions in consideration of a certain future benefit expressly contracted for ; namely, a given amount of annuity, when my payments should be completed. This future and stipulated benefit can only by the regulations of the fund be defeated by an express contingency, namely, my dismissal from the service *whilst a subscriber.* I say, *whilst* a subscriber. because the regulations, individually and collectively, make it imperative that every individual concerned, shall have *ceased to be a subscriber* for one

twelvemonth at least, and shall have satisfied a specific claim which the fund has upon him *at parting*, before he can be paid as an annuitant; or in other words, be put into possession of the benefit contracted for. Now, this *contingency* had not occurred when I had fulfilled all the terms of the trust-deed; and when, having paid my parting adjustment money, and having for four years actually received my annuity, I had not only *ceased* to be a subscriber, but if there is meaning in words, I had fully *entered* on the benefit of *my contract.*

When I had thus entered on the final benefit, the *contingencies* of the contract had inevitably ceased, *and as the Court were parties* to all these acts, with what pretence of justice or honour can they, at this period, again call me "a subscriber," attempt again to revive these very *contingencies*, and by a kind of *ex-post facto* law, deprive me of the stipulated benefit of which, by the express terms and unquestionable intention of the same contract, I had been for four years in *absolute* possession.

The Court which I am addressing, I know to be composed of gentlemen of the highest personal honour, and I now beg to be allowed most respectfully to request each individual among them to imagine such a case as mine to have occurred within his own private dealings.

Let him suppose himself, in consequence of having for many years accepted an annual portion of the earnings of his domestic servants, to stand pledged to pay to each of them a stipulated annuity for the rest of their lives. Let him further suppose the payment of these annuities to be nevertheless contingent upon two circumstances; the one, that the servant should not have been dismissed his service for misconduct: the other, that on *voluntarily quitting it after a given number of years*, he should further pay down a certain principal sum, which sum, calculated in reference to the gross amount of the whole annual subscriptions of the servant, the master should only be entitled to demand, upon this voluntary dissolution of the contract of service. Would the master upon some suspicion (however strong) instilled into his mind, of the previous misconduct of any one of these servants who had not been dismissed up to the time when he performed all these stipulated acts,—would the master, I ask, feel himself, *after having received that servant's parting money*, and paid his annuity for four years, justified in withholding it for all future time, upon the sole plea that he could, and did now, dismiss him from his service? Will any individual of your Honourable Court rise in his place and say, that he himself would, on such a plea, retain in his own pocket the amount of which he thus deprived the annuitant? Would not his conscience demand of him how he could withhold the annuity on the ground that the annuitant had been in his service up to the *present* date, and, at the same time, keep possession of that very sum, which he was only entitled to receive on the express ground that the service was relinquished, and the man's title to the annuity made good four years ago, when that sum was paid? Is there an individual of your Honourable Court who would stoop to minister to his own benefit, in the face of such a contradiction in terms, and in violation of so plain an agreement?

If there be not one, who, in his individual capacity, would hesitate to consider such a course inconsistent with his private honour and integrity, I call upon your Honourable Court, composed as it is of such individuals, to consider, what there is in their collective capacity, to give them a different view of the principles which should regulate the discharge of their public duties. Does the principle of private honour differ from that of public faith? Is a public body exempted from the sacred ties which bind the consciences and feelings of individuals? Is each man to lay down his own private sense of right the moment he finds himself, and only *because* he finds himself, incorporated with others, who may nevertheless be equally imbued in private with similar principles to his own? Or, is he at liberty, when he finds the part which he is called upon to take as a public man, offend the integrity of his private feelings, to shelter himself under the reflection that he is only one among many who commit the act of injustice? If not; if the principles which are to regulate both our public and our private conduct be alike founded upon one comprehensive and unerring law, I earnestly implore your Honourable Court to carry their high feelings, as individuals, into the reconsideration of the question, whether, in withholding the payment of my annuity, they do not, in truth, break the solemn faith they had pledged to me? I was not dismissed when I laid claim to the annuity. I was not dismissed when my claim was officially notified to the Court. I was not dismissed during the whole time I was a subscriber. I was not dismissed when nearly £5,000 was accepted from me as a *parting* payment. I was not dismissed for four years after this claim had been so completely conceded by the Court; that payment was regularly made by them upon it. What then was there to hold the contract in suspension? The terms of it were already satisfied, and as I have already said, the contingencies which alone could break it were long since annulled.

There is now but one point more to urge upon the notice of the Court: It is this; that even the strongest moral conviction in their own minds, that I was guilty of these unproved accusations, would not justify the Court in treating me as if they were proved. The Court have condemned me in secret, upon a case of suspicion only. They have never called on me to *rebut any sort of evidence* whatever. They have not even gone so far as to pretend that the case against me was backed by testimony worthy of credit. I was once indeed, before I quitted India, called on by the Governor-General, *to prove the contrary of a mere assertion,* and because I indignantly refused so *illegal* and unjust a test of innocence, they professed, in their published extract from their despatch on the subject, to take this refusal as a positive acknowledgement of guilt. Against such a deduction I protest;—common sense, the interests of society revolt at it—according to the wise principles of British jurisprudence, justice is not allowed to strike its victim, until his guilt has been proved, *according to rules of evidence and forms of Court.* Divested of such rules and forms, the character of justice is lost. Forming, as these do, the only machinery by which the principle itself can work, they become the main security and guarantee for the integrity of it. In all cases, therefore, even those of the strongest suspicion, guilt must be judicially *proved,* before punishment can be awarded. The spirit of our laws, and indeed their letter, enjoins that individual guilt should be rather suffered to escape, than that, in order to reach a particular case of it, the flow of justice should be so violently diverted, that the image of it should be lost by the disturbance of those pure fountains in which alone it can be reflected.

But in seeking my condemnation, the Court have allowed their *own* laws to be overlooked, their *own* forms to be abandoned; they have given an unforeseen and untenable interpretation to the spirit as well as to the letter of an agreement, involving the highest principles of faith between a governing body and their servants. They have entangled themselves in a manifest contradiction in terms; and have been driven to treat the position in which I stood at a given time towards them, as different to that of others whose circumstances were precisely similar to mine.

I submit to the Court, that to persevere in inflicting a penalty on me, which has been awarded under such a violation of justice, of honour, and of good faith, would constitute a public and private wrong, of which they will not, I am sure, be consciously guilty.

In adopting the line of argument which I have taken in this letter, I plead as a ruined man for nearly the last remaining provision for a rising family. But I beg it to be understood, that this part of the question has nothing to do with the defence of my character, which lies elsewhere. The grounds which I now urge for the restoration of my property, are independent of that on which I defend my innocence. That innocence I have elsewhere established, and my present argument refers entirely to the impropriety of *the mode* by which the Court have caused so heavy a penalty to be inflicted on me.

This argument is a valid one when urged upon men of honour: and I beg the Court to believe, that, in stating it, I have not wished to say anything offensive to their feelings as individuals; I have urged it in the full conviction that the Court have not seen the matters I have pressed upon their notice, in the light and under the bearings in which I have now put them, and though I have been forced to state plainly, the various acts of injustice, by which I have been made to suffer; yet, so far has it been from my intention to impugn the individual integrity of the members of the Court, that it is to that very integrity that I appeal, for the redress of my wrongs, when a reconsideration of my case shall have exhibited the real nature of them.

I have the honour to be, &c.

MORDAUNT RICKETTS.

Lake House, Cheltenham, 12th May, 1836.

East-India House, 1st July, 1836.

SIR,—The Court of Directors of the East-India Company have considered your letter dated the 12th May last, stating the grounds upon which you request the Court to revise their proceedings in your case, and to rescind their resolution dismissing you from the Company's service, by the operation of which, you are excluded from the benefits of the Annuity Fund; and I am commanded to inform you in reply, that the Court decline to depart from the decisions which they have passed on your case.

I am, Sir, your most obedient, humble servant,

JAMES C. MELVILL, *Sec.*

M. Ricketts, Esq.

𝔐𝔦𝔰𝔠𝔢𝔩𝔩𝔞𝔫𝔦𝔢𝔰, 𝔒𝔯𝔦𝔤𝔦𝔫𝔞𝔩 𝔞𝔫𝔡 𝔖𝔢𝔩𝔢𝔠𝔱.

PROCEEDINGS OF SOCIETIES.

Royal Asiatic Society.—2d of July, 1836.—A general meeting was held this day; the Right Hon. Sir Alexander Johnston in the chair.

Among the donations laid on the table, were the following:—From Brian H. Hodgson, Esq., the Honourable East India Company's Political Resident in Nepál, a second series of original Bauddha works, in Sanscrit MS., collected by him in Nepál. From C. M. Whish, Esq. a large collection of palmleaf and paper MSS., principally in the Sanscrit language, written in the Malayalama character, and consisting of the *Védas,* and other standard works of the Hindús. This collection was made by Mr. C. M. Whish, of the Madras Civil Service, deceased. From the Asiatic Society of Bengal, several Arabic and Sanscrit works, being part of those, the printing of which the Society had undertaken to complete, in consequence of the operations of the Education Committee at Calcutta having been suspended by order of Government. From Lord Prudhoe, four spears, used by different tribes of the island of Sennar. From the Rev. C. Gutzlaff, of Canton, two Japanese coins. (The Chairman announced that Mr. Gutzlaff was engaged in collecting coins of Japan for the purpose of illustrating the history of that country.) From Sir Charles Forbes, Bart., portraits of Jamsetjee Bomanjee, and his son, Nowrojee Jamsetjee, the well-known shipbuilders of Bombay, and the first who constructed vessels at that place in the European style.—Eight new members were elected.

The Secretary read the following papers to the meeting:—1st. The personal narrative of the Taleb Sidi Ibrahim Mohammed el-Messi, of the province of Sús, including some statistical and political notices of that extreme southwest country of Morocco; translated from the original Berber MS. into Arabic; and afterwards translated into English by W. B. Hodgson, Esq.

Mr. Hodgson described the Berber language as being spoken in North Africa, from the banks of the Nile to the Atlantic ocean; and considered that it merited investigation from its great antiquity, and from its connexion with the geography and history of North Africa and Egypt. The original text of the present narrative would supply an example of the language; and the narrative itself would furnish some information respecting a remote province of Morocco, very little known to Europeans. Mr. Hodgson knew of only three

Berber MSS. in existence: one was the narrative of the Taleb; the next, a version of the Evangelists, made under his own superintendance, and now in the possession of the British and Foreign Bible Society; the other, a book of religious faith and practice, written for the use of the natives of *Wad Draa*, a copy of which the enterprising traveller, Mr. Davidson, then in Morocco, had promised to endeavour to procure for him. 2. The translation, by the late Sir Charles Wilkins, of an inscription on an ancient Hindu seal; with observations, by Professor Wilson. The interpretation of this inscription had in vain been attempted by pundits in India.

16th of July.—The Right Hon. C. W. Williams Wynn, M.P., the President, in the chair.

Walter Elliot, Esq., presented two MS. volumes, containing 595 inscriptions, principally in Sanscrit, written in the Canarese character, copied from the original monumental stones, pillars, walls, &c., in the southern Mahratta country, and in other parts of India. These volumes were accompanied by an analytical account of their contents, and of the dynasties to which the inscriptions had reference. Also, three copies of his alphabet of the ancient Canarese character; and an original grant, or deed, engraved on copper-plates, in the same character.

The following native gentlemen of Bombay were balloted for, and elected non-resident members of the Society:—Jugonathjee Sunkersett, Esq.; Jamsetjee Jeejeebhoy, Esq.; Curzetjee Cowasjee, Esq.; Dadabhoy Pestonjee, Esq.; Dhakjee Dadajee, Esq.; Bomanjee Hormajee, Esq.; Framjee Cowasjee, Esq.; Cursetjee Ardaseer, Esq.; Nowrojee Jamsetjee, Esq.; Mahommed Ali Rogay, Esq.; Cursetjee Rustomjee, Esq.; Mahommed Ibrahim Muckba, Esq.; and Hormarjee Bhiccajee, Esq. The Imâm of Muscat was elected an honorary member. Thomas Teed, and John Macvicar, Esqs., were elected resident members.

The Meetings were adjourned till December.

Asiatic Society of Bengal—At the meeting of 6th January, the Rev. Dr. Mill, W. H. Macnaghten, Esq., Sir J. P. Grant, and Sir B. Malkin, were chosen Vice-presidents for the ensuing year; and Messrs. H. T. Prinsep, J. R. Colvin, C. E. Trevelyan, C. H. Cameron, D. Hare, Ram Comul Sen, Captains Forbes and Pemberton, and Dr. Pearson, members of the Committee of Papers.

The resolution of the Government to make over the library of the College of Fort William to the "Public Library" lately instituted in Calcutta, was coupled with a reservation of all the works exclusively oriental, of which it is known that the college possesses a very extensive and valuable collection, comprising the whole library of Tippu Sultan. These, it was generally understood, the Government would be willing to transfer to the Asiatic Society, should a request be expressed by this body to obtain them. As their possession would necessarily involve an increase of establishment, the Committee of Papers had hitherto hesitated making any application on the subject, but it was evidently desirable that such an opportunity of enriching its collection should be hailed with eager desire by a body devoted to the cultivation and study of Indian literature and history.

The Secretary apprised the meeting, that he has received from Mr. W. H. Smoult, the box of papers of the late Mr. Moorcroft, which were in possession of the late W. Fraser, Esq., and which he was willing to place at the disposal of the Society, on the conditions expressed by the deceased, *viz.*, that any profit accruing from their publication should go to the benefit of Mr. Moorcroft's relatives in England.

The Society, entirely concurring in this view, resolved, that they should be immediately forwarded to Professor Wilson, in England, to be made use of along with the former manuscripts, on the conditions specified.

A letter from the Vicar Apostolic of Cochin China was read, requesting the Society to forward the specimen of the dictionary, which he regretted to hear could not be printed in Calcutta, to the Oriental Translation Fund in England, in case that body should be inclined to patronize its publication.

A letter was read from Captain C. M.Wade. transmitting a second memoir, by Mr. Charles Masson, on the ancient coins discovered at Beghrám in Kohistán, at Jelálábád and Kábul.

The memoir had been detained in Captain Wade's possession, since the month of June last, in consequence of some official correspondence with Colonel Pottinger, to whom the coins to which it relates have been finally forwarded for the Bombay Government.

The present memoir adds the names of Diomedes, Palerkos, Alooukenes (?), to those already known, and gives some valuable information on the sites of the *Alexandria ad caleem Caucasi, &c.*

CRITICAL NOTICES.

The Madras Journal of Literature and Science. Published under the Auspices of the Madras Lit. Soc. and Aux. R.A.S. Edited by the Secretary. Madras.

THIS work was commenced in October 1833, with a view of affording a channel of immediate publicity for communications to the Madras Literary Society, a branch of the Royal Asiatic Society. Under the able editorship of Mr. Morris, it has been already the vehicle of some valuable papers, one of which we have this month transferred to our pages.

Observations on the Commercial and Agricultural Capabilities of the North Coast of New Holland, and the Advantages to be derived from the Establishment of a Settlement in the vicinity of Raffles' Bay. By GEORGE WINDSOR EARL. London, 1836. E. WILSON.

THE observations and suggestions of Mr. Earl, being the fruit of local experience, are valuable. He has personally conversed with commanders of Bugis prahus, who have been to New Holland and Raffles' Bay.

Observations on the Advantages of Emigration to New South Wales, &c. London, 1836. Smith, Elder, and Co.

THIS little work consists of extracts of the evidence of various persons examined before a committee in the colony, and other documents, useful to the emigrant.

A Warning; in a Letter addressed to John Poynder, Esq., pointing out the Importance of the Vernacular Dialects of India, and suggesting the Expediency of an Explicit Law, declaratory of Religious Liberty in the East. By NATHANIEL SMITH, Esq. B.C.S. London, 1836. Richardson.

MR. SMITH contends, that the disuse of the vernaculars in India, "through the influence of the literary party," operates as a draw-back to popular education, secular or evangelical ; that the enactment of an explicit law in favour of converts to Christianity, is necessary, and might be safely introduced ; and that by indirect means Hindooism might he speedily abolished : " already is there a great disposition amongst the *cestuy qui trust's*, to misapply funds devoted to superstitious purposes ; and if, either by a direct law, or by an enactment *obiter* introduced into any other law, we could strike a blow at such ' uses,' Hindooism would speedily be annihilated by the people themselves. This might be effected either by embroiling the remedy, when trusts in mortmain are abused, or by at once turning such estates into fee-simple, discharged of the use, under enactments framed to assist alienations by way of compromise between the heirs of the grantors and grantees." Of the morality of this course, Mr. Smith does not say any-thing,—nor shall we.

A History of Greece. By the Rev. CONNOP THIRLWALL. Vol. III, being vol. LXXX. of Dr. Lardner's *Cabinet Cyclopædia.* London, 1836. Longman and Co. Taylor.

IN this volume, the affairs of ancient Greece are brought down to the Sicilian expe-dition, B. c. 413. The contents include the administration of Pericles, and the state of science, literature, and the arts, in Athens, at that period, and the history of the Pelo-ponnesian war. We discover the same comprehensive research, and originality of ob-servation, in this as in Mr. Thirlwall's former volumes.

Travels and Adventures in Eastern Africa; descriptive of the Zoolas, their Manners and Customs, &c., with a Sketch of Natal. By NATHANIEL ISAACS. Two vols. London, 1836. Churton.

THIS is a plain, modest, unobtrusive narrative of a visit to the tribes to the northward of Cape Natal, and to the dreaded King Chaka. The manners and habits of the people are described with apparent fidelity, our security for which consists in the strong marks of ingenuousness in the writer, who is a young man, a nephew of the well known Mr. S. Solomon of St. Helena.

Schloss Hainfield; or, a Winter in Lower Styria. By Captain BASIL HALL, R.N F.R.S. Edinburgh, 1836. Cadell.

CAPTAIN Basil Hall is so entertaining a writer, that we always take up a work of his with a kind of prepossession. The Schloss, or Castle, of Hainfield, about six hours from Gratz, was the scene of Capt. Hall's sojourn, in the year 1834, and the historical and other incidents connected therewith, and with the dowager Countess Purgstall, make up the amusing contents of this volume, which we are glad to find is the harbinger of more.

Jerningham; or, the Inconsistent Man. Three vols. London, 1836. Smith, Elder, and Co.

THIS is an attempt to expose the fallacies of the Shelley and ante-establishment school; we cannot speak much in praise of the execution.

Report on the Commerce of the Ports of New Russia, Moldavia, and Wallachia, made to the Russian Government in 1835. Translated from the original, published at Odessa, by T. F. TRIEBNER. London, 1836. E. Wilson.

THIS is a very valuable report, by M. de Hagemeister, attached to the Government of " New Russia," to Count Woronsow, of a personal visit, in 1834, to the northern parts of the Black Sea, and the sea of Azoff, from the Danube to the Don. Appended are Tables of Imports and Exports.

General Statistics of the British Empire. By JAMES McQUEEN, Esq. London, 1836. Fellowes.

A COMPENDIOUS view of the immense property, capital, industry, produce, trade, and resources of the British Empire. The facts will surprise those who have paid but a superficial attention to the subject. They are extracted generally from official sources, but they are mostly of a long past date. The section devoted to the East-Indies gives imperfect (not to say erroneous) details.

Observations on the Curiosities of Nature. By the late WILLIAM BURT, Esq. Edited by his Nephew, T. SEYMOUR BURT, Esq., Bengal Engineers. London, 1836. W. H. Allen & Co.

THIS work affords a fresh proof of Mr. Burt's taste and talents.

Wilson's Historical, Traditionary, and Imaginative Tales of the Borders. Edinburgh, 1836. Sutherland.

A HIGHLY amusing work, published in monthly parts, price sixpence!

Finden's Ports and Harbours of Great Britain. Part I, London, 1836. Tilt.

THIS is a magnificent work, intended to give correct views of our principal Ports and Harbours, and remarkable places and objects on the coast, with local descriptions, and a history of each port. The present Part contains four such views (besides the vignette of Tynemouth Priory and Lighthouse), namely, Tynemouth Castle, Culiercoats (near Tynemouth), Shields Harbour, and Berwick Bridge.

Stanfield's Coast Scenery. Smith, Elder and Co.

THIS work is brought to a close by the publication of the Tenth Part. It contains forty plates, and we may, without exaggeration, say, that it is a work which will do honour to the state of English art.

Syria, the Holy Land, Asia Minor, &c., illustrated in a Series of Views drawn from Nature, by W. H. Bartlett, William Purser, &c., with Descriptions of the Plates, by JOHN CARNE, Esq. London, 1836. Fisher and Son. Parts I. and II. 4to.

MESSRS. Fisher, with an enterprize which deserves the warmest public encouragement, have sent out artists of talent into Syria and Asia Minor, to take upon the spot drawings for a series of views to illustrate sacred and profane history, and to furnish accurate representations of those countries into which European commerce is endeavouring to penetrate. The two Parts we have seen (each containing four large engravings, price 2s.) promise that the work will fulfil all that the most sanguine expectation could look for.

The Shakspeare Gallery, containing the Principal Female Characters in the Plays of the Great Poet, &c. London, 1836. Tilt. Part I.

THE object of this work is to embody the female characters of Shakspeare; and if Mr. Charles Heath, who has the superintendence of the work, proceeds as he has begun, he will delight the lovers of the poet as well as of the arts. Shakspeare himself could not desire to see his ideal creations more happily represented in reality of shape and expression than Mr. Meadows has done in " Viola " and " Anne Page."

Observations on the Present State of Naval Architecture in Great Britain; together with a popular View of the Application of Science to Ship-Building. By JAMES CAULFIELD BEAMISH. Cork, 1836. London, Boone.

MR. BEAMISH has given a very clear and concise view of the scientific principles of ship-building in this little pamphlet; and we join with him (and we believe a great many more) in deeply regretting the injudicious *reforms* which have been made in our national ship-yards.

The Magazine of Health. Conducted by a Practising Physician. London, Tilt.

A USEFUL addition to our periodical works; ably conducted, and cheap.

College=Examination.

EAST-INDIA COLLEGE, HAILEYBURY.

GENERAL EXAMINATION, *May,* 1836.

On Friday, the 27th of May, a Deputation of the Court of Directors proceeded to the East-India College at Haileybury, for the purpose of receiving the report of the College Council as to the result of the general examination of the students.

The Deputation, upon their arrival at the College, proceeded to the principal's lodge, where they were received by him and the professors. Soon afterwards, they proceeded to the hall, accompanied by several distinguished visitors, where (the students being previously assembled) the following proceedings took place:—

A list of the students who had gained medals, prizes, and other honourable distinctions, was read.

Mr. Archd. R. Young read an English Essay.

The students read and translated in the several Oriental languages.

The medals and prizes were then presented by the Chairman, (Sir James Rivett

Carnac, Bart.,) according to the following report, viz.

Medals, prizes, and other Honourable Distinctions of Students leaving College. May, 1836.

Fourth Term.

Alexander Penrose Forbes, medal in classics, medal in mathematics, medal in political economy, medal in law, medal in Sanscrit, and prize in Arabic.

George Berkeley Seton Karr, prize in Persian, prize in Hindustani, and highly distinguished in other departments.

Sir Charles Metcalfe Ochterlony, Bart., was highly distinguished.

William Young passed with great credit.

Third Term.

Edward Peters, prize in mathematics, prize in political economy, prize in Sanscrit, prize in Persian, prize in Arabic, and highly distinguished in other departments.

George Fergusson Cockburn, prize in law, prize in Bengali, and prize in Hindustani.

Robert Bensley Thornhill, and Henry Mountford Reid, were highly distinguished.

Second Term.

Cecil Beadon, prize in classics, prize in mathematics, prize in law, prize in Bengali, prize in Arabic, second prize essay, and highly distinguished in other departments.

Archibald Roberts Young, prize in political economy, prize in Hindustani, prize essay, and highly distinguished in other departments.

Charles Edward Fraser Tytler, prize in Persian, and highly distinguished in other departments.

William Fisher, prize in Sancrit, and with great credit in other departments.

Hew D. H. Fergusson was highly distinguished.

Prizes and other Honourable Distinctions of Students remaining in College.

Third Term.

William Edwards, prize in classics, and with great credit in other departments.

Arthur St. John Richardson was highly distinguished.

Second Term.

Henry James Turquand was highly distinguished.

First Term.

William Muir, prize in classics, prize in law, prize in Bengali, and with great credit in other departments.

Alexander Ross, prize in Persian, prize in Hindustani, prize in Arabic, and with great credit in other departments.

Arthur A. Roberts, prize in Sanscrit,

and highly distinguished in other departments.

Alexander M. Sutherland, prize in Sanscrit, and with great credit in other departments.

Coutts T. Arbuthnot, prize in mathematics.

C. B. Thornhill, Dawson Mayne, and George Edmonstone, were highly distinguished.

William Wynyard, Henry Vansittart, R. C. Raikes, and Arthur H. Cocks passed with great credit.

Rank of Students leaving College, as determined by the College Council, viz.

BENGAL.

First Class.

1. Cecil Beadon.
2. G. F. Cockburn.
3. R. B. Thornhill.
4. H. M. Reid.
5. H. D. H. Fergusson.

Second Class.

6. Sir C. M. Ochterlony, Bart.
7. William Young.

(No Third Class.)

MADRAS.

First Class.

1. Alexander P. Forbes.
2. E. Peters.
3. William Fisher.

(No Second or Third Class.)

BOMBAY.

First Class.

1. A. R. Young.
2. G. B. S. Karr.
3. C. E. F. Tytler.

(No Second or Third Class.)

It was then announced, that the certificates of the College Council were granted, not only with reference to industry and proficiency, but also to *conduct;* and that this latter consideration had always *the most decided effect* in determining the order of rank.

It was also announced, that such rank would take effect only in the event of the students proceeding to India within six months after they are so ranked; and " should any student delay so to proceed, he shall only take rank amongst the students classed at the last examination previous to his departure for India, and shall be placed at the end of that class in which rank was originally assigned to him."

The Chairman then addressed the students, expressing the very great gratification which the deputation felt at the very favourable result of the examination, as well as the excellent conduct of the whole body of the students; and the business of the day concluded.

ASIATIC INTELLIGENCE.

Calcutta.

LAW.

SUPREME COURT.—November 23.

In the matter of Alexander and Co.—
This was an appeal from an order made
the court for the relief of insolvent
rs in India, on the petition of A.
m.*

unsel having been heard and the case
argued during the term, the court this
ronounced its decision. There being
erence on the bench, the judges deli-
their opinions *seriatim.*

B. Malkin—This is an appeal from
rder made on the 3d of January last,
ir. Justice Grant, in the Insolvent

It is, necessarily, with some hesi-
that I come to a conclusion, especi-
n a question principally of fact, at
ce with that formed by the judge
heard the evidence in the case; but,
having had the advantage of a full
nunication of the reasons given by the
ed judge for the opinion he enter-
d, and of hearing the case argued with
itmost force and ability in support of
opinion, I cannot feel that the order
t to be supported. In its present
, it does not appear to me to have been
which the Insolvent Court had power
iake; and I cannot collect from the
ence any state of facts which calls for
substitution of any other.

The first question in the case is, whether
order made was one which the Insol-
t Court had jurisdiction to make. And
must turn entirely on the construction
the 49th sec. of the stat., 9th Geo. 4. c.
for, except under the special provisions
that act, the Court could have no such
wer. The order originally applied for,
rather that part of the application which
in substance granted, was to set aside
le, treated as actually made, on the
nd of negligence or fraud; the order
departed in form from that applied
and corresponds with that made in
-parte Bennett," 10 Ves. J. 331. But
case is an express authority to show
such an order could not be made,
ias by consent, by the Lord Chancellor
ng in bankruptcy; and of course it
ld not be made by the Insolvent Court
except under the express provisions of
nsolvent Act. The same principle is
recognized by the other cases cited in
ment on the subject. The application,
ir as this portion of it is concerned,
lves itself completely into an applica-
on to set aside the sale, or render it

* See vol. xvii. p. 79, and last vol. p. 238.

inoperative. on the ground of legal or
actual misconduct, and such an application,
on the authority of " *Ex parte* Bennett,"
ought, independently of the special provisions of the Insolvent Act here, to be
made to a Court of Equity. It appears
to me that the Insolvent Act does not give
the court the power which it has exercised.
The only sections which materially bear on
the question are the 49th, 50th, and 56th.
The 56th is only so far important on this
point, that, by giving other relief in cases
of improper or improvident sales, when
any actual damage has accrued, it makes
it unnecessary, for the purposes of justice,
to attempt to extend the operation of the
other sections by any strained construction.
And on the most obvious and natural construction both of the 49th and 50th
sections, I think that they contemplate
future sales only: that they are merely
prospective in their operation.

The power of this court is not merely to
confirm or dismiss the order of the Insolvent Court, but to inquire into the matter
of the petition and of the proceedings
petitioned against, and "to make such
order thereon as to the same court shall
seem meet and just." Now, the original
petition was not merely to set aside the
sale, or to restrain a conveyance, but it
prayed that, if the court could not cancel
the sale, it should be referred to the
examiner of the court to inquire and report
whether the factories could have been sold
to any, and what greater, advantage, had
they been duly advertised for sale, and exposed to sale by public auction, or that the
court should grant such other order as the
circumstances of the case might require.
The Insolvent Court, therefore, was at
liberty, under that petition, to proceed
under the 56th section of the statute; and
if the circumstances of the case would warrant such a proceeding, it would be the
duty of this court to adopt it. It is, therefore, necessary to inquire into the circumstances of the case, and it would indeed be
material to do so, even if it were not
required for the actual decision of the
cause, because the character of the assignees has been attacked, and they are
officers whom it would be our duty, as we
have the power, immediately to remove, if
some of the imputations cast on them were
supported. With respect to Mr. Hurry,
indeed, as far as personal conduct and character are concerned, he is out of the question; having had nothing to do with the
sale, he cannot have incurred any censure
with respect to it. He may, indeed, be
implicated with Mr. Burkinyoung in the
charge of negligence, in not advertising

(A)

and looking out for purchasers in the early part of the year 1834; but any such negligence in a single instance can furnish no imputation on his character, though it might render him liable to make good any loss sustained by reason of it. With respect to such negligence, however, I think that no charge can be supported; that the disputes existing between the Bank of Bengal and the assignees, and the proceedings pending in the court, with respect to the general principle on which the mortgaged property was to be disposed of, were abundantly sufficient to justify the assignees in not incurring any expense by advertisements, and in waiting to see the result of the controversy. And if so, there can be no remedy on that account under the 56th section, which only makes them liable in cases where there is both injury and fault. It has been suggested, indeed, that the assignees ought to have accepted the offer of Rs. 70,000 made in January for the three factories constituting the Moisurah concern, notwithstanding the pending disputes, which had reference to the general management of the estates, but would not have affected a single transaction of this kind. I am far from being convinced that, even on this single point, the conduct of the assignees was censurable; but on this, at all events, no claim of remedy can be supported, for there is nothing to show injury, nothing to raise any presumption that the assignees, who still retain the Moisurah and Gungadhurpore factories in their own hands, and who have sold Neeschunderpore for the full value at which they estimated it in making the aggregate value of Rs. 70,000 for the whole, have subjected the estate to any loss by not complying with that offer.

The question, therefore, resolves itself entirely into that which has always been treated as the main question in the case, the character of the transaction of the 25th of August; and it becomes necessary for me, as there is some variation in the evidence on that subject, to state distinctly the view which I entertain of the facts of the case. I need not for this purpose enter fully into the details of the evidence; but may state shortly the conclusions of fact which I collect from it: the inferences of law resulting from them are plain and simple when the facts are once ascertained.

It appears, then, that, long before the date of this transaction, the factories had been valued by persons very competent to the office, who raised a former valuation of the three factories at Rs. 60,000 to the sum of Rs. 70,000, and who in that enhanced value rated Neeschunderpore at Rs. 15,000, and no more. On this valuation, Saupin was then willing to purchase Neeschunderpore, and the assignees to sell; but the Bank refused their consent. An argument was raised from this refusal,

that the price was inadequate. I do not see, however, why the opinion of the Bank is to be taken as conclusive, and that of the valuers rejected: and the opinion of the Bank may have rested, as it is alleged that it did, chiefly on a temporary fluctuation in the value of indigo, and it seems at all events to have been so far renounced shortly afterwards, that in January they were willing to accept for the three factories that sum of Rs. 70,000, of which, according to the estimate of the assignees, the fair proportion of Neeschunderpore was only Rs. 15,000. I see nothing, therefore, in this transaction to hinder the assignees from fairly considering this a reasonable price for Neeschunderpore, even at that time.

At the period of the actual sale, however, the circumstances were considerably altered. The lease, or *izara*, had expired, and a considerable advance was demanded for the renewal. The circumstances connected with this *izara* require careful consideration, because a great deal of erroneous argument has, in my opinion, been founded on them, on each side. On the one side, it has been treated as if the advance required was equivalent to an addition to the price, so that the sale for Rs. 15,000, and the transferring the necessity of making the advance from the assignees to Saupin, was a transaction as beneficial to the estate as a sale for Rs. 25,000 would have been, if the assignees still had to secure the *izara* themselves. On the other hand, it is contended that the advance for the *izara* being a mere loan, to be deducted out of the rent, and bearing interest, was no prejudice at all to the estate, and deserves no consideration whatever, except as to the minor exactions of the *salammie* fees, and the small additional sums finally advanced on less favourable terms than the principal sum of 8,000 Rs. The truth, as in most cases, lies between the two extreme statements. The advance required undoubtedly cannot be treated as any material enhancement of the price, or diminution of the value, of the lands. On the other hand, the assignees appear to me to have formed a just opinion, that it would be very undesirable for them, situated as they were, to make such an advance, and that probably the court would not sanction it. Their duty is to sell, with all reasonable expedition—to sell, unless there is good cause for delay; and I cannot think it would have been desirable for them to encumber themselves with a transaction of advance, from which the estate, whether it continued in their own hands, or was transferred by them to others, could not be completely extricated in less than three years. It is also material to observe that the bargain for the *izara* was not completed: in fact, it was not finally concluded exactly on the terms then expected. And it is admitted that the value of the factory almost entirely depended on the obtaining the *izara*. Under these circumstances, if the assignees could sell the factory, they cast the risk of failure in obtaining the *izara* on the purchaser, and they delivered themselves from the necessity of making advances, undesirable in their situation, though, perhaps, immaterial to more independent speculators. The *value* of the factory might not be seriously affected by these considerations; but they would furnish good reason why the assignees should be peculiarly ready to accept any thing which they considered as a fair offer. They would furnish some reason also for a *private* sale; for, on the announcement of a public one, any speculator in the neighbourhood might have been induced to secure the *izara* on unreasonable terms, in the confidence that he would have the means of finally reimbursing himself the sum lent to the zemindar by stopping it out of the rents; so that the magnitude of the advance would produce temporary inconvenience only, and not final loss, and in the expectation that the Neeschunderpore factory would fall into his hands at a very low price, when he had secured the only means of rendering it valuable to a purchaser.

In this state of things, Mr. Burkinyoung proposed to Mr. Saupin that he should renew his former offer, and become the purchaser at the valuation price of Rs. 15,000. This offer Mr. Saupin accepted, on condition that he should be allowed to divide his purchase, and with a stipulation for liberty to consult Mr. Rogers, by whom he expected to be supplied with the means of completing it. Mr. Rogers agreed to the proposal, and the bargain was made. The bargain, however, is sought to be impeached on three grounds:—that Saupin was an agent for sale, and not a buyer, and that a purchase by Rogers for him, he being such agent, was fraudulent and void in law : that the purchase was actually fraudulent on Saupin's part, from suppression of knowledge which he possessed as to the likelihood that other parties would purchase: and that there was great negligence on the part of the assignees in concluding a sale without making further inquiries. It is further said, that loss has accrued in consequence of that negligence, for that Messrs. Gregg and Donaldson were willing to give Rs. 20,000 for the factories at that time; that they even offered Rs. 22,000 to Saupin shortly afterwards; and that at all events there was great neglect at the very time of the sale, for that the assignees knew that Mr. Storm would have purchased Autpara at an advance on the price for which Mr. Bell was to have it.

With respect to the question of agency, I have already intimated my opinion that the transaction was one between Burkin-

young and Saupin, and a purchase by the latter. If so, the objection, as to the agency, falls to the ground. There is, undoubtedly, some confusion in the evidence, arising both out of various statements as to what passed at the time, and out of some expressions contained in the subsequent letters. If those only are to be dwelt on, the transaction looks like an agency for sale; but the evidence of Mr. Burkinyoung and of Mr. Saupin is distinct that it was a bargain made with Saupin for a sale either directly to him, or directly from the assignees to Rogers for Saupin's benefit. In either case, it is substantially a dealing with Saupin as the purchaser, and if so, it is immaterial whether the conveyance was to be made directly to him, or, for any reason unexplained to us, but understood among the parties, to Rogers, for his benefit. One fact seems to me conclusively to shew that this was the real understanding of the transaction : I mean the circumstance, that the sale was a mere renewal of a former negotiation, in which it is not even suggested that Saupin was not dealing completely and directly for himself; though at that time, also, Rogers was expected to furnish him with the means of fulfilling his contract. If it were so,—if the sale were notoriously for Saupin's benefit, I cannot see that it is void on any ground of agency; if it were, all sales would be void in which the bargain was made by a person who preferred having his conveyances made to a trustee for him, and himself arranged with the trustee that he should become so.

It is true, that there are expressions in Mr. Alexander's letters (hardly in his evidence, for, while he speaks of considering Rogers as the purchaser, he speaks also of considering the bargain as concluded with Saupin, and clearly under circumstances which, if they made Saupin an agent at all, made him the agent for Rogers as the purchaser, not for the assignees as the sellers, a relation of which the legal consequences would be widely different), which seem rather to represent Saupin as the agent for sale of the assignees. Thus he talks of the " power of selling being given to Saupin, and that he has secured purchasers " (Alexander's letter to Storm, August 26) ; and generally in his correspondence uses similar phrases. And it would seem that Mr. Burkinyoung himself thought it necessary to be satisfied by Mr. Rogers, that he was willing to take the factory at the price stipulated, and that he thought it likely (though there is some confusion on this subject), that Mr. Storm would be in time with his amended offer. It is always perplexing and unfortunate when facts are at all loosely dealt with, or carelessly stated ; I cannot, however, see in these circumstances, especially when viewed with reference to the rather com-

plicated and confused nature of the transaction, any thing to make me discredit the
positive assertion of Burkinyoung and Saupin, that they considered their dealing as
a bargain made; and the question of fact
is, what was their understanding? Mr.
Alexander's is only material as evidence, even if it differed more substantially
from their statement than I think it does.
Even the intimation to Storm, assuming it,
too, to be correctly represented, might
almost as well correspond to a belief that
he would be in time to get his offer accepted by Saupin, as that the assignees
still had the power of interfering. On the
whole, therefore, it seems to me that the
transaction is not void on any ground connected with Saupin's agency for sale:
that the fact is not made out in proof. It
is not necessary, therefore, to discuss any
questions of law arising on it.

The next objection is, that fraud was
actually practised by Saupin, and that a
sale to him, obtained by his fraud, cannot
be allowed to stand. I have already said,
that the Insolvent Court has not, in my
opinion, the power of interfering with a
sale actually made to a stranger. It is,
therefore, unnecessary to inquire into Mr.
Saupin's conduct, for the purpose of fixing
him, unconnectedly with the assignees,
with any imputation of fraud: and it
would be improper, if unnecessary, as he
has not had the opportunity of proving his
own case in answer to any such charge.
Without pretending to say whether there
are not circumstances which it would be
desirable, in another proceeding, that Mr.
Saupin should account for, it is quite clear
that there are none which might not very
well admit of explanation. But, at all
events, if Mr. Saupin was not the agent of
the assignees in this matter, it is impossible
that they should be responsible for any
frauds committed by him, unless it were
by reason of their own negligence that such
frauds were successful.

Now, with reference to the last question of negligence, I have already expressed my opinion, that the assignees were
fully justified, under the circumstances,
in making a private and sudden sale, if
they could obtain a fair price for the property; and I am not aware of any thing in
the evidence to shew that they had any
reason to be dissatisfied with the price of
Rs. 15,000. It was the price at which
their valuers had appraised it; it was the
price, as far as they could understand at the
time, at which Gregg and Donaldson
estimated it. It is true, that those gentlemen had made an offer of Rs. 20,000
for the factory to the Bank; but that is
distinctly shewn never to have been communicated to the assignees, nor was it
likely that it should, as the Bank at that time
would not consent to a sale, except of the
whole Moisurah concern. The offer of

Rs. 70,000 *was* communicated, but that
aggregate corresponded with their own valuation, and in considering it the assignees
would, of course, suppose that the portions would be estimated as they had estimated them; for no explanation was given
of the manner in which Donaldson and
Gregg computed their value. Even if
the letter of the 15th January from Gregg
and Donaldson ever reached the assignees,
of which there is no proof at all, but a denial, it would have conveyed no further
information; for it communicated the offer
of the ·Rs. 70,000 only; and although it
refers to Saupin's offer of Rs. 15,000, and
the refusal of it by the Bank, on the ground
that the price was too small, and ought to
be raised to Rs. 20,000, it does not give
any intimation that the parties had ever
proposed to give Rs. 20,000, or even that
they thought it a fair value; unless, indeed, this is to be concluded by a specu-
lative inference from the words, that, in
making the price Rs. 70,000, the Bank
had added "in the same ratio" to the other
two divisions. But it is not merely that
the assignees had no reason to think the
price of Rs. 15,000 inadequate; there is,
in fact, no evidence that it really was so.
There are offers, undoubtedly, of higher
prices; but with the single exception of
the temporary opinion of the Bank, there is
nothing to shew a higher estimate of value.
Gregg distinctly declares, and so does
Storm, that they offered above the value;
that there were local and personal circumstances which made them willing to give
more than it was worth. If the assignees
knew this, they ought to have used the
knowledge for the benefit of the estate;
but as they did not, it seems impossible to
hold them culpable (and if not culpable
they are not responsible) for selling the
estate *bonâ fide* for as much as it was really
and generally worth.

This brings me to the only remaining
part of the case—the question whether
Burkinyoung was not guilty of negligence
in not communicating to Saupin the offer
of Storm to advance on the price to be
given by Bell. I have felt more doubt on
this part of the case than on any other;
and perhaps, in this particular, there was
some little want of that diligence which is
due from the assignee of an insolvent
estate, to do every thing in his power for the
benefit of the creditors. Still I am of opinion that no order can be made on this
ground. If I am right in thinking that
there was a sale to Saupin, he, and not
the assignees, would have had the benefit
of Storm's advance; for it is clear, that
the sale to him was of the whole property.
Or, even if this were otherwise, he had at
all events so far the disposition of Autpara, that the assignees could not refuse to
carry into effect the sale to Bell unless he
could do so himself. And he was bound

to Bell even before the sale to himself; having fully contracted with him to allow him to have Autpara at Rs. 5,000, if he himself obtained the whole Neeschunderpore concern at Rs. 15,000. On both grounds, therefore, if Storm's offer had been communicated to him, the *estate* would not have been benefited; and thus, even if there were some slight neglect in this one particular, there has been no loss in consequence of it; and no remedy, therefore, is required.

It follows that the order obtained must, in my opinion, be discharged; and with whatever regret I may come to such a conclusion in a case of sufficient difficulty to have produced conflicting decisions, and still to divide the opinion of the court, it seems to me that it ought to be discharged with costs. If it is sought to be supported on the ground that the original order was correct, the majority of the court being of opinion that such an application was made to an incompetent jurisdiction, the order would be discharged with costs, of course: and the same results would seem to me to follow on the other part of the case also. The application proceeds entirely on the imputation of grave charges of fraud and misconduct; and a party who prefers such, not merely without being able completely to prove their truth, but when they are in point of fact unfounded, as they appear to me to be in the present case, must in my opinion abide by the consequences of his rashness. It would obviously be impossible, with the view which I entertain of the case, to allow the assignees to bear personally the expense of defending themselves against unfounded charges; and it certainly would not be a proper result of a proceeding, brought ostensibly for the benefit of the estate, that the estate should be prejudiced, by having to bear the costs of opposing an application which ought not, if my view of the facts is correct, ever to have been made.

Sir *J. P. Grant* maintained his former opinion (as usual) at enormous length. In conclusion, the learned judge expressed himself as follows :—

There are three things, however, which I am desirous of adverting to, mentioned in the petition of appeal.

1. That the assignees, or rather Mr. Burkinyoung, the only assignee at the time capable of acting, acted *bọnâ fide*, and with the best intentions.

It will be recollected that in my former judgment I stated that sales in such circumstances might be invalid, either in respect of the relation the purchaser stood in to the seller, or upon the ground of fraud, and that the whole of my argument proceeded upon the first consideration only. I did not, nor do I now, impute to this gentleman, whom I believe from what I have heard of him to be a very respecta-

ble person, any fraudulent or unfair intention. I did, and I do, impute to him a negligence and want of due consideration in making the sale of these factories, which has brought loss upon the estate. Nor can I see that I was wrong in saying that that, which it is now alleged was done, was a different thing from that which from the terms in which the transaction was concluded was to appear to have been done. That this was meant, and fraudulently, by the assignee I did not say, nor do I believe.

2. That the order, after being passed, was altered upon the petition of one of the parties which it ought not to have been. This was not so; a verbal intimation of the judgment was given from the bench. From notes of this the clerk drew up the draft of an order, and furnished a copy to the parties, on which they might have submitted observations on points within the general scope of the judgment, and, if they chose, through the clerk. I believe one of the parties did so; I am informed by way of petition. But there was no order, and no terms of any order settled or authorised by me; but they are appealed from.

3. It was said, in support of the allegation, that the judgment contains orders which the appellants had no means to enforce; that the parties concerned are subject to another jurisdiction, before whom the appellants may be unable to succeed in recovering possession of the estate. But I, for one, cannot listen to a suggestion that the jurisdiction will not enforce justice and right, and will not take the same view of justice and right with this court; I entertain no suspicion of the kind, and if I did it would not relieve me from the necessity of deciding in the case before me according to what I believe to be the law of the court in which I sit, whether of common law, or equity, or of insolvency.

The *Chief Justice.*—I regret that there should be a difference of opinion on the bench, but after the best consideration I can give to this case, and after listening to the able argument of the Advocate-General, and reading the judgment of the learned judge, I cannot concur in the order which he has made.

The first question in this case is, whether the Insolvent Court, under the 49th sect. of the 9th Geo. IV. c. 74, has the power to delay and postpone a sale, on the application of a creditor, where the assignees have entered into a contract to sell, and have received a moiety of the purchase-money, on the ground of the contract being void for fraud, or that the price agreed on was inadequate to the value of the property: the purchaser, it should also be observed, not being any party to the proceeding in the Insolvent Court, or shown to be subject to its jurisdiction. If the court has not this power, then, in no view of the facts of the present case, can this order be supported. I am clearly of opinion that the 49th section does not confer this power on the Insolvent Court, and that where an actual sale has taken place, with whatever circumstances its validity may be effected, such circumstances cannot be a ground for that court making any order under this clause of the Act of Parliament, and that if the creditors desire to question the validity of the sale, they must do so in some court that has the power to try that question. It has been contended at the bar, that this court has a power analogous to that exercised by the Chancellor when sitting in bankruptcy, and that the Chancellor would, in a case of fraud or negligence in a sale by an assignee, on petition, declare such sale to be void. "*Exparte* Bennett," 10 Ves. Jun. has been cited as an authority to support this position; but when the case is examined it will be found to have expressly decided that in bankrupcy the Chancellor has no jurisdiction, and that the order which he did make in that case for a resale was only because the purchaser appeared and consented to abide by the decision of the Chancellor, who even then doubted whether he should accept the offer of the parties. The fact, however, as stated by Mr. Sugden in his book of Vendors and Purchasers, is that the Chancellor has never exercised this jurisdiction with the express decision of Lord Eldon, is in my mind ample authority to show that the Chancellor in bankruptcy has no such jurisdiction. It should be observed, that in bankruptcy the Chancellor rarely interferes, even to postpone or delay a sale, and in "*Exparte* Montgomery," 1 Glyn and Jameson's Rep., the Chancellor said, the court ought not to interfere to stay the sale, because the assignees act at their own risk and upon their own responsibility, and they and not the court are to be judges of the propriety and expediency of the sale. The question therefore reverts to the construction that is to be put on this 49th clause, and that, I am satisfied, applies only to delaying and postponing of sales about to take place. What I have already stated is sufficient to dispose of the present order, but the validity of that order is not the only matter before the court; the 4th section of the Insolvent Act, which allows an appeal, directs that this court shall inquire into all the matters of the petition and of the proceedings and evidence, and make such order as to them may seem meet and just. It is necessary therefore to consider whether the proceedings and evidence before us would justify our making an order under the 56th section of the Act; and independent of this duty which the Act imposes upon us, I think, as the character of persons who may be considered in the light of officers of the Insolvent Court has been attacked, and to whom conduct has been

imputed that would, in my opinion, if substantiated, make it incumbent upon us to remove them from their office, it is necessary that the whole of the case should be looked into, to see if these charges rest upon any foundation. I am prepared to go into the facts, but I think it unnecessary as they have been entered into so fully by Mr. Justice Malkin; and I so entirely agree with him in the view he has taken of them and in the conclusions he has drawn, that it would be but a needless repetition if I were to go over the same ground. One or two matters, however, I think it necessary to notice. The imputation of fraud, or, as it has been termed, legal fraud, has been applied to that part of the transaction in which it is alleged that Saupin was held out to the world as the agent of the assignees, and as employed in that capacity to act for them, and consequently, if a purchaser himself, the sale would be vitiated on the common principle, which is so well established, that it requires no authority to be cited in support of it, that an agent employed by a vendor to sell cannot become a purchaser himself. I need hardly observe that in this sale Mr. Hurry is in no way implicated; he was absent and ill at the time. It appears from Mr. Alexander's evidence, that he supposed Rogers and Bell to be purchasers, and was not aware, for some time after the sale, that Rogers purchased for Saupin; and the letters which were subsequently written by him, and, as he states, approved of by Mr. Burkinyoung, might induce those who were ignorant of the facts to draw the same conclusion. This inaccuracy and looseness of expressions, in the letters, were probably sanctioned by Burkinyoung from the understanding that existed as to Rogers advancing the money for Saupin. But where is the fraud? and what could be the motive or inducement to Mr. Burkinyoung for any concealment or contrivance? It is indisputable on the evidence, and not disputed on either side, that Saupin bought, and Burkinyoung sold, with a full knowledge that Rogers, as the agent of Saupin, was to advance the money for Neeschunderpore, and that Bell was to purchase Autpara. It was, in fact, only the renewal of an offer that had been made by Saupin in September 1833. How then can Saupin be considered as an agent, and how can the principle, upon which all the cases of purchase by agent are founded, apply here?

But besides the ground of fraud, upon which I have observed, the conduct of the assignees is complained of as culpably negligent, in allowing of a private sale without having duly advertised the property, and in selling one of the divisions of the Neeschunderpore factory for a less sum than they could, with proper diligence and enquiry, have obtained for it. These questions have been so fully considered by Mr. Justice Malkin, that I shall not enter upon them at length; but, as to advertising, it is clear that, from the October preceding, when they were repeatedly advertised, all persons possessing factories in the neighbourhood, and in any way likely to become purchasers, must have been aware that they were for sale, and the disputes between the Bank and assignees fully account for their not incurring an useless expense, when there was little probability that they could effect a satisfactory sale. This would account for their not advertising before the order of 26th of July was obtained. But it is alleged that they refused in January an offer of Rs. 70,000 for the whole of the Neeschunderpore concern, and that neglecting to advertise after the order of 26th of July was obtained, they consented to a private sale of a portion of this concern at a less price than could have been obtained. The rejection of the offer of the Rs. 70,000 is accounted for by the pending disputes between the Bank. Mr. Udny did not communicate to the assignees the offer of Donaldson and Gregg until the 18th of January; the order of the Insolvent Court was obtained on the 1st of February, and at the time of Mr. Udny's communication, the assignees were aware of the intention of the Bank to apply to the court. As to the offer of Rs. 20,000 by Donaldson and Gregg for the Neeschunderpore concern on the 28th of December 1834, and which the Bank rejected, it is clear that the assignees had no notice of it. In the private sale without further advertisement, on the 24th of August, to Saupin, the culpable negligence of the assignees, it is contended, is apparent. Mr. Alexander states, that after the order of the 26th of July, he had frequent conversations with Mr. Burkinyoung on the necessity of something being done with reference to the advance for renewing the *izara*, to prevent the factory from going to ruin, and the conclusion that Birkinyoung and Alexander came to, *prior to Saupin's arrival at Calcutta*, was, that it was better to sell the factory at once than to go to the court to ask for liberty to make so large an advance, which they thought the court would not sanction: with this impression on the mind of Burkinyoung, Saupin renews his offer to purchase at the value fixed upon Neeschunderpore by those most competent to form an opinion on the subject, and up to which time no offer had been made to the assignees of an advance upon this estimated value; for the offer of Rs. 70,000 by Donaldson and Gregg in January, for the whole concern, was only the sum which the assignees had fixed, estimating the Neeschunderpore division at the sum at which Saupin purchased it for Rs. 15,000: a sale then is effected, and Mr. Alexander swears that, at the time, neither the assig-

nees or he had any reason to expect they could have obtained better prices, and when it was doubtful as to the terms on which the *izara* could be renewed, when publicity might have thrown difficulties in the way of the renewal, and when this risk was thrown upon the purchaser, it being clear that, without the renewal of the *izara*, the property would have been worthless; I cannot therefore say, that a private sale at the estimated value, under such circumstances, proves negligence. The only remaining matter that I think it necessary to notice, after the full discussion this case has received, is the question of costs; I entirely agree with Mr. Justice Malkin in thinking that this order must be discharged with costs. I regret that there should be a difference of opinion on the bench, and that, owing to the different views which have been taken on this subject, the costs will be enhanced. But with every deference and respect for the learned judge who originally made this order, I am bound, in the view I have taken of this case, to think that the creditor who originally made the application to the Insolvent Court should have well considered whether, in the result, the insolvents' estate was likely to reap any advantage by the application which he made. As the estate is not benefited by the proceedings which have been had, I think it would not be just to the creditors generally, to oblige them to pay the costs of a particular creditor who has been mistaken in his views—certain I am that it would not be right to charge the assignees personally with these costs, when they are acquitted by the court of all misconduct and negligence; upon the party, therefore, who has unadvisedly caused all these proceedings, the expense must fall, and, under the powers which this court possesses under the 4th section of the Act, and which the Insolvent Court at present has not—we direct that Mr. Lingham shall pay the costs of all the proceedings both in the Insolvent and the Supreme Court.

When the Chief Justice had delivered the judgment of the court, Sir John Grant said:—

Being not of opinion that this judgment ought to be reversed, I need not say that I do not concur as to the costs. But I desire to say, that even if I were of opinion the judgment ought to be reversed, I should not concur in giving costs.

November 24th.

Calder v. *Halkett.*—The court to-day delivered its judgment in this case.[*]

The *Chief Justice.*—The general points of this case the court will now determine; one question and that the main question upon which the case depends, we will reserve for further consideration; the other

[*] See last vol. pp. 93 & 239.

points are: First, as regards the motion for a nonsuit, on the ground that of the connection between the defendant and the perwannah, there was no evidence to go to a jury. Mr. Justice Grant and myself, at the trial, were of opinion that there was evidence, and I remain of the same opinion. Looking at all the circumstances of the case, we must conclude, that the arrest was caused by the defendant, and that the perwannah which was produced in the course of the trial was issued by him, and that it was under that instrument that the arrest took place. In respect to the pleas of justification, if the arrest was effected under the seal of the Fouzdary Court, and not by the defendant in his capacity of magistrate or justice of the peace, such pleas of justification could not be maintained, as the plaintiff was a British subject and not liable to the jurisdiction of zillah court. Now, notice was given to the defendant to produce the perwannah at the trial. Mr. Reid, the registrar of the Sudder Dewanny, was served with a *subpœna duces tecum*, and then out comes Reid's declaration that the defendant had acknowledged, that there was such a perwannah, and that he issued it. I see, therefore, no grounds for a nonsuit on account of absence of sufficient evidence to go to a jury, nor do I think the pleas of justification an answer to the action. The only and main question that remains is, whether this court is, or is not, precluded from jurisdiction in such cases as the present, by the 24th section of the stat. 21st Geo. III. c. 70. On this point the court will take time to consider.

Mr. *Justice Grant* and Mr. *Justice Malkin* concurred generally in the opinion delivered by the Chief Justice.

November 30.

The same.—The court gave final judgment in this case. There being a difference of opinion on the bench, the judges severally delivered their judgments.

Mr. *Justice Malkin.*—This question mainly depends upon the construction of the statute 21 Geo. III. c. 70, sec. 24—and whether, under the provisions of that enactment, this court is or is not precluded from exercising jurisdiction in this and similar cases. I am of opinion, that if a perwannah be an order of the court out of which it issues, this court is so precluded. The words of the Act are—

And whereas it is reasonable to render the provincial magistrates, as well natives as British subjects, more safe in the execution of their office, be it enacted, that no action for wrong or injury shall lie in the Supreme Court against any person whatsoever, exercising a judicial office in the country courts, for any judgment, decree, or order of the said court, nor against any person for any act done by, or in virtue of, the order of the said court.

In regarding this provision, we are to look to the history of the period at which it was enacted. The object which the Legislature contemplated at that period was to restrain and set limits to the jurisdiction of the Supreme Court. This Act was passed with that view, and must receive an interpretation consistent therewith. It appears to me, therefore, that we are excluded by the terms of this section of the 21 Geo. 3. c. 70, from entertaining an action grounded upon an order issuing out of the court wherein the defendant sat in a judicial capacity, and, consequently, that the verdict in this case ought to be set aside, and a verdict entered up for the defendant.

Mr. *Justice Grant* expressed great regret that a difference of opinion should subsist upon the bench, the more especially on a question of such magnitude, affecting the due and right construction of a most important Act of Parliament; and of the greatest consequence to the happiness and well-being of a considerable body of inhabitants in the Mofussil.

Previously to the Act of 21 Geo. 3. c. 70, this court constantly entertained actions for damages, brought against persons acting in a judicial character in the country courts. It was to remedy this mischief that that Act was passed, and the object of it was to afford these magistrates, in respect of such actions, the same protection as is afforded to magistrates at home. That law was very necessary to those judicial officers, but it cannot be construed to extend beyond the mischief calling for correction; far less to convey immunities not possessed by the judges of the highest courts of record. An act to fall under the protection or exclusion of this clause of the statute must be done judiciously; must be done in the exercise of a judicial office in the country court; or the order in question must be an order of the said court. But because an illegal act is done by one who is a magistrate, it is not, therefore, an act done officially. An act, to become an order of the court, must be done officially; but, in order to this, there must be a judge, and in order to give his actions a judicial character, he must be acting in a matter judicially before him, which cannot be unless there be accuser, accused, and a cause before him to be determined. Where there are no parties, there can be no judge, and it is a manifest contradiction to say that this purwannah is an order of the country court. It is a mere illegal act, emanating from a party who happens to be a judge of a country court. I, therefore, am of opinion that this verdict ought to stand.

Mr. *Justice Ryan.*—This is an action of trespass and false imprisonment. The only question remaining now to be determined is, whether, under the 21 Geo. 3. c. 70, the court is precluded from jurisdiction in this case. We have already expressed our opinion as to the defendant being at liberty to take advantage, under the general issue, of giving matter of justification in evidence. I am of opinion that this court is entirely and completely precluded from taking cognizance of the subject matter of this suit. The words of the statute are expressly to that effect; and the only jurisdiction intended to be left to this court in such cases, was a criminal jurisdiction upon occasions of corruption or malicious abuse of the process of the country court.

The order of the court, therefore, is, that a verdict be entered for the defendant, with costs.

MISCELLANEOUS.

THE SELECT VESTRY.

To the Venerable T. Dealtry,
				Archdeacon of Calcutta.

Venerable Sir,—The Governor of Bengal has perused the report of the proceedings in the vestry of the cathedral church of St. John's, at this place, contained in your letter dated the 29th ult.

It appears that the orders of this department, dated 19th August last, issued with a view to associate with the bishop and his clerical assistants a body of laymen, elected from among those who attend divine service in the cathedral church, have failed to answer the ends contemplated, and that, on the contrary, discord and dissension have continued.

In consequence of the part taken by those who attended to make the election, and of the irregularities by which it was distinguished, the Hon. the Governor of Bengal has come to the conclusion, that it will not be possible to conduct the affairs of the cathedral with harmony and effect under the arrangement now existing. It has accordingly appeared to him necessary to transfer so much of the adminstration of this church as it is in the power of government to regulate, to the ecclesiastical officers of the presidency, provided by government, subject to the orders and control of the Lord Bishop.

The Hon. the Governor, has, therefore, determined, that the monthly payments heretofore made from the Treasury, on account of establishments, &c. of the cathedral church of St. John's, and placed at the disposal of the presidency chaplains and vestry, shall henceforward be paid to the receipt of the bishop, or, in his absence, or under his authority, the archdeacon, to be by him distributed according to usage, and the patronage, i. e. the right of selecting persons to fill the offices paid from those allowances, will devolve, of course, on the bishop, or on the archdeacon, subject to approval and sanction by his superior, the lord bishop. The allowances appropriated to the free school will be made payable to the order of the directors or governors of that institution.

The two presidency chaplains, attached

to the cathedral church of St. John's, will perform its duties as ministerial officers, subject to the orders of the lord bishop, and, in his lordship's absence, to the orders of the archdeacon. To the same authority, that is, to the lord bishop and archdeacon, is given the right of determining as to the making collections in the church. The amount collected will, of course, be appropriated to the purposes and in the manner declared at the time of collection.

With respect to the administration of the trust charities, heretofore committed to the clergy and churchwardens of St. John's, or to the select vestry, the advocate-general has authority to apply to the Supreme Court, to provide for such of these trusts as are paid under the authority and orders of the court, in order that due provision may be made for their distribution. Until the Supreme Court shall have made this provision, the archdeacon and the government chaplains will, of course, give their assistance in the partition of these, as of all other, charitable funds, in order that the poor of Calcutta, who depend upon the charities for their subsistence, may suffer no interruption in the receipt of their respective allowances.

You will perceive that it is not the desire of the Hon. the Governor of Bengal, to interfere with the rights of property, or of possession, which any persons may consider themselves to enjoy; but that he would prefer leaving all such questions to be decided by the courts of law.

The Hon. the Governor of Bengal, accordingly, issues no orders as to the property of the church, and the effect and interpretation of the trust-deed, executed at the time of its first erection. If it should be found hereafter that these questions are beset with difficulties, such as to prevent their proper adjudication in the courts of law, it will then be time to consider of the expediency of providing for their adjustment, by a reference to the legislative council of India.

You will be pleased to convey to the reverend the presidency chaplains such orders as may be necessary, according to the contents of this letter; and it is the desire of the hon. the Governor, that neither they nor yourself should again officially meet the lay gentlemen claiming to have been elected members of the vestry of St. John's, either at the cathedral or elsewhere.

I have the honour to be, Venerable Sir,
				your most obedient servant,
				(Signed) H. T. Prinsep.
Fort William, the 4th Nov. 1835.

To Mr. Llewelyn, Vestry Clerk.

Sir,—We have read with much surprise the accompanying letters, and will take an early opportunity of communicating with the presidency chaplains on the subject of them.

Whatever may be the right of the lord bishop, archdeacon, and presidency chaplains, to be considered members of the vestry, it is not competent for them to allege that our claim is not fully as valid, we having been chosen in the manner laid down in the rules which received the sanction of the Governor-general in Council on the 19th day of August last; by the authority of which only (if a mere rule be an authority) the bishop and archdeacon can pretend to claim a right of acting. We, therefore, desire that you, as vestry clerk, will not call any meeting of that body without including us in the notice.

We likewise request that you will forward to us the letter of the 29th ult., in reply to which the enclosed letter from Mr. Secretary Prinsep appears to have been written. Should there be no copy in your possession, you will communicate our request to the venerable the archdeacon, stating our desire to be furnished with the document.

We are, Sir, your obedient servants,
T. E. M. TURTON.
LONGUEVILLE CLARKE.
JOSEPH SPENCER JUDGE.
Calcutta, 24th Nov. 1835.

The *Hurkaru* observes, on the foregoing letter from the Government secretary: "This is precisely the course we expected things to take. We never supposed, that if independent lay members of the vestry were elected, they would be suffered to act. The archdeacon is following in the footsteps of his superior and patron, and grasping at power, it would seem; and the Governor, approving of a despotism in church matters, supports his pretensions! The orders of the 19th August, referred to in the letter of the Governor of Bengal now before us, are expressly stated, in the official paragraph which introduces them, to have 'received the sanction of the Governor-general in Council,' and yet we find the Governor of Bengal, in the letter before us, coolly setting them aside, in that 'free and easy' style of autographic legislation, which solves every difficulty by cutting the Gordian knot which it cannot unloose; in other words, by the simple process of a *sic volo!* We suspect that his honour will find, however, that in annulling orders of the Governor-general *and* Council, he has exceeded his powers."

Poor Sir Charles Metcalfe!

THE BANK OF BENGAL.

A special meeting of proprietors was held at the Bank of Bengal, on the 1st December, for the purpose of considering certain propositions for modifying the division of the shares, so as to have them represented in even thousands of Company's rupees. Of the two plans, No. 1 divided the capital into shares of 4,000 Company's rupees, and No. 2 into shares of 5,000. The following resolutions were carried *nem. con.*

"That the capital stock of the Bank of Bengal, in the proposed new charter, be expressed in Company's rupees, and that the conversion be made in such a manner as to preserve the division of the shares in even thousands."

"That the plan No. 1 of the circular be adopted."

The Chairman then observed, that the cases of shares already divided would require a special provision, which had been suggested in a letter from Government then before them, but which would only have application in one case, there being but one divided share on the register.

Mr. Cockerell proposed that, in consequence of the present vote adopting the division of 4,000 Company's rupees, the following scale of votes be adopted:

A holder of 1 share to have 1 vote.
        5 shares...... 2 votes.
     10 — ...... 3 —
     15 — ...... 4 —
     20 — ...... 5 —
     30 — ...... 6 —
     40 and upwards, 7 —

This proposition was carried *nem. con.*

THE GLO'STER MILLS.

The Glo'ster Mills were put up this day in one lot, which was knocked down to Mr. Allan, the attorney, for two lakhs and a-half. There were three *bona fide* competitors present; possibly more. The first cost of the various property conveyed by this sale is believed to have exceeded ten lakhs. It comprises a freehold estate of about 500 biggahs, a splendid cotton spinning-mill, with 20,000 spindles, in a very complete state, a range of power-looms, a printing-work with copper cylinders—all these in one pile of buildings; an excellent iron-foundery; a rum-distillery; a very complete oil-mill, with the best steam-machinery and hydrostatic presses from England; a sugar-boiling concern, and a capital residence in one of the most delightful situations upon the river. The impression in the room was, that the purchaser had made a very good bargain. The stock of cotton and goods on hand was reserved by the seller, and also all machinery indented for and not actually arrived. We are glad to entertain the opinion that the buyer has a prospect of making the cotton-mills yield a good return for the capital he has invested in the purchase.—*Cal. Cour.*, *Dec.* 1.

THE LATE WOONGYEE OF RANGOON.

Having been furnished with a translation of a letter addressed to the king of Ava by the late woongyee of Rangoon, just before his demise, we give it a place in our columns to-day, as a curious document. The letter was forwarded to Ava by the officers of the Rangoon Government, in an express-boat, immediately after the death of their chief. We learn also, that the king of Ava refused to grant the dying request of his servant, but ordered the whole of the arms to be taken up to him at Ava, and the last accounts from Rangoon relate, that the lady woongyee, and a deputation of officers, had arrived there from the capital to burn the body of the late woongyee, which had been preserved in honey, and that her ladyship had already begun to dispute with her rival, the subordinate but favourite wife, about the division of the property.

" Your majesty's slave, the woongyee of Henzawadee, Mengyee Maha Maulha Yaza, humbly submits. Your majesty, reposing especial trust and confidence in your slave, appointed and delegated him as commissioner, with full powers, to take charge of all the country to the southward of Prome, as well as of the thirty-two districts of Henzawadee. In accordance with the favour received from your majesty, and with his bounden duty, your slave has exercised superintendence and authority for nearly nine years, without consulting his own profit, but bearing in mind only the advantage of your majesty, of the empire, and of religion. Under the protection of your majesty's, power, arms and men have been collected for the purpose of being immediately available if the royal service required them. In addition to the 2,000 muskets in the town (of Rangoon), your slave possesses 100 French muskets, 100 English muskets, twenty English fusils, with twisted guards, twenty English fusils, with plain guards, and six English muskets, with swords attached, making altogether 246 stand of arms, the whole of which your slave presents to your majesty. With respect to some twenty or thirty guns which remain, may your majesty graciously bestow them on the four sons of your slave, and make them hereafter serve your majesty. To your majesty your slave also presents a canoe-bottomed boat, ten fathoms long, and carrying fifty-four oars. To her majesty the queen, he presents a canoe-bottomed boat of Thengan wood, nine and a-half fathoms long, and carrying fifty oars :— and to the princess Tsoo Phaya, he presents a canoe-bottomed boat, of the hill Pein wood, nine fathoms long, and carrying forty-nine oars.

" In the event of your majesty's slave not recovering from his present illness, but removing to another state of existence, let not the property belonging heretofore, whilst he was well, to each, to the lady woongyee, and to the wife Mi-Tsee, be mixed up together. The lady woongyee's property has been separated and kept distinct by her own steward; let her not interfere with, or give trouble to the wife Mi-Tsee, but let her (the latter) live quietly with the four sons of your majesty's slave. Let the lady woongyee also present twenty viss (2,000 ticals) of silver, and Mi-Tsee five viss, to the mother who bore your majesty's slave, for her own use, and for the purpose of making charitable offerings."—*Bengal Herald, Nov. 29.*

ECCLESIASTICAL INTELLIGENCE.

The lord bishop of Madras has brought out the new patents. The bishop of Calcutta is to be Metropolitan, with the same authority over the other bishops as an archbishop in England. New South Wales is withdrawn from the see of Calcutta, and is to constitute a separate see. Ceylon is joined to Madras. The arrangements for the new bishopric of Bombay were not completed, when the *Exmouth* left England. The archdeacon there is still subject to the bishop of Calcutta. The nomination of the archdeacon of Calcutta rests with the bishop of Calcutta, as before.—*Christ. Intell. for Dec.*

JUDICIAL ANOMALY.

Mr. Shuttleworth, indigo planter, of Nundalalpore Factory, Commercolly, and certain natives, were charged by one Parbuttychurn Roy, the naib of Goluckmony Deby, with breaking open the treasury-chest and taking away the papers of a zemindary, and firing a musket. Mr. G. T. Shakespear, the magistrate who investigated the case, held that nothing was proved against the accused planter, but that he went to the house of the complainant and fired off a musket, by which he frightened the said plaintiff and his neighbours, and for this offence he was fined 200 rupees, and the native defendants imprisoned. Mr. Shuttleworth paid the fine; but appealed against it to Mr. R. H. Tulloh, the commissioner of circuit, Bhauleah, who called on the joint magistrate for the record, and, deeming the evidence wholly unsatisfactory, ordered, that the decision of the joint magistrate be reversed; that he be instructed to return to Mr. Shuttleworth the fine, if already received; that, should the money be still unpaid, it be not demanded; that the other persons be released; that Mr. Shuttleworth be informed that, if he should be injured by people of the neighbourhood, he should prefer a complaint at the police. Previous to the receipt of the order, the fine had been transmitted to the clerk of the crown, in the Supreme Court, and the joint magistrate could only refer the party to that quarter. Mr. Shuttleworth applied to the commissioner, who sent him an official letter; but that would not suffice—he found that the money could not be paid to him without an order from the Supreme Court, and that that could not be obtained without filing a copy of the commissioner's order, and as the expenses were likely to exceed the amount of the fine, of course Mr. Shuttleworth did not adopt it. He appealed to the Supreme Government, and was informed, that the commissioner was not authorized to reverse the order of the magistrate. The Government declined interfering, and the grievance of which Mr. Shuttleworth complained, according to the commissioner's view of the case, with reason, remains to this day unredressed; nor, although he has been declared by the decision of that authority to have been entitled to redress, is there any tribunal to which he can appeal for it, according to the recent judgment in the Supreme Court, in the case of " Calder *v.* Halket."—*Hurk., Dec.* 18.

PRESS AND SOCIETY OF CALCUTTA.

A writer of a series of letters on Indian affairs, published in the *Hurkaru*, draws the following picture of the press and public of Calcutta:—

" The inhabitants of Calcutta, who are now, like the inmates of the fabled Castle of Indolence, reposing in fancied security, under the influence of their old delusion, may continue to dream on, and scatter the produce of their dreams around the sphere in which they move; but, happily, this does not extend so widely over the European public in India as they are apt to imagine. When the press was confined to Calcutta, they were enabled to put forth pretensions which were supposed to be admitted, because no one had the means of denying them, and a solitary visitor from the interior was overwhelmed by their congregated members in the city itself. The establishment of the provincial press has had the effect of reducing the standard of Calcutta authority on the subject of Indian affairs: and though it may yet be as high as ever in its own estimation, facts and opinions from better authenticated sources have lowered the height of its pretensions, and, on some essential points, changed its tone. The severity with which it has been handled by its Mofussil contemporaries, has created an irritability and sensitiveness on its part, which might have been anticipated, though, I think, without sufficient reason. The absurdity was in arrogating to itself qualifications for which there could possibly be no foundation. The inhabitants of Calcutta could not, had they reflected a moment, be expected to have acquired, by instinct, a knowledge of Indian affairs, on which, beyond the mere

routine of official business by the few so employed, scarcely any one in Calcutta has hitherto deigned to bestow the slightest attention. In Calcutta society, a man who should start any part of Indian affairs as a topic for conversation, would be considered a bore; almost all literature or information on Indian subjects is thrown aside, as dry and tasteless, nor is it possible that those whose Indian career has been spent in Calcutta, should possess any sound or solid views thereupon. Of the majority of the Calcutta public, I believe it will scarcely be too severe to assert, that the arrival of a fresh cargo of prime Yorkshire hams, hermetically sealed salmon, or raspberry jam; a squabble between two fiddlers of the theatre, and consequent postponement of an opera, would create a greater sensation among them, than the rebellion of half-a-dozen of the western provinces. I appeal to those who were in Calcutta in 1819, to testify, whether or not this be exaggeration. At that period, the number of professional musicians was just sufficient, if all were *d'acord*, to get up a good concert; but the two principal performers quarrelled, as to a share of the profits, and refused to unite their forces, thus preventing any concerts being held. The Calcutta public, instead of declining to patronize either until they should have agreed—by which means the musicians would have come to their senses in a week—actually formed two parties in favour of their respective heroes. Judges of the Supreme Court, judges of the Sudder, members of council, secretaries, and, indeed, almost the whole of the society, espoused the cause of either side; even the governess-general did not stand aloof: the petty animosities of the fiddlers' squabble seemed, as it were, to afford a vent for all the *mens irritabile* which the atmosphere of Calcutta is said so peculiarly to engender; and one could hardly enter a house without encountering the fury or spite of some partisan of the conflicting rivals. And yet, with all this eagerness and vivacity upon a point, in which mere amusement or pleasure is concerned, there is a cold, unsocial heartlessness in the society of Calcutta; a haughty pomposity, and a parvenu grandee notion of splendour and dignity, (particularly among the officials and their ladies), accompanied with a reluctance to exertion, even for their own interests, if the benefit be not immediate. It is with the greatest difficulty, for instance, that any public institutions can be established, or even preserved, under the apathy which exists among the English in Calcutta. Even English news is, in reality, little cared for: the attention of the greater number seems to be almost entirely devoted to their own little daily comforts, and they are only to be excited by a ball or a dinner. The remarks of a celebrated writer on the state of society in Paris, before the revolution, will, with a slight variation, but too well apply to them. ' They danced and sung to the emperor, they danced and sung to King Louis, and they would have danced and sung to King Satan, if he would have given them a fête or a spectacle;' so will the Calcuttites flatter and feast in honour of Governor Bentinck, flatter and feast in honour of Governor Metcalfe, and they would flatter and feast in honour of Governor Satan, if he would only give them a dinner or a ball, and occasionally 'honour the theatre with his presence,' at seven o'clock precisely, so as not to keep the audience waiting."

OUTRAGE ON A BRITISH OFFICER.

Neemuch.—An incident lately occurred in the neighbourhood of this station, which is now-a-days neither rare nor surprising. An officer of the 46th N.I., while out in the district, was seized by some insignificant zumeendar, and forced, at the point of a spear, to enter a house, where he was confined for more than an hour; during his imprisonment, a mob of all the disorderly ruffians around collected, insulted and threatened him in every possible way, pointing to a *siklee gur*, or needy knife-grinder, sharpening swords, making faces at and addressing him with every epithet of abuse their simple vocabulary afforded. The particulars of his release have not transpired.—*Agra Ukhbar, Dec. 5.*

THE BENGAL CLUB.

An insult of an atrocious nature is about to be put upon the members of the Bengal Club by some of the gentlemen composing the committee of management. We say some, because we have too great confidence in the honour, the independence, and the high feeling of a certain number of that body, to believe that they would lend themselves to a transaction which must be so offensive to every member, whose feelings are not warped, and whose judgment is not biassed, by individual partialities, and professional or family connection. It is, we are informed, the intention of the majority of the committee to call a general meeting, to determine whether a certain member of the club shall not receive a refund of his subscription, and be requested to withdraw from that institution, for the gratification of the spleen of some three or four venerable *qui hies!* The parties, at whose instance a portion of the committee are about to act, are, we have strong reason to believe, three *anciens militaires.* The obnoxious individual, whose ejection is demanded as the price of the continuance

of these individuals as *subscribers* to the club (for visitors they can scarcely be called), is the editor of the *Englishman.— Englishman, Dec. 11.*

The *Englishman* has a long editorial upon a subject that has taken us somewhat by surprise, for we had no idea that such a proceeding was in contemplation, namely, a proposition to be brought forward by Mr. Longueville Clarke, supported by Col. Beatson and a few other officers of high rank, to eject Mr. Stocqueler from the Bengal Club, on the ground (so we make out from the article before us), of his having published the *Military Mouth-Piece* in the *Englishman.* The series of articles or letters (for we never regarded them as editorials), under that head, have been full of severe comments upon the character and capacity of Col. Lumley, which from the first we regarded as wanton defamation. Indeed, from the repeated attacks upon him, and the strong language employed, an impartial reader could not but suspect there must be some private motive for these endeavours to prejudice the mind of the commander-in-chief against that respectable officer. Whether Colonel Lumley was the very fittest man that could have been selected for the Adjutant-generalship, we are not competent to form an opinion; but we are satisfied that his Excellency is the very best judge of such matters, and not at all likely to be swayed by the passionate declamations or prejudiced views of any anonymous writer. The publication of the *Military Mouth-Piece* in the columns of the *Englishman* must, therefore, naturally have given offence, not only to the friends of Col. Lumley, but also, we believe, to every right-thinking person in the army, more especially as these articles were put forth in avowed defiance of Gen. Watson's late order respecting anonymous writings.—*Cal. Cour., Dec. 11.*

Our *Courier* contemporary has, of course, his little characteristic say upon the subject of the Lumley Club business, and, as usual, contrives to evade the real point at issue. The *Courier*, than whom, from his demi-official connection, no one can possibly better judge of the character of the various attacks that have been directed against the Adjutant-general, takes upon himself to think, that the comments published in the *Mouth-Piece* were " wanton defamation." Suppose they were—what is that to the purpose? The question now in debate is, whether an editor of a public journal is disqualified, by the discharge of what he conscientiously believes to be his duty, for the society of a certain set of gentlemen—and whether the efforts of a *clique* to ride over the press are to be tolerated for a single moment.—*Englishman, Dec. 12.*

The *Englishman* asks what, if the comments in the *Military Mouth-Piece* were wanton defamation, "what is that to the purpose?" To which we reply—a great deal. It will scarcely be denied, we presume, that, if a member of the club indulges in wanton defamation of other members, that is a circumstance likely to disturb the harmony of the institution; and, if so, according to the spirit and letter of the rules of the Bengal Club, the member who indulges in such defamation is liable to be expelled. If the answer should be, that the party indulging in such defamation has done so in his capacity of journalist, and has considered it his duty, the rejoinder is obvious—if he should consider it his duty in *any* capacity to do that which does disturb the harmony of the institution, he must make his election between abandonment of such duty—and resignation of the club—and he has no right to complain, if, in following that course which he holds to be most popular and most advantageous, he loses the advantages of an institution which requires from members a different line of conduct. —*Hurk.*, Dec. 14.

A correspondence has taken place on this subject, between the secretary of the club, and the editor of the *Englishman*. The former states:—" I am directed by the committee to request, that you will state, on what grounds you have considered yourself authorized to make this severe and public attack on the conduct of the members of the committee, in particular, and on the affairs of the club in general. The committee of management have directed me to inform you that they have no hesitation, in explicitly declaring, (whatever may have been the private opinions of some gentlemen,) that they have never entertained, either directly or indirectly, any such proposition, as that alluded to in the article above-noted; *viz.* to request you to withdraw from the institution. The committee have also directed me to request, that you will state the nature and character of the communication made to you by Mr. Osborne on behalf of Mr. Longueville Clarke or Colonel Beatson, that the committee may be able to judge, whether this occurrence is likely to disturb the order and harmony of the club." The editor states in reply, that " Mr. Osborne, the barrister, called on me and stated that he came on the part of Mr. Longueville Clarke, to intimate that it was in contemplation to call a general meeting of the members of the Bengal Club for the purpose of proposing my ejection; that Col. Beatson was to move the necessary preliminary measure in committee; and that Mr. Longueville Clarke 'who had been called in and consulted,' was to bring the motion forward at the general meeting. Mr. Osborne added, that I was to consider

his message as ' official,' and he desired my answer, adding that the intimation to me was one which Mr. Clarke had insisted on as the condition of his agreeing to act at the general meeting. My reply was, that as it was thus intended undeservedly to put an insult upon me, I should make use of the instrument at my command to repel it."

Our impression as to this matter (which has excited much controversy) is, that the club, having admitted an individual known to be the editor of a newspaper, cannot, without manifest injustice, eject him on that ground. The majority may adopt a rule of disqualification for future cases.—ED. A. J.

ESTATE OF FERGUSSON AND CO.

Statement of Transactions of the Assignees, from 1st June to 31st October 1835.

Payments.

By Indigo Advances .... Sa. Rs.	4,37,303
Advances on account of other Goods ..	3,71,961
Sundry Advances	13,947
Dividend paid	3,56,268
Amount paid in Anticipation of Dividend	4,839
Amount of Acceptances received for Property sold, credit for which is given *per contra*, although not yet Realized	1,59,613
Amount borrowed Repaid	94,000
Amount paid, being refund of so much received on Account parties not indebted to the Estate	14,917
Amount paid on account Law Costs....	7,119
Premium paid on Life Insurances	1,09,064
Company's Paper purchased	3,35,818
Repairs and other Charges on Property belonging or mortgaged to Fergusson and Co.	190
Sundry Charges connected with the Estate	1,586
Refund of Amount received on Sale of house at Barrackpore since cancelled	3,851
Loss by exchange on sale of Bills taken in payment of Debts	535
Charges on Goods	683
Postage paid	495
	19,12,189
Balance in hands of Assignees	61,721
Sa. Rs.	19,73,911

Receipts.

Balance of last Statement 1st June 1835 Sa. Rs.	55,798
Outstanding Debts recovered	3,313,018
Sale of Indigo	7,46,879
Sale of other Goods	4,98,135
Sale of Company's paper	1,80,903
Sale of Union Bank shares	7,900
Received on Account Sale of *India Gazette* Press	6,000
Received on Account Sale of indigo factories	94,011
Received on Account Sale of houses, &c.	1,68,692
Paid on Account Law Costs refunded ..	1,000
Paid in anticipation of Dividend refunded	11,137
Received dividend from Estate of Mc Quodi, Davidson, and Co., in which other parties are interested	11,719
Indigo Advances refunded	13,896
House and Godown rent received	415
Interest received	2,608
Commission received	2,353
Charges on Goods paid by Estate refunded	291
Sa. Rs.	19,73,911

In possession of Assignees, Company's
Promissory Notes, belonging to Estate,
amounting to .... Sa. Rs.   1,87,800

ESTATE OF COLVIN AND CO.

Statement of Transactions of the Assignee
from 1st to 31st October 1835, published
(as filed by the assignee) by Order of the
the Court.

Payments.

Indigo Advances .... Sa.Rs.	17,631	
Dividends to Creditors	4,073	
Refund of Surplus Receipts	287	
Law Charges	213	
Assessments on Houses	37	
Redemption of Mortgage in part	2,373	
Company's Paper purchased for		
Sa. Rs.	20,000	
		19,845
Balance Cash in hand .... Sa.Rs.	13,239	
Ditto in Bank of Bengal	300	
		13,539
	Sa. Rs.	57,998

Memorandum.

Company's Paper of 4 per cent. Sa.Rs.	100,000	
Bank of Bengal	300	
Cash in hand	13,239	
	Sa. Rs.	1,13,539

Receipts.

Balance of last statement ...... Sa.Rs.	19,047	
Outstanding Debts recovered	38,951	
	Sa. Rs.	57,998

Statement of the Transactions of the Assignee from 1st to 30th November.

Receipts.

Balance per last Statement .... Sa.Rs.	13,539	
Outstanding Debts recovered	48,760	
Recoveries on Account of others	3,017	
Interest on Company's paper	1,254	
Sale of Goods	132	
	Sa. Rs.	66,702

Payments.

Indigo Advances ....Sa.Rs.	13,828	
Dividend paid to Creditors	5,570	
Ditto in Anticipation	100	
Payments on Account of Others	3,294	
Postage for September...............	51	
Law Charges in Mofussil Courts	140	
Charges, Advertisements, &c.	36	
Mortgage redeemed in part	9,575	
Purchasing 4 per cent. loan Sa.Rs.	20,200	
		20,982
Balance Cash on hand	8,826	
Bengal Bank	4,300	
		13,126
	Sa. Rs.	66,702

Memorandum.

Company's Paper	1,90,900	
Bank of Bengal	4,300	
Cash................	8,826	
	Sa. Rs.	1,33,396

UNIVERSAL ASSURANCE COMPANY.

The Directors of the Universal Assurance Society laid before the proprietors
and policy-holders, at their first annual
meeting, yesterday, one of the most favourable reports we remember to have met
with. Up to the end of November, 225
policies have been issued by the Indian
branch of the Society, covering 27,35,740

sicca rupees. At home, according to the
last statement, there have been issued 127
policies, covering £130,661, making the
total annual transactions 40,42,358 sicca
rupees. But what is most extraordinary,
not a single lapse has occurred since the
formation of the society. — *Englishman,
Dec.* 15.

FREQUENCY OF COURTS-MARTIAL.

We think we should be neglecting our
duty, if we did not earnestly invite the
attention of the army to some admirable
remarks of the Commander-in-Chief, on
the endless number of courts-martial in
the Indian army, which he ascribes to
the obstinate adherence of individuals to
their own opinions, in defiance of the
unbiassed judgment of superior authorities to whom they may have appealed.
Whatever may be the cause, the effect is
sufficiently deplorable, and is calculated to
~~~~~ discredit on the Indian army, wher-
e~~~~ it is known. We sincerely hope,
the~~~~re, that the officers will listen to the
app~~~~ thus made to them, and feel that
sam~~~~ individual opinion are de-
~~~~ still alike by a sense of duty, and a re-
g~~~~ for the character and interests of the
service to which they belong.—*Hurkaru.*

OPIUM CULTIVATION.

Extract of a letter from Tirhoot, dated
7th December :—

" We are very much bothered now-a-days
with the opium, for W. is sending out his
people to all the Assamies, to send in
complaints against us, and some of our
Assamies, whose lands we have prepared
for the last two months, and to whom
we have made advances for the same, are
giving in complaints against us."

This clashing of the opium with the
indigo trade is a matter which merits the
most serious attention of the government.
We are informed that there is a wide
difference between the penalties which
attach to a ryot's violation of his engagement to cultivate opium and his engagement to grow indigo. If he breaks the
latter, he may, under a recent regulation,
be sued in a civil court for *damages;* but,
if he disregard the former, he is liable to
be treated as a felon! Surely, it never
can be intended that so wide a distinction
should subsist between the two parties.
—*Englishman, Dec.* 15.

COPPER COINAGE.

An Act passed the legislative council
on the 7th December, by which it is
enacted, that from the 20th of that
month, a new copper coinage was to be
issued from the Bengal mint, consisting
of a *pie*, weighing 33½ grs. troy, and
nearly corresponding to the piece of 5
cash, or 1 pice of the Madras currency;

a *pice*, weighing 100 grs. troy, about 1½ doodie—15 cash, or ¾ anna; and a *double pice*, weighing 200 grs. troy, equal to 30 cash, 3 doodies, or half-anna. There is no allusion made in the Act to the copper currency of the Madras or Bombay presidencies, but it is provided that " no copper coin shall be a legal tender in any part of the Company's territories except for the fractional part of a rupee."

The following devices for the new coin are announced in an order of the 16th :—

For the *pice*—on the obverse, the armorial bearings of the East-India Company; on the reverse, the value of the coin in English—*one quarter anna*—and in Persian يك پائي , encircled by a wreath, with the words " East-India Company" round the margin. For the *double pice*—on the obverse, the same armorial bearings, with the words " East-India Company" round the margin; on the reverse, the value of the coin in English—*half-anna*—and in Persian دو پائي ,

For the *pie*—on the obverse, the armorial bearings, as in the pice; on the reverse, the value in English ¹⁄₁₂ *anna*—and in Persian ثلث پائي , with a wreath, and the words " East-India Company " round the margin.

The above pice, being a legal tender for any fraction of a Company's rupee, will be received and issued at the rate of 64 to the said rupee.

The *Calcutta Courier* remarks : " We had hoped to see some notice tending to remove, if not immediately, at least at a period not far distant, the strange anomaly of the same pice passing for equal divisions of rupees of different values. Instead of this, we find an apparent endeavour to force equality where no equality exists ; for the new pice are to be received and issued at the rate of 64 to the Company's rupee, and also are to be received in all the public departments at the same rate for the fractions of the sicca, indiscriminately with the pice now current ; the effect of which, it appears to us, will be not only to retard the return of the old coin and encourage that of the new, which it should be the endeavour to force out rather than to force in, but also to create a most unnatural traffic, quite foreign to the legitimate purposes of currency. The new pice will be purchased from the treasury with Company's rupees, and they will be immediately retailed to persons having payments to make in siccas at the public offices, whereby government will sustain a loss of four pice in every sicca rupee so represented."

INTELLECTUAL CONDITION OF INDIA.

It is lamentable to observe, that, after having so long held India, we have made no definite impression on native society. Notwithstanding the compliments which pass and repass between Calcutta and Leadenhall-street, it is a fact, which no man acquainted with the country will deny, that the British government in India has neither produced any ameliorating change in the *people*, nor adopted any measures which might lead to the hope, that the foundation of such a change had been laid, and that time only was required to develope it. We have wrought no improvement in India in the remotest degree correspondent with the extent of our own acquirements, or the advantages which we have long enjoyed in the country. We have protected the country from foreign enemies ; and this is, we fear, nearly the sum and substance of our achievements. But we owed this to our dignity, peace, and character ; other duties, which we owed to the country, we have yet to think of. The benefits which the natives have derived from our own advent, have arisen simply from the *existence* of a powerful and vigorous administration among them; from any exertions of that administration, the intellectual condition of the people has obtained no benefit. Burke, in a strain of bitter invective, said, half a century ago, " Were we to be driven out of India this day, nothing would remain to tell that it had been possessed, during the inglorious period of our dominion, by any thing better than the orang outang or the tiger." The censure is now* inapplicable ; but it may be said, with the strictest truth, that, if we were this day driven out of India, there would not remain any thing to testify that it had been held for seventy years, in undisputed sovereignty, by the most active and civilized people on earth. In fact, the entire structure and complexion of our government appear utterly unadapted for making any permanent, civilizing impression on the mass of the people; for laying deep the foundations of new institutions, calculated to elevate the natives. Every thing about our government is transient and fugitive ; there is nothing permanent. The scene flits before the eyes of the natives, and the actors appear and disappear on the stage with all the rapidity of dramatic representation. From the highest to the lowest officer, we see nothing but perpetual change. No sooner do the natives begin to understand the character of a governor general, and the governor general to understand them and their country, than he removes to his native land, and is succeeded by another, who has no sooner completed the term of his " ap-

* And always was.—ED.

prenticeship," and become initiated in the craft and mystery of Indian government, than he also disappears. The same principle of change pervades all the subordinate offices. Take the civil stations all round, and it will be found that the functionaries are changed about every three years. In scarcely a single instance, is there time for a judge, magistrate, or collector to become intimately acquainted with the people under him. He seems always in a hurry to be gone, first from one place to another, and eventually from India to England. Is it possible that any permanent institutions for the benefit of India can be founded and matured, in so changing a scene?"

———

A writer in the *Calcutta Courier*, treating upon the education of the natives, expresses himself thus: "What, then, is the proximate cause of the want of improvement and nearly stationary condition of India? What can it be but the comparative indolence and want of enterprize characteristic of the people? But whence comes this indifference? Does it exist where a *certain* and *immediate* prospect of advantage lies open to their perception? This can scarcely be said. The inactivity complained of must, therefore, originate, in a great measure at least, in the want of a full and distinct understanding of the advantage of pushing enterprize into other than the customary channels. And how is it that such perception is wanting? Custom, long and deeply-rooted, prejudice, and ignorance (connected no doubt, in part, with the physical character of the people, but attributable still more to the nature and effects,—which have been operating for ages,—of the religion they profess and the civil institutions arising from it), have obscured the reasoning powers of the nation, and blunted the measure of ingenuity which they undoubtedly possess, so as to debar them from the attainment of just principles in philosophy, from the discovery of truth in the sciences, and as a consequence, in some degree necessary, from a knowledge of the simplest and most effectual processes in the mechanical and other arts. In the meanwhile, the almost total want of intercourse with more enlightened foreigners, until a recent period, rendered it impossible that the valuable knowledge, of which,—as long experience had shewn,—there were no indigenous germs, could be introduced from other quarters. The ultimate principle, it appears, then, to which we are conducted by this analysis, is the ignorance of the people, which disables them from perceiving, and profiting by, those means of bettering their condition and augmenting the national wealth, which their interest would other-

wise render them quick to seize upon and turn to advantage. What, then, are those agents which would operate most powerfully in advancing the civilization of India, of which its people are yet ignorant? and by what obstacles are they prevented from becoming acquainted with, and availing themselves of them? These questions would lead to a wide discussion. In the mean time, they can only be answered briefly and partially.

"A knowledge of the principles of science and their application to the arts, is the particular agent, in the improvement of this country, which it is at present intended to insist on. The consideration of the means by which such a knowledge could be imparted, is closely connected with the general subject of education. The preparation of books in the vernacular tongues, on the principles of the several sciences most applicable to the common purposes of life, and on the practice of the most extensively useful arts, would be one important means of disseminating the required information; but still more important, nay absolutely essential, towards the attainment of the end here proposed, (*viz.* the excitement of a desire to know and to employ improved methods in the arts), is the appointment of practical professors at each of the large cities of Hindoosthan, to instruct the most intelligent artisans of all descriptions, especially young men, in the theory and practice of the simplest and most effectual processes in their several departments. No body of men, especially a people in the situation of the Hindoos and other inhabitants of this country, can be expected to innovate largely without the expectation, nay, the clear prospect, of some tangible profit. A measure like that just indicated, the operation of which, by displaying to them the palpable and material advantages of improvement in knowledge, would strongly attract them to its acquisition, would, therefore, undoubtedly prove an effectual agent in advancing the civilization of the nation. A perception of the vast benefits of knowledge in a material point of view, as well as the improvements so effected by its agency, would, in the natural course of things, introduce a higher order of civilization, and promote the cultivation of knowledge, in all its departments, for its own sake."

———

CULTIVATION OF INDIGO.

From our enquiries, we learn there is no disposition to extend the cultivation of indigo, and advances are restricted to factories which can produce indigo at the cheapest and lowest cost. We do not hear of any increased capital being applied to the cultivation of this article:

(C)

but, on the contrary, we learn there are at this time many planters who are unable to get assistance to carry on their factories, where the cost appears to exceed the ordinary average.—*Englishman, Dec.* 3.

___

THE PHILOSOPHER'S STONE.

The river Soan, which intersects the military road leading from Calcutta to Benares, is famed for its pebbles. In the rainy season, the stream is full three miles across, but, during the remainder of the year, the greater portion of its bed is dry, and abounding in quicksands. It is believed by the credulous, that the *philosopher's stone* lies somewhere in the bed of the river; and the belief is founded on the following *fact*. In the days when Sasseeram and Rotus Ghur were flourishing places, a chief (Shere Shah, I think), with his whole paraphernalia, crossed the Soan in progress to Bengal; and, on arriving at the eastern bank, it was discovered that a chain attached to the leg of one of the elephants, instead of being of iron, was composed of pure gold! The sages, on being summoned to account for such a phenomenon, questioned the mahout, and on his declaring he had not put the chain on the animal's leg, unanimously declared, that a transmutation had taken place by the " *Parus Puthur*" having come in contact whilst the elephant was crossing. Such an opportunity for securing the long-looked and long-wished for talisman was not, of course, to be neglected. An order was instantly issued for each person in the camp to collect a heap of pebbles from the bed of the river. In this occupation patricians and plebeians eagerly joined, gold being the stimulus. The next process was for the people to arrange themselves, with their collections, along the water's edge, every one having a piece of iron, with which they were to touch each pebble. If the desired effect was not produced, the pebble was to be thrown into the water as useless. Away then to work they went, touching and throwing; and this scene continued for several days. At last, the folks grew tired and careless, and the operation of ' touch-and-go' was carried on at the rate of thirteen miles an hour. Fortune is said to be blind, and unluckily she here stumbled on a poor grass-cutter, who got hold of the desired object of search. His piece of iron no sooner came in contact with it, than the base metal was turned into gold! But he having been so accustomed to the touch-and-throw movement, the ,real pebble shared the fate of its predecessors; into the water it went. The hue and cry was soon made, that the " *Parus Puthur*" was found, but like Pat's tea-kettle at the bottom of the sea—it was *not lost*—the

grass-cutter knew where it was, and that's all! The chief, on finding what had occurred, and vexed at his disappointment, had the unfortunate grass-cutter bound hand and foot and thrown into the river for his stupidity. Many fruitless endeavours were made to fish up the cast-away article; but, as good-luck seldom visits one twice in the twenty-four hours, it was never found again—there the " *Parus*" remains, and will for ever remain, unless the same grass-cutter who first discovered it finds it again!— *Central Free Press, Nov.* 28.

___

LAW COMMISSION.

The Law Commissioners have issued a circular calling for information regarding the state of slavery in India.

___

NATIVE PATRONAGE.

The anxiety of the natives to obtain situations under Government seems to be out of all proportion to the amount of the salaries attached to them. Even where the pay is contemptibly insignificant, there is the most eager competition for them, and men of the most respectable and wealthy families in the country scruple at no means to obtain them. These official posts appear valuable in their eyes, from the dignity and standing which they give in society, and from the opening which they afford for indirect gains to an unlimited extent. A good situation in the judicial, revenual, or commercial line is moreover considered as a provision for a whole family, since a native who may have obtained one always pushes his own relatives into every employment within his reach. A flock of hungry, needy connections attends on his movements, to seize upon these posts as they fall vacant. And however the right of presentation to them may belong to the European functionary at the head of the office, the patronage does, some how or other, invariably fall to the disposal of some native on his establishment, who has contrived to make himself useful or necessary. To the attainment of this great object, that of subjecting their European master to their own influence, the uninterrupted attention of the most ambitious natives in the office is constantly directed; and, sooner or later, their efforts are crowned with success. They lead, by appearing always to follow. It is quite amusing to see, as is often the case, a European functionary of firmness and integrity, boasting of his own complete independence of all the natives around him, while at the same time every thing is eventually done exactly as his influential native servant desires. A native who has thus succeeded in obtaining the ear and the confidence of his master, enjoys therefore, in addition to the dignity and emoluments of his own station, the patronage of almost all the inferior situations in the department. It is also a fact worthy of note, that the public situations of government, which are filled by natives, carry with them a very large share of influence, more especially in the country. In England, a country gentleman of large property, and of an ancient family, enjoys far more consideration than a simple justice of the peace, or an ordinary functionary of government. In this land of sycophancy, it is generally the reverse. A subordinate native officer of the court, or of the collectorate, enjoys greater distinction in many parts of the country than a wealthy zemindar. His opinions carry more weight; his example extends to a wider range, and he exercises a more decided influence upon the opinions and practice of the people. It is, therefore, not surprising that posts in the public service, even where the stipulated salary does not exceed twenty or thirty rupees monthly, should be considered as valuable prizes, and eagerly sought after by natives of every rank and denomination.— *Friend of India, Nov. 19.*

JEYPORE AFFAIRS.

Major Alves and Captain Thoresby are to proceed, immediately, to Dewsa, for the express purpose of instituting a *vivá voce* investigation, in which Jotha Ram is to be personally confronted, and exposed to the ordeal of a strict examination, by which, it is confidently expected, his guilt will be established, and the whole "mystery of iniquity" be brought to light. Some of the questions to be put to him are said to be real *posers;* which, if answered at all, must, very shortly, terminate this tedious affair."—*Delhi Gazette, Dec. 2.*

We understand that a new corps of local cavalry is about to be raised at Ajmere, the expenses of which are to be defrayed by Maun Sing, of Joudpore, in lieu of the contingent which he has hitherto furnished, according to the treaty, which has proved itself more than useless, and almost openly hostile to our welfare.

Capt. Downing, of the 3d N. I., it is said, will have the command of it; though others are of opinion, that that officer's services are placed at the disposal of Major Alves, in order to his employment as political agent in Shekawattee. Capt. Thoresby, we hear, will remain at Jeypore.

The *Hurkaru* has recanted and apologized for its unfounded censure of Major Alves. In the paper of Nov. 26th, it says:—" Our object, in all our strictures on the Jeypore tragedy, has been to promote the ends of justice. The inference that the tumult must have been known at

the palace soon enough to have enabled the authorities to interfere in time to prevent the murder of Mr. Blake, seemed to us inevitable, from all the accounts of the case which had been published, when we made the remarks, to which our correspondent refers. Undoubtedly, the case assumes a different aspect now, that the source of the treachery is discovered, and Lieut.-Colonel Alves stands exonerated from the blame which has been heaped upon him by those who, it appears, were less capable of judging of its real character. We sincerely regret that our journal should have been the vehicle of much undeserved severity of censure directed against the gallant officer, though in any remarks of our own, we believe, we have not rendered ourselves liable to the reproach of harshness in our strictures on his measures; but, although it appears that the resident was right in not imputing the treachery to the executive authorities at Jeypore, and although it may be now known that there was no sufficient ground for suspicion of them, we still think, that, in the circumstances previously known, such suspicion was extremely natural."

It was stated in a late number of this journal, that the Jeypore ranee had sent *choories and pugrees* to the several thakoors. Naringhun Loll, vakeel to the Nawab of Thonk, in reply stated, that he was at the ranee's command, and ready to bring his forces whenever she might desire him to do so! Ubah Singh has arrived with his troops at Jeypore.— *Delhi Gaz, Dec. 9.*

THE NEW CURRENCY.

It would appear that disinclination, and in some instances refusal, to accept the new rupee, have been experienced at the presidency. This state of confusion and uncertainty demands the immediate attention of government. If the currency is depreciated 2-4 per cent., we conceive batta to that extent is in justice due by the government. No security is, moreover, given that this depreciation shall be final. A new Governor-general may take a fancy to a new rupee of a new device, when a second reduction of its value may take place, we therefore strongly advocate the *obsta in principio* to such encroachments.—*Meerutt Obs., Nov. 12.*

" I am certain that you would oblige a great many in the upper provinces by noticing the effect on the finances of all stationed above Dinapore by the late change in the currency. Whilst we are *actually* paid in the same coin as heretofore, it has virtually lost in its comparative value with the Calcutta sicca rupee, Rs. 2-2-8 per cent., thus adding to the difficulties of all who may labour under pecuniary embarrassments, Rs. 2-2 per cent. on their debts. It equally affects all who have to remit to Europe for their families, as though Calcutta and Company's siccas principally are remittances makeable, it enhances by the same ratio the prices of all Calcutta articles, whilst the sicca is permitted to continue current in Calcutta. I have fortunately no debts to pay, but sending a draft for sicca rupees 300 to Calcutta a few days ago, I had to pay *in the same currency* as would a few months ago have amounted only to 313.8—Rs. 320; merely because they were *then* called Sonauts, and are *now* designated Company's rupees."—*Hurkaru, Dec.* 19.

Our *Courier* contemporary doubts the accuracy of the statement inserted in the *Englishman,* regarding the intention of government to make up the difference to the non-commissioned officers and troops of the army, occasioned by the recent alteration in the coinage. We can only say, that our authority is a civilian, high in the service—that the fact was mentioned at a meeting of the first merchants in Calcutta, and in the presence of an officer holding a high staff situation. Since which, we have heard military men say, they have seen a government letter to the presidency paymaster, authorising the measure.—*Englishman.*

Our contemporary is, nevertheless, not more correct in this instance than when a high staff officer was once before quoted as authority for imaginary murmurs at Barrackpore. The simple fact is merely, that for the present it is ordered that the new coin shall not be issued at the presidency pay-office until siccas shall have ceased to be issued from any other public office, and the former obtain more general circulation—perhaps not until the new pice (if there are to be new pice), shall make their appearance.—*Calcutta Cour.*

MILITARY ITEMS.

The late order by the Commander-in-chief, on the subject of the dress of the officers of the army, though conceived in strict accordance with military usage, is still not in unison with either the spirit of the times, or the climate under which we live, and is, moreover, expressed with a quaintness and affectation of wit, seldom leavening the mass of the orders issuing from the Adjutant-general's office of the Indian army. By a citizen's plain blue frock-coat, we are inclined to gather one that is not strictly according to orders,— one that is not emblazoned with gilt buttons, and covered with silk braid. Now, if our memory deceives us not, the plain blue frock-coat was introduced and almost invariably worn with the foraging-caps by Lord Combermere, and has been since

continued from experience of its greater comfort and less expense. Had his Excellency inquired the reason of the capes (*and collars*) of jackets being turned down, he would have found it to be the extreme discomfort and inconvenience of the cloth jacket in a climate like Calcutta, to obviate which, and, as much as in the wearer's power, to catch the breeze of heaven, induced him to adopt this slovenly habit. Swords are, no doubt, very military, but hardly a necessary appendage in the theatre or ball-room, and if insisted on during the hot season, will deprive the places of public resort of encouragement from military men. The order might bear the complexion of enforcing unity and propriety, while reprobating the solecism often observed in the union of the two costumes, military and civil:—if such the intention, we shall not regret the loss of green and gold velvet waistcoats, on which our eyes have oft reposed as relief from the fiery scarlet coats often superadded.—*Meerut Obs., Dec.* 10.

Sir H. Fane, it seems, does not issue orders for the sake of filling the columns of a contemporary; he means that they should be obeyed to the letter. Yesterday, some officers went to the cathedral in demi-military costumes—or at least in costumes forbidden by the general orders. An aide-de-camp was desired to invite them to Sir Henry's presence, whither they repaired, and received a gentle lecture upon their breach of regulations.— *Englishman, Nov.* 30.

A general court-martial has been sitting at Barrackpore, for seven days, for the trial of Ensign Smith, of H. M.'s 38th, for sending Capt. Souter (also of H. M.'s 38th) a challenge to fight a duel. This is a charge seldom brought before a court-martial, but there are particular circumstances attending it. The same court met yesterday morning for the trial of a private of the 38th, for striking an officer on parade. As soon as this is over, we understand the same court is to try Capt. Horne, of H. M.'s 44th, for "willingly absenting himself from parade," &c.—*Ibid, Dec.* 1.

NATIVE MARRIAGE.

The son of Rajah Juswunt Singh of Naubab, accompanied by a force of fifteen thousand men, consisting of suwars and sepoys, proceeded last week to Bhullumghur, the residence of Rajah Naeb Singh, to whose sister he was married. Upwards of 200,000 people assembled, amongst whom 10,000 four and eight-anna pieces were thrown; in the attempt to secure some of them, twelve men were killed; another instance of the bad effects of indiscriminate charity. Eight-anna pieces were afterwards distributed. The total expense attendant upon this marriage, conducted as it was upon the grandest scale of eastern magnificence, exceeded *six lacks of rupees*; a sum which, if judiciously administered to the suffering natives, might have been productive of lasting good.—*Delhi Gaz., Dec. 9.*

NATIVE STATES.

Lahore.—Runjeet Sing has written to the Hakim of Sinde, requesting him to forward, without delay, the amount of the nuzeranna. The latter, with more courage than prudence, returned a spirited answer, to the purport "that as a soldier he would not pay until forced to do so," and has, accordingly, prepared his forces, consisting of 10,000 or 12,000 men, horse and foot, for immediate action.—*Delhi Gaz., Dec. 9.*

Delhi.—A letter from Delhi, received yesterday. mentions that Dewan Kishen Loll has been imprisoned on suspicion of being concerned in a conspiracy to murder Mr. Simon Fraser. Our readers are aware that Kishen Loll is the man of Baraiteh and Jyepore fame.—*Englishman, Nov. 9.*

Gwalior.—Capt. Ross has gone over to Futtyghur to the Baiza Baee. She is at last about to proceed by Benares to the Dekhan, with six lakh of rupees a-year for life. Major Sutherland, it is said, will wait on her at Allahabad, as a mark of respect on her leaving this part of India. —*Agra Akhbar, Dec. 5.*

Ludakh.—Zoorawur Sing in the service of Goolab Sing, having effected a footing in the country, and taken possession, and repaired the fort, the prince of Ludakh, with his son and minister, have fled to Puttun, near Rampore, and there prevent people from going to Ludkah, stating, that Zoorawur Sing, seizing travellers and merchants, employs them on the works of the fort; moreover he has stopped the transit of shawls, and restricted it to Shoroo and Murroo, with the exception of a small quantity sent by the road to Jumoon, which, being reported to Runjeet Sing of Lahore, he immediately sent orders to remedy this, by not allowing the shawls to enter Umritsur.—*Englishman.*

Rajah Golab Sing, of Jummoo, has at last sent his son with a reinforcement in aid of Zaruour Sing, who has taken up his quarters on the mountain of Secundria, with 15,000 horse and foot, and where he has been joined by the rajah's son. The rajah of Ludakh, on being apprized of this junction, caused the passes to be completely blocked up. On seeing this, Zuruour Sing, alarmed, applied to Rajah Joy Sing, of Muhulmoonee, for assistance, who put him in a condition to meet his enemy in the field. The rajah of Ludakh, in conjunction with the troops of Yarkhund and Thibet, combated the troops of the Sing and routed them completely, after having killed a number of them and wrested their arms. The vanquished have again taken shelter at the beforementioned mountain; making preparations for a third combat.—*Jami Jehannamah.*

Hyderabad.—By recent Ukbars, it appears that Rajah Chundoo Loll commands every thing, and carries the day on his palm. The Nawab Asif Jah is a mere tool in his hands. A Rohilla Patan, in the service of Seraj Doulah, the nominal minister, having had large arrears of pay due to him, tried every possible means for the recovery of the same, in an amicable manner; but seeing no possibility of getting it, he has had recourse to the last alternative of sitting *Dhurna*, with a naked sword in his hand, at the entrance of Seraj Dowlah's residence, opposing the ingress and egress of every body. Seeing this, his master promised to pay off his arrears by a certain day; upon which the Patan was pacified. But no sooner had he left his post, than it was occuped by a considerable number of tailors, who made a hideous outcry in demanding the arrears of their wages. The Nawab Asif Jah, on hearing this, said, in an air of contempt, ' what! does Seraj Dowlah not keep sufficient money in his purse so as to pay the arrears of the tailors?'

Intelligence was conveyed to the nawab that the moon-faced ladies of Mugferuth Manzil, being considerably in arrears, had formed the resolution of breaking through the zenanahs, for the purpose of personally representing their grievances to the " *Huzzoor Blund Eckball.*" In order to avert this disgrace, the nawaub directed their arrears to be forthwith discharged, with an injunction that the entrance leading to the ladies' apartments might be entirely blocked up, so as never to admit of their coming out upon any future occasion, when they may be so inclined.

The state of the Hyderabad police is still in as bad state as ever, and scarcely a day passes but what brings the intelligence of some robberies and murders.

Ulwar.—The rajah of this principality, Buxhee Sing, being excessively fond of the society of young females and musicians, has entirely abstracted his attention from the administration of state affairs; consequently, the zemindars have began to take advantage of the same, in refractorily withholding the payment of their stipulated revenues, which circumstance has reduced Baney Sing to the utmost distress and want. Seeing this state of affairs, Suntram, a wealthy banker of Ulwar, submitted a proposition to the rajah, that if he would give him the farm of his territories, he was willing to engage himself to defray all the expenses of the civil and military department, as well as every other miscellaneous expense; and moreover he would let his rajahship have eighty thousand rupees for his privy purse per annum. The rajah rapturously embraced the proposition, conceiving it a very advantageous one for himself, as it relieved him from the trouble, anxiety, and vexation of government, and consigned his territories to the charge of the former for a period of five years, and immersed himself the more deeply into the pleasures of the seraglio.—*Englishman.*

Herat.—By the latest Ukbars, it appears that the Persian prince, Kye Khusru Meerza, has removed his camp in the vicinity of Herat; and that Comran Shah, conceiving peace and tranquillity more conducive to his true interests and welfare than hostility, took upon himself the rather humiliating task of waiting upon the Persian Shazadah in his own camp, who is said to have received the ruler of Herat with great attention; so much so, that he actually rose from his musnud on the approach of the Herat prince, and embraced him, making him sit down on the same musnud with himself. Comran Shah, after passing a long interval in the company of the Persian prince, took leave, and, instead of returning to his capital, proceeded by forced marches to Seistan, and upon his arrival at that principality, he sent for Ally Khan, the son of the ruler, and Mohumed Saleh, the governor of the fort of Lash, under the plea of some important business, and upon their complying with his message, he shewed them every kingly favour and indulgence by investing them with splendid honorary dresses, which lulled these simple and unsuspecting sirdars into a perfect confidence of personal safety, and they therefore hesitated not to pass the night in the camp of the shah; but, in the morning, they found themselves delivered into the custody of the kuzzulbash, enchained on the leg, and halters put round their necks for the purpose of conveying them to Herat, and there being no one to oppose the treacherous prince, he took possession of Seistan. It seems to be the determination of the perfidious Comran to possess himself of the forts of all the neighbouring minor chiefs in this manner, with the aid of the Persian Biree, who is said to have promised him his assistance in the time of need. The ruler of Candahar, on being apprized of this trea-cherous deed of Comran, became extremely agitated and alarmed, and has caused his family, with all the valuable effects, to be removed to Curshack, the fort of which is undergoing repairs.—*Ibid.*

Cabul.—One of the Ukbars from this quarter, dated the 2d of September, states that prodigious numbers of Patans are daily coming to Cabul from Jullalabad and Deyrah Khyber, with the design of aiding and assisting Dost Mohamed in his projected expedition against the subah of Peshawur. On the assemblage of the Patans, amounting to several thousands, they expressed an ardent desire to have a personal interview with the head of the Khan clan, and were introduced to him by Attah Khan, who had previously invited all the principal chiefs of Cabul to be present at this grand meeting. Dost Mohamed, seeing that the Patans were extremely eager to engage with the Seiks, received them with very great kindness, and held out to them promises of great wealth and renown, and the Patans, in their turn, declared their readiness to sacrifice their lives in the cause of Mohamedanism, and further assured the sirdar, that since the period the subah of Peshawur has been possessed and governed by the Seiks, they have been subjected to great distress and mortifications. This address of the Patans tended so much to impassion Dost Mohamed, as to induce him to determine upon sending his son, Afzal Beg Khan, with 15,000 horse, and a much larger body of infantry, against Peshawur; assuring the Patans that he will follow himself with reinforcements, as originally resolved on by him. Mohamed Afzal Beg is to encamp his troops at Jullalabad, where the father has promised to meet him with all practicable expedition.—*Ibid.*

Peshawur.—A *quasid,* or messenger, having lately arrived at Ludianah, represented that, from the commencement of the present cold season at that soobah, the Patans have been occasioning great annoyances to the Seiks on their nocturnal depredations. Almost every night these marauders commit thefts in the camp of the Seiks; and these miscreants are so very skilful in the art of stealing, that the poor Seiks find it most difficult even to preserve their turbans from the plunder of these night robbers, notwithstanding every possible precautionary measure adopted by the skilful General Ventura: but with all his efforts and exertions, he has not been able to put a stop to the predatory visits of these wretches, and really conceives himself to be involved in serious misfortunes in having the government of Peshawur bestowed on him. The Patan zemindars of this province are so much lost to all feelings of honour and integrity, that they do not hesitate to come before Gen. Ventura in the daytime, and make most solemn asseverations of allegiance and submission, while, in the night, they barefacedly send in their partizans to rob the Seiks; and these zemindars are so full of duplicity and deceit, that notwithstanding the great vigilance and penetration of Gen. Ventura, he has been more than once imposed upon by these miscreants, in conferring khelats on them, believing them to be faithful subjects of the state.—*Ibid.*

THE SURAOGEES AND VISHNOVEES.

An official correspondence has been published concerning the dispute between the Suraogees and Vishnovees, two sects of Hindoos, in Hatrass. The former are a class of Sikhs.

Mr. E. F. Tytler, joint magistrate of Ally Ghur, writes (24th Nov. 1834) to Mr. R. B. Boddam, the commissioner of circuit at Agra, reporting his proceedings in respect to the dispute, which took place in the Hatrass bazaar, observes that the cause originated in the attempt of the Suraogees to lead out in procession the image of Parusnath, within the town, such exposure of the idol (which had been confined to the temple by order of the magistrate) being offensive to the other sect. Mr. Tytler says, that he could see no satisfactory reason for the image being thus confined to the temple, merely to gratify the caprice of a few individuals, and, therefore, passed his final order that it should be allowed egress, directing in person (conformably to previous orders of the Nizamut Adawlut) that, to prevent disturbance, the procession should be confined to the outer walls of the bazaar. This decision, however, he says, was opposed by the Vishnovees, "whose party spirit runs so high, that, while they tolerate all other Hindoo processions, and that of the Mahomedan *tazeeas*, yet are most violently opposed to the religious practices of the Suraogees. Not that their objections are reasonable; on the contrary, they are opposed to the usages of the country, and to that system of tolerance that all sects should, I conceive, accord to others of a different persuasion. In a word, the Vishnovees of Hatrass are a most troublesome set; they treat with contempt every order of this court, and are not to be satisfied unless they are allowed uncontrollable and unlimited power in the Hatrass town and bazaar." He concludes with expressing his opinion, "that some decided measures should be at once adopted to bring the several troublesome characters to a proper understanding; I have therefore summoned

them to Ally Ghur, where I shall take security for their good conduct, and the keeping the peace."

Mr. Boulderson, the officiating commissioner (Dec. 6, 1834) declares, that the orders issued by Mr. Tytler are directly opposed to those issued by the late commissioner, and as such proceedings are very irregular, he requests the officiating magistrate (Mr. Davidson) to revoke the orders issued by the acting joint magistrate, and enforce those of the commissioner.

On the 31st, however, Mr. Boulderson writes again to Mr. Davidson, stating that the question of the dispute between the sects having been again submitted, with Mr. Tytler's letter, to the Nizamut Adawlut, the orders of the late commissioner, which appear to have been issued under a misapprehension, have been altered. He adds: "Were the dispute to be decided by strict justice, the Suraogees should have full liberty to parade their idol when and where they pleased; but probably all purposes may be answered—the dispute set at rest, by allowing liberty to the extent mentioned in Mr. Tytler's letter, and I request the favour of your carrying that gentleman's views into effect."

Mr. Davidson deputed Mr. A. U. C. Plowden, the officiating magistrate, to make arrangements for securing the public peace on the day of the procession (11th February 1835), with a force of 200 sepoys, under Capt. McQueen.

Mr. Plowden, accordingly, undertook all the precautions he considered necessary and practicable, and the result is stated by him in his report, dated the day after the affair:

" Sir,—I have the honour to inform you, that yesterday being the day appointed for the image of the Suraogees to make its egress out of the town, I proceeded down at day-break to the city, with a detachment of the 45th and 32d N. I. under Capt. McQueen. On our arrival there, we barricaded the different entrances leading into the main street through which the procession had to pass, and placed parties of sepoys not only at the barricades but on the tops of the houses; precautions were also taken to barricade the street, in which the temple of the Suraogees was situated, by placing a couple of backeries with a party of the police at the top of the lane, and twenty sepoys at the bottom. The people appeared to be very peaceably inclined until the *dooly* approached, for the conveyance of the image out of the town, when they commenced throwing bricks and setting fire to the *choppers* of their own houses. Upon seeing that the people were determined to do all the mischief that laid in their power, and refusing to listen to any remonstrances, I requested Capt. Mc-Queen to act as he might think proper, when he immediately cleared the street with a party of sepoys. Whilst we were preserving peace in the main street, intimation was brought us that the temple of the Suraogees was set on fire. We lost no time in proceeding to the spot, where we succeeded in seizing four men occupied inside the temple in plundering and polluting the idol, two of whom afterwards unfortunately escaped. I have not the slightest doubt, had Dowlutt Ram and his party used their endeavours to preserve order, that no breach of the peace would have taken place."

Dowlutt Ram, here mentioned, is one of the leading men of the Vishnovees, and described by Mr. Tytler, with his confederates, as " the most troublesome class in the Ally Ghur divison."

A letter from Mr. Davidson to Mr. Boulderson, dated 14th February, enters into a fuller exposition of the affairs. He states, that the Suraogees had been induced to concede to the other party that their image should be conveyed in a *palkee* instead of a *rath*, or carriage, unattended with tom-toms, and that this arrangement appeared to satisfy both parties. When the palkee was traversing the narrow streets, towards the temple, a crowd suddenly collected, to the number of about 400, who had been concealed in their houses or compounds, who set fire to the *choppers*, whilst the military were pelted with brickbats from the roofs of the houses. The Suraogees, alarmed, dared not take their image from the temple. The deputy collector, having left the spot, a number of men, till then in concealment, let themselves down from the houses opposite to the temple, and set fire to the *chopper* which covered it; this frightened the horses of the sowars, who were guarding the upper entrance of the lane; the crowd at that end then either removed or clambered over the hackery barricades, destroyed the palkee, beat the attendant Suraogees, and entered and plundered the temple, the roof of which fell in when the rafters which supported it were burnt. No life was lost nor serious injury sustained, nor property destroyed, save what was in the temple. There was no serious affray; the crowd in the street did not attack the sepoys, nor were there above two or three individuals who appeared to have arms, though some sticks were observable. " The whole, however," he says, "was evidently a concerted plan of the opposing Vishnovee party to prevent the exit of the palkee and Suraogees' image, and the criminality of the influential men of that party is not the less, that their measures did not result in bloodshed. In further evidence of violent intention on the part of the Vishnovees, I have to state that, the night before the intended procession, the zemindars and villagers of the surrounding country, to the number of some thousands, assembled close to the town with their bullocks, intended, it is said, to be introduced into the streets to create confusion. As it appeared to me, beyond all reasonable doubt, that the leading characters among the Vishnovee party had acted throughout in direct opposition to the terms of the recognizance which I had taken from them on the 17th December, I deemed the same to be forfeited, and have accordingly called on the parties to pay into court the respective amounts, viz. 5,000 rupees each, from Dowlutt Ram, Sookbanund, Choonnyloll and Permanund. It is well known, that the wealthy men of this party had determined to go to any cost in gaining their object against the Suraogees, and I consider them justly liable to suffer the above penalty." The Suraogees succeeded in carrying out their idol on the 14th.

The opinion of the Government on the affair is conveyed in the following extract of a letter from the Secretary to the Government of Agra, dated 27th February 1835.

" It is the opinion of the Governor, in all matters in which religious prejudices are concerned, the right course is to follow established usage. The party which deviates from that, becomes the cause of any disturbance that ensues: in this view, he would have been better pleased if the local officers had dissuaded the Suraogees from attempting any innovation contrary to the known feelings of the Vishnovite inhabitants of Hattrass. Had they done so, no injustice would have been done to the Suraogees, and the Vishnovites, having no cause of complaint, would have made no opposition Instead of this, the local officers appear to have encouraged and supported the Suraogees in the performance of a ceremony, in a manner never before performed in the same place; and thus the employment of a military force became necessary to support the order which the magistrate had given."

THE TRADE OF CABUL.

The hon. the Governor-general of India in Council has been pleased to direct the following paper, describing the trade of Cabul, to be published for general information:

Kabul, the capital city of an extensive kingdom, is not only the centre of a large internal traffic, but, enjoying eminent advantages of locality, ought to possess the whole of the carrying trade between India and Turkistan. A trade has ever existed besween India and Afghanistan, the latter deriving from the former a variety of commodities foreign to the produce of its own soil, climate, and manufactures, while she has little to return beyond fruits of native growth. Afghanistan is dependant upon India for articles indispensable for the convenience of her inhabitants, and the carrying on of her few manufactures, as fine calicos, indigo, spices, drugs, &c. Of late years, the introduction of British manufactured goods, as fine calicos, muslins, chintzes, shawls, &c., has produced a new era in this trade, superseding, in great measure, the inferior importations as to quality from India, and the more expensive fabrics from Kashmir. The consumption of these manufactures at Kabul, although extensive and increasing, will from causes have a limit, but to what extent they might be transmitted to the markets of Turkistan, cannot be so easily defined. At the same time that British manufactured goods have found their way to Kabul, so have also Russian, and what is singular, even British manufactured goods may be found at Kabul which have been imported from Bokhara.

The anarchy reigning in Afghanistan for a long period, and the ambiguous political relations of the several petty governments at the present time established in it, have not been favourable to the prosecution of its commerce; yet it would appear that during the last few years the trade of Kabul has considerably increased, the custom-house of Kabul, under the Suddozie princes being farmed for only twenty-five thousand rupees per annum, and that of Ghazni for only seven thousand rupees per annum, whereas the last year (1834) the former was farmed for one lac and forty thousand rupees, and the latter for eighty thousand rupees, —while the duties levied are at the same rate: viz. a chabalek, (one in forty) or two and half per cent. ad valorem. With respect to the value of the trade of Kabul, it may be observed, that there are six points within its territories where duties on merchandize are levied: viz. Kabul, Ghazni, Bamian, Charreekar, Loghar, and Jalalabad. The transit duties at these places in 1834 were farmed as follows:

Kabul.		£.
1,40,000×40=56,00,000		466,666+
Ghazni.		
80,000×40=32,00,000		266,666+
Bamian.		
50,000×40=20,00,000	12 Rs. per £. sterling.	166,666+
Charreekar.		
10,000×40= 4,00,000		33,333+
Loghar.		
6,000×40= 2,40,000		20,000
Jalalabad.		
12,000×40= 4,80,000		40,000

2,98,000 { Total Duties.	Value Merchandize. }	993,331

This table only correctly shews the amount of benefit to the state, derived from direct duties on merchandize, as duties are levied on the same goods frequently at two places, as at Ghazni and Kabul, &c.; yet, when it is considered that the farmers of them reap, or expect to reap, a profit, and that smuggling to a very great extent prevails, while there is a constant evasion of payment of duty, through favour, power, or other circumstances, the calculation that the trade of Kabul, with her neighbours, may be of the value of one million sterling, is likely to fall short of, rather than to exceed, the truth. Of this sum, £200,000 will be the value of its trade with Turkistan.

The opening of the navigation of the Indus, and the establishment of British factories at Mithankot, cannot fail to have a salutary effect in increasing the extent and facility of commercial transactions between India and Kabul, and of inducing a much larger consumption of British manufactured goods both in Kabul and Turkistan. Perhaps no spot could have been selected for a mart on the Indus offering equal advantage with Mithankot, being at once the key to the rivers of the Panjab, and the point nearly at which the merchandize of India is at the present day transmitted to Afghanistan by the medium of the Lohani merchants. It was no trivial point gained, that, by the selection, a great portion of the extended trade will be confined to them, as the limited trade is now. Independently of the wisdom of causing no unnecessary innovation in the established usages and practices of a people, the commercial Lohani tribes may be expected to lend every assistance to measures which decrease their labours and lengthened journeys, and increase, consequently, their gains. They have long engrossed the trade between Kabul and Multan, and the monopoly was and is due to their integrity, valour, and industry. No other men could travel, even in kaflas, from Kabul to Darband. The Lohanis pass *vi et armis*, and as they pay no duties on the road, and the camels (the beasts of burthen employed) are their own property, no other traders can afford to bring or carry merchandize at so cheap a rate, and they have, therefore, no competitors, in the markets they frequent, able to undersell them. Moreover, at Kabul and Ghazni, on account of being Afghans, and in conformity to ancient right or indulgence, they pay duties on a lower scale than other individuals. But the Lohanis, a patient and persevering class of men, accustomed to a regular routine of trade, are, from their habits, little likely to embark in any new speculations, unless encouraged and invited to do so. Their caution, and, perhaps, apathy, cause them to form their investments of such goods as they know will sell, and by no means of such as may sell—seeming to prefer a certain, but small profit, to a larger, but doubtful one. These reasons, I apprehend, account for the non-appearance of very many articles of British and Indian produce and manufactures in the Kabul market, while many articles are found there brought from Russia, *viá* Bokhara, which might be procured better in quality, and cheaper in price, from India.

In proportion to the extent and variety in the assortment of goods at Mithankot, will of course be the facility of introducing and disposing of them. At Qandahar, whose commerce is very short of that of Kabul, but whose merchants generally proceed to Bombay, where there is no want of allurement to purchase from deficiency in the abundance, variety, and display, of goods, there are an infinity of articles to be found, which are in vain sought for at Kabul. Of the commodities of India, and manufactures of Great Britain, which would find sale in Afghanistan and Turkistan, the former are well known, and would remain as at present, the demand being only increased, as spices, indigo, muslin, fine sugar, drugs, &c., were diminished in price by the additional facilities which would be given to commerce, but of the latter, a great variety of new articles might be introduced. Chintzes, fine calicoes, muslins, shawls, &c., of British manufacture, have now become fashionable, and investments of broad cloth, velvet, paper, cutlery, China ware, gold and silver lace, gold thread, buttons, needles, sewing silks, and cotton thread; iron bars, copper, tin, brass, and quicksilver, iron and steel wire, looking glasses, with a multitude of various little articles, conducive to comfort and convenience, would be readily disposed of. It is singular, that not a sheet of English manufactured writing-paper can be found in the bazaar of Kabul, while Russian foolscap, of coarse inferior quality, abounds, and is generally employed in the public departments.

It may not be improper to enumerate some of the articles which form the bulk of the exports from Russia to Bokhara, specifying such thereof as find their way to Kabul.

Broad cloth re-exported to Kabul in large quantities.
Fine linens and calicoes.
Silk goods re-exported to Kabul in large quantities.
Velvets, ditto, ditto, ditto.
Chintzes, rarely to Kabul.
Sewing thread and Silk.
Gold and silver lace re-exported to Kabul.
Gold and silver thread re-exported to Kabul.
Needles, re-exported to Kabul.
Steel and Copper wire re-exported to Kabul.
Leather of Bulgar re-exported to Kabul.
Paper re-exported to Kabul.
China-ware rarely to Kabul.
Glass-ware.
Cutlery.

Loaf sugar, very rarely.
Iron in bars.
Steel in bars.
Tin in plates.
Copper in plates, re-exported to Kabul.
Brass re-exported to Kabul.
Quicksilver re-exported to Kabul.
Cochineal re-exported to Kabul.
Tea re-exported to Kabul.
Honey.
Wax, white and yellow.

In glancing over this imperfect list, it will be obvious, that many of the articles of Russian manufacture, most largely imported to Kabul *viá* Bokhara, ought to be superseded by similar ones from Bombay. From Orenburg, the point whence traffic between Russia and Bokhara is principally conducted, there are sixty-two camel or kafla marches, and from Bokhara to Kabul, thirty-five camel or kafla marches, being a total of ninety-seven camel or kafla marches, independent of halts. In the distance travelled, duties are levied at Khiva, Bokhara, Balkh, Muzzar, Khulam Hybuk, Qunduz, Kahmerd, Sohghan, Bamian and Kabul. That the supplies from Bombay to Kabul have been hitherto inadequate for the wants of the market, is, in a great measure, owing to the sluggishness of the Afghan merchants; that they will cease to be so, may be hoped from the opening of the navigation of the Indus, and the conversion of Mithankot into a mart, which will bid fair to become a second Bombay for the merchants of these countries.

Broad cloth, largely imported from Bokhara, is a regular article of consumption at Kabul, being used for the chupkuns, kabahs, sinabunds, &c. of the opulent, as coverings to the holster-pipes of the military, and as jackets for the disciplined troops. Dark colours are generally preferred, but blue, scarlet, and drab, are also in vogue, and fine and coarse qualities are alike saleable.

In fine linens and calicoes, the Russian fabrics are unable to contend with British manufactures at Kabul, either in quality or price, and some of the latter even find their way to Bokhara. Russian chintzes are esteemed more durable than British, as being of coarser texture, but with less elegant or fast colours, and although occasionally brought to Kabul, afford no profit to induce further speculations.

Silk goods, which are brought to Kabul from Bokhara, of Russian manufacture, and in large quantities, would appear to have every chance of being superseded by better and cheaper importations from Mithankot or even Bombay, where certainly the fabrics of Bengal and China, if not England, must be abundant. Amongst a variety of modes in which silk goods are consumed at Kabul, permanent ones are in the under garments of both male and female inhabitants, who can afford it. The colours most prized, are red, blue, and yellow. Silk handkerchiefs of various colours, and even black ones, would probably meet a ready sale, as would some articles of silk hosiery, as socks, and even stockings. Silk gloves, lace, ribbons, &c. might not be expected to sell, there being no use or idea of them. Kabul has its own silk manufactures, introduced some twenty-five years since, by artizans from Harat, under the patronage of Shah Mahmud. At present, there are eighty-eight looms in employment, each of which pays an annual tax to the state of twenty-three rupees. The articles manufactured are plain silks, called kanavaiz, red, yellow, and purple. Durahee, of slighter texture, less width, and of the same colours. Suja khannee, of large and small width, a red ground, with perpendicular white lines. Dushmals or handkerchiefs, black and red, with white spots, bound by females around their heads, and loonghees hummama, or for the bath. Raw and thrown silks are imported from Bokhara, Qandahar, and Harat, and raw silk is procured from Tauhow, the districts of the Sufaid Koh, Koh Daman, and the neighbourhood of Kabul: the thrown silk of Harat is preferred to that of Bokhara, and the latter to that of Qandahar, while silk thrown at Kabul, from native produce, is preferred to all of them.

Velvets and satins, of Russian manufacture, are brought from Bokhara to Kabul, where there is a small, but regular, consumption : velvets being employed sometimes for kabahs, and to cover saddles, &c. This year, the battalion soldiers were furnished with caps of velvet, all of Russian fabric. For kabans, black velvet is most in request, but red and green are also used. Satins are employed sometimes to form articles of dress, most frequently as facings and trimmings.

Sewing threads and silks, I should suppose, would be as saleable at Kabul as at Bokhara, but I have never before observed any of European manufacture here. They are brought from Bombay to Hydarabad, and may be seen in the shops there. Gold and silver lace is brought from Bokhara to Kabul, of Russian manufacture, in large quantities ; they are also brought from India, both of Indian and British manufacture. The quantity brought from Bokhara exceeds that brought from India.

Steel and copper wire, very largely exported from Russia to Bokhara, is introduced at Kabul. I am not aware of the uses or extent of consumption of these articles, but the former, I believe, is used for musical instruments. Leather, churm of Bulgar, is brought from Bokhara to Kabul, of Russian preparation, and in large quantities, being consumed in the construction of military and riding-coats, horse furniture, and mattarrahs or flaskets,

for holding water, which every horseman considers a necessary part of his equipments. Leather is also largely prepared at Kabul, and hides are imported from Bajore, Peshawr, &c. Paper, of Russian fabric, is brought from Bokhara to Kabul in very large quantities, and is much in demand. It is of foolscap size, and of stout inferior quality, and both white and blue in colour, as well as both glazed and unglazed. The blue glazed paper is preferred, ung'azed paper being even submitted to the operation of glazing at Kabul. Quantities of Russian paper, both glazed and unglazed, are annually exported from Kabul to Qandahar ; at the latter place is also found ordinary white foolscap (perhaps brought from Bombay), but which, from the watermarks, would appear to be of Portuguese fabric ; the same article is also plentiful at Hydarabad, and may, perhaps, be manufactured at Daman. Paper for the Kabul market should be stout, to allow facility of erasure, and on this account, and with reference to the nature of the ink employed, glazed paper is most prized, which is prepared by saturating the unglazed fabric in a composition of starch, and, subsequently, polishing it. No duty is paid on paper at Kabul.

China-ware is sometimes exported from Bokhara to Kabul, but generally of ordinary Chinese fabric. It is also in a certain demand, which is likely to increase from the growing habit of tea-drinking, &c. Articles of British china-ware are occasionally seen, but they have been brought (probably from Bombay) rather as presents than as objects for sale. In the same manner, tea-trays and other conveniences are found. China-ware, stoneware, and even the superior kinds of earthen-ware, would no doubt, find a sale at Kabul, if the charges on their transmission from Bombay or Mithankot would allow of the speculation ; but the articles should be of a solid nature, and fitted for the uses of the purchasers, as plates, dishes, basins, bowls, tea-pots, tea cups, jugs, &c. China-ware, as well as being in quest for use, is employed for ornament and display, every room in a respectable house having its shelves furnished with sets of basins, bowls, &c. &c , and these are generally of the coarse fabric of Kabul ; China-ware being scarce, and too high in price. The earthen-ware of Kabul manufacture is very indifferent, although the country abounds with excellent materials.

Glass-ware, exported from Russia to Bokhara, is not brought to Kabul for sale, nor is any of British manufacture to be found, although many articles, applicable to ordinary and useful purposes, would probably sell. To Hydarabad, imports from Bombay are in a greater or less degree made, and glass decanters, with drinking-glasses, are common in the shops. During the last five or six years, attempts have been made, generally by Persians, to establish a glass-manufactory at Kabul, but the success has not been complete in a profitable point of view. The articles fabricated are bottles, drinking-glasses, &c. ; the glass made is slight, and not very clear, but, upon the whole, of tolerable quality.

Cutlery, of Russian manufacture, exported to Bokhara, is not brought to Kabul, nor has English cutlery ever been a subject of trade there. Hydarabad, and also Qandahar, derive many articles of cutlery from Bombay, as razors, scissors, clasp-knives, &c., which would, no doubt, as readily sell at Kabul. These are manufactured at Kabul of inferior kinds and of more esteemed quality at Chahar Bagh or Lughman, but they are still indifferent articles.

Loaf sugar, largely imported from Rustia to Bokhara, is rarely brought to Kabul, where are manufactures of a coarse article prepared from the finer raw sugars imported from India, from which also sugar-candies are prepared. In the districts west of Jalalabad, as Chahar Bagh and Balla Bagh, the sugar-cane is extensively cultivated, and the products in sugar and goor to a large amount are disposed of at Kabul; but whether from the circumstances of soil, climate, cultivation, or preparation (more probably the latter) both the cane and its produce are inferior articles. Sugars also find their way to Kabul from Peshawr, where the plant thrives better, or is cultivated with more attention, and the products consequently are of a richer and finer grain than those of Jalalabad. The sugars of India are exported from Kabul to Bokhara to a limited extent, but no British loaf-sugar has ever arrived at Kabul, and the experiment remains untried whether it might be profitably carried to Bokhara, or be able to compete with that of Russian manufacture at that city, where, from the universal habit of tea-drinking, it is in general demand and consumption. The chances are in its favour ; but certainly, were the communications such as they might and ought to be, between India and Kabul and Turkistan, the latter, or at least her provinces south of the Oxus, ought not to be dependent for saccharine products on Russia.

Iron in bars, largely exported from Russia to Bokhara, does not find its way to Kabul, nor does iron of British produce, although exported from Bombay to Kalát of Bilochistan and Qandahar. Kabul derives its iron from the mines of Bajore, and re-exports it to Turkistan, generally in the form of horse-shoes, large quantities of which are annually sent over

the Hindu Kosh mountains from Charreekar of Kohistan. Iron is not abundant at Kabul, and high-priced, one and a half seer of unwrought iron selling for the current rupee, and for the same sum half the quantity (three charruks) of wrought iron.

Steel of Russian fabric exported to Bokhara is not introduced at Kabul, which, independently of her own manufactures, derives supplies of Indian steel *viá* Peshawr and Multan, and British steel from Bombay *viá* Qandahar.

Tin plates or white iron is largely brought to Bokhara from Russia, but not re-exported thence to Kabul. This article is exported from Bombay to Qandahar, where there are several dokans or shops of whitesmiths.

Copper in plates and bars, very extensively exported from Russia to Bokhara, is also largely exported from the latter place to Kabul, where there is a constant and important consumption of it, for the ordinary household utensils of the inhabitants, for the copper coinage of the government, and for other various purposes. Copper from Bombay is largely introduced into Sindh, Bilochistan, and more to Qandahar. Whether it might be profitably brought to Kabul will be best determined by the prices obtained for it there. New unwrought copper is retailed for eight rupees the seer Kabul, wrought or fashioned into vessels eleven rupees Kabum, broken copper purchased by the mint at seven rupees the seer. Notwithstanding the existence of copper in many of the mountains of Afghanistan and Bilochistan, there is not a single mine worked in them, or indeed in any region between the Indus and the Euphrates, the Persians deriving their copper *viá* Erzerum from Asia Minor, the Uzbeks, and partially the Afghans from Russia, while Qandahar and the maritime provinces of Sindh and Bilochistan are supplied from Bombay.

Brass, exported from Russia to Bokhara, is sparingly introduced into Kabul, where there is a limited but constant consumption of it in the ornaments of horse furniture, military arms and equipments, bells for the necks of camels, pestles, mortars, &c., &c.; occasionally for the casting of guns. Brass utensils are little used by Mohammadans, but largely by Hindus. and these are brought prepared to Kabul from the Panjab.

Quicksilver is exported from Russia to Bokhara, and thence to Kabul, and is employed to plate looking-glasses, in medicines, &c.; its consumption is but limited, and it is also brought from India.

Cochineal, exported from Russia to Bokhara, is brought thence to Kabul, where its consumption is by the silk-dyers. It sells for seventy rupees Kahum the maund Tabrizre, or two and a-half charruks of Kabul.

Tea is exported largely from Russia to Bokhara, of a kind called there "kooshbooee;" this is rarely brought to Kabul, but large quantities of ordinary kinds of black and green tea are brought there from Bokhara, which seem to be imported from China *viá* Kokan and Yargand. A superior kind of tea called "Bankah" is sometimes to be procured at Kabul, but not as an article for sale. The consumption of tea will, in the course of time, be very considerable at Kabul, the habit of drinking it being a growing one. At Qandahar it does not prevail, and tea. I believe, is seldom or ever carried there for sale. As a beverage, it is also nearly unknown in Bilochistan and Sindh. It is considered cheap at Kabul at six rupees the charruk or one-fourth of a seer.

Honey and wax, exported largely from Russia to Bokhara, are not introduced to Kabul, which is plentifully supplied with excellent qualities of these articles from its native hills, as those of Bungush, Khonur, and the Sufaid Koh range.

The trade between Russia and Bokhara yields to the government of the latter a yearly revenue of 40,000 tillahs, collected from the kafias passing to and fro. As khiraj or duty is levied at the rate of two and a-half per cent. *ad valorem*, the whole amount of the trade will not be less than 1,600,000 tillahs, or about 12,500,000 rupees, a large excess to the amount of trade between Kabul and Bokhara, which would seem to be about 2,500,000 rupees.

The merchants of Kabul have many of them commercial transactions with Russia itself, and their agents or gomashtahs are resident at Orenberg and Astracan, while their intercourse with India seems to exist rather from necessity than choice. The reason for the traffic of Kabul inclining towards Russia for articles of European fabric may perhaps be discovered in the remoteness from it of any great mart for British manufactures ; Bombay, until lately the nearest, being to be reached by sea, if *viá* Karáchi Bunder, or through countries unknown even by name here, if by a land route from Hyderabad. Sea voyages are generally much dreaded, and a journey to Bombay is seldom performed by an inhabitant of Kabul, unless as a consequence of one of the last and most desperate acts of his life, the pilgrimage to Mecca. It may also in part be ascribed to the comparative facility and safety of the communications between Kabul and Bokhara, which, excepting one or two points, are tolerably secure, while the rulers of the intermediate regions are content to levy moderate badj or duty upon merchandize, the governments of Bokhara being in this respect singularly

lenient and liberal. The routes between Kabul and India are, with the exception of the dreary and desolate one of the Gomul, impracticable to any kafia of whatever strength ; and this can only be travelled by the Lohanis, who are soldiers as well as merchants. But these being also a pastoral community, for the convenience of their flocks, make but one visit to India during the year, and the route is closed, except at the periods of their passage and return. The Lohani, born and nurtured in the wilderness, and inured from infancy to hardship and danger, will encounter from custom the difficulties of the Gomul route ; but the merchant of Kabul shrinks from them, and the route is likely ever to be monopolized by the Lohanis, and never to become a general one for the merchants of Kabul. The intercourse between Kabul and India would be exceedingly promoted by opening the anciently existing high road from Kabul to Multan, &c. *viá* Bungush and Bannu. This route is very considerably shorter, leads chiefly through, a level fertile, and populous country, is practicable at all seasons of the year, and no doubt could be rendered safe were the governments on the Indus and of Kabul to co-operate.

The traders of Russia appear very accurately to study the wants and convenience of the people with whom they traffic, and to adapt their exports accordingly. The last year (1834), a species of Russian chintz was brought as an experiment from Bokhara to Kabul. It was of an extraordinary breadth and of a novel pattern, and was sold for three rupees the yard. In like manner was brought nankah, or linen stamped with chintz patterns ; and the readiness with which these articles were disposed of, will probably induce larger exports. The last article is one calculated to supplant the present large importations of British chintzes or stamped calicoes. The advantage of superior machinery enabled the skilful and enterprising artisans of Great-Britain to effect a memorable revolution in the commerce of Asia, and their white cottons and printed calicoes have nearly driven from its markets the humbler manufactures of India. Slight cotton fabrics are, of course, eminently calculated for so sultry a climate as that of India, but less so perhaps for one so variable in temperature as that of Afghanistan. Its inhabitants, while from necessity they clothe themselves in calicoes, will naturally prefer the better fabrics of Britain ; but if they were offered linens of equally fine web and beauty of printed patterns, there can be no doubt which would be selected. It is not improbable but that, sooner or later, manufactures of flax and hemp will in some measure supersede those of cotton for general use in Afghanistan.

I shall close these remarks, which principally turn on the trade between Russia and Kabul, *viâ* Bokhara, by observing that the Russian merchants so nicely study the wants and even disposition of the people with whom they traffic, that multitudes of the inhabitants of Kabul are to be seen with chupans of nankah on their backs, actually got up and sewn at Orenberg, while all the shops in the city may be searched in vain for a single button of British or indeed any other manufacture, when one, two, three, or more, are required for the dress of every individual; as substitutes for which, they are compelled to use thread simply twisted into a spherical shape.

ZOOLOGY OF ASSAM.

Compared with those of most other jungly countries, there is scarcely any peculiarity in the animals of Assam. Wild elephants are plentiful, and move in large herds. Great numbers are caught every year, and transported to other countries; but the speculation is very precarious, as many of them die before they are domesticated. A few are shot in their wild state, merely for their ivory. They are frequently very dangerous, and many of the natives are annually killed by them. The rhinoceros inhabits the densest and most retired parts of the country. The young ones are a good deal looked after, but so difficult to be found, that a party with two or three elephants don't succeed in catching above one or two in a season, and these, when caught, frequently die in the nursing. The mode of taking them is first to shoot the mother, and then the calf is easily secured. Frequently the mother, in her dying agonies, lays hold of her young one with her teeth, and lacerates it so severely, that it dies of its wounds. In those books of natural history, of which I am in possession, the *rhinoceros indicus* is described as having no canine teeth; but on an inspection of a skull, a few days ago, I found two very stout canines, one on each side of the two incisors of the lower jaw. The upper jaw was so incomplete, that I could determine nothing respecting their existence in it. The old rhinoceroses are frequently killed for the sake of their horns alone, to which the natives attach a great deal of sanctity; so much so, that the general belief is, that there is no more certain way of insuring a place in the celestial regions, than to be tossed to death on the horn of a rhinoceros. These horns are as hard as bone, very stout and broad at the base, and seldom longer than eight or ten inches. They have a slight curvature towards the forehead, and in colour are as black as the buffalo's. The horn is not a process of the bone of the nose, but united to it by a concave surface, so as to

admit of being detached by maceration, or by a severe blow. It has no pith, but the centre is a little more cellular than the rest. Considering the wild and sequestered habit of these animals, it is surprising how very easily they are tamed. With a little training, a young one, a few months after being caught, may be turned loose to feed, and be ridden by children. They contract a strong affection for their keeper, and come at his call, and follow his steps wherever he goes.

Tigers, leopards, and bears, are numerous, but though they occasionally carry off a bullock, accidents to human life are rare. There is a reward of six rupees a-head allowed by government for their destruction; certain castes adopt this as their profession, and make a good livelihood by it. They destroy them by means of poisoned arrows. Having found out a recently frequented track, they fix a strong bamboo bow (a modification of the cross bow) horizontally, upon three forked sticks, driven firmly into the ground, and just so high as to be on a level with the tiger's shoulder. The bow being bent, and the poisoned arrow fixed, a string connected with the trigger is carried across the path in the same direction with the arrow, and secured to a peg. The tiger in passing along, comes in contact with this string, the bow is instantly let off, and the arrow is lodged in his breast. So very active is this poison that the animal, though not otherwise mortally wounded, is commonly dead within one hundred yards of the place where he was struck.

Wild buffaloes abound in all parts of Assam. They are not much sought for unless by some classes for eating. They are too fierce and formidable to be robbed of their young with impunity; and as they are seldom found solitary like the rhinoceros, the calves could not be secured even at the expense of the parent's life. It is the common practice to breed from the wild buffalos; no males are kept by the feeders: the tame herd is driven towards the jungle, where they are joined by the wild males, who continue in the flock during the season.

Of all the animals that roam the forest, not even excepting poisonous serpents and beasts of prey, the buffalo is the most formidable, and the most to be dreaded when defenceless; and more inhabitants are destroyed by his gore than by all other animals put together. Scarcely a month passes, without some person being attacked in this district, and gored to death. A man was lately brought in to me, with the whole of his stomach protruding through a small wound in the epigastric region. The horn had entered the stomach, and a small hole existed, like the mouth of a purse, into which I could introduce my finger. He had two other wounds in his body, both of which seemed mere scratches; but one of them entered the thorax, and the other the abdomen. He had been gored the day before I saw him, and been conveyed from a distance on a hurdle; but with all my care, he died next morning. The only thing remarkable in this case was his living so long with wounds in such vital parts.—*India Jour. Med. Science for Nov.*

Madras.

MISCELLANEOUS.

THE GOVERNOR.

The Madras papers inform us that Sir Frederick Adam left that presidency for the Nilgherries, on the 25th ult. A proclamation in the *Fort St. George Gazette*, issued upon the occasion announces, that "the administration at the presidency will, in his absence, be conducted by the remaining members of the government, and that all official correspondence is to be carried on as usual, and the resolutions of the government will continue to be passed in the name of the Governor in Council." We are particular in referring to this notice, as there has been some discussion, both at Bombay and Madras, about the propriety, and even about the legality, of a governor absenting himself from the seat of his government for purposes other than the public service, and continuing to perform the functions, and draw the salary of his office, during such absence. Undoubtedly, the prolonged residence of a governor at any place but the seat of the public offices, must be attended with so much inconvenience, that it could not have been the intention of the British legislature to allow the comfort of the individual, rather than the *salus populi* to be the *suprema lex* in this case; and whether authorised or not by the strict letter of the act, we should conceive that the controlling authorities at home would not fail to put their *veto* upon such discretionary absences, if often repeated, although they could not desire altogether to deny their governors the opportunity of visiting the hills for the renovation of their health, when enfeebled by the labours of council at a sultry presidency. But unless the word "presidency" be interpreted in its most restricted sense, we do not find in the act any such prohibition as some writers have assumed, much less any stipulation that a portion of the salary shall be forfeited during the governor's absence. We heard of a scheme some time ago to remove the seat of government from Bombay to Poonah, and Lord William Bentinck, when he planned his first visit to Simlah, actually made arrangements for conducting the government of the Bengal provinces temporarily at that place. In-

deed, in a great measure, he did conduct it there. His lordship has since pronounced judgment against the existing seats of government of all the presidencies, and we may therefore expect, if he obtain, and for any time hold, the office of President of the Board of Control, that some Utopian scheme will be suggested by that board to turn things upside down in this matter, and give us all those *benefits* of change,—change for itself,—which, to some few tastes, produces a pleasing excitement, while the admiring multitude are apt to grumble at the trouble of moving, when they find themselves comfortable where they are, and see no particular advantages for them in the land of promise.—*Cal. Cour., Dec. 7.*

CONVERSION OF A BRAMIN.

Last Sunday morning, at the Wesleyan Chapel, a bramin was baptized by the Rev. Robert Carver, in the presence of many ladies and gentlemen and other Hindoos; a rare circumstance indeed. The conversion of this bramin was through the instrumentality of a catechist of the Wesleyan Society. The bramin and three others of his own creed set out from a village in Travancore, called Trevandrum, with a view of making a pilgrimage to Cashee (Benares). No sooner had they left Travancore and commenced their journey than the catechist came in their way, preaching and conversing with the travellers. These men out of curiosity lent their ears to the sayings of the catechist, who, after the conversation was over, put into their hands a part of the Gospel, and left them to make what good they could with it. After they journeyed for three or four days together, one of them became ill and died. On this catastrophe, they resolved with greater diligence to proceed to the place of their pilgrimage, and one manifested an anxious desire to know the Christian religion, and he therefore persuaded the other two to read the book he had with him; but they abused him for his folly, and went their own way. The man, who arrived at Madras a few months ago, put himself under the instructions of Mr. Carver, and afterwards hesitated not to become a Christian, and was baptized. This is the whole statement of his conversion. We are indeed, astonished at this brahmin's conduct, and to find that in the space of a few months he should have appreciated the Christian religion more than his own.—*Carnatic Chron., Dec. 2.*

COMPUNCTIOUS VISITINGS.

The *Fort St. George Gazette* contains the following official announcement:

" *Fort St. George, 11th December* 1835. —The accountant General has received a communication, of which the following is a copy : ' Sir, The accompanying fifteen bank notes, amounting to 4,500 rupees, are sent to be placed to the credit of the Government by one who is thankful for the means of making restitution.' "

In the *Gazette* of the 19th is another similar announcement of the receipt of 10,000 rupees.

SUICIDE AMONGST NATIVES.

A Hindu correspondent of the *Courier*, with reference to the frequency of suicides by natives, makes the following remarks :

" In Madras, there are, I doubt not, lacs of souls, say half Christians and half heathens, and, ever since the Coroner's Department was established, which perhaps now is more than forty years, was it ever heard that a Christian, East-Indian, or Native, ever took away his own life wilfully ;* that life which God gave and which he alone has a right to take away ? whereas, on the contrary, the Hindoos (heathens), for every trivial thing, make away with their lives, either by drowning in a tank or well, by hanging, or cutting their throats, or by poisoning themselves, &c. I would wish any of my Hindoo brethren to tell me how comes this difference, that Hindoos are for every trivial thing ready to perpetrate self-murder, and that Christians, Native, or East-Indians, for worse offence, shrink from such a crime. I would, therefore, very respectfully, and with great submission, recommend to the legislative council and to our present much esteemed Governor-general, Sir C. Metcalf, to enact a law to the effect following : " That, from and after this date, all persons committing suicide, either by hanging, drowning, or otherwise, and it be proved on evidence that the crime was wilful—that the bodies of such person be not given over to the family or relations of the deceased, but that the coroner or magistrates shall, in all such cases, at the expense of government, send such carcasses to the nearest jungle, there to be thrown for a prey to the wild beasts of the forest, and that the property of such deceased persons, either of land or otherwise, shall be confiscated for the use of the crown."

SIR RALPH PALMER.

The Literary Society gave a dinner, on the 9th December, to their retiring president, Sir Ralph Palmer ; the Hon. Mr. Oliver in the chair.

After dinner, the Chairman proposed the health of Sir Ralph, highly eulogizing his mildness, affability, and social virtues.

* Surely the writer was not ignorant of a remarkable instance of suicide by an European holding a judicial appointment.

Sir Ralph Palmer expressed his regret at parting with a society from which he had received so much kindness ; but could not deny that this regret was counterbalanced by the hope and pleasure of returning to the land of his birth, where he might superintend in retirement the education of his children. He had always looked to the bright side of life's picture, and his experience had borne him out in so doing. He had for many years enjoyed happiness here, and was now returning with every prospect of happiness to his own family, in whose circle death had not made a single vacancy since his departure from England. Sir Ralph mentioned the choice of his successor as the most prudent that could have been made. He reprobated the scandal vented by certain periodicals against the Literary Society ; and concluded by praising the secretary, Mr. Morris, for his zeal, talents, and diligence.

RIGHT AND LEFT HAND CASTES.

M. Navariah Bramin writes thus to the *Standard :* " It has often struck me, and many respectable members of the Hindoo class have also suggested to me, the desirableness of putting an end to one of the most disgusting evils—the distinction of the *right hand and left hand castes*, —which has for a long series of years disturbed the tranquillity and good understanding of the whole Hindoo community. If there is any tangible evidence that this division has its existence coëval with the creation of the world, or when the *vadums*, &c. were written, it would be far from my intention to suggest its abolition ; but, from history and unquestionable tradition (an outline of which I have drawn in the shape of a memorandum, which is herewith sent), the origin is traced to discontented persons ; and I am therefore, particularly solicitous that it should receive a death-blow by one concordant voice from the whole Hindoo population. To effect this most devoutly to-be-wished-for consummation, I beg to propose that a meeting be called for at the Hindoo Literary Society, or elsewhere, to consider upon the matter, so as to take the most effectual step to rend it asunder."

AFFAIR OF HONOUR.

A meeting took place on the 29th November between Capt. J. Smith, of the 2d Light Cav., and Capt. C. Taylor, of the artillery, arising out of a correspondence in the newspapers. A letter bearing Capt. T.'s signature having appeared in the *Madras Times*, which Capt. S. considered to couple his name with dishonourable proceedings, sent a friend to demand an apology, or a meeting.

Capt. T. offered to express regret if Capt. S. would disavow the authorship of certain letters, signed "Manly Safeguard," making attacks upon Capt. Fryer, with reference to his recent appointment, which he considered wanton and dishonourable. Lieut. Thomson, the friend of Capt S., considered that this demand was, under circumstances, out of the question. Mr. Grant then tendered from Capt. Taylor the following :—"Although Capt. Taylor still retains his opinion, as expressed in the letter in question, of the person who wrote that under the signature of ' Manly Safeguard,' and considers all the epithets used to that person most justly applied ; yet, with the advice of his friend, he is willing to admit that he was not justified in coupling Capt. Smith's name with the dishonourable and unmanly conduct which he reprobates ; with this admission, Capt. Taylor does not hesitate to express regret at having so used Capt. Smith's name." This was refused by Lieut. Thomson as insufficient, and Mr. Grant was informed that nothing short of an apology, without reference to the letter of " Manly Safeguard," could possibly be received. Capt. Taylor having refused to make any apology, the parties met ; when, after an exchange of shots (Capt. Taylor's pistol missing fire), the seconds considered the shot rendered Capt. Taylor's expression of regret (again repeated), *but without allusion* to the letter signed " Manly Safeguard," sufficient without an apology, and the parties shook hands.

CAPT. RICHARDSON.

We learn from the *Madras Times*, that there is a prospect of Capt. Richardson being restored to the appointment of which he was lately deprived. An order to that effect would, we feel persuaded, give much satisfaction ; but, much as we might feel gratified with seeing such an order in the official gazette, we incline to think Capt. R. is entitled to something more if to any consideration at all ; his conduct has been represented as disgraceful, at least that we infer from the letter which led to his removal being designated " a misrepresentation of a digraceful nature," and, in our humble opinion, a court-martial only is competent to remove or confirm the reproach that epithet conveys.—*Cour., Dec.* 10.

THE BISHOP OF CALCUTTA.

A private letter from Cochin of the 25th inst., states that the bishop of Calcutta had been indisposed the day before, in consequence of eight hours' exposure to the sun in boats and palunquins, going to visit the Syrian churches in the vicinity of Timpootra, the residence of the Cochin rajah. The *Hatrass* sailed on the 24th

for Choughaut, for which place the bishop's party were about to embark, proceeding by Backwater, on the afternoon of the 25th. There was full service morning and evening on the 24th, when about fifty persons were confirmed. We are happy to be able to add, from the same source, that his lordship had quite recovered on the morning of the 25th.—*Conservative, Nov.* 28.

THE MINT.

We understand that those who are likely to be best informed on the subject, confidently anticipate that the Madras Mint will be speedily re-established. It appears that a very considerable rise in the value of the current coin has already taken place in the bazaars ; and as this has occurred before any scarcity, strictly so speaking, could have been felt, we are not surprised that government should at length begin to doubt whether the change will not have a very prejudicial effect on the revenues of the country. That government, for the probable saving of a few thousand rupees only annually, should have incurred even the risk of injuriously affecting the commercial interests of Madras, to say nothing of prejudicing their own interests, is hardly to be believed. We trust, however, that they will endeavour to repair the injury which they have already inflicted as speedily as possible; and verify the old proverb, " better late than never."—*Mad. Gaz., Dec.* 12.

THE COORG PRIZE MONEY.

Accounts have been received of the warrant for the distribution of the Coorg prize-money having been signed on the 22d of June.—Sir P. Lindsay receives 1-16th of the whole amount, and the other officers share as follows :—

Colonels	Rs. 25,000	each.
Lieut. Colonels	„ 15,000	do.
Majors	„ 10,000	do.
Captains	„ 5,000	do.
Subalterns	„ 2,500	do.

The distribution will take place almost immediately.— *Cour., Nov.* 12.

CASE OF SOOBROYAH MOODELLY.

Would we could say there is a prospect of Soobroyah's trial being speedily brought to a close ; but there are frequent adjournings of the court, arising out of difficulties and sickness of members. On the court opening, on the 17th inst., a certificate of ill-health from the deputy judge-advocate-general was read, which set forth that he would not be able to resume his duties for some time, and in consequence, the court was closed till further orders. This is the third or fourth time the court has been adjourned since our last account of its proceedings, while Soobroyah continues all the time under confinement, and may so continue, if the

(E)

form of trial which has been adopted is persevered in, until he shall be worried out of life—when there are other courts by which he could be tried, and, if found guilty, be as effectually punished, as by a court-martial, and without the delay which attends the present course.—*Mad. Cour.*, Dec. 21.

THE GOOMSUR RAJAH.

The following is an account of operations in the Goomsur country.

Col. Hodgson's field force advanced into the Goomsur zemindary on the 3d November, and took possession of the town, which was deserted. Ensign Stuart, who was sent to take possession, by a judicious movement, with a small party of his men, secured the zemindar's dewan. The force was at Goomsur on the 4th, but could not move, owing to the weather, until the 8th, when it proceeded towards Coladah, a place reputed to be strong by nature and art. Major Low was detached with four companies of the 8th to take possession, as it was deserted. Leaving a company under Ensign Yates, to keep the place and protect the houses, the colonel advanced, on the 12th, towards Dugerprasoud, some twenty or thirty miles further in the hills, the last tenable position of the rajah's to the westward, and on the ground of encampment on this day, he was fired upon by matchlock-men from the jungle contiguous to the camp. A party of the 21st, under Capt. Butler, drove them away, without loss. The rajah having, by this act of aggression, forfeited all claim to further indulgence, he was declared a rebel, and martial law was proclaimed in the zemindary.—*Cour.*, Dec. 3.

Col. Hodgson returned from his pursuit of the rajah on the 18th, to the neighbourhood of Goomsur, and is now encamped in an open plain, at Nougaum : he was much annoyed by the fire of the rebels on both days' march, and had five more men wounded. On passing Coladah, he left a detachment to occupy it, under Lieut. Taynton of the 8th, who set to work to destroy the defences; the enemy did not allow him to do his work quietly, but kept up an incessant fire, which did not, however, do much execution. Taynton succeeded in bringing a howitzer to bear upon a party collected behind a bamboo clump—several of the enemy were killed on this occasion, and in the course of the day, and it has had the effect of keeping these gentry at a more respectful distance. The place was afterwards evacuated, for the inhabitants to return.—*Ibid.*, Dec. 7.

It is stated that the rajah of Goomsur has fled to the Nagpore territories, and that his chief-men have come into the English camp.—*Mad. Gaz.*, Dec. 12.

General Taylor has applied for reinforcements. It is also stated that the Hon. Mr. Russell is about to be again deputed as special commissioner to the Northern Circars.

Bombay.

SLAVE-TRADING IN KATTYWAR.

Some time ago we gave insertion to a letter, which alluded to the fact of slaves being an article of extensive traffic in the Kattywar country, and we have now been favoured with some particulars which go to prove the assertion, and the further fact of the matter having not escaped the notice of the late political agent in that country.

It would appear that, so late as the last monsoon, instructions had been given by the authority then at Rajcote to an officer stationed at Porebunder, to turn his attention particularly to the conduct of the Porebunder authorities with regard to the traffic in slaves, as there were reasons for suspecting that a great many of those poor wretches, from Africa, the Red Sea, and Persian Gulf, had been or were about to be landed at that port for the purpose of sale.—The rana of Porebunder and his durbar had some time before entered into an engagement with the British authorities, to use every exertion for the suppression of the trade in slaves ; but, as much reliance could not be placed in a promise which was made more from compulsion than choice, it was considered necessary to keep a vigilant eye over their conduct. Perhaps, indeed, the temptations to a violation of their engagements were such as would soften the scruples of greater casuists than they profess to be. Dependant as they are in a great measure on the little trade to and from the port of Porebunder, their exchequer was very likely to suffer a diminution from any check or embargo they might attempt to place on the vessels entering the harbour, and there is no doubt but that any thing like a rigid search, or seizure on finding, would have frightened the shippers, and induced them to find a port elsewhere for the landing and sale of their sooty cargo. Be this as it may, however, it was well known that several slaves had been purchased for the use of the ranee, and were in her employment, subsequent to the date of the engagement which had been entered into for the suppression of the trade.—The officer at Porebunder, with a zeal which was very creditable to him, on receipt of Mr. Willoughby's instructions, adopted every means in his power (those means were rather limited, and, if we are rightly informed, were represented as such) to put an effectual stop to the trade in slaves at that port, or at any other within his limits, and in the prosecution of this very laudable object, he discovered, about the beginning of last month, that three Arab boats or bungalows had arrived at Pore-bunder, each carrying. as a portion of the trade, a number of slaves. This officer lost no time in communicating with the rana and his advisers on the subject of the importation of the slaves. They acknowledged the engagement they had entered into with the political agent at Rajcote, and immediately volunteered to seize the commanders and crews, take charge of the boats, and deliver the slaves to the officer, to be kept under his charge until instructions should be received from Rajcote as to the disposal of them. Search was immediately made, and seventy-four naked half-famished wretches were found stowed away in chests. boxes, and in other places of concealment. There were forty-three boys, and thirty-one girls, all of them of about the age of ten years.—*Bombay Gaz.*, Dec. 16.

THE COOLIES.

Extract of a letter from Baroda.—" The Coolies are disaffected to the northward, and again busily plying at the trade of their ancestors, and it seems very probable that a strong force will be soon required to put them down. The troops in Guzerat have suffered so severely from sickness this year, that at present no addition could be easily made to the force which marched from Baroda last September, under command of Cap. More, 24th, and which now garrisons Ahmednugur. A party of the Auxiliary Horse, under Lieut. Skinner, 9th regt., have been ordered up by forced marches to assist in quelling the disturbance there, arising from the clamorous demands made by a large body of Puttans enlisted in the Joudpoor country, by the emissaries of the raja, for arrears of pay. It appears that these vagabonds have been permitted to enter the town by the raja's people, and that another detachment of several hundred are now on their march down. We have native reports here of a bloody battle having been fought near Panora, in the hills, by the mercenaries employed by the Pinora and Gorawa thakoors ; about fifty of the Pinora man's Mukranees were left dead in the valley, and the rest fled. Mr. Erskine has taken up his appointment as resident at Baroda. —*Bombay Gaz.*, Dec 2.

NATIVE SERVANTS.

The revenue commissioner deserves great praise for having appointed a committee of natives at Poona, for the examination of all candidates for situations in the revenue department. It is composed at present of Ballajee Punt Natoo, the dufturdar of the revenue commissioner, the native judge of Poona, and one or two others, all of them the most respectable servants of Government, and men of well-known integrity. Many advantages to the public service are likely to result from the scrutiny which the committee will exercise upon the appointments of carkoons and shekdars, so that there would remain very little chance of those situations being given to persons unfit to hold them. It has also been directed that the present carkoons should pass an examination before this committee, previous to their being promoted to higher offices ; and instances have come to our knowledge in which persons have resigned their places from a reluctance to appear before this body: a reluctance which amounts to a diffidence in their own abilities and fitness. This has created a sensation among the native servants of Government.—*Durpun, Nov. 20.*

Ceylon.

At about two o'clock P.M., on Saturday, a loud noise, resembling thunder, was heard in the fort, which proceeded from the king's house, the tiles on the roof of which fell in. The accident appears to have been caused by the removal of some tiles for the purpose of repair at the lower part, when all those above gave way ; the reapers were also broken, in consequence of which, a considerable quantity of the tiles went through between the rafters, but no further than the first ceiling, the strong beams of which enabled it to support the weight. The inmates, amongst whom were the Governor and Lady Horton, as may be imagined, were greatly alarmed, and took refuge by flight (those above-stairs in the balconies, and those below in the gardens), until it was discovered they might return in safety. The broken materials of the roof were immediately removed, and tarpaulings spread over.—*Colombo Observer, Nov. 3.*

Ava.

The *Christian Observer* of Calcutta, for December, has some very interesting intelligence regarding the progress of English among the Burmese.

Col. Burney, the British resident at Ava, on his recent return from Calcutta to Ava, took with him a lithographic press, from which, in the presence of the principal inhabitants, he took off impressions of printing and writing. Their attention was thus excited, and, in consequence, Col. B. was requested to procure a press for the late woongee (a man, in most respects, very superior to his country-men, and had no doubt but that when he reached Ava (which he has done ere now), he should receive similar orders from other noblemen.   Col. Burney is also a friend to the introduction of the English lan-guage, as far as practicable; and with this view, made arrangements, on his late visit to Calcutta, for the publication of Johnson's Dictionary in English and Bur-mese, originally commenced by the late Rev. Dr. Price, and completed by the prince of Mekra (the king's uncle), and Mr. Lane, an intelligent merchant at Ava. When published, the work will give great facilities to the higher class of Burmans to acquire our language, of which, from their growing conviction that in scientific acquirements, as well as in warlike prowess, the British are superior to them, many will avail themselves.   Mr. Blun-dell, the commissioner in the Tenasserim provinces, is ardent for the diffusion of English. The Supreme Government hav-ing placed a sum of money at his disposal for the purposes of education, he has determined upon the establishment of English schools at Moulmein, Tavoy, and Mergui.   The school at Moulmein is under the superintendence of Mr. and Mrs. Bennet, of the American mission. It contained 100 children of various castes and countries.   The first class have made considerable progress in arithmetic and geography, and are also taught grammar, the use of the globes, and English com-position.   The chief difficulty consists in getting the children to *speak* English. The language of the country is not neg-lected.   The interest which the natives have manifested as regards the education of their children in European science, is much greater than could have been ex-pected. Mrs. Bennet has not yet suc-ceeded in inducing the people to send their females to school.

Siam.

The barque *Pyramus*, Capt. Weller, ar-rived here on the 13th inst. from Siam, bringing advices from Bangkok down to the 25th ult.   The disputes with Cochin China were still pending, and the Siamese were busy preparing for war.   A small brig of war of about 200 tons, built un-der the direction of a young Siamese noble-man at Chentaboon, a small port near the mouth of the Meinam, had just arrived at Bangkok, and we understand that, in point of model and workmanship, she reflects great credit on the builder.   This vessel, it seems, is to be employed against the Cochin Chinese, with whom, how-ever, his Siamese majesty considers him-self unequal to cope by sea, and is very anxious that the English should send an

expedition to his assistance!   By land, he thinks himself sufficiently powerful, and in the event of receiving the required aid from the British, his majesty is cer-tain of soon being able to subject the whole of Cochin China to his sway: and as a reward for their services he promises to give to the English the sea-ports along the east coast of Cochin China.—*Sing. Free Press, Nov.* 19.

Persian Gulf.

"*Bagdad, Oct* 12th.—A few days ago we were within an ace of being all mur-dered, through the madness of a mis-sionary—a fanatic called Jacob Samuel, a Prussian jew, converted to Christianity, and, unaccountably, converted at the same time into an Englishman!   This indivi-dual went into the bazaar, followed by two hamals, loaded with religious tracts and books reflecting upon Mahomed and Mahomedanism.   These he distributed to the people, and, as you may suppose, a mob immediately collected, crying out vengeance upon all Christians.   The pasha, at the time, was out with his troops two days from here, but his lieu-tenant acted nobly.   He first ordered all the people to keep quiet, and sent parties of the nizam into every street.   These put the people down on this side of the river; but on the other they had arrived, and were gathering with the most awful determination for revenge.   However, the tophanjchee basshee, with the Alba-nians, gained the bridge, and having once crossed, by threats and determined con-duct, the mob was dispersed without bloodshed.   In the mean time, the unfor-tunate cause of the disturbance was put into Col. Taylor's boat, and packed off to Bussora snug enough; but some thou-sands of poor harmless unoffending Ar-menians and Catholics were obliged for several days to skulk in their houses and neglect their business; for, whenever they dared shew their faces, they were insulted in every direction.   The cazee and moof-tee, however, notwithstanding the termi-nation of the affair, issued sentence of death against Mr. Samuel, and, as they could not get at him, collected all his books, and had them publicly burnt amidst all sorts of indignity.   As for ourselves, personally, at the residency, we did not care two straws for the mob; for, as long as they had not the Government on their side, they could not get cannon to blow us up, and with their swords and muskets alone, I think their courage would soon have been cooled by a few shots from our Indian sepoys.   The Bag-dad government, I have only to add, de-serves a great deal of credit for their cool-ness in this affair.

" This place is much as you left it, except that upwards of 3,000 regular troops from Constantinople have arrived, and affairs are going on much better. The Arabs are now quiet, and the nizam are remarkably steady well-behaved men; and, were they well taken care of, would be excellent soldiers.

" Chesney is, I suppose, still at Bir, for we have neither heard of nor from him for an age. Mahomed Ali is underhand doing all he can to prevent the expedition, though any child can see that the Russians are the mainspring at work."—*Bomb. Cour*, Dec. 5.

China.

THE EMPEROR'S EDICT AGAINST FOREIGN BOOKS.

The following is a translation of an edict, issued by the late Governor Loo, and privately obtained by an influential friend. There can be little doubt but the emperor was greatly surprised at the appearance of the *Chinese Magazine*. This singular fact, that a book written by an European in the Chinese language, printed from Chinese blocks by a native, and published by the author, and brought to the notice of the great officers of state, and even of H. I. M. himself, stands alone in the history of literature and of China.

" To Woo-tun-yuen, How-qua, and the rest of the hong merchants, for their full information, from the governor and foo-yuen, who, on the 21st day of the 6th moon of the 15th year of Taou-kwang, received and in council opened a despatch from the great officers of the military council, saying that, on the first day of the 6th moon, 15th year of Taou kwang, they received the imperial edict—as follows:—

" ' Lo-shen (foo-yuen of Füh-këen), and the others have forwarded a foreign book to the office of the military council, from English foreigners, which has been presented to me for my inspection. I, the emperor, have carefully turned it over, and looked at it; the title-page bears the date—Taou-kwang, *Kea-woo* (the name of the 31st year of the Chinese cycle, 1834) ; it is dated in the summer months, and sealed with a private seal. The book contains questions from the five classics. It is most certain that an outside foreigner did not print the book. The said nation frequents Canton for the purposes of trade ; assuredly, in the interior, there must be traitors among the people, who unite together to print and circulate (the book) : this is most detestable. If this book was printed in last year, how is it that, this spring, it can be circulated from the said nation as far as Füh-këen province ?—This affair must, most decidedly, be investigated to the bottom, and it will not be difficult to ascertain the

real facts. I order the said governor and foo-yuen (of Füh-këen), and the others, to institute immediate secret inquiries. The shopmen, who printed the foreign book, must be seized and sent before the magistrates, and strictly examined as to what person prepared this foreign book, and who gave it to the said shopmen to print, and the facts and persons concerned must be clearly proved and pointed out, and elicited by examination ; there must not be the least tergiversation or glossing over, which will be a most heavy and perverse offence. Let this edict be communicated to Loo and Kee (the governor and foo-yuen of Canton) ; and also send it to Pang (the hoppo) for his information. And I order the volumes of foreign books to be both sent at once (from the military council to the above officers at Canton). Respect this.'

" The imperial will has been received ; and we have written a dispatch, communicating the above circumstances.

" I (Loo. the governor of Canton) have examined, and find, that the governor of Füh-këen and Che-keang has transmitted a document, stating that foreigners distributed foreign books in Füh-këen province, &c. We, the governor and foo-yuen, fear that the said foreign vessel has entered into Canton province ; we have already ordered the *Sze* officers (the treasurer and the judge) to commence inquiries as to whether any foreign books have been distributed in Canton. Afterwards, we received the edict containing the imperial will, ordering the examination of the shopmen who printed the foreign books ; and we have already respectfully obeyed the orders, for instituting an enquiry : this is on record. Now, we have respectfully received the foregoing directions, as well as the two volumes of foreign books ; and we, the governor and foo-yuen, with extreme care, have looked them over, and it is clearly the case that they are Chinese-printed books ; they are got up, as to appearance, fashion, paper, and title-page, exactly the same as the story-books, song-books, &c. that are sold in the streets. Canton is the place which the English foreigners frequent for the purposes of trading ; certainly, there must be native traitors amongst the people, who link themselves on (to the foreigners) and print (their books). We have also communicated to the two *Sze* officers, the treasurer and criminal judge, to immediately direct the Kwang-chow-foo and the two *hëens* of Pwan-yu and Nan-hae, to search about the provincial city, inside and out, as well as Macao and other places ; and, moreover, to give secret orders to all the hong merchants, secretly and quickly, to ascertain the facts by examination. The shopmen, who printed the foreign books, must be taken, and subjected to the severest examination before the magistrates ; that the man who prepared these foreign books, and who delivered them to the said shopmen to be printed, may be discovered ; and at what time and place they were printed ; all these circumstances must be drawn out by grinding torture ; for the real facts must be obtained. If the blocks are still in the country, immediately seize them, and deliver them up, altogether, to await our (the governor and foo yuen) personal inspection, in order to send them (to the emperor). Thus, we respectfully obey the edict containing the imperial will, ordering us to examine into this important business.

" It certainly cannot be reported back from Canton, that there are not any cutters (of blocks for the characters). It is absolutely requisite for the said *foo* and *häen* officers to deliberate and examine, and obtain the facts. It is expected that they will certainly make a seizure. If the district officers have been guilty of the fault of circumstances in enquiring, yet, if they pursue and seize the printing criminal, they may beg for some indulgence ; but, if they shrink from and avoid their duty, or are careless and slur over the business, and the criminals are seized by other persons, the said *foo* and *häen* officers may fear the difficulty of bearing the consequences of so heavy a crime. It is absolutely necessary that the utmost secrecy and sincerity be used to prevent the matter from being known abroad, so that the traitors may not be able to conceal themselves at a distance, and the guiltless be implicated. It is proper, respectfully to record (the edict) and the documents (connected with it), to be respectfully obeyed.

" These orders for examination having, with secrecy and haste, come before me, the hoppo, on receiving them, besides sending secret messengers to examine, I, with haste, unite with and give secret orders to the said hong merchants to obey accordingly, and, after having examined, to inform me of the facts by petition ; thus I respectfully obey the edict containing the imperial will respecting this examination. The said hong merchants must not be guilty of the offence of evading their duty. A special edict.

" Taou-kwang, 15th year, 6th moon, 28th day (23d July 1835.")—*Canton Reg.*, Oct. 6.

Australasia.

NEW SOUTH WALES.

THE EXPEDITION INTO THE INTERIOR.

. The report of Major Mitchell of the result of the expedition to explore the course of the Darling river, is published by the local government. It is dated " West of Harvey's Range, 4th Sept."

He states that he set out from Buree, on the 7th April, by an unexplored route, intending to proceed along the high ground between the Rivers Lachlan and Macquarie, hoping to avoid the necessity for crossing any rivers, or incurring any risk of delay from floods, and to extend his trigonometrical survey as far as possible along these heights into the interior. He reached the Darling, near the junction of New Year's Creek, in thirty-one days, from Buree ; " having found the country so favourable that it was never necessary to unload a dray or cut a way through scrub, or to pass a night without water." On the right were the waters of the Bogan, and on the left, a connected chain of heights, whereof New Year's Range is the last.

A grievous misfortune befel the expedition in the loss of Mr. Cunningham, the colonial botanist, who wandered from the party near the head of the river Bogan, on the 17th of April. After an anxious search, continued for twelve days, during which the party halted, his horse was traced till found dead, having still the saddle on, and the bridle in its mouth. It appeared that Mr. Cunningham, after losing his horse, had directed his steps northward ; they were traced into the Bogan, and westward along the bed of that river for twenty miles, and until they disappeared near a recent encampment of natives. There a small portion of the skirt of his coat was found, also some fragments of a map in his possession. There were two distinct tribes of natives on the Bogan, from whom nothing could be learned of his fate.

" We found the interior country," Major Mitchell says, " parched by such excessive drought, that the swamp under Oxley's Table-land, mentioned by Capt. Sturt, was completely dry, and only a few ponds remained in the river Bogan (which is New Year's Creek of that traveller). Indeed, for three hundred miles below that creek, we drank no other water than that of the Darling. In this river there was a slight current, the quantity flowing in rapids, being about as much as might be required to turn a mill. The water was in all parts as transparent as that of the purest spring well, and it entirely lost all brackish taste below an extreme point of Dunlop's Range, where a hill, consisting of a very hard breccia, closes on the river so as to separate the plains above it from those lower down."

When the party first arrived on the Darling, the Major was induced, from the favourable appearance of the reaches, to try at what rate he might proceed on the river with the boats ; and on the 1st of June proceeded down the river in the boats, with the greater portion of the party ; but they found too many shallow and rocky places in the river. On the 8th of June they proceeded along the left bank of the Darling.

"As the cattle became weaker, the country, as we descended, became much more difficult for them to travel upon. It consisted chiefly of plains of naked earth, too soft to retain roots, yet just tenacious enough to open in deep cracks, across which it was not always safe to ride. Impassable hollows (covered with *polygonum juncium*) at length skirted the river so extensively, that we could seldom encamp within a mile of it, and sometimes not within three. Still we could not have existed there without the river, which contained the only water, and had on its banks the only grass for our cattle. I had proceeded thus about 300 miles down the Darling, when the weakness of the bullocks, and the reduced state of our provisions, obliged me to consider the expediency of going forward, with a small party only, and a faster rate, while the exhausted cattle might in the meantime be refreshing for the homeward journey. But before deciding on the separation of the party, in the presence of several powerful tribes of natives, I halted it to rest the animals, while some preparations were going forward for setting out. In two days I was convinced, from the movements I observed amongst the native tribes, that in proceeding further at so great a risk of compromising the safety of the stationary party, I should have acted contrary to the 9th article of His Excellency's instructions, and thereupon I abandoned the intention."

The natives now became very troublesome ; the conduct of several of these tribes was very extraordinary. To conciliate them was quite hopeless, but not from any apprehension on their part. "On the contrary," he says, " the more we endeavoured to supply their real wants, and shew good-will towards them, the more they seem to covet what was utterly useless to them, and the more they plotted our destruction. Some of their ceremonies were different from those of any other aboriginal tribes nearer the colony, such as waving the green bough, first setting it on fire, with furious gestures at us ; throwing dust at us with their toes, and spitting at our men." Of the three parties most offending, two were killed, and one (the chief) shot through the groin. The only injury done, on our side, was the blow of a waddy by that chief, who knocked a man down while carrying water, in order to take his kettle."

They now retrograded, and as the track of the drays had formed a road, which was much easier for the cattle in returning, by short marches, and occasional rests, they reached their former depôt (about twelve miles below the junction of New Year's Creek), on the 10th of August.

"The interior country, westward of the Darling, is diversified with detached groups of hills, and low ranges, broken into portions, resembling islands, but the general aspect thereof afforded no indication of its having then any water on its surface. From two different hills, each about twelve miles west of the Darling, and distant from each other about seventy miles, I obtained extensive views across the country, but from neither of these heights could I perceive any smoke, or even any appearance of trees, the whole country being covered with one kind of bush, forming a thick scrub, with intervals rather more open, but strewed with smaller bushes. During the four winter months just past, no clouds gathered to any particular point of that horizon ; no rain has fallen, neither has there been any dew, and the winds from the west and north-west hot and parching, seemed to blow over a region in which no humidity remained."

The Darling did not, in a course of 300 miles, receive a single river or chain of ponds from either side. Such was the extent of the plains on its banks, and the depth and absorbent quality of the soil, that much of the waters of high floods appear to be retained therein, besides all the drainage from the back country. Thus the springs appear to be supplied, by which the river is sustained during the present season of drought. These absorbent plains extend to about five miles, on an average, from the river on each side, hills of soft red sand bound them, and recede about three miles further. Undulations of diluvial gravel (of a very hard siliceous breccia) succeed, and skirt the base of the heights, which generally consist of primary sand-stone. The country, eastward of the river, rises gradually backwards towards the hills, by which I advanced to the Darling. There the higher grounds are more connected, and send down chains of ponds, which appear to be absorbed in the plains. The same kind of bush, however, covers the first region of high ground back from the Darling on both sides, and the character of features, and direction of valleys, were not very apparent from heights near this river. The general course of the Darling, as far as I had explored it (which was to the latitude of the head of Spencer's Gulf), is somewhat to the west of south-west (variation $8°\ 27'$). This would tend to the westward of the head of Gulf St. Vincent, if the longitude of the Upper Darling were correct ; but I make the longitude of that river, on the parallel of $30°$ south, nearly a degree more to the eastward, and from that longitude, the general course tends much more nearly towards the supposed junction below, although still considerably to the west of that point, as laid down on maps.

" From Fort Bourke (long. 145° 52′ 12″ E., lat. 30° 7′ 4″ S) I continued the survey of the Darling, by actual measurement, corrected by intersecting distant points, and also by observations of latitude, to the termination of my journey, in lat. 32° 24′ 20″ S., and I make the longitude of that point, as deduced from this survey, 142° 24′ 26″ E.

" Having ascertained the most westerly of the two creeks crossed by Capt. Sturt on his journey beyond the Macquarie to be the Bogan; and being desirous to discover the origin of the other, named Duck Creek, I sent Mr. Larmer to survey it. Mr. Larmer traced Duck Creek upwards to a large lagoon on the margin of that river, from which other lagoons and channels also led into this creek. Mr. Larmer found in Duck Creek extensive reaches of excellent water; but the bed of the Macquarie was dry where he made it. Thus it appears that, as the dip of the whole country is to the westward, the surplus waters of the Macquarie are conveyed to the Darling by Duck Creek, a separate channel altogether to the westward of the marshes."

Cape of Good Hope.

The *Grahams-town Journal* gives an account of a great meeting, King William's Town, on the 7th January, of all the Caffree chiefs, now under British jurisdiction, for the purpose of administering the oath of allegiance to the magistrate and people, for initiating the chiefs and other heads of Kraals in the office of magistrates, full commandants, and field cornets: and for explaining to those functionaries the duties they are expected to perform.

The Caffres were bivouacked on the slopes of the hills. The tribes of Macomo and Tyrali presented a very imposing appearance, mounting about 600 men on horseback, besides about 1,000 foot. The other Caffres came up with great order and regularity—some of the tribes singing their war-song. On the ground were the commissioners, some missionaries, several gentlemen from India, &c. The *coup-d'œil* was exceedingly interesting; it had a character altogether new, and was rendered highly picturesque by its wildness. In the centre was the tent of the commander-in-chief of the province; on his right hand sat Macomo, on his left Tyrali, each dressed in a suit of blue cloth. Next sat Sutu, Gaska's queen wife; next Nonube—then came Cobu, Congo, Pato, and William Kama.

The business of the day was opened with an impressive prayer in the Caffre language, by the Rev Mr. Chalmers. Before reading the address, Col. Smith waving his hat, called out, " Long live our good King William the Fourth," which was responded to by a shout from the Caffres; they raised their hands high in the air, snapping their fingers, as they yelled, with singular effect; they then sat down, and it appeared incredible that 2,000 men could be stowed away in so small a compass. Colonel Smith then read the important document. When it was finished the Colonel said, " Macomo and Tyrali, and the other magistrates, I now wait to hear any thing you have to say." After a short pause, Macomo turned round, and said, " Although my people are stupid, ignorant, and naked, I and they are perfectly sensible when good words are said to us. I will always tell you if anything happens among my people, as you are the representative of the king and the governor; and I will obey your instructions." To which the governor replied, " Macomo, you have shewn yourself to-day the same man I ever found you, and I again urge you to remember these words—you are now British subjects." Tyrali then spoke briefly: he thanked Col. Smith for all he had done for him and his people.

Thus ended this remarkable meeting: the parties quietly dispersed, each tribe of Anglo-Caffres marching off to their places of occupation.

Madagascar.

The queen of Madagascar has, by an edict, suppressed the profession of Christianity among her subjects, and strictly prohibited, on the head of religion, any departure from the customs of their ancestors. This princess, the widow and successor of the celebrated Radama, reigns over nearly four millions of people, from whom she has withdrawn, in her folly, the means which were freely offered to them, of raising themselves to a level with the most prosperous and powerful nations.

In her edict she expresses her willingness to receive European arts, and such inventions as tend directly to augment the wealth and power of her kingdom, being ignorant of the fact, that all the useful arts, both in their birth and application, as the supporters of national greatness, are inseparably connected with the intellectual and moral condition of the human mind. The arts of Christian Europe speedily become unfruitful, and perish utterly, when left in the hands of a heathen and depraved community.— *South Afr. Advertiser, Feb.* 10.

REGISTER.

Calcutta.

GOVERNMENT ORDERS, &c.

DRESS OF OFFICERS.

Head-Quarters, Calcutta, November 8,
1835.—1. The Commander-in-Chief finds
it impossible to abstain from remarking
upon the improprieties which he too frequently sees in the dress of officers at the
presidency.

2. He cannot pass on the public drives
about the city without observing military
caps worn with citizen's plain blue frock
coats : the capes of jackets turned down in
a most unsoldier-like and slovenly manner :
at the theatre, officers in red jackets without sash or sword, or any thing to indicate
that they belong to the army ; and he has
even seen an officer in a morning, with
sash and sword on, and shoes with bows
of ribbon !

3. The Commander-in-Chief is fully
aware that officers may be just as good,
and just as brave, under these circumstances : but, as such proceedings happen
to be contrary to *orders*, and obedience to
orders is the very life of discipline in an
army, he feels obliged to desire that the
officers will refer to his Majesty's Regulations and the circular letter and General
Orders addressed to this army on the 30th
of July and 31st of October 1854 on this
subject, and conform to the same.

4. It is to be understood, that he does
not desire at all to interfere with their
comforts in their *early* morning rides before breakfast ; or in any of their sports
or amusements ; but he insists that when
they appear in public, as officers, they
shall be dressed as such, in conformity to
the orders which are in existence.

5. Cloth trowsers will be worn on all
parades by the staff, after the 30th instant.

6. He calls on the heads of the staff to
check improprieties where they observe
them : and to obviate the necessity for any
further reference to this subject on the part
of the Commander-in-chief.

APPOINTMENTS TO THE GENERAL STAFF.

Fort William, Nov. 30, 1835.—In obedience to instructions received from the
Hon. the Court of Directors, the Governor-
General of India in Council is pleased to
revive and republish the Rule laid down
in paragraph 21 of General Orders, dated
the 12th Aug. 1824, relative to appointments to the general staff.

" No officer shall be eligible to hold
the situations of adjutant-general, quarter-
master-general, military auditor-general,
or commissary-general, who has not previously attained the rank of major in the

army, unless he shall have actually served
twenty years in India. The deputies in
those departments must have attained the
rank of captain in the army, or have served
twelve years in India ; and the assistants,
if they have not attained the rank of captain, must have served ten years in India."

The above revived rule cancels the regulation published in General Orders by
the government of India, under date the
24th Sept. 1834.

COURTS MARTIAL.

ENSIGN J. W. S. SMITH.

Head-Quarters, Calcutta, Nov. 30, 1835.
—At a general court-martial held at Barrackpore, on the 18th Nov. 1835, Ensign
J. W. S. Smith, H.M. 38th Foot, was
arraigned on the following charge :—

Charge.—" Ensign John William Sydney Smith, of H.M. 38th regt., placed
under arrest by me, and charged as follows :

" For conduct unbecoming the character of an officer and a gentleman, and
subversive of military discipline, in having,
on the 20th Sept. 1835, endeavoured to
force me to fight a duel with him ; without
any sufficient cause for it, or just provocation on my part.

(Signed)   " J. J. LOWTH,
            " Capt. H.M. 38th regt."

Upon which charge the court came to
the following decision :

Finding.—That the prisoner, Ensign
J. W. S. Smith, of H.M. 38th regt., is
guilty of so much of the charge preferred
against him, as extends to the simple sending of the challenge, in breach of the Articles of War, but acquit him of the rest.

Sentence.—The court having thus found
the prisoner guilty of so much of the
charge as is above particularized, do therefore sentence him to be reprimanded.

Approved,

(Signed)   H. FANE, General,
                Commander-in-chief.

Remarks by his Excellency the Com-
            mander-in-Chief.

1. The commanding officer of H.M.
38th regt. will summon Ens. Smith to his
presence, and point out to him the error
of his conduct, in breach of the 60th Article of War ; reprimand him as directed
by the above sentence ; and inform him,
that he must consider the early reparation
which he was prepared to make for his
offence, to have been the means of his
salvation from ruin.

2. The Commander-in-chief is of opinion, that he should neglect his duty to
the army, if he failed to offer some remarks
grounded upon this court-martial.

(F)

3. He will candidly state to the army, that the endless numbers of courts-martial in *India*, is a general topic amongst military men in England, and is the subject of general condemnation amongst soldiers.

4. Until he was placed in his present position, he was at a loss to account for this peculiar circumstance; but this court-martial, and many similar examples which have been brought before him, since he has had the honour to command this army, have fully explained how this evil arises.

5. Capt. Lowth's proceedings afford him a perfect elucidation of his view of the case, and he will make it the occasion of explaining that view.

6. In this instance, two brother officers of H.M. 38th regt. fall out about a matter in itself trifling, which leads to a certain crisis.

The affair is brought to a point which requires a decision; and Capt. Lowth forms his own judgment about what is right and necessary for the vindication of his honour.

Two captains (A. Campbell and W. Campbell, as is shown in the proceedings of the court-martial) are of opinion, that what is offered as an apology by the offender, is quite sufficient to render unnecessary any further proceedings.

The commanding officer of the regiment is of opinion, that what is offered is sufficient.

The Commander-in-chief is of opinion, that what is offered is sufficient; and Major-general Watson, who commands the division, hopes that "the sentiments of the Commander-in-chief may be respected."

All this will not do!

The opinions of the four superior authorities named, are not sufficient to suit Capt. Lowth's ideas; but, obstinate in his own opinion, he solicits to be permitted to appeal to the last resort, namely, a court-martial.

7. Let the army take another case.

An officer has a dispute with his brother officers about a matter relating to the mess of the regiment.

His brother officers decide against him; he is not content.

The commanding officer of his regiment decides against him; he is not content.

The brigadier decides against him.

The general of division decides against him, and he is still not content. At last he comes to the Commander-in-chief, who also decides against him, (probably with no better result!)

8. He could produce many other instances of this unbending and *obstinate perseverance* in the opinion of the correctness of the individual's *own views*, and the utter disregard of the opinions of those superiors who stand in a position to look calmly and without bias on the cases laid before them.

9. How this has grown up it is difficult to say, but that it ought to be corrected, all who wish well to the harmony and the reputation of the army must feel.

10. The Commander-in-chief solicits the officers to reflect upon what he has said, and to aid him in getting rid of that bane to the service, and to the character of the army, "the endless calls for court-martial."

The injury to the army is lamentable from the number of officers withdrawn from their regimental duties, month after month, to investigate the quarrels and squabbles of individuals: and the personal inconvenience to the officers themselves is a very important object for consideration.

11. With the general assistance of the officers of the army, all this may be easily corrected; but unless the Commander-in-chief receive such aid, that blot upon OUR character as an army (which he so much desires to remove) cannot but remain attached to US.

Ensign Smith is to be released from arrest, and will return to his duty.

CAPT. R. A. MCNAGHTEN.

Head-Quarters, Calcutta, Dec. 19, 1835. —At an European general court-martial hold at Kurnaul, on the 21st Nov. 1835, Capt. R. A. McNaghten, 61st regt. N.I., was arraigned on the following charge:—

Charge.—" I charge Capt. Robert Adair McNaghten, of the 61st regt. N.I., with scandalous conduct, in having, in a note to the address of Capt. E. C. Windus, H.M. 11th Lt. Drags., dated 29th April 1835, made the following assertion : *viz.*

" ' As we' (meaning Capt. McNaghten and Capt. Monke) ' know that he' (meaning Lieut. Low, when a witness on the trial of Lieut. Wallace, 39th regt. N.I.) ' has sworn to what is not the truth;' such assertion being false and unwarrantable, and tending to destroy my character as an officer and a gentleman.

(Signed) " JOHN HANDCOCK Low,
" Lieut. 39th regt. N.I.
" Junior Assist. Agent Gov. Gen."
" Landour, 5th Sept. 1835.''

Finding.—The court, from the evidence before them, are of opinion, that Capt. Robert Adair McNaghten, 61st regt. N.I., is not guilty of the charge exhibited against him, except of writing the note set forth in the charge, and to which they attach no criminality; the court do therefore fully and honourably acquit Capt. Robert Adair McNaghten, 61st regt. N.I., of the same accordingly.

Approved.
(Signed) H. FANE, General, Commander-in-chief, East-Indies.

Remarks by the Court.

The court feel it no more than justice to Lieut. Low to record that, in the opinion of every individual member of it, he stands acquitted of any wilful or intentional departure from the truth, in giving his evidence on the late trial of Lieut. Wallace, 39th regt. N.I.

Capt. McNaghten is released from arrest, and directed to return to his duty.

CIVIL APPOINTMENTS, &c.

BY THE GOVERNOR-GENERAL.

Judicial and Revenue Department.

Nov. 21. Mr. G D. Wilkins to be an assistant under commissioner of revenue and circuit of 11th or Patna division.

Mr. E. F. Radcliffe to be an assistant under commissioner of ditto ditto.

24. Mr. Wm. Blunt to be a judge of courts of Sudder Dewanny and Nizamut Adawlut.

Mr. H. C. Metcalfe to exercise powers of a joint magistrate and deputy collector at Jessore, and to conduct current duties of office of magistrate and collector at sudder station, during absence of Mr. Donnelly in the interior.

Mr. F. Lowth to officiate as magistrate and collector of zillah Backergunge, during absence of Mr. H. Stainforth.

26. Mr. C. R. Barwell to officiate as a judge of courts of Sudder Dewanny and Nizamut Adawlut.

Mr. J. H. D'Oyly to officiate as additional judge of zillah 24-Pergunnahs.

Mr. J. Staniforth to officiate as magistrate and collector of Midnapore, in room of Mr. D'Oyly.

Mr. H. P. Russell to officiate as additional judge of zillah Nuddeah.

Dec. 1. Mr. N. J. Halhed to officiate as a judge of courts of Sudder Dewanny and Nizamut Adawlut.

Mr. R. P. Nisbet to officiate as additional judge of zillah Midnapore.

Mr. W Tayler to officiate as magistrate and collector of Burdwan.

Mr. W. J. Allen to be assistant to magistrate and collector of Tipperah, with authority to exercise powers of joint magistrate and deputy collector of that district.

Mr. R. F. Hodgson to be an assistant under commissioner of revenue and circuit of 12th or Bhaugulpore division, and stationed at Monghyr.

Mr. Wm. Bell to be an assistant under commissioner of revenue and circuit of 15th or Dacca division.

Mr. J. B. Ogilvy to officiate as joint magistrate and deputy collector of Pubna, in room of Mr. Allen.

8. Mr. Wigram Money to officiate as special commissioner, under Reg. III. of 1828, of Moorshedabad division, in room of Mr. C. R. Barwell.

Mr. W. J. H. Money to conduct current duties of office of civil and session judge of Beerbhoom, in room of Mr. Money.

Mr. H. Nisbet to officiate as commissioner of revenue and circuit of 12th or Bhaugulpore division.—Mr. G. G. Mackintosh, on Mr. Nisbett's vacating, to conduct current duties of civil and session judge of Purneah.

Mr. W. Travers to be deputy collector of Bhaugulpore, in addition to his appointment of same grade at Monghyr.

Mr. C. Steer to officiate as head assistant to magistrate and collector of Bhaugulpore.

Lieut. P. Mainwaring, 33d N.I., to conduct current duties of office of superintendent of Cachar, during absence of Capt. Fisher.

15. Mr. J. Lowis to be special commissioner, under Reg. III. of 1828, for district of Sylhet.

Mr. E. A. Samuells to officiate as magistrate of zillah Hooghly, in room of Mr. Gilmore.

Mr. F. Skipwith to officiate as joint magistrate and deputy collector of zillah Burdwan.

Mr. J. S. Torrens to be an assistant under commissioner of revenue and circuit of 15th or Dacca division, with authority to exercise powers of joint magistrate and deputy collector in zillah Furreedpore.

Lieut. J. R. Lumsden, adjutant to Arracan local battalion, to officiate as a junior assistant in Arracan, during absence of Lieut. Rainey.

16. The Hon. R. Forbes to officiate as joint magistrate and deputy collector of Maldah.

General Department.

Nov. 25. Mr. R. H. Alexander to act as first assistant to collector of customs, in room of Mr. Thornhill.

Dec. 9. Mr. C. F. Young to officiate as assistant to Board of Customs, salt and opium, v. Mr. H. R. Alexander.

Political Department.

Nov. 23. Capt. A. McLeod, 5th Madras L.C , to officiate as an assistant to commissioner for government of territories of H.H. the Rajah of Mysore.

Dec. 7. Lieut. J. R. Lumley, 9th N I., to be an assistant to general superintendent of operations for suppression of thuggee, v. Ensign Russell dec.

Capt. Richard Budd, 32d Madras N.I., to officiate as an assistant to commissioner for government of territories of H.H. the Rajah of Mysore.

Law Department.

Dec. 7. Richard Howe Cockerell, Esq., to be sheriff of Calcutta during ensuing year.

Miscellaneous.

Mr. A. G. Macdonald, having exceeded the period within which, under the orders of the Hon. the Court of Directors, he ought to have qualified himself for the public service by proficiency in the native languages, has been ordered to return to England; date 25th Nov. 1835.

Messrs. R. T. Tucker and Alfred Turnbull reported their arrival as writers on this establishment, the former on the 25th, and the latter on the 29th November.

Mr. R. T. Tucker has been permitted to proceed to Azeemghur, and prosecute his study of the Oriental languages at that station.

Major J. Morison assumed charge of the duties of resident in the Persian Gulf on the 24th of September last.

Lieut. C. Davidson, of the 66th Bengal N.I., now on the personal staff of the Governor of Bombay, is placed at the disposal of the resident at Hydrabad.

BY THE GOVERNOR OF AGRA.

Judicial and Revenue Department.

Nov. 10. Mr. R. Neave to officiate as civil and session judge of Cawnpore.

Mr. E. H. C. Monckton to be an assistant under commissioner of 5th or Benares division.

21. Mr. G. W. Bacon to receive charge of office of civil and session judge of Suharunpore from Mr. Biscoe, who has obtained leave of absence on med. certificate.

Dec. 3. Mr. R. J. Tayler to officiate as civil and session judge of Futtehpore.

8. Mr. W. H. Benson to officiate as commissioner of revenue and circuit of 4th or Allahabad division, during Mr. Turner's absence on leave.

Miscellaneous.

The Hon. the Governor of Agra is pleased to authorize the undermentioned officers to continue to officiate in their respective appointments, until further orders: *viz.*—Nov. 11. Capt. P. Latouche, 7th N.I., military secretary to the governor; Ens. H. M. Barwell, 59th N.I., private secretary to the governor; Capt. A. Wheatley, 5th L.C., town and fort major and aide-de-camp to the governor; Lieut. F. P. Fulcher, 67th N.I., aide-de-camp to the governor; and Civil Assist. Surg. A. Beattie, surgeon to the governor.

Capt. J. K. M. Causland received charge of the office of political agent at Sabathoo, from Capt. C. P. Kennedy, on the 2d November.

The appointment of Mr. E. F. Radcliffe, under date the 10th September last, to be an assistant under the commissioner of the 3d or Bareilly division, is cancelled.

ECCLESIASTICAL.

Nov. 18. The Rev. E. White, in conformity with orders of the Government of India, removed from his situation of district chaplain at Cawnpore.

Dec. 2. The Rev. R. Chambers to officiate as chaplain at Agra, v. the Rev. Dr. Parish on leave.

MILITARY APPOINTMENTS, PROMOTIONS, &c.

Head-Quarters, Nov. 18, 1835.—The following removals and postings to take place in Regt. of Artillery:—1st-Lieuts. G. Campbell, from 4th tr. 3d brig. to 2d tr. 1st brig.; G. Larkins, from 2d tr. 1st brig. to 3d tr. 2d brig.; R. R. Kinleside, from 2d comp. 3d bat. to 2d tr. 3d brig.; F. C. Burnett (on furl.), from 1st tr. 1st brig. to 6th comp. 7th bat.; F. W. Cornish (on staff employ) from 2d tr. 3d brig. to 2d comp. 3d bat.; A. Broome, new prom. to 4th comp. 3d bat.; A. Huish, new prom., to 4th tr. 3d brig.—2d-Lieuts. T. Edwards (on furl.) from 5th comp. 7th bat. to 4th tr. 3d brig.; F. Wall (on furl.) from 3d comp. 7th bat. to 2d tr. 3d brig.; R. Walker (on staff employ) from 1st comp. 7th bat. to 3d tr. 1st brig.; E. W. S. Scott, from 4th comp. 5th bat. to 1st comp. 7th bat.; T. Bacon, brought on strength, to 3d comp. 7th bat.; J. Abercrombie, brought on strength, to 2d comp. 7th bat.

Nov. 19.—The following station orders confirmed:—Surg. J. Johnstone, M.D., 67th N.I., to afford medical aid to staff at Dinapore, from 9th Nov.—Assist. Surg. C. J. Macdonald, 29th N.I., to afford medical aid to prisoners in jail and to Nujeeb corps at Jubbulpore, during absence, on duty, of Surg. G. G. Spilsbury; date 27th Oct.

Nov. 20.—Capt. T. E. Sampson, 22d N.I., to officiate as deputy judge advocate-general to western division, from date of departure of Capt. C. G. Ross, on sick cert.

Assist. Surg. H. M. Tweddell removed from 52d and posted to 31st N.I. at Bancoorah, v. Assist. Surg. Bowron app. to civil station of Jessore.

Nov. 21.—The following orders confirmed:—Capt. T. Des Voeux, 44th N.I., to officiate as major of brigade to Malwah field force, during absence, on leave, of Capt. and Brigade Major C. Cheape; date 2d Nov.—Lieut. J. C. Haslock to act as adj. to 39th N.I., in room of Ens. H. Howorth permitted to resign the app., and during absence, on med. cert., of Lieut. and Adj. G. Pengree; date 1st Oct.

Surg. Morgan Powell removed from 57th to 64th N.I., at Saugor.

Surg. A. K. Lindesay removed from 58th to 57th N.I. at Secrole, Benares, and directed to join on being relieved from medical duties of garrison of Chunar by Garrison Surg. James Clarke.

Lieut. Col. G. E. Gowan, 4th bat., to continue in command of artillery division at Neemuch, until further orders.

Fort William, Nov. 23, 1335.—Capt. Philip Jackson, regt. of artillery, at his own request, transferred to invalid establishment.

Nov. 30.—*Regt. of Artillery.* 1st-Lieut. and Brev. Capt. P. T. Cautley to be capt., and 2d-Lieut. L. Smith to be 1st-lieut., from 23d Nov. 1835, in suc. to Capt. P. Jackson transf. to invalid estab.—Supernum. 2d-Lieut. R. Warburton brought on effective strength of regt.—Supernum. 2d-Lieut. J. S. Phillips brought on ditto, in room of 2d-Lieut. P. Bridgman dec., 7th April 1835.

5th N.I. Ens. A. F. C. Deas to be lieut., from 13th Nov. 1835, v. Lieut. Chas. Terraneau dec.

Lieut. R. M. Hunter, 73d N.I., permitted to resign his appointment to Assam Sebundy corps.

Head Quarters, Nov. 27.—Ens. G. Shairp to act as adj. to left wing 15th N.I.; date 2d Nov.

Ens. F. S. Paterson removed from 55th to 54th N.I. as junior of his rank.

Nov. 28.—Lieut. S. J. Tabor to be adj. to 7th L.C., v. Master, who resigns the appointment.

Unposted Ens. E. T. Dalton to do duty with 43d N.I. at Barrackpore.

Dec. 1.—Capt. Robert Campbell, 43d N.I., to be an aide-de-camp on personal staff of Commander-in-chief.

Cornet H. Y. Basett to do duty with 3d L.C., on march of the 9th from Kurnaul; date 17th Nov.

Dec. 2.—*64th N.I.* Lieut. W. F. Campbell to be interp. and qu. master.

Ens. W. R. Mercer removed from 58th to 57th N.I., as junior of his rank.

Unposted Cornet H. G. C. Plowden permitted to do duty with 5th instead of 10th L.C.

Dec. 4.—Capt. G. S. Lawrenson, 1st comp. 5th bat., to proceed to Lucknow, and relieve Capt. H. Delafosse from command of artillery at that station, until further orders; date 26th Nov.

Capt. J. Hall, 8th N.I., to act as brigade major to Rajpootanah field force, in room of Capt. J. Wilson, 17th N.I., whose corps moves in present relief, during absence of Capt. P. La Touche, on detached employment.

Capt. T. Bolton, 47th N.I., to act as brigade major in Oude, during absence, on leave, of Capt. W. Parker.

Dec. 5.—Lieut. J. R. Younger, 56th N.I., to act as station staff at Dinapore, during absence, on duty, of Capt. D. Thompson, deputy assistant adjutant general; date 27th Nov.

Fort William, Dec. 7.—*Infantry.* Lieut. Col. and Brevet Col. J. Simpson to be colonel from 23d June 1835, v. Col. A. Stewart dec.—Major H. M. Wheeler to be lieut. col., v. Lieut. Col. J. Simpson promoted, with rank from 13th Aug. 1835, v. Lieut. Col. R. C. Faithful dec.

6th L.C. Capt. J. B. Hearsey to be major, and Lieut. F. Coventry to be capt. of a troop, from 19th Nov. 1835, in suc. to Major R. W. Smith dec.—Cornet G. Scott to be lieut., from 16th Nov. 1835, v. Lieut. W. H. Hall dec.—Cornet J. R. Burt to be lieut., from 19th Nov. 1835, in suc. to Lieut. F. Coventry prom.

Supernum. Cornets J Staples and H. Brougham brought on effective strength of cavalry.

48th N.I. Capt. R. A. Thomas to be major, Lieut. and Brevet Capt. T. Fisher to be captain of a company, and Ens. H. Palmer to be lieut., from 13th Aug. 1835, in suc. to Major H. M. Wheeler prom.

Col. G. Becher, of L.C., to command Dinapore division of army, with rank of brigadier, during absence of Brig. Gen. W. Richards, c.s., on leave to the Hills, or until further orders.

Lieut. W. O. Young, regt. of artillery, to officiate as a commissary of ordnance, v. Lieut. Day.

Cadets of Infantry J. C. Brooke and Fletcher Shuttleworth admitted on establishment and promoted to ensigns.

Superintending Surg. W. Findon, being junior of that rank, to revert to grade of surgeon, agreeably to existing regulations, consequent on Sup. Surg. S. Ludlow's return to his duty.

Lieut. Mellish, 10th L.C., to take charge of invalids, &c., of H.C. service, under orders of embarkation for Europe on ship *Duke of Buccleugh.*

Major C. A. Munro, 74th N.I., permitted, at his own request, to retire from service of Hon. Company, on pension of his rank, from 15th Dec.

Capt. H. B. Henderson, 1st-assistant, to be deputy military auditor-general, v. Lieut. Col. Kennedy permitted to proceed to Europe on medical certificate.

Capt. J. Pyne, 2d-assistant, to be 1st-assistant military auditor general, v. Capt. Henderson.

Lieut. R. G. MacGregor, of artillery, to be 2d-assistant military auditor-general, v. Capt. Pyne.

Dec. 14.—Cadets of Infantry A. W. Onslow and A. H. Kennedy admitted on estab., and prom. to ensign.

Major Wm. Buckley, 5th L.C., permitted, at his own request, to retire from service of Hon. Company, on pension of his rank.

Head-Quarters, Dec. 8.—The following removals and postings of medical officers made:—Surgeons George Govan, M.D. (on furl.), from 37th to 12th N.I.; Robert Brown from 36th to 37th do., at Agra; John Griffiths from 8th to 59d do.—Assist. Surgs. E. T. Downes from 37th to 49th N.I., at Neemuch; Samuel Winbolt from 49th to 8th do., at Nusseerabad; C. J. Davidson, on being relieved from medical charge of 10th N.I., to proceed and do duty under superintending surgeon of Benares.

Dec. 9.—Capt. J. D. Douglas, dep. assist. adjutant-general of Benares division, to conduct duties of department during indisposition of Brev. Major D. D. Anderson, assist. adj. gen.; date 29th Nov.

Superintending Surg. Samuel Ludlow posted to presidency division.

Surg. W. Findon to officiate as superintending surgeon to Benares division, during employment as a member of medical board of Superintending Surg. J. Sawers.

Surg. D. Renton, 18th N.I., officiating superintending surgeon to Benares division, to rejoin his corps on arrival of Officiating Superintending Surgeon Findon within Benares circle of superintendence.

Lieut. G. B. Reddie, 29th N.I., to officiate as interp. and qu. mast. to that regt., from 16th Nov., in room of Lieut. F. C. Marsden, who has obtained leave, on med. cert.

Lieut. H. R. W. Ellis, 23d N.I., to officiate as interp. and qu. mast. to 28th N.I., during absence, on med. cert., of Lieut. Interp. and Qu. Mast. R. Smith.

Assist. Surg. R. Christie to proceed to Katmandoo, and to place himself under orders of resident at Nepaul.

Unposted Ensigns J. C. Brooke and F. Shuttleworth to do duty with 14th N.I. at Moradabad.

Dec. 11.—Unposted Cornet J. A. D. Fergusson, doing duty with 6th L.C., to act as adj. to corps during indisposition of Cornet (now Lieut.) and Adj. J. R. Burt; date 14th Oct.

The following postings and removals made:—Col. John Simpson, new prom. (on furl.), to 58th N.I.—Lieut. Col. John Craigie (member military board), on leave to Cape of Good Hope, from 48th to 69th N.I.—Lieut. Col. H. M. Wheeler, new prom., to 48th N.I.

The following removals and postings to take place in Regt. of Artillery:—Capts. G. R. Crawfurd (on furl.) from 1st comp. 7th bat. to 3d comp. 3d bat.; H. Rutherford (on staff employ) from 2d comp. to 1st comp. 7th bat.; D. Ewart (on temporary staff employ) from 3d comp. 3d bat. to 2d comp. 7th bat.; P. T. Cautley (on staff employ), new prom., to 6th comp. 6th bat.—1st-Lieuts. G. F. C. Fitzgerald (on staff employ) from 4th comp. 4th bat. to 7th comp. 7th bat; L. Smith, new prom., to 4th comp. 4th bat.—2d-Lieuts. E. R. E. Wilmot (on furl.) from 2d comp. 4th bat. to 4th tr. 2d brig. horse artillery; R. Warburton, brought on strength, to 4th comp. 4th bat.; J. S. Phillips, brought on strength, to 2d comp. 4th bat—2d-Lieut. Warburton to continue to act as qu. mast. to 6th bat., during absence, on sick leave, of Lieut. and Qu. Mast. J. L. Mowatt.

Dec. 12.—Surg. A. Ross, 4th L.C., to have medical charge of artillery detachment under command of Lieut. Col. C. P. King, at Jeypore; date 23d Nov.

Dec. 15.—Assist. Surg. Wm. Rait, doing duty with 1st brigade horse artillery, to proceed to Mussoorie, and afford medical aid to officers of civil and military services residing there, until relieved by Assist. Surg. John Magrath; date 2d Dec.

Dec. 16.—Lieut. and Brev. Capt. H. Clerk, of artillery, to act as adj. to division of artillery at Neemuch, during absence, on duty, of Lieut. W. O. Young.

Cornet E. K. Money, 7th L.C., to act as interp. and qu. mast. to corps, from 29th Nov.

Dec. 18.—Surg. R. Brown to afford medical aid to detachment of 4th L.C. at Nusseerabad, under command of Capt. S. Nash; date 1st Dec.

Ens. R. A. Herbert to act as interp. and qu. mast. to 46th N.I., during absence, on leave, of Lieut. Drake; date 1st Dec.

Examinations. — The undermentioned officers having been declared by the examiners of the College of Fort William to be qualified for the duties of interpreter, are exempted from further examination in the native languages, *viz.*— Nov. 24. Lieut. F. W. Birch, 41st N.I.—Lieut. G. A. Mee, 58th do.

The undermentioned officers having been pronounced qualified in the Persian and Hindoostanee languages by a district committee, are exempted from further examination, except by the examiners of the College of Fort William, which it is expected they will undergo whenever they may visit the presidency, *viz.*—Dec. 2. Lieut. J. C. Sai-

keld, 5th N.I.—Lieut. G. B. Reddie, 29th do.—Lieut. W. F. Campbell, 64th do.—5. Ensign J. W. Carnegie, 15th do.—Lieut. R. S. Simpson, 27th do.

Returned to duty, from Europe.—Nov. 23. Lieut. T. H. Shuldham, 52d N.I.—Dec. 7. Col. F. V. Raper, 42d N.I.—Capt. R. Gardener, 13th N.I.—Capt. D. Simpson, 29th N.I.—Lieut. C. W. Haig, 5th N I.—Surg. M. Nisbet, M.D.—Superintending Surg. S. Ludlow.—14. Assist. Surg. C. B. Handyside, M.D.

FURLOUGHS.

To Europe.—Nov. 23. Capt. James Croudace, 11th N.I.—Lieut. B. Kendall, left wing European regt.—Lieut. John Graham, 55th N.I., for health. —2d-Lieut. E. W. S. Scott, artillery, for health.—Ens. C. A. Hepburne, 51st N.I., for one year, for health.—Capt. R. R. Hughes, 62d N.I., on private affairs.—30. Capt. Thos. Seaton, 35th N.I., on ditto.—Surg. Joseph Duncan, on ditto.—Lieut. Roderick Macdonald, 69th N.I., for health.—Lieut. Joseph Chilcott, 74th N.I., for health.—Ens. W. H. L. Bird, 12th N.I., for health.—Dec. 7. Lieut. Col. W. Kennedy, 16th N.I., and deputy military auditor general, for health.—Lieut. H. P. Voules, 3d L.C., for health.—Lieut. D. G. A. F. H. Mellish, 10th L.C., on private affairs.—Lieut. F. C. Marsden, 29th N.I., on ditto.—14. Capt. A. J. Fraser, 56th N.I., on ditto.—Capt. H. O. Frederick, 67th N.I., on ditto.—Lieut. J. H. Blanshard, 63d N.I., on ditto.—Assist. Surg. Alex. Chalmers, M.D., for health.—Assist. Surg. D. W. Nash, for health (to proceed from Bombay).

To visit Presidency (preparatory to applying for furlough to Europe).—Nov. 20. Lieut. J. B. Lock, 5th N.I.—14. Assist. Surg J. Esdaile, M.D.

To Bombay.—Nov. 23. Capt. John Moule, 23d N.I., for four months, on private affairs.

To Cape of Good Hope.—Nov. 30. Col. Wm. Hopper, regt. of artillery, for two years, for health.—Dec. 7. Capt. R. G. Roberts, of artillery, for ditto ditto.

Cancelled.—Dec. 14. The furl. to Europe granted to Lieut. T. B. Studdy, 8th L.C., on 31st Aug.

His Majesty's Forces.

To Europe.—Lieut. W. Ellis, 16th Lancers.—Lieut. J. W. Audain, 3d Foot.—Brev. Capt. R. S. Ridge, 13th L. Drags.—Lieut Lord C. Kerr, 6th Foot.—Lieut. J. B. Chalk, 54th Foot.—Lieut. P. P. Neville, 26th Foot.—Capt. Allan Stewart, of the Buffs, for six months, and to report himself at the Horse Guards (having been absent without leave from 16th Jan. to 19th Nov. 1835).

SHIPPING.
Arrivals in the River.

Nov. 25. *Ernaad*, Hill, and *Ruby*, Warden, both from China and Singapore; *Irma*, Benard, from Havre de Grace.—26. *Ararat*, Wyatt, from Penang.—27. *Lucullus*, Duranteau, and *Eucharis*, Maksin, both from Bordeaux; *Elizabeth*, Baker, from Rangoon; *Octorava*, Fairfour, from Philadelphia.—28. *Windsor*, Henning, from London; *St. George*, Thomson, from Bristol, Cape, and Madras.—29. *Lady Clifford*, Masson, from Moulmein; *Nerbudda*, Patrick, from China, &c.; *Highland Chief*, Hullock, from Penang.—Dec. 4. *Syed Khan*, McKinnon, from China and Singapore.—5. *Bombay Packet*, Garnock, from Bombay; *Hero*, Morris, from Moulmein.—9. *Lady Grant*, Jeffreys, from China and Singapore.—10. *Duke of Bedford*, Bowen, from London.—11. *Red Rover*, Clifton, from China.—12. *Hope*, Fleming, from Philadelphia.—13. *Euphrates*, Hannay, from Liverpool.—15. *Lord Hungerford*, Farquharson, from London.—17. *Bresbornebury*, Chapman, from London and Cape; *Diana*, Hawkins, from Liverpool; *Adelaide*, Steele, from Hobart Town; *Washington*, Taylor, from Philadelphia; *Florence*, Russell, from Boston; *Alexander*, Ramsay, from Sydney.—18. *Salamandre*, Debia, from Bordeaux and Pondicherry; *Water Witch*, Henderson, from China and Singapore.—19. *Collingwood*, Hookey, from China, Penang, &c.—23. *John Woodall*, Arnold, from Liverpool.—*Isabella*, Brown, from Liverpool—*London*, McLean, from London. — 26. *Duke of Northumberland*, Pope, from London and Cape.—27. *Indien*, Truquelet, from Havre de Grace.—28. *Resolution*, Seagar, from Padang.—30. H.M.S. *Victor*, Crozier, from Penang.

Departures from Calcutta.

Nov. 23. *Mount Vernon*, Scoble, for Boston.—Dec. 15. *Edward*, Land, for Philadelphia.—21. *Thetis*, Clark, for China.—25. *Duke of Buccleugh*, Martin, for London.—27. *Lonach*, Jellicoe, for Bombay; *Eliza*, Campbell, for London —Jan. 3. *Duke of Bedford*, Bowen (proceeding down the river), for London.

Sailed from Saugor.

Nov. 24. *Hooghly*, Teansolon, for Marseilles.—26. *Attaran*, Smith, for Madras.—27. *Isadora*, Hodson, for Madras.—30. *Sir Archibald Campbell*, Robertson, for Bombay.—Dec. 4. *Barretto Junior*, Saunders, for Madras and England.—7. *Will Watch*, Bristow, for Madras and Pondicherry.—9. *Marion*, Richard, for Singapore and China.—11. *Lawrence*, Gill, for Liverpool.—12. *Bland*, Callan, for Liverpool.—13. *Sir Herbert Taylor*, Wemyss, for Mauritius.—15. *Elizabeth*, McNair, for Liverpool.—16. *Solon*, Allan, for New York.—18. *Helen*, Macalister, for Penang and Singapore.—23. *Bolton*, Compton, for London.—24. *Mountstuart Elphinstone*, Toller, for London.—25. *Fairlie*, Ager, for London.—28. *Earl of Clare*, Scott, for China — *Georgiana*, Thoms, for London.—*Fortitude*, Lambert, for Boston.

To Sail.—Robert Small, for Cape and London, on 3d Jan.; London, for London, 4th Jan.; Lord Hungerford, for London, 8th Jan.; Herefordshire, for London, 10th Jan.; St. George, for Bristol, 15th Jan.; Cornwall, for London, 18th Jan.; Euphrates, for Liverpool, 20th Jan.; Windsor, for Cape and London, 20th Jan.; Broxbornebury, for London, 28th Jan.

Freight to London (Dec. 31)—Sugar and saltpetre, £5; rice, £5. 5s. to £5. 10s.; linseed, £5. 15s.; indigo and silk, £6. to £6. 10s.

BIRTHS, MARRIAGES, AND DEATHS.

BIRTHS.

Oct. 28. At Neemuch, the lady of Capt. Aitchison, of a son.

Nov. 3. At Kyook Phyo, the lady of Lieut. John Erskine, 40th N.I., of a son (since dead).

5. At Sultanpore, Oude, the lady of Lieut. Samuel Toulmin, 63d N.I., of a son.

8. At Mussoorie, the lady of Capt. E. Wintle, 71st regt., of a son.

10. At Seetapore, Oude, the lady of Capt. D. Sherriff, 48th N I., of a son.

15. At Muttra, the lady of Capt. G. L. Trafford, 10th L.C., of a son.

16. At Kidderpore, the lady of J. P. Maillard, Esq., of a son.

18. At Allahabad, Mrs. Hoff. of a son.

— At Monghyr, the lady of C. C. Fussell, Esq., of a daughter.

— Mrs. M. Gonsolves, of a son.

— Mrs. J. S. Dover, of a son.

19. At Cawnpore, the lady of Lieut. Wm. Ashmore, H.M.'s 16th regt., of a daughter.

21. At Meerut, the lady of the Rev. J. C. Proby, chaplain, of a son.

23. At Gowhatty, in Assam, the lady of Capt. William Simonds, commanding the local bat., of a daughter.

— Mrs. B. Macmahon, of a son.

25. At Gorruckpore, the lady of Hugh Gibbon, Esq., of a daughter.

26. At Ramnaghur factory, Barasett, Mrs. F. W Lidiard, of a son.

27. At Ishapore, Mrs. Briton, of a son.

28. At Dacca, the lady of Capt. Thomas Fisher, superintendent of Cachar, of a son.

30. Mrs. L. Fraser, of a son.

Dec. 1. At Agra, the lady of Brevet Capt. Havelock, adj. H.M. 13th L. Inf., of a daughter.

2. At Chowringhee, the lady of A. Liddell, Esq., of a daughter.

— At Mozufferpoor, Tirhoot, the lady of Dr. K. Mackinnon, of a daughter.

— Mrs. J. Weaver, of a son.

3. At Bubadoorgunge, in zillah Poorneah, the wife of Mr. J. B. Rondeau, of a son.

4. At Oya, the lady of F. Gouldsbury, Esq., C.S., of a daughter.

5. At Allahabad, the lady of R. H. Scott, Esq., C.S., of a son.

6. At Cawnpore, the lady of Lieut. Gascoyne, 5th Cavalry, of a daughter.

7. At Monghyr, the lady of A. Lang, Esq., of a son.

— At Allahabad, Mrs. E. G. Fraser, of a son.

— Mrs. Mark D'Cruze, of a son.

9. Mrs. N. S. Sweedland, of a daughter.

10. At Calcutta, the lady of Capt. John Macdonald, 61st N.I., of a son.

— At Meerut, the lady of Lieut. Stewart, H.A., of a son.

— At Benares, Mrs. J. A. B. Campbell, of a daughter.

— Mrs. John Russell, of a son.

11. At Burdwan, the lady of G. N. Cheek, Esq., civil surgeon, of a son.

— Mrs F. La Valette, of a daughter.

12. At Calcutta, the lady of F. Millett, Esq., C.S., of a daughter.

13. At Noacolly, the lady of F. J. Halliday, Esq., of a son.

— At Ballygunge, the lady of Capt. Prole, 37th regt., N.I., of a son.

14. At Calcutta, the lady of the late Capt. J. E. Debrett, of artillery, of a daughter.

— Mrs. M. A. Pereira, of a daughter.

— Mrs. George Higginson, of a son.

15. The lady of Dr. Graham, of a daughter.

16. At Kishnaghur, the lady of C. W. Fuller, Esq., civil surgeon, of a daughter.

— Mrs. John Muller, of a son.

17. At Serampore, the lady of J. Davidson, Esq., of a son, which expired a few minutes after its birth.

18. At Chowringhee, the lady of Major Archd. Irvine, C.B., engineers, of a son.

— Mrs. J. S. Dover, of a son.

— Mrs. M. Gonsalves, of a son.

20. At Calcutta, the lady of Mr. Wm. Sinclair, of a son.

MARRIAGES.

Nov. 12. At Meerut, E. C. Monckton, Esq., C.S., to Miss C. R. Woodcock.

14. At Saugor, Lieut. F. W. Burkinyoung, 5th N.I., to Charlotte Maria, eldest daughter of Col. and Mrs. Salmon.

— At Calcutta, Mr. James Ellison to Mary Louisa, second daughter of the late Lewis Namey, Esq.

16. At Calcutta, John Brown, Esq., of Burresaul, to Elizabeth Cecelia, eldest daughter of L. F. Pereira, Esq., of the General Post Office.

18. At Calcutta, Wm. Gordon, M.D., to Margaret, eldest daughter of Alex. Johnston, Esq., Newmill, Elgin, Scotland.

22. At Jessore, Henry C. Metcalfe, Esq., C.S., to Miss Madeline Catania.

23. At Cuttack, C. L. Babington, Esq., of Sumbhulpoor, to Miss H. Robinson, niece of Col. F. Walker, commanding 33d regt. N.I.

— At Calcutta, E.W. Brightman, Esq., to Eleanor Caroline, fifth daughter of the late Joseph Hodges, Esq.

— At Howrah, Mr. Thos. Reeves to Miss Elizabeth Amelia Farrow.

— At Seetapore, Ensign H. D. Van Homrigh, 48th N.I., son of the late Peter Van Homrigh, Esq., M.P. for Drogheda, to Caroline Louisa, daughter of Capt. R. A. Thomas, 48th N I.

— At Calcutta, Lawrence D'Silva, Esq., of Backergunge, to Miss A. Eassan.

24. At Calcutta. Lieut. James Sissmore, 23d N.I., to Miss Sophia Jane Dick, eldest daughter of Col. Dick, B.N.I.

— At Calcutta, Mr. John Thomas Mitchell to Miss Elizabeth Portray Aubray.

25. At Calcutta, Capt. J. M. Higginson to Miss Louisa Mary Ann Shakespear.

— At Calcutta, W. W. Glass, Esq., to Eliza Cordelia Emily, third daughter of Mark Leckersteen, Esq.

Dec. 1. At Calcutta, George Loch, Esq., C.S., to Louisa, only daughter of the late Major Robert Gordon, Bombay engineers.

— At Calcutta, George Chisholm, Esq., to Mrs. Caroline Kellner.

2. At Calcutta, Capt. Peter Mitchell to Miss Elizabeth Clementina Bason.

3. At Calcutta, Mr. John Childs, H.C. marine, to Miss E. B. Laine.

3. At Calcutta, Mr. John Wm. Peterson to Miss Susannah Thomas.

5. At Delhi, Humphrey Howorth, Esq., 59th N.I., to Louisa Catherine, second daughter of Brigadier Fast, commanding at Delhi.

7. At Calcutta, George Gordon MacPherson, Esq., surgeon at Moorshedabad, to Charlotte, eldest daughter of the late Wm. Leycester, Esq., of the civil service.

8. At Calcutta, George Wilding Chisholm, Esq., to Mrs. Elizabeth Harrold.

16. At Calcutta, Mr. Walter Witchlow to Mrs. Maria Rebeiro.

DEATHS.

Nov. 1. Mrs. Hosannah Joaquim, aged 42.

7. At Cawnpore, Ensign Edward Brabason, of H.M. 16th regt. of Foot

12. The Rana of Dhoulpore. His son Bhugwant Singh, thirteen years old, succeeds him.

13. At Etawah, Eliza, wife of Lieut. Edmund Talbot, adjutant 53d regt. N.I., aged 25.

— At Saugor, Lieut. Charles Terraneau, of the 5th regt. N.I.

14. At Calcutta, Mr. Wm. Christian, of the ship *Robert Small*, aged 94.

17. Master George Jones, aged 12.

19. At Mundlesir, Major R. W. Smith, of the 6th regt. L.C.

23. At Joudhpore, Assist. Surg. W. H. Rogers, of the 4th regt. L.C.

94. At Calcutta, Sarah, lady of J. P. Maillard, Esq., army agent, aged 27.

27. At Monghyr, Mrs. C. C. Fussell, second daughter of the Rev. Wm. Moore, aged 19.

28. At Allahabad, in his 31st year, J. A Greenway, Esq., proprietor of the *Central Free Press* at that station. He was sitting up correcting proof sheets until midnight, and the next morning at five was a corpse.

— Capt. Alexander Broughton Fraser, late of the country service, aged 40.

30. Mrs. Eliza Matilda Gee, aged 27.

Dec. 1. At Patna, Sarah, relict of the late Ross Jennings, Esq., aged 83.

— At Cuttack, Mrs. J. C. Pritchard, of the Cuttack salt agency, aged 23.

— Mr. Thomas Smith, aged 42.

5. Mr. John Turner, superintendent of Hooghly Point, Semaphore station.

6. At Calcutta, Mrs. A. G. Aviet, aged 16.

— Mr. Samuel Gomes, aged 20.

7. At Calcutta, Capt. James Masson, commander of the bark *Lady Clifford*, aged 23.

— Mrs. John Landeman, aged 34.

— Mrs. Charles Arrandal Sealy, aged 37.

9. At the residence of Mrs. Ross, Sulkea, Allen Robertson, Esq., aged 39.

12. At Calcutta, of consumption, Harriet, wife of Mr. B. Macmahon, aged 33.

— Master George Aris, aged 13.

13. At Calcutta, Mr. Wm. Johnson, of the ship *Mountstuart Elphinstone*, aged 22.

— At Calcutta, Joseph Pereira, Esq., aged 65.

14. At Calcutta, Susana, widow of the late Mr. Manuel Cardoso, aged 46.

16. At Balloo Ghaut, on board his boat, Major Edward Whitty, paymaster H.M. 26th regt., an hour after his arrival from Meerut, on medical certificate, to proceed to Europe.

Madras.

GOVERNMENT ORDERS, &c.

OCCUPATION OF PUBLIC QUARTERS.

Fort St. George, Oct. 2, 1835.—The 6th paragraph, page 368, of the Code of Pay Regulations, is cancelled, and all officers, without distinction, in command of divisions or stations, who shall occupy public quarters, will be subject, from the 1st proximo, to stoppage or payment of rent on the scale laid down in G. O. G. 29th March 1831 : colonel to be subject to the same charge as field officers.

DEPÔT AT POONAMALLEE.

Fort St. George, Nov. 24, 1835.—The Right Hon. the Governor in Council is pleased to direct, that from the 31st of December next, the depôt at Poonamallee be discontinued as a government command ; and that from the 1st January 1836 the duties shall be conducted by the senior officer for the time being, assisted by the staff officer and paymaster.

The present establishment will be disposed of as follows, from the same date :

Officer commanding—discontinued as a government command, staff pay to cease.

Staff Officer and Paymaster—to remain as at present.

Assistant Surgeon—to remain upon the same staff allowance as for the charge of a regiment.

Garrison Serjeant Major—to remain as at present.

Cantonment Serjeant Major—to remain as depôt serjeant major.

Ditto as Drill Serjeant—discontinued, staff pay to cease.

Commissariat Staff Serjeant—at the disposal of the commissary general.

Barrack Serjeant—to remain and perform the duties of key serjeant ; a serjeant of 2d class to be appointed on the occurrence of a vacancy.

Key Serjeant—discontinued, the present incumbent available for transfer to another station on a vacancy.

Hospital Serjeant—to remain as at present.

Librarian—to remain as at present.

Serjeant in charge of great coats—discontinued, staff pay to cease.

Store Serjeants, one for each of his Majesty's regts.—to remain as pay and store serjeants on the same allowance as pay serjeant of a company ; present staff pay to cease.

Store Corporals, one for each of his Majesty's regts.—discontinued, staff pay to cease.

Barrack Conicopoly—discontinued, to be discharged.

The present permanent establishment of the commissariat department, both for King's and Company's troops, will be discontinued from the same date ; and the number and description of barrack attendants will in future be regulated, according to the provisions of the G. O. G. 24th Jan. 1812, by the number of European troops actually present : arrangements to be made for these regulations to be in effect on the 1st January 1836. The scavenger's cart upon the same scale as at St. Thomas's Mount (Rs. 14 per mensem), will be kept up under charge of the staff officer.

The detail of store lascars will be recalled by the Military Board.

CIVIL APPOINTMENTS, &c.

Dec. 8. W. A. Forsyth, Esq., to act as assistant judge and joint criminal judge of Malabar, during absence of Mr. Strange.

15. Malcolm Lewin, Esq., to act as 2d judge of provincial court of appeal and circuit for northern division, v. Mr. Nicholls permitted to proceed to Europe.

Patrick Grant, Esq., to act as collector and magistrate of Rajahmundry, during employment of Mr. Lewin on other duty.-

W. A. Neave, Esq., to act as collector and magistrate of Guntoor, during employment of Mr. Grant on other duty.

H. V. Conolly, Esq., to be assistant to the sub-treasurer.

F. N. Maltby, Esq., to act as head-assistant to principal collector and magistrate of Canara.

29. C. E. Oakes, Esq., to act as assistant judge and joint criminal judge of Guntoor.

J. Rohde, Esq., to act as assistant judge and joint criminal judge of Ganjam, during absence of Mr. Arbuthnot.

H. D. Phillips, Esq., to resume, at his own request, his appointment of register to zillah court of Nellore.

J. C. Taylor, Esq., to act as head assistant to principal collector and magistrate of Nellore, during employment of Mr. Smollet on other duty.

D. White, Esq., to act as sub-collector and joint magistrate of Malabar, during absence of Mr. Smith.

———

J. Goldingham, Esq., acting judge and criminal judge of Salem, took charge of the zillah court at that station, on the 1st Dec.

H. V. Conolly, Esq., resumed his duties as cashier of the Government Bank on the 10th Dec.

George Garrow, Esq., was, on the 22d Dec., sworn acting civil auditor.

The following gentlemen have accepted annuities from the Civil Fund:—The Hon. Wm. Oliver, Esq.; Solomon Nicholls, Esq.; Edward Smalley, Esq.; and Henry Gardiner, Esq.; date 24th Nov. 1835.

Henry Gardiner, Esq., and S. Nicholls, Esq., have been permitted to resign the service of the Hon. Company.

The following gentlemen have returned to duty, viz.—Hatley Frere, Esq., from Europe.— Rev. John Hallewell, chaplain of Cuddalore, from Cape of Good Hope.

———

Attained Rank.—W. Douglas, as senior merchant, on 6th Oct. 1835; E. Storey, as factor, on 27th do.

MILITARY APPOINTMENTS, PROMOTIONS, &c.

Fort St. George, Dec. 8, 1835. — Lieut. (Brev. Capt.) S. Hicks, of 35th N.I., permitted to resign appointment of adj. to that corps.

Lieut. C. Woodfall, 47th N.I., to officiate as paymaster in northern division, on Capt. Duff's responsibility, during his absence.

Dec. 11.—4th L.C. Cornet James Norman to be lieut., v. Maitland dec.; date of com. 3d Dec. 1835.

Adjutant General's Office, Dec. 2, 1835.—Lieut. S. F. Mackenzie, 2d L.C., permitted to rejoin his regt. vid Madras.

Dec. 8.—Ens. Edward Dumergue, left wing European regt., removed, at his own request, to 27th N.I., and will rank next below Ens. John Mylne.

Ens. P. F. Thorne, 16th N.I., removed, at his own request, to left wing European regt , and will rank next below Ens. Andrew Walker.

Dec. 9.—Lieut. P. Oliphant to act as adj. to 35th N.I., v. Hicks resigned.

Assist. Surg. James Shaw removed from Madras European regt. to 2d L.C.

Dec. 11.—Lieut. Col. W. K. Ritchie (late prom.) posted to 2d N.I.

Dec. 12.—Ensigns J. F. Erskine and F. F. Warden removed from doing duty with 29th to 18th N.I.

Lieut. John Cooke, horse artillery, to act as qu. mast. of that corps, during absence on duty of Lieut. and Qu. Mast. Showers.

Dec. 14.—Cornet E. C. Curtis, 3d L.C., permitted to join his corps at Bellary.

Dec. 17.—Assist. Surg. C. Don removed from 3d bat. artillery to do duty with Madras European regt.

Dec. 18.—Assist. Surg. J. Kellie placed at disposal of officer commanding northern division, for employment with force in Goomsoor.

Dec. 19 to 22.—Capt. W. P. Macdonald, 41st N.I., with sanction of government, to do duty with 3d L.Inf., and to join detachment in Ganjam district.

2d-Lieut. W. M. Gabbett to act as qu. mast. and interp. to 4th bat. artillery, during absence of Lieut. Rowlandson, or until further orders.

Assist. Surg. J. E. Porteous, 39th N.I., to afford medical aid to detail of H.M. 41st Foot, and all public followers proceeding from Poonamallee to join regimental head-quarters at Arnee.

Assist. Surg. T. White to proceed to Aska.

Assist. Surg. W. G. Davidson, 43d N.I., to proceed to Aska and receive his orders from officer commanding northern division.

Assist. Surg. R. H. Buchanan to proceed and take medical charge of 43d N.I., during absence of Assist. Surg. Davidson.

Lieut. Col. S. S. Gummer removed from 14th to 8th N.I., and Lieut. Col. G. Muriel from latter to former corps.

Capt. T. E. Geils removed from 3d to 4th bat. artillery; 2d-Lieut. F. B. Ashley from 2d to 4th do.; 2d-Lieut. W. M. Gabbett from 2d to 4th do.; and Supernum. 2d-Lieut. R. Bromley from 3d to 4th do.

Fort St. George, Dec. 22.—Assist. Surg. Hugh Cheape, of horse artillery, to be attached to Hon. G. L. Russell, Esq., during his employment in Goomsoor.

Dec. 23.—Cadet of Cavalry Henry Hall admitted on estab., and prom. to cornet.—Cadets of Infantry G. Fitzmaurice and Robert Woolley admitted on ditto, and prom. to ensigns.

Assist. Surg. D. Macdougall permitted to resign his appointment on Neilgherries.

Dec. 29.—Surg. W. E. E. Conwell, M.D., to act as superintending surgeon in ceded districts during absence of Sup. Surg. J. Macleod at presidency, preparatory to applying for leave to return to Europe on sick certificate.

Surg. George Meikle to act as superintending surgeon in northern division of army, during absence of Sup. Surg. Haines on sick certificate at Neilgherries.

Adjutant-general's Office, Dec. 24 to 29.—The following young officers to do duty:—Cornet H. Hall with 2d L.C.; Ens. G. Fitzmaurice with 9th N.I.; and Ens. R. Woolley with 28th do.

The services of Lieut. G. A. Marshall, 18th N.I. and Ens. T. L. Place, 44th do., placed at disposal of officer commanding northern division, to be employed with a corps in that division serving in the field.

Returned to duty, from Europe.—Dec. 11. Lieut. K. E. A. Money, 4th L.C.—23. Lieut. W. D. M. Lys, 22d N.I.—Lieut. J. M. Macdonald, 1st L.C.

Rewards.—The following officers have been deemed by the Commander-in-chief entitled to the reward authorized by the Hon. the Court of Directors for proficiency in the Oriental languages, viz. —*In Persian :* Lieut. J. Haplin, 30th N.I.; Lieut. D. C. Campbell, 9th do.—*In Hindoostanee:* Lieut. C. M. Macleane, acting qu. mast. and interp., 43d N.I.

———

FURLOUGHS.

To Europe.—Dec. 4. Lieut. F. Gottreux, 1st N.I., for health (to embark from western coast).— Maj. C. O. Fothergill, Carnatic European Vet. Bat. (to embark from Vizagapatam).—11. Surg. W. H. Richards, for health.—Capt. J. T. Brett, 4th L.C. (to embark from western coast).—Capt. J. Fullerton, 17th N.I., for health.—18. Major C. M. Bird, 31st L.Inf., for health.—Lieut. G. Freese, 12th N.I., for health.—Assist. Surg. James Hamlyn, for health.—22. Maj. H. W. Hodges, 34th L. Inf., for health.—Major G. Stott, 11th N.I.—23. Lieut. Thomas Bayles, 52d N.I., for health (to embark from western coast)—Lieut. T. W. Jones, European Regt.—Assist. Surg. J. Bell, for health.—29. Lieut. H. Pereira, 43d N.I., for health —Capt. R. Gordon, 26th N.I., for health.—Lieut. A. R. Rose, 50th N.I., for health.—Lieut. Col. John Morgan, 28th N.I., for health.

To visit Presidency (preparatory to applying for furlough to Europe).—Dec. 11. Superintending Surg. J. Macleod, ceded districts.—8. Lieut. Col. J. Kitson, 23d L.Inf.—18. Lieut. Col. H. G. Jourdan, 10th N.I.—29. Lieut. E. J. Taynton, 8th N.I.

To Neilgherry Hills.—Dec. 11. Superintending

Surg. Wm. Haines, northern division, until 31st July 1836, for health.

To *Calcutta*—Dec. 18. Ens. G. H. Eckford, 12th N.I., until 15th June 1836.

To *Sea.*—Dec. 22. Lieut. H. A. Kennedy, 14th N.I., for two years, for health (also to Cape of Good Hope).

SHIPPING.

Arrivals.

Dec. 1. *Attaran*, Smith, from Calcutta.—4. *Eugene*, Couman, from Bourbon and Mauritius.—5. *Louisa*, De la Combe, from Tavoy.—8. *Sir Archibald Campbell*, Robertson, from Calcutta.—16. *Barretto Junior*, Saunders, from Calcutta.—13. *Will Watch*, Bristow, from Calcutta.—17. *Isadora*, Hodson, from Calcutta, Vizagapatam, &c.—21. *Wellington*, Liddell, from London, Madeira, and Cape.—23. *Tawse*, Paulier, from Masulipatam.—27. *Annandale*, Hill, from Bombay; *Bland*, Callan, from Calcutta.—28. H.M.S. *Hyacinth*, Blackwood, from Trincomalee; *Charles Stewart*, Davis, from Rangoon.—29. *Lady Flora*, Ford, from London; *Bassein Merchant*, Snowball, from Nicobar.—31. *Rubarts*, Wake, from London (off Madras).

Departures.

Dec. 14. *Charles Dumergue*, Hery, for Coringa and Vizagapatam; *Attaran*, Smith, for Pondicherry.—16. *Sir Archibald Campbell*, Robertson, for Cannanore and Bombay; *Will Watch*, Bristow, for Pondicherry and Ceylon.—27. *Louisa*, De la Combe, for Ganjam.—29. *Barretto Junior*, Saunders, for London.—30. *Blond*, Callan, for Liverpool.—31. *Heroine*, MacCarthy, for London.

BIRTHS, MARRIAGES, AND DEATHS.

BIRTHS.

Oct. 16. At Kamptee, the lady of Major Cleveland, commanding 38th regt., of a daughter.

Nov. 24. At Pondicherry, Mrs. Joyan, of a son.

25. At Kamptee, the lady of Capt. F.W. Hands, 38th N.I., of a daughter.

— At Madras, Mrs Hugh Ross, of a son.

Dec. 2. At Chicacole, the lady of Capt. J. W. Yaldwyn, 21st regt., of a daughter.

3. At Cochin, the lady of Asist. Surg. R. Oliphant, of a son.

— At Masulipatam, the lady of Capt. George Burn, 14th N.I., of a son.

— Mrs. Hugh Meredith, of a son.

— 4. Mrs. John Ritchie, of a daughter.

— At Vellore, the lady of Lieut. C. A. Cosby, 25th N.I., of a daughter.

8. Mrs. Burgess, of a daughter.

11. Mrs. A. L'Fleur, of a daughter.

13. At Trichinopoly, the lady of Brevet Capt. John Stoddart, H.M. 54th regt., of a daughter.

14. At Vizianagram, the lady of Major Leggett, commanding 3d L. Inf., of a on.

19. At Secunderabad, the lady of Lt. and Qu. Mast. Hughes, 39th N.I., of a son.

— Mrs. Thos. Wilmott, of a daughter.

20. At Nellore, Mrs. Maria Louisa Summers, of a daughter.

22. At Madras, the lady of Henry Chamier, Esq., of a son

23. At Madras, the lady of Major Ross, corps of engineers, of a daughter.

MARRIAGES.

Nov. 23. At Madras, Mr. John Xavier to Roza, daughter of the late Mr. Antonio Munis.

Dec. 8. At Tanjore, Henry Forbes, Esq., civil service, to Isabella, youngest daughter of Lieut. Col. Macleane, resident at Tanjore.

DEATHS.

Nov. 4. At Bangalore, Capt. G. C. Borough, of H.M. 39th regt. of Foot, youngest son of Sir Richard Borough, Bart., in his 28th year.

25. At Wallajabad, Mr. Burnella Peters, aged 96.

26. At the Club House, Madras, Mark Moore, Esq., of the civil service.

29. At Nagpore, Isabella, wife of Capt. William Warde, assistant resident at Nagpore, aged 36.

Dec. 1. At Pondicherry, Mrs. Joyan, aged 17.

3. At Secunderabad, Lieut. J. Maitland, of the 4th regt. Light Cavalry.

— At Trichinopoly, Mrs. Eliz. Kemp, aged 71.

— Mrs. Mary Magdaline Trutwein, aged 59.

7. At Madras, Mr. Francis Brisson, aged 56.

19. At Berhampore, Capt. Thos. Swaine, of the 49th regt. or W.I.

Bombay.

GOVERNMENT ORDERS &c,

STUDY OF THE NATIVE LANGUAGES BY MEDICAL OFFICERS.

Bombay Castle, Nov. 7, 1835.—The attention of government having been drawn to the necessity which exists, that medical officers, whose duties bring them into constant intercourse with the natives of the country, should possess some colloquial knowledge of the Hindoostanee, Mahratta or Guzerattee languages, the Right Hon. the Governor in Council is pleased to declare as follows :—

No medical officer shall henceforth be permanently appointed to the medical charge of a native regiment, to that of a civil station, to the office of vaccinator, to that of surgeon to any of the political residencies, or to any other medical charge, with the exception of those in the naval branch of the military service, without having passed an examination in one at least of the Hindoostanee, Mahratta, or Guzerattee languages.

It not being in contemplation to insist upon a greater knowledge of the native languages than is required for the efficient discharge of the duties confided to the medical officer, the examination will have in view such a colloquial command of the language as may suffice for that object, and will not include any of the exercises prescribed as tests of a higher degree of proficiency.

At whatever station two or more qualified interpreters are present, there, by order of the general commanding the division, a committee may be assembled for the purpose of such examination as aforesaid ; such committee to consist of two interpreters, and of the commanding officer of the regiment.

These regulations will not interfere with the temporary appointment of medical officers to any charge when the exigencies of the service require it ; but a medical officer so appointed, will be removed from such charge after a lapse of six months, should he not then be able to pass the requisite examination, and should there be a qualified officer to take his place.

The operation of these regulations will be entirely prospective, and will not now, or at any future time, affect the medical officers at present permanently posted to native regiments, or any of the other situations above specified.

These regulations are not to be under-

(G)

stood as lessening the inducement to medical officers to submit themselves to the higher examination, as now constituted, at the presidency. An examination, passed before the committee there, will remove the necessity of going before any other committee, and will, in addition, be considered by the Right Hon. the Governor in Council as highly to the credit of the individual.

All former regulations on this subject are cancelled.

UNFOUNDED IMPUTATION ON OFFICERS.

Marine Department, Bombay Castle, Nov. 10, 1835.—Captain Simpson having published a pamphlet, containing strictures on the proceedings of a committee which sat in 1834, for the purpose of enquiring into certain frauds committed in the Indian naval department, and having in that work ascribed to feelings of personal hostility against himself, the conduct of the committee alluded to, and especially of two of its members, Capt. Wilson, of the Indian navy, and Lieut. Pope, of the commissariat department, those officers some time since applied to the government to protect them against aspersions for acts performed in the discharge of a public duty.

The Right Hon. the Governor in Council feels that he cannot but admit the appeal thus preferred to him; while he, at the same time, thinks proper to abstain from any further reference to the publication in question.

Having minutely examined the alleged grounds of the imputation complained of, and having received, and considered the explanatory statements of Capt. Wilson and Lieut. Pope, the Governor in Council is pleased to declare, that he deems the imputation on those officers to be altogether unfounded, and is satisfied that, in the execution of a very invidious service, cast on them by an authority which they were bound to obey, they fulfilled their part most conscientiously, and under the influence of none but the purest and most honourable motives.

In reporting to government opinions unfavourable to Capt. Simpson, they knew that their report, which was confidential, could not possibly affect that officer, either in situation or in character, excepting as far as the government itself, to whose inspection every part of their proceedings was submitted, should choose to give it effect or notoriety.

The measure that followed of displacing Capt. Simpson for a time from the office, to which, in the sequel, he was, on a fuller investigation of his conduct, triumphantly restored, was obviously the act of the government alone.

In recurring, and, as he trusts, for the last time, to discussions which ought now to be for ever forgotten, the Governor in Council assures Capt. Wilson and Lieut. Pope, that he reposes the fullest and most unshaken confidence in their talents, public spirit, and integrity.

SEARCH FOR COAL IN CUTCH.

Bombay Castle, Nov. 14, 1835.—The Right Hon. the Governor in Council has been pleased, by a resolution passed in the general department, under date the 13th instant, to discontinue the office of superintendent for search of coal in Cutch, in which Lieut. G. B. Munbee, of the Engineers, is at present acting.

PARKUR PRIZE MONEY.

Bombay Castle, Nov. 17, 1835.—The Rt. Hon the Governor in Council is pleased to publish, for the information of all concerned, the following statement, exhibiting the scale of distribution of the Parkur prize property, and to intimate that abstracts should be preferred to the general prize committee's office for payment.

	Amount for each rank.		
Lieut.-Col. commanding (1) ⅛ of the whole	735	9	10
Major (1)	350	0	0
Captains, Surgeons, Major of Brigade, Dep.-Quart.-Mast.-Gen. (9)	175	0	0
Lieuts., Assist.-Surgeons, Ensigns, and Cornets (20)	87	8	0
Conductors (1)	21	14	0
Sub-Conductors, Line and Provost Serjeant, Serjeant-Major, and Assistant-Apothecary (6)	4	6	0
Subedars (10)	10	3	4
Jemedars (15)	4	6	0
Havildars (62)	1	15	1
European Corporals, Drummers, Bombardiers, and Gunners (44)	1	7	4
Native Naiks, Drummers and Trumpeters, Farriers, Sepoys, Puckalies, 2d Tindals, Lascars, and Hospital Assistants (1,093)	0	15	6

Total amount to be distributed, 5884*l*. 14*s* 11*d*.

Roll of regiments and detachments entitled to share in the property captured at Parkur, *viz.* :—Staff ; 2d regt. L. C. ; Artillery ; 21st regt. N. I. ; Poona Auxiliary Horse ; and Irregular Horse of H. H. the Rao of Cutch.

MEDICAL CHARGE OF TROOPS ON THE INDIA VOYAGE.

Bombay Castle, Nov. 21, 1835.—The following extract from a letter from the Hon. the Court of Directors, dated 26th June 1835, is published for general information.

1. " Referring to our dispatch in this department, of the 15th Nov. 1826, which allowed to surgeons of our chartered ships, the option of receiving in this country, the amount due to them for professional attendance on military that were from time to time to be embarked for your presidency, we have to direct, now, that the surgeon's responsibility ceases, upon the disembarkation of the military,

and his journal is deposited with your medical board, that claims of this nature, be in future settled at your presidency.

2. " It has been our invariable practice not to make any allowance for the wives and children of military officers and to pay upon such number of military only as were *landed*, rules which it is our desire should on all occasions be observed by you."

COURT MARTIAL.

LIEUT. J. BEEK.

At a General Court Martial assembled at Ahmedabad, on the 7th Sept. 1835, and of which Major T. Bailie, of the 24th regt. N.I, is president, Lieut. John Beek, of the 9th regt N.I., was tried on the following charge, viz. :

For highly unofficerlike and disgraceful conduct, in abandoning a party escorting himself and baggage, after the said party had been attacked on the march towards Ahmednuggur in Guzerat, and while it was engaged with a body of insurgents near the village of Huglore, on the morning of the 7th of May 1835.

Upon which charge the court came to the following decision :

Finding and Sentence.—That the prisoner, Lieut. John Beek, of the 9th regt. N.I., is guilty of the charge preferred against him, with the exception of the word " disgraceful," as the court do not consider his conduct to have arisen from personal cowardice ; and they do therefore adjudge him, the said Lieut. John Beek, to be dismissed the Hon. Company's service.

Recommendation.— The court having thus performed the duty of awarding the above punishment, beg leave, under the peculiar circumstances of the case, strongly to recommend the prisoner, Lieut. Beek, to the merciful consideration of his Exc. the Commander-in-chief.

(Signed)   T. BAILIE, Major and President.

Approved and Confirmed.—In consideration, however, of the recommendation of the court, and of the high character which Lieut. Beek has hitherto borne as an officer and gentleman, in his regiment and in the service, and taking also into consideration the high principles of honour by which, in my experience of the officers of the Bombay army, I have found them to be actuated and guided, I do not deem it necessary to make an example, by carrying into execution the sentence awarded by the court in this instance, and I therefore extend a full pardon to Lieut. Beek, of the 9th regt. N.I., in the confident anticipation, that his future career will be such as to reflect credit upon himself, and to occasion me no

regret at having extended this leniency towards him.

(Signed) J. KEANE, Lieut.Gen. Commander-in-chief.

Lieut. Beek is to be released from arrest, and ordered to return to his duty.

CIVIL APPOINTMENTS, &c.

Political Department.

Nov. 10. Mr. J. P. Willoughby, political agent in Kattewar, to be secre ary to government in political, secret, and judicial departments, in room of Mr. Norris

11. Lieut. W. Lang to be acting political agent in Kattywar.

Dec. 17. Capt. Ward to have charge of residency in Cutch, during absence of the resident to presidency on sick certificate.

General Department.

Dec. 29. W. H. Wathen, Esq., to be chief secretary to government, in suc. to C. Norris, Esq., who proceeded to England on 10th Nov.

Territorial Department—Revenue.

Nov. 7. Mr. A. W. Jones to be assistant to principal collector of Poona, and placed in charge of Barsee talooks.

Mr. C. Price to act as second assistant to collector of Rutnagherry.

Nov. 27. Mr. M. Larken to act as third assistant to collector of Candeish, under provisions of 22d clause of Absentee Regulation.

Dec. 15. Mr. W. Courtney to act as second assistant to collector of Kaira.

29. Mr. A. Hornby to be supernumerary assistant to collector of Tannah, as a temp. arrangement.

Territorial Department—Finance.

Nov. 20. Mr. B. Noton to resume his appointment of assay master of mint at this presidency.

Judicial Department.

Nov. 19. Mr. Henry Roper to be acting advocate-general and ex-officio president of committee for management of House of Correction, during absence of Mr. Le Messurier on sick certificate.

Dec. 16. Mr. W. C. Bruce, of the civil service, to be sheriff for ensuing year.

Mr. J. Little to be coroner of Bombay, in succession to Mr. Noton.

29. Mr. G. Grant to be acting judge and session judge of Surat, during absence of Mr. W. Lumsden, on leave.

The following gentlemen have returned to duty from Europe:—Mr. Wm. Courtney ; Mr. Arthur Hornby.

Furloughs, &c.—Nov. 19. Mr. A. S. Le Messurier, advocate general, to Cape of Good Hope, for twelve months, for health.

ECCLESIASTICAL.

Dec. 24. The Rev. A. Goode, chaplain of Bhooj, to be chaplain of Ahmednuggur and Mallegaum, in suc. to the Rev. C. Jackson, LL.B., proceeding to England.

Furlough.—Nov. 19. The Rev. G. C. Jackson, to Europe.

MILITARY APPOINTMENTS, PROMOTIONS, &c.

Bombay Castle, Oct. 29, 1835.—*18th N.I.* Ens. A. Macdonald to be qu. mast. and interp. in Hindoostanee ; date 15th Oct. 1835.

Nov. 3.—The following temporary arrangements confirmed:—Lieut. J. F. Frederick, 18th N.I., to conduct duties of commissariat department at Kulladghee, from 18th Oct.—Ens. E. Baynes, 20th, to act as adj. to left wing of 12th N.I., and to receive charge of remount depôt at Rajcote, from 1st Oct., during absence of Lieut. Baldwin on sick certificate.

The following officers, cadets of season 1819, to have brevet rank of captain, viz.—Lieut. T. H.

Ottley. 20th N.I.; Lieut. H. H. Hobson, 20th do.; and Lieut. N. Strong, right wing European regt., all from 6th Oct. 1835.

17th N I. Lieut. D. Davidson to be capt., and Ens. C. Manger to be lieut., in suc. to Billamore dec.; date of rank 20th Aug. 1835.

Nov. 9.—Lieut. T. H. Brown, fort adj. at Asseerghur, to act as second in command of Bheel corps, during Capt. Outram's absence in Guzerat.

Nov. 16.—Capt. J. W. Stokoe, of invalids, to be paymaster of pensioners in Northern Concan, in suc. to Lieut. Jackson dec.

Ens. C. Burnes, of 21st, transferred, at his own request, to 17th N.I., taking rank next below Ens. C. F. Sorrell, as 4th ensign.

The following temporary arrangement confirmed :—Capt. J. Clunes, 12th N.I., to assume command of station of Baroda, from 24th Sept. last.

Ens. Jones to act as qu. mast. to 12th N.I., from date of Ens. Brown's departure to Bombay; date 12th March 1835.

26th N.I. Ens. L. Scott to be interp. in Mahratta language; date 15th Oct. 1835.

Nov. 17.—Lieut. Col. T. Stevenson, horse artillery, to accompany Commander-in-chief on his Excellency's tour of inspection to Southern Mahratta country.

Nov. 20.—Capt. Scott to complete the public works now in progress at Sholapoor, before proceeding to join his appointment in Candeish.

Nov. 23.— The following temporary arrangements confirmed :—Surg. H. Johnston to perform duties of acting staff surgeon at Ahmedabad from 1st Sept.—Ens. H. W. Evans, 9th N.I., to act as adj. to field detachment of that regt. stationed at Ahmednuggur, consisting of upwards of 300 rank and file, from 20th Oct.

2d L.C. Lieut. W. J. Ottley to be qu. mast. and interp. in Hindoostanee; date 10th Nov. 1835.

Ens. R. N. Meade, 12th N.I., to act as adj. to left wing of that regt. at Rajcote, on departure of Lieut. Jessop on med. cert., until arrival of Lieut. Fisher.

Lieut. A. Nash, of engineers, to superintend operations of boring for water in the Deccan.

Lieut. G. B. Munbee to be assistant to superintending engineer at presidency.

Assist. Surg. J. F. Cullen, doing duty in Indian Navy, placed at disposal of Commander-in-chief.

Lieut. E. A. Guerin, 14th N.I., to be aide-de-camp to Brig. Gen. W. Gilbert, commanding southern division of army, from 13th Sept.

Cadet of Infanty A. P. Hunt admitted on estab., and prom. to ensign.

Nov. 24.—Assist. S. Fraser to act for Assist. Surg. Heddle as storekeeper of European General Hospital.

Nov. 26.—1st. Gr.N.I. Ens. H. C. Rawlinson to be lieut., v. Stuart dec.; date of rank 26th Feb. 1835.

Capt. W. Ogilvie, 26th N.I., to be paymaster of Poona division of army, v. Stark dec.

Lieut. Wingate, of engineers, appointed to a special duty under orders of Mr. Goldsmid the assistant collector in charge of pergunnahs of Indapoor and Mahole.

Nov. 30.—Assist. Surg. Prichard placed at disposal of superintendent of Indian Navy for duty in that branch of service.

Surg. J. Bird, 19th N.I., to act as surgeon of European General Hospital, during absence of Acting Sup Surg. Henderson.

The following temporary arrangements confirmed :—Lieut. T. Eyre, 3d L.C., to act as adj. to that regt., during period Lieut. and Adj. Mallet may be in charge of regt.—Ens. T. R. Prendergast, 10th N.I., to act as adj. to detachment of that regt. proceeding to Vingorla, Warree, and Malwan, consisting of 300 rank and file.

Cadet of Infantry A. N. Aitchison admitted on estab., and prom. to ensign.

Dec. 1.—Assist. Surg. Winchester to afford medical aid to Bhonj residency, during illness of Assist. Surg. Nicholson.

Dec. 10.—Capt. J. Outram, 23d N.I., to be an assistant in Thuggee department in Western Malwa and Guzerat; and Lieut. J. Hale, 23d N.I., to

act for him in that department, during his absence on a special mission to Mahee Caunta.

Assist. Surg. J. Don to act as occulist, during absence of Mr. Jeaffreson, on leave to Europe.

Maj. E. F. Hamilton, 21st N.I., permitted to retire from Hon. Company's service on pension of his rank.

Dec. 14.—Capt. C. Waddington, inspecting engineer S. D. of army, his duty at presidency having been completed, to return to his station.

Dec. 15.—Lieut. J. Pope, 17th N.I., to act as interp. in Hindoostanee and Mahratta languages to left wing 1st L.C., from 24th Nov., as a temp. arrangement.

Lieut. and Acting Adj. J. Holmes, 12th N.L., to act as qu. mast. to that regt., during absence of Ens. Brown, on sick cert., as a temp. arrangement

Assist. Surg. J. F. Cullen permitted to resign his commission in Hon. Company's service.

Cadet of Engineers John Hill admitted on estab., and prom. to 2d-lieut.—Cadets of Infantry W. E. Evans and R. Lane admitted on ditto, and prom. to ensigns.

Dec. 17.—Assist. Surg. R. Frith, M.D., civil surgeon of Rutnagherry, and Assist. Surg. J. J. Lawrence, civil surgeon of Sholapore, permitted to exchange respective appointments.

Assist. Surg. P. Hockin, doing duty with detachment of cavalry, to administer medical aid to European and native servants of sub-collectorate of Bagulkota, v. Surg Bird ordered to Poona.

Consequent on departure of Capt. Reynolds and Maj. Holland for Cape of Good Hope, on sick cert., the following arrangements are directed until their return, or until further orders :—Capt. Payne to be acting assist. com. gen. northern division of army; Capt. Davidson, acting assist. com. gen. Poona division of army; Lieut. Whichelo, acting deputy assist. com. gen. at Dessa; Lieut. Hartley, acting deputy assist. com. gen. at Belgaum; and Capt. Hallett, 3d N.I., to act as assist. com. gen. at Ahmednuggur.

Capt. A. F. Johnson, 17th N.I., to be military secretary to Right Hon. the Governor, v. Major Havelock resigned.

Brev. Capt. G. Jameson to be first assistant auditor-general, v. Johnson.

Lieut. Thornbury, 4th N.I., to be second assistant auditor general.

Capt. P. M. Melville, 7th N.I., to be deputy judge adv. gen. to northern division of army, v. Ogilvie appointed paymaster to Poona division of army.

Dec. 19.—Ens. H. Lavie, 13th N.I., to receive charge of ordnance department at Deesa, on departure of Lieut. Forster, from 1st Dec., or until further orders.

Maj. D. Capon, 2d or Gr. N.I., to assume command of station of Sholapore, from 1st Dec., during absence of Brigadier Litchfield, on med. certificate.

Assist. Surg. B. P. Rooke, 5th N.I., to act as staff surgeon and deputy medical storekeeper at Poona, v. Don appointed to act as oculist.

Lieut. G. O. Reeves, 3d L.C., to act as adj. to that regt. on departure of Lieut. and Adj. Eyre on detachment duty to Kusha.

17th N.I. Ens. A. J. Jukes to be lieut., v. Leavins dec.; date of rank 29th Nov. 1835.

Cornet W. C. Hailes to rank from 1st June 1835, and posted to 2d L C.

Assist. Surg. Sullivan placed at disposal of Superintendent of Indian Navy, to relieve Assist. Surg. Clarke, who is placed at disposal of Com.-in-chief.

Dec. 24.—21st N.I. Capt. E. Mason to be major, Lieut. C. Clarke to be capt., and Ens. J. L. Hendley to be lieut., in suc. to Hamilton retired; date 20th Dec. 1835.

Dec. 23.—Brev. Capt. G. J. Jameson, 4th N.I., and first assistant to mil. auditor gen., to be secretary to Military Fund, from 18th Dec., v. Johnson resigned.

Dec. 25.—Lieut. Edmunds, 3d N.I., to command detachment of Poona Auxiliary Horse, serving under orders of Capt. Outram in Myhee Caunta, during absence of Lieut. Erskine.

Returned to duty, from Europe.—Nov. 16. Capt. C. J. Conyngham, 1st L.C.—Lieut. W. J. Ottley, 2d L.C.—30. Capt. G. St. B Brown. 7th N.I.— Lieut F. Ayrton, artillery.—Dec. 15. Surg. J. Howison.—Capt. B. Crispin, 16th N.I.—Surg. W. Carstairs.—Assist. Surg. P. Gray.—Assist. Surg. W. J. Ferrar.—19. Surg. A. Graham.

FURLOUGHS.

To Europe.—Nov. 3. Brev. Capt. J. Hobson, European regt.—Lieut. H. Stamford, horse artillery.—5. Capt. C. H. Delamain, 3d L.C., for health.—9. Capt. W. C. Manesty, 8th N.I., for health.—12. Deputy Assist. Commissary A. Gourley, for health.—Lieut. C. Manger, 17th N I., for health.—14. Assist. Surg. H. T. Chatterton, for health.—16. Maj. P. D. Ottey, 11th N.I, for health —23 Assist. Surg. D. W. Nash, Bengal estab., for health.—30. Capt. T. C. Parr, 7th N.I.— Dec. 10. Capt. J. S. C. Jameson, 18th N.I.—15. Lieut. J. Macdonell, 19th N.I.—Capt. J. T. Molesworth, 11th N.I., for health.—19. Lieut. Wm. Chambers, 13th N.I.—24. Assist. Surg. B. A. H. Nicholson, for health.—28. Lieut. E. W. Cartwright, 23d N.I., for health.

To Egypt.—Dec. 28. Capt. H. Macan, 17th N.I., for twelve months, for health.

To New South Wales.—Dec. 24. Assist. Surg. A. H. Leith, for two years, for health.

To Neilgherries.—Nov. 13. Lieut. S. Turnbull, artillery, for six months, for health.

MARINE DEPARTMENT.

Nov. 9.—Commander J. Wilson to be controller of the dock yard, boat master, and agent for transports.

Lieut. Williams to act for Commander Wilson, during his absence.

Leave of Absence.—Nov. 30. Lieut. F. Whitelock, for eight months, to proceed into interior of Arabia and Persia, for purpose of perfecting himself in languages of those countries.

SHIPPING.

Arrivals.

Nov. 23. *John Adam*, Roche, from Socotra; *Arethusa*, Canning, from Calcutta.—25. *Malabar*, Tucker, from London.—27. *Rupurell*, Wilson, from Calcutta.—28. *Cornwallis*, Clark, from China and Singapore; *Theodore Eugene*, Beck, from Bordeaux and Colombo.—Dec. 1. *Carnatic*, Brodie, from London and Cape; *Edmonstone*, McDougall, from China and Singapore.—7. *Wm. Nicoll*, Rincaid, from Greenock.—8. *Lady Raffles*, Pollock, from London; *Charlotte Melville*, from China and Singapore.—9. *Huddersfield*, Noakes, from Liverpool and Rio de Janeiro.—10. *Cashmere Merchant*, Edwards, from Calcutta.—11. *Nerbudda*, Careless, from River Indus.—13. *Corderey*, Rays, from Penang and Cochin; *Hattrass*, Clarke, from Calcutta, Quilon, Cochin, Goa, and Vingorla (with Lord Bishop of Calcutta).—14. *Clifton*, Bushby, and *Tury*, Reid, both from Liverpool.—15. *Theodosia*, Coleman, from Liverpool.—17. *Col. Newall*, Kall, from Calcutta; *Medora*, Dixon, from Liverpool.—22. *Triumph*, Green, from London.—24. *Sultana*, Evans, from China and Aleppy.—25. H.C. brig *Tigris*, Lowe, from Mocha and Socotra. —31. *Oriental*, Allen, from Sydney.

Departures.

Nov. 24. *Morley*, Douglas, for Malabar coast, Ceylon, and London.—25. *Lady Wilmot Horton*, Jacob, for China.—26. *Regia*, Kemp, for Cochin; *William Rodgers*, Crawford, for China.—30. H.C. brig *Palinurus*, Haines, for Persian Gulf.—Dec. 2. *La Marie*, Briole, for Malabar coast and Bordeaux.—4. American ships of war *Peacock*, Strehling, and *Enterprise*, Cambell, both to sea.—6. *Shepherdess*, Kinaman, for Colombo and New York; H.M.S. *Rattlesnake*, Hobson, to sea.—8. *John Adam*, Roche, for Calcutta.—10. *Emma*, Hudson, for Cork.—16. *Hero of Malown*, Grundy, for Cork.—18. *Sandada*, De Costa, for Rio de Janeiro.—19. *Albion*, M'Leod, for Liverpool.—20. *Theodore Eugene*, Beck, for Malabar coast and Bordeaux.—21. *Cornwallis*, Clark, for Madras.— 24. *Sir Herbert Compton*, Simmons, for China; *Hattrass*, Clarke, for Calcutta.—25. *Gilmore*, Lindsay, for London.—27. *Arethusa*, Canning, for

Calcutta.—Jan. 1, 1836. *Huddersfield*, Noakes, for Liverpool.

To Sail.—*Clifton*, for Liverpool, 5th Jan.; *Marquis Hastings*, for London, 10th Jan.; *Malabar*, and *Carnatic*, for Cape and London, 10th Jan.; *Lady Raffles*, for London, 20th Jan.; *Triumph*, for London, 25th Jan.

Freight to London (Dec. 31)—£4. 4s. to £4. 10s. per ton.

BIRTHS, MARRIAGES, AND DEATHS.

BIRTHS.

Nov. 17. At Aurungabad, the lady of Lieut. Chas. Macleod, Nizam's cavalry, of a son.

— At Surat, the lady of Assist. Surg. T. Waller, 6th N.I., of a daughter.

21. At Upper Colabah, the lady of H. W. K. Beyts, Esq., of a son.

26. At Malligaum, the lady of S. J. Stevens, Esq., 21st N.I., of a son.

Dec. 4. At Colaba, the lady of Lieut. S. H. Buckler, I.N., of a still-born daughter.

11. At Malligaum, the lady of Capt. Forbes, major of brigade Kandeish, of a son.

13. At the Esplanade, the lady of C. A. Stewart, Esq., of a daughter.

20. At Bombay, the lady of John Wedderburn, Esq., C.S., of a son.

— At Bombay, the lady of W. C. Bruce, Esq., C.S., of a daughter.

22. At Poona, the lady of Capt. Bulkley, acting paymaster Poona division, of a son.

MARRIAGES.

Dec. 3. At Calicut, John Doig, Esq., Bombay medical service, to Mary Catherine, widow of the late C. M. Bushby, Esq., M.C.S.

6. At Ahmednuggur, Lieut. D. C. Graham, B.M.S., to Mrs. H. Tracy.

15. At Bombay, Major P. Marshall, 25th N.I., nephew of the late Gen. Marshall, of this establishment, to Louisa Emilia Young, eldest daughter of the late B. H. T. Young, Esq., of the Madras civil service.

18. At Byculiah, Capt. James Outram, of the Bombay N.I., Bheel agent in Candeish, &c. &c., to Margaret Clementina, second daughter of James Anderson, Esq., Brechin, N.B.

DEATHS.

Nov. 8. At Callana, on Salsette, the Rev. Mr. Francisco de Annunciacaō.

16. At Bombay, Lieut. W. H. Hall, of the 6th regt. Bengal L.C.

18. At Colaba, aged 33, Frances, wife of Lieut. Clendon, Indian Navy, and youngest sister of Capt. W. A. Bowen, of the *Duke of Bedford*.

Dec. 25. At Bombay, H. P. Hadow, Esq., of the firm of Messrs. Remington and Co., aged 36.

Lately. At Bombay, in his 49th year, Hormasjee Bhickajee Mehrjee, senior partner in the late firm of Bhickajee Mehrjee and Co.

— In China, or on his way there, Major Jameson.

Ceylon.

SHIPPING.

Arrivals.—Dec. 12. *Clifton*, from London.—14. *Zoe*, from Liverpool and Mauritius.—15. American ships of war *Peacock* and *Enterprise*, from Bombay.—18. *Colombo*, from London and Cape.— 19. *Fairy Queen*, from ditto.—*Morley*, from Bombay.

BIRTHS.

Oct. 23. At Colombo, the lady of the Rev. J. H. De Saram, Chingalese colonial chaplain, of a daughter.

Nov. 23. At Kandy, the wife of Capt. Hutchison, 97th regt., of a son.

DEATH.

Oct. 26. At Colombo, in the Fort, James Smyth, Esq., in the 36th year of his age.

Penang.

BIRTH.

Oct. 9. The lady of George Scott, Esq., of a daughter.

Singapore.

SHIPPING.

Arrivals.—Nov. 12. Eliza Heywood, from London.—Dec. 3. Jean Graham, from London.—4. Vansittart, from Madras.

BIRTH.

Nov. 23. The lady of T O. Crane, Esq., of a son.

Batavia.

SHIPPING.

Arrivals.—Nov. 26.—Singapore, from Greenock. —Dec. 18. Hector, from Hobart Town.—19. Margaretha, from London; Rosab-lla, from Cape.— 23. Zeno, from Liverpool.—27. Monarch, from Liverpool.

Manilla.

MARRIAGE.

Aug. 1. W. R. Paterson, Esq., to Matilda, youngest d-ughter of Thos. Colledge, Esq., of Kilsby, county Northampton.

China.

SHIPPING.

Arrivals.—Dec. 1. Enmore, from Liverpool and Madras; Lady of the Lake, from Manilla.—2. General Gascoygne, from Liverpool.—3. Fairee Queen, from Liverpool; Patriot King, from Bombay; Charles Forbes, from Madras.—13. Severn, from Calcutta.—Victory, from Madras and Singapore.

DEATHS.

June 27. At Canton, Woo Ping-keen, Howqua's fourth brother. Hitherto he had attended to the tea department of the hong. Howqua, seeing himself to be old, and on the verge of life, his posterity useless as far as the affairs of the hong are concerned, is deeply afflicted, and it is thought he will soon die; and there is nobody to whom the management of the trade of the hong can be entrusted.—Canton Reg.
Sept. 22. At Whampoa, of fever. Mr. E. J. S. Hill, chief officer of the ship Ernaad, aged 30.
24. Loo, the governor of Canton. The immediate cause of his death was constipation. He has left three sons, a widow, and three concubines.
Nov. 10. At Macao, Sir Andrew Sjungstedt, a native of Sweden, aged 81.

New South Wales.

SHIPPING.

Arrivals.—Oct. Backwell, from Cork; Orwell, from Singapore; Maria, from London; England, and William, both from Portsmouth.—19. Fortune, from Singapore; Argo, from Mauritius.— 23. Mary Ann, from Sheerness; Lady M'Naghten, from Dublin.—Nov. 2. Lotus, from London.—3. Eagle, from Swan River.

Van Diemen's Land.

SHIPPING.

Arrivals at Hobart Town.—Oct. 14. Aurora, from London.—15. Richard Walker, from Liver-

pool.—20. Perthshire, from Leith; Hector, from London.—24. Kinnear, from London; Mary Sharp, from Greenock; Grecian, from China.— 31. Rachael, from Liverpool; Augustus Cæsar, from London.
Arrivals at Launceston.—Oct. 15. Crusader, from London.—19. Ann, from London.—Nov. 15. Charles Kerr, from London.

Swan River.

DEATH.

Aug. 7. At Perth, aged 43, Capt. Daniell, of H.M. 21st regt., senior member of the councils of this colony, and commander of the troops.

Mauritius.

SHIPPING.

Arrivals.—Jan. 4. Atlas, from London.—7. Cognac Packet, from London; Paragon, from Bristol.—8. Apprentice, from London.—11. Thomas Dougall, from Bordeaux; Cheshire, from Rio— Annab-lla, from London; William Thompson, from Cape.

BIRTH.

Dec. 19. At Port Louis, the lady of the Hon. James Wilson, chief judge of the Mauritius, of a son.

Cape of Good Hope.

APPOINTMENTS.

Dec. 31. Mr. Thomas Mitchell, surgeon, to be health officer at Simon's Town.
Jan. 4. John Steuart, Esq , to be sheriff of this colony and its dependencies, for one year from this date.

SHIPPING.

Arrivals.—Jan. 25. Lord Hobart, and Antelope, from St. Helena.—Feb. 7. Briton, from St. Helena; Gondolier, from Liverpool (since struck on Robbin Island. cargo discharging.—14. Childe Harold, from London.

BIRTHS.

Jan. 5, 1836. Mrs. Dobie, of a daughter.
6. Mrs. Hodgskin, of a son.
Feb. 4. At Cape Town, the lady of Capt. B. T. Phillips, 7th Bengal L.C., of a son.
5. At Feldhausen, the lady of Sir J. F. W. Herschell, K.H., of a son.

MARRIAGE.

Jan. 1. At Cape Town, D. G. Van Renen, Esq., eldest son of Daniel Van Renen, Esq., of the Brewery, Newlands, to Maria Martha Dirkina, only child of George Cadogan, Esq., registrar of the Court of Vice Admiralty.

DEATH.

Feb. 6. On board the bark Eagle, Dr. James Shaw, aged 68 years.

Persia.

DEATHS.

Sept. 22. In Bushire Roads, Persian Gulf, Mr. F. T. Hard, of the H.C. brig of war Euphrates.
Dec. 16. At Shiraz, of fever, Capt. D. Ruddell, of the Bengal establishment, Secretary of Legation, and a most accomplished scholar.

POSTSCRIPT TO ASIATIC INTELLIGENCE.

CALCUTTA and Madras papers to a somewhat later date than are quoted in the preceding pages have been received, but they contain no local news of any importance.

Bombay papers to the 29th of December state that the *Tigris* had arrived with the London mail of the 1st September. The only news she brought from the Red Sea was, that the Pasha of Egypt was determined to carry on the war against the Arabians, notwithstanding his recent reverses. When the *Tigris* left Suez, 12,000 troops were waiting to be transmitted to Judda, and 4,000 were at Cossier, to be conveyed to the same destination. The coffee monopoly at Mocha had been partly relaxed, it having been determined that one-half only should be appropriated to the account of the government, and the remainder to be exported. Lieut. Burnes, who had been ordered up the Sinde, to adjust some difference amongst the Ameers, had returned, after fully completing his mission, besides having removed many obstacles in the way of the expedition which was about to proceed up the Indus. He had also gained permission from the Ameers to survey the mouth of the river.

The Lord Bishop of Calcutta arrived at Bombay on the 13th of December, on his primary visitation. On his way thither he landed at Goa, where he was received with marked respect, and visited the churches and monasteries of that interesting city.

Singapore *Chronicles* report that the dispute between Cochin China and the Siamese was assuming a very serious aspect: the latter were making preparations for active hostilities. The king of Cochin China is said to have applied to the British residents for the assistance of their government, and promised in return the free entry of the eastern ports of Cochin China.

The advices from Philadelphia give an abstract of a treaty between the United States and Siam, by which the citizens of the former are permitted to enter and depart from any port of the kingdom, with cargoes of whatever description ; and to buy and sell, without restriction, except that they are not to sell munitions of war to any other person than the king, or to import opium, or export rice.

At Malacca, Count Vou Ranzow, his son Daniel Detloff Van Ranzow, and his servant Augustino, had been convicted, the former for stabbing, cutting, and wounding, with intent to kill and murder a Mr. de Wind ; the two latter for aiding and abetting. Death was recorded against all, but commuted for the Count to imprisonment for one year ; for his son to six calendar months, and for his servant to three calendar months.

Advices from Canton to the 16th of December have been received. The linguist, Hopun, had been banished to slavery in the green-tea district for not reporting and preventing Lord Napier's arrival in Canton. The *Register* of the 11th December contains a letter, which refers to the seizure of the second officer of the *Fairie Queen*, and states that he was in a Chinese boat, and his person and letters were detained, because he refused payment of 500 drs. This letter adds, that this vessel was bound direct for Whampoa, with a full cargo of British goods ; there is no allegation of smuggling. It concludes by calling upon the British residents to go to the city gate, and let them say, " If full apology and reparation is not instantly made, they will make reprisals against the government officers of China afloat, until they get redress. We have the physical power," says this letter ; " the moral right is with us ; why not use it ?" There is, however, an impression that the officer of the *Fairie Queen* had infringed the rule laid down by the Chinese authorities, by going up to Canton in a Chinese boat, instead of waiting till he could proceed with the ship's boat under British colours.

The *Singapore Chronicle* says, that " Howqua has been in prison for several days, and the contest is, whether he will declare himself liable for his hong's debts, or not. If the hong goes on, it does so with the plain declaration of its senior, that nothing except personal torture induced him to become liable for the hong debts."

Advices were received at Lloyd's from the Sandwich Islands, of 1st of December. Most of the crews of the English whalers that had arrived there were in a mutinous state. The agent states that the ship *Awashontas*, on the 6th of October last, whilst off Baring's Island, in lat. 6° 30′ N., long. 168° 52′ E., was boarded by the natives, who suddenly commenced an attack, killed Capt. Coffin, the first and second mates, three seamen, and wounded several others, and got possession of the deck. The remaining officers, with the crew, however, having obtained their arms, and killed some of the savages, they abandoned the ship, which was brought into Howlulu by the third mate.

New South Wales papers to the 22d of Oct. have been received. The colony continues flourishing and tranquil. Great ridicule is thrown, in these papers, on the centralization scheme of colonization which the South Australian Commissioners have been appointed here to carry into effect. The New South Wales settlers had just heard, in October, of the scheme, and they pronounce it impracticable.

HOME INTELLIGENCE.

MISCELLANEOUS.

COURT OF DIRECTORS.

On the 13th April a ballot was taken at the East-India House for the election of six Directors, in the room of Wm. Astell, Esq., Wm. Bayley, Esq., Russell Ellice, Esq., Richard Jenkins, Esq., Campbell Marjoribanks, Esq., and John Masterman, Esq., who go out by rotation. At six o'clock the glasses were closed and delivered to the scrutineers, who reported that the election had fallen on John Cotton, Esq., John Forbes, Esq., John Loch, Esq., Charles Mills, Esq., Henry Shank, Esq., and Henry St. George Tucker, Esq.

On the 14th a Court of Directors was held, when the new directors took the oath and their seats. Sir J. R. Carnac, bart., was chosen chairman, and John Loch, Esq., deputy chairman, for the year ensuing.

JUDICIAL APPOINTMENTS.

His Majesty has appointed Sir Edward Gambier, knt., to be one of the puisne justices of the Supreme Court of Judicature at Madras, in the room of Sir R. B. Comyn, promoted to the office of chief justice; and Sir Wm. Norris, knt., now chief justice of the Supreme Court of Judicature at Ceylon, to be recorder of Prince of Wales Island, in the room of Sir Edward Gambier, knt.—*Morn. Her.*

GOVERNOR OF MADRAS.

On the 30th March a Court of Directors was held at the East-India House, when the Right Hon. Lord Elphinstone was appointed Governor of the Presidency of Fort St. George.

COMMANDER-IN-CHIEF AT MADRAS.

On the 20th April a Court of Directors was held at the East-India House, when Lieut.-Gen. Sir Thomas Peregrine Maitland, K.C.B., was unanimously appointed Commander-in-chief of the Company's forces on the Fort St. George establishment.

GAZETTE APPOINTMENTS.

South Australia.

James Hurtle Fisher, Esq., to be resident commissioner of public lands in the Province of South Australia; date 18th April 1836.

Van Diemen's Land.

Sir John Franklin, Knt., captain in the Royal Navy, to be lieutenant-governor of the Island of Van Diemen's Land and its dependencies; date 9th April, 1836.

The Rev. William Hutchins to be archdeacon of the Island of Van Diemen's Land; date 16th April 1836,

HIS MAJESTY'S FORCES IN THE EAST.

PROMOTIONS AND CHANGES.

4th L. Drags. (at Bombay), Capt. F. D. Daly to be major by purch., v. Byne who retires; Lieut. John Harrison to be capt. by purch., v. Daly; and Cornet Wm. Perse to be Lieut. by purch., v. Harrison (all 27 Oct. 35); Cornet H. W. Knight to be lieut. by purch. v. Perse, whose prom., as dated 29th Dec. 35, has not taken place (29 Dec.); Geo. Cornwall to be cornet by purch., v. Knight (25 March 36).

11th L. Drags. (in Bengal), Lieut. Col. J. T. Lord Brudenell, from h. p. unattached, to be lieut.-col., v. M. Childers, who exch., rec. dif. (25 March 36).—Serj. Wm. Betson to be regimental qu.-mast., v. Henderson dec. (1 Nov. 25.

13th L. Drags. (at Madras). Assist. Surg. P. Brodie, from 13th F., to be assist. Surg., v. Stephenson, prom. in 54th F. (8 April).

3d Foot (in Bengal). Lieut. R. H. Peel, from h.p. 1st garrison bat. to be lieut. v. Clarke app. to 17th regt. (1 April).—Ens. Chas. Sawyer to be lieut. by purch., v. Peel, who retires; C. J. Foster to be ens. by purch., v. Sawyer (both 8th April).

9th Foot (in Bengal). D. Perie to be ens. by purch., v. Brooke, prom. in 23d regt. (18 March 36).—Maj. H. Fane, from h. p. unattached, to be major, v. Wm. Seward, who exch., rec. dif. (12 Nov 35).

13th Foot (in Bengal). G. W. Barnes, M.D., to be assist. surg., v. Brodie app. to 13th L. Drags. (8 April 36).

20th Foot (in Bombay). F. Raikes, to be ens., v. Le Couteur prom. in 31st regt. (1 April).

31st Foot (in Bengal). Ens. P. Le Couteur, from 20th regt. to be lieut. v. Dickson app. to 17th regt. (1 April).

39th Foot (at Madras). H. Gray to be ens., v. Morris dec. (25 March 36)—Ens. Wm. Munro to be lieut. by purch., v. Hassard who retires; H. Newcomen to be ens. by purch., v. Munro (both 1 April).

41st Foot (at Madras). Major Gore Brown, from 28th regt., to be major, v. Cotton, who exch. (25 March 36); Lieut. Wm. Barnes to be capt., v. Ellis dec. (14 Sept. 35); Ens. A. C. Melk to be lieut., v. Barnes (14 do.); James Eman to be ens., v. Melk (25 March 36).

44th Foot (in Bengal). Ens. Arthur Hogg to be lieut., v. Wetherall app. to 17th regt.; Ens. Wm. Mac'Mahon, from 81st. regt., to be ens., v. Hogg, (both 1 April).

54th Foot (at Madras). Ens. John Cameron, from h. p. 92d regt., to be ens., v. Phillips app. to 17th regt. (2 April).—Assist. Surg. T. G. Stephenson, M.D., from 13th L. Drags, to be surgeon, v. Chas. Hamilton, who retires upon h. p. (8 April).

55th Foot (at Madras). 2d Lieut. H. T. Butler, from 23d regt., to be lieut. by purch., v. Denhame, who retires 18 March 36.

62d Foot (at Madras). Aug. Harris to be ens. by purch., v. Stacpoole who retires; Assist. Surg. John Dempster, M D., from 44h regt. to be surgeon v. Radford app. to 17th regt. (all 4 March 36). —Ens. R. Shearman to be lieut. v. Hodgson. dec. (29 Aug. 35); Ens. F. E. Scobell to be lieut. by purch., v. Shearman, whose prom. by purch. has not taken place (11 March 36).—Ens. James M'Carthy, from h. p. 96th regt., to be ens. v. F. E. Scobell, prom. (17 March 36); T. E. Mulock to be ens. by purch., v. Scott who retires (18 do.)— G. Mackay to be ens. by purch. v. M'Carthy who retires (25 do.).

63d Foot (at Madras). H. Pilleau to be assist.-surg., v Russell app. to 73d F. (23 Jan. 36).—Ens. T. L. K. Nelson, from 94th F., to be lieut., v. Morphett, prom. in 40th F. (29 Jan.).—Ens. P. Lindesay to be lieut. by purch. v. Nelson app. to 40th F.; and J. B. Leatham to be ens. by purch., v. Lindesay (both 5 Feb.)

INDIA SHIPPING.

Arrivals.

MARCH 28. *Freak*, Smoult, from China 31 Oct.; at Cork.—*Brothers*, Hall, from Batavia 10th Dec.; off Falmouth.—*Statesman*, Quiller, from China 20th Nov.; off Bristol.—30. *Cumbrian*, Latimer, from Mauritius 29th Dec., and Cape 19th Jan.; at Deal.—*Duchess of Clarence*, Hutchinson, from Bombay Nov. 17th; off Cape Clear.—*Mary Bibby*, Neale, from China 29th Nov.; off Liverpool.—31. *Favourite* Ford, from South Seas; *Africa*, Hammond, from Mauritius 17th Dec.; both at Deal.—*Cordelia*, Creighton, from China 2d Dec.; off Liverpool.—APRIL 1. *Hepworth*, Pritchard, from Mauritius 10th Dec.; at Deal.—2. *Fortitude*, Wilson, from Mauritius 19th Dec.; off Margate.—*Venelia*, Miner, from South Seas; at Deal.—*Jean Wilson*, Hood, from Mauritius 18th Dec.; at Falmouth.—4. *Eleanor* Mann, from Mauritius 28th Dec., and Cape 23d Jan.; at Deal.—*Princess Charlotte*, M'Keen, from Bombay 11th Nov., and Allepy 30th do.; at Liverpool.—*Arnold Wells*, Stanwood, from Manilla 10th Oct.; off Dover (for Antwerp).—5. *Eliza*, Harris, from Mauritius 6th Jan.; at Bristol.—*Elizabeth*, Folkens, from Batavia; off Dover (for Rotterdam).—*Warblington*, Crosby, from Mauritius 13th Dec.; off Folkstone.—6. *Charles*, Hawkins, from South Seas; at Deal.—8 *Boyne*, Richardson, from Bombay 15th Nov., Allepy 5th Dec., and Cape 7th Feb.; off Portland.—*Duke of Lancaster*, Hargraves, from China 12th Dec.; at Deal.—9. *Barretto Junior*, Sanders, from Bengal 4th Dec., Madras 29th do., and Cape 4th Feb.; off Dover.—*Lawrence*, Gill, from Bengal 11th Dec., and Cape 7th Feb.; off Holyhead.—*Rossendale*, Friend, from China 16th July, and Singapore 21st Nov.; *Mountstuart Elphinstone*, Tolier, from Bengal 24th Dec.; both off the Wight.—*Jean*, Goldie, from Singapore 25th Nov., and Cape 30th Jan.; at Deal.—11. *Sophia*, M'Nair, from China 17th Dec.; off the Wight.—*Arab*, Sparkes, from China 16th Dec.; off Cork.—14. *Bland*, Callan, from Bengal 12th Dec., and Madras 30th do.; off Liverpool.—15. *Flinn*, Collard, from Mauritius 27th Nov., and Cape 27th Jan.; *Sandwich*, Hall, from Muscat; both at Deal.—*Gilmore*, Lindsay, from Bombay 23th Dec., and Cape 10th Feb.; off Portsmouth.—16. *Emma*, Hudson, from Bombay 10th Dec., and Cape 5th Feb.; off Cork.—*Albion*, M'Leod, from Bombay 19th Dec.; off Holyhead.—18. *Heroine*, MacCarthy, from Madras 31st Dec.; Portsmouth.—19. *Trusty*, West, from China 12th Dec.; at Deal.—*Huddersfield*, Noakes, from Bombay 1st Jan.; off Liverpool.—*Margaret and Ann*, Buck, from Cape 4th Feb.; off Dartmouth.—*Susanna*, Grim, from Batavia; off Dover.—25. *Demerara*, Thorn, from Mauritius 6th Jan. at Liverpool.—26. *Britannia*, Leith, from Mauritius 6th Jan., and Cape 6th Feb.; at Deal.—*Emerald*, Crawford, from Mauritius; off Liverpool.—27. *Spence*, Hardie, from N. S. Wales 24th Oct.; *Cognac Packet*, Spittal, from Mauritius 30th Jan.; both off Brighton.

Departures.

MARCH 21. *Imogen*, Riley, for China; from Liverpool.—APRIL 2. *Castle Huntly*, Jolly, for Bombay and China; from Torbay.—*Alfred*, Jameson, for Batavia and Singapore; from Greenock.—3. *Viscount Melbourne*, Thomas, for Madras, Bengal, and China; *Iris*, Mackwood, for Ceylon; *Artemis*, Sparkes, for Madras and Bengal; *Prince George*, Chilcott, for Bombay (ballast); *Lord Goderich*, Wetherell, for N. S. Wales; *Cygnet*, Rolls, for South Australia; *Ambassador*, Attwood, for Mauritius; all from Deal.—4. *Crown*, Ponsonby, for Bengal; from Liverpool.—*Adelaide*, Guthrie, for Bombay; from Portsmouth.—*Margaret Wilkie*, Smith, for Cape; from Deal.—5. *Peter Proctor*, Terry, for Mauritius; from Deal.—*Juliet*, Wilson, for Rio and Batavia; from Liverpool.—6. *Orwell*, Lancaster, for Madras, Bengal, and China (having put back on 25th March, with loss of main-yard); *Achilles*, Duncan, for Mauritius; both from Falmouth.—6. *Ganges*, Broadhurst, for Mauritius, Madras, and Bengal; from Cowes.—*John Pirie*, Martin, for South Australia; from Dartmouth.—8. *Reliance*, Bowen, for Bombay; from Liverpool.—9. *Parkfield*, MacCauley, for Bombay; from Liverpool.—10. *Hashemy*, Hyde, for Bombay and China (having put back on 1st April after being damaged in a hurricane); from Portsmouth.—*Asia*, Pearson, for Bengal and China; from Weymouth.—*Mary Ann Webb*, Lloyd, for Bengal; *Red Rover*, Currie, for V.D. Land and N. S. Wales; both from Cowes.—*Duke of York*, Morgan, for South Australia; from Torbay.—*Princess Victoria*, Bissett, for Bombay, from Greenock.—11. *Isabella Cooper*, Currie, for Bengal; from Portsmouth.—*Inglis*, Wise, for Bombay and China; *Eliza Stewart*, Miller, for China; *Perseus*, Howlett, for N. S. Wales; *Symmetry*, Riley, for Mauritius and Bombay; all from Deal.—*Tweed*, Smith, for Bombay; from Liverpool.—12. *Senator*, Grindley, for Cape and Mauritius; *Planter*, Abdoll, for Batavia and China; both from Deal.—15. *Biboo*, Brook, for Bengal; from Liverpool.—16. *Thames*, Hornblow, for Madras, Straits of Malacca, and China; from Portsmouth.—*Eliza Jane*, Canney, for Batavia and Singapore; from Deal.—17. *Hindoo*, Driscoll, for Bombay; *Kirkman Finlay*, Russell, for Bombay; *Goshawk*, Laing, for V. D. Land and N. S. Wales; *Reform*, Selkirk, from Cape and Algoa Bay; *Fair Barbadian*, Lott, for Cape; all from Liverpool.—*Batavia*, Blair, for Batavia; from Cowes.—18. *Gloucester*, Brooks, for Bengal, via Bordeaux; *Avoca*, Boadle, for V D. Land and N.S. Wales; *Bachelor*, Ellis, for Cape and Algoa Bay; all from Dea.—*Arcturus*, Oliver, for Mauritius and Ceylon; from Plymouth.—*Lord Lyndoch*, Baker, for V. D. Land (convicts); from Sheerness.—*Heywood*, Jones, for China; from Liverpool.—19. *Craigevar*, Ray, for N. S. Wales; *George and Mary*, Roberts, for Mauritius and Ceylon; both from Deal.—*Visitor*, Moppett, for Cape; from Liverpool.—24. *Bengal*, Wilson, for Bengal; *Lord William Bentinck*, Hutchinson, for Cape, Bengal, and China; *Rio Packet*, Dench, for Muscat; *Emma*, Nelson, for Cape and South Australia; all from Deal.—24. *Orient*, White, for Madras and Bengal; from Portsmouth.—24. *Hellas*, Scanlan, for Bengal; *Blake*, Thompson, for Bombay; *Trio*, White, for Batavia, Singapore, and China; all from Liverpool.—*Ajax*, Brenton, for Mauritius; from Bristol.—27. *Bussorah Merchant*, Moncrieff, for China; from Deal.

PASSENGERS FROM INDIA.

Per Heyworth, from Mauritius: Mr. R. Jenner.

Per Boyne, from Bombay: Mrs. Young and three children; Mrs. Scott and two children; Lord Charles Kerr, lieut. H. M. 6th Foot; Capt. Manesty, 8th N. I.; Lieut. Bennett, H. M. 16th Foot; Lieut. Manger, 17th N. I.; Dr. Chatterton and two children; two servants.—From Cannanore: Mrs. Church; Capt. Sullivan, H. M. 57th Foot.—From the Cape: Rev. Mr. and Mrs. Halbeck and two children; Mrs. Clemans; Mrs. Harvey; Mr. Charles Pillans; Misses Meyer, Nantons, Landeman, Luttringe, and Grant; Masters E. and S. Lehman, Stein, and Meyer.

Per Memnon, from Bengal: Capt. Duhn; Mr. Cocklin.

Per Gilmore, from Bombay: Mrs. Hamilton; Miss Parsons; Miss Jefferys; Col. Morgan, 14th N.I.; Major Hamilton, 21st N.I.; Capt. Jameson, 18th N.I.; Capt. Molesworth, 11th N. I.; Capt. Tyson, H. M. 4th L. Drags.; Mr. and Mrs. Rutherford; Mr. Munro; Mr. Laudby, from Cape; Mr. La Bougue, from Mauritius.—(Dr. Keith was left at the Cape).

Per Jean, from Singapore: Mrs. Goldie; Mr. Taylor; three children.

Per Mountstuart Elphinstone, from Bengal: Mrs. Denton and four children; Mrs. Gogerly and five children; Mrs. Leighton and two children; Mrs. Martin and two ditto; Mrs. Hobson and four children; Miss Marnell; Samuel Denton, Esq.; Capt. Alex. Stuart, H. M. service; Capt. Fraser, B. N. I.; Lieut. Audain, H. M. 3d Foot; Lieut. J. Graham, 55th N. I.; Rev. Mr. Gogerly; two Misses Ferris; two Misses McDormind; two Misses Husband; Misses Logie, Hulse, and Hope.

Per Emma, from Bombay: Mr. Walker, late of Indian navy; Mr. Rooke.

Per Bland, from Bengal and Madras: Mrs. Callan; Miss Byrne; Miss Craigie; Dr. J. Duncan. Lieut. Macdonald, 69th N.I.; Lieut. Marsden, 29th do.; Lieut. E. W. S. Scott; Bengal artillery; Cornet Hepburne, 5th Bengal L. C.; Ens. Hepburne, 51st Bengal N.I.; Mr. Duce, H.C. pilot service.

Per Barretto Junior, from Bengal and Madras: Mrs. Smith; Mrs. Hughes and child; Mrs. Horner ; Mrs. Cooke ; G. J. Waters, Esq., Madras C. S. ; Major G Stott, 11th Madras N.I. ; Capt. Hughes, 63d Bengal N.I. ; Capt. Horner, H. M. 55th Foot ; Capt. Fullerton, 17th Madras N.I. ; Ens. R. O. Gardner, 50th do. ; Rev. J. Hands ; Rev. W. Campbell ; six children.

Per Albion, from Bombay : Mrs. Laurie ; Mrs. C. Laurie ; Mrs. Barnes ; three Misses Laurie ; two Misses Clendon ; Masters Laurie, Poole, Swanson, and Wilson ; two sergeants' wives ; two servants.

Per Heroine, from Madras : Mrs. Eger ; Dr. Andrew ; Lieut. Trapaud ; Mr. Thorp.

Expected.

Per Hero of Malown, from Bombay : Mrs. Hughes and child ; Mrs. Billamore and two children ; Lieut. Col. Hughes, C.B. ; Mr. Moore, H.M.40th regt. ; Alli Agha, governor of Bussorah, Mahomed Bey, and four servants ; Mons. Powowski ; J. S. Sturg.

Per Pyramus, from Singapore : Mrs. Ricketts and four children ; Mrs. Collie ; Miss Collie ; Capt. Schildknecht.

Per Morley, from Bombay, Malabar Coast, &c. Francis Pryce, Esq. ; Capt. Browne, H.M. 57th regt. ; Lieut. Gottreux, 1st Madras N.I. ; Ens. E. Pereira, 26th do. (from Quilon).

Per Malabar, from Bombay : Hon. Mrs. Grant and two children ; Mrs. Havelock and two children ; Mrs. Hayman ; Mrs. Salter ; Mrs. Ottey ; Mrs. Rydge ; Mrs. Collier and child ; Mr. Grant ; Mr.Cassamaijor, resident at Mysore ; Major Ottey, 11th N.I. ; Capt. Rydge ; Capt. White ; Lieut. Scott, in charge of invalids ; Masters Griffiths and Duckett.—For Cape : Mr. Le Messurier, advocate-general ; Capt. Reynolds.

Per Eagle, from Mauritius : Rev. Mr. and Mrs. Freeman ; Mrs. Davis ; Capt. Cock. (Dr. Shaw died at sea.)

Per Penyard Park, from Mauritius : A. B. Consell, Esq. , Mr. and Mrs. Gilbert ; Mrs. Mason ; Mr. and Mrs. Geslin and three children.

Per Eliza, from Bengal : Mrs. Munro and children ; Mrs. Hope Dick and children ; Mrs. Allan ; Mrs. McLeroth and child ; Mrs. Crickett ; Mrs. Grant and children ; Mrs. Dalton and children ; Mrs. Stephenson and children ; Miss Munro ; Major Munro, 74th N.I. ; Capt. A. L. Campbell, 1st Cavalry ; Lieut. Dalton, 3d Buffs ; Lieuts. Mc Leroth, Grant, and Crickett, H.M. 38th Foot ; Lieut. Voules, 3d L.C. ; Lieut. Campbell, Madras army ; J. Stephenson, Esq. ; J. N. Lyall, Esq. ; W. L. McDowell, Esq.—For the Cape : Capt. Roberts, artillery ; Mrs. Roberts.

Per Duke of Buccleugh, from Bengal : Mrs. Greenway and two children ; Miss Stone ; Capt. Seaton ; Mr. Mellish ; Master Davidson.

Per Georgiana, from Bengal and Mauritius : Mrs. Wise ; Mrs. Crawford and son ; J. Day, Esq. ; Mr. Beard ; three servants.

Per Mary Ann, from Ceylon and Mauritius : Capt. Hawks, late of the *Adonis ;* Lieut. Kelly.

PASSENGERS TO INDIA.

Per Orient, for Madras and Bengal : Mrs. Lamb ; Mrs. Austin ; Mrs.White ; Mrs. Spence ; Mrs.Callagher ; Mrs. Cragg ; three Misses Lamb ; two Misses Ward ; Misses Young, Holbrow, Butts, Humphreys, Bowyer, and Crommelin ; Lieut. Timmins ; Lieut. Remington ; Mr. Cragg ; Mr. Burkinyoung ; Mr. Fanshaw ; Mr. Hall ; Mr. Youngson ; two Messrs. Wilson ; Mr. Arthur Lattey ; Mr. Collett ; Mr. Montgomery.

Per Bussorah Merchant, for China : Mr. Wallace ; Mr. Dalrymple ; Mr. Kerr.

Per Thames, for Madras, Straits, &c. : W. R. Taylor, Esq., and family ; Capt. Anderson and lady ; Capt. Haines and lady ; Capt. Howison and lady ; Capt. Young and lady ; Rev. Mr. Cottrell and lady ; Rev. Mr. Schreyvogel and lady ; Rev. Mr.Walpole and lady ; Mr. Millar and lady ; Miss Anderson ; Capt. Deas ; Capt. Dunsmure ; Capt. Hutton ; Mr. Binney ; Dr. Desormeaux ; Dr. Wyllie ; Rev. Messrs. Hole, Heswell, Hardy, and Hubbard ; Messrs. Hunter, Saumares, Ogilvy, Barrow, Magrath, Knoll, and Macvicar.

Per City of Edinburgh, for Mauritius and Madras : Lieut. and Mrs. Lys and child ; Mr. and Mrs. Kelsey and child ; Mrs. Sturt ; Mrs Frazer ; Miss Pinson ; Miss Gufford ; two Misses Symes ;

two Misses Bayley , Messrs. Taylor, Clunie, O'Brien, and Clarke.

Per Lord William Bentinck, for Cape and Bengal ; Hon. Capt. Stockenstrom, lieut. governor eastern division of Cape of Good Hope ; Mrs. Stockenstrom and child ; Dr. Barry ; Ens. Gall ; Assist. Surg. Batson and lady ; Mr. Morgan ; Mr. Alexander.

BIRTHS, MARRIAGES, AND DEATHS.

BIRTHS.

March 31. At her house, No. 11, Cumberland Terrace, Regent's Park, the lady of Wm. Scott Binny, Esq , of Madras, of a son.

April 1. The lady of Lieut. J. S. Harris, 30th Bengal N.I., of a daughter.

13. At Paris, the lady of Lieut. Col. Napier, of a son.

15. In Collet-place, the lady of Robert Jobling, Esq., late Hon. Company's service, and of Newtonhall, Northumberland, of a son.

16. At South-lodge, near Air, the lady of Major Wm. Cunningham, Bengal army, of a son.

17. In Gloucester-place, New Road, the lady of Donald S. Young, Esq., head surgeon in H. H. the Nizam's service, Hyderabad, of a son.

19. At Balgarvie, the lady of Col. Webster, Hon. E. I. Company's service, of a daughter.

MARRIAGES.

March 28. At the British Embassy at Paris, William Ricketts Parker, Esq., to Anna Maria, daughter of the late H. Taylor, Esq., of the civil service, Madras.

29. At Edinburgh, the Rev. Alexander Stewart, A.M., of the Scottish Church, Stafford, to Mrs. Margaret Sheriff, relict of the late Lieut. Col. Davies, of the Hon. E. I Company's service.

April 5. At Tuxford, Buchan Warren Wright, Esq., Madras medical service, to Sarah, youngest daughter of the late Sir Thomas Woollaston White, Bart., of Tuxford Hall, Notts., and Wallingwells, Yorkshire.

— At St. Paul's, Bedford, John Humphrey, Esq., M.D., to Annie Maria Jane, second daughter of the late James Dyson, Esq., and niece of Col. J. F. Dyson, of the Bombay establishment.

6. At Edinburgh, James Strachan, Esq., of Manilla, to Mary Catherine, second daughter of John Mowbray, Esq., of Hartwood, W. S.

7. At Tretherne, in Gloucestershire, Charles Avery Moore, Esq., third son of the late Rev. Dr. Moore, to Mary, relict of Thomas Townshend, Esq., senior judge of the Zillah Court in Madras, and youngest daughter of the late John Tripp, Esq., of Iwood-House, Somersetshire.

12. At St. Mary's Marylebone, Robert Plumbe, Esq., of the Hon. E.I. Company's service, Madras, to Louisa Mary Anne, only surviving daughter of the late R. Davies, Esq., of the Bengal medical establishment.

— At Cricklade, Wilts, Henry M. Becker, of the Hon. E. I. Company's service, to Lydia Catherine, second daughter of the late Rev. Wm. Read, of Ston Easton, Somerset.

21. At Cheltenham, Capt. Frobesher, of the Bengal army, to Rose, youngest daughter of John Helsham, Esq., of Leadstruth, county of Kilkenny, Ireland.

DEATHS.

Jan. 9. At the Island of Ascension, on board H. M. S. *Liverpool,* John James, son of J. W. Christie, Esq., late of Bombay.

16. At Kensington, Isabella Anne, and on *March* 29, Amelia, daughters of the late Rev. Wm. Neale, of Essendon and Bayford, Hertfordshire, and sisters of the late Lieut. Col. George Neale, of the Madras Cavalry.

March 25. At Edinburgh, Mrs. Elizabeth Thomas, relict of the late Capt.David Thomas, Bengal Native Infantry.

26. At Ryde, in the Isle of Wight, Parke Pittar, Esq., of John Street, Adelphi.

27. At Tenny Park, near Kilkenny, Jane, relict of Maj. Gen. Francis Ryan, of the Hon. E.I. Company's service.

28. At his seat, Nursted House, Hants, General Hugonin, in his 86th year, colonel of the 4th. or Queen's Own Light Dragoons, in which regiment he had served sixty-eight years.

29. At Edinburgh, Capt. D. P. Wood, of the 17th Regt. Bengal N. I.

30. At Dundee, Charles Rait, Esq., late captain in the Marine of the Hon. E. I. Company.

April 7. At Poplar, Loretta, widow of the late Capt. Edward Foord, H. C. S., aged 68.

10. In York Terrace, Regent's Park, Capt. A Gordon Duff, late of the 14th Light Dragoons

12. At Taunton, aged 17, William Thompson, eldest son of William Spencer, Esq., of the Hon. E. I. Company's service.

18. At Kirkaldy, Henry, infant son of Henry Beveridge, Esq., late of the Hon. Company's maritime service.

19. At Casterton-house, Mid-Lothian, Col. Alex-ander Cumming, East-India service, colonel of the 4th Bengal L.C., third son of the late Colonel Sir John Cumming, of the same service.

20. At Irvine, Dumfriesshire, the seat of Sir Pulteney Malcolm, Miss Malcolm, aged 73.

21. At the Hotel Mirabeau, Paris, in the 53d year of his age, Robert Mitford, Esq., late of the Bengal civil service.

24. At Taunton, Mary, wife of John Norris, Esq., of Thorncombe-house, Somerset, and daughter of Wm. Grant, Esq., late of the Hon. E. I. Company's civil service.

Lately. At Tiverton, Devon, Mrs Harriet Evans, grand-daughter of the late William Butterfield, Esq., of Lancaster, and sister of the late Sir W. D. Evans, Recorder of Bombay, and formerly of Manchester.

— At Edinburgh, Essex Kerr, daughter of Col. Turner, Bombay Cavalry.

— At Canton, in his 17th year, on board the *General Gascoyne,* of Liverpool, James, eldest son of the late Rev. Adam Hayes, St. Mary's, Edge-hill.

A List of the Directors OF THE EAST-INDIA COMPANY For the Year 1836.

Director	Finance and Home	Political and Military	Revenue, Judicial, and Legislative	Years to serve
Sir James Rivett Carnac, Bart. (Chairman), 21, *Upper Harley St.*		FM		3
John Loch, Esq. 8, (Deputy Chairman), *Upper Bedford Place.*		FM		4
William Wigram, Esq. 6, *Upper Harley Street.*				3
Hon. Hugh Lindsay, 2, *Berkeley Square.*		FM		2
John Morris, Esq., 3, *Baker Street.*	FH			2
William Stanley Clarke, Esq. *Elm Bank, Leatherhead.*	FH			1
John Thornhill, Esq. *Bedford Hill.*	FH			1
George Raikes, Esq. *Fellbridge.*				1
Sir Robert Campbell, Bart. 5, *Argyll Place, Argyll Street.*			RJL	2
John Goldsborough Ravenshaw, Esq. 9, *Lower Berkeley Street.*			RJL	2
Josias Du Pré Alexander, Esq. 7, *Grosvenor Square.*		FM		2
Neil Benjamin Edmonstone, Esq. 49, *Portland Place.*		FM		2
Charles Mills, Esq. *Camelford House, Oxford Street.*			RJL	4
John Petty Muspratt, Esq. 9, *New Broad Street.*	FH			3
Henry Alexander, Esq. *Wickham Park.*	FH			1
Henry St. George Tucker, Esq. 3, *Upper Portland Place.*		FM		4
James L. Lushington, Esq. C.B., 13, *York Street, Portman quare.*			RJL	3
Sir William Young, Bart., 24, *Upper Wimpole Street.*	FH			1
George Lyall, Esq. 17, *Park Crescent.*			RJL	3
John Forbes, Esq. 15, *Harley Street.*			RJL	4
Henry Shank, Esq. 62, *Gloucester Place.*			RJL	4
John Cotton, Esq. 30, *Upper Harley Street.*			RJL	5
Patrick Vans Agnew, Esq. C.B., 32, *Lower Brook Street.*	FH			
John Sheppard, Esq. 44, *Gloucester Place, Portman Square.*	FH			1

THE FOLLOWING GENTLEMEN ARE OUT BY ROTATION:

Wm. Astell, Esq. *Everton.*

William Butterworth Bayley, Esq. 71, *Broad Street.*

Russell Ellice, Esq. 5, *Portman Square.*

Richard Jenkins, Esq. 19, *Upper Harley St.*

Campbell Marjoribanks, Esq. 3, *Upper Wimpole Street.*

John Masterman, Esq. *Nicholas Lane, Lombard Street.*

N.B. *The letters P.C. denote prime cost, or manufacturers' prices; A. advance (per cent.) on the same; D. discount (per cent.) on the same; N.D. no demand.—The bazar maund is equal to 82 ℔. 2 oz. 2 drs., and 100 bazar maunds equal to 110 factory maunds. Goods sold by Sa.Rupees B. mds. produce 5 to 8 per cent. more than when sold by Ct.Rupees F. mds.—The Madras Candy is equal to 500℔. The Surat Candy is equal to 746½ ℔. The Pecul is equal to 133⅓ ℔. The Corge is 20 pieces.*

CALCUTTA, December 31, 1835.

	Rs.A.		Rs. A.		Rs.A.		Rs. A.
Anchors ....Sa.Rs. cwt.	13 0	@	19 8	Iron, Swedish, sq...Sa.Rs. F.md.	5 1	@	5 3
Bottles 100	9 4	—	9 12	—— flat ....do.	5 0	—	5 2
Coals ....B. md.	0 7	—	0 8	—— English, sq. ....do.	2 10	—	2 12
Copper Sheathing, 16-32 ..F. md	33 6	—	33 14	—— flat ....do.	2 9	—	2 11
—— Brasiers', ...do.	32 4	—	32 12	—— Bolt ....do.	2 11	—	2 13
—— Thick sheets..........do.	—			—— Sheet ....do.	5 0	—	5 6
—— Old Gross..........do.	32 4	—	32 8	—— Nails ....cwt.	11 0	—	15 8
—— Bolt ....do.	32 0	—	32 4	—— Hoops..........F.md.	5 0	—	5 6
—— Tile ....do.	31 6	—	31 12	—— Kentledge ....cwt.	1 4	—	1 6
—— Nails, assort. ......do.	30 0	—	36 8	Lead, Pig ....F.md.	6 0	—	6 2
—— Peru Slab.......Ct.Rs. do.	27 4	—	29 12	—— unstamped.........do.	5 14	—	5 15
—— Russia ....Sa.Rs. do.	—			—— Millinery	15 to 35 D.&P.C.		
Copperas ....do.	4 0	—	4 2	Shot, patent ....bag	2 10	—	3 8
Cottons, chints ....pce.	—			Spelter ....Ct.Rs. F. md.	6 8	—	6 9
—— Muslins, assort. ......do.	1 4	—	13 0	Stationery	5 to 25 D.&P.C.		
—— Yarn 16 to 170 ......mor.	0 7	—	0 9½	Steel, English....Ct.Rs. F. md.	5 14	—	6 4
Cutlery, fine..............	5 to 10A. & P.C.			—— Swedish ....do.	6 12	—	7 2
Glass.....................	5A.	—	10A.	Tin Plates ....Sa.Rs. box	14 12	—	16 8
Hardware.................	20 D.	—	45D.	Woollens, Broad cloth, fine ..yd.	5 0	—	9 8
Hosiery, cotton..........	15 to 45A.&P.C.			—— coarse and middling....	1 7	—	4 0
Ditto, silk	20 to 35 D.&P.C.			—— Flannel fine..............	1 2	—	1 14

MADRAS, November 18, 1835.

	Rs.		Rs.		Rs.		Rs.
Bottles 100	12	@	14	Iron Hoops ....candy	21	@	22
Copper, Sheathing ......candy	265			—— Nails ....do.	110	—	115
—— Cakes ....do.	—			Lead, Pig ....do.	42	—	45
—— Old ....do.	230	—	240	—— Sheet ....do.	38	—	40
—— Nails, assort. ......do.	350	—	370	Millinery	10A.	—	15 A.
Cottons, Chints........... piece	6	—	7	Shot, patent ....bag	3	—	3¾
—— Ginghams ....do.	2	—	3	Spelter ....candy	40	—	42
—— Longcloth, fine .....do.	10	—	15	Stationery	Overstocked.		
Cutlery, coarse	P.C.		10 A.	Steel, English.........candy	50	—	55
Glass and Earthenware	10A.		25A.	—— Swedish ....do.	70	—	75
Hardware..............	10A.		—	Tin Plates ....box	19	—	20
Hosiery.................	25A.	—	30A.	Woollens, Broad cloth, fine	10A.	—	15A.
Iron, Swedish ....candy	40	—	50	—— coarse	Wanted		
—— English bar ....do.	21	—	22	—— Flannel, fine	10to12Ans.pr.yd.		
—— Flat and bolt.........do.	21	—	22	—— Ditto, coarse	6to8Ans. do.		

BOMBAY, December 19, 1835.

	Rs.		Rs		Rs.		Rs.
Anchors ....cwt.	10	@	12	Iron, Swedish ....St. candy	49	@	—
Bottles ....doz.	1.4	—	—	—— English ....do.	23		—
Coals ....ton	10	—	12	—— Hoops.............cwt.	5.8		—
Copper, Sheathing, 16-32 ....cwt.	49		—	—— Nails ....do.	12		13
—— Thick sheets ....do.	52		52.8	—— Sheet ....do.	5.8		—
—— Plate bottoms ....do.	51		—	—— Rod for bolts ......St. candy	27.8		—
—— Tile ....do.	45		45.8	—— do. for nails ....do.	26	—	28
Cottons, Chints, &c., &c.........	—		—	Lead, Pig.............cwt.	10		—
—— Longcloths	—		—	—— Sheet ....do.	9.8		—
—— Muslins	—		—	Millinery	10 D.		—
—— Other goods	—		—	Shot, patent ....cwt.	10		—
—— Yarn, Nos. 90 to 100 ...lb.	10	—	1.6	Spelter ....do.	7.13		—
Cutlery, table............	10A.		—	Stationery	P. C.		—
Glass and Earthenware	10 D.		20D.	Steel, Swedish ....tub	10	—	10.4
Hardware..............	P. C.		—	Tin Plates ....box	16	—	16.8
Hosiery, half hose..........	P.C.		—	Woollens, Broad cloth, fine ..yd.	4	—	7
				—— coarse	1.12	—	7
				—— Flannel, fine	1.8		—

CANTON, December 8, 1835.

	Drs.		Drs.		Drs.		Drs.
Cottons, Chints, 28 yds.........piece	3	@	4	Smalts ....pecul	30	@	80
—— Longcloths ....do.	3	—	11	Steel, Swedish ....tub	4	—	—
—— Muslins, 20 yds..........do.	—	—	—	Woollens, Broad cloth ....yd.	1	—	1.40
—— Cambrics, 40 yds ....do.	3	—	4	—— do. ex super ....yd.	2.50	—	3.75
—— Bandannoes ....do.	1.25	—	1.45	Camlets................pce.	28	—	30
—— Yarn, Nos. 16 to 50.........pecul	44	—	51	Do. Dutch ....do.	34	—	37
Iron, Bar ....do.	2.25		—	Long Ells ....do.	9	—	10
—— Rod ....do.	3	—	3½	Tin, Straits..............pecul	16	—	16½
Lead, Pig ....do.	6½	—	—	Tin Plates ....box	10	—	—

SINGAPORE, December 5, 1835.

	Drs.	Drs.		Drs.	Drs.
Anchors............pecul	6	@ 7½	Cotton Hkfs. imit. Battick, dble...dos.	2½	@ 4
Bottles 100	—	—	—— do. do Pullicat..........dos.	1½	— 2
Copper Nails and Sheathing ......pecul	36	— 37	—— Twist, 30 to 40 ....pecul	58	— 60
Cottons, Madapollams, 24yd. by 36in. pcs.	2	— 3½	Hardware, and coarse Cutlery..........	scarce.	
—— Imit. Irish .....24......	34-36 do.	2	—— 2½ Iron, Swedish ....pecul	3½	— 3½
—— Longcloths 38 to 40	34-36 do.	4½	—— 4½ —— English ....do.	2½	— 2½
—— —— do. do....	36fine do.	5	— 5½ —— Nail, rod ....do.	2½	— —
—— —— do. do....	40-44 do.	4	— 6½ Lead, Pig ....do.	5½	— 5½
—— —— do. do...	44-54 do.	5	— 9 —— Sheet ....do.	5	— 5½
—— —— —— 54	do.	—	— Shot, patent ....bag	—	—
—— Prints, 7-8. *single colours* .....do.	2	— 2½ Spelter ....pecul	5½	— 6
—— —— 9-8. ....do.	2½	— 2½ Steel, Swedish ....do.	4½	— 4½
—— Cambric, 12 yds. by 45 to 50 in...do.	1½	— 2½ —— English ....do.	—	—
—— Jaconet, 20 ......40 — 44 ...do.	2	— 2½ Woollen, Long Ells ....pcs.	9	— 10
—— Lappets, 10 ......40 — 44 ...do.	1	— 1½ —— Camblets ....do.	25	— 30
—— Chints, fancy colours ....do.	3	— 5½ —— Ladies' cloth ....yd.	1	— 2

REMARKS.

Calcutta, Dec. 31, 1835.—The amount of business done in Cotton Goods throughout the past week has not been large, indeed the demand, excepting for Books and Lappets, of which the market is again bare, has been far from urgent—this period of the year is of course always the least active for the light Cottons, but the usual backwardness of the buyers at present arises to a great extent, no doubt, from the expectation which they continue to entertain, that by the time the warm season sets in, both stocks and imports will be increased—importers, however, do not appear to be apprehensive on this head, and are consequently firm in their demands.—The only sale of Cotton Yarn quoted is 60 bales, average 49, at 6-11 per morah; buyers continue to hold back, and sales could hardly be effected at the rates current two weeks ago.——There have been several purchasers of Woollens going about, principally requiring the lower kinds of cloth, of which 392 pieces have been sold.—The transactions in Copper have been trifling; they, however, shew a slight improvement in the prices of the qualities sold.—In Iron there is no change to note, nor indeed is there in any other description of metals.—*Pr. Cur.*

Bombay, Dec. 5, 1835.—There has not been much business transacted in Europe Goods during the week, and the only sales which appear on our returns are the following:—Fine Prints, 550 pieces, at Rs. 9 per piece ; Iron Hoops, 750 cwt., at Rs 5-1 per cwt. ; Twist, 3,000 lbs., average No. 30, at 12 annas per lb.—*Pr. Cur.*

Singapore, Dec. 5, 1835.—There has been very little doing during the week in Cotton Piece Goods.—Cambrics are still without inquiry, but a good demand is anticipated for the Siam market in the course of a few months.—Longcloths, nearly all the inquiry is for good ordinary to fine qualities; present stock moderate. — The transactions in Woollens have been trifling, Scarlet cloth is in moderate demand at Dr. 1 per yard.—Camlets and Bombasetts, nothing doing.—Long Ells will not be in demand until the arrival of the Cochin China ships.—Cotton Twist, Grey Mule, no transactions to notice, there being no suitable numbers now in the market.—Metals, altogether confined to retail.—*Pr. Cur.*

Canton, Dec. 8, 1835.—Cotton Yarn is rather dull of sale at our quotations.—Woollens, no improvement.

INDIA SECURITIES AND EXCHANGES.

Calcutta, Dec. 31, 1835.
Government Securities.

	Rs. As.		Rs. As. [Sell.
Buy.] Rs. As.			
Prem. 17 0 Remittable	....	16	8 Prem.
Prem. 0 4 Second 5 per cent.....	2	8	
2 12 Third 5 per cent.	2	8	Prem.
Disc. 2 5 Four per cent. Loan··	2	9	Disc.

Bank Shares.

Bank of Bengal (10,000) .... Sa. Rs. 15,550 a 15,600
Union Bank .. (2,500) .... 2,500 ——

Bank of Bengal Rates.

Discount on private bills .... 7 0 per cent.
Ditto on government and salary bills 4 0 do.
Interest on loans on govt. paper .... 5 0 do.

Rate of Exchange.

On London and Liverpool, six months' sight, to buy, 2s. 2d. ; to sell, 2s. 3d. per Sa. Rupee.

Madras, Nov. 18, 1835.
Government Securities.

Remittable Loan, six per cent.—16 per ct. prem.
Non-Remittable—Old five per cent.—1½ prem.—3 disc.
Ditto ditto of 18th Aug. 1825, five per cent.—1½ prem.—3 disc.
Ditto ditto last five per cent.—1½ prem.—3 disc.
Ditto ditto Old four per cent.—5 per cent. disc.
Ditto ditto New four per cent.—5 per cent. disc.

Exchange.

On London, at 6 mths, 1s. 11d. to 2s. 1d. per Md. R.

Bombay, Dec. 19, 1835.
Exchanges.

Bills on London, at 6 mo. sight, 2s. to 2s. 1½d. per Rupee.
On Calcutta, at 30 days' sight, 108.4 to 108.12 Bom. Rs. per 100 Sicca Rupees.
On Madras, at 30 days' sight, 103 to 103.12 Bom. Rs. per 100 Madras Rs.

Government Securities.

Remittable Loan, 125 to 125.4 Bom. Rs. per 100 Sa. Rs.
5 per cent. Loan of 1822-23, according to the period of discharge, 108.4 to 108.12 per ditto.
Ditto of 1825-26, 108 to 111.8 per ditto.
Ditto of 1829-30, 111 to 111.8 per ditto.
4 per cent. Loan of 1832-33, 106 to 106.4 per ditto.

Singapore, Dec. 5, 1835.
Exchanges.

On London, 4 to 6 mo. sight, 4s. 4d. to 4s. 5d. per dollar.
On Bengal, gov. bills 206 Sa. Rs. per 100 dollars.

Canton, Dec. 8, 1835.
Exchanges, &c.

On London, 6 mo. sight, 4s. 10d per Sp. Dol.
E. I. Co's Agents for advances on consignments, 4s. 8d.
On Bengal. — Private Bills, 212 Sa. Rs. per 100 Sp. Dols.—Company's ditto, 30 days, 210 Sa. Rs.
On Bombay, ditto Bom. Rs. 220 to 222 per ditto.
Sycee Silver at Lintin, 3½ to 4 per cent. prem.

LIST of SHIPS Trading to INDIA and Eastward of the CAPE of GOOD HOPE.

Destination.	Appointed to sail.	Ships' Names.	Tons	Owners or Consignees.	Captains.	Where loading.	References for Freight or Passage.
	1836.						
Bengal	May 15	Arab	378	John S. Sparkes	John S. Sparkes	St.Kt.Docks	Sir Chas. Cockerill, Bart., & Co.
	June 1	Jean	340	Thomas Hamlin	Peter Goldie	Lon. Docks	Gregson, Melville, & Co.; Phillips & Tiplady.
Madras	May 20 Ports.	Royal William	451	Arbuthnot & Latham	George Ireland	W. I. Docks	Arbuthnot & Latham; Alves,Steele, & Harrison, Lime-st sq.
do.	5	Sesostris	540	Alexander Yates	Alexander Yates	W. I. Docks	Tomlin, Man, & Co., Cornhill.
	15	Thomas Grenville	886	Robert Thornhill	Robert Thornhill	E. I. Docks	Sir Chas. Cockerill, Bart., & Co.; T. Haviside & Co.
	do.	Theresa	550	James Thomas Hay	Walter Young	W. I. Docks	Rickards, Little & Co.; T. Haviside & Co.
	June 90	Repulse	600	Toxalin & Pryce	Henry Pryce	E. I. Docks	Tomlin, Man, & Co.
Madras and Bengal	June 1	Roxburgh Castle	600	Wigrams & Green	Wm. Cumberland	E. I. Docks	John Pirie & Co.
	1 Ports.	Duke of Lancaster	565	J. Gladstone & Co.	J. Hargraves	St.Kt.Docks	Arbuthnot & Latham; Alves, Steele, & Harrison.
		Heroine	650	Gledstanes & Co.	R. Mac arthy	St.Kt.Docks	Thos. Haviside & Co.
	8 Ports.	Mauri. Elphinstone	611	Joseph L. Heathorn	William Toller	W. I. Docks	Joseph L. Heathorn, Change Alley.
	15 Ports.	True Briton	600	Money & Henry Wigram	Charles Reed	E. I. Docks	John Pirie & Co., Freeman's-court.
	11	Baretto Junior	600	Reid, Irving, & Co.	Richard Saunders	W. I. Docks	T. Haviside & Co.
	July 10 Ports.	Scotia	700	Walkinbaw & Co.	John Campbell	E. I. Docks	Lyall, Brothers, & Co.; John Pirie & Co.
	May 10 Ports.	Euphrates	600	William Tindall	William Buckham	E. I. Docks	Lyall, Brothers, & Co.; John Lyney, Birchin-lane.
	16 Ports.	George Canning	400	Richard Fenwick	Thomas Winn	Lon. Docks	Sir C. Cockerill, & Co.; Arnold & Woollett.
	25	Walmer Castle	700	Richard Green	William Bourchier	E. I. Docks	John Pirie & Co.
Bombay		Bengal	400		John J. Marjoram	Lon. Docks	J. Cockburn & Co.; Waddell, Beck, & Co., Leadenhall-st.
	June 5	Gilmore	550	Reid, Irving, & Co.	H. H. Lindsay	W. I. Docks	Reid, Irving, & Co.; Thos. Haviside & Co.
	July 1	Boyne	619	Thacker, & Mangles&Co.	George Richardson	E. I. Docks	Thacker & Price, Leadenhall-st.; James Barber.
	May 7	Fama	980	William Purvis	William Purvis	Lon. Docks	William Martin, St. Mary Axe.
Cape and Batavia	90	Trusty	350	Thacker, & Mangles &Co.	James B. West	E. I. Docks	Hill & Wackerbath; Thacker & Price; Edmund Reed.
China	10	Agrippina	322	John Allan	William Rodgers	W. I. Docks	John Lyney, Birchin Lane.
Ceylon	10	Miranda	300	Thomas Joyce	Robert Hopper	W. I. Docks	Barclay, Brothers, & Co.; John Chapman, & Co.
Mauritius	10	Indemnity	168	Gardner & Urquhart	George Roberts	Lon. Docks	Mac Ghie, Page, & Smith, Abchurch-lane; J. Groves.
Mauritius and Ceylon	June 10 23	Harvey	400	Wigrams & Co.	H. N. Parkinson	St.Kt.Docks	Gregson, Melville, & Co.; Gardner & Urquhart.
Mauritius, Penang, & Singapore	May 16	Eagle	290	Nixon & Co.	Charles Patterson	Lon. Docks	John Pirie, & Co.
Cape and Mauritius	5 Conv. S.	Sea Witch	341	Thomas Ward	William Baker	Lon. Docks	Edward Luckie.
St. Helena	4 Conv. S.	Atwick	414	T. Brocklebank	Hugh Mackay	St.Kt.Docks	Carter & Bonus, Leadenhall-street.
Hobart Town	16 Emig.S.	Waterloo	390	John Todd	John Cow.	Dub.& Cork	Lachlan, Sons, & M'Leod.
New South Wales	15 Conv. S.	Cæsar. of Durham	463	Buckles & Co.	John Todd	Lon. Docks	Arnold & Woollett, Clement's-lane.
	18	Hooghly	540	John Pirie & Co.	George Bayly, jun.	St.Kt.Docks	Buckles & Co.; Devitt & Moore.
V'n D Land & New South Wales	90 Conv. S.	D.o/Northumbld.	360	Robert Henderson & Son	David Roxburgh	Lon. Docks	John Marshall, Birchin-lane.
		Scotia	383	Thomas Dobson	W. Randolph	St.Kt.Docks	Buckles & Co.; Devitt & Moore.
New South Wales	25 do.	Tam O'Shanter	684	Thomas Ward	W. Freema	St.Kt.Docks	Godwin & Lee; Thos. Dobson.
Van Diemen's Land	June 1 do.	Lady Kennaway	451	James B. Gordon	Robert P. Davidson	Sheerness	Lachlan, Sons, & M'Leod, Alie-street, Goodman's-fields.
New South Wales		Captain Cook	485	N. Griffiths	George Brown	Cork & Dub.	Lachlan, Sons, & M'Leod
	May 90	Henry Porcher	452	Goodwin & Lee	John Hart	Portsmouth	Lachlan, Sons, & M'Leod.
Hobart Town and Launceston		Florentia	350	Goodwin and Lee	W. S. Deloitte	St.Kt.Docks	Godwin & Lee.
Hobart Town	11	William Bryan	320	Domett & Co.	John Roman	Lon. Docks	Domett, Young, & England.
		Albatross	400	Phillips, King, & Co.	W. Westmoreland	St.Kt.Docks	Godwin & Lee
		Wave			Edw Goldsmith	St.Kt.Docks	Phillips, King, & Co.; Arnold & Woollett.
Cape and Sierra River	10	Joshua Carrol	143	William Bruce	Jacob Toby	St.Kt.Docks	F. & C. E. Mangles; Edmund Read.

EAST-INDIA AND CHINA PRODUCE.

	£. s. d.		£. s. d.
Coffee, Batavia ......cwt.	2 12 0	@	3 5 0
—— Samarang	2 8 0	—	2 11 6
—— Cheribon	2 16 0	—	3 4 0
—— Sumatra	2 6 0	—	2 8 0
—— Ceylon	2 13 0	—	2 14 6
—— Mocha	3 2 0	—	6 0 0
Cotton, Surat............lb	0 0 6¼	—	0 0 8½
—— Madras	0 0 6¼	—	0 0 8½
—— Bengal	0 0 5¾	—	0 0 7
—— Bourbon	none		——
Drugs & for Dyeing.			
Aloes, Epatica......cwt.	9 10 0	—	15 0 0
Anniseeds, Star..........	5 0 0		——
Borax, Refined..........	3 3 3		——
—— Unrefined	3 10 0		——
Camphire, in tub	12 10 0	—	13 0 0
Cardamoms, Malabar ..lb	0 3 0	—	0 3 1
—— Ceylon	0 1 2	—	0 1 6
Cassia Buds ....cwt.	3 10 0	—	4 0 0
—— Lignea	3 2 0	—	3 6 0
Castor Oil ....lb	0 0 4	—	0 0 10
China Root..........cwt.	17 0 0	—	18 0 0
Cubebs..................	2 5 0	—	2 12 0
Dragon's Blood.	10 0 0	—	25 0 0
Gum Ammoniac, drop ..	6 0 0	—	8 0 0
—— Arabic	2 10 0	—	4 5 0
—— Assafœtida	1 10 0	—	4 0 0
—— Benjamin, 3d Sort..	3 10 0	—	10 0 0
—— Animi..............	5 0 0	—	8 0 0
—— Gambogium........	5 0 0	—	15 0 0
—— Myrrh	2 0 0	—	14 0 0
—— Olibanum..........	0 6 0	—	2 18 0
Kino....................	12 0 0		——
Lac Lake..............lb	nominal		
—— Dye................	0 2 10		——
—— Shell ....cwt.	5 10 0	—	7 15 0
—— Stick	3 10 0	—	3 17 0
Musk, China ....oz.	0 10 0	—	1 5 0
Nux Vomica ....cwt.	0 8 0		——
Oil, Cassia ....oz.	0 8 6		——
—— Cinnamon..........	0 4 0	—	0 6 0
—— Cocoa-nut......cwt.	1 11 0		——
—— Cajaputa ....oz.	0 0 4	—	0 0 6
—— Mace	0 0 2	—	0 0 3
—— Nutmegs	0 1 2	—	0 1 5
Opium..................	none		——
Rhubarb................	0 2 6	—	0 3 6
Sal Ammoniac ......cwt.	8 8 0		——
Senna ....lb	0 0 3	—	0 1 2
Turmeric, Java ....cwt.	0 9 0	—	0 18 0
—— Bengal	0 12 0	—	0 16 0
—— China..............	0 16 0	—	1 2 0
Galls, in Sorts	4 0 0	—	4 5 0
——, Blue	5 0 0	—	5 5 0
Hides, Buffalo ....lb	0 0 2½	—	0 0 3½
—— Ox and Cow........	0 0 3	—	0 0 4
Indigo, Blue and Violet....	0 6 6	—	0 7 1
—— Purple and Violet....	0 5 2	—	0 6 6
—— Fine Violet	0 5 2	—	0 6 6
—— Mid. to good Violet ..	0 5 8	—	0 6 1
—— Violet and Copper	0 5 4	—	0 5 10
—— Copper	0 5 2	—	0 5 6
—— Consuming, mid. to fine	0 4 11	—	0 5 8
—— Do. ord. and low	0 4 3	—	0 4 10
—— Do. very low	0 3 9	—	0 4 2
—— Madras, mid. to good	0 4 10	—	0 5 3
—— Do. very low to ord ..	0 3 9	—	0 4 8
—— Oude, good mid. & good	0 4 6	—	0 4 11
Mother-o'-Pearl Shells, China ...cwt.	3 5 0	@	4 15 0
Nankeens ....piece	——		——
Rattans 100	0 2 9	—	0 6 6
Rice, Bengal White....cwt.	0 12 0	—	0 15 0
—— Patna	16 0	—	0 18 0
—— Java..................	10 0	—	0 12 0
Safflower..................	1 0	—	9 0 0
Sago......................	9 0	—	0 10 6
—— Pearl	13 0	—	0 16 0
Saltpetre..................	0 5 6	—	1 9 6
Silk, Company's Bengal lb	0 16 0	—	1 8 0
—— Novi	——		——
—— China Tsatlee	1 5 6	—	1 9 6
—— Bengal Privilege......	0 15 6	—	1 1 0
—— Tayaam	1 2 0	—	1 4 6
Spices, Cinnamon..........	0 5 0	—	0 9 6
—— Cloves	0 0 9½	—	0 1 3
—— Mace	0 6 0	—	0 9 0
—— Nutmegs	0 5 0	—	0 7 0
—— Ginger ....cwt.	1 16 0	—	2 14 0
—— Pepper, Black......lb	0 0 4¾	—	0 0 5
—— —— White	0 1 4	—	0 1 8
Sugar, Bengal ....cwt.	1 16 0	—	1 19 0
—— Siam and China	1 15 0	—	2 0 6
—— Mauritius (duty paid)	3 0 0	—	3 9 0
—— Manilla and Java	1 13 0	—	2 0 6
Tea, Bohea..............lb	——		——
—— Congou	——		——
—— Souchong	——		——
—— Caper	——		——
—— Campoi	——	See Sale.	——
—— Twankay	——		——
—— Pekoe, (Orange, &c.)..	——		——
—— Hyson Skin	——		——
—— Hyson................	——		——
—— Young Hyson	——		——
—— Gunpowder, Imperial	——		——
Tin, Banca............cwt.	4 17 0	—	4 19 0
Tortoiseshell ....lb	1 1 0	—	1 18 0
Vermilion ....lb	0 3 3	—	0 4 0
Wax ....cwt.	7 0 0	—	7 7 0
Wood, Saunders Red ..ton	7 0 0		——
—— Ebony	13 0 0		——
—— Sapan................	6 0 0	—	13 0 0

AUSTRALASIAN PRODUCE.

	£. s. d.		£. s. d.
Cedar Wood............foot	0 0 6	—	0 0 7
Oil, Fish................tun	37 10 0	—	40 0 0
Whalebone ....ton	150 0 0		——
Wool, N. S. Wales, viz.			
Best....................lb	0 2 3	—	0 3 6
Inferior	0 1 0	—	0 3 2
—— V. D. Land, viz.			
Best......................	0 2 0	—	0 2 8
Inferior	0 1 0	—	0 1 9

SOUTH AFRICAN PRODUCE.

	£. s. d.		£. s. d.
Aloes ....cwt.	1 10 6	—	1 13 0
Ostrich Feathers, und ....lb	——		——
Gum Arabic............cwt.	1 5 0	—	1 10 0
Hides, Dry ....lb	0 0 4¾	—	0 0 6½
—— Salted	0 0 3½	—	0 0 5
Oil, Palm ....cwt.	1 14 6		——
Raisins	——		——
Wax	7 0 0	—	7 5 0
Wine, Cape, Mad., best ..pipe	17 0 0	—	19 0 0
—— Do. 2d & 3d quality	14 0 0	—	15 0 0
Wood, Teak ....load	9 5 0	—	10 10 0
Wool ....lb.	0 1 6	—	0 2 6

PRICES OF SHARES, April 26, 1836.

	Price.	Dividends.	Capital.	Shares of.	Paid.	Books Shut for Dividends.
DOCKS.	£.	£.	£.	£.	£.	
East-India..............(Stock)....	105	— p. cent.	496,667	—	—	March. Sept.
London ....(Stock)....	58½	2½ p. cent.	3,238,000	—	—	June. Dec.
St. Katherine's	88½	3 p. cent.	1,352,752	100	—	Jan. July
Ditto Debentures	—	4½ p. cent.	——	—	—	5 April. 5 Oct.
Ditto ditto	102	4 p. cent.	——	—	—	5 April. 5 Oct.
West-India ....(Stock)....	109	5 p. cent.	1,380,000	—	—	June. Dec.
MISCELLANEOUS.						
Australian (Agricultural)............	40	——	10,000	100	26½	——
Bank (Australasian)	59	——	5,000	40	40	——
Van Diemen's Land Company......	14½	——	10,000	100	17	——

Wolfe, Brothers, 25, *Change Alley.*

THE LONDON MARKETS, April 26.

Sugar.—The stock of West India sugars is now 10,078 hhds. and trs., being 520 less than last year. The stock of Mauritius is now 89,009 bags, which is 27,110 less than last year. The delivery of West India last week was 2,373 hhds. and trs., which is 371 more than last year. The delivery of Mauritius was 8,768 bags, being 145 less than the corresponding week of last year. A further improvement in the prices of Mauritius of 6d. to 1s. has taken place, and the demand has been very brisk by private contract. There is a good disposition shown to buy East-India sugars, but owing to the supply at market being small, extensive transactions have been prevented.

Indigo.—The quarterly sale commenced on the 19th April without briskness, but as the sale proceeded, the biddings became more animated, particularly for ordinary and middling sorts, of which there was only a limited quantity put up. The prices obtained are above those of the last sales, say 9d. to 1s. for ordinary and low middling sorts, 8d. to 10d. for middling and good, and 6d. to 8d. on fine quality. The proprietors were firm, and have bought in considerably. The sale will finish on the 27th. The quantity declared was about 5,500 chests.

Coffee.—There has been very little doing in British plantation, owing to the large arrivals from the West Indies. One reason for the decline in the prices of Ceylon coffee is ascribed to the letters from that place, stating two vessels loading with certificate for coffee, and would sail the end of January, and of course entitled to entry at the low duty.

Tea.—The tea market is heavy, occasioned by the large quantities advertised for sale, still the holders are firm, and to purchase small profits must be paid on the prices of the late sales; the sales advertised are 30,776 packages on the 17th of May, and 44.000 packages to follow the Company's sale in June, making a total of 74,776 packages, exclusive of the Company's sale. The large public sales of free trade teas commenced on the 12th April, and ended on the 19th; the quantity brought forward was about 60,000 packages. The sale was well attended by the trade, but the biddings were very languid. A great proportion of the quantity brought forward has been bought in, but the quantity sold has found buyers at an advance upon the prices of the last public sales. The improvement is principally in common congou and bohea, the former 2½d. to 3d. higher, the latter 1½. higher.

The East-India Company have issued their declaration for the June sale, and it consists of 600,000lbs. of bohea; 2,600,000lbs. of congou, campoi, &c.; 700,000lbs. of twankay and hyson skin; and 100,000lbs. of hyson—total 4,000,000lb.

Cotton.—The cotton market is dull.

DAILY PRICES OF STOCKS, *from March 26, to April 25,* 1836.

Mar.	Bank Stock.	3 Pr. Ct. Red.	3 Pr. Ct. Consols.	3½ Pr. Ct. Red.	New 3½ Pr. Cent.	Long Annuities.	India Stock.	Consols for acct.	India Bonds.	Exch. Bills.
26	Shut	Shut	91⅝ 91¾	Shut	99⅞ 100	Shut	Shut	91¾	6 8p	21 23p
28	—	—	91⅝ 91¾	—	99⅞ 100	—	—	91¾	6p	20 23p
29	—	—	91⅝ 91¾	—	99⅞ 100	—	—	91⅝ 91¾	6 8p	20 22p
30	—	—	91⅝ 91¾	—	99⅞ 100	—	—	91⅝ 91¾	5 7p	19 21p
31	—	—	91½ 91¾	—	99⅞ 100	—	—	91⅝ 91¾	7p	19 21p
Apr.										
2	—	—	91½ 91¾	—	100⅛	—	—	91⅝ 91¾	5 6p	18 20p
4	—	—	91⅝ 91¾	—	100⅛	—	—	91¾	6 7p	19 21p
5	—	—	91⅝ 91¾	—	—	—	—	91¾	6 8p	19 21p
6	215 215½	90⅞ 91	91¾ 91⅞	98⅞ 99⅛	100 ⅛	16 16 1/16	—	91¾ 91⅞	—	19 21p
7	215	90⅞ 91	91¾ 91⅞	99 ⅛	100 ⅛	16 16 1/16	—	91¾ 91⅞	6 8p	19 21p
8	214	91 91⅛	91⅞ 92	99⅛ ¼	100⅛ ¼	16 16⅛	—	91⅞ 92	6 8p	20 22p
9	213¾ 214½	91⅛ 91¼	91⅞ 92	99⅛ ¼	100⅛ ¼	16 16⅛	—	92	6 8p	20 22p
11	214 214½	91⅛ 91¼	91⅞ 92	99⅛ ¼	100¼ ⅜	16 16 1/16	—	91⅞ 92	—	20 22p
12	213 213¾	91⅛ 91¼	91⅞ 92	98⅞ 99⅛	100⅛ ⅜	16 16 1/16	—	91¾ 91⅞	5 8p	19 22p
13	—	91 91⅛	91¾ 91⅞	99 ⅛	100⅛ ¼	16 16 1/16	—	91⅞ 92	7p	19 21p
14	213½	90⅞ 91⅛	91⅝ 91⅞	98⅞ 99⅛	100⅛ ¼	15 15/16 16 1/16	258¼ 9	91¾ 91⅞	5p	18 21p
15	213¼	90⅞ 91	91½ 91¾	98⅞ 9	100⅛ ¼	15 15/16 16	258 9	91⅝ 91¾	7p	18 20p
16	213	90¾ 90⅞	91⅜ 91⅝	98⅝ ⅞	100 ⅛	15 15/16 16	—	91½ 91⅝	5 7p	18 20p
18	212½ 213	90¾ 90⅞	91½ 91⅝	99½ ¾	99⅞ 0⅛	15 15/16 16	258¼ ½	91½ 91⅝	5p	18 20p
19	212½	90¾ 91	91½ 91¾	99⅝ 99¾	100⅛ ¼	15 15 15/16	258 ¼	91 91⅝	7p	18 20p
20	212	90¾ 90⅞	91½ 91⅝	98¾ 98⅞	100⅛ ⅜	15 15/16 16	257½ 8¼	91⅝ 91¾	5 7p	19 21p
21	211½ 212	90¾ 91⅛	91⅝ 91⅞	98¾ 9	100⅛ ⅜	15 15/16 16	258 ¼	91⅝ 92	5 6p	18 21p
22	211¼ 211¾	91⅛	91¾ 91⅞	98⅞ 9	100¼ ⅜	15 15/16 16	257½ 8	91⅝ 91⅞	5 7p	19 21p
23	211½	90⅞ 91	91⅝ 91⅞	98⅞ 9	100⅛ ⅜	15 15/16 16	—	91¾	5 7p	19 21p
25	211	90⅞ 91	91⅝ 91¾	98¾ ⅞	100⅛ ¼	15 15/16 15⅞	—	91¾	6 7p	19 21p

FREDERICK BARRY, Stock and Share Broker, 7, Birchin Lane, Cornhill.

ASIATIC INTELLIGENCE.

Calcutta.

MISCELLANEOUS.

CIVIL SERVICE ANNUITY FUND.

The meeting on the 1st January was attended by 31 members; Mr. H. T. Prinsep in the chair.

After passing the accounts of the year and re-electing the managers, the circular of the secretary, communicating the Court's modifications of the fund to the service, was read; and it appearing that, of 263 answers, 258 were assents, including 9 of a more or less conditional nature, and only 5 dissents (namely, those of Messrs. Hughes, Deane, Lushington, W. Young, and Houston,), it was resolved, "That the propositions submitted to the service in the despatch of the Hon. Court, dated May 1835, having been accepted by the service, their acceptance be recorded accordingly."

Mr. Melville then moved the following: " That it be an instruction to the committee, in preparing the rules, to give effect to the propositions of the Hon. Court, to look to the permanence of the institution, and to guard the funds from any appropriations likely to interfere therewith."

Mr. Prinsep explained, that the directions of the Court could not be literally carried into effect, because, if the words of their despatch were taken literally, the third of the unappropriated pensions, instead of being reserved, as clearly intended by the Court, would have to be thrown back into the fund, and counted in the division for appropriation over again from year to year, till reduced to a single one; and further, it was the Court's object, in their scheme of modification, to apply the surplus funds only; but how was the surplus to be ascertained? not by the original calculations, for these contemplated a yearly receipt of a lakh of rupees from fines, after the fund should have run on for 25 years, and a capital of 26 lakhs: but now this resource of the fines was entirely taken away by the new limitation of the contributions, and it would happen consequently that, when Sir C. Metcalfe and Mr. Ross should retire, and also in some other cases, the fund would have to pay back large sums to those members for the excess of their contributions. Besides, it was impossible to foresee how many applicants for pension would step forward during the three years of experiment allowed by the Court. There were now 51 unappropriated annuities, and 14

applications were already before the managers. The calculations for the stability of the fund were also affected by the donations and modified pensions to persons retiring on sick certificate. For these reasons, he considered it necessary that a committee should examine the whole subject. They ought to proceed upon the principle of establishing at once the permanent stability of the fund. This they had now abundant means of doing, and he would therefore suggest that, of the 60 lakhs now at credit of the fund, they should set apart 35 lakhs to provide for the loss of the one lakh per annum of fines, as well as to make up a sufficient capital in reserve as originally contemplated. They would still have 25 lakhs available for the annuities in excess of the regular annual number.

After some discussion *pro* and *con*, respecting the stability of the fund,

Mr. Colvin considered it unnecessary to take means to secure the permanency of the fund, having the Court's guarantee to their original bargain for the nine pensions of £1000; he accordingly proposed the following amendment:

" That the proposition already carried is a sufficient instruction to the committee of managers;" which was carried by 19 to 12.

The Hon. Mr. Elliot then drew attention to the last paragraph of the letter of the managers to the Court, which had led to these modifications in the fund, and pointed out that the Court had omitted to notice the suggestion it contained, that members of the service, retiring immediately after the date of the letter, should have all the benefit of any modifications that should be allowed by the Court. He thought it only just that the managers, in answering the Court's letter, should re-urge this point, for two or three gentlemen had retired on the faith of being so admitted, who would probably otherwise have awaited the issue. He therefore moved the following proposition, which was carried unanimously:

" That the case of the servants who have retired subsequent to the transmission of the memorial of the service, in which their claim to benefit by any prospective modification was submitted to the Hon. the Court of Directors, not having been noticed in the despatch now before the meeting, it be again recommended to the consideration of the Hon. Court, those servants having retired in the confident belief that the service had pledged themselves to support their claim to participate in the benefits now about to be enjoyed by those immediately about to retire."

Mr. Mangles observed upon the hardship of the second clause in the Court's letter, requiring that persons retiring on medical certificate should be re-examined by the Court's physician in England: which rule might cause men to be sent back to India, whose constitutions might not be able to stand the climate, in spite of apparent restoration to health while in Europe; and upon his motion it was unanimously resolved:

" That it be an instruction to the managers, to solicit the Hon. Court to re-consider the clause in the rules relating to confirmation of certificate of the Court's examining physician, after a residence in England, on the part of the absentee, of at least twelve months, with reference to the hardship which such rule may probably be the means of inflicting."

Mr. John Trotter requested the attention of the gentlemen present to a scheme he wished to bring forward, with a view to increase promotion in the service. It contemplated the establishment of a supplementary fund, independent of the other and of the Company, to be supported by subscriptions of the service, which fund to be devoted to increasing the amount of the pensions from the present annuity fund.

The following letter, signed by two of the gentlemen on the dissentient list, was read at the meeting, and excited a good deal of amusement:

" To the Chairman of the Special Meeting, to be held on the 1st of January, 1836.

" Sir,—Having taken into the fullest consideration the proposals contained in the Hon. Court of Directors' letter of the 27th May 1835, I am compelled most reluctantly to withhold my assent from the proposals referred to, under the impression that a more advantageous mode is offered to us of applying the large unappropriated balance. In a case recently brought before the Supreme Court, a considerable fine was imposed on Mr. Halkett, the acting magistrate of Nuddeah, in order, it may be presumed, to mark the dissatisfaction of the judges at that gentleman's conscientious discharge of his duty. With reference, then, to this case, particularly, I suggest that the unappropriated balance may be set aside as a fund for the payment of such fines as the judges of the Supreme Court, in the exercise of an authority not wisely delegated, may impose, from time to time, on the imprudence of official integrity. A great benefit will thus be conferred on those members of the service who may fall into the natural, but mistaken, notion, that obedience to the orders of the Government, from which alone they derive their authority, is not likely to be the

means of subjecting them to pecuniary loss.

" I have the honour to be, &c.
     " H. W. DEANE.
" I concur: H. LUSHINGTON.
" Bijnour, 19th Nov. 1835."

The *Courier*, noticing this letter in its report of these proceedings, states : " we are informed it is the intention of Government to reimburse Mr. Halkett for all the charges he has incurred in defending the action brought against him by Mr. Calder."

NEW HINDU SECT.

Allusion is made by one of the correspondents of the *Christian Intelligencer* for December, to a new sect, founded by the late Baboo Joynarayun Ghosaul, formerly of Kidderpore, latterly of Benares, where he endowed a college. Their numbers are said to amount to about a hundred thousand. They are called *Kurta Bhoja*, or worshippers of the creator, and deny that Brahmins are gods, reject all idols, perform no *shraddha* or any ceremony connected with idol worship. Their creed is, that there is but one God, and that to think of him constitutes worship; that this was the way the Vedants had pointed out. They are blamed by their neighbours for being slothful and neglecting their families; they never cut their hair, shave their beards, nor pare their nails : and they are abhorred and persecuted by the orthodox Hindus.— *Beng. Herald, Jan. 3.*

Since our attention has been directed to this subject, we have had several opportunities of obtaining farther information respecting the Kurta Bhoja sect, and reviving our recollections of what we had previously heard. We are satisfied that a mistake has been committed in attributing the institution of this sect to Joynarayun Ghosal, although it is very probable that he may have attached himself to it, and contributed to its extension. We have at Serampore native Christians, of long established character, who were connected with the Kurta Bhojas before they embraced Christianity, nearly thirty years ago; and there are others, younger men, whose parents belonged to the sect. Some of our pundits, being natives of the district where the sect first originated, have likewise given us information respecting it, which coincides with that derived from our Christian friends.

The real founder of the sect was Ramchurun Ghose, a Sudgopa, (the caste of Cowherds, of whose services brambuns avail themselves), of Ghospara, on the opposite side of the river near Hooghly. He appears to have instituted his sect about forty or fifty years ago; and his son to this day enjoys the distinction which at first belonged to his father as head of the Kurta Bhojas. We are inclined to think that, although idleness and licentiousness may be the chief characteristics of this party, at first, at least, there was something better amongst them—a dissatisfaction with the grossness of image worship, an impatience of bramhunical pretention to deity, and perhaps some approach to a recognition of the one living and true God, and the spirituality of his worship. It is a certain fact, that a considerable number of those who first received the Gospel in Jessore, were in a measure prepared to do so by an acquaintance with the religionists of Ghospara. Nevertheless, even then, the excesses which the Kurta Bhojas indulged in appear to have been so abominable as to shock such as were with any sincerity desirous of finding the truth. A chief pretence of the sect has been to substitute an actual vision of the gods of every individual for material images: for each one is allowed to retain the deity he has been accustomed most to honour. We have received different accounts of the means by which this pretence was established. All agree that a secret and darkened apartment is chosen for the purpose. Some imagine that the worshippers have the forms of their gods brought before them in such situations by some inexplicable sort of *black art*, resembling, as we were gravely told, the experiments of chemistry. Others give a much simpler explanation by saying, that the worshippers are made first to look steadfastly upon a strong light, and then turn their faces to a dark recess, where, out of the dazzling confusion left upon their eyes, their imaginations may conjure up something they can call the appearance of their god. It is also one of the tenets of the sect to reject the use of all medicine, instead of which they have recourse in sickness of every sort to some charms of their own. The story goes, that the founder of the sect made friendship with a muhapooroosh, who gave him a *kulsee* of water, of which whoever partook would be cured of whatever disease he might be affected with. The water, however, is now spent; and we have not heard what substitute has been obtained for it.

In Jessore, in particular, the sect is very widely diffused. Many of its adherents conceal their connection with it; but even those who make no secret of it do not lose caste, because no openly manifest distinction or observance is required of them which is in violation of the rules of caste; and their promiscuous feasting of all castes, Hindoos, Moosulmans, and even Portuguese, is always so secret as to be unseen by those who are in caste: and what is unseen is in respect of caste harmless. The sect have not yet produced any written account of their doctrines. Indeed they hold pens, ink and paper in contempt: they are too material for them. Their doctrine is therefore wholly traditional, and is propagated by initiated disciples, in correspondence with the chief at Ghospara.—*Friend of India, Jan.* 14.

UNION BANK.

An Annual General Meeting of the Proprietors of the Union Bank took place yesterday. The accounts exhibited a most favorable out-turn of the last half year's transactions—the profit realized being 13¼ per cent. of which 10 per cent., or 125 Sa. Rs. per share, were ordered to be paid to proprietors as dividend, and about 2¾ per cent., or Sa. Rs. 314 per share, being retained and added to the value of shares, making them Company's rupees 2,700 instead of Sa. Rs. 2,500 as formerly.—*Hurkaru, Jan.* 15.

THE KHASIAS OF CHERRAPOONJEE.

Mr. Lish, the missionary from Serampore stationed at Cherrapoonjee, having come to Calcutta a short time ago, brought with him a company of Khasia youths, who, from the reports of their companions who had accompanied him on a previous occasion, were eager to see the wonders of the capital. Amongst them were two young princes, the nephews of the present Raja of Cherrapoonjee, who have both been Mr. Lish's pupils ever since he went to reside at his station. One of them has been particularly studious, and has added a considerable acquaintance with English, and facility of conversation in it, to the use of his native tongue in Bengalee characters; for it has no character for itself, and it had no readers until Mr. Lish commenced his schools. Several others have made attainments but little inferior to those of this young man.—*Friend of India, Jan.* 14.

ESTATE OF ALEXANDER AND CO.

Abstract of Cash Receipts and Disbursements, for October and November, 1835, filed by the Assignee.

Receipts.

Cash Balance, 30th September		4,120
Sale of Indigo Factory		3,500
Ranneegunge Colliery		30,263
Rents of Landed Property		736
From the Union Bank	65,629	
Less paid	65,000	
		629
Remittances from Dr. Constituents		95,495
Interest on Government Paper		60
Loan for Indigo Advances		31,000
	Sa. Rs.	1,65,803

Disbursements.

Advances for manufacture of indigo		1,31,538
Ranneegunge Colliery		8,579
Peergunge Saltpetre Concern		1,200
Law Charges		15,373
Office Establishment		5,153
Incidental Charges		251
Assessments, Ground Rent, Durwan's Wages, &c., for Landed Property		297
Refund to Creditors of Sums realized since failure		1,279
	Sa. Rs.	1,63,670
Cash in hand		2,133
	Sa. Rs.	1,65,803

Memorandum.

Cash in hand	2,133	
Ditto Union Bank	12,011	
Government Securities	2,500	
Unrealized Acceptances	1,44,243	
		1,60,887
Deduct Loans payable		41,000
	Sa. Rs.	1,19,887

The estate of Alexander and Co. will pay its creditors, in March next, a dividend of three per cent. on all proved claims. Three years ago, oaths were taken that the estate had assets to the value of eight annas in every rupee of claims. The first dividend will be a payment at the rate of one per cent. per annum; one-eighth of the mere interest formerly allowed; and a proportion that, even if there were the amount of assets sworn, would take fifty years to liquidate the reduced claims! The chief source of this dividend is said to be the profits of the factories belonging to the estate; so that even the paltry sum, now to be disbursed, has been created since the property was declared on oath to be then sufficient to pay off half the claims. We would ask Sir Edward Ryan, who, before his elevation to the chief seat on the bench, was said to possess a tolerable share of radical sense, and who may still see the matter in its popular light, whether he was not deceived by a fraud when this matter was brought before him in its early stages in the Insolvent Court? If there was not a legal, no one can doubt, that there was a moral, fraud. And, further, whether he would have considered the case cognizable in that court, if no other oath had been made than such as represented the circumstances of the broken firm to be as they have now proved?—*Central Free Press, Jan. 2.*

ESTATE OF FERGUSSON AND CO.

Statement of Transactions of the Assignees, for November, 1835.

Payments.

Indigo Advances	Sa. Rs.	49,959
Advances on account of other Goods		34,963
Sundry Advances		3,083
Dividend paid		35,869
Amount paid in Anticipation of Dividend		75
Amount of Acceptances received for Property sold, credit for which is given *per contra*, although not yet Realised		3,07,416
Amount paid, being refund of so much received on Account parties not indebted to Estate		499
Amount Bills of Exchange taken in payment of Debts and remitted to London for recovery		34,744
Premium paid on Life Insurances		3,520
Company's Paper purchased		21,442
Sundry Charges connected with Estate		729
Postage paid		95
		4,92,394
Balance in hands of Assignees		62,473
	Sa. Rs.	5,54,867

Receipts.

Balance of last Statement furnished 1st November	Sa. Rs.	61,722
Outstanding Debts recovered		3,71,933
Sale of sundry Goods		18,902
Sale of Company's paper		31,123
Amount Received on Account Sale of indigo factories		55,217
Amount received on Account Sale of houses, &c.		1,027
Amount received on Account of an outstanding debt, but in which other parties are interested		1,347
Indigo Advances refunded		11,013
Interest received		2,583
	Sa. Rs.	5,54,867

In possession of Assignees, Company's Promissory Notes, belonging to Estate, amounting to	Sa. Rs.	1,77,080

ESTATE OF MACKINTOSH AND CO.

Abstract of Receipts and Disbursements for October and November 1835, filed by the Assignees.

Receipts.

Cash Balance, 30th September	2,08,356
Sale of Landed Property	11,009
Rents of Landed Property	1,991
Steamer *Forbes*	13,860
Refund of Payments in anticipation of Dividend	59
Sale of Office Furniture	62
Remittances from Dr. Constituents	45,226
	Sa. Rs. 2,80,564

Disbursements.

Advances for manufacture of Indigo	98,300
Steamer *Forbes*	7,951
Life Insurance Premiums	4,179
Repairs, Assessments, Durwans' Wages, &c. of Landed Property	4,895
Law Charges	5,279
Office Establishment	2,473
Incidental Charges	97
Refund to Creditors of Sums realized since the failure	270
Payment in anticipation of Dividend	500
Cost of a 4 per cent. Government note for Rs. 500	486
Balance of T. Graham's London account	500
Loans at interest	41,000
Dividends paid	10,136
	1,05,987
Cash in hand and in Union Bank	1,74,577
	Sa. Rs. 2,80,564

Memorandum.

Government Securities	53,500
Unrealised Acceptances	3,00,645
Loans at Interest	41,000
Cash Balance in Union Bank	1,74,577
	Sa. Rs. 5,69,722

ABOLITION OF OATHS.

The Indian Law Commissioners have proposed the following question, relative to judicial evidence, for the consideration of the judges of the Sudder Dewanny and Nizamut Adaulut:

" If oaths and declarations, containing appeals and imprecations of a religious kind, were altogether abolished in criminal proceedings—all the legal penalties of false testimony being retained—would the effect on the administration of justice be on the whole salutary or pernicious?"

The commissioners request that the

question may be circulated to the commissioners of circuit, the civil and session-judges, and the magistrates and joint magistrates, for their opinions, and any facts which their experience may enable them to furnish in explanation of them; and likewise to such of the Principal Sudder Ameens, Sudder Ameens, and Hindoo and Mahomedan law officers, as the courts of Sudder Dewanny and Nizamut Adaulut think may be consulted with advantage.

THE AGRA COLLEGE.

We have lately had an opportunity of perusing the report of the superintendent of the Agra College, on the last half-yearly examination. The difficulties hitherto complained of in the propagation of education, and especially of English education, in this country, are said to have proceeded from the opposition of prejudices, or at least from indifference to the benefits proposed for them on the part of those to be instructed—the natives themselves. The present report, however, affords gratifying evidence of such obstacles having in a great measure vanished, at least in this quarter, and would seem to show, that any deficiency or weakness in the practical effect of this institution is more attributable to the want of *materiel* of instruction, books and teachers, than to any lukewarmness on the part of the natives. Whether this greater readiness to acquire our language and science has its source in the loaves and fishes scented afar off,—that is, in the expected favour thereby of the European functionaries, and the attainment of office through the language, whose adoption is said to be in contemplation,—it matters not; the desired result will be not less certain. At all events, it will be conceded that they should at least have that best encouragement to acquirement, the ready and effective means. The Agra Local Committee of Education, we believe, are of the same opinion, and have minuted strongly to that effect.—*Agra Ukhbar, Dec.* 19.

TRADE OF CABUL.

In an official notification is published the following extract of a letter from Mr. Masson (the writer of the paper inserted in p. 24), addressed to Captain Wade, from Cabul, May 31:

" On arrival at Cabul, I made enquiries as to the chance of disposing of indigo, and exhibited the samples sent. The quality was admitted by all, but it was asserted that the indigo was of a kind not in use here or at Bokhara. There were many consumers who would have taken a small quantity, say 1 or 2 maunds, and have experimented upon it; but that it could be advantageously sold in Cabul is not evident. The indigo of the vale of the Indus is now selling at Rs. 80 per maund,

and the brokers say is likely to fall to Rs. 60 Kábum, it being known that the Lobánis have purchased their indigo this season at the low rate of Rs. 28 per maund. The kisht or brick-like form of the musters is objected to; the dump form being preferred. The indigo received from the vale of the Indus is packed first in a cotton bag, then cased with untanned skin, and covered with *júāl* or *summad.* Three maunds are put into each package, and two of them are a load for a camel. Occasionally, the packages are of four maunds each. The hire of a camel from Multán to Cabul is 16 Rs., and duty is collected at the two Derahs, at Ghazní and Cabul. Two kafilas from Turkistan remain at Khalam, fearful to advance to Cabul; and a third is at Koshan, in the same predicament. From the latter, a quantity of gold thread and tillahs of Bokhara have been sent to Cabul. Gold is very cheap; the tillah current for 8 Rs., and the ducat for 5½ Rs.; the former Rupees Kahum. Chintzes, black pepper, and drugs from Bombay have been received at Cabul *via* Kandahar. The chintzes sold at low prices, and are retailed at ½ R. the yard. Black pepper was at first sold for 44 Rs. pukhtab per maund, ready money; afterwards fell to Rs. 40; then advanced to 44, 48, and 50 Rs., successively, and is in demand. Shirkhirst, or manna, sold for Rs. 50 pukhtah, per maund Tabrezi—ready money. Some camphor also arrived, but has not yet been sold."

THE SANSCRIT COLLEGE.

The native managers of the Government Sanscrit College have succeeded in proscribing the study of the English language and sciences there (which were introduced a few years ago), on the ground that it is not compatible with the shastras; that it deteriorates the value of oriental acquisitions, renders the students unfit for sacerdotal duties, and plants mistrust in their minds. The *Friend of India,* with great warmth, censures this proceeding; observing that " the expulsion of English during the administration of Ramkomul Sen shows the inveteracy of the prejudice against it. If any man was likely to have used the utmost exertion to restrain the bigots of the college from this act of suicide, it was Baboo Ramkomul Sen. That native gentleman derives his weight in society from European associations. He is himself one of the best English scholars in the country, and his reputation is founded on the English and Bengalee Dictionary with which he has favoured the public as the result of ten years of assiduity. With all his predilections in favour of this language, with a strong attachment to the sciences which ennoble the European world, and with an ardent desire to raise his own countrymen, he has been obliged to yield to the current of Hindoo prejudice, and to become the instrument of expelling the language of the rulers of India from an institution which is supported by their bounty. The step which has now been taken by the directors of the college will not, however, be found unserviceable, after all, to the progress of truth, because it serves fully to develope the genuine character of Hindooism. We have now the most unequivocal proof that it is incapable of advance or elevation. It stands aloof from all the improvements of the age, and refuses all association with them. It will not accommodate itself to the progress of society. To the scientific errors which have been embodied in its sacred books, it clings with the most tenacious grasp. It will not permit its literati to adorn their minds with the knowledge of the nations, or to form part of the great communion of intellect throughout the world, of which the first principle is *progression.* They are never to go beyond the wisdom of their ancestors. They are to admit no ideas into their minds which would place them ahead of their creed. They are always to continue in the belief that the world is flat, and that the sun revolves round it.[*] They are never to doubt the existence of the seas of clarified butter and curds. They are for ever to continue to draw their history from their poets, and their chronology from their astronomers. Such are the facts which have been laid open, by the discussions to which the exclusion of English from the Sungskrit College has given rise. The Sungskrit College is now employed, therefore, exclusively in teaching Hindoo learning, on Hindoo principles, for Hindoo objects; and there is no prospect of its ever being incorporated with any plan of national improvement. It is a nursery for the Hindoo priesthood. The question touching the support it shall continue to receive from funds which ought to be sacred to higher objects, is now reduced within a very narrow compass. We doubt not the subject will receive the attention which it merits, from the public authorities both in this country and in England. And we would venture to express our humble opinion, that the principle laid down by the Court of Directors should be strictly kept in view in all future arrangements; and that the rule of Lord William Bentinck, which cuts off all future exhibitions, be rigidly maintained. The present incumbents, both teachers and pupils, have a claim upon government, with which it would be unjust to interfere. Let the college last their

[*] The writer of this appears to affect ignorance of the fact, that the Hindoo astronomical writers have as just notions of the motions of the heavenly bodies as our own.—ED. A. J.

time. The students will gradually drop off, through the withdrawal of support from all new applicants; and the professors will in time be left without duties. To give it a fresh lease of life, by reviving the stipends of the students, after its unequivocal declaration of hostility to every species of scientific and literary improvement, would be, to use the expression of the Court, ' an act of folly.' "

Those who take a more temperate view of the subject than this writer, will perceive, in this step of the directors of the Sanscrit College, nothing more than a fair retaliation against the late unjust and unwise proscription of oriental literature by the Indian government.

RAJAH RAJNARAIN ROY.

The Governor-General gave a private audience to-day to Rajah Rajnarain Roy, at which the Rajah was presented with a large gold medal of honour, bearing the following inscription:—On the obverse, the Company's arms, richly chased, with the motto upon a dark ground in a circle—" *Auspicio Regis et Senatus Angliæ* "— and on the reverse, the words " Presented by the Hon. Sir Charles T. Metcalfe, Bart., Governor-General of all India, to Rajah Rajnarain Roy Behadur, A.D. 1835." The medal is fitted with a clasp to be worn upon the breast, like a star; and we have no doubt the young rajah will value this appendage to his dress as a more honourable distinction than the jewels with which a wealthy inheritance has hitherto adorned his person.—*Cal. Cour.*, Dec. 29.

NATIVE EDUCATION.

Upon the list of donations to the fund for the education of natives, under the direction of the Committee of Public Instruction, are the following:

Rajah Buddyanath Roy	Rs. 50,000
,, Nursing Chunder Roy	20,000
,, Cally Sunker Roy	20,000
,, Benwari Lal Roy	30,000
,, Gooroo Presaud Roy	10,000
,, Hurry Nath Roy	20,000
,, Salb Chunder Roy	20,000

Making an aggregate of 1,70,000 Rs., or nearly £200,000, contributed by seven individuals. Every contributor to the extent of 10,000 Rs. is entitled to the privilege of admitting one pupil to the Hindoo College. The *Gyananeshan* (native paper), noticing these munificent donations, and another of 10,000 Rs. by Rajah Bijoy Govind Sing, of Purnea, asks—" What are the Debs, the Mullicks, the Seals, and other wealthy natives, doing? Surely they cannot exercise their charity in a nobler object than that of being the means of bestowing upon their countrymen that most inestimable gift— the gift of moral and intellectual education."

GANGES INSURANCE OFFICE.

There was a meeting of the members of the Ganges Insurance Company yesterday, called chiefly for the purpose of considering the means to meet the recent call on the society, on the policies effected on the *Lady Munro.* After some discussion, it was resolved to call on the shareholders, who, on a recent occasion, advanced Sa. Rs. 1,000, to make an additional advance of Sa. Rs. 500, and those who on the same occasion advanced Sa. Rs. 500, are now to be called on for Sa. Rs. 1,000, and those who did not pay at all are to advance Sa. Rs. 1,500. It was also agreed that Mr. J. Low and Mr. J. Allan be requested to take the management of the society's affairs, with a view to the final winding up of the Insurance Office.—*Englishman, Dec.* 21.

DELHI.

Much discord is now prevalent in the palace of the king of Delhi. The eldest son of his Majesty is nominated as the heir-apparent. Mirza Saleem, the younger son, of an aspiring disposition, has, in consequence of this arrangement, raised much dissension, and his improper exertions have been supported by many of the court adherents. Baboo Rada Presaud, son of the late Raja Rammohun Roy, has advised Mirza Saleem to provide him with documents under the seal of the relations of the king, and he will proceed to Calcutta to make intercession for him. Shuja ool Moolk, who arrived from Mecca on the 17th ult., has been married to the daughter of Walleeaubud. The king presented him with many valuable presents, and so enraged was Mirza Saleem, at his brother's fortunate disposal of his daughter, that he absented himself for three days, at the expiration of which his Majesty sent for him, and commanded him to offer the customary presents to his nephew. To this proposal the son thought fit to concede, and accordingly forwarded the usual gifts. The general opinion of the court is, that the king would do well to resign in favour of his eldest son, and by that means, secure for him the possession of the crown previous to his own decease. His Majesty is completely in the hands of Mirza Saleem's party, who have just made him perpetrate an affront on Walleeaubud. It appears that Walleeaubud had solicited a title for his son-in-law, Shuja ool Moolk, and that his Majesty had agreed to confer one—but when that individual attended, on the day appointed, to receive it, he was put off by frivolous and evasive excuses, at the instance of the party already named, upon whose proceedings we trust our worthy agent, Mr. T. Metcalfe, will keep an eye.—*Delhi Gaz., Dec.* 30.

GRAND CRICKET MATCH.

A very spirited cricket match was played on new year's day, and yesterday, on the Esplanade. Eleven Etonians against all Calcutta. The Eton men won the throw for innings—and the Calcutta men went in, and scored 133 runs, 19 byes, and 2 wide balls; total 154. The Eton men then went in, and two of their crack wickets went down immediately without a run. " Them Eton men seems bothered," exclaimed a voice on the ground. The odds seemed heavily against them; but they were now on their mettle, and to it they went in right earnest, and, at half past two, had scored 147 runs, 7 byes, and 3 wide balls; total 157. The Calcutta men now went in for a second innings, which ended a little before sunset, they having marked 110; thus leaving the Eton men 107 to make up in their second innings. The Eton men went in again yesterday afternoon, and won the match, having 4 wickets to go down. It was an exceedingly good match. The Calcutta men are the best fielders and their two bowlers are superior; but the Eton men have here an advantage over their opponents, as they have four bowlers, and all excellent. The Calcutta men, moreover, possess a most admirable second stop. It must be observed that the Eton men had never played together before the match, and some had never handled a bat or thrown a cricket ball for years. As matches with Etonians possess some interest beyond Calcutta, we subjoin the names of the players on each side.

CALCUTTA.

Mr. G. Udny, Mr. S. Palmer, Mr. Urquhart, Mr. E. Deedes, Mr. W. Crawford, Mr. W. Hay,	} Civil Service.
Mr. B. Waddington, Mr. W. H. L. Frith, Mr. W. Frith,	} Members of the Calcutta Club.
Mr. Oakes, junior,	
Mr. H. Atkinson,	Madras.

ETON.

Mr. C. H. Cameron,	Law Commissioner.
Captain Mitchell,	A. D. C.
Mr. J. P. Grant, Mr. P. Taylor, Mr. H. V. Bayley, Mr. G. Battye, Mr. A. G. Macdonald, Mr. H. Alexander,	} Civil Service.
Mr. H. Holroyd,	Barrister.
Captain Brownrigg,	H. M. 9th.
Captain T. J. Taylor,	Madras Cavalry.

—*Beng. Herald, Jan.* 3.

INDIAN JAILS.

We understand that a committee, of which the three Judges, Mr. Macaulay, Mr. Shakespear, and six other gentlemen, are members, has been formed to enquire into the state of the Indian Jails and prepare an improved plan of prison discipline; the junior member, Mr. J. P. Grant, to act as Secretary.—*Cour. Dec.* 30.

ABOLITION OF CUSTOM HOUSES.

Our mercantile readers will learn with pleasure, that the abolition of the custom-houses of Benares, Ghazeepore, Allahabad, Cawnpore, Furrukhabad, and Bareilly has been determined on, and will take place, as soon as the present collectors are provided for elsewhere. The immediate cause of this important determination, is, we have heard, a " surplus revenue ;" but we are willing to suppose that it is based on some sounder principle, and that a desire to relieve the trade of the country from the incubus of custom-houses, has given rise to it. The custom-houses of Agra, Mirzapore, and Meerut are to be continued, for granting and registering passports, receiving the duties, &c. ; but as the great preventive line will prevent the illegal transit of goods, and defeat all attempts at fraud, the business at these custom-houses will be simplified to the mere issue of passes. The detention, search and vexation, which under the old system were so oppressive, will now be as light as the levying of transit duties, in any shape, will admit of, and the evil be at least reduced to a minimum. From the lower range of the Himalaya to the Vindaya hills, we shall then have a line of posts, with four principal currents of the trade of North Western and Central India, instead of the country being studded with places of search and detention.—*Agra Ukhbar, Dec.* 19.

We wish the editor had been more explicit in his statements on a subject so full of interest, and had informed us more particularly what he meant by the " surplus revenue," the acquisition of which has led to this arrangement. We are almost inclined to believe that the new preventive line, in the first year of its operation, has been found to afford a larger revenue than the custom-houses and chowkeys, which studded the country, yielded to the treasury ; and that this generous policy has already been found as advantageous to Government as it cannot fail to be beneficial to the people. Enough, however, is told us in the extract to shew, that the whole country, from the Himalaya to Patna, embracing perhaps 2000 miles of commercial navigation, is to be immediately freed from the vexations of the custom-house system ; and this agrees with the information we have received from other quarters. This is, indeed, an important and decisive measure. It places the question of transit duties in a new position. It is so exhilirating a procedure that it would perhaps be ungracious to enquire how it happens that, while a committee now sitting in Calcutta is investigating the subject with care and caution, the great majority of the custom-houses have slipped through their fingers and expired ; while they are deliberating on measures of relief which are to embrace

all the Presidencies, the custom-houses at one entire Presidency have become extinct. It is sufficient for those who cannot see behind the curtain, and who know nothing but what passes before their eyes on the public stage of action, to be informed that the Governor of Agra has cut the gordian knot, and swept away these obnoxious custom-houses from his own jurisdiction. This bold and judicious measure combines in itself two advantages. It affords immediate relief to the trade of the forty millions of people who inhabit the Western Provinces, and it brings the prospect of relief in Bengal nearer to accomplishment.—*Friend of India, Jan.* 7.

NATIVE SERVANTS.

We learn from the *Sumachar Durpun*, that the commissioner of the district of Hooghly has commenced an investigation into the conduct of the amlahs of the court, in consequence of complaints of their corrupt and oppressive practices. The commissioner, in order to remove every obstacle in the way of this object, has issued a proclamation stating, that he has heard of the oppression and corruption of the amlahs ;—that he is about to enter into examination of these charges,—and that, as many, who have suffered from amlahs, refrain from complaining through fear of their honour and of being obliged to make oath, they may bring forward their charges without entertaining any such apprehension. Those, who are aware of the difficulties in the way of preferring complaints before magistrates of the conduct of native functionaries, will perceive, that, however much the course adopted by the commissioner deviates from ordinary rule of British justice, it is the only one most likely to lead to a full discovery of the misdeeds, if there be any, of the amlahs.—*Englishman, Jan.* 19.

AURUNGABAD.

A correspondent describes this district as fast going to ruin, by the oppression and mismanagement of the Nuwab, Noor Oolla Khan, the Governor appointed by the Nizam. No means of violence or deceit are left unresorted to, to acquire possession of money, whether it belongs to rich or poor : the consequences are, that the whole social machine is broken up, a moral pestilence has fallen upon the place, and robbery and riot, the immediate results of the people's misery and despair, are of daily occurrence. The merchant refuses to expose for sale to such a rabble the necessaries he commands ; and famine is added to the rest, so that, says the correspondent, unless some arrangement be made to remove or check the Nuwab, the people will be driven to insurrection, and then butchered by the troops disciplined by English knowledge.—*Agra Ukhbar, Dec.* 12.

THE OPIUM-TRADE WITH CHINA.

The opium trade with China has been hitherto carried on by advances from private capitalists, who found in it a far more lucrative way of employing their money than any other means equally secure. Besides the interest they got on these advances, they profited by the difference of exchange. Especially in these times, when mercantile credit is but just recovering from the shock it lately received, this means of employing capital afforded great advantages. We are now given to understand, on good authority, that government are engaged in considering the propriety of making advances on opium investments to China at a rate more advantageous to the speculators than that at which they have hitherto obtained the assistance of capitalists. This measure will no doubt injure the interests of the capitalists; but as capitalists form only a very small portion of the public, the question proper for our consideration is, how the proposed change is likely to affect the country at large, and the mass of the people. We perceive both advantages and disadvantages involved in this measure.—*Bengal Herald, Jan.* 3.

DAWK-TRAVELLING.

The conveyance by steam, on our principal river, has of late engaged so exclusively the public attention, as to throw our more ancient mode of dawk-travelling rather out of sight. The river-navigation, however, when brought to perfection by the improvements of science, will never entirely supersede the conveyance by land, partly because the water distance between Calcutta and Allahabad is more than 800 miles, while the distance by land is less than 500 miles; and partly because it is to be doubted whether steam-travelling by night in our uncertain rivers will ever be feasible.

The distance between Calcutta and Benares by the old route, through Dwarhatta to Bancoorah, is 420 miles. The road between Calcutta and Bancoorah, which comprizes one-fourth of the entire distance, not having been repaired for many years, has now become utterly impassable, and travellers are obliged to proceed a long round-about way through Burdwan, by which the distance is increased twenty-six miles, the expense Rs.13. By the old route, then, upon which all the published tables of charges are founded, the expense of travelling is at the rate of eight annas a mile (Rs.210), which sum the traveller is required to deposit before he starts on his journey, and with it one-half the sum for prospective demurrage. The stages are, we be-

lieve, forty-five. A full dawk includes ten men for the day stages, and twelve for those which are traversed by night; so that, upon the most accurate calculation, 500 bearers are employed through the entire route. These men receive from government at the rate of four annas a man for each stage. The trip, therefore, for which the traveller pays Rs.210, costs the public treasury in actual outlay about 125, say Rs.130, leaving a surplus of Rs.80. Out of this sum is to be provided the expense of two servants at each bungalow, and the dawk-writers and moonshees at the various stages; but the charge of these items can bear no proportion to the aggregate surplus. Hence we feel confident, that, if the profits of dawk-travelling be not estimated as part of the public revenue, a revision of the present system would enable the postmaster to reduce the charges twenty, if not twenty-five per cent., without incurring any risk of loss. Any individual who may start for Benares, without laying a public dawk, and take his chance of finding bearers on the route, may effect the journey for about Rs.130. We believe it has been done for less. Bearers may be obtained in abundance; and they will always be found more ready to serve the chance travellers, who pay ready money at the close of each stage, than the individual who travels under the patronage of the post-office.

This readiness on their part to serve private individuals, grows out of the grievances of the government system. The traveller pays his fare, with a heavy deposit for demurrage, in advance; but the poor bearers are not paid for two or three months, and every day's delay lessens the chance of their being paid in full. They are at the mercy of the dawk moonshees on the line of communication, who, being public servants, armed with public authority, may command their services, however tardy or insufficient may be their remuneration. As to any complaint on the part of the poor bearers, it is out of the question; in India, the poor man does not readily complain against those who are in power. The bearers are miserable beings, with barely a rag to cover them, living in huts, which they contrive to shelter from the elements by the branches and leaves of trees. A more destitute, abject, wretched race can scarcely be imagined. They seem almost to occupy a kind of midway station between the rational and the brute creation. They can neither read nor write; whenever, therefore, there is any arrear of accounts, and this is always the case, they are sure to be the losers. Hence they afford a rich harvest for plunder to the dawk moonshees. Paid, as they are, so long after the money has been earned, they must obtain food on

(K)

credit, which the dawk moonshee is always benevolent enough to give them. The bearers more than suspect that the shops, at which their wants are so liberally supplied, are under the control of the moonshees, and are possibly carried on for their benefit; and this suspicion is strengthened by the two facts, that the food is sold to them at a much higher price than they could procure it for at any other shop, and that they cannot resort to any other store, without incurring the serious displeasure of the moonshee. The fact is, that, wherever native agency is employed, there is such a complication of machinery, that the keenest European finds himself baffled in his attempts to discover all the secret wheels of private interest which are brought into play. No wonder, then, that the bearers leap for joy at the idea of being paid four annas a-piece, in shining coin, into their own hands, without deduction and without delay, as they bring the traveller to the end of the stage. This little four-anna piece, thus punctually paid, is worth full thirty per cent. more to the poor fellows, than the four annas which the traveller pays to government, and government to the post-master, and the post-master to the deputy post-master, and the deputy post-master to his baboo, and the baboo to the dawk moonshees in the interior, and the dawk moonshees to the bearers, one, two, or three months after the money has been earned, and long after it has been all anticipated by the food which has been sold at an extravagant rate at the dawk moonshee's favourite shop.—*Friend of India, Dec.* 31.

GROWTH OF TEA IN INDIA.

Whilst we admire the spirit of enterprize and improvement in our government, we think it necessary to consider the prospects which these experiments afford of ultimate benefit to the country. It will be readily admitted that, so long as India remains under the domination of Great Britain, she must, in some shape, continue to pay her tribute. This is at present accomplished without involving her in any considerable difficulty: her opium and other productions are taken to China, and thence remittances made to England. If China were ever to cease supplying her tea, her profits would lessen, her luxuries decrease, and the consumption of our opium be consequently diminished. Trade ultimately depends on its original basis of barter; and though gold and silver supply a convenient medium of conducting the details of business, yet, considered as the circulating medium, they can never uphold the commerce of two countries, which cannot barter their produce, either directly or through any circuitous channel. If, then, India were to supply England with

tea, that commodity would not be taken from China, and China would, in the same ratio, become unable to consume our opium. Now, even if the tea of India succeed so well as to drive the tea of China out of the markets of Europe, our advantages in this will be greatly moderated by our losses consequent on the diminished demand for our opium. But if, after all, which we think to be the more likely result, India will not be able successfully to compete with China in the production of tea, all the expense now incurred in the experiments must be carried to profit-and-loss account. The signal defeat in the experiments made here on the coffee plant, the quality of the fruit of which is not equal to that of the coffee which we get from Arabia, is well known to all. The fact is, that the soil of India, though perhaps the most prolific in the world, is not fitted for the production of every kind of plant. We may grow here, both coffee and tea; but the question is, will the quality, the quantity, and the expenditure of growing be equally favourable here as they are in the countries to which these plants are indigenous?—*Bengal Herald, Jan.* 10.

PROGRESS OF THE ENGLISH LANGUAGE.

An evidence of the progress of the English language in Anglo-India appears in the following letter of the young Raja of Bhurtpore, to some of his political acquaintance:

" My dear friend,—Allow me to congratulate you on the occasion of the approaching Christmas and New Year, and to wish you the compliments of the season, and many happy and prosperous returns of the same. I hope you are in the enjoyment of good health, and that I shall have the pleasure of hearing the same from you. I am happy to say that I have myself been perfectly well, and trusting that you will ever continue to regard meas your devoted friend and well-wisher, I remain, your's very sincerely."

THE NEPAUL EMBASSY.

All Calcutta swarmed upon the maidaun yesterday, to witness the landing of the Nepaul embassy. While the *Hooghly* steamer was towing the *Soonamookee*, with the Nepalese general and suite on board, along the strand, the troops of his escort were firing away with their little muskets, in boats ranged on either side. After the landing, we were entertained for nearly an hour with the discordant blasts of a dozen trumpets with enormous mouths, followed at a short distance by a regular band of Nepalese, playing English tunes in very good time. The old general, Martubbar Sing, who was conveyed to government-house in Mr. Trevelyan's carriage, was dressed in an elegant uniform, with English epaulettes, and is a fine-looking man. The troops of the escort (there seemed to be full 800 of them) were also very smart-looking fellows, small of stature, but very active, and, no doubt, good soldiers for mountain service. Their muskets were the smallest we have ever seen, and the bayonets upon them were in all manner of shapes. Altogether, the sight was extremely interesting. The escort were marched off to Balligunge. The general and some of his officers made their appearance at the theatre in the evening.—*Cal. Cour.*, *Jan.* 16.

BABOO JOYKISSUN DOSS.

A wealthy banker of Benares, Baboo Joykissun Doss, died in Calcutta on the 30th ult., and left property to the amount of about *eight lakhs*, by will, to his wife and a daughter now seven years old; with reversion to this government if the latter die without issue. The government, and in case of their refusing to act, Mr. Smoult, is appointed executor. Whatever might have been the motive which led this individual to dispose of his property in the manner he has done, the result cannot but be such as every properly constituted mind will rejoice in seeing. If the daughter has issue, the property will of course go to the rightful owner, and be saved from the hands of the enemies of a helpless female; if not, it will come to this government, which, we have no doubt, will make such proper use of it as will be most beneficial to the country and creditable to itself.—*Reformer, Jan.* 1.

THE LIBRARY.

The *Calcutta Courier*, on the subject of the Public Library, observes, "We are afraid about the accomplishment of the one thing still wanting, the filling up the requisite number of a hundred proprietors. We hear that more than twenty are still wanting, that is, more than 6,000 of the requisite 30,000 rupees are still to seek. We fear they will not easily be found, for the last twenty names have been slowly collected, in six or seven weeks; and every body, conversant with subscription-lists knows, that, as the list fills, the difficulty of enlarging it increases in a geometrical ratio."

SHOJA-OOL-MOOLK.

Several applications have been sent to the ruler of Scinde, by Runjeet Sing, requesting Shekarpore. Noor Mohumed Khan, the ruler of Hyderabad, did not seem inclined to pay attention to this; but Runjeet wrote to assure the Khan that, unless he complied with his request, he would resort to arms, but strongly recommended the Khan to give it up amicably.

Noor Mohumed could neither think of giving up Shekarpore to his inveterate enemy, nor face his troops, so he offered Shekarpore to Shah Shoojah, as the legitimate sovereign of the province; but the Shah replied that he did try his fortune once, and the recollection of the troubles he experienced in the experiment, had taken away from him all desire to attempt regaining his lost kingdom.—*Mofussil Paper.*

THE BENGAL CLUB.

The affair referred to in our last Journal (p. 13), namely, the meditated ejection of Mr. Stocqueler, the editor of the *Englishman*, from the Bengal Club, on the ground of certain strictures in that paper, calculated to disturb the harmony of the club, continues to provoke controversy; the last papers from the presidency are full of the subject. The following proceedings have taken place in the club.

On the 30th December, a meeting took place at the club-house, which was attended by between forty and fifty members; the Hon. Mr. Melville in the chair. Mr. Longueville Clarke moved the following resolution, which was seconded by Mr. W. Bracken, and supported by Capt. Sewell, Mr. Dickens, Col. Beatson, and Mr. J. P. Grant:

" That the statement contained in an article of the *Englishman* newspaper, of the 11th inst., wherein it is alleged, that the manner in which the invitation to the Commander-in-chief was preferred, was obviously to subserve selfish and slavish purposes, is untrue, and conveys a scandalous imputation on some of the members of the club."

Mr. Pattle moved the following amendment, seconded by Mr. Osborne:

" That the very reprehensible editorial article of the *Englishman* newspaper, of the 11th inst., has not disturbed the harmony and order of the club."

A very animated debate took place, in which Mr. Clarke, Mr. Dickens, Col. Beatson, and others, spoke in favour of the original motion; and Mr. Pattle, Mr. O'Hanlon, Mr. Osborne, Mr. Mackinnon, and others against it On a division, Mr. Pattle's amendment was carried by a majority of twenty-two votes against seventeen.

When the matter had been decided,[*] Mr. Stocqueler stepped forward, and declared that, though he had determined not to apologize, further than he had done in his letters, while any question was before the meeting—lest it should be said, that he made concessions in order to shirk the discussion—he could have no hesitation. now that the matter was decided in his favour, in apologizing to the committee at large, and to Colonel Beat-

[*] We cite this statement from the *Englishman.*

son in particular, for imputing to them improper motives of action, which did not appear, by the statements now put forth, to have guided them.

The *Calcutta Courier* states that, among the majority were two (it appears that there were three) of the members of the committee, who had, on the 17th inst., joined their colleagues in unanimously coming to the following resolutions:

" The committee, having proceeded to take the above papers into consideration, are of opinion that several of the paragraphs in the editorial article contained in the *Englishman* of the 11th inst., are, as far as regards the intentions of the committee of management, altogether unfounded; that other paragraphs commenting on the votes of certain members of the club, recorded at the last general meeting, and on the dinner that was given by the members of the club to Sir Henry Fane, are extremely offensive and unwarrantable; and that the conduct of Mr. Stocqueler (as a member of this club), in inserting the whole of the above article in his paper (the *Englishman*) of the 11th December, is not only calculated to be very prejudicial to the best interests of the club, but is entirely subversive of the order and harmony of the institution."

On the 19th January, an extraordinary general meeting was convened by regular requisition and advertisement, signed by the secretary, to consider the propriety of adopting the following new rules:

" Any member of the club, publishing remarks on matters connected with the institution, or making statements in the newspapers regarding subjects that have taken place within the club-rooms, until the committee of management shall have enquired into and disposed of the alleged grievance or complaint, in the first instance, and afterwards a general or extraordinary general meeting, shall be deemed to have come under clause 7, rule vii. of the rules of this club."

" Any member, or committee of members, who shall violate, or cause to be violated, any rule of the club, shall be expelled, and no qualification to this rule shall be admitted."

" No editor of a newspaper shall henceforth be eligible for election as a member of this club."

" The amount of entrance to the club shall be reduced from Sa. Rs. 250 to 160 Company's Rupees, or 10 gold mohurs of the new currency."

The result of this meeting is thus stated by the *Hurkaru*, a paper adverse to Mr. Stocqueler:

" About fifteen members met at the club-house to discuss the proposed new rules. Dr. Ranken was called to the chair, which he at first declined, pleading that he could not consistently preside over the introduction of measures which he had come there to oppose; but, on finding nobody else willing to be chairman, he consented to act, on condition that he might speak and vote as he pleased. A good deal of irregular discussion took place on the first proposition, and various amendments, which were successively put, and all rejected. An adjournment was then moved, which the chairman objected to, until given to understand that the remaining propositions would in that way be ' cashiered' and not revived. The meeting then dispersed, in considerable merriment at the expense of those who had suggested the calling of it. " As you were !" was the cry, and it seems to express fully the result of this odd effort of some ·person or persons unknown in club-legislation. Those who had signed the requisition, with few exceptions, disclaimed approbation of the proposed rules, though they meant to consent that a meeting should be held to consider them."

THE JEYPORE AFFAIR.

The *Delhi Gazette* has published another version of the Jeypore affair, on the faith of "certain facts and particulars, hitherto unknown to the public, by a talented and intelligent member of the community, on whose judgment it places the greatest reliance;" which, if true, sets the affair in a new light, and proves unequivocally that the atrocious murder of Mr. Blake, and the attack on Major Alves, were planned by the public authorities of the state, and executed by their connivance, if not by their direction. It is there stated that the rawul was highly displeased at having others associated with him in the management of the raj, and the ranee was openly opposed to the rawul being sole manager, to which she knew his ambition looked ; and Rhymutoolah Khan, the rawul's vakeel, was known openly to say that, so long as Major Alves and Mr. Blake had influence at Jeypore, his master had no chance of attaining his wishes. The other ranees, the widows of the two preceding rajas, combined together to get possession of the young raja, under the idea that whoever had charge of him would possess the consequent authority of the affairs of the country; and were, therefore, jealous of Ranee Chundrawut's influence, who had been, by direction of the British Government, constituted sole malik on behalf of her son, who was to remain in her charge. On the night during which these women first proceeded to act openly against the ranee, there was a state party given to the European gentlemen, at the palace. After the *zeafut*, and towards the close of the nautching, the suroee walla kanee, the wife of Jysing Suway, who was, with many other women, behind purdahs, addressed herself to Major Alves, and, in an angry, menacing tone, told him she would never submit to be under the influence of Ranee Chundrawut; that he (Major Alves) had, under cover of the British Government, taken the Sambhur country, and got possession of Shekawat, which was highly improper and unjust; and he had further evinced the spirit which actuated him, by affording protection to Joota Ram, with whom, he well knew, she had a long account to settle in the shape of a demand of at least twenty lakhs of rupees, but more particularly on account of her late husband's blood, which called aloud for vengeance; and she called upon him to give up Joota Ram, or punish him himself—if not, she could assure him there were three hundred thousand of her tribe forthcoming, and they would seek vengeance, if it were to be had. Major Alves endeavoured, in a mild, conciliating manner, to appease and persuade her; but finding the little effect it had, he took his departure.

The result of this evening's proceedings, and the negative countenance given to them by the rawul, caused an immediate report all over Jeypore, that the intention of massacreing the Europeans was too evident to leave a doubt on the subject, and the general opinion was, that they had had a narrow escape *that* evening.

On the following day, all the other ranees combined to prevent articles of food, &c. being delivered as usual to Ranee Chundrawut's outhul, and proceeded to various acts of outrage; towards evening, the rawul went to Major Alves, and requested he would proceed to the palace and quell the riot, otherwise the women would proceed to serious acts of violence. Major Alves gave for answer, that it was then too late in the day; requested the rawul would go back and exert himself to keep them quiet; saying that it was no part of his business to interfere on such occasions as this; but that, as he seemed to press the necessity of it so strongly upon him, he would go to the palace next morning.

Major Alves went accordingly, on the following morning, accompanied by Mr. Blake, Lieut. Macnaghten and Captain Ludlow, and, when they arrived at the palace, they were ushered into the inner apartments by Rawul Byree Saul, Hunwunt Singh, Buhadoor Singh, and Luchmun Singh, sirdars, and they endeavoured to persuade the women not to molest the ranee and young raja, but to continue to enjoy all their former incomes, &c., and leave affairs in peace and quietness. Ranee Chundrawut, with the young raja, confined herself, during these disturbances, strictly to her own suite of apartments. After many ineffectual attempts to appease the growing wrath of these women, Major Alves and the whole party left the apartments, with the purpose of going to the residency.

It is customary, on the visits of the political agent to the palace, for the highest officer of state present to lead him to his conveyance, and then to take his leave; on the present occasion, the rawul complained of severe pain, which prevented his performing this customary piece of etiquette, and all the other sirdars present made equally frivolous excuses to evade it, and Major Alves and his party proceeded to their conveyances unattended.

Major Alves was attacked only thirty yards from the spot where the rawul was standing. The sirdars, when expostulated with and threatened by Mr. Blake, were heard to call out to their people, "Take care he does not escape," and then went into the palace.

When Pirthee Singh, the man who wounded Major Alves, was questioned, three days afterwards, as to his reasons for the act, and who it was that advised him to it, he deposed that Rajoo Lall, Ameer Chund, &c., had planned it, and induced him to commit the act—but, when these individuals were placed before him, he could not recognize one of them, and Major Alves returned him to the rawul. On being questioned by Major Alves, the rawul said that the mob of the city had murdered Mr. Blake, without his knowledge, though, at the moment Pirthee Singh, a follower of Bhyra Singh, made his attack on Major Alves, the rawul was an eye-witness of it, at a distance of thirty yards, and that, at the time Mr. Blake left the palace, i.e. turned his back on it to go away—orders were heard to issue from the palace, in a distinct, audible voice, to release Pirthee Singh from the charpoy, and on no account to let Mr. Blake escape. It is also well ascertained that his eldest son, Luchmun Singh, was standing on a part of his house, commanding a full view of the acts committed upon Mr. Blake, without in any measure attempting to render him assistance.

These are the material facts in this statement. It is to be regretted that some official or accredited account of the affair is not put forth to stop these contradictory details.

———

On the 8th inst. Sunghee Hookum Chund and Futtey Lall, the brother and nephew of Dewan Jootaram, left Agra under the escort of a detachment commanded by Capt. Lloyd, 36th N.I., on their way to Rajgurh, in Alwar, the civil authorities of Agra having been directed to make over the prisoners to Major Alves, with the view to their being put to trial by the Jeypore state, as accomplices in the crimes committed on the 4th of June last, at Jeypore. It is not generally known what is the object of Major Alves in ordering over the prisoners to Alwar. Native rumour, however, reports that the rawul is to accompany the resident to Rajgurh, and the motive of examining these parties out of the Jeypore territories, is to prevent the possibility of any unhappy collision or disturbance, at a time when the minds of all parties at Jeypore are naturally in a state of fever, and when men of all classes, from the dupe to the knave, are throwing difficulties in the way of a calm judicial enquiry.—*Agra Ukhbar, Jan. 9.*

THE BAIZA BAEE.

This lady, with excusable vanity, loves to measure her importance by the interest she excites, and the employment she affords to the civil and military authorities. For the last two or three months, she has daily promised to leave Futteghur; but as often her ingenuity devises some pretext to evade this promise. The consequence is, that she finds the troops of the station set in motion to expel her, the civil authorities perplexed, her own importance magnified, and ample opportunity afforded her followers to gratify their hatred and contempt by laughing at the simplicity of the *Feringee Log*, who are thus foiled by a woman's insincerity, or what to them seems wit. Lately, the 71st N.I. was ordered out by the session-judge, and their presence intimidated the lady into a promise of going within six or seven days. Seven and more days having elapsed without a symptom of preparation, far less of departure, appearing in her camp, the entire troops of the station were ordered out, cavalry and infantry. When the force had approached within a-quarter of a mile of the camp, the civil authority which had brought them stopped them, from an apprehension that their nearer approach would lead to a collision with her highness's troops. At this juncture, Appa Sahib presented himself to the judge, and inquired the nature of the procession, whether it was ceremonious or religious. The judge quickly explained the nature of it, and presented a paper, stating that it was an engagement which he should sign, promising, on the part of the baee, to leave Futtegurh on the 25th. To sign the paper was the work of a moment. The affair being thus satisfactorily settled, the civilian intimated to the officer commanding the ejecting party, that he might withdraw. The officer was chagrined at the part given to him in this melodrama; and, instead of availing himself of the permission thus granted, proposed that, as he had every thing prepared, he should encamp where he was, and thus more conveniently

escort the baee, on her departure. The pacific judge reiterated his objection, that such might lead to a "collision," and the officer marched back again, wondering, very naturally, why he had been called out at all. The 24th came, and with it fresh orders to the troops to hold themselves in readiness to escort the baee on the succeeding morning. On that morning a despatch was received from Government, directing the local authorities to meddle no further with her highness, for that Mr. Ross had been ordered from Gwalior to' *persuade* her to go to Bunarus. Thus were abruptly terminated all the agreeable proceedings which had afforded, for such a length of time, the utmost amusement to the natives. Her highness regards the whole as a signal victory, to celebrate which, she has given a triumphal *natch*. To describe the magnificence of it, "language is inadequate;" it lasted two days and a night, amid the most uproarious mirth and exultation, at the success of her highness.—*Mofussil Paper.*

The Baiza Baee has at length fairly gone; her objections to move were quickly overruled by Captain Ross, of whose tact and delicacy in this difficult affair the whole station speaks warmly. Unlike the civil authorities, when asked if he required military assistance, he replied, no—the only lever he used was judicious persuasion.—*Meerut Ukhbar.*

SELECTION OF NATIVE SERVANTS.

The *Guyannaneshun* has some remarks on the selections made by Government of natives for public offices of trust. It complains that, instead of the educated youths of the Hindoo College being selected for these appointments, men of the old school, without any pretensions to intelligence, and whose notions of morality are squared by the beautifully accommodating rules of Hindu orthodoxy, or rather bigotry, have been preferred. The complaint is just. It may be observed also, that in European society, natives have been counted rather for their wealth than their character and attainments. Many of these young men, educated at the college, are qualified, as well by'their gentlemanly conduct and manners, as by their acquaintance with general literature, especially with that of our country, to do credit to any society; but while these are kept in the back-ground and meet with little encouragement, wealthy baboos or pretended *littérateurs*, who get books written for them in English, which they do not comprehend, are honoured with special notice.—*Bengal Hurk., Nov. 26.*

THE BEGUM SUMROO.

Our little Semiramis, the Begum Sumroo, had been suffering from another attack of that incurable disease, old age, but rallied a little, and is now convalescent. The fright awoke a spirit of religion and charity in her, and she now practises on a very large scale—these kindred virtues. To heaven she has made, in the most handsome manner, a very liberal present of a lakh of rupees, to be appropriated to the erection of places of worship, and her charity is shewn in a less ostentatious, if not more useful, way, by giving annuities to all the faded beauties of her court—those virgins, whose looks and age deter any of the other sex from raising them to the dignity of matrimony.—*Agra Ukhbar, Nov. 28.*

THE MOFUSSIL PRESS.

We cannot really help laughing at the harmony that prevails among Mofussil editors. Each successive journal that comes to hand, contains a severe hit at its neighbour. Thus the *Agra Ukhbar* never loses an opportunity of exposing the *Cawnpore Free Press.* The *Meerut Observer* and the *Delhi Gazette* do not seem to bear one iota of regard for each other. The *C. F. P.* re-echoes all the witticisms of the *Delhi Gazette;* the *Delhi Gazette* insists upon it that *we* are hostile to his undertaking ; and the *Ukhbar* and *Omnibus* are at daggers drawn.

In the last number of the *M. O.* we find a specimen of the Delhi editor's wit—nothing more or less than a play on the word " Allahabad" (*All-aha-bad !*) which struck us as being considerably above par. The *Meerut Observer* should not be so severe towards his Delhi contemporary, for the latter has quite enough to do with the *Agra Ukhbar, Central Free Press,* and *Cawnpore Omnibus,* without " entering the lists" against his near neighbour of Meerut ; and, besides, what will grandpapa *Hurky* say to all this ? No, no, let these gentlemen henceforth establish an era of cordiality and good-fellowship, which the effects of time itself shall never be able to eradicate, and which will be handed down from generation to generation.—*Cawnpore Omnibus, Nov. 28.*

COURTS-MARTIAL.

We understand that court-martial duty is pressing very heavily on the officers at the presidency, owing to the number of trials actually in progress, or on the *tapis.* The fact affords another strong reason why the army should endeavour to give effect to the salutary advice of the Commander-in-chief. Every body of officers, we take it, possesses the moral power of repressing that obstinate adherence of individuals to their own views of their own cases, which the Commander-in-chief has justly depreciated ; and that power, for the good of the service, it is surely their duty to exert.—*Bengal Hurk., Dec. 7.*

JUNGYPORE INDIGO-FACTORY.

The celebrated Jungypore indigo concern, which in former days yielded so large a fortune to Mr. Ramsay, and the elder Mr. Maseyk, was brought to the hammer last week, by the assignees of Cruttenden and Co., and bid up to 3,70,000 rupees, at which price it was bought in.—*Friend of India, Nov. 26.*

FRONTIER PREVENTIVE LINE.

From the following communication, published in the *Agra Ukhbar,* we learn, that the great frontier preventive line, which is to extend from the Sutledge to the Vindya hills near Mirzapore, and which is to free the navigation of the Jumna from all the vexation of custom-house chowkeys, is nearly completed :

" The great frontier preventive line will extend to a short distance beyond Mirzapore, where it will terminate in the Vindya hills. It has already been completed, as far as the conjunction of the Jumna and Chumbul, by Mr. Blunt, from whence it will be continued by Mr. Bowring, civil service. This officer has already commenced his preparations, and in the course of a week or so, the arrangements for forming his portion will be in full train. Mr. Blunt has left Agra ' to put himself in communication ' with Mr. Bowring, and convey the results of his experience. On the completion of Mr. Bowring's portion of the line, a chain of posts will exist, extending from the Sutledge to the natural barrier of the Mirzapore hills, and commanding all access between Central and the Company's portion of Western India."

DEPUTY COLLECTORS.

We perceive from the last *Calcutta Gazette,* that five natives have just been appointed deputy-collectors, of whom three are Musulmans, and two Hindus. It is understood to be the intention of Government to reserve these situations almost exclusively for natives. This is, indeed, very kind towards the natives, and we have to thank the authorities for their goodness. But, whilst we do so, we must express our unqualified objection to all exclusive measures. We would have every branch of the service, from the highest to the lowest, thrown open to all classes of the people. Why not admit Christians, and even Englishmen, to the deputy collectorates? Nothing but good moral character and aptitude for business should decide the question of preferment to office. This principle is fully recognized in the Company's charter, and practice ought to conform to it ; otherwise it is a farce to enact laws, and the charter should be thrown into the fire, rather than remain as a monument of inconsistency for the derision of future ages.—*Reformer, Dec. 13.*

MISCELLANEOUS MOFUSSIL NEWS.

Lahore.—Our latest accounts from Lahore state, that Runjeet Singh was again dangerously ill. Kunwur Shere Singh had arrived at Lahore from Cashmere, in expectation of his father's death, and it is generally believed he will dispute, or rather contest, his brother Kunwur Kurruck Singh's title to the guddee. —*Delhi Gaz.*, Dec.

Cholera is making fearful havoc among the people in Lahore, about a hundred individuals daily falling victims to this baneful pestilence. The richer class of inhabitants have fled across the Hydraotes to escape the plague.

Jullalabad.—Dost Mahomed has moved a considerable force, commanded by his second son, on this town, with a view to invade the Sheik territories on the expected demise of Runjeet Singh. He has also directed his eldest son to collect and organize new troops with all possible speed, and to join his brother.

Cabul.—By the last accounts received from Cabul, it appears that both Dost Mahomed's sons were both encamped near Jullalabad, within a march of each other, awaiting instructions to attack Peshawur, and that they had been joined by numbers of the Mulkeeah Putans, and several other Mahomedan chiefs. Dost Mahomed Khan had left Cabul to join his sons. He has been fortunate enough to recover jewels to the amount of several lakhs of rupees from banditti, who were afraid to dispose of them in the market, and has appropriated the money accruing from the sale of them to the expenses of the expedition against Peshawur. The khan has dismissed the greatest part of the Affghan soldiery in his employ, and has substituted the kuzzal bash for them, who now constitute the main force of his army. Twenty thousand of these soldiers had been sent to Jullalabad, ten thousand of whom had succeeded in surprising the nazim of Peshawur (who was on his way to invest Bysool, which place had been taken by the khan's troops) at the gates of Peshawur, and forced him to retire into it with the loss of many of his followers. —*Bengal Herald, Jan.* 10.

Bhurtpoor.—A Cawnpoor Feringee merchant has just speculated a *little-go* into this district, consisting chiefly of English glass in the shape of looking-glasses, shades, &c., &c., of which the raja alone purchased 10,000 rupees' worth. Here is a new field opened for mercantile enterprize.—*Agra Ukhbar.*

Delhi.—The late Shumshoodeen's estates and other property are to be sold by public auction. The Putteahlah and Khitul rajas are expected to be the principal purchasers.—*Delhi Gaz.*, Dec. 23.

Gwalior.—The raja is so debilitated, either from illness or the customs of eastern princes, that his recovery is looked on as distant and doubtful. The administration is, however, vigorous under the mamajee, and nothing impaired by his highness's illness.—*Agra Ukhbar, Dec.* 12.

THE NEW CURRENCY.

The government, in reply to a memorial from the uncovenanted servants, on the subject of their losses through the new currency, observes: —" It would be a great mistake to suppose that the government contemplates gain by this change, or proceeds on the unjust principle of paying at one rate, and receiving at another. Whatever may be the incidental effects either way, there has been no other object than uniformity in the currency, and an equable consideration for all classes of public servants. The government will have to sustain loss in many instances. The large amount of debt, which is borrowed at the old established rate of conversion, or 104.8, it will have to pay at the higher intrinsic rate of 106.11-8. With the servants of the state in the Bengal and Agra presidencies, with regard to their allowances, it continues to pay and receive at the rate of conversion always hitherto established in such transactions in those presidencies, and could not do otherwise without great confusion and inequality, or a total new modelling of the pay of all the servants of the state throughout India. In all other transactions the government pays and receives at the rate of the intrinsic difference. For the reasons above explained, the Governor-general in Council is compelled, with great regret, to avow, that he sees no feasible means of complying with the petition of the memorialists; but he confidently trusts that the loss of which they complain is only apparent or temporary, for there is little doubt that, when the momentary anxiety produced by the change in the currency has subsided, and prices and wages become adjusted according to the new currency, the memorialists will find that the increased numerical amount of their receipts will, in the aggregate, go practically as far in their expenditure as the greater intrinsic value of the smaller quantity hitherto received now does, and that, on the whole, they will not ultimately suffer any perceptible loss."

A correspondent of the *Courier* says :— " The Company's rupee and the Sonat

rupee are intrinsically of the same value. The popular mistake, which ascribes a higher value to the sonat rupee, arises, I conceive, from the long established rate of exchange in its favour equal to 1 rupee 15 annas sicca per cent. The Company's servants, both civil and military, in the Upper Provinces, whose allowances are fixed in sonat or Furruckabad rupees (of equal value), were paid in Furruckabad rupees without any loss. If desirous of a bill on Calcutta, they were allowed to tender 104.8 (exclusive of premium or office fee) for 100 sicca rupees, although the intrinsic rate of exchange would have been 106.10.8 Furruckabad rupees per 100 sicca rupees; and Company's officers in the Lower Provinces, whose allowances were fixed in sonat rupees, received 95.11 sicca rupees per 100 Sonat rupees; which latter, however, (sonata) were intrinsically worth only 93.12 siccas; thus gaining 1 rupee 15 annas sicca per cent."

Much inconvenience has arisen from the mode of introducing the new copper coin. The *Courier* of December 23 states, " that the greatest confusion prevails in the bazaar on the subject of the pice; and the notice in last Saturday's *Gazette* (we cannot call it a proclamation, for there appears to have been no proclamation by the usual method of *tom-tom* in the bazaar) seems only to have made matters worse. A letter in the *Englishman* says, that the shroffs and podars refuse to take the new pice at all, for want of the usual *tom-toming* notice; and we heard, yesterday, that a gentleman's servant, wishing to get change for a Company's rupee, tendered it in vain. If some remedy be not quickly applied to put the copper currency upon a rational consistent footing, there is danger that the doubts and difficulties attending it may seriously contract the circulation."

The *Hurkaru,* of January 8, adds:— " The poor are suffering very heavy loss from the want of an abundant supply of the new copper coinage. The money-changers have got hold of what is extant, and are making an enormous profit of it. The new rupee is declared equivalent to 16 annas of the new pice, that being, we suppose, the true relative value of the coinage; but the shroffs will not give more than 14 annas and three pice—one pice is the usual batta for changing. but the one-anna and three-pice is downright extortion, and the people cannot help themselves. For the benefit of the poor, and to defeat this conspiracy of the shroffs. many householders and others would be at the trouble of getting new pice from the mint, and supplying it to the poor people at 16 annas to the rupee; but they cannot be had. The poor people are suffering severely. We know that some indi-

viduals succeeded in obtaining pice from the mint, which they have been able to supply to their servants and other natives; but now they cannot be got, it seems, and a heavy tax is levied on the poor in consequence."

The *Bengal Herald,* of January 17, says, " that Mr. Gomes, a public-spirited individual, has entered into an arrangement with government for supplying pice to the lieges, with a view to defeat the conspiracy of the shroffs against the poor. He has obtained the sanction of government to be supplied with five hundred rupees' worth of pice at a time from the mint, which he proposes supplying to the public at the rate of fifteen annas and two pice for the Company's rupee, deducting two pice to defray the expense of opening shops in various places, and to remunerate himself."

Madras.

LAW.

SUPREME COURT, *Dec.* 31.

Retirement of Sir Ralph Palmer.—The Court met specially, for the purpose of administering the oaths to the Hon. Sir Robert Comyn, as Chief Justice, in succession to Sir Ralph Palmer.

After the ceremony was over, Mr. Norton, the advocate general, proceeded to address the late chief justice, on his retirement from the bench, and, in a short speech, happily expressed and full of feeling, tendered him the united regard, gratitude and good-will of himself and all the members of the legal profession at Madras, the bar, the officers of the court, and the solicitors.

" If I might venture to particularize," he observed, in the course of his address, " I should be led to select that elaborate care and solidity, which have distinguished all your decisions on the equity side of this court. The whole profession, and those who come after us, must always feel that, in the pronouncing those judgments, your mind has been actuated by wider and nobler objects than the mere disposal of the questions before the court, or even the dispensing requisite and ample justice, as between the parties. They have been made the vehicles of sound professional instruction; they have been made a boon, and a valuable and lasting contribution to the just administration of the national law. The practitioners in this court, and, indeed, the public at large (for their interests must ever be bound up with those of the efficient and pure administration of justice in the national courts), must owe a perpetual debt to your lordship for those decrees, which have formed a mass of precedents in judicial equity, the best-digested, perhaps, of any the Indian courts can boast of, and which cannot fail of the most beneficial effects in rendering the paths of right clear and even. But, my lord, I should forget a most particular duty due from me to those around me, due to my own feelings, due most eminently to your lordship, if I should omit to mention our sense of the undeviating urbanity, which has throughout characterized your demeanour to every member of our profession. We, my lord, in the conflicts, and agitations, and anxieties, almost inseparable from a zealous performance of our duties to those clients who have entrusted their essential or dearest interests to our advocacy—we may, in some passing and occasional moments, have swerved from that respect which is not only due to the court, but has by us always been felt so to be. But your mind has never, on these or any other occasions, been shaken, from its just propriety—it has never been moved from an indulgent bias towards us. We have always experienced the utmost patience in scrutiny, and the utmost kindness and consideration in manner. It may be a gratification to your lordship's reflection, as it surely is to us who testify it, that the dignity of the court, so far from having been thereby impaired or compromised, has by nothing been more maintained and upheld—and, with it, as a necessary consequence, the respectability, the reputation, and the honour of our profession."

Sir Ralph's reply is described as most affecting. He expressed his high satisfaction to find that, on his retirement from this bench, he carried with him the good wishes and kind feelings of those with whom he had co-operated in the administration of justice in this country. He added: "with regard to what you have been pleased to attribute to me as urbanity; if any thing, deserving that term, has been evinced in my conduct on this bench, am I not bound to confess that the courtesy, the kindness, and the respect that I have uniformly received from the bar, the solicitors, and every officer of this court, have demanded such a return from me, as of right—that it has been yours not *de gratia* but *de jure?* In other professions,—in some at least,—there are two leading principles, of constant command on the one hand, and obedience on the other. With us, there is one principle pervading all alike—independence of opinion and freedom of speech. To make those qualities, however, essentially useful,—that they may conduce alike to the promotion of substantial justice, and to the creating and cherishing that good-feeling and harmony which ought to exist among all the members of a court—and which, when it does exist, adds not only to the comfort and

happiness of those who practise in it, but cannot fail to win also the respect of the public,—they must ever be accompanied by a proper, not servile, but gentlemanly, deference for the opinions of others, and a mutual forbearance towards those infirmities of our common nature, which, in spite of the very best endeavourrs to the contrary, will break forth, whether to be seen in the impatience, or perhaps sometimes the petulance, of the judge, or in the overstrained zeal, and sometimes hasty expressions, of the advocate. ' *Damus hanc veniam petimusque vicissim*,' was the maxim which I endeavoured to lay down for myself, upon taking my seat on this bench;' and if I have, as from the terms in which you have expressed yourself this day, I may hope has been the case, at all acted up to that maxim on my part, I am sure that there has been many and many a time when I have had occasion to seek it on yours, and I am equally sure that I have never sought it in vain."

MISCELLANEOUS.
OPERATIONS IN GOOMSUR.

A communication from the camp in the Goomsur Zemindary, dated December 16th, published in the *Madras Herald*, gives an account of the operations in that country.

The field force having assembled at Askah on the 1st November, two companies of the 40th N.I., with the rifle company, advanced towards Goomsur, and one company, under ensign Stuart, pushed on to occupy the fort, which was nearly deserted, and taken without opposition. The following day, the rajah's dewan and his two sons gave themselves up. The force marched from Askah on the 3d, under Col. Hodgson, reached Goomsur on the 5th, where a halt was called for some days. Proceeded to Nowagaum on the morning of the 10th, on which day a wing of the 8th, under Major Low, with Lieuts. Taynton and Napleton, received orders to take possession of the fort of Coladah. They arrived there without opposition, though several lancers were seen scouring the jungle in their front, and voices were heard from behind a strong barrier and bamboo defence, which impeded their progress for a short time. The troops followed the next morning and halted about two miles in advance, at a place called Baroda, whence Ensign Yates was sent to relieve the wing under Major Low (with one company), to keep the place, and forward supplies; and where he remained till the 19th. The force reached Gullary on the 13th, where gingal and matchlock sounds were heard for the first time; martial law was proclaimed, and a reward of Rs. 5,000 offered for the head of Dunjee-Bungo, the rajah. Next morning, advanced to Rumlah, under a sharp fire from the heights, kept up during day and part of the night. On the 15th, arrived at the dark cave, or strong hold, of the rajah; shouting in all directions from the jungle. It was supposed that this dark cavern, and the principal defences, lay to the front; but the brigadier, soon discovering the mistake, ordered a movement to the left, and advanced by a defile, two or three abreast. On reaching the gateway, which was found to be blocked up, the sappers and miners were called into play; the rascals scudded off, leaving a few old guns. The fort is situated at the top of a ghaut about 1,500 feet high, and enclosed by an irregular mud and stone wall. The force countermarched the next morning to Gullary. The rear guard, under Lieut. Napleton, was much harassed that morning. There was a good deal of firing the whole way. Lieuts. Taynton and MacCally distinguished themselves on that morning, while in command of the rear-guard, and received the thanks of the brigadier in orders for their gallant behaviour, &c., having killed three men with their rifles, and wounded a number of others. On the 18th, the force returned to Nowagaum, leaving Lieuts. Taynton and Napleton, and Ensign Yates, with 200 men and a howitzer, at Coladah, a nasty place, thickly surrounded by jungle, and where lots of rebels harbour to this day. The rear-guard of the force had no sooner passed the village (of Coladah), than a host of vagabonds, armed with matchlocks and swords, &c. followed them pretty closely, thinking, perhaps, as the buildings were on fire, that the place was deserted. However, they very soon discovered their mistake, as some of the party sallied forth, and having placed themselves in a very sweet spot, under a bank covered with bamboo jungle, and near the main road, quietly awaited their approach, and peppered them right well. After about an hour, finding the fellows still impudent, the big gun was brought to the front, and having been placed, unobserved, in a capital spot, a few rounds of grape and round astonished their weak minds. They had no sooner made their post secure against night attacks, &c., when they received the *hookum* to join the main body, at Nowagaum. After halting at the latter place a day or two, the head-quarters returned to the old spot of Goomsur (where they still remain), leaving Lieut. Napleton and Ensign Yates there as the advanced post. Nothing particular has transpired there, or in our camp since the 25th of November, with the exception of Lieuts. MacCally, Grimes, and Ensign Stuart

having captured several excellent characters, who are now about to be tried by martial law.

The following is a letter from Berhampore, dated the 20th December :

" At present, the force under the command of Col. Hodgson is encamped one mile to the northward of the town of Goomsur; it consists altogether of the 8th regt., the 49th regt., three comps. of the 3d Lt. Inf., three comps. of the 10th regt., one comp. of artillery (Native), two comps. 21st regt., and sappers and miners. The force is now pretty healthy, but, a short time ago it was quite the contrary, having, on an average, 220 men in the hospital, principally fever. The wounded men are doing well in the field hospital, at Aska. Constant parties are sent out from head-quarters, to surprise the enemy, and have in many instances been successful, and brought in many prisoners, found with arms in their possession ; the trials of these men commence in camp to-morrow by court-martial ; there are about seventy or eighty to be brought before the court. General Taylor is present with the force, as also Mr. Stevenson, the collector. The march of the 49th regt. to Nagpore is, it is said, countermanded, it being required in the disturbed Zemindary for some time longer."—*Herald*, *Dec.* 30.

We have received a communication from the camp at Goomsur, which states that there is scarce a doubt of the rajah's death. This will not, however, relieve us from the necessity of taking the country, and of keeping it till the whole family submit, as well as the chiefs who support them. A good many men have been taken in arms by our officers at the outposts ; and four incendiaries have been hanged by sentence of the special court-martial. Their fate was partly expedited by an atrocity of the deepest dye that recently occurred. A party of these wretches (who, we understand, are quite distinct from the fighting men) attacked a small defenceless village, consisting of about ten houses, which, of course, were, as usual, burnt to the ground ; killed three men, and desperately wounded two little girls, of about ten and seven years old. One arm of the latter, with brutal ferocity, they had cut clean off, and the other child was half decapitated. The poor little things have been taken by Gen. Taylor under his special care, and our medical men think that they are likely to recover. Pardon to such fiends in human shape would be almost criminal.—*Ibid. Jan.* 20.

SUPERSTITION IN THE NEELGHERRIES.

A circumstance took place about a year

ago, in which some fifty or sixty persons of the Kooromar caste were massacred by the Thodars of the Blue Mountains, for having caused a mortality among the buffaloes of the latter, by means of witchcraft. The Thodars, we understand, have been tried at Coimbatore, but the sentence passed upon them is, to us, unknown.—*Standard, Dec.* 15.

IRON WORKS AT PORTO NOVO.

We understand that the Porto Novo iron works are proceeding with much activity. We had an opportunity of seeing some iron railing yesterday which was made there, apparently equal to any thing of the kind which is manufactured in England.—*Mad. Gaz., Jan.* 13.

NATIVE MEDICAL STUDENTS.

A gratifying report has appeared in the Madras papers, of an examination, lately held there, of the pupils of the Medical School of that presidency. This school, it appears, was recently instituted by government, for the instruction of apprentices in the subordinate medical department. The pupils are between 25 and 30 in number, of whom about one-half are East-Indians; and, with the exception of one Moosulman, the rest are Hindoos. They have been studying only for three months; and their studies have been confined to the classification of medicines, and the first branch of anatomy, which treats of the bones. On this branch of science they were examined methodically, and also in a still more satisfactory and practical way. In one part of the room stood a skeleton, and on a table lay a collection of bones. From the latter, the pupils were required to take any one that first came to hand, and name it; show the character by which they were able to distinguish it from the rest, and then show its place in the skeleton. They sustained the examination in a most creditable manner. Their instructors are Dr. Mortimer and Dr. Harding.

THE BREAKWATER.

It appears that the work of the breakwater at Madras has been suspended by order of the Supreme Government; for this reason, that the amended estimate of the committee was nine times as large as the original one.

THE MADRAS CLUB.

In the revised rules of the Madras Club, a rather important alteration has been made with respect to eligibility. According to the old rule, the test was being " on the government list;" in the new rules the words, "gentlemen received into general society " have been substituted for the foregoing.

MILITARY FUND.

The following circular has been issued by the Directors of the Military Fund :—
" To the officer commanding.—Sir, referring to our circular letter of the 25th June last, we have the honour to communicate, for the information of the subscribers in the corps under your command, that the proposition therein submitted, for admitting the widows and legitimate children of all subscribers to the benefits of the fund, without reference to their extraction, has been carried by a number of votes exceeding two-thirds of that received, as shewn in the margin,* and that, in consequence, sec. 3d has been cancelled, and the following regulation adopted by the army substituted in lieu, from the 25th ult. *viz.*—

" ' That the fund be hereafter open to widows or orphans, under the rule that governs admission of cadets to the army, and that all existing marriages (hitherto excluded under the old) be recognized and admitted under the new rule, by paying up all arrears of subscription, &c. according to the existing rates, from the date of marriage, with interest at 8 per cent., accumulated half-yearly.'

" We beg to state, for general information, that the period for admission under the foregoing rule is limited to six months from this date, applicable equally to non-subscribers, as those at present subscribing as unmarried, at the expiration of which they will be excluded ever joining the institution. The arrears of new subscribers to be liquidated within three years, and all others on or before the expiration of twenty-four months."

" A copy of the letter to government, communicating the result of the above reference, is transmitted herewith for the information of the subscribers."

" Military Fund Office,
" Fort St. George, 17th Oct. 1835."

" To His Exc. Lieut. Gen. the Right Hon. Sir Frederic Adam, K.C.B., Governor in Council, &c. &c. &c.

" Right Hon. Sir:—As the most satisfactory mode of demonstrating the course pursued on the despatch from the Hon. the Court of Directors, received with minutes of consultation, the 30th January last, we have the honour to submit extracts from our proceedings on the several dates noted in the margin, by which it will be observed, that the exclusion clause has been cancelled by the voice of the army, and that widows and orphans, without distinction of extraction (including those of existing marriages where the husbands may think proper to subscribe

In favour	577
Against	220
Majority in favour	357

and conform in every essential to existing regulations) are henceforth eligible to all the benefits of the Madras Military Fund. It will, we doubt not, afford unqualified satisfaction, equally to your hon. board as to the home authorities, to find that this benevolent measure has been at length effected in deference to the Court's anxious solicitations ; and the Court may be confidently assured that the opposition which for so many years has been maintained to the change was founded mainly on a conviction that its adoption would entail additional burdens sufficient to impoverish, if not altogether to wreck, the pecuniary interests of this most valuable institution, which already requires many material sacrifices to insure its stability.

"We may be permitted to say, that the army were not less grieved than unprepared for the Court's threat to deprive this charitable institution of the support of the state, should a clause of its regulations coeval with its foundation, that has been operating for a series of years under the express sanction of the Court, be not abrogated: and since this occurrence even more than implies a right in the Court at pleasure to alter the rules or constitution of the fund against the sense of a numerous body of its contributors, by withdrawing the pecuniary support of the state, should the right not be conceded, we trust it will not be considered out of season, or otherwise wanting in that respect or gratitude which is due to the home authorities, our redeeming a pledge that we conceive has been not without its influence in the favourable issue of this important question on a renewed application (more in detail) for the votes of the army. On that occasion, as will be seen by our proceedings, dated 5th June last, we pledged ourselves, should the measure be carried, to solicit from the justice and liberality of the Hon. Court, a guarantee of existing immunities upon the rules or regulations (graced by the present provision of not hereafter recognizing any distinction of extraction), and moreover that the fund may be encouraged to hope for some further pecuniary aid, proportioned to the additional burdens that this measure of the Hon. Court will certainly entail upon its resources, but which cannot at present be accurately estimated until its working (in an experience of years) shall have been ascertained: meanwhile it may be the pleasure of the home authority to anticipate the wants of the fund, by an increase to the annual donation, or any other mode of compensation that might be deemed preferable, subject to reduction or extension, as future experience may point out to be necessary.

"We have the honour to be,
"Right Hon. Sir,
"Your most obedient servants,

(Signed) "G. WAUGH, Col.
"G. CADELL, Lieut.-Col.
"W. CULLEN, Lieut.-Col.
"H. WALPOLE, Lieut.-Col.
"W. STRAHAN, Major.
"P. WHANNELL, Major.
"T. K. LIMOND, Major.
"T. B. FORSTER, Capt.
"T. SEWELL, Capt.
"Directors."
"Military Fund Office,
"Fort St. George, 30th Sept. 1835"

Bombay.

LAW.

SUPREME COURT, *Dec.* 6.

Mahomed bin Suggur was indicted for piracy committed in the Persian Gulf. The indictment contained two counts : 1st. That on the 25th March 1835, the prisoner, with force and arms, upon the high seas, distant about two leagues from the island of Huneya, within the Admiralty jurisdiction of the court, did piratically and feloniously enter a bugalow called the *Deriah Dowlut*, the property of Hajee Mahomed Ali Suffur, a British subject, and did piratically and feloniously assault certain mariners in the bugalow ; and did piratically take away certain property then under the care, custody, and possession of the said mariners, and belonging to Hajee Mahomed Ali Suffur : 2d. For piratically stealing goods of the value of 2,000 rupees on board the same bugalow, the property of Abbas bin Abdul Kurreem, and under the care and in the custody and possession of the said mariners.

The *Advocate General* opened the case, and called

Abbas bin Abdul Kurreem, who said he was a merchant, and made a voyage from Bombay to Bushire about ten months ago, on board the bugalow *Deriah Dowlut;* there was a naqueda, passengers, merchants, and several others, on board. "When we left the port of Bunder Abas for the island of Huneya, we saw four vessels, about nine in the morning. The land was then in sight. These vessels were near the port of Huneya, and were at anchor. We were in this situation for about an hour, when we saw them hoist their sails. We found they were coming after us. We passed their vessels, and they afterwards followed. They soon overtook us, and when they came near, they ordered us to lower down our sail. Our naqueda said 'we shall not do so; why should we? We are going on our way.' They then said, 'if you will not do so, you must prepare yourself for battle.' The naqueda said, ' we are not disposed for fighting ; we sail under the English flag, and you must not interfere with us.' The English flag was then flying at the mast-head. I knew it to be the English flag, as I have seen it flying at the mast-head of the English Government ships. They then said, ' do not be afraid of us ; we are friends of the government.' On their informing us of this, we were satisfied, and we lowered down our sails. The naqueda then desired one of our men to lower down the jolly boat and go to the bugalow and show our pass. The boat was lowered, and the pass was sent to them. I saw the pass shown them. They tore it in pieces and threw it into the sea. Afterwards, the large bugalow came alongside our ship. All persons on board her had swords and spears in their hands. There were about 200 persons on board her. Our vessel was larger than their's. Those persons then rushed into our bugalow, and ordered us to deliver up our clothes to them, and throw ourselves into the sea. We, through fear, delivered up all our clothes to them. Then we heard them desire one of our passengers, who was a nuwaub, to deliver up his clothes. He refused to do so, and they immediately gave him a blow with a sword on the shoulder. The nuwaub fell down, and they then gave him several other blows with daggers and spears. When the nuwaub received three or four wounds, he threw himself into the sea. When I saw the nuwaub do so, I immediately, through fear, did the same. When I was in the sea, I saw the naqueda, passengers, and crew also had thrown themselves into the sea. At this time, I saw the nuwaub swimming about, and after about a-quarter of an hour, he was drowned. We all were also swimming about. I went towards the naqueda and said, we must try to gain the shore. We swam some short distance, but we got fatigued. I then recommended that we should return towards the buga- low. As we neared the bugalow, one of the Arabs, who was standing on the forecastle, told us, ' you are deserters ; why do you come here? go away;' and he fired at us with a musket. The naqueda was wounded by the shot. He then called for assistance, and I and another went to him, and we both held him by the arms. As we again approached the vessel, an Arab said, ' we will forgive you ; come into the bugalow.' On this, some of us went into their vessel, others into our own vessel. I and the naqueda went into the ship of the Arabs. About fifteen persons altogether went into her. I was in the water about three-quarters of an hour or an hour. When we got on board the Arab's ship, we saw them go to our ship and take out goods, and bring them to their own. The goods were chintz, long-cloths, piece-goods, and others. The Arabs on board the ship pointed out a

man on board to us, and said, ' he is our chief man ; you must go and kiss his hand.' On which, I asked him the name of his chief man, and they said his name was Mahomed bin Suggur ; this man was then in the cabin; he could not hear what was said. Several of our men were wounded, and could not get up, and we said ' the shaik should come to us.' At this time, the shaik came up on the poop where we were. On his approach, all the Arabs said ' here is our shaik.' The per- son pointed out as such was quite close, and could hear. We, through fear, went up and kissed his hand. The per- son whose hand we had so kissed then assured us that ' we will not kill you nor plunder your property;' saying ' what is done is done.' The goods brought from our ship were then lying about the deck of the Arab ship. An order was then given to hoist the sail of the ship. About sixty or seventy persons from the Arab ship went on board our ship, with swords and other instruments, and hoisted up her sails. We then asked, where they were going to take us; when they said, ' we shall put you ashore on an island :' we then sailed in company with the fleet. After a day and night's sailing, we came in sight of an island, and about eighty persons were landed in a boat from the *Deriah Dowlut.* A boat came to the ship on which we were, and we were put into it, and sent ashore. We requested a boat to be left with us, as there were no provisions on the island ; but they would not give it, saying there was water to be found on the island. They then said, ' we shall give you a boat and two robins of rice, and you can go where you like.' They gave us the rice and some dates, and told us to go. We then left the Arabs, and landed on an island, called Tum. The eighty persons who landed on the island were all belonging to the *Deriah Dowlut.* Some were of the crew and some were passengers. All the ves- sels then sailed away." The witness then identified the prisoner as the man whose hand he kissed, and added that they went from Tum to Bassadore, and thence to Bombay. There had been 130 or 135 persons on board the bugalow, and about 100 were landed at Tum.

Two of the sailors, who were on board the *Deriah Dowlut,* gave evidence con- firmatory of that given by the preceding witness. They both identified the prisoner as being the leader of the pirates.

Hajee Mahomed Ali Suffur had been for about forty years trading to and from Bombay. Had resided in Bombay for the last thirteen years. Is the sole owner of the *Deriah Dowlut.*

Lieut. Kempthorne, I. N., was em- ployed in April last on board the *Amherst,* in the Persian Gulf, as second lieutenant.

About the end of April, the vessel was on the coast of Arabia. Aboth-a-bee is on the coast of Arabia. He recollects the Shaik of that place coming on board his ship and delivering up two prisoners. The prisoners were Arabs. They were taken to Bassadore. The prisoner is one of them.

Commander John Sawyer, I. N., commanded the *Elphinstone* in May last. There came two Arabs as passengers in her to Bombay. They were placed on board by order of Capt. Pepper, senior officer in the Gulf. The prisoner is one of them. Witness brought the two to Bombay and gave them over to the police.

No evidence was offered in defence.

Mr. *Roper* took objections to the indictment on two or three grounds,—that of the jurisdiction of the court over the criminal and the offence committed by him,—that of the indictment not averring that the parties to whom the vessel and goods belonged, or the mariners who sailed in the vessel, were in the peace of "our Lord the King," and the parties, prosecutors, therefore not being entitled to the protection of the British.

As a defence, the possibility was urged of the attack having been made by the authority of the chief of the tribe to which the prisoner belonged, and if made under such authority, that the act was not a piratical act, but one of hostility by that tribe, against the state to which the mariners of the *Deriah Dowlut* owed allegiance ; and it was urged that the prisoner, being a shaik, or chief, might, as such, have the power of ordering or leading in such acts of hostility, without being amenable to a court of law, or chargeable with the crime of piracy.

Sir *John Awdry* reserved consideration of some of these points, (chiefly, that of the jurisdiction of the court over the criminal,) and in alluding to the averment in the second count—that the goods of Abbas bin Abdul Kurreem were "under the care and in the custody and possession of the said mariners," and to the evidence given by that witness that the goods were under his own charge,—his lordship pointed out to the jury that that count could not be sustained, as the evidence showed that the goods were in the care and custody of the witness himself, and not of the mariners, as averred. With regard to that portion of the defence which related to the crime being an act of hostility, and not piracy, his lordship, while admitting that the power to order acts of hostility to be committed might be in those chiefs, as chiefs, stated that it was incumbent on the prisoner to prove that any such order or authority had been given, and that the act complained of had been committed under such order. No proof of the kind had been offered, and it remained therefore for the

jury to judge, under all the circumstances, whether the acts charged against the prisoner were piratical or not.

The jury immediately returned a verdict of " Guilty."

On the 9th, the prisoner was placed at the bar, when his lordship passed sentence of death on him, but respited it until the pleasure of his Majesty is known.

The *Bombay Gazette*, with reference to this trial, states that the prisoner is supposed to have been the leader of the Pirate fleet with which the Company's cruizer *Elphinstone* met, sometime ago, in those seas. " The circumstances detailed in the evidence given on the trial, with those which occurred at the time the *Elphinstone* met them, shew this pirate and his followers to have been a set of cold-blooded, desperate, and daring characters. It will be recollected that they had all but attempted to take the *Elphinstone* by boarding, but the shot from the vessel so thinned their crew, and marred their scheme of operations, that they were compelled to look to their own safety."

MISCELLANEOUS.

SLAVE-DEALING.

By the shipping report of the H. C. brig *Thetis*, it appears this vessel has brought sixty-five slaves from Porebunder. These unfortunate people were conveyed to that port in an Arab vessel from Maculla, from which they were exported in consequence of a famine. The laws here regarding slaves are well known to the Arabs, and Porebunder seems to have been selected in the present instance from its being without the jurisdiction of the Company. The speculation however has failed ; for the rana of Porebunder, being under stipulations similar to those entered into with the Imaum, to put a stop to slave-dealing, has either been forced, or has come forward voluntarily, to give them up. Slave-dealing, however, notwithstanding occasional checks like this—and there have been several of them within the last year or two —seems to be carried on to a considerable extent on this side of India. Nor is there much prospect of its being stopped under existing regulations, since no inducement is held out to individuals to bring it to the notice of the British authorities, and the feelings of the natives are by no means hostile to it. The facilities for it, at the same time, are very great. In both Goa and Demaun, we believe, it may be carried on almost openly, as well as in all the small and nominally independent states along the coast, such as Angria's Colaba; and from these slaves may be, and, are introduced clandestinely into the Company's territories at all times. The remedy, however, is simple. A small reward in cases of detection would bring forward informers in abundance, and render the traffic throughout the country dangerous, instead of being, as it is now, even in this island, comparatively secure.—*Courier, Jan. 5.*

TRADE AND NAVIGATION OF THE INDUS.

A commercial communication has this year commenced on the Indus; in accordance with the treaty, boats have both begun to ascend and descend the stream. It seems desirable, therefore, to record some of the earliest information of a practical nature regarding the river, the vessels on it, and the trade itself.

It is imperatively necessary to adhere to the mould of boats now in use on the river. Science may, in time, improve them, but disappointment will, I believe, follow all attempts at it, till further experience is obtained. A boat with a keel is not adapted to the river Indus.

Though the Indus is accessible, after November, the labour of tracking up against the stream is, at that time, great. The river is then, and for the three successive months, about its lowest, which prevents the boatmen from seeking the still water, and drives them to the more rapid parts of the current. The northerly winds, which blow till February, make the task more than ever irksome, and extra-trackers are required. The treaty too encourages large boats more than small ones, the toll on both being alike, and those unwieldy vessels require many hands which adds to the expense. After February, the voyage, from the sea to Hydrabad, which would previously have occupied nearly a month, may be performed in five days, the expense of trackers is avoided, the river has less dangers, and the merchant thus saves his time, labour and interest. The swell of the Indus does not prevent vessels ascending to the Punjab; for, at that time, the southerly winds prevail. It is these southerly winds which give to the Indus, in its navigation, advantages over the Ganges. The course of the one river is about east and west, that of the other, north and south. Use must, therefore, be made of this natural advantage to make merchandize profitable by the route of the Indus.

The obstacles to navigating the Indus at its mouth are, no doubt, great, but they have been magnified. Above Calcutta, for a considerable part of the year, there is no greater depth in the rivers Bhagruttee and Jellingee, which lead from the Hoogly to the Ganges, than two and three feet. In the Indus, a greater depth than this will always be found somewhere, to lead from the sea ports to the great river. This, then, is a decided advantage in the inland navigation, though the Indus has not a mouth accessible to large ships like the Ganges. It proves too, that a portage or

even a canal (were it possible to cut one) is unnecessary, as it must never be forgotten that the largest boats of the river draw but four feet when heavily laden.

Much stress has been laid upon a place being fixed for unshipping the cargoes of the sea-going, into the river-going, boats. Anxiety on this point is useless, for it will vary every two or three years, and the utmost reliance may be placed on the people now in the trade. In 1831, the mouth leading to Vikkur had four fathoms of water; in 1835 it had but one and-a-half in most places, and, in one, but six feet, terminating in a flat. The estuary was also quite changed. Sea-boats can always ascend one mouth of the Indus, and the navigators find it out without difficulty. From four to five hundred sea-going boats sailed out of the port of Vikkur alone last year. They are the common boats of western India, drawing from nine to twelve feet of water, and which convey all the coasting trade of the country, valuable as it is. If traders will not place reliance upon these boats, experimental vessels for the Indus must, of course, be made at their own risk. In the navigation upwards, after leaving the sea, a trader will experience little or no inconvenience in a boat of the country. Let him make his agreement with *the proprietor* of the boat, and avoid, if possible, engaging one of the vessels belonging to Ameers (of which there are about forty), and which, it seems, may be had for hire. If he does so, the agreement will be better fulfilled, since the trade in Sinde, as in Egypt, will receive but little benefit by the rulers sharing in it. If this practice is ever carried to any great extent by the Ameers, it will be necessary to try and stop it. For the present, there are so few boats that it is best to put up with it.

The depth of the river is doubtless variable—in some places great, in others less; but this is of very small consequence to flat-bottomed vessels. Sand-banks are numerous, and would perplex an European navigator; but the native pilots have a good eye and manage to avoid them. In the Delta there are also sand-banks, but the streams there are much narrower and deeper and more free from them, though I only speak comparatively. These sand-banks are a marked and general feature of the Indus, and seem to be formed by backwater or eddies. A dry bed of the Indus shews that they rise up without regularity, but that there is always a deep channel, though sometimes intricate, through them.

In December, I descended the Indus from Hydrabad, and though then near its lowest, the soundings in the great river were never under two fathoms or eleven feet, and the boatmen did not always keep in the strength of the stream. While in the river, we never grounded, and many heaves of the lead gave five and eight fathoms, but two and two-and-a-half predominated. In the cold season, the Indus, in the Delta, shrinks into a narrow and deep channel, which disappoints a stranger who has heard of the magnitude of this river;—many of the inferior branches even dry up. The natives attribute this to cold. The evaporation is great. The channel of the Sata, which supplies most of the branches in the Delta, had, this year, at the last sounding which I took, eight fathoms; but less than half that gives about its usual depth. It was about 400 yards broad. This is a feature more favorable to navigation than otherwise, yet this branch must be entered by a circuitous channel, and is not accessible to boats from the sea, though in the end of September last, the water out from it was fresh in a depth of seven fathoms, and a Cutch boat filled up its tanks from it.

It appears that there is much error abroad, regarding the trade on the Indus. Enterprise will doubtless do much to *create and improve* commerce, but, for the present, it is a trade *by* the Indus, and not *on* the Indus. It is, in fact, a transit trade to western and central Asia, a line, however, which ought to supersede that by Sonmeeanee to Candahar, and by Bownuggur to Pallee and Upper India. If the mercantile community hope for any increased consumption of British goods in Sinde itself, they will be disappointed; the time may come, but, at present, the bulk of the people are miserably poor, and there are really no purchasers. The courts of Hydrabad and Khyrpoor, however, will, no doubt, take a good part of some of the investments, and both these chiefs and their families have already sued for a first sight of the goods that have reached Sinde. This might appear objectionable in another country and under other circumstances, but the treaty will protect all traders, and they need not fear imposition or oppression. A few of the Beloochee chiefs have also expressed their readiness to purchase, and the good work is in a state of progression.

To the exports, by way of the Indus, it is unnecessary to allude, as they have been fully spoken of, and we have now no additional particulars of a practical nature to communicate. As the price of wages is, in most, if not in all, countries, regulated by the price of grain, the effect of opening the river Indus, on Bombay and Western India, ought to be most important. The immense advantages which the great body of the population will derive, I leave others to estimate; but I may affirm, that the European community ought by it, to be able to bring down their expenses, nearly to the standard of the Bengal presidency. ALEX. BURNES.

Sinde, Dec. 12, 1835.

THE RAJA OF SATTARA.

The raja of Sattara has lately issued an order for appropriating 50,000 Rupees for making good roads through his territory. The first road selected is that between Sattara, and the Neera Bridge, to which a road leads from Poona. The road between Sattara and Mahoolee, which was out of order, has been lately restored to its former state.—*Durpun, Dec.* 4.

THE COLABA CAUSEWAY.

After a monstrous deal of delay, the proceedings and investigations connected with the Colaba causeway, we understand, have been brought to a close. The sanction of the Court of Directors for the outlay necessary for the work was obtained nearly two years since, and preparations were made for it soon after. A question, however, arose among the officers employed at different times upon it, as to the site it was to occupy, which was not settled until a few days since. When the causeway was first proposed, serious fears were entertained of its injuring the defences of the Fort, and the eastern line for it, which corresponds nearly with that of the present road, was, therefore, preferred, from being commanded by the guns on the ramparts. This line, also, avoided the deep sand which is found on the other, and was, consequently, looked upon as more likely to give stability to the structure. It was subsequently decided, however, by the late Major Hawkins of the engineers, who paid great attention to the subject, that the sand offered no real ground of objection to the shorter route, and a plan of his for it was forwarded to the Court of Directors, and submitted to Mr. Telford, and upon his approval of it, sanctioned by them. Its advantages over the plans for the other route are, its greater economy and the distance it saves. A similar plan, therefore, notwithstanding the military objections to it—which, however, are considered as greatly overrated at present—has met with the support of a committee recently appointed to examine all the plans made for the same purpose, and we believe is to be forthwith acted upon.

The expense of the causeway, as at present contemplated, is estimated at Rs. 1,21,000, which includes the cost of an iron aqueduct from the esplanade to Colaba. The work is to be of loose stones throughout, and will connect, in a nearly direct line, the present road along the esplanade with the road at the boat house in Colaba. Its effect upon the latter place, and especially upon the value of landed property in it, as well as upon this island generally, is too obvious to require notice. It is only surprising, when the latter circumstance is considered, that the undertaking was not commenced and finished long ago.—*Cour.* Nov. 28.

(M)

THE PARSEES.

Curæetjee Cowæejee, Esq , one of the justices of the peace, has assigned over to the punchayet of his caste, an oart belonging to him, situated on the Chowpatee Road, for the purpose of erecting buildings thereon, as an asylum for the Parsee poor, infirm and decrepit. The punchayet have resolved on making the outlay necessary for carrying this plan into effect, from the funds accumulated by the levy of fees, fines, &c. from among the Parsees. The inmates are to be supplied with provisions from the same funds. The monthly expenses of the establishment will amount to about 500 rupees.—*Durpun.*

SOCOTRA.

The H. C. S. *Coote* arrived yesterday from Socotra. The detachment there embarked for Bombay two days before the *Coote* left, the attempt made to purchase the place having failed. The number of sick was very great, but no deaths had occurred. The high grounds of the island had been occupied by the detachment since its arrival there; and as the period of its stay was the most favourable season of the year, the result proves that Socotra, though perhaps less unhealthy in some parts than in others, has still a bad climate every where.—What has become of the coal landed on the island does not appear. —*Cour. Nov.* 21.

STEAM-NAVIGATION ON THE INDUS.

With regard to the little steamer, our latest accounts represent every thing to be going on as well as could be expected. The force of the current in the Delta was almost too much for her small power; but she overcame it and arrived safely at Hyderabad, using wood the whole of the way. At this place she was visited by the Ameers, and the result of their examination is, that they have applied formally to the Bombay government to procure a vessel of the same kind, but of a larger size, for them from England. Her trip, therefore, cannot fail to have a good effect. By awakening the Ameers to a sense of the advantages of a more intimate connexion with the British Government, it will secure their co-operation in extending the trade through their territories, and must thus hasten considerably its progress.—*Bomb. Cour.,* Dec. 26.

The attempt of the *Indus* steamer to ascend the Indus has failed, owing to the shallowness of the stream; she lighted herself by every possible means, discharging her coal, and was notwithstanding unable to go beyond Tatta. Dr. Heddle was left at Hyderabad. Another attempt was made by the Company's cutter the *Nerbudda* to enter the river, but, owing to some unexpected change of the usual channels, was obliged to return, and until a good chart is made of the fluctuating mouths of this river, a passage must always be uncertain.

Col. Pottinger was, by late accounts, suffering from indisposition, and had determined on proceeding to Bombay.— *Agra Ukhbar, Dec.* 26.

AGRICULTURAL CAPABILITIES OF INDIA.

A letter addressed to the Agricultural and Horticultural Society of Western India, by Dr. Chas. Lush, of the Bombay Medical Staff, contains some valuable hints on the agricultural capabilities of India.

After expressing some surprise at the absence of the colonists, and " British skill and capital," that were waiting the alteration of the Company's charter, to be embarked in various schemes for the improvement of Indian cultivation, he observes:

" There can be little amelioration in the dry land agriculture of this country; and it is even questionable whether that little is worth the attempt, unless in that most important article, cotton. Perhaps the coarse implements of the Hindoo may answer better in the end, or at any rate, until a general improvement in manufacture has preceded the change, so as to allow improved tools to be mended when out of order, instead of becoming only wood or old iron, lying about the fields after the slightest accident. But with regard to irrigated crops, there is a better prospect, especially for introducing machinery for raising and conveying water. Even the less promising Deccan valleys may admit of a change, by attention to the course of the rivers, to the erection of dams or bunds, especially across the smaller rivers, before their junction with larger streams; securing the banks by stone-work, preventing the waste of water, by contracting the channels, so as to keep them flowing throughout the year, instead of being allowed to be imbibed over an irregular and extended surface. Another word on the banks of the Deccan rivers. Of all those parts not given up to cultivation, a portion should in every village be set apart and inclosed, for the growth and protection of Babool timber.

" An economical method of raising water, by machinery, is the very first thing required towards advancing cultivation in the Deccan. The machinery must be simple, easily made, and repaired; the supply of water constant, with but little aid from cattle or manual labour. Every attempt should be encouraged; and he whose endeavours should be completely successful, would deserve no mean reward. In this country (the Deccan plains) of high wages and expensive fodder, we have little chance of participating in any extension of the growth of sugar, silk, &c. unless we can turn to account, at a cheaper rate than at present, the overflowings of the upland rivers.

" Now, setting aside what may be done in the *interior* of a country like the Deccan, let us proceed to consider in what manner superabundance of cheap labour, especially that of the wandering gangs of well and tank-diggers, may be made available for the *permanent improvement* of a tract of mountainous country, where the rains are most abundant—the edges of the table-lands towards the sea, usually called the tops of the ghauts.

" No one can have visited our mountain districts without being struck by the quantity of water which runs down the sides of hills, forming many unwholesome swamps in the villages below. Few of these torrents are taken advantage of. Yet we here and there see terraces cut and embanked in squares for second or irrigated rice-crops, while quantities of spare water flow beyond into the river, nullah or swamp, below, as the case may be, even during the hottest season. A want of capital—want of demand for the produce of irrigated land in such situations—want of the spirit of enterprise among the natives—their unwillingness to quit the busier haunts of men, are causes, which severally concur to prevent these natural resources from being turned to account.

" If we can make our hills productive of something exportable, as well as new descriptions of food, a new population may be supported having new wants which will add to the wealth of the state; while the greater part of the cultivation, being independent of precarious monsoons, an additional resource may be found against those famines, to which the interior hill-country is so frequently subject, from deficiency of rain. To compass these objects, I propose to introduce, upon all favourable spots, a system of *terrace-cultivation*.

" I believe the range of western ghauts, the hills of the Conkan and Southern Maratha country, to be extremely well adapted for terracing. The preference would be given to the Laterite formation. Wherever that extends, of course there is room for the roots of trees of any size. It is so easily worked, that wells are dug without blasting. The terrace-system is in operation in parts of Italy, especially for vineyards, where the vines are supported by mulberry-trees.

" The command of water flowing over terraces would enable the cultivator, besides the usual crops of the low land, sugarcane, rice—perhaps indigo and mulberries —to cover his hills with plantations, which would form a succession of products, gradually increasing in value from the interval of two years to that of a century. I need scarcely urge the importance of planting and preserving the best kind of timber,

considering that the provinces of this presidency are not only destitute of coal, but possess comparatively few forests of importance; yet there is plenty of jungle land convertible into good forests under proper management. Now, it is next to impossible that the Government of India, under existing circumstances, can be expected to make direct sacrifices of revenue for the distant prospect of felling timber, yet to be planted. A strict conservation of woods and forests now existing, might be troublesome and expensive, and lead to an inconvenient monopoly. And yet, unless something is done in the way of planting, a few generations will see the country bare of shelter, and no fuel remaining, excepting that staple commodity of the Deccan plain, cow-dung. Planting timber to a proprietor of a hill farm, with secure possession, would be an affair extremely easy to arrange with the Government. The planter might confine himself to three important species; the teak, the jack, and the sandal-wood. The two former need no comment. The benefit of a plentiful supply of jack-fruit, in times of scarcity of grain, is obvious. With regard to sandal-wood, which is so valuable as an export to China, &c., it is time that public attention should be called to its gradual diminution, and threatened extinction, on this side of India. It forms an important article of revenue, wherever it is found. It is easily raised on red and sandy soil in the up-country, skirting the ghauts. A remarkable circumstance connected with it is, that when grown at the level of the sea, the wood, having scarcely ever the red heart or centre (which constitutes what is called sandal-wood in commerce), is useless. The formation of sandal-wood plantations on the highest parts of the mountain estate, should be one of the first objects of attention. The other two kinds of timber would occupy parts of the terraces, as well as the waste land below. These with coco-nut-trees and betle palms, may form, as it were, the skeleton and framework of the terrace plantation, while the following trees and plants constitute the mass, alternately or otherwise, as most convenient; or, accordingly as the exposure, soil, and breadth of terrace may indicate.

" *Coffee* will be found to succeed in a red soil. With a little shelter from the sun, and severe winds, it will give but little trouble and a fair share of profit, while it will associate very well with other trees.

" *Vines* will prove profitable where there is an abundant supply of water during the cold season. Grapes are in great demand throughout India, and as they will keep sound to a great distance, are a pretty sure speculation.

" *Mulberries.*—If these will, under any circumstances, repay 'the growth as standard trees, it will be probably in the form of pollards, placed, as in many parts of Italy, as props for vines. Wherever the leaves can be employed on the spot, as food for the silk-worm, the white mulberry must be more profitable than the useless Erythrina, and other quick growing spongy wooded trees, in common use in the vineyards of the Deccan. This manner of growing mulberry-leaves can, however, be only considered as auxiliary to the more abundant crops obtained from small plants grown in fields, frequently cut down and renewed. The latter, *i. e.* the Bengal system, is more in conformity to the quick succession of the worms, as you have the crops, as it were, on demand. If the worms become scanty at intervals, you may cease to water, and give a rest. Besides, it will be found that, even in such moist climates as the Wynaad (to say nothing of the Deccan), mulberry-trees of four or five years old, without cutting or irrigation, are very deficient in leaves— they run to fruit. The tops of hills being considered most favourable to the health of the silk-worm, and to the fineness or quality of the silk, this commodity may be fairly set down in the catalogue of the productions of a mountain farm.

" Cardamons, black-pepper, and the betle vine, or pepper, are all grown in similar situations to the above, and present a choice to the cultivator. The two latter (the black-pepper especially), by climbing over timber-trees, scarcely occupy extra space.

" The Cassia-bark tree and Malabar cinnamon, though inferior to Ceylon cinnamon, are articles of trade not to be despised. They are wild in some of our jungles, and when cultivated may turn to account : as is actually the case in Malabar. These, with the growth and preparation of various dying drugs for exportation, collecting the skins and horns of wild animals, are among the minor resources which may be brought into play.

· " Pernambuco or Kidney Cotton.—This cotton, unlike most others of long staple, preserves its length of fibre in this country. It is already naturalized, but not grown for a crop, the ordinary cotton-soil and mode of cultivation not being adapted to it. I have found it a total failure on the same land where other perennials succeeded. Seeing it grow spontaneously in red soil, in high situations, without watering, and propagate itself in neglected gardens, I confidently anticipate a favourable result from a trial in newly-cleared land about the ghauts. This cotton is in great demand in England, while some other long-fibred kinds, as the Bourbon, are declining. Added to this, it appears that the supply from Brazil is decreasing. Thus it is a matter of no small importance.

" Oranges and limes are almost the only remaining kinds of fruit that secure good returns to the grower, at the same time that they are adapted to the situations in question. As it is only my purpose to shew what is likely to be of exchangeable value, I may be excused giving the long catalogue of fruits that may be grown, and the same may be observed of all other horticultural produce, and of the many kinds of vegetables that especially "rejoice," (as the old English writers on gardening would say) on the tops of hills. It may be added, that the irrigation between the trees of the watered portion of the terraces will afford space for cold and hot weather crops, of all kinds of vegetables,—Asiatic and European, Guinea grass, lucerne for fodder, maize, or Indian corn, &c. Some resource against the famines of the interior may be found in the preparation of Arrow-root, as it is commonly called, that is to say the fecula, or starch, of the roots of all those species of Curcuma and other Scitamineous plants, which do not contain too much aromatic or other foreign principles. These grow wild in inexhaustible abundance in most mountainous jungles. The cultivation of the real West-Indian arrow-root recently introduced here, *viâ* Bengal, may assist. But above all, the Cassada, or Tapioca plant (Jatropha manihoot) should be recommended. Although naturalized by the Portuguese, who brought it from Brazil or Mozambique, it has not been adopted by the natives as an article of food in our provinces ; nevertheless, it may be seen here and there in the pepper-gardens of Malabar. Its great productiveness is too well known every where (excepting in India) to require any comment.

" Now, however hastily and imperfectly the above details are drawn up, I trust I have made out a *primâ facie* case, and have shown the possibility of rendering a tract of cultivated mountain, a valuable property both in present possession, and future prospect."

Ceplon.

The legislative council assembled on the 14th December, when the right hon. the governor delivered the session address, in which he stated that Mr. G. H. Boyd, who had been nominated senior un-official member of council, had declined to accept the appointment. His excellency then stated the subjects of certain ordinances which he was about to propose, and which were laid upon the table. He observed, in conclusion, " that the doors of the council room are thrown open to the public ; a general report of the discussions that have taken place within these walls has hitherto been given to the public, and will continue to be given : The public, therefore, both here and in England, will possess the means of conclusively judging for themselves as to the manner in which our legislative duties are executed."

A discussion of some of the ordinances then took place between the governor, the chief justice, Sir John Wilson and the auditor general, which is reported in the *Government Gazette.*

Malacca.

LAW.

Court of Judicature, Nov. 28.—Count von Ranzow (late resident at Rhio), his son, and servant, were indicted for, and convicted of, stabbing, cutting, and wounding with intent to murder, Mr. De Wind, a magistrate. Sentence of death was recorded, but was commuted to imprisonment in the gaol of Malacca, the first for a year, the second for six months, and the last for three months.

A letter from Malacca states: " On our arrival here, we found every one full of the poor old count's trial. Most people here think he has got off cheaply, and, if all reports are true, many there are who would not have objected to his being hanged. For myself, I think his punishment not too severe ; but I think he ought not to have been indicted for *murder* at all, but only for a violent 'assault ' to do grievous bodily harm,' &c. as the law phrase goes: as far as human reason can guide people in coming to a conclusion, it appears altogether absurd to fancy that any man would go out with such an ' intent ' on a road, nearly as public as your Campong Glam road. The facts, from all I can learn, where every one appears strongly prejudiced against Count Von Ranzow, are, that the assault committed on him in Rappa and Co.'s shop, when he was entirely alone, and without a single witness, rankled strongly in his mind, and he most unjustly came to the conclusion that he had a right to retaliate in the same way, and went out with the intention of giving De Wind a sound thrashing, where he thought there would be no witnesses, without reflecting that a big Caffre's blows might be dangerous.

" There is one thing that appears to me strange, that Mr. De Wind, who committed certainly a breach of the peace in attacking Von Ranzow, should be continued a magistrate."

Siam.

Extract of a letter from Bankok, dated 16th November : " The Siamese government do not exactly know, at present, what course to pursue with regard to Co-

chin China. They are evidently afraid of the Cochin Chinese ; but the ambitious ruler of Siam cannot bear the idea of sitting down quietly under his late defeats. He is perfectly aware they have hitherto had the worst of it, but will by no means acknowledge it. The Siamese, in fact, in all cases, invariably claim a victory; and the king pretends to fancy his forces are able to conquer the world. The army, however, if it deserves the name, is the most wretched imaginable. Sir John Falstaff, with half-a-dozen of his ragged recruits, would put to flight a thousand of them. The great body of the able-bodied men in the country are priests, and if they were let loose upon the Cochin Chinese, each with a stick in his hand, they would produce more effect than the present invulnerable army. Bankok alone contains 15,000 priests, and the old city called Juthia, 8,000, besides the out-posts and villages, which contain 17,000, making in all 40,000 yellow-robed, lazy, able-bodied priests, or talapoins. Among them, it is true, there are some old men, but they are comparatively few.

" It is much to be desired that the Siamese would decide on either making war or peace: as it is, the country is in a state of excitement, and the government appear to have no definite object in view. I asked the minister for foreign affairs, the other day, if they had any just grounds for going to war ; and, from the surprise he evinced, it was evident he had not of late given the subject much consideration. After chewing his betel, and reflecting for some time, he replied : ' O yes ! we have abundant cause. The governor of Sigon had dared to open a letter from the king of Siam to the king of Cochin China, and had taken the liberty to introduce an alteration that made the former style the latter *Emperor,* which in itself was a sufficient cause.' He then proceeded to relate the misunderstanding regarding Cambodia, which he adduced as another good and sufficient reason for making war on the Cochin Chinese. My own opinion is, that this war has been purposely got up, to keep the public mind excited, and not to allow the people time to reflect on the wretched condition to which they are reduced by the measures of government. The country is heavily oppressed by a system of grinding taxation, for no other purpose, apparently, than to raise money for the king to squander away in the building of enormous and expensive pagodas ; in which he is profusely liberal, but in every other respect penurious in the extreme.

" Some alteration ought to be made in the treaty of commerce at present existing between the East-India Company and his Siamese majesty. If a British vessel comes here to trade, and is only able to sell a few packages of goods, she is subjected to the same heavy measurement-duties of 1700 ticals (about 1000 Sp. dollars) per fathom, as if the whole cargo had been sold, and a full and complete one taken in return, which is manifestly unjust. The duty ought to be arranged to meet cases of this kind, two of which have recently occurred. The treaty operates very injuriously in other repects, which I shall point out to you on a future occasion. The Chinese pay a measurement, import, or export duty, saving a duty on the produce in the interior, which we also pay, besides the above measurement-duty. Considering the services rendered to the Siamese by the British, particularly during the Burmese war, and in the late affair with Quedah, we have every right to expect, and indeed to insist on, being permitted to trade here on the footing of the most favoured nation. An ambassador coming here ought to have a moderate naval force, and he would experience no difficulty in concluding such a treaty as is required."

China.

MISCELLANEOUS.

Diffusion of Knowledge in China. — The first report of the Society for the Diffusion of Useful Knowledge in China contains the following details :

"Those, if such there were, who expected that ' treatises in the Chinese language, on such branches of useful knowledge as are suited to the present condition of the people of this empire,' could in a few months be prepared and published, will not find their expectations realized ; nor will they, we trust, after considering all the circumstances of the case, see cause to regret the formation of this society, or to complain either of the measures which it has adopted or of the incipient labours which it has performed.

" Your committee have felt that the responsibility of the society must depend very much on the measures which it adopts, and the manner in which it carries them into effect. Every plan should be well matured ; and every publication prepared in the best style. As yet, the committee have not sent forth to the Chinese a single publication ; but, having surveyed the ground before them, they see occasion for a great variety, and very arduous labours ; and they cherish the hope that the time may not be very distant when, encouraged and countenanced by the most enlightened and liberal of this country, the society will be enabled to send forth its standard and periodical publications freely through all the provinces of the empire, and to all who speak the same language in the surrounding countries.

" Considering that much of what the society will have to communicate to the Chinese will be new to them, requiring many new names in geography, history, and science, your committee early took measures for preparing a Chinese nomenclature, which shall conform to the pronunciation of the court (or mandarin) dialect, but embrace, as far as possible, names that are already in use. Considerable advances have been made in this work, and the characters for expressing a large number of names of persons, places, &c. have been selected. Years, however, will be needed to carry this work to that state of perfection which the exigencies of the case require. It can only be perfected as the terms are from time to time needed for use. In a description of a steam-engine, for instance, or of the manipulations of a laboratory, in order to convey full information of the necessary apparatus and modes of operation, many new terms will be required. Your committee have not contemplated the publication of this work ; but they are desirous that a standard should be fixed, to which all their works may conform. The advantages of this will be obvious to every one. Terms, such as *Hung-maou kwei,* ' red-haired flower-flaged devils,' now commonly used for the English ; *Hwa-ke-kwei,* ' Flower-flaged devils,' for the Americans ; *Keang-koo-kwei,* ' old story-telling devils,' for preachers of the gospel ; and all similar epithets, as they are calculated to create and perpetuate bad feelings, will be discountenanced. Nor, when speaking of the Chinese, or of aught that belongs to them, will any but the most correct and respectful language be employed. Let there be given in this, as in all other cases, honour to whom honour is due.

" Three works are being prepared for the press ; 1st, a general history of the world ; 2d, a universal geography ; and 3d, a map of the world. These have been several months in hand, and will be carried forward, and completed with all convenient despatch. They are designed to be introductory works, presenting the great outlines of what will remain to be filled up. The history will be comprised in three vols., the geography in one. The map is on a large scale, about eight feet by four feet, presenting, at one view, all the kingdoms and nations of the earth. These three works the committee expect will be published in the course of the coming year ; and it is hoped they will soon be followed by others, in which the separate nations, England, France, &c., their history and present state, shall be fully described.

" In the absence of works already prepared for the press, an edition of the *Chinese Magazine*, 1,000 copies, each in two vols., has been contracted for. These are intended for the Chinese in the Indian Archipelago,—Batavia, Singapore, Malacca, Penang, &c. The progress of this work has been interrupted; it is expected, however, that it will be resumed in the course of a few months. Mr. Gutzlaff has offered the Magazine to the society, in order that its publication may be continued under its auspices; and the committee have expressed their willingness to undertake the work. whenever it can be done with a fair prospect of success.

" The expediency of procuring metallic type, for printing Chinese books, has engaged the attention of the committee. They have heard with satisfaction of the efforts of M. Pauthier, Paris, and of the Rev. M. Dyer, Penang. In both these places the type is being prepared by the means of punches, and at a very moderate expense; yet in such a manner as to render the type perfect and complete,— equalling. if not surpassing, the best specimens of Chinese workmanship."

The late Governor Loo.—Loo, governor of the two Kwang, minister of state, guardian of the prince, &c. &c. &c., died this morning (Sept. 24th), at one o'clock. The immediate cause of his death was constipation. Dr. Fan-laou-luh, a native of Keang-se, and long resident in Canton, wished to give the governor rhubarb, to allay the internal inflammation; but he replied, that an old man could not bear the operation of such a *strong* medicine, and that he was afraid to take rhubarb. He afterwards ate some *ginseng*, to strengthen him, which aggravated his complaint, and rendered useless all attempts to save him. He has left three sons, the youngest is in his own office; a widow and three concubines; No. 3 is said to be young and beautiful.

Governor Loo was a native of Shantung, the native province of Confucius. He was formerly the foo-yuen of this province; afterwards the governor of the two Hoo province, Hoo-pih and Hoonan; and then was promoted to the governorship of the two Kwang. On Sunday last, his *Yin-tsih*, ' secret narrow house,' in which he is to dwell, was burnt in his office. These *Yin-tsih* are made of paper and bamboo.—*Canton Reg.*

The Canton papers of 12th of January mention that great commotion had been caused amongst the Chinese authorities, by the *Jardine* steamer having effected a passage to Macao, notwithstanding the firing of the ports on both sides of the river. It appears that the merchants are particularly desirous of effecting a steam passage to Macao, but the local arrangements of the Chinese strictly prohibit it. Another attempt was to be made, although a decree had appeared, desiring the governor of the Bogue, if the " foreigners' smoke-ship arrives, to open and attack her hull with a thundering fire, and those who succeed in knocking her to pieces shall certainly be promoted." If the orders are disobeyed, and she enters, the least guilty shall be reported to the emperor, degraded from office, and wear the wooden collar; the most guilty shall be punished according to military law,— namely, exiled to the frontiers as slaves to the army. The Hong merchants had also requested that all boats and their crews which came up to Canton should return as speedily as possible to Whampoa, to prevent disturbances and quarrelling with the natives. This was considered a very prudent suggestion, as a disturbance might lead to serious consequences, there being at that moment no foreign commercial officer, excepting the French and Dutch consuls, to protect the trade.

Tahiti.

A writer in the *Singapore Free Press*, who has visited this island frequently, and had considerable traffic with the natives, gives the following account of them :

" Attempts have been made to initiate the natives into the mystery of several mechanic arts. There are many passable carpenters among them, as the new church at Papata Bay, built entirely by them, will testify. A person was sent out from the society, with machinery, on purpose to instruct them in the art of spinning and weaving cotton, the spontaneous growth of which afforded every facility. Some few did learn, and could make very good cloth, all things considered ; but, naturally of an indolent disposition, they must be paid for learning, and, seeing no possible advantage to be derived from making cloth, when they could procure it from the shipping at much less trouble, the project was and has been long abandoned. Many are owners of sugar plantations, and manufacture a considerable quantity of sugar, which they dispose of to shipping that visit them. It is not long since a Spanish gentleman came there from the Sandwich Islands, with the intention of purchasing a plantation, and cultivating sugarcane. His intention having been made known to ' government' (at the head of which stand the missionaries, who have sugar-plantations of their own), he was ordered to depart as he came, and not land on the island. But the vessel being bound to a distant port, permission was granted him to land, provided he agreed to leave in the first vessel bound to the Spanish Main or Sydney. He did so, and left about four weeks after. The natives have an inveteracy against the whites, which proceeds from nothing but envy and a love of gain. Formerly, they encouraged the whites to reside among them, ' but the times are greatly altered now ;' no white man is allowed to remain on the island without permission from the queen, and no one allowed to marry a native woman. This island, with the best of harbours, might be made a fine place ; but, if it continue for any length of time as it now is, it is probable their wish will, ere long, be gratified, in having the island to themselves—many of the whites having left since their 'new laws' have been in force, and those that remain will continue but a short time longer. When I last left the island, two gentlemen of the Friends' Society were there, on a visit. They came in a small vessel, chartered expressly for the purpose, and left England as agents on behalf of their society, with orders to visit the different mission-stations in the South-Sea Islands, to examine into the proceedings of the missions, and report if such were worthy the support of their society. How these gentlemen may succeed, and what may be their opinions concerning the object of their voyage, will before long be made public ; their intention being to publish the journal of their voyage when completed. One anecdote I cannot forbear relating. One of these gentlemen informed me that one day a party of natives came on board of his vessel, and inquired if he had blunderbusses for sale. ' I was much shocked,' said he, ' for I thought they were peaceful people, and of course had no call for such weapons.' "

Cape of Good Hope.

The Cape papers of February state that

the expedition under Dr. Smith, for exploring central Africa, had returned, and a general meeting of the subscribers had been summoned to hear the report. It was considered so successful, that a proposition was made to the meeting, by Sir John Herschel, " that this association should not dissolve, but continue to exist as a permanent institution for the further prosecution of its original object."

The governor had addressed a circular to the different civil commissioners of the colony, with a view of apportioning certain parts of the country to the Hottentot families.

Persia.

Constantinople, April 17.—Despatches from the Turkish ambassador, Essad Effendi, have been received, in nineteen days from Persia. The Shah has resolved to reduce Herat and Khiva, and 30,000 Persians were advancing against Khorasan. Tranquillity prevailed in the whole empire; the influence of the Russians was very great. The Shah, in order to give a proof of the advancement of civilization, had suddenly thrown open the gates of his harem, and given their liberty to all the females it contained. The great men of the empire followed the example, and the inhabitants of Tehran could scarcely believe their eyes when they saw the gates of the palace opened, for the first time, for the unhappy victims. This news causes an extraordinary sensation here ; it was believed in Pera that the Sultan would follow the example.—*Hamburgh Paper.*

Mr. Ellis arrived at Tehran about the middle of October. He was received with great kindness by the Shah, who was prodigal of his expressions of gratitude to the King of England, for the assistance rendered him by the British government.

Postscript.

An overland communication has been received, with advices from Calcutta to the 4th, and Bombay to the 18th, of March, which announce the arrival out of Lord Auckland, the new Governor-general. No other intelligence of any importance has transpired.

The *Malta Gazette* quotes letters from the Euphrates expedition, dated the 20th of March, mentioning that the two steamers, after considerable difficulty, had at last got afloat, manned and equipped,

without loss or injury to the machinery. The larger one, the *Euphrates*, had made a trip, up a rapid, to Bir, and there saluted the Grand Sultan's authority with 21 guns, to the astonishment of the native population. The *Tigris* was detained for some stores lately carried to Syria by His Majesty's sloop *Columbine*, but it was expected that, in a day or two, Col. Chesney, with both the steamers, would commence his course down the river.

REGISTER.

Calcutta.

GOVERNMENT ORDERS &c,

SUDDER AMEENS, MOONSIFFS, &c.—TRADING SPECULATIONS.

Fort William, Judicial and Revenue Department, Dec. 29, 1835.—The principal sudder ameens, sudder ameens, and moonsiffs, and the Mahomedan and Hindoo law officers of the zillah and city courts, and of the sudder Dewanny Adawlut under this Presidency, are hereby prohibited, under pain of dismissal from office, from being engaged in any trading speculations.

If any principal sudder ameen, or other of the officers above-mentioned, shall be now engaged in trading speculations, or any such speculations shall devolve on him by inheritance, it shall be incumbent on him, within one month, to make known the circumstance to the zillah or city judge, or to the register of the court of sudder Dewanny Adawlut; and to terminate his connexion with such transactions at the earliest practicable period. Should he be unable to do so within one year, he shall either resign his situation, or submit a report of the circumstances of the case to the judge or register, who will forward it to the Government or Court of Sudder Dewanny Adawlut, as the confirmation of the officer may be vested in one or other of these authorities; with his own opinion as to the propriety of allowing the officer a further period for the purpose of bringing his transactions to a close. If any of the officers, above-mentioned, shall fail to conform to the above rule, the same penalty shall attach to him, as if he had engaged in trade subsequent to the publication of this order.

Candidates for any of the offices above-mentioned shall certify in their applications that they are not engaged in any trading speculations; and in the event of their being appointed, and of its being subsequently discovered that they were so engaged at the time of making their application, they shall be liable to be dismissed from office.

CONDUCT OF LIEUT T. BELL.

Head-Quarters, Calcutta, Jan. 6, 1836.—1. Lieut. Interp. and Qu. Master T. Bell, of the 2d N. I., fancying that the adjutant of that regt. had improperly interfered with some of the details of the quarter master's business, made an appeal against what he supposed to be the misconduct of the adjutant, to Lieut. Col. D. Dowie, commanding the regiment.

2. The consequent line of conduct, adopted by Lieut. Col Dowie, led to a correspondence between him and Lieut. Bell; and as the Lieut. deemed that Lieut. Col. Dowie, in this correspondence, had not done him, or his office of quarter master, due justice, he desired to appeal from his commanding officer's decision, and to submit the affair to the superior judgment of Brigadier General Smith, commanding the Saugor division.

3. Brigadier General Smith, having considered the case, ordered a severe and well-merited censure to be addressed to Lieut. Bell for his conduct, and for the insubordinate and highly disrespectful style of a letter, which the Lieut. had addressed to his commanding officer.

4. Lieut. Bell has thought proper to appeal from this decision of Brigadier General Smith to the Commander-in-chief.

5. The Commander-in-Chief, having looked carefully at the case, and deeming that Lieut. Bell was in error from the very commencement of his proceeding, and concurring entirely in the view taken of the case by Brigadier General Smith, and quite approving the censure which he had expressed, His Excellency called on Lieut. Bell to assign his reasons for his appeal.

6. In his reply, the Lieut. has so entirely overlooked the relative position of himself and Brigadier General Smith in the army, as to presume to set up his (the Lieutenant's) opinion, that the General's decision ' is at variance with existing regulations,' and that the General's censure of him was as 'unjust' as 'unmerited;' and he winds up this highly disrespectful and insubordinate series of conduct, by putting it as a questionable point, whether the decision of the General was given from ' an error of judgment,' or from ' partiality !'

7. In order to mark the Commander-in-Chief's strong disapprobation of such a total absence of subordination and respect to superiors, he directs that Lieut. Bell shall be dismissed from the staff situation of quarter master and interpreter of the 2d regiment.

8. If Lieut. Col. Dowie has officers in the corps fit to fill up the vacancy, he will send in their names. If not, an officer will be appointed from another corps.

9. This, and another case which has recently been brought under the consideration of the Commander-in-Chief, occasion him to feel it necessary to call the attention of quarter masters of regiments to section 4 of the standing orders of this army, pages 17 and 18, in which their duties are clearly defined.

10. It would seem, from the instances to which he alludes in the last paragraph, as if some fancied, that the quarter master's department in a regiment formed something distinct, and differently circumstanced from other parts of the corps, and as if they considered themselves in some degree independent of the control of their senior officers. They must learn, therefore, that their duties are merely executive, under the orders and control of the commanding officer of the regiment, and that it is that officer who is the responsible person to the Commander-in-Chief, for every article issued by the quarter master to a regiment, and consequently, that every thing issued must meet his entire satisfaction and approval.

11. Lieut. Bell appears also to have quite mistaken the duties of the adjutant of a regiment, when he talks of his (the adjutant's) ' presuming,' in having sent to Lieut. Col. Dowie a turban, which was placed on the head of a recruit of the 2d regiment.

It is the duty of an adjutant, to observe all that is wrong in any department of his regiment, and to bring the same to the notice of his commanding officer ; and in reporting upon the turbans, which were in possession of the recruits on this occasiou, the adjutant did no more than was strictly his duty.

SINGFOES.—BRAVERY OF NATIVE SOLDIERS.

Head-Quarters, Calcutta, Jan. 12, 1836. —1. A hostile irruption having been made by a powerful neighbouring chief of the Singfoes into our territories on the Assam frontier, hostilities have been for some time in progress against him.

2. Major A. White, commanding the Assam Light Infantry, has succeeded, after much praiseworthy exertion, in bringing the chief to action, and in capturing some very strong stockades, in which the said chief had intrenched himself and followers, and in driving them over the frontier of our states.

3. In the last attack, Subadar Joynundeen Sing and two Sepoys of the Assam Light Infantry much distinguished themselves by their courage and devotion.

4. The Commander-in-Chief therefore recommended their conduct to the notice of his Honor the Governor-general in Council, who has been pleased to sanction the immediate promotion of Subadar Joynundeen Sing to the distinguished situation of Subadar Major of his corps, and the two sepoys to be made naicks.

5. The good conduct of these brave soldiers is thus made known to the army, and the Commander-in-Chief has much pleasure in announcing their reward by the Government.

DRESS OF STAFF OFFICERS.

Head-Quarters, Calcutta, Jan. 12, 1836. —His Exc. the Commander-in-Chief is pleased to signify to those officers of the general staff, who are required by the regulations of the service to conform in dress with the same ranks in His Majesty's army, that certain alterations in their uniform have been directed in a G. O., dated Horse Guards, 1st of Aug. 1834.

A memorandum of these alterations has been forwarded to officers commanding divisions and districts, and to heads of departments, for their guidance, and for the information of those under their orders.

The Commander-in-Chief does not desire to involve officers in unnecessary expense by a hasty conformity to the new regulations, but the sooner perfect uniformity is established, the better for the appearance of the army. He will name the 30th of June as the last day for any of the old pattern uniforms being worn in Bengal, and 30th of August in Madras and Bombay.

MOVEMENT OF CORPS.

With the sanction of Government, the 21st regiment native infantry will be cantoned at Kurnaul.

COURTS MARTIAL.

ENSIGN M. V. ABBOTT.

Head Quarters, Calcutta, Dec. 29, 1835. —At a general court-martial assembled at Cawnpore, on the 4th Dec. 1835, Ensign Montague Vernon Abbott, of H.M.'s 16th regt. of Foot, was arraigned on the following charge, *viz.*—

Charge.—" For conduct highly unbecoming an officer and a gentleman, and prejudicial to good order and military discipline, in familiarly associating and drinking with Sergeant William Perrin and Private Bernard Levy, of the same regiment, and one James Hack, in the bungalow of the said Ensign M. V. Abbott, on the night of the 5th and morning of the 6th Oct. 1835, notwithstanding that he, the said Ensign M. V. Abbott, had been twice warned of the consequences of his persisting in such improper conduct."

Upon which charge the court came to the following decision :

Finding.—" That the prisoner is guilty of the charge preferred against him, with the exception of the word ' twice,' of which they do acquit him."

Sentence.—" The court, having found the prisoner guilty as exhibited above, do sentence him, Ensign M. V. Abbott, of H.M.'s 16th regt. of Foot, to be dismissed from his Majesty's service."

Recommendation.—" The court, having awarded a sentence that they deem commensurate to the offence that the prisoner has been found guilty of, respectfully beg leave to recommend him to the clemency of his Exc. the Commander-in-chief, in consequence of the deep contrition that he has expressed, and with reference to his having alleged that he purchased his commission."

Approved.
(Signed)   H. FANE, General,
                      Commander-in-chief.

Remarks by the Commander-in-chief.

The Commander-in-chief regrets that he cannot see any grounds which could justify his attending to the recommendation of the court.

Ensign Abbot is to be struck off the list of the 16th regt. of Foot, from the date of this communication being made known to him, which the commanding officer will specially report to the adjutant-general of his Majesty's forces in India, and to the military secretary to his Exc. the Commander-in-chief.

CAPT. P. O'HANLON.

Head-Quarters, Calcutta, Dec. 31, 1835. —At a general court-martial, re-assembled in Fort William, on the 27th Oct. 1835, of which Brigadier Penny was president, Capt. Pringle O'Hanlon, of the 1st regt. L.C., was arraigned (by order of his Exc. the Commander-in-chief) on the following charge, *viz.*

Charge. — " That the said Capt. P. O'Hanlon (being then under suspension) was made officially aware, in July 1835, of the publication of a letter, dated 18th April, in the newspaper denominated the *Meerut Observer,* of the 23d April 1835, which letter was signed with his name, ' Pringle O'Hanlon,' and purported to have been written by him to the editor of the said paper, for the purpose of being laid before the public, and which contained false and scandalous charges against Col. Stephen Reid, of the 10th L.C., his former commanding officer, and also against Capt. John Augustus Scott, of the 1st regt. L.C.; and after being so made officially aware of the said letter, Capt. P. O'Hanlon never offered any contradiction to, or disavowal of, the same, but allowed the same letter to continue to appear before the army and the public as written by him, Capt. P. O'Hanlon, to the great detriment of the said Col. Stephen Reid and the said Capt. John Augustus Scott; such conduct being unbecoming the character of an officer and a gentleman, and subversive of military discipline."

Finding.—" The court, upon the evidence before them, are of opinion, that the prisoner, Capt. P. O'Hanlon, of the 1st regt. L.C. (being then under suspension), was made officially aware, in July 1835, of the publication of a letter, dated the 18th April, in the newspaper denominated the

Meerut Observer, of the 23d of April 1835, which letter was signed with his name, ' Pringle O'Hanlon,' and purported to have been written by him to the editor of the said paper, for the purpose of being laid before the public, and which contained scandalous charges against Col. S. Reid, of the 10th L.C., his former commanding officer, and also against Capt. J. A. Scott, of the 1st regt. L.C.; and that, after being so made officially aware of the said letter, Capt. P. O'Hanlon never offered any contradiction to, or disavowal of, the same, but allowed the said letter to continue to appear before the army and the public as written by him, Capt. P. O'Hanlon, to the great detriment of the said Col. S. Reid and the said Capt. J. A. Scott; such conduct being unbecoming the character of an officer, and subversive of military discipline: but the court acquit the prisoner, Capt. P. O'Hanlon, of the remainder of the charge."

Sentence.—" The court sentence the prisoner, Capt. Pringle O'Hanlon, of the 1st regt. L.C., to lose a portion of his rank in the regiment to which he belongs, by being placed on the list of captains in the said regiment next below Capt. John F. Bradford, and to be severely reprimanded in such manner as the Commander-in-chief may deem proper."

Remark by the Court.—" The court cannot close their proceedings without recording a just tribute to the deputy judge advocate-general who has conducted them, for the assiduity and dispassionate conduct displayed by him throughout this long, perplexing, and painful trial ; nor can the court sufficiently estimate the able advice he has afforded them in all points upon which he has been called upon so to do, as their law adviser."

The court re-assembled on the 28th Dec. 1835, in obedience to General Orders by his Exc. the Commander-in-chief, to re-consider their former verdict.

Revised Finding and Sentence.—" The court adhere to their former finding ; and, in doing so, beg respectfully to explain to the Commander-in-chief, that they consider it unbecoming an officer to resort to the public newspapers in which to state his grievances; but they do not think it ungentlemanly in this instance, inasmuch as the court acquit Capt. O'Hanlon of having stated any falsehood in the letter he published; and, under this explanation, the court adhere to their former sentence."

Remark by the Court.—" The court also desire to cancel their remark on the contents of the Meerut paper of the 18th Dec. 1834, and, with much deference to the Commander-in-chief, they would observe that, in their opinion, Capt. O'Hanlon's letter of the 18th April 1835 does not appear to adopt the charges in the editorial remarks of December 1834. In finding upon the case, the court abstain from pronouncing any opinion on the charges preferred by Capt. O'Hanlon against Col. Reid and Capt. Scott in January last, which, in the court's opinion, are not brought before them by the letter signed ' Pringle O'Hanlon.' The court, in deference to the Commander-in-chief, withdraw their remark on the conduct of Col. Reid."

Confirmed,

(Signed) H. FANE, General,
Commander-in-chief.

Remarks by his Excellency the Commander-in-Chief.

1st. Although I have " confirmed " I do not approve either the " finding or sentence " of this court-martial.

2d. My view of what is due from one officer and gentleman to another, is dissimilar to that adopted in this instance by the court.

3d. I deem that Capt. Pringle O'Hanlon had placed himself between the horns of this dilemma ; *viz.* he wrote the letter of the 18th April, or he did not. If he wrote it, he was bound, as an officer and a *gentleman*, to meet the charge of having done so, and to justify the act to the injured party as he best could; if he did not write it, then was he bound, when it appeared before the army and the public, under the sanction of his name, to disavow it. Such is my conception of the conduct becoming an *officer* and a *gentleman ;* and as the court have given a verdict that, in the course pursued, Captain Pringle O'Hanlon has lapsed from the former character, so, in my opinion, ought they to have decided with reference to the latter.

4th. I think their conclusion unsatisfactory also, as respects Col: Reid and Capt. Scott. The court permitted Col. Reid to go into a great mass of evidence to shew the falsehood of the allegations which were circulated against him and Capt. Scott, in the *Meerut Observer* of the 18th Dec. 1834, and which formed so much of the basis of the letter signed " P. O'Hanlon," of the 18th April 1835 ; and yet they conclude their revised proceedings by saying, they " abstain from pronouncing any opinion upon the charges preferred by Capt. O'Hanlon against Col. Reid and Capt. Scott in January last, which, in the court's opinion, are not brought before them by the letter signed ' Pringle O'Hanlon';" although in the letter itself, it is said, on the data referred to in the *Meerut Observer* of the 18th of Dec. 1834, " I framed and forwarded against Col. Reid four charges, and two against Capt. J. A. Scott," &c. &c. I am at a loss to understand for what purpose the great quantity of evidence, which has reference to the truth or falsehood of those charges, was permitted to take up so many days of the court's time, if, in the end, the court was to abstain from pronouncing an opinion.

5th. But since the court profess not to pronounce any opinion on the truth or falsehood of those charges, I feel it due to Col. Reid and Capt. Scott to say, that from what appears on the face of the proceedings, the charges were based upon foundations, which were formed upon very exaggerated views of the circumstances, and such as were little worthy of being brought forward as grounds upon which to wreck the reputation of two officers of the rank of Col. Reid and Capt. Scott; and, in justice to those officers, I must state my opinion that the gravamen of those charges is disproved.

6th. With reference to the " sentence," I think the measure of punishment quite inadequate to the amount of the military offence found to have been committed.

7th. I think the example which it affords to the army is calculated to lead to much mischief, by shewing to junior officers at how small an amount of punishment they may vituperate their superiors, and to what an extent they may attach obloquy to the names and characters of those who, in the enforcement of discipline, may happen to offend them.

8th. I am of opinion that harmony and good-will towards each other are more desirable and essential amongst the officers of the army of India than in any other of which British officers form a part ; and I am greatly apprehensive that neither one or the other will be in any degree forwarded by the award of this court-martial, which punishes such an act as that of which they have declared the prisoner " guilty," with the loss of one step of regimental rank only, and reprimand from the Commander-in-chief.

9th. Capt. P. O'Hanlon will receive what is said in the preceding remarks as a portion of the reprimand ordered by the court to be addressed to him. I further desire, that he will look at the results of his conduct, as respects his brother officers and the service.

10th. On his three courts-martial, *thirty* officers, exclusive of witnesses, have been withdrawn from their ordinary duties ; *eighty* days have been spent (either in sittings or adjournments) in investigating his misconduct and disputes, and the expenses to the government, and the inconveniences to individuals, have been very great.

11th. I am not aware that there has been in Capt. O'Hanlon's military services, or that enough may be expected from them, to compensate either to the army or the government for the evil which his conduct is thus shewn to have produced.

12th. His name is to be transposed in the army list, according to the sentence of the court. He is to be released from his arrest, and to join and do duty with the 9th regt. L.C. until further orders, since it is impossible that his services can be useful in the 1st Light Cavalry.

———

LIEUT. S. B. GOAD, CORNET J. IRVING, AND LIEUT. W. MARTIN.

Head-Quarters, Calcutta, Jan. 6, 1836. — At a general court-martial, assembled in Fort William, on the 21st Dec. 1835, Lieut. Samuel Boileau Goad and Cornet James Irving, of the 1st regt. L.C., were arraigned on the following charge:

Charge. — " For conduct unbecoming the character of officers and gentlemen, in having, at Meerut, on the 9th July 1835, upon frivolous and unjust pretences, refused to make adequate reparation to Lieut. William Martin, of the 52d regt. N.I., after he had acknowledged himself to be the writer of a letter signed ' Vindex,' in the *Meerut Observer* of the 2d July 1835, whom Cornet Irving had designated, in his reply to that letter, published in the *Meerut Observer* of the 9th July 1835, as a ' coward, who, sheltering himself under the imagined bulwark of a false signature, hesitates not to launch forth his venomed falsehoods.' "

Finding. —" The court, upon the evidence before them, are of opinion, that the prisoner, Cornet James Irving, of the 1st regt. L.C., is not guilty of the charge preferred against him, of which the court do therefore acquit him.

" The court also find the prisoner Lieut. S. B. Goad, of the 1st regt. L.C, not guilty of the charge, and they do accordingly acquit him."

Approved,

(Signed)   H. FANE, General,

Commander-in-chief.

———

Before the same court-martial, on the 24th Dec. 1835, Lieut. William Martin, of the 52d regt. N.I., was arraigned on the following charge :

Charge. —" For conduct prejudicial to good order and military discipline, in having, at Meerut, on the 9th July 1835, written, and sent to Cornet Irving, of the 1st L C., a paper containing the following expressions : ' I hereby denounce him (Cornet Irving) as a cowardly poltroon, and desire that he will consider himself as posted and horsewhipped.' "

Finding. —" The court, upon the evidence before them, are of opinion, that the prisoner, Lieut. Wm. Martin, of the 52d regt. N.I., is guilty of the charge preferred against him."

Sentence. —" The court sentence the prisoner, Lieut. Wm. Martin, of the 52d regt. N.I., to be reprimanded in such manner as the Commander-in-chief may be pleased to direct."

Recommendation by the Court. —" The court, taking into consideration the evidence before them, cannot abstain from attracting the attention of the Commander-in chief to the great provocation given by Cornet Irving to Lieut. Martin, as a ground on which the court recommend Lieut. Martin to the leniency of the Commander-in-chief."

Approved.

(Signed)   H. FANE, General,

Commander-in-chief.

Remarks by the Commander-in-chief.

1st. I willingly listen to the recommendation of the court in this case, because the prisoner, in his defence, has fairly and honourably acknowledged, that " on subsequent reflection he has convinced himself, that the terms which he made use of towards Cornet Irving were unbecoming him to use, and derogatory to the person himself who uses them," and he " acknowledges his error," and " submits himself to the reproof of the court."

2d. I will therefore say no more in reprobation of Lieut. Martin.

3d. I much disapprove of the conduct of Assist. Surg. Tweddell, who appears, from the proceedings of the court-martial, to have acted as Lieut. Martin's friend. Had he proceeded with moderately good judgment, he must have felt, that as " Vindex " was the aggressor, " Vindex " ought to have been the first to have unsaid what he had stated wrongfully, in which case (as it would seem) all matters might have been settled satisfactorily, and all the subsequent proceedings have been avoided.

4th. This is the third court-martial which has recently been concluded, growing out of the very unsoldier-like, and, as I think, improper proceeding of officers, endeavouring to write down the characters of others in the public newspapers.

I appeal to the army whether any particle of *good* has arisen from what has passed in these cases ; and I beg of them to reflect whether it is not better that such feuds and disagreements as arise amongst ourselves, should be adjudicated and settled by ourselves only, rather than that they should be cast before the public on *exparte* statements, there to be commented upon for months before the real merits can be decided, and to be made topics for conversation in every reading-room in India, or perhaps the British empire, under the imperfect view which an *exparte* statement is sure to afford.

Lieut. Goad and Cornet Irving, of the 1st L.C., and Lieut. Martin, of the 52d N.I., are to be released from arrest, and to return to their duty.

CIVIL APPOINTMENTS, &c.

BY THE GOVERNOR-GENERAL.

Judicial and Revenue Department.

Dec. 22. Mr. J. Donnithorne to be collector of Calcutta as well as of the 24-Pergunnahs.

The Hon. W. H. L. Melville to officiate as special commissioner, under Reg. III. of 1828, of Calcutta division, in room of Mr. N. J. Halhed.

Mr. J. A. O. Farquharson to conduct current duties of office of civil and session judge of Purneah, instead of Mr. G. G. Mackintosh.

Mr. G. L. Martin to be an assistant under commissioner of revenue and circuit of 19th or Cuttack division.

29. Mr. W. A. Pringle to be civil and session judge of Purneah.

Mr. H. Nisbet to be civil and session judge of Sarun.

Mr. T. R. Davidson to officiate as civil and session judge of zillah Sarun during Mr. H. Nisbet's employment as officiating commissioner of 12th or Bhaugulpore division.

Mr. H. B. Beresford to officiate as magistrate and collector of Purneah, upon being relieved by the Hon. Mr. Forbes at Maldah.

Mr. R. B. Garrett to exercise powers of joint magistrate and deputy collector in district of Balasore.

Mr. A. G. Macdonald to be an assistant under commissioner of revenue and circuit of 13th or Bauleah division.

Jan. 5. Mr. R. Williams to officiate as civil and session judge of zillah Behar, in room of Mr. Cuthbert.

Mr. John Hawkins to officiate as civil and session judge of zillah Shahabad.

Mr. R. Houstoun to officiate as collector of Calcutta and the 24-Pergunnahs.

Lieut. F. W. Birch, 41st N.I., to be superintendent of police of town of Calcutta, v. Capt. Steel resigned.

12. Mr. H. S. Oldfield to officiate as collector of Calcutta and the 24-Pergunnahs, in room of Mr. Houstoun.

Capt. James G. Burns, 3d N.I., to be superintendent of Upper and Lower Cachar and Jynteea, in room of Capt. T. Fisher.

Mr. James Young to be clerk of the peace, in room of Mr. W. H. Smoult resigned.

Mr. J. Lowis to be commissioner of revenue and circuit of 15th or Dacca division, v. Mr. J. A. Pringle.

Mr. A. J. M. Mills to be magistrate and collector of central division of Cuttack.

Mr. J. B. Ogilvy to be joint magistrate and deputy collector of Puhna.

Mr. R. J. Loughnan to exercise full powers of a collector in district of Behar.

Mr. R. B. Garrett to be an assistant under commissioner of revenue and circuit of 15th or Dacca division, with authority to exercise powers of joint magistrate and deputy collector in zillah Furreedpore.

Mr. J. S. Torrens to be an assistant under commissioner of revenue and circuit of 19th or Cuttack division, with authority to exercise powers of ditto ditto in zillah Balasore.

Mr. C. Steer to be invested with full powers of a joint magistrate and deputy collector in zillah Bhaugulpore.

Mr. A. Grote to be assistant under commissioner of revenue and circuit of 13th or Bauleah division.

Mr. F. D. Rosario to be deputy collector in district of Monghyr.

Mr. J. Dunsmure to be sudder ameen in zillah Rungpore.

General Department.

Dec. 22. Mr. G. J. Siddons, collector of customs at Calcutta, to take charge of office of postmaster-general from the Hon. Mr. Elliott.—Mr. C. C. Hyde to take charge of office of collector of customs from Mr. Siddons.—Mr. C. Mackenzie to take charge of commercial residency at Bhaulea.—These appointments to take permanent effect on departure of the Hon. J. E. Elliot for Europe.

30. Mr. L. Magniac to officiate as salt agent of Bullooah and Chittagong, during absence of Mr. Blagrave.

Jan. 6. Mr. C. F. Young, officiating second assistant to Board of Customs, salt and opium, to take charge of office of superintendent of stamps from Mr. Saunders, proceeding to Europe.

Assist. Surg. T. Corbet appointed to office of 1st-assistant to opium agent at Behar, in room of Dr. Clark resigned.

13. Lieut. F. W. Birch, 41st N.L., to receive charge of Calcutta salt chokies, with same powers as those possessed by Capt. Steel resigned.

Political Department.

Dec. 14. Capt. J. D. Stokes, 4th Madras N.I., to be resident at Mysore, on reduced consolidated allowance of 30,000 Company's rupees per annum, in suc. to Lieut. Col. Fraser. This appointment to take effect from date of Lieut. Col. Fraser's appointment to residency of Travancore and Cochin.

Lieut. Col. Cubbon, commissioner for government of territories of H.H. the Rajah of Mysore, to be also commissioner for affairs of Coorg, in suc. to Lieut. Col. Fraser.

21. Assist. Surg. A. Walker, Bombay establishment, placed at disposal of resident at Hydrabad.

28. Ens. Walter Caddell, 36th N.I., placed at disposal of resident at Hyderabad.

Jan. 4. Capt. C. G. Dixon, of artillery, to be superintendent in Mhairwarrah, and to command Mhairwarrah battalion, in suc. to Lieut. Col. Hall, proceeded to Europe.

Capt. P. A. Reynolds, 38th Madras N.I., to officiate as general superintendent of operations for suppression of Thuggee, during absence, on leave, of Capt. W. H. Sleeman.

Lieut. C. E. Mills, regt. of artillery, and Lieut. J. Sleeman, 73d N.I., to be assistants to general superintendent of operations for suppression of Thuggee.

Lieut. J. H. Smyth, Bengal artillery, placed at disposal of resident at Gwalior, for employment in Sindia's Reformed Contingent.

Capt. A. Macarthur, 41st Madras N.I., to be superintendent of a division under commissioner for government of territories of H.H. the Rajah of Mysore, v. Hunter appointed to Silladar horse.

11. Capt. N. Lowis, 63d N.I., to be an assistant to general superintendent of operations for suppression of Thuggee.

Cornet H. G. Chichely Plowden, 5th L.C., placed under orders of resident at Hydrabad.

18. Lieut. Col. James Caulfield, c.b., 9th L.C., placed at disposal of Government of Bengal.

Lieut. Fraser, 1st L.C., and attached to revenue survey, to officiate as assistant to resident at Nagpore.

Ens. T. G. St. George, 17th N.I., placed under orders of resident at Gwalior.

Financial Department.

Dec. 19. Mr. C. Trower, collector of Calcutta, to take charge of office of civil auditor, and to succeed eventually on departure of Mr. Tulloh to Europe. (The office of collector of Calcutta, held by Mr. Trower, will be abolished from the same date, and its duties will be annexed to the office of collector of the 24-pergunnahs.)

30. Mr. J. Dewar to have temporary charge of commercial residency of Bauleah, during Mr. Mackenzie's absence.

Miscellaneous.

The undermentioned gentlemen have, at the request of government, formed themselves into a committee for the purpose of inquiring into the state of the Indian gaols, and of preparing an improved plan of prison discipline:—The Hon. H. Shakespear, Esq., president; Hon. Sir E. Ryan; Hon. T. B. Macaulay, Esq.; Hon. Sir J. P. Grant; Hon. Sir B. H. Malkin; C. H. Cameron, Esq.; J. M. Macleod, Esq.; G. W. Anderson, Esq.; C. R. Barwell, Esq.; D. McFarlan, Esq.; J. P. Grant, Esq., junior member and secretary.

Mr. A. G. Macdonald having passed an examination on the 16th Dec, and being reported qualified for the public service by proficiency in the native languages, the order issued on the 25th Nov., for that gentleman's return to Europe, is cancelled.

Mr. G. L. Martin is reported qualified for the public service by proficiency in two of the native languages.

Mr. J. M. Hay having exceeded the period within which, under the orders of the Hon. the Court of Directors, he ought to have qualified himself for the public service by proficiency in the native languages, has been ordered to return to England : date 13th Jan. 1836.

Mr. David Cunliffe has been permitted to proceed to Chuprah and prosecute his study of the Oriental languages at that station.

Messrs. R. H. Tulloh and J. A. Pringle, of the civil service, have been permitted to return to England in order to retire upon annuities of the year 1836.

The following gentlemen have reported their return from furlough :—Messrs. J. A. Craigie and H. S. Oldfield, and are assigned to the Agra presidency ; Mr. J. A. F. Hawkins, and is assigned to the Bengal presidency ; Mr. R. B. Garrett.

Furloughs, &c.—Dec. 23. Mr. Edward Deedes, to Europe.—30. Mr. M. Malcolm, to sea, for six months, for health.—Jan. 6. Mr. G. R. B. Berney and the Hon. J. E. Elliot, to Europe.—Mr. H. Saunders, leave of absence for one month, preparatory to proceeding to Europe.—Lieut. Col. T. A. Cobbe, agent to Governor-general at Moorshedabad, to visit presidency, preparatory to proceeding to Cape of Good Hope.

BY THE GOVERNOR OF AGRA.

Judicial and Revenue Department.

Dec. 16. Mr. G. Todd to officiate as collector of customs and town duties at Mirzapoor.

Political Department.

Dec. 19. Mr. M. P. Edgeworth to be first assistant to political agent at Umballa for management of the Jheend territory.

Mr. R. Money to be second assistant to ditto.

The Hon. the Governor of Agra has placed the following junior assistants at the disposal of the Hon. the Governor of Bengal :—Messrs. J. T. Mells, W. T. Trotter, R. Hampton, W. P. Goad, R. H. Snell, E. H. C. Monckton, E. Bentall, C. Todd, R. R. Sturt, and A. Forbes.

The services of Messrs. J. H. Young and R. J. Loughnan have been placed at the disposal of the Bengal Government.

ECCLESIASTICAL.

Dec. 23. With reference to orders under date the 29th April 1835, appointing the Rev. John Vaughan to officiate as district chaplain at Dinapore, and the Rev. Charles Wimberley to officiate as garrison chaplain of Fort William, each for six months from that date, the Hon. the Governor of Bengal is pleased to confirm the exchange of appointments by those gentlemen respectively.

Jan. 13. The Rev. H. Parish to officiate at St. John's Cathedral during absence of the Rev. Henry Fisher.

MILITARY APPOINTMENTS, PROMOTIONS, &c.

Fort William, Dec. 21, 1835.—*5th L.C.* Capt. Wm. Warde to be major, Lieut. C. E. T. Oldfield to be capt. of a troop, and Cornet J. D. Macnaghten to be lieut , from 14th Dec. 1835, in suc. to Major Wm. Buckley retired on pension of his rank.

Supernum. Cornet J. H. L. M. Toone brought on effective strength of cavalry.

74th N.I. Capt. James Johnston to be major, Lieut. A. Charlton to be capt. of a comp., and Ens. T. W. Oldfield to be lieut., from 15th Dec. 1835, in suc. to Major C. A. Munro retired on pension of his rank.

Lieut. A. K. Agnew, 6th N.I., to be capt. by brevet, from 16th Dec. 1835.

Cadets of Infantry Archibald Campbell, A. D. Cauldfield, C. R. Larkins, and W. H. Larkins admitted on estab., and prom. to ensigns.

Assist. Surg. Donald Campbell to be surgeon, v. Surg. Geo. Skipton dec., with rank from 15th Oct. 835, v. Surg. John Allan, M.D., dec.

Surg. John Sawers, officiating 3d member, to be 3d member of Medical Board, from 3d Oct. 1835, v. Surg. Skipton dec.

Officiating Superint. Surg. D. Renton to be a superintending surgeon on estab., from 3d Oct. 1835, v. Surg. Sawers app. 3d member of Medical Board.

Consequent on return of Superint. Surg. S. Ludlow from furlough, Superint. Surg. Renton reverts, from 7th Dec., to grade of surgeon, agreeably to existing regulations.

That part of G. O., of 7th Dec., directing return of Superintending Surg. Findon to his former rank, cancelled.

Lieut. Col. J. Craigie (having reported his return from Cape of Good Hope) to resume his duties as a member of Military Board, and Colonel W. Battine, principal com. of ordnance, to receive charge of arsenal of Fort William from Lieut. Col. Powney, officiating in that appointment.

Surg. A. R. Jackson, M.D., to relieve Surg. John Grant, and to officiate as apothecary to Hon. Company during latter officer's absence at Cape of Good Hope.

Lieut. J. F. Egerton, regt. of artillery, placed at disposal of Hon. the Governor of Bengal for survey duty.

In consequence of the paucity of senior officers present with 48th N.I , Capt. Fisher, of that corps, lately prom. to a company, placed at disposal of Commander-in-chief for regimental duty.

Dec. 28.—Cadets of Infantry H. Strachey and R. M. Franklin admitted on estab., and prom. to ensigns.

Supernum. 2d-Lieut. J. H. Smyth, regt. of artillery, brought on effective strength of regt., v. 2d-Lieut. J. D. B. Ellis dec., 14th Dec. 1835.

Lieut. R. M. Hunter, 73d N.I., to continue to do duty with Assam Sebundy corps ; his resignation published in G. O. of 30th Nov. accordingly cancelled.

Lieut. R. G. Macgregor, 2d-assistant, to be 1st-assistant military auditor general, v. Capt. Pyne permitted to proceed to Europe on furlough.

Capt. James Roxburgh, 39th N.I., to be 2d-assistant military auditor-general, v. Lieut. Macgregor.

Lieut. R. Hill, corps of engineers, to officiate as assistant superintendent of Coel division of Delhi and Allahabad road, during period that Lieut. Anderson shall officiate as assistant superintendent of Dooab Canal.

Head-Quarters, Dec. 21, 1835.—The following orders confirmed :—Cornet and Adj. M. R. Onslow, 4th L.C., to officiate as detachment staff at Jeypore, v. Lieut. and Adj. F. W. Burroughs, 17th N.I. ; date 28th Nov.—Lieut. F. G. Beck to act as adj. to 13th N.I., during absence, on leave, of Brevet Capt. and Adj. G. H. Edwards ; date 1st Dec.

Dec. 23.—Surg. Mathew Nisbet, M.D., removed from 61st to 48th N.I., at Seetapore ; and Assist. Surg. James Davenport, M.D. (on furl.), from 8th L.C. to 21st N.I.

Dec. 24.—Superintending Surg. W. Findon posted to Benares division.

The following unposted Ensigns to do duty :— A. H. Kennedy with 4th N.I., at Berhampore ; W. H. Larkins and C. R. Larkins with 43d N.I., at Barrackpore ; A. D. Caulfield with 4th N.I., at Berhampore.

Dec. 26.—The following removals and postings made :—Lieut. Cols. C. P. ing from 4th to 10th L.C.; D. Harriott, from K10th to 6th do. ; A. Warde from 6th to 3d do. ; W. Pattle from 3d to 4th do.

Dec. 28.—The following division order confirmed :—Capt. J. Leeson, 42d N.I., and Lieut G. Cautley, 8th L.C., to do duty at convalescent dépôt at Landour, during winter months ; date 13th Dec.

Col. J. S. Harriot (on furl.) removed from 70th to 42d N.I., and Col. F. V. Raper from 42d to 70th ditto.

Ens. A. C. Boswell removed from 59th to 19th N.I., as junior of his rank.

Dec. 29.—Capts. W. Hough and F. Angelo, of the judge advocate-general's department, permitted to exchange divisions (Sirhind and Benares).

The following unposted Ensigns to do duty :—Arch. Campbell, R. M. Franklin, and Henry Strachey, with 57th N.I., at Benares; A. W. Onslow with 4th do., at Berhampore.

Dec. 31.—Assist. Surg. C. B. Handyside, M.D., of 49th N.I., to proceed and do duty under superintending surgeon at Meerut.

Fort William, Jan. 4, 1836.—Lieut. R. S. Tickell, 72d N.I., to be sub. assist. com. general, to fill an existing vacancy.

Lieut. John Gilmore, corps of engineers, to be executive engineer, Ramghur division, department of public works.

Cornet C. G. Becher, of L.C., to officiate as adj. of Governor-general's body guard, during absence of Lieut. Baker, on med. cert.

Cadet of Infantry John Plunkett admitted on estab., and prom. to ensign.

Under circumstances brought to notice of government by his Exc. the Commander-in-chief, the operation of G.O. No. 7, of 1834, is suspended in the case of Capt. O'Hanlon, of 1st L.C., so long as his Exc. may deem it necessary that that officer should do duty with 9th L.C.

The following officers confirmed in appointments in which they are at present officiating :—Capt. G. D. Stoddart, 8th L.C., as paymaster at presidency and to King's troops.—Lieut. Chas. Campbell, 42d N.I., as deputy paymaster of Cawnpore circle of payment.

Jan. 11.—*Infantry.* Major David Crichton to be lieut. col., from 7th Jan. 1836, v. Lieut. Col. Wm. Kennedy dec.

69th N.I. Capt. Henry Norton to be major, Lieut. and Brev. Capt. R. D. White to be capt. of a comp., and Ens. Geo. Hutchings to be lieut., from 7th Jan. 1836, in suc. to Major D. Crichton prom.

Lieut. Wm. Macgeorge, 71st N.I., to be a deputy judge adv. gen. on estab., v. Lieut. R. G. McGregor, who has been app. to audit department.

The following officers to be Capts. by brevet :—Lieut. R. J. H. Birch, 17th N.I.; Lieut. F. W. Birch, 41st do.; and Lieut. J. Woodburn, 44th do.; all from 7th Jan. 1836.

Capt. J. A Scott, 1st L.C., permitted to rejoin his corps at Neemuch, *via* Bombay.

Assist. Surg. R. J. Brassey, officiating garrison assist. surgeon at Allahabad, placed at disposal of Government of Agra, for purpose of being confirmed in that appointment.

Infantry. Major James Stuart to be lieut. col., from 7th Jan. 1836, in suc. to Lieut. Col. Wm. Stirling retired on pension of his rank.

34th N.I. Capt. Robert Low to be major, Lieut. and Brev. Capt. Richard Angelo to be capt. of a comp., and Ens. P. J. Chiene to be lieut., from 7th Jan. 1836, in suc. to Major James Stuart prom.

Lieut. Edward Buckle, regt. of artillery, deputy commissary, to be commissary of ordnance, v. Capt. C. G. Dixon app. superintendent in Mhairwarrah.

Lieut. W. O. Young, regt. of artillery, to be deputy commissary of ordnance, v. Lieut. E. Buckle.

Assist. Surg. George Craigie, M.D., to be assistant marine surgeon, v. Spens. dec.

Assist. Surg. J. S. Login, M.D., to be 2d assist. garrison surgeon of Fort William, v. Craigie.

Assist. Surg. John Jackson app. to medical duties of civil station of Howrah, v. Login.

Assist. Surg. A. Vans Dunlop, M.D., app. to medical duties of civil station of Furreedpore.

Head-Quarters, Jan. 1, 1836.—Lieut. and Brev. Capt. Colin Troup to be adj. to 48th N.I., v. Lieut. and Brev. Capt. F. C. Smith, permitted to resign the appointment.

Lieut. and Brev. Capt. H. Garbett to be adj. and qu. mast. to 3d brigade horse artillery, v. Lieut. W. M. Shakespear dec.

Capt. T. B. P. Festing, inv. estab., permitted to reside and draw his allowances at presidency.

Jan. 4.—The following division orders confirmed :—Assist. Surg. J. S. Sutherland to assume medical charge of left wing 3d N.I.; date 20th Dec.—Assist. Surg. Thos. Smith, M.D., 8th L.C., to proceed to Azimgurh, and perform medical duties,

civil and military, at that post, in room of Assist. Surg. James Eslaile, M.D., proceeded to presidency on med. cert ; date 21st Dec.

Ens. J. S. D. Tulloch, 17th, to act as interp. and qu. mast. to 63d N.I.

Jan. 6.—29th N.I. Lieut. G. B. Reddie to be interp. and qu. mast., v. Marsden gone to Europe on furlough.

Jan. 7.—Capt. J V. Fo:bes, 15th N.I., to act as major of brigade at Cawnpore, during absence of Capt. R. Wyllie; date 1st Nov. 1835.

Jan. 8.—Lieut. Col. J. Hunter removed from 17th to 51st N.I., and Lieut. Col. G. Hawes, from 51st to 17th do.

Unposted Ensign John Plunkett to do duty with 4th N.I. at Berhampore.

Jan. 9.—Lieut. Interp. and Qu. Mast. A. Mackintosh, 52d N.I., to act as detachment staff at Jeypore; date 20th Dec.

Cornet E. K. Money removed from 7th to 2d L.C., as junior of his rank.

Jan. 12.—Lieut. and Brev. Capt. H. Clerk, regt. of artillery, permitted to resign situation of acting adj. and qu. mast. to Neemuch div. of artillery.

The following orders confirmed :—Lieut. J. W. V. Stephen to act as interp. and qu. mast. to 41st N.I., during employment, on detached duty, of Lieut. F. W. Birch; date 1st Jan.—9d-Lieut. W. Paley to act as adj. to artillery at Neemuch, during absence, on detached employment, of Lieut. W. O. Young; date 24th Dec.

The following removals and postings made:—Lieut. Cols. J. Craigie (member Military Board) from 69th to 41st N.I.; W. W. Moore (on furl.) from 41st to 16th do.; D. Crichton (new prom.) to 69th do.; J. Stuart (new prom.) to 34th do.

Fort William, Jan. 13.—Assist. Surg. Roger Foley app. to medical duties of political agency at Harowtee, v. J. Corbet app. assistant opium agent in Behar.

Assist. Surg. R. C. McConnochie to officiate as civil assist. surgeon at Sylhet.

The following officers to be Capts. by brevet :—Lieut. James Mackenzie, 8th L.C., from 13th Jan. 1836; Lieuts. H. Clayton and Wm. Benson, 4th L.C., from 16th Jan. 1836; Lieut. John Butler, 3d N.I., from 12th Jan. 1836; Lieuts. C. Chester, 2d N.I., O. W. Span, 53d do., and R. McNair, 73d do., from 13th Jan. 1836; Lieuts. B. Bygrave, 5th N.I., James Maclean, 11th do., S. Long, 40th do., and E. J. Betts, 7th do., from 16th Jan. 1836.

Lieut. R. C. Macleod, of engineers, acting assistant engineer Delhi division, permitted to rejoin corps of Sappers and miners.

Head-Quarters, Jan. 15.—15th N.I. Ens. J. W. Carnegie to be interp. and qu mast., from 5th Dec., v. Ogilvy app. adjutant.

Assist. Surg. H. M. Green, 25th N.I., on leave at presidency, app. to medical charge of a detachment of volunteers of H.M. service proceeding to Bombay on ship *Adelaide.* Assist. Surg. Green will afterwards proceed to Mhow, and do duty with artillery at that station.

Ens. C. F. M. Mundy removed from 1st to 34th N.I., as junior of his rank.

Jan. 16.—The following station order confirmed :—Assist. Surg. A. C. Duncan, M.D., medical storekeeper at Neemuch, to receive medical charge of 37th N.I. from Assist. Surg. E. T. Downes removed to 49th regt.; date 28th Dec.

Jan. 18.—41st N.I. Lieut. J. W. V. Stephen to be interp. and qu. mast., v. Lieut. and Brev. Capt. F. W. Birch app. superintendent of police, Calcutta.

Permitted to Retire from Hon. Company's Service.—Dec. 21. Lieut. Col. Wm. Stirling, 34th N.I., on pension of his rank.—Lieut. Col. W. C. L. Bird, invalid estab., on pay of his rank.—Jan. 4. Capt. Philip Jackson, invalid estab., on half-pay of his rank, subject to confirmation of Hon. the Court of Directors.—11. Capt. James Johnson, regt. of artillery, on pension of his rank.—13. Maj. C. P. Kennedy, regt. of artillery, on pension of his rank.

Examination. — The undermentioned officer having been declared by the examiners of the College of Fort William to be qualified for the duties of interpreter, is exempted from further examinaing.—3. *Gironde*, Lagrauere, from Bordeaux.— nation in the native languages, *viz.* — Jan. 9. Lieut. C. Graham, 55th N.I.

Returned to duty, from Europe.—Dec. 21. Lieut. Col. Arthur Warde, 6th L.C.—Capt. C. E. T. Old-field, 8th L.C.—Lieut. C. J. H. Perreau, 58th N.I. —Lieut Col. and Brev.Col. James Caulfield, c.b., 9th L.C.—Capt. G. Hicks, 8th N.I.—28. Lieut. Col. W. G. Mackenzie, 15th N.I.—Lieut. G. Kennaway, 5th L.C.—Lieut.W. J. B. Knyvett, 38th N.I.

FURLOUGHS.

To *Europe.*—Dec. 21. Lieut. and Brev. Capt. G. Griffiths, 13th N.I., for health. — Lieut. J. K. Phibbs, 41st N.I., for health.—Lieut. E. T. Erskine, 63d N.I., for health. — Capt. J. T. Croft, 34th N.I., on private affairs —Lieut. the Hon. R. V. Powys, 12th L.I., on ditto.—Lieut. Wm. Jervis, 42d N.I., on ditto.—Lieut. J. B Lock, 5th N.I., for health.—26. Capt. A. L. Campbell, 1st L.C., on private affairs.—28. Maj. George Kingston, 52d N.I., on ditto.—Capt. F. J. Simpson, 55th N.I., on ditto. — 1st-Lieut. and Brev. Capt. H. Humfrey, artillery, on ditto — 1st-Lieut. George Campbell, artillery, for health.—Lieut. Col. Henry Hall, 42d N.I., political agent in Mhairwarrah, for health.—Ens. J. G. Gaitskell, 26th N.I., for health.—Capt. John Pyne, 32d N.I., on private affairs.—Lieut. W. L. L. Scott, 1st I.C., on ditto. —Lieut. R. H. De Montmorency, 65th N.I., on ditto.—Jan. 2. Assist. Surg. W. P. Andrew, M.D., for health.—4. Capt. and Brev. Maj. E. A. Campbell, 3d L.C., for health.—Supernum. 2d-Lieut. John Trail, corps of engineers, for health.—Capt. Charles Griffiths, 37th N.I., for one year, on private affairs.—Surg. Ewen Macdonald, on private affairs.— Capt. James Steel, 41st N.I., superintendent of Calcutta police, for health.—Ens. J. W. Chalmers, 43d N.I., for one year, on private affairs.— 11. Capt. Wm. Grant, 27th N.I., for health.—Capt. John Martin, 41st N.I., for health. —Lieut. and Brev. Capt. F. C. Smith, 48th N.I., for health (*via* Van Diemen's Land).—Surg. Thos. Stoddart, for health.—Assist. Surg. James Esdaile. M.D., for health.—Maj. H. L. Worrall, 1st I.C., on private affairs.—Maj. Thos. Reynolds, inv. estab., on ditto.—Capt. Henry Monke, 39th N.I., on ditto.—Lieut. A. Tucker, 9th L.C., for health. —13. Lieut and Brev. Capt. A. C. Scott, 70th N.I., for health.—18. Lieut. Col. John Craigie, 41st N.I., on private affairs.—Maj. E. J. Honywood, 7th L.C., superintendent of Mysore princes, &c., on ditto.—Capt. John Mathias, 33d N.I., on ditto.—Capt. J. W. H. Turner, inv. estab., on ditto.—Lieut. Wm. Little, 3d N.I., on ditto.— Lieut. Wm. Martin, 52d N.I., on ditto.—Surg. J. J. Paterson, on ditto.—Capt. John Platt, 23d N.I., for health.—Lieut. T. S. Price, 8th N.I., for health.

To *visit Presidency* (preparatory to applying for furlough to Europe .—Dec. 29. Lieut. Interp. and Qu. Mast. G. D. Davies, 54th N I.

To *Cape of Good Hope.*—Dec. 21. Lieut. Wm. Baker, 9th L.C., for two years, for health.—Jan. 4. Capt. and Brev. Maj. D. D. Anderson, 29th N.I., for ditto ditto.—11. Major R. Fernie, 27th N.I., for ditto ditto.—18. Surg. John Grant, apothecary to Hon. Company, for ditto ditto.

To *Van Diemen's Land.*—Jan. 18. Lieut. J. R. Revell, regt. of artillery, for two years, for health.

His Majesty's Forces.

To *Europe.*—Capt. T. E. Wright, 29th Foot.— Lieut. C. Paterson, 11th L. Drags.—Lieut. G. S. Fitzgerald, 26th Foot.—Lieut. H. Croly, 63d Foot. —Capt. S. O Goodwin, 31st Foot.—Brev. Capt. H. W. Hassard, 39th Foot.—Lieut. A. Harper, 9th Foot.—Lieut. C. B. Roche, 45th Foot.—Capt. F. Blundell, 11th L.Drags—Lieut. P. D. Streng, 13th L.I.

SHIPPING.

Arrivals in the River.

Dec. 31. *Swallow*, Adam, from China, Singapore, &c.—Jan. 1. *Anna*, King, from Madras, &c. —2. *Gaillardon*, Bowman, from Macao, Singapore, &c.—3. *Bright Planet*, Richardson, from China.— 4. *Oriental*, Pigareaux, from Bordeaux; *Jessy*, Auld, from Penang.—7. *Trescott*, Lindsay, from Boston; *Corsair*, Cooke, from Singapore and Pe-

nang.—8. *Gironde*, Lagrauere, from Bordeaux.— 10. *Sophia*, Rapson, from China, Singapore, and Penang.—12. *William Gray*, Bartoll, from Boston.—13. *Tartar*, Rough, from the Straits.—15. *Sulimany*, McFarlane, from China and Singapore. —16. *Gabrielle*, Guesenec, from Bordeaux; *Amelia*, Hurcade, from Bourbon. — 19. *La Lucie*, Garignon, from Bourbon.—27. *Montrose*, Wall, from Liverpool.—Feb. 1. *Zenobia*, Owen, from London; *William Salthouse*, Roberts, from Liverpool.—2. H.M.S. *Raleigh*, Quin, from Madras; *William Harris*, Terry, from Sydney.—3. *Roberts*, Wake, from London and Madras; *Dauntless*, Pinder, from Bombay.—6. *Mary*, Simpson, from Sydney.—8. *Dennison*, Poole, from Liverpool.— 9. *Vestal*, Taylor, from Sydney; *Thistle*, from ditto.—17. *Joanna*, Denniston, from Greenock.— 28. *Mary Dugdale*, Worthington, from Liverpool. —29. *Larkins*, Ingram, from London; *Coromandel*, Boyes, from London, Cape, and Madras.— March 1 *Stirlingshire*, Scoby, from Liverpool.— 3. H.M.S. *Jupiter*, from England (with the new Governor-general) ; *Donna Carmelita*, Gray, from Bombay; *Consolation*, Demoly, from Nantes.

Departures from Calcutta.

Jan. 20. *London*, McLean, for Liverpool.— Feb. 3. *Salamandre*, Debia, for Bordeaux; *Hope*, Hughes, for Madras and New York.—7. *Washington*, for Philadelphia.—13. *Hero*, for Singapore and China.—25. *Montrose*, Wall, for London.—27. *Indien*, for Havre; *William Harris*, Terry, for Sydney; *Lucullus*, Durunteau, for Bordeaux; *Mary*, Simpson, for Sydney.—March 2. *Gabrielle*, for Havre; *Fanny*, Sherriff, for China.

Sailed from Saugor.

Jan. 1. *Earl Grey*, Talbert, for London. — 2. *La Petite Nancy*, De Trelo, for Bourbon.—Lunach, Jellicoe, for Bombay.—6. *Herefordshire*, Isaacson, and *Duke of Bedford*, Bowen, both for London.—7. *London*, Wimble, and *Robert Small*, Fulcher, both for London.—8. *George*, Balch, for Boston.—9. *Bombay Packet*, Garnock, for Liverpool.—11. *Lord Hungerford*, Farquharson, for London; *Vestal*, for Muscat; *Thistle*, for Rangoon; *Red Rover*, Clifton, for China.—12. *Water Witch*, Henderson, for China.—15. St. *George*, Thomson, for Bristol; *Exmouth*, Warren, and *Cullingwood*, Hookey, both for London; *Hindostan*, Mitchell, for Maldive Islands; *Elizabeth*, Baker, for Rangoon, &c.—17. *Cornwall*, Bell, for London; *Diana*, Hawkins, for Liverpool.—23. *Windsor*, Henning, for London; *Euphrates*, Hannay, for Liverpool.—Feb. 4. *Alexander*, Ramsay, for Sydney; *Resolution*, Jellicoe, for Bombay; *Broxbornebury*, Chapman, for London.—6. *Duke of Northumberland*, Pope, for London.—18. *Isabella*, Brown, for London.—20. *Irma*, for China. —28. *Emily*, Kilby, for London.—29. *William Salthouse*, Roberts, for Liverpool; *Oriental*, Pigareaux, for Bordeaux.

Freight to London (March 3)—Sugar and saltpetre, £5. to £5. 10s.: rice, £5. 5s. to £6.; indigo and silk, £6. to £7. 10s.

BIRTHS, MARRIAGES, AND DEATHS.

BIRTHS.

Nov. 21. At Powie, in the Azimgurh district, Mrs. Gould of a daughter (since dead).
30. At Mhow, in Malwah, the lady of Capt. C. G. Macan, 16th N.I., of a son.
Dec. 7. Mrs. R. Crofton, of a daughter.
8. At Dinapore, the lady of P. G. Cornish, Esq., 10th N.I., of a daughter.
9. At Futtyghur, Mrs. M. S. Hennessy, of a daughter.
— At Calcutta, Mrs. Ducas, of a son.
10 At Cawnpore, the lady of J. Reid, Esq., of a still-born son.
— At Cawnpore, the lady of C. M. Caldecott, Esq., C.S., of a son.
11. At Jubbulpore, the lady of C. R. Browne, Esq., 60th regt., assistant agent, Governor-general, of a son.
— At Cawnpore, the lady of Capt. Wm. Burlton, deputy com. general, of a son.
— At Kurnaul, the lady of Lieut. C. S. Reid, artillery, of a son.

15. At Chittagong, the lady of Capt. R. H. Jellicoe, 55th N.I., of a daughter.
19. At Lucknow, the lady of Lieut. Col. Monteath, 35th regt., of a daughter.
— At Dinapore, Mrs. J. H. Love, of a son.
20. At Chowringhee, the lady of E. Macnaghten, Esq., of a daughter.
22. At Calcutta, the lady of Capt. Wm. Boothby, of the *Emily Jane*, of a daughter.
— At Garden Reach, the lady of John Cowie, Esq., of a son.
— Mrs. Thomas Fraser, of a son.
— At Jounpoor, Mrs. Pushong, of a daughter.
23. In camp, near Jessore, the lady of Capt. T. P. Ellis, 52d regt. N.I., of a son.
— Mrs. F. H. Peterson, of a daughter.
— Mrs. C. F. Gwatkin, of a still-born son.
25. At Garden Reach, the lady of J. Dougal, Esq., of a daughter.
— At Calcutta, the wife of Capt. R. W. Wiseham, commander of the H. C. iron steamer *Lord William Bentinck*, of a son.
— At Chandernagore, the lady of W. Y. Woodhouse, Esq., of a son.
26. At Allahabad, the lady of F. Stainforth, Esq., C.S., of a son.
— Mrs. F. S. Bruce, of a son.
28. At Mynpooree, the lady of Capt. G. N. Prole, of a daughter.
— Mrs. J. B. Levesay, of a son.
29. At Calcutta, the lady of Capt. Clapperton, master attendant's department, of a son, still-born.
— At Calcutta, the lady of J. A. Terraneau, Esq., of a son.
30. At Lucknow, the lady of Brev. Capt. H. T. Raban, 47th N.I., of a daughter.
31. At Patna, the lady of J. C. Dick, Esq., C.S., of a son.
Jan. 1. At Mosufferpore, the lady of George Gough, Esq., C.S., of a son.
— At Bandel, Mrs. M. Godinho, of a son.
— At the Mussoorie Seminary, Mrs. Mackinnon, of a daughter.
2. At Sultanpore, Oude, the lady of J. J. M'C. Morgan, Esq., 63d N.I., of a daughter.
4. Mrs. C. Lefever, of a daughter.
6. At Nusseerabad, the lady of Brev. Capt. Naylor, 8th N.I., of a son.
7. At Dum-Dum, the lady of Capt. W. R. Maidman, artillery, of a son, still-born.
8. At Arrah, the lady of T. Sandys, Esq., C.S., of a daughter.
— Mrs. Wale Byrn, of a son.
— At Barrackpore, the wife of Mr. J. C. Robertson, of a son.
9. At Chowringhee, the lady of Ross D. Mangles, Esq., C.S., of a son.
10. At Barrackpore, the lady of Lieut. Col. Swinhoe, of a daughter.
11. Mrs. Richard Parmer, of a daughter.
— At Fort William, the lady of R. B. McCrea, Esq., H.M. 44th Foot, of a son.
12. At Allipore, the lady of George Dougal, Esq., of a son.
— At Howrah, Mrs. Jas. Carter, of a son.
13. At Calcutta, the lady of G. Evans, Esq., of a daughter.
— Mrs. James Wood, of a daughter.
14. At Neemtullah factory, the lady of T. B. Rice, Esq., of a son.
17. Mrs. J. Hullock, of a daughter.
18. At Calcutta, the lady of Lieut. W. Martin, 59d N.I., of a daughter.
19. Mrs. H. F. King, of a daughter.
Lately. At Cawnpore, the wife of Mr. James Flatman, of a daughter.
— At Meerut, the lady of Lieut. H. A. Stewart, of a son.

MARRIAGES.

Dec. 21. At Calcutta, Henry Thuillier, Esq., of the regiment of artillery, to Susanne, relict of the late W. H. Steer, Esq.
— At Calcutta, J. R. Lumsden, Esq., lieut. 63d regt. N.I., to Sarah Swain, only daughter of the Rev. G. H. Hough.
— At Berhampore, Mr. Wm. Hyde to Miss Mary Burford.
23. At Dacca, Lieut. John Macdonald, 50th regt. N.I., to Anne, daughter of the late Capt. Gardner Boyd, of the same regiment, and niece of Major Blackall, commanding the corps.
— At Bankipore, Robert N. Farquharson, Esq.,

to Marian Doyly, eldest daughter of Charles Tucker, Esq.
30. At Calcutta, Mr. Noah Davies to Mrs. Lavinia Rooney.
Jan. 1. At Chandernagore, Mr. A. A. Dassies, indigo planter, to Miss E. M. Blouet, second daughter of the late J. B. Blouet, Esq., of Furridpore.
— At Delhi, Lieut. R. H. Seale, 20th N.I., to Miss Taylor, daughter of J. H. Taylor, Esq.
2. At Calcutta, J. M. Manuk, Esq., to Hurripsimah Matilday eldest daughter of G. A. Aviotick, Esq.
4. At Calcutta, J. Oman, Esq., indigo planter, to Maria Jane Helena, eldest daughter of C. E. Eweler, Esq., indigo planter, both of Jessore.
— At Calcutta, Mr. John Hammerdinger to Miss C. F. D'Rosario.
5. At Calcutta, Mr. H. Williams to Mrs. Maria Jones.
7. At Calcutta, John Gale, Esq., Pundoul factory, Tirhoot, to Mary, second daughter of M. Stalkart, Esq., of Calcutta.
9. At Calcutta, Capt. W. H. Halford, 41st regt., to Mrs. Anna Gibbs, youngest daughter of the late Col. Innes Delamain, Bengal army.
12. At Calcutta, the Rev. A. B. Lish, of Cherrapoonjee, to Eliza Sophia, youngest daughter of the late S. Marston, Esq.
14. At Calcutta, W. P. Palmer, Esq., of the civil service, to Ellen Olympia, youngest daughter of the late Robert Thomas, Esq., of Calcutta.
— At Calcutta, Lieut. Francis Dashwood, horse artillery, to Jane, daughter of the late Major Skyring, Royal Artillery.

DEATHS.

Dec. 8. At Nusseerabad, after a long and trying illness, Elizabeth, wife of the Rev. W. Palmer, district chaplain.
14. At Futtehgurh, in his 24th year, Lieut. J. D. B. Ellis, of the Bengal artillery.
19. At Mundlaisir, near Mhow, Major R. W. Smith, commanding 6th L.C., Bengal estab.
— Mrs. Ann Creighton, aged 23.
20. At Calcutta, Mark Anthony Lackersteen, junior, Esq., aged 33.
— At Calcutta, W. V. Bennett, Esq., proprietor of the classical seminary, aged 38.
— At Chandernagore, Harriot, relict of the late J. J. Goodlad, Esq., of Commercolly, aged 33.
— At Chandernagore, F. Albert, Esq., indigo planter, aged 56.
21. At Kurnaul, Capt. Greene, of H.M. 31st regt. of Foot.
22. At Calcutta, Mr. George Williams, aged 26, son of Samuel Williams, Esq., head assistant to the court of Sudder Dewanny Adawlut and Nizamut Adawlut of Fort William.
— At Calcutta, John Francis Chopin, Esq., indigo planter, aged 59.
23. At Lucknow, the lady of Lieut. Col. George Moore, commanding the 59th regt N.I., aged 31.
24. At Calcutta, Thos. Colvin, Esq., indigo planter, aged 36.
25. At Calcutta, Elizabeth Lydia, wife of Mr. Wm. Cornelius, aged 33.
30. At Allahabad, Eliza, wife of Frederick Stainforth, Esq., of the civil service, and daughter of John Thornton, Esq., of Clapham.
31. At Seebpore, Master George G. D. S., fifth son of the late Mr. John Chew, H. C. Marine, aged 15.
Jan. 4. At Calcutta, Mr. Thos. Haycock, aged 32.
5. At Calcutta, Thos. Spens, M.D., assistant marine surgeon, aged 33.
7. On board the *Cornwall*, off the Botanical Gardens, Lieut. Col. Wm. Kennedy, deputy military auditor general, aged 49.
— Mrs. Anna Maria Brooks, aged 46.
— At Calcutta, aged 60, Mrs. Mary Evans, relict of the late Mr. Robert Evans.
9. Mr. Thomas J. Conran, aged 34.
10. Mr. A. Robinson, aged 17.
14. At Calcutta, Mr. John Voss, aged 43.
15. At Dacca, Mrs. Beglar, wife of Mr. D. M. F. Beglar, in her 50th year.
16. At Calcutta, Mr. William Kent, of the ship *Brosbornebury*, aged 26.
17. At Calcutta, Mr. C. J. Jones, aged 40.
18. At Intally, Master Chas. Wilson, aged 16.
Recently. At Canton, Capt. Baker, late of the country service.

Madras.

GOVERNMENT ORDERS, &c.

BRITISH SUBJECTS ARRIVING AT MADRAS.

Fort St. George, Oct. 20, 1835.—The Right Hon. the Governor in Council, with reference to Act 3rd and 4th of William IV., cap. lxxxv., clause lxxxi., is pleased to appoint the superintendent of police and chief magistrate, as the officer to whom all natural born subjects of his Majesty, not in the King's or Company's service, and not being natives of India, must report themselves on their arrival at Madras, from any port or place not within the Company's territories. At out-stations, the report is to be made to the nearest justice of the peace.

ALLOWANCES TO KING'S OFFICERS.

Fort St. George, Dec. 8, 1835.—The Governor in Council is pleased to publish the following extract from the Bengal regulations, and to declare the law laid down applicable to this presidency :

" Officers of his Majesty's service, promoted in India by the Commander-in-chief, draw, from the date of such promotion, Company's allowance of the advanced rank so long as they continue to do its duty.

" Officers of his Majesty's service, belonging to corps in India, promoted by his Majesty, draw Company's allowances from the date on which their promotion is notified in general orders by the Commander-in-chief, from which date their performance of duty of the advanced rank commences."

FEES ON COMMISSIONS.

Fort St. George, Jan. 5, 1836.—The Governor in Council is pleased to direct, that the aggregate amount of fees leviable on commissions issued to the Company's officers under this presidency, one moiety of which is credited on account of the Company's, and the other moiety on account of the King's commissions, according to the scale laid down in the G. O. by government No. 243, dated Aug. 5, 1834, shall, hereafter, be levied at once on the issue of the Company's commission, the King's commission being subsequently furnished to the party concerned so soon as received from the office of his Ex. the Commander-in-chief in India.

CONDUCT OF LIEUT. WEST.

Head Quarters, Choultry Plain, Jan. 15, 1836.—A case has recently occurred so peculiarly illustrative of that inclination to petty disputes, combined with a spirit of insubordination and contempt for authority, which has, of late, lowered the discipline of this army, and produced an endless succession of trials by courts-martial, equally inconvenient to the public service and discreditable to the parties implicated, that the Commander-in-chief has decided upon holding up the offender, in general orders, as an example to his brother officers.

Lieut. West, of the 32d regt. N. I., having purchased certain articles, the property of Mr. Nicholls of the civil service, acting second judge of the Western Division, allowed several months to elapse without any offer of payment. Mr. Nicholls, being about to embark for Europe, addressed a perfectly unobjectionable note to Lieut. West on the subject, to which the latter made no reply. Mr. Nicholls then appealed to the officer commanding the 32d regt. N. I.; a measure forced upon him by a disregard of the common courtesy of society, and of which Lieut. West, therefore, had no reasonable cause to complain; but he, nevertheless, saw fit to address a letter, extract of which is annexed in the margin,* to Mr. Nicholls, who thereupon brought the whole transaction to the notice of the Commander-in chief.

His excellency, after an attentive consideration of the whole correspondence, expressed his decided disapprobation of Lieut. West's conduct, and, trusting that calm reflection would have led him to perceive his error, required him to make a fitting apology, and to withdraw the insulting expressions, so improperly addressed to Mr. Nicholls. Lieut. West, however, has obstinately persevered in error, and disregarded the Commander-in-chief's instructions, upon the mistaken assumption, that, having once expressed his opinion of Mr. Nicholls, he could not conscientiously retract it with honour to himself!

Lieut. West will do well to avoid *hereafter* the discredit which attaches to the offer of gratuitous insult, to remember that stubbornness is not firmness, and to consider that the head of the army is the appropriate judge of that which regards the honour of officers serving therewith. It will require a long course of good and obedient behaviour to relieve Lieut. West from the imputation of insubordinate misconduct, under which he at present labours; and the Commander-in-chief trusts that he will profit by the lesson, and reflect upon the risk to which he would have been subjected, had not the departure of the complainant precluded his conduct being investigated by a general court-martial.

* " Having now concluded my pecuniary affairs with you, I cannot refrain from remarking, that I consider the means you have resorted to, as very indelicate and ungentlemanly. At present, I dare not take further notice of it, without you waive your commission. However, as I trust to meet you in England when *out* of the service, we shall *then* have an opportunity of speaking more fully on the subject."

This order to be read to Lieut. West by the officer commanding the provinces of Malabar and Canara, in the presence of the officers stationed at Cannanore, who are to be assembled for the purpose, and also to every corps and detachment of this army on its public parade.

CIVIL APPOINTMENTS.

Dec. 29. J. Rohde, Esq., to act as assistant judge and joint criminal judge of Chicacole, during absence of Mr. Arbuthnot.

Jan. 5. Lieut. Col. J. S. Fraser, 36th N.I., to be resident at Travancore and Cochin, from date of Mr. Casamaijor's embarkation for England.

A. F. Bruce, Esq., to act as collector and magistrate of Guntoor, instead of Mr. Neave, whose appointment to act has not taken place.

Hatley Frere, Esq., to be an assistant to principal collector and magistrate of Malabar, and to act as head assistant while Mr. White officiates as sub-collector in Mr. Smith's absence on leave.

19. W. H. Babington, Esq., to be sub-collector and joint magistrate of Cuddapah.

W. A. Morehead, Esq., to be assistant judge and joint criminal judge of Chingleput, v. Mr. Neave proceeded to Europe.

C. H. Hallet, Esq., to be sub-collector and joint magistrate of northern division of Arcot.

C. Whittingham, Esq., to act as registrar to zillah court of Combaconum, during absence of Mr. Tracy.

P. Irvine, Esq., to be an assistant to collector and magistrate of Vizagapatam.

W. A. Forsyth, Esq., acting assistant judge and joint criminal judge of Malabar, took charge of the auxiliary court at Tellicherry, on the 28th Dec., from G. Sparkes, Esq.

J. Rohde, Esq., acting assistant judge and joint criminal judge of Chicacole, took charge of the auxiliary court at Vizagapatam, on the 8th Jan.

M. Lewin, Esq., delivered over charge of the collectorate of Rajahmundry to C. Dumergue, Esq., head assistant collector of that district, on the 13th Jan.

Hugh Montgomerie, Esq., has reported his return to this presidency from Europe.

H. D. Cook, Esq., is admitted a writer on this establishment from the 28th Dec.

Attained Rank.—T. J. W. Thomas, as senior merchant, on 24th Dec. 1835.

Furlough.—Jan. 19. R. H. Williamson, Esq., to Europe, for three years, on private affairs.

ECCLESIASTICAL.

ARCHDEACONRY OF MADRAS.

The Right Rev. the Lord Bishop of the Diocese has been pleased to appoint the Rev. Henry Harper, M.A., to be archdeacon of the archdeaconry of Madras, v. Robinson resigned; date 8th Jan. 1835.

MILITARY APPOINTMENTS, PROMOTIONS, &c.

Fort St. George, Dec. 31, 1835.—*49th N.I.* Lieut. (Brev. Capt.) E. Roberts to be capt., and Ens. P. E. L. Rickards to be lieut., v. Swaine dec.; date of coms. 19th Dec. 1835.

Cadet of Cavalry W. N. Mills admitted on estab., and prom. to cornet.—Cadets of Infantry T. G. Oakes and S. G. G. Orr admitted on ditto, and prom. to ensigns.

Jan. 5, 1836 —*Infantry.* Maj. H. W. Hodges, from 34th L.Inf., to be lieut. col., v. Ritchie dec.; date of com. 1st Jan. 1836.

34th L.I. Capt. J. R. Haig to be major, Lieut. T. R. Crosier to be capt., and Ens. George Singleton to be lieut., in suc. to Hodges prom.; date of coms. 1st Jan. 1836.

Lieut. Col. J. Hanson, qu. mast. gen. of army

(having returned to presidency), to resume charge of his office and his seat at Military Board.

Lieut. A. B. Jones, 3d L.C., permitted to resig service of Hon. Company.

Jan. 8.—*5th L.C.* Lieut. Lorenzo Moore to be qu. mast. and interpreter.

7th N.I. Lieut. H. C. Goaling to be qu. master and interpreter.

12th N.I. Lieut. (Brev. Capt.) H. A. Hornsby to be qu. mast. and interpreter.

43d N.I. Lieut. C. M. Macleane to be qu. mast. and interpreter.

46th N.I. Lieut. Chas. Yates to be adjutant.

3d L.C. Cornet H. F. Siddons to be lieut., v. Jones resigned; date of com. 5th Jan. 1836.

Surg W. H. Richards permitted to retire from Hon. Company's service, from 8th Jan. 1836.

The services of Capt. G. P. Vallancy, 38th N.I., placed at disposal of Supreme Government, with view of his being employed in department of operations for suppression of Thuggee.

Head Quarters, Jan. 4, 1836.—Ensigns C. H. G. Roberts, 47th N.I., and H. D. Innes, 40th do., permitted, at their own request, to exchange corps.

The following young officers to do duty :—Cornet W. N. Mills with 3d L.C.; Ensigns T. G. Oakes and S. G. G. Orr with 12th N.I.

Ens. R. Wallace, 51st, to continue doing duty with 46th N.I., until 15th April, when he will proceed to join his corps.

Lieut. J. Fitzgerald, 42d N.I., to be a member of the committee assembled at Fort St. George for investigation of claims to pensions.

Jan. 7.—Assist. Surg H. S. Brice, of 30th regt. directed to rejoin his corps.—Assist. Surg. J. E. Porteous, of 39th, to do duty with 44th regt.—Assist. Surg. J. Cardew, M.D., to do duty with 45th regt.

Assist. Surg. D. Trail to have medical charge of detachment of sappers and miners, and convicts employed at Guindy under orders of Lieut. Cotton of engineers.

Jan. 8.—Lieut. George Foster, 49th N.I., to act as qu. mast. and interp., v. Roberts prom.

Jan. 9.—Ens. T. G. Oakes removed from 12th to do duty with 25th N.I.

Fort St. George, Jan. 12.—Maj. William Stewart, Madras European regt., permitted to return to Europe, and to retire from Hon. Company's service, from date of his embarkation.

Jan. 15.—Assist. Surg. John Ricks, M.D., to be surgeon, v. Richards retired; date of com. 8th Jan. 1836.

Assist. Surg. James Supple permitted to enter on general duties of army.

The periods of service of members of Medical Board directed to be calculated from following dates, when they should, respectively, have succeeded in regular tour :—Mr. T. H. Davies from 22d Feb 1831 ; Mr. J. Hay from 18th June 1831 ; and Mr. J. Annesley from 18th Jan. 1833.

Jan. 19.—Lieut. W. H. Budd, 31st L.Inf., to act as sub. assist. com. general, during absence of Lieut. Taylor, deputy assist. com. general.

Assist. Surg. John Richmond to be medical officer to zillah of Guntoor, v. Edgcombe permitted to proceed to Europe.

Deputy Assist. Commissary Wm. Brookes, to have rank of lieut. on non-effective estab.; date of com. 19th Jan. 1836.

2d N.I. Lieut. Robert Shirreff to be capt., and Ens. Arthur Wyndham to be lieut., v. Jeffries dec.; date of coms. 9th Jan. 1836.

Ens. R. Fletcher, 7th N.I., transferred to pension establishment.

Jan. 22.—*42d N.I.* Lieut. James Fitzgerald to be adjutant.

Lieut. Col. H. G. Jourdan, 10th N.I., permitted to retire from service of Hon. Company, from date of his embarkation for Europe.

Head-Quarters, Jan. 12.— Assist. Surg. Colin Rogers, M.D., of 44th, to proceed and take medical charge of 43d N.I., during absence of Assist. Surg. Davidson.

Jan. 14.—Ens. F. S. Gabb, 59d N.I., to act as qu. mast. and interp., v. Bayles proceeded to Europe.

Jan. 15 to 18.—Lieut. W. Gordon, 6th N.I., to be a member of committee assembled at Fort St. George for investigation of claims to pensions, in room of Lieut. J. Fitzgerald relieved from that duty.

Asst. Surg. C. Ferrier to do duty with H.M· 63d regt., until an opportunity offers for him to join H. M. 63d regt. at Moulmein.

Lieut. Col. H. W. Hodges (late prom.) posted to 2d regt. N.I.

Jan. 19 to 22.—*Horse Artillery.* Lieut. Hall to be adj. to C troop, v M'Nair.—Lieut. G. Briggs to be adj. to B troop, from 11th Jan. 1836.

Capt. M. Davies, 11th N I., relieved as a member of Clothing Committee assembled at Fort St. George.

Capt. R. Watts, 48th N.I., to be president, and Capt H. Roberts, 9th do., a member of above committee.

The following orders confirmed:—Lieut. Nicolay to act as adj. to Madras Europ. regt., during absence of Lieut. and Adj. W. M. Gunthorpe, 6th N.I., as adj.; Ens. H. F. Gustard, 6th N.I., as qu. mast. and interp.

Asst. Surg. W. G. Davidson removed from 43d to 49th regt.; and C. Rogers, M D., from 44th to 43d do.

1st-Lieuts. T. K. Whistler removed from 3d bat. to horse brigade artillery; and J. and C. McNair from horse artillery to 3d bat. do.

Lieut. W. Brookes, of non-effective estab., posted to 1st Nat. Vet. Bat.

———

Reward.—The following officers having passed the prescribed examination in the Hindoostanee language, are deemed by the Commander-in-chief entitled to the reward authorized by the Hon. the Court of Directors:—Lieut. and Adj. W. M. Gunthorpe, 6th N.I., as adj.; Ens. H. F. Gustard, 6th N.I., as qu. mast. and interp.

———

Returned to duty, from Europe.—Dec. 31. Capt. J. T. Baldwin, artillery.—Capt. C. E. Faber, engineers—Capt. A. C. Wight, 8th N.I.—Capt. M. Davies, 11th do.—Capt. R. W. Sparrow, 18th do. —Lieut. Jas. Fitzgerald, 42d do.—Lieut. John Millar, 43d do.—Jan. 5. Capt. Wm. Stokoe, 10th N.I.

———

FURLOUGHS.

To Europe.—Dec. 31. Capt. A. Derville, 31st L.Inf.—Jan. 5. Lieut. Col. J. Kitson, 23d N.I.— Maj. C. Maxtone, 1st N.V.Bat., for health.—Capt. E. T. Hibgame, 29th N.I., for health.—Lieut. D. Scotland, 7th N.I., for health.—g. Ens. E. H. Impey, 31st L.Inf., for health.—Superintending Surg. J. Macleod, for health.—Asst. Surg. G. Edgcome, for health.—Lieut. E. J. Simpson, 37th N.I. — 12. Lieut. J. F. Leslie, 13th N.I., for health. — 2d-Lieut. H. Lawford, artillery, for health.—19. Capt. Alex. Grant, 5th L.C.—Capt. C. H. Græme, 5th L.C.

To visit Presidency (preparatory to applying for furlough to Europe)—Jan. 7. Lieut. Col. M. Riddell, 2d L.C.—Lieut. J. S. Du Vernet, 24th N.I.— 11. Lieut. W. E. Lockhart, 45th N.I.

To visit Cannanore (preparatory to ditto).—Dec. 31. Lieut. H. Beaver, 3th N.I.

To visit Western Coast (preparatory to ditto.)— Lieut. W. Russell, 18th N.I.

To Sea.—Dec. 31. Lieut. Col. W. K. Ritchie, 2d N.I., for two years (since dead).—Jan. 5. Ens. H. Metcalfe, 29th N.I., until 31st Dec. 1836, for health.—8. Capt. A. G. Hyslop, com. of ordn., Nagpore subsidiary force, for twelve months (also to Cape of Good Hope).

To Bengal.—Jan. 22. Lieut. W. Darby, 45th N.I., from 1st Feb. to 31st July 1836, on private affairs.

To Benares.—Jan. 22. Lieut. Thos. Snell, 7th L.C., from 20th Feb. to 31st Aug. 1836, on private affairs.

To Neilgherry Hills.—Jan. 8. Capt. W. E. Litchfield, 6th L.C., for six months (also to Bombay).

SHIPPING.

Arrivals.

Dec. 30. *Clorinde,* Superville, from Coringa.— 31. H.M.S. *Algerine,* Thomas, from Penang.— Jan. 1. *John Wm. Dare,* Towle, from Moulmein. —4. *Jane,* Wilkins, from Coringa, &c.—5. H.M.S. *Andromache,* Chads, from Mauritius.—6. *Edward,* Land, from Calcutta. — 12. *Charles Dumergue,* from Vizagapatam.—13. *Cecelia,* Roy, from Port Louis.—14. *Premier,* Byron, from China, &c.— 17. H.M.S. *Raleigh,* Quin, from Trincomallee; *Joseph Victor,* Le Cour, from Bourbon.—19. *Mary Ann,* Tarbutt, from London.—22. *Napoleon,* Barbot, from Padang.

Departures.

Jan. 3. *Isadora,* Hodson, for Northern Ports.— 7. *Duke of Buccleugh,* Martin, for London.—10. *Edward,* Land, for Philadelphia. — 12. *Bolton,* Compton, for Cape and London.—13. H.M.S. *Andromache,* Chads, on a cruize.—14. *Cecelia,* Roy, for Covelong.—16. *Wellington,* Liddell, for Cape and London.—17. *Prince George,* Shaw, for London.—20. *Robarts,* Wake, for Calcutta.—22. *Joseph Victor,* Le Cour, for Calcutta.—25. *Lady Flora,* Ford, for London.

———

To Sail.—*Mary Ann,* for London, 15th Feb.

———

BIRTHS, MARRIAGES, AND DEATHS.

BIRTHS.

Dec. 10. At Hingolee, the wife of Mr. D. Alexander, of a daughter.

28. The lady of Lieut. Rowlandson, Persian interpreter at head-quarters, of a daughter.

— At Trichinopoly, the lady of Capt. E. J. Butcher, deputy assist. com. gen., of a son.

29. At Hingolee, the lady of Capt. G. W. Onslow, of the artillery, of a son.

31. At Guindy, Mrs. J. E. Cashart, of a son.

Jan. 1 At Secunderabad, the lady of Capt. Eades, 39th regt., N.I., of a son.

— At Vepery, Mrs. W. Axelby, of a son.

3. At Bangalore, the wife of the Rev. John Smith, of a daughter.

— At Nungumbaukum, the lady of Capt. Ely, deputy qu. mast. gen., of the centre division, of a son.

5. At Berhampore, near Ganjam, the lady of Lieut. Col. S. I. Hodgson, 49th regt., of a daughter.

— At Bangalore, the lady of Capt. Henry Bevan, 27th N.I., of a daughter.

— At Kamptee, the lady of Capt. Edward Simpson, Madras Europ. Regt., of a son.

8. At Waltair, the lady of Capt. Reece, 10th regt., of a son.

11. At St. Thomé, the lady of J. F. McKennie, Esq., of a son.

———

MARRIAGES.

Dec. 21. At Waltair, the Rev. W. T. Blenkinsop, chaplain, to Louisa, third daughter of the Rev. W. Chester, chaplain of Visagapatam.

Jan. 1. At Trichinopoly, J. M. D. Minto, captain of the 5th regt. N.I., to Miss C. M. Hichens.

6. At Calingapatam, John Campbell, Esq., of the 21st regt., to Miss Maria Henrietta Davis, niece of Capt. R. S. Dirkss, master attendant at that place.

8. At Madras, Lieut. H. C. Armstrong, engineers, to Eliza, youngest daughter of the late Lieut. Col. Rundall, of this establishment.

20. At Madras, Mr. Bernard Quintual, of the civil auditor's office, to Miss Caroline Gordon.

———

DEATHS.

Dec. 31. At Hyderabad, Mrs. Lee, wife of Capt. George Lee, of the 8th Madras N.I.

Jan. 1. At Cannanore, Edward Chamier, Esq., of the Bombay civil service.

— At Madras, Lieut. Col. W. K. Ritchie, of the 2d regt. N.I.

— At Madras, Capt. C. A. Kerr, late of the Hon. Company's service, who has lately taken so active a part in the Neilore copper mine speculation.

9. At Mangalore, Capt. A. H. Jeffrics, of the 2d regt. N.I.

Bombay.

GOVERNMENT ORDERS, &c.

ARMY RANK.

Bombay Castle, Nov. 27, 1835.—The Right Hon. the Governor in Council is pleased to direct, that, in conformity to the instructions of the Hon. the Court of Directors, bearing date the 28th Dec., 1832, and published to the army on the 31st May, 1833, army rank be assigned to the several officers promoted to the grade of ensign, under the operation of the rule here referred to, as well as prospectively to all others, from the date of their respective arrivals, and not, as at present, from the date upon which they may be finally posted to corps in succession to vacancies.

OFFICE ALLOWANCE.

Bambay Castle, Nov. 28, 1835.—In lieu of the office allowance (King's and Company's) at present drawn by paymasters of his Majesty's regiments on this establishment, the Right Hon. the Governor in Council is pleased to authorise, from the 1st proximo, the same scale as is drawn by the corresponding grade of his Majesty's service in Bengal.

A paymaster of Light Drags. Rs. 65 5 4
A paymaster of a regt. of Foot   78 10 8

The above allowances are inclusive of office rent and office tentage, and in lieu of writers, stationery, and all contingencies.

STEAM POSTAGE.

General Department, Nov. 28, 1835.—The Right Hon. the Governor in Council is pleased to republish the following scale of steam postage, fixed on the 6th inst., on letters sent to England *via* the Red Sea, exclusive of inland postage; and to announce, for the information of the public, that the same rates of steam postage will be collected on letters received from Europe, viz.

		Rs.	As.
On letters not exceeding a sicca weight, or ½ a tolah	....	0	8
1 ditto	....	1	0
2 ditto	....	1	8
3 ditto	....	2	0
4 ditto	......	3	0

and so on, one rupee being charged for every sicca weight or tolah.

CHARGE OF TROOPS.

Bombay Castle, Dec. 5, 1835.—Doubts having arisen as to what officer is in certain cases entitled to the charge of troops and companies, the Right Hon. the Governor in Council is pleased to establish the following rules on the subject, which are in accordance with the practice that obtains in Bengal:—

A cavalry officer returning, whether from furlough to Europe, leave beyond sea, or staff employ, is not entitled to the benefits of the troop contract until he rejoins his regiment.

An officer holding temporary charge of a troop, will lose the contract emoluments if absent, from any cause, for a period exceeding the 30 days in six months allowed, without forfeiture of such emoluments, by the regulations.

PIONEERS.

Bombay Castle, Dec. 15. 1835.—The Right Hon. the Governor in Council is pleased to direct, that the G. O. dated the 10th ultimo, for disbanding three companies of pioneers of the engineer corps, be suspended until further orders.

CONTROL OVER ENGINEER OFFICERS.

Bombay Castle, Dec. 19, 1835.—In order to prevent any misunderstanding, as to the degree of control to be exercised over engineer officers, while civilly employed, by their military superiors, the Right Hon. the Governor in Council is pleased to declare, that, although the military authorities have no power to interfere with the *duties* of any officer civilly employed, or to communicate any orders that can in any manner control their separate and distinct duties, still, as far as the general orders and usage of the service affect all classes, as in the case of regulations regarding dress, at the presidency or at military stations, or reporting their arrival at or departure from those stations, all engineer officers are strictly bound to obey those regulations, and the military authorities to enforce them, reporting to government, through his Exc. the Commander-in-Chief, any breach of them on the part of engineer officers civilly employed.

BHEWNDY CANTONMENT.

Bombay Castle, Dec. 28, 1835.—With reference to the G. O. of the 16th of April last, it is hereby announced that Bhewndy is no longer to be considered as a cantonment, and its military limits are abolished accordingly.

SIGNAL AT BOMBAY.

Notice.—Marine Department—The established signal at the several flag-staffs on the island of Bombay, for a schooner or a cutter, is a cylinder painted red.

CIVIL APPOINTMENTS, &c.

Political Department.

Jan 5. Mr. James Erskine to be political agent in Kattywar.

9. Mr. Arthur Malet to be first assistant to political commissioner for Guzerat and resident at Baroda.

Mr. Wm. Courtney to be second assistant to ditto ditto ditto.

Capt. James Outram, 23d N.I., to be acting political agent in Mahee Caunta.

Lieut. R. Wallace, superintendent of Guicowar contingent at Sadra, to officiate as assistant to political agent in Mahee Caunta.

Territorial Department—Revenue.

Jan. 13. Mr. George Waddell to be supernumerary assistant to principal collector of Poona.

Mr. D. Davidson to be assistant to collector of Tanna.

Mr. A. A. C. Forbes to be assistant to collector of Ahmednuggur.

Judicial Department.

Nov. 27. Capt. James Outram and Lieut. Joseph Hale to be assistant magistrates in the several zillahs comprehended within Bombay presidency.

Dec. 5. Mr. Chamier, acting assistant judge of Poona, to be acting assistant to agent for Sirdars in Deccan.

Jan. 14. Mr. J. L. Philips to act as master in equity, and Mr. D. B. Smith to act as clerk of the small causes, Supreme Court, during absence, on leave, of Mr. Wm. Fenwick.

20. Mr. J. L. Philips to act as examiner on the equity side, and Mr. O. W. Ketterer to act as ecclesiastical registrar of Supreme Court of Judicature, until return of Mr. M. T. West. Mr. J. L. Philips also to act as clerk of the crown, clerk of the indictments, clerk of the arraigns, and register on the admiralty side in criminal department of Supreme Court.

General Department.

Dec. 31. Mr. W. C. Bruce to act as deputy civil auditor and deputy mint master, during absence of Mr. Gregor Grant.

Separate Department.

Jan. 18. Mr. J. R. Morgan to place himself under orders of acting collector at Ahmedabad.

19. Mr. H. R. Stracy to place himself under orders of collector at Rutnagherry.

Mr. E. M. Stuart was examined in the regulations of government on the 31st Dec., by a committee assembled for that purpose, and was found quite competent to enter on the transaction of public business.

Furloughs, &c.—Dec. 9. Mr. J. D. Inverarity, to sea, for six months, for health.—Jan. 7. The furlough to Europe granted to Mr. H. W. Reeves on 7th Oct. last cancelled.—14. Mr. Wm. Fenwick, master in equity, leave of absence for one year, for health.

MILITARY APPOINTMENTS, PROMOTIONS, &c.

Bombay Castle, Dec. 2, 1835.—Capt. A. C. Peat to be executive engineer at Belgaum, v. Capt. C. W. Grant proceeding to England on sick cert.

Dec. 3.—Cadet of Infantry W. H. C. Lye admitted on estab., and prom. to ensign.

The services of Assist. Surg. A. Walker, M.D., placed at disposal of Supreme Government for employment in military service of H.H. the Nizam.

Dec. 4.—Capt. Foquett's appointment as commissariat agent at Rajcote cancelled, from date of delivering over charge to Lieut. Hartley.

Dec. 5.—The following temporary arrangements confirmed:—Lieut. A. Morison, 3d N.I., to act as fort adj. at Asseerghur, during absence of Lieut. Brown on duty.—Lieut. H. C. Morse, 8th N.I., to act as adj. to that regt., during absence of Lieut. F. Cristall.—Lieut. C. Rooke, 22d N.I., to act as qu. mast. and paym. to that regt., during period Lieut. Hart may be in charge of commissariat at Ahmedabad.—Ens. J. R. Kelly, 20th, to act as interp. in Hindoostanee and Mahratta to left wing 12th N.I., during absence of Lieut. Ash.—Capt. W. J. Browne, brigade major at Baroda, to assume command of that station on departure of Capt. J. Clunes.—Capt. C. Denton, 24th N.I., to act as major of brigade at Baroda, during period Capt. Browne may remain in command of station.

Dec. 7.—Lieut. D. C. Graham, second in command of Bheel corps in Candeish, to act for Capt' J. Outram, as commanding officer of that corps, during his absence on duty in Guzerat.

Dec. 25.—31st N.I. Capt. E. Mason to be major, Lieut. C. Clarke to be capt., and Ens. J. L. Hendley to be lieut., in suc. to Hamilton retired; date 20th Dec. 1835.

Dec. 29.—Assist. Surg. Hamilton to take charge of duties of civil surgeon of Rutnagherry, from 5th Dec., in consequence of the civil surgeon having been obliged by illness to leave his duties.

Dec. 31.—Lieut. J. Macdonell, 19th N.I., to command invalids of the season of H.C. service, proceeding to Europe.

Ens. H. Fenning, 23d, transferred, at his own request, to 21st N.I., he entering latter corps as junior of his grade.

Lieut. C. Shirt, 20th N.I., to act as adj. to left wing of that regt. on departure of head-quarters from Rajcote to Baroda, as a temp. arrangement.

Lieut. J. P. Major, 11th N.I., to be commissariat agent at Bhooj.

Jan. 4, 1836.—Lieut. T. Cleather, of Golundauze Bat., to act as interp. in Hindoostanee to 4th N.I., from 23d Dec., as a temp. arrangement.

Jan. 5.—Assist. Surg. Kirk, at present doing duty in Indian Navy, placed at disposal of Com.-in-chief.

Assist. Surg. Hughes placed at disposal of superintendent of Indian Navy, for duty in that branch of service.

Jan. 7.—Lieut. Ayrton, regt. of artillery, placed under orders of chief engineer, for performance of a special duty.

The recent G. O. placing Assist. Surg. Sullivan at disposal of Superintendent of Indian Navy cancelled; and in his room Assist. Surg. Winchester placed at disposal of superintendent.

Jan. 11.—3d L.C. Capt. J. Sutherland to be major, Lieut. D. C. F. Scott to be capt., and Cornet M. R. Daniel to be lieut., in suc. to Jameson dec.; date of rank 19th Oct. 1835.

Assist. Surg. David Forbes to be surgeon, v. Cockerill dec.; date of rank 24th Dec. 1835.

The following temporary arrangements confirmed:—Capt. J. Farquharson, 9th N.I., to assume command of station of Baroda, from 4th Dec.—Lieut. T. T. Christie, 17th N.I., to act as qu. mast. to that regt., during period Lieut. J. Pope may be in temporary charge of regt.—Capt. E. M. Earle, 24th N.I., to act as Mahratta interp. to that regt., from 5th Dec.—Lieut. J. C. Anderson, line adj. at Rajcote, to receive charge of commissariat department at that station from 7th Dec.

Lieut. and Brigade Major A. R. Wilson to act as assistant in qu. mast. general's department N.D.A., and to accompany Brig. Gen. Salter on his tour of inspection, during absence of Lieut. Del Hoste on duty at Tankaria Bunder; date 1st Dec.

Lieut. T. Christie, 17th N.I., to be commissariat agent at Hursole.

Capt. A. Maclean, commanding detachment of 8th N.I., at Tannah, assumed temporary charge of office of paymaster of pensioners in Concan on 4th Jan., in consequence of death of Capt. Stokoe.

Returned to duty, from Europe.—Dec. 3. Lieut. Col. J. Shirreff, European regt.—Capt. E. Stanton, artillery.—Capt. A. C. Peat, engineers.—Capt. J. D. Browne, 10th N.I.

To Europe.—Dec. 2. Capt. C. W. Grant, corps of engineers, for health.—Brev. Col. T. Morgan, 7th N.I., for health.—Jan. 4. Capt. J. S. Grant, executive engineer at Poonah.—7. Lieut. J. Anderson, 17th N.I., for health.—Lieut. G. N. Prior, 21st N.I., for health.—11. Ens. R. Jeffery, 19th N I., for one year (without pay), on private affairs.—15. Surg. J. M'Morris.—Assist. Surg. D. Gilerson, for health.

To Cape of Good Hope.—Dec. 2. Capt. J. Reynolds, 1st assist. com. gen., for eighteen months, for health.—Jan. 9. Capt. J. Gunning, 17th Madras N.I., for ditto ditto.—12. Col. Ballantine, for health (eventually to Europe).

To Neilgherries.—Dec. 2. 2d Lieut. G. K. Bell, regt of artillery, for two years, for health.

MARINE DEPARTMENT.

Jan. 4. Capt. E. W. Harris to be senior naval officer at Surat, from 19th Jan.,"in suc. to Capt. Brucks, whose time of service in that appointment, as limited by regulations, will have then expired.

SHIPPING.
Arrivals.

JAN. 1. H.C. brig of war *Thetis*, Harvey, from Porebunder, &c.: *Hannah*, McGregor, from China and Singapore.—8. *Lady Rowena*, Main, from Rio de Janeiro.—9. *Java*, Todd, from London.—16. *Lord Castlereagh*, Tonks, from China, Singapore, &c.; H. C. new cutter *Margaret*,' Gardiner, from Porebunder.—17. *Sophia*, Farahan, from Bushire and Muscat.—18. *Sir Archibald Campbell*, Robertson, from Bengal and Cannanore; *Quill*, King, from Salem (America).—19. *Caledonia*, Lancaster, from China.—22. *Seine*, Lemarie, from Havre de Grace and Cochin.—23. *William Metcalfe*, Philipson, from London.—FEB. Buckinghamshire, Hopkins, from London.—13. *John Campbell*, from Greenock.—14. *Centrian*, Killock, from Liverpool. —*Grenada*, Sulivan, from Liverpool.—21. *Trinculo*, Jeffs, from Liverpool.—MARCH 8. *Canton*, Gibson, from Liverpool; *Lord Lowther*, from China.—16. *Palmira*, Loader, from London.

Departures.

DEC. 31. *Cashmere Merchant*, Edwards, for Calcutta.—JAN. 1. H. C. cutter *Nerbuddah*, Carless, for Scinde.—3. H. C. brig of war *Thetis*, Harvey, for Surat.—4. *Malabar*, Tucker, for London.—10. *Marquis of Hastings*, Clarkson, for London.—12. H.C. sloop of war *Amherst*, Sawyer, for Vingorla. —16. *Carnatic*, Brodie, for London.—17. H.C. cutter, *Margaret*, Gardiner, for Surat.—23. *Tory*, Reid, for Liverpool.—30. *Lady Raffles*, Pollock, for London.—FEB. 15. *Java*, Tod., for London. —25. *William Metcalfe*, Philipson, for London.— MARCH 15. *Buckinghamshire*, Hopkins, for London.

Freight to London (March 18).—In consequence of the price of cotton getting up, freight has fallen to £6.

BIRTHS, MARRIAGES, AND DEATHS.
BIRTHS.

Dec. 7. At Girgaum, Mrs. W. Turner, of a daughter.
19. At Deesa, the lady of J. Bowstead, Esq., of a son (since dead).
21. At Baroda, the lady of Lieut. A. N. Ramsay, 24th N.I., of a son.
23. At Malligaum, the lady of Wm. Gray, Esq., surgeon, 21st N.I., of a daughter.
Jan. 2. At Bombay, the lady of H. Hebbert, Esq., C.S., of a son.
— At Dharwar, the lady of A. N. Shaw, Esq., of a son.
3. At Belgaum, the lady of Capt. Deshon, H.M. 20th regt., of a son.
5. At Deesa, the lady of Lieut. Williams, 13th N.I., of a son.
10. At Broach, the lady of Dr. W. B. Barrington, civil surgeon at that station, of a daughter.

MARRIAGE.

Jan. 14. At Bombay, Capt. Melville, deputy judge advocate-general of the army, to Catherine Mary, youngest daughter of John Robertson, Esq., of Tweedmouth, Berwick-upon-Tweed.

DEATHS.

Dec. 22. At Mazagon, Catherine, wife of Mr. Wm. Waddington, aged 27.
Jan. 2. At Fort George Barracks, Bombay, Capt. T. W. Stoccoe, of this establishment, aged 65.
6. In Colaba Barracks, Lieut. J. T. Latham, of H.M. 6th regt. of Foot.
12. At Bombay, Mr. Joseph Hannah, aged 70.

Ceylon.
SHIPPING.

Arrival.—Jan. 21. *Tigris*, from London.

BIRTHS.

Nov. 30. At Colombo, Mrs. J. C. Gerhard, of a son.
Dec. 27. At Kandy, the lady of Lieut. Roddy, Ceylon Rifles, of a daughter.

DEATH.

Nov. 25. At Colombo, Mr. G. R. Herft, interpreter of the Supreme Court, aged 51.

China.
SHIPPING.

Arrivals.—Dec. 24. *Neptune*, from London; *Coromandel*, from Liverpool.—28. *Derwent*, from Rio and Batavia.—JAN. 4. *Macclesfield*, from N.S. Wales.—5. *Canton*, from N. S.Wales; *Ann*, from Cochin; *Irt*, from Liverpool.

DEATH.

Nov. 18. At Canton, whilst bathing, Wm. Miller Jackson, Esq., third son of the late Col. G. J. A. Jackson, of the Hon. East-India Company's service.

Penang.
MARRIAGE.

At St. George's Church, Capt. James Rapson, of the barque *Sophia*, to Miss Anne Thompson.

New South Wales.
SHIPPING.

Arrivals.—Oct. 9. *Dawson*, from London.—Nov. 20. *Warrior*, from Calcutta.—28. H.M.S. *Zebra*, from Madras.—30. *Frances Charlottes*, from London.—Dec. 11. *Royal Sovereign*, from London.— *Jessie*, from Liverpool.

Van Diemen's Land.
SHIPPING.

Arrivals at Hobart Town.—Nov. 13. *John*, from London.—15. *Brothers*, and *Eldon*, both from London.—Dec. *Psyche*, from Calcutta.
Arrivals at Launceston.—Dec. 2. *Isabella*, from London.—20. *Protector*, from London.

Mauritius.
SHIPPING.

Arrivals.—Jan. 15. *Africanus*, from London and Ascension —Feb. 14. *Vicissitude*, from London.

Cape of Good Hope.
APPOINTMENTS.

Feb. 24. Hougham Hudson, Esq., to be agent-general for whole of the Kaffir tribes and families now under British jurisdiction. Mr. Hudson also to act as resident magistrate of district of Albany.

Theophilus Shepstone, Esq., to be Kaffir interpreter and clerk to the agent-general.

SHIPPING.

Arrivals.—Feb. 21. *Commodore*, from Liverpool. —24. *Upton Castle*, from London.—25. *Feejee*, from Liverpool.—March 9. *William*, from Greenock.— 10. *Courier*, and *Andromache*, both from London.
Departures.—Feb. 28. *Commodore*, for Ceylon.— 29. *Upton Castle*, for Bombay.—March 1. *Childe Harold*, for Bombay.—14. *Feejee*, for Manilla.

BIRTH.

Feb. 10. The lady of Martin West, Esq., of a daughter.

DEBATE AT THE EAST-INDIA HOUSE.

East India House, May 6.

A *Special* General Court of Proprietors of East India Stock was this day held at the Company's house, in Leadenhall-street.

EQUALIZATION OF SUGAR DUTIES.

The minutes of the last Court having been read,

The *Chairman* (W. S. Clarke, Esq.) said, he had to acquaint the Court that it was specially summoned, in consequence of the following letter, which had been addressed to the Court of Directors:

To the Honourable the Court of Directors of the East India Company.

Hon. Sirs,—We, the undersigned proprietors of East-India Stock, being duly qualified, request you will be pleased to call, at your earliest convenience, a Special General Court of the East-India Company, to take into consideration the propriety of petitioning the Honourable the Commons House of Parliament for the equalization of the duty on East and West-India sugar.

We have the honour to be,
Honourable Sirs,
Your obedient servants,

Thomas Weeding, Charles Forbes, John Locke, C. Fletcher, James Mackenzie, Henry Rowles, John Deans Campbell, T. Shore, R. Durant.

London, April 28, 1836.

Mr. *Weeding* said, he would, in the first instance, read to the Court a copy of the resolution which he meant to propose for their approbation, and which was as follows:—" That a petition be presented to the House of Commons, praying that sugar, the production of the British territories in the East-Indies, shall be admitted into the United Kingdom at an equal rate of duty with sugar imported from the British settlements in the Mauritius, America, and the West-Indies." The hon. proprietor then proceeded to observe, that this was a subject which had oftentimes been brought under the consideration of the Court, and, as its importance deserved, had met with the most serious attention. There was on these occasions, with very few exceptions, a general concurrence of opinion in the Court of Proprietors as to the justice and policy of equalizing the duties on East and West-India sugars. The present was a very favourable period for again demanding an equalization of those duties. The West-India interest was in a more prosperous state than it could boast of for many years; and this circumstance, independently of the large sum which Parliament had granted to the planters for the abolition of slavery, rendered the present time, of all others, the most fitting to call the attention of government to the claim which they were about to make—that claim being, that equal justice should

be extended to India. (*Hear, hear!*) He hoped that it was not necessary to go at length into a question which had been so often discussed; but still there were a few leading points, which were of such vital importance, and pressed so irresistibly on the subject, that he deemed it necessary briefly to notice them. In the first place, India consumed more of the manufactures of this country than any other British settlement. That was a fact which could not be controverted. Another important circumstance was, that India paid for her own protection. Did any other British settlement, he would ask, do the same? (*Hear, hear!*) Again, India, with a population of almost 100,000,000, was governed by England, and paid her governors for their care and assiduity in administering her affairs with a most generous and liberal hand. (*Hear, hear!*) But, not content with that, after they had retired from the service, they were remunerated with ample pensions, as the cheering reward of their past labours (*hear, hear!*),—and, he believed, there was scarcely a province in the United Kingdom that did not, in consequence, possess some of the wealth arising from that source. (*Hear, hear!*) These facts being admitted, was there not strong ground for them to call on the imperial Parliament to do speedy justice to India? That country admitted the woollen fabrics of England free of duty, and cotton and silk piece-goods of British manufacture at a duty of 2½ per cent. He asked, in return, to be allowed the importation of her manufactures into Great Britain on equal terms. At present, her manufactured cotton was loaded with a duty of 10 per cent. *ad valorem*, and her manufactured silk of 20 per cent. *ad valorem*. In calling for a system of reciprocity, she desired only to attain that which was strictly just and equitable. When she admitted our manufactures at a duty of 2½ per cent., had she not a right to demand that her sugars should be received on the same terms as those of the West-Indies? Under these circumstances it was that he wished her case to be clearly laid before the hon. the House of Commons. The voice of that Court would, he confidently hoped, reach the ears of those who were anxious to consult the general good. Let it not be forgotten, that the manufactures of India (for she once was a manufacturing country, though she did not stand in that position now) had been superseded by the superior skill and enterprize of the British manufacturer. (*Hear, hear!*) That circumstance alone surely afforded a suffi-

(P)

cient plea for sympathy and condolence—that circumstance alone afforded the strongest possible claim on the justice of the Legislature—and India asked for nothing more than equal justice. (*Hear, hear!*) These were a few points upon which he deemed it necessary to touch, as regarded the claims of India. He would next look at the subject as it regarded England. He contended that the equalization of the duties on sugar would be extensively beneficial to this country. If sugar were allowed to be imported from our Eastern possessions on the same terms that were imposed on its importation from the West-Indies, the effect would be a very great extension of British and Indo-British shipping. Sugar being a necessary of life, would be imported in large quantities—it would be received as payment for assorted cargoes—and thus employment would be afforded for ships to a much larger degree than at present, to the great benefit of the shipping interest. Again, as regarded the manufacturing interest, the alteration would operate most favourably. Give to the natives of India an opportunity of paying for your manufactures with their sugar, and they will infallibly purchase a much larger quantity of goods than they were now enabled to do under the exclusive system by which their produce was shut out. Why should they not be allowed, like other nations, to pay for our manufactures in produce, if they are not able to pay for them in specie? If this were permitted, they would take a much larger quantity of British goods, and thus the people of this country would be greatly benefitted, in a two-fold point of view—a more extensive market would be opened for manufacturing industry, and sugar would be obtained at a more moderate price. If the natives of India were allowed to make returns in kind, he was convinced that the export of British cotton manufactures would greatly increase; but that could not be expected so long as their sugars were kept out of the British market. He thought that it was perfectly clear, from the reasons which he had adduced, that the British ship-owner and the British manufacturer were deeply interested in the equalization of those duties, as that equalization was manifestly calculated to afford increased employment and activity to both. Now, he should be glad to know what the British ministers could say in opposition to this appeal on behalf of the natives of India. If they asserted—" We are prevented from agreeing to this proposition, because we are bound to protect another interest:" he would answer to that—" No, you are not; for you have given to that interest a very large sum of money, as an indemnity for any loss they may sus-

tain under the new order of things—the cultivation by free labour. If that be so, then we call on you, as a matter of justice, to act fairly and impartially towards India. We, therefore, desire to know, and we hope that you will be able to give us a good reason, if any such exist, why you do not think proper to interfere. But if you can advance no reason at all, then we demand at your hands the accomplishment of that promise which has so often been made, and which has as often been forgotten or evaded." (*Hear, hear!*) Before he went farther, he would read to the Court the petition which he had drawn up. In the first place, he should propose a resolution, that which had been read, pledging the Court that a petition should be presented to the House of Commons, praying that East-India sugar imported into the United Kingdom should only be liable to the same rate of duty as was levied on sugar the produce of the Colonies; and the following was the petition which he meant to submit to the Court:

> To the Honourable the Commons of the United Kingdom of Great Britain and Ireland in parliament assembled:
>
> The petition of the East-India Company respectfully sheweth—
>
> That your petitioners being invested with the sacred trust of the government of British India, deem it to be their duty to bring to the notice of your Hon. House:
>
> That sugar, the production of the British possessions in the East-Indies, is subjected to a duty of 32s. per cwt. in its importation into the United Kingdom; while sugar, brought from the Mauritius and the British Colonies in the West-Indies, pays a duty only of 24s. per cwt.
>
> That this difference of 8s. per cwt. imposed upon East-India sugar operates as a prohibition on the importation of it.
>
> That the natives of India being thus deprived of the best market for a great and valuable production of their soil, their industry is thereby impeded, the cultivation of their land is discouraged, and the general prosperity of the British empire, in its commercial relations with the most important foreign settlement of the British crown, is baffled, injured, and oppressed.
>
> In its effect, it tends largely to deprive the British and Indian shipowner of the opportunity of obtaining profitable employment for their ships; it narrows the means of making returns for British manufactures; it contracts the channels of remittance, wanted alike for the purposes of the Indian government and for its civil and military servants; while it exposes the people of the United Kingdom, the consumers of sugar, to the chance of paying an undue price for an article of the first necessity, by confining its importation to the West-India Colonies, and denying to the people of India their fair and unquestionable title to participate in the supply of it.
>
> Your petitioners therefore submit, that the inequality of the duty on sugar is detrimental and unjust to India as well as to Britain, and they implore your Hon. House to take immediate steps for the removal of it.
>
> And your petitioners will ever pray, &c.

The hon. proprietor then observed, that the natives of India were sensitively alive to this question, and were most anxious to obtain the concession asked for. In order to prove this, he would just read, with the permission of the court, a petition on this subject which had been recently put into his hands. It was a petition from the native and European inhabitants of Bombay, and had been presented a few days since to the House of Lords, by the Earl of Clare. The hon. proprietor then read the petition. The petitioners expressed themselves " deeply impressed with a sense of the disadvantages under which the products of India now laboured, in consequence of the application of a system of discriminating duties on various articles, which prevented them from entering into competition with more favoured British settlements. They complained, that while British manufactures were admitted at 2½ per cent., articles of Indian manufacture were subject to a charge of from 100 to 150 per cent. They declared that this system militated against the commercial interests of both countries, and they submitted that one more in accordance with the true principles of trade ought to be substituted. They observed, that, if their representation were not attended to, they should feel that they no longer had that claim on the consideration of the British Legislature which they had always believed that India possessed." This petition was signed by a great number of the European and native population of Bombay, and he had only troubled the court with it to prove that the natives of India were perfectly alive to this subject, and were most anxious to have their just claims allowed. If, therefore, it was their duty, at all times, to endeavour to procure justice for India, under existing circumstances, it still more behoved that court and the Company to take every opportunity of petitioning, and even of remonstrating, if necessary, with the Government on this subject. (*Hear, hear!*) If redress were refused, he knew not what remedy they had, except, as governors of India, sending out to that country, and saying, " We must place a countervailing tax on British manufactures. (*Hear! from Sir C. Forbes.*) They must demand justice from the people of England ; and if they refused to relieve the natives of India from the burdens of which they complained, it would be necessary that they should extend equal and even justice to them, by laying on British manufactures an impost to the same amount as was levied on the products of India. (*Hear, hear!*) This, he knew, was a very delicate and difficult point. He, however, only wished to give fair protection to India. We had destroyed the muslin manufacture of that country, and it was only just that our market should receive, on an equitable footing, the sugars and other produce of the Indian soil. It was on this principle of fair dealing that commerce ought to be bottomed, and it was clearly the only principle by which the prosperity and comfort of the natives of India could

be secured. This was a subject which had heretofore been frequently discussed in that court, and he dared to say that there would be no dissenting voice from the proposition which he was about to submit for their approbation. If, however, any hon. proprietor should oppose it, he would reserve to himself the right of answering his objections in the best manner he could. He hoped, however, that the feeling of the court would be unanimous as to the necessity of carrying the point which the petition had in view, that of doing justice to India, and, at the same time, rendering essential service to this country.

The resolution and petition having been read by the clerk,

Mr. *D. Campbell*, in seconding the motion, said, he would take that opportunity of expressing the great pleasure he felt at the agitation of this most important question in the Court of Proprietors. The liberal principles which the petition embraced, and which had, on different occasions, been so ably advocated on both sides of the bar, must command the approbation of every unprejudiced mind. As the Company were now relieved from the incongruous situation of traders, the Directors would have a full opportunity to devote their time and attention to the welfare of India, and he hoped that they would fulfil with anxious care and attention the important interests that were entrusted to them. When the natives of India learned the deep interest which the Company took in their prosperity, it could not fail to inspire them with a just feeling of the advantages which must result from their connection with this country. He viewed this effort to open a market for the products of India as the first movement of the key of that casket in which was locked up the brightest jewel of the British crown ; and, at no distant period, they would see that—the most precious gem of the world—sparkling in all its native brilliancy. The real value of India did not consist in what was collected from its hundred millions of inhabitants ; it was to be sought for in the bowels of its fertile soil, and in the extent and variety of its products. These formed the real treasures of India ; and skill, capital, and enterprize were only wanted to render them available, and thus to add to the power and wealth of both India and England. They were now in a condition to petition the Legislature—and, he trusted, with a good prospect of success—for the concession to India of privileges that should never have been withheld. The Company required millions annually, to meet the dividends, interest on loans, salaries, pensions, warlike stores, &c., which must be supplied by India. And how, he would ask, was that country to meet the demand, when we had nearly annihilated her industry, by inundating India with our manufactures, which we could afford to dispose of at very moderate charges? They could not be met, unless we afforded a market for the products of India. Under these circumstances, to deny to India the means of disposing of her produce, was to do an act of positive injustice and oppression. We complained of restrictions placed on our trade by the Chinese; but what was our connection with China, as compared with the relation in which we stood to India? The natives of India, whose produce we refused, had much more reason to complain of us, than we had to complain of the Chinese. The latter did not insist on our admitting their teas, and, therefore, they had a right to deal, as best suited them, with our manufactures. But we acted differently towards India. We sent to that country an immense quantity of manufactures; but we refused, in return, to receive the produce of India. The Chinese did not expect any thing from us—they did not ask us to trade with them. Why then should we complain of any restriction which they imposed, at the moment when we were treating India upon a principle of policy which was not only absurd but unjust! He trusted that this would be the last time they should be obliged to supplicate the Legislature to grant as a boon that which could not be 'without injustice denied,—namely, the admission into Great Britain, upon equitable terms, of the staple produce of their Indian territories. He should like, in common fairness, to ask, whether the West-India interest could put forth any fair claim for the continuance of these discriminating duties? No less than £20,000,000 had been granted to that interest, for the very tardy and reluctant annihilation of the slave trade. But, on the other hand, far from doing any thing for India, whose manufactures they had destroyed, they were constantly draining that country of large sums of money. He would say, let India, which possesses so many advantages, be properly encouraged—let her be treated as other British possessions were treated, which did not possess any such powerful claim for favour and protection. He was perfectly sure, that, by pursuing such a course of policy as he was pointing out, India would be rendered prosperous and happy, and England would reap a proportionate benefit. India, wealthy and prosperous, would indeed, as he had already observed, be hailed as the brightest jewel in the British crown. The details of the question had been so well brought forward by the hon. mover, that he did not deem it necessary to detain the Court

with any farther observations. He entirely concurred in the true and eloquent statements contained in the petition; and he entertained a confident hope that the Court of Directors would use their most strenuous exertions, to impress on the Legislature the necessity of complying with its just and moderate prayer. By that means the people of India, whose claims had been too long resisted, would be induced hereafter to place confidence in the justice and wisdom of the British Legislature. Impressed with these sentiments, he most heartily seconded the motion. (*Hear, hear!*)

Mr. *Fielder* said, though he had on many occasions stated his opinions on the subject of the sugars of India, still he could not refrain from availing himself of every opportunity to do justice to the natives; and he therefore requested the Court's attention while he offered a few observations on a question most important to the natives of India, and equally so to the character and the real interests of the India Company, and of the British nation. It had been repeatedly urged by the enemies of India, that its Company seeked benefit at the expense of the West-India colonies, and it had been also roundly asserted, that the East, after having borrowed the sugar-cane from the West, was now endeavouring to monopolize the whole of the English sugar market, and, in fact, to effect the total ruin of the West-India colonies. Such being the case, he deemed it a duty to refer to a most elaborate treatise and report in 1792—a work hardly equalled by the heart and pen of man for its humanity, usefulness, and sound policy. He referred to it to show that, notwithstanding the existence at that time, and for many years before and subsequent thereto, of what was termed the Company's monopoly of tea and other Eastern productions, it was always considered that the discriminating duties as regarding the produce of the cane, was any thing but sound English policy, humane or just. If these sentiments were well-founded under such circumstances, what, he would enquire, must be considered the conduct of the English government towards India since the act of 1833, which deprived the Company of its commercial pursuits in both India and China, and, consequently, of its means and power in aiding and assisting India in its necessary remittances for payments in England. (*Hear, hear!*) He would show that the cane was not a native, but an exotic of the New World—that the East had not robbed the West of it—but that the latter was indebted to the former for an article which had been from time immemorial the staple commodity of Bengal, and a source of great commerce and wealth throughout India. It appeared by this excellent report, and also by other works, ancient and modern, that the Eastern world had justly claimed the truly valuable cane plant as her own, as a native of her own soil. (*Hear, hear!*) It is traced from India to Cyprus; from thence, in the 12th century, to Sicily; and, early in the 15th century, it took root in the soil of Madeira and of the Canaries. It afterwards found its way to the American continent, and so much was it appreciated by the Portuguese, so well aware were they of its intrinsic value, that it became a subject of their first consideration, in so much as to enable them from Brazil alone to supply all Europe with the useful and nutritious article of sugar. In the beginning of the 16th century, the cane was first planted in Hispaniola, Mexico, Chili, and Peru, where it rapidly flourished to a great extent. At this period, and for more than a century after, the cane was entirely unknown to the English, at least it was not planted by them in any one spot in the west, for it is distinctly averred that the first cane ever planted by the English in that quarter was in Barbadoes, and then not until the year 1641. (*Hear, hear!*) He deemed it only just to state, that owing to discriminating duties, most unjust to India, the West-India colonies had, year after year, been hindering India, who had first supplied Europe and America with her native plant, from putting forth her gigantic strength in industry and commerce, and preventing her thereby from adding to those resources which were necessary, not only to carry on her own government, but to enable her to make the great annual remittances of millions for payments in England. (*Hear, hear!*) He felt warranted in stating this much, for he found in every work he had read that India, if put on a footing with the West-India colonies in point of duties, notwithstanding the great difference as to distance and freight, that the cane would be multiplied, as it formerly had been, to that extent as to meet every demand, and thereby enable England to command the sugar market throughout Europe. (*Hear!*) It appeared that the East-India sugars were preferred to those of China, Manilla, and Batavia, and that they had been for a very long period the staple articles of Bengal, whereby such a considerable trade was carried on, that there flowed into Bengal alone in 20 years no less a sum in specie than 60 lacs of rupees. He said it was lamentable that the great trade of the Dutch in Batavian sugar rose only on the decline, or rather on the ruin of the sugar trade of India, nothing less than by English unjust conduct, a Dutch colony flourished on the ruins of the best colony England ever had, or ever will possess. All writers

agreed that if the cane did not meet with due encouragement, the trade of India would, as a matter of course, be drawn into foreign hands; moreover, that the sugar trade of India was vitally essential to the British consumer, and to the prosperity of the public revenue. It, therefore, appeared clear, that the cane had not only been a blessing to India, as respecting industry, commerce, and wealth, but equally so to the British dominions for more than two centuries. (*Hear!*) He regretted to say that the introduction of the cane into the western world had been far from a blessing; it had been the bane of the Spaniard, and looking to the waste of blood and of treasure in St. Domingo, it had been a curse to the French nation. And as respecting the British West-India colonies, he sincerely hoped that the cane there planted would not be attended with the same consequences to England as it had been to Spain and France. This he must say, that the cane in the West-India colonies was not, and he feared never would be, to England a blessing, cultivated as it was by forced and unnatural labour; while the natives of the East were, at the same time, by the imposition of unjust and partial duties, prevented from cultivating the cane on its own soil, in a way that was most natural, most beneficial, and most pleasing to themselves. (*Hear, hear!*) Mr. Fielder said that he had no doubt, if proper exertions were made, that Parliament would now do justice to India, not for the sake of the natives only, but for the character and for the real interests of the English nation at large, as every reflecting person well knew that the remittances from India in favour of England must entirely depend upon the industry of the Hindoo, and upon opening a market for the produce of his native soil—and though last, most material, also depend upon the convincing all India that the English nation, instead of wishing entirely to ruin the manufactures, and to limit the productions of their country, would put her on equal footing with the other colonies—in short, treating England and India as one country, and the English and Hindoos as one people; thus so firmly cementing with England a country of more than half a million of square acres in extent, with a population of 100 million of inhabitants, as to defy the rest of the world to separate them. (*Hear, hear!*) In alluding to Parliament, he would make mention of the hon. ex-Director, Mr. Fergusson, and, with the Court's permission, he would give an extract of his speech in 1834, on the subject of India and her sugars:

He (Mr. Fergusson) complained that, while this country had voted 20 millions to the West-India planters, the trade and the general interests of

India had been so very much neglected by his Majesty's government. The duty upon East and West-India sugar was very different—this difference always being in favour of the West-Indies. While the country was making so many sacrifices for the West-Indies, the interests of India should not have been neglected as they hitherto had been. This house had cast additional burdens upon the people of India by the bill of last year, and he did expect that something would have been done for their relief before the present day. It was a gross injustice to India that her sugars should not be imported at as low a rate of duty as those of the West-Indies. The time was rapidly advancing when the interests of India must be considered. The productions of India should be equally favoured with those of our other colonies, for at present, while we were conceding a reciprocity to foreign nations, we positively denied it to India. He trusted the interests of India, particularly as to the sugar trade, would be fully considered, for it really was too bad that India should be depressed in consequence of the financial policy of this country. It was a scandal that an undue preference should have been so long given to the West-Indies at the expense of India.

Mr. *Fielder* said, such was the manly and honest declaration of Mr. Fergusson at his post in the British senate, on behalf of the natives of India, at the same time to confer a lasting benefit to the English nation. He would also advert to the language of Mr. Hume, an hon. proprietor, and also a member of the House of Commons, who in that place last year openly declared—

That for the last fifteen years he had heard, year after year, promises of justice being done to India, and he hoped they would now be speedily fulfilled. We had by our policy been ruining the commerce of India, and he feared that, unless a more liberal course were promptly adopted, we should be unable to maintain that empire and the necessary establishments there. He hoped the session would not pass without the subject being fully brought under the consideration of the house, that all parties might know what was to be done hereafter. If the government should not do justice to India, he should be happy to join his hon. friend (Mr. Ewart) in forcing that tardy measure of justice, which had been so long delayed. No colony belonging to any country had ever been treated by the mother country as India had always been treated by England, and he hoped the injustice would at length be put an end to.

He (Mr. *Fielder*) said, he felt it to be his bounden duty to state these facts; to show that for the last sixty years, notwithstanding the Company's alleged monopoly, it had been invariably deemed essential to encourage the sugar cane of India, not only to give full employ to the industrious and faithful Hindoo, but also to continue India to be such a colony as to be of the first importance to the mother country. He had ever understood it to be an admitted maxim, that impoverishing the colony, by taxation or otherwise, tended also to weaken the home dominions. This maxim in modern times had been painfully illustrated and realized with respect to Old and New Spain, England and America, France and St. Domingo. On the other side is seen, that colonies progressing in industry and fruitfulness naturally return for just and impartial management a mine of character and wealth to their parent countries. (*Hear, hear!*) Mr. Fielder then observed, that as the commercial charter had been wrested from the East-India Company, the proprietors, and others having claims upon the Company, were in a great measure reduced to depend on the good management of India for their dividends, capital, stock, and annuities; only holding that empire, not by the handful of Europeans, but by possessing the confidence, good-will and opinion of the natives. The proprietors present were assembled not merely for themselves, but on behalf of upwards of 3,000 absent proprietors, including the widow and the orphan, and were bound to use every honest means to render justice to the natives of India, and in so doing India would be well enabled to raise herself again high in the estimation of other nations; and by giving full employment to her numerous population, she would make the large annual remittances necessary for payments in England, with ease to herself, and with great benefit to the British nation. (*Hear!*) He earnestly called on the Court of Directors to exert themselves with members of parliament to give their support to the petition, in order that justice might be done to India. He earnestly entreated the Court of Directors not only to cause the petition to be presented, but that they would exert all their parliamentary and other interest, for the purpose of carrying it into effect. From 1792 up to the present time, a period of 44 years, it had been an admitted maxim, that that which was now prayed for ought to be conceded. Such being the case, the proprietors would not be doing their duty if they did not call on the Court of Directors to exert every nerve, in order that justice might be rendered to the finest colony England ever possessed—to the finest colony that belonged to any power in Europe. (*Hear, hear!*)

Colonel *Sykes* said he had, for a long period, carefully considered this question; and three or four years back he had stated his views with reference to it in that court. He was clearly of opinion that in the removal of the heavy India duty on East-India sugar and other Indian products, was involved the welfare of the manufacturing interests of this country. In the observations he had to make he would confine himself to two chief points: the *injustice* of discriminating duties as they affected the people of India; and their *impolicy* as they affected the productive industry of Great Britain. He perceived, with reference to the first point, as was manifested by official documents, that we received from India an excessively small quantity of cotton and silk goods, upon which a very large duty was payable; while we sent out an immense quantity of our manufactured cottons and silks, on which a duty of only two and a-half per cent. was charged. Was there, he would ask, a shadow of justice in such a proceeding? We imposed a duty of ten per cent., *ad valorem*, on the manufactured cotton of India, and twenty per cent., *ad valorem*, on manufactured silk; while we exported our silk and cotton fabrics to India at a duty of two and a-half per cent.; treating, in fact, India as a foreign country, indeed worse than a foreign country, for we should not have the temerity to venture upon the same practice where retaliation was to be expected. This was, indeed, an unfortunate type of that *recipocrity* in commercial relations for which England was so clamorous at the present moment! Oh, it was no doubt just to crush the manufactures of India by an almost prohibitory impost, while we inundidated the country with our own manufactures nearly duty free! Indeed so reckless were we of the consequences of our selfish policy, that, not satisfied with having reduced the silk and cotton manufactures of India to the greatest state of depression, (the importation of cotton piece goods having diminished from 1,245,722 pieces in 1829, to 268,877 pieces in 1834,) that we were now taking away the very means of subsistence, trifling as they were, from the poor; we were depriving the aged and infirm female of her spindle, by which she had been accustomed to earn a scanty livelihood, for in 1833 and 1834 respectively, there were exported to India 4,783,794 and 4,267,653 pounds weight of cotton twist and yarn. (*Hear, hear!*) The operation of the discriminating duties of thirty-two shillings per cwt. on the sugar of British India, while that of the West Indies and Mauritius was charged only twenty-four shillings, drove the former nearly out of the market. He held in his hand a detailed account of the importation of sugar from the Mauritius and India, from the years 1827 to 1834, inclusive: the duty on Mauritius sugar being twenty-four shillings, and that on East-India sugar thirty-two shillings:—

IMPORTS OF RAW SUGAR.

	MAURITIUS.	INDIA AND CEYLON.
	Cwts.	Cwts.
1827	204,344	166,086
1828	350,569	155,346
1829	297,452	188,722
1830	485,326	252,029
1831	516,076	185,572
1832	527,904	131,654
1833	525,017	153,994
1834	553,889	101,997

It was thus seen that the sugar imported from the Mauritius was 204,344 cwt. in 1827, but in 1834 it had increased to

553,889 cwt. The sugar imported from India and Ceylon in 1827 was 166,086 cwt., and in 1834 it had fallen to 101,997 cwt. Here it appeared that there had been imported from the Mauritius, a mere speck in the Indian Ocean, more than five times the amount of sugar imported from the immense territory of India; the light duty had proved an annual stimulus to industry in the Mauritius, and the heavy duty had paralyzed industry in India. Of an analogious character were the duties on coffee. West-India coffee paid sixpence per pound, and until 1835 East-India coffee paid ninepence per pound duty; in 1835 it was reduced to sixpence. By the returns made up to the 5th of January 1835, it appeared that 9,951,141 pounds of coffee were imported into Great Britain from the East-Indies and the Mauritius, but of this quantity it was necessary again to send out of the country 6,303,562 pounds, the high duty disabling the importer from selling it at a profit. Here the humble classes in England had good cause for complaint (as well as the people of India), by having been disabled from *extending* their consumption of a most salutary berry by an impolitic impost. With regard to the second point of his argument, if the people of India could not dispose of their produce to us, they must, of necessity, send it to foreign countries, and he would ask, would such a proceeding be for the benefit of the people of England? Commerce, he contended, could only exist by barter, and merchants sending their goods to India must receive Indian produce in return, and the prosperity of such an intercourse would be commensurate with the amount of the products interchanged. It appeared that the shipments to India had fallen off for several years. Why had these shipments decreased? Simply because the produce of India could not be received in return for our goods. The declared value of all shipments of British and Irish produce and manufactures to the Company's territories and Ceylon (China being excluded) in 1827, was £3,662,012, while in 1834, the value had decreased to £2,578,569, exhibiting a difference of £1,083,443. For the intermediate years between 1827 and 1834, China is *included* with India and Ceylon in the returns, and the decline for each year cannot be stated; but in the following table of all exports from Great Britain to *all* places eastward of the Cape of Good Hope (*except China*) there is sufficient evidence of a gradual diminution:—

EXPORTS.

1827.	1828.	1829.
£4,636,190	£4,467,673	£4,100,264

1830.	1831.	1832.
£4,087,411	£3,635,051	£3,750,286

Shewing a difference of £885,904 between 1827 and 1832. It might be attempted to account for this difference by a fall in prices, the quantities exported remaining the same, but the returns would not support such an attempt:—

BRITISH WOOLLEN MANUFACTURES EXPORTED TO ALL PLACES EASTWARD OF THE CAPE OF GOOD HOPE (EXCEPT CHINA):

1829.		1830.	
Pieces.	Value	Pieces.	Value.
96,460	£372,497	97,223	£344,398

1831.		1832.	
83,412	£281,438	71,809	£2,37,509

In cotton manufactures the same results are seen:—

COTTON MANUFACTURED GOODS EXPORTED TO INDIA AND CEYLON.

1833.

Total declared.	Value.	£. 1,497,992
Twist and Yarn.	Value.	£. 326,353
	lbs.	4,783,794
Hosiery and small Wares.	Value.	£. 24,153
Printed Cottons, &c.	Value.	£. 333,408
	Yards.	11,529,460
White or Plain Cottons.	Value.	£. 819.078
	Yards.	32,226,450

1834.

Total declared.	Value.	£. 1,274,804
Twist and Yarn.	Value.	£. 315,183
	lbs.	4,267,650
Hosiery and small Wares.	Value.	£. 15,717
Printed or Dyed Cottons, &c.	Value.	£. 221,317
	Yards.	7,983,527
White or Plain Cottons.	Value.	£. 722,187
	Yards.	30,988,532

The several imports from Great Britain into the presidencies of Bengal, Madras, and Bombay, from 1828-9 to 1831-2 inclusive, exhibits the same features. In the first period they amounted to £3,362,227, and in the last to £2,592,531, and the total imports into those presidencies for the same periods from Great Britain, foreign Europe, and North and South America, show a difference between £3,992,420 and £3,133,401; whilst, therefore, foreign countries, in their intercourse with India had a diminished demand for their products to the value only of £89,329, Great Britain experienced a diminished demand of the value of £769,696. The difficulty of obtaining produce from India compelled the English merchants engaged in the direct trade with India, to take treasure instead of produce; in 1822-3 the sum of £943,095 was withdrawn from India, and in the preceeding year, including money sent to England by the Company, the sum was £7,611,669; the whole amount from 1811-12 to 1832-33 being between seven and eight millions. Now, although treasure is merely a commodity for barter like other commodities; it is not reproducible periodically like cotton from a shrub, indigo from a herb, or saltpetre from the earth; and the draining a country of its precious metals was inflicting upon it a serious injury, by deranging its inter-economical relations, and undermining its commerce. In fact India could not have stood the drain upon it so long, but for the importations of treasure from foreign Europe, North and South America, and China. Great difficulties might be experienced in providing specie to meet the demands of those who exported their goods from England. It was plain, therefore, that the system was not a healthy one, nor likely to be permanent. Merchants would not send their goods to India, unless assured of a profitable re-return. If, however, there were an equalization of duties, interchangeable products would be multiplied, and commerce extended; but, if the present system were continued, the exports to India must go on diminishing, as they had done, and those who supported discriminating duties must be looked upon as adhering to them on selfish grounds alone, and not with reference to the general welfare of this country, or the interests of its manufactures, which they evidently were not calculated to promote. In the *Quarterly Review* for December 1835, there was an elaborate article to prove that sugar could not be imported from Bengal at a less cost than forty-three to forty-three and sixpence per cwt. ; while in March, June, and September 1834, West India sugar was selling in the English markets at from twenty-nine shillings and five-pence to thirty shillings and a halfpenny per cwt. He only noticed it to show the absurdity of protective duties for the West India sugar, in *case the Reviewer was right*, as the cost of the protection of the India sugar was a sufficient protection. We were the natural protectors of India,—no, he would not say the *natural* protectors, because the annals of all nations showed nothing so *unnatural*, as that a portion of the inhabitants of a small island should be the protectors of 100,000,000 of people, at the distance of a quarter of the globe,—but he would say, that they, being the *legal* protectors of India ought to apply themselves seriously to a due consideration of the interests of that country, in order that they might procure long-withheld justice for an ill-treated people. They ought not to take up this subject in a cold and apathetic spirit, but with that energy, zeal, and perseverance, that resulted from a philanthrophic stimulus. He had formerly expressed a hope in that court, and he did not hesitate to express it again, that the growing intelligence of the people of India might speedily enable them to give that moral force to the manifestation of their

Asiat. Journ. N. S. Vol. 20. No. 78.

just wishes, that no party, or local interest in Great Britain, could safely resist.

Sir *C. Forbes* said he should take up the time of the court for a very few minutes ; but he should be sorry to allow this question, which possessed so much interest, to be brought to a conclusion without stating his sentiments upon it. After what had been said on the subject by the honourable mover and seconder, as well as by his honourable friend on the right, (Col. Sykes,) it was not necessary for him to occupy much of their time, and the more especially as he sincerely hoped and believed that no difference of opinion would be found to exist on the question, but that the court would be unanimous on the present occasion. The observations made by Mr. Weeding as to what the Company ought to do, provided the representation of that court had no effect, deserved the most serious consideration; and he would go so far as to call on the Court of Directors, and on the Court of Proprietors, in the event of the failure of their petition, at once to proceed to the adoption of the principle which Mr. Weeding had proposed. It appeared to him to be the only mode which they could properly pursue for protecting India, and procuring for her that justice which he feared the government and the parliament were by no means willing to grant. (*Hear, hear.*) It had been justly observed by Mr. Hume, in the speech which had been quoted, that for the last fifteen years promises of justice to India had been repeated by the Tories, by the Whigs, and by—(he did not know what to call them, but he would say)— the managers of the Whigs, all alike imposing, but all alike ending in nothing. (*Laughter.*) Yes, they all spoke of relief to be given to India, but nothing was done, and he sincerely wished that the same thing might not occur in the present session. He hoped that he might not be a true prophet, but he believed that nothing would be done this session. Another promise would be given, but no relief would be granted. (*Hear, hear.*) The sooner, therefore, the executive body did their duty, and prepared a dispatch to the Bengal government, directing them to lay on countervailing duties, equal to those which this country imposes upon the produce and manufactures of India, the sooner would they obtain redress from the British government. By taking this step they would rouse the manufacturing interests of this country, and they would also call up the mercantile interest with their respective representatives in Parliament on the subject. The manufacturing interest would of course complain of the new duties, and they would request that measures should be taken to remove them ; but what would be the natural answer to their application

(Q)

On the part of those who supported the interests of India? Why they would say —" Undoubtedly we have outhoused the increased duties, but let us have fair play, if you will remove the duties imposed on East-India produce and manufactures, we will remove the duties on goods sent out to India from this country." If they adopted that bold course, they would have a power arrayed in the House of Commons in favour of the interests of India which unfortunately they did not now possess. India was not represented in the House of Commons. (*Hear, hear!*) There were but two or three individuals in that house who cared any thing about India. Beyond those few individuals, where was the man who noticed what was going on in India? Indeed India was scarcely ever mentioned, except perhaps to ask a question about hanging a nabob, or something of that kind (*laughter*), which he did not mean to touch on now, although he might be allowed to express a hope that no more exhibitions of such a nature would take place. No interest was taken in the House of Commons with reference to Indian subjects. What they wanted was, that India should be represented and supported with such power as the great agitator for Ireland wielded in behalf of that country. That was the man they wanted for India. (*Cries of No, no!*) Such he repeated, was the man India wanted; and he only wished they could enlist in her cause a man with such power, such perseverance, and such talents, for then they might hope to wrestle with the government, and successfully to oppose those whose private interests were arrayed against the prosperity of the people of India. He expressed himself warmly on this subject, because perhaps it was the last time that he should address the court with reference to it. He was so disgusted with the conduct of government in relation to the question, that he should probably in future decline taking any part in its discussion. He however would recommend, as he had before done when the subject was under consideration, though his recommendation was not attended to, that they should follow the example of the Native and European inhabitants of Bombay, (he said the Native and European inhabitants, because he thought the natives should take precedence) and send a copy of this petition to the House of Lords as well as to the House of Commons. He knew very well that the House of Commons must originate any measure introduced on this subject: but finally that measure must come up to the House of Lords. If, however, this were not the case, still there were many noble lords in that house who took a much greater interest in the affairs of India than the members of the House of Commons generally did. He would therefore give those noblemen an opportunity of stating the case of the natives of India ably in the House of Lords. He would let their sentiments go forth to the public, and he was sure that their opinions would produce a strong moral effect. He only feared that all they did on this occasion might be considered as mere waste of paper or parchment. He confessed, his impression was, that nothing would be done, for he feared that the West-India interests would be too powerful for that of the East-Indies, and that the former would be enabled successfully to contend against the latter as they had hitherto done. God knows, the sop thrown out to them was not a trifling one. No less a sum than twenty millions was given to them. For what? Why, to emancipate their slaves. But those poor creatures were, in fact, as much slaves as ever, and must continue to be so, if not worse than slaves. (*Cries of " No, no!"*) They must continue to labour; and when sickness or old age renders them incapable, the planters were no longer compelled to support them. He was informed that the compensation granted to the planters of the Cape of Good Hope and Mauritius far exceeded their most sanguine expectation. He presumed that the West-India planters had taken good care to get their full share of the grant, and they were right in doing so. He never wished to press on them, or any other body of men; but while the country was taking care of the West-India interest, he thought that the native population of the East-Indies should not be neglected or forgotten. He understood that the West-India planters were taking measures to make up for any deficiency of slave labour. They were, he had heard, employing some of the most intelligent of the negroes to go to Africa, and engage others to go to the West-Indies to serve as apprentices for five years, after which they were to be sent back to their own country. He hoped that this plan would succeed, as it might do under proper regulations. Why might not that be done, as well as employing people from this country or from China? The West-Indies were in a better situation now than for the last ten or fifteen years. The produce was now fifty per cent. higher than it was a few years ago, and was daily rising in value. He understood, that persons connected with the West-India interest, speaking of this petition to the House of Commons said, that its success depended on them. "We will," they observed, "agree to it on one condition—but on that we shall insist—namely, that the same freedom of the foreign market shall be given to us as to the East-India grower." Now he had no objection to that. Why should not the West-Indians carry their produce to any part of the world they pleased."

Mr. *Lyall.*—They may do so.

Sir *C. Forbes.*—I understand they must first bring their sugar here in English ships.

Mr. *Lyall* said, that foreign ships might proceed to the West-Indies and convey the produce to their respective countries. The rule did not apply to English ships.

Sir *C. Forbes* said, it was a West-India merchant who had made the observation to him, and he could not see why full latitude should not be allowed to the West-India planter to dispose of his produce as he could either in British or foreign vessels. However that might be, he would again say, that the East-India Company were morally bound to protect the interests of the people of India, and to take those measures, which finally they must take, (and the sooner the better,) to shew that they would no longer be trifled with, otherwise they might rest assured, no relief would be granted to the East-Indies. He most strenuously advised the sending out a dispatch, directing the Government of India to lay on such countervailing duties as would force the question fairly before Parliament, on the ground of reciprocity. If 10 per cent. duty is to be exacted on India cotton goods imported into England, the same should be imposed on the importation of English cottons into India; and, if 20 per cent. is to be charged here on Indian manufactured silks, the same ought to be levied on English manufactured silks sent into the Indian market. Every description of produce and manufactures, such as woollens, metals, and hardwares, exported from England ought also to be subjected to a duty of at least 10 per cent. instead of being free as at present. This, he admitted, was a course exceedingly to be deprecated, if it could be at all avoided; but he felt that the first obligation of the East-India Company was to watch over and advance, by every possible means, the welfare and happiness of the people of India. There was also a very large pecuniary interest connected with this question; and, when they looked at what had been done for the West-Indians, it would be well to recollect, that, from four to five millions annually must be drawn from India, to whose people no relief had been extended; indeed, looking to all the expenses to which India was subject—the discharge of part of the 6 per cent. loan, the payment of the dividends to the proprietors of £630,000, &c., and the total annual drain from India could be little short of five millions sterling. How was this to be realized? How could they expect to supply the home treasury from

India, when they destroyed her manufactures and refused to receive the produce of her soil? While they were, in fact, plundering the people of India day after day, and year after year, to an extent horrible to be contemplated! In fifty years they had exacted from India more than would be sufficient to pay off the national debt, as shewn by a calculation made by Mr. Montgomery Martin. The European party, both here and in India, took good care of themselves, but the people of India were left to shift as they could. He hoped, however, that the day was approaching when the latter would be able to take care of themselves, and to compel those to do them justice who now refused to attend to their complaints.

Sir *P. Laurie* said, that the statement made by the gallant officer (Col. Sykes), as to reduction within a given time, of one million in the amount of their exports to India, was both important and alarming, and he should like to have more information on the subject. If their exports were thus diminishing one year after another, it was a subject that required immediate legislative consideration. The true way to rouse the attention of Parliament, was to shew that the English exports were rapidly falling off. They were, he was sorry to say, in that extraordinary position at present, in which, he believed, the Company was never before placed—they were wholly unrepresented in Parliament; (*hear, hear!*) such had been the effect of the alterations in the law of election in this country, that there was not one Director who had it in his power to state his opinion in the House of Commons on any question which affected the East-India Company. He regretted that the hon. bart. should have expressed a disposition to withdraw his services from the Company, because he felt it was important that the hon. bart. should attend for the purpose of occasionally agitating in that Court, questions connected with the interests of the East-India Company and of the people of India. It could now be done in that Court only, since they had no representative in the House of Commons—(*hear, hear!*)—and, therefore, he hoped that his excellent friend would never relax in his attendance or in his exertions. (*Hear, hear!*) Whether successful or not, he hoped that he would still persevere. He thanked him for his instrumentality in calling the Proprietors together; and he trusted that Courts would be occasionally called for the purpose of considering important questions; for they might depend on it, that, without agitation of this kind, it would soon be forgotten that there was such a body in existence. (*Hear, hear!*) He hoped therefore that his hon. friend would not think of retiring. (*Hear, hear!*) He trusted that the petition would be placed in the hands of Mr. Fergusson, who understood the subject thoroughly; and who felt, as they knew from the sentiments which he had expressed in that Court, a deep and zealous interest for the welfare of India. (*Hear, hear!*)

Mr. *Marriott* said, that the interests of the natives of India ought, in the estimation of the Company, to be paramount to all other interests. He considered that they were trustees, whose imperative duty it was to protect the best interests of the people of India. They ought to adopt every means that appeared calculated not merely to advance their commercial prosperity, but that was likely to prove conducive to their moral and spiritual interests. (*Hear, hear!*)

Sir *H. Willoughby* said, he felt a considerable degree of pleasure in agreeing to the motion. He was, it was true, very much concerned in the continuance of the discriminating duties; but he considered it to be his paramount duty—a duty superior to all others—to support any proposition which had for its object the preservation of the interests of their native subjects. (*Hear, hear!*) He should, therefore, most cordially assent to the motion of the hon. proprietor. (*Hear, hear!*)

The *Chairman.*—It is hardly necessary for me to detain the Court for any length of time, or to indulge in many observations, as there appears to be no difference of opinion on the proposition which has been submitted to us for consideration. (*Hear, hear!*) Neither would it be necessary for me to claim the attention of the Court, if I were competent to enter upon the subject, considering the great ability which has been displayed by those who have already spoken on this question. I perfectly concur in what has been stated by those who have addressed the Court, that it is quite an anomaly in legislation, to see two regions, which ought, in the eye of the parent state, to be viewed with the same degree of favour, distinguished by discriminating duties on the same article of commerce. (*Hear, hear!*) I agree perfectly in an observation that has been made by a gentleman on the other side of the bar, that the agitation of this question is likely to influence the decision of the legislature, and to accelerate the removal of this crying injustice to India. (*Hear, hear!*) Not a day passes in which the public is not rendered more alive to the fact that the interests of England and of India are intimately connected; and means will be taken, I trust, by persevering in the course now adopted, to relieve India from its present oppressed situation. (*Hear, hear!*) We, the Directors, have been earnestly called on to do our duty, collectively and individually,

with zeal and spirit. In answer, I beg to assure our constituents, that no occasion has ever presented itself, in which the Court of Directors has not most warmly represented and supported the interests of India—not merely with reference to the duty on sugar, but our efforts have always been directed to obtaining an equality for India in all respects. (*Hear, hear!*) I do hope that these representations, backed by the urgent statements contained in this petition, will be responded to by the legislature in that spirit of justice which has been too long neglected. I shall only say farther, that no opportunity shall be lost on my part, or on that of my honorable colleagues, in requiring for India that justice, which I think, I have always thought, has been too long denied. (*Hear, hear!*) Such an alteration of policy is not only necessary for the interest of that country, but is equally essential for the welfare of England; and, I trust, that, while the proprietors deem it necessary to resort to temperate agitation on this question, it will be found, that, so far from feeling any reluctance at their assembling for the purpose in this Court, we shall be happy to meet their views, for devising the best means to secure the welfare and prosperity of India. (*Hear, hear!*)

Mr. *Twining* did not mean to occupy the attention of the Court for many minutes on the present occasion, seeing that a perfect unanimity of sentiment prevailed on the question. Indeed he should have remained silent, if he had not, on a former occasion, when the subject was brought forward, felt it to be his duty to state his opinion. That, therefore, having been the case, he should be sorry not to take this opportunity again to record his opinion. That opinion remained unaltered, as to the justice and propriety of endeavouring to effect the great object which had been brought under their consideration. He thought, from all the experience which they had, that the act of justice which they had long sought for, might now be carried into effect, without injury to the West India interest or to the interest of any other party. No ground now remained to enable any set of persons to allege, as had formerly been done, that if this concession were made, they were likely to suffer injury. He believed, that, in the present state of the commerce of this country, the object which they had in view, if granted, would not operate prejudicially to any interest whatever, but would prove beneficial to all parties, and would have the effect of promoting the interests of India and the prosperity of the country at large. (*Hear, hear!*) It would be a most important object to secure unanimity of exertion in pressing on the consideration of Parliament, the justice, necessity, and propriety of the measure which they were now seeking. He trusted that, on this important occasion, they would not be deprived of the exertions, the zealous and honest exertions, of Sir Charles Forbees (*Hear, hear!*) He was extremely sorry to hear any allusion from him as to his withdrawal from that scene where they had derived so much benefit from his disinterested services; and, though, with Sir Peter Laurie, he greatly regretted that there were, at present, no members to state the opinion of the East-India Company, in the House of Commons. still he did hope, that an occasion, would, ere long, present itself, when the zeal, integrity, and intelligence of the honorable bart. would again enable him to act in the legislature for the benefit both of the Company and of the empire at large. (*Hear, hear!*)

Colonel *Sykes* read an official account of our exports to India, in 1831—32—33, and 34, to show the decrease which had gradually taken place.

Mr. *Weeding* said, as perfect unanimity prevailed, it was unnecessary for him to address any farther observations to the Court. The anomalous situation in which the Indian trade was placed, operated as a bounty to all foreign nations to compete with us; and every one knew how much the Americans had availed themselves of the circumstance. The additional quantity of sugar imported from the Mauritius after the reduction of the duty from 32s. to 24s. proved clearly the great benefit which India must derive from a similar reduction of duty. They ought to call on ministers to give some reason for the preference which they shewed to the West-India interest, if they persisted in the present system. As the ministers of a great country, they were bound to do this, or to yield to the reasonable representations that were addressed to them.

Mr. *H. St. George Tucker* said, he had so often experienced the indulgence of that Court, when he had addressed the proprietors on this subject, that he would not have thought of offering himself to their notice on the present occasion, had he not felt a wish to excite and stimulate those who had not yet stated their opinion, and who, from their experience, knowledge, and talent, were likely to throw new light on this question, to declare their sentiments. Some points had been very ably treated by the hon. mover and other gentlemen who had taken part in the discussion: but there were other points of great importance, which, he conceived, ought to be prominently introduced. He meant especially the effect of the present system on the agriculture of India, and on the revenue derived from that agriculture. The commercial, manufacturing, and shipping part of the question had been extremely well argued; but he should like the subject of the agriculture of India, and the effect which the existing system had on the remittances of that country, which were necessary to meet its political and other debts, to be introduced to their consideration; and there was a right hon. friend of his in that room who was peculiarly competent to give them the best information on all these questions. His opinion was of very great value; and they had so few friends who advocated their cause in Parliament or elsewhere, that he could not lose the opportunity of taking his most valuable evidence, he would call it, on this question. They had no means of applying to Parliament, except through the medium of that Court. Petition after petition had been presented to the legislature on this subject, but hitherto without effect. Last year a petition from that Court, unanimously carried, had been presented to parliament, fruitlessly as it would appear. On that occasion, and indeed for the last fourteen or fifteen years he did every thing that lay in his power to further the object which they had now in view; an object not more important to the interests of India than it was to those of the mother country; for, if they did not allow the produce of India to be imported into this country, India would have no means of paying her debt. The hon. baronet had said, that the Company, if their representations were not successful, ought to undertake a war with the custom-house. He confessed that he was not in favour of such a proceeding. He wished for reciprocity. He was anxious that India should be placed on a fair and equal footing with other British possessions. Unfortunately, if they wished to act as the hon. baronet advised them, they had not the power. They could not send out a dispatch ordering additional duties to be levied. The right of imposing duties was never vested in the government of India; and a vast deal of jealousy would be excited in this country if any attempt were made to place a check upon her manufactures. The Company, he repeated, had no such power. All they could do was to require redress for their own particular grievance —to call on the legislature for equal justice. They had a right to demand that fair and equal duties, the same duties that were imposed on the produce of other British settlements should be imposed on similar produce imported from India He had made these few observations to excite his right hon. friend to give the Court the benefit of his evidence.

Mr. *Holt Mackenzie* said, he would be very happy to assist, in any way, in attaining the object of the petition then before the Court. He had, however, been called on by his hon. friend, not exactly to speak to the subject, but to give evidence. He feared, however, that he would be found a very partial evidence (*hear, hear!*); for, he confessed, that all his partialities leaned towards the interests of India, (*hear hear!*) and he would be ashamed of himself if he could consider a question that affected those interests, quite impartially. (*Hear, hear!*) His views and feeling, however, on this occasion, impelled him to take that course which was, he thought, best calculated to support the interest of India, as well as the interest of the West-India proprietors. Some individuals said, that the West-India interests would suffer if the Company were successful. Now his opinion decidedly was, that they would not suffer. He believed, that if the market were thrown open, there would be so great an accession of wealth consequent on the encreased consumption of manufactures, that the demand for sugar would be fully equal to the produce of both the East and West-Indies. It was only necessary to make the reduction in the duties now called for, and such would inevitably be the result. The population of England, as the population of returns shewed, were increasing every day in number, and he hoped in comfort. A large proportion of that population consisted of manufacturers, and if the duties were equalized, there was nothing to prevent the manufacturers of England from consuming the produce of both the East and the West-Indies. Those who took a just view of the subject must hail with satisfaction the general principle which they wished to establish, that being the principle of free-trade. As an ex-financial secretary he well knew the importance of this question. The Company's records were, in truth, full of facts, that proved the great importance of this subject to the revenue of England. In all that had been said as to the propriety of encouraging the growth of sugar in India, he entirely concurred. Indeed, the result of all inquiries shewed, that precisely in proportion as the cultivation of sugar was extended, in the same proportion wealth was enlarged. (*Hear, hear!*) As a proof of this fact, he would point to Bengal, where sugar was extensively grown. Those who had been in that country must remember how carefully sug r was there cultivated, and they must be delighted to recollect the comfort which the persons employed in that species of labour enjoyed. It was most gratifying to see them in the Indian spring (a very different sort of spring from that which they were now experiencing in this country), cheerfully engaged in this favourite occupation.

Sugar, in fact, throughout a large part o the Company's possessions, was that article on which every thing connected with the revenue must depend. In order to collect their revenue, they must necessarily have a certain supply of the precious metals. Now, India had no mines of her own; and if it were required to export a quantity of the precious metals, where were they to be found. They could not depend for the realization of their revenue; they could not depend on the common grain of the country. It was impossible for them to look to that as the great source of revenue. They must, therefore, turn their attention to those agricultural and commercial productions which might be most advantageously exported, and amongst these sugar certainly held the highest place. If, therefore, they were not allowed to export it profitably, they could not procure the necessary supply of the precious metals, and therefore he arrived at this conclusion, that the very solvency of India depended on extending the growth of sugar, and exporting it profitably. But, farther, there was another very important circumstance to be taken into consideration; they were requiring from India very large remittances for a variety of purposes. Those remittances they must take as they could get them. Now, if sugar was saddled with a duty, amounting almost to a prohibition, India was thereby deprived of paying its debt. (*Hear, hear!*) He had heard mention made of a recurrence to a war of duties. Now, he would rather keep duties for a moment in the back ground. He wished to regard India as an integral part of the British empire, and its people as forming a portion of the subjects of that empire. (*Hear, hear!*) He had no doubt that the people of England would daily become better acquainted with the claims of India to their sympathy and affection. He would not have India treated as a foreign dependency of this country, but as a part of this great empire. Looking to the subject in that light; viewing India as a part of the empire; he must enter his protest against a war of duties. (*Hear, hear!*) He would have no angry agitation, but just so much agitation as would serve the fair interests of the Company, and what was more, the interests of England, which were clearly bound up with the question. He would hold out no threat, but calmly show, that by taking the course proposed, government would be adopting the true means of increasing the wealth of India, and with it the wealth of the United empire. The English manufacturer might be assured, that it was in vain for him to look for a market, if the produce of India were not received in return for his goods. The system of a policy which had been pursued for so long a time, tended to render the great ocean of Indian population as unproductive as the real ocean. The only thing necessary to correct this evil was, that India should be allowed to pay by a return of her produce; and the only way to effect that object was, to regard that country as a part of this empire. He would not demand any angry kind of justice, but he would call for as full a measure of justice as they would yield to Scotland. He wished to see the same principle applied to India, as had been applied to Scotland, but not the same principle that had been applied to another country which had attracted so much of their attention lately. He should like to encourage the produce of India as that of Scotland had been encouraged—by extending the knowledge of scientific agriculture—by introducing a liberal system of education among the people—and by disseminating all that information which practical men could give, with reference to the interests of India. He would afford greater facilities for men of science spreading abroad their knowledge, and by that means uniting more closely together, not only England and India, but the different parts of India itself. This was the species of agitation of which he approved. That agitation which did not disseminate sound knowledge amongst the people was not good, and it could not be denied that the agitation of angry passions banished, instead of assisting, the acquirement of knowledge. As a witness, he would say, that if they wished to maintain their revenue, they must continue to give protection to agriculture; for agriculture and revenue were nearly linked together, and if they wished to raise the character of the people, it was merely necessary to provide for their comfort and happiness. To effect these objects they ought to encourage the growth of sugar; for, in proportion as the cultivation of that article was discouraged, in the same proportion was India deprived of her wealth, and the character of her people lowered. In proportion as they protected agriculture, they would add to those blessings which England had bestowed upon India, and for which the people of that country owed, and were willing to pay, a kind and grateful return. (*Hear, hear!*)

Sir *Charles Forbes* wished to say one word in explanation, with reference to the " war of duties," which had been alluded to by the two last speakers. He should never have thought of recommending such a measure, but as a last resource; indeed, under any other circumstances, he should greatly deprecate it; but they ought not to forget that, in order to obtain advantageous terms of peace, they ought to be prepared for war.

The motion was then put, and unanimously agreed to.

Mr. *Weeding* said that an hon. gentleman, for whom he felt the greatest respect, had been mentioned as the individual most fitted to discharge the task of presenting the petition to House of Commons. He thought, however, that some little difficulty might be felt in asking the gentleman, to whom he alluded, to perform that office, as he was a member of his Majesty's government. Besides, he thought it better that the petition should be entrusted to one, who was a member of that court, and independent of place.

Sir *Peter Laurie* suggested that it would be desirable to leave the selection of a gentleman, to present the petition, to the discretion of the Court of Directors.

Mr *Weeding* thought the nomination of the individual should proceed from his (Mr. W.s) side of the bar. He should, therefore, propose that Joseph Hume, Esq., be requested to present the petition to the House of Commons; and he would leave it to the chairman to select Lord Clare, or any other nobleman, to present it to the House of Lords.

Sir *C. Forbes* begged to second the proposition. He had perfect confidence that Mr. Hume would take up the question in a warm manner. He and Mr. Hume differed with regard to politics, but they had always agreed on questions relating to India

Colonel *Sykes* had the highest respect for Mr. Hume; but he thought that if an individual, in such an ostensible position as a member of the government, were allowed to present the petition, that circumstance might induce the ministers to take the matter up in a strong way, and perhaps effect the desired equalization of duties.

Mr. *Fielder* would name Mr, Ewart, as a fit person to present the petition; but he thought they could not do better than leave the selection with the Court of Directors, who would, doubtless, be able to obtain the co-operation of several influential individuals in advocating the claims of the East-Indies.

Mr. *Twining* said, there was something like an impression on his mind that Mr. Cutlar Fergusson had made something like an offer to present such a petition as the one just adopted: and he wished to know from the chair whether or not that was the fact.

The *Chairman* was not aware that Mr. C. Fergusson had made any offer that year, but he had certainly made an offer last year; and he advocated the cause of the East-Indian with all that ability which had been described.

Sir *P. Laurie* said that, since it was Mr. Fergusson who presented the last petition, not to allow him to present the present one, would seem like the withdrawal of the confidence of that court from the hon. gentleman. He should, therefore, move an amendment to the original proposition.

Mr. *Weeding* said it was his wish to render the proposition of any amendments unnecessary, and he would give up his original motion, and instead, thereof,

would move, "That the petition be presented to Parliament by such noble lord, and such honourable member, as the Court of Directors might deem proper to select." (*Hear, hear!*)

This motion having been carried, the court adjourned.

HOME INTELLIGENCE.

MISCELLANEOUS.

SIR P. MAITLAND.

On the 21st May the Directors of the East-India Company gave a dinner, at the Albion Tavern, Aldersgate-street, to Lieut.-General Sir Peregrine Maitland, K.C.B., who is about to take his departure for Madras, to assume the appointment of commander-in-chief of the forces on the Fort St. George establishment. The Directors were honoured on this occasion with the company of several officers of high military rank, and other distinguished personages.

PRINCES OF PERSIA.

Three Persian princes, sons of the present Shah of Persia, have arrived in England, to visit the King. Their names are Shah Zadeh Rhoda Kóli Meerza, who bears the title of Naib-ul-Moolk; Shah Zadeh Najaf Kóli Meerza, who bears the title of Wadi; and Shah-Zadeh Tamoor Meerza, who is styled Hossam-ul-Dawleh.

Their ostensible visit to this country is stated to be one of curiosity; but it is supposed their mission has other objects in view.

GENERAL ALLARD.

Our Paris correspondent writes that General Allard is about to return to the court of Runjeet Sing, in a French vessel of war, which is to bear the artillery and other presents, which the general has been the means of obtaining for the Maharajah. As the aim of the expedition is, in part, scientific, to honour Allard, the attempt will be made to ascend the Indus. —*Morn. Chron.*

GAZETTE APPOINTMENTS.

George Stoddart, Esq., to be his Majesty's consul in the islands of Madeira; date 12th April 1836.

Mr. Lewis de Drusina, approved of as consul at Port Louis, in the island of Mauritius, for the Republic and Hanseatic city of Hamburgh; date 10th May 1836.

James Brant, Esq., sometime British vice-consul at Trebisonde, to be his Majesty's consul at Erzeroom; date 29th April 1836.

HIS MAJESTY'S FORCES IN THE EAST.

PROMOTIONS AND CHANGES.

4th L. Drags. (at Bombay). Lieut.-Gen. Lord R. E. H. Somerset, G.C.B., from 1st Drags., to be

col., v. Gen. Hugonin dec. (1 March 36).—Lieut. R. D. Campbell, from 15th L. Drags., to be lieut., v. Vernon, who exch. (29 April)—Cornet H. St. G. Priaulx to be lieut. by purch., v. Dalgleish, who retires; Ens W. W. W. Humbley, from 2d W.I. regt., to be cornet by purch., v. Priaulx (both 6 May).

13th L. Drags. (at Madras). Capt. George Weston, from 15th F., to be capt., v. Magan, who exch. (30 April).

3d Foot (in Bengal). H. C. A. Clarke to be ens., v. Nugent, app. to 59th F. (22 April).

9th Foot (in Bengal). Lieut. Wm. Dean, from 38th F., to be lieut., v. Glasse, who exch. (2 Dec. 35).

21st Foot (in V. D. Land). Lieut. Alex. Mackenzie to be capt. v. Daniell, dec. (9 Aug 35); Lieut. Chas. Lonsdale to be capt. v. Williams app. to 24th regt. (11 Dec.); 2d Lieut. J. R. Stuart to be 1st lieut. v. Mackenzie (9 Aug.); B. C. Crookshanks to be 2d Lieut., v. Stuart (25 March 36).

28th Foot (in N. S. Wales). Maj. S. J. Cotton, from 41st regt., to be major v. Browne who exch. (25 March 36).

31st Foot (in Bengal). Ens. A. Du Bourdieu to be lieut., v. Fortune, dec. (27 March 36); Jos. Greenwood to be ens. by purch., v. Du Bourdieu (6 May).

39th Foot (at Madras). Lieut. H. C. Scarman to be capt., v. Borough, dec.; Lieut. S. Philips, from 17th F., to be lieut., v. Scarman (both 22 April).

44th Foot (in Bengal). Lieut. C. K. Macan, from 48th F., to be lieut., v. Riley, who exch. (22 April).

58th Foot (in Ceylon). Lieut. John Guthrie, from h. p. Chasseurs Brittaniques, to be lieut., v. Pack, prom.; C. Dreing to be ens. by purch., v. Jephson prom. in 9d regt. (both 19 Feb. 36).—Ens. W. H. Collins to be lieut. by purch., v. Guthrie who retires; and Moore Hill to be ens. by purch. v. Collins (both 26 Feb.); Ens. and Adj. O. Gorman to have rank of lieut. (27 do.).—Lieut. Wm. Fisher, from 78th regt., to be lieut., v. Watson app. to Ceylon regt. (1 April).

69d Foot (at Madras). Ens. Robert Gibson, from 36th regt., to be lieut. by purch., v. Day, who retires (15 April)—Staff Assist. Surg. George Carr to be assist. surg., v. Knox, app. to staff (22 April).

78th Foot (in Ceylon). Lieut. Wm. Morris, from 97th regt., to be lieut., v. Fisher app. to 58th regt. (1 April).

97th Foot (in Ceylon). Lieut. O. Keating to be capt. by purch. v. Layard who retires; Ens. C. J. F. Denshire to be lieut. by purch., v. Keating; and H. C. M. Ximenes to be ens. by purch., v. Denshire (all 11 March 36); cadet W. Boyd to be ens., v. Ximenes app. to 16th regt. (12 do.)—Lieut. Robert Lisle, from Ceylon regt., to be lieut. v. Morris app. to 78th regt. (1 April).

Ceylon Rifle Regt. 2d-Lieut. H. Smith to be 1st-lieut., v. Morris, dec. (15 July 35).—2d-Lieut. Wm. Hardisty to be 1st-lieut., v. Hulgate, dec. (8 Jan. 36).—Ens. W. L. Domenichetti, from h. p. 96th regt., to be 2d-lieut., v. Smith (11 Feb.)—E. J. Holworthy to be 2d-lieut. by purch., v. Domenichetti who retires (12 Feb.)—Cadet P. L. McDougall to be 2d-lieut., v. Hardisty (13 Feb.)—Lieut. Albert Watson, from 58th regt., to be lieut., v. Lisle app. to 97th (1 April).—Lieut. Alexander Tomkins, from 2d W.I. regt., to be 1st lieut., v. Jefferson, app. paymaster; Lieut. R. Jefferson to be paymaster, v. J. Boustead, who retires on h. p. (both 6 May).

Brevet.—Capt. B. B. Shee, 47th M.N.I., to have

local rank of lieut. col. on a particular service in Persia (25 April 36).

Capt. Maconochie, the secretary of the Royal Geographical Society, has been appointed secretary to Sir John Franklin, the new governor of Van Diemen's Land, and will proceed with him to his destination in July.

INDIA SHIPPING.

Arrivals.

APRIL 30. *Batavia*, Scharper, from Batavia; off Penzance.—MAY 2. *Hero of Malown*, Grundy, from Bombay 17th Dec., and Cape 16th Feb.; off Cork.—7. *Lady Nugent*, Fawcett, from China 25th Nov.; off Portsmouth.—9. *Royal Admiral*, Fotheringham, from China 13th Nov.; off Plymouth.—10. *Mary Ann*, Anderson, from Ceylon 6th Oct., and Mauritius 22d Jan.; off Falmouth.—12. *Duke of Sussex*, Horsman, from China 14th Jan.; off Penzance.—*Windsor*, Henning, from Bengal 23d Jan., and Cape 13th March; *Duke of Buccleugh*, Martin, from Bengal 25th Dec., and Madras 7th Jan.; *Arethusa*, Jane, from Manilla 20th Nov., and Cape 5th Feb.; *Malabar*, Tucker, from Bombay 4th Jan., and Cape 11th March; all off Plymouth.—*Elizabeth*, M'Nair, from Bengal 17th Dec.; off Cork.—13. *Herefordshire*, Isaacson, from Bengal 6th Jan., and Cape 5th March; *Wellington*, Liddell, from Madras 16th Jan., and Cape 4th March; and *London*, Wimble, from Bengal 7th Jan.; all off Falmouth.—*Cornwall*, Bell, from Bengal 17th Jan., and Cape; off Penzance.—*Euphrates*, Hannay, from Bengal 23d Jan.; off Liverpool.—14. *General Kyd*, Aplin, from China 13th Jan.; *Lord Hungerford*, Farquharson, from Bengal 11th Jan., and Cape; *Fairlie*, Ager, from Bengal 25th Dec.; *Scaleby Castle*, Sandys, from China 17th Jan.; *Edinburgh*, Marshall, from China 15th Jan.; *Robert Small*, Fulcher, from Bengal 7th Jan.; *Lady Flora*, Ford, from Madras 25th Jan.; and *Duke of Bedford*, Bowen, from Bengal 7th Jan; all off Plymouth.—*Morley*, Douglas, from Ceylon 5th Jan., and Cape 28th Feb.; off Falmouth.—*Claremont*, Stephens, from China 8th Jan.; *Arab*, Lowe, from China 28th Dec., and Cape 12th March; *Bethaven*, Crawford, from China 4th Jan.; *Mary Somerville*, Jackson, from China 1st Jan.; *Gipsy*, Highat, from China 3d Jan.; *Fatama*, Feathers, from China 6th Jan.; and *Herculean*, King, from China 3d Jan.; all off Holyhead.—*Collingwood*, Hookey, from Bengal 15th Jan., and *Malabar*, Dunlop, from Mauritius 27th Jan.; both off Cork.—*Arabian*, Brown, from China 31st Dec.; at Bristol.—16. *Susannah*, Ridley, from N. S. Wales 7th Dec.; *Grecian*, Smith, from V. D. Land 29th Dec.; *Georgiana*, Thoms, from Bengal 28th Dec., and Mauritius 1st Feb.; *Earl Grey*, Talbert, from Bengal 1st Jan.; *Exmouth*, Warren, from Bengal 15th Jan., and Cape 13th March; *Carnatic*, Brodie, from Bombay 16th Jan.; and Cape 17th March; *Clifton*, Worsall, from Ceylon 8th Jan.; *Henry Bell*, Wesley, from Mauritius 3d Feb., and Cape 6th March; *Royal George*, Richards, from China 3d Jan.; and *Prince George*, Shaw, from Madras 17th Jan.; all off Plymouth.—*Bolton*, Compton, from Bengal 23d Dec., Madras 19th Jan., and Cape 15th March; *Marquis of Hastings*, Clarkson, from Bombay 10th Jan.; *Jacob Cats*, Ingeram, from Batavia 5th Jan.; *Anna Bella*, Anstruther, from Mauritius 16th Feb.; *Olive Branch*, Shirling, from Cape 26th Feb.; *Mary Taylor*, Early, from Mauritius 12th Jan.; and *Emma Eugenia*, Milbank, from China 24th Dec.; all off Falmouth.—*Tory*, Reid, from Bombay 23d Jan.; and *Bombay Pack t*, Garnock, from Bengal 9th Jan.; both at Liverpool.—*Mary Walker*, Pollock, from China 24th Dec., and Cape 5th March; *Dominica*, Huntley, from Mauritius; and *Salma*, Adams, from China 30th Dec.; all off Cork.—*Pestonagee Bomanjee*, Thomson, from China 8th Jan.; *Columbia*, Underwood, from China 8th do.; both off Fowey.—*St. George*, Thompson, from Bengal 15th Jan., and Cape 1st March; and *Paragon*, Cook, from Mauritius 1st Feb.; both at Bristol.—*Penyard Park*, Middleton, from Mauritius 18th Jan., and Cape 10th Feb.; off Penzance.—*Lady Faversham*, Webster, from Bombay 15th Nov., Aleppy, and Cape 11th Feb.; off Swanage.—H. M. hired transport *Muitland*, Marshall, from St. Helena 13th March, and Ascension 20th do.; off Portsmouth.—*Renown*, M'Leod, from Mauritius 5th Feb.; in the Clyde.—17. *Neptunia*, Kray, from Batavia 19th Jan.; off

Portland.—*Frances*, Kirkus, from Mauritius 30th Jan.; off Falmouth.—*Sterling*, Burnett, from Mauritius 31st Jan., and Cape 24th Feb.; off Plymouth.—18. *Westmoreland*, Brigstock, from V. D. Land 30th Dec.; off Hastings.—19. *William*, Dunn, from Cape 27th Feb.; at Deal.—*Vasco de Gama*, from Batavia, &c.; off Portsmouth.—20. *Diana*, Hawkins, from Bengal 13th Jan.; at Liverpool.—21. *Velocity*, Withicomb, from Muscat; at Deal.—*Troughton*, Thomson, from China 20th Dec.; off the Wight.—24. *Pyramus*, Weller, from Singapore 5th Dec., and Cape 14th Feb.; off Falmouth.—25. *Manchester*, Hawks, from Mauritius; off Dartmouth.

Departures.

APRIL 5. *Medora*, Tweedie, for V. D. Land and N. S. Wales; from Deal.—15. *Augusta Jessie*, Edenborough, for N. S. Wales; from Portsmouth.—27. *City of Edinburgh*, Frazer, for Mauritius and Madras; from Portsmouth.—28. *Rio Packet*, Dench, for Muscat; from Torbay.—30. *Mary Bibby*, Cumming, for Bombay; from Liverpool.—MAY 1. *Tiger*, Searight, for Bombay; *Tigris*, Titherington, for Bengal; and *Regulus*, Vasmer, for China; all from Liverpool.—2. *Nelson Wood*, Robinson, for Batavia and Singapore; from Liverpool.—4. *Rapid*, Light, for South Australia (with emigrants); from Deal.—5. *John Bagshaw*, Blyth, for Madras and Bengal; from Deal.—*Royal Saxon*, Renner, for Batavia, Singapore, and China; from Liverpool.—6. *Duchess of Clarence*, Hutchinson, for Bombay; from Liverpool.—*Jannet*, Chalmers, for Mauritius; and *Amelia Thompson*, Tomlinson, for Launceston (with emigrants); both from Deal.—7. *Muffat*, Bolton, for N. S Wales (with convicts); from Portsmouth.—8. *Clorinda*, Mitchell, for N. S. Wales; *William Glen Anderson*, Dobson, for ditto; *Morning Star*, Linton, for Cape and Algoa Bay; and *Duchess of Northumberland*, Roxburgh, for N. S. Wales (with convicts) *via* Cork; all from Deal.—*Agnes*, Broadfoot, for Bengal; and *Sarah Birkett*, Atkin, for Singapore; both from Liverpool.—9. *Gulnare*, Henderson, for V. D. Land and N. S. Wales; from Liverpool.—10. *Eudora*, Addison, for Hobart Town; and *Thomas Snook*, Baker, for Cape; both from Deal.—*Enterprise*, Roberts, for Batavia and China; from Liverpool.—11. *Thomas*, Harmer, for Cape; *Cordelia*, Creighton, for Bengal; *Australia*, Forrister, for Bombay; and *Samuel Winter*, Rodger, for Batavia and China; all from Liverpool.—12. *Duke of Clarence*, Sandford, for Cape; from Deal.—14. *Jane Brown*, Dunlop, for Batavia and Singapore; from Clyde.—15. *Euphrates*, Buckham, for Bombay; and *Welmer Castle*, Bourchier, for ditto; both from Portsmouth.—*Malabar*, Forbisher, for Bombay; from Liverpool.—16. *Alexander Baring*, St. Croix, for China; from Deal.—17. *Theresa*, Young, for Madras and Bengal; from Portsmouth.—*Arabian*, Cain, for Launceston; and *Mary Catherine*, Campbell, for Cape and Bengal; both from Deal.—*Lawrence*, Gill, for Bengal; and *Italy*, Commerals, for China; both from Liverpool.—18. *Allerton*, Evans, for Bengal; from Liverpool.—*Eliza*, Harris, for Mauritius; from Bristol.—19. *Sesostris*, Yates, for Cape, Madras, and Bengal; from Portsmouth.—*Douglas*, Hamilton, for N. S. Wales; from Deal.—20. *Memnon*, Ekin, for Bengal; from Liverpool. 21. *Anna Robertson*, Hamilton, for China; from Deal.—*Waterloo*, Cow, for N. S. Wales (with convicts); from Cork.—23. *Royal William*, Ireland, for Madras; from Portsmouth.—*Margaret*, Taylor, for Algoa Bay; from Deal.—*Orixa*, Clover, for China; *John O' Gaunt*, Robertson, for Batavia and China; and *Emerald*, Crawford, for Mauritius; all from Liverpool.—24. *Royal George*, Wilson, for Bombay; and *Indemnity*, Roberts, for Mauritius and Ceylon; both from Deal.—*Jumna*, Pinder, for Batavia and China; from Liverpool.—25. *Jean*, Goldie, for Bengal; *Trusty*, West, for China; *George Canning*, Winn, for Bombay; and *Hersey*, Parkinson, for Mauritius, Penang, and Singapore; all from Deal.—27. *Fama*, Purvis, for Cape, Batavia, and China; from Deal.

PASSENGERS FROM INDIA.

Per Windsor, from Bengal: Mrs. Longueville Clarke; Mrs. De Brett; Mrs. Boyd; Mrs. Simpson; Miss Killett; Misses J. and F. Boyd; J. A. Pringle, Esq., C. S; R. H. Tulloh, Esq., C. S.; Chas. Beecher, Esq., C. S.; Maj. E. A. Campbell, 2d L. C.; Geo. Boyd, Esq.; Wm. Patrick, Esq.;

J. W. Sutherland, Esq.; R. Spiers, Esq.; A. A.ford, H.M. 16th F.; A. Spiers, Esq., Bengal C.S.; Mackay, Esq.; Misses Clarke, De Brett, A. Boyd, P. Boyd, A. Simpson, and H. Simpson; two Masters Boileau; two Masters Simpson; Master De Brett; Master Crawford.—From the Cape: A. Horak, Esq.; two Misses De Witt.—Landed at the Cape: Dr. John Grant, Mrs. Grant, and children.

Per Spence, from N. S. Wales: Capt. Moxey, late of the *George the Third*; Mr. and Mrs. Jourdaine; Mrs. Caville.

Per Edinburgh, from China: Capt. John Templeton; Mr. D. L. Brown; Mr. Kennedy; Mr. Geo. Coles; Mr. E. H. Burgh.

Per Duke of Sussex, from China: James N. Daniell, Esq.; Mrs. Daniell and five children; J. A. Pereira, Esq; Mr. W. F. Dry.

Per Hero of Malown, from Bombay: Alli Agah, Governor of Bussorah; Capt. Poweakl; Dr. Moore. —From St. Helena: Brigadier Gen. Dallas, late governor; Mrs. and Miss Dallas; Capt. Spiller; Mrs. Lewis; Miss McCutcheon.

Per Elizabeth, from Bengal: Mr. and Mrs. Aitchison; Mr. Barclay and child.

Per Duke of Buccleugh, from Bengal and Madras: Mrs. Storey and two children; Mrs. Maxtone; Mrs. Warner and two children; Mrs. Kerr and two ditto; Mrs. Greenway and two ditto; Miss Stone; Miss Davidson; the Venerable Archdeacon Robinson; W. A. Neave, Esq., C. S.; Col. Morgan; A. F. Arbuthnot, Esq.; Maj. Maxtone; Capt. Boileau; Capt. Seaton; Lieut. Mellish; Lieut. Kennedy, 14th N. I.; thirty-eight invalids; five servants.

Per Malabar, from Mauritius: Mrs. Pereira and child; Lieut. Graves; Dr. Owen; Mr. Morgan.

Per Sterling, from Mauritius: Mr. and Mrs. Blackburn and three children; Miss Southcote; Dr. Henderson; two servants.

Per Fatuma, from China: Mr. J. A. Stewart.

Per Herefordshire, from Bengal: Mrs. Col. Piper and four Misses Piper; Mrs. Gordon; Miss Vernon; Col. Piper, H. M. 38th regt.; Majors Hopper and Young, ditto; Capts. Carr, Campbell, Grimes, and Blennerhassett. ditto; Lieuts. Campbell, O'Halloran, Irvine, Green, Lecky, Horsley, Frith, and Glass, ditto; Ensigns Smith, O'Connell, Stowell, Brace, and Anderson, ditto; Surg. Roe, ditto; Assi't. Surg. Foss, ditto; 300 men, 25 women, and 52 children of H. M. 38th regt.

Per London, from Bengal: Hon. Mrs. R. Forbes; Mrs. Archdeacon Dealtry; Mrs. Stalkart; Mrs. Kingston; Mrs. Ross; Mrs. Jackson, Miss Stalkart; Col. Stirling, 74th N. I.; Maj. Kingston, 52d N. I.; Lieut. Chilcott, 74th N. I.; Rev. Mr. Eteson; Wm. Thacker, Esq.; John Browne, Esq.; two Misses Forbes; two Misses Davidson; two Misses Ross; Misses Barton, Jackson, and Ramsay; Masters Stalkart, Shakspeare, Stewart, Jackson, Goodwyn, Ennis, Watts and Griffin; eight servants.

Per Wellington, from Madras: Lady Palmer; Mrs. Armstrong; Mrs. Briggs; Mrs. Wahab; Mrs. Harriott; the Hon. Sir Ralph Palmer, Knt.; Maj. Gen. T. Hawker; Capt. G. Manners, H. M. 13th L. Drags.; James Webster, Esq.; Lieut. Campbell, H. M. 13th L. Drags.; Lieut. H. Lawford, Artillery; Mr. J. Berenbruck; Rev. H. Page; three Misses Palmer; Misses Blair and Wahab; Masters Palmer, Hawker, Bell, three Horsley's, Watkins, and Briggs; ten servants, (Mrs. Gen. Hawker died on 21st March.)

Per Morley, from Ceylon: Capt. and Mrs. Charvel; Mr. and Mrs. Barnett and two children; Mrs. Douglas; Capt. Beverhout, H. M. 56th regt.; Mr. Coulfield, C. S.; Dr. Fitzmaurice; Lieut. Gottreux; Mr. Cockburn; five children.— From the Cape: Rev. Dr. Phillip; Mr. Phillip; Mr. Read; Jan Tsatsee and Andre Stoffel, Caffre chiefs; Mrs. Smith; Mrs. Gibbs.

Per Prince George, from Madras: Mrs. Macleod and child; Mrs. Norfor and child; John Macleod, Esq.—From St. Helena: Mrs. Solomons and son.

Per Cornwall, from Bengal: Mrs. Kennedy; Mrs. George Bird; Mrs. Steel; Mrs. Seppings; Mrs. Richy; Mrs. Smith; Mrs. Bell; Mrs. Goodwin; Maj. Reynolds, invalids; Capt. Johnson, Beng. Artillery; Capt. Goodwin, H.M. 31st F.; Capt. Simpson, 55th N.I.; Capt. Lowth, H.M. 28th regt.; Capt. Steel, 41st N.I.; Capt. Humfrey, Artillery; Lieut. Phibbs, 41st N.I.; Lieut. Craw-

L. A. Richy, Esq.; J. D. Smith, Esq.; fifteen children.—From the Cape: Mrs. Brown, two Masters Brown, and two Misses Brown.—Landed at the Cape: Mrs. R. Bird and four children; Major Anderson. (Master Harrington died at sea, 4th Feb.)

Per Robert Small, from Bengal: Mrs. C. Plowden; two Misses Plowden; the Hon. Capt. and Mrs. Powys and five children; Capt. and Mrs. Steer and four children; Mrs. Maj. Frushard and child; Miss Church; three Misses Langstaff; J. Church, Esq.; F. Trower, Esq; Capt. Ellis, H.M. 16th Lancers; Capt. Croft, Bengal Army; Capt. Frederick, ditto; Capt. Croudace; Lieut. Blanshard; Lieut. Jervis and child.

Per Euphrates, from Bengal: Mrs. Griffiths and two children; Mrs. Moore and four ditto; Mrs. Hutchins and two ditto; Capt. Griffiths, 37th N.I.; Capt. Griffiths, 13th ditto; John Moore, Esq. (house of Tulloh and Co.); two Masters Macleod; two Masters Sterndale.

Per Marquis of Hastings, from Bombay: Mrs. Nicholls. Mrs. Gunning; J. Nicholls, Esq, Madras C.S.; Wm. Lumsden, Esq., Bombay C.S.; W. Fenwick, Esq., ditto; Capt. C. W. Grant, Engineers; Capt. Gunning, Madras est'b.; two Misses Fenwick; two Misses Brown; two Misses Gunning; Misses De Silva, Graham, and Sayer; Messrs. Gunning, Minchin, &c.; six servants.

Per Lord Hungerford, from Bengal: The Hon. Mrs. Elliot; Mrs. Dunlop; Mrs. D'Aguilar; Mrs. Russell; Mrs. Hughes; Mrs. De Montmorency; Mrs. Smoult; Miss Philp; the Hon. J. E. Elliot; Dr. Macdonald; Capt. Campbell; Capt. Hughes; Capt. De Montmorency; Mr. Smoult; three Masters Smyth; two Masters Russell; Masters Chambers, Turnbull, Masters, Dick, Mytten, and De Montmorency; two Masters Hughes; two Misses Dunlop; three Misses Young; Misses Smith, D'Aguilar, Chambers, Macdonald, Mytten, and De Montmorency.

Per Lady Flora, from Madras: Mrs. Eden; Mrs. Col. Fraser; Mrs. Highmoor; Mrs. Stewart; Mrs. Cuppage; Mrs. Montgomerie; Mrs. Chambers; Mrs. Humfreys; Mrs. Pearce; Mrs. Bell; Mrs. Harvey; Miss Hutchinson; Miss Pearce; Lieut. Col. Hodges, private sec. to Right Hon. the Governor; Major Stewart, Madras European regt.; Capt. Derville, 31st L. Inf.; Capt. Montgomerie, 7th L.C.; Capt. O. Driscoll, late of the *Lanach*; Lieut. Jones, Madras E.R.; Lieut. Simpson, 37th N.I.; W. Hart, Esq.; J. Bell, Esq; P. Slaney, Esq.; J. Brown, Esq.; Wm. Lambe, Esq.; Mr. Dandeville; thirty-two children and servants. (Lieut. Pereira died at sea).

Per Lady Faversham, from Bombay: Capt. and Mrs. Kerr and two children; Lieut. Chalk.

Per General Kyd, from China: Capt. and Mrs. Neish and family.

Per Earl Grey, from Bengal: Capt. Williams, 73d B. N. I.; Mr. Mc Keen; Mr. Logan.—From St. Helena: Mrs. Capt. Ricketts and four children, from the *Pyramus.*

Per Duke of Bedford, from Bengal: Mrs. Hall; Mrs. Shuldham; Mrs. Cooper; Mrs. Andrew; G. R. B. Berney, Esq., C.S.; Major Buckley, Bengal Cavalry; Capt. Morse Cooper, H. M. 11th L. Drags; Lieut. Gaitakell, Bengal army; R. H. Strong, Esq., H. M. 26th regt.; Dr. Andrew, Bengal L. C.; eight children; five servants. (Mrs. James Millar died at sea 8th Jan.)

Per Maitland (transport), from St. Helena: Mrs. Armstrong; Miss Armstrong; Misses Mary Lydia and Harriett Clementina Younge; Capt. A. A. Younge, Hon. E. I. Company's St. Helena regt., commanding the detachment; Lieut. S. F. Armstrong, St. Helena Artillery; Lieut. J. B. Alexander, St. Helena regt.; 2d Lieuts. F. N. Greene and F. M. Baker, St. Helena Artillery; Surg. A. C. Ross; 2 serjeants, 5 corporals, 14 bombardiers, 1 drummer, 123 gunners, 95 soldiers' wives, and 56 children, of the Hon. E. I. Company's St. Helena Artillery; 4 serjeants, 5 corporals, 1 drummer, 190 privates, 95 soldiers' wives, and 87 children, of the Hon. E. I. Company's St. Helena regt.

Per Westmorland, from V. D. Land: Mr. C. B. Hine; Mr. Thomas Berrand.

Per Bombay Packet, from Bengal: Mrs. Stocqueler and child; Mr. Limond, Mr. Turner.

Per Exmouth, from Bengal: Mrs. Col. Bird; Mrs. Chalmers and family; Mrs. Eckford and family; Mrs. Warren and family; Mrs. Sherer; Mrs. Spens and child; Mrs. Phillips; Col. Bird; Dr. Chalmers; Capt. Warren, late of the *Sherbourne;* Capt Pine; Mr. Bird; two Misses Campbell; two Misses Battye; two Masters Campbell; two Masters Battye; Master Angelo.—Landed at the Cape: Col. and Mrs. Hopper; Mr. Hopper; Capt. Baker.—Landed at St. Helena: Capt. and Mrs. Alexander; three Misses Alexander.

Per Sealeby Castle, from China: Mr. William M'Killigan; Mr. S. Holbrook.

Per Bolton, from Bengal and Madras: Mrs. Johnstone and two children; Mrs. Edgcombe and two ditto: Mrs. Sheppard; Lieut.-Col. Kitson, 23d M.N.I.; Major Johnstone; Capt. Hibgame, 39th M.N.I.; Dr. Richards; Dr. Bell and two children; Dr. Edgcombe; Lieut. Kendall, Beng. Europ. Regt.; Lieut. Channer, Bengal Artillery; Lieut. Rose, 50th M.N.I.; Lieut. Scotland, 7th ditto; Ens. Impey, 31st ditto; 52 invalids of H.M. service, 1 woman, and 6 children—(Lieut. Froese, 12th M.N.I., died at sea).

Per Carnatic, from Bombay: Mrs. and Miss Hobson; Mrs. Farquharson; Mrs. and Miss Macleod; Mrs. Stevens on and four Masters ditto; Mrs. Moore; Mrs. Grierson; Mrs. Brodie; Capt. Hobson, Bombay army; Dr. Grierson, ditto; Lieut. Ralph, Queen's, in charge of invalids; Lieut. M'Leod, Madras army; Lieut. Stewart, H.M. 57th regt.; two Masters Hobson; Masters Malcolm and Flower.—From the Cape: Mrs. Blair; Mrs. and Miss Dickson; Wm. Dickson, Esq.; Mr. Ross; Mr. Burrows; Master and Miss Lindsay; 45 invalids; 8 servants.

Per St. George, from Bengal: Mrs. Cardew and two children; Mrs. Stainforth and six ditto; Mrs. Clark and two ditto; Mrs. Marshman and child; Mrs. Rankin; Mrs. Blenkin and child; Mrs. Stephenson and four children; Mrs. Patten and child; Mrs. Harjette and two children: Miss Williams; C. Cardew, Esq., C.S.; Major Worrall, B.C.; Capt. Jackson, B.A.; Capt. Martin, 41st regt. B.I.; Lieut. Streng, H.M. 13th Lt. Inf.; Lieut. Holder, ditto; Lieut. Lock, 15th B.N.I.; Lieut. Trail, Engineers; Mr. Pogson, Esq.; Mr. Harjette; Dr. Blenkin; Mr. Stephenson; Mr. Patten; Miss Sophia Monckton; Masters Fred. Inglis and John Monckton; 10 servants.—Miss Wheatley was landed at the Cape.

Expected.

Per Broxbornebury, from Bengal: Hon. Mrs. Lindsay; Mrs. Henry Lushington; Mrs. Col. Faithfull; Mrs. Capt. Fell; Mrs. Blundell; Mrs. W. W. Bell; Mrs. Low; Mrs. Campbell; Miss Halcott; Robert Saunders, Esq., C.S.; G. W. Traill, Esq., C.S.; Capt. Blundell, H.M. 11th Lt. Drags.; Capt. W. Grant, 27th N.I.; Capt. J. H. Low; Lieut. Harper, H.M. 9th Foot; Misses Davidson, two Robinson, two Kennedy, two Dashington, two Millett, two Robertson, Metcalfe, Wilkinson, Traill, and Faithfull; Masters Blundell, two Robinson, Holland, Hindants, Metcalfe, Borough, two Farrington, Fell, Low, two Blair, and Davidson.

Per Florentia, from N.S. Wales: Mrs. Baines and son; Mrs. Perkins; Dr. Savage; Capt. Petrie; Messrs. Watt, Denton, Denton, jun., M'Kinlay, Clark, Porter, Corrobine, Maiber, Craig, and Brown; Masters Aspinall, Forbes, and two Dickson.

PASSENGERS TO INDIA.

Per Sesostris, for Bengal: Mrs. Yates; Mrs. Bell; Miss Britton; Miss Home; Capt. Bell; Mr. Muir, C.S.; Lieut. Carter.—For Madras: Mrs. Thomson; Mrs. O'Brien; Miss Daunt; Miss O'Brien; Mr. Stokes, surgeon; Lieut. Pratt; Mr. Pilleau. assist.-surg.; Rev. Mr. Thomson; Ens. Ramsbottom; Mr. O'Brien, quar.-mast. H.M. 39th regt.; Mr. O'Brien.—For Cape: Mrs. Stigmann; Major Cloeté; Rev. Mr. Stigmann.

Per Royal George, for Bombay: Miss George; Miss Leonard.

Per Theresa, for Madras and Bengal: Mr. Anderson and family; Capt. M'Cartney; Lieut. Watt; Lieut. M'Kenzie; Mr. F. Stoddart; Mr. Strachey; Mr. Martin; Mr. Smith; Mr. Young; Mr. Sowerkroop; Mr. Kettlewell.

Per Walmer Castle, for Bombay: Col. Osborne and lady; two Misses Osborne; Major Penycuicke and lady; Capt. Hancock and party; Capt. Newport and lady; Dr. Cahill and lady; Major Little

(in charge of troops); Major Romney; Lieut. Holdsworth; Ens. Jephson; Mr. Hadow; Mr. Steuart; Mr. Jackyl; Mr. Howard; Mr. Munro.

Per Euphrates, for Bombay: Mr. and Mrs. Mills; Mr. and Mrs. Wilson; Dr. and Mrs. Sproule; two Misses Watkins; Miss Cole; Lieut. Broadhurst; Mr. Wilson; Messrs. Nelson; Mr. Perfect.

Per Royal William, for Madras: Mr. and Mrs. G. A. Smith; Major and Mrs. M'Pherson; Capt. Gray and family; Mrs. MacCloud; Miss Chrystie; Miss Macdonald; the Misses Prendergast; — Pringle, Esq., Madras C.S.; Capt. Pcchell; Lieut. Butler, Madras army; Mr. Raikes, C.S.; Mr. Fraser; Mr. Grant, H.M. 63d regt.; Mr. Wahab, Madras army; Mr. Money, ditto; Mr. Gordon.

BIRTHS, MARRIAGES, AND DEATHS.

BIRTHS.

Feb. 15. At Sea, the lady of Capt. W. Bell, Ship *Cornwall,* of a daughter.

April 23. At Brabœuf, Surrey, the lady of Major Arthur Wight, H.C.S., of a son and heir.

May 5. In Manchester Square, the lady of Winthrop M. Praed, Esq., M.P., of a daughter.

9. In Somerset Street, Portman Square, the lady of Henry Stahman, Esq., of a son.

MARRIAGES.

April 29. At Bath, the Rev. William Littlehales, third son of Rear-Admiral Littlehales, to Elizabeth, eldest daughter of the late Capt. W. H. Cleather, of the 1st Ceylon regt., many years deputy judge advocate in that island.

May 11. At Saham, Norfolk, D'Urban Blyth, Esq., nephew to Maj. Gen. Sir Benjamin D'Urban, governor of the Cape of Good Hope, to Ann, daughter of William Farrer, Esq., of Saham.

12. At Kensington, J. H. Whiteway, solicitor, eldest son of Samuel Whiteway, Esq., of Oakford House, Kingsteinton, Devon, to Frederica Gimbert, daughter of the late Capt. Wm. Wilkinson, of the Hon. E. I. Company's Service.

17. At St. Mary's, Marylebone, Capt. C. S. Maling, of the 68th regt. Bengal N. I., to Wernyss Jane, relict of the late Maj. C. H. Campbell, and daughter of the Hon. L. G. K. Murray, youngest son of the late Earl of Dunmore.

19. At Bathwick Church, Charles Rowlandson, Esq., of the Madras army. third son of the late Rev. M. Rowlandson, D.D., Vicar of Warminster, Wilts., to Ellen, second daughter of C. F. Sorensen, Esq., of Bathwick-hill.

25. At St. Mary's, Bryanston Square, Barré Wm. Goldie, Esq., of the Bengal Engineers, to Julia Harriett, only child of the late James Gosling, Esq., formerly of Clay Hall.

Lately. At Dingwell, R. Mackenzie, Esq., major E. I. Company's service, to Katherine, daughter of the late Alex. Mackenzie, Esq, of Burton-Crescent.

DEATHS.

Feb. 24. At Sea, on board the ship *Bolton,* homeward bound from Madras, Lieut. George Freese, of the 12th regt. Madras N. I., second son of the late Col. J. W. Freese, of the Madras army.

March 21. At Sea, on board the *Wellington,* on the passage from Madras, Mrs. Gen. T. Hawker.

May 3. At Pisa, L. F. Cottrell, Esq., Lieut. in the 8th regt. Madras L. C., in the 27th year of his age.

5. On board the Ship *Lady Flora,* on the passage from India, Lieut. H. Pereira, of the 43d regt. Madras N. I.

6. At Loam-pitt hill, Mrs. Rebecca Grey, relict of the late Capt. Robert Grey, of the Hon. E. I. Company's service.

— At the settlement of the Moravian Brethren, Fairfield, near Manchester, the Rev. Christian Ignatius La Trobe. This venerable man (who died in the 79th year of his age), had been for nearly fifty years secretary of the Brethren's

Society for propogating the Gospel. In 1814, he visited the Missions in South Africa, and published an interesting account of his travels.

8. At Grove-place, the lady of Capt. John Fawcett, of the Bombay army.

10. At Edinburgh, the Hon. Robert Lindsay, of Balcarras, second son of James 5th Earl of Balcarras.

11. At the East-India College, Herts, in his 65th year, David Shea, Esq.

13. At his house in Baker Street, Portman-Square, Sir Charles Wilkins, K.H., LL.D., F.R.S., aged 85. (A Memoir of this gentleman will appear in next month's journal.)

14. At his residence, Herne-hill, Surrey, in his 74th year, James Horsburgh, Esq., hydrographer to the East-India Company.

21. In Upper Harley Street, in her 38th year, Penelope, wife of John Cotton, Esq.

26. At Bath, in the 25th year of her age, Cecilia, eldest daughter of the late A. G. J. Tod, Esq., of the Bengal Civil Service.

Lately. On board the *Duke of Bedford*, on the passage from Bengal to England, Mrs. Millar.

— At Madehurst Lodge, Sussex, of consumption, Lady Ellen Dalzell, second daughter of the Earl of Carnwath.

— At Dover, Catherine, relict of Capt. John Boyce, Hon. E. I. Company's service, aged 71.

LONDON PRICE CURRENT, May 24, 1836.

EAST-INDIA AND CHINA PRODUCE.

	£.	s.	d.		£.	s.	d.
Coffee, Batavia ....cwt.	2	12	0	@	3	9	0
— Samarang	2	7	0	—	2	10	0
— Cheribon	2	16	0	—	3	4	0
— Sumatra	2	2	0	—	2	8	0
— Ceylon	2	11	6	—	2	13	0
— Mocha	3	0	0	—	5	0	0
Cotton, Surat ....lb	0	0	6¼	—	0	0	8½
— Madras	0	0	6¾	—	0	0	8½
— Bengal	0	0	5¾	—	0	0	7
— Bourbon		none				—	
Drugs & for Dyeing.							
Aloes, Epatica ......cwt.	9	10	0	—	15	0	0
Anniseeds, Star	5	0	0			—	
Borax, Refined	3	3	0			—	
— Unrefined	3	10	0			—	
Camphire, in tub	12	10	0	—	13	0	0
Cardamoms, Malabar ..lb	0	3	0	—	0	3	1
— Ceylon	0	1	2	—	0	1	6
Cassia Buds ....cwt.	5	0	0	—	5	5	0
— Lignea	3	6	0	—	3	8	0
Castor Oil ....lb	0	0	4	—	0	0	10
China Root ....cwt.	17	0	0	—	18	0	0
Cubebs	2	5	0	—	2	12	0
Dragon's Blood	10	0	0	—	25	0	0
Gum Ammoniac, drop	6	0	0	—	8	0	0
— Arabic	2	10	0	—	4	5	0
— Assafœtida	1	10	0	—	4	0	0
— Benjamin, 3d Sort	3	10	0	—	10	0	0
— Animi	5	0	0	—	8	0	0
— Gambogium	5	0	0	—	15	0	0
— Myrrh	4	10	0	—	4	15	0
— Olibanum	0	6	0	—	2	18	0
Kino	12	0	0			—	
Lac Lake ....lb			nominal				
— Dye	0	2	10	—	0	3	0
— Shell ....cwt.	5	10	0	—	7	15	0
— Stick	3	10	0	—	3	17	0
Musk, China ....oz.	0	10	0	—	1	5	0
Nux Vomica ....cwt.	0	8	0			—	
Oil, Cassia ....oz.	0	8	6			—	
— Cinnamon	0	4	0	—	0	6	0
— Cocoa-nut ......cwt.	1	11	0			—	
— Cajaputa ....oz.	0	0	4	—	0	0	6
— Mace	0	0	2	—	0	0	3
— Nutmegs	0	1	2	—	0	1	5
Opium		none				—	
Rhubarb	0	2	6	—	0	3	6
Sal Ammoniac ......cwt.	3	8	0			—	
Senna ....lb	0	0	3	—	0	1	2
Turmeric, Java ....cwt.	0	9	0	—	0	18	0
— Bengal	0	12	0	—	0	16	0
— China	0	16	0	—	1	2	0
Galls, in Sorts	4	0	0	—	4	5	0
—, Blue	5	0	0	—	5	5	0
Hides, Buffalo ....lb	0	0	2½	—	0	0	3¼
— Ox and Cow	0	0	3	—	0	0	4
Indigo, Blue and Violet	0	7	0	—	0	7	5
— Ex. fine Bl. and Violet	0	7	6	—	0	7	8
— Purple and Violet	0	6	8	—	0	7	0
— Fine Violet	0	6	8	—	0	7	0
— Mid. to good Violet	0	6	3	—	0	6	7
— Violet and Copper	0	6	0	—	0	6	4
— Copper	0	5	8	—	0	6	0
— Consuming, mid. to fine	0	5	6	—	0	6	3
— Do. ord. and low	0	5	0	—	0	5	5
— Do. very low	0	4	6	—	0	4	11
— Madras, mid. to good	0	5	1	—	0	5	6
— Oude, good mid. & good	0	3	8	—	0	3	11
Mother-o'-Pearl Shells, China ....cwt.	3	0	0	@	4	2	0
Nankeens ....piece		—				—	
Rattans 100	0	2	9	—	0	6	6
Rice, Bengal White ....cwt.	0	12	0	—	0	15	6
— Patna	0	16	6	—	0	18	0
— Java	0	10	6	—	0	13	0
Safflower	5	1	0	—	9	0	0
Sago	0	9	0	—	0	10	6
— Pearl	0	13	0	—	0	16	0
Saltpetre	1	8	6	—	1	11	0
Silk, Company's Bengal lb	0	16	0	—	1	8	0
— Novi		—				—	
— China Tsatlee	1	5	6	—	1	9	6
— Bengal Privilege	0	15	6	—	1	1	0
— Taysam	1	2	0	—	1	4	6
Spices, Cinnamon	0	6	0	—	0	10	0
— Cloves	0	0	9½	—	0	1	2
— Mace	0	5	0	—	0	9	0
— Nutmegs	0	5	0	—	0	7	0
— Ginger ....cwt.	1	16	0	—	2	10	0
— Pepper, Black ......lb	0	0	4¾	—	0	0	5½
— — White	0	1	4	—	,	1	8
Sugar, Bengal ....cwt.	1	16	0	—	2	1	6
— Siam and China	1	14	0	—	2	2	0
— Mauritius (duty paid)	3	0	0	—	3	9	0
— Manilla and Java	1	13	0	—	2	2	0
Tea, Bohea ....lb		—				—	
— Congou		—				—	
— Souchong		—				—	
— Caper		—				—	
— Campoi		—		See Sale.		—	
— Twankay		—				—	
— Pekoe, (Orange, &c.)		—				—	
— Hyson Skin		—				—	
— Hyson		—				—	
— Young Hyson		—				—	
— Gunpowder, Imperial		—				—	
Tin, Banca ....cwt.	5	15	0	—		—	
Tortoiseshell ....lb	1	1	0	—	1	18	0
Vermilion ....lb	0	4	5	—	0	4	10
Wax ....cwt.	7	0	0	—	7	7	0
Wood, Saunders Red ..ton	7	0	0			—	
— Ebony	13	0	0			—	
— Sapan	6	0	0	—	13	0	0

AUSTRALASIAN PRODUCE.

	£.	s.	d.		£.	s.	d.
Cedar Wood ....foot	0	0	6	—	0	0	7
Oil, Fish ....tun	36	0	0	—	39	0	0
Whalebone ....ton	120	0	0	—	140	0	0
Wool, N. S. Wales, viz.							
Best ....lb	0	3	3	—	0	3	6
Inferior	0	1	0	—	0	3	2
— V. D. Land, viz.							
Best	0	2	0	—	0	2	8
Inferior	0	1	0	—	0	1	9

SOUTH AFRICAN PRODUCE.

	£.	s.	d.		£.	s.	d.
Aloes ....cwt.	1	10	6	—	1	13	0
Ostrich Feathers, und ....lb		—				—	
Gum Arabic ....cwt.	1	5	0	—	1	10	0
Hides, Dry ....lb	0	0	4½	—	0	0	6½
— Salted	0	0	3½	—	0	0	5
Oil, Palm ....cwt.	1	17	0			—	
Raisins		—				—	
Wax	7	0	0	—	7	5	0
Wine, Cape, Mad., best ..pipe	17	0	0	—	19	0	0
— Do. 2d & 3d quality	14	0	0	—	15	0	0
Wood, Teak ....load	9	5	0	—	10	10	0
Wool ....lb.	0	1	6	—	0	2	6

N.B. *The letters* P.C. *denote prime cost, or manufacturers' prices;* A. *advance (per cent.) on the same;* D. *discount (per cent.) on the same;* N.D. *no demand.—The bazar maund is equal to* 82 lb. 2 oz. 2 *drs., and* 100 *bazar maunds equal to* 110 *factory maunds. Goods sold by Sa. Rupees B. mds. produce* 5 *to* 8 *per cent. more than when sold by Ct. Rupees F. mds.—The* Madras Candy *is equal to* 500lb. *The* Surat Candy *is equal to* 746½ lb. *The* Pecul *is equal to* 133⅓ lb. *The* Corge *is* 20 *pieces.*

CALCUTTA, January 21, 1836.

Article	Unit	Rs. A.		Rs. A.
Anchors	Sa.Rs. cwt.	12 8	@	19 0
Bottles	100	8 12	—	9 4
Coals	B. md.	0 7	—	0 8
Copper Sheathing, 16-32	F. md	34 0	—	34 8
—— Braziers',	do.	34 12	—	35 0
—— Thick sheets	do.	——		——
—— Old Gross	do.	32 6	—	32 10
—— Bolt	do.	32 12	—	33 8
—— Tile	do.	31 4	—	32 0
—— Nails, assort.	do.	32 8	—	38 0
—— Peru Slab	Ct.Rs. do.	27 12	—	29 12
—— Russia	Sa.Rs. do.	——		——
Copperas	do.	4 0	—	4 2
Cottons, chints	pce.	——		——
—— Muslins, assort.	do.	1 2	—	13 0
—— Yarn 16 to 170	mor.	0 6½	—	0 9
Cutlery, fine		5 to 10A. & P.C.		
Glass		7A.	—	12A.
Hardware		20 D.	—	50D.
Hosiery, cotton		20 to 50 A.&P.C.		
Ditto, silk		20 to 35 D.&P.C		
Iron, Swedish, sq.	Sa.Rs. F. md.	5 1	@	5 3
—— —— flat	do.	5 0	—	5 2
—— English, sq.	do.	2 10	—	2 13
—— —— flat	do.	2 9	—	2 11
—— Bolt	do.	2 11	—	2 13
—— Sheet	do.	5 4	—	5 10
—— Nails	cwt.	11 0	—	15 8
—— Hoops	F. md.	5 3	—	5 6
—— Kentledge	cwt.	1 2	—	1 5
Lead, Pig	F. md.	6 1	—	6 3
—— unstamped	do.	5 14	—	6 0
Millinery		15 to 35D.&P.C.		
Shot, patent	bag	2 6	—	3 4
Spelter	Ct.Rs. F. md.	6 9	—	6 10
Stationery		5 to 25 D.&P.C.		
Steel, English	Ct.Rs. F. md.	5 14	—	6 4
—— Swedish	do.	6 8	—	7 0
Tin Plates	Sa.Rs. box	15 0	—	15 8
Woollens, Broad cloth, fine	yd.	5 0	—	9 8
—— coarse and middling		1 7	—	4 0
—— Flannel fine		1 2	—	1 14

MADRAS, January 6, 1836.

Article	Unit	Rs.		Rs.
Bottles	100	12	@	14
Copper, Sheathing	candy	265		——
—— Cakes	do.	——		——
—— Old	do.	230	—	240
—— Nails, assort.	do.	350	—	370
Cottons, Chintz	piece	4	—	5
—— Ginghams	do.	2	—	3
—— Longcloth, fine	do.	9	—	14
Cutlery, coarse		15A.		20A.
Glass and Earthenware		10A.		25A.
Hardware		10A.		—
Hosiery		25A.	—	30A.
Iron, Swedish,	candy	40	—	50
—— English bar	do.	19	—	20
—— Flat and bolt	do.	19	—	20
Iron Hoops	candy	19	@	20
—— Nails	do.	110	—	115
Lead, Pig	do.	42	—	45
—— Sheet	do.	38	—	40
Millinery		20A.	—	25 A.
Shot, patent	bag	3	—	3½
Spelter	candy	30	—	35
Stationery		Overstocked.		
Steel, English	candy	50	—	55
—— Swedish	do.	70	—	75
Tin Plates	box	18	—	19
Woollens, Broad cloth, fine		10A.	—	15A.
—— —— coarse		Wanted		
—— Flannel, fine		12to14Ans.pr.yd.		
—— Ditto, coarse		8to10Ans. do.		

BOMBAY, January 16, 1836.

Article	Unit	Rs.		Rs.
Anchors	cwt.	12	@	13
Bottles	doz.	1.4		——
Coals	ton	10	—	12
Copper, Sheathing, 16-32	cwt.	48	—	49
—— Thick sheets	do.	52		52.8
—— Plate bottoms	do.	50		——
—— Tile	do.	44.8		45
Cottons, Chintz, &c., &c.		——		——
—— Longcloths		——		——
—— Muslins		——		——
—— Other goods		——		——
—— Yarn, Nos. 20 to 100	lb.	0.11	—	1.7
Cutlery, table		10A.		——
Glass and Earthenware		10 D.		20D.
Hardware		P. C.		——
Hosiery, half hose		P. C.		——
Iron, Swedish	St. candy	48	@	——
—— English	do.	23		23.4
—— Hoops	cwt.	5.4		——
—— Nails	do.	12		13
—— Sheet	do.	5.8		——
—— Rod for bolts	St. candy	23	—	24
—— do. for nails	do.	26	—	28
Lead, Pig	cwt.	10		——
—— Sheet	do.	9.8		——
Millinery		10 D.		——
Shot, patent	cwt.	10		——
Spelter	do.	7.12		——
Stationery		P. C.		——
Steel, Swedish	tub	10.4		——
Tin Plates	box	16		——
Woollens, Broad cloth, fine	yd.	4	—	7
—— —— coarse		1.12	—	7
—— Flannel, fine		1.8		——

CANTON, January 12, 1836.

Article	Unit	Drs.		Drs.
Cottons, Chintz, 28 yds.	piece	3	@	4
—— Longcloths	do.	3	—	11
—— Muslins, 20 yds.	do.	—		—
—— Cambrics, 40 yds	do.	3	—	4
—— Bandannoes	do.	1.25	—	1.45
—— Yarn, Nos. 16 to 50	pecul	44	—	51
Iron, Bar	do.	2.25		——
—— Rod	do.	3	—	3½
Lead, Pig	do.	6	—	—
Smalts	pecul	30	@	60
Steel, Swedish	tub	3.75		—
Woollens, Broad cloth	yd.	1.30	—	1.40
—— do. ex super	yd.	2.50	—	2.75
—— Camlets	pce.	28	—	30
—— Do. Dutch	do.	34		37
—— Long Ells	do.	9	—	9½
Tin, Straits	pecul	16	—	16½
Tin Plates	box	8		——

SINGAPORE, December 5, 1835.

		Drs.		Drs.			Drs.		Drs.
Anchors	pecul	6	@	7½	Cotton Hkfs. imit. Battick, dble.	doz.	2½	@	4
Bottles	100	—		—	—— do. do Pullicat	doz.	1½	—	2
Copper Nails and Sheathing	pecul	36	—	37	—— Twist, 30 to 40	pecul	58	—	60
Cottons, Madapollams, 24yd. by 36in.	pcs.	2	—	2½	Hardware, and coarse Cutlery		scarce.		
—— Imit. Irish /24 34-36	do.	2	—	2½	Iron, Swedish	pecul	3½	—	3¾
—— Longcloths 38 to 40 34-36	do.	4¼	—	4¾	—— English	do.	2¾	—	3½
—— —— do. do. 36 fine	do.	5	—	5½	—— Nail, rod	do.	2½	—	—
—— —— do. do. 40-44	do.	4	—	6½	Lead, Pig	do.	5¼	—	5¾
—— —— do. do. 44-54	do.	5	—	9	—— Sheet	do.	5	—	5½
—— —— 54	do.	—		—	Shot, patent	bag	—		—
—— Prints, 7-8. *single colours*	do.	2	—	2½	Spelter	pecul	5½	—	6
—— —— 9-8.	do.	2¾	—	2½	Steel, Swedish	do.	4¼	—	4½
—— Cambric, 12 yds. by 45 to 50 in.	do.	1½	—	2½	—— English	do.	—		—
—— Jaconet, 20 40 .. 44	do.	2	—	2¾	Woollens, Long Ells	pcs.	9	—	10
—— Lappets, 10 40 .. 44	do.	1	—	1½	—— Camblets	do.	25	—	30
—— Chintz, fancy colours	do.	3	—	5½	—— Ladies' cloth	yd.	1	—	2

REMARKS.

Calcutta, March 4, 1836.—The market for Piece Goods is in a healthy condition. The late arrivals from Liverpool and Glasgow found the bazaar bare of several descriptions of light goods, more particularly Lappets, Books, and Mulls, which accordingly met, and would still experience, a ready and profitable sale. Jaconet Muslins, likewise, have had a good demand, and continue to be enquired for, the stock being moderate. The more heavy Cottons, say Shirtings, and Cambrics, are abundant, and less saleable. Of printed Goods, Bengal Stripes, and single coloured Plates, meet with buyers, but recent sales have been effected at rates not generally remunerative. Other description of prints are without enquiry.—The market for Cotton Yarn may be considered in a very uncertain and unsatisfactory state.—The Woollen market offers little subject for remark; the sales for the last two months have certainly been greater, and at better rates than for some time before, but the amount altogether has not been large.—The Copper and Spelter market may be considered in an encouraging state.—English Iron, large imports, and market looking low.—The market continues to be quite bare of Beer.—Wine and Spirits, the market is quite overstocked.—*Extra Exch. Price Current.*

Madras, Jan. 6, 1836.—A small rise has taken place in White Twist, which is beginning to look up; in Orange, the prices have declined a little; the sales have, however, not been very considerable in both qualities. German dye and Turkey-red maintain former prices.—Large quantities of Iron, Copper, Spelter, and Tin-plates have come to market, but we have not heard of any sales having been yet effected.—The recent arrivals from England have brought a good supply to the market of Hoisery, Select Millinery, &c., which have realised between 30 and 40 per cent.

Bombay, Jan. 21, 1836.—The following sales of Piece Goods have been reported: Grey Madopollams, 1,000 pieces, at Rs. 3-3 per piece; Mull Muslins, 2,100 ditto, at Rs. 4½ to 9-1 per ditto; Zebra Dresses, 1,200 ditto, at Rs. 2-1 per ditto.—Metals are in limited demand.

Canton, Dec. 29, 1835.—Iron has declined in price a little.—Camlets and Long Ells are in good demand.—*Jan.* 12, 1836: Sales of Woollens are being made at our quotations, but there is little tendency to any improvement.—Cotton Piece Goods in moderate demand.—Cotton Yarn rather dull.—The importations of Tin Plates having lately been considerable, the price has fallen to 8 dols. per box.

INDIA SECURITIES AND EXCHANGES.

Calcutta, Jan. 21, 1836.

Government Securities.

Buy.]	Rs.	As.		Rs.	As.	[Sell.
Prem.	15	8	Remittable	15	0	Prem.
Prem.	0	4	Second 5 per cent.	2	8	
	2	12	Third 5 per cent.	2	8	Prem.
Disc.	2	5	Four per cent. Loan	2	9	Disc.

Bank Shares.

Bank of Bengal (10,000) .... Sa. Rs. 15,550 a 15,600

Union Bank .. (2,500) .... 150 to 200 prem.

Bank of Bengal Rates.

Discount on private bills .... 7 0 per cent.

Ditto on government and salary bills 4 0 do.

Interest on loans on govt. paper .... 5 0 do.

Rate of Exchange, *March* 4.

On London and Liverpool, six months' sight, to buy, 2s. 2d.; to sell, 2s. 2½d. per Sa. Rupee.

Madras, Jan. 6, 1836.

Government Securities.

Remittable Loan, six per cent.—15 per ct. prem.

Ditto ditto of 18th Aug. 1825, five per cent.—1 prem.—2 disc.

Ditto ditto last five per cent.—1 to 1½ prem.

Ditto ditto Old four per cent.—4½ to 5 disc.

Ditto ditto New four per cent.—4½ to 5 disc.

Exchange.

On London, at 6 months,—to buy, 2s.; to sell, 1s. 11d. per Madras Rupee.

Bombay, Jan. 21, 1836.

Exchanges.

Bills on London, at 6 mo. sight, 2s. 1½d. to 2s. 1½d. per Rupee.

On Calcutta, at 30 days' sight, 108.12 to 109.4 Bom. Rs. per 100 Sicca Rupees.

On Madras, at 30 days' sight, 103 to 103.8 Bom. Rs. per 100 Madras Rs.

Government Securities.

Remittable Loan, 124.8 to 125 Bom. Rs. per 100 Sa. Rs.

5 per cent. Loan of 1822-23, according to the period of discharge, 108.8 to 109 per ditto.

Ditto of 1825-26, 109.12 to 111.8 per ditto.

Ditto of 1829-30, 111 to 111.8 per ditto.

4 per cent. Loan of 1832-33, 106 to 106.4 per ditto.

Singapore, Dec. 5, 1835.

Exchanges.

On London, 4 to 6 mo. sight, 4s. 4d. to 4s. 5d. per dollar.

On Bengal, gov. bills 206 Sa. Rs. per 100 dollars.

Canton, Jan. 12, 1836.

Exchanges, &c.

On London, 6 mo. sight, 4s. 10d per Sp. Dol.

E. I. Co's Agents for advances on consignments, 4s. 8d.

On Bengal. — Private Bills, 212 Sa. Rs. per 100 Sp. Dols.—Company's ditto, 30 days, 210 Sa. Rs.

On Bombay, ditto Bom. Rs. 220 to 222 per ditto.

Sycee Silver at Lintin, 3½ to 4 per cent. prem.

LIST of SHIPS Trading to INDIA and Eastward of the CAPE of GOOD HOPE.

Destination.	Appointed to sail.	Ships' Names.	Tons.	Owners or Consignees.	Captains.	Where loading.	Reference for Freight or Passage.
	1836.						
	June 1	Arab	378	John S. Sparkes	John S. Sparkes	St.Kt.Docks	Sir Chas. Cockerill, Bart., & Co.
	— 20	Java	1200	R. Scott, Fairlie & Co.	Robert Joblin	E.I. Docks	R. Scott, Fairlie, & Co.; John Pirie & Co.
	— 25	Herefordshire	1335	Thacker, F&CE Mangles	H.S.H. Isaacson	E.I. Docks	Thacker & Price; F. & C. E. Mangles; Leary &Thompson.
	July 10 ..Ports.	Mstu. Elphinstone	611	Joseph L. Heathorn	William Toller	W.I. Docks	Joseph L. Heathorn; Leary & Thompson; James Barber.
Bengal	— 10	Cornwall	872	Palmers, Mackillop&Co.	William Bell	W.I. Docks	Thomas Haviside & Co.
	— 16 ..Ports.	London	62n	Money Wigram	John Wimble	E.I. Docks	John Pirie & Co.
	June ..Ports.	Earl Grey	600	Marjoribanks & Ferrers	James Talbert	E.I. Docks	Majoribanks & Ferrers; Waddell, Beck, & Co.
	Aug. 1	Lord Hungerford	724	Charles Farquharson	C. Farquharson	E.I. Docks	Sir Chas. Cockerill, Bart., & Co.; T. Haviside & Co.
	— do.	Windsor	700	Richard Green	Alex. Hemming	E.I. Docks	Thomas Haviside & Co. [Co.
	— 5	Scotia	740	Thomas&William Smith	John Campbell	E.I. Docks	Walkinshaw & Co.; Lyall, Brothers, & Co.; John Pirie &
Bengal and China	— 1	Tartar (N.S.)	250	William O. Young	Wm. O. Young	Blackwall	Palmers, Mackillop, & Co.; Capt. Young, Jerus. Coffee-[house.
	June 1	Repulse	1424	Tomlin & Pryce	Henry Price	E.I. Docks	Tomlin, Man, & Co., Cornhill.
	— 1 ..Ports.	Duke of Lancaster	565	J. Gladstone & Co.	James Hargraves	W.I. Docks	Arbuthnot & latham; Alves, Steele, & Harrison.
	— do.	Roxburgh Castle	600	Wigrams & Green	Wm. Cumberland	E.I. Docks	John Pirie & Co., Freeman's court.
Madras and Bengal	— 5	Thomas Grenville	896	Robert Thornhill	Robert Thornhill	E.I. Docks	Sir C. Cockerill, & Co.; T. Haviside & Co.
	— 7 ..do.	Exmouth	6nn	Reid, Irving, & Co.	Richard Saunders	W.I. Docks	Forbes, Forbes, & Co.; Jopp & Scarr; Tomlin & Man.
	— 11	True Briton	75n	Forbes, Forbes, & Co.	Charles Beach	E.I. Docks	John Pirie & Co.; James Barber, Leadenhall-street.
	— 13 ..Ports.	Robert Small	70n	Money & Henry Wigram	William Fulcher	E.I. Docks	Small, Colquhoun, & Co.; John Pirie & Co.
Cape, Madras, and Bengal	— 20 ..do.	Heroine	650	Gledstanes & Co.	R. M'Carthy	St.Kt.Docks	Thos. Haviside & Co.
Madras and Bengal	July 1	Duke of Buccleugh	650	Richard Green	R.F. Martin	W.I. Docks	Thomas Haviside & Co.
	June 1	Prince George	500	Francis Shaw	Francis Shaw	St.Kt.Docks	Tomlin, Man, & Co., Cornhill.
	Aug. 15	Lady Flora	755	Robert Ford	Robert Ford	E.I. Docks	Crawford, Colvin, & Co.; Tomlin Man, & Co.
Madras	July 1	Wellington	500	Gustavus Evans	James Liddell	W.I. Docks	MacGhie, Page, & Smith, Exchange-buildings.
	Aug. 1 ..Ports.	Great Hartwood	421	William Bottomley	MacGowan	Llanelly	Lachlan, Sons, & M'Leod.
	— 8	Pestonjee Bomanjee	600	Turner & Co.	James Thompson	W.I. Docks	Stewart & Westmoreland; Jas. Thomson, Billiter-square.
	June 15	Bengal	400	John Wright	John J. Marjoram	Lon. Docks	J. Cockburn & Co.; Waddell, Beck, & Co.
	— 15	Gilmore	550	Reid, Irving, & Co.	H. H. Lindsay	W.I. Docks	Reid, Irving, & Co.; Thos. Haviside & Co.
	— 3	Boyne	619	Thacker, F&CE Mangles	George Richardson	E.I. Docks	Thacker & Price, Leadenhall-st; James Barber.
	— 20	Scalely Castle	400	James Walkinshaw	Thomas Sandys	E.I. Docks	John Pirie & Co.
Bombay	— 11	Carnatic	650	Richard Green	John Brodie	E.I. Docks	John Pirie & Co.
	— 30	Malabar	630	Richard Green	William Tucker	E.I. Docks	John Pirie & Co.
	July 6 ..Ports.	Mary of Hastings	500	John Clarkson	John Clarkson	W.I. Docks	T. Haviside & Co.
	— 20 ..do.	Lady Feversham	430	Robert Barry	George Webster	E.I. Docks	Capt. Clarkson, Jerusalem Coffee-house.
	June 15	Royal Admiral	414	William Bottomley	D. Fotheringham	E.I. Docks	Lachlan, Sons, & M'Leod.
China	— 18	Clifton	350	Thomas Heath	Thomas Worsell	Lon. Docks	Thos. Heath, Fenchurch-street; Read, Cornhill. [Tiplady;
	— 11	Edinburgh	1414	John Macvicar	David Marshall	E.I. Docks	Gregson, Melville, & Co.; Gardner & Urquhart; Phillips&
Cape	June	Caroline	200	W. Abrahams	William Holmes	Lon. Docks	Thomson & Edwards, King's Arms-yard.
	— 3	Olive Branch	217	Phillips King, & Co.	C. A. Warring	St.Kt.Docks	Walter Hawkins, Fowlke's-buildings, Tower-street.
St. Helena	— 25	Mary Ann	130	E. Luckie	D. Shirling	Lon. Docks	Edward Luckie.
New South Wales	— 16	William Bryan	329	Domett & Co.	John Roman	Lon. Docks	Domett, Young, & England, George-yard.
South Australia	— 10	Arricane	316	Thomas Finlay	John Duff	Lon. Docks	Henry Toulmin.
Cape and Seven River	— 7	Joshua Carrol	143	William Bruce	Jacob Toby	St.Kt.Docks	F. & C. E. Mangles; Edmund Read.

THE LONDON MARKETS, May 24.

Sugar.—The large arrivals near at hand of British plantation sugar caused the demand from grocers and refiners to be very moderate last week. The stock of West-India sugars is now 6,490 hhds. and trs., being 7,511 less than last year. The stock of Mauritius is now 73,701 bags, which is 48,216 less than last year. There has been a good enquiry after Bengal sugar by the grocers and shippers. In Manilla, Siam, or Java, scarcely any thing done, the supply being still scanty and indifferent, and for which the holders ask extreme quotations, which prevents business of the least consequence from being transacted; these descriptions are much wanted.

Coffee.—There has been no alteration in the prices of East-India—Ceylon has been taken by the home trade in small parcels at 52s. to 53s.; Mysore has secured a good sale for shipping.

Lac Dye.—There is a good and regular demand for this article at late prices. In lac lake a good deal has been done for home use and on speculation.

Indigo.—There has been more enquiry, but the limited business done in the indigo market at present have been confined to small parcels of old quality, at the rates of the late quarterly sale. Accounts have been received from Calcutta to the 4th March, stating the crop at 108,000 maunds, out of which only 55,000 maunds would be shipped to England; the prices there have risen 10 per cent. for the ordinary qualities.

Cotton.—The arrivals from the East-Indies still continue to come in freely; the prices still remain nominal, scarcely any thing being done. Liverpool market dull.

Rice.—Although the arrivals of East-India have been large, still the demand has been brisk, principally for exportation.

Spices.—In spices there has been little done.

Saltpetre.—The brisk request which existed for this article in the middle of last week has been suddenly checked by the extensive arrivals.

Tea.—The tea sales, which commenced on the 17th inst., concluded yesterday; of the 42,000 pkgs. offered, about 36,000 have been taken by the trade with more spirit than has hitherto been witnessed. Canton boheas have supported the prices which previously ruled in the market; Fokien boheas and common congous 1d. per lb. higher; the mixed blackish leaf kinds have advanced 1½d. to 2d. per lb.; those of wiry blackish leaf and pekoe flavour have sold 2d. below the rates of the sales which took place in April. Souchongs and pekoes have maintained their value. Twankays of the common kinds are 1d. per lb. higher; the fine ones rather cheaper. Hysons have hardly supported their previous value towards the close of the sales. Imperials and gunpowders sold freely at the quotations. The Company's June sale contains a large quantity of fine blackish leaf kinds, as well as some between these and the common kinds, with full flavour, altogether about 4,000,000lbs.; which will be followed by about 36,000 pkgs. of Free Trade. There have been immense arrivals since this day week, in all 85,801 packages, or nearly 6,100,000lbs.; large public sales are advertised, mostly of congou, 36,000 pkgs. to follow the Company's June sale, and 35,000 pkgs. for the 5th July.

The question as to the time when the 2s. 1d. duty on boheas comes into operation is still unsettled.

DAILY PRICES OF STOCKS, *from April 26, to May 26*, 1836.

April.	Bank Stock.	3 Pr. Ct. Red.	3 Pr. Ct. Consols.	3½ Pr. Ct. Red.	New 3½ Pr. Cent.	Long Annuities.	India Stock.	Consols for acct.	India Bonds.	Exch. Bills.
26	210½ 211	90⅞ 91	91⅝ 91¾	98⅝ ⅞	100⅛ ⅜	15 13/16 15⅞	257	91⅝	5 7p	19 21p
27	210	90⅞ 91	91⅝ 91⅞	98⅝ 98¾	100⅛ ¼	15 13/16 15⅞	257½	91¾	5 7p	19 21p
28	210	90⅞ 91⅛	91⅝ 91⅞	98⅝ 98⅞	100⅛ ⅜	15⅞ 15 15/16	257½	91⅞	5 7p	19 21p
29	209¾ 210	90⅞ 91	91¾ 91⅞	98¾ 98⅞	100¼ ⅜	15⅞ 15 15/16	257	91⅞	4 7p	19 21p
30	209¾ 210¼	90⅞ 91	91¾ 91⅞	98¾ 98⅞	100¼ ⅜	15⅞ 15 15/16	257½ 8	91¾	4 6p	18 20p
May										
2	210¼ 210¾	90⅞ 91	91¾ 91⅞	93¾ 98⅞	100¼ ⅜	15 15/16	258	91¾	4 5p	18 20p
3	210 210¼	90¾ 90⅞	91¾ 91⅞	98⅝ 98⅞	100⅛ ⅜	15⅞ 15 15/16	257½ 8½	91⅝ 91¾	3 5p	18 20p
4	210¼ 210¾	90⅞ 91	91¾ 91⅞	98¾ 98⅞	100¼ ⅜	15⅞ 15 15/16	258¼	91¾	3 5p	18 20p
5	210½ 210	90¾ 91	91⅝ 91⅞	98⅝ 98⅞	100¼ ⅜	15⅞ 15 15/16	—	91⅝ 91⅞	3 5p	16 19p
6	209¾ 210¼	90¾ 91	91⅝ 91⅞	98⅝ 98⅞	100⅛ ⅜	15⅞	257½ 8	91¾ 91⅞	4 5p	17 19p
7	210 211	90⅞ 91	91⅜ 92	98¾ 99	100¼ ½	15 13/16 15 15/16	—	91⅞ 92	5p	17 19p
9	210½ 212	91¼ 91⅛	92 92¼	98⅞ 99⅛	100½ ⅝	15 15/16	259	91⅞ 92¼	3 5p	17 19p
10	212 212½	91¼ 91⅛	92 92⅛	98⅞ 99	100⅜ ⅝	15⅞ 15 15/16	259½	92 92⅛	3p	16 19p
11	—	91⅛ 91⅜	92⅛ 92¼	98⅞ 99	100⅜ ⅝	15⅞ 15 15/16	—	92⅛ 92¼	2 5p	13 17p
12	212 212½	91⅛ 91⅜	92⅛ 92¼	98⅞ 99	100⅜ ⅝	15 13/16 15⅞	258½ 9	92 92⅛	1 4p	13 16p
13	212 212½	91⅛ 91⅜	92⅛ 92¼	98⅞ 99	100⅜ ½	15 13/16	259 9¼	92 92⅛	par 3	13 15p
14	212 212½	91⅛ 91¼	92 92⅛	98⅞ 99	100⅜ ½	15 13/16 15⅞	259 9¼	92 92⅛	2 3p	13 15p
16	212 213	91⅛ 91¼	92 92⅛	98⅞ 99	100⅜ ⅝	15 13/16 15⅞	259 9¼	—	1 3p	13 15p
17	212 213	91⅛ 91¼	92 92⅛	98⅞ 99⅛	100⅜ ⅝	15 13/16 15⅞	259 9½	—	—	14 16p
18	213	91⅛ 91¼	92 92⅛	98⅞ 99	100¼ ⅜	15 13/16 15⅞	259 9¾	92 92⅛	4p	16 17p
19	212½ 213	91 91⅛	91⅞ 92	98⅞ 99	100¼ ⅜	15 13/16 15⅞	259	91⅞ 92	2 4p	15 17p
20	212½ 212¾	90⅞ 91⅛	91¾ 92	98⅞ 99	100⅛ ⅜	15 13/16 15⅞	—	91¾ 91⅞	1 3p	15 17p
21	212	90¾ 90⅞	91⅝ 91¾	98¾ 98⅞	100½ ⅝	15¾ 15 13/16	258¾ 9	91⅝ 91¾	par	12 15p
23	—	90⅞ 91	91¾ 91⅞	98⅝ 98¾	100⅜ ⅝	15¾ 15 13/16	—	91¾ 91⅞	par 2p	13 15p
24	212	90⅞ 90¾	91¾ 91⅞	98¾ 98⅞	100⅛ ⅜	15¾	258¼ ¾	91¾	par 2p	13 15p
25	211 211½	90⅝ 90⅞	91⅝ 91¾	98⅝ 98¾	100⅛ ¼	15 11/16 15¾	257½ 8	91⅞	par 1p	12 14p
26	210½ 211	90½ 90¾	91½ 91¾	98½ 98¾	100 ⅛	15 11/16 15¾	257¼ 8	91¾ 91⅞	1ds. par	11 14p

Frederick Barry, Stock and Share Broker, 7, Birchin Lane, Cornhill.

ASIATIC INTELLIGENCE.

Calcutta.

LAW.

INSOLVENT DEBTORS' COURT, *Jan.* 23.

Cruttenden & Co.—A petition from Mr. Donald Macintyre, sole assignee to the estate of Cruttenden, Mackillop, and Co., praying to be allowed to vacate the assignment on the ground of ill-health, accompanied with a certificate from Dr. Nicolson, stating the necessity of his immediately proceeding to sea, was presented by the Advocate General. The petition contained a sketch of the progress made towards liquidating the estate—the total amount of claims was found to be about Sa. Rs. 1,11,00,000, and the present net value of the assets was estimated at about 42 lakhs, after deducting various liens upon the property. As, however, the greater proportion of the Indigo factories were unsold, which formed the principal property out of which the dividends can arise, it had been impossible hitherto to make any dividend. The factories had yielded 7,800 maunds of indigo, during the season just expired, valued at Sa. Rs. 10,41,685, of which 3,06,215 were already realized. The cash balance in hand amounted to Sa. Rs. 2,30,935; but deducting from these assets Sa. Rs. 5,72,000, the amount for which they were pledged, there would remain only Sa. Rs. 3,94,401 available for a dividend, equal to about 3⅜ per cent., while, on the other hand, the indigo factories, if carried on, would require an outlay of Sa. Rs. 8,96,200 for the ensuing season, including Sa. Rs. 3,02,252 already disbursed. The petition further represented, that the assignee had incurred expenses, during the two years since the failure, to the amount of Sa. Rs. 75,429-3-5, and not having made a dividend, he had no opportunity of covering these out of the stipulated commission of 4 per cent. thereon, which rate of commission he had accepted in lieu of other compensation, in the belief that he should be able to remain in charge of the estate until its final liquidation—that he still thought the commission of 4 per cent. upon all the dividends an adequate remuneration for the trouble and expenses of winding it up; but, situated as he was, he prayed for permission to have his disbursements considered a charge upon the estate, and to be allowed a monthly stipend for himself for the past period of his assigneeship.—A petition was also put in, praying for the appointment of Mr. Thomas Holroyd in the room of Mr. Macintyre. This petition was stated to be signed by nearly all the creditors now in Calcutta, and altogether by or on behalf of 225

creditors, whose joint claims amounted to about Sa. Rs. 43,07,000.

The Court ordered the assignment to be vacated as regarded Mr. Macintyre, and appointed Mr. T. Holroyd in his place as sole assignee to the estate of Cruttenden, Mackillop, and Co., and directed the assignee to call a meeting of the creditors, for the purpose of suggesting what remuneration should be given.

Dividends were declared on the following estates, namely Fergusson and Co., 10 per cent., (this estate has already paid 10 per cent.)—Colvin and Co. 5 per cent., (making, with former dividends, 20 per cent., and it is expected there will be 17 or 18 per cent. more).

Mr. Colville, one of the unpaid assignees of Fergusson and Co., was allowed to retire from the trust.

MISCELLANEOUS.

MR. ADAM'S REPORT ON THE STATE OF EDUCATION IN BENGAL.

This highly interesting report has at length issued from the press, under the auspices of the General Committee of Public Instruction. It contains much well-digested information, of which a great part was either never before published, or was scarcely accessible to the public in general; and the spirit in which it is written is exactly that which is proper for such a document. It is in one sense impartial; for all parties whose efforts in promoting education are noticed, are treated with uniform candour. In another sense it may be considered partial, inasmuch as it shews a just and generous desire to allow and exhibit to the fullest extent the merits of all parties.

The publication of this report is to be considered as a pledge of "more extended and systematic efforts for the promotion of native education," on the part of Government; and we have, therefore, the more reason to hail it with satisfaction. It is the first step towards ascertaining what the country really needs of Government in this respect. Mr. Adam has embodied in it all the information which could be collected respecting education in Bengal proper, otherwise than by personal examination in a tour through the country. As might be expected, it presents nearly a complete view of all that is done by European instrumentality, since the greater part of what is so done may be known from annual reports, or other accessible documents: but in respect of strictly indigenous education, it is of necessity very defective. Much, however, even of that, of great interest, is brought to light, and the existing deficiency Mr. Adam is now diligently supplying, through his tour in the Mofussil.

Mr. Adam observes, that, in collecting and compiling his materials, he has endeavoured to keep the following three considerations in view ; that the sufficiency of the means of education existing in a country depends, first, upon the nature of the instruction given, secondly, upon the proportion of the institutions of education to the population needing instruction, and thirdly, upon the proper distribution of those institutions. The report, therefore, includes a brief account of the course of instruction pursued in each large class of schools, or in single institutions, whose importance entitles them to separate notice; and some idea is conveyed of the relative distribution of the means of education to the wants of the country, by comparing its several districts with each other. But, as the estimates of the population of the different districts are still for the most part merely conjectural, and in most districts there must be many native institutions of which no known record exists, much remains to be ascertained, as we have already observed, by minute local investigation.

The various institutions for education are classified, first, according as they are elementary or learned ; secondly, as they are strictly native or instituted and conducted by Europeans ; and lastly, as they are intended for male or female youth. The several classes thus formed are designated as Indigenous Elementary Schools, Elementary Schools not Indigenous, Indigenous Schools of Learning, English Colleges and Schools, and Native Female Schools. The report conducts us from district to district, and shews, as far as could be done from the sources at command, to what extent each is supplied with the different classes of seminaries before mentioned. In the first section we have this sort of view of the twenty-four Purgunnas, including Calcutta ; and, as is natural, this section contains not only an enumeration of the particular institutions in the district to which it is devoted, but also the general description of the several classes into which they and all the rest throughout the country are divided. The following is Mr. Adam's description of the Indigenous Elementary Schools:

" By this description are meant those schools in which instruction in the elements of knowledge is communicated, and which have been originated and are supported by the natives themselves, in contradistinction from those that are supported by religious or philanthropic societies. The number of such schools in Bengal is supposed to be very great. A distinguished member of the General Committee of Public In-

struction, in a minute on the subject, expressed the opinion, that if one rupee per mensem were expended on each existing village school in the Lower Provinces, the amount would probably fall little short of 12 lakhs of rupees per annum. This supposes that there are 100,000 such schools in Bengal and Behar, and assuming the population of those two provinces to be 40,000,000, there would be a village school for every 400 persons. There are no *data* in this country known to me by which to determine, out of this number, the proportion of school-going children, or of children capable of going to school, or of children of the age at which, according to the custom of the country, it is usual to go to school. In Prussia it has been ascertained, by actual census, that in a population of 12,256,725, there were 4,487,461 children under fourteen years of age, which gives 366 children for every 1000 inhabitants, or about eleven-thirtieths of the nation. Of this entire population of children, it is calculated that three-sevenths are of an age to go to school, admitting education in the schools to begin at the age of seven years complete, and there is thus in the entire Prussian monarchy the number of 1,923,200 children capable of receiving the benefits of education. These proportions will not strictly apply to the juvenile population of this country, because the usual age for going to school is from five to six, and the usual age for leaving school is from ten to twelve, instead of fourteen. There are thus two sources of discrepancy. The school-going age is shorter in India than in Prussia, which must have the effect of diminishing the total number of school-going children ; while, on the other hand, that diminished number is not exposed to the causes of mortality to which the total school-going population of Prussia is liable from the age of twelve to fourteen. In want of more precise *data*, let us suppose that these two contrary discrepancies balance each other, and we shall then be at liberty to apply the Prussian proportions to this country. Taking, therefore, eleven-thirtieths of the above-mentioned 400 persons, and three-sevenths of the result, it will follow that in Bengal and Behar there is, on an average, a village school for every sixty-three children of the school-going age. These children, however, include girls as well as boys, and as there are no indigenous girls' schools, if we take the male and female children to be in equal, or nearly equal proportions, there will appear to be an indigenous elementary school for every thirty-one or thirty-two boys. The estimate of 100,000 such schools in Bengal and Behar is confirmed by a consideration of the number of villages in those two provinces. Their number has been officially estimated at 150,748, of which, not all, but most have each a school. If it be admitted that there is so large a proportion as a third of the villages that have no schools, there will still be 100,000 that have them. Let it be admitted that these calculations, from uncertain premises, are only distant approximations to the truth, and it will still appear that the system of village schools is extensively prevalent; that the desire to give education to their male children must be deeply seated in the minds of parents, even of the humblest classes; and that these are the institutions, closely interwoven as they are with the habits of the people and the customs of the country, through which primarily, although not exclusively, we may hope to improve the morals and intellect of of the native population. It is not, however, in the present state of these schools, that they can be regarded as valuable instruments for this purpose. The benefits resulting from them are but small, owing partly to the incompetency of the instructors, and partly to the early age at which, through the poverty of the parents, the children are removed. The education of Bengalee children, as has been just stated, generally commences when they are five or six years old, and terminates in five years, before the mind can be fully awakened to a sense of the advantages of knowledge, or the reason sufficiently matured to acquire it. The teachers depend entirely upon their scholars for subsistence, and being little respected and poorly rewarded, there is no encouragement for persons of character, talent, or learning to engage in the occupation. These schools are generally held in the houses of some of the most respectable native inhabitants, or very near them. All the children of the family are educated in the vernacular language of the country; and, in order to increase the emoluments of the teachers, they are allowed to introduce, as pupils, as many respectable children as they can procure in the neighbourhood. The scholars begin with tracing the vowels and consonants with the finger on a sand-board, and afterwards on the floor, with a pencil of steatite or white crayon; and this exercise is continued for eight or ten days. They are next instructed to write on the palm-leaf with a reed-pen, held in the fist, not with the fingers, and with ink made of charcoal, which rubs out, joining vowels to the consonants, forming compound letters, syllables, and words, and learning tables of numeration, money, weight, and measure, and the correct mode of writing the distinctive names of persons, castes, and places. This is continued about a year. The iron style is now used only by the teacher in sketching on the palm-leaf the letters which the scholars are required to trace with ink. They are next advanced to the study of arithmetic and the use of

the plantain leaf, in writing with ink made of lamp-black, which is continued about six months, during which they are taught addition, subtraction, multiplication, and division, and the simplest cases of the mensuration of land and commercial and agricultural accounts, together with the modes of address proper in writing letters to different persons. The last stage of this limited course of instruction is that in which the scholars are taught to write with lamp-black ink on paper, and are further instructed in agricultural and commercial accounts, and in the composition of letters.' In country places, the rules of arithmetic are principally applied to agricultural, and in towns, to commercial accounts; but in' both town and country schools the instruction is superficial and defective. It may be safely affirmed that in no instance whatever is the orthography of the language of the country acquired in those schools; for, although in some of them two or three of the more advanced boys write out small portions of the most popular poetical compositions of the country, yet the manuscript copy itself is so inaccurate, that they only become confirmed in a most vitiated manner of spelling, which the imperfect qualifications of the teacher do not enable him to correct. The scholars are entirely without instruction, both literary and oral, regarding the personal virtues and domestic and social duties. The teacher, in virtue of his character, or in the way of advice or reproof, exercises no moral influence on the character of his pupils. For the sake of pay, he performs a menial service in the spirit of a menial. On the other hand, there is no text or school-book used, containing any moral truths or liberal knowledge; so that education being limited entirely to accounts, tends rather to narrow the mind, and confine its attention to' sordid gain, than to improve the heart and enlarge the understanding. This description applies, as far as I at present know, to all indigenous elementary schools throughout Bengal. The number of such schools in Calcutta is considerable. A very minute inquiry respecting them was instituted, when the Calcutta School Society was formed, in 1818-19. The result was, that the number within the legal limits of Calcutta was 211, in which 4,908 children received instruction. Assuming the returns of the Hindoo and Mohammadan population of Calcutta, made in 1822, to be correct, this number is about one-third the number of native children capable of receiving instruction, the other two-thirds being without the means of instruction in institutions of native origin. In 1821, of these schools 115, containing 3,828 scholars, received books from the School Society, and were examined and superintended by its officers and agents; while 96 schools, containing 1,080 scholars, continued entirely unconnected with that Society. In 1829, the date of the fifth Report of the School Society, the number of schools in connection with it had been reduced to 81; and since that date there has been no account given to the public of the Society's operations. There is no reason to suppose that the indigenous schools unconnected with it are less numerous than when their condition was first investigated, in 1818-19: on the contrary, the impulse which education has since received in Calcutta, has most probably increased both their number and efficiency. The improvements introduced by the School Society into the schools in immediate connection with it are various. Printed, instead of manuscript schoolbooks, are now in common use. The branches formerly taught are now taught more thoroughly; and instruction is extended to subjects formerly neglected, viz. the orthography of the Bengalee language, geography, and moral truths and obligations. The mode of instruction has been improved. Formerly, the pupils were arranged in different divisions, according as they were learning to write on the ground with chalk, on the palm-leaf, on the plantain leaf, and on paper, respectively; and each boy was taught separately, by the schoolmaster, in a distinct lesson. The system of teaching with the assistance of monitors, and of arranging the boys in classes, formed with reference to similarity of ability or proficiency, has been adopted; and, as in some instances it has enabled the teachers to increase the number of their pupils very considerably, and thereby their own emoluments, it is hoped that it will ultimately have the effect of encouraging men of superior acquirements to undertake the duties of instructors of youth. A system of superintendence has been organized by the appointment of a pundit and a sircar, to each of the four divisions into which the schools are distributed. They separately attend two different schools in the morning, and two in the evening, staying at least one hour at each school, during which time they explain to the teachers any parts of the lessons they do not fully comprehend, and examine such of the boys as they think proper in their different acquirements. The destinations of the pundits and sircars are frequently changed, and each of them keeps a register, containing the day of the month; the time of going to, and leaving, each school; the names of the boys examined; the page and place of the book in which they were examined; and the names of the schoolmasters, in their own handwriting—which registers are submitted to the Secretaries of the Society every week, through the head pundit. Further examinations, both public and private, yearly, half-yearly, or quarterly, as necessity or convenience dictated, have been held in the presence of respectable European and Native gentlemen, when gratuities were given to deserving teachers, and prize books to the best scholars, as well as books bestowed for the current use of the schools. The tendency of all these measures to raise the character and qualifications of the teachers must be apparent, and it is with reference to this tendency that the labours of the Calcutta School Society have received the special approbation of the Court of Directors. In 1825, the Court, in confirming the grant of Rs. 500 per month, which had been made to this Society by the local Government, made the following remarks: —"The Calcutta School Society appears to combine with its arrangements for giving elementary instruction, an arrangement of still greater importance, for educating teachers for the indigenous schools. This last object we deem worthy of great encouragement, since it is upon the character of the indigenous schools that the education of the great mass of the population must ultimately depend. By training up, therefore, a class of teachers, you provide for the eventual extension of improved education to a portion of the natives of India, far exceeding that which any elementary instruction, that could be immediately bestowed, would have any chance of reaching." In consequence of the reduction of the Society's means, the examinations have been discontinued since 1833. Unequivocal testimony is borne to the great improvement effected by the exertions of the School Society, both in the methods of instruction employed in the indigenous schools of Calcutta, and in the nature and amount of knowledge communicated; and I have thus fully explained the operations of this benevolent association, because they appear to me to present an admirable model, devised by a happy combination of European and Native philanthropy and local knowledge, and matured by fifteen years' experience; on which model, under the fostering care of Government, and at comparatively little expense, a more extended plan might be framed for improving the entire system of indigenous elementary schools throughout the country. In these schools, the Bengalee language only is employed as the medium of instruction; but the children of Mohammadans, as well as the various castes of Hindoos, are received without distinction. Mohammadans have no indigenious elementary schools peculiar to themselves, nor have they any regular system of private tuition. Every father does what he can for the instruction of his children, either personally or by hiring a tutor; but few fathers, however qualified for the task, can spare from their ordinary avocations the time necessary for the performance of such duties; and hired domestic instructors, though unquestionably held in more honour than among Hindoos, and treated with great respect by their pupils and employers, are always ill-paid, and often superannuated—men, in short, who betake themselves to that occupation only when they have ceased, from age, to be fit for any other. There are, moreover, few who are qualified to intrust their children, and fewer who are able to employ a tutor."—*Friend of India, Jan.* 14.

ESTATE OF CRUTTENDEN AND CO.

A meeting of the creditors of this estate was held at the Exchange on the 30th January, to take into consideration the amount of remuneration to be allowed to Mr. Donald Macintyre, whose ill-health has obliged him to retire—and to suggest to the Insolvent Court the nature and amount of the remuneration to be allowed to Mr. T. Holroyd, the assignee appointed in the room of Mr. Macintyre. Capt. Vint was called to the chair.

Mr. Macintyre being too ill to attend the meeting, Mr. Wilson, his solicitor, attended on his behalf, and read the following report of the management of the estate since the insolvency.

" You must all be aware that, from the circumstance of the late firm of Cruttenden & Co., being the last of the large houses of agency which was compelled to have recourse to the Insolvent Court, and from the great glut in the market of property belonging to the other estates of a similar description to that which belonged to this estate, it was necessarily placed in a more unfavourable position than they were, as regarded a speedy realization of the assets. This remark applies not only to the disposal of the indigo factories, but also to the recoveries from debtors to the estates; for in many instances, the same persons being debtors of the other estates, had been compelled to make arrangements with the assignees of them, and were either under stoppages to these assignees to the full amount of what they could possibly give, or to those who had enabled them to effect compromises by paying a certain sum down. The consequence has been, that the recoveries from debtors in this estate has been extremely small, although the strongest threats have been used from the beginning to intimidate them into some kind of arrangement. Latterly, a great number of writs have been issued, and it may reasonably be expected, as well from that circumstance, as also from the gradual completion of their other payments, that the realizations from this quarter will now be considerably increased. In regard to the sale of the indigo factories, it must be admitted that the realizations from that source have been less than the creditors could at the time of the insolvency have contemplated; at the same time, I am perfectly satisfied that they will

find that the slightest blame is not attachable to the late assignee on this point. I can speak from personal knowledge, that the utmost anxiety has all along been felt by him to get them disposed of, provided he got any thing like a fair price, but for very few of them has he ever received any offer at all, and he has certainly never refused one offer without being assured from those capable of advising him, that it was an inadequate one. It is said by some, that he ought to have accepted an offer made last year for the Belnaberry concern, and as matters have turned out, it is perhaps unfortunate that he did not do so; but at the same time, you will find, from the facts, that no blame is attachable to him in the circumstances. They were simply these. He was on the 17th of January last applied to, to name the lowest price for the concern, which he stated in reply to be four lacs; an offer was thereupon made of 2,80,000, which he declined; on the 20th of the same month, the same party advanced his offer to 3,20,000, which was also declined; but Mr. Macintyre, in order to meet the difference between them, offered to take 3,50,000. Some communings then took place between the parties, and the assignee was fully convinced that the sum he asked would be given: that he had good reason to believe so, or at any rate that he would not then have been justified in lowering the price he had fixed, will fully appear to you from the following letter, dated the 5th of February, being fifteen days after the date of the previous offer.

' We are in receipt of yours of yesterday, with last year's statement of the Belnaberry concern, which we herewith return: *as we are not yet prepared to state our final determination*, we would by all means recommend that the operations of this important season should proceed the same as if we were not at all in treaty.'

" After this, the party changed his mind, and made no further offer; but you will readily perceive that Mr. Macintyre did nothing that each of you would not have done in his own case, and that he is entirely without blame in respect to the treaty having closed as it did.

" It has also been stated, as a ground of complaint against Mr. Macintyre, that he had purchased in factories at the public sales at prices for which he ought to have allowed them to go; but the short answer to that accusation is, that at all the public sales referred to, he was the only bidder, there having been no *bonâ fide* offer by any person. I shall not trouble you with further explanations as regards past proceedings, but shall now direct your attention very briefly to the present situation of the estate, and to the circumstances which have endered the present meeting necessary.

" On the first point, I shall scarcely do more than refer you to the several accounts and documents which are now on the table; these were prepared for the information of the Insolvent Court, and they show, upon the most moderate valuation that could be put upon the assets, that there is about forty-two lacs of rupees to meet the claims against the estate, which amount to about 1,11,00,000. According to these statements, there appears at the date they were made out to be cash in hand the sum of sicca rupees 230,935

The gross value of the Indigo of the present season is valued at........ .... } 10,41,685

Deduct already received.................. } 3,05,215

Leaving for realization......... 7,35,470
Making, together with the cash balance,............. } Rs. 9,66,405,
which would be now available for a dividend if no preferable claims existed. The assignee, however, in order to redeem various valuable premises, and also to render available certain postponed securities which the late firm held over indigo factories, has been obliged to pledge the assets of the estate to the amount of Sa. Rs. 5,72,000, which ought to be paid before any dividend, and which would, therefore, only leave a sum available for a dividend to the amount of Rs. 3,94,405. I believe calculations have been made to a later period than when these statements which I produce were made out, and that they show that a larger dividend can be made at present without detriment to the interests of the estate; to these I therefore beg to refer you without further remark. The only object I had in view was, to show that, up to this date, it has been impossible to declare a dividend. Now you are aware that, when Mr. Macintyre was appointed assignee of this estate, the mode of remuneration fixed upon was a commission of four per cent. upon the declared dividend, including allowance to Messrs. Brown and Cullen of Sa Rs. 600 per month, and all other charges, with the exception of law charges. No dividend having yet been declared, Mr. Macintyre has not had an opportunity of deriving any remuneration whatsoever for his services, nor even of defraying the charges for the office establishment. These charges amount to Sa. Rs. 75,529, and have, from time to time, as they were paid, been debited to the estate, and carried to a separate account, for future adjustment between the estate and the assignee, out of the commission on dividends. I need scarcely state, that in fixing the allowance at 4 per cent. upon the amount of dividends, and in the assignee having accepted of it as sufficient remuneration, it was supposed and taken for granted by all parties, that he would be able to manage the estate until it was finally wound up, and in such case he might

finally have been remunerated for his services, as the expenses of the establishment are gradually capable of being diminished, until they amount to a mere trifle; but in the change which Mr. Macintyre's state of health renders so indispensably necessary—a state which I am fully convinced has been greatly caused by the laborious and harassing duties to which he has been obliged to submit in this estate,—I am sure that you will readily and liberally take the hardship of his case into consideration. It is impossible to deny that the charges are large : but I beg of you to consider, that at least Rs. 1,200 a month were fixed upon him by the court as salaries to the insolvents; and further, that the whole of them were incurred, while not a doubt could exist in Mr. Macintyre's mind that they were all to go out of his own pocket. Judging, therefore, from the ordinary rules by which man is governed, it may with propriety be taken for granted, that the expenses have been no greater than what was actually required for the efficient carrying on of the business of the estate.

" The questions now referred to you by the court, as regard the late assignee, are that of considering, 1st, whether the charges of the establishment shall continue at the debit of the estate, as they now stand charged to it ; and, 2dly, what amount of remuneration ought to be allowed to the assignee in lieu of commission. Upon the first point, I do not anticipate any difference of opinion amongst you ; upon the second, there may probably be a difference as to the amount. Upon that question, it would be against Mr. Macintyre's wishes if I were to say a word ; he leaves it entirely to yourselves, and will be perfectly satisfied with your determination, whatever it may be. The consideration of what allowance ought to be made to Mr. Holroyd will also be matter for your consideration ; but I submit that that gentleman ought to succeed to the management of the estate entirely unconnected and unincumbered with the situation of his predecessor. I would, therefore, humbly submit that you should, before proceeding to his case, first determine the questions as regards Mr. Macintyre ; and I beg to submit the following resolution to your consideration, leaving it to any of the creditors either to suggest alterations, or any other which may appear to him more fitting in the circumstances of the case. The resolution I would suggest as follows :—

" ' The creditors, having considered the state of affairs submitted to them, and the precarious state of Mr. Macintyre's health, which has rendered his retirement from the assigneeship absolutely necessary, do humbly suggest and recommend to the court, that the charges of establishment incurred since his appointment be allowed to remain at the debit of the estate, and that he be allowed the monthly sum of Sa Rs. —— as a remuneration for his services during the period he has acted as assignee, in lieu of the commission on declared dividends formerly fixed as the mode of his remuneration.'"

Mr. Cockerell considered the charges for establishment much too great, and objected to a salary being allowed to Mr. Macintyre.

Mr. Bagshaw also demurred, and suggested that the documents on the table, from which Mr. Wilson stated he had compiled his report, should be circulated amongst the creditors.

It was finally proposed by Mr. Cockerell, and carried unanimously,

"That the assignee's accounts be submitted to the following gentlemen : — Messrs. Mackillop, John Allen, Geo. Vint, J. Dow, and R. H. Cockerell, to report to a meeting, to be called for Thursday next, as to the general state of the affairs of the insolvent estate, and also upon the question of remuneration to the late and present assignee."

After which, the meeting broke up.

The following documents were laid on the table : —

Synoptical view of the present situation of the Estate of the late Firm of Cruttenden, Mackillop, and Co.

Assets.

Landed Property 'exclusive of Premises in Raneemoody Gully, mortgaged for their full value) ....Sa Rs.	5,16,800
Indigo Factories	15,21,000
Indigo	7,30,470
Outstanding Debts	10,00,000
Ships................................	1,00,000
Docks	1,50,000
Shares in the Asiatic Annuity Company.	30,000
Final Dividend on 48 lapsed shares in the Laudable Society	40,000
Surplus Remittances to England	33,000
Proceeds of the *Ruby* at London	50,000
Jungypore Indigo, of Season 1833-4, in London	50,000
Bills Receivable	1,55,888
Cash	2,30,935
	Sa. Rs. 46,08,093

Deduct.

Mortgaged to Browne's Trustees ....Sa. Rs.	3,17,000	
Mortgaged on Jungypore Concern.......................	1,50,000	
Received in part of purchase money of Landed Property sold	1,09,500	
Estimated value of J. Price's Annuity, secured by mortgage over Tank Square Estate	10,000	
Payable to C. Birch .... 85,000 Less his share of outlay for Jungypore Concern.............. 43,500	41,500	
Balance of Advances required for carrying on Indigo Factories, for the current season	6,37,448	
Money borrowed or realized on account of parties not debtors to Estate, and to be refunded	63,500	13,38,948
		Sa. Rs. 32,69,145

Add,

The coming crop of Indigo taken at amount of outlay ··	8,68,000	
Payment made in anticipation of Dividends...............	56,212	9,24,212
	Total....Sa. Rs.	41,93,357
	To meet Sa. Rs.	1,11,00,000

Factories sold in 1835.

Kishnaghur Concern three-fourth Sa. Rs. 1,16,250 Less received ....,........... 58,125		58,125
Chauleah ditto, purchase money received. Nesindpore ditto......... 80,000 Less received, Sa. Rs. 30,000		50,000
Comlapore ditto		10,000
Packedanga ditto, ¼th········ 6,500 Less received 3,500		3,000
Included in Statement of Bills receivable ···· ··········· ..... Sa. Rs.		1,21,125

N. B. Factories sold in 1831.
Toradah Concern ···· Sa. Rs. 2,10,000
Amount received.

Since making up the list of indigo factories sold last year, we understand the Belnaberry concern has been sold for about Rs. 2,65,000—*Courier.*

PROPOSED NEW WHARF.

It is in contemplation to erect a wharf in Calcutta for loading and unloading the shipping of the port, which shall extend the whole length of the Custom-House, 800 feet. Two plans have been submitted ; of which the one is calculated to cost about a lakh and a half of rupees; the other about four lakhs.

PROGRESS OF THE ARTS AND TRADE.

As we are in the habit of noticing the progress of the arts and manufactures in this City of Palaces, we must record the opening of another Flour Mill at Cossipore lately, on the same principle, and established for the same purpose, as the Mills of Messrs. Smithson and Co. on the Strand. There is also a large building now rising from the ground, near Messrs. Jessop's establishment, in Clive Street, intended for cotton crews.—The stagnation of demand for house property too has almost disappeared—quite so with respect to some descriptions of it ; and the increasing commercial prosperity of the place has filled every building suited to an office, and given a new stimulus to building plans wherever favourable sites are discovered.— *Englishman, Jan.* 29.

CIVIL SERVICE ANNUITY FUND.

A Quarterly General Meeting of the Subscribers to the Civil Fund was held on the 25th of January; the Hon. W. L. Melville in the chair.

The following report from the Managers was read : —

"With reference to the resolutions passed at a special meeting of the subscribers
to the Civil Fund, held on the 14th Nov.
1835, the Managers of the Civil Fund beg
to report to the quarterly general meeting, that 117 subscribers have recorded
their votes in favour of the Hon. Mr. Melville's original motion, 'that the Resolutions of the 27th April 1835, admitting
Mr. Sutherland, be rescinded,' and only 67
have voted in favour of Mr. D. C. Smyth's
amendment, ' that the proceedings of 27th
April 1835, admitting Mr. Sutherland, be
upheld."

" In like manner, the Managers have to
report, that 135 have voted against the admission of Mr. Elliott, and only 43 have
voted in favour of the admission of that
gentleman."

The Managers of the Civil Service Annuity Fund had a meeting to-day, to elect
a secretary in place of Mr. Alexander,
deceased, and the choice fell upon Mr. G.
F. McClintock, by a majority of one, including the vote of Mr. Trower, an *ex-
officio* manager, but not a member of the
fund. Hence a question of his title to
vote, which is to be referred to a meeting
of subscribers, called for the 17th March,
to consider of the above nomination. Mr.
H. Torrens and Mr. J. Grant were also
candidates for the secretaryship.—*Cal.
Cour., Jan.* 30.

PRESIDENCY OF AGRA.

It is stated that letters have been received by the *Zenobia*, announcing the abolition of the Agra presidency, but that the
government is to be administered by a
deputy governor, to be appointed by the
Governor General; and that, in consequence of this intimation, Sir Charles Metcalfe has determined upon proceeding
home.

M. CORDIER.

We hear that the venerable governor of
Chandernagore, M. Cordier, is about to
retire from the government he has held for
many years, and to return to Europe.—
Cal. Cour., Jan. 12.

INDIAN JAILS.

A native correspondent of the *Reformer*,
referring to the committee appointed to inquire into the state of Indian jails, gives
the following description of their character
and discipline :—

" The great evil, in all the jails of this
country, is the venality and extortion of
the officers of these institutions. It is by
such individuals that tyranny and oppression are exercised upon the poor and the
helpless, and every sort of comfort and
assistance afforded to the powerful and the
opulent. The way in which the jail-da-
rogahs and guards effect their purpose is

too well known to many of the natives of
this country. Whenever a person is confined, the officers of the jail raise a simul-
taneous cry, ' let's have something.' The
prisoner readily perceives the necessity of
complying with their request. He accurately balances the inconveniences and the
hardships to which he would otherwise be
subjected, against their heavy demands, and
finding no alternative, cannot but submis-
sively obey their commands. But if he
be poor, and his circumstances do not permit him to give them what they want, his
condition must be as wretched as possible.
If the person is confined for any debt, or
by virtue of any civil writ, he must be sent
to the Dewanny jail, and there doomed to
pass his days and nights amidst the threats,
sneers, and insulting rebukes of the officers,
and deprived of those advantages which he
is entitled to enjoy. But if he is confined
for any crime or misdemeanor, or by virtue
of any criminal writ, he is immediately
shut in a gloomy cell of the Fowzdary jail,
and drags a miserable existence during the
whole period of his imprisonment. The
moment he enters the jail, and tells the
daroga and his subordinates that be has
nothing to give, they hasten to load him
with irons. The poor prisoner trembles
with fear, and yields to their cruelty. The
guards laying hold of him, pour volleys of
abuse, and bind his hands together, and
strike him as often as they are actuated by
whim or caprice. He is suffered to live
amidst the horrors of the dungeon, and is
entirely cut off from every sort of communication whatever. No brother, no friend,
no relation, nor even a servant can have
access to him, and no eatables and drink-
ables can be sent him for his support and
maintenance. The prisoner, placed as he
is in such a deplorable situation, is soon
reduced to a state of misery and starvation,
and is thus made to suffer more than the
law directs. I have heard from a respectable zemindar, of the Twenty-four Pergunnahs, that, when two of his gomashtas
were lately confined in the Twenty-four
Pergunnah jail, in a case of some ryots, they
fasted for a day and a half, and in sending
them a rupee or two to buy the necessaries
of life, he had to bribe the jail-guards
almost double the sum, and unless that was
done, the gomashtas would have starved
them and perhaps left their bones where
they were confined. Numberless instances
of this sort can be easily given by any native who is at all acquainted with the conduct of the jail officers, and there can be
but one opinion as to their venality, extortion, and ill-treatment. It is a matter
of notoriety, that they behave most liberally
towards those who pay them well; they
not only endeavour to increase their comforts, but sometimes expressly permit them
to indulge in sensual pleasures. To the
rich they look up as their protectors, or

ged, and always serve them as their
menial servants. The poor, and the poor
only, fall victims to their rapacity, and are
punished ten times more than the wealthy
prisoners. This distinction of punishment
has entirely emanated from the corruption
of the jail officers, and cannot but be considered an anomaly in such an enlightened
age as this."

CHAMBER OF COMMERCE.

The Chamber of Commerce has accumulated upwards of 13,000 rupees from
subscriptions, in excess of its current
charges; and as the fund is likely to go
on increasing, a suggestion was offered by
an influential member, at the last meeting,
to procure or erect an appropriate building
for the business of the Chamber, which at
present is carried on, not very conveniently,
in two or three hired rooms at the Exchange.—*Cour.*, Feb. 1.

SEVERITY OF THE COLD.

The accounts we have heard from several
places, of the severity of the cold during
the night of the 17-18th of January, are
sufficiently remarkable to merit some record. The ice observed in the Botanic
Garden was found in small pools. At one
of the Soonderbun estates, ice was obtained
in a saucer simply exposed upon the
ground. At Dum-Dum and Barrackpore
there was hoar-frost. At Sook Saugor,
ice was formed of considerable thickness in
a plate or basin placed in an open verandah, and some injury was done to a coffee
plantation in that neighbourhood by the
frost.—*Ibid.*

PRESENTS FROM NATIVE CHIEFS.

The *Reformer* has some remarks on the
practice of putting up the presents of native chiefs to the British Indian Government for public sale. There can be no
doubt that this practice arises out of the
prohibition against receiving presents; but
it is extremely undignified, the motive of
it can never be appreciated by the native
rulers, and it is not at all indispensable, nor
even useful, as a check upon corruption.
There is the obvious course pointed out by
the *Reformer*, of sending the presents to
be deposited in a museum, which would
equally prevent any appropriation of them
to private purposes. The course actually
pursued lowers us in the estimation of the
natives, to whom it must of course appear
the result of the sordid spirit of a trading
government, while in some cases it may
wear the semblance of insult. What would
a native ruler say, for example, if he
should learn that his portrait, set with
diamonds, had been sold at public auction,
to be trafficked about in the bazaar like a
bale of goods? The presents of the Nepa-

lese envoy are said to have been purposely
insignificant, with reference to this practice
of selling them, and his Excellency is
too intelligent not to trace it to its true
course; but he is a case of exception—for
in general the practice will be viewed in
the most odious light.—*Hurk.*, Feb. 2.

ENGLISH EDUCATION.

Baboos Rajkissen and Prawnkissen Roy
Choudree, two very opulent and respectable zemindars in the 24-Pergunnas, and
residents of Puneeattee, have, from the
laudable desire of seeing the children of
their countrymen educated in English,
and brought on a level with their enlightened fellow natives, established a seminary
on the banks of the river, near Cook's stables, which is just half way to Barrackpore. The baboos have, for the present,
given up their Raus nautch-house for the
school, and engaged a very deserving and
fully-qualified European teacher, Mr. L.
M'Donnell, who, with the assistance of a
Portuguese usher, well acquainted with
the Bengalee language, is getting on fa-
mously with the boys entrusted to his
tuition. The number now in the school
amounts to forty boys and upwards. From
the shortness of the time since the establishment of the school to the present, and
from the almost daily flocking-in of new
boys, the institution promises fair. The
children therein are taught reading, writing, arithmetic, grammar, geography, the
use of the globes, astronomy, translation,
and composition, for the very trifling
charge of two rupees, or somewhat less,
per boy. So that the baboos will, for some
little time to come, be obliged to defray
the additional expenses of the establishment after realizing what the school yields.
The Puneeattee baboos have, in this instance, like the Takee baboos, set a noble
example to their wealthy countrymen, who,
where there is no English academy, nor
even the likelihood of one being established
without their aid, should not hesitate to afford it, feeling, as every reasonable man
conscientiously must, that the only good
that can be done by a man to his fellow
creatures, is either to aid in their education
or to extend a liberal hand for their wants
—these constitute charity which will bring
its own reward.—*Cal. Cour.*, Jan. 19.

ORIENTAL LITERATURE.

Several respectable natives have formed
themselves into a club at Allahabad, for
the purpose of selecting and printing scarce
Eastern works. This attention to the literature of their country, and the use to which
the press is to be devoted, will be a redeeming point in the modern history of the natives of Hindoostan.—*Central Free Press*,
Jan. 16.

THE KING OF DELHI.

In order to prove that we were quite correct in stating that an intrigue was going on in the palace here against the heir-apparent, we give the following curious address of his Majesty the king of Delhi, which was put forth some time ago, and which, we hear, obtained the names of even some of our European functionaries! We shall not lose sight of the subject—for the poor old king is quite in his dotage. The parties who are now deluding, and extracting money from him, are quite well known to us.

" To our fortunate Brothers,—to the well-beloved members of our illustrious House—to the honorable gentlemen of the English Nation—to the supporters of our eternal empire—be it known—that the Most High Creator, whose glory is overcoming, has rendered that apple of his Sovereign's eye—that lustre of his Monarch's brow—that light of the Goorgan Race—that lamp of the house of Timur—that well directed—happy, son,—the core of our heart and the engraft of our being, Sultan Mahomed Selim Bahadoor, the subject of universal praise; so that one of his countless virtues is sufficient passport to all the human heart can desire here or hereafter. Influenced by the fear of God, —the pursuit of truth—rectitude and purity of mind—by natural kindness and moral habits—he is just, equitable, and humane—seeing and practising that which is right—He is experienced—discreet—kind—benevolent—wise—brave ; in fact, for his inestimable qualities, God blesses him—and for his liberality, mankind adore him. The felicity to which he has attained by his attentions to us, has seldom been the lot of another—we would purchase him with our heart and soul. If we called him the ' soul of our existence,' the epithet would become him—if the ' solace of our life,' it would be apposite—indeed he is our very being itself, for our soul places her unbounded reliance in him—and our life and soul drawing their comforts from him, our pure spirit is his. All the English gentlemen are grateful to him, for his politeness to them—and how could it be otherwise, when it is the chief aim of this illustrious son to gain their suffrage? He often assures us of the cordial attachment of the English gentlemen to our person—and declares that all their professions tend to our weal. The Right Honourable the Governor General Lord Amherst,—apprised of the real character of this Prince, styles him, in this letter, ' The cream of the race Timur ;'—and His Excellency the Earl Dalhousie, commander-in-chief, who had formed a proper estimate of his qualifications, declares in his petition to us, —' that to the latest moment of life, he must remain under obligations to this Prince,' which also is a very suitable ex-

pression of his worth. The pillars of our everlasting Monarchy act properly in contemplating his advancement. To ask ' is the public anxious to witness his administration of justice and munificence'—is an idle question. Worthy of supreme power, this Prince thro' the plausibility of his manners, has attained the satisfaction of rendering the hearts of men obedient. Such alone deserves to adorn the universe. Excelling in mercy and bountifulness, he is worthy of becoming the asylum of the world. Gratitude is due to him from every rank for his recent exertions in procuring for the general comfort an augmentation of our peshkush—and for his affording satisfaction to every class before that event. Although the world may deem this beloved of every heart as merely the *Uzeez i misr* (the title of the Egyptian Wuzeers), yet our warm affection for him and his own fortune exceed those of Jacob and Joseph. The sincerity of this light of our eye adds to the splendour of all the gems of his prosperity—this natural amenity is an invaluable jewel. Though the brilliancy of these virtues appears to us mortals wondrous rare, its emanation is from the mercy of God, who has shed a ray of His light upon his heart. If a servant can be acceptable, the Deity will surely exalt this Prince to the pinnacle of greatness—for it is said,

If his servants are kind to mankind,
God will forgive their sins in the day of judgment,
And place them on the seats of honour,
Making them partakers of his secrets.

" Although all our sons are dear to us, the excellency of this son is a divine gift, and God has rendered him in rank and birth more honourable than all our other offspring—seeing that his mother was of noble parentage and united to us in the bonds of matrimony, agreeably to the holy laws of the Prophet, which distinction and the sanction of our laws, conferred on that Lady a pre-eminence over all our other virtuous Queens.

" The object of this address—unalterable as fate—is that those who are acquainted with, or have been witnesses of, the foregoing particulars, which are conspicuous as the noonday sun, will, in that faith which shall serve them in the day of judgment, testify to the truth of the contents of this document, by affixing their seals and signatures—avoiding all envy and malice, which are contrary to religion and the hopes of salvation. The bat does not become the glorious sun ; by envying its rays, the brightest day is still to her but a night of darkness."—*Delhi Gaz. Jan.* 13.

Rookin Oodowah, a doctor in the service of her majesty the queen of Delhi, has been requested by his royal mistress to proceed to Allahabad, in order to arrange matters in her behalf, in case of the king's demise. As a compensation for this trouble, he is to receive a gratuity of twenty-five thousand rupees, provided his services are satisfactory.—*Central Free Press, Jan.* 16.

MILITARY FUND.

At the annual meeting for the election of directors, in answer to a question from the Rev. Mr. Wimberley, why no statement was published beforehand, in order to give members an opportunity of knowing something about the accounts they were called upon to pass at these meetings, Capt. Young explained, that there would be no advantage in doing so, since, by the constitution of the fund, in case any one should wish to make a proposition, it could not be entertained at a meeting, but must be circulated throughout the army. The accounts of the year, after being passed, were printed and circulated to every station, and opportunity was thus given to every one interested to study them at leisure.

When this Fund was re-constituted in 1824, the balance in hand, we are informed, was little more than eight lakhs of rupees. Its capital has since swollen to nearly twenty-eight lakhs; but the fund is supposed to be still far from having reached its maximum of capital and incumbrances.

The following is an abstract of the receipts and disbursements during the past year:

Receipts.

Balance on 31st December 1834, Sa. Rs.		26,75,093
Donations from Subscribers····	93,519	
Subscriptions·················	2,10,110	
The Company's Donation ····	22,965	
Difference of Exchange between 1s. 11d. and 2s. 4d············	68,699	
Interest on Government Paper,	2,10,016	
Donations and Subscriptions in England····················	15,779	
Sundries····················	1,250	
		6,22,329
	Sa. Rs.	32,97,422

Disbursements.

Office ·························	5,064	
Pensions in India.·············	56,719	
Passage money to Officers paid in India ·····················	19,500	
Ditto to 8 Widows ·············	15,200	
Outfit to Officers paid in India,	12,000	
Drafts from England··········	356,549	
Interest on ditto, at 5 per cent. paid to the Company········	21,127	
Donations, &c. in England, remaining there ·············	15,776	
Sundries·····················	5,856	
		5,11,391

Balance 31st December, 1835, Sa. Rs. 27,86,031

RESUMPTION OF RENT-FREE LANDS.

We learn that measures are now in progress for carrying into effect the orders of the Court, as to the adjudication of the resumption suits, and that Mr. Millett, the secretary to the Law Commission, is preparing a law for the purpose. It is some consolation to us to learn, that meanwhile, wherever the resumption laws are actively

enforced, separate officers, instead of the collectors, have been appointed to carry them into effect. This just arrangement has been carried into effect, we understand, in the districts of Patna, Benares, Sarun, Shahabad, Tirboot, Monghyr, Bhaugulpore, Tipperah, Bullooah, and Chittagong, and the system is to be extended as fast as fit men for such delicate and important work can be found.—*Hurk. Jan.* 26.

SLAVE TRADE IN DINAGEPORE.

A Correspondent of the *Bengal Herald* states: " In Rungpore, women and children are sold at a less price than brutes. But what excites our pity most is, that there are some rogues, in its northern portion, bordering on the Bhootan territories, whose profession it is to wheedle some of their neighbours, whether young or old, male or female, to accompany them to certain neighbouring places, and there, having got them out of the British dominion, deliver them up to some Bhootanese, with whom a previous bargain has been made, while the unhappy victims, in the midst of confusion, are at a loss to comprehend how they were sold to a stranger, by one who had no right over them, and in vain struggle to escape from the hands of their cruel master, who immediately sends them to some of his adjacent kellahs or castles.* In the mean time, the fictitious owner of the slaves receives the settled price, and returns home triumphantly, transported with the success of his traffic. Such is the conduct of these knaves, who, not being satisfied with the plunder of moveable property, carry away human beings, and sell them like dogs in the market."

TEA PLANTS.

Several thousands of tea plants have arrived at Ghurmucteesur Ghaut from the Botanical Gardens, and are intended to be planted in the Hills. The plants are now in excellent condition, and have apparently sustained little or no injury from their removal.—*Delhi Gaz., Jan.* 13.

IMPROVEMENT OF THE DAK.

The effects of the late arrangement to expedite the Bombay dâk are beginning to appear, the last Bombay mail having reached Agra within ten days, a degree of quickness which we do not remember ever to have known before.—*Agra Ukhbar, Jan.* 16.

THE NEPAUL EMBASSY.

The first interview between the Nepaul Envoy and the Governor General took

* " A Bhootan kellah or castle is composed, so far as I have seen, of bamboos only, and resembles rather an enclosure for the fight of beasts than any. thing like a fortification."

place on the 21st of January. The ceremony was very imposing, and attracted a
large concourse of spectators. The Nepalese ambassador having been met by
Mr. Trevelyan and Major Honywood, on
his way from Ballygunge, arrived at
Government House with his suite, consisting of two young sons, and five Goorkha
officers, preceded by a battalion of his
troops, which, with drums beating, colours
flying, their national trumpets and Scotch
bagpipes braying, drew up for exhibition
within the enclosure. The Governor General's body-guard received his Excellency
as he passed along in a carriage, but did not
present arms. A company of Europeans
from the fort formed the guard of honour,
in front of which the party passed in the
corridor of the first story, whence the ambassador ascended to the hall of audience,
where he found the Governor General, the
Commander-in-chief, and Members of
Council, with the secretaries to Government, and a great number of official gentlemen seated, waiting his arrival. The
whole of them rose up, as Sir Charles
Metcalfe advanced to meet the Nepalese
general, and embraced him, according to
eastern custom. The Governor General's
band ranged along the corridors, struck
up several appropriate airs in succession,
as the parties took their seats, Europeans
on the right and Goorkhas on the left of
the head of the government. Sir Charles
Metcalfe and his visitor entered into conversation for about a quarter of an hour,
when the ambassador proposed an adjournment to the balcony, opposite to which
his warriors were drawn up in line, with
their band playing English tunes. After
a brief inspection of the mountaineers in
their European costume, the party returned
to the corridor behind the audience room,
where the presents from the Rajah of
Nepaul were displayed. These consisted
chiefly of magnificent furs and embroidered dresses, kookries, and some enormous
tushes of elephants. There were also a
leopard and a tiger, said to have been
nursed by a woman! The rhinoceros,
which was brought from Nepaul, escaped
the first day. After resuming their seats
in the hall of audience, the Governor
General presented *utar* and *paun* to the
ambassador and his sons, who then took
leave.

The manners of the general are frank
and engaging. He shakes hands in genuine English fashion. His costume was
extremely splendid; a long robe of crim-
son-velvet, trimmed with fur, and richly
ornamented with gold, secured round the
waist by a band of the same material, fastened by a clasp studded with diamonds,
and large gold epaulets, and a turban of
rich materials, with bandeaus of fine pearls,
and a tiara of brilliants in front. The
costumes of the officers of the suite were

also exceedingly rich. The embassy, it is
said, will ultimately proceed to England.

JOHN PALMER.

It is our melancholy duty to record the
death of John Palmer.

Mr. John Palmer was, we believe, the
youngest son of the late Major Palmer, so
well known in his day as the confidential
private secretary, in fact, the confidential
minister of Warren Hastings, who died a
lieutenant-general, at Berhampore, on the
20th of, May 1816, after having filled the
highest offices in the diplomatic line in
India for more than twenty years, and
finished his career as an officer on the
Bengal staff. He was acknowledged to
be second to no one in the Company's service for talent, experience, and that honourable independence of mind for which
his son was distinguished. General Palmer
entered the Bengal army, from the king's
service, in 1770, rather later in life than is
the usage of the present day, and his children, we believe, were born in America or
the West-Indies. * Two found employment in the Bengal army, and died field-
officers.

John Palmer was brought up for the
navy, which he entered at a very early age,
in which he served several years, until he
obtained his commission, having, during
that time, been in a vessel which engaged
the celebrated Suffrein. Mr. Palmer,
however, left the navy when his prospects
of advancement were destroyed by the general peace of Paris, in 1793.

He first entered into business in Calcutta,
about fifty years ago, in the retail line, in
partnership with Mr. St. George Tucker,
now a director of the East-India Company;
afterwards conducted it by himself, and
subsequently joined Mr. Barber, with whom
he carried on business, under the firm of
Barber, Palmer, and Co. Mr. Palmer
afterwards entered into partnership with
Mr. Traill, whose partners, Messrs. Paxton
and Cockerell, had proceeded to Europe.
Mr. Traill himself, shortly afterwards, retired from the Calcutta firm, and Mr.
Palmer continued the business under the
well-known firm of Palmer and Co.,
which in 1830 failed, and drew down with
it, within a few years, all the long-esta-
blished agency-houses of this place, which
could not withstand the universal shock to
credit and confidence which the fall of
such a house, and such a man at the head
of it, produced.

The great success which for so many
years attended the house of Palmer and Co.,
and the almost unparalleled credit that
house commanded, have been justly ascribed more to the liberality and kindness

* A correspondent in the *Calcutta Courier* states,
that John Palmer was both born and brought up
in England, and was also for some time a resident
in France, a considerable part of which he visited.

of heart of the head of that firm, even than to his intelligence and enterprizing spirit; but, unfortunately for himself and for those who became afterwards associated with him, an excess of that generosity, which had won for him the gratitude of so many, led in later times and altered circumstances to the disastrous result we have mentioned, and which has been the source of so much distress. His inability to refuse applications for pecuniary aid, and his reluctance to question the integrity of others, were mainly instrumental in producing the failure—an event which Mr. Brownrigg's attempts to retard by the adoption of the opposite course, so far from retarding, we believe, accelerated. There probably never was a more unhappy period in Mr. Palmer's life than that in which, while efforts were made by his partners to retrieve the affairs of the firm, his liberality was entirely restrained, and he was reduced in his own office, as he expressed it, to a cipher. When the failure took place, such was the confidence of the natives in Mr. Palmer, such their respect for him, that many came forward with offers of liberal assistance; but the case was too desperate to admit of any relief of that kind. The creditors in general, to mark their sense of Mr. Palmer's merits, placed his name at the head of the list of assignees. The Chief Justice, when the list was presented to him, regretted that a legal objection existed to such a nomination; but he seized the occasion to pay a feeling tribute to the character of Mr. Palmer, and to express deep sympathy in his misfortunes.

About three years ago, Mr. Palmer was enabled to re-establish himself in a business, which is, we believe, in a most flourishing condition; and out of the profits of this concern, Mr. Palmer supported and assisted many distressed creditors of the late firm —a fact more to his honour than any recorded in his history.

Mr. Palmer's name was to be found at the head of every association for resisting wrong and supporting right. Mr. Palmer was, in short, an independent citizen, a generous and steady friend; he has lived esteemed and beloved, and his death will be deeply lamented by all who had an opportunity of estimating his virtues.

He lived to a good old age; but his strong constitution, and the good health he generally enjoyed, gave promise of much longer life. The immediate cause of his death was quinsy. He expired about two o'clock in the morning, in the 70th year of his age, and his remains were carried to the grave yesterday morning, followed by a more numerous concourse of friends, and others who respected his memory, than perhaps has ever attended any funeral in Calcutta. —*Bengal Herald, Jan.* 24.

He possessed a mind of the first order. He was not only liberal, but patriotic. His enlarged views embraced as well the present condition, as the prospective amelioration, of the country in which his lot was cast. He saw clearly how much the welfare of future generations in India was dependent on the progress of liberal institutions, and he laboured to promote them, not merely by pecuniary donations, but by active exertions. Though only a private citizen, he rendered eminent service in this respect to the state, by promoting to the utmost extent of his influence the growth of liberal and enlightened sentiments. Though associated in the bonds of an intimate and long-connected friendship with many who had risen through the gradations of the service to the direction of public affairs, he fearlessly opposed their views when they appeared inimical to the march of improvement; and in the struggles for the freedom of the press, his name appears foremost in the lists, as the uncompromising champion of this safeguard of every other free institution. He entered with equal ardour into every plan for alleviating distress, and promoting education. To enumerate his various donations, would be to name every institution which was set on foot for the welfare of India during his prosperity.

His mind was amply furnished with various and valuable information. His conversation was a rich feast, in which it was difficult to determine which most to admire, the elegance of his diction, or the solidity of his judgment. Though he had not enjoyed the benefit of an education at the great seats of learning in England, his composition was distinguished by a peculiar ease, strength, and chasteness. His letters we have always considered models of style, the effusions of an accomplished mind and a finished gentleman.

But it was after his fall from power and influence, that the excellencies of his character shone with peculiar lustre. In the fugitive state of society in India, individuals pass from the scene with such rapidity, that we have few opportunities of contemplating a great character, from its commencement to its close. John Palmer moved and acted in this country for more than half a century. After his reverses, he did not quit the sphere of which he had so long been one of the brightest ornaments, but he continued to reside among us; and as he had blessed society with his liberality in prosperity, so he afforded to it the benefit of his example in adversity. To him was given, we may almost call it, the rare felicity of passing through the two extremes, of wealth and penury, in which human character is tried; and his acquired only additional brightness from the ordeal to which it was subjected. His magnanimity in adversity was, if possible, even more conspicuous than his generosity in the days of affluence. The serenity with which he bore his reverses, the benevolence with which he palliated the ingratitude of those who had once basked in the sunshine of his favours, bore ample evidence to the sterling stamina of his character; and many whom we could name felt a kind of revulsion of feeling, that they should at all be in prosperity, when so much greatness of soul was in adversity. In re-establishing a house of business, his chief delight was to contemplate it as affording him the means of assisting the poorer classes, who had suffered most severely by his insolvency: and it is among the most delightful associations of life, that we were among those whom he honoured by his selection to distribute, month after month, the small sums which he scrupulously devoted to their relief from the profits of his labour. —*Friend of India, Jan.* 28.

A Meeting invited by Sir Charles D'Oyly, of the European and Native private friends of the late John Palmer was to take place on the 6th February, "for the purpose of taking into consideration the most appropriate mode of testifying their respect and affection for his eminent private virtues, and the deep regret which his loss will inflict on all who have had the happiness to appreciate them."

SALE OF SHUMSOODEEN'S PROPERTY.

Extract from a letter from the Upper Provinces: — "Shumsoodeen's personal property is to be sold. The Ulwar Raja offered six lacs for his sporting establishment of elephants, guns, and dogs, and it is wondered why Government did not take it. Shumsoodeen's whole property, of every description, is confiscated; this part of the sentence will frighten the natives properly, and have much more effect than the hanging."—*Englishman, Jan.* 25.

SMUGGLING ACROSS THE JUMNA.

The smuggling across the Jumna is carried on to an amazing extent, in spite of the large establishment of preventive service; in consequence of the large quantity of water expended by the canals, the Jumna twenty miles north of Delhi is in many places not above knee-deep, which accounts for the smuggling. On Christmas night an immense run was made all along the line; the principal trade is cotton from the Jumna to the Ganges, with sugar in return. The principal smuggling is in salt.—*Ibid.*

MILITARY ITEMS.

We hear that the troops are to be removed from Islampoor in Shekhawatee immediately; and it is supposed the two forts will be restored to their mistress, the Ranee of Sikar. It is reported that Capt. Forster's corps of Shekhawatee Kuzzaks,

now at Jhoonjboo, will be retained on the present footing, to insure the peace of the country after the Company's troops have quitted it. It is as yet uncertain whether the latter will be distributed; some imagine they will return to cantonments; while a native report says their destination is Jeypoor, at which city it is intended by Government to station one regiment of cavalry, two of infantry, besides artillery.

The new cantonment will probably be at Sanganeer about 6 miles south of the city.

Captain Thoresby's appointment. as political agent in Shekhawatee, will of course be cancelled.

The most recent and authentic information from Jeypoor is, that Major Alves has no longer the remotest suspicion but that Jotha Ram is the guilty party, and that the Rawul had no share in the attack, but on the contrary, was to have been destroyed himself! The natives, however, seem generally to believe that Luchmun Singh, son of the Rawul, was the person who instigated the mob to the murder of Mr. Blake.—*Delhi Gaz., Jan.* 24.

Neemuch, January 10. — "The 37th N. I. are under orders to march, and reports are afloat that we shall be required at Jeypore: another rumour, and one generally credited is, that this force has been applied for by the Bombay Government, to co-operate with other troops in quelling an insurrectionary Rajah."— *Hurk., Jan.* 26.

We understand that, in consequence of Col. Cragie's taking his furlough to England, Capt. Gavin Young, formerly secretary and acting member of the Military Board, succeeds the colonel as a permanent member. We have not heard who is to succeed Capt. Gavin Young as judge-advocate general.—*Englishman, Feb.* 1.

MILITARY DISCUSSIONS IN THE NEWS-PAPERS.

The *Meerut Magazine* has an article on this subject, from which we extract a few passages:—

"The first question is, whether those who have the power to *check* military discussion, would do wisely to resort to the *only means* available for the detection of offenders; whether the strong hand of power should be unceasingly stretched out to inflict summary punishment, with the chance of failing nine times out of ten in hitting on the right person,—we think not. For we see plainly what the result must be.

"Within the last three years, the press has been deluged with letters of all sorts and descriptions—a few have been excellent, the mass execrable; good, perhaps, in intention, but bad in style, in grammar, and in argument. These productions have been laughed at by ninety-nine men out of a hundred, and lost the relish, the piquancy,they had at first,—people became tired of the endless disputes, and the good sense of the majority would soon have found a correction, had not the press found assistance, where it was least to be expected, and the Scrutator's, Fiat Justitia's, Miles', &c. &c. &c., re-stamped by the hand of authority for a fresh term, enabled to pass current. Admitting that the adoption of vigorous measures drive this host of small fry from before the public, what will be the result? As we may be supposed to have some knowledge of the actual situation of the press, our explanation, given in good faith, may be not uninteresting to those who view the present struggle with interest.

" Throughout India there are a certain number of military men, well known to the editors of newspapers and conductors of magazines, not only for their forcible style of writing, but also for the correctness of their views, and their intimate knowledge of the feelings entertained by the army on peculiar questions. Now, it must be self-evident, that so long as the editors open the all-powerful ' we' to these gentlemen, the most determined persecution will never reach them ; besides which, by reducing the supply, the demand will be increased, and the ponderous talent of some we could name, no longer alloyed by the trash of the many— will create a thousand-fold greater effect on readers than it now does. The number of literary men in India is not great, and though, perhaps, not personal acquaintance exists, yet we find them in constant correspondence with each other. This eventually gives them a power, for good or evil, as it may turn out, according to the active measures employed *against them.* The subsidiary forces may be destroyed, but authority will be left to contend with well-disciplined writers, small in number, it is true, but formidable from talent and experience."

Madras.

MISCELLANEOUS.

COCHIN.

Extract of a letter from Cochin, Jan. 7.—" The trade of the place has also fallen off within the last few years. What little there is, is in the hands of the natives chiefly. This appears strange, considering the fertility of the country and the advantageous position of the town, situated on a considerable river (which has 16½ feet water on the bar at low water), where ships can lie in security all the year round The inland water communication is also extensive, rivers and

salt lakes leading to Coimbatoor, Quilon, Alepee, &c. The native Christians at Cochin are numerous, but in their dealings not a bit more honest than the Bengalees, and far inferior in rectitude to the natives of upper India. Those Christians we saw at Point de Galle are the greatest extortioners I ever met with—only to be equalled by the Cochin gentry, who, in celebrating the rites of the Christian religion, indulge in all kinds of Brahminical idolatry and superstition. The bishop remained here three or four days, but I do not think he could have been much edified with his Cochin flock. The immorality and ignorance of these native Christians, shows the absolute necessity of imparting knowledge first; religion must follow :—at all events, idolatry would cease, and the standard of morality become purer—great points, surely. Although the trade of Cochin has declined, the ship-building business is pretty active — one ship of 560 tons is now building for a Muscat buneeah, and four or five buggalos for the Arabs. A pretty little barque of between 200 and 300 tons, belonging to the Bao-naggur Rajah (near Surat), was lately launched, and is now ready for sea. These vessels are all built of the best teak, and at moderate expense. The 560 tons ship will not cost more, when completed, than 60,000 to 70,000 rupees. Mr. Powney is the chief, if not the only, builder."—*Hurk.*, *Jan. 26.*

REV. MR. ROTTLER.

A monument to the memory of the late Rev. J. Rottler, D. D., is to be erected in Vepery Church, by subscription. Of this pious and aged divine it may with truth be said, he was a walking commentary of the principles he inculcated and doctrines taught. At his grave were tears of sincere and heartfelt sorrow shed, and evidences of bitter grief shown. The following is from the *Christian Observer* :—" We are glad to learn that a monument to this good man's memory is to be erected in Vepery Church, by subscription, and that any excess in the amount of the sums subscribed, over the cost of the monument, is to be applied to the founding of one or more Rottler's Scholarships."—*Cour.*, *Feb. 12.*

KURNOOL.

We observe, from the *Madras Herald*, that there is a probability of hostilities taking place shortly, at Kurnool. Kurnool is a strongly-fortified town, chiefly inhabited by Patans and Arabs, on the south bank of the Toombudra river, about 130 miles south of Hyderabad. It is the capital of a small independent state, abutting, to the north, on the territories of the Nizam, and to the south-east and west on those of the Company. It is well known, that for some years past the prince had actively engaged in procuring supplies of arms from the presidency of Madras; and one invoice, of 600 muskets, packed and marked as " glass *en route* to Hyderabad," was last year seized in the Cuddapah district. But, before this discovery was effected, upwards of 1,400 muskets had already been conveyed in a similar manner, and had reached Kurnool in safety. The rightful prince of this state is a state-prisoner in the hill fortress of Bellary, having been set aside and confined for life for the murder of his wife, under circumstances of great atrocity, in 1823, in our territories, only the day before he was to have ascended the musnud. The next nearest relative was, we believe, then elevated to that dignity, by our authority; but he has long borne the character of a most debauched and profligate ruler.—*Hurk., Feb. 2.*

TINNEVELLY MISSION.

We extract a few passages from a letter of the Rev. Mr. Rhenius, published in the *Madras Herald,* with reference to a letter from the Committee of the Church Mission Society, dated 13th Feb. 1835, on the subject of Mr. Rhenius' disconnexion with the Society, on account of his review of the Rev. Mr. Harper's work on the Church.

Mr. Rhenius first endeavours to shew, that the act was *unnecessary,* although " Bishop Wilson, at the last visitation of this presidency, in December 1834, threw out in his charges to the clergy, some very hard expressions against us, *viz.* that ' the missionaries in Tinnevelly carry on a system, destructive of the holiness and peace of the Christian converts,—a system threatening the ruin of Christianity itself among them.' The Committee's secretary, the Rev. Mr. Tucker, at his visit in Tinnevelly, in April 1835, took particular care to ascertain the true state of the mission, and he not only found the assertion of Bishop Wilson to be unfounded, but could rejoice in all that he saw and heard. He had the kindness even to tell us that the Tinnevelly mission ought to be ' the nursery of missionaries,' &c. and, upon his return to Madras, published in the *Missionary Record,* for May, the following testimony respecting this mission, introductory to our report, for 1834 :—' That he had no hesitation in saying, that, as far as he was able to judge, the particulars published (in our report) do not convey to the mind of the reader an adequate idea of the prosperous state of this mission, and the reality of the work which God is working in this district ;' and, at the end, calls it ' this extensive and well conducted mission ;' and this he said and published, while he was aware, and saw with his own eyes,

that the Church of England forms were not strictly observed ; he declared, however, that if there was a leaning towards any church establishment, it was to that of the Church of England." Mr. Rhenius then states—

" But, secondly, the act was, in my opinion, also *unjust.* This will appear when it is considered, that I was in nowise bound to the Church of England, but came out to the mission field in the capacity of a Lutheran clergyman, who had no other bonds upon him but those of the word of God, and who had full right to carry on the mission work, according to the German evangelical church, just like the many German missionaries who before me had been sent out to India by the Society for Promoting Christian Knowledge. The committee in England never laid before me the regulations of the Society to observe the discipline and constitution of the Church of England ; I never gave them any pledge to that effect ; nor did they ever afterwards demand any such thing from me; those regulations of the Society were brought to my notice only lately, when the ordination question came to be discussed.

" But, lastly, it was also *highly injurious* to the cause of Christ in Tinnevelly. I will not speak of injury done to myself, because, not being conscious of having published any thing contrary to the word of God, I felt persuaded that my heavenly Master would not forsake me, but continue his gracious care over me and my family as before, only in a different manner. By leaving the Society and Tinnevelly, I did not change my Master's service, but only the place of service. But what must the people of Tinnevelly have thought of this measure? The Christians regarded me as the chief instrument by whom they were brought out of the darkness of Heathenism into the light of the Gospel, and by whom they were nourished for so many years with the pure milk of the Divine word, and whom they loved and revered. Suddenly, I am torn away from them ; and when they inquire, Why? what answers can be given to them? If a charge of immorality or false doctrine could be fixed upon me, then the matter would be plain to them. But, as this cannot be done, what must they think when they understand the true cause, viz. that I published a little book, pointing out certain errors in the forms of the Church of England, in the same way as I have published many other little books against errors in other bodies of men? What must they think of the Church Mission Society, when they learn that simply on that account they removed their beloved and conscientiously walking teacher from them? What must they think of the

Christian church in general? How greatly must their confidence—I will not say in Christianity, but in their new teachers—be shaken?

"Those injurious effects upon the Christians have, alas! already fully appeared. Hardly two months elapsed, when the majority of the catechists and congregations loudly and voluntarily desired and called me and my brethren back to Tinnevelly. That I had no idea of returning, is fully proved by my proceeding to occupy a new mission-field at Arcot, with all my brethren, at a considerable expense. I took even a house there for a whole year. Had I had any idea of returning to Tinnevelly, or had I so early given them hints to that effect, it would have been the greatest folly, or the basest hypocrisy, in me, to have made all that expense, and to undergo all that trouble, of removing to Arcot."

ARCHDEACON ROBINSON.

To the Ven. Archd. T. Robinson, M. A.

Venerable Sir,—We, the inhabitants of John Pereira's and others, forming the congregation of Trinity Chapel, feel it to be our most pleasing duty, on the occasion of your departure to your native land, to express our sense of obligation for the readiness with which you heard our prayer for a minister, and our unfeigned gratitude for your personal attendance, and for the pastoral anxiety and pious sympathy with which you regarded us during the brief period of your valuable ministration among us. Permit us, Venerable Sir, without flattery, to assure you that your absence will be severely felt by us. But we sincerely hope and trust, through your kind exertions, to be blest with a successor, whose unassuming piety, ardent zeal, and affectionate solicitude for our spiritual welfare, shall perpetuate your memory among a people who highly respect and esteem you as a successful minister of God.

"And now, may the Lord preserve and bless you, direct and prosper you in all your undertakings; and whersoever Providence shall call you to labour, may your ministry be crowned with abundant success, and may you find a people whose esteem and affection shall be as ardent, and more worthy your regard, than

"Rev. and Ven. Sir.

"Your Reverence's most humble and obedient servants,"
(190 *Signatures*.)

The Lodge of Perfect Unanimity, No. 1, met on the 21st December, at a dinner given to their worshipful master, Archdeacon Robinson, previously to his departure for England; the worshipful master elect, J. C. Morris, Esq. was in the chair.

After the toasts of "The King and the Craft," "The Duke of Sussex, and the Lodges working under him,"

The chairman rose and said: "You are all doubtless aware that we are met here this evening to welcome and do honour to our worshipful brother Robinson, who for the last twelvemonth has filled the office of worshipful master of the Lodge of Perfect Unanimity, No. 1. Brother Robinson's career in masonry has been short, but it has been proportionably distinguished. With him, the usual apprenticeship and lengthened practice were by no means requisite to render him perfect. His giant mind grasped the whole subject almost at a thought, and his learning and research have enabled him to clear up many points in our mysteries which had become obscure by the lapse of ages, and have rendered our beautiful system perfect in all its parts, from the commencement of time to the very depths of eternity. To the great grief of the Lodge we are about to part with this distinguished mason, but we have determined not to do so without presenting him with some testimonial of our admiration, respect, and regard. The record of his services was too precious to be committed to such perishable articles as paper and parchment; we have, therefore, determined to have them inscribed in gold. In pursuance of this resolution, worshipful Sir, I am about to present you with this medal; and I cannot resist saying, that I can recall to my mind few occurrences of my life which have afforded me greater satisfaction and delight than I now feel in paying this well-merited compliment to one whom I revere as a minister of my God, whom I respect for his talents and learning, and whom I love, dearly love, as a brother and a friend. There is the medal, Sir—wear it as a proud trophy which you have won in the pursuit of masonic knowledge. Preserve it as a token of the love and affection of those who have been proud to call you by the endearing name of brother, and by whom your loss will be long and deeply felt. You are leaving us—happily returning to your family and native country; and oh! in the warmth of my friendship, and in the fulness of my heart, I cannot breathe a more ardent wish for you, than that your worth may be as well known and appreciated by those among whom you are going, as they have been by the Lodge of Perfect Unanimity, No. 1."

The Archdeacon, in returning thanks, said that the noviciate might be startled at the apparent mysterious darkness which prevailed in the entrance to the arcana; and he could not deny that curiosity had in part contributed to his at first becoming an apprentice; but each stage

(U)

had its own proper contribution of light and wonder; and he would avow that, as he advanced in his masonic career, he felt less cause for wonder that so many great and excellent men had, to the world at least, appeared to throw a dignity on Masonry, to which its own intrinsic worth did not appear to entitle it. But when he arrived at the highest ranks in its orders, he was sure that the very best and ablest men, themselves gathered the light and advantages which the world believed the institution itself derived from them; and, instead of being surprised that it should have existed for 6,000 years —aye, 6,000 years, he said, fearlessly, the Society of Masonry had existed—he was quite sure that it was founded on principles which must preserve it to the latest ages of the world. The medal which had been given to him he should guard near his heart as his richest treasure, until his death, and then bequeath it his children. He then took a rapid view of the services of Masonry to the world, in the preservation of moral truth, the promotion of science, and the interchange of kindness —particularly in softening down the horrors of war, drying the tears of the widow, and training the orphan to the imitation of his father's virtues.

At a meeting of the subscribers to the "Robinson Testimonial," held in the College Hall, on the 30th December, adverting to the amount of subscriptions up to this date, it was resolved,

"That this amount be appropriated to the purpose of presenting to the Venerable Archdeacon Robinson, a breakfast-service of plate, and a silver stand-dish; and that the plate be inscribed as follows: "Presented to the Rev. Thomas Robinson, A. M., Archdeacon of Madras, in testimony of the esteem and affection, with which he was regarded by the Clergy and Laity of his Archdeaconry."

Bombap.

MISCELLANEOUS.

GRAND BALL BY JAMSETJEE JEEJEEBHOY.

"I know of nothing," said Sir John Malcolm, in speaking of the natives of India, "which will more effectually attach them to our Government, than friendly intercourse with Europeans, and an interchange of those petty civilities which draw men together every where— which invariably pave the way to that unrestrained expression of their inmost thoughts, their hopes, their fears, and their capabilities:—a course, in fact, which has raised the people of the west to their present eminent rank in the scale of civilization."

Where the natives themselves are for-

ward to promote such intercourse, it is impossible that any benevolent mind should look on, and be insensible to the ultimate consequences, if the opportunities be rightly improved.

Our society has been convened on many interesting occasions, since the period of Mr. Elphinstone's accession to this government, but none, we believe, when our fellow subjects of India have displayed greater hospitality, magnificence and urbanity, than on the evening of the 14th inst., when Jamsetjee Jeejeebhoy entertained the Right Hon. the Governor, Lady Grant, and about 350 gentlemen and ladies, at a ball and supper, on the occasion of the marriage of his two sons. His splendid and elegantly furnished mansion was thrown open at an early hour. The music struck up shortly after the arrival of Sir Robert and Lady Grant; and our fair country women displayed their unabated fondness for the dance, to which the present unusually cold season gave a zest that is seldom felt under a tropical climate. These festivities were kept up till 12, when the party adjourned to a supper, which had been laid out in an adjoining structure, put up for the occasion, on the opposite ramparts. The elegance, the grandeur, and the taste evinced in this instance, reminds us of those beautiful fabrics described in the Arabian nights. Imagine a hall, 170 feet in length and 40 in breadth, supported on either hand by fourteen octagonal columns, and beyond these a colonnade fifteen feet in width all round, the architraves decorated with blue ornaments on a white ground, and over all, festoons of scarlet and gold, to which eleven chandeliers and a variety of lights communicated a brilliancy surpassing description.

After the accustomed pledges of loyalty to our most gracious Sovereign had been greeted with enthusiastic cheers, Jamsetjee rose and addressed the assembled company as follows:—

"I am persuaded there are many in this assembly who will rejoice to hear, at the lips of one born and educated in India, that their host considers it his highest privilege to be counted a British subject—and that he cannot but consider it a pledge of those common ties, by which he, and every native of British India, are bound to this great nation;—that he cannot but esteem it a proof also, that the councils of this nation, and our most gracious Sovereign, are sensible to the claims of India on the mother country, that Great Britain has been so scrupulous in its selection of our successive governors. Who is there here who will not remember—each as he may have had opportunities of knowing their virtues and their talents—an Elphinstone—a Malcolm— and a Clare? With what associations will he not call to mind, that we have at this time, and here present, the son of that excellent individual, whose whole life was devoted to the interests of this remote land;—that we are honoured with the presence of the brother of that distinguished statesman, to whom India may one day acknowledge herself to be mainly indebted for the development of its ample resources, moral, natural, and intellectual? To those ·of Britain's sons, whether Indians or Europeans, who are called to the exercise of any public functions under such rulers, the mother country sets forth these men as examples of benevolence, rectitude, and moral worth; that we also may concur with them, in proclaiming her high character to the farthest parts of Asia. I am sure that indulgence will be shewn for this imperfect but honest expression of my gratification on seeing his Excellency the Governor, and so many of my friends, at an entertainment, on the celebration of the marriage of my two sons – and that my friends will join with me in wishing Sir Robert Grant health, and abundant opportunity to carry on the good work of improvement, which this country so much needs, and Britain has such great facilities in accomplishing."

Sir Robert, in returning thanks, adverted with great feeling, to those of his family who have done so much to raise India to its proper place, amidst Britain's numerous dependent colonies. He dwelt on "recollections at once melancholy and grateful to him," briefly, but eloquently, showing that he was evidently moved by his host's kindness.

We looked in vain for some gentleman to exhibit his powers of oratory in behalf of the ladies; but we presume they were too much engaged in digesting the concluding words of Jamsetjee's address, and the party shortly returned again to the dance, which they prolonged to a late hour, and every one, we believe, took leave of his host with one unqualified expression of delight and gratification.— *Bombay Cour. Jan. 23.*

INDIAN PRODUCTS.

At the annual meeting of the Agricultural and Horticultural Society of Western India, on the 5th Jan., the secretary read a letter from Mr. Mutti, of Kootoor Bagh, near Poona, detailing the result of his experiments in the culture of the mulberry tree as a standard; which Mr. Mutti states to succeed so well in this country, that in two years the mulberry becomes so large, that trees planted at sixteen feet from each other would touch with their branches, and that each young tree will yield from eight to ten pucca seers of leaves (a pucca seer is about two pounds avoirdupois); and that they do not re-

quire to be watered more than once a month. It may, therefore, be anticipated, that, when full grown, in four years, they will not require any water. Mr. Mutti then adverts to the endeavours he has made, and proposes making, to induce the natives themselves to adopt a more improved method of growing mulberries, rearing silk-worms, winding silk, and manufacturing silk piece-goods. Two natives, whom Mr. Mutti got to make silk for a manufacturer in Poona, obtained Rs. 13½ the pucca seer for the silk which was pronounced of excellent quality. Mr. M also got a native to make silk handkerchiefs, and intends establishing, at Kootoor, a regular manufactory of similar kinds of cloth.

Another letter was read from Mr. Mutti, detailing the success which has hitherto attended his silk undertaking. The mulberry preferred by Mr M. is the St. Helena species, given to him by Dr. Lush, which he rears as standards. Mr. M. has trees of 27 months' growth, four of which yielded respectively 23½, 19 16, and 15 pucca seers of leaves, the branches of which are strong enough to bear six men climbing among them at the same time. Of silkworms, Mr. Mutti says,—" I have tried the small Chineseworm of four stages, which makes a sulphur cocoon generally in 30 days; answers remarkably well, and continues to breed all the year round without interruption." It requires about 12 pucca seers of leaves (more or less) of the St. Helena mulberry to nourish 1,000 worms. Generally from 9,245 to 16,000 cocoons are required to make one pucca seer of silk, but as the natives become more expert in winding silk, waste of cocoons will not be so great.

A letter from J. S. Law, Esq., dated Surat, 24th Sept. 1835, notices a tree he had met with, a specimen of the *pterocarpus marsupium*, from which gum kino may be obtained by incisions in the bark, but more expeditiously from a strong decoction of the bark and evaporating it in the sun. "The European market," adds Mr. Law, "is chiefly supplied from the west coast of Africa with this drug, and it is there obtained from the *pterocarpus erinaceus.*

A letter from the superintendent of the Ashtagram division of Mysore notices a palm tree, from which a considerable quantity of meal, resembling sago, has been obtained. This palm is the *mhurr* of the natives, or the *caryota urens*, regarding which the late Dr. Roxburgh has the following observations: *Flor. Ind.* vol. iii., pp. 625-626, " It is a native of the various mountainous parts of India, where it grows to be one of the greatest and most charming of this beautiful tribe or natural order. It is highly valuable to the natives of the countries where it grows in plenty. The pith or farinaceous part of the trunk of old trees is said to be equal to the best sago. It forms a part of the diet of the natives, and during a a famine they suffered little while those trees lasted. I have reason to believe this substance to be highly nutritious, and think it as fully palatable as the sago we get from the Malay countries." The tree is not uncommon in the ghauts of the Concan. There are several in different parts of this island and Colabah.

NATIVE EDUCATION SOCIETY.

The anniversary meeting of this society was very numerously attended. The Right Hon. the Governor was in the chair; among the persons present were the Hon. the Chief Justice, the Members of Council, the Chief Secretary, &c. The native company included nearly all the most eminent members of the community, and presented an agreeable mélange of costume, language, and religion: Parsees, Hindoos, Jains, Sunnees, Sheeyas, all sat amicably intermingled. There were some names too of historical association; the descendant of the Nuwab of Bednore, who fought and suffered for the British in the war with Tippoo Sahib; the sons of Gungadbur Shastree, whose assassination in some measure led to the last Mahratta war; and the representative of Naroba Autya, in whose possession the treasure of the Peshwa was seized after the capture of Poona, all called up recollections, curiously contrasting with the peaceful purpose of the present meeting.

Capt. Pope, the secretary of the society, read the report of the committee for the past year. In addition to a satisfactory statement of the society's finances, this document noticed the completion of a new range of school-rooms for the accommodation of the English school; the arrival of the Elphinstone professors of science and belles-lettres; the satisfactory progress in all the schools of the institution; and the election of four new "West" and two "Clare" scholars. It also alluded to an offer made to the society by government, to make an arrangement for employing some of its most qualified students in the public service in the districts, under the revenue commissioner; which arrangement, on mature consideration, it was thought not advisable to enter on immediately, as those whose qualifications would have entitled them to be selected—the old West scholars,—could not be spared from the school till those recently elected were sufficiently advanced to supply their places. In noticing the English school, the report stated that the progress made had surpassed the warmest anticipations entertained at the last meeting. The master, in addition to the usual school-hours, had

instituted evening meetings, for examinations in science and general studies. These meetings were open to the public, and excited considerable interest: they were well attended by the natives; and several European gentlemen, who had made a habit of attending, and themselves examined the scholars, had expressed their warmest admiration at the extent and solidity of the information evinced. So great and so evident was the improvement in this school, both in the scientific and the general department, that the directors considered the warmest commendations and thanks of the society due to the masters, Mr. Bell and Mr. Henderson, for their zealous and most successful labours.

The pupils of the Mahratta, Guzerathee, and Hindoosthanee schools were then successively examined by the Rev. Mr. Wilson and the Rev. Mr. Stevenson. They read portions of works in these several languages, explanatory of the system of English jurisprudence and similar practical matters; and answered very readily a strict cross-examination of the sense and grammatical construction of the passages. The result, in the opinion of the examiners, evinced a very decided improvement on the last year. The mathematical department of the English school, under Mr. Bell, was next examined; then the general department under Mr. Henderson. The examinations are diversified with speeches, recitations, &c. by the scholars. The report in the *Gazette* states: "What rendered the matter still more interesting, was to find the same individual foremost in every exercise; thus the little lad Narayun Dinanath, who distinguished himself at the public examination both in mathematics and civil law, was, in the private meetings, the best orator and the most skilful chemist."

At the close of the examination, his excellency distributed prizes to a great number of boys who had distinguished themselves in the different schools: after which a resolution was passed, thanking Sir Robert Grant for his kindness in taking the chair.

His excellency expressed the warm gratification he had felt, and should ever feel, while in office, in seeing on this occasion so many of this great community, of all castes and classes and religious persuasions, assembled around him, and heartily co-operating in support of the cause of native education. The most sanguine anticipation indulged in on that occasion by his illustrious friend the Earl of Clare, had been, he would not say realized, but far surpassed, by the results of this day's examinations. Of the progress of the scholars in the languages of India he was himself not competent to speak, but he had been informed by the learned gentlemen who had examined them, that there was a very decided improvement upon last year. Of the progress of the English school in all its departments, those who had heard the astonishing display of information, both in quantity and quality, which had just been made, could entertain but one opinion: for his own part, he would acknowledge, that he sometimes found it difficult to follow the scientific students in the rapid and easy manner in which they performed the several tasks assigned them; and that it was not merely a matter of rote, a part got up for display on this occasion, must be evident from the manner, the expression of countenance, the tones of voice, the intelligence and emulation, which marked the whole examination. Gratifying as this exhibition eminently was, he was anxious to impress upon the students that they must not rest there, but must press onward with renewed ardour to perfect the work so happily begun; they must not mistake the means for the end. He would wish it to be impressed on the native community generally, that success in this institution would be a passport to success elsewhere. He did not think *that* the most healthy state of public education, where government was obliged to hold out its patronage as an inducement and a reward; here was a state beyond, where education was prosecuted for its own sake, and knowledge sought for its intrinsic worth; and he hoped that state would ere long come to pass. But there was an intermediate stage, where the fostering hand of government was necessary, and he would say, "shame on the government which then held back from affording its encouragement." Under this view, he was willing to offer all the aid to native education that was in his power, and with this idea that offer had been made by the government to this institution, which he had no doubt would be eventually made available in one shape or other. He hoped, however, the day was not far distant when the members of this important community would seek to educate their children, not with a view of obtaining thereby a passport to subordinate employment under government, but of qualifying them for taking that part in public life, and filling worthily those high offices, to which every great people should aspire.

The *Friend of India*, adverting to the closing remarks of Sir R. Grant, observes: " This is the first distinct assurance given to the native community by government, that the ranks of the public service in the native department, will be replenished from the higher classes in the colleges. Two great advantages are likely to flow from such an arrangement: in the first place, the public offices will gradually be filled with a superior class of functiona-

ries; and in the second place, the highest stimulus will be afforded to the native community, to persevere in the acquisition of sound knowledge;—a stimulus sufficiently strong to overcome hereditary prejudice, and even national apathy. Sir Robert Grant hopes that the time will come when learning will be pursued for its own innate dignity. Nothing will tend so much to hasten this period as the public encouragement of learning, by holding forth the rewards which the state can bestow. In the absence of superior motives, we must work with those which are within our reach. When the public service has thus been filled with men who are imbued with European knowledge, when the most influential men in the native community are enlisted in favour of the literature and science which we value, the general tone of native society will be raised, and superior motives will grow up of their own accord."

Ceylon.

LEGISLATIVE COUNCIL.

On the 21st December, a rather warm discussion took place in the council, on a draft of an ordinance for the protection of landed property from the depredations of stray cattle.

Major-colonel Sir *John Wilson* complained that no protection was afforded by the ordinance to fortified works and their dependencies. Was this because they were deemed less worthy of protection than other public property? He might, perhaps, be told that the rights of his Majesty, in respect to military works, were sufficiently guarded by the common law, and that an enactment by the legislative council for their protection was unnecessary, and would bear the character of presumption. He was not prepared to deny this being the case; but he was able to assert from his own knowledge, that the military authorities had sought redress from the common law, and that their efforts had been in vain. He now held in his hand an official communication with respect to one case of this nature, and, as it would throw more light on the matter than any observations from him, he would with permission of the council read it.

The major-general here read a letter from Lieutenant Jones, commandant at Ruanwelle, complaining of the damage done in the fort and works by stray cattle; that a herd of buffaloes, belonging to a Cingalese, which he had placed in the government *crawl* (or pound), had been forcibly released; that the staff-sergeant had received instructions from the district judge to bring an action on behalf of the government against the owner, for the trespass and damage; the case was tried in the district court, and the judge decreed that the defendant should pay the damage and costs : but by an appeal to the supreme court, the decree was set aside, and the plaintiff directed to pay the costs of suit. Lieut. Jones added: " The chief justice, Sir Charles Marshall, having stated in his remarks, that it was an illegal proceeding to seize cattle at Ruanwelle for trespass, it not being one of the places named in the Regulation No IX, of the 23d September 1833, and that, should the public works at Ruanwelle require protection from the encroachment of cattle, a specific clause for that purpose must be applied for."

The major-general asked whether the military authorities were to take the law into their own hands? He proposed a proviso : " That nothing in this ordinance shall be construed to give a right to interfere with or trespass upon any of the military works or their dependencies in this island, which by law and usage are under the care and control of the competent military authorities."

Mr. *Marshall* seconded this amendment. The council had, on a former occasion, been told by the chief justice (whose absence he regretted), that "they should be laughed at in England for presuming to pass laws on subjects already provided for by the common law." The case now brought before them afforded proof that the local and common law are not in unison, and of the futility of the assertion that no local legislation is necessary, where the common law is already in force. If matters were permitted to remain in this state of uncertainty, the complaints would be innumerable.

Mr. *Anstruther* objected to the proviso as unnecessary; the words conveyed no meaning whatsoever, and if he did not imagine, from the major-general's observations, that more was meant to be inferred from them. he should not wish to oppose them. An additional clause had been inserted, which gave the fullest protection to the principal military posts, and if it could be shewn that any other station required similar protection, he was ready to add them to the enumeration. The object of the major-general might be effected by fencing the minor posts.

The *President* had witnessed the injury done to the works at Ruanwelle, but thought the minor posts would be protected by fence.

Mr. *Anstruther* moved an amendment, instead of the major-general's, adding the words, " or in any other land properly enclosed, whether public or private."

The major-general's amendment was negatived, and Mr. Anstruther's carried.

On the 29th, on the motion for confirming the proceedings of the last sitting,

The *Chief Justice* complained of the misrepresentation of the major-general (who was not now present), in the case he had referred to. The council, be was quite sure. would agree with him in thinking, that judgments of courts of justice, and he spoke of all courts, high and low, civil or military, ought to be held sacred—not from discussion and animadversion, for which he was an advocate in the largest and severest sense of the words—but from perversion and distortion. He sought no exemption from free and fair discussion; but he did claim immunity from misrepresentation. Sir Charles then read notes of the major-general's statement, namely :—that a serious trespass and damage had been proved on the military ground at Ruanwelle;—that in an action on behalf of government, to recover compensation for the injury, the district court had awarded damages;—that the Supreme court had set aside that decision, and remitted the damages;—that the reason assigned for that remission was, that Ruanwelle was not included in the Regulation of 1833;—and, that he, the chief justice, had declared generally, that it was illegal to seize cattle trespassing at Ruanwelle. The council would not be a little surprised to hear that every one of these positions was absolutely false; not intentionally so, he hoped and believed; but that each of them was unfounded in fact. An action was brought, on the civil side of the district court, by some serjeant-major, for certain penalties alleged to have been incurred. by the cattle of the defendant having been found on the ground attached to the fort at Ruanwelle. The evidence of the bare trespass was very scanty; but of real injury or damage occasioned thereby, or even of the reason why the cattle had been impounded. no sufficient evidence was offered. A fine was, however, imposed of a certain sum for each head of cattle so impounded. The defendant appealed against this decision to the supreme court. And the question which naturally suggested itself to the chief-justice on that occasion, independently of the anomaly of imposing a fine in a civil action, was, by what law this fine had been imposed. Accordingly, by an order of reference of the 1st July, it was " Ordered, that the proceeding be referred back to the district court of Ruanwelle, in order that it may be stated by what law the fine decreed against the defendant was awarded." No evidence was offered of damage sustained by the prosecutor ; and it is therefore to be presumed that some law exists, by which a specific penalty is imposed on the owners of all cattle found trespassing In obedience to that order, the district judge wrote a letter in substance as follows :—

" That the fine was awarded according to a district order, which has been in existence ever since this has been a military post, by which a specific penalty is imposed on the owners of all cattle found trespassing on the government works and esplanade." And the district judge added, "that the Regulation of government No. IX, of 1833, had been acted upon by his predecessors, and was acted upon now in this district." The final judgment of reversal was read to this effect :—"If it were possible for this court to recognize any authority, except that of the Legislature, by which specific penalties could be imposed on specific offences, it would have been necessary to send for the 'district order' alluded to. But no such authority can be recognized as vested any where, except in the legislative power of the island. And if any such law had emanated from that quarter, it would be to be found, as regards Ruanwelle, among the proclamations relating to the Kandian provinces. No such enactment, however, is to be found. If by 'district order' be meant an order issuing from any local authority of the province or district, whether civil or military, such order can be considered of no force whatever, at least in legalizing the infliction of penalties. The district judge, however, adds that 'the Regulation of government, No. IX, of 1833, has been acted upon by his predecessors, and is acted on now in this district.' The supreme court is bound to observe that any conviction under that regulation is wholly illegal, except for offences committed within the gravets of the towns therein enumerated. Where there is no law on the subject in force, in the place in question, the owner of cattle found trespassing can only be sued civilly for the damage which may have been done, including any expense or reasonable charge for trouble which may be incurred in securing the animals, and preventing their doing further mischief; and to this demand, therefore, the present action should have been limited. If it be necessary to protect the public works at Ruanwelle, or elsewhere, by positive law, recourse must be had to the proper quarter for that purpose. Another irregularity appears on the face of the present proceedings. If the penalty could legally be enforced, in the course of proceeding, according to the practice of the courts in this island, would be on the criminal side of the court, by which the defendant would not have been put to the expense of stamps. As they have been incurred, and as it is not just that the defendants should bear any portion of costs to which they have been put, in defending an action which cannot legally be supported, it is further ordered that the plaintiff do pay the costs of both defendants."

He would now ask whether he had not shewn that every one of the positions taken by the major-general's speech, and by the letter of the commandant of Ruanwelle, was utterly unfounded? No damage had been proved, no damages had been awarded; it was scarcely necessary to say, therefore, that no damage had been, or could have been, remitted by the supreme court. The fine had been remitted, as illegally imposed; but not for the reason assigned by the commandant and the major-general, viz. that Ruanwelle was not included in the regulation of 1833, but because the "district order," on which, and not on the regulation, the conviction in the district court proceeded, was a mere nullity. The doctrine conveyed in the judgment of the supreme court, which was couched in language intelligible to the meanest understanding, was, that no fine or penalty could be imposed for acts innocent and harmless in themselves, unless by sanction of a duly constituted legislative authority. The doctrine attempted to be imputed to that judgment was, that even though damage should be proved, there still was no law in Ruanwelle which would award reparation to the party injured, for the trespass. The two propositions were too distinct to be confounded together; and he should suppose that scarcely a non-commissioned officer could be found in the service, who would not be ashamed of not at once perceiving the difference. The major-general had asked whether the military were to take the law into their own hands? To this question a very short answer presented itself :—that if they did, it would very soon be taken out of them. But it would appear that, this was the very thing they had been doing. What might be thought of this discussion in other places, or what had now fallen from himself, he, (Sir C. M.) knew not, and certainly cared as little. But he had a pretty strong opinion of what ought to be the answer to any representation, which the major-general might make on the subject. He would be told, " It was your business, Sir, it was your bounden duty, to have made yourself acquainted with the state of the forts, and with any deficiency, real or imaginary, which was supposed to exist in the law, for their protection ; it was your duty to have brought such alleged defect to the notice of the legislature, as recommended by the judgment of the supreme court, in proper time, and in proper manner;—in proper time, by taking care that all judicial decisions, affecting the interests of his Majesty's military service, should be communicated to you as soon as passed, and by laying this particular decision before the executive council, of which you are yourself a member, without delay, instead

of waiting, as you have done, till all the
other amendments had been passed, and
till a moment when the only member of
the legislative council, capable of explaining the effect of the decision, was absent ;
—in proper manner, by consulting one of
the law officers of the crown, as to the
best mode of introducing the necessary
protection, who would have told you that,
instead of the unmeaning ineffective proviso, which you with such tardy zeal introduced at the last moment, three words
would have placed the minor forts in precisely the same situation, if it had been
considered necessary so to do, as the cinnamon plantations, and other government
ground. You have neglected your own
duty in allowing yourself to remain uninformed on this subject for so many
months, and by not using your information, when obtained, to any useful purpose ; and you are now endeavouring to
make the supreme court and the legislative council responsible for that neglect."

MISCELLANEOUS.

The Governor, in a letter dated " King's
House, January 7th," and signed by his
private secretary, has addressed the following remonstrance, respecting the ani-
madversions passed upon his Excellency
in the press of the colony, to Mr. Read,
one of the principal merchants :—

" The Governor, in the official answer
which he directed Mr. Anstruther to return to the letter of the merchants of the
29th December ult., has not thought fit
to introduce therein a serious complaint
which he has to make against that body,
of which you are the senior member.

" It is notorious that the merchants
have been, and are, the chief proprietors
of the *Observer* newspaper, and that its
columns have been made the vehicle of
anonymous and slanderous abuse of Sir
Robert Horton and his Government. Of
abuse of this nature, the Governor considers that, as a public man, he has not
the slightest right to complain, as long as
it only affects his public character, and is
genuinely anonymous; and, for this reason, that, if anonymous charges, of the
nature of those brought against him, were
sustainable, it would be the duty of complaining parties to come forward in their
own persons to sustain them, and their
omission so to come forward is the most
conclusive refutation of the charges themselves. But the complaint that the Governor has to make is, that the merchants
have resorted to, or at least encouraged
by their tacit sanction, an expedient,
which combines the effect of a secret
anonymous accusation with that of an
overt complaint. There have appeared
in the *Observer* of the 7, 11, and 25th
August, 1st September, and 2d October,
five letters, signed ' A Merchant.' These
letters accuse the Governor of various
instances of misconduct. ' Think you,
sir,' says this writer, 'that the Executive
wish that a member of the Legislative
Council should be permitted to express
openly his opinions of the local Government? 'Tis too ridiculous to waste a
thought upon. Oh, how my fancy revels
in the mere idea of the numberless acts of
Government, the gross jobs we have witnessed, the tyranny exercised, which an
honest member would rise up to condemn
and demand satisfaction for!' Of these
expressions, taken by themselves, or even
expressed under the signature of ' A
merchant,' the Governor would have
considered that he had no sort of right to
complain, inasmuch as they are vague and
unspecific. The writer must not be a
merchant, he might only express his personal sentiments ; but when formally put
forward as being undoubtedly ' the sentiments of the whole mercantile body of
Ceylon,' of the limited extent of which
body the public, elsewhere, are perfectly
ignorant, the character of these expressions is utterly changed. This ' merchant' had previously committed the
whole body of merchants ; he volunteered
as their representative ; he had quoted
their participation in his opinions, and
had assigned a special reason for their
omitting to memorialize the Secretary of
State for redress. In speaking of his
opinions generally (*Observer*, 11th August) he says, ' I must, however, premise
that, although I have not the slightest
doubt that the whole mercantile body
participated with me in the opinions I
put forth, still they may not be the precise opinions which, as a collective body,
they would adopt in an official remonstrance. He then deliberately states,
with all the force of delegated authority,
what are the sentiments of the merchants.
' That they do not proceed (he says) to
official remonstrance is, because they are
disgusted with the present Government,
have no respect for or confidence in the
present Council which advises its head,
and can readily conceive that the distracted position of the parent state leaves
them no room to hope for the attentive
consideration of complaints from any
colony which has not the moral power to
make itself heard.' No species of contradiction to this exposition of the sentiments of the merchants of Colombo has
ever appeared. The Governor, however, could still not have felt it necessary
to make the slightest allusion to the subject, had it not been for the senseless and
absurd nature of the opinion itself, contained in the latter part of this paragraph
just quoted. Whether that opinion is or
is not entertained by the body of Colombo
merchants, the Governor has no knowledge, and as they have at last come for-

ward with a memorial, he trusts that they have ceased to entertain such an opinion, if ever they did entertain it. But, if a writer in the *Observer* had signed himself ' A merchant,' and had stated an opinion that a double export or import duty ought to be imposed on any article, or had advanced any other proposition, prejudicing the interests of the mercantile body, as a proposition in which ' he had not the slightest doubt the whole mercantile body of Ceylon participated,' the Governor does not entertain the slightest doubt, but that there would have been an absolute and early contradiction of such an assertion.

" His Excellency feels it, however, to be his duty to inform you, sir, who are at the head of the body to whom doubts are imputed of the willingness of the King's Government, and of the imperial Parliament, to redress grievances, that such doubts are of a highly disrespectful nature. Complaints, suitably brought forward, will ever be duly considered by the British Government ; but neither Government nor Parliament will condescend to receive anonymous complaints as matter of crimination against any public functionary. Even accusers, who deal, in their own persons only, in vague generalities and undefined complaints, will, sooner or later, discover that their accusations will be disbelieved and their motives suspected. The public are also liable to suffer, as real abuses have a strong chance of being passed over, after the public mind has for a length of time been disgusted with unfounded complaints."

Penang.

The *Gazette* of the 12th Jan. contains an account of several daring acts of piracy, committed in the immediate vicinity of Penang, during which, it is said, upwards of fifty persons, on several occasions, were carried off, in the space of three or four days, besides property taken at different places in Province Wellesley, where the pirates had landed. The admiral, who was then at Penang, hearing of their depredations, sent out the boats of the *Winchester* in quest of the pirates ; and two prahus were sent in, one with twelve, and the other with five men. We learn, however, from a private source, that, though strong suspicions were attached to these men, yet they were likely to be liberated, as the charge of piracy could not be proved, those who had escaped from pirates not being able to identify any of them.

Singapore.

MISCELLANEOUS.

Duties on Imports and Exports.—Governor Murchison, in a letter to the mer-

cantile community of this settlement, dated 13th January, apprizes them, " that the supreme Government has directed him to submit the draft of an act and schedule, for levying a duty on the sea exports and imports of the three settlements, to meet the expense of effectually protecting the trade from piracy. The above comprises the directions of the supreme Government,—the *rate* of the duties will be regulated by the estimated expenses of a flotilla and a custom-house, on neither of which points can I, at present, give you any precise information. I may, however, state, that, on the best procurable information, I am of opinion that a duty of 2½ per cent. on the articles enumerated in the annexed list, (square-rigged vessels under foreign colours being liable to double duties) will raise a sufficient fund to meet the objects in view."

List of articles chargeable with import and export duty of 2½ per cent : vessels importing and exporting the same under a foreign flag to pay double duties.

Imports.—Cotton twist; iron and steel; beer, wines and spirits ; gunpowder ; arms; canvas ; cordage ; copper sheathing ; anchors, cables, &c.; earthenware; glassware; hardware ; cotton goods, India and Java ; do. British ; gunnies ; saltpetre ; tobacco, China and Java ; cotton ; cotton goods, from Continental Europe ; opium at 10 rupees per chest.

Exports.—Sugar ; cotton ; pepper; tin ; tortoise-shell ; spices ; cigars ; hides ; mother-o'-pearl shell ; rattaus ; grain (rice and wheat) ; bees' wax ; benjamin ; sapan wood.

Java Bank.—" I have just received advices from Java, that our friends there are not without anxiety as to the intentions of Government with respect to the bank, the charter of which expires in 1837 ; and it is yet undecided whether it will be renewed, or whether, if renewed, it may not be on terms neutralizing those beneficial effects that well-conducted establishment has hitherto produced. The prosperity of the Java bank, if not entirely unexampled, has few parallels in the history of such institutions, and there is no doubt but that that trading Government looks with some avidity on the profits realized, and would seek to appropriate them, could it insure public confidence, in a bank of its own formation, governed by its own functionaries, and under no control save the *sic volo* of the Governor. It is not, however, supposing our neighbours to have made much progress in political wisdom, to believe they have already discovered that in such hands these establishments have hitherto proved failures, or, at least, of very doubtful utility to the public, however convenient to a

(X)

short sighted financier. The presumption, therefore, at present, is, that they will not attempt it unless the shareholders of the bank refuse the terms which may be proposed. It is not, I am informed, yet ascertained what these terms are likely to be, nor is it forgotten that the late commissioner's ire was excited by the refusal of the bank directors to co-operate with him in a measure affecting the currency, which, as far as can be learnt of official secrets, would have gone the length of an entire change of the standard of value in Java, from silver to copper."
—*Corr. Sing. Free Press.*

Sir Stamford Raffles.—At a meeting of the subscribers to the monument, intended to be erected to the memory of Sir Thomas Stamford Raffles, convened by public advertisement, and held in the Reading-room, on the 1st inst., for the purpose of consulting on the best means of employing the funds already collected, as well as other matters connected with that undertaking ; it was resolved :

" That it is the opinion of this meeting, they will best perpetuate the remembrance of the eminent services rendered to this settlement, and the commercial world generally, by this distinguished individual, by endeavouring to complete the institution founded by him for the purposes of education."

" That, as the meeting find the funds already collected for the monument amount to Drs 1,827, and that there is nearly Drs. 1,000 more subscribed, which, it is expected will be paid immediately on application, it was, therefore, further resolved—that as soon as it is found a sufficient sum can be raised, by additional subscription, for the purpose of completing the buildings, and making them fit for schools on an extended scale, they will place at the disposal of the trustees of the institution, the whole sum subscribed for the erection of the monument."—*Sing. Chron. Jan 2.*

Burman Empire.

Letters from Rangoon give a very favourable account of the first proceedings of the new woonggee. He seems to be anxious to settle justly and expeditiously all such law-suits as have yet been brought before him ; and, although not very quick and intelligent, he is patient, and honest, and firm. Before his departure from Ava, he was well schooled and cautioned. He made an attempt, however, to re-introduce the ceremony of unslippering, which no Englishman has observed at Rangoon since the late war. One of the most respectable English merchants there, Mr. Trill, on whom the demand was first made, resisted it with determination, but with great good humour, and soon persuaded the woonggee to give up the point. Mr. Trill deserves the thanks of all his countrymen. Another letter adds :

" The Resident has had a battle to fight with the Court, on the subject of the aggression committed by a large party of the wild tribe, called Singfos, who entered our territory to the southward of Suddiya, in Assam, and burnt and plundered a village, occupied by another set of the same race. Here, no one seems to know or care anything about these Singfos ; but it was necessary to prevent their troubling our frontier, and, after some battling, the Resident persuaded the Court to send a strong party, and an officer of rank, to the offending Singfos, and allow Captain Hannay, the officer commanding the Resident's escort, to accompany the mission. They left Ava on the 22d ult., and are to go by water to Mogoung, and thence across the country, nearly due north, to the vicinity of Suddiya. Captain Hannay will have an opportunity of seeing Baman, Mogoung, the amber mines, and a tract of country to the north of Ava, which, perhaps, no European has ever before visited ; and it is satisfactory to know that he is every way qualified, not only possessing good instruments and some science, but good temper, judgment, and some knowledge of the Burmese, to gather, during his journey, all such information as may be useful and interesting. By the bye, I may mention, that on the 12th of last month he calculated the quantity of water discharged by the Erawadi River ; it amounted then to so much as 211,140 cubic feet in a second of time. By two trigonometrical observations, one on the Ava side, near the British Residency, and the other on the opposite Tsagain bank, he made the breadth of the river there 1,244 yards ; the average depth was 23 feet, and the average velocity 150 feet in a minute. A good section of the river, however, cannot be taken near Ava, as the depth varies very much, from 8½ fathoms to a cubit, and less."—*Beng. Hurkaru, Feb. 8.*

Cochin China.

Accounts have been received at Singapore from Cochin China, which state that the insurrection and disturbances, which had prevailed there for the last three or four years, are quelled, and that the country is quiet and in a good state of defence.

Siam.

A visit of three individuals, of the American mission, to Chantibun, proved highly interesting. They were favoured with the friendship of the prah-klang and his son ; the latter of whom afforded them all necessary facilities for exploring the country, and even prompted them to it. The town is fifteen miles from the mouth of the river of the same name, and contains about 10,000 inhabitants, nine-tenths of whom are Chinese and Cochin-Chinese. The latter are numerous, and entirely under the influence of the Romish priests; who, without being able to read a word in them, pronounced the books of the missionaries to be most pernicious. The country around the city, to the distance of twenty or thirty miles, contains many villages, of 3 000 or 4,000 inhabitants each. The scenery is pleasant, and much of the soil of a superior quality, but not well cultivated, and the markets are but poorly supplied with provisions. There are evidences of the cultivation having formerly been more extensive than it is at present. The prah-klang is building an extensive fortification eight miles below the town. He politely invited the missionaries to make him a visit, which they gladly did. It was a very pleasant interview. He took not a little pains to make it agreeable to us. He had a band of fifteen female musicians, playing upon as many different kinds of instruments, for our amusement. I must say, the music was admirable, exceeding any music I have heard since I left America. The missionary physician, Dr. Bradley, returned to Bankok, after seven or eight weeks' absence, with improved health, and, at the date of my intelligence, was about to commence medical operations again, in a house built upon the water. He can, therefore, " pull up stakes," and move to another place, without trouble, if the Siamese dignitaries think he is doing " too much good." One of the missionary ladies had gathered a few girls around her, and was hoping to collect a flourishing school; but the Romish priests took the alarm, and ordered the parents and guardians of the children, who happened to be all Roman Catholics, to remove them, on pain of excommunication, which they, of course, did not dare to expose themselves to."—*Corr. Sing. Free Press.*

A rumour is now current here, that the King of Siam is about to give his favourite daughter in marriage to Chan-fah, and elevate him to the rank of " Second King."—*Sing. Free Press, Jan. 7.*

China.

We have been informed by late arrivals from China, that the whole foreign European community did proceed to the city-gate to demand the release of the officer of the *Fairy Queen*, and after some opposition from the troops, skirmishing with clubs and bamboos, giving and receiving

broken pates, and which would in all probability have proceeded to greater extremities, had not orders at length arrived from the Canton authorities to release the prisoner at once, with all his papers, into the possession of the foreigners. A proclamation it is stated was also issued, that further aggressions of a similar nature against foreigners were to be thereafter strictly prohibited, and that the offending mandarin on this occasion should be flogged and degraded from his rank and honours. We trust that this demonstration of spirited and determined opposition, on the part of the foreign community, to any thing like uncalled for oppression by the subjects of the celestial empire, will operate as a check upon such insolence in future, and may have a much more salutary effect than a thousand undignified and degrading supplications for favour or redress, under the cloak of political or commercial expediency.—*Sing. Chron., Jan. 2.*

Australasia.

NEW SOUTH WALES.

LAW.

Supreme Court, Feb. 5—Jack Congo Burrell, a native black, was arraigned on an indictment for the murder of Jabengi, another black, by hitting him with a tomahawk, at Windsor. The indictment and plea, being of a novel description, excited much interest. The plea was a special one, and demurred to the jurisdiction of the Court, setting forth that the prisoner was not liable to the laws of England, and did not recognise any authority of the King of England, or the laws in force in the Colony—he being an aborigine of the Colony, and governed by laws peculiar to his tribe, which were in existence before the English law was introduced into the Colony; and that, if any charge was against him, he was liable to stand punishment by having so many spears thrown at him by the relatives of the deceased, which was the law of the tribe.

The *Chief Justice* remarked, that it was a very ingenious plea, and asked the Attorney General what course he intended to pursue, to which the latter replied, that he did not know, but must consider of it.

MISCELLANEOUS.

Patriotic Association.—On the 8th December, a General Special Meeting of this Association took place at its rooms in Sydney; Sir James Jamison in the chair. The chairman stated, that he had felt it his duty to call the meeting, to discuss the information necessary to instruct Mr. Bulwer respecting the qualifications of representatives and voters for a Legisla-

tive Assembly. His view of the matter
was, that this point should be left to the
British government. If this was agreed
on, Mr. Wentworth would draw out two
bills. One bill would consist of two
Houses, an Upper and Lower House;
the Upper to consist of fifteen members,
five elected by the government, and ten
by the people; and the other of fifty members, elected by the people, and would
form a Commons or Lower House.
Another form proposed, was the junction
of the Executive and Legislative, or
Upper and Lower House, in one body, to
be composed of fifty members, ten appointed by the government, and forty
elected by the people, which would be a
House of Lords and Commons blended.
The only exclusion that he (Sir John)
would propose was, the Clergy. He
thought the population ought to be the
criterion in fixing the number of members
to be chosen from the free male population
of the colony above twenty-one years of
age.

Dr. Bland suggested, that the first step
was to obtain an elective representation;
it should include all classes, who should
be properly represented.

Mr. Falwasser said, if the qualifications
of members and voters were fixed by the
British Parliament, the local legislature
could not alter them, if the system did
not work well.

Mr. Poole proposed a scheme, under
which the government would consist of
three estates,—the Governor, the Upper
House of Assembly, and the Lower House
of Assembly. The Upper House to consist of sixteen members, selected from the
unpaid magistrates, exclusive of the Chief
Justice (as speaker), Colonial Secretary,
Commander-in-Chief, and Treasurer; the
Lower House to consist of fifty members,
including six *ex-officio* members; all persons qualified for special jurors to be
eligible as members, and the election to be
by ballot; the qualification of voters to be
freedom, majority, 10*l.* freeholders, or 15*l.*
householders.

Some discussion took place as to the
number of members, some recommending
fifty, others eighty.

The Chairman stated, that the number
of the free male population of the colony,
above twenty-one, was 17,542.

Mr. Stephen proposed, that the constitution should be formed of a Council,
and an Assembly, nominated jointly by
the government and the people.

Captain Biddulph and Mr. Hipkiss
objected to this; the admission of the
nominees of government into the Assembly would give a preponderance to the
government, which would be fatal to the
interests of the public.

Dr. Bland was averse to having two
houses; he was for one house, giving

government the nomination of one-fourth
of the members. In Canada, it was proved
that two houses did not work well; there
was perpetual jarring.

Mr. Falwasser concurred with Dr.
Bland.

Mr. Carmichael thought it inconsistent
to send home two bills, one for one house,
and a second for two houses. He thought
the British Parliament would laugh at
such a measure.

Dr. Bland explained, that the intention
of the two bills was to be prepared with
an alternative, in case of a refusal of the
first bill. A new form of government,
intended to obviate the evils which arose
from the Upper House in Canada, was
proposed; if this was refused, then the
Colonists prayed for the form of government which had been obtained in the
other Colonies.

Captain Biddulph moved that persons
possessed of £1,000 in real property,
should be eligible as members, and that
£15 rental should qualify voters.

Mr. Levy thought it ridiculous to look
to wealth alone as a qualification of members. He knew many persons possessed
of thousands, who could not write their
names, and who scarcely knew B from a
bull's foot; were they fit persons for legislators? It was not money made the man,
but man that made the money.

Mr. Keith considered it would be hard
for persons of the highest talent and experience to be shut out from a voice in
the legislature, merely by a disqualification of not possessing money. He would
propose that the qualification of voters
should be fixed at £5 rental for Sydney,
and 40s. for country voters.

Mr. Carmichael suggested that Mr.
Keith had omitted moral qualification.

Dr. Bland asked how that was to be
ascertained.

After a long discussion, which was adjourned, and resumed on the 19th, it was
resolved that the first bill should be printed, omitting Van Diemen's land.

Jurors.—It is a matter of much regret
that any indisposition to attend the supreme court, for the despatch of criminal
business, should be at all evinced by persons properly qualified, and duly summoned, to act therein as jurors. No later
than Thursday last, the court was detained above two hours from the total absence
of a sufficient jury; and it was not without difficulty, we hear, that "twelve good
men and true" could at last be mustered
and empanelled. If this were caused by
positive numerical insufficiency—by a
paucity of properly qualified jurors to be
found in the colony, or rather within the
limits prescribed by the act in council,—
we would deem such absence, however, to
be regretted, yet excusable, from the

necessity of the thing; but with the *directly contrary* fact staring us in the face, it must be pronounced as most unpardonable.—*Sydney Gaz.*, Feb. 6.

———

Emigration Settlers.—We very much approve of the plan, which the lieutenant-governor has lately adopted, of settling some of the more respectable and industrious labouring emigrants and their families; that of giving each family a small spot of ground in the neighbourhood of rising and populous towns and villages, in which there is a demand for labour. The experiment was first tried, last year, in the township of Blandford; a number of emigrant families sent out by Lord Egremont were settled, by the government, in the immediate vicinity of the new and very trifling village of Woodstock, in that township, and the experiment succeeded well. The advantages of the plan are obvious. Labour of every description being in great demand in these rising villages, every member of a family, whether male or female, labourer or mechanic, who is old enough, and able to go out to work, can get employment on the spot, while the female head of the family and children can be employed in the domestic affairs, or in the cultivation of the little plot of ground assigned to them, upon which also the older branches of the family, when out of employment, can always profitably employ themselves.—*Ibid.*, *Feb.* 11.

———

VAN DIEMEN'S LAND.

A most extraordinary discovery has taken place at Port Philip. Some of Mr. Bateman's men were, one fine morning, much frightened at the approach of a white man, of immense size, covered with an enormous opossum-skin rug, and his hair and beard spread out as large as a bushel measure—he advanced with a number of spears in one hand, and a waddy in the other. The first impression of Mr. Bateman's men was, that this giant would put one under each arm, and walk away with them. The man shewing signs of peace, their fear subsided, and they spoke to him. At first, he could not understand one word that was said, and it took a few days before he could make them understand who he was and who he had been—his story is very remarkable. This man's name is William Buckley; he was formerly a private in the 4th, or King's own; he was transported to New South Wales, and accompanied governor Collins, in the year 1804, to the settlement of Port Philip. Whilst the new colony was being established, Buckley with three others absconded, and when the settlement was abandoned, they were left there, supposed to have died in the bush. It might be imagined that there is some hoax about the affair, and we should not have credited the story, had not two of the leading members of the new company gone to one of the old settlers, who was also one of those forming the expedition of governor Collins. After asking a few particulars respecting the country, the question was put, whether any of the party remained after the settlement was broken up, when the party applied to immediatey said, that four men were left —one of whom he particularly recollected, because he was much taller than Lieut. Gunn, and his name was Wm. Buckley; he added, they were never heard of afterwards. It appears, Buckley has never seen a white man for upwards of thirty years. He has been living on friendly terms with the natives, and has been considered as a chief. He says he does not know what became of the other three runaways. Curiosity induced Mr. Bateman's party to measure this Goliah; his height is six feet five inches and seven-eighths; he measures, round the chest, three feet nine inches; the calf of his legs, and the thick parts of his arms, are eighteen inches in circumference. By all accounts, he is a model for a "Hercules." He is more active than any of the blacks, and can throw a spear to an astonishing distance. He refused to leave the natives. This man may be made most useful to the new settlement; and, we trust, every precaution will be taken to conciliate the blacks, and bring them by degrees to industrious habits, through the medium of this man.—*Col. Times, Aug.* 25.

════════

SUPPLEMENT TO ASIATIC INTELLIGENCE.

Calcutta.

LAW.

Supreme Court, Feb. 4.—Shaw v. Freeman. This was an action for libel. The plaintiff, Mr. W. A. Shaw, is an indigo-factor at Bhaugulpore: the defendant lives in the same district. The latter had taken a pottah of some chur lands, which were claimed by Mr. Shaw. A suit in the Mofussil Court decided the question in favour of Mr. Shaw; and Mr. Freeman then wrote to Mr. Shaw the following letter:

"Mr. Freeman begs to repeat, that, in the event of Mr. Shaw persisting in breaking his agreement, he, Mr. Freeman, will be driven to the unpleasant necessity of taking the first opportunity of making public to every one at Bhaugulpore and elsewhere his (Mr. Shaw's) want of faith and honesty in his engagements, written or verbal, his disregard to truth, and his non-repugnance in forfeiting his character as a gentleman; and this, if Mr. Shaw persists in endeavouring to evade the said verbal agreement, Mr. Freeman will undertake to prove to the satisfaction of any one who may wish to enquire as to the truth of Mr. Freeman's charge "

Mr. Freeman proceeded to carry his threats into execution, by sending a circular round to the society at Bhaugulpore, as follows :

" To the Residents at Bhaugulpore.— Gentlemen, however painful and repulsive the task, Mr. Freeman feels it a duty he owes to the society at Bhaugulpore, to expose in their true light the principles and character of one of its members; *viz.* Mr. W. Shaw. Mr. Shaw having forfeited his word and written engagement, and having violated the terms of a most solemn written agreement with Mr. Freeman, Mr. Freeman holds himself bound by his promise held out to Mr. Shaw, under date the 4th instant, to put every man upon his guard against such a character, and to publish that the said' Mr. Shaw is a man void of all sense of honour, faith, integrity, or shame; and, as such, Mr. Freeman takes this opportunity of posting him as a person void of all honourable principle, in having broken through his engagements, both verbal and written, —in having violated his most sacred written pledge,—as the inventor of the most wanton falsehoods,—and as having forfeited all claim to the character of a gentleman, and a member of a respectable society. The above facts, Mr. Freeman undertakes to prove to any person who may be inclined to enquire into them."

The parties were bound over to keep the peace.

The *Court.*—There can be no doubt, but that there must be a verdict for the plaintiff. This libel is not of so light a character as the counsel for the defendant has described it; on the contrary, the words are strong, the plaintiff being described as a man void of all honour and integrity, and without pretentions to the character of a gentleman. It is alleged that no damage has been proved; but it is quite impossible to say that the circulation of the libel must not have had a very injurious effect. Taking into consideration the letter written by Mr. Shaw, as going in some degree to lessen the amount of damages, we cannot give a verdict for a less amount than Rs. 1,000.

MISCELLANEOUS.

Mr. Ricketts.—Mr. Mordaunt Ricketts has appealed to the Managers of the Civil Service Annuity Fund against the refusal of the Court of Directors to continue the payment of his pension, since they recorded against him a dismissal from their service in 1834. We doubt whether his original letter to the managers has yet been received; but, in the mean time, a lithograph copy having reached us, we do not hesitate to give insertion to it, as well as to some remarks upon his case in the *Cheltenham Journal* and in *Alexander's Magazine,* which, we are assured—(and we readily believe it with respect to the latter, which always assumes the Company to be in the wrong), express the spontaneous opinions of the writers. We have not yet seen the pamphlet alluded to—possibly it may shake the opinions we formed long ago upon the question of Mr. Ricketts' guilt or innocence of the charges brought against him. But we cannot help remarking that the Press in England has done but little good, if he has found no better advocate than the journals we have quoted, whose reasoning appears to us but a tissue of sophistry and an evasion of the question altogether. We certainly entertain very different sentiments from those professed by Mr. Ricketts and his two feeble advocates, as to the course which an innocent man in most cases would, and in all cases ought, to pursue, when his character is at stake. Mr. Ricketts lays much stress upon the inconvenience he would have been put to, had he accepted the alternative offered him by the Government here, of giving up his passage when already engaged, and personally meeting the investigation into his conduct, which was then decided upon. It was undoubtedly great weakness in this Government, to let the alternative of an investigation in his presence or in his absence rest with him. He ought to have been, and we understand it was proposed in council that he should be, peremptorily ordered to wait the issue on the spot, whether the evidence against him was then considered sufficient to go to trial, or whether it was only in course of collection—supposing (as we must suppose) that a *prima facie* case of criminality had been made out sufficient to warrant further proceedings. Why so much consideration was had for the personal convenience of a public functionary under strong suspicion at least of high crimes and misdemeanors, we cannot comprehend; but surely the evasion of an accused party, after notice of the charges against him, can never be admitted as an argument in his favour, and as invalidating all inquiry, and Mr. Ricketts could not hope to be exculpated by the world because he let judgment go by default. In the army, when but a slight is put upon an officer, affecting his professional character, it is the practice of every high spirited man to *demand* enquiry, not to wait for it,—to demand to be personally confronted with his calumniators and accusers. What would be thought of an officer who (if permitted to do so) should go out of the way, beyond the jurisdiction of the Court before which he had notice that his conduct would be arraigned, and, when found guilty of the charges, keep himself still out of reach, refusing to disclose circumstances of the highest importance to his own justification, the disclosure of which would be no breach of confidence and no possible injury to any other person whatever? If Mr. Ricketts be an innocent man, he has acted like a man who wished the world to think him otherwise. Let the reader mark the last paragraph quoted by the *Cheltenham Journal* from Mr. Ricketts's pamphlet. He declares that, on the evening before his embarkation for England, he was required by Lord William Bentinck to shew his accounts with his agents, and he makes it a sort of boast that he " did not commit the baseness of acceding to so tyrannical a command." What *baseness* could there be in acceding to the command, even though it were tyrannical? He was not required to expose the private affairs of other persons, but invited to abide by a test, in the case of his own, that *ought* to have been a very conclusive as well as very simple means of proving his innocence of the bribery and peculations of which he then stood suspected or accused. Still, there might be matters affecting others in his agents' accounts, which he might properly object to disclose without their sanction. But no such objection could exist to his shewing, or at least declaring, what was the amount of his own funds in his agents' hands. The insolvency of all the great houses has since revealed the state of his affairs in that particular. He has proved his debt upon Alexander and Co. in the London Bankrupt Court, and the amount of it has appeared in all the newspapers. And the schedules of the fallen houses being filed in the Insolvent Court here, every creditor has a right to inspect them, and to know the amount upon which another creditor is allowed his dividends. Concealment is no longer possible. Mr. Ricketts, therefore, has no longer the same or any good plea for declining explanation, how it happens that he appears in Alexander and Co.'s books as a creditor for Sa. Rs. 4,00,573. 5. 4; and in those of Fergusson and Co. for Sa. Rs. 3,37,853. 10. 7; upon which latter sum he has received the first dividend; while his family is also creditor in a trust account with Palmer and Co. for Sa. Rs. 1,05,413. 11. 0; and he does not appear as a debtor in the schedules of any of the late firms. We do not consider ourselves at liberty to notice what we have heard or may privately know about his remittance transactions to England, or any other facts connected with his pecuniary affairs.

On the Annuity question, there will be differences of opinion unconnected with the culpability or innocence of Mr. Ricketts. In equity, if he did that which ought to have deprived him of his right to pension from the first, he could have no better right to it by having enjoyed it for four years—rather, he should be made to refund what he has unduly received. But the point of right seems to turn upon the interpretation of a particular section in the rules of the fund, and upon a question of fact, whether Mr. Ricketts's *resignation* was or was not a *retirement*. We have heard that, on the eve of his departure from Calcutta, he substituted a tender of resignation for his first application for furlough, and that an answer accepting his resignation was designedly not given. —*Cal. Cour. Feb. 5.*

Cruttenden and Co.'s Estate.—A meeting of the creditors of the late firm of Cruttenden and Co., took place on the 4th February; Capt. Vint in the chair. The following report of the committee appointed at the last meeting was read :

" The committee beg to report that, for the short time that has been afforded them to look into the affairs of the late firm of Messrs. Cruttenden, Mackillop, and Co., they have come to the conclusion, that the statement of the present value of the assets exhibited at the last meeting, estimating the amount at 42 lakhs of rupees, is a fair and reasonable expectation of the probable outturn of the estate.

" With reference to the meeting of creditors on the 10th January 1834, at which it was stated that the estimated amount of assets was 128 lakhs (although the books exhibited a much larger amount), exclusive of 26 lakhs to meet mortgage claims and sets-off that could not be disputed, the committee have endeavoured to ascertain the cause of the extraordinary difference between the amount of assets stated as being good at that period and the present estimated value.

" The statement, upon which the former estimate was made up, not being forthcoming, the committee's examination into this matter cannot be rendered with that accuracy they could wish; but it appears to them that the deficiencies principally arise under the following heads, *viz.*

	Lakhs.
' Loss on working indigo factories, although the previous two years shewed a gain of about 12 lakhs ...	2½
' Over estimated value of ditto ..	28
' Ditto of Landed Property	6
Carry forward	36½

Brought forward	36½
' Ditto recoveries from book debts	23
' Ditto of recoveries from indigo planters, on account, independent of the value of their factories, but which shew a loss of about 2½ lakhs	16
' Apparent loss on Commercial accounts	35,000
' Expended by Mr. Macintyre for establishment, &c.	75,000
' Interest paid on sums borrowed......................	1
' Arrears of salary, brokerage on indigo and contingent charges 30,000	0½
' Law Charges 20,000	
	78

which being deducted from 128 lakhs, leaves the present value of the assets at 50 lakhs, instead of 42 lakhs, of which details were given at the last meeting."

After the report was read, Mr. Dickens wished to ask, whether Mr. D. Macintyre was a certified bankrupt at the time of his appointment to the assigneeship of Cruttenden and Co.'s estate, of whom Palmer, Mackillop, and Co., the London correspondents of Cruttenden and Co., or *some one* of the partners, were assignees?

Mr. James Mackillop replied, that *he* was one of the assignees, but that the firm of Palmer, Mackillop, and Co, were *not*, and therefore that what Mr. Dickens had stated, was *not a fact;* and further, that Mr. Macintyre's former firm had paid 20*s.* in the pound.

Mr. Dickens said, that if a partner of of Palmer, Mackillop, and Co., was an assignee of Mr. Macintyre, it was in substance the fact, that Messrs. Palmer, Mackillop, and Co., of London, were the assignees of Mr. Macintyre; and that, as to any private explanations arising out of matters not matters of business, they had better be pursued elsewhere.

Mr. Dickens then asked of Mr. Mackillop, " Was the dividend of 20*s.* in the pound before the appointment of Mr. Macintyre ?"—Answer, No.

Mr. Dickens continued. The fact of Mr. Macintyre's being a bankrupt, and that a partner of Messrs. Palmer, Mackillop, and Co.'s was his assignee, did not disqualify him, nor was he qualified *though he had not* paid 20*s.* in the pound until after his appointment, for being assignee of any other firm; but he was peculiarly disqualified for being the assignee of Cruttenden and Co. It must be obvious to every man of sense among the merchants and creditors of the Calcutta firm, that it gave Mr. Macintyre an opportunity and an interest in prolonging the *mercantile character of his assigneeship;* that if, as there were *two* or more rates of commission, on sale of consignments to London, he would and *must* send

to London consignments to Palmer, Mackillop, and Co., and at probably the highest rates; but whether in fact he did so or not, was quite immaterial; for, as an honest man, he was bound to state to the creditors on the 11th January 1834, when they appointed him, that he laboured under this disqualification; and the partners were also bound to state it. If he had stated it, and every creditor had consented, the court *could not have appointed him.* Mr. Dickens moved the following resolution :—

" That, in the opinion of the creditors assembled, there is no ground whatever for departing from the terms of the order of the 11th January, 1834, by which Donald Macintyre was appointed assignee, with liberty to pay himself a commission of 4 per cent. on all declared dividends; including the allowance to James Cullen and Robert Browne, and in lieu of all charges but law charges."

Mr. Dickens stated his reasons for moving this resolution. It was a contract voluntarily made by Mr. Macintyre, himself a merchant connected with this firm, dependent to some degree upon it, mixed up with its trusts; he knew what he was about; next he entered into expenses which no sane merchant or assignee would have submitted to (unless he were dependent), for his expenses, 75,000 for two years, were not all, and there were some charges for principal sums not brought to account, and no interest whatever allowed; now, as he had, with full knowledge, accepted a commission of four per cent. in lieu of all charges, except law charges, the result was this, *viz.* that if (having twenty-three lakhs of mortgages, besides law charges to pay, and only 1,10 lakhs of nominal assets to receive) he had calculated on receiving in five years fifty lakhs to make a dividend of (to do which he must have received sixty-five lakhs out of the 1,10 lakhs), he had gone on knowingly on a scale of expense, by which he could not have received a sixpence at the end of five years, even if he had realized and paid in dividends fifty lakhs ! He had paid 600 Rs. to Mr. Browne monthly, up to the month he embarked for England. Mr. Browne was a gentleman with a very handsome income, in right of his wife, if not of his own, and having from £1,500 to 2,000 a year in England. Mr. Cullen,* another gentle-

---

* Mr. Cullen has published a letter, with reference to these two statements, wherein he asserts as follows :—" Mr. Browne left India in January 1835, and, although he continued labouring for the estate up to within a few days of his departure, he drew no allowance for services subsequent to the month of September preceding, and his receipts in all, amount, I find, to Sa. Rs. 5,400 only ! As to my own case, I have simply to state, that I have not received a sixpence from the estate, or Mr. Macintyre, for the past seven months, although daily employed in its business; and my average income

man, borne on the assignee's books, at 600 Rs. a month, from the month of January 1834, was a gentleman in this situation, *viz.* that, a little after that time, he had been appointed to the secretaryship of the Laudable Societies: for the purposes of his appointment, and as an electioneering manœuvre, the commission formerly received by secretaries had been reduced to one-half by Messrs. Cockerell, Ouseley, Forbes, Greenlaw, Harding, Turton, and others, whose names were not recollected: after the point was carried, the former commission was restored! consequently, Mr. Cullen was a gentleman, who had been receiving from January 1834, as near as could be estimated, about 1,800 Rs. a month. Baboo Russomoy Dutt had received, up to June 1834, 800 a month, from thence 500 a month, his son 200 a month. The result was that, out of these three salaries, all paid to opulent men, about 40,000 Rs. of the 75,000 had been expended. When the creditors agreed to Mr. Macintyre's paying this, it was to be presumed, that they had no objection to his performing an act of liberality; it came to a different question when Mr. Macintyre asked the *creditors,* some creditors for themselves, some creditors for others much poorer than any of those who asked, directly or indirectly, for this boon. He had shewn that no sane man could calculate on having more than fifty lakhs to distribute; he had shewn also that, having spent more than 75.000, without interest, Mr. Macintyre had in effect spent at the rate of every sixpence he could spend, supposing he had received his rateable proportion of 200,000, which was the utmost he could receive. On what ground did he come—not only to ask for liberty to charge this sum of 75,000 on the estate. but for an *an additional reward?* (Here Messrs. Cockerell and Wilson intimated that the resolution Mr Wilson suggested was not pressed.) Be it so; then Mr. Macintyre only claims 75,000 of his expenses to be charged to the creditors, because he has paid 600 Rs. to Mr. Browne, who did not want it till he went away; because he has paid 600 Rs. to Mr. Cullen to this hour, who did not want it—and had 1,800 Rs. at least a month—but let me stop—(said Mr. D.) before we come to the question of refunding, there may be one obstacle; Mr. Holroyd, the assignee of the private estate of Mr. Cullen, is here. I ask you, sir, have you received the 600 Rs. a month paid by the general creditors, or rather which Mr. Macintyre now asks the general creditors to pay, for the benefit of the *private* creditors of Mr. Cullen? (Mr. Holroyd said, No, he had income for the two past years has barely reached a moiety of Mr. Dickens's estimate, while latterly it has fallen considerably short of a third part of it!"

Asiat. Journ. N.S. Vol. 20. No. 79.

not.) Mr. Dickens continued: it would really have been pleasing to have thought or believed this, even though it could not be reconciled with strict justice; but it seemed it was not so. If Mr. Macintyre were a poor man, if he wished to be reimbursed, he had a plain course; let him go to Mr. Browne, to Mr. Cullen, to Russomoy Dutt, all opulent men, and say to them, " out of the 75,000. I have paid and charged to the estate, in breach of my original contract, full 40,000 and more has been paid to you, who can repay; then repay me, for I cannot in decency, I cannot in honesty, ask the creditors to do so."

Mr. Mackillop disclaimed all previous knowledge of the appointment, with which he had nothing to do or say; although he thought Mr. Macintyre was unfortunate in some of his transactions, he considered that he had exerted himself to his utmost for the estate; that he deserved at least that his actual expenses should be paid by the estate, even if they refused him any personal allowance, which was not insisted on. He added that, though the expenses of the management had been heavy, he did not believe they were greater than had been incurred in the other estates; a fact which could be ascertained by reference to the assignees; that Mr. Elliot Macnaghten, who deservedly possessed the public confidence for his management as assignee, had estates three times greater, and it would be found he had incurred similar expense.

Mr. Holroyd felt it incumbent on him to remove an erroneous supposition which appeared to exist, that he was willing to accept the rate of commission offered to him, which he declared he was not, and that he should object to the same at the first meeting of the insolvent court at which it was proposed.

Mr. Dickens' motion was lost by a majority of 10 to 7.

It was then proposed by Mr. Cockerell and seconded by Mr. R. Davidson, that the recommendation of the committee be adopted.

Upon which Mr. Dickens moved as an amendment:

" That the report now read be rejected, and that, in the opinion of this meeting, no interest on the sum of 75,000 charged by the said Donald Macintyre to the estate in account, in breach of the terms, ought to be insisted on, provided the principal be repaid in three months; but that, otherwise, interest at the rate of five per cent. be insisted on."

Messrs. Cockerell and Mackillop answered Mr. Dickens, and Mr. Dickens replied.

The amendment was then put and lost, by a majority of 7 to 5.

The recommendation of the committee was accordingly adopted.—*Hurkaru.*

Rammohun Roy.—Since we spoke of the Rammohun Roy testimonial, we have been favoured with information, which, however it may reflect upon certain parties in England, at all events exonerates the late Rajah's friends in this country from any imputation of indifference to his memory. It seems that the sum subscribed down here being insufficient to the satisfactory execution of the purposes of the Memento-committee, they have been induced to apply to wealthy natives at a distance, who held Rammohun Roy in great regard, for such contributions to the general object as they might be disposed to furnish ; and as soon as the replies of these parties shall have been received, something decisive will be arranged.

With regard to the biography of the remarkable Hindoo refoi mer, we are informed that all papers belonging to Rammohun Roy, including the interesting memorandum of his visit to Great Britain, are now in England, and that efforts have been fruitlessly made to induce the party in whose possession they are, to send them out to India. As soon as these papers are received, some competent individual will be employed to prepare a sketch of the life of the great deceased, and we have not the smallest doubt that they will furnish a volume not less instructive to the natives than interesting to the general reader. — *Englishman, Feb.* 1.

Municipal Taxation.—The following statement was produced at the meeting of the magistrates in Quarter sessions, on the 3d February, and exhibits (as remarked) "but a sorry answer to their call upon the public spirit of the inhabitants :"

Assessment—gross collections of the past year	Sa.Rs. 250,870
Charges	27,476
Net Receipts	Sa. Rs. 2,23,394

Disbursements.

Repairs of Roads .. Sa.Rs.	41,447
Cleansing of town	76,336
Repairs of drains	8,229
Sundry charges············	8,946
	134,958
Establishment············	145,242
	280,200
Excess of disbursements .... Sa. Rs.	56,805

" which deficiency of receipts," Mr. Blacquiere observed, " he should be very glad to see some good suggestion offered by the public to extinguish."

The Begum Sumroo.—The *Meerut Observer* announces the death of her Highness the Begum Sumroo, at Sirdanha, on the 27th ult.—as much celebrated of late for the munificence of her charities and other pious donations, as she was formerly for acts in which christian charity

was not very conspicuous. By the death of this princess, her valuable jagheer falls in to the Company. The net revenue of the jagheer is said to be about ten lakhs. They have no interest in the personal property. The amount of the latter is guessed to be very large, perhaps sixty or eighty lakhs ; but there is not a tithe of this sum invested in Company's paper in the Begum's name

The *Meerut Observer* contains a long account of the funeral of the Begum, whose remains were escorted with due honours to a vault in the centre of the cathedral ; 87 minute guns being fired during the procession. The article concludes with the following information :

" As soon as the family had retired into the palace, the magistrate of Meerut proceeded with the officers of his establishment, to proclaim the annexation of the territories of her late Highness to the British government, proclamation was made throughout the town and vicinity of Sirdhannah, by the government authority, and similar ones at the principal towns, in different parts of the jaghire, according to previous arrangement, so that this valuable territory became almost instantaneously incorporated with the Zillah Meerutt, to which it will remain annexed : the introduction of the police and fiscal arrangements having been specially intrusted to Mr. Hamilton, by orders from the government of India, received so far back as August 1834. The whole of the landed possessions of her late Highness revert to the British, but the personal property, amounting to near half a crore, devolves by will to Mr. Dyce Sombre, with the exception of small legacies and charitable bequests, the particulars of which we are not informed."

Mr. John Palmer.—A crowded meeting of the friends of the late Mr. Palmer assembled this morning, at the Town Hall, and unanimously agreed to raise a subscription, for a marble bust of the deceased ; to be considered a private affair, among Mr. Palmer's friends ; and, in case the sum collected should be more than sufficient for the bust, the mode of appropriating the surplus to be determined hereafter. A committee of thirteen gentlemen, including two natives, was appointed to carry the object of the meeting into effect.

Under a misconception of the private nature of this meeting a letter was addressed to the chairman, by Mr. T. B. Scott, suggesting the establishment of a school, under the name of *La Palmiere*, of which the master and mistresses should be chosen from among the second class sufferers by the failure of Palmer and Co. The letter was accompanied with a bank note of fifty rupees, as a subscription.

There was also a letter from a native, named Gungapursaud Mozendar, who described himself as a poor writer, in Mr. Palmer's employ for the last twenty years, and willing to work extra hours, in order to save something by way of contribution, to commemorate the virtues of his lamented master. The letter contained a bank note of ten rupees, and suggested that the subscriptions of the natives should be kept distinct from the rest,—which, the chairman observed, could only be effected by the natives getting up a separate subscription, managed by a separate committee, if they wished to do so.—*Cour., Feb. 6.*

Tiger-Hunting.—Extract from a letter from Dacca:—" We arrived last night in Dacca, after a melancholy winding up of our shooting excursion. We had intelligence of an immense tiger, which had killed several bullocks, &c. On Saturday, we hunted him for several hours, but could not get him. On Sunday, Mr. C., Mr. B., Mr. E., sen., and Mr. E., jun., went out and sprung the tiger, and wounded him severely. He charged the elephants six times, wounded three of them, and pulled poor E., sen., from the howdah, and killed him instantly. There are half-a-dozen deep wounds on the neck, at the juncture of the spine, and several on his face and breast. Although the body was picked up by the rest of the party immediately, the vital spark had fled. This is a dreadful business, and almost enough to satisfy any one of tiger-shooting, and has thrown all Dacca into a ferment."—*Englishman, Feb. 6.*

In the *Meerut Observer*, a correspondent writes :—" In a few years, there will not be a tiger found in the Khadur, for this new practice of murdering the hog-deer so unmercifully will drive the tigers where their staple commodity can be found. I recollect when tigers were as plentiful at Unoopshuhur as they are now at Jogewala ; they have disappeared, and so have the hog-deer, as far up as Ghurmukteesur, and if you go on, they will be driven back to the Hills. About two years ago, a party of you did for most of the Muha, and very few indeed are now to be found ; it is absolutely necessary, therefore, for restraint, and hereafter I trust you will be more moderate, otherwise your conduct will be noticed as unsportsmanly. Your boasting of the numbers you have killed, is a vain-glorious trait, peculiar to your class ;—but, depend upon it, there is no credit in knocking over a hog-deer rising at your foot, or pouring five or six bullets in the side of a poor muha, as big as an ox ; besides, it is not the number brought to bag ; the number wounded is at least equal, and

they generally die of their wounds. The numerous herd of antelope in the district affords sufficient legitimate sport in deer-shooting, and an excellent trial for the gunner with his rifle, but, how seldom is this sport pursued ! No, you are all for quantity, and care nothing for the quality of the sport, which you pretend to enjoy. I call upon all true sportsmen to aid and abet in putting a stop to the practice I have noticed, and so injurious to the fair sportsman, by setting their faces against it, and to endeavour to establish a little rule :—for instance, it should be considered unsportsmanly to shoot the doe of either hog-deer or muha, or any wild boar or sow, or to bag more than five brace of black partridge in one day, or to fire at a hare within ten miles of any cantonment or station where greyhounds are kept."

A tiger paid a visit to Horel lately, where he wounded a man severely, and killed a cow ; but ere the sportsmen in that neighbourhood could get their elephants ready, and go in pursuit, the cunning animal had stolen a march upon them ! It appears, and we have it on the best authority, that the moment the tiger sprung out upon the man, who received the wound, a herd of buffaloes, hard by, rushed down to his rescue, beat off the tiger, and saved the man's life.—*Delhi Gaz., Feb. 21.*

Agra Bank.—We copy from the *Agra Ukhbar* the report of the Agra bank for the last half year, and rejoice to find that institution in so flourishing a condition, as to exhibit a net profit at the rate of twenty per cent. per annum. The bank, until lately, was working upon a capital of two lakhs and a half, divided into 1,000 shares, which being found insufficient for its increasing business, the subscription books have been re-opened for another 1,000 shares, which appear to be filling up fast.—*Cour. Feb. 9.*

Dr. Bryce.—Letters were received yesterday from the Rev. Dr. Bryce, dated 23d January, from Major Alves' camp at Alwar. The reverend gentleman has visited many of the stations in the upper provinces ; he officiated in the churches of Meerut and Agra ; and has been actively engaged in soliciting attention and aid, from his countrymen and others, to the General Assembly's school and missions. The establishment of a branch of the institution in Upper India, conjoined with the object of affording divine service after the forms of the Church of Scotland, to her members in those distant quarters, will, it is hoped, be the result of Dr. Bryce's mission. Dr. Bryce expected to reach Nusserabad in eight or ten days, and Neemuch before the middle of February, proceeding from that place after the 28th February with all speed, to reach the steamer before she starts from Bombay.—*Cal. Cour. Feb. 6.*

Agricultural Society.—At a meeting of this society, it was resolved to invest 1,000 rupees in the purchase of Upland Georgia cotton seed, and to write to the President of the Board of Trade at home to secure a direct channel for the regular supply of fresh seed from America. A smaller sum is applied to the purchase of Egyptian seed.

Reports were read of the successful experiments with Indian corn and the Otaheite sugar cane.

Smuggling.—A serious affray occurred during the past week at Mahim, a village of considerable extent, in the Hurriana line, within the beat of Mr. Gwatkin, patrolling officer. It appears that a considerable body of smugglers, amounting, by the most limited computation, to 1,000, had determined *vi et armis* to carry their goods across the line, the duties being unpaid. Mr. Gwatkin having received timely intimation of their design, boldly resolved to carry into execution, at all hazards, the duty entrusted to him, and accordingly proceeded to make the legal seizure. This patrol establishment only consisted of about fifty men, together with his daroga, and, upon the refusal of the smugglers to deliver up their goods, an affray ensued, in which two of the offending party were killed. We regret to add, that the daroga is severely wounded, together with two Government chuprassies. Mr. Smith, the collector of customs, has, with his usual promptitude, ordered an additional number of men to be attached to Mr. Gwatkin's establishment.—*Delhi Gaz., Jan. 20.*

Akyab.—As our recent letters from Akyab contain further information respecting the insurrection which has broken out in these parts, we hasten to lay it before our readers. For some time back it seems there has been a disposition among some of the principal inhabitants of Akyab town to resist the Government and plunder the Treasury. Some intimations of their plans was discovered, so far back as Nov. 1834, but they were considered too chimerical to attract the attention of the authorities. From time to time, however, the ringleaders of the present rebels have been collecting muskets and ammunition, and sending them into the interior; and, having at length got one of their number, of a desperate character, to head the insurrection, they collected a large body of men in the interior of the district,

and entered on their work of indiscriminate plunder; and, in four or five places, close to Arracan, they have committed very serious depredations on the poor ryots. When the news reached Akyab, which was about the beginning of January, the commissioner immediately ordered two lieuts. with a party of Mugh sepoys, and Burkundauzes, to go into the interior and quell the disturbance. When they arrived at the spot they were joined by the Thannadar of the old town and his party; but the number of the insurgents was so great that they were almost immediately overpowered, and obliged to retreat to Long-grah. We regret to say, that the poor Thannadar was shot through the body, and died a few days afterwards in the Akyab hospital. A stronger party was then sent, with better success. The ringleaders, we are happy to state, have been taken.—*Friend of India, March 3d.*

China.

Advices from Canton, dated the 24th January, state, that another fire has taken place there, not to the extent of the former one, but still very formidable to foreigners, as being nearer to their factories. The last great fire was inside the city wall; this occurred in the suburb adjoining the foreign factories, but without the wall. It broke out on the morning of the 24th, and before any steps were resorted to, it had assumed a fierce and dangerous head, burning before a strong north wind, through Carpenter-square, right down on the foreign factories. At about five o'clock, a flake of fire, carried by the wind, fell on the shingle roof of a small Hoppo-house, just on the east bank of the creek, and it was instantly in a flame, and communicated fire across the creek to No. 2, a foreign factory. Thus a portion of the foreigners and their property were for a period placed in the utmost peril. Great exertions were made by the neighbours to get the fire quenched in No. 2, and to open the communication with the river. Vast numbers of Chinese could be seen tearing down and stripping off the roofs from the houses not on fire, judiciously resigning those they were not able to save. At the same time, sheets of water from twenty well-supplied fire-engines were pouring on the flames, and drenching all in the dangerous vicinity. "This skill, coolness, and activity, met with its reward in the extinction of the fire, after all hope of rescuing their property had left many a foreign breast. It was universally noticed how much the Chinese had learned from us barbarians these few last years, in their mode of resisting and extinguishing conflagrations."

New South Wales.

Revenue.— Between 1st January and 31st December 1835, the sum total of the revenue of New South Wales, ordinary and extraordinary, has been £273,744. During the like period in 1834, it was £205,535; thus the gross increase on the former year has been £71,119; or, deducting a few items of decrease, of which fees of public offices form the greater part —£68,209 net increase. If the yet unpublished statement of expenditure do not much exceed the probable sum of £210,000, there remains a clear surplus of above £60,000 towards the service of the current year!—*Gazette, Jan.* 19.

Prisoners.—In 1835 the number of prisoners received in the Sydney gaol was 1,788 males, and 1,079 females; of the males 614 were for felony, and 1,014 for misdemeanours. The number of females who arrived pursuant to sentences was 695, while 132 were for trial; of the males, 732 were tried and 1061 untried. There were 590 cases of sickness in the course of the year, and one natural death. During the year 36 prisoners were executed.— *Monitor, Jan.* 13.

Western Australia.

The accounts received by the present opportunity from Swan River are far from encouraging. Though the newspapers give a favourable report of the new country, which has been explored by the governor in person, private accounts give a lamentable picture of the individual distress endured by many respectable worthy families. The state of utter destitution to which some are described to us as being reduced is indeed heart-rending and sufficient to excite our warmest sympathies. Families accustomed from their infancy to the usual comforts of affluence and civilization, are driven to have recourse to the most arduous and precarious means to obtain a subsistence; and even young ladies, clothed in the worn-out remains of their English attire, imitate the natives in their modes of catching fish to preserve life. — *Hobart Town Courier, Jan.* 4.

The aforegoing is from a hostile source; on the other hand, letters and papers have been received from Swan River to the 23d of January, which state that the colonists were prospering much more rapidly than was anticipated at the commencement of the last year. The number of acres of land under cultivation, at the close of 1834, was 900; but at the commencement of this year 1,500 were in cultivation. The harvest was expected to be abundant; and shipments of grain were making to New South Wales and Van Diemen's Land. During the last year, twenty-seven merchant vessels had arrived at the colony, of which, however, only seven were British. Money continued scarce; and the supply of goods was so abundant, that a portion had been re-shipped to the river Plate. The stock of cattle and flocks of sheep had increased. In the population there had been a marked increase. The natives were friendly, and many in the employ of the colonists.

Cape of Good Hope.

Cape papers to the end of March state, that all was quiet on the Eastern frontier, with the exception of some few petty feuds between the Finuoes and the Caffres. Public attention of the Cape inhabitants has been drawn to a proclamation of the Governor, directing the peremptory withdrawal of the circulation of the whole rix dollar currency from the 9th of April, in the Cape and Stellenbosch districts, and from the 30th of April in all parts of the colony; such notes to be exchanged by the Treasurer-General and Cashier of the Bank, until the 31st of May next; and from that period till the 30th of July rix dollar notes, in government sterling notes, or British silver, no other being received in payment at any government office. After the 30th of July, such notes as shall be exchangeable under the aforementioned conditions shall be exchangeable at the Treasury in Cape Town only, on a government order, indorsed on a written application to that effect, to be presented at the Colonial Office.

Netherlands India.

Journals from Java to the 30th of December, give a detailed account of the effects of the late earthquake at Amboyna. During three weeks in October, the air was obscured by a thick sulphurous fog; and on the 1st November, at three in the morning, a very severe shock of an earthquake was felt in Amboyna and the neighbouring islands, which was succeeded on the 4th by many other shocks. In Amboyna, the earthquake had done dreadful mischief; fifty-eight men, women, and children, were killed in one of the barracks in Fort Victoria; sixty-six persons were wounded. The government buildings have suffered much, as well as the two churches; and almost all the dwellings of the natives are much damaged. The distress of the inhabitants is extreme. The oldest do not remember such an earthquake. A rough estimate of the damage done makes it amount to 300,000 florins.—*Dutch Paper.*

Advices from Sumatra state, that the Dutch government had not been able to suppress the insurrection of the natives in the interior, but had lost many troops, and affairs in that colony wore a serious aspect.

REGISTER.

Calcutta.

GOVERNMENT ORDERS, &c.

FULL TENTAGE.

Fort William, Jan. 18, 1836.—Under instructions from the Hon. the Court of Directors, the Governor-general of India in Council has the satisfaction to announce, that full tentage will be granted to the commissioned officers of the European regiments, stationed at Ghazeepore, Dinapore, and Hazareebaugh, from the 15th instant, the date of receipt of the Hon. Court's despatch.

REGIMENTAL DUTY.

Head-Quarters, Calcutta, Jan. 19, 1836. —His Exc. the Commander-in-chief is pleased to direct, that officers who are members of general or other courts martial, assembled at the station where their regiments are quartered, shall, during the adjournment of such courts, when the period of adjournment exceeds one day, discharge their regimental duties.

GOORKAH OR HILL CORPS.

Fort William, Feb. 8, 1836.—All the officers and men at present belonging to the three Goorkah or Hill Corps, who came over to the British army from that of the Nepaul Government during the campaign of 1815, having now completed twenty years' service, and being consequently entitled to transfer to the pension establishment when unfit for local service, agreeably to G. O. No. 9, of the 2d May, 1823; the Governor-general of India in Council is pleased, at the recommendation of his Exc. the Commander in-chief, to abolish the denomination of garrison company, authorized in G. O. No. 78, of the 31st July 1823, and to direct, that the company considered the garrison company, be simply numbered the 8th in succession with the others.

His Excellency is requested to take measures for transferring to the pension establishment, all such men of the garrison companies of the Nusseeree, Sirmoor, and Kemaon local battalions, as have served the prescribed period of 20 years, and may be considered unfit for active local service.

MUSKETS FOR ARTILLERY REGIMENT.

In conformity with instructions from the Hon. the Court of Directors, the Commander-in-chief is pleased to direct, that the substitution of muskets for fuzils, in the equipment of the artillery regiment, be notified in general orders; the arrangement to have effect in the gradual order

that the fuzils now in use, become unserviceable.

COURT MARTIAL.

ENS H. W. ROWEN.

Head-Quarters, Calcutta, Jan. 23, 1836.—At a general court martial, assembled at Dinapore, on the 30th Dec. 1835, Ensign H. W. Rowen, of H. M. 49th regt., was arraigned on the following charge, *viz:*

Charge.—" For conduct unbecoming the character of an officer and a gentleman, in that he, Ensign Henry William Rowen, did, on the evening of Tuesday the 29th Sept. 1835, appear at the mess of H. M. 49th regt., at Hazareebaugh, in a state of intoxication; he being at the time on duty as orderly officer of the day."

Upon which charge, the court came to the following decision :

Finding.—" The court, upon the evidence before it, finds Ensign H. W. Rowen, of H. M. 49th regt., guilty of the charge preferred against him.

Sentence.—" The court sentences Ensign H. W. Rowen, H. M. 49th regt , to be cashiered."

Approved,
(Signed)   H. FANE. General.
Commander-in-chief.

Ensign Rowen is to be struck off the list of H. M. 49th regiment, from the date of this communication being made known to him, which the commanding officer will specially report to the Adjutant-general of His Majesty's forces in India, and to the military secretary to His Exc. the Commander-in-chief.

CIVIL APPOINTMENTS, &c.

BY THE GOVERNOR-GENERAL.

Judicial and Revenue Department.

Jan. 19. Mr. Charles Smith to officiate as civil and session judge of zillah Sylhet.

Mr. J. C. Brown to officiate as civil and session judge of zillah Behar.

Mr. R. Williams to officiate as civil and session judge of zillah Cuttack.

26. Mr. M. W. Carruthers to be deputy collector of zillah Mymunsing.

Feb. 2. Mr. R. W. Maxwell to be civil and session judge of zillah Backergunge, from date of departure of Mr. C. Cardew for Europe.

Mr. H. B. Brownlow to officiate as magistrate and collector of zillah Shahabad.

Mr. W. Luke to officiate as magistrate and collector of zillah Sarun, in room of Mr. Brownlow.

Mr. W. P. Good to be an assistant under commissioner of revenue and circuit of 12th or Bhaugulpore division.

Mr. C. B. Quintin to be head assistant to magistrate and collector of zillah Behar.

Mr. G. P. Leycester to conduct current duties of office of civil and session judge of Moorshedabad, in addition to his own.

9. Mr. Henry Ricketts to be commissioner of

revenue and circuit of 19th or Cuttack division, in room of Mr. J. Master.

Mr. F. J. Halliday to be magistrate and collector of northern division of Cuttack.

Mr. James Grant to be magistrate and collector of zillah Dacca.

Mr. T. C. Scott to be joint magistrate and deputy collector of central division of Cuttack, but to officiate, until further orders, as joint magistrate and deputy collector of southern div. of Cuttack.

Mr. W. A. Law to be joint magistrate and deputy collector of Dacca.

Mr. A. C. Bidwell to be head-assistant to magistrate and collector of Sylhet.

Mr. T. Bruce to officiate as joint magistrate and deputy collector of Bullooah, in room of Mr. Halliday.

Mr. J. C. Brown to be civil and session judge of zillah Behar, in room of Mr. S. T. Cuthbert.

Mr. R. Williams to be civil and session judge of zillah Cuttack.

Mr. R. Torrens to be magistrate and collector of Moorshedabad.

The Hon. R. Forbes to be joint magistrate and deputy collector of Maldah.

Mr. W. Taylor to be joint magistrate and deputy collector of Burdwan.

Mr. E. E. H. Repton to be head assistant to magistrate and collector of central division of Cuttack.

Mr. E. M. Gordon to be civil and session judge of Moorshedabad, in room of Mr. H. J. Middleton.

Mr. J. F. G. Cooke to be magistrate and collector of Nuddeah.

Mr. J. H. D'Oyly to officiate as civil and session judge of zillah Beerbhoom, in room of Mr. Wigram Money.

Mr. E. Bentall to be an assistant under commissioner of revenue and circuit of 18th or Jessore division.

Mr. R. H. Snell to be ditto ditto under ditto.

Mr. J. T. Mellis to be ditto ditto under commissioner of 14th or Moorshedabad division.

Mr. W. T. Trotter to be ditto ditto under commissioner of 12th or Bhaugulpore division.

Mr. E. H. C. Monckton to be ditto ditto, under ditto ditto.

Mr. C. Todd to be ditto ditto under commissioner of 13th or Bauleah division.

Mr. R. Hampton to be ditto ditto, under ditto.

Mr. R. R. Sturt to be an assistant to commissioner of revenue and circuit of 15th or Dacca division.

Mr. A. Forbes to be ditto ditto under commissioner of 19th or Cuttack division.

Political Department.

Jan. 25. Lieut. Col. Caulfield, c.b., 9th L.C., to officiate as agent to Gov.-gen at Moorshedabad.

Lieut. G. A. Mee, 58th N.I., to accompany Goorkha corps which escorted Napalese envoy to Calcutta, on its return to Catmandhoo.

Feb. 1. Capt. Vallancy, 36th Madras N.I., to be an assistant to general superintendent of operations for suppression of thuggee.

23. Lieut. Col. Caulfield, c.b., 9th L.C., to be superintendent of the Mysore Princes, v. Major Honeywood resigned, from date of departure of that officer for Europe.

Capt. J. Higginson, 58th N.I., to be agent to Governor-general at Moorshedabad, v. Lieut. Col. Cobbe resigned, from date of departure of that officer for Europe.

— Col. H. T. Tapp, commanding 1st N.I., to be political agent at Subathoo, and to command Nusseeree battalion, v. Maj. Kennedy, who has retired from the service.

Financial Department.

Jan. 20. Mr. J. W. Sage to take charge of remaining filatures of Radnagore residency from Dr. Stuart on his vacating the office.

27. Mr. G. F. McClintock to be 1st-assistant in office of accountant-general in room of Mr. J. W. Alexander dec.

Mr. H. R. Alexander to be 2d-assistant to accountant-general and to sub-treasurer, in case his services should be required by this officer, v. Mr. McClintock prom.

Mr. C. Trower to be civil auditor, in room of Mr. R. H. Tulloh, to take effect from 23d Jan., the date of his departure for Europe.

Feb. 3. Capt. W. N. Forbes to be mint master and superintendent of government machinery, to take effect from date on which Mr. R. Saunders embarked for Europe.

Mr. J. W. Sage to take charge of Radnagore residency during absence of Mr. Stuart.

General Department.

Jan. 27. Mr. John Campbell to officiate as 1st-assistant to collector of government customs at Calcutta, in room of Mr. J. B. Thornhill, v. Mr. H. R. Alexander.

Mr. A. J. M. Mills to be salt agent in central division of Cuttack, v. Mr. Lowis.

Feb. 3. Mr. H. B. Brownlow to be deputy opium agent at Shahabad.

Mr. W. Luke to be deputy opium agent at Sarun, to take effect from 2d Feb.

Mr. R. Houston to officiate as deputy secretary to board of customs, salt and opium, and superintendent of stamps.

Mr. S. G. Palmer, 1st-assistant in board of customs, salt and opium, to be deputy secretary to that board, and superintendent of stamps.

Mr. H. Palmer, 2d-assistant to board of customs, salt and opium, to be collector of Calcutta stamps, and superintendent of Sulkea salt chokies.

———

Messrs. Charles Becher, G. W. Traill, and S. T. Cuthbert, have been permitted to return to Europe in order to retire on annuities, from the 1st May 1836.

Mr. T. C. Loch reported his arrival as a writer on this establishment, on the 7th Feb.

Mr. Ross is appointed Governor of the Western Provinces.—*Beng. Hurk., March* 3.

Furloughs, &c.—Jan. 19. Mr. B. Golding, to Cape of Good Hope, for two years, for health.—27. Mr. Robert Saunders, to England, in the present season.—Mr. T. P. B. Biscoe, of the Agra presidency, to New South Wales, for two years, for health.—Feb 2. Mr. H. J. Middleton, to visit presidency, preparatory to his applying to retire upon an annuity of the year 1836.—3. The leave granted to Mr. Edward Deedes, on 23d Dec. last, to proceed to Europe on furlough, cancelled at his own request.—10. Mr. John Master, to Europe, in the present season.

———

BY THE GOVERNOR OF AGRA.

Political Department.

Jan. 27. Assist. Surg. A. C. Gordon, attached to Umballa agency, to be extra assistant to political agent at Umballa.

General Department.

Feb. 3. Capt. J. M. Heptinstall, 31st N.I., to be deputy post-master at Meerut, v. Major Campbell resigned; to take effect from 18th Jan.

ECCLESIASTICAL.

Feb. 3. The Rev. E. White to officiate as district chaplain at Barrackpore.

———

MILITARY APPOINTMENTS, PROMOTIONS. &c.

Fort William, Jan. 18, 1836.—Capt. Gavin Young, 70th N.I., to be a member of military board, from date of departure of Lieut. Col. Craigie for Europe.

Jan. 25.—*Infantry.* Major Hugh O'Donel, 13th N.I., to be lieut. colonel, in suc. to Lieut. Col. Hardy retired.

13th *N.I.* Capt. Edward Gwatkin to be major, Lieut. and Brev. Capt. J. E. Bruere to be capt. of a company, and Ens. G. F. Whitelocke to be lieut., in suc. to Maj. H. O'Donel prom.

Regt. of Artillery. Supernum. 2d-Lieut. E. K. Money brought on effective strength, v. 2d-Lieut. H. H. Cornish resigned 15th July 1835.

Assist. Surg. Hezekiah Clark to be surgeon, v,

Surg. Wm. Hamilton, M.D., resigned, with rank from 15th Oct. 1835, v. Surg. John Allan, M.D.

Assist. Surg. Andrew Vans Dunlop, M.D., placed at disposal of Agra government.

Assist. Surg. Coll Macintyre appointed to medical charge of civil station of Furreedpore, v. Dunlop.

Assist. Surg. J. H. W. Waugh, now officiating for Assist. Surg. Macintyre at Akyab, confirmed in that appointment.

Brev.Capt. E. C. Archbold, 8th L.C., permitted, at his own request, to resign service of Hon. Company, from 1st Feb.

The following officers to do duty with Assam Light Infantry:—Lieut. James Wemyss, 44th N.I.; Ens. A. P. Phayre, 7th do.

Feb. 1.—*Regt. of Artillery.* Capt. C. H. Bell to be major, 1st-Lieut. and Brev. Capt. C. McMorine to be capt., and 2d-Lieut. G. L. Cooper to be 1st-lieut., from 17th Jan. 1836, in suc. to Major C. P. Kennedy retired on pension of his rank.—1st-Lieut. and Brev. Capt. C. Grant to be capt., and 2d-Lieut. T. Edwards to be 1st-lieut., from 17th Jan. 1836, in suc. to Capt. J. Johnson retired on pension of his rank.—Supern. 2d-Lieuts. W. Maxwell and H. M. Conran brought on effective strength of regt.

Allahabad, Jan. 15, 1836.—Ens. H. M. Barwell, 59th N.I., to officiate for Lieut. F. P. Fulcher, 67th do., as aid-de-camp to Governor of Agra, from this date, until return of Lieut. Fulcher to his duty, or until further orders.

Jan. 27.—Assist. Surg. R. J. Brassey to be assistant to garrison surgeon of Allahabad.

Feb. 3.—Assist. Surg. A. Reid placed at disposal of Commander-in-chief.

Assist. Surg. A. Vans Dunlop appointed to medical duties of civil station of Azimgurh.

Head Quarters, Jan. 19, 1836. — Lieut. J. T. Lane to be adj. and qu. mast. to Neemuch division of artillery, v. Lieut. W. O. Young app. to ordnance commissariat department.

Assist. Surg. W. E. Watson removed from 1st brigade horse artillery, and posted to 69th N.I.

Jan. 20.—Assist. Surg. Andrew Henderson (on furl.) removed from 41st to 50th N.I.; and Assist. Surg. J. V. Leese removed from 4th to 41st do., at Barrackpore.

Assist. Surg. Chas. McCurdy to afford medical aid to artillery at Agra, during absence of Assist. Surg. Wm. Gordon, M.D.; date 25th Dec. 1835.

Jan. 21.—*8th L.C.* Lieut. Thomas Moore to be adj., v. Mackenzie gone to Europe on furlough.

Jan. 26 —Lieut. W. O. Young, regt. of artillery, lately appointed a deputy commissary of ordnance, posted to Ajmere magazine.

Lieut. G. Cautley, 8th L.C. (doing duty at convalescent depôt) to act as station staff at Landour, during absence, on leave, of 1st-Lieut. G. H. Mc Gregor.

Jan. 27.—The following Benares division orders confirmed.—Surg. Wm. Jackson, 8th L.C., to receive charge of records, &c. of superintending surgeon's office, from Surg. D. Renton; date 11th Jan.—Surg. Thomas Forrest, 25th N.I., to perform medical duties of civil station of Mirzapore, from date of Surg. Andrew Wood's departure to join 5th bat. of artillery; date 16th Jan.

Jan. 30. — Lieut. Col. Hugh O'Donel (lately prom.), posted to 13th N.I.

Capt. G. H. Cox, of invalid estab., permitted to reside in north-western hills, and draw his allowances from Meerut pay-office.

The following division orders confirmed:—Lieut. R. Macdonell, 10th L.C., to take charge of remount horses from Hissar and Hauper studs allotted to Madras army, as far as Nagpore; date 6th Jan.—Lieut. B. C. Bourdillon, 2d L.C., to receive charge of thirty-one remount horses from Hissar stud for that corps, and to await arrival of his regt. at Meerut in course of relief; date 8th Jan.—Cornet G. Buist, 10th L.C., to receive charge of remount horses from Hissar stud from Lieut. H. Lawrell, 3d L.C., on his arrival at Muttra, and proceed with them to Neemuch and Mhow; date 16th Jan.—Assist. Surg. J. V. Leese, now of 41st N.I., to proceed to Bhaugulpore, and receive medical charge of that station from Assist. Surg. A. B.

Webster, M.D., who will rejoin detachment of H.M. troops proceeding by water to Upper Provinces; date 22d Jan.

Feb. 2.—Assist. Surg. A. Mackean to proceed to Islampore, and relieve Assist. Surg. John Magrath from medical charge of 22d N.I.; date 18th Dec.

Surg. Andrew Wood to join and resume medical charge of left wing of 5th bat. artillery, at Saltanpore, Benares, and accompany it to Cawnpore.

Feb. 5.—2d-Lieut. and Adj. Henry Rigby to resume duties of his office; date 1st Feb.

The following removals and postings of medical officers ordered:—Surgeons W. E. Carte. A.B. (in medical charge of 1st local horse), from 70th to 40th N.I.; James Atkinson from 43d to 70th do., at Barrackpore; James Duncan (on furl.) from 15th to 8th do.; Donald Campbell, new prom., to 15th do., at Cawnpore; Thos. Stoddart (on furl.) from 22d to 33d do.; Hezekiah Clark, new prom., to 22d do., at Islampore.

Assist. Surg. K. M. Scott to do duty with H.M. 44th regt. at Fort William.

Fort William, Feb. 8.—*Infantry.* Lieut. Col. and Brev. Col. Sir Jeremiah Bryant, Kt., to be colonel, from 6th Aug. 1835, v. Col. (Lieut. Gen.) George Prole dec.—Maj. W. H. Hewitt, 40th N.I., to be lieut. col., in suc. to Lieut. Col. Sir J. Bryant prom.

40th N.I. Capt. M. A. Bunbury to be major, Lieut. and Brev. Capt. Samuel Long to be capt. of a company, and Ens. G. F. Ritso to be lieut., in suc. to Maj. W. H. Hewitt prom.

European Regiment (right wing). Lieut. Chas Jorden to be capt. of a company, and Ens. J. W. Bennett to be lieut., from 16th Dec. 1835, in suc to Capt. David Ruddell dec.

Cadets of Artillery C. A. Green and Edward Kaye admitted on estab., and prom. to 2d-lieuts.—Cadets of Infantry H C. James and E. W. Hicks admitted on ditto, and prom. to ensigns.

Lieut. H. A. Boscawen, 54th N.I., to officiate as secretary to clothing board during absence of Capt. J. H. Simmonds, who has obtained leave to Cape of Good Hope.

The appointment, in Nov. last, of Assist. Surg. A. B. Webster, M.D., to officiate at civil station of Bhaugulpore, hereby cancelled.

Head-Quarters, Feb. 6.—Lieut. J. Millar, 29th N.I., attached to Assam L.Inf., to act as second in command during absence of Capt. and Second in Command A. Charlton; date 9d Jan.

Ens. Geo. Jenkins, 47th, at his own request, removed to 21st N.I., as junior of his rank.

Feb. 8.—Lieut. and Brev. Capt. Robert McNair 73d now acting interp. and qu. master to 43d N.I.) appointed interp. and qu. master to his own corps, and directed to join.

Removal from Staff.—G.O.C.C., Feb. 9, 1836.— The insufficiency of Lieut. J. R. Burt, as adjutant of the 6th L.C., was called to the observation of the Provincial Commander-in-chief in 1835, but it was then determined to allow him a further trial. It having now been reported by the brigadier commanding the Malwah field force, that Lieut. and Adj. Burt, "from his natural apathy, and the little interest he evinces in what is going on, and being naturally devoid of activity of thought and action, never will be an efficient staff officer," his Exc. the Commander-in-chief is pleased to remove him from the adjutancy of the regiment.

Capt. R. S. Phillips, 67th N.I., is transferred to the invalid estab., which promotes Lieut. and Adj. W. Hicks and Ens. R. Price.

Capt. A. Gerard, 27th N.I., has retired, which promotes Lieut. L. W. Gibson and Ens. H. Laing.

Lieut. and Brev. Capt. A. K. Agnew, 16th N.I., is promoted to the captaincy of a company, in suc. to Birkett deceased.

The death of Capt. E. N. Townsend, 21st N.I., promotes Lieut. H. J. Guyon, now on furlough, and Ens. Newbolt, of the commissariat department.

Lieut. Col. G. Gibbs, invalid estab., has been appointed commandant of the fortress of Buxar, in the room of Lieut. Col. W. C. L. Bird retired.

Lieut. Col. G. Hawes, 17th N.I., has retired.

Returned to duty, from Europe.—Feb. 8. Assist. Surg. Wm. Bogie, M.D.

FURLOUGHS.

To Europe.—Jan. 25. Capt. F. E. Manning, 16th N.I., on private affairs.—Lieut. Samuel Smith, 9th L.C., for health.—Lieut. J. H. Low, 39th N.I., senior assist. to agent in Saugor and Nerbudda territories, for health.—Lieut. N. Palmer, 54th N.I., for health.—Lieut. S. J. Grove, 68th N.I., for health.—Feb. 1. Capt. B. Y. Reilly, corps of engineers, on private affairs.—Lieut. G. C. S. Master, 4th L.C., on ditto.—Lieut. G. W. Master, 4th L.C., on ditto.—Assist. Surg. James Hervey, for health.—8. Capt. J. A. Fairhead, 28th N.I., for health.—Lieut. Ralph Smith, 28th N.I., for health. —Lieut. Geo. Turner, 38th N.I., for health.— Capt. F. Rowcroft, 1st N.I, on private affairs.— Major Horsburgh, 46th N.I., for health.—Lieut. Charteris, 65th N.I., for health.—Capt. W. Parker, 10th L.C., for health.—Lieut. Townshend, 9th N.I., on private affairs.—Lieut. R. Wright, 26th N.I.—Maj. W. Gairdner, 14th N.I.

To visit Presidency (preparatory to applying for furlough to Europe).—Jan. 22. Capt. W. Ewart, 54th N.I.—Capt. J. F. May, 72d N.I. (since dead).

To Van Diemen's Land.—Feb. 23. Capt. R. C. Johnson, for two years, on private affairs.

To Cape of Good Hope.—Feb. 8. Capt. J. H. Simmonds, 55th N.I., and sec. to clothing board, for two years, for health.—Surg. James Hutchinson, sec. to medical board, for ditto ditto.

To Singapore.—Jan. 27. Lieut. and Brev. Capt. E. J. Betts, 70th N.I., for eight months, for health.

His Majesty's Forces.

To Europe.—Brev. Capt. Manners, 13th L. Drags., for health.—Maj. Taylor, 20th Foot, to precede his corps.—Surg. W. Daunt, 44th Foot, for health.— Lieut. H. Cooper, 62d Foot, on private affairs.— Paym. H. C. Forster, 63d Foot, on ditto.—Lieut. R. S. Boland, 39th Foot, for health.

Cancelled.—The leave to England granted to Lieut. G. Fitzgerald, 26th Foot.

SHIPPING.

Arrivals in the River.

JAN. 26. *India*, Snow, from New York; *Mermaid*, Stavers, from China, Singapore, and Penang; *John Adam*, Roche, from Bombay.—28. *Frasquita*, Hervietor, from Bourbon.—29. *Forth*, Landers, from China and Singapore; *Elisabeth*, Shepherd, from Singapore and Penang.—FEB. 3. *Haidee*, Randle, and *Elisabeth*, Spooner, from Singapore, Malacca, &c.—4. *Louvre*, Brown, from Boston; *Salaryce*, Williams, from Mauritius.—5. *Carnatic*, Proodfoot, from China and Rangoon; *Messager des Indes*, Verspecke, and *Sinius*, Hugues, from Bourbon.—6. *Virginia*, Smith, from Singapore and Penang.—7. *Joseph Victor*, Le Cour, from Bourbon and Madras.—12. *Finette*, Ducross, from Mauritius. — MARCH 3. *Hibernia*, Gillies, from London and Madras; *Discovery*, Hawes, from Bombay.—4. *Argyle*, M'Donald, from London and Madras.—*Tapley*, Tapley, from Madras.

Departures from Calcutta.

JAN. 24. *Nabob*, Putream, for Boston.—FEB. 3. *Nerbudda*, Patrick, for Bombay; *Ernaad*, Hill, for Gulph; *Lady Clifford*, Steward, for Straits and China; *Octorava*, Fairfour, for Philadelphia.—6. *Allalevie*, Clarke, for Bombay.—MARCH 4. *Zenobia*, Owen, for London.

Sailed from Saugor.

JAN. 23. H.M.S. *Victor*, Crozier, for Madras.— 26. *George Gardiner*, Smith, for Philadelphia.— 27. *London*, M'Lean, for Liverpool.—29. *John Woodall*, Arnold, for Liverpool.—MARCH 1. *Indien*, Irequehet, for Havre.—3. *Lucullus*, Duruntesu, for Bordeaux.

To Sail.—For London: *Dauntless*, about 9th March; *Robarts*, 10th March; *Larkins*, 23d March; *Coromandel*, 4th April.—For Liverpool: *Mary Dugdale*, 16th March. — For Greenock: *Joanna*, 10th March.

BIRTHS, MARRIAGES, AND DEATHS.

BIRTHS.

Dec. 15. At Delhi, the lady of Capt. Farmer, 21st N.I., of a still-born child.

Jan. 4. At Petooaghur, Kumaon, the lady of Capt. G. Holmes, 7th N.I., of a son.

9. At Muttra, the lady of John Free, Esq., of a daughter.

11. At Kurnaul, the lady of Capt. H. L. McGhie, H.M. 31st regt., of twin daughters.

14. At Ghazeepore, Mrs. Threipland, of a son.

15. At Meerut, the lady of Capt. Mylne, of H.M. 11th Dragoons, of a daughter.

16. At Mirzapore, the lady of W. H. Woodcock, Esq., C.S., of a son.

— At Allahabad, Mrs. John Babanoe, of a son.

17. At Hauper, the lady of Capt. J. Hoggan, 53d N.I., of a daughter.

19. Mrs. A. W. Stone, of a daughter.

20. At Nudjuffghur factory, near Cawnpore, the lady of W. Vincent, Esq., of a daughter.

21. At Cawnpore, the lady of Major Carter, H.M. 16th regt., of a son.

— Mrs. R. Mortimer, of a daughter.

— Mrs. J. Stark, of a daughter.

22. At Barrackpore, the lady of Capt. J. Cumberlege, 41st N.I., of a daughter.

23. At Elambazar, the lady of John Erskine, Esq., of a son.

24. In Fort William, the lady of Lieut. J. E. Codd, H.M. 44th regt., of a daughter.

25. At Cossipore, the lady of Major G. Hutchinson, engineers, of son.

— At Kurnaul, the lady of Capt. H. J. Wood, horse artillery, of a son.

— At Neemuch, lady of Capt. Chester, of a son.

26. In Mission Row, the lady of H. C. Watts, Esq., of a son.

— At Dinapore, Mrs. F. Smyth, of a son.

27. Mrs. George Gill, of a daughter.

29. At Dinapore, the lady of James Johnstone, Esq., M.D., surgeon 67th N.I., of a son.

— At Semulbarree factory, the lady of G. Walker, Esq., of a son.

— Mrs. J. Hypher, of a daughter.

30. At Ghazeepore, the lady of R. W. Barlow, Esq., C.S., of a son.

— Mrs. H. A. Andrews, of a son.

— Mrs. Wetherill, of a daughter.

31. At Calcutta, the lady of M. S. Owen, Esq., of a son.

Feb. 1. Mrs. C. J. Sutherland, of a daughter.

— At Cossipore, Mrs. G. Rogers, of a son.

2. At Chattac, Mrs. H. Inglis, of a son.

4. At Calcutta, the lady of J. W. Macleod, Esq., of a son.

5. At Sulkea, the lady of James Mackenzie, Esq., of a daughter.

— Mrs. A. Baptist, jun., of a son.

7. At Chowringhee, the lady of J. H. Crawford, Esq., Bombay C.S., of a son.

10. At Allahabad, the lady of Henry Byng Harrington, Esq., of a son.

— At Dum-Dum, the lady of Capt. Torckler, artillery, of a son, still-born.

— Mrs. R. Locken, of a daughter.

17. At Government Place, the lady of John Peter Grant, Esq., C.S., of a son.

25. At Chinsurah, the lady of Lieut. Edmond, H.M. 9th regt., of a daughter.

28. At Alilpore, the lady of Alexander Rogers, Esq., of a son.

Lately. At Chowringhee, the lady of Dr. John Swiney, of a son.

MARRIAGES.

Dec. 21. At Cawnpore, Mr. P. W. Powers to Mrs. H. C. Melhuish, relict of the late Mr. J. Melhuish, chemist and druggist.

Jan. 9. At Mhow, Henry C. Bagge, Esq., civil service, to Margaret, second daughter of Brigadier Bowen, commanding Malwa field force.

16. At Calcutta, Mr. Samuel Fisher, mariner, to Miss Lydia Pereira.

18. At Allahabad, the Rev. Frederick A. Dawson, A.M., district chaplain at Lucknow, to Louisa, daughter of the late Wm. Lowther, Esq., C.S.

22. At Calcutta, Mr. Edward Williams to Miss Charlotte Henrietta Bowler.

— At Berhampore, Mr. Garret Hanscap, of Purniah, to Miss A. M. S. Jenkinson.

(Z)

23. At Kurnaul, Rowley Hill, Esq., 4th regt. N.I., to Caroline, second daughter of Col. Sale, C.B., 13th Light Infantry.

25. At Calcutta, J. A. F. Hawkins, Esq., of the civil service, to Margaret Edmonstone, youngest daughter of Col. D. McLeod, of engineers.

— At Monghyr, M. Chardon, Esq., to Hannah, third daughter of the Rev. Wm. Moore.

— At Calcutta, John Seton Chisholm, Esq., to Miss Isabella Sarah Dobson.

— At Calcutta, Mr. F. Des Bruslais, to Miss Caroline Delamougerode.

26. At Calcutta, Cornet J. M. Loughnan, 10th L.C., fort adjutant, Fort William, to Marion, relict of the late Lieut. Robertson, Bengal army.

— At Calcutta, Edmund W. Johnson, Esq., indigo planter, Purneah, to Miss Frances Egerton.

Feb. 1. At Calcutta, Mr. Wm. Masters, head master of the La Martiniere, to Caroline Louisa, youngest daughter of the late R. F. Crow, Esq., of Calcutta.

— At Calcutta, Charles Mackinnon, Esq., indigo planter, Tirhoot, to Miss Henrietta Studd.

3. At Calcutta, James Colquhoun, Esq., to Louisa Barbara, eldest daughter of J. C. C. Sutherland, Esq.

4. At Calcutta, J. H. Patton, Esq., of the civil service, to Mary Louisa, youngest daughter of the late George Chapman, Esq., county Kildare, Ireland.

— At Chinsurah, the Rev. J. G. Linke, of Burdwan, to Charlotte Elizabeth, eldest daughter of Lewis Betts, Esq.

6. At Calcutta, A. H. Arrathoon, Esq., to Catherine Catchick, eldest daughter and heiress of the late Catchick Sethagassee, Esq., of Dacca.

— At Calcutta, Mr. M. D'Silva, of Salt Golahs, to Mrs. M. P. Goodwin, widow of the late Capt. J. H. Goodwin.

12. At Calcutta, Mr. Peter Emmer to Miss Grace Elizabeth Crump.

13. At Meerut, Mr. Owen, the special commissioner, to Miss Graham.

— At Calcutta, Mr. George Thomas to Miss Ann Casey.

15. At Calcutta, D. Brown, Esq., of Tirhoot, to Mary Anne, youngest daughter of Major T. Hall.

18. At Calcutta, P. G. E. Taylor, Esq., of the civil service, to Sophia Marian, orphan daughter of Capt. L. M. Shawe, Company's service.

22. At Allahabad, Alfred William Begbie, Esq., of the civil service, to Margaret, eldest daughter of the late Isaac Watt, Esq., of Logie, Anguashire, Scotland.

29. At Calcutta, Sir James Anburey Mouat, Bart., of the engineers, to Louisa Caroline, youngest daughter of H. R. Montgomery, Esq., late of the Ceylon civil service.

DEATHS.

Jan. 7. Mrs. E. L. Turnbull, aged 24.

10. At Bilsa, Assist. Surg. J. Dallas.

16. At Delhi, Mrs. Farmer, wife of Capt. C. Farmer, of the 21st regt. N.I.

22. At his residence in Chowringhee, John Palmer, Esq., aged 69 years.

— Mr. Francis Esperança, aged 76.

23. At Calcutta, aged 39, J. W. Alexander, Esq., of the civil service, son of R. Alexander, Esq., of Gloucester Place, Portman Square.

24. Mrs. J. T. Williams, aged 46.

26. At Calcutta, Mr. R. L. D'Oliveira, aged 63.

27. At Meerut, aged 89. Her Highness Fuzund Azuzai, Oomdootoul Urraikeen, Zeiboul Nissa, Begum Sumroo, the events of whose life are related in the 15th volume of the *Asiatic Journal.*

28. At Dinapore, Mr John Havell, founder and proprietor of Deegah Farm, aged 66.

30. At Cawnpore, Elizabeth, wife of Assist. Surg. D. Mensies, H.M. 16th Foot.

31. At Meerzapore, Dacca, while on a hunting excursion, John Demetrius Ellias, Esq., aged 36.

Feb. 1. At Meerut, the lady of Capt. Mylne, of H.M. 11th Light Dragoons.

— At Calcutta, Mrs. G. F. Bowbear, aged 26.

2. At Calcutta, Mr. James Reid, late of Culen, in Banffshire, Scotland.

4. At Calcutta, Mrs. A. Carlow, aged 55.

5. At Calcutta, Elizabeth Clements, daughter of Mr. Mathew Johnston, registrar of the Board of Customs, aged 27.

10. At Delhi, Mr. Hetsler, whose death was caused by his falling from a balcony.

— Mrs. Flora Gonsalves, aged 85.

13. At Barrackpore, Capt. Thomas Birkett, of the 6th regt. N.I.

15. On the river, near Allahabad, Capt. E. N. Townsend, of the 31st regt. N.I.

17. At Allahabad, Mr. H. Barnfield, aged 23, son of W. Barnfield, Esq., of Brixton.

20. At Allahabad, the lady of F. Stainforth, Esq., C.S., aged 27 years.

23. At Calcutta, Capt. J. F. May, of the 73d regt. N.I., aged 36.

March 4. At Calcutta, Henry Paulin, Esq., the Hon. Company's solicitor on the Bengal establishment.

Lately. At Calcutta, Mr. V. Holcroft, aged 34, eldest son of the late T. Holcroft, Esq., author of *The Road to Ruin,* and other works.

— Capt. Neville, paymaster to H.M. 11th regt. of Light Dragoons.

Madras.

GOVERNMENT ORDERS, &c.

DATE OF FURLOUGHS.

Fort St. George, Dec. 8, 1835.—The following extract from a letter from the Hon. the Court of Directors, in the military department, under date the 18th March last, is published for the information of the army.

Para. 1. "We observe from the list of officers on furlough, dated 1st July 1834, that the furloughs of officers of your establishment who embarked at Bombay, have been dated as commencing from the period of their embarkation, and not (according to the rules established in Bengal and Bombay) from the time of quitting the frontier station of their own presidency.

2. "We desire that your practice in this respect may be assimilated to that which obtains at the other presidencies."

CONDUCT OF LIEUT. HUMPHREYS.

Head-Quarters, Choultry Plain, Jan. 18, 1836.—Lieut. Humphreys, of the 23d Light Infantry, having been ordered for trial by a general court-martial, upon the complaint of Mr. Bilderbeck, an inhabitant of Madras, is necessarily released from arrest in consequence of the death of the complainant, who was also the principal witness against him.

As, however, Lieut. Humphreys declined to offer any explanation of his conduct, before a court of inquiry previously assembled; and as the written statement originally sent in by Mr. Bilderbeck is entirely clear and explicit as to the whole proceeding, the Commander-in-chief considers it expedient thus publicly to notify his marked reprobation of the wanton and unjustifiable nature of the attack made by Lieut. Humphreys, in the public street, without provocation, upon an individual utterly unknown to him, and then labouring under a malady which has since brought him prematurely to the grave.

This is not the first occasion on which this officer has been placed in peril of his commission; for he had but a few days previously to this offence been released from the police jail for an aggravated assault on a police officer. His Excellency can, therefore, only hope that Lieut. Humphreys, instead of being hardened by impunity, may profit by the narrow escape which he has made; and resolve to place his future conduct in honourable contrast to his past behaviour, which has been so little creditable either to the service or to himself.

Lieut. Humphreys is released from arrest, and will leave the presidency forthwith to join his regiment.

INDIAN ALLOWANCES.

Fort St. George, Jan. 26, 1836.—The Governor in Council is pleased to announce that officers of this establishment, serving in the Eastern settlements, proceeding to Calcutta for the purpose of embarking thence to Europe on medical certificate, will not be entitled to Indian allowances posterior to the date of their embarkation from those settlements, except when in cases of certified sickness a passage to Madras could not be procured, of which a certificate from the chief civil or military authority will be required.

MOVEMENTS OF CORPS.

The 30th regt. N. I. to march from Madras to Secunderabad, to be there stationed.

The 17th regt. N. I. to proceed to Madras, to be there stationed.

COURT MARTIAL.
LIEUT. W. S. NORTON.

At a General Court-Martial, held at Bellary on the 30th Dec. 1835, Lieut. W. S. Norton, of H. M. 55th Foot, was arraigned on the following charge, *viz.*

" For scandalous and disgraceful conduct, unbecoming the character of an officer and a gentleman, in having, at Bellary, on the 1st Oct. 1835, made use of grossly abusive, obscene, and threatening language to his wife, Mrs. Jane Whitely Norton."

Finding.—Guilty.

Sentence.—To be ' Cashiered.'

Approved.

(Signed)　　H. FANE, General, Commander-in-chief.

Calcutta, 3d Feb. 1836.

Recommendation by the Court.—" The court having performed the painful duty of awarding the punishment made imperative on them by the Articles of War, for the crime of which the prisoner Lieut. Norton has been found guilty, beg, in consequence of the extraordinary nature of the case, most respectfully to recommend him to such mercy as his Exc. the Commander-in-chief may deem consistent with upholding the honour of his Majesty's service.

Remarks by His Exc. the Commander-in-chief.—Although the language proved to have been used by Lieut. Norton, coupled with his subsequent proceedings, would bespeak him to be little fit for the position amongst gentlemen which he occupies, yet the Commander-in-chief is unwilling to turn a deaf ear to the recommendation of the members of a general court-martial, when he can make any excuse to himself for listening to it.

He, therefore, will allow it to have its weight in this case; and will meet the wishes expressed by the court, in the only way in which the members must have known he could meet them, namely, by remitting the punishment they have awarded.

He would have felt, however, much more satisfaction in attending to their recommendation, and in extending his pardon, had any testimonies of the general good conduct of the officer under sentence been laid before him.

Lieut. Norton is pardoned, and is to return to his duty.

CIVIL APPOINTMENTS, &c.

Jan. 23. Lieut. M. J. Rowlandson, 32d N.I., to act as government agent at Chepauk, and paymaster of Carnatic stipends, on embarkation of Lieut. Col. Hodges for England.

26. J. Haig, Esq., to be second judge of provincial court of appeal and circuit for northern division, v. Mr. Nicholls proceeded to Europe; but to continue officiating as second judge of provincial court of appeal and circuit for centre division, for Mr. Casamajor.

H. T. Bushby, Esq., to act as judge and criminal judge of Bellary.

J. J. Cotton, Esq., to be assistant to principal collector and magistrate of Bellary.

W. B. Hawkins, Esq., to be assistant to princi. pal collector and magistrate of Bellary.

C. H. Woodgate, Esq., to be assistant to principal collector and magistrate of Coimbatore.

R. W. Chatfield, Esq., to be assistant to principal collector and magistrate of Canara.

B. Cunliffe, Esq., to be assistant to collector and magistrate of Guntoor.

29. A. E. Angelo, Esq., to be judge and criminal judge of Bellary, v. Mr. Boileau.

T. E. J. Boileau, Esq., to be third judge of provincial court of appeal and circuit for northern division. v. Mr. Waters proceeded to Europe.

C. E. Oakes, Esq., to be assistant judge and joint criminal judge of Guntoor, v. Mr. Angelo.

Feb. 2. G. M. Ogilvie, Esq., to act as principal collector and magistrate of northern division of Arcot, during absence of Mr. Roberts, who has been permitted to proceed to Neilgherries on sick certificate.

W. Harrington, Esq., to officiate as second judge of provincial court of appeal and circuit for southern division, during employment of Mr. Ogilvie on other duty.

R. Nelson. Esq., to act as third judge of ditto ditto, during period Mr. Harrington officiates as second judge of that court.

E. B. Glass, Esq., to act as judge and criminal judge of Combaconum, during absence of Mr. Lewin.

E. P. Thompson, Esq., to act as judge and criminal judge of Malabar, during employment of Mr. Nelson on other duty.

Hatley Frere, Esq., to act as head assistant to principal collector and magistrate of Coimbatore, during absence of Mr. Roupell.

9. B. Cunliffe, Esq., to act as an assistant to

principal collector and magistrate of southern division of Arcot.

12. Mr. J. Wilkins to be master attendant at Negapatam, v. Honner dec.

Attained Rank.—George Sparkes, as junior merchant, on 1st Jan. 1836; S. I. Popham, ditto, on 30th Jan. 1836; F. N. Maltby, C. T. Kaye, T. H. Davidson, T. W. Goodwyn, J. C. Taylor, G. A. Harris, G. F. Beauchamp, and Henry Forbes, as factors, on 12th Jan. 1836.

Furloughs, &c.—Jan. 26. A. E. Angelo, Esq., to Europe, for three years, on private affairs.—Feb. 12. T. B. Roupell, Esq., to Europe, for health.

MILITARY APPOINTMENTS, PROMOTIONS, &c.

Fort St. George, Jan. 26, 1836. — Ens. John Campbell, 21st N.I., to be an assistant surveyor-general of 1st class.—Ens. Campbell to take charge of Trichinopoly survey during absence of Lieut. Hill.

Brigadier Vigoureux, C.B., of H.M. 45th regt. to be a brigadier-general on staff of army and to command Mysore division until further orders.

Lieut. Col. J. T. Trewman to command Hyderabad subsidiary force, until further orders.

Cadet of Engineers C. C. Johnston admitted on estab., and prom. to 2d-lieut.—Cadets of Infantry W. P. Devereux and W. A. Lukin admitted on ditto, and prom. to ensigns.

Jan. 22.—*European Regt.* (left wing). Capt. St. J. B. French to be major, Lieut. J. C. Hawes to be capt., and Ens. Andrew Walker to be lieut., v. Stewart retired; date of coms. 25th Jan. 1836.

Capt. C. E. Faber, corps of engineers, to act as civil engineer in 4th division; and Lieut. S. Best to resume his appointment of 1st-assistant to civil engineer of 3d division.

The services of Lieut. J. Inverarity placed at disposal of Com.-in-chief, with a view to his being posted to corps of sappers and miners, and placed in charge of boring party in southern division.

Lieut. H. C. Armstrong, corps of engineers, to take charge of superintending engineer's department in northern division, during absence of Lieut. Bell.

Head-Quarters, Jan. 22, 1836.—Capt. J. Smith, 2d L.C., permitted to reside and draw his pay on Neilgherries, from 16th Feb. until further orders.

Jan. 25.—Assist. Surg. J. E. Mayer removed from H.M. 39th Foot, and posted to 20th N.I.

Assist. Surg. C. Ferrier removed from H.M. 63d Foot to do duty with H.M. 13th Lt. Drags.

Veterinary Surg. W. H. Wormsley removed from E to B troop horse artillery, and directed to join at St. Thomas's Mount.

Jan. 27.—The following young officers to do duty:—Ensigns W. P. Devereux, with 18th N.I.; W. A. Lukin, with 45th do.

2d-Lieut. C. C. Johnston, of engineers, posted to corps of sappers and miners.

Fort St. George, Feb. 5.—Assist. Surg. Robert Power to be surgeon, v. Reid retired; date of com. 15th Jan. 1836.

Assist. Surg. W. Middlemass to act as medical storekeeper at presidency, during absence and on responsibility of Surg. White permitted to proceed to Neilgherries.

Feb. 9.—Capt. G. C. Whitlock, 36th N.I., to be deputy assistant adj. gen. Mysore division, v. Derville proceeded to Europe.

Capt. W. Johnstone, 1st N.V.B., appointed to charge of native pensioners at Chingleput, v. Gaitakell resigned.

7th N.I. Ens. C. A. Browne to be lieut., v. Nixon invalided; date of com. 5th Feb. 1836.

Head-Quarters, Feb. 1.—Surg. John Ricks, M.D. (late prom.) posted to 1st bat. artillery.

The services of 2d-Lieuts. Rundall, Inverarity, and Chapman, of engineers, having been placed by government at disposal of Commander-in-chief, they are posted to corps of sappers and miners.

Capt. Woodburn, deputy judge adv. gen., posted to III district; and will also, in addition, conduct duties of I district until further orders.

Lieut. McGoun, deputy judge adv. gen., to remain in V district during absence of Capt. Nepean on sick certificate; and will also, in addition, conduct duties of VI district until further orders.

Capt. Osborne, deputy judge adv. gen., to conduct duties of VIII district, in addition to his own, until further orders.

Feb. 2.—Assist. Surg. P. Roe, M.D. (having been reported qualified for treatment of acute cases of disease) removed to do duty with H.M. 63d Foot.

Feb. 8.—Cornet W. N. Mills removed from 2d to do duty with 8th L.C.

Capt. H. Roberts, 9th N.I., relieved from duties of clothing committee assembled at Fort St. George.

Lieut. John Nixon, recently transf. to invalid estab., posted to Carnatic European Vet. Bat.

Returned to duty, from Europe.—Jan. 26. Major J. R. Godfrey, 1st N.I.—Maj. John Tod, 33d N.I.—Capt. H. Millington, 1st N.V.B.—Lieut. R. R. Scutt, 52d N.I.—1st-Lieut. S. W. Croft, artillery.—Supernum. 2d-Lieut. R. H. Chapman, engineers.

Permitted to Retire from Service of Hon. Company—Jan. 26. Surg. Thos. Williams, from 1st March 1836.—Feb. 2. Surg. David Reid, M.D., from 15th Jan. 1836.—12. Maj. J. R. Godfrey, 1st N.I., from 10th Feb. 1836.—Maj John Tod, 33d N.I., from 14th do.

Transferred to Invalid Establishment.—Feb. 5. Lieut. John Nixon, 7th N.I., at his own request. —12. Capt. Robert Francis, 45th N.I., ditto.

FURLOUGHS.

To Europe.—Jan. 26. Lieut. J. W. Strettell, 1st L.C.—29. Assist. Surg. Wm. Rose, for health.—Feb. 2. Lieut. W. E. Lockhart, 45th N.I., for health.—9 Lieut. Col. M. Riddell, 2d L.C., for health.—Lieut. H. Thatcher, 43d N.I., for health. —Lieut. H. Beaver, 5th N.I., for health (to embark from western coast).—Lieut. W. H. Welsh, 26th N.I. (to embark from ditto)—12. Capt. P. Henderson, 42d N.I., for health (to embark from ditto).

To visit Presidency (preparatory to applying for furlough to Europe).—Jan. 26. Lieut. W. S. Ommanney, 2d L.C.—Feb. 2. Lieut. J. G. B. Bell, artillery.—19. Lieut. A. J. Hadfield, 37th N.I.

To Neilgherries.—Feb. 5. Surg. J. White, medical storekeeper at presidency, for six months, for health.—Lieut. Col. W. Garrard, chief engineer, from 20th Feb. to 30th Nov. 1836, for health.

SHIPPING.

Arrivals.

JAN. 23. *Cecelia,* Roy, from Covelong. — 25. *Cornwallis,* Clark, from Bombay —26. *Eleanor,* Timms, for Moulmein: *Catherine,* Walker, from Vizagapatam, &c.; and H.M.S. *Wolf,* Stanley, from Trincomallee and Pondicherry.—29. *Margaret,* Spain, from Rangoon —FEB. 9. *Napoleon,* Barbot, from Pondicherry.—10. H.M. brig *Victor,* Crozier, from Kedgeree.—*George Gardiner,* Smith, from Calcutta.—13. *Isadora,* Hodson, from Vizagapatam, &c.—17. *Orontes,* Currie, from London; H.M.S. *Andromache,* Chads, from Colombo; and *Louisa,* De la Combe, from Coringa.—18. *Swallow,* Adam, from Calcutta—19. *Duke of Argyll,* Bristow, from London and Cape; *La Bella Alliance,* Arckoll, from ditto ditto; and *Edmond Castle,* Fleming, from Mauritius.—26. *Elizabeth,* Kelso, from Mauritius.—*Argyle,* Mc Donald, from London.—*Hibernia,* Gillies, from London and Cape.—MARCH 8. *Hindostan,* Redman, from London.

Departures.

JAN. 22. *John William Dare,* Towle, for northern ports.—26. *Charles Dumergue,* Hery, for Coringa.—27. *Cecilia,* Roy, for Calcutta.—30. *Annandale,* Hill, for Liverpool; H.M.S. *Wolf,* Stanley, for Malacca; and *Courier de St. Pierre,* Basque, for Coringa.—FEB. 7. *Margaret,* Spain, for Coringa and Calcutta.—8. *Eleanor,* Timms, for Moulmein.—13. *Napoleon,* Barbot, for Karrikal and Singapore.—16. *Mary Ann,* Tarbutt, for

London.—Hibernia, Gillies, for Calcutta.—*Argyle,* McDonald, for Calcutta.

To Sail.—Orontes, for London, on 5th March; La Belle Alliance, for London and Cape, on 5th do.

BIRTHS, MARRIAGES, AND DEATHS.

BIRTHS.

Dec. 25. At Moulmein, the lady of Brevet Capt. T. G. E. G. Kenny, 13th regt., of a son.

Jan. 7. At Bangalore, the wife of the Rev. J. Guest, Wesleyan missionary, of a daughter.

15. At Hingolee, the lady of Lieut. T. Davies, 4th Nizam's service, of a daughter.

18. At Cannanore, the lady of D. White, Esq., C.S., of a daughter.

— At Vepery, the lady of R. Walter, Esq., of a daughter.

21. At Mangalore, the lady of H. F. Dumergue, Esq., of a son.

23. At Bellary, the lady of Assist. Surg. A. B. Morgan, H.M. 55th regt., of a son.

25. At Madras, the lady of Dr. Milligan, H.M. 63d regt., of a son.

26. At Secunderabad, the lady of Major Mac Farlane, 10th N.I., of a daughter.

27. Mrs. E. Jones, of a daughter.

28. At Madras, the lady of A. P. Onslow, Esq., of a son.

29. At Cuddapah, the lady of Lieut. McCally, 28th N.I., of a daughter, still-born.

30. At Kamptee, the lady of Lieut. and Adj. C. Ireland, 11th regt., of a daughter.

Feb. 2. At Chittoor, the lady of T. Onslow, Esq., C.S., of a son.

15. At Madras, the lady of Arthur Freese, Esq., C.S, of a daughter.

MARRIAGES.

Jan. 25. At Cannanore, Lieut. J. Martyr, 36th N.I., to Mary Jane, second daughter of J. Mac Donell, Esq., M.D., surgeon H.M. 57th regt.

27. At Madras, Lieut. G. W. Y. Simpson, adjutant of artillery, to Mary Helen, eldest daughter of George Meikle, Esq., acting superintending surgeon northern division.

28. At Vepery, Mr. Robert Cornelius Hart to Miss Sarah Roberts.

DEATHS.

Jan. 14. At Vepery, in her 27th year, after giving birth to a still-born child, Mary Ritchie, wife of Mr. John Maddox, coach-maker.

24. At Madras, after a few days' illness, which commenced with paralysis, the Rev. Dr. J. P. Rottler, missionary, aged 86. For above sixty years he laboured as a missionary in India, formerly in the Danish mission at Tranquebar, and since 1804, in the mission of the Society for the Propagation of the Gospel at Vepery.

26. At Madras, Mr. J. Honner, acting master-attendant at Cuddalore and Porto Novo.

— At Vepery, in her 21st year, Ann Caroline, wife of Mr. Wm. Edwards.

29. Suddenly, Capt. the Hon. W. T. O'Callaghan, of H.M. 41st regt., military secretary and aide-de-camp to his Exc. the Commander-in-chief.

Feb. 4. Mr. R. M. B. D'Cruz, aged 21.

7. Mrs. M. Spencer, aged 36.

24. At Madras, Capt. W. Walker, of the 1st regt. Light Cavalry.

Lately. On the Neilgherry Hills, Mrs. Macleane, wife of the Resident of Tanjore.

Bombay.

GOVERNMENT ORDERS, &c.

TOUR OF INSPECTION—POONAH DIVISION OF THE ARMY.

Head Quarters, Poonah, Jan. 16, 1836.— The Commander-in-chief having returned from his tour in the Southern Mahratta country, has a pleasing duty to perform in recording his opinions on the actual state in which he found the troops stationed in the southern division of the Poonah division, with which he commenced his inspections.

The admirable state in which the horse artillery at Poonah appeared before his Exc. in the field, the celerity with which all the movements that belong to the exercise of that arm, their firings, &c. were performed, was such as to reflect the highest credit upon Lieut. Col. Stevenson, the officers, and men under his orders.— The soldierlike appearance and movements in the field of the 5th and 19th regts. N. I., the former under the command of Major Spiller, and the latter under Major Stalke, afforded his Exc. the highest satisfaction.

To Col. Lodwick, commanding at Sattara, the thanks of the Commander-in-chief are in an especial manner due. In addition to the creditable state of the station in a military point of view, the satisfactory way in which he conducted the official visits of his Highness the Rajah, and the Commander-in-chief, and the general information relative to that part of the country which he gave, merit his Excellency's acknowledgments.

The splendid appearance of the 23d N.I., which possesses a remarkably fine body of men. attracted the Commander-in-chief's peculiar notice, and their movements in the field were equally satisfactory; a proof to his Exc. that Major Wilson had bestowed much attention upon his duties, and was rewarded by finding himself at the head of a regiment of which he has reason to be proud.

The Commander-in-chief has every reason to speak in high terms of Brigadier-general Gilbert, for his management of the troops stationed in the Southern Division of the Army, and his Exc. requests the Brigadier-general will accept his thanks for his exertions in upholding discipline, and the respectability of character of those placed under his orders.

The 10th N. I., furnishing large detachments at out-stations, had not more than about 200 men in the field at the inspection. It was evident, even from so small a number, that much is wanting to put the regiment on an equality with others of the native army, from which, the Commander-in-chief is sorry to observe, it widely differs in point of appearance and efficiency. When the regiment arrived at Belgaum last year, under the command of the senior captain, its discipline and interior economy appeared to have been much neglected. Brigadier-general Gilbert has however, assured the Commander-in-chief, that since Colonel Morse has assumed the command of the 10th N. I., a very great improvement has taken place, and the Lieut. General relies with confidence upon the exertions of

Col. Morse, to perfect the work he has so well begun.

Sir John Keane has long known and served with his M.'s 20th Regt., and he has ever found it, as he did at this inspection, under the command of Lieut. Col. Green, a credit to itself and to the British army. Its couduct in the field has always been a proud example of steady discipline and valour ; and now that its period of service is nearly completed in India, and that it is about to leave this command on its return to England, the Lieut. General feels it to be due to the regiment, and it is to him a pleasing duty to state, that its fair fame has been well supported by its uniform soldierlike conduct, during the time it has served in the Bombay presidency.

The well regulated state of the arsenal at Belgaum, and the manner in which the duties of ordnance store-keeper appear to be conducted by Capt. Gibson of the Artillery, reflect credit upon that officer. —From Lieut. Holland, assist. qu.-mast.-general, and from Capt. C. W. Grant, executive engineer at Belgaum, the Commander-in-chief derived useful information on the points he had occasion to refer to them.

The Commander-in-chief was happy to perceive that the 1st or Grenadier Regt. N. L, under the command of Capt. Billamore, at Dharwar, retains the soldierlike appearance, and high state of discipline and efficiency, which it was his pleasing duty to compliment the regiment upon at Poonah last year.

Of the 18th N.I., under the command of Capt. Worthy, at Kulladghee, the Commander-in-chief cannot speak in terms of too much praise. The regiment is composed of a fine body of men ; their soldierlike appearance and steadiness under arms was remarkable ; their movements in the field were done with celerity and correctness. Their marching in line, in column, and echellon, was such as to call forth the expression of his unqualified approbation. The state of Capt. Brook's troop of the 2d Lt. Cav. at Kulladghee, met with Sir John Keane's approbation.

The Commander-in-chief derived much gratification from the inspection of the troops stationed at Sholapoor. The state of Capt. Cocke's troop of horse-artillery is highly praiseworthy in every particular, and the Lieut. General compliments that officer on the admirable practice in round shot, grape, and spherical case (or shrapnell) made on the morning of the inspection, which equalled in correctness any the Commander-in-chief had ever before witnessed.

The appearance of the 2d Lt. Cav. in the field, whether taken as regarded the men, the condition of their horses, or the state of their equipments, together with the movements they performed, in strict conformity to the new book on cavalry drill, also with what came before his Exc. in connexion with the interior economy of the regiment, was greatly to be admired, and reflected much credit upon Capt. Wilson, the commanding officer, who possesses zeal and a good feeling for the respectability of his regiment, which could not prove otherwise than pleasing to the Commander-in-chief.

The 2d or Grenadier Regt. N. I., seen by his Exc. for the first time, affords him the opportunity of recording his opinion, that it is in every respect a fine regiment. Its appearance in the field, and its movements under the command of Capt. Graham, holding it temporarily during Major Capou's exercise of the command of the Sholapoor station, was such as proved highly satisfactory to the Commander-in-chief.

Sir John Keane will always retain a pleasing recollection of the able assistance he received, throughout this tour, from Lieut. Col. Stevenson, of the horse-artillery, who accompanied him, and whose experience and proverbial zeal, combined with his knowledge of the country and its usages, and every thing relating to the native army, rendered him a most useful as well as a desirable companion to His Excellency, and the Lieut. General requests Lieut. Col. Stevenson will accept his best thanks upon the occasion.

In conclusion, Sir John Keane begs to compliment the officers of this portion of the Bombay army, upon the well-conducted and good style of their regimental messes, than which nothing tends more to the respectability of a corps of officers, or is more conducive to the promotion of good feeling, and the gentlemanly demeanour which can never be dispensed with in the military profession, and is inseparable from the exercise of a high and proper degree of discipline.

COMMAND ALLOWANCES.

Bombay Castle, Jan 25, 1836.—The allowance of Rs. 120 per mensem, granted under existing regulations to the senior regimental commanding officer at the head-quarters of a division, during the absence of the general officer on duty within his division, is extended to cases of authorized absence on leave.

Should the head-quarters be, with the sanction of government, temporarily established at any head-quarters of two or more corps, it becomes a cantonment command, and the senior officer draws the full allowance of Rs. 520 per mensem, giving over the regimental command to the next senior officer.

BRIGADIER L. C. RUSSELL.

Bombay Castle, Feb. 1, 1836.—On occasion of the departure of Brigadier Russell (commandant of artillery) from the presidency, the Right Hon. the Governor in Council feels bound to record the deep sense which he entertains of the qualifications and services of that officer.

With the praise of gallantry in the performance of active duty in the field, and conspicuous ability in fulfilling the functions of a regimental command, Brigadier Russell has united that of devoted and successful assiduity in the less ostensible sphere of an official charge; and these merits, eminent in themselves, have been enhanced by that high and soldierly spirit, which has stamped itself in every act of his service.

In the retirement to which the state of his health compels him for a season to withdraw, Brigadier Russell will find comfort in the consciousness that he carries with him the warm regard of the profession to which he belongs, and the sincere esteem of the government for whose benefit his high qualifications have been exercised.

WARRANT OFFICERS.

Bombay Castle, Jan. 9, 1836.—The Right Hon. the Governor in council is pleased to rescind such part of art. 57, section 47, of the military regulations, as directs that warrant officers, absent in Europe on furlough, be borne on the strength as supernumeraries, and to direct that the following rules be substituted :—

" When a warrant officer proceeds to Europe on medical certificate, the senior of the next inferior grade, if of unexceptionable character, and if recommended by the proper authorities, will be appointed to officiate in the rank and with the pay and allowances of the absentee, during his absence."

SIGNAL AT BOMBAY.

Notice. — Marine Department. — The established signal at the several flag-staffs on the island of Bombay for a schooner or cutter, is changed from a cylinder painted *red*, to a cylinder painted *bright yellow.*

COURT MARTIAL.
ASSIST. SURG. T. HUNTER.

Assist. Surg. T. Hunter, of H. M.'s 2d or Queen's Royal regiment, has been tried at Bombay on the following charges:

1st. Highly unofficer-like and disgraceful conduct in being intoxicated and incapable of performing his duty as a medical officer, in charge of invalids proceeding from Poonah to Bombay, on the 26th, 27th, 28th, and 29th Oct. 1835.

2d. Highly unofficer-like conduct and neglect of duty, in quitting the detachment without leave at Carli, on the 28th October, proceeding in advance, and affording no medical aid to the invalids during the remainder of the march to Bombay, *viz.* from the 29th Oct. to the 2d Nov. 1835.

3d. Scandalous and disgraceful conduct unbecoming an officer and a gentleman : *First*—In appearing intoxicated before a board of officers, assembled at Poonah, on the 25th Nov. 1835, to investigate into the above conduct. *Second*—Appearing in the regimental hospital on the mornings of the 20th, 21st, and 22d Nov. [and the evening of the 20th Nov.] in a state of intoxication.

Finding — Guilty, except of words within brackets.

Sentence— To be Cashiered.

Approved by the Commander-in-Chief in India.

Remarks by the Commander-in-Chief.

1. The Commander-in-chief desires to point the attention of the army to the case of Mr. T. Hunter, as it is but three months since this very individual was before tried for a similar offence.

2. The ruin of the man strongly elucidates the dangerous results of the habit of drunkenness, when once given way to.

3. It is with much regret that his Excellency has to observe, that this is the *third* officer of H. M.'s army who has been cashiered for this odious offence, within the last two months, so that he can little wonder that thoughtless private soldiers should give way to the pernicious vice, when such examples are set before them.

4. He has the utmost confidence in the commanding officers of his Majesty's regiments, that they will aid him in his endeavours to root out this evil from the army, and that they will oblige the officers under their command, not only to assist in preventing drunkenness amongst their men by personal exertions, but also by setting a proper example to those under them.

CIVIL APPOINTMENTS, &c.

Territorial Department—Revenue.

Jan. 27. Mr. E. G. Fawcett to act as sub-collector of Bagulcotta, during Mr. Shaw's absence on sick leave.

Mr. Henry Liddell to act as first assistant to collector in Candeish.

Judicial Department.

Jan. 26. Mr. Arthur Hornby to be assistant to judge and session judge at Tannah.

Lieut. J. Hale, 22d N.I., to officiate as an assistant to general superintendent of operations for suppression of Thugee in Western Malwa and Guzerat, during absence of Capt. Outram.

Mr. Hart was examined in the printed regulations of government, by a committee appointed for the purpose, on the 25th January, and reported to have passed a very creditable examination.

Leave of Absence.—Jan. 23. Major J. Morison, resident in Persian Gulf, to presidency, for one month, on private affairs.

MILITARY APPOINTMENTS, PROMOTIONS, &c.

Bombay Castle, Jan. 19, 1836.—Lieut. N. H. Thornbury, 4th N.I., to act as interp. in Hindoostanee to that regt., from 14th Oct. last, during absence of Lieut. Lucas; confirmed as a temp. arrangement.

Jan. 21.—Lieut. E. Pottinger, of artillery, to proceed in command of a detachment of auxiliary horse from Cutch.

Capt. Goodfellow to be executive engineer at Poona, v. Capt. Grant.

Lieut. T. M. B. Turner to be executive engineer at Ahmednuggur, v. Goodfellow.

Lieut. C. H. Boye to be paymaster of pensioners in Concan, v. Stokoe.

Lieut. C. Threshie, sub-assist. com. gen. in charge of bazaars at Deesa, to act at Rajcote during time that Lieut. Hartley is employed at Belgaum.

Lieut. P. K. Skinner, 9th N.I., to act as sub-assist. com. gen. in charge of bazaars at Deesa.

Jan. 23.—Capt. D. Forbes and Lieut. J. Ramsay placed at disposal of Com.-in-chief (the commands of Nandode and Veerpoor being placed on same footing as Porebunder).

Jan. 25.—Lieut. D. Davidson, 18th N.I., to assume temporary charge of duties of commissariat department at Kulladghee, from 6th Jan.

The undermentioned officers, cadets of season 1830, to have brevet rank of captain, from dates specified, *viz.*—Lieuts. M. F. Willoughby, artillery; W. Brett, horse artillery; C. Lucas, artillery; H. W. Trevelyan, do.; and T. E. Cotgrave, do.; all from 19th Dec. 1835.—Lieuts. J. Hale, 22d N.I.; R. Hutt, 14th do.; and W. Wade, Europ. Regt.; all from 4th Jan. 1846.

The following appointments made in Qu. Mast. General's Department, consequent upon death of Major Hart, to have effect from 30th May 1835:—Capt. N. Campbell, assist. qu. mast. gen., to be deputy qu. mast. gen., with official rank of major, v. Hart.—Lieut. E. P. De l'Hoste, deputy assist. qu. mast. gen., to be assist. qu. mast. gen., v. Campbell.—Lieut. W. S. Adams, 10th N.I., to be deputy assist. qu. mast. gen., v. De l'Hoste.

2d-Lieuts. Henry Creed and C. R. Dent, former to act as qu. mast. and latter as interp., to 1st bat. artillery, during absence of 2d-Lieut. Gaisford, on leave.

Jan. 28.—Capt. M. Stack to be superintendent of government stud, v. Maj. Jackson dec.

Capt D. Cunningham, 2d L.C., to command Poona auxiliary horse, in suc. to Capt. Stack.

Feb. 1.—The following temporary arrangements confirmed:—Lieut. A. M. Haselwood, 3d N.I., to act as adj. to that regt., during absence of Lieut. Edmonds.—Ens. J. D. Leckie, 22d N.I., to act as qu. mast. to that regt., during absence of Lieut. Rooke, on sick cert.

Lieut. Col. J. G. Griffith to be commandant of artillery, consequent on departure of Col. Russell for Europe.

Capt. J. Lawrie to receive temporary charge of arsenal from Lieut. Col. Griffith, who vacates his appointment as senior commissary of stores on becoming commandant of artillery.

FURLOUGHS.

To Europe.—Jan. 19. Lieut. W. Wade, European regt.—25. Lieut. W. Jones, 20th N.I.—26. Brev. Capt. J. E. Lang, 20th N.I., for health.—Lieut. J. E Frederick, 18th N.I., for health.—Feb. 1. Brigadier L. C. Russell, commandant of artillery, for health.

To Neilgherries.—Jan. 25. Lieut. G. H. Bellasis, 24th N.I., for twelve months, for health.—Feb. 1. Ens. W. Brown, 12th N.I., for eighteen months, for health.

To Mahabuleshwar Hills. — Feb. 1. J. Orton, Esq., member of medical board, for six weeks, on private affairs.

To Cape of Good Hope.—Jan. 25. Surg. J. Walker, medical storekeeper at presidency, for one year, for health.

MARINE DEPARTMENT.

Bombay Castle, Jan. 19, 1836. — The following

promotions made in supercession of those announced under dates 4th June, 14th July, 29th Sept., and 26th Oct. last:— Midshipman J. J. Bowring to be lieut., v. Harrison dec.; date of com. 30th Jan. 1835.—Midsh. J. F. Prentice to be lieut., v. Rowband prom.; date 17th Feb. 1835.—Midsh. J. W. Young to be lieut., v. Peters dec., date 23d May 1835.—Midsh. J. Buckle to be lieut., v. Wells prom.; date 18th June 1835.—Midsh. C. F. Warden to be lieut., v. Rose dec.; date 29th Nov. 1835.

Furlough.—Jan. 28. Capt. Brucks, to Europe, for three years, agreeably to regulations.

SHIPPING.

Arrivals.

JAN. 23. H.M.S. *Winchester*, Sparshott (bearing flag of Rear-Admiral Sir T. B. Capel), from Trincomallee; H.M. brig *Algerine*, Thomas, from the coast.—24. *Fanny*, Rutler, from Bencoolen, &c.—26. *Royal Family*, Fernandes, from China.—27. H.C. armed cutter *Margaret*, Powell, from Surat. —31. H.C. sloop of war *Amherst*, Sawyer, from Vingorla.—FEB. 2. *Pascoa*, Morgan, from China, Manilla, &c.—3. *Triton*, Ducom, from Bordeaux and Bourbon.—4. *Lonach*, Jellicoe, from Calcutta and Cochin (dismasted 18th Jan. in Gulf of Manar). —FEB. 10. *Hugh Lindsay*, from Red Sea.—28. *Fort William*, Fraser, from China and Singapore. —MARCH 8. *John Bannerman*, Daly, from China; *Nerbudda*, Patrick, from Calcutta.

Departures.

JAN. 18. *Clifton*, Bushby, for Liverpool.—28. H.C. brig of war *Tigris*, Rowband, for Surat; *Theodosia*, Coleman, and *Medora*, Dixon, both for Liverpool.—31. *Triumph*, Green, for London.— FEB. 1. *Oriental*, Allen, for Liverpool; H.C.'s sloop of war *Onote*, Low, for Persian Gulf.—3. *Betsey*, Jones, for China.—6. *Lady Rowena*, Main, for Liverpool.—10. *William Nicol*, for China. 14. *Governor Findlay*, for China.—MARCH 5. H.C. brig *Tigris*, Iggleadon, for Torres Straits. —8. H.M.S. *Algerine*, Thomas, to sea.

BIRTHS, MARRIAGES, AND DEATH.

BIRTHS.

Jan. 9. Mrs. C. W. Allen, of a daughter.
— Mrs. A. Cuthbert, of a son (since dead).
17. At Ahmednuggur, the lady of Capt. J. D. Hallett, 3d N.I., of a son.
21. At Kulladghee, the lady of Capt. J. Worthy, 18th N.I., of a daughter.
24. At Ellichpoor, the lady of Lieut. Meadows Taylor, H.H. the Nizam's army, of a daughter.
27. At Bombay, the lady of Lieut. Col. Griffith, regt. of artillery, of a son, still-born.
29. At Bombay, the lady of Capt. Laurie, artillery, of a daughter.
Feb. 22. At Bombay, the lady of the Right Hon. Sir Robert Grant, of a son.

MARRIAGES.

Jan. 27. At Poona, James Erskine, Esq., eldest son of David Erskine, Esq., of Cardross, Perthshire, to Mary Eliza, second daughter of Brigadier C. S. Fagan, C.B.
Feb. 3. At Byculiah, Capt. G. J. Mant, of the Bombay army, commanding the marine battalion, to Mary Emily, third daughter of James Anderson, Brechin, N.B.
March 3. At Poona, George Hicks Pitt, Esq., of the civil service, to Wilhelmina Petrie, second daughter of Lieut. Gen. Bell, of the Madras artil.

DEATH.

Jan. 1. At his jagghire, Vinchoor, the Rajah Wittul Rao Nursing Vinchoorkur.

Ceylon.

BIRTHS.

Jan. 8. At Cotta, Mrs. W. Ridsdale, of a son.
9. The lady of Capt. Parke, H.M. 61st regt., of a son.
12. At Kandy, the lady of L. Kelly, Esq., M.D., of a son.

MARRIAGE.

Dec. 28. At Jaffna, Edmund James Wood, Esq., district judge of the Wanny, to Sarah Ann, eldest daughter of the late Lieut. Burke, Ceylon Rifle Regt.

Penang.

BIRTH.

Jan. 20. The lady of Capt. G. Middlecoat, commanding the artillery in the Straits, of a daughter.

Singapore.

BIRTHS.

Dec. 19. The lady of G. F. Davidson, Esq., of a still-born son.
. 24. Mrs. Moor, of a daughter.
Jan. 10. The lady of Simon Stephens, Esq , of a daughter.

DEATHS.

Dec. 20. Mr. G. S. Concannon, aged 28.
30. The Rev. Dominick Anthony Jeremiah, late missionary apostolic of Siam, aged 63.

China.

SHIPPING.

Arrivals.—Jan. 17. *Mary Ann*, from Sydney.—28. *Louisa Campbell*, from London and Batavia; *Mangles*, from Sydney; *Children*, from Samarang.—Feb. 2. *Vansittart*, from Madras and Singapore.
Departures.—*Irt*, and *Panther*, both for Manilla.—Jan. 30. *Lady of the Lake*, for Hobart Town and Sydney.
Freight to Great Britain (Jan. 30)—£4. 10s. to £5.; large ships, £6.

BIRTH.

Jan. 24. At Macao, the lady of Thos. R. Colledge, Esq., of a son.

DEATHS.

Jan. 30. At Macao, Mr. Richard Markwick.
Lately. At Macao, Mr. Arthur Hamilton Mc Cally, youngest son of the late Col. Whitney McCally, of the Madras army.

New South Wales.

SHIPPING.

Arrivals.—Dec. 10. *Augustus Cæsar*, from Hobart Town.—26. *Minerva*, from Downs; *Psyche*, from Calcutta and Hobart Town.—Jan. 1. *Salacea*, from London.—9. *Gem*, and *Elizabeth*, both from Launceston; *Auriga*, from Hobart Town.—11. *Siren*, from ditto; *Rhoda*, from London.—12. *Leda*, and *Layton*, both from Hobart Town.—13. *Derwent*, from ditto.—17. *Lord William Bentinck*, from London; *John Barry*, from Torbay; *Dart*, from Launceston.—18. *Magnet*, from Downs; *Edinburgh*, from Liverpool.—19. *Tamar*, from Manilla.—20. *Orissa*, from Hobart Town; *Exporter*, from Mauritius.—27. *Integrity*, from London and Cape.—Feb. 7. *James Pattison*, from Cork; *Henry Wellesley*, from London; *Bardaster*, from London and Hobart Town; *Clyde*, from Liverpool; *Susan*, from Portsmouth; *William*, from Launceston.—*Governor Harcourt*, from London.—14. *Platina*, from London.—24. *Giraffe*, from London.—25. *Recovery*, from Portsmouth; *Roslyn Castle*, from Cork; *Harriet*, from Canton.—26. *Samuel Cunard*, from Dartmouth.

Van Diemen's Land.

SHIPPING.

Arrivals at Hobart Town.—Jan. 18. *Ellen*, from Liverpool. — 28. *Eldon*, from Sydney.—Feb. 1.

Vansittart, from Cowes —4. *Boadicea*, from London (with female emigrants).—*North Briton*, from Cork ; *Janet*, from Greenock ; *Margaret Graham*, from Clyde.

Cape of Good Hope.

SHIPPING.

Arrivals.—March 18. *Abberton*, and *Kerswell*, both from London ; *Munster Lass*, from St. Helena.—19. *Fergusson*, from London.—20. *Juliana*, from London ; *Palinure*, from Norfolk.—22. *Columbine*, and *Henry*, both from London. — 25. H.M.S. *Atholl*, from St. Helena.—29. *Comet*, from London, at Algoa Bay.—April 11. *Madras*, from London.—13. *Lynher*, from Liverpool.
Departures.—March 21. *Abberton*, for Madras and Calcutta.—29. *Fergusson*, for ditto ditto.

BIRTHS.

March 10. At Fort Wiltshire, the lady of Capt. R. D. Halifax, 75th regt., of a daughter.
11. At the parsonage of Swellendam, Mrs. Robertson, of a son.
20. At Sea Point, the lady of the Hon. Mr. Justice Menzies, of a son.
21. Mrs. George Thompson, of a daughter.

MARRIAGE.

Feb. 29. Alex. Brown, Esq., surgeon, to Susan Margaret, youngest daughter of J. C. Fleck, Esq., justice of the peace, and late member of the court of justice.

DEATHS.

March 2. At the Paarl, Mr. Henry Thomas Hitchcock, aged 46.
9. At Cape Town, Jane Rumsey, wife of Mr. A. W. Walter, of the customs.
19. Capt. George Keir, of his Majesty's service, aged 49.
22. On board the *Fergusson*, Mr. W. H. Brown, midshipman, aged 16.

Swan River.

DEATH.

Dec. 31. William Trimmer, Esq., of H.M. 17th regt., in his 40th year. He was drowned near Bassendean, by the upsetting of a sailing-boat, while proceeding on an excursion up the river.

St. Helena.

MEMBERS OF THE COUNCIL.

Major General Middlemore, as governor, having brought with him a commission to elect his own council, has chosen Thomas H. Brooke, Esq., and Thomas Greentree, Esq., as such, to form the new constitution of government, and to officiate as usual in their judicial capacity. — *Extract of Letter.*

NEW CIVIL ESTABLISHMENT.

Secretarial Department.—Mr. R. F. Seale, secretary and registrar, &c.—Mr. W. H. Seale, chief and treasury clerk.—Mr. J. Doveton, junior clerk.—Mr. G. W. Melliss, surveyor and collector of rents and revenues.—Mr. W. Seale, office-keeper.
Audit Office.—Mr. F. E. Knowles, auditor.
Customs, &c.—Mr. John Young, collector and register master.—Mr. Stephen Pritchard, clerk and warehouse-keeper.
Judicial Department.—Chief justice and King's advocate (vacant).—Mr. W. H. Seale, clerk of the peace.—Mr. George Weston, marshall.
Police Department.—Mr. C. R. G. Hodson, judge and magistrate of Summary Court.—Mr. G. A. Den Taffe, county magistrate. — Mr. Thomas Baker, town magistrate.—Four Provosts.
Emancipation Department.—Mr. George A. Den Taaffe, reporter.

LATEST INTELLIGENCE.

Our correspondent at Calcutta has forwarded us, by steam and overland conveyance, the following *resumé* of the contents of the Calcutta papers down to the 5th March. By continuing this system, our reader will be furnished with the latest possible intelligence.

Major Alves returned to the *Mahajee-barhang*, at Jeypore, on the 6th inst., accompanied by Hookhum Chund, the brother, and Futteh Lell, the son of Jotha Ram, under strong guard. Jotha Ram is to be taken immediately from the fort at Dewsa to Jeypore. Koonwur Hurruck Sing, Runjeet Sing's eldest son, informed his father, that Rutton Sing had an extremely beautiful daughter, whom he was anxous to obtain in marriage. Runjeet having called the jageerdar to "the presence," desired him to bestow his daughter on the Koonwur, but Rutton Sing having excused himself on the plea that his daughter had been already betrothed, Runjeet cast him into a dungeon, and confiscated his jageer.

The *Lahore Ukhbars* say, that Runjeet having brought Sooltan Mahomed Khan to Lahore, under the express promise of appointing him agent at Peshawur, and having failed in that promise, the brother of Sooltan Mahomed, Dost Mahomed Khan, assembled 15 or 20,000 mulkeeas, &c. at Jellallabah, whence he intends marching forthwith on Peshawur, and taking vengeance upon Runjeet.—*Delhi Gaz., Feb* 10.

Baron Hugel, who is now on his way down from Cashmere, will reach Delhi in the course of this day.—*Ibid.*

The whole of the troops and establishments belonging to her late highness the Begum Sombre, have been paid up and discharged, without the smallest disturbance.—*Meerut Obs., Feb.* 11.

It is with the greatest satisfaction we this day announce the abolition of the last of the custom-houses, that of Allahabad, and the abandonment throughout the Agra presidency of the system of inland and transit duties.—*Central Free Press, Feb.* 13.

Dividends were declared of 10 per cent. on the estate of Fergusson and Co.; five per cent. on that of Colvin and Co.; and three per cent. on Mackintosh and Co.—*Englishman, Feb.* 22.

The *Forbes* was sold yesterday by public auction to Messrs. Carr, Tagore, and Co., for Rs. 1,10,000. We understand that Messrs. Cockerell and Co., Messrs. R. C. Jenkins and Co., and several other firms have taken shares in this vessel

and the new Emulous which will soon be finished.—*Bengal Herald, Feb.* 21.

A public sale of landed property belonging to the firm of Cruttenden and Co., was held yesterday at Messrs. Jenkins, Low, and Co.'s, which attracted many purchasers, and excited much competition. Six lots were submitted, for each of which there were bidders; but three of them, (two in the Bow Bazar and one at Howrah,) were more actively competed for than the rest, and realized much more than the upset prices.—*Englishman, Feb.* 24.

Two acts of our legislature are published to-day, or rather an act and a proposed act, which deserve attention. The latter affects the indigo planters, and contains a provision which will afford them some protection against the violence of a zemindar, or other intruder attempting to deprive them of their plant. The former is an extension of that exquisite piece of legislation, the present insolvent act *for three years* from the 1st of March next, when it expires.—*Cour., Feb.* 24.

Col. Parker passed through *en route*, to Simlah. Mr. Hamilton has returned from Sirdannah, having completed the arrangements immediately necessary for the district.—*Meerut Obs., Feb.* 18.

Our troops in Shekawattee expects to move, about the end of the present month, in the neighbourhood of the city of Jeypore, where it is said a new cantonment will be formed. Lieut. Trevelyan and Doctor Mottley were expected to arrive at Thoonjhnoo, on the 2d or 3d instant, *en route*, from Bukaneer to Jeypore.—*Delhi Gaz., Feb* 13.

A private letter from the vicinity of Benares states, " we have had a tremendous hail-storm, which has destroyed the grain almost entirely for twenty miles in length, and four in breadth. Some of the masses of ice were a seer in weight.

Col. Tapp is likely to succeed Major Kennedy in his political office and military command at Subathoo.—*Hurkaru, Feb.* 25.

The affairs of the public library are going on very satisfactorily. and although the proprietary list has received but few additional names for some time, there will be above Rs. 11,000 available for the purchase of books, after paying all expences, when the next instalment is collected.—*Cour., Feb.* 24.

Government had determined to do away with the salt sales. A price is to be put upon each description of salt in the government golas, and any person

.may buy as much or as little as he pleases at any time. By this method the speculation, which has hitherto taken place at the periodical sales will be put an end to, for no capitalists will be foolish enough to buy for an advance when his powerful competitor is always ready to undersell him.—*Hurkaru, Feb.* 25.

The lottery committee have either recommended or about to recommend to government, the abolition of the government lottery, which has hitherto been carried on with the ostensible object of improving the city of Calcutta.—*Gyan-sune Shun, Feb.* 24.

" Goomsur, 30th January :—The late operations carried on, on the western side of the seminary, have been the means of entirely clearing away the strong range of hills of the rebels."—*Madras Herald, Feb.* 13.

The last accounts from Goomsur state that there is now no doubt of the death of the rajah. The country, however, will be taken, and the power of the chiefs destroyed. Several men have been taken in arms at our outposts, and four incendiaries, who had also committed murder, have been hanged by sentence of a special court-martial.

The appointment of Lieut. Higginson to the political office of agent to the Governor-general at Moorshedabad, and the removal of Col. Caulfield the officiating agent, have given very great offence.—*Englishman, Feb.* 27.

The 38th regt. N. I., under the command of Lieut.-Col. Nott, reached Delhi on the morning of the 12th inst., and the 42d N. I., commanded by Major Ross, quitted Delhi on Monday morning last in progress to Bareilly, where it is to be stationed.

The *Ukbars* say, that the Hakeem of Sinde, Meer Nour Mahomed Khan, has invited the ex-king Shah Shooja-ool-Moolk, to resume the government of Shikarpore, and that the ex-king has accepted the offer.

The mussulman population at Lahore, are, it appears, in a state of considerable excitement. Monsieur Ventura has been ordered by Maharajah Runjeet Sing, to appropriate a certain worshipping place for the purpose of holding his Kutcherry. Remonstrance against this insult was, of course, useless ; the circumstance, however, has produced great dissatisfaction in the minds of the " faithful *Delhi Gaz.*"

. One of the ameers of Scind has expressed a desire to have a steamer built for him at Bombay to navigate the Indus, and the Court have been requested to send out engines for her.

· The tax on the Hindoo devotees who bathe at the junction of the Ganges and Jumna, near Allahabad, amounted on the 25th ult. to about Rs. 64,000.

An earthquake was felt on the 24th ult. at Chandernagore and Sook Saugor, where the shock was so considerable is to bring down the plaster from the houses.

Messrs. Spence and Wetherill have proposed establishing a coffee-house : the plan has met with so much encouragement that they have commenced carrying it into effect.—*Reformer, Feb.* 7.

A faqueer, by name Ramtullah Khan, was fortunate enough to discover a vessel containing five hundred mohurs. Dost Mohummud Khan having been informed of this circumstance, ordered the faqueer into his presence, and having obtained an acknowledgment of the discovery, dismissed the faqueer, with a remark which would do credit to a more enlightened governor. " As you have," said the sirdar, " without equivocation, confessed you found the coin, I now confirm you in the possession, which would not have been the case had you uttered any untruth."—*Delhi Gaz., Feb.* 17.

The *fiat* has at last gone forth to abolish transit duties throughout the Bengal provinces. The abandonment of these duties in the Agra presidency, could not but be followed by their abandonment in Bengal.— *Cour., March* 2.

Enquiries recently instituted have, we understand, elicited some very curious facts relative to the operation of the transit system in various parts of India. Among other singularities we learn that the following mode of collecting transit duties existed some years in the province of Berar, but has been since abolished. " A transit duty was levied on all women travellers *enciente*, and on all animals great with young !" We do not know to whose ingenuity government were indebted for this most atrocious tax, but as a measure of revenue we conceive it to be quite unique—a sort of prospective poll-tax.—*Hurkaru, March* 2.

Brigadier Brown has been left a legacy of seventy-five thousand rupees, and is now on his way to Sirdanha, being an executor to the will.—*Agra Hurkaru, Feb.* 20.

We announced yesterday, by an extra, the arrival of the Right Hon. Lord Auckland in the *Jupiter*, and as the vessel passed Kedgeree in tow of the *Ganges*, with a spring flood, we expected that his lordship would land about two o'clock ; but, in the course of the day, we were informed by Sereaphom that the *Jupiter* had anchored at Diamond Harbour at one o'clock, and soon afterwards we learned that his lordship would not land until this evening. Of course this is an arrangement of his lordship's choice, not of necessity, since there being a steamer with the vessel, his lordship might, by leaving the ship, have landed yesterday evening, or at latest early this morning. All was bustle and activity yesterday at the government-house, and Sir Charles Metcalfe issued cards to some of the elite of society here, inviting them to a dinner in the evening to meet Lord Auckland. Of course they were disappointed of the honour. This evening, however, his lordship will land, and be greeted by the usual honours.—*Hurkaru, March* 4.

The new Native Medical College is to be opened on the 10th inst., when Principal Bramley will deliver an appropriate address. We gave, some time ago, a sketch of the examination of the pupils of the Native Medical College, and of the new building, which is on a scale worthy of the government; and the very important objects which it is the object of the institution to receive.

Some of the merchants were about to propose to the Chamber of Commerce to thank Sir Charles Metcalfe, by deputation or by address, for the abolition of the transit duties; but just after voting the proposition, the matter was necessarily suspended by the news of the *Jupiter's* arrival.—*Cour., Mar.* 3.

At a meeting of merchants and others desirous of establishing a steam-tug association for running the *Forbes* and a new vessel upon the river Houghley; resolved:—That an association be formed from this date, to be called the Calcutta Steam-tug Association. That a deed be prepared for the signature of every shareholder to the following effect:—1st. Term of association to be five years, with half-yearly meetings for passing accounts and declaring dividends. 2dly, Capital to consist of two lacks of rupees, invested in the purchase of two vessels. The *Forbes* of 279 tons at 1,10,000 rupees. New vessel of 236 tons at 90,000. 3d. Shares to be one thousand rupees each, with other minor resolutions.—Secretaries *pro tem.* Messrs. Carr, Tagore, and Co.

The *Hattrass* pilot vessel is leaving town with Capt. Bell, the superintendent of public buildings, on board. That officer is instructed to take down Point Palmiras' light-house, which is in danger of falling, in consequence of the island of Mypurrah, on which it is situated, washing away. As a substitute for the light, rockets are to be fired at stated periods. —*Hurkaru, Mar.* 2.

A full attendance of the inhabitants of Calcutta and its neighbourhood is requested at the meeting convened by the sheriff of Calcutta for this morning at the Town-hall, for the purpose of taking into consideration the present state of the important question of a steam communication between England and India by way of the Red Sea. The meeting

has been called by 470.—*Englishman, March* 5.

Major Pew, of the artillery, met with a serious accident a few days ago, when at an awkward and narrow part of the road, leading to his residence, his horse suddenly started, and he was thrown with great violence from his buggy, by which the acromion process of the left shoulder was fractured, and other injury sustained.—*Delhi Gaz.*

On further examination of the documents seized from the possession of Hookura Chund and Futteh Lol, it has become apparent that Chimun Singh, the chief of Saewar, was a confederate in the conspiracy which ended in the massacre of June last at Jeypoor; he has consequently been formally cited to appear at Jeypore, and defend himself; but has very wisely and positively declined doing so. This polite invitation having failed to entrap the wily sirdar, recourse is now to be had to force, and by this time a corps d'armée of the Jeypore troops, amounting to about 5,000 men, has probably marched from the capital to invest the places, and render themselves masters of his person, which perhaps, should they succeed, is destined to " point a moral or adorn a gibbet," in company with the rest of the crew. Knowing this, he will no doubt make the best resistance he can, and as Saewar is a hill fort, he will probably keep the Jeypore rabble at bay for a month or two. Saewar will, or more probably will *not*, be found on the map about ten miles north of Monohurpoor, and as much S.W. of Baberd, that is, about thirty miles north from Jeypore. Rumours of the assembly of the troops for this expedition have for some time prevailed in the Shekawattee, but sadly distorted; for it has been very generally said that Luchmun Singh of Choomooah, who is to command the force, was collecting them on his own account, in anticipation of being very speedily placed himself in the same predicament as Chimun Singh now stands in, and this both high and low in Shekawattee seem generally persuaded is really his true position. This occurrence will probably delay for some time longer the final settlement of affairs at Jeypore, if such a period be ever destined to astonish the world.—*Delhi Gaz.*

We understand from a native gentleman of rank, that it is in contemplation to get up a native address to Sir Charles Metcalfe, to thank him for the benefits conferred upon the country under his administration.—*Cour., March* 4.

Although we are no patrons to the Calcutta lotteries, yet while they continue to figure in the list of ways and means for raising the revenue, we derive some degree of satisfaction from their success in effecting their object. We are therefore glad to hear that our forebodings of a considerable loss on the out-turn of the last lottery have not been followed by a corresponding result, and that instead of a heavy loss, there has actually been a net gain of nearly 36,000 rupees, notwithstanding the large number of unsold tickets (about 1,200). — *Courier, Mar. 4.*

The shareholders of the Universal Life Assurance will be glad to hear that their shares already bear a premium of 20 per cent. in the London market. It has been determined at home to apply for a charter for this association, as soon as the consent of the proprietors in India shall have been obtained.

Calcutta.

GOVERNMENT ORDERS, &c.

AGRA.—WESTERN PROVINCES.

Political Department.—Feb. 29, 1836.— In conformity with instructions from the Hon. the Court of Directors, the execution of the provisions of the Act of the 3d and 4th William IV. cap. 85, so far as they relate to the creation of the Government of Agra, and to the division of the territories formerly subject to the government of the presidency of Fort-William, into two distinct presidencies, is hereby suspended.

As a temporary arrangement, and until further orders, the Hon. Alex. Ross, Esq. is appointed to be lieutenant-governor of the Western Provinces, with the same powers as have heretofore been exercised by the Governor of Agra.

MERCANTILE PURSUITS.

Head-Quarters, Calcutta, Feb. 27, 1836. —It has occurred more than once within a short period, that officers of the medical department, who have been attached to civil stations, when restored by the civil to the military department, have pleaded their entanglement with mercantile or agricultural pursuits, as reasons for demanding long periods of leave of absence, instead of forthwith taking on themselves the military duties, to the discharge of which they are nominated.

2. His Exc. the Commander-in-chief therefore deems it necessary to give this public notice to military surgeons, that he considers their entering into any pursuits which prevent their being immediately available for the duties of the service to which they belong, as contrary to what is right, and that he will not in future listen to such pleas as are alluded to in the antecedent paragraph.

MILITARY APPOINTMENTS, PROMOTIONS, &c.

Fort William, Feb. 29, 1836.—*27th N. I.* Lieut. L. W. Gibson to be capt. of a comp., and Ens. H. Laing to be lieut., from 15th Feb. 1836, in suc. to Capt. Alexander Gerard retired.

31st N. I. Lieut. H. J. Guyon to be capt. of a comp., and Ens. George Newboldt to be lieut., from 15th Feb. 1836, in suc. to Capt. E. N. Townsend dec.

72d N.I. Lieut. St. G. D. Showers to be capt. of comp., and Ens. R. J. Graham to be lieut., from 22d Feb. 1836, in suc. to Capt. J. F. May dec.

Regt of Artillery. Supern. 2d-lieut. A. W. Hawkins brought on effective strength of regt., v. 2d-lieut. F. Wall dec., 17th Sept. 1835.

Surg. James Ranken, M.D., to officiate as a presidency surgeon, v. Surg. Simon Nicholson, who resigns that situation.

Assist.-Surg. J. C. Smith app. to temporary medical duties of civil station of Purneah, during absence on leave of Assist.-Surg. T. Chapman, M.D.

Lieut. E. R. Lyons, 37th N.I., to be second in command of Sylhet Light Infantry, v. Lieut. Townsend, who has obtained furlough to Europe.

Infantry. Lieut. Col. and Brev. Col. C. W. Hamilton to be col., from 10th Nov. 1835, v. Col. T. D. Broughton dec.—Major Hugh Caldwell to be lieut.-col. in suc. to Lieut. Col. and Brev. Col. C. W. Hamilton prom.; date of rank to be adjusted hereafter, with reference to retirement from service of Lieut.-Col. Abraham Hardy.

49th N. I. Capt. R. C. Macdonald to be major, Lieut. F. C. Elwall to be capt. of a comp., and Ens. J. T. Wilcox to be lieut.; date ditto ditto.

Lieut.-Col. George Hawes, 17th N.I., permitted to retire from service of the Hon. Company on pension of his rank.

Lieut. James Brind, regt. of artillery, placed at disposal of Government of Agra, with a view to his being appointed to revenue survey department.

10th L.C. Lieut. W. Wingfield to be capt. of a troop, and Cornet J. M. Loughnan to be lieut., from 17th Feb. 1836, in suc. to Capt. G. L. Trafford dec.

Supernumerary Cornet Alfred Harris brought on effective strength of cavalry.

The following appointments made by Hon. the Governor General on his personal staff:—Brev. Col and Lieut.-Col. James Caulfield, C.B., 9th L. C., to be an aide-de-camp, from 24th Feb.—Lieut. W. M. Smyth, corps of engineers, to be an aide-de-camp, from 12th Jan. last.

Lieut. G. B. Michell, 9th N.I., and Lieut. J. C. Lumsdaine, 58th do., placed under orders of Resident at Gwalior.

Ens. Humphrey Howorth, 39th N.I., placed under orders of Resident at Hydrabad.

Assist.-Surg. W. A. Green app. to medical duties of civil station of Ghazeepore, in suc. to Assist. Surg. Jackson, M.D.; date of Agra order 10th Feb.

Head Quarters, Feb. 26, 1836.—Lieut. Charles Graham, 55th N.I., to act as interp. and qu.-mast. to 58th do., during absence on duty of Lieut. and Qu.-mast. G. A. Mee.

Unposted Ens. G. U. Law, lately admitted, to do duty with 50th N.I., at Dacca.

Feb. 27.—*8th N.I.* Lieut. and Brev. Capt. C. H. Naylor to be interp. and qu.-mast., v. Price.

The retirement of Lieut.-Col. G. Hawes, 17th N.I., promotes Major J. Howe (60th) to be lieut.-col., Capt. A. Dickson to be major, Lieut. G. Cox to be capt., and Ens. J. E. Verner to be lieut.— *Englishman.*

FURLOUGHS.

To Europe.—Feb. 29. Surg. J. N. Rind, of inv. estab., and Superintendent of Gov. lithographic press, for health.—Capt. Wm. Ewart, 54th N.I., for health.

To Cape of Good Hope.—Feb. 29. Capt. A. Charlton. 74th N.I., second in command of Assam Light Infantry, for 18 months, for health.

DEBATE AT THE EAST-INDIA HOUSE.

East-India House, June 22d.

A quarterly General Court of Proprietors of East-India Stock was this day held at the Company's house in Leadenhall-street, pursuant to the charter.

EQUALIZATION OF DUTIES ON SUGAR.

The minutes of the last Court having been read—

The Chairman (Sir James R. Carnac) said, " I have to acquaint the Court, that the petitions agreed to by the Proprietors on the 6th of May last, to be laid before the Houses of Lords and Commons, relative to the equalization of the duties on East and West-India sugars, which were committed respectively to the care of the Earl of Clare and Lord W. Bentinck, have been presented accordingly. I feel much pleasure in stating to the Court that the Directors have been in communication with his Majesty's ministers on this most important and interesting subject, and it affords me great satisfaction to lay before the Court a letter which has been received from the President of the Board of Control, which I have no doubt will prove very gratifying to the proprietors. (*Hear, hear!*)

The letter was then read by the clerk, as follows:

" Berkeley Square, June 22, 1836.
" My dear Sir,—The Chancellor of the Exchequer will explain his plan to-night.* It is this:—that all sugars coming from India with a certificate of origin, will, in point of duty, be assimilated with West-India sugars. Steps must however be taken, entirely to prohibit the introduction of foreign sugars into the sugar-growing and exporting provinces of India, although such restrictions need not apply to the other parts of that empire. The whole system of drawback will be subject to future modification. I trust that this plan will be quite satisfactory. " I remain, &c.
(Signed) " J. C. HOBHOUSE."
" Sir James Carnac, Bart."

* The following is the resolution moved by the Chancellor of the Exchequer, and agreed to in the Committee of Ways and Means (relative to the sugar duties), on Wednesday, the 22d of June:

That, towards raising the supply to be granted to his Majesty, the following duties shall be paid on the importation of sugar, on and from the 5th day of July 1836, for a time to be limited, and under such regulations and conditions as shall be provided for by any act to be passed in this session of parliament; (that is to say),

SUGAR, viz.	£	s.	d.
Brown, or Muscovado, or Clayed Sugar, not being refined, the cwt	3	3	0
The growth of any British possession in America, and imported from thence, the cwt	1	4	0
The growth of any British possession within the limits of the East India Company's charter (into which the importation of foreign sugar may be prohibited by law), and imported from thence, the cwt	1	4	0

Sugar.

Sir *C. Forbes* said, he took the earliest opportunity to express the sincere pleasure he felt at finding that he was mistaken in his view of the course which ministers were likely to pursue on this subject, when he addressed the last General Court. (*Hear, hear!*) He was now ready to give ministers full credit for their conduct on this occasion; the more especially as he confessed he was but little prepared to expect it. (*A laugh.*) He hoped however that the Proprietors would not stop here, but that they would remonstrate until all other duties which affected the produce and manufactures of India, were equalized. (*Hear, hear!*) For his own part, he would not be satisfied until full and complete justice was done to India. So long as any thing remained to be conceded, he conceived that they ought to continue loudly to demand it. He thought that that which had occurred, afforded a pretty clear proof that they could only obtain justice through the medium of agitation, and therefore he recommended that they should proceed in the same course.

Mr. *Weeding* was greatly pleased with the communication which had just been made. The equalization of the duties would be beneficial both to this country and to India. It would open to the latter the best market for her staple produce, while to the former it would extend the employment of the shipping interest. He differed from the hon. bart. in supposing that angry agitation was called for, in order that justice might be done to India; his idea was, that it was only necessary to state the reason of the thing calmly, constantly, and perseveringly, in order to accomplish that object. By adopting that course, he thought that, in the end, they would succeed in procuring full and entire relief. He could not but express the utmost pleasure at finding that this, the first important point, was carried. Sugar formed the great staple commodity of India; and the duty on it having been equalized, the same thing would follow with reference to other Indian productions. In effecting that object, their great endeavour should be, to interest the

SUGAR, viz.	£	s.	d.
The growth of any other British possession, within those limits, and imported from thence, the cwt	1	12	0
Molasses, the cwt	1	3	9
The produce of, and imported from, any British possession, the cwt	0	9	0
Refined, the cwt	8	8	0
Candy, Brown, the cwt	5	12	0
White, the cwt	8	8	0

Bill ordered to be brought in by Mr. Baring and the Chancellor of the Exchequer.

people of this country in favour of their Indian fellow subjects, by proving to them that any measure which was favourable to the prosperity of the latter, must be beneficial to the empire at large.

Mr. *Fielder* hoped that he might be allowed to say a few words on this occasion. He was extremely glad that ministers had acted so promptly in complying with the wishes of the Company. (*Hear, hear!*) He was rejoiced that they had acted without hesitation, and without endeavouring to throw any additional obstacle in the way of the attainment of the object which the Company had so long and so fruitlessly sought. He conceived that every praise was due to them for their conduct on this occasion. Having effected this object, there were others to which the attention of the proprietors ought now to be drawn; and he had no doubt that, with proper perseverance, the equalization of other duties would follow in due time; therefore he exhorted his brother proprietors to proceed in the same straightforward and determined course.

Mr. *H. St. George Tucker* wished to enquire whether by the word "*assimilation,*" which was used in the letter of the President of the Board of Control, that right hon. gentleman meant "*equalization?*" It was very important that they should come to a right understanding upon that point, because things might be assimilated without being equalized.

The *Chairman* said, no man could explain the meaning or intention of the word better than his hon. friend himself. If, however, his hon. friend had any doubt on the point, and would refer to the whole context of the communication, he would see the inference was, that "*equalization*" was meant. (*Hear, hear!*) He would now take the liberty of observing that, willing as he was to give every credit to the government for agreeing to this assimilation of duties, still he could not yield the whole and entire credit to them; because he must in a considerable degree ascribe the success which the Company had met with to the repeated remonstrances of the Court of Proprietors (*Hear, hear!*) supported as they had always been by the executive body. (*Hear, hear!*) He considered that, independently of the justice of the case, the continued remonstrances which they felt it to be their duty towards the people of India to press on the government with respect to this question, was the main cause of their ultimate success. (*Hear, hear!*)

Mr. *Fielder* said he did not mean to detract from the merit of the Court of Directors or Proprietors. The former, he knew, had had a most arduous task to perform, and they had executed it in a very able manner; (*Hear, hear!*) they therefore deserved the highest degree of credit. All he meant to observe was, that when the government appeared to be ready to do an act that would greatly benefit India, they, on their parts, ought not to be backward in saying, "thank you" for it.

The Hon. *Hugh Lindsay* said, that if what appeared in this day's paper was correct, ministers had gone farther than the prayer of their petition. It was stated in this day's paper that the Chancellor of the Exchequer last night gave notice, that it was the intention of his Majesty's government to move for the assimilation of the duties on all the produce of our East-India territories.* (*Hear, hear!*) Now he apprehended that it was only on the subject of the sugar duties that that Court had addressed Parliament. It was left to the Chancellor of the Exchequer to propose the assimilation of all other duties, and if he had taken up the subject, special thanks were due to the government. (*Hear, hear!*)

Mr. *Wigram* said, it was useless to calculate upon what might be done with respect to other points, on which they had no official information. For himself, he was extremely glad to get the boon which Government had conceded by assimilating the sugar duties.

Here the conversation ended.

PARLIAMENTARY PAPERS.

The *Chairman* said, that certain Papers which had been laid before Parliament since the last General Court, the titles of which should be read, were now submitted to the Proprietors, in conformity with the By-law, cap. 1, sec. 4.

The titles of the papers were then read, as follows:

"Lists specifying compensation proposed to be granted to certain persons late in the service of the East-India Company.—(Nos. 47, 48, 49, and 50.)
"Lists specifying the particulars of the compensation proposed to be granted to certain persons late in the maritime service of the East-India Company, under an arrangement sanctioned by the Board of Commissioners for the Affairs of India.—(Nos. 41, 42, 43, 44, 45, 46, and 47.)
"Resolutions of the Court of Directors of the East-India Company, being warrants or instruments granting any pension, salary, or gratuity.
"Minutes and Resolutions of the Court of Directors of the East-India Company, as to the amount of compensation granted to Mr. Arnot, in consequence of his deportation from India by the Government there.
"Copy of the Order of Sir Edward Paget, issued from Fort William, Calcutta, respecting the infliction of corporal punishment on the native soldiery."

HALF-YEAR'S DIVIDEND.

The *Chairman* said, "I have to inform the Court, that the warrants for the half-

* The notice of the Chancellor of the Exchequer, given in some of the morning papers, was "to assimilate the duties on East and West-India *produce.*" This was an error. The notice, as it appears on the parliamentary votes, is—"Annual sugar duties; and to assimilate the duties on *East and West-India sugars.*—(Committee of Ways and Means)."

year's dividend on the Company's stock will be ready for delivery (pursuant to the eleventh section of the 3d and 4th William 1V., cap. 85), on Wednesday, July 6th."

Sir *C. Forbes* said, he would take that opportunity of adverting to a subject which he considered to be of very great importance to the Company. The matter in question arose out of a discussion, which it appeared had taken place some nights ago in the House of Commons, when the case of certain maritime officers, late in the service of the East-India Company, was brought under the notice of that House.

The *Chairman* rose to order. He was very sorry to interrupt the hon. baronet, but the hon. baronet was entering into a statement, when there was in fact no motion before the Court. The business of the day was not over; but when it was over, he would be most willing, on the question of adjournment, to hear any observations which the hon. baronet might think proper to make.

Sir *C. Forbes* submitted, that he was perfectly in order on the present occasion. The communication just made to the Court had reference to the dividend on their stock; and he wished to draw the attention of the Court to a statement, said to have been made by one of his Majesty's ministers, which seemed to countenance the opinion that they might dispense with that form. He understood that it was stated by the President of the Board of Control, in a speech delivered by him in the House of Commons, on Friday night last, that the proprietors had nothing else to do, but to look to the receipt of their dividend; that they had no right to trouble themselves about the revenues of India, how it was expended, or what grants were charged upon it. In fact, the speech of the right hon. gentleman went to this point, that the Court of Proprietors was to be considered as a mere nullity. That being the case, he believed that he was perfectly correct in rising at that moment, for the purpose of bringing the subject under the consideration of the Court, the more especially as he considered it to be one that very materially concerned their rights and privileges. If they were to submit to be spoken of by any of his Majesty's ministers, in the terms in which it appeared Sir John Hobhouse did speak of them on Friday night last —if this were to be submitted to without observation or reprehension—then he would say that their functions were gone, and there was no longer any use to be derived from their meeting in that court. He should now speak of the report to which he alluded, as it had appeared in a public paper.

Sir *J. R. Carnac*—In what paper?

Sir *C. Forbes* said, he held the *Times* in his hand; but, what perhaps would be more satisfactory to his hon. friend, he had the *Morning Chronicle* in his pocket (*laughter*). The hon. baronet then handed the extract from the *Times* to the clerk, who read as follows:—

" The hon. gentleman had referred to the decision of the Court of Proprietors, but he (Sir J. Hobhouse) must say, that that decision did not carry, in his opinion, much weight with it. They were not a fit body to entertain a question of the kind. They had no power over the revenues of the Indian empire, and the source of their incomes would not be at all affected by the decision of such claims as this, one way or the other. He doubted very much that the interpretation put by his hon. colleague (Lord Glenelg) on the Act of Parliament was correct. He thought that the Court of Proprietors, strictly speaking, had no right to discuss questions of this kind."

Sir *P. Laurie* said, he should like to have the passage from Sir John Hobhouse's speech read from the other paper also,—he could not be satisfied with the report of one paper only.

Sir *C. Forbes*—There is much more to be read yet.

The clerk then proceeded with the extract:—

" He (Sir J. Hobhouse) begged to assure the hon. gentleman opposite, that there was not a single instance where commanders who had gone in Company's ships five voyages, had afterwards taken up freighted ships. What the act of Parliament intended to guard against was, the infliction of prospective loss on any individuals. They had nothing whatever to do with the former circumstances of these gentlemen; all that the Board of Control had to inquire was, whether their claim could have a prospective force. It was just possible that they might have again been called into service; but he had no control over that. They had derived all the advantage they had a right to expect from employment in the Company's service, and, being in possession of that, they had no right to attempt to prove a prospective loss, on which ground alone they had any claim to compensation. He contended that the arguments advanced in support of the claim were founded on a total misapprehension of the act of Parliament. His hon. friend was quite mistaken if he supposed that Parliament could exercise any power in granting compensation, or in any particular, except in distributing it. If they were to undertake the settlement of the various claims which were urged by individuals, the time of the house would be entirely taken up in considering them. He had given the most careful attention to this case, as well as to all that had come before him, and if he could fancy for a moment that injustice had been done, he would not hesitate to reconsider it. But he conceived that Lord Ellenborough was right; that the gentlemen concerned had not proved a prospective loss; and that, not having proved it, they had no right to claim compensation. The argument pressed by the hon. member for Essex in favour of the claim was, that other parties had received sums of money, not as pensions, but gratuities, larger, perhaps, than those gentlemen would think it just to claim. He replied, that he was not responsible for the scale on which those gratuities were granted. It was, in his opinion, an extremely improvident one. (" *Hear, hear!*" from Sir C. Forbes.) Any gentleman who could prove that there would have been a certainty of his being employed as captain of a Company's ship, not having been so previously, was entitled to a gratuity of £5,000, and a pension of £200 a-year, that is, for giving up his chance of the advantage to be derived from five voyages, he was entitled to what was equivalent to £7,000. His hon. friend admitted that the profits, on an average of five voyages, did not amount to a great deal more than £7,000. He thought the compensation was unnecessarily large; but, comparing it with the alleged amount of profit, certainly no ground of complaint could be advanced by the parties. He had to apologize to the house for entering into this detail; but he thought he had made out such a case as proved he had come to a correct decision, and that this was not a case which Parliament should consider, or in which the House of Commons ought in any way to reverse the decision to which the Commissioners for Managing the Affairs of India had, after due deliberation, arrived."

Now, he had the *Morning Chronicle* report in his possession. It was substantially the same, but was not so fully given as in the *Times;* and he had heard, from gentlemen who were present on the occasion under the gallery of the House of Commons, that the report in the *Times* was most correct. Indeed, it appeared on the face of it, and from the course adopted by Sir John Hobhouse, that such was the line of argument he was likely to take up. The decision of the Court of Proprietors was treated as a matter of no importance, and he supposed that the decision of the Court of Directors would be looked upon as worth little more. It would appear, indeed, according to the doctrine laid down, that the

Government alone had the power of acting with reference to grants of money out of the Indian revenues. Such, at least, was the interpretation which must be put upon Sir J. Hobhouse's speech, in which the acts of the Proprietors were treated as if good for nothing—as if they were not recognized by law. In fact, he thought that he had not for a long time seen, in a speech which occupied so short a space, a greater number of offensive observations, than were contained in the speech of Sir J. Hobhouse. Before he proceeded to offer a very few remarks on the situation in which they were placed, he would endeavour to shew, and, he trusted, successfully, that Sir J Hobhouse was entirely wrong in his assertion. He might be again permitted to observe, with respect to the speech, that there were gentlemen present under the gallery when it was delivered, who spoke to the general correctness of the report of the *Times.* Indeed, the general accuracy of the reports in that paper, and their perfect impartiality, was a sufficient guarantee for the fact in this instance. How, then, was he to deal with the speech to which he had alluded? He thought that the best way would be, to place in opposition to the speech of the President of the Board of Control, certain by-laws of the Company, founded on Acts of Parliament. The by-laws to which he referred were very short; he should, therefore, read them, and thus their letter and spirit might be at once compared with the statement contained in the speech of Sir J. Hobhouse. He would first call their attention to the by-laws, cap. 6, sec. 17. It set forth,

" *Item, it is ordained,* That no new office, either at home or abroad, shall be created by the Directors, with any salary exceeding the sum of 200*l.* per annum, without the approbation of two General Courts, to be summoned for that purpose."

And yet (said Sir C. Forbes) they were told by Sir John Hobhouse. that the Proprietors of East-India Stock had not, " strictly speaking," a right to discuss questions of this kind, which had for their object the granting of sums of money. What, he would ask, was that by-law meant for, except as a check on the Court of Directors, a check which was very properly placed in the hands of the Proprietors. The Court of Directors could not. without the approbation of the Court of Proprietors, make such a grant as that by-law contemplated. No not even with the sanction of the Board of Control; a sanction which, he was sorry to say, had been lately obtained for grants of money, before those grants were submitted to the Proprietors. Again; he would refer to the by-law, cap. 6, sec. 18, which ran thus.

(2 B)

" *Item, it is ordained,* That no additional salary, exceeding in the whole two hundred pounds per annum, shall be annexed to any office, without the approbation of two General Courts, to be summoned for that purpose."

Now, he thought that this was very strong. That by-law, like the proceeding, was founded on the Act of Parliament. The statute expressly admitted their right to deal with these grants; and, looking thus to the provision contained in the by-laws, founded, as they were, on the enactments of the Legislature, he was astonished that any one could tell the proprietors that they had no right " strictly speaking," (be it remembered) to discuss questions of this nature. He should now advert to cap. 6, sec. 19, which said—

' " *Item, it is ordained,* That every resolution of the Court of Directors for granting a new pension, or an increase of pension, exceeding in the whole 200*l.* per annum, to any one person, shall be laid before, and approved by, two General Courts, specially summoned for that purpose, before the same shall be submitted to the Board of Commissioners for the Affairs of India, in the form of a report, stating the grounds upon which such grant is recommended, which resolution and report shall be signed by such Directors as approve the same : and that the documents upon which such resolution may have been formed, shall be open to the inspection of the Proprietors from the day on which public notice has been given of the proposed grant; and that such allowances, in the nature of superannuations, as the Court of Directors are empowered to grant to their officers and servants in England, by 53 Geo. III., cap. 155, sec. 93, shall be laid before the next General Court."

Here was another confirmation of his argument. But again, what said cap. 6, sec. 20? It was there set forth—

" *Item, it is ordained,* That every resolution of the Court of Directors for granting to any person, by way of gratuity, any sum of money, exceeding in the whole 600*l.*, shall be laid before, and approved by, two General Courts, specially summoned for that purpose, in the form of a report, stating the grounds upon which such grant is recommended, which resolution and report shall be signed by such Directors as approve the same : and that the documents on which such resolution may have been formed, shall be open to the inspection of the Proprietors, from the day on which public notice has been given of the proposed grant."

Now, having said thus much, he thought that it was quite unnecessary for him to advance anything further, for the purpose of impressing the Court with the propriety of impugning and resisting any declaration that called in question the power of the Proprietors to entertain and to discuss any proposition, having for its object the grant of money to individuals. He trusted that the Court of Proprietors would strenuously maintain their by-laws. If they did not he would say again, as he had often said before, that their meeting there was really nothing more than a farce! He confidently hoped, however, that they would firmly maintain their rights; (*Hear, hear!*) and farther, that the Court of Directors would assist them in maintaining and supporting those rights.

(*Hear, hear!*) They were bound to call on the Court of Directors to support them; since, on many occasions, the Directors had found their best bulwark against the incursions of the crown, through the medium of ministers, in the earnest support which they received from the Court of Proprietors. (*Hear, hear!*) If the Directors and Proprietors agreed together, then he should like to see any of his Majesty's ministers daring to act on the principles laid down in the speech to which he had referred. Taking the report of that speech to be correct, it contained a gross attack upon their privileges. —He did not hear the speech delivered; but, looking to the acknowledged correctness of the reports in the *Times*— looking also to the fact that he had spoken to gentlemen who were under the gallery and in the gallery when the speech was delivered—(and he believed that he might point to some of the Directors, who had also heard Sir J. Hobhouse on the occasion)—he could not come to any other conclusion but that the right hon. gentleman had uttered the sentiments imputed to him; but it was evident to him, that that right hon. gentleman, in stating his idea of the law, and of the application of acts of parliament, had made a very great mistake. He could not suppose that that right hon. gentleman was acquainted with all the facts of the case on which he was speaking, and the bearing of the law upon it, or he never would have made such a statement; and it was proper that the right hon. gentleman's views of the matter should be strongly and decidedly contradicted; for the doctrine laid down by him was (so far as their rights were affected) of a very dangerous nature;— that doctrine being, that the Proprietors had no right to interfere with the appropriation of the Indian revenues, in the granting of pensions and gratuities. Indeed, he had heard that the Court of Directors and the Board of Control had already taken upon themselves to grant, not a vote of £600, but of £8,000, without coming to the Court of Proprietors for their approbation—without calling on them for their sanction. For what purpose was that grant made? Why to throw it away upon the Euphrates job—upon that silly steamnavigation project. What! were the Directors to be restricted under the by-laws from giving away a sum of £600 and were they, at the same time, to be at liberty to appropriate thousands without the sanction of the Court of Proprietors? If they proceeded thus, where was the act of parliament to justify such a proceeding? Yet he heard that the Directors had actually granted

£8,000 towards that wild goose scheme; and that, too, in addition to £6,000 formerly lent on the security of the machinery, which would never be forth-coming, making a sum total of £14,000, which they might as well have thrown into the sea.   Now if this were really the case—if such a sum were granted with-out any application to that Court—then indeed it would appear that Sir J. Hob-house had some ground for thinking that the Court of Proprietors had nothing to do with the application of the Company's funds.   If the Court of Directors and the Board of Control could thus give away £14,000, without the sanction of the Proprietors, then, perhaps, it might be said, that they had nothing to do with the compensation to be granted to meri-torious individuals who had applied for remuneration; and whose application was rejected by the Board of Control, after having been unanimously approved of by the Court of Directors and the Court of Proprietors.   He here alluded par-ticularly to the case of Captains Newell, Glasspoole, and Barrow.   The claims of those officers had obtained the sanc-tion of both the Directors and the Pro-prietors, for they came under the plain and fair construction of the regulations under which compensation was to be granted.   They demanded, and were entitled to, £200 a year each, making in the whole £600 per annum.   Now, that £14,000, which was to be squan-dered in the manner he had mentioned, would have been sufficient to purchase an annuity of £600 for those meritorious officers whose claims had been rejected by the Board of Control.   He hoped, however, that justice would yet be done to them, and that the matter would be hereafter introduced as a subject well worthy the consideration of the Court. The question was, as he said before, whether the Court of Proprietors were to be put down in this manner by the Government, and to be told, forsooth, that they had nothing to do with their own financial concerns.   He did not agree in the view taken by the president of the Board of Control, as to the case of these officers, or as to his interpretation of the act of parliament.   In his opinion, the decision and judgment of Lord Glenelg, which had been impugned by Sir J. Hob-house, were correct, and those of Lord Ellenborough, on the other hand, appear-ed to him to be erroneous.   He left it, however, to Sir J. Hobhouse to defend as he best could the opinions which he had laid down.   He did not mean to conclude with any motion, but he had felt it necessary to draw the attention of the Proprietors to a case vitally affecting their rights and privileges.

Mr. *Wigram.*—" I am really surprised that the hon. Chairman has not long be-fore this called the hon. bart to order. The hon. bart. has been proceeding to ad-dress us at great length, without any question being before the court.   If the hon. bart. had any motion to make, he should have waited till the business of the Court had terminated; he would then have been regular in proceeding.   But the course he has taken is perfectly irregu-lar.   I thought that the hon. Chairman would have suggested to the hon. bart. that he was entirely out of order, and that he ought to have postponed his observa-tions till the regular business was at an end."

Mr. *Mills* said, that as there was no question before the court, the hon. bart. could not regularly go on.   As the sub-ject was however of importance, it might be introduced at the close of the business.

Sir C. *Forbes* conceived that he was perfectly right in introducing this impor-tant subject at the present moment. The hon. Chairman had announced when the warrants would be ready for their dividend, and therefore he had taken that opportunity, as the subject was one which related to the Company's revenues, to introduce it then.

Mr. *Weeding* said, he was much obliged to the hon. Chairman for having dispensed with the formality of calling the hon. bart. to order.   There was what might be called a money declaration, though not a motion, before the court, and therefore he considered the present to be a fit time to notice such a subject as this.   If the re-port which had been quoted were correct —if it could be substantiated, then he thought that his Majesty ought to be called on to remove from his councils the gentleman who had asserted such an opinion; because it was evidently a blow at the rights and privileges of the Pro-prietors.   He knew very well that vague words, spoken in warmth and haste, could often be softened down and explained; but to say that the Proprietors had nothing to do with the appropriation of the Com-pany's revenue was most preposterous, and ought not to pass unnoticed.

Mr. *Mills* said, that they could not be certain whether any such declaration had been made or not.   The words were said to have been spoken in Parliament,—a fact which, at present, they had no means of accurately ascertaining.   He would say, that if such an assertion had been made, it was in direct violation of an ex-press act of Parliament.

Mr. *Weeding* said, he felt himself called upon to notice the statement which had been brought before them by the honour-able baronet.   He cared not whether it was spoken at Charing Cross or elsewhere. He viewed it as a declaration of a minister of the crown, and as such they ought to deal with it. Had they not a right to examine the justice of an opinion delivered by a minister of the crown—by a responsible officer? They had a right to inquire whether that minister held such an opinion as was described; which they knew, if acted on, would involve a vital breach of their privileges. He called on the hon. Director who had last spoken, knowing as he did that hon. Director was alive to the importance of public opinion, to allow the Proprietors to proceed in the course they were then pursuing. He thought it would be proper that the President of the Board of Control should be asked whether he really did make any declaration of this nature; but, in the mean time, he conceived that it was the duty of the Proprietors to express a strong opinion upon what had gone abroad. By former acts of Parliament, a gratuity of £600 could not be granted unless approved of by that Court. By that rule they had heretofore been guided, and sorry and ashamed would he be if they ever departed from it, under any pretext whatever. The honourable baronet had adverted to a grant of £8,000 for steam navigation. That he believed was a perfectly legal grant, for the purpose stated. It was, in fact, a part of the Government expenditure, and was as much a charge, to be included within that expenditure, as the cost of fitting out the steam-boat to Bombay; because those who administered the affairs of the Indian government were authorized to expend money at their discretion, for such purposes as that government deemed necessary. He agreed with the hon. baronet as to the folly of the expedition in furtherance of which the sum of £8,000 was granted; but he denied that the grant was in any respect illegal. The Government said, "here is an experiment set on foot, and as there is some hope of its succeeding, we will bear part of the expense;" and this they had an undoubted right to do. There was another matter, with respect to which he disagreed from the honourable baronet. He said that Lord Glenelg—

Mr. *Marriott*—"I rise to order. I do feel, and the Court must feel, that the whole of this proceeding is uncalled-for and irregular."

Mr. *Weeding* said, he did not conceive that he was out of order, and he requested the honourable proprietor to allow him to proceed, as he felt himself called on to do, without interruption.

Mr. *Wigram* said, he would listen with a great deal of pleasure to the honourable proprietor, if he would confine himself within the rules of order, and state his sentiments at a proper time. There was at present no question before the Court; there was merely a communication before the Court, on which there could be no vote, and no debate. The honourable baronet, however, had thought fit to get up, and having observed on a speech attributed to Sir J. Hobhouse, he then went to the case of Captain Glasspoole, and finally introduced the Euphrates expedition. He should be very glad to hear these questions discussed—not then, but when the question was moved " that this Court do now adjourn." He, therefore, called on the honourable proprietor, for the sake of order, to allow them to finish the business upon which they were summoned. (*Hear, hear!*) After that was disposed of, no man would be more willing than himself to hear the honourable proprietor. (*Hear, hear!*)

Sir *C. Forbes* said, that he introduced this subject as a question deeply affecting the rights and privileges of the Company; and he thought that the Court ought to be obliged to him, instead of censuring him, for taking the earliest opportunity to bring it before them.

Mr. *Fielder* said, he thought that the honourable baronet would have been wanting in his duty, if he had not come forward and stated the fact, that a minister of the crown had, in another place, made such a declaration as they had heard. (Cries of *Hear, hear!* and *Order.*)

The "*Chairman.*—The honourable director who lately spoke, has stated with perfect correctness, that there is no question before the Court, and that therefore, the whole of this discussion is out of order. When the honourable baronet rose, I submitted to him that there was no question before the Court, and therefore that that was not the proper time for him to make his observations. The honourable baronet, however, proceeded to address the Court; and unwilling as I always am to interrupt any honourable proprietor, I acceded to his wishes, though it was not in order to do so. It will be competent to him, or to any other honourable proprietor, to make what observations he pleases, when the question of adjournment is before the Court; and, therefore, I trust that the discussion will now be suffered to terminate." (*Hear, hear!*)

BY-LAWS.

The *Chairman.*—"I have now to acquaint the Court that it is ordained by the by-laws, sec. 2, cap. 3, that the by-laws shall be read in the first General Court after every annual election."

The by-laws were then read short, *pro forma.*

The *Chairman.*—" I have now the ho-noor to acquaint the Court, that it is made special for the purpose of receiving a report from the Committee appointed to inspect the East-India Company's By-laws, proposing an alteration in one of the said laws."

Mr. *Twining* (being called on as Chairman of the Committee of By-laws) presented the Report of that Committee, which was read as follows:—

The Committee appointed to inspect the East-India Company's By-laws, and to make enquiry into the observance of them, and to consider what alteration it may be proper to make therein, have proceeded to the discharge of their duty, and have agreed to the following Report—

The result of the enquiry instituted by your Committee, affords them the satisfaction of being enabled to report to the General Court, that the By-laws have been duly observed and executed during the past year.

In consequence of the consolidation of the offices of Secretary and Financial Secretary, your Committee have had under consideration the By-law chapter 12, relating to the custody of the Company's seal, and they beg to recommend to the General Court, that the words "Examiner of India Correspondence," be substituted for the words "Financial Secretary," in the said By-law.

The By-law, as altered, will then be as follows; viz.—

"*Item, it is ordained,* That the common seal of this corporation shall be kept under three locks. That the key of one of the said locks shall be kept by the Chairman or Deputy Chairman for the time being; that the key of another of the said locks shall be kept by the Secretary or his Assistant; and that the key of the third lock shall be kept by the Examiner of India Correspondence or his Assistant. That in case of the indispensable absence of the Chairman and Deputy Chairman, they be authorized to place their key in the custody of such other officer as they may select for that purpose, and that the said seal shall not be set to any writing or instrument, but by an order of the Court of Directors, first had for that purpose; and in the unavoidable absence of the Chairman and Deputy Chairman, not to be affixed but in the presence of the Secretary and the Examiner of India Correspondence, or their respective Assistants, and of the officer who may be in charge of the Chairman and Deputy Chairman's key."

(Signed)   RICHARD TWINING. -
         JOHN CARSTAIRS.
         JAMES SHAW.
         JOHN HODGSON.
         WILLIAM BURNIE.
         ALEXANDER ANNAND.
         A. W. ROBARTS.
         J. WOOLMORE.
         LEWIS LOYD.

East-India House, 19th May 1836.

The Report having been read,

The *Chairman* said, "I beg to move that the said by-law, as proposed to be altered, be approved, subject to the confirmation of another General Court."

The motion, which was seconded by the Deputy Chairman (John Loch, Esq.) was agreed to unanimously.

The *Chairman.*—"I have next to state that it is ordained by the by-law, cap.3, sec.1, that at the General Court to be held in the month of June, a committee of fifteen shall be elected, for the inspection of the by-laws."

The *Chairman* then proceeded to propose, *seriatim,* the members who composed the committee last year, viz.

Richard Twining, Esq.
Robert Williams Esq.
Benjamin Barnard, Esq.
Sir Henry Strachey, Bart.
John Carstairs, E-q.
Sir James Shaw, Bart.
William Burnie, Esq.
John Hodgson, Esq.
Abraham Wilday Robarts, Esq.
Sir John Woolmore.
William Gill Paxton, Esq.
Lewis Loyd, Esq.
Edward Goldsmid, Esq.
Colonel Blackburne.
Alexander Annand, Esq.

Sir *C. Forbes* asked whether Sir H. Strachey attended regularly, or whether any intimation had been given of his intention to resign.

The *Chairman* said, he had received no communication as to the hon. baronet's reluctance to serve on the committee.

Mr. *Twining* said, that Sir H. Strachey had expressed a wish to make himself as serviceable as possible, and had been regular in his attendance.

Sir *C. Forbes* said, that in his opinion such members of the committee as did not attend regularly, ought to withdraw.

The *Chairman* said, he was not aware of any gentleman not attending. Of course, on a vacancy occurring, in consequence of the death or resignation of a member, it was open to any proprietor to propose any gentleman he might think proper.

Sir *C. Forbes* said, in his opinion, it would be better if the members were elected generally from the body of the court, instead of being re-elected in this manner from year to year.

The whole of the committee was re-elected without a dissenting voice.

The *Chairman* then moved that the Court do adjourn.

Mr. *Mills* said, that the Court were much indebted to the hon. Bart. (Sir C. Forbes) for having brought this subject under the notice of the court, as it was one in which they were greatly interested. He thought that if the observations attributed to the right hon. bart, had been really used by him, he need not be slow to acknowledge them; and if he did admit that he had used them, it could not be denied that he had made a most serious attack on the rights and privileges of the whole body of proprietors. It scarcely was necessary for him to add, that if that spirit existed amongst the proprietors which he believed did exist, they would not be slow in asserting their independence, and in doing so he was sure they might calculate upon the cordial aid and support of the gentlemen at that (the Directors') side of the bar. (*Hear, hear!*) The Directors felt that without the support of the proprietors, they would be useless as a body, and be placed in a position in which they could not discharge their duties. They would, in fact, be little more than a body to record the acts of the Board of Control. (*Hear, hear!*) If this was the intention of the right hon. bart. and of the government, it would be much better that it should be openly avowed; that the directors and proprietors might know what course to take. If the government intended that the Company should be mere ciphers and exercise no control over the affairs of India, it ought to be avowed, so that the Company should take those measures which would bring the question of their rights to an issue. He was sure that the Company would not give up their rights tamely —they would not allow them to be frittered away by the dictum of any individual, however high in rank or station. (*Hear, hear!*) All he desired was, that the opinions of those who made so light of the rights and privileges of the Company should be openly avowed; the proprietors would then know what course to take.

Sir P. Laurie said, he was sure there must be some mistake as to the observations of the right hon. bart. (Sir J. Hobhouse), but, however, the Court of Directors must know from their communications with the right hon. bart. as president of the Board of Control, whether the opinions attributed to him in the report of his speech in the House of Commons, were consistent with those which he expressed to the Directors. If he did express himself as he was reported to have done, no doubt he would avow it; but until it was explained, there could be no doubt that a serious attack had been made on the rights and privileges of the proprietors.

Mr. Weeding hoped that an opportunity would be given to Sir John C. Hobhouse to express his regret, either that he was mistaken in what he said, or that he was mis-reported. He (Mr. Weeding) could scarcely believe that the right hon. baronet had expressed himself in the terms in which he had been reported: but be that as it might, an opportunity would occur for the right hon. bart. to state what it was he did mean. The great importance of our East-India colonies to this country was now admitted on all hands. By the manner in which those colonies were governed —a government which was an anomaly of itself—a government directed by twenty-four gentlemen selected from the middle classes; there was secured to England a domination over a larger portion of the human race than ever belonged before to any country in the world as a mother country over colonies. From a state of semi-barbarism, or at least from a state of half civilization, there was raised a civilized colony; in fact, a paradise was

raised out of a desert, and a degree of civilization was given to heretofore uncivilized countries, which probably would last to the end of the world. Was it not, then, he would ask, most important that the power and the form of government which had produced those happy results, should be continued? The government of our East-India possessions as regarded this country, partook more of a republican character than any other form of government of the present day; it had achieved its great object; it brought a hundred millions of men under the control of law; it had imparted to them the means of well regulated social intercourse. Why then, let him ask, should that system of government which had produced so many good effects, be now disturbed for another system of which they had no experience? He differed widely from the right hon. bart. (Sir. J. C. Hobhouse) on another point, in which the right hon. bart. appeared to think that his predecessors in office were improvident in their allowance of pensions and compensation to others employed in the Company's maritime service; he thought this was a slur on the predecessors of the right hon. bart. which was by no means justifiable. The right hon. bart. seemed to think that there was no prospective loss: but he seemed to forget that those captains who had some voyages to go, would have been benefited by those voyages. He made no distinction between those who had got compensation, and those who had a clear right to get it.

Mr. Wigram said, that he could not allow this discussion to close without offering a few words. Of the observations of the right hon. bart. in the House of Commons he could know nothing personally, as he was not a member of the house, and was not present at the discussion, but if he were to take for granted the correctness of the observations attributed to the right hon. bart., there could be no doubt that they involved a serious attack upon the rights and privileges of the Company; this was not the first occasion on which the right hon. bart. had said that which was an infringement upon the rights of the Company, and what was in fact directly illegal. The right hon. bart was decidedly opposed to the opinions given by Lord Glenelg as to the powers and privileges of the Company; he (Mr. Wigram) took a totally different view of the case, for he thought that the Court of Proprietors had the right to discuss and give their opinion upon all matters connected with the expenditure of the Company. When he expressed his opinion against that of Sir John Hobhouse, he must also say that he thought the opinion of Lord Ellenborough when president of the Board of Control, was equally hostile to the rights and privileges of the Company. From the letters of Mr. C. Grant, (now Lord Glenelg,) to the Company, and from the letters to Sir J. Malcolm, there could be no doubt that all the rights and privileges of the Proprietors were to be continued the same as they had been before the passing of the bill; the Proprietors had the same right to meet and discuss all questions of expenditure in that room, as they had under their former charter. The letter of Mr. C. Grant said, "I must however add, in reference to this subject, that while the government deeply feel the obligation of providing for every fair and just claim that can be preferred on the part of the proprietors, it is from other and higher considerations that they are led to attach peculiar value to that part of their plan, which places the proprietors on Indian security. The plan allots to the proprietary body important powers and functions in the administration of Indian affairs; and in order to ensure their properly exercising such powers and functions, his Majesty's ministers deem it essential that they shall be linked and bound in point of interest, to the country which they are to assist in governing." The measure, therefore, of connecting them immediately with the territory of India, is evidently not an incidental or immaterial; but a vital condition of the arrangement: and in proportion as this condition is dispensed, the advantages of the arrangement are sacrificed. If the proprietors are to look to England rather than to India, for the security of their dividend, their interest in the good government of India, and consequently their fitness as one of the principal organs of Indian government, will in the same degree be impaired. He differed from his hon. friend (Sir C. Forbes) in one point; for there was no doubt that if the right hon. bart. Sir C. Hobhouse had refused the sanction of the Board of Control to certain propositions of the Court, be had an equally good right to state the reasons on which he grounded that refusal. No doubt the right hon bart. had the right to state what was his opinion on the subject: but if what he said was correct, the constituent body of the Company would be worse than useless; it would be mischievous, and the Directors and Proprietors could appear only as the agents of the government of India; for his own part, he would rather give up his situation as a director, and let the whole of the affairs of India be managed under the responsibility of the government, than consent to have a nominal power given to the Company, where no efficient exercise of that power was permitted. On this point he might quote the letter of Mr. Charles Grant to the Chairman, in which he alluded to that part of the late bill, in which it was

the intention of government to continue the powers of the proprietary body. In that letter the right hon. gentleman stated, that it was the intention of government to connect and bind up the interests of the Company with the country which they were to assist in governing. The right hon. gentleman added, that if the Company looked to this country rather than to India for the payment of their dividends, their interest in the government of that country would, to a great extent, cease; but if they were to look to India for the payment of those dividends, their interests would be bound up with those of that country. These were the sentiments of the right hon. gentleman, Mr. C. Grant, and it was to be fairly presumed they were the sentiments of the government with which he was then connected; and it was not unreasonable to infer that they were also the opinions of the present government; and if that were so, he was not unreasonable in assuming that the opinions of the right hon. baronet were incorrectly given, or that if they were correctly reported, the right hon. baronet himself was mistaken in what he said. If, however, what was reported of the right hon. baronet were correct, all he had to say upon it was, that the Company might as well at once give up their nominal powers, for they had no real power to interfere in the government of India. He would be no party to such a proposition; he would resist it to the utmost of his power in that court; for he was firmly convinced that the principle assumed by the right. hon. baronet was decidedly illegal.

Mr. *Twining* said, it was not usual in that court, nor did he know there was any precedent for founding any of their proceedings on the reports of debates in newspapers. He fully agreed in the sentiments expressed by the hon. baronet (Sir C. Forbes), as to every thing connected with the interests of our Indian possessions, and as to the right of the Company to interfere, and to exercise its authority in every matter connected with those interests; —but, at the same time he must say, that the Court ought not to take any step upon the mere newspaper report of what had been said by Sir John Hobhouse, or any other member of Parliament. For his own part, he could not believe that it was the intention of the Government, in the late bill, to take away the authority of the Court of Proprietors, in matters relating to the government of India; and, as to the opinion of Sir J. Hobhouse, as stated in the report mentioned by the honourable baronet, he would only observe, that in the confusion that frequently took place in the discussions in the House of Commons, it would be wrong to rely on the reports of the proceedings. Gifted and able as he admitted the reports for the daily press in that house were—and he admitted to the fullest extent the talents and abilities which they displayed—and, even adding the authority of persons who were placed under the gallery in support of the correctness of those reports, still he must say, that the reports were not authorities on which that Court could rely in founding any proceedings. If, however, he should find, from any official communication, or from any document which could be considered official, that Sir John C. Hobhouse had asserted and laid down those principles which were attributed to him in the report, be had no doubt that that Court would soon be crowded with Proprietors, ready and anxious to defend their rights—rights which they held under the express authority of an act of Parliament, and which nothing less than another act of Parliament could abrogate. In the mean time, he thought that this conversation should drop, and that the Court should not found any resolution upon a mere newspaper report. He was sorry to find that the Board of Control had not admitted the principle which the Court of Proprietors had agreed on, as to the compensation of some of its maritime officers; but he admitted that the present was not the time for discussing that question, and he hoped that no further notice would be now taken of it.

Mr. *Weeding*, adverting to what had been said on the assimilation of the sugar duties, observed, that the great increase of the culture of sugar in our Indian possessions had resulted from the encouragement given to that culture in the year 1822. There was no doubt that the encouragement of that culture would be most important to India, and he was sure that the Directors would give their attention to that important branch of East-India produce. He trusted also that they would direct their attention to other matters connected with East-India produce, such as the growth of cotton-wool, and the culture of silk and indigo, and other valuable productions of our East-India possessions. If the Court would allow him, he would submit a motion; or if there was any objection, he would give it as a notice; but he should wish to move that the Court of Directors be requested to give their attention to the culture of cotton-wool, and also to the culture of silk and indigo, and the other produce of India, with the view to promote an increase in the growth and quality of those articles.

Colonel *Sykes* said, he would support the motion of his hon. friend. From his own experience he could state, that where attention had been given to the culture of cotton-wool in India, it had been followed by great success. In Calcutta, Mr. Pen-

drick had embarked a large capital in the growth of cotton; he had cultivated the Orleans cotton, and had been so successful in its cultivation that his cotton sold for 19½d. per lb.; and Mr. Pendrick stated, that if proper attention were paid to the culture of cotton, it might be produced in India to any extent that the consumption of this country required. It was said that American cotton plants, when grown in India, deteriorated in quality; this, however, was disproved by the experiments made by the gentleman to whom he alluded. In some parts where the Orleans cotton had been planted, the tide flowed in and swept away many of the plants; but some knolls had remained, and, after a lapse of fourteen years, when nobody thought the plants could be productive, they had shot out, and produced a large crop of cotton, equal in quantity and quality to any American cotton. He trusted that these circumstances would induce the Directors to give their attention to this subject.

Mr. *St. George Tucker* assured the court, that the Directors had not been inattentive to this subject; he himself had published a paper on the matter, in which he would not say there was much information, but, at all events, the reception it had met showed that the Court of Directors was not inattentive to the improvement of the culture of cotton, as well as the other produce of our Indian possessions. Under the direction of the court, cotton seeds of all kinds had been sent out to India. Improved machinery had also been sent there. Rewards had been offered for improved culture, and such other encouragements had been given for the growth of cotton, that he was led to hope, that at no very distant day the Company might compete with the United States of America in the produce of that article. Such steps had been taken to improve the cultivation of cotton in India, that he hoped that we might soon, not only rival other countries in the production of that article, but that it might also be made the means of affording larger remittances from India; and he likewise trusted that the improved culture of silk and indigo might afford an increased means for those remittances.

Colonel *Sykes*, in explanation, observed, that he did not impute any want of attention to the subject to the Court of Directors; on the contrary, he had reason to believe that they had given their attention to the subject.

Sir *C. Forbes* said, that cotton plants which were laid in the ground thirty years ago at Bombay, had sold at half-a-crown a pound, which was higher than any American cotton; and he had no doubt that, if pains were taken to improve the culture of cotton, the effect would be, that many tracts of land which were now barren might be improved to a paradise.

The *Chairman* said, that the Court of Directors had paid a great deal of attention to this subject, and they were willing to give every information which they had collected respecting it. The honourable proprietor had moved, that the Court of Directors be requested to give their atten-tion to the matter, and that they should investigate it. Now they had investigated the subject fully, and he would suggest to the hon. gentleman, that he should alter his motion to this effect, that instead of investigating, the Directors should be requested to lay before the court the information which they had collected respecting the cultivation of cotton, silk, and indigo. The Court of Directors was most anxious to lay before the proprietors all the information they had collected on these points, and if the hon. proprietor would frame his motion so as to call for that information, he would not oppose it; but from the reduced state of the establishment, the documents might have been ready before now.

Mr. *Weeding* said, that he was glad to learn that the attention of the Directors had been called to this subject, and he was quite willing to frame his motion in the way which had been suggested by the hon. Chairman.

The following motion was then put and agreed to:

*Resolved:—*That the Court of Directors be requested to communicate to this court any information which they may possess regarding the production of cotton-wool and the culture and manufacture of silk and indigo in British India.

ATTENDANCE IN THE PROPRIETORS' ROOM.

Sir *C. Forbes* said that he had now to call the attention of the court to a subject which he considered of some importance. The hon. Chairman had just alluded to the reduced state of the Company's establishment, and, for his (Sir C. Forbes') part, he could not see why the Directors should incapacitate themselves by reductions, from being of that use to the Company which they could otherwise be. He believed that many of the reductions that had been made did not originate with the Directors themselves, but, in sanctioning those reductions, they lent themselves to a system which detracted from their utility. See how the proprietors suffered from these reductions. Look at the proprietors' room, and see the situation in which they had been placed; they had, on the ground of what he could not but call a very mistaken economy, been deprived of the services of a very able and efficient servant, who had for many years been in the Company's employment. He (Sir C. Forbes) went to-day to the proprietors' room, and asked for Mr. Sheppard, to whose zeal

Asiat.Journ. N.S. Vol. 20. No.79.

and ability in attending on the proprietors, and procuring them any documents for which they sought, he could bear testimony. When he entered, he saw a paper stuck on the glass, on which was written "Please to ring the bell." He did ring the bell, and one of the messengers made his appearance to know what it was he wanted. He said he wanted to see Mr. Sheppard: but was told that he was gone away, and was now residing in Aberdeen, having been pensioned off. Other proprietors came and rang the bell, and received a similar answer to their enquiries. Now he owned he could not see the propriety of such economy as that, which got rid of the service of a man so useful to the proprietors as Mr. Sheppard had been. The proprietors had a right to be attended in their room, and certainly no man could have been better fitted for that situation than Mr. Sheppard had been. He believed that that gentleman had been twenty years in the Company's service, and, at the time of his removal, was in the receipt of an income of £300 a-year. What sort of economy, he would ask, was it to get rid of his valuable services, in order to save one-third of his income? He did trust that the Directors would reconsider the subject, and recall a gentleman, whose services were so useful to the Company.

Mr. *Weeding* said, he could add his testimony to that of the hon. bart. as to the efficient services of Mr. Sheppard, who was on all occasions most active and most willing to give to the Proprietors every information which they required. He himself had had occasion recently to go to the proprietors' room to enquire for a particular document. He rang the bell, and a porter made his appearance, and in answer to his enquiries, said he would go to the Secretary's Office and call down one of the clerks. He did so, but on the arrival of the clerk, he seemed to know nothing whatever of the document which was required. He (Mr. Weeding) did not dispute the right of the Directors to make any arrangement they thought proper with respect to their clerks—but, without attempting to interfere with those arrangements, he did hope that the Court would reconsider the matter, and if it was not inconsistent with any rules they had laid down, that they would restore Mr. Sheppard to the situation which he had so ably filled.

Col. Sykes and two other proprietors also bore testimony to the zeal and ability with which Mr. Sheppard had discharged his duties in the Proprietors' room.

The *Chairman* was glad to hear so many testimonies borne to the efficiency of one who had been so long in the Company's service. With respect to Mr. Sheppard he should observe, that his removal came within a general rule for the removal of certain extra clerks, and he could not have

(2 C)

been retained without doing injustice to others. The clerk in the proprietors' room had not any thing to do for more than eight or nine months in the year, and it was thought that a person permanently to attend was not necessary, as a clerk from the Secretary's Office would attend when required. However, after such a general expression of the opinion of the proprietors on the subject, he would take the matter into consideration, and mention it to the Court of Directors. (*Hear, hear !*)

Mr. *Weeding* was glad to hear this expression from the hon. Chairman. He thought that the payment of an very efficient a servant of the Company, would be a much better application of the Company's funds, than spending £8,000 on the expedition to the Euphrates.

The Court then adjourned.

HOME INTELLIGENCE.

IMPERIAL PARLIAMENT.

House of Commons, *June 7.*

Mr. Buckingham's Case.—Mr. *Tulk* once more brought forward what are termed Mr. Buckingham's "claims," which were again opposed by the government and negatived by the house, by a majority of 92 against 66. Sir John Hobhouse alluded to the "threatening letters" which had been sent round the country on this subject.[*]

June 17.

Capts. Newall, Barrow and Glasspoole.— Mr. *Young* presented a petition from these gentlemen, complaining that the compensation to which they were entitled under the Act 3 and 4 of Will. IV., 84., had been withheld from them.

Sir *J. Hobhouse* said, that no man esteemed the value of the services of the officers of the East-India Company more than himself; but, having seen the petition, and inquired into the case of the individuals, he felt it his bounded duty to state, that they were not entitled to the compensation which they claimed.

Mr. *Young* gave notice of a motion for the 7th July, to refer the petition to a Select Committee, and it is to be hoped it will be acceded to.

June 22.

Sugar Duties.—Mr. S. *Rice*, in a Committee of Ways and Means, announced the intention of government to equalize the duty on East and West-India sugar, and that the equalization would not be gradual, but immediate.

MISCELLANEOUS.

STEAM NAVIGATION.

An experiment in steam navigation, on a grand scale, is about to be made under the direction, and at the sole expense of the East-India Company. Two vessels of the largest class have been for some time preparing, and are now nearly completed,

with which it is intended, at intervals of about a month each, that the voyage to Bengal shall be made by the Cape of Good Hope. The steam-engines of each vessel will be of two hundred horse power. Arrangements have been made for providing a supply of coals at stated places, for which 3,000 tons have been ordered, and they are said to be so well chosen as to allow the power of steam to be kept up with very little intermission during the whole distance. To what use these vessels are to be put at the termination of the voyage, does not appear to be yet fully settled.— *Times.*

THE CHINA TRADE.

On the 13th June, a meeting of the merchants and others connected with the importation of tea from China, was held at the City of London Tavern, for the purpose of receiving a report from those members of the East-India and China Association, who had had interviews with Government for the purpose of obtaining, if possible, an extension of the period fixed for the payment of the present duty upon Bohea teas. Mr. G. G. de H. Larpent took the chair. Mr. Palmer moved the appointment of a committee of twelve gentlemen, for the purpose of considering the best means of bringing the question before a committee of the House of Commons. Mr. Bates seconded the resolution, which was carried unanimously, and the committee was nominated.

THE PERSIAN PRINCES.

The three young Persian princes have made their *début* in the fashionable world. In the absence of any received envoy, however, from the court of Tehran, no arrangements have yet been completed for the introduction of the princes at court.

GAZETTE APPOINTMENTS.

John M'Neill, Esq. (whose appointment as His Majesty's Minister Plenipotentiary to the Shah of Persia, was notified in the Gazette of the 9th Feb. last) to be His Majesty's Envoy extraordinary and Minister Plenipotentiary to the Shah of Persia dated 25th May, 1836.

---

[*] A meeting took place on the 15th June at the Freemason's Hall, at which it was resolved to open a subscription to compensate Mr. Buckingham for his losses. Lord William Bentinck was present, and spoke in favour of the project.

INDIA SHIPPING.

Arrivals.

MAY 30. *Jane Elisa*, Jones, from South Seas; in the River.—JUNE 3. *Elisa*, Campbell, from Bengal 1st Jan.; off Penzance.—4. *Sarah and Elisabeth*, Swain, from South Seas; off Plymouth.—6. *Abercrombie Robinson*, Scott, from China 30th Jan.; *Neptune*, Stockley, from China 5th Feb.; both at Deal.—*Fairy Queen*, Douthwaite, from Ceylon 23d Jan., and Cape 16th March; in the River.—H. M. S. *Atholl*, Karley, from Cape 1st April, and St. Helena, 15th do.; at Portsmouth.—*Brankew Moor*, Honey, from Manilla 17th Nov.; off Swanage.—7. *Lady Ruffles*, Pollock, from Bombay 30th Jan., and Cape 7th April; off the Wight.—*Marquis of Huntly*, Mollison, from China 13th Feb.; off Brighton.—*Courier*, Palmer, from Cape 12th April; at Deal.—*Patriot King*, Clark, from China 20th Jan.; *William Thompson*, Wild, from Mauritius 7th Feb.; both at Bristol.—8. *Cœur de Lion*, Wamesley, from China 23d Jan., *Theodosia*, Coleman, from Bombay 20th Jan.; *Medora*, Dixon, from Bombay 20th Jan., and Cape 1st April; *Annandale*, Hill, from Madras 30th Jan.; *Faires Queen*, Holmes, from China 23d Jan.; all at Liverpool.- *William Barras*, Norie, from Mauritius, 20th Feb.; off Brighton.—*Brasbornebury*, Chapman, from Bengal 4th Feb.; off Portland.—*Ann Lockerby*, Johnstone, from China 22d Jan.; off Dover.—9. *Triumph*, Green, from Bombay 31st Jan., and Cape 4th April; at Deal.—*Vibilia*, Stephenson, from V. D. Land 6th Jan.; off Dover.—*Duke of Northumberland*, Pope, from Bengal 6th Feb.; *Mary Ann*, Tarbutt, from Madras 16th Feb., and Cape 7th April; both at Portsmouth.—10. *Norfolk*, Gatenby, from N. S. Wales 11th Feb.; *London*, M'Lean, from Bengal 27th Jan.; both at Liverpool.—*Lady Rowena*, Main, from Bombay 6th Feb.; off Holyhead.—*Margaretha*, Barcham, from Sourabaya; *Warren*, Creaton, from South Seas; *Fenella*, Bosworth, from Cape 27th March; all at Deal.—*Minerva*, Templer, from China 6th Feb.; off Lyme.—*Tyrer*, Ellis, from China 16th Jan.; off Dover.—*Diligence*, Boss, from Batavia; off the Wight.—11. *General Palmer*, Down, from China 22d Jan.; at Deal.—*Rubicon*, Lennington, from V. D. Land 29th Jan.; off Portsmouth.—*Urania*, Ainly, from China 19th Jan.; *Clifton*, Bushby, from Bombay 18th Jan.; both at Liverpool.—13. *Glenalvon*, Skinner, from Mauritius 28th Feb., and Cape 31st March; off Swanage.—*John Dennistoun*, M'Kie, from V. D. Land 19th Feb.; off Dover.—*Mary and Jane*, Winter, from Cape 18th March; in the River.—*Oriental*, Allen, from Bombay 1st Feb.; at Liverpool.—*James M'Inroy*, Cleland, from China 21st Jan. (for the Clyde); *Derwent*, Hewett, from China; *Clyde*, Kerr, from China 7th Feb., and Ascension 18th April; all off Cork.—15. *Macassar*, Poppin, from Batavia; off Dover.—*Isabella*, Robertson, from China 12th Jan.; at Leith.—16. *John Woodall*, Arnold, from Bengal 29th Jan.; off Liverpool.—17. *Atlas*, Hunt, from Mauritius 13th March, and Cape 13th April; off Penzance.—*Royal William*, Smith, from Mauritius 24th Feb.; off Holyhead.—*Enmore*, Swainson, from China 20th Jan.; off Cork.—*Colombo*, Mackellar, from Ceylon 15th Feb.; off Plymouth.—18. *Isabella*, Brown, from Bengal 17th Feb., and Cape 13th April; *Ann*, Vertue, from V. D. Land; both off Plymouth.—*Phenomene*, Hoed, from Batavia; off Dartmouth.—20. *Mary*, Jacks, from V. D. Land 29th Jan., and Rio de Janeiro; off Margate.—*Suffolk*, Smith, from Manilla 7th Feb.; at Cowes.—*George*, Oppenheim, from St. Helena 16th Jan., and Bahia 30th March; *Columbia*, Booth, from China, in Feb.; both at Deal.—22. *Fortune*, Lester, from N. S. Wales 5th Feb.; at Deal.—23. *Jessie*, Bell, from N. S. Wales 4 h March; at Liverpool.—24. *Marie Thereue*, Geoffry, from Batavia; off Scilly.

Departures.

MAY 24. *Elephanta*, Buchanan, for Bengal; from Greenock.—26. *Huddersfield*, Hall, for Bombay; from Liverpool.—27. *Hope*, M'Callum, for N. S. Wales; from Liverpool.—*Duchess of Northumberland*, Roxburgh, for N. S. Wales, with emigrants); from Cork.—28. *Agrippina*, Rodgers, for Ceylon; from Deal.—*Tarquin*, Hunt, for Batavia and China; from Liverpool.—29. *Cognac Packet*, Spittall, for Mauritius; *Jane*, Churchward, for N. S. Wales; both from Deal.—31. *Princess Charlotte*, M'Kean, for Bombay; *Alexander*, Penneger, for

China; both from Liverpool.—JUNE 1. *Jamaica*, Martin, for Bombay; from Greenock.—*Tory*, Reid, for Bombay; from Liverpool.—*Paragon*, Cooke, for Mauritius; from Bristol.—*Cumbrian*, Paul, for Johanna and Madagascar (with Company's coals; from Llanelly.—*Miranda*, Hopper, and *Ludlow*, Firth, both for Mauritius; from Deal—2. *Alice*, Scales, for Bengal; from Liverpool.—5. *Courier*, Dixon, for Cape (with troops); from Cork; *Fanny*, Taylor, for Manilla; from Liverpool.—6. *Norfolk*, Gildowny, for Mauritius; from Deal—8. *Mary Somerville*, Jackson, and *Africa*, Croughham, both for China; from Liverpool.—9. *Belhaven*, Crawford, and *Fatima*, Fethers, both for Bengal; from Liverpool.—11. *Arab*, Sparkes, for Bengal; *Lady Kenmuwry*, Davison, for N. S. Wales (with convicts); *Sea Witch*, Huson, for Cape; all from Deal.—13. *Repulse*, Pryce, for Madras and Bengal (with troops); from Torbay.—14. *Duke of Lancaster*, Hargraves, for Madras and Bengal; from Portsmouth.—14. *Heroine*, M'Carthy, for Cape, Madras, and Bengal; *Houghlay*, Bayley, for N. S. Wales; *Caroline*, Holmes, for Cape; *Captain Cook*, Brown, for N. S. Wales, via Dublin (with convicts); all from Deal.—*Columbia*, Hooton, for Bombay; and *Canton*, Garbutt, for Mauritius (with Company's coals); both from Llanelly.—15. *Thomas Grenville*, Thornhill, for Madras and Bengal; from Portsmouth.—*William*, Thomas, for Bengal; from Liverpool.—16. *Arab*, Lowe, for Singapore; from Liverpool.—*Arabian*, Brown, for Batavia and China; from Bristol.—17. *Esmouth*, Warren, for Madras and Bengal; *Margaret and Ann*, Buck, for Cape and Mauritius; both from Deal.—*Patriot King*, Clarke, for China; from Bristol.—18. *Roxburgh Castle*, Cumberland, for Madras and Benga; from Portsmouth.—*Manchester*, Hawkes, for Mauritius; from Deal.—*Ann Baldwin*, Crawford, for China; *James Matheson*, Milward, for Singapore; *Orleana*, Cameron, for Bombay; all from Liverpool.—*Renown*, M'Leod, for Mauritius; from Greenock.—19. *Annabella*, Anstruther, for Mauritius; from Deal.—20. *Bengal*, Marjoram, for Bombay; *Joshua Carroll*, Toby, for Cape and Swan River; both from Deal.—*William Jardine*, Highat, for Batavia and China; from Liverpool.—23. *Clifton*, Worsell; for China; from Deal.—26. *True Briton*, Beach, for Madras and Bengal, from Portsmouth.—*Richard Alsop*, M'Michael, for China; *Countess of Durham*, Todd. for N. S. Wales; *Velocity*, for Muscat; *Olive Branch*, Shirling, for Cape; all from Deal.—27 *Boyne*, Richardson, for Bombay (with Company's troops); *Pestonjee Bomanjee*, Thompson, for Bombay; *William Barras* Norrie, for Mauritius; *Florentia*, Deloitte, for N. S. Wales; *Elizabeth*, Austin, for ditto (with convicts); *Scotia*, for V. D. Land; all from Deal.

PASSENGERS FROM INDIA.

Per Clifton, from Ceylon: Mrs. Jeffery and two children; Mrs. Worsell.

Per Abercrombie Robinson, from China and St. Helena: Major and Mrs. Hunter; Capt. Gaskell.

Per Neptune, from St. Helena; Lieut. MacLane; Mr. James Matthews.

Per Fairy Queen, from Ceylon: Mr. and Mrs. Ackland; Mr. and Mrs. Mackay; Mr. Young; Lieut. Jones; seven children; three servants.

Per Lady Raffles, from Bombay; Mrs. Campbell; Mrs. Grierson; Col. Russell, artillery; Maj. Havelock, H. M. 4th L. Drags.; Capt. M'Duff, H. M. 40th regt.; Capt., in charge of invalids; Capt. Lang, 20th N. I.; Lieut. Prior, 21st ditto; Lieut. Jones, 20th ditto; Lieut. Frederick, 18th ditto; Ens. Jeffries; Mr. Sparshott, H.M.S. *Winchester*; 30 invalids H. M. 40th regt.; 2 children; 2 servants.—From the Cape: George Greig, Esq.; Mrs. Greig; two Misses and two Masters Greig; Miss Dixie; Mr. Hodgkins and two children; two servants.

Per Mary Ann, from Madras: Mrs. Harper; Mrs. Maidman; Mrs. Major Crisp; Mrs. O'Neill; Mrs. E. Crisp; Mrs. Cochrane; Mrs. Wright; Mrs. Hosmer; Mrs. Maitland; Lieut. Col. H. G. Jourdan, 10th N. I.; Maj. J. Tod, 33d N. I.; Capt. R. Gordon, 26th N. I.; Capt. J. Cochrane, H. M. 41st regt.; Capt. T. E. Wright, 27th ditto; Capt. C. H. Graeme, 5th L. C.; Capt. Hassard, H. M. 39th regt.; Lieut. Lockhart, 45th N. I.; Lieut. Leslie; Rev. E. Crisp; Assist. Surg. Rose; Rev. Father Louis; Misses Calder, Garnault, two Crisps, and O'Neill; Masters T. and E. O'Neill,

Cochrane, Wright, Harper, and Crisp; 10 servants; 9 invalids.

Per Eliza Haywood, from Singapore: Mr. Gordon; Mr. Cornish.

Per Triumph, from Bombay; Mrs. Hadow; Mrs. White and child; Col. Ballantyne, Bombay army; Dr. Ramsay, H. M. 49th regt.; Lieut. Macdonell, 19th N. I., in charge of invalids; Lieut. Anderson, 17th N. I.; Surg John M'Morris; two Misses Forbes; Master M'Morris; 40 H. C. invalids, &c. —From the Cape: Mrs. Harvey; Mrs. Hughes; Misses Gibbs and Hughes; William Harvey, Esq.; Lieut. Col. Hughes, C. B. Bombay army; three Masters Harvey.— Joseph Harvey, Esq., died at sea).—Left at the Cape: A Shaw, Esq., C. S.; Mrs. Shaw; Master and Miss Shaw.

Per Broxbornebury, from Bengal (additional): Mrs. Thomas Kennedy.

Per Norfolk, from Sydney: Dr. Boyter; Dr. Pines; Mr. Flower; Mr. Nicholson, Mr. Waddell.

Per Elizabeth, from Bengal: Mr. and Mrs. Aitchison; Mr. Barclay and child.

Per Duke of Northumberland, from Bengal: Mrs. Col. Walker; Mrs. Cumming; Mrs. Daunt; Mrs. Platt; Mrs. Holmes; Mrs. Chalmers; Mrs. Goad; Capt. Manning, 16th N. I.; Capt. Platt; Dr. Daunt; Dr. Stoddart; Lieut. Tucker; Lieut. Smith; Ens. Chalmers; F. Bathie, Esq.; — Parish, Esq.; Rev. F. Holmes; 13 children; seven servants.— From St. Helena: Dr. M'Ritchie; (Maj. Fernie was landed at St. Helena for the Cape.)

Per Minerva, from China: Dr. Hardwicke.

Per London, from Bengal: H. L. Blandford, Esq.; Capt. P. Neville.

Per Annandale, from Madras; Capt. Wetherall, 41st regt.

Per H. M. S. Atholl, from St. Helena: Mrs Knipe and two children; Mrs. Lester; Lieut. T. B. Knipe, St. Helena regt., commanding detachment; Lieut. Lester, St. Helena regt.; Mr. W. Mulhall, conductor of Ordnance; Mr. G. Armstrong; Mr. A. Eyre; Mr. J. Wright; 138 men of the artillery and infantry; 37 soldiers' wives; 80 children of ditto.

Per Rubicon, from V. D. Land: Mr. A. Murray.

Per Colombo, from Ceylon; Mrs. Selkirk; R. M. Sneyd, Esq., and children; Lieut. Col. Vavasour, Lieut. B. Layard.

Per Atlas, from Mauritius; Mr. and Mrs. Pearson; Miss Pearson; Mr. and Mrs. Rowlandson; Capt. and Mrs. Andrews; Mr. and Mrs. Luce; Mr. and Mrs Gilbert; three Misses Gilbert; Mr. A. Gilbert; Mr. M. Noncomp; Mr. Blane; Mr. Sangery and Master Sangery; Mr. Duval; Masters West and Vicrange; four servants.

Per Isabella, from Bengal: Mrs. Brown; Mrs. Silver; Mrs. Graham; Miss Robson; Miss Watkins; Capt Vernon; Capt. Warner; Capt. Reilly; Capt. Rogers; Lieut. Little; Rev. Mr. Anderson; J. F. Sandys, Esq ; Master Robson.

Per Vibilia, from V. D. Land: Mrs Stopford; Mr. and Mrs. Dyus and child; Mr. T. Walker; Mr. N. Solomon; Mr. E. Martin; Mr. W. Roberts.

Per Mary, from V. D. Land: Mr. and Mrs. Cameron; Mr. and Mrs. Robson; Mr. Duncan; Mr. Lonsdale; Mr. Stoddart.

Expected.

Per Emily, from Bengal: Capt. H. Monke, 39th N.I.; Capt. E. C. Archbold, 8th L. Cav.; Lieut. R. Wright, 26th N.I.; Andrew Peterson, Esq.; Misses Sicker and Fisher; Masters Fisher and Lloyd.

Per Zenobia, from Bengal: Mrs. Turner and two children; Mrs. Ainslie; Mrs. Rowcroft and two children; Mrs. Cowie and two ditto; Mrs. Martin and two ditto; Miss Dougan; J. Master, Esq., C. S.; J. G. Lawrell, Esq., C. S.; T. B. C. Bayley, Esq., C. S.; Major Gairdner, 14th N.I.; Capt. A. C. Scott, 70th ditto; Capt. Rowcroft, 1st ditto; Capt. Matthias, 33d ditto; Lieut. W. Martin, 52d ditto; Lieut. Master, L. Cav.; J. Cowie, Esq.; D. Ainslie, Esq.; — Joseph, Esq.; Lieut. Edwards.

Per Hercules, from N. S. Wales: Mrs. Bouverie; Mrs. Barnes; Mrs. Fowler; Major Bouverie, 17th regt.; Dr Loar; Messrs. Varley, Crocker, Smith,

Cæsar, Dean, Eagan, Grey, O'Brien, Macklin, and Rady.; 98 invalids of 17th regt.; 8 women and 15 children of ditto. (Mr. Tytler and Mr. Tobin, died at sea).

Per Gabrielle, from Bengal (for Havre): Mons. Cordier, governor of Chandernagore; Madame Cordier; Mons. Cordier, fils; Madame de Mornet and two children; Madame de Arbolles; Mons. Arbolles, Faudon, and Boltier; Dr. Paterson; P. S. Barber, Esq.; Mons. Morel, Aubin, and Moulon.

Per Orontes, from Madras: Mrs. M'Master and family; Mrs. Hay; two Misses Hay; Sir Patrick Lindesay, C. B.; Lieut. Col. Townsend; Lieut. Col. Kyd; Major Poole; Maj. C. M. Bird; W. Lavie, Esq.; Dr. Hay; Lieut. Ommaney, 2d L.C.; Lieut. Boland, H. M. 39th foot; Lieut. Swyny, H. M. 63d foot.

PASSENGERS TO INDIA, &c.

Per Courier, for Cape, &c. (from Cork): Lieuts. Vereker and Tousel, 27th foot; Capt. Gowan, and Ensigns Pollard and Sherson, 72d foot; Ensigns Ellis and Guise, 75th foot; detachments for H. M. 27th, 72d, and 75th regts.

Per Repulse, for Madras and Bengal: Lieut. Col. Gummer; Major and Mrs. M'Donald; Capt. Wake; Lieut. Prescott; Lieut. Walker; Dr. Balfour Mr. and Mrs. Brae; Mr. and Mrs. Heyland; Rev. Mr. Brotherton and lady; Miss Reddish; Mr. Horneman; Mr. Ibbetson; Mr. Glascott; Mr. Heyland; Mr. Greathed; Mr. Le Bas; Mr. Marquis; Mr. Harris; Mr. Cummins; Mr. Johnston; Mr. Forsyth; Mr. Alexander; Mr. Maginnes; Mr. Pryce; Mr. Ford; Mr. Griffin; Mr. Sutherland; Mr. Gedge; Mr. Harris; Mr. Cooper

Per Exmouth, for Madras and Bengal: About fifteen King's officers; troops, &c.

Per True Briton, for Madras and Bengal: Sir P. Maitland, new commander-in-chief at Madras, and family; Major and Mrs. Wardlaw; Capt. Conway; Capt. Godfrey; Capt. Justice; Capt. V. Hughes; Capt. Weston; Lieut. Short; Assist. Surg. Carr; Rev. Mr. Peckenham and family; Mr. F. Hughes; Mr. Blunt; Mr. Tucker; several troops.

Per Arab, for Bengal: Mr. and Mrs. Bourke, &c.

Per Roxburgh Castle, for Madras and Bengal: Mr. and Mrs. Roussac and party; Mr. and Mrs. Anderson and family; Miss Paddon; Capt. Austin; Ens. James; Mr. Hardiman; Mr. Foster; Mr. Harrison.

Per Boyne, for Bombay: Capt. and Mrs. Saunders; Miss Dingwall.

Per Thomas Grenville, for Madras and Bengal: Mrs. E. Strahan; Mrs. Polwhele; Mrs. Cock; Col. Cock; Lieut. Raleigh; Mr. Richards; Mr. Fullarton.

Per Duke of Lancaster, for Madras and Bengal: W. Chatfield, Esq.; Mr. and Mrs. Symes; J. E. Arbuthnot, Esq.; Mr. Curtis.

Per Mountstuart Elphinstone, for Bengal: Mrs. Col. Littler; Mrs. Lane; Mrs. Fergusson; Mrs. Bunce; Mrs. Thomas; Miss Bunce; two Misses Elphinstone; Miss Pratt; Miss Davidson; Miss Thomas; Col. Littler; H. S. Lane, Esq.; W. H. Fergusson, Esq.; Charles Thomas, Esq.; Ens. M'Mahon; Messrs. Russell, Forbes, Bennet, Turnbull, Davis, Fergusson, and Dyce.

BIRTHS, MARRIAGES, AND DEATHS.

BIRTHS.

May 28. The lady of Lieut. James Remington, Bengal army, of a son.

31. At Edinburgh, the lady of Assist. Surg. D. Grierson, M. D., of the Bombay medical establishment, of a son.

June 2. At Kensington, the lady of Capt. R. R. Ricketts, of the 48th Madras N. I., of a daughter.

5. The widow of the late Colonel Delamain, of a son.

6. In Woburn Square, the lady of Col. Pereira, of the Madras army, of a son.

7. At Catisfield, near Fareham, Hants., the lady of Henry Gardiner, Esq., late of the Madras civil service, of a daughter.

7. At Bath, the lady of Major Havelock, of P. M. 4th Lt. Drags., of a daughter. The infant died on the 9th.

17 At Ryde, Isle of Wight, Mrs. T. T. Harington, of a son.

MARRIAGES

May 10. At the Church of the Sœurs Grises, in Posen, Elisa Margaret Dickens, eldest daughter of the late John Dickens, Esq., Judge of Prince of Wales' Island, and also at Calcutta, to Louis de Zakrzewski, eldest son of Charles de Zakrzewski, of Osick Nielagowo, &c., in the circle of Kosten.

31. At St. George's, Hanover Square, J. Lindsay, Esq., of Loughry, in the county of Tyrone, to Harriott Hester, daughter of the Right Hon. C. W. W. Wynn.

June 1. At Bury St. Edmund's, J. W. Langford, Esq., of the Bombay civil service, to Susanna, eldest daughter of S. W. Hicks, Esq. of Ilfracombe, in the county of Devon, and grand-daughter of the late Thomas Mills, Esq., of Great Saxham Hall, Suffolk.

— At Putney, F. H. Lindsay, Esq., to Sophia, eldest daughter of the late Claud Russell, Esq., of the Bengal civil service.

4. At Liverpool, John Ponsonby Vero, Esq., eldest son of John Vero, Esq., of the county Wexford, to Caroline, fifth daughter of S. Walmsley, Esq., of Great Crosby, and niece of Major Sneyd, of the Hon. East-India Company's service.

14. At St. Pancras, Joseph Bonsor, Esq., of Polesden, Surrey, to Eliza Denne, youngest daughter of Major Alexander Orme, Fitzroy Square.

16. At Edinburgh, Capt. Charles Wahab, Hon. E. I. Company's service, to Janet, second daughter of Duncan Gowan, Esq.

— At St. James's Church, the Rev. Henry Malthus, rector of Poughill, Devonshire, only son of the late Rev. Robert Malthus, Professor of Political Economy at the East-India College, to Sophia, eldest daughter of the Rev. William Otter, Principal of King's College.—And at the same time, Alexander Trotter, Esq., third son of Alexander Trotter, Esq., of Dreghorn, N.B., to Jacqueline, third daughter of the Rev. William Otter, Principal of King's College.

20. At Worcester, Thomas C. Loughnan, Esq., of the Hon. East-India Company's civil service, Bombay, to Harriet Strickland, youngest daughter of the late Nicholas Power, Esq., of Queen Square.

DEATHS.

Feb. 14. On his passage home from New South Wales, on board the *Hercules*, Lieut. Wellington Tobin, of the 17th regt., second son of Thomas Tobin, Esq., of Liverpool.

March 12. Washed overboard in a gale at sea, and drowned, on his passage home from Van Die-

men's Land, on board the *Hercules*, George Grant Fraser Tytler, Esq., late of the 4th regt., eldest surviving son of W. F. Tytler, Esq., of Belnain, sheriff of Inverness-shire.

April 26. At sea, on board the *Triumph*, on the passage from the Cape of Good Hope, Joseph Harvey, Esq., treasurer general.

May 30. At Heavitree, near Exeter, of apoplexy, Colonel John Delamain, C. B., of the Hon. East-India Company's service.

— On board the East-India ship *Eliza*, off Scilly, James Napier Lyall, Esq., of Calcutta, after an absence of twenty years.

June 1. At Lyon Terrace, Edgeware Road, in her 29th year, Margaret, eldest daughter of the late .Col. Mignon, of Bombay, and relict of Mr. Wm. Woodd, youngest son of the late Rev. Basil Woodd, surviving her husband only four months, and leaving four infant orphan children unprovided for.

4. At Chiswick, in the 66th year of his age, W. D. Jennings, Esq., of Doctors' Commons, and for many years King's proctor at the Cape of Good Hope.

6. After a few hours' illness, William Augustus, youngest son of the late Lieut. Col. Sir David Ogilby, of the Hon. East-India Company's service, and lately of Fromer Lodge, Friern-Barnett.

9. At his house on Cambridge Terrace, Edgeware Road, of erysipelas on the head, terminating in brain fever, Barry Edward O'Meara, Esq., late surgeon to the Emperor Napoleon, author of *A Voice from St. Helena*, &c.

14 At Broomhouse Mill, Mrs. Slight, widow of Capt. Stephen Slight, Bombay engineers.

18. At his house in Woburn Square, Edward Turner, Esq., late of the Hon. East-India Company's service.

20. At Edinburgh, Col. John Simpson, of the 66th regt. Bengal N. I.

22. In Hertford Street, Mayfair, in the 46th year of his age, Colonel Mackinnon, of the Coldstream Guards.

23. At his house in Kensington, James Mill, Esq., author of the "*History of British India*," "*Elements of Political Economy*," "*Analysis of the Human Mind*," and other works. He fell a victim to consumption, after nearly one year's lingering illness, during which time he was disabled from attending to the duties of his most important office, that of chief examiner to the East-India Company, which duties were those of preparing despatches and other state papers submitted for the consideration of the Court of Directors. He has left a widow and nine children, five of whom are grown up. His eldest son holds an important office in the same department as his father.

Lately. On board the *Eliza*, on the passage from Calcutta, Mrs. Pitt.

THE LONDON MARKETS, June 24.

Tea.—The East-India Company's quarterly sale finished on the 6th June. The entire quantity offered (4,000,000 lbs.) found ready purchasers at an advance upon the March sale costs of 3d. per lb. on Fokien Boheas; 1d. per lb. on common Congous; 2d. per lb. on Twankays; 2d. to 3d. per lb. on common Hysons. Fine Congous have declined 1d. to 1½d. per lb. Fine Hysons have sold quite as cheap as in March sales.

The East-India Company have issued a notice, dated the 15th June, that they will be prepared to advance on account of the buyers of Bohea at their last sale, the duties which may be payable on those teas that may be required to be entered for home consumption previously to the 1st July.

The following is an extract from the Minute of the Lords of the Treasury on the subject of the 1s. 6d. Bohea tea duty :—

" The Chancellor of the Exchequer stated to the Board that he had received a great many applications on the subject of the postponement of

the duty, and, wishing to relieve the mercantile interest, he submitted a postponement of the duties till after the payment of the July dividends, but in order to afford similar relief to the trade in the country, he considered the time should be extended for one month.

" ' My Lords concur in this opinion, provided the postponement of duty should take place in respect of such Bohea teas as are actually entered for home consumption before the 1st of July; these teas to remain under the King's locks, and the duty of 1s. 6d. per lb. to be paid before the 1st of August.' "

Indigo.—The market for East-India has become quiet, but the late advanced rates are fully maintained. There has not been so much demand, it being expected that the public sales to be brought forward on the 12th of July will contain an unusually large amount; it will consist mostly of goods of the recent importations.

N.B. *The letters P.C. denote prime cost, or manufacturers' prices; A. advance (per cent.) on the same; D. discount (per cent.) on the same; N.D. no demand.—The bazar maund is equal to 82 ℔. 2 oz. 2 drs., and 100 bazar maunds equal to 110 factory maunds. Goods sold by Sa. Rupees B. mds. produce 5 to 8 per cent. more than when sold by Ct. Rupees F. mds.—The Madras Candy is equal to 500℔. The Surat Candy is equal to 746½ ℔. The Pecul is equal to 133⅓ ℔. The Corge is 20 pieces.*

CALCUTTA, February 11, 1836.

	Rs. A.		Rs. A.		Rs. A.		Rs. A.
Anchors ....Sa. Rs. cwt.	12 8	@	19 0	Iron, Swedish, sq...Sa. Rs. F. md.	5 1	@	5 3
Bottles 100	8 12	—	9 4	—— flat ....do.	5 0	—	5 2
Coals ....B. md.	0 7	—	0 8	—— English, sq. ....do.	2 9	—	2 11
Copper Sheathing, 16-32 ..F. md	34 0	—	34 8	—— flat ....do.	2 7	—	2 9
—— Brasiers', ...do.	34 0	—	34 8	—— Bolt ....do.	2 9	—	2 11
—— Thick sheets ....do.				—— Sheet ....do.	5 4	—	5 10
—— Old Gross ....do.	32 4	—	32 8	—— Nails ....cwt.	11 0	—	15 8
—— Bolt ....do.	33 0	—	33 8	—— Hoops..........F. md.	5 2	—	5 5
—— Tile ....do.	31 6	—	32 2	—— Kentledge ....cwt.	1 0	—	1 3
—— Nails, assort. ....do.	30 0	—	36 0	Lead, Pig ....F. md.	6 1	—	6 3
—— Peru Slab......Ct. Rs. do.	28 4	—	29 12	—— unstamped...........do.	5 13	—	5 15
—— Russia ....Sa. Rs. do.				Millinery.......................			5 to 25 D.&P.C.
Copperas ....do.	3 0	—	3 5	Shot, patent ....bag	2 6	—	3 4
Cottons, chints ....pce.				Spelter ....Ct. Rs. F. md.	6 9	—	6 10
—— Muslins, assort. ....do.	1 5	—	13 0	Stationery			5 to 25 D.&P.C.
—— Yarn 16 to 170 ....mor.	0 6³	—	0 8½	Steel, English......Ct. Rs. F. md.	5 14	—	6 4
Cutlery, fine..................			5 to 10A. & P.C.	—— Swedish ....do.	6 8	—	7 0
Glass...............			7A. — 12A.	Tin Plates..........Sa. Rs. box	14 10	—	15 2
Hardware....:....			25 D. — 50D.	Woollens, Broad cloth, fine ..yd.	5 0	—	9 8
Hosiery, cotton.................			20 to 50A.&P.C.	—— coarse and middling....	1 4	—	4 0
Ditto, silk			20 to 35 D.&P.C	—— Flannel fine.........	1 0	—	1 12

MADRAS, January 20, 1836.

	Rs.		Rs.		Rs.		Rs.
Bottles 100	12	@	14	Iron Hoops ....candy	18	@	19
Copper, Sheathing ....candy	265			—— Nails ....do.	110	—	115
—— Cakes ....do.				Lead, Pig ....do.	42	—	45
—— Old ....do.	230	—	240	—— Sheet ....do.	38	—	40
—— Nails, assort. ....do.	350	—	370	Millinery	20A.	—	25 A.
Cottons, Chintz..........piece	4	—	5	Shot, patent ....bag	3	—	3½
—— Ginghams ....do.	2	—	3	Spelter ....candy	40	—	
—— Longcloth, fine ....do.	9	—	14	Stationery			Overstocked.
Cutlery, coarse	15A.		20A.	Steel, English...........candy	56	—	55
Glass and Earthenware	10A.		25A.	—— Swedish ....do.	70	—	75
Hardware......................	10A.			—— Tin Plates ....box	18	—	19
Hosiery......................	25A.	—	30A.	Woollens, Broad cloth, fine......	10A.	—	13A.
Iron, Swedish, ...candy	40	—	50	—— coarse			Wanted
—— English bar ....do.	18	—	19	—— Flannel, fine.........			12 to 14 Ans. pr. yd.
—— Flat and bolt..........do.	18	—	19	—— Ditto, coarse			8 to 10 Ans. du.

BOMBAY, March 12, 1836.

	Rs.		Rs		Rs.		Rs.
Anchors ....cwt.	12	@	14	Iron, Swedish ....St. candy	51	@	
Bottles ....doz.	1.4	—		—— English ....do.	23	—	23.8
Coals ....ton	10	—	12	—— Hoops................cwt.	5.4	—	
Copper, Sheathing, 16-32 ..cwt.	51	—		—— Nails ....do.	12	—	13
—— Thick sheets ....do.	55	—		—— Sheet ....do.	5.8	—	
—— Plate bottoms ....do.	53	—		—— Rod for bolts ......St. candy	23	—	24
—— Tile ....do.	44	—	45	—— do. for nails ....do.	28	—	30
Cottons, Chintz, &c., &c.........				Lead, Pig ....cwt.	10.4	—	
—— Longcloths...........				—— Sheet ....do.	10	—	
—— Muslins				Millinery	10 D.	—	
—— Other goods				Shot, patent ....cwt.	10	—	12
—— Yarn, Nos. 20 to 100 ...lb.	0.11	—	1.12	Spelter ....do.	7.8	—	
Cutlery, table..............	10A.	—		Stationery			P. C.
Glass and Earthenware	10 D.	—	20D.	Steel, Swedish ....tub	10	—	
Hardware..................	P. C.	—		Tin Plates ....box	15.8	—	
Hosiery, half hose...........	P. C.			Woollens, Broad cloth, fine ..yd.	4	—	7
				—— coarse	1.12	—	7
				—— Flannel, fine...........	1.4	—	2

CANTON, February 2, 1836.

	Drs.		Drs.		Drs.		Drs.
Cottons, Chintz, 28 yds..........piece	3	@	4	Smalts ....pecul	30	@	80
—— Longcloths ....do.	3	—	11	Steel, Swedish ....tub	3.75	—	
—— Muslins, 20 yds...........do.				Woollens, Broad cloth ......yd.	1.30	—	1.40
—— Cambrics, 40 yds ....do.	3	—	4	—— do. ex super............yd.	2.50	—	2.75
—— Bandannoes...............do.	1.25	—	1.45	—— Camlets ....pce.	23	—	31
—— Yarn, Nos. 16 to 50........pecul	44	—	51	—— Do. Dutch ....do.	34	—	37
Iron, Bar ....do.	2.95	—		—— Long Ells ....do.	36	—	41
—— Rod ....do.	3	—	3½	Tin, Straits................pecul	16	—	16½
Lead, Pig ....do.	5½	—	6	Tin Plates ....box	3	—	

SINGAPORE, January 30, 1836.

		Drs.		Drs.			Drs.		Drs.
Anchors	pecul	6	@	7½	Cotton Hkfs. imit. Battick, dble.	doz.	2¼	@	4
Bottles	100	—		—	—— do. do Pullicat	doz.	1½	—	2
Copper Nails and Sheathing	pecul	36	—	37	—— Twist, 30 to 40	pecul	55	—	57
Cottons, Madapollams, 24yd. by 36in.	pcs.	2	—	2½	Hardware, and coarse Cutlery	scarce&wanted			
—— Imit. Irish 24 34-36	do.	2	—	2¼	Iron, Swedish	pecul	3¼	—	3½
—— Longcloths 38 to 40 34-36	do.	4¼	—	4½	—— English	do.	2½	—	2¾
—— ———— do. do. 36fine	do.	5	—	5¼	—— Nail, rod	do.	2¾	—	3
—— ———— do. do. 40-44	do.	4	—	6½	Lead, Pig	do.	5½	—	5¾
—— ———— do. do. 44-54	do.	5	—	9	—— Sheet	do.	5	—	5½
—— ———————— 54	do.	—		—	Shot, patent	bag	—		—
—— Prints, 7-8. *single colours*	do.	2	—	2½	Spelter	pecul	5¾	—	6½
—— ——— 9-8.	do.	2¼	—	2½	Steel, Swedish	do.	4¼	—	4½
—— Cambric, 12 yds. by 45 to 50 in.	do.	1½	—	2½	—— English	do.	—		—
—— Jaconet, 20 ...... 40 .. 44	do.	2	—	2½	Woollens, Long Ells	pcs.	9	—	10
—— Lappets, 10 ...... 40 .. 44	do.	1	—	1½	—— Camblets	do.	25	—	30
—— Chints, fancy colours	do.	3	—	5½	—— Ladies' cloth	yd.	1	—	2

REMARKS.

Calcutta, March 4, 1836.—The market for Piece Goods is in a healthy condition. The late arrivals from Liverpool and Glasgow found the bazaar bare of several descriptions of light goods, more particularly Lappets, Books, and Mulls, which accordingly met, and would still experience, a ready and profitable sale. Jaconet Muslins, likewise, have had a good demand, and continue to be enquired for, the stock being moderate. The more heavy Cottons, say Shirtings, and Cambrics, are abundant, and less saleable. Of printed Goods, Bengal Stripes, and single coloured Plates, meet with buyers, but recent sales have been effected at rates not generally remunerative. Other description of prints are without enquiry.—The market for Cotton Yarn may be considered in a very uncertain and unsatisfactory state.—The Woollen market offers little subject for remark; the sales for the last two months have certainly been greater, and at better rates than for some time before, but the amount altogether has not been large.—The Copper and Spelter market may be considered in an encouraging state.—English Iron, large imports, and market looking low.—*Exch. Price Current.*

Madras, Jan. 20, 1836.—Cotton Twist maintains former rates, and sales continue to be made in small parcels both in White and Orange, which are getting into good request. About 100 tons of Iron realised last week between 18 and 19 Rs. the candy; the market has since received a further supply of that article with Tin-plates, &c.,

Singapore, Jan. 30 1836.—The demand for Cotton Piece Goods, plain and coloured, is improving, though the transactions since our last have been only trifling.—We have no transactions in Woollens to notice at present. Long Ells of assorted colours will shortly be in some request by the Cochin Chinese, who are the only purchasers of the article. We are still without any further importations of Cotton Twist, and the stock in the market consisting of low unsuitable numbers, does not exceed 40 peculs: a rather brisk demand is now shortly anticipated.—The stock of Bar Iron in first hands amounts to about 180 tons, and our present quotations are likely to be maintained. In Spelter and Lead there is no alteration, both are scarce and wanted.—Copper Nails and Sheathing, only a trifling stock in first hands, and prices firm at our quotations.

Penang, Jan. 4, 1836.—Our market continues bare of produce, and much in activity in the demand for Europe manufactures.

Canton, Feb. 2, 1836.—Trade, as usual at this period of the approach to the Chinese new year, is very dull, and we have no observations to make on any particular articles.

Manilla, Jan. 6, 1836.—The market is well supplied with Cotton goods, and overstocked with some descriptions, also with Woollens, and prices are low.—Freights to Europe, nominal.—Exchange on London, 6 months' sight, 4s. 8d. to 4s. 9d. per dol.

INDIA SECURITIES AND EXCHANGES.

Calcutta, Feb. 11, 1836.

Government Securities.

Buy.	Rs. As.		Rs. As.	Sell.
Prem.	15 8	Remittable	15 0	Prem.
Prem.	0 4	Second 5 per cent.	2 8	
	2 12	Third 5 per cent.	2 8	Prem.
Disc.	2 5	Four per cent. Loan	2 8	Disc.

Bank Shares.

Bank of Bengal (10,000) .... Sa.Rs. 15,550 a 15,600
Union Bank .. (2,500) .... 250 to 300 prem.

Bank of Bengal Rates.

Discount on private bills .... 7 0 per cent.
Ditto on government and salary bills 4 0 do.
Interest on loans on govt. paper .... 5 0 do.

Rate of Exchange, *March* 4.

On London and Liverpool, six months' sight, to buy, 2s. 2d.; to sell, 2s. 2½d. per Sa. Rupee.

Madras, Jan. 20, 1836.

Government Securities.

Remittable Loan, six per cent.—15½ per ct. prem.
Ditto ditto of 18th Aug. 1825, five per cent.—2 prem.—3 disc.
Ditto ditto last five per cent.—2 prem.
Ditto ditto Old four per cent.—4½ disc.
Ditto ditto New four per cent.—4¼ disc.

Exchange.

On London, at 6 months,—to buy, 2s.; to sell, 1s. 11d. per Madras Rupee.

Bombay, March 12, 1836.

Exchanges.

Bills on London, at 6 mo. sight, 2s. 1¼d. to 2s. 1½d. per Rupee.
On Calcutta, at 30 days' sight, 108.4 to 108.8 Bom. Rs. per 100 Sicca Rupees.
On Madras, at 30 days' sight, 102.8 to 103 Bom. Rs. per 100 Madras Rs.

Government Securities.

Remittable Loan, 125 to 125.4 Bom. Rs. per 100 Sa. Rs.
5 per cent. Loan of 1822-23, according to the period of discharge, 109 to 109.4 per ditto.
Ditto of 1825-26, 109 to 111.12 per ditto.
Ditto of 1829-30, 111.12 to 112 per ditto.
4 per cent. Loan of 1832-33, 106.4 to 106.8 per ditto.

Singapore, Jan. 30, 1835.

Exchanges.

On London, 4 to 6 mo. sight, 4s. 4d. to 4s. 5d. per dollar.
On Bengal, gov. bills 206 Sa. Rs. per 100 dollars.

Canton, Feb. 2, 1836.

Exchanges, &c.

On London, 6 mo. sight, 4s. 10d per Sp. Dol.
E. I. Co's Agents for advances on consignments, 4s. 8d.
On Bengal. — Private Bills, 212 Sa. Rs. per 100 Sp. Dols.—Company's ditto, 30 days. 210 Sa. Rs.
On Bombay, ditto Bom. Rs. 220 to 222 per ditto.
Sycee Silver at Lintin, 3½ to 4 per cent. prem.

LIST of SHIPS Trading to INDIA and Eastward of the CAPE of GOOD HOPE.

Destination.	Appointed to sail.	Ships' Names.	Tonnage.	Owners or Consignees.	Captains.	Where loading.	Reference for Freight or Passage.
							1836.
Bengal	July 4	Mstrs. Elphinstone	611	Joseph L. Heathorn	William Toller	W.I. Docks	Joseph L. Heathorn; Leary & Thompson.
	10	Isabella	570	Dunbar and Sons	David Brown	E.I. Docks	Lyall, Brothers, & Co.; John Mason, Lime street square.
	10	Cornwall	872	Palmers, Mackillop&Co.	William Bell	W.I. Docks	Thomas Haviside & Co.
	16	London	620	Money Wigram	John Wimble	W.I. Docks	John Pirie & Co., Freeman's-court.
	25	Duke of Bedford	726	Sir C. Cockerill, Bt. &Co.	W.A. Bowen	W.I. Docks	Sir C. Cockerill, Bt., & Co.
	20	Robert Small	655	Thomas &WilliamSmith	William Fulcher	E.I. Docks	John Pirie & Co.; Small, Colquhoun, & Co.
	31	Bolton	600	T.B. Oldfield	William Compton	W.I. Docks	Sir C. Cockerill, Bt., & Co.; Jopp & Scarr; Noel, T.Smith,
	Aug. 1	Lord Hungerford	724	Charles Farquharson	C. Farquharson	E.I. Docks	Sir C. Cockerill, Bt., & Co.; T.
	1	Windsor	700	Richard G. ...en	Alex. Heming	E.I. Docks	T. Haviside & Co.
	5	Scotia	700	Thomas & Wm. Smith	John Campbell	E.I. Docks	Walkinshaw & Co.; Lyall,
	15	Duke of Buccleugh	660	Richard Green	R.F. Martin	W.I. Docks	Thomas Haviside & Co.
	90	Duke of Northumb.	650	William Langley Pope.	Wm. L. Pope.	W.I. Docks	Thomas Haviside & Co.
Bengal and China		New Ship	250	William O. Young	Wm. O. Young	Hull	Capt. Chapman, Birchin-lane, or Jerusalem Coffee-house.
Cape and Bengal	July 3	Broxbornebury	750	Alfred Chapman	Alfred Chapman	W.I. Docks	Thomas Haviside & Co.
Madras and Bengal	Aug. 1	Barretto Junior	690	Reid, Irving, & Co.	R. Saunders	Portsmouth	Crawford, Colvin, & Co.; Tomlin Man, & Co.
Madras	Sept. 1	Lady Flora	755	Robert Ford	Robert Ford	E.I. Docks	Charles Moss & Co., Mark-lane.
		Mary Ann	500	...les & Co	Chas B. Tarbutt	St.Kt.Docks	Gledstanes & Co.; Smith, Exchange-buildings.
Cape and Madras	July 13	Wellington	500	Gustavus Evans	Jnes Liddell	W.I. Docks	MacGhie, Page, & Smith, Exchange-buildings.
	Aug. 1	Gilmore	550	Reid, Irving, & Co.	H.H. Lindsay	W.I. Docks	Reid, Irving, & Co.; Thos. Haviside & Co.
	July 30	Scauby Castle	255	Jues	...le Robertson	E.I. Docks	John Pirie & Co.
Bombay		Melador	650	Richard ...en	Edward des.	E.I. Docks	John Pirie & Co.
	25	Mary of Hastings	540	John Gilkson	John Clarkson	W.I. Docks	Capt. ... ham, Birchin-lane; Crawford, ...n, & Co.
	25	Triumph	600	Robert & Thomas Green	...lias Green	W.I. Docks	Robert ...; Tomlin and Man.
	Aug. 1	Herefordshire	1335	Thacker,F&CE.Mangles	H.S.H. ...am	E.I. Docks	Thacker & Price; F. & C.E. Mangles; Jopp & Scarr.
Cape and Bombay	16	Lady Raffles	647	...ard Green	Robert Pollock	E.I. Docks	John Pirie & Co.
China	July 1	Carnatic	630	Thacker,F&CE.Mangles	John Brodie.	E.I. Docks	Phillips & Tiplady; Edmund Read, Cornhill.
	15	Neptune	250	...rge R.	Thomas Williams	E.I. Docks	E. & A. ...le.
Ceylon	Aug. 1	Fairy Queen	490	...Walkinshaw & Co.	G.R. Douthwaite	E.I. Docks	...aw & Co.; John Pirie & Co., Freeman's court.
Cape	July 7	Colombo	755	...lias Winter	...ean Mackellar	St.Kt.Docks	Cookes & Long.
Cape, V.D.L., and Sydney	Aug. 1	Mary and Jane	940	...as Ward	Thomas Winter	Lon. Docks	...hn Marshall, Birchin-lane.
Algoa Bay	July 10	Fairlie	755	N. Griffiths	Henry Ager	St.Kt.Docks	Cookes & Long.
		Grace	160	Joseph Somes	Thomas U. Gull	St.Kt.Docks	Cookes & Long.
Van Diemen's Land	3	Lady Nugent	583	N. Griffiths	J.H. Ret	Sheerness	Lachlan, Sons, & M'Leod, Great Alie-street.
	3	Henry Porcher	485	William Bottomley	John Hart.	Portsmouth	Lachlan, Sons, & M'Leod, ditto.
	10	Westmoreland	405	Joseph Somes	J. Brigstock	Woolwich	Lachlan, Sons, & M'Leod, ditto.
	30	Bengal Merchant	583	W.E. Ferrers	William Campbell	Sheerness	Lachlan, Sons, & M'Leod, ditto.
	30	Earl Grey	571	John Pirie & Co.	James Talbert.	Kingstown & Cork	Lachlan, Sons, & M'Leod, do.
New South Wales	1	Pyramus	389	Domett & Co.	James Weller	Cork	John Pirie & Co.
	30	William Bryan	390	Godwin & Lee.	John Roman	Lon. Docks	Domett, Young, & England, George-yard.
	31	Spartan	500	William Lockerby	Orlando Bull	St.Kt.Docks	Godwin & Moore.
Hobart Town	16	Ann Lockerby	400	Phillips, King, & Co.	Thomas Watson	St.Kt.Docks	Buckles & Ub.; Devitt & Moore.
South Australia	9	Wave	400	Thomas Dobson	Edw. Goldsmith	St.Kt.Docks	Phillips, King, & Co., Poultice-buildings; Amld & Woollet.
		Tam O'Shanter	383		Whitman Freman St.		...twin ...ee; Thomas Dobson.

ASIATIC INTELLIGENCE.

Calcutta.

LAW.

INSOLVENT DEBTORS' COURT, *Feb. 6.*

Assignee of Cruttenden and Co. Mr. *Leith,* on behalf of Mr. D. Macintyre, late assignee to the estate of Cruttenden, Mackillop and Co., drew the attention of the Court to the facts of the case.

In January 1834, on the insolvency of this firm, Mr. Macintyre was appointed assignee, at the recommendation of the creditors, after much discussion and consideration. It was known at the time that he had been a bankrupt in England, and that he possessed a certificate from his creditors, and that Mr. Mackillop was one of his assignees; but it was also known, that since his arrival in this country, he had paid 20*s.* in the pound—he mentioned this in testimony of his high moral feeling, no legal obligation requiring him to do so. Mr. Macintyre had produced to this court the certificate of Dr. Nicolson, which states the absolute necessity of his quitting Calcutta, the only chance of saving his life.

Mr. *Dickens,* as trustee for an infant estate, as a creditor, and so registered in the schedule of the estate, wished to point out to Mr. Leith where he was inaccurate in his statement of facts—he wished to be permitted to see the papers which formed the grounds of Mr. Leith's case, or any affidavit setting forth that Mr. Macintyre was known and stated to be a bankrupt, at the period of his appointment as assignee to this estate.

These papers being handed to Mr. Dickens, and not bearing out Mr. Leith's assertion, he acknowledged he was wrong.

Mr. *Leith* proceeded ; a sum of Rs. 75,000 had been expended by Mr. Macintyre in the management of the estate, for which purpose a large establishment was necessary. The chief objection that would, as he understood, be raised, was to the allowance made to Mr. Robert Browne, and Mr. James Cullen—an allowance recommended by a very large public meeting of creditors and confirmed by this Court. By the same authority and recommendation, it was also agreed that the assignee should be paid by a commission of 4 per cent. on dividends ; the allowance to the partners above named to be paid out of this commission. Mr. Macintyre had continued to perform his duties as assignee, until the date of his application to this Court, on account of his illness. He now asked to be allowed to charge his expenses to the estate, as recommended by the creditors. It is true that these expenses had been provided for by the commission, and, had not

Asiat. Journ. N.S. Vol. 20. No. 80.

the state of Mr. Macintyre's health compelled him to quit his post, this application would not have been made : but as he had been compelled to vacate the assigneeship by the visitation of God, and not by any fault or desire of his own, he appealed to this court, as a court of equity, in the execution of a sound legal discretion, to sanction this modification of the original order. The claims of the minority of creditors, who dissented from the recommendation of the committee, only amounted to Rs. 5,80,000, while the claims of the majority, which recommended that Mr. Macintyre's expenses be charged to the estate, amount to Rs. 46,00,000.

Mr. *Dickens* opposed the prayer of the petition of the late assignee, and objected to Mr. Leith's obtaining any order to confirm his application. The grounds on which he proceeded were informal and incorrect. He insisted, in the first place, that Mr. Macintyre had not complied with Section 30 of the Act, which directs that, on a new assignee being appointed, the outgoing assignee shall transfer to him the whole of the effects belonging to the estate ; whereas it was not shown that Mr. Macintyre had delivered over one farthing of the property. In the next place, there was great informality and irregularity in the petition signed by Mr. Holroyd and Mr. Macintyre. It was not made known to the creditors, or to this court, that, when appointed assignee, Mr. Macintyre was a bankrupt, and Mr. Mackillop, a partner of the London firm of Palmer, Mackillop and Co., one of his assignees—P. M. and Co. having been the London correspondent of the late firm of Cruttenden, Mackillop and Co. Mr. Dickens insisted on the moral and legal impropriety and the peculiar disqualification of Mr. Macintyre to act as assignee to *this* estate, under the circumstances of the case, even though he thought it might be no disqualification to his becoming assignee to any other. He objected strongly to the impropriety of Mr. Macintyre now (he the assignee and agent of the creditors) asking the court to pay to Mr. Browne and Mr. Cullen each Rs. 600 per month, the former being a man of large private fortune by right of his wife, and the latter being in the receipt of at least Rs. 1,000 per month, as Secretary to the Laudable Society—of which circumstances Mr. Macintyre was fully aware. Mr. M. was, of course, at perfect liberty to pay them as much as he pleased out of his own funds, out of his 4 per cent. on dividends—out of which alone he can take his expenses. These expenses appeared to him to be enormous, amounting to nearly

(2 D)

Rs. 30,000 or 40,000 per annum, while the expenses of the estate of Colvin and Co. (similar in other respects), for three years, had been only Rs. 47,000 ! Mr. Macintyre was not entitled to draw his expenses from the funds of the estate, and if he were, he ought to have allowed interest on such sums, up to the time of declaring a dividend. Mr. Macintyre had not shown any disposition or means to repay this large sum, and his extravagant expenditure and disqualification by the bankrupt laws, gave him no title to ask for indulgent consideration, either from this court or the creditors. Besides it appeared, from his own accounts, that he had not more than four lakhs towards making a dividend, and these four lakhs he could not rationally apply towards making a dividend, while the unprovided outlay, according to his own estimate, for carrying on indigo factories for the current year, was six lakhs; and, even if he did, the commission on it, at 4 per cent., would be only about Rs. 18,000 to meet the Rs. 30,000, or thereabouts, with which he desired to burden the estate. To this application, a breach of direct contract, he strongly objected as a creditor, and he hoped the court would not sanction such a waste of the slender assets of the estate.

Mr. *Leith*, in reply, observed that Mr. Dickens' objections appeared to class themselves under two heads—1. Extravagant expenses; and 2. Appointment void *ab initio*. As to the charge of extravagance, there was nothing before the court to show that it was unnecessary or improper, and in a recent appeal to the Supreme Court, in the case of Lingham, it was established that this court could not interfere with the discretion of an assignee in the management of an estate. In this case, the assignee's honesty was not impugned—on the contrary, Mr. Dickens had stated that he imputed no blame to Mr. Macintyre for paying, or Mr. Browne or Mr. Cullen for receiving the money. As to the charge of the appointment being void *ab initio*, by reason of the assignee being a bankrupt— (the Commissioner here observed that Mr. Dickens had stated that there was no objection to a bankrupt being an assignee generally—but objected to his being so in this particular case)—in a particular bankruptcy; if the appointment was not legal, it ought to have been objected to at the time, and not now, two years after, as a charge against a man, who, he could not show had acted otherwise than fairly and conscientiously. Mr. Dickens had argued that Mr. Macintyre, in accepting the assigneeship on the terms of a commission of 4 per cent. on dividends, had entered into a deliberate contract, and must abide by the terms of it; but he (Mr. Leith) would beg to draw the attention of the court to the circumstances under which Mr. Macintyre has been compelled to retire from his contract. It is not by his own choice that he does so. An act of God rescinds all contracts, and this such a case. Mr. Macintyre's life is in danger, and has mainly arisen from excessive anxiety of mind, and fatigue and disease of body—he is under an absolute necessity to withdraw. There is no imputation attempted to be cast upon him; but he is unable from sickness to fulfil his contract, and for this shall he be visited with a penalty of Rs. 75,000 ? Had he not benefitted the estate, and is he to suffer for so doing? In the first period of management, the expenses are ten-fold what they would be when affairs are brought into a proper train. In reference to Mr. Macintyre not having declared a dividend, Mr. Leith urged that he had done better; he had preferred paying off mortgages to declaring a dividend—he preferred the interest of the estate to his own interest.

Mr. *Dickens* observed that, not the assignee, but this court, declares the dividend, when it is informed that the means of so doing have been accumulated by the assignee. But he desired to know what mortgages had been paid off—he denied that there was any evidence before the court to show that any had been so paid.

Mr. *Leith* insisted upon it that mortgages to a large amount had been paid off; he was surprised at Mr. Dickens's objections, which however showed the absence of better grounds of opposition. Mr. Leith averred that Mr. Macintyre was possessed of means ten thousand times more than the Rs. 75,000 in dispute.

Mr. *Dickens* produced the Committee's Report, by which it appeared that the mortgages are *not* paid off.

Mr. *Leith* admitted he was mistaken —he was deceived in his grounds, which had misled him.

The *Commissioner* (Sir B. Malkin) said, he could take no notice of what was not verified and before the court.

Mr. *Dickens* admitted that only Rs. 5,72,000 of mortgages now appears due.

Mr. *Leith* added that there was due at the time of filing the schedule Rs. 25,00,000, making a difference paid to mortgagee creditors, of twenty lakhs of rupees.

Mr. *Dickens* again objected to this as an inaccurate statement. On reference to the Report, it appeared that there had been an amount of twenty six lakhs of *mortgages and sets-off*, but nothing to show the amount of each.

Mr. *Leith* proceeded ; he repeated that Mr. Macintyre's conduct was such as must be approved by all, in paying off mortgages instead of declaring dividends and obtaining his commission. With reference to Mr. Macintyre being a certified bankrupt, Mr. Leith observed that he could see no legal or moral defect. He could not understand in what way Mr. James Mackillop's being an assignee to Mr. Macintyre, can affect his (Mr. M.'s) being assignee to Cruttenden, Mackillop and Co. If, on mere moral grounds, Mr. Dickens imputes dishonest conduct to Mr. Macintyre, he is bound to prove it; but he imputes no blame to him for the allowances to the partners of the late firm. Mr. Leith adverted to the fact that Mr. James Mackillop was not in India at the time Mr. Macintyre was appointed assignee. Suppose Mr. Macintyre had died, would you make his estate pay the expenses incurred in the management of the insolvent estate, because no dividend had been declared? He is in the next state to death—he is incapable of further labour by the visitation of God; and shall he be visited with this additional affliction, contrary to the principles that govern transactions between man and man?

The *Advocate General*, on behalf of Mr. Holroyd, the assignee appointed to succeed Mr. Macintyre, briefly drew the attention of the Court to the circumstances of the case, as above detailed. It was true that, on appointing Mr. Holroyd to succeed Mr. Macintyre as assignee to the estate, the Chief Justice had referred it to the creditors to recommend what the former should receive; but he thought they had stepped out of their way to recommend a new method of remuneration, before they had applied to quash the order by which the old method had been established. The creditors had recommended that Mr. Holroyd should receive 1 per cent. on the "forthcoming" dividend, and 2½ per cent. in all future dividends; but he could no where find that it had been referred to the creditors to recommend so novel a course. Mr. Holroyd ought to succeed according to the terms of the former order as a matter of course, relieving Mr. Macintyre of both his profits and his troubles at the same time. It had been stated that nothing remained to be done but to distribute the accumulations: he thought differently. The disposable sum appeared to be only nine lakhs. How could a dividend be expected when there are yet nearly six lakhs of mortgages to be paid off and six lakhs of advances to be made for next year's indigo cultivation? As it is, money must be borrowed for these purposes, and if a dividend be declared, it must be paid, in fact, out of borrowed funds. All trouble of collecting and laying out, is yet to be gone through, and there is not a shadow of reason to make any difference in the rate of commission formerly allowed. Besides, it is well known that the first dividend is always the most troublesome and most difficult. A thousand things happen in making a first dividend, that will never happen again, and yet only 1 per cent. is to be allowed for the first, but 2½ per cent. for all future dividends! Several instances have occurred

in this Court which can determine what is a reasonable rate of remuneration for an assignee. The rate of allowance to the assignee of the estate of Colvin and Co., an estate said to be similar in its features to the one now before the Court, is a good example. In that estate, the allowance was 5 per cent on dividends—and a salary of Rs. 1,000 per month for the first year. All the labour of a first year has yet to be gone through in this estate, and yet the committee think 1 per cent. a sufficient remuneration. It rests with the Court to decide whether this remuneration is reasonable. Mr. Advocate General believed that the members of this committee were chiefly merchants. He had heard, he was not quite sure, but he believed, there were certain rates of commission, by which *they* were authorized to charge 2½ per cent. for only *receiving* and taking charge of money, without any trouble or expense of collection, or responsibility in dividing and deciding on claims. The Advocate General concluded by observing, that *there was no chance of any dividend for some time to come*—that it appeared to him that 4 per cent. on dividends, when they did come, was not one atom too much, and he trusted the Court would confirm the existing order.

Sir B. Malkin enquired if there was any order of Court making it imperative in the late assignee to continue the services of the late partners at the expense of the estate. Being answered in the negative, he stated his intention to take time to look over his notes, as it was a case of importance, at all events, whether it were one of any difficulty or no, and that he would give his decision on both subjects the next Court day.

The Same. Feb. 20. Sir *B. Malkin* stated, that he found it not possible to pronounce a decision in the matter before the Court last court day, relative to the estate of Cruttenden and Co., without further information. His lordship proposed in the first instance, that it should be referred to Mr. Macnaghten, to report what would be a fair remuneration to Mr. Holroyd; secondly, what would be the probable out-turn of the estate, and the probable time that would elapse before the business of the insolvent firm might be brought to a final close; thirdly, whether the expenses incurred by Mr. Macintyre are reasonable and fair; and what would have been a reasonable remuneration to the original assignee, had he continued in the appointment until the final winding up of the estate. Sir Benjamin explained, that Mr. Macnaghten was not an officer of the Court, but he thought it probable that gentleman had more experience in the affairs of insolvent agency houses than the court's own officer, and, in the event of parties consenting, he thought it would be desirable that Mr. Macnaghten should also have authority to inquire into and report on all circumstances connected with the estate which he might think necessary for the information of the Court. To this arrangement, Mr. Dickens and counsel immediately acceded, and the matter stands over for Mr. Macnaghten's report.

Fergusson and Co. An application of much importance was made in the matter of Fergusson aud Co. Prior to the failure of Alexander and Co., the firm, in anticipation of an expected pressure, applied to the other four large agency houses for assistance, and they agreed to afford it to the extent of twenty lakhs. Subsequently, one of the firms withdrew from the agreement; but the other three drew, or accepted, or indorsed bills to the extent of seventeen lakhs, for which they obtained indigo factories and other landed property as security. These bills were afterwards discounted by the Bank of Bengal, and the indigo factories, &c. handed over to the bank as a collateral security. Subsequently, all the agency houses became in the same condition, and the assignees obtained an order to redeem certain of the securities at a sum at which they were valued by competent persons. The bank at the same time obtained an order for the sale of the indigo factories. The whole of the proceeds, &c., about fourteen lakhs, was paid to the Bank of Bengal, but still there remained unpaid six and a-half lakhs, or rather more. For this sum the Bank now applied for an order *nisi* to prove on the estate of Fergusson and Co., and no doubt, if the rule is made absolute, a similar application will be made for leave to prove on all the other estates, unless the dividends from one or more of them, discharge the whole of the Bank of Bengal's claim.

Dividends were declared of 10 per cent. on the estate of Fergusson and Co., 5 per cent. on that of Colvin and Co., 3 per cent. on Mackintosh and Co., and 2 per cent. on that of Frith and Gordon.

MISCELLANEOUS.

POLYGAMY OF THE KULIN BRAHMANS.

Above the Bansha brahman, rises the Khetriya, and over him the Kulin—the proudest of the proud—who, if not disgusted by the servility of parasites, may live as a prince not among beggars, but among princes of his own tribe. How niggardly soever his habits; how despicable soever his literary attainments, and contemptible his manners; how filthy soever his person, and disgusting his costume; how rapacious soever his disposition, and mean his conduct, to be a Kulin is to be divine. To be regarded with venera-

tion, and flattered by adulation; to be privileged with a home in the bosom of every brahman family; aye, and to be bribed with money for consenting to eat of the bounty of his fellow brahman, are the usurped prerogatives of the Kulin. His visits are welcomed, his stay solicited, his departure regretted, as the removal of a divine being, whose presence confers the *summum bonum* of temporal and eternal blessings.

Notwithstanding his divine origin, as he eats, sleeps, and dies, like other men, we may suppose him to possess the dispositions, appetites, and passions incident to human nature; to be attracted, at least in some period of his life, by connubial happiness; and when married, to seek a settled home, that he may confer on his offspring an education suited to their rank: but, in tracing the path of the divine Kulin, such a supposition would mislead us. Though originally restricted to two wives, with one of whom only he should cohabit, unless she be sterile, he now defies all moral restraints, and multiplies his wives more rapidly than he numbers the years of his life: aye, and has been known at the verge of death, when his friends were bearing him to his long home, anxious lest the ebb of life should bear him beyond their reach ere they could lave his body in the sacred stream, to have married two wives on the last evening of his existence.

One of the least evils arising from this practice is, that other brahmans are compelled to purchase their wives; and brahman daughters, as other cattle in the market, are vended, according to their beauty, youth, and connexions, at from 200 to 400 rupees a-head.

From the *Kula Shastra* alone (an unorthodox work), we learn the origin of the Kulin.

Ballál Sena, a raja, by descent a sudra, and by birth illegitimate, in the 63d year of his age, (about A. D. 904,) appears to have assembled around him the most reputed of his subjects for wisdom and morality; and to have dignified those who possessed decision, meekness, learning, character, love of pilgrimage, aversion to bribes, devotion, love of retirement, and liberality, with the appellation of *Kulin:* thus strewing the walks of literature, science and morality, with the attractions of honour and wealth. Whatever were the reasons for his conduct, whether we suppose the learning of the age to have been a mere gossamer of sophistry; and morality, by a continuous ebb, to have left the exhalations of a putrid marsh to poison the intellectual atmosphere, until the energies of the sovereign were required to rescue his people from crime and barbarity; or whether, taking for our guide the fabled traditions of the times, we admit, that whilst the rest of mankind were sunk in ignorance, India was the only country exalted by wisdom, and that Ballál Sena was nobly ambitious to elevate his subjects still higher in moral excellence ; whatever the circumstances of the age, or the motives of the sovereign, the measure commends itself as calculated to found an empire of knowledge on the ruins of ignorance, give stability by equitable laws to the throne, and encircle so wise a ruler with a halo of glory, which malevolence could not obscure, and which future generations should venerate.

All must regret that the advanced age of Ballál Sena did not permit him to complete his noble design. Had he lived to disrobe of their father's honours those Kulin sons, whom neither paternal example nor the sovereign favour could stimulate to morality ; and to remand individuals so unworthy of their father's distinctions back to poverty and neglect ; he would at its first setting in have arrested a tide of arrogance and wickedness, which without opposition has rolled on through subsequent ages.

To pursue the gradations through which Kulin polygamy obtained its present abominable excess, would neither interest nor profit. Human nature, unbridled, rapidly advances in the path of crime ; and the brahman and Kulin mutually stimulated, this by covetousness and lust, that by fame, would agree to trample down every obstacle to the attainment of their wishes. The Kulin, denuded of moral sensibilities, had much to gain by multiplying his wives; and the brahman, inflated with the pride of exalting his family, forgot the solicitudes of a father when, by giving his daughter to the *nominal* embraces of a Kulin, he inclosed her in an iron cage of necessity, dammed up the streams of domestic comfort, and consigned her to solitude worse than that of widowhood ; a prey to passions, designed by the beneficent Creator to make her an affectionate wife, and the happy mother of a contented family; but which by this unnatural custom, as fires smothered up, consumed by slow degrees her constitution, or breaking out into flames, constrained her to fly to illicit intercourse while under the paternal roof, or to the abode and degradation of a prostitute.

Were a census taken of that unhappy class of beings just alluded to, it would perhaps he ascertained, that the majority is composed of Hindu females, not by nature more frail, nor by disposition more disposed to go astray, than others ; but whose calamity has been to be wedded in infancy to infants like themselves, and whose husbands died before they had attained the age of manhood ; and who, being bound by their shastras to remain in widowhood, never tasted domestic happiness. After allowing for the disparity of numbers between the Kulin and other tribes, were a second census taken, may we suppose that the majority obtained would be made up of Kulin wives. We cease therefore to wonder, when a Kulin's wife, unless a Kulin born, becomes a mother, that her offspring is regarded as illegitimate ; and fear that a mere tithe of such children arrive at manhood. Neglect, not to say wilful murder, can put a speedy termination to their existence. That the destruction of such infants, however frequent, escapes detection may be accounted for, by the reputed sanctity of a brahman's house, and the seclusion of brahmanis from the rest of mankind. The pregnancy of a brahmani reaches not the ear of a Musalman neighbour, till after parturition ; but this, if dishonourable, is of course never announced. Should a whisper breathe reproach on a brahman, a Hindu's bosom is the sacred deposit of such scandal; we may as easily extract water from a flint as elicit the secret from him : veneration for the brahman hermetically seals his lips ; and did it not do so, his caste, his reputation, his livelihood, his family, his home would all be placed in jeopardy by the disclosure. Thus a fountain of iniquity is opened, the streams of which, though concealed from the eye of others, are imbibed more or less by the whole Hindu race, and demoralize them till, *horrible dictu !* they brutalize the father, debase the mother, mock the bride, prostitute the daughter, and murder the infant.—*Cal. Christ. Obs.*

<hr>

EXTORTION.

The *Hurkaru* publishes a letter from a correspondent, giving the following particulars of a case of "Jubburdustee" on the part of the Girdwaree Chowkee, at Moneerampore :—

" On the night of the 21st instant (January), I drove to Moneerampore (a place adjoining to Barrackpore and subject to the Allipore Cutchery), to cross over to Buddibatty, a village opposite to it. It was nearly ten P. M. when I took a boat at Ganty Ghaut, situated between Moneerampore and Barrackpore, but had not proceeded far when some people who were in a boat, said to be of the Girdwaree Chowkee, subject to the thana of Nabobgunge, called out to us to stop. Our boatmen did so, and I observed that they were in good numbers. They demanded of me in angry language what I was about at that time of night. I stated I was going home to my house at Buddibatty, and that it was not an unusual circumstance for men to go on the river at that time of night. They said you must be a dacoit and we cannot let you pass on. No remonstrance prevailed, they would not let us go, and it would have been folly to have attempted to get off by force ; to persuade them of the injustice of their act was equally vain ;—neither could I remain out in the cold in the exposed boat at their command. I was therefore obliged to meet the alternative of a douceur, on giving which I was allowed to go."

LEGISLATION FOR INDIA.

Mr. Charles Thackeray, of Howrah, has addressed a letter to Mr. T. B. Macaulay, in his "legislative capacity," on the "gross absurdities" committed in the acts of the council, for which he holds that gentleman responsible. "You, sir," he says, "have so far forgotten your function, as to promulgate notifications of intended laws, which are as dangerous and illegal in their intent, as they are absurd, contemptible, and abortive in their terms. If you look to the 46th sec. of the Act of Arrangement, the 3d and 4th Wm. IV. c. 85, you will find that it is there provided that the Governor-general of India in Council is precluded, ' without the previous sanction of the Court of Directors,' from *abolishing* ' any of the courts of justice established by his majesty's charters.' Now, sir, I have long had my eye upon those words, ' without the previous sanction of the Court of Directors,' as contained in this clause, and have long been watching for a fit occasion to bring them before the public. Sir, you must know, the most ignorant must know, that a court of appeal is, or is presumed to be, ' a court of justice,' and when you repeal the 107th clause of the 53d of Geo. III. c. 155, which makes the Supreme Court a court of appeal from the mofussil courts, you *abolish a court of justice.* You will, perhaps, say, it is not a court of justice established by his majesty's charter; no; but by a far higher authority—the giver of the power to give charters; and will any Englishman dare to say, that the British legislature intends to protect the court which is constituted by the power they entrust to the king, whilst they leave to the mercy of your hasty and slovenly legislation, the court which it constitutes by its own original authority? None; I will answer for you, no Englishman existing will or dare answer otherwise than—none. Then, sir, I ask you, have you the Court of Directors' previous sanction for the measure in contemplation? If you have *not,* you must perceive that you contemplate a measure of a *rebellious* character, and of the *most* rebellious character, inasmuch as you thereby contemplate, not to overturn the authority of the king, but the authority of king, lords, and commons.

"Legislation, sir, is, or ought to be, a work of deliberation; but I grieve to see that men, whose every word affects the happiness, or rather misery, of some eighty or ninety millions of human beings, should manifest such gross negligence in the structure of their legislative language, as in some instances to utter nonsense, in others to utter worse than nonsense, *viz.*

language tending to give protection and indemnity to the most absurd exercise of the power of nomination to judicial appointments that imagination can fancy in its wildest moods. Why, sir, you are preparing a law of indemnity for the nomination by the governor of Bengal or Agra to the situations of principal sudder ameen, sudder ameen, and moonsiff, of a cooley, a cook, a syce or an old woman—not figuratively, but literally—an old woman. Now, sir, it may not be that the governor or government contemplate such a provision for their burthensome dependents, but if it be not so, you really should not have allowed the governors of Bengal and of Agra to incur the scandal which will necessarily arise from their procuring an indemnity, I should rather say indulgence, to make principal ameens *et cetera* (you know the value of an ' &c.') of old women, children, knaves, fools, or, in your own legislative language, ' any person whatever.* Really, sir, for a gentleman who will legislate after this manner, to take upon himself to repeal acts of the British parliament, and render British subjects amenable to mofussil law, without appeal to the laws of their country, is ' too bad,' and such legislation is founded upon a gross want of knowledge of your own weakness, and of our strength. Sir, you are not legislating for children, when you take in hand to legislate for British-born subjects in India, and we are not used to obey the dictation of nonsense,—nor will we."

The section referred to in the beginning of Mr. Thackeray's letter is the following:—

" Provided also and be it enacted, that it shall not be lawful for the said Governor-general in Council, without the previous sanction of the said Court of Directors, to make any law or regulation whereby power shall be given to any courts of justice other than the courts of justice, established by his Majesty's charters, to sentence to the punishment of death any of his natural-born subjects born in Europe, or the children of such subjects, or which shall abolish any of the courts of justice established by his majesty's charters."

It has extorted the following remarks from the *Hurkaru* :—

" Now we ask our readers, each and all of British birth, whether they can read the above clause, without a feeling approaching to horror, at the bare thought of a Court of Directors having or exercising the right to nominate a tribunal empowered to pass sentence of death upon a British-born subject? But what will our readers

* The following will be found in the *Calcutta Gazette* of the 3d Feb, a rich specimen of loose legislation :—
" It is hereby enacted, that from the—day of—it shall be lawful for the governor of Bengal and for the governor of Agra, to appoint *any person whatever* to the situation of principal sudder ameen, sudder ameen, or moonsiff."

say when they find, that whilst this clause subsists, the government of India are preparing an act, by which the whole ordinary power and authority of the sudder adawlut, and the courts of nizamut adawlut, shall be vested in any and every single judge of those courts; in capital cases in two of those judges. If this be not too bad, we know not what is, or can be. The government, in a word, are about to ' taboo' all India; for what Englishman would consent to hold his life at the disposal of a tribunal established by a Court of Directors of any Company whatever? We earnestly entreat the Government to put forth some assurance that may quiet the alarm which the steps in progress will most undoubtedly spread through the interior; for who can tell that the ' sanction ' is not already obtained; who can say that to-morrow, if we step beyond the precincts of the Supreme Court, we may not be tried for our lives, before a mofussil judge? Nay, more, who can tell whether the government may not extend the jurisdiction of the sudder or other Company's court to Calcutta itself, and give a concurrent jurisdiction with the Supreme Court in criminal as well as civil matters? Let us look to ourselves then, the evil is at the door; let us care for own dwelling—*proximus ardet.*"

The new acts, the drafts of which are published, are on the following subjects :—

The first abolishes the appeal from the Company's Courts to the Supreme Court.

The next ordains that the governor of the two presidencies may appoint any person whatever to the situation of principal sudder ameen, sudder ameen, and moonsiff.

The last act provides that a single judge of the chief civil and criminal court in the country, shall, in every stage of a judicial proceeding, exercise the whole powers of the court, with this proviso, that a single judge shall not reverse the orders of another judge, and that the concurrent opinion of two judges shall be necessity to decree capital punishments.

ESTATE OF MACKINTOSH AND CO.

Abstract of Receipts and Disbursements appertaining to the Estate, for December 1835 and January 1836, filed by the Assignees and published by order of the Court.

Receipts.

Cash balance 30th November	1,74,577
Sale of Landed Property	43,000
Ditto of a Bank of Bengal Share, including arrears of Dividends	17,468
Ditto of Government Notes	63,463
Ditto of Office Furniture	58
Steamer *Forbes*	13,400
Recoveries from Life Insurance	9,738
Rents of Landed Property	1,408
Refund of payments in anticipation of dividends	3,110
Carried forward ..	3,26,222

Brought forward ..	3,26,222
Refund of Loans at Interest	41,000
Interest realized on Loans, &c.	816
Remittances from Dr. Constituents	2,03,871
Sa. Rs. ..	5,71,909

Disbursements.

Advances for the manufacture of Indigo.	22,455
Steamer *Forbes*.....	7,149
Life Insurance Premiums.............	7,031
Repairs of Landed Property, and Durwans' wages	2,965
Law Charges··········	4,180
Office Establishment	3,567
Incidental Charges	100
Government Notes purchased	24,746
Payment in anticipation of dividend ..	251
Dividends paid·····	47,134
	1,19,578
Cash in hand and in the Union Bank ..	4,52,331
Sa. Rs. ..	5,71,909

Memorandum.

Government Securities	13,700	
Unrealized acceptances	2,09,641	
Cash balance and in Union Bank	4,52,331	
Sa. Rs. ..	6,75,672	

ESTATE OF ALEXANDER AND CO.

Abstract of Receipts and Disbursements appertaining to the Estate of Alexander and Co., for December 1835 and January 1836, filed by the Assignees and published by order of the Court.

Receipts.

Cash balance 30th November	2,133
Sales of Indigo	3,66,618
Ditto of Indigo Factories..............	48,500
Refund of Indigo Advances for the Bansbareah Concern, for the Current Season	13,884
Sales of Government Notes	2,316
Ranneegunge Colliery	29,440
Rents of Landed Property	2,420
Remittances from Dr. Constituents	68,628
Sa. Rs. ..	5,33,929

Disbursements.

Advances for the manufacture of Indigo		1,53,609
Ranneegunge Colliery		8,137
Peergunge Saltpetre Concern		544
Law Charges.......................		18,006
Office Establishment		6,182
Incidental Charges		162
Assessments, Durwans' wages, &c. for Landed Property.............		241
Refund to Creditors of sums realized since the failure		2,318
Loan for Indigo advances paid off with Interest		41,376
To the Union Bank..........	4,55,492	
Deduct, drawn	1,58,943	
		2,96,549
		5,27,124
Cash in hand......................		6,805
Sa. Rs. ..		5,33,929

Memorandum.

Cash in hand	6,805	
Ditto Union Bank	3,08,559	
Unrealized Acceptances	3,94,056	
Sa. Rs. ..	7,09,420	

ESTATE OF COLVIN AND CO.

Statement of Transactions of the Assignee of the late firm of Colvin and Co., from

1st to 31st December 1835, filed by the Assignee and published by order of the Court.

Receipts.

Balance on hand per last statement	13,127
Outstanding debts recovered	25,702
Charges for sale of office furniture	27
Indigo sales realized	48,062
Company's 4 per Cent. Paper for Rs. 15,000 realized	14,711
Interest on Company's Paper	1,278
Sale of Indigo Factories...............	45,037
Sa. Rs. ..	**1,47,944**

Payments.

Advances on account of Indigo		14,351
Dividends paid to Creditors............		383
Payment on Life Insurance		855
Postage for October....		31
Payment in part redemption of mort-gage		82,867
Law Charges for Court Fees		8
Printing and other Charges		12
Repairs and Assessments on Houses....		1,133
Purchase of five Government Notes of 5 per Cent. for Rs. 30,000		30,414
Balance in hand this day, *viz.*		
In Cash	13,590	
In the Bank of Bengal	4,300	
		17,890
Sa. Rs. ..		**1,47,944**

Memorandum.

Cash in hand	13,590
Cash in Bank of Bengal	4,300
Cash in Company's 4 per Cent. Paper	1,05,200
Cash in Company's 5 per Cent. Paper	30,000
Sa. Rs. ..	**1,53,090**

From 1st to 31st January 1836.

Receipts.

Balance per last statement	17,890
Outstanding debts recovered	1,01,696
Indigo sales realized	1,27,018
Sa. Rs. ..	**2,46,534**

Payments.

Indigo Advances		18,571
Life Insurance for Premiums paid......		12,390
Charges for Advertisements, &c.		24
Dividends paid in anticipation		5,474
Law Charges in the Insolvent and Mo-fussil Courts		177
Mortgage redeemed in part		14,381
Refund of surplus Receipt		5
Postage account for November last		36
Government Notes purchased, amount to Sa. Rs. 47,600		48,873
Dividend to Creditors		7
		99,868
Balance in Cash .... Sa. Rs.	4,757	
Balance in Bank of Bengal ..	1,36,909	
		1,46,666
Sa. Rs. ..		**2,46,534**

Memorandum.

Cash in hand .... Sa. Rs.	9,757
Cash in the Bank of Bengal ..	1,36,909
In 4 per Cent. Paper	1,05,200
In 5 per Cent. Paper.........	77,600
Sa. Rs. ..	**3,29,466**

ESTATE OF CRUTTENDEN AND CO.

Mr. Dickens has addressed a letter to the creditors of the estate of Cruttenden and Co., with reference to the denial pub-lished by W. Cullen, mentioned in p. 168, in which are the following passages :

" As to what I said of Mr. Browne's allowance, I stated the amount which he had received, but, to the best of my recol-lection, inaccurately ; I think I stated it at 5,200. Mr. Cullen says, and correctly, it was 5,400. I further said, that I be-lieved he had drawn it within a month of his departure. I was wrong in a month and some days. Mr. Cullen himself is in error in saying Mr. Browne drew no al-lowances for services subsequent to the month of Sept.; he was paid up to 10th Oct., though the payment in the assignee's account is entered under date 6th Oct., when four days' allowance was not due. Mr. Browne left India in January 1835, says Mr. Cullen; I hear it was on the 1st January 1835; but really it is scarcely worth while to go into this detail on such a point; from the 10th January 1834 up to the 16th Dec., a period of eleven whole months, Mr. Browne received his allow-ance for nine whole months. I never blamed Mr. Browne for receiving it; I blame the assignee for asking the creditors to pay it. I said, if there be any good reason why it should be repaid, let him go to Mr. Browne, who can repay it. Now, as to what I said of Mr. Cullen's income, it was this : I believed he must have had from 1,600 to 1,800 rupees during the pe-riod, from 10th January 1834, to the time I was speaking. Mr. Cullen says, he has not received his 600 a-month from Mr. Macintyre for the last seven months; to which I reply, that I think, writing from a recollection of the assignee's accounts, be makes a mistake of a month even in this ; but allowing it to be very true, he is *en-titled* to receive it, and Mr. Macintyre is *ordered* to pay it; and this amount and two months' house-rent, at 375 a month, must be added to the 75,000 and some hundred rupees already paid for charges, and so I stated it to the meeting; for I said that, adding these, without interest, the real charge would be full 80,000 for two years. Mr. Cullen's 'simple statement' of his own case is (without affectation I may say it) a very serious puzzle to me : observe, we both speak of the same period of time, *viz.* two years and some days; Mr. Cullen says, ' my *average* income for the two past years has barely reached a *moiety* of Mr. Dickens's estimate (that is, half of 1,800 or 900 a-month), while *latterly* it has fallen *considerably* short of a *third* part of it :' that is, as I understand the matter, an averment that an *average* of 900 a month, during twenty four months, is an *average* during some of the latter of these months ; that is, considerably less than 600 a-month. The solution of this enigma I leave in despair. What I take Mr. Cullen really to mean is this, a quibble on the signification of the words *income* and *receipts :* for instance;

be has *not received* seven months' allowance, or 4,200; therefore, that is not *income* during the '*two past years;*' I make no comments on what I do not understand, but, I submit to your understandings, gentlemen, that, as Mr. Cullen was entitled to receive, and Mr. Macintyre ordered to pay, 600 rupees a month, from 16th January 1834 up to this date, it is no great inaccuracy to estimate that Mr. Cullen has had an income of 600 rupees a month from this source during this period. I have not heard that Mr. Cullen has given this up, or that Mr. Macintyre has refused to pay; if he have refused, he has no right to do so, nor can he legally resist the demand of payment until he gets rid of the order.'

THE NIZAMAT COLLEGE AT MURSHIDABAD.

The Madrissa of his highness the Nizam was instituted by government in 1824. It was designed to relieve the members of the Nizamat family from the expense of private tutors; but more especially to insure them a good moral education. To render it more generally useful, other youths, not connected with the family, were gradually admitted, and an allowance of from six to ten rupees a-month was allotted to some who were expected to persevere in a course of Arabic and Persian for seven years. Maulavi Faizlurahman, a man of integrity and erudition, was appointed first mudarras, with eight professors. During the first two years, 500 students were in regular attendance; after which, their number diminished to 100, but never sunk below that standard. Twelve young men have been honoured with certificates of proficiency, and an additional twelve having passed through the accustomed routine of oriental literature, are expecting the same reward of merit.

It must be a source of regret, that an institution, supported by the highest native authorities, and patronized by the government, has not produced that moral effect on the inhabitants of Murshidabad which the friends of education might have anticipated. In 1833, two young men, who had been educated at the Hindu College, were sent up from Calcutta to form an English class. One died shortly after his arrival, and the other carried on the duties by himself. Though a person of good attainments, the circumstance of his being a Hindu so excited national antipathy, that he could not obtain the esteem of the Musalmans (for whose sole benefit the Madrissa was originally established), and, consequently, in May last, he resigned. The establishment is now under the general superintendance of Mr. Jones; the English department entirely so, in which he has the aid of two native assistants. At his appointment, the English class, in number about thirty, (which consisted entirely of Hindus), increased in one week to eighty, and was

composed both of Hindus and Musalmans. Observing their prejudices, he divided them into classes; the first consisted of Sahibzadas, the second of Mahammadans, and the third of Hindus. This arrangement gave general satisfaction.

Two causes, namely, illness and the festivals, materially reduced the English class during the months of September and October. It has, however, since rallied; eighty-five are now on the muster-roll, and the number steadily advances. It is pleasing to observe, that, as they progress in English, their sectarian differences appear to decrease. In the first class, which is large, Mahammadans and Hindus now promiscuously assemble and read together with as much good will, as if they were all of the self-same caste. The number of students in English consists of fifty-five Musalmans and thirty-five Hindus. The first class read Marshman's Brief Survey of History, the English Reader, No. IV., and Grammar of History. They have commenced arithmetic and geography, and translate from Hindustani and Bengali into English. The students in the Arabic and Persian are 112; the first class read *Baizavi, Hidava,* and *Sharah Viqava,* in Arabic; *Allami, Bahar Danish, Niamat khun Ali,* with all the first authors, in Persian. They also study arithmetic and geometry in Arabic.—*Cal. Christ. Ob.*

MUNICIPAL AFFAIRS.

It must be confessed, there was not very much gained by the two hours of desultory discussion yesterday at the Quarter Sessions. To be sure, we had a public avowal by the whole body of the magistracy (for the only absentee, Mr. McFarlan, has already proved himself a friend to publicity), that the rate-payers have a clear right to know the amount of the taxes they have to pay, and the manner in which the money is laid out. But this right does not appear to have been ever denied; the statements periodically produced at these magisterial meetings, were as much open to the public as to the inspection of their worships; and if they were signed and passed without notice by the one, and without examination by the other (as Mr. O'Hanlon observed, he found himself obliged, in his capacity of examiner to another court, to sign many papers which he really did not examine), it must not be alleged that concealment and mystery were the order of the day, because nobody took the trouble to look into the accounts when exhibited. One point, however, does appear to require clearing up; the present chief magistrate seems to look upon it as his exclusive province to order and regulate all municipal money-matters; and yet his colleagues in Quarter Sessions are expected to put their names to the abstract of the collector's payments and receipts. For ourselves, we approve the principle of a division of labour, and like to fix individual responsibility upon public officers: but let the extent of their powers and responsibility be properly understood, and let things be done in a consistent manner.

Our morning contemporaries are urging the expediency of petitioning for a corporation here, on the reformed principles of the English bill. We should readily join in the request, if we could persuade ourselves that our aldermen or common-councilmen would really attend to the duties expected of them. Past experience is against any such hope; and if you must have paid functionaries because competent persons either will not or cannot devote their time to such duties gratuitously, nothing is gained by taking the municipal business out of the hands of persons under the control of government. Better organization and more zeal are the general consequence of that control, as compared with the usual imbecility of a muncipal corporation.—*Cal. Cour.*, *Feb.* 4.

Statement of Receipts and Disbursements for 1832-33.

Receipts.

House Tax, Gross Collections ......Rs.	2,37,806
Less Commission, and Charges	28,479
Net Collections ·· Rs.	2,09,326

Disbursements.

Thannadaree Establishment ··········	1,13,610
Conservancy Establishment, *viz.* Superintendent of Roads and Executive Officer, and their Subordinate Establishment, Overseers, Sircars, Peons, &c.	32,028
Cleansing the Town ·····················	79,942
Repairing { Roads ·····················	39,608
Drains ·····················	7,335
Buildings·····················	1,116
Rent to Constables, &c.··············	4,321
New Dung Carts·····················	1,389
Petty Charges ·····················	3,941
	1,36,951
Total Disbursements ·· Rs.	2,82,589
Net Receipts ·· Rs.	2,09,326
Excess paid by Government ·· Rs.	73,263

For 1833-34.

Police Thannadars, Burkundasses and others ···················· Rs.	1,45,652
Materials for repairing Roads ··········	16,267
Labour in ditto ditto ··········	12,184
Repairing Cross Bridges, &c. ··········	10,667
Sundry charges, including Thannah Rent, new Carts, Rollers, repairs of Buildings, Office Charges, &c. &c. ··	12,946
Labour in cleansing the Town··········	66,749
Feeding Bullocks for cleansing, &c. ····	6,206
Total Disbursements ·· Rs.	2,69,971
Net Receipts ·· Rs.	1,95,500
Excess paid by Government ·· Rs.	74,171

RENT-FREE LANDS.

The resumption of *lakhiraj*, or rent-free lands, is the subject of discussion in the Calcutta papers. The *Gyannaneshun*, native paper, counsels their resumption, on the ground

that the government pledged themselves in "error or ignorance," a dangerous principle: "If, therefore,"—the writer says, "the time has arrived, when these prodigious errors in legislation are to be rectified by a body of law commissioners imbued with the enlightened spirit of the age, and judging for themselves, not through the misty veil of imperfect official records at a distance of 14,000 miles, but on the spot, and with the country before them, it shall not, we hope, be the good fortune of interested parties to succeed in screening those gigantic abuses with the plea of 'sacred pledges,' or 'undisturbed possession!' As well may the oppressor allege, I ought not to be deposed—I've sat firmly on the throne, though by sufferance, and my children look to it after my death? When the interests of a vast country, like India, are jeopardized by treaties executed by penury-struck parties, under the exultant feelings incidental to the acquisition of exhaustless wealth, it is positively ridiculous to bring forward claims founded on grants from men who could not grant, but blinded by prosperity, looked on the people and their property like a herd of cattle, and disposed of them likewise. In olden times, the Pope of Rome granted the possession of countries to be explored, to his vassal kings and dependents. But history has long since verified the impotency of his fiat, and the inherent right of man to judge and dispose of his own by himself."

LAW OF PRIMOGENITURE.

A writer in one of the Calcutta papers, in replying to an article in the *Reformer*, calling for the introduction of a law of primogeniture in India, observes: "And what is there in India that should make it so particularly desirable to have a law of primogeniture? It is alleged that two or three brothers, who inherit a small landed estate of thirty or forty begahs, or even less, either keep it undivided and live upon it together, or divide it among themselves, and each cultivates his share, content to live on the most wretched pittance. But what would be the difference if the estate descended to the eldest brother? Why, the others would either assist him as servants, or serve other cultivators. What would there be in this more advantageous and beneficial to agriculture? The law of caste, combined with the absence of manufactures, necessarily leaves no other resources but agricultural employments to an immense proportion of the Hindoos. No. It is no law of primogeniture that is required in India. It is instruction and protection from individual tyranny she mostly needs. Let her have a good system of civil, criminal, well administered laws; let her taxes be judiciously levied and moderate; let England deal with her in her commercial regulations, as with an independent and friendly state, and India will prosper! India is at present an agricultural country, and she will remain so until the people require something more than a miserable rag to cover their nakedness, and a wretched hovel for a house to shelter them."

THE " CHARLES EATON."

Advices have at length been received of the appearance of a part of the crew of the ill-fated ship *Charles Eaton*, which, it was conjectured, had been lost in Torres' Straits on 15th August, 1834. It seems that five of the men have arrived at Batavia from Amboyna, whither they had made their way from Timor-laoet, where they had remained for thirteen months. The account the men give of themselves and of the rest of the ship's company and passengers is any thing but satisfactory, and in some particulars is contradicted by facts which have come to light through other, and more credible sources. According to the story told by these fellows, the *Charles Eaton* went to pieces very soon after they left her, and all hands must have perished immediately. In contradiction of this, however, it has been ascertained, that on 5th of last August, the ship was seen hard and fast ashore (on the spot where she is said to have been wrecked), and standing in such a position, that the passengers and others might have maintained themselves alive as long as their provisions lasted. Moreover, we have information, that some Europeans are residing on some of the islands in the straits, and either cannot or will not come away, or communicate with those who have touched there—thereby warranting the inference that they form part of the crew of the unfortunate ship, and that some foul play has been practised in respect to the wreck. The Batavian government is most laudably exerting itself to learn further particulars, and we do not despair of the whole of the circumstances connected with the wreck and the passengers, &c. being brought to light sooner or later.—*Englishman, Feb.* 17.

The *Singapore Chronicle* of December 12, contained the following particulars of this vessel :

" We learn that accounts have been received from the ship *Mangles*, at Lombock, dated 10th October last, that when passing through Torres' Straits she touched at Murray's Island, where eight Europeans, part of the crew of the long missing bark, *Charles Eaton*, were discovered, and who were then under enslavement. The fate of all on board that vessel has, for about two years, been a subject of the most intense interest and anxiety to many in India, particularly to those who had relatives as passengers. The *Charles Eaton* is supposed to have been lost on the Barrier Reef, in Torres' Straits, in

prosecution of her voyage from New South Wales to Madras; but until now, no intelligence has been received as to the certain fate of those who might have escaped from a watery grave, only to a prolonged and dreary existence of servitude and slavery, among a barbarous and savage people, such as the natives of Murray's Island are represented to be."

Among the government notifications, is a communication from " His excellency the Governor of Batavia," describing the measures his excellency had adopted, in consequence of the application of his Honour the Governor-General of India, relative to the survivors of the bark *Charles Eaton*, and embodying a report of the examination of some of the crew of that vessel who had reached Batavia. Not only is the evidence of these men at variance with unequivocal testimony as to the condition of the vessel, but there are other circumstances with which it is equally irreconcileable. The commander of the *Mangles*, or some of his people, according to a statement we recently published, had been informed by some of the crew of the *Charles Eaton* on Murray's Island, that they and the rest of *all* the crew and passengers were detained, as slaves, on the island. Now, supposing that the Timor Laut of the people examined at Batavia, should be Murray's Island, which we believe it is not, still they have not alluded at all to the *Mangles* touching at the island. We hear, moreover, that government has received information, that the *Mangles* in Torres' Straits, fell in with a boat manned by natives, in which there was a European, who refused to come to them when hailed; and that when they sent a boat after him, he jumped overboard and made his escape. Altogether, the circumstances which have transpired relative to this case are very mysterious; and unless there has been a mistake as to the vessel seen upright on the Barrier Reef, "with royal yards across," being the *Charles Eaton*, the men examined at Batavia have sworn to a false statement. We trust a vessel has been despatched to Murray's Island, or that the captain of H. M. S. *Rose*, to whom the commander of the *Mangles* addressed one of his circulars, will have proceeded there. The matter must not be suffered to rest where it is.—*Hurk, Feb.* 29.

INDIA COTTON.

The second volume of the Transactions of the Agricultural and Horticultural Society of India, contains ample proof of the activity with which the improvement of India cotton is sought. There are twenty-seven papers on the subject in the volume, detailing the character and the mode of culture of the plant in different parts of India. The natives are so anxious to adopt the improvements and to obtain seeds and plants. Major Colvin even says, that the zemindar *stole* some of his cotton (Upland Georgia), to secure the seed! In the Akra farm, Upland Georgia has been made to yield the same return as country cotton.

ROADS AND CANALS.

The roads and canals that are to be met with in India, are not only few in number, but most of them exhibit a condition truly miserable. Witness, for instance, the road from Calcutta to Benares. This road is in a good and efficient state as far as Bankoorah; but what terrible obstacle has the traveller to encounter in his passage thence to the holy city. In some places he is obliged to rise up some eighty or ninety feet high, in others he is shoved to a depth, the descent of which is, perhaps, greater than the height he had ascended, and then, perhaps, he meets with a stream, in which he will reckon it his good fortune, if he finds a dinghy to carry him across. In fine, such is the dangerous state of this road, that though Benares is but 436 miles distant from the metropolis by land, people find it more safe to travel nearly double that distance by the circuitous route of the river. The state of the canals is, we apprehend, equally wretched, and it cannot be denied that they are still fewer in number. In the time of our late esteemed Governor-General, the attention of his lordship was directed towards this important subject. Not only, if we remember right, was the construction of one or two roads undertaken at the expense of the state, but private individuals were encouraged to engage in these useful works. Since his lordship's departure, however, the subject has, we are afraid, been altogether lost sight of. No efforts, that we are aware of, have been made to repair the roads that are now being decayed, or to construct new ones to increase the facilities of communication. This state of things is a matter of deep regret.—*Gyannaneshun, Feb.* 17.

EXECUTION OF DECREES.

A few weeks since, the draft of an Act for empowering Principal Sudder Ameens to execute decrees, was read for the first time in the Legislative Council. This proposed enactment naturally led to the supposition that the existing arrangements had been found insufficient for that purpose, and also to the hope that this new provision would effectually prevent the accumulation of arrears in future. The extent of those arrears, however, was not known beyond the limits of the courts, before the publication of the *Agra Ukhbar* of the 90th Jan. In that journal we have a memorandum of the number of decrees remaining unexecuted on the 1st of October, last year, in the seventeen courts embraced within the jurisdiction of the Allahabad Sudder Court, and the account stands thus:

Of the Judge's decrees, there remained unexecuted on that date ... 3,413
Of those of the Principal Sudder Ameens 4,116
Of those of Sudder Ameens .:.... 5,043
Of those of Moonsiffs............... 8,637

Total...... 21,209

If such was the state of the file in the courts under the western presidency, there is no reason to suppose that it was in a more improved state in the lower provinces. Indeed, we have credible information, that in some of the courts, the number of unexecuted decrees is even greater than in the most backward courts under the new presidency. Assuming, however, that there exists the same general average of delay throughout both presidencies, we shall have:

Unexecuted decrees in the seventeen courts of the Agra Presidency 21,209
In the twenty-six courts of the Bengal Presidency at the same ratio................................. 32,400

Total...... 53,609

It is singular that in the courts enumerated in the *Agra Ukhbar*, there should be one court, that of Allyghur, in which no decrees remain unexecuted. That journal ascribes this expedition to the character of the judge. Are we then to ascribe to the same cause the fact, that in the district of Furruckabad, there should be more than a thousand decrees of the judge's court unexecuted? We rather think there must be some other cause for this relative disproportion.

The frightful arrears of unexecuted decrees in the two lower courts, those of the Sudder Ameens and Moonsiffs, shows that the new judicial system requires improvement. The Moonsiffs have to deal with the causes of the very poorest class, and if possible, greater expedition should be used in the final settlement of their cases than even in those of the wealthy; yet forty per cent. of the unexecuted decrees belong to these destitute beings.—*Friend of India, Feb.* 18.

THE MELA.

The tax on the Hindoo devotees who bathe at "the meeting of the waters" during the mela, had produced, on Monday last, about sixty-four thousand rupees. This is a large sum, but we believe it is much less than might have been expected, considering the collections of former years. The amount of revenue collected (the tax being a rupee a head) shows the number of persons who, up to the time stated, had arrived for the purpose of bathing; but though this great influx of people must prove highly beneficial to the trade of the station, as well as profitable to the government, we would rejoice were the pilgrim taxes, by which our rulers countenance and encourage the rites of idolatry, at once abolished for ever.—*Central Free Press, Jan. 30.*

TRADE OF CABUL.

Political Department, Fort William, 8th Feb.—The hon. the Governor-general of India in Council has been pleased to direct the publication of the following paper on the trade of Cabul, in continuation of the extracts already published under date the 16th November last :

" Extracts of letters from Mr. Masson to Captain Wade, dated the 16th of July 1835. On the 10th of July, a kaffila arrived from Qandahar, about twenty yabus (ponies). They were laden with black pepper, salep, saffron, manna, and silk. Up to this date, only the Kurohti Lohanis have ventured with their merchandize to Cabul. The Mir Khels, the most opulent, are shortly expected, as they will have heard that the Shikarpurians have returned to their kotis ; and Mulla Badaruddin has sent them many encouraging letters. It is ascertained that the Lohanis have brought quite, or nearly, 2,500 loads of merchandize, of which 1,500 are of indigo, besides which 600 loads of indigo have been sent to Qandahar. In last year, it is said, not above 800 loads of indigo arrived at Cabul. About 800 loads of linens and cottons are computed to be forthcoming, with 200 loads of sugar, drugs, and sundries."

Accompanying is a statement of the prices at which sales of Indian and other goods are now effected at Cabul.

THE BEGUM SUMROO.

In our last week's paper, it was our painful task to announce the death of her highness the Begum Sombre, on the 27th, at her residence at Sirdhannah.

Her highness had, some days previously, been attacked by indisposition, from which she had perfectly recovered ; when on the night of the 25th, she was suddenly seized with an alarming attack. Dr. Drever had not quitted the house ; his patient was then speechless and apparently senseless ; the applications resorted to had the effect of relieving her. In the course of the 26th, she lapsed into a state of torpor, and early in the morning of the 27th her spirit fled from its earthly tenement.

No time was lost in despatching an express to the magistrate at Meerut and the agent to the governor at Delhi : the former of these officers reached Sirdhannah by noon, and immediately proceeded to the palace, where he was received by Mr. Dyce Sombre, Dr. Drever, and other members of the family. Necessary arrangements were immediately made for the funeral and other ceremonies ; and it being announced that Colonel Dyce had repaired to Sirdhannah, Mr. Hamilton had an interview with that officer, who shortly after returned to Meerut.

The crowds assembled outside the palace walls, and on the roads, were immense, and one scene of lamentation and sorrow was apparent ; the grief was deep and silent, the clustered groups talked of nothing but the heavy loss they had sustained, and the intensity of their sorrow was pictured in their countenances, nor did they separate during the night ; according to the custom of the country, the whole of the dependants observed a strict fast ; there was no preparing of meals, no retiring to rest ; all were watchful, and every house was a scene of mourning.

At nine, the whole of the arrangements being completed, the body was carried out, borne by the native Christians of the artillery battalion, under a canopy, supported by the principal officers of her late highness' troops, and the pall by Messrs. Dyce Sombre, Solaroli, Drever, and Troup, preceded by the whole of her highness' body guards, followed by the bishop, chaunting portions of the service, aided by the choristers of the cathedral. After them, the magistrate, Mr. Hamilton, and then the chief officers of the household, the whole brought up by a battalion of her late highness' infantry, and a troop of horse, the procession preceded by four elephants, from which alms and cakes were distributed amongst the crowd, passed through a street formed of the troops at Sirdhannah, to the door of the cathedral, the entrance to which was kept by a guard of honour from the 30th N. I., under the command of Capt. Campbell. The procession passed into the body of the cathedral, in the centre of which the coffin was deposited on tressels. High mass was then performed in excellent style, and with great feeling, by the bishop. The body was lowered into the vault. Thus terminated the career of one who, for upwards of half-a-century, has held a conspicuous place, in the political proceedings of India. In the Begum Sombre the British authorities had an ardent and sincere ally, ever ready, in the spirit of true chivalry, to aid and assist, to the utmost of her means, their fortunes and interests.

As soon as the family had retired into the palace, the magistrate of Meerut proceeded, with the officers of his establishment, to proclaim the annexation of territories of her late highness, to the British Government ; proclamation was made throughout the town and vicinity of Sirdhannah, by the government authority, and similar ones at the principal towns, in different parts of the jaghire, according to previous arrangement, so that this valuable territory became almost instantaneously incorporated with zillah Meerut, to which it will remain annexed. The introduction of the police and fiscal arrangements having been especially intrusted to Mr. Hamilton, by orders from the government of India, received so far back as August 1834.

The whole of the landed possessions of her late highness revert to the British; but the personal property, amounting to near half-a-crore, devolves by will to Mr. Dyce Sombre, with the exception of small legacies, and charitable bequests.—*Meerut Obs., Feb. 4.*

A writer in one of the Calcutta papers, complains of the fulsome article in the *Meerut Observer*, which we have so greatly retrenched, and observes of the Begum:—

"With the exception of a few old women at Sirdhannah, who were the objects of her charity, her death is hailed as a blessing throughout her territories. The zemindars, who were shamefully screwed and oppressed, are rejoicing that her reign is over. She was about ninety years of age, completely in her dotage, and her affairs were entirely managed by her heir, young Dyce, who takes the name of Sombre and succeeds to all the wealth of the old lady. There must be at least half a crore of rupees at Sirdhannah in palaces, bungalows, elephants, camels, horses, guns of all calibres, &c. &c. &c., and thirty-three lacs were transferred to Company's paper in the four per cent. last year: all this Dyce Sombre will get; but he is only to have the interest of it until he is thirty years of age. He is now about 26. The begum has left all her old and faithful servants, many of whom have served her from twenty to forty years, totally unprovided for. To her physician she bequeathed twenty thousand rupees; to Mr. Troup, who married Dyce's sister, fifty thousand; and to Mr. Salaroli who also married a sister of Dyce, and has a family, eighty thousand. She also left seventy-five thousand rupees to an old officer in the Company's service, who, compared with all her old faithful followers, was quite a stranger to her. These, I understand, are all her legacies, and the remainder goes to Dyce. Old Colonel Dyce, the father of this young man, who was formerly in her service, and quarrelled with her, has not got a fraction. The begum's revenue, including customs and duties of all kinds, amounted to about ten lacs per annum, and her expenditure was not above six. On her death the commissioner and the magistrate of Meerut went to Sirdhannah and took possession of the country in the name of honourable John. This was done simply by proclamation, the people being too ready and willing to acknowledge a new master."

The following passage, in the *Reformer*, native paper, in an article on "the Spirit of the Age," indicates the growing political tone of the native press:—

"In every civilized country, where knowledge shines with its brilliant lustre, where the people value the truth of education, where the educated are stimulated by splendid reward for their talents and learning, merit is, save in India, crowned with success. It is a stimulus highly desirable for the proper cultivation of knowledge. It is for this that prizes are often given to the best of the school boys, that they may diligently cultivate the seeds of early education. Happy, thrice happy are the people of England!! The learned professions, the public service, the highest offices of state, even the senate house, hold out innumerable brilliant prospects to raise the ardour of the youthful student. Invited by these prizes ever kept in public view, thousands of new candidates for fame and promotion, are daily pouring forth from our seminaries in the west and pressing forward, while thousands more advance in successful ranks behind them, to supply their places. How different is the case in India, where the learned have no prospect of 'rising in the world;' where foreigners are enjoying that degree of political privilege, which is the birthright of every Hindu; where the British rulers are so *partial* that they ever sacrifice the interest of the many for the sake of a few of their own race! This is an undeniable fact, and can be demonstrated by several practical instances. To speak the truth, our brethren of England are as mere *birds of passage*. They look on India as a patrimony granted to them for the support of their families in the west. It is an indelible disgrace to Britain to allow her sons thus to plunder the riches of India for the mere satisfaction of the India Company. Hundreds of millions of money are remitted every year to the East-India stock, merely for the discharge of the debts contracted by the Company in the character of merchants—hundreds after hundreds of persons come from that quarter of the globe to fill high situations *here* in India. Amazing policy! Excellent, laudable is the method adopted for the exaction of money! Surely such a straightforward course of social justice at once bespeaks the well-being of the Indian community! It, however, becomes a convincing proof that the power exercised by the British nation in India is a political phenomenon; indeed, our rulers, with all their liberal professions, do not allow the natives to enjoy any degree of political privilege; learned men are denied rewards or honours due to their talents, and none of the educated Hindus are admitted into lucrative situations, as if their talents were treason against the BRITISH INDIAN GOVERNMENT. The line of conduct embraced by our rulers is exceedingly striking, when we consider that even the barbarous Mahamedans allowed the natives to enjoy every kind of political privilege pursuant to their talents, while a nation by far the more civilized and prosperous, scruple to place the aboriginal inhabitants in high dignities. It is a mere mockery to delineate the characteristics of our *enlightened* rulers. Suffice it to say that they can well appreciate their *own* interest and the interest of *their* countrymen. The slight vestiges of labours that have been made by the Anglo-Indian government, for the welfare of the Hindus, bespeak how much good they have done to England and to India."

MR. WAGHORN.

Mr. Waghorn has come out to Egypt, where he has established himself to facilitate the progress of passengers by the steamers. He writes, that the railroad across the Isthmus is actually to be made. The ironwork is in progress at home. When it is finished, the journey to Cairo will be performed in about six hours! By this means, books and parcels may reach Bombay with facility at moderate charge; but while the communication is limited to that port, all India, except Bombay and its immediate vicinity, will be deprived of this advantage; and as for passengers, of course, they cannot avail themselves of steamers at Bombay, unless they are located near that port, since they can only reach it from the interior by land journies, frequently difficult and costly, and at one season, that very season when they would be most anxious to go by steam, impracticable—*ergo* we must agitate for the comprehensive plan and no monopoly. —*Bengal Herald, Feb. 28.*

INSOLVENT ACT.

An Act of our legislature is published today, an extension of that exquisite piece of legislation, the present Insolvent Act, *for three years* from the first of March next, when it expires. When we recollect the many instances in which this act has been condemned by every member of the bar here, and by every judge who has had occasion to refer to it; and when we recollect also, that the reason assigned in England for giving the Act a short extension without amendment, in 1833, was that it had been determined to leave the duty of amending it to the law commission, we may well ask how it happens that so faulty a law should now be extended for another term of three years, without any alteration whatever? how it happens that, while lawmaking has been going on at a steam pace for some time back in advance of the public

wants, a most important matter, especially recommended to the attention of the commissioners by the authorities at home, should have been utterly neglected till the very moment when the Act was about to expire? And now, what occasion is there for a three years' renewal? Why not renew it for six months or a year, and in the mean time set about revising its provisions? The task ought not to be very long, since the working of the Act has made its defects sufficiently notorious.—*Cal.Cour., Feb. 24.*

NEW FORM OF OATH.

In the Supreme Court, February 22. Baboo Russick Krishna Mullick, the editor of the *Gyananneshun*, being one of the petit jury, prescribed a form of the oath that he wished should be administered to him. It was worded nearly thus:—" I call heaven to witness that, between my sovereign lord the king, and the prisoners at the bar, I shall give a verdict according to the evidence I bear." The oath was accordingly administered to him by Mr. Blacquiere, the chief interpreter, under the sanction of the judge on the bench.

DEFENCE OF POLYGAMY.

The discussions in the Calcutta papers, on the subject of polygamy, has brought forth the following plausible defence of it, by a native:—

" Sir,—You English gentlemen are very fond of complaining against the natives of this country, because they marry many wives. If your religion and the customs of your country don't allow you to have more than one woman as wife, why should we be guided by you, who are of another nation and religion? It is a true thing, which every body acquainted with Asia knows, but how it happens nobody knows, that there are more women than men in this country, whether because more females are born, or because you Englishmen kill the males in battle, magician only can tell. Then, in this case, giving one woman to every man, what is to become of the remaining many women? They must have somebody to love them. The plain truth is, we are destined by nature to have many wives and much happiness—it is our good fate to have many wives—it has been so from the beginning of the world. Don't then, I pray, interfere with the decree of nature."

SALE OF HOUSE PROPERTY.

We are happy to hear from several quarters, that there is a demand for landed property, and that purchasers will come forward, if they are satisfied that there is any disposition to sell at market rates. Hitherto there has been so strong a determination to stand up for old prices, that no person, whose time was valuable, would throw it away by attending sales, when there appeared no inclination to sell. Such was the case with the frequent mock sales of the landed property of the estate of Cruttenden, Mackillop, and Co., under the former Assignee.

The new Assignee, with prompt and sound judgment, is fast turning indigo, ships, waste ground, and old bricks, into sicca rupees. The ruinous premises in Cossitollah, formerly Duckett's coach manufactory, and subsequently James Lamb and Co.'s auction, were yesterday sold by Jenkins, Low, and Co., for 32,200 rupees; and considering that it must cost 7 or 8,000 rupees to put them in good repair, they have, we think, brought a good price; more, indeed, than it was generally thought they would sell for.

We trust for the sake of the creditors of the late firm of Cruttenden and Co., that all the other houses, belonging to this estate, will be speedily offered for sale at moderate upset prices, when there will be no want of bidders. Competition and the disposition to buy, which appears to prevail at present, will realize fair prices, and assist in making a speedy dividend.—*Hurkaru.*

ABOLITION OF SALT SALES.

We understand that government has determined to do away with the salt sales. A price is to be put upon each description of salt in the government golas, and any person may buy as much or as little as he pleases at any time. By this method, the speculation which has hitherto taken place at the periodical sales, will be put an end to; for no capitalist will be foolish enough to buy for an advance, when his powerful competitor is always ready to undersell him. If, indeed, the stock in the golas were to be reduced to something near the means of an individual, it might be all purchased at once; but this it is easy for the Board to prevent, as the regulation of the supply is in their own hands.—*Hurk.,* Feb. 26.

ABOLITION OF LOTTERIES.

We are very glad to learn, that an abomination against which we have long raised our voice, is at last likely to be done away with, by the act of government. The *Gyanunneshun* tells us, that the lottery committee are recommending the abolition of the government lottery. Sorry, however, are we to say, in announcing the cessation of this national disgrace, that we can neither compliment the government upon the occasion, as for an act of virtue; nor can we flatter ourselves with the gratifying reflection, that our humble efforts contributed to the long called-for measure; seeing that the government are not leaving off the lottery, but as is said of old rakes, in respect of their vices, the lottery is leaving off the government. In other words, the committee have reported a "loss," and humble individuals, not to speak of governments, are rarely guilty of practising vices from which they derive neither pleasure nor profit; far less where such vices are merely odious and expensive. We cannot but congratulate the public at large in this instance, upon being far in advance of government, both in virtue and in good sense.—*Ibid.*

SUPERINTENDING SURGEONS.

We have just heard it rumoured, that intelligence has been received by government, that superintending surgeons are to be allowed to retire on the pay of lieut.-colonels, immediately on their promotion, instead of serving two years in that grade, as formerly; also that the three additional annual retirements from the Medical Fund have been sanctioned.—*Journal Med. and Phys. Science.*

AGENT AT MOORSHEDABAD.

The Calcutta papers are full of letters and "editorials" on the subject of the appointment of Capt. J. Higginson, 58th N. I. (announced in our last Register), to the post of Agent to the Governor-General at Moorshedabad, which is stigmatized as "the Moorshedabad Job." Capt. Higginson is stated to be a relation of Sir C. Metcalfe; he entered the service in 1826. On this subject, the *Hurkaru* observes:— "With reference to some recent appointments, we have heard an opinion expressed that delicacy precludes a successor of a governor-general from rescinding the appointments of him to whom he succeeds. We cannot admit the force of this plea, more especially if it is to be urged in bar of a just regard for the interests of the public service in any case, and still more when it applies to appointments made at a period when the successor was hourly expected; for surely then delicacy is at least as much violated by such appointments, as by the rescindment of them."

TRANSIT DUTIES.

We have at last the satisfaction of announcing, that the *fiat* has gone forth to abolish the transit duties throughout the Bengal provinces.* While, however, we rejoice that Sir Charles Metcalfe has not quitted the helm without conferring upon

* "*Fort William General Department,* 1st *March,* 1836.—Notice is hereby given, that from and after the 1st of April next, the several custom houses and chokeys, established for the collection of inland or transit duties at the stations and in the districts of Patna, Moorshedabad, Dacca, and Hooghly, shall be discontinued; and from that date forward, all articles of merchandise, goods and commodities, shall pass through the provinces and districts of the Bengal presidency, without payment of any duty, tax, or fee whatsoever, and shall not be required to be covered by a ruwana or pass, or by any other document as a protection from the demand of duty."

us this great benefit to the commerce and industry of the country, we must take leave to remind the Governor-General, that the measure is not yet complete. So long as the town duties are continued, a large portion—we may say the most vexatious portion—of the trammels upon internal trade will continue, and with them all the abuses of a complicated system of thanahs and passes, which there is the less motive to maintain for the collection of a reduced revenue. We have always held, that it was idle to treat the question of the two descriptions of duty separately. Both must go together, and we trust, as reason has been victorious in one part of the field, she will not delay to drive her enemy from the rest of his position. There is still another important respect in which this measure is incomplete. The transit and town duties of the Madras and Bombay presidencies remain to be extinguished. Surely, Sir Charles Metcalfe will not mar a liberal act by presenting it with a character of partiality, as if its aim were merely to win golden opinions at the seat of his own government, instead of consulting alike the welfare of the whole country.

Possibly it may create some surprise to see these obnoxious taxes removed, without any announcement of other taxes in their place, it being known that the Customs' Committee have been some time charged with the consideration of a substitute in augmented duties upon external trade. Their first report, we understand, is before government; but whether or not it embraces that department of their investigation, we are unprepared to say—we believe not. Of course, it will not be expected, that so important a resource as the Inland Customs of the four presidencies should be given up gratuitously. But the necessity of an equivalent is not so pressing as is commonly supposed. We are informed upon good authority, that, after very careful investigation, it has been discovered, that the finances of India are at this time yielding a real surplus, instead of exhibiting a deficit, all the home charges inclusive.—*Cal. Cour. Mar.* 1.

The *Hurkaru* states, that " Enquiries recently instituted, have elicited some very curious facts relative to the operation of the transit system in various parts of India. Among other singularities, the following mode of collecting transit dues existed for some years in the province of Berar, but has since been abolished : ' A transit duty was levied on all women travellers *enceinte*, and on all animals great with young,' "

POWER OF THE COMMANDER-IN-CHIEF.

The *Bengal Herald*, in a controversy respecting the power of the head of the army in India, alluding to " the disposition of high military authorities in India occa-

sionally to overstep their powers," adduces the following illustrations :

" Among the financial arrangements of the Bengal government, a few years ago, was the abolition of the King's depôt at Chinsurah. Against this measure the commander-in-chief had strongly protested, but was overruled; the depôt was dissolved, and its inmates ordered into Fort William. The governor-general and commander-in-chief at this period were both on the Hills. No sooner did the latter hear of the abolition of the depôt, than he resolved on its re-establishment, and sent orders to the officer commanding the presidency division, to direct the staff and others to return to Chinsurah, resume their appointments at the depôt, and conduct the duties, pending a reference to the Horse Guards. This order reached the officer commanding the division, Col. Ximenes, in due course. Sir Charles Metcalfe was then vice president in Council, and simply forbade Col. Ximenes to issue the order at his peril, and interdicted any officer or man recently employed at the depôt, from quitting Fort William. Col. Ximenes was too old a soldier to hesitate which to obey —he bowed to the civil authority, and the military mandate was thus treated as ' waste paper!' Still worse, his Excellency had the option of rescinding the order, or of resigning his command. After a struggle, he accepted the less ruinous alternative, and withdrew the order.

" It happened, some years ago, that, on casting his eye over the present state of his Majesty's corps in this country, the commander-in-chief in India observed, that in a certain dragoon regiment there were 100 horses ' wanting to complete.' This seemed to his Excellency objectionable; but what was the course pursued ? Instead of bringing the omission to the notice of Government, and requesting respectfully that measures might be adopted to rectify the same, he directed the adjutant-general to lay his commands on the commander of the forces in that presidency to complete the regiment forthwith. The mandate went its errand. It found its way at length to the Council-table, and great was the surprise and wild the laughter, when its tenor was promulgated. ' His Excellency commands that the corps should be completed,' ' orders from the Horse Guards,' &c.! The government were much obliged to him, but they recognised neither his Excellency nor the Horse Guards, as any authority for their proceedings. The appropriation of the revenue of a local presidency did not rest with the commander-in-chief in India, but with the local government. As an economic measure, that government had resolved the said regiment should be kept 100 horses short of its complement, and to change those orders they did not intend, and this was quietly

(2 F)

intimated to the commander-in-chief. His mandate was thus considered as so much ' waste paper,' and the corps is 100 horses short of its complement to this very day.''

UNION OF THE REVENUE AND JUDICIAL FUNCTIONS.

An official circular appears in the Calcutta papers, the object of which is to elicit reports on the result of the system of uniting revenue and judicial functions. The enquiry is instituted by desire of the Court of Directors, who think that the question of the advantage or disadvantage of the system will be determined by the increase or diminution of crime. The Sudder, in their circular to the magistrates, appear to consider it as involving such a mixture of fact and opinion, that it will be no easy task to separate one from the other. " One district may exhibit under the actual system, a great diminution of crime for the period of comparison—another an equal increase; and these two results of the same system must obviously be referred to some other cause than that of the system itself, and the results, be they what they may, be influenced by circumstances which no tabular form can exhibit."

MANOOLA, THE DACOIT OF JESSORE.

" At last, through the zeal of our magistrate and collector, Mr. A. F. Donnelly, Manoola, the Robin Hood of Jessore, has been apprehended and lodged in the jail of this district. This desperate character has hitherto eluded and laughed at the many attempts made by Mr. Donnelly's predecessors to capture him. Indeed, in the different societies of indigo planters in which I have mingled (men of experience and nerve too), I have always heard even the idea of its being possible to capture Manoola quite laughed at and ridiculed.'' —*Corres. Hurk.*

NEW MEDICAL COLLEGE.

We had the gratification to be present for the first time, to-day, at one of the ordinary examinations of the students at the new Medical College. The number of scholars present exceeded fifty, including not more than three or four Christians, a large portion of them quite boys. The manner in which, one after another, these native youths explained chemical affinities, and answered the many difficult questions put to them by Dr. O'Shaughnessy, was sufficiently surprising, and we were about to note the names of one or two of the boys who seemed to us distinguished by their intelligence; but we soon found that we should but be doing injustice to others, for as the still more difficult portion of the examination proceeded, boys who had hitherto escaped notice, showed themselves able to meet a severe examination on the construction of

the human form, the names and uses of the bones and nerves, &c. &c., and two of them, without the least embarrassment, explained the various dislocations of the shoulder, the effect and appearances thereof, the nature of a dislocation in the thigh, and the manner in which it was to be distinguished from a fracture in the neck of the thigh bone. We really were in no small degree delighted at the great and rapid proficiency of the students, which certainly reflects very great credit upon Principal Bramley and his assistants, as well as upon the attention and talents of the pupils themselves, considering that the lectures only commenced in June last.—*Cal. Cour. Feb.* 13.

NATIVE FEMALE EDUCATION.

In Mr. Adams's report, it is stated that in Rangpur it is considered highly improper to bestow any education on women, and no man would marry a girl who was known to be capable of reading; but as girls of rank are usually married about eight years of age, and continue to live with their families for four or five years afterwards, the husbands are sometimes deceived, and find, on receiving their wives, that after marriage, they have acquired that sort of knowledge which is supposed to be most inauspicious to their husbands. Although this female erudition scarcely ever proceeds further than being able to indite a letter and to examine an account, yet it has been the means of rescuing many families from threatened destruction. The women of rank live much less dissipated lives than the men, and are generally better fitted for the management of their estates, on which account they are considered intolerable nuisances, by the harpies who seek to prey on their husbands and to plunder their estates. Mr. Adams mentions, that there were at one time several schools for native girls in Beerbhoom, but they have all been formed into one central school, which is in connexion with the Calcutta Baptist Female School Society. Until lately it contained upwards of eighty girls, but since the hurkaree employed to collect them was dismissed, and especially since the employment of Christian instead of non-christian teachers, the school has fallen away one-half, there being at the date of the last report only forty girls on the list. Almost all attend in the morning, but there is always a considerable deficiency in the afternoon.

MOFUSSIL MISCELLANEOUS NEWS.

(From various Journals.)

Cawnpoor.—This station, as the Guide books would say, is the ancient Kanb, or city of the cupid of the Hindoos, a name given to it probably from the devotion to gallantry shewn by its inhabitants, and which, whether arising from the soil or atmosphere, is in as active operation now as it was centuries ago. Old maids and scandal are not more naturally associated than Cawnpoor and gallantry, nor is there, in Gangetic India, any station where you can be deprived of a mistress or wife with more despatch or *eclât*. This gallantry, which frequently expresses itself by an elopement, sometimes in a stage trick, by dropping a letter, is, however, sometimes equivocally shewn in a 'jocular remark,' as may be gathered from the following recent anecdote. A number of charitable ladies announced, in the following circular, a sale of all the pretty toys they had beguiled the tediousness of the hot months in making :—

" The Ladies of the Committee of the Native Female Orphan Asylum beg to notify, that the sale of fancy articles (for the benefit of the above institution) will take place on Tuesday next, the 2d February, between noon and 3 P. M.—Cawnpoor, January 30th, 1836.''

And with it was forwarded the following note to the Brigade-Major, Capt. Forbes :—

'' My dear Sir,—The ladies of the Committee of the Native Infantry Asylum will be obliged by your encouraging the writers of the corps to copy the annexed notice, in order that it may be generally known.— Jan. 30th, 1836.''

A copy of the notice, the circulation of which was thus provided for, was, of course, laid before Brigadier Churchill, *pro forma*, for his sanction for the meeting. The Brigadier, however, was disposed to treat the subject in jest, and across the circular wrote as follows :— " Who, in the name of all that is holy or unholy, is this Committee ? Who is the President ? Mrs. Vaughan or Mrs. Ram Chunder Pant ?"

This remark did of course, created a considerable sensation in the Cawnpoor circle; some contended that Brigadier Churchill's " minute'' was intended for a jest, a mere joke, though the gallant and gallant writer had forgotten the point; while others maintained that it had some connection with the cause of Mr. White, which was espoused generally by the station at large, particularly by the members of the Female Asylum Society. The agitation subsided, by the Brigadier withdrawing his refusal, and disclaiming all intention of being wanting in courtesy by the " Jocular Observation.''

Bhurutpoor.— His Highness the Raja has just proceeded on a Battue to Roobas, accompanied by his dewan Bolanath, and a large cortége. Among the other amusements which occupy the time of royalty, is that of flying kites. Seated at their tent

doors, the Rajah and his prime minister, fatigued with the cares of the state, amuse themselves in flying and endeavouring to cut the strings of each other's kites, in which the skill of the Rajah, or the deep respect of the minister, generally inclines the victory to the former.

Lahore.— Raja Ruttun Sing, one of the principal and favoured chiefs of Runjeet, has forfeited the favour of his master and his jagheers, for his unreasonable and traitorous conduct. No Nihil, the amorous grandson of Runjeet, had fallen in love with the reputed beauty of the daughter of Rutton Singh, and demanded her in marriage ; the father, however, refused to send his daughter to the royal menagerie, as she had long been betrothed to the son of a fellow sirdar. He even resisted the solicitations and orders of Runjeet himself, who, by virtue of his royal prerogative, confiscated his property, and threw him into prison. The Raja, however, has effected his escape, and will probably " turn rebel'' for his uncourteous treatment.

It is stated that Runjeet, having brought Sultan Mahomed Khan to Lahore, under the express promise of appointing him agent of Peshawer, and having failed to keep that promise, the brother of Sultan Mahomed, Dost Mahomed Khan, assembled 15,000 or 20,000 Mulkeas, &c. at Jullalabad, whence he intends marching forthwith on Peshawer and taking vengeance upon Runjeet.

The Mussulman population at Lahore are, it appears, in a state of considerable excitement. Monsieur Ventura has been ordered by Maharaja Runjeet Sing, to appropriate a certain worshipping place for the purpose of holding his kutchery. Remonstrance against this insult was, of course, useless ; the circumstance, however, has produced great dissatisfaction in the minds of the " faithful.''

Agra.—Baron Hugel was at Hansi on the 10th of January, and proposes to leave Delhi for Jeypore on the 17th, where he expects to arrive about the 20th. The lateness of the season compels the baron to run through Rajpootana to Bombay as quickly as possible, with the view to embark at once for Europe. The tour to Cashmere is described by the baron as interesting, but fatiguing. In going, he took the hill-route by Belaspoor, Jualamooki, and Tommoo, and in returning followed the Jeelam to Mayufferad, and went from thence to Attock, to make some observations on the Indus.

Delhi.—Mr. Cowley, the artist, is employed on an historical painting of the King of Delhi, representing his Majesty and four sons, a species of grouping in high estimation among the kings of the east.

The kidnappers of Delhi continue to steal young children, both within and without the walls of the city, and, it is said, find a ready sale for them in the palace of the Great Mogul.

Allahabad.—The Baza Baee arrived here on the 11th instant, *en route* to Benares, where she goes on a pilgrimage.

Jeypore.—Hookum Chund and Futteh Lol were delivered over to Major Alves at Raja Ghur, by Captain Lloyd, of the 36th N. I. The former was brought up for examination before Major Alves, Captains Thoresby, political agent at Shekawattee, Ludlow, and Conolly. His examination was suspended, or, as it is reported, concluded: nothing was elicited from him to corroborate the documentary evidence, which we hear fixes clearly the affair of the 4th of June on Joota Ram and his party. His answers to the various questions proposed were all in the *non mi ricordo* style. The examination of the younger prisoner, Futteh Lol, was to commence, and on the close of it, Major Alves would return to Juepoor. Both prisoners are to be confined in a gurry outside Juepoor, and close to the Residency, being separated, to prevent collusion.

The Ulwur Raja received the Furingees with all his country's hospitality; he entertained Major Alves, his suite, and the officers of the different escorts, at a sumptuous English dinner, and on the succeeding days amused them with displays of the favoured sports of the Rajpoots—the death of a tiger, cheeta hunting, elephant fights, wrestling, &c. &c. The Raja is stated to be a fine specimen of the Rajpoot himself.

Our troops in Shekawattee will shortly move to the neighbourhood of the city of Jeypore, where, it is said, a new cantonment will be formed.

Loodianah.—Dr. Henderson has arrived here from his travels in the Punjab and Hills, and in conformity with the orders of the Commander-in-chief, has been placed under arrest, until he gives a satisfactory explanation of his unauthorized passage across the frontier. His arrest is, of course, merely formal; and on the receipt of his explanation at head-quarters, he will probably be released, when we may expect to get some account of his interesting expedition.

Herat.—The carrier traders, who conduct the trade between this and Eeran, Russia, Mazinderan, and Toorkistan, have lately been so harassed and pillaged by the marauding Belochees, that they one and all represented their case before the Heerat ruler, Sha-Kamren, a son of the unfortunate Shah-Zuman, who derives no inconsiderable income from this trade. Urged

by their solicitation, and the fear of his revenue being impaired, he sought out the Beloches, and coming on them unawares, a sanguinary conflict ensued, which terminated in the slaughter or capture of the principal leaders of these hordes. The victory has been followed up by the Shah, who is now investing one of their strongest holds, the fort of Las.

Aurungabad.—The power of an exposing press is felt at even this remote and semi-barbarous state. The Nuwab Viceroy, whose illegal and arbitrary conduct was noticed in a former paper, on the receipt of it at Aurungabad, was so conscience-stricken or terrified, as suddenly to convene an assembly of his Omlah, to whose agency or connivance he attributed the wrongs complained of; and before them to state, that the first act of injustice or oppression brought before him should be summarily punished. This exhortation was followed up by an instant removal of some of the most corrupt of them, and the substitution of others of better character.

Madras.
MISCELLANEOUS.
AFFAIR OF SOOBROYAH.

The case of Soobroyah, late of the commissariat department at Bangalore, and now a prisoner for trial by court-martial, is not likely to be brought to a speedy conclusion. Some time has now elapsed since the court-martial first convened to try him was dissolved, and another ordered; but, strange as it may appear, up to the present date, no advance whatever has been made in the trial—the court has not yet been once opened. The proceedings of the former court,—embracing the investigation into one of the charges preferred, and having occupied the attention of the court nearly two months, but without any thing being established against him deserving of bonds or imprisonment—have been to no purpose whatever; the present court will have to proceed as if no investigation had been entered upon; and Soobroyah be still a prisoner in the main guard. Will this be tolerated? Is there no power to which this persecuted individual can appeal, and demand either to be put on his trial, or discharged from further restraint and responsibility?—if not, in what consists the dearly-purchased privilege of the *habeas corpus?* So severely had Soobroyah been made to feel he was a prisoner, that he had not been permitted to perform the last solemn service to an aged parent, or to be near her in her last moments to receiving her dying commands and benediction:—nay more, a British officer, whose heart was not steeled against every tender emotion, for having been less rigorous in the discharge of his duty than it was desirous he should be—for having granted some trifling indulgence to Soobroyah during his mother's sickness, we have been told, was severely reprimanded for the feeling and sympathy he had shown! —It has also been communicated to us, that more than one appeal has been made by persons, supposed from their rank and standing in the service to have influence, to the head of the Madras government, for some relaxation in the severity of the confinement to which that unfortunate and ill-used man had been so long subject—but without avail. Did Soobroyah know less of the private history of some few, than we have been informed he does, and of the way in which they have discharged the duties pertaining to the appointments they hold, and amassed the fortunes they possess, it has been said, the way in which he acquired his own wealth would never have excited suspicion, much less been subject-matter for enquiry.—*Mad. Cour. Feb.* 8.

GOOMSUR.

Letters from Goomsur, dated the 30th January, state, that in the western side of that country, a strong range of hills had been cleared of the rebels. The destruction of their granaries, and some night attacks made on the rebels, had completely intimidated them. The young Rajah has since expressed a desire to deliver himself up to the commissioner, who has gone to Nowgaum, and hostilities had in consequence ceased.

MARINE EXCURSION.

An excursion of a novel description for the Madras Roads, but which is likely to be of frequent occurrence if the break-water prove successful, took place this day. A party of ladies and gentlemen, not having the fear of the surf before their eyes, went on board the *Wellington* for a cruise, passed astern of H. M. ship *Andromache*, proceeded to sea, and returned a few hours afterwards, highly gratified, we understand, with their short but very agreeable voyage.—*Mad. Gaz. Jan.* 26.

Bombay.

MISCELLANEOUS.

THE ELPHINSTONE COLLEGE.

Our presidency readers must have observed with delight an advertisement, announcing the opening of the first term of the Elphinstone College. They ought to be congratulated for the establishment of this and other seminaries, intended to give superior knowledge of European science and literature, as it is not quite ten years ago, when Bombay could not

boast of a single respectable school for the education of natives; and when children were obliged to beg for the little knowledge of the English language, necessary to gain employment in public offices of Government. Now, then, as it is in the power of even the poorest of them, to bestow the blessings of sound instruction on his children, we repeat that the opportunity will be embraced as widely as possible, and that no parent will neglect to perform the important duty which he owes to himself, to his children, and to the community generally, of sowing the seeds of knowledge in their minds.—*Durpun, Feb.* 19.

MALWA OPIUM.

The quantity of Malwa opium exported from Bombay to Canton in 1835, was valued in a late number of the *Courier* at Rs. 1,25,00,000. Fifteen years ago, not a single chest was exported of this article. To the enterprize of the British merchants and the British Government this new traffic is solely attributable. It has proved highly advantageous to the agricultural interests of Malwa, and promises soon to make it one of the richest provinces of India. A correspondent, on whose local knowledge we can safely rely, states, that "it has contributed to raise the rents of every village in Malwa most considerably. In some villages, the rents, owing to the increased cultivation of opium, have been more than doubled within the last fifteen years."—*Ibid.*

CULTIVATION OF COTTON.

The following is a comparative statement of the cultivation of cotton in the Surat district, during the present and the preceding years:—

Pergunnahs.	A. D. 1834-35. Begahs.		A. D. 1835-36. Begahs.
Burdolee	86		57
Boharee	67		107
Chicklu	20		30
Chorassee	4,151		4,363
Kurode	2,084		2,158
Mota	782		853
Colpar	2,708		3,000
Khoorasud	19,656		23,985
Parchol	2,157		3,690
Parnura			8
Soopa	2,791		4,171
Surbohon	3,416		3,979
Turkesur	3,532		3,775
Walor	2,458		3,620
	43,912		53,799

From this it appears that the quantity of ground under cultivation in Surat is about 25 per cent. greater than it was last season. In the Broach districts, the increase is upwards of 30 per cent. In Dhargar and Candeish, it may, at a low estimate, be placed at 20 per cent. From the rest of the Bombay territories, accounts are yet wanting; but as they have been received from the principal cotton districts, and as the extension of cultivation is proportionably greater in the larger than in the smaller ones, we shall, we believe, be rather under the mark in placing the average increase of cotton cultivated throughout the presidency this year at 25 per cent. —*Cour. Feb.* 16.

TRAVELLERS IN ARABIA.

By the last arrival from Muscat, letters have been received from Lieuts. Wellsted and Whitelock, of the I. N., who are attempting to penetrate the Arabian peninsula to the capital of the Wahbees, Derhia. These enterprising travellers have made a short journey in the hill country lying westward of Muscat, and thus describe this hitherto unvisited tract :

" The country in general is very fertile, and in some spots fruits of nearly every kind met with in India, are to be seen. The native Bedouins have behaved to us with an hospitality of conduct, that indeed has been aught but very pleasant, as we have no way of returning it but by reiterated thanks. We are now lodged in the Shaik's house of the village of Neizma, who supplies us from his own table with every kind of dressed food, vegetables, and fruits ; and he is so pressing for our stay, that one of us is obliged to remain here at least a week for fear of offence. The house is situated in the midst of a forest of vegetable luxury. Every kind of fruit clusters in at the windows, and when oppressed by the slightest thirst, we have no more to do than pluck one of the golden oranges or clustering bunches of grapes, that hang ready to our hands. This is an Arcadia I was not prepared for in Arabia. The sides of the hills are terraced, and sown with wheat. The lower parts of the hills are thickly set with vines and pomegranate, and the other fruits are grown in gardens.

" The thermometer at night we felt as low as 44°, and by day it only rises to 60°, which has again sown the English bloom upon our cheeks, and put us in rude health for our long journey. The inhabitants of the hilly district are a fine athletic race, and the best sample I have seen of the sons of Ishmail ; and need I add, that the women are remarkably fine, and possess an intuitive grace, that has quite put all idea of civilization from our minds. The natives distil a wine from the grapes, which they drink in great quantities ; but as it is not of a very intoxicating quality, they don't think much of breaking the first precept of their religion."

Further, they speak of the scenery as exceedingly grand ; and their comforts of travelling have in every way been provided for, by the kind attention of the Imaum. Matters of a pecuniary nature have obliged the return of one of them to Muscat, whence they proceed to the capital Derhia ; not to proceed empty-handed to the presence of the barbaric chief, they are providing themselves with a few presents, which at least may tend to their safety on their journey there.

As this is a journey fraught with much peril, and highly interesting to enquiring minds, we only hope it may prove successful, and that the two travellers who have so nobly offered their services for such an undertaking, may return in safety, to reap the rewards of a liberal government, and the thanks of their gratified countrymen.

This system of making journeys into the interior is connected with the survey of the coast ; who it originated in I don't know, but the design is a grand one, and from a mind of no common draught. Our geographical knowledge of the countries around us is very scant, and not at all creditable to us from the long time we have held sway in these countries. It is now that the English traveller has the best chance of penetrating those countries, that have bid defiance to the traveller for many centuries, when our name as a nation is respected, which it certainly is by the most barbarous ; when the most petty boat from the smallest places on the Afric and Arabian coast visits our ports unmolested, and receives the rights of the greatest ; they return marvelling at the greatness of our justice, and they are thus made ready to treat us, when we visit them, with kindness and hospitality. The journeys of Lieut. Wellsted along the Arabian coast have proved this, and his journals when printed, or his observations when added to the stock of general knowledge, will tend more to the honour of the service he belongs to, than the sheets of chart paper that have been compiling for ages.—*Bomb. Gaz. Jan.* 20.

STEAM-NAVIGATION.

A letter from Bombay mentions, that one of the Ameers of Sinde has expressed a desire to have a steamer built for him at Bombay, to navigate the Indus, and that the Court have been requested to send out engines for her.

Ceylon.

The Governor and the Merchants.—The *Colombo Observer*, of January 12th, has the following comments upon the Governor's letter to the Merchants (p. 160) :—

" Our astonishment at the receipt of his Excellency's communication could only be equalled by our regret, that so injudicious and ridiculous a production could proceed from the head of the government under which we live. We leave it to Mr. Read and his younger brethren to answer the ' serious complaint ' brought against their body.

"In entering upon our own defence against the gross charge, made so undeservedly against us by Sir R. Horton, we beg leave to call the attention of our readers to a specimen of the difficulties we are at times placed in, of discriminating between public and private character. We are here accused of *corruption*, involving the integrity of our entire reputation, and in a manner too which might make us question the same in our hon. opponent: we shall, however, rather suffer wrong than follow his example, further than our duty to society demands.

"'It is notorious,' as his Excellency remarks, 'that the merchants have been and are the chief proprietors of the *Observer* paper,' that is, numerically speaking, but even not so much so as is generally supposed; but whatever 'slanderous' insinuations these words are intended to convey, the public may remember that we have already given them the terms on which the editor of this journal holds his office, and well does the Governor know them, as we could easily prove; but, to refresh the memory of our readers, and particularly of him who so carefully peruses our columns, we refer to our 4th No, where they will be found. From this the real state of the case is seen; that a few independent men, who were desirous that the liberties of the colony should not be trampled on with impunity or in silence, determined to have an organ which would, as far as they could insure, equally protect the rights of the *many* as well as of the *few*, and accordingly established this press, and committed the charge of it to the present object of Sir R. Horton's displeasure, and who is alone responsible for what appears in its columns. Whether the individual so intrusted has performed his duty honestly, however imperfectly, he leaves to a higher tribunal than the Governor to determine. The second part of the charge against us is certainly specific, namely, that our 'columns have been made the vehicle of anonymous and slanderous abuse of Sir R. Horton and his government;' but the evidence adduced in support of this accusation most lamentably fails. We must here premise, that the writer, 'A Merchant,' whose voluminous letters appear to have produced such a salutary effect upon his Excellency, as not to have been forgotten in the long and intervening lapse of time since they appeared, is known to us in *propria persona*, and we pledge ourselves as to his high respectability, his being fully entitled to the signature assumed, and to his possession of a judgment capable of forming conclusions, such as he has ever favoured the public with, upon the very ample data within his reach. This correspondent, therefore, could not be considered an *ano-*

nymous writer, in the full acceptation of the term.

"The Governor says, that 'as a public man, he has not the slightest right to complain, as long as it only affects his public character, and is genuinely anonymous;' and although he quotes from five of these (to him) galling letters, he does not mention a single instance in which he is spoken of but 'as a public man.' But his Excellency adds, that we 'have been made the vehicle, &c.' although he possesses, at this moment, in various ways, proofs that, whatever course we have adopted, we have acted as voluntary a part as any individual in a social compact could do."

Address of the Natives.—A deputation of the Natives, consisting of J. L. Perera Modliar, D. J. Dias Modliar, E. De Saram Modliar, and L. De Lewera Modliar, waited on the Right Hon. the Governor, on the 8th January. There were present on the occasion more than 400 persons, being native chiefs, and other principal natives of all classes. The object was to present an address to the Governor, which had been carried unanimously at a meeting held on the 8th of September last. Mr. L. De Lewera read the address, as follows:

"We, whose names are hereunto affixed, his Majesty's Singhalese and other native subjects, residing in the various provinces of this island, take this opportunity of requesting your Excellency to convey to the foot of the British throne this most humble but sincere expression of our gratitude, for the very important privilege of being represented by our own countrymen in the Legislative Council of Ceylon, which has been recently granted to us by his Majesty's most gracious and paternal care.

"Various as were the disadvantages under which we were hitherto placed, in the absence of a public share in the legislative administration of our country, we cannot but hail this privilege as an event which affords abundant cause of satisfaction and thankfulness—an acquaintance with the peculiar resources of the natives, a sympathy with their feelings and habits of thinking, a knowledge of their religious and other rites and customs, are so essential in legislating for the natives, that no council can be perfect in which these requisites are wanting.

"Alive as we are to the important practical benefits immediately to result to us, from a voice of our own by native representation in the legislative council, our view, however, is not confined to those benefits alone; we look upon this privilege (placed as the native representatives are, with reference to precedence, on an equality with the European members) as an earnest given to us of many future privileges, and, what we prize above all, as a public and lasting recognition of our political existence, calculated at once to strengthen our interests, and enhance our importance in the estimation of the world.

" In conferring so great a boon upon us, our gracious Sovereign has at once commanded our admiration, and imposed on us obligations of the most lasting gratitude,"

Mr. Lewers informed his Excellency that there were 19,800 signatures attached to the Address—that they had written to the out-stations to send in the signatures of such persons as might be desirous of joining with them in the Address, so as to be here on the last day of December ultimo—that they had not as yet heard from several of the out-stations—and that as soon as the signatures shall have been received from them, they shall take another opportunity, with his Excellency's permission, to submit them to him for the purpose of being attached to the Memorial.

The Governor, in his address to the deputation, said :—

" I am bound to take this opportunity of stating, that the services rendered by the native members in the last session of the Legislative Council hold out an earnest of future assistance of the most valuable nature. I am gratified at the sentiments which you express in your Memorial, when you declare that you consider the privilege of having a voice of your own by native representation in the Legislative Council, to be an earnest given to you of many future privileges, and what you prize above all—a public and lasting recognition of your political existence, calculated at once to strengthen your interests, and enhance your importance in the estimation of the world. As His Majesty's Representative I can venture to assure you, that you have taken a correct view of the consequences which may be justly expected to result from the boon which His Majesty has conferred upon you. And that you may not suppose that these are mere empty words, I am happy to inform you that a prospectus will probably appear in to-morrow's Gazette, of a seminary for the education,—the liberal education,—of children of all classes of His Majesty's subjects of this island. This will afford to the natives a complete opportunity of qualifying themselves for public stations—and a career is open to you which can only be frustrated by your negligence."

Singapore.

PIRACY.

The Malayan Archipelago has been long noted as the haunt of pirates, so much so that with many persons, a Malay and a pirate are synonymous terms. The natural

formation of this region, being divided into numerous islands, which are distributed over an area of such vast extent, affords secure means to the rude and uncivilized inhabitants who live on the shores, and lurk in the numerous creeks, protected by mangrove-jungle, to waylay and prey on the peaceful trader ; and it is well that these marauders, though treacherous and rapacious, are, at the same time, indolent and unenterprising, as, otherwise, these seas would be impassable for the general class of traders who frequent them. It is to be remarked that those tribes who follow agriculture or commerce as regular pursuits—such as the native of Java,—portions of Sumatra,—Borneo,—Celebes,—and the Malayan Peninsula, are not addicted to piracy ; while the idle and least industrious, who appear to have no other means of subsistence than fishing, are the most notorious for their depredations. Among these latter, are the inhabitants of several islands in our vicinity—the Carimons, Pulo Soojee, Timiang, Galang, Moro, Sekana, all which belong to the Bintang and Lingin groupes— Pulo Tingih off the E. coast of the Peninsula, and several petty places on the coast, such as Johore and Kemaman. Pirates prevail also at the northern entrance of the Malacca straits, frequenting the Sembilans, Dindings, Arroa, and other islands. They are to be found also in the straits, principally about Salengore and Lingie, and not unfrequently they lurk about Pulo Pisang and Cocob. There is another class of pirates, distinct from and more enterprising and formidable than Malays, who likewise infest these parts—the Illanoon or Lanun—a race inhabiting the Sooloo groupe, between Borneo and the Philippines. These extend their predatory excursions as far as the Spice Islands to the eastward, and the Straits of Malacca to the westward, during the favourable monsoons. They are said to possess establishments not far hence,—one at Ritti, near Indragiri, in Sumatra, and another on the island close to Lingin. The Malayan piratical prahus are generally from 6 to 8 tons burden, from 50 to 60 feet in length, and 11 to 13 in breadth ; they commonly carry one or two small guns, three or four rantakas or brass swivels, with a crew of 20 to 30 men, who are armed with spears, krises, and often with muskets. They have likewise a fence called ampelan, made of thick plank, and placed across the fore part of the boat, behind which they fire their guns, and shelter themselves when attacked. The Illanoon pirates have larger boats, manned generally by 40 to 80 men, and carry a proportionate number of guns and arms. It has been remarked that Malayan pirates are more cruel and sanguinary in their attacks than the Illanoon, as they seldom spare the lives of their captives, probably from fear of recognition at a future time in some European port.—*Sing. Free Press.*

Trade to Batavia.—A meeting to petition the governments in India and this country, on the subject of the duties proposed to be levied here, was about to be convened, and it was suggested, that at the same time, the exactions of the Dutch at Batavia should be taken into consideration. These are described to be such as must press very seriously on British trade. The *Singapore Chronicle* says:—" The duty now levied at Batavia on woollens and cotton goods, is by virtue of an edict published in February 1824, not a month before the ratification of the treaty in London, but never rescinded after the treaty had been proclaimed through Netherlands' India. All duty beyond what is sanctioned by that treaty, and levied upon British goods after its promulgation, must be obviously illegal, and forms a claim against the Dutch, which the British government ought to insist upon as a penalty for the violation of the treaty. This claim we have heard computed as amounting to nearly a million sterling, dating the exactions from the time that the Belgian goods came first into play, about the end of 1827. During the existence of the former Melbourne ministry, we are informed that strong representations had been made to the Dutch and Colonial Minister as to the infraction of the treaty, and that matters had advanced so far, that the Dutch Minister answered the remonstrance by a threat to levy a duty of 25 per cent. on all Dutch goods, and double that rate upon British, in the event of the British government insisting upon the fulfilment of the treaty to the letter."

Persia.

A Tartar arrived at Constantinople on the 21st June, with despatches and letters from Teheran. Their contents are gratifying and important. Mr. Ellis had, on the eve of his departure from the capital, succeeded in obtaining the same privileges for English commerce as those enjoyed by Russia. All duties on exports and imports were to be limited to 5 per cent. On taking leave of the Shah, Mr. Ellis received some valuable presents, consisting of a horse, shawl, and a portrait of the Shah, set in brilliants. He had reached Tabreez on the 3d June, and is there awaiting the arrival of Mr. M'Neil.

China.

Canton papers to the 8th of March have been received. It was reported, that in the district of Shaow-chow-foo, disturbances

had broken out between two of the tribes, and that many on both sides had been slain. Ke, the foo-hëen, intended to go immediately to the spot to inquire into the affair. Eleven British vessels were lying at the port of Lintin, and five at Canton.

Australasia.
NEW SOUTH WALES.

Major Mitchell's Exploratory Tour.— It gives us much pleasure to be enabled to adduce any proof of the activity of the Executive Authorities in this colony having useful scientific objects in view— one of which decidedly is the expedition of discovery of the interior now in progress under the conduct of Major Michell, the surveyor general. Yesterday morning, Major Mitchell set out from Sydney. It is his intention to proceed first to Bathurst, and thence to Wellington Valley, where a depôt of boats and other necessaries has been formed. He then proposes to embark upon the Murree and ascend the Murrumbidgee, tracing those rivers, their branches, and tributary streams, as far as practicable, with the country for some distance inland from their banks, and so return to headquarters in about four months. He is well supplied with mathematical and astronomical instruments. The expedition carries with it about one hundred live sheep. We look anxiously for information as to its progress.—*Syd. Gaz.* March 10.

Steam Navigation.—It gives us much pleasure to state, that the whole of the shares in the projected Steam Conveyance Company, as open to be subscribed for here, are now taken up, and the two hundred reserved for Van Diemen's Land will, in all likelihood, shortly be so. If not, there are plenty of speculators in New South Wales who will snatch at them.—*Ibid.*

Penal Discipline in 1835.—Under this head, the *Sydney Herald* has a long report of the proceedings before the Police Court, in reference to charges made against William Watt, a convict, holding a ticket-of-leave, and reputed Editor of the *Sydney Gazette*, which had occupied the Court and the time of fourteen magistrates for several days. The *Herald*, in order to save their " English friends" from the necessity of wading through this "mass of low matter," presents the following abstract of the proceedings :—
" About fifteen months ago, two slips of printed matter were stolen by a convict compositor from our office, at the suggestion of Watt, for the receipt of which he paid. He then sent them through the
(2 G)

post-office, in a disguised hand, to a man named Haldane, and Haldane commenced a prosecution against the printers, although the slips had not been published, and the offensive matter might have been corrected. For a long period, evidence could not be obtained to convict Watt and the other convict; at last it was got, and Watt was committed for trial by a full bench of magistrates. The trial came on upon the 17th of August, and Watt was acquitted, not because he was not guilty, but because the jury dared to do what no jury in the history of the world had ever done before, decided that the article stolen was of *no value*. The Judge, it is understood, wrote to the Governor on the subject, and Watt's ticket was transferred to Port Macquarie, a free part of the colony, while the aggrieved parties were left without redress, and all the rogues and vagabonds of the country were in ecstacy at this first attempt to introduce a new policy, in reference to penal discipline. Watt in his defence made some most improper, untrue, and unjust statements, particularly in reference to Mr. Mudie, a magistrate of the territory. Mr. Mudie, unwilling to submit to the most horrifying imputations, which, if true, affected his life and property, and happiness in this and every other country, brought Watt before the Bench of Magistrates for summary punishment. Will it be credited in England, that a transport, who in a court of justice in New South Wales, branded an individual as a murderer of five men, and as a virulent persecutor, himself a prisoner of the crown, against whom no proceeding for damages or reparation of any kind can be instituted, should have possessed unseen influence enough to protract the case day after day, while the avowed acknowledgments that he made, the statements were sufficient to authorize, and imperatively require the Government to act with prompt and decisive measures against this convict disturber of the public peace."

VAN DIEMEN'S LAND.

A number of respectable persons, with large families, amounting altogether to nearly one hundred, have engaged a schooner, with whale-boats, to make an excursion up the Huon, for the purpose of searching for good land, with a view of settling themselves thereon. As most of these persons have not the means of supporting their families in Hobart Town, the Lieut. Governor has wisely intimated that he will assist them in their project, to the utmost of his power, by granting them extended leases, at a nominal rent, and in the mean time call the attention of the British Government to the propriety of allowing them to purchase their re-

spective locations at a low rate. For if the good old system of forming a peasantry, by some means, be not speedily adopted, by holding forth an incentive to industry to those deluded and disappointed emigrants, that distress, which has so long been felt in Hobart Town, from its unnatural population, will end in irretrievable misery and ruin. Bye-laws are being framed, in which are many judicious regulations, such as the prohibition of spirituous liquors being used in the settlement, with many more equally conducive to human felicity.—*Bent's News.*

St. Helena.

From St. Helena we learn, by a private letter, that the East-India Company's establishment is dissolved; " the corps of artillery and infantry having been disbanded—most of the men sent to their own parishes—others having enlisted as volunteers for His Majesty's service in the East-Indies. The officers are all pensioned on the following scale, *viz.*—Lieut. Colonels, £460 per annum; Majors, £365; Captains, £255; and Subalterns from £90 to £120. The civilians have likewise been provided for, but not to the extent it was expected. A few are re-employed by His Majesty's Government."—*Cape Paper, March 30.*

Cape of Good Hope.

Papers from the Cape, to the 1st of May, mention that all the frontier country beyond the Keishama was perfectly tranquil. Some temporary excitement was occasioned at Fort Waterloo on the 12th of April, in consequence of the unintentional infringement of a military order by one of the native chiefs, but it soon subsided. It appears, that the chief Umhala attempted to walk into the commissariat stores without permission, was stopped by the sentinal, and upon Umhala seizing the soldier's firelock by the muzzle, the latter drew his bayonet and wounded him. Umhala made a formal complaint, and the soldier was tried, but acquitted, while the chief was satisfied no premeditated injury was intended. Capt. Stockenstrom had been appointed Lieut.-Governor, with a view of directing exclusively the affairs of the eastern and newly-acquired provinces. By the report of the committee of the Commercial Exchange which was read at a general meeting of shareholders on the 25th of April, it appears that the exportation of wine to Great Britain and other places from the colony, between the 6th of April 1835, and the 5th of January 1836, three quarters of a year, was 7,458 pipes, the declared value of which was £75,875; grain, 26,475 muids, equal to £19,373; flour and bran, 1,277,350lbs. equal to £10,150; wool, 117,634lbs., equal to £8,517; tallow and candles, 230.213lbs., equal to £4,231; beef and pork, 849 casks, equal to £2,049; hides, 35,794, equal to £18,764; skins, 172,844, equal to £12,291; and horns, 88,629, equal to £2,336; the declared value of the exports from Table and Simon's Bays being £242.170, and from Port Elizabeth £24,373, making a total of £266,543. The value of the imports at Table and Simon's Bays, according to the same document, was £327,672, and £32,984 at Port Elizabeth, making a total of £360,656 during the three quarters, ending the 5th of January 1836.

———

Mr. Wilberforce Bird died on the 19th inst., at his residence at Wynberg, in the 78th year of his age.

For the last twenty-nine years, Mr. Bird has been a distinguished member of the civil service of this colony, a steady friend and able supporter of our public and benevolent institutions, and one of the most agreeable and instructive of those ornaments of social life, known by the name of companionable gentlemen. In his early years, he served in Parliament, for the borough of Coventry—the cotemporary of Fox, Burke, and Sheridan; and when listening to him at the Cape, even in his seventieth year, we have heard language and marked sentiment and manner, so peculiarly English, that for a time we could fancy ourselves carried back to that period of classic eloquence To Mr. Bird we owe one of the best works that has yet been published on the Cape of Good Hope. With some things on which we differed from him, it exhibits in a just light the character of our government, laws, customs, and manners. He anticipated most of the improvements we have since seen; and dealt in candour and characteristic mildness with what was amiss, and could only be remedied by time. The style is perspicuous, simple, and uniformly elegant; and the day-light of good-humour and perfect urbanity pervades the whole composition. Mr. Bird was amongst the last remaining members of that circle, which rendered Cape Town for several years so attractive to accomplished strangers. In few colonies, perhaps in very few capitals, could such men be met with at the same table, as Thomas Sheridan, Henry Alexander, and the author of the *State of the Cape in* 1822. " *Requiescat in pace!*" says one who crossed swords with him perhaps once too often; but who lays this sincere tribute of esteem and respect upon his tomb, with feelings which he would have been proud to excite in the breast of him who is now beyond the sphere both of private

friendship and political opposition!—*South Afr. Com. Adv., April 23.*

———

Asiatic Russia.

News has arrived by way of Odessa from Taganrock, throwing some light on the state of affairs in the Caucasus, a subject upon which the Emperor Nicholas does not allow any thing to be published, and which explains the orders previously sent to despatch for Kertself and the sea of Azof a good number of light vessels fit for the service of the coast. It appears, that the most considerable of the tribes of the Caucasus have again formed a confederation of war, and that they have profited by the previous advantages with a skilfulness of tactic and of combination, such as they were not supposed capable of employing. It cannot be estimated with precision how many men these tribes have on foot, but the Russians find them everywhere numerically superior to themselves, and think they cannot be calculated at less than eighty thousand fighting men, not comprising the bands which, though out of the grand league, are still in a state of permanent stability. The Russians, after having lost their positions of the Kouban, run the risk of not being able to keep those of the Don, unless their army is promptly reinforced, or rather renewed; because the terror inspired by the Tcherkesses, and the incredible rapidity of their marches, have greatly demoralised their troops, already much reduced, and unable to count upon the aid of the ordinary Cossacks, who cannot contend against the cavalry of the insurgents. What is the most inconvenient to them, in the actual state of things, is that their communications are cut off in all directions, and that those with the army of Georgia can no longer take place without regular expeditions attended by loss of men, arms, and money.—*Courrier Francais.*

Much injury has been done in many parts of the Crimea by night frosts. On the 7th of May, seven houses, fourteen barns full of corn, and a public house, were destroyed by fire at Astrachan. The damage is estimated at 200,000 roubles, Bank assignats.

———

Asiatic Turkey.

It would appear, by reports from the Turkish army in Asia, that its irregular troops have been exposed to a sudden and vigorous attack by between 30,000 and 40,000 Kurdish horsemen. The Turks were unable to withstand the shock, and were obliged to retreat in great confusion. The affair took place in the province of Diarbeki (Mesopotamia) and the disciplined troops of Reshid Pacha were not engaged in it. The Kurds are so independent in their ideas, and so alike in their habits, that neither the Sultan, nor his immediate successors, are likely to see their complete subjection.—*Extract of Letter from Constantinople, June 22.*

Egypt.

The Viceroy still remains in Lower Egypt, and has seen with his own eyes the misery to which the province is reduced by his civil and military system of government. The fields are untilled for want of labourers, and Mahomet Alli has been so forcibly struck with the deplorable state of the country, that he has actually been induced to distribute succour. He has even, to the astonishment of those who are with him, desisted from levying the taxes. He is going from village to village, taking a generous interest in the most unfortunate, and has deferred his return for six weeks. Nothing proves the cruel situation of the provinces of Lower Egypt, which have been depopulated by a long succession of wars, so much as a firman promulgated by the Pasha on May 2, enjoining every Egyptian who is married, without having any children, to take a second wife. If his fortune is not sufficient to maintain her, the firman directs the government to make provision for the second wife, and such children as she may have.—*Suabian Mercury.*

Eleven cargoes of iron rails, for the railroad across the Isthmus of Suez, have arrived at Cairo. The work will be commenced immediately.

A private letter from Alexandria repeats the report that the Pasha had determined, in consequence of the high price of stone required to make dams across the river Nile, at the head of the Delta, to pull down one of the small pyramids of Gheza.

The progress of the plague had created little alarm either at Alexandria or at Cairo, although it raged violently in many of the villages, where the inhabitants suffered greatly; among others at Sieret, and two or three places in that district.

The Rev. Joseph Wolff was at Suez on the 13th April, being about to embark for Jiddah, in the steam-vessel which was then awaiting the Indian mail from Alexandria. He intended to go as far as Mocha, thence cross over to Mosawah, Adwah, Gondar, and Shoah, in Abyssinia. He had with him a M. Bethlehem, a clever Armenian, who is servant to the King of Abyssinia.

Syria.

By the last accounts from Syria, Ibrahim Pasha and his numerous legions were employed in destroying locusts, myriads of which were threatening destruction to every thing green in the province. To destroy them ere they could take the wing was his only chance, and Ibrahim had set not only all his army to pursue them, but every village had been called upon to send out parties against the common enemy.

The last accounts from Colonel Chesney left him at Beles, about 140 miles from Bir, down the Euphrates, and he had inspired the Arabs with such a friendly disposition and admiration of his powers, that they looked on him as a magician whom nothing could resist.

Spanish India,

By the Spanish brig *La Fama*, from the Spanish settlement of Samboanga, we had received intelligence that there had been, on the 3d January, a severe earthquake at Mindanao, the largest of the Phillipine Islands, next to Luçonia. As yet, beyond mere report, we have been unable to ascertain the extent of the damage which this earthquake had occasioned; but it was rumoured at Samboanga when the *La Fama* left, that many lives had been lost. Besides the volcanic mountain in the southward of Mindanao, which is represented to be in constant eruption, there are besides others in different parts of the island which occasion earthquakes to be of no unfrequent occurrence.—*Singapore Chron., March 5.*

Sandwich Islands:

Extract of a letter from Mané, 24th Dec. 1835:—The *Awashouks* arrived in November, under the command of her third officer, Mr. Jones. Capt. Coffin, the first and second officers, and some of the seamen, were killed by the natives of Baring's island, on October the 5th. This is in about 6° 30′ N. and 168° 32′. The natives came off in canoes, and soon after coming over the sides, they seized the cutting spades, and made attack. Capt. Coffin fell the first victim; the mate, after killing the native who struck the captain, was himself killed by a spade. The third officer jumped overboard, and was killed in the water by a native with a paddle. A seaman leaped overboard, and was drowned. The third officer, after being overpowered on deck, sprang into the forehold, from whence he made his way between decks into the cabin, where he hunted up the muskets and loaded them. Several of his men joined him, and by firing through the cabin gangway they killed some of the natives. The chief got possession of the helm, and was trying to head the ship towards the shore, about two miles distant, when he was shot by a musket ball, which came through the binnacle. Mr. Jones and his seven men now made ready for a rush upon deck, determined to clear them and retake the ship. Just as they were ascending the gangway, however, the men from aloft cried out that the decks were clear. On losing their chief all the natives jumped overboard. Thus the vessel was rescued, and the rest of the crew were saved by a kind Providence from an impending and awful destruction. One seaman died of his wounds on the passage; and one is still confined to his bed. A handsome subscription has been got up for him. The *Awashouks* belongs to Falmouth.

" January 4th, I add a line to tell you sad news. The schooner *Hondurus* of Boston, which sailed from this place on a shelling expedition to the southern groupes, under command of Capt. Scott, arrived to-day from Strong's Island, where Capt. Scott and thirteen of his men were massacred by the natives. Capt. Scott went on shore with eight of his men, soon after coming to anchor. In a short time he was seen by the mate on board running towards the beach, calling to him to load the guns and fire upon the natives. But at this time there were some twenty or thirty natives on board, who also commenced an attack. All the company on board were killed, excepting the mate and a boy. The mate seized a cutlass and killed several natives, when two, being overpowered, went below into the only cabin, loaded four muskets and cleared the decks. These two, the only survivors, slipped the cable, and by help of a light breeze, which providentially sprung up at the time, escaped. They navigated the vessel to Ascension Island in eleven days, where they had left the supercargo. The white vagabonds upon the island instigated the natives to take the vessel ; but the king, a personal friend of the supercargo, sent him word that he was not safe, and actually sent off 150 natives to remain on board his vessel to defend her against the infamous plot of the white men. The supercargo returned to Strong's Island, but could neither see nor hear any thing of Capt. Scott, though he sailed about the island for a month. He then saw one of the *Waverley's* boats, and was twice fired upon from a large gun : too certain evidence that she too with her twenty-three souls had been cut off at the island.

" Mr. Young, an Englishman, the oldest foreign resident on the islands, died recently in Honolulu. He was about ninety-three years old, and had lived upon the islands forty-seven years. He was an honorary chief, having attended Tamehaeha through all his wars."

The love of plunder seems to have emboldened these savages, and the possession of fire-arms putting them on an equal footing in this cruel warfare with the Europeans and their descendants, renders them doubly anxious to possess themselves of the virgin mines of silver with which the country abounds. At present they are in undisputed possession of the mountains and forests, though lately a company of fourteen adventurers have established themselves in a rich mining district, well provided, however, with fire-arms for their defence.—*Canton Reg., Feb. 23.*

Postscript.

INTELLIGENCE from Alexandria, *via* Malta, announces the following melancholy accident, which has befallen the Euphrates expedition :—The expedition, with the *Euphrates* and *Tigris*, was descending the river prosperously. The state of the river was so favourable, that the *Tigris*, the smallest vessel, was in the habit of leading, having a native pilot on board. On the 21st May, they had brought up at mid-day to a bank for fuel, and after the people had dined, cast off, meaning to steam to Annan, distant about eighty miles. Scarcely, however, had they commenced the voyage, when a cloud of dust was seen to rise on the right bank, threatening a squall. The *Tigris* was rounding to make fast, the *Euphrates* following. As they neared the left bank, the *Tigris* failed to bring up. The *Euphrates* was now obliged to back her paddles to give room, an operation full of danger, lest she should be unable to gather way upon herself again against the current and violence of the gale. Her consort, however, drove down the stream, unable to bring her head to the gale, and she upset to leeward about three quarters of a mile, and instantly after went down. A party was sent off along shore to render what assistance they could, and another went by boat. Some of the officers, namely, Col. Chesney, Lieut. Lynch, Mr. Eden, Dr. Staunton, Mr. Staunton, and Mr. Thompson, swam and dived ashore. Some seamen and natives also followed them ; but fifteen Europeans, of whom three were officers, namely, Lieut. Cockburn, Royal Artillery; Mr. Lynch, a passenger, and brother to Lieut. Lynch ; and Mr. Sarded, an interpreter, were lost, besides five natives. The hull of the vessel has never been found. She filled and turned bottom up. All sounding has been in vain. Besides the loss of life, it is much feared that Colonel Chesney's valuable papers were in the *Tigris*.

PRESENT DISTRIBUTION OF THE INDIAN ARMY.

COMMANDERS-IN-CHIEF:

Bengal—His Exc. Gen. Sir Henry Fane, G.C.B.
Madras—His Exc. Lieut. Gen. Sir T. P. Maitland, K.C.B. (now on his way out),
Bombay—His Exc. Lieut. Gen. Sir John Keane, K.C.B., G.C.H.

BENGAL ESTABLISHMENT.

King's Troops.

Regts.	Stations.
11th Lt. Drags.	Meerut.
16th do.	Cawnpore.
3d Foot	Meerut.
9th do.	Chinsurah.
13th do.	Kurnaul.
16th do.	Cawnpore.
26th do.	Ghazeepore.
31st do.	Dinapore.
44th do.	Fort William.
49th do.	Hazareebaugh.

Company's Troops.

Regts.	Stations.
1st Lt. Cav.	Neemuch.
2d do.	Meerut.
3d do.	Kurnaul.
4th do.	Kurnaul.
5th do.	Cawnpore.
6th do.	Mhow.
7th do.	Cawnpore.
8th do.	Sultanpore.
9th do.	Nusseerabad.
10th do.	Muttra.
Europ. Regt.	Agra.
1st Nat. Inf.	Cawnpore.
2d do.	Saugor.
3d do.	Mynpoorie.
4th do.	Berhampore.
5th do.	Benares.
6th do.	Barrackpore.
7th do.	Almorah.
8th do.	Nusseerabad.
9th do.	Barrackpore.
10th do.	Barrackpore.
11th do.	Goruckpore.
12th do.	Allahabad.
13th do.	Nusseerabad.
14th do.	Moradabad and Shahjehan- [pore.
15th do.	Cawnpore.
16th do.	Delhi.
17th do.	Loodhianah.
18th do.	Benares.
19th do.	Cuttack.
20th do.	Delhi.
21st do.	Kurnaul.
22d do.	Nusseerabad.
23d do.	Neemuch.
24th do.	Midnapore.
25th do.	Mirzapore.
26th do.	Meerut.

Regts.	Stations.
27th Nat. Inf.	Kurnaul.
28th do.	Neemuch.
29th do.	Banda.
30th do.	Meerut.
31st do.	Bancoorah.
32d do.	Allyghur.
33d do.	Jubbulpore.
34th do.	Futtehghur.
35th do.	Lucknow.
36th do.	Agra.
37th do.	Agra.
38th do.	Delhi.
39th do.	Neemuch.
40th do.	Arracan.
41st do.	Barrackpore.
42d do.	Bareilly.
43d do.	Barrackpore.
44th do.	Mhow.
45th do.	Muttra.
46th do.	Gurrawarrah.
47th do.	Lucknow.
48th do.	Seetapore.
49th do.	Neemuch.
50th do.	Dacca.
51st do.	Agra.
52d do.	Nusseerabad.
53d do.	Bandah and Etawah
54th do.	Meerut.
55th do.	Chittagong.
56th do.	Dinapore.
57th do.	Benares.
58th do.	Jumaulpore.
59th do.	Lucknow.
60th do.	Mhow.
61st do.	Kurnaul.
62d do.	Loodianah.
63d do.	Sultanpore (Oude).
64th do.	Saugor.
65th do.	Allahabad.
66th do.	Baitool.
67th do.	Dinapore.
68th do.	Mhow.
69th do.	Saugor.
70th do.	Barrackpore.
71st do.	Cawnpore.
72d do.	Saugor.
73d do.	Barrackpore.
74th do.	Bareilly.
Artillery	Dum Dum (hd. qu.)
Engineers	Fort William (hd. qu.)

MADRAS ESTABLISHMENT.

King's Troops. [1835.]

Regts.	Stations
13th Lt. Drags.	Bangalore.
39th Foot	Bangalore.
41st do.	Arnee.
45th do.	Secunderabad.
54th do.	Trichinopoly.
55th do.	Bellary.
57th do.	Cannanore.
62d do.	Moulmein.
63d do.	Fort St. George.

Company's Troops.

Regts.	Stations
1st Lt. Cav.	Nagpoor.
2d do.	Arcot.
3d do.	Bellary.
4th do.	Secunderabad.
5th do.	Arcot.
6th do.	Trichinopoly.
7th do.	Secunderabad.
8th do.	Bangalore.
Europ. Regt.	Nagpore.
1st Nat. Inf.	Quilon.
2d do.	Mangalore.
3d do.	Visianagrum.
4th do.	Bangalore.
5th do.	Dindigul.
6th do.	Trichinopoly.
7th do.	Bellary.
8th do.	Berhampore.
9th do.	Vellore.
10th do.	Vizagapatam.
11th do.	Kamptee.
12th do.	Bangalore.
13th do.	Moulmein.
14th do.	Vizianagrum.
15th do.	Penang and Malacca.
16th do.	Secunderabad.

Regts.	Stations
17th Nat. Inf.	Madras.
18th do.	Palaveram.
19th do.	French Rocks.
20th do.	Bangalore.
21st do.	Chicacole.
22d do.	Secunderabad.
23d do.	Trichinopoly.
24th do.	Secunderabad.
25th do.	Vellore.
26th do.	Paulgautcherry.
27th do.	Bangalore.
28th do.	Cuddapah.
29th do.	Masulipatam.
30th do.	Secunderabad.
31st do.	Secunderabad.
32d do.	Cannanore.
33d do.	Palamcottah.
34th do.	Secunderabad.
35th do.	Trichinopoly.
36th do.	Coorg.
37th do.	Secunderabad.
38th do.	Kamptee.
39th do.	Secunderabad.
40th do.	Vellore.
41st do.	Salumcottah.
42d do.	Nagpore.
43d do.	Bellary.
44th do.	Madras.
45th do.	Palaveram.
46th do.	Trichinopoly.
47th do.	Masulipatam.
48th do.	Singapore and Malacca.
49th do.	Nagpore.
50th do.	Ellore.
51st do.	Cannanore.
52d do.	Hurrygbur.
Artillery	St. Thos.'s Mount (hd. qu.)
Engineers	Fort St. George (hd. qu.).

BOMBAY ESTABLISHMENT.

King's Troops.

Regts.	Stations
4th Lt. Drags.	Kirkee.
2d Foot	Poonah.
6th do.	Bombay.
17th do.	Expected from N.S. Wales.
20th do.	Belgaum (ordered home).
40th do.	Deesa.

Company's Troops.

Regts.	Stations
1st Lt. Cav.	Rajcote and Hursole.
2d Foot	Sholapore.
3d do.	Deesa.
Europ. Regt.	Poonah.
1st Nat. Inf.	Dharwar.
2d do.	Sholapore.
3d do.	Asseergbur.
4th do.	Ahmednuggur.
5th do.	Poonah.
6th do.	Bhewndy.
7th do.	Ahmedabad.

Regts.	Stations
8th Nat. Inf.	Bombay.
9th do.	Baroda.
10th do.	Belgaum.
11th do.	Bhooj.
12th do.	Rajcote.
13th do.	Deesa.
14th do.	Ahmedabad.
15th do.	Bombay.
16th do.	Bombay.
17th do.	Hursole.
18th do.	Kulladghee.
19th do.	Poonah.
20th do.	Baroda.
21st do.	Malligaum.
22d do.	Belgaum.
23d do.	Sattara.
24th do.	Baroda.
25th do.	Dapoolie.
26th do.	Malligaum.
Artillery	Poonah, Bombay, &c.
Engineers	Seroor (hd. qu.)

REGISTER.

Calcutta.

GOVERNMENT ORDERS, &c.
COMPANY'S RUPEES.

Fort-William, Financial Department,
Feb. 10, 1836.—Notice is hereby given,
that from and after the 1st May 1836,
all Government Accounts will be kept in
Company's Rupees.

The same arrangements will take effect
from and after the same date (1st May
1836), at the Presidencies of Madras and
Bombay.

ARTILLERY WITH THE ASSAM LIGHT INFANTRY.

Head-Quarters, Calcutta, Feb. 13, 1836.
—1. His Exc. the Commander in Chief
is pleased to direct, that the artillery,
which forms a part of the establishment of
the Assam light infantry battalion, shall,
as soon as practicable after the receipt of
this order, be organized as specified in the
margin.*

2. A subaltern of artillery will be attached to the corps. His duty will be
(under the officer commanding the battalion) to take charge of the instruction of
the officers and soldiers selected for the
artillery service, in all their especial exercises and duties as artillery-men; and to
have the particular care and superintendence of the ordnance, and all its stores and
equipments of every kind.

3. He is to understand that he is attached to the corps for the purpose of giving instruction in, and superintendence
over, the particular branch of the service
to which he belongs; but that he is in
every respect under the commanding
officer of the battalion he is attached to.

4. The native officers, non-commissioned and gunners, &c., should be carefully chosen from amongst those whose
strength and activity render them most
eligible; and the Commander in Chief
has no doubt, that the artillery selection
may be rendered very popular, by judicious measures on the part of the commanding officers of the battalion.

5. The establishment of the corps is to
remain as at present; and the officer of
artillery will be accounted for in third
page of the return, as " attached, doing
duty."

6. The commanding officer will use his
own discretion in teaching any number of
extra men of his corps the duties of artillery-men, to prepare them for filling
vacancies.

* 1 Subaltern, Bengal artillery, 1 Gun Sergeant,
1 Gun Corporal, 1 Jemadar, 2 Havildars, 2 Naicks,
96 Sepoys, 1 Tindal, and 8 Gun Lascars, for 2
pieces of field artillery.

7. The Commander in Chief recommends, that the artillery should be retained as much as possible with the head-
quarters of the corps, and move with the
main body; as the detaching of artillery
with small bodies of light troops always
interferes with the active and energetic
movements, which specially belong to
their particular branch of the service.

CIVIL APPOINTMENTS, &c.
BY THE GOVERNOR-GENERAL.
Judicial and Revenue Department.

Feb. 16. Mr. E. Deedes to officiate as joint magistrate and deputy collector of Moorshedabad,
during absence of Mr. J. G. B. Lawrell, or until
further orders.

Lieut. Thomas Simpson, 57th N.I., to officiate
as junior assistant to agent to Governor-general,
under Reg. XIII. of 1833.

Mr. R. T. W. Betts to be deputy collector, under
Reg. IX. of 1833, in zillah Jessore.

23. Mr. H. B. Beresford to be deputy collector in
zillah Purneah and in Maldah.

Mr. G. P. Leycester to exercise powers of a joint
magistrate and deputy collector in Moorshedabad.

Mr. W. C. S. Cunninghame to be an assistant
under commissioner of revenue and circuit of 19th
or Cuttack division.

26. Mr. C. R. Barwell to be a judge of courts of
Sudder Dewanny and Nizamut Adawlut.

Mr. Wigram Money to be special commissioner
under Reg. III. of 1828, for division of Moorshedabad.

Mr. J. H. D'Oyly to be civil and session judge of
zillah Beerbhoom.

Mr. J. Stainiforth to be magistrate and collector
of zillah Midnapore.

Political Department.

Feb. 8. Ens. H. C. Jackson, 45th N.I., placed
under orders of resident at Hyderabad.

15. Lieut. G. J. Fraser, 1st L.C., to be assistant
to resident at Hyderabad, v. Major Warde resigned.

Cornet E. I. Robinson, 7th L.C., to be an assistant to general superintendent of operations for
suppression of thuggee.

22. Lieut. G. B. Michell, 9th N.I., and Lieut. J.
C. Lumsdaine, 58th do., placed under orders of
resident at Gwalior.

Ens. H. Howorth, 39th N.I., placed under orders of resident at Hydrabad.

Financial Department.

Feb. 17. Mr. J. W. Sage to take charge of records and remaining works of late Radnagore commercial residency from date of Mr. Stuart's departure.

Mr. Chas. Herd to be superintendent of western
salt chokies, under Act IX. of 1835, and attached
to office of board of customs, salt and opium.

General Department.

Feb. 24. Mr. F. J. Halliday to be salt agent of
northern division of Cuttack, in room of Mr. H.
Ricketts.

Mr. C. F. Young to officiate as salt agent during
absence of Mr. Plowden.

Messrs. R. B. W. Ramsay and W. C. S. Cunninghame, writers, are reported qualified for the public service by proficiency in two of the native languages.

Mr. J. M. Hay having passed an examination on
the 15th February, and being reported qualified
for the public service by proficiency in the native
languages, the order issued on the 13th Jan., for
that gentleman's return to England, is cancelled.

The Hon. the Governor-general is pleased to attach to the Bengal presidency, Messrs. J. M. Hay, R. B. W. Ramsay, and W. C. S. Cunninghame, writers, reported qualified for the public service.

The Right Hon. Henry Ellis, his Britannic Majesty's ambassador to the court of Persia, having reached Teheran, Sir John Campbell, Kt., resigned his functions as envoy on the 4th of Nov. last.

Mr. James Pattle, senior member of the sudder board of revenue, resumed charge of his duties on the 16th February.

Furloughs, &c.—Feb. 23. Mr. C. Grant, commissioner of the Soonderbuns, to Cape of Good Hope, for eighteen months, for health.—24. Mr. J. B. Lawrell to England.—Mr. T. B. C. Bayley, to England, for health.

BY THE GOVERNOR OF AGRA.
Judicial and Revenue Department.

Feb. 6. Mr. E. H. Morland to be joint magistrate and deputy collector of Allahabad.

Mr. J. A. Craigie to be an assistant under commissioner of 4th or Allahabad division.

8. Mr. T. P. B. Biscoe to be magistrate and collector of southern division of Delhi territory.

Mr. G. W. Bacon to be civil and session judge of Seharunpore.

Mr. R. J. Tayler to be magistrate and collector of northern division of Delhi territory.

Mr. S. Fraser to be civil and session judge of Bundlecund.

Mr. C. Fraser to officiate as ditto ditto at Cawnpore.

17. Mr. W. B. Jackson to officiate as civil and session judge of Juanpore.

Mr. G. Lindsay ditto as additional judge at Ghazeepore.

Political and General Department.

Feb. 13. Mr. R. H. Scott to conduct duties of office of secretary to Government of Agra in political and general departments, during Mr. Bushby's absence on private affairs.

The Hon. the Governor is pleased to place the services of Mr. H. C. Halkett at the disposal of the Hon. the Governor of Bengal.

MILITARY APPOINTMENTS, PROMOTIONS, &c.

Fort William, Feb. 15, 1836.—8th L.C. Cornet George Murray to be lieut., from 1st Feb. 1836, v. Lieut. and Brev. Capt. E. C. Archbold resigned.

Supernum. Cornet A. W. C. Plowden brought on effective strength of cavalry.

20th N.I. Capt. W. C. Denby to be major, and Lieut. Thos. Gear (dec.) to be capt. of a comp., from 20th May 1834, in suc. to Major Wm. Price retired.—Lieut. J. H. Craigie to be capt. of a comp., and Ens. J. K. Spence to be lieut., from 11th Oct. 1834, in suc. to Capt. Thos. Gear dec.

Assist. Surg. Nathaniel Morgan to be surgeon, v. Surg. George Govan, M.D., retired, with rank from 15th Oct. 1835, v. Surg. John Allan, M.D., dec.

Lieut. R. P. Pennefather, 3d L.C., to be capt. by brevet, from 14th Feb. 1836.—Lieut. Wm. Wise, 29th N.I., to be ditto, from 14th Feb. 1836.

Lieut. Col. John Gibbs, inv. estab., to be commandant of fortress of Buxar, in room of Lieut. Col. W. C. L. Bird; to have effect from Jan. 15th.

Lieut. W. J. B. Knyvett, 38th N.I., to officiate as adj. of Calcutta Native Militia during period Lieut. Boscawen shall officiate as secretary to clothing board.

The services of Lieut. W. H. R. Boland, 7th N.I., placed at disposal of Agra government.

Mr. R. W. Wrightson admitted on establishment as an assist. surgeon.

The services of Lieut. Thos. Simpson, 57th N.I., placed at disposal of Hon. the Governor of Bengal, for purpose of being appointed to officiate as a junior assistant to agent to Governor-general on south-western frontier.

Assist. Surg. Alex. Reid, attached to civil station of Bolundshuhur, having resigned that appointment, placed at disposal of Commander-in-chief.

Feb. 22.—*6th N.I.* Lieut. and Brev. Capt. A. K. Agnew to be capt. of a comp., and Ens. Robert Mathison to be lieut , from 15th Feb. 1836, in suc. to Capt. Thomas Birkett dec.

67th N.I. Lieut. J. W. Hicks to be capt. of a comp., and Ens. Robert Price to be lieut., from 15th Feb. 1836, in suc. to Capt. R. S. Phillips, transf. to invalid estab.

Surg. James Ranken, M.D., to officiate as secretary to medical board, during absence, on leave to Cape of Good Hope, of Surg. James Hutchinson.

Assist. Surg. T. C. Hunter appointed to medical duties of civil station of Gowalpara.

Cadet G. U. Law admitted on establishment, and prom. to ensign.

The transfer and appointment, in April 1835, of Lieut. W. H. Graham, executive engineer at Mhow, to be executive engineer at Balasore, cancelled.

Capt. Francis Wheler, 2d L.C., appointed to situation of brigade major at Meerut, vacant by return to Europe of Brev. Maj. E. A. Campbell.

The undermentioned officers placed at disposal of Governor of Agra:—Col. H. T. Tapp, lieut. col. 1st N.I.; Lieut. Col. G. E. Gowan, regt. of artillery; and Assist. Surg. W. Gordon, M.D., medical department.

Surg. Thomas Drever, M.D., late in service of her Highness Begum Sombre deceased, placed at disposal of Commander-in-chief.

Head Quarters, Feb. 10, 1836.—The following young Ensigns to do duty:—H. C. James, with 58th N I., at Jumaulpore; E. W. Hicks, with 67th N.I., at Dinapore.

Feb. 12.—Surg. D. Renton removed from 18th to 57th N.I., and Surg. A. K. Lindesay, from latter to former corps.—Mr. Lindesay to proceed forthwith to Chunar, and officiate as garrison surgeon at that station, until further orders.

Assist. Surg. C. B. Handyside, M.D., to perform medical duties at Simla, v. Dallas dec.

Feb. 13.—Ens. E. W. Bristow, 71st, at his own request, removed to 1st N.I.

Feb. 15.—Ens. M. T. Blake, 56th N.I., to act as adj. to corps of Hill Rangers, during absence, on leave, of Lieut. and Adj. Don; date 14th Jan.

Col. Sir Jeremiah Bryant, Knt., lately prom. (on furl.), posted to 14th N.I.

Lieut. Col. and Brev. Col. J. H. Littler (on furl.) removed from 40th to 19th N.I.

Lieut. Col. W. H. Hewitt, lately prom., posted to 40th N.I.

Assist. Surg. Matthew Lovell removed from 9th L.C. to medical charge of 3d Local Horse.

Assist. Surg. James Barber, now officiating garrison assist. surg. at Chunar, confirmed in that appointment.

Feb. 15.—The following removals and postings to take place in regt. of artillery:—Majors R. B. Fulton (on staff employ) from 5th to 3d bat.; C. H. Bell, new prom., to 5th bat.—Captains W. Bell (on staff employ) from 3d comp. 1st bat. to 1st tr. 3d brig.; G. Twemlow (on staff employ) from 3d comp. 5th bat. to 3d comp. 1st bat.; G. S. Lawrenson from 1st comp. 5th bat. to 2d comp. 3d bat.; C. McMorine, new prom., to 1st comp. 5th bat.; C. Grant, new prom., to 3d comp. 5th bat.—1st-Lieuts. J. R. Revell from 1st comp. 2d bat. to 3d comp. 5th bat.; F. Dashwood (on staff employ) from 4th tr. 1st brig. to 4th tr. 3d brig.; G. H. Swinley from 4th comp. 6th bat. to 4th tr. 1st brig.; F. B. Boileau from 1st tr. 2d brig. to 3d tr. 3d brig.; F. Gaitskell from 3d comp. 5th bat. to 4th comp. 3d bat.; A. Humfrays (on furl.) from 3d tr. 2d brig. to 4th comp. 6 h bat.; Z. M. Mallock from 2d comp. to 3d comp. 7th bat.; A. Broome from 4th comp. 3d bat. to 1st tr. 1st brig.; A. Huish from 4th tr. 3d brig. to 4th tr. 1st brig.; C. L. Cooper, new prom., to 3d tr. 2d brig.; T. Edwards, new prom. (on furl.), to 1st comp. 2d bat.—2d-Lieuts. J. Innes (on furl.) from 1st comp. 4th bat. to 4th tr. 1st brig.; E. G. Austin from 1st comp. 1st bat. to 1st tr. 3d brig.; M. Mackenzie from 4th tr. 1st brig. to 4th tr. 3d brig.; T. J. W. Hungerford (on furl.) from 3d tr. 3d brig. to 7th comp. 7th bat.; J. Abercrombie from 2d comp. 7th bat. to 3d tr. 3d brig.; J. H. Smyth, brought on strength (on staff employ) to 2d comp. 7th bat.; E. K. Money, brought on ditto, to 1st comp. 1st bat.; W. Maxwell, brought on ditto, to the 4th comp. 3d bat.; H. M. Conran, brought on ditto, to 1st comp. 4th bat.—Supernum. 2d Lieut. A. W. Hawkins to join and do duty with 4th tr. 3d brig. at Neemuch.

Lieut. and Adj. H. Le Mesurier, 61st N.I., to officiate as station staff at Kurnaul; date 2d Feb.

Lieut. J. Liptrott, 30th N.I., to be adj. to Kemaoon local bat., v. Lieut. C. Campbell app. deputy paymaster of Cawnpore circle.

Feb. 17.—Ens. J. D. McPherson, interp. and qu. mast. 22d N.I., to act as detachment staff at Shekawatt; date 27th Jan.

Surg. J. Griffiths, 52d N.I., to have medical charge of artillery detachment at Jeypore under Capt. J. Rawlins; date 29th Jan.

Capt. W. Hoggan, 63d N.I., doing duty with Ramgurh light infantry bat., directed to join his regiment.

Feb. 20.—Assist. Surg. J. S. Sutherland to relieve Assist. Surg. C. McKinnon, M.D., from medical charge of 71st N.I.; date 5th Feb.

Unposted Ens. G. G. Bowring to do duty with left wing of 53d at Bandah, until arrival of 29th N.I. at that station.

Lieut. George Hutchings, 69th, to act as interp. and qu. master to 2d N.I.

Feb. 22.—The undermentioned officers to do duty at convalescent depôt at Landour, during ensuing season:—Capt. B. P. Browne, H M. 11th L. Drags.; Capt. G. Myllus. H.M. 16th Foot; Capt J. Leeson, 42d N.I.; Lieut. A. Huish, 4th tr. 1st brig. horse artillery; Lieut. G. Cautley, 8th L.C., officiating station staff, Landour.

Feb. 24.—Major Isaac Pereira, regt. of artillery, to command artillery division at Neemuch, in room of Lieut. Col. G. E. Gowan, whose services have been placed at disposal of Agra government.

Assist. Surg. William Rabit, on being relieved from his present charge, to proceed to Nusseerabad, and join 13th N.I.

Assist. Surg. J. C. Smith, arrived at presidency with 4th comp. 1st bat. artillery, directed to do duty with artillery at Dum Dum.

FURLOUGHS.

To Europe.—Feb. 15. Lieut. J. S. Davies, 32d N.I., on private affairs.—22. Lieut. Col. T. A. Cobbe, 37th N.I., agent to Governor-general at Moorshedabad, for health.

To visit Hills north of Deyrah (preparatory t⁰ applying for furlough to Europe).—Feb. 20. Assist. Surg. C. Finch, M.D., 13th N.I.

Cancelled.—Feb. 15. The furlough to Europe granted to Capt. J. W. H Turner, inv. estab., on 18th Jan. (since permitted to proceed to Meerut on private affairs).

SHIPPING.

Arrivals in the River.

FEB. 15. *Telaire,* St. Quantin, from Nantes, St. Dennis, and Mauritius; *Sumatra,* Hermanin, from Batavia and Malacca.—16. *Drongan,* Mackenzie, from Cochin and Colombo; *Georgia,* Saunders, f om Boston; *Hattrass,* Clark, from Bombay.— 22. *L'Egod,* Pellier, from Nantes and Bourbon.— 26. *Indian Oak,* Worthington, from Mauritius.— 28. *Cashmere Merchant,* Edwards, from Bombay.

Departures from Calcutta.

FEB. 13. *Hero,* Hughes, for Singapore and China.—19. *Sophia,* Rapson, for Straits and China. —20. *Cavendish Bentinck,* Eales, for Persian Gulf; *Jos ph Victor,* Le Cour, for Bourbon.—26. *Gaillardon,* Bowman, for Singapore and China.— 27. *Virginia,* Hullock, for Bombay; *Elizabeth,* Shepherd, for Masulipatam and Madras.—29. *Salazes,* Williams, for Mauritius and Bourbon; *Frasquita,* Hervietor, for Nantes; *Ann,* King, for Penang.

BIRTHS, MARRIAGES, AND DEATHS.

BIRTHS.

Jan. 29. At Neemuch, the lady of Capt. R. F. Vac Vitie, 49th N.I., of a son.

Feb. 8. At Calcutta, Mrs. J. Previte, of a son.
13. At Calcutta, Mrs. W. Bonaud, of a son.
15. Mrs. J. A. Lorimer, of a son.
16. At Chowringhee, the lady of Wm. Moran, Esq., of Tirhoot, of a son.
19. At Dacca, the lady of W. A. Peacock, Esq., of a daughter.
20. Mrs. George Clarke, of a son.
23. Mrs. J. P. Namey, of a daughter.
24. Mrs. James Black, of a daughter.
28. Mrs. E. Nash, of a daughter, still-born.

MARRIAGES.

Jan. 28. At Gwalior, Major Owen Jacob, son of Col. Jacob, to Miss Salome, daughter of P. Carapiet, Esq.
Feb. 13. At Calcutta, Mr. George Reston to Miss R. M. D'Cruz.
15. At Howrah Church, James Ilbery, Esq., to Henrietta, second daughter of John Thomas, Esq., of Howrah.
— At Calcutta, Mr. J. Castello, jun., to Miss Rose P. Cornelius.
16. At Meerut, Henry Travers Owen, Esq., of the civil service, to Catherine Nicholson, daughter of Alexander Graham, Esq., of Glasgow.
— At Calcutta, Mr. Charles Martin Wickens to Miss Harriet Herman.
20. At Calcutta, W. B. Tytler, Esq., superintending engineer, H C. steam department, to Charlotte, youngest daughter of Richard Rose, Esq., of Kent.
— At Calcutta, Joseph Agabeg, Esq., eldest son of the late Aviet Agabeg, Esq., to Salome, eldest daughter of the late C. J. Malchus, Esq.

DEATHS.

Jan. 12. At Arooab Factory, near Chuprah, John MacLachlan, Esq., aged 33.
Feb. 5. At Buchour, in Tirhoot, Mr. Kennedy Huggins, aged 58.
7. At Muttra, of an apoplectic attack, Capt. Trafford, of the 10th regt. L.C.
10. At Calcutta, Mrs Elizabeth Da Cruz, aged 27.
12. On board the bark *Lady Clifford,* on the passage to Singapore, Donald Macintyre, Esq., of Calcutta.
18. Suddenly, Mr. John D. Price, aged 22.
21. At Calcutta, Julia, wife of Mr. G. Clermont.
26. Mr. Clementi D'Paiva, aged 43.
27. At Calcutta, Mrs. F. Hypher, wife of Mr. J. Hypher, aged 23.
29. Mrs. B. Pereira, aged 29.

Madras.

CIVIL APPOINTMENTS, &c.

Feb. 16. M. Murray, Esq., to act as register to zillah court of Canara, during employment of Mr. F. N. Maltby on other duty.

The appointment, under date 12th Feb. 1836, of Mr. Wilkins to be master-attendant at Negapatam, is cancelled; and the master-attendantship of Nagore and Negapatam are united and placed under the charge of Capt. Hindes, the master-attendant at the former station.

MILITARY APPOINTMENTS, PROMOTIONS, &c.

Fort St. George, Feb. 16, 1836.—1st N.I. Capt. J. E. Williams to be major, Lieut. H. W. Hadfield to be capt., and Ens. R. Hamilton to be lieut., v. Godfry retired; date of coms. 10th Feb. 1836.

33d N.I. Capt. J. Campbell to be major, Lieut. H. Marshall to be capt., and Ens. R. A. Bruere to be lieut., v. Tod retired; date of coms. 14th Feb. 1836.

45th N.I. Lieut. W. R. A. Freeman to be capt., and Ens. R. Crew to be lieut., v. Francis invalided; date of coms. 12th Feb. 1836.

Surg. J. Hay, 2d member of Medical Board, permitted to return to Europe, and to retire from Hon. Company's service from 25th Feb.

Infantry. Lieut. Col. J. S. Fraser to be col. v. Lieut. Gen. R. Mackay dec.; date of com. 28th Sept. 1835.

34th N.I. Maj. W. T. Sneyd, from 39th regt., to be lieut. col., v. Ritchie dec.; date of com. 1st Jan. 1836.

39th N.I. Capt. W. Taylor to be major, Lieut. (Brev. Capt) F. Eades to be capt., and Ens E. Norman to be lieut., in suc. to Sneyd prom ; date of coms. 1st Jan. 1836.—Maj. W. Strahan, from 37th regt., to be lieut. col., v. Jourdon retired; date of com. 15th Feb. 1836.

37th N.I. Capt. G. Storey to be major, Lieut. (Brev. Capt.) P. Bedingfield to be capt., and Ens. W. Hake to be lieut., in suc. to Strahan prom.; date of coms. 15th Feb. 1836.

2d-Lieut. J. W. Rundall, of engineers, to be adj. of corps of sappers and miners.

Bombay.

GOVERNMENT ORDER.

SERVICES OF CAPT. BRUCKS.

Marine Department, Bombay Castle, Feb. 11, 1836.—With reference to the G. O. of the 28th ultimo, permitting Capt. Brucks to proceed to Europe on furlough, the Right Hon. the Governor in Council takes this opportunity to express his high sense of the value of that officer's services, and will have much pleasure in bringing the same to the favourable notice of the Hon. the Court of Directors.

COURTS-MARTIAL.

MIDSHIPMEN H. H. HEWITT, W. E. CAMPBELL, AND B. HAMILTON.

Bombay Castle, Jan. 22. 1836.—At a general court-martial assembled at Bombay, on the 27th Nov. 1835, Mr. Midshipman H. H. Hewitt, mate of the Indian navy, was tried on the following charges, *viz.* :—

Charges preferred by Commander, late Lieut. J. H. Rowband, in charge of the H. C. sloop of war *Ternate*, against Mr. Midshipman H. H. Hewitt, mate of the said ship.

First Charge.—" For a breach of discipline, and undue assumption of authority, and disrespect towards Lieut. Frushard, in the evening of the 27th instant, in the following instance :—In reprimanding Mr. Castle, acting boatswain, while in the execution of his office, under the immediate orders, and in the presence of Lieut. Frushard, his superior officer, such being at variance with the 28th article of the general instructions to captains.

Second Charge.—" For highly disrespectful and grossly insubordinate conduct towards me, his commander, in the following instance:—In addressing me as follows, when directed to pursue a different line of conduct from that mentioned in the first charge:—" Then, Sir, I will not do duty in the fore-top again," and repeating the same words on my desiring to be assured of what he had uttered.

" Such conduct being grossly insubordinate, and highly disrespectful to me his commander.

(Signed)   " J. H. ROWBAND, Commander, late Lieut , in charge of the H. C. ship, *Ternate.*"

H. C. sloop of war, *Ternate,* } at sea, 27th April, 1835. }

Upon which charges the court came to the following decision :

Finding and Sentence.—With respect to the first charge, that the prisoner Mr. Midshipman H. H. Hewitt, is guilty of the whole and every part thereof.

With respect to the second, that he is guilty of the whole and every part thereof.

The court having found the prisoner guilty as above specified, in breach of the articles of war in such cases made and provided, do sentence him (the said Mr. Midshipman Hewitt) to be dismissed the Hon. Company's service.

(Signed)   JOHN SAWYER, Commander I. N. and President.

Approved and Confirmed.—But in consideration of the strong and correct recommendation of the court, the length of arrest, the previous good conduct of the prisoner, and above all, the contrition Mr. Hewitt has expressed since, at his deviating from it, leads the Commander-in-chief to meet the wishes of the court, in the hope that M. Hewitt's future services will shew that in zeal and obedience to the orders of his superiors, he is grateful for such indulgence.

Mercy is therefore extended to Mr. Hewitt ; he is released from arrest, and placed at the disposal of Sir Charles Malcolm, superintendant Indian Navy.

(Signed)   JOHN KEANE, Lieut. Gen., Commander-in-chief.

In continuation of the proceedings of the same court-martial re-assembled at Bombay on the 3d Dec. 1835, Mr. W. E. Campbell, midshipman of the Indian Navy, was tried on the following charges, *viz* :—

Charges preferred by Commander, late Lieut. J. H. Rowband, in charge of the H. C. sloop of war *Ternate*, against Mr. W. E. Campbell, midshipman of the said ship.

First Charge.—" For wilful neglect of duty, and disobedience of orders, in the following instance : — In quitting his post, during his watch upon deck, at about 7 P. M. on the 25th of April 1835, without permission, and under the pretence of taking tea, when he had absented himself from the deck for that purpose at four P. M., the appointed hour, and had even remained below longer than the prescribed time.

Second Charge.—" For wilful neglect of duty, disobedience of orders, and contempt of authority, in the following instance :—In not relieving the deck in his watch at four P. M. this day, although twice sent for by Lieut. Frushard, and further treating him, the said Lieut. Frushard, his superior officer, with contempt, by not coming upon deck when sent for, or taking the slightest notice of that officer's communication.

Third Charge —" For disobedience of orders in the following instance:—In not conforming to the regulations of the ship, in taking his meals at the periods appointed by me for that purpose.

(Signed) " J. H. ROWBAND,
Commander,
late Lieut. in charge H. C. Ship
Ternate."

H. C. sloop of war *Ternate,*
at sea, 25th April, 1835.

Upon which charges the Court came to the following decision :

Finding and Sentence.—That with respect to the first charge, the prisoner Mr. W. E. Campbell, midshipman in the Indian Navy, is guilty of having quitted his post during his watch upon deck at about seven P. M. on the 25th April, 1835, without permission, and under the pretence of taking tea, when he had absented himself from the deck for that purpose, at four P. M. the appointed hour, and had even remained below longer than the prescribed time ; but as the Court are of opinion, that in quitting his post under the circumstances he did, the prisoner did not act contrary to the custom of the service, they attach no criminality to his having done so, and they do therefore acquit him of wilful neglect of duty and disobedience of orders.

That with respect to the second charge, he is guilty of the whole and every part thereof, with the exception of the words " or taking the slightest notice of that officer's communication."

That with respect to the third charge, it is not proved.

The Court having found the prisoner guilty to the extent above specified, in breach of the articles of war in such cases made and provided, do sentence to him, the said Mr. W. E. Campbell: midshipman in the Indian Navy, to lose three (3) steps in the list of midshipmen, so that his standing shall be immediately below Mr. Midshipman W. Fell, and next above Mr. Midshipman A. Offer.

(Signed) JOHN SAWYER,
Comdr. I. N. and President.

On a full consideration of this whole case, I approve and confirm the finding on the 2d and 3d charges, and the sentence of the Court accordingly ; but I dissent entirely from the opinion of the Court on the first charge, although, under all the circumstances, I do not deem it

necessary to direct a revisal.—It appears clearly from the evidence brought forward, that Mr. Midshipman Campbell's conduct was directly at variance with the orders issued a few days previous by his commander, Capt. Rowband, of which order he was reminded by the first Lieut. Pool, and was even threatened with being reported to his captain at the moment he was about to act in direct opposition to it. That the practice assigned by Mr. Midshipman Campbell for quitting his post, appears to have been entirely groundless, and the distinctions he has attempted to draw in the course of his defence, regarding the meals of tea and supper, (which he himself appears by his letter of complaint, and every naval man well knows, are one and the same) serve only to shew more clearly the spirit by which he was actuated in opposing the wishes and orders of his commander, and that he deserves even a heavier punishment than that which the Court has awarded him.

(Signed) JOHN KEANE, Lieut.-Gen.
Commander in Chief.

In continuation of the proceedings of the same court-martial re-assembled at Bombay on the 16th Dec. 1835, Mr. B. Hamilton, midshipman of the Indian Navy, was tried on the following charge, viz.—

Charge.—" For conduct highly prejudicial to good order and naval discipline, while on board the H. C. sloop of war *Ternate,* in the following instances :—

1st. " In taking part in a personal conflict between the gun-room cook and midshipman's servant, and striking the former, on or about the 22d of April, 1835.

2d. " For addressing to the late Commodore Elwon two letters, one dated 21st April, another dated 3d May 1835, being in their tone and spirit insulting and disrespectful towards me his commander, and unbecoming his (Mr. Hamilton's) situation as a midshipman ; also reflecting upon my character as an officer, in his appeal against arrangements which I had found it necessary to make in carrying on the duties of the vessel, and against my enforcing the regulations of the ship with regard to the hours for the meals of the midshipmen.

(Signed) " J. H. ROWBAND.
Commander, Indian Navy."
Bombay, 30th Nov. 1835.

Upon which charge the Court came to the following decision :

Finding and Sentence.—With respect to the 1st instance of the charge, the prisoner, Mr. Midshipman B. Hamilton, is not guilty, and the court do therefore acquit him.

With respect to the 2d instance of the

charge, that he is guilty of all and every part thereof.

The court having found the prisoner guilty to the extent above specified, in breach of the articles of war in such cases made and provided, do sentence him, the said Mr. Hamilton, to lose two steps, so that his future standing in the list of midshipmen in the Indian Navy, shall be immediately below Mr. C. Hewitt, and next above Mr. C. J. Cruttenden.

(Signed)   JOHN SAWYER,
Commander I. N. and President.
Approved and Confirmed,
(Signed)   JOHN KEANE.
Lieut. Gen. Commander in Chief.

Remarks by the Commander in Chief.— I regret that I cannot see in these proceedings a sufficient reason for complying with the recommendation of the Court, to remit the penalty awarded; the sentence is lenient, and again, the concluding remark of the Court does not appear borne out by the evidence adduced either on this or the previous trials, and is in fact rather inconsistent with the findings on them all, particularly that in the present case.

CIVIL APPOINTMENTS, &c.

Territorial Department.

Feb. 9. Mr. A. Campbell to be fourth assistant to principal collector of Dharwar, from 1st Jan. 1836, and to act as third assistant.

Mr. Simpson to act as collector of Tannah from 20th Feb.

Judicial Department.

Feb. 12. Mr. E. Grant (having reported his arrival from Cape of Good Hope) permitted to resume charge of his duties of judge and session judge at Ahmedabad.

Mr J. G. Lumsden, assistant session judge at Surat, to take charge of Adawlut at Broach, during absence of Mr. W. Richardson allowed to proceed to presidency in consequence of ill-health.

Furloughs, &c.—Feb. 10. Mr. A. Elphinston, to Neilgherries, for twelve months, for health.

MILITARY APPOINTMENTS.

Bombay Castle, Feb. 4, 1836.—Lieut. E. Farquharson to act as senior deputy com. of ordnance during such time as Capt. Laurie may be in charge of arsenal, as senior commissary of ordnance.

Assist. Surg. Bourchier to be acting residency surgeon in Cutch, during Assist. Surg. Deacon's absence on sick cert. to Cape of Good Hope.

Assist. Surg. Ferrar to act in medical charge of Auxiliary Horse in Cutch during employment of Assist. Surg. Bourchier as residency surgeon.

Lieut. W. Massie to act as junior deputy commissary of stores at presidency.

2d L.C. Capt. P. P. Wilson to be major, v. Rybot retired; date 14th July 1834.—Lieut. W. Trevelyan to be capt., and Cornet R. C. Le Geyt to be lieut., in suc. to Urquhart dec.; date 19th do.

The following appointments confirmed:—Maj. C. W. Shaw, 20th N.I., to assume command of station of Baroda, from 30th Dec. 1835.—Capt. A. F. Bartlett, 26th N.I., to act as major of brigade in Candeish, from date of departure of Capt. Forbes to presidency.—Capt. A. T. Reid, 12th N.I., to act as interp. to that regt. from 22d Dec. 1835.—Ens. J. R. Keilly, 20th N.I., to act as adj. to that regt. during absence of Lieut. and Brev. Capt. J. E. Lang on sick cert. to presidency.— Capt. C. Denton, 24th N. I., to act as adj. to that regt. during absence of Lieut. Ramsay on sick cert.

1st Gr. N.I. Capt. J. Reynolds to be major, Lieut. A. C. Harrington to be capt., and Ens. R. R. Moore to be lieut., in suc. to Morse dec.; date of rank 23d Aug. 1835.

13th N.I. Ens. N. I. McDougall to be lieut., v. Cooke dec.; date 9th Nov. 1835.

Feb. 11.—Capt. S. Robson, European regt., to assume command of Poona brigade, from date of departure of Lieut. Col. Stevenson to presidency on duty, as a temporary arrangement.

Feb. 15.—Maj. F. Schuler, regt. of artillery, to be senior commissary of stores, in suc. to Lieut. Col. Griffith.

Maj. C. Ovans, right wing European regt., to be quarter-master general of army, with official rank of lieut. col., v. Morse dec.; date of app. 23d Aug. 1835.

The following temporary arrangements confirmed:—Lieut. A. F. Rowan, regt. of artillery, to receive charge of deputy commissary of ordnance at Deesa, until arrival of Lieut. Webb.—Lieut. and Brev. Capt. H. Hobson, 20th N.I., to act as adj. to that regt., during absence of Lieut. and Brev. Capt. J. E. Lang on sick cert. to Bombay.— Capt. J. Cooper, 7th N.I., to command station of Ahmedabad, on departure of Capt. Clarke on 19th Nov. last.

Lieut. T. Studdert to act as executive engineer at Deesa, during absence of Capt. Harris.

2d-Lieut. J. B. Woosnam, horse artillery, to act as interp. to H.M. 4th L. Drags., v. Lieut. E. Scott proceeded to Europe.

FURLOUGHS.

To Neilgherry Hills.—Feb. 8. Lieut. G. K. Erskine, 1st L.C., for twelve months, for health.

To Bombay.—Feb. 15. Capt. W. Harris, engineers, for two months, for health.

SHIPPING.

Arrival.

FEB. 17. *Richard Walker*, Fidler, from Sydney.

BIRTH, MARRIAGE, AND DEATHS.

BIRTH.

Lately. At Bombay, the lady of William Courtney, Esq., late of Plymouth, of a son.

MARRIAGE.

Feb. 2. At Bombay, Assist. Surg. R. A. J. Hughes, to Kate, fifth daughter of the late W. T. Green, Esq., of Henrietta Street, Brunswick Square, London.

DEATHS.

Feb. 7. At Seroor, Mr. Thomas Griffiths, a pensioned assist. dep. com. of ordnance, aged 70.

11. At his residence, Breach Candy, in his 44th year, Thos. M'Carthy, Esq., son of the late Jeremiah McCarthy, Esq. surveyor to the Hon. East-India Company.

Ceylon.

BIRTHS.

Feb. 4. Mrs. E. M'Carthy, of a son.
7. Mrs. P. Brohier, of a son.

MARRIAGE.

Jan. 18. At Colombo, Christopher Elliott, Esq., surgeon, to Miss Jessie Clark.

DEATH.

Feb. 14. At Point de Galle, aged 19, Gerald Benjamin, only son of the late Lieut. Gicsler, second Ceylon regiment.

Dutch India.

SHIPPING.

Arrivals at Batavia.—Feb. 16. *Olympus*, from

London and Cape.—22. *Vanguard*, from Singapore.—23. *Clifford Wayne*, from Rio de Janeiro.

Departures.—Feb. 15. *Cherub*, for Singapore.—16. *Charles Kerr*, for China; London, for Sourabaya.—18. *Potomac*, for China.

BIRTH.

Sept. 6, 1835. At Batavia, Mrs. James B. Gray, of a son.

DEATH.

Oct. 26. At Sourabaya, Mr. Alex. Gray, late of the Cape of Good Hope, aged 31.

China.

SHIPPING.

Arrivals.—Jan.—*Dawson*, from Manilla.—27. *Timor*, from Manilla.—Feb. 1. *Navarino*, from Calcutta.—13. *Champlain*, from Liverpool; *Commerce*, from Manilla.—18. *John Gilpin*, from Manilla.—19. *Rassalas*, from Sandwich Islands; *Levant*, from Batavia; *William Wilson*, from Singapore.—24. *Aurelius*, from London; *William Rodger*, from Bombay.—26. *Syed Khan*, from East Coast; *Lady Grant*, from Calcutta.—28. *Walter Scott*, from Batavia.—29. *Hector*, from Hobart Town.—*Fairy*, from East Coast.—*Rosalind*, from London.—March 1. *Mavis*, from Singapore.—4. *Bombay Castle*, from Calcutta; *Lady Hayes*, from Lombock; *Virginia*, from Batavia; *Colon*, from Manilla.

Departures.—Jan. 30. *Penelope*, for London.—Feb. 2. *Lord Lowther*, for Bombay; *Columbia*, for London.—5. *Charles Forbes*, and *Golconda*, both for Bombay.—6. *Alfred*, for London.—8. *Severn*, for London; *Earl of Balcarras*, for Madras.—11. *Oberlin*, for New York.—12. *Ann*, for London.—14. *Victory*, for Madras.—15. *Morrison*, for Manilla; *Cynthia*, for New York.—16. *Macclesfield*, for Sydney.—20. *Jardine* (steamer), for Singapore.—22. *Bombay*, and *Sarah*, both for London.—23. *Louisa*, for Monte Video.—25. *Red Rover*, for Calcutta.—26. *Canton*, for Batavia.—29. *Watkins*, for Singapore.—March 2. *Marquis Camden*, and *George IVth*, both for London.—3. *Coromandel*, for London; *Children*, for Singapore.—4. *Syed Khan*, and *Aurelius*, both for Bombay.—5. *Mangles*, for Straits; *Hellespont*, for Manilla.—14. *Balgueric*, for Bordeaux.—17. *Louisa Campbell*, for London.

Freight to London (March 2)—£4. 10s. to £5. per ton.

DEATH.

Feb. 13. Mr. Charles Reynell, late purser of the *Earl of Balcarras*.

New South Wales.

SHIPPING.

Arrivals.—Feb. 26. *Sydney Packet*, from New Zealand.—28. *Dryade*, from Newcastle; *Vansittart*, from London and Hobart Town.—March 1. *Richard Reynolds*, from London.—*Joseph Weller*, from New Zealand.—9. *Elizabeth*, from Launceston; *Royal William*, from Hobart Town; *Nimrod*, from Launceston.—10. *Brougham*, from Mauritius and Hobart Town.—13. *Fanny*, from New Zealand.

Departures.—Feb. 12. *Layton*, for Manilla; *Royal Sovereign*, for Penang.—17. *Orissa*, for Singapore.—18. *Minerva*, for Manilla; *Salacea*, for King George's Sound; *Sir David Ogilby*, for New Zealand.—March 1. *Mediterranean Packet*, for New Zealand.

BIRTHS

Aug. 3, 1835. At Norfolk Island, the lady of Major Anderson, 50th regt., of a daughter.
20. At Clydesdale, the lady of Mr. John Johnstone, of a daughter.
25. At Sydney, the lady of George Weller, Esq., of a daughter.
Sept. 16. The lady of John Nicholson, Esq., harbour-master, of a son.

Oct. 9. At Sydney, the lady of Major Croker, 17th regt., of a daughter.
Nov. 23. At Sydney, the lady of Capt. Ebbart, of a son (since dead).
25. At Denham Court, the lady of T. V. Bloomfield, Esq., of a son
28. At Sydney, the lady of John Thompson, Esq., of a daughter.
Dec. 17. At Concord, the lady of Montague Rothery, Esq., of a son.
23. At Moreton Bay, the lady of I. S. Parker, Esq., of a daughter.
Jan. 3, 1836. Mrs. Rust, of a daughter.
8. The wife of the Rev. Charles Price, Port Stephens, of a son.
9. At Kirkham, the lady of Charles Cowper, Esq., of a son.
— Mrs. Robert Cooper, of Juniper Hall, South Head Road, of a daughter.
17. At Annandale, the lady of Thomas Collins, Esq., of a daughter.
18. At Marian, Field of Mars, the lady of D. A. C. G. Bowerman, of a daughter.
Feb. 27. At Lake Bathurst, Mrs. E. S. Hall, of a son.
March 5. At Annandale, the lady of Robert Johnston, Esq., of a son.

MARRIAGES.

Sept. 1. At Parramatta, his Honour James Dowling, Esq., one of the judges of the Supreme Court, to Harriet Mary (relict of A. M. Ritchie, Esq., formerly of Calcutta), eldest daughter of John Blaxland, Esq., M.C., of Newington.
2. At Maitland, Helenus Scott, Esq., J. P., of Glendon, Hunter's River, to Sarah Anne, eldest daughter of the Rev. G. K. Rusden, chaplain of Maitland.
3. At Sydney, A. B. Lowe, Esq., lieut. of the Royal Navy, to Margaret, eldest daughter of S. G. Irwin, Esq., also a lieut. of the Royal Navy.
15. At Windsor, Frederick Garling, Esq., of Sydney, to Sarah, third daughter of T. W. Wilkinson, Esq., of Stonehouse, near Plymouth, Devon, formerly of the 4th regt., and now of the ordnance department.
16. At Sydney, Robert, second son of Robert Campbell, M. C., to Anne Sophia, eldest daughter of the late Edward Riley, Esq.
22. At Windsor, George Pitt, Esq., of Richmond, to Miss Julian Johnson, of the same place.
Oct. 29. At the Field of Mars, Dudley, brother of Frederick North, Esq., M.P., of Rougham Hall, Norfolk, and Hastings Lodge, in the county of Sussex, to Sarah, eldest daughter of Edmund Lockyer, Esq., of Ermington.
Nov. 28. At Sydney, George Bennett, Esq., F.L.S., surgeon, to Julian Ludavina, second daughter of the late Lieut. Col. Charles Cameron, of the 3d regt. or Buffs.
— At Sydney, Mr. H. H. Vintnam to Elizabeth, youngest daughter of James Curry, Esq., of Southead, Essex.
Dec. 30. At Sydney, L. Spyer, Esq., to Miss Juliana De Metz.
Jan. 7, 1836. At Parramatta, Nelson Lawson, Esq., of Mudgee and Prospect, to Honoria Mary, second daughter of the Rev. Charles Dickinson, of the Field of Mars.
25. At Maitland, P. W. Mallon, Esq., surgeon, to Catherine, third daughter of S. G. Irvine, lieut. R.N.
Feb. 17. At Maitland, Wakefield Simpson, Esq., merchant, to Miss Winder, eldest daughter of T. W. M. Winder, Esq.
March 8. At Sydney, J. G. Colyer, Esq., of Sutton Forest, to Elizabeth Ann, daughter of Wm. Elyard, Esq., R.N.

DEATHS.

Aug. 7. At Sydney, Elizabeth, wife of Deputy Assist. Commissary General Howard.
23. At Baulkham Hills, Mary, wife of John Smith, Esq., aged 67.
26. At Sydney, aged 63, Mrs. Walker, widow of the late John Walker, Esq., of the city of Cork, Ireland.
30. At his residence, Darlinghurst, James Laidley, Esq., deputy com. general.
Sept. 14. At Norfolk Island, Mr. John Leach.
Oct. 2. At the Parsonage House, Parramatta, Mrs. Marsden, wife of the Rev. Samuel Marsden, senior chaplain to the colony, aged 63.
Nov. 6. At Parramatta, James Orr, Esq.

25. Mr. Jacob Wyer, for many years the principal rope-maker of Sydney.

Jan. 2, 1836. At Sydney, Capt. Potter, of the ship *Rachel*, of Liverpool. He died suddenly, of apoplexy.

4. At Sydney, Mr. John Pitman.

7. At Sydney, aged 18, Anne, daughter of the Hon. James Dowling, judge of the Supreme Court.

8. Charles S. Johnson, aged 18, third officer of the *Royal Sovereign*, son of James Johnson, Esq., M.D., surgeon R.N.

12. At the parsonage, Parramatta, of consumption, Frances, wife of the Rev. H. H. Bobart, M.A., who arrived in November 1835, in the *Lotus*, to join the church mission in New Zealand.

15. At Newcastle, H. W. Radford, Esq., surgeon of H.M. 62d regt., now in India.

Feb. 21. At Sydney, Charles Pittman Skelton, Esq., of the Madras civil service, second son of Maj. General Skelton.

23. At Sydney, Mr. Charles White.

March 4. At Sydney, R. Smith, Esq., R.N., only brother of Dr. C. Smith, Pitt Street.

7. At Bathurst, Major John Masseter, of H.M. 50th regt. of Foot.

10. At Sydney, to which place she had proceeded for the benefit of her health, Margaret, wife of Thomas Wood Rowlands, Esq., of Hobart Town, aged 31.

Lately. Capt. Bragg, of the schooner *Industry*. He was murdered by his own crew, who had mutinied, on the passage from Launceston to New Zealand.

— At sea, John Watson, Esq., commander of the barque *Lynx*.

Van Diemen's Land.

APPOINTMENT.

Jan. 4. John Beamont, Esq., to be sheriff of Van Diemen's Land, for current year.

SHIPPING.

Arrivals at Hobart Town.—Feb. 12. *Matchless*, from Sydney—21. *Asia*, from London; H.M.S. *Zebra*, from Sydney.—22. *Bencoolen*, from London.—23. *Stirling Castle*, from London.—March 2. *Alice*, from Liverpool.—3. *Merope*, from Twofold Bay.—5. *Ulysses*, from Mauritius and Launceston.—8. *Thomas Laurie*, from London.

Departures from ditto.—Feb. 25. *Francis Freeling*, for Sydney.—March 2. *North Briton*, for ditto.

Arrivals at Launceston.—Feb. 12. *Frances Charlotte*, from Sydney.—16. *Dart*, from Sydney.—18. *Chili*, from London.

BIRTHS.

Oct. 25. At Glen Esk, Mrs. Aitkin, of a son.

28. At New Norfolk, the lady of W. S. Sharland, Esq., of a daughter.

Dec. 17. Mrs. Ludbey, of a daughter.

31. Mrs. H. Miller, of a daughter.

Jan. 15, 1836. Mrs. James Smith, of a daughter.

21. At Ellenthorpe Hall, Mrs. J. Knight, of a daughter.

Feb. 18. At Tullochgorum, Mrs. Archibald Mc Intyre, of a son.

March 3. At Hobart Town, the lady of P. Murdoch, Esq., of a son.

MARRIAGES.

Oct. 24. At Hobart Town, Charles C. Innes, Esq., to Elizabeth Cunninghame, youngest daughter of the late John Haldane, Esq., of Edinburgh.

Nov. 5. At Evandale, Mr. Wm. Roberts, of Hobart Town, to Mary, eldest daughter of Joseph Solomons, Esq., of Launceston.

11. At Launceston, Charles Henty, Esq., managing director of the Cornwall Bank, to Susan, eldest daughter of the late Charles Boniface, Esq., of Kinfield, Sussex.

16. At Launceston, G. B. Skardon, Esq., J.P., of Little Hampton, lieut. R.N., to Mary, second daughter of the late John Hearn, Esq., R.N.

27. At Cawood, T. H. Patterson, Esq., of Calton Hill, to Martha Reeves, niece of D. W. Harvey, Esq., M.P. for Southwark.

Dec. 2. At Launceston, J. L. Deane, Esq., of

H.M. customs, Sydney, to Elizabeth, third daughter of the late Wm. Fisher, Esq., of Aylesbury, Bucks.

10. Mr. Wm. Blyth, of Fenchurch Street, London, to Elizabeth, only daughter of Mr. Crowther, surgeon.

21. At Weobley, near Campbell Town, Theophilus Swifte, Esq., to Jane Eliza, daughter of Henry Keach, Esq., of Weobley.

22. At Hobart Town, Mr. Edw. Carr Shaw, to Anne, second daughter of the late James Fenton, Esq., Dunlavin, county of Wicklow, Ireland.

— At Launceston, F. Y. Wilmore, Esq., of Blackwood-hill, West Tamar, to Eliza, eldest surviving daughter of Mr. Wrentmore, of London, solicitor.

31. At New Town, Mr. Benj. Perry (of the firm of Crookes and Perry, Hobart Town), to Eliza, eldest daughter of Mr. Samuel Banks, of Tottenham, Middlesex.

Jan. 14, 1836. At Hobart Town, Edward Bedford, Esq., to Mary, daughter of the late William Selby, Esq., of Welmington, Kent.

23. At Hobart Town, Mr. Wm. Giblin, second son of R. W. Giblin, Esq., of New Town, to Marian, eldest daughter of the late John Falkinor, Esq., of Mount Prospect, county Tipperary, Ireland.

Feb. 16. Mr. Henry Ransome, second son of James Ransome, Esq., Rushmere, Suffolk, to Ann, second daughter of the late Francis Patten, Esq., many years alderman of the city of Rochester.

DEATHS.

Aug. 9. At Mill's Plains, Thomas Pitcairn, Esq.

16. Mary, wife of Mr. John Nash, of Glenorchy, late of the Royal Veteran corps.

— At Douglas Park, Anne Rankine, wife of Temple Pearson, Esq.

Nov. 3. Of apoplexy, Sarah, wife of Mr. J. W. Scott, collector of indigenous seeds.

4. At Hobart Town, Mr. David Nuthall, aged 44, many years a resident in Calcutta.

Dec. 1. Capt. Sergeantson, late of H.M. 40th regt. He was found murdered in the bush near Campbelltown. Capt. S. had been a very distinguished officer, and had signalized himself on many occasions in the Peninsular war, and served in the 28th regt. at Waterloo. He was on the point of returning to England with his family.

17. Mr. Henry Parkinson, aged 23, tutor in the family of J. T. Gellibrand, Esq.

Jan. 1, 1836. At Hobart Town, aged 19, Mary, wife of Mr. De Villiers, and second daughter of James Cox, Esq., Clarendon.

17. At Allanvale, suddenly, Thomas Martin Fenton, Esq., J.P., aged 48.

Feb. 24. At Elphin, near Launceston, Mrs. Dry, wife of R. Dry, Esq.

New Zealand.

BIRTH.

Sept. 28, 1835. At the Bay of Islands, the wife of James Busby, Esq., British resident, of a daughter.

Persian Gulf.

DEATH.

Lately. The Imaum of Senna. He has been succeeded by his son Ally-bin-Abdoolla Munsoor, who is about twenty-five years of age.

Cape of Good Hope.

APPOINTMENT.

March 28. The Rev. Thomas Reid to be minister of Dutch Reformed Church at Colesberg.

SHIPPING.

Arrivals in Table Bay.—April 13. *Morven*, from Bristol.—15. *Ann*, from Downs.—16. *David Scott*, from Torbay; *Sanguenay*, from Liverpool.—17. *Addingham*, from London; *Mary*, from Rio de Janeiro.—19. *Lord Hobart*, from St. Helena.—22.

Midlothian, from Leith.—23. *Sir Edward Paget,*
from London.—25. *True Love,* from London.—26.
Thomas Harrison, from Cork.—29. *Guiana,* from
Downs: *Dorothya,* from Milford Haven.—May 11.
Matilda, from Downs.

Departures from ditto.—April 8. *Munster Lass,*
for Algoa Bay.—10. *Eleanor,* for ditto.—16. *Madras,* for Madras; *Juliana,* for Madras, &c.—21.
Palinure, for N.S.Wales.—23. *Kerswell,* for Mauritius.—25. *David Scott,* for Madras and Calcutta.
—26. *Sir Edward Paget,* for Madras.—29. *Thomas
Harrison,* for Sydney.—May 1. *Midlothian,* for
N.S. Wales.—4. *Highlander,* for ditto: *Guiana,*
for V.D. Land.—5. *Addingham,* for Swan River.—
8. *Henry,* for Mauritius.

Arrival at Port Elizabeth.—April 15. *Maria,*
from Falmouth.

BIRTH.

April 16. At the Gardens, the lady of John Jack-

son, Esq., East-India Company's service, of a
daughter.

MARRIAGES.

April 19. At Cape Town, Augustus Smith Le
Mesurier, Esq., advocate-general of Bomb·y, to
Sarah Anne Taylor Morley, widow of the late
James Morley, Esq.
22. At Rondebosch, Thomas Baylis, Esq., captain in the Madras artillery, to Frances, eldest
daughter of the late George Napper, Esq., assistant surgeon, Royal Artillery.

DEATHS.

April 3. At Graham's Town, in consequence of
a fall from his horse, Mr. John Watkins, surgeon,
aged 25, son of Mr. Thomas Watkins, of Cardiff.
He was attached to the army medical staff.
19. At Wynberg, in the 78th year of his age,
William Wilberforce Bird, Esq., many years comp-
troller of his Majesty's customs at the Cape of
Good Hope.

SUPPLEMENT TO ASIATIC INTELLIGENCE.

ESTATE OF CRUTTENDEN, MACKILLOP, AND CO.

At the request of Mr. Browne, who is
in England, we insert the reply of Mr.
Cullen (part of which we have already inserted) to the statements, in reference to
the estate of Cruttenden, Mackillop, and
Co., made by Mr. Dickens; that Mr.
Browne had drawn or received his allowance of Rs. 600 per mensem, from the
estate of the asignee up to the date of his
departure for England, and, moreover,
that he (Mr. Cullen) had continued to
draw or receive a similar sum " up to this
hour,"—which, with the Laudable Societies' allowances, yielded an income, for
the past two years, of " at least" Sa. Rs.
1,800 per mensem. Mr. Cullen says · " Mr.
Browne left India in January 1835, and
although he continued labouring for the
estate up to within a few days of his departure, he drew no allowance for services
subsequent to the month of September
preceding, and his receipts, in all, amount
I find, to Sa. Rs. 5,400 only ! As to my
own case, I have simply to state, that I
have not received a sixpence from the estate or Mr. Mac Intyre for the past seven
months, although daily employed in its
business; and my average income for the
two past years has barely reached a *moiety*
of Mr. Dickens's estimate, while latterly
it has fallen considerably short of a third
part of it !" He adds : " In drawing the
Court's appointed allowance from Mr.
Mac Intyre, both Mr. Browne and myself
never could have dreamt that the estate of
the late firm was to bear the cost, and I
have the satisfaction of thinking even now
that, if justice be done to the property,

and the late Committee's suggestions be
adopted, the expenses incurred will eventually be satisfied without injury to any
one, and the acting assignee amply remunerated at the same time."

Mr. Browne has appended the following
note to this letter :

" That the English public may know
from what motives, and with what consistency, Mr. Dickens denounces the salaries
paid to Mr. Cullen and Mr. Browne, and
challenges Mr. Mac Intyre's charges, it
is only necessary to state, that Mr. Dickens
is one of the asignees of Palmer and Co.,
and to ask whether, in that capacity,
without the sanction of the creditors and
without the authority of the Court, be
concurred with the other assignees in
maintaining the following establishment :
viz. House-rent, Sa. Rs. 1,000 per mensem ; secretary 1,000 ; four partners 700
each, or 2,800 ; together, Sa. Rs. 4,800
monthly, or annually Sa. Rs. 57 600, exclusive of large subordinate European
and native establishments ? in short, during the first twelve months, Mr. Dickens was an approving party to the expenditure of upwards of Rs. 80,000, on account of Palmer and Co's. estates. All
this Mr. Dickens must know to be true,
though he, now, not only quarrels with
Mr. Mac Intyre's expenditure of a much
smaller sum, in *more than double the period;*
but absolutely proposes to allow nothing
at all for management. It is to be lamented that Mr. Mac Intyre's expenses have
proved so heavy ; but before assailing his
neighbours, Mr. Dickens should have explained his own apparently reckless waste
of the funds of another estate."

DEBATE AT THE EAST-INDIA HOUSE.

East-India House, July 11.

A special General Court of Proprietors of East-India Stock was this day held, pursuant to requisition, at the Company's house in Leadenhall-street.

PARLIAMENTARY PAPERS.

The minutes of the last court having been read,—

The *Chairman* (Sir J. R. Carnac, Bart.) said : " I am to acquaint the Court, that certain papers which have been laid before Parliament since the last General Court, the titles of which shall be read, are now submitted to the Proprietors, in conformity with the by-law, cap. i. sec. 4."

The clerk then read the titles of the papers, as follow :

Lists, specifying compensation proposed to be granted to certain reduced servants of the East-India Company.— (Nos. 51, 52, 53. and 54.)

Lists, specifying the particulars of compensation proposed to be granted to certain persons late in the maritime service of the East-India Company, under an arrangement sanctioned by the Board of Commissioners for the Affairs of India.—(Nos. 53 and 54.)

Annual home accounts of the East-India Company, pursuant to the 3d and 4th William IV., cap. 85.

Accounts of the territorial revenues and disbursements of the East-India Company, for the years 1831-32, 1832-33, and 1833-34, with an estimate for the succeeding year.

SUGAR DUTIES.

The *Chairman.*—" I have to state that this Court has been specially convened, in consequence of a requisition, signed by nine proprietors duly qualified by law, for the purpose of taking into consideration the subject referred to in that requisition, which shall now be read."

The clerk then read the following requisition :—

" To Sir James Rivett Carnac, Bart., Chairman of the Honourable the Court of Directors of the East-India Company.

" SIR : We, the undersigned Proprietors of East-India Stock, duly qualified, referring to chap. 1, sec. 3, of the By-laws, which ordains, that 'all proceedings of Parliament, which, in the opinion of the Court of Directors, may affect the rights, interests, or privileges of the East-India Company, shall be submitted by them to the consideration of a General

Asiat.Journ. N.S. VOL. 20. No. 80.

Court, to be specially summoned for that purpose, before the same shall pass into a law,' request that a Special General Court may be summoned without delay, to take into consideration the bill for the equalization of duties on East and West-India sugars, now about to pass into a law, considering that the stipulations of the bill, as it now stands, will prove injurious and unjust towards a large portion of the British territory in India, but particularly those under the presidencies of Madras and Bombay.

We have the honour to be, Sir,

Your obedient servants,

" CHARLES FORBES,
GEORGE ARBUTHNOT,
THOMAS WEEDING,
P. LAURIE,
JOHN DEANS CAMPBELL,
W. H. SYKES,
E. E. CAMPBELL,
JAMES MACKENZIE,
P. LAURIE, JUN.,
CHARLES GRANT,
GEORGE FORBES,
ALFRED LATHAM.

" London, July 4, 1836."

Mr. *Weeding* then rose and said, that the requisition which had just been read, would apprize the Court of the important nature of the question which the Proprietors were now assembled to discuss, and which he would endeavour, as briefly as possible, to bring under their particular notice. It would, in the first place, be necessary for him to call their attention to what had already taken place with reference to an equalization of the duties on East and West India sugar. It would be recollected that, on the 6th of May last, the Court had agreed to petition both Houses of Parliament, praying that sugar, the produce of British India, might be imported into this country at the same rate of duty as was imposed upon sugar the produce of other British settlements. At their last meeting, on the 22d of June, it was announced to them, that the Directors had been in communication with his Majesty's ministers on this subject, and that the hon. Chairman had received a most satisfactory letter from Sir John Hobhouse with respect to it. He, in common with the whole court, was extremely gratified on receiving this intelligence; and he had hoped that the principle laid down in the letter of Sir J. Hobhouse would have been carried out to the fullest extent, and that it would include sugar the produce of every part of the Company's Indian territory. This hope was, however, unfortunately disappointed. A bill was brought into the House of Commons for the equalization of the sugar duties on the 23d of June, and he was surprised to find, that while it granted the privilege of exporting sugar from Bengal at a reduced rate of duty, it excluded Madras and Bombay from the like privilege. On the 2d of July, that bill passed both Houses of Parliament; and, on the 4th of July, it received the royal assent. The bill took no notice whatever of the claims of Madras and Bombay, but was confined to Bengal alone. There was no doubt that, in the last-named presidency, a more considerable portion of land was employed in the cultivation of sugar, from' natural as well as artificial causes, than in the other presidencies; but that afforded no reason for refusing to grant a privilege to Madras and Bombay, which would encourage them hereafter to cultivate that species of produce. One of the great causes which operated to encourage the manufacture of sugar in Bengal, was that in the old time, when the East-India Company were traders, they were in the habit of bringing large quantities of that article, in conjunction with saltpetre, to this country, those articles forming the dead-weight of their shipping, by which means great benefit accrued both to the natives of India and to the Company; and his anxious wish was, that the benefit to be derived from the growth and exportation of sugar under the altered duty, should be extended equally to all the presidencies, instead of being confined to Bengal. This, however, was not contemplated by the measure recently passed. By the 3d section of that bill it was enacted, "that from and after the 1st day of December 1836, it shall not be lawful to import into any part of the presidency of Fort-William, in Bengal, or of any dependency thereof, being a British possession, any foreign sugar, nor any sugar the growth of any British possession into which foreign sugar can be legally imported, save and except into such districts or provinces of the said presidency, or of the dependencies thereof, as shall be appointed by the Governor-General of India in Council." Here no notice whatever was taken of Madras or Bombay, and a power was given to the Governor-General in Council to declare into what districts of the presidency sugar might or might not be imported. The act however went farther; for by the 4th section it was provided, "that no sugar, the produce of any district or province, in respect of which any such order or orders shall be issued, shall be imported into any part of the United Kingdom, at the lower rate of duty proposed by this act." The meaning of this was, that sugar, allowed to be imported into those

districts, from which the Governor-general in council might take upon himself to remove the inhibition, could not be imported into the United Kingdom except at a heavy rate of duty. Thus it appeared that the advantages which were granted to Bengal, were not to be extended to Madras or Bombay. It was his wish, however, that the same option should be given to those two presidencies as was granted to Bengal; and, at the same time, that the foreign trade in sugar, which Madras and Bombay now enjoyed, should be preserved to them. If it were alleged that the revenue might suffer if this system were allowed, he would say, in answer to that allegation, that the revenue officers would have little or no difficulty, by demanding a certificate, properly authenticated, of acquainting themselves with the fact, as to sugar being the production of Guzerat or of any other particular place. This, he conceived, would afford sufficient security for the revenue. Taking this view of the subject, he thought it was their duty to appeal to his Majesty's government, and to impress on them, that the only way to carry the principle of the law into beneficial effect, was by extending its operation to all the presidencies. If he had made himself understood on this subject, he trusted the Court would agree with him in the necessity of petitioning the House of Commons for an alteration of the law; and he saw that it was provided, by the last clause of the bill recently passed, "that this act may be altered, amended, or repealed, by any act to be passed, in this present session of Parliament." He was of opinion that the foreign trade in sugar, from whatever place carried on, whether from Manilla, Siam, or the Eastern Archipelago, should be continued to the merchants of Bombay and Madras; and if such trade were under the regulation of a bonding system, which might easily be adopted, the districts or dependencies subject to the presidencies of Bombay and Madras could enjoy the privilege now granted to Bengal, without violating the principle laid down in the Act of Parliament. To the merchants of Bengal ought to be allowed, under the same regulation of entrepôt or bonding system, the benefit of a foreign trade in sugar. He conceived that it was necessary for the prosperity of India, and was of great importance also to England, especially when it was recollected, that Bombay was the great mart for piece goods, the consumption of which the merchants would be enabled to extend, if greater protection were given to the trade, and more encouragement to the productions of the soil of India. Believing, as he did, that the government wished to encourage the industry of the natives of India, he conceived that the most beneficial course they could pursue to effect that object would be, to carry into operation the principle on which this bill proceeded to its fullest and fairest extent. Every facility ought to be afforded to India, to enable the natives of that country to cultivate and to export, to the greatest possible extent, not only sugar, but cotton and other valuable articles of produce. If the growth and exportation of sugar were encouraged, it would render still more profitable the exportation of cotton wool, since it might be used as ballast to those vessels that were employed to transport cargoes of the latter article. It was well known that, at present, English ships going to Bombay for a cargo of cotton wool, were obliged, in the first place, to take on board a cargo of stones as ballast. They would not be considered sea-worthy if, carrying a cargo of cotton wool, they were not first supplied with a cargo of stones. If, therefore, they encouraged the growth of sugar, which could only be done by allowing every facility for its exportation, it might be beneficially and profitably substituted as dead weight, or ballast, instead of stones. He would give every encouragement to the cultivation of land in India; and he would receive, at the lowest possible rates, the produce of that country, whether it was sugar, silk, or cotton. He would do strict justice to the natives of India; and, by pursuing a fair and liberal line of policy, he would connect England and India still more intimately by one common union of objects and interests. (*Hear, hear!*) He hoped that the words which he had addressed to the Proprietors, would force on them the same impression which he himself felt; and with that hope he should now read to them the petition which he meant to propose for their adoption.

The hon. proprietor then read the following petition:—

To the Honourable the Commons of the United Kingdom of Great Britain and Ireland in Parliament assembled.

The Petition of the East-India Company.

Respectfully showeth,

That an Act has been passed in the present Session of Parliament by your Honourable House, in concurrence with the Right Honourable the Lords Spiritual and Temporal, and with the sanction of his Majesty, for granting certain duties on sugar imported from the British possessions in the East-Indies into the United Kingdom.

That the said Act, while it declares that "sugar, the growth of any British possession within the limits of the East-India Company's charter, into which the importation of foreign sugar may be by this Act prohibited, and imported from thence, shall be subject to a duty of 24s. per 100 weight," confines the operation of the Act to the presidency of Fort William, in Bengal, and the dependencies thereof.

That the subordinate presidencies of Fort St George and of Bombay, and their dependencies, are excluded from the benefit of the said Act.

Your petitioners submit, that while they believe it was the intention of the legislature to render equal justice to India, and to encourage the industry of its people, this justice is denied to them, and their industry is checked, while Madras and Bombay, and the dependencies thereof, are excluded from the beneficial operation of the said Act.

And as it is enacted that the said Act may be altered, amended, or repealed by any Act to be passed in this present Session of Parliament, your petitioners entreat your Honourable House to pass a Bill, which may secure to the districts and dependencies of Madras and Bombay, the same option or privilege which is now given to Fort William and its dependencies.

They intreat also that your Honourable House will permit Bengal sugar to be imported into the United Kingdom from Madras and Bombay, as well as from Fort William, reserving to Bombay and Madras the benefits of the foreign trade in sugar which these places now carry on.

This is most important for the encouragement of the manufactures and trade of Great Britain, as well as of India. Sugar forms a necessary article of dead weight for ships, and by allowing the British merchant to import it from Madras and Bombay at the lower duty, he will be enabled to bring the general produce of those presidencies, especially cotton wool, more readily and more cheaply for the use of the manufacturers of this country.

Under present circumstances, the British merchant is obliged to take on board a cargo of stones as ballast for his ship, before he can venture to take on board his cotton wool. Sugar, if permitted at the lower duty, a duty of equalization only with West-India sugar, would afford sufficient ballast in lieu of stones, and this would benefit not only the shipowner, merchant, and manufacturer of Great Britain, but would encourage the production of the soil of India, enlarge its revenues, and enrich its people.

Your petitioners, therefore, entreat your Honourable House to grant to Madras and Bombay the privilege which is conceded to Bengal, of exporting to the United Kingdom at the lower rate of duty, sugar which is produced in the British territories subject to the said presidencies.

And your Petitioners will ever pray.

The Hon. proprietor then proceeded to observe, that in introducing this petition he was actuated solely by a desire to benefit both England and India. He could see no reason, if Bombay and Madras had any sugar to spare, why those presidencies should not be allowed to export it at the lower rate of duty; and although the cultivation of sugar at these presidencies might at present be small, yet, he doubted not, that by extending the principle of the Bill to them, it would soon be considerably increased. By refusing the right of exporting at the lower rate of duty, they did so far prohibit the increased cultivation of sugar. He considered it to be of great advantage to the British manufacturer, that the foreign trade of Bombay and Madras should be preserved. It could only be opposed on the fallacious principle that they were to reject the useful for fear of its being abused. Now, he would contend, that they ought to adopt the useful, guarding strictly and properly against its abuse. If it were said, that the continuance of this trade would open the door to smuggling, he would answer, that he could not subscribe to any such proposition. And why? Because there was no reason whatever for supposing, but exactly the contrary, that the gentlemen to whom the government of India was entrusted, would betray their duty, and would not carry into effect the law as it was laid down, strictly, fairly, and honestly. Why, then, should not that which he contended for be conceded? He hoped that no idle fear on the part of his Majesty's Government, would prevent the principle which was applied to Bengal from being extended to Madras and Bombay. He would not take up the time of the court further, but would move " That the petition which he had read be approved of." The petition, as given above, was then read by the clerk.

Sir *Charles Forbes* said, that, in rising to second the motion of his hon. friend Mr. Weeding, he felt with him, that it was right to call the attention of his Majesty's Government, and of Parliament, to the great importance of this subject. He was far from blaming Government, or supposing that it was the intention of the Chancellor of the Exchequer, in bringing in his Bill, to deal hardly by the presidencies of Madras and Bombay. On the contrary, he was convinced that his right hon. friend was anxious to do justice to India generally, and he thanked him for what he had done; but it did appear to him, that sufficient explanation could not have been given, and that the situation of the excluded presidencies had not been clearly understood. He trusted that no one who had heard the petition which had just been read, would refuse his assent to the correctness of its positions; and he could not believe that the Chancellor of the Exchequer (with whose candour and fairness he was well acquainted), when put in possession of the facts, would hesitate in conferring upon Madras and Bombay the same facilities and advantages as were granted to Bengal. It did seem to him that the other two presidencies were overlooked; that they could not have been properly represented in the interviews which had taken place with the Chancellor of the Exchequer, and that their interests had been strangely neglected. It might be said, that the Bill was framed with a view to the protection of the West-Indian interest. But the chief object which the petition contended for at present was, that sugar, the produce of Bengal, should continue to be imported into England from Madras and Bombay as heretofore, at the same rate of duty as if imported from Bengal direct. Now the fact was, that this would not affect the West-Indies unfavourably, but the contrary; because Bengal sugar so imported from Bombay or Madras must come by a circuitous route, and would be loaded with such additional freight, insurance, and other charges, as would afford a protection to the West-India grower, equal to the reduction of duty; and therefore those presidencies ought rather to be favoured than otherwise on the score of duty. It was his wish, however, to do justice to the

West-India interest as well as to the East-India interest; he did not desire unfairly to benefit the one at the expense of the other, but unfortunately, the former always had the advantage of the latter. He had made inquiries as to their relative situations; and he had, that very morning, heard the sentiments of an eminent West-Indian merchant on this subject, who assured him, that he could not see any reason whatever why Bengal sugar should not be imported from Madras and Bombay. The article would be warehoused at Madras and Bombay, and, if required, consumed at those presidencies; but if not wanted there, he could see no reason why it should not continue to be sent to Great Britain, as well as to any other part of the world, as at present. Would it be said, that any danger was to be feared from the fraudulent exportation of sugar the produce of China, or Siam, or Java, or of any other foreign country whatever? He would contend, that, under proper regulations, no such danger was to be apprehended, the usual certificate of growth being required on importation into the United Kingdom; and, besides, the peculiar quality of Bengal sugar was so well known at the Custom-house here, that no imposition could take place. He was convinced that not a pound of Java sugar found its way to any part of British India: and why was it so? Because the Dutch Government imposed a high export duty on that article if it were not sent to Holland. America was the only exception to this rule; between which country and Java, trade to a great extent was now carried on. He would ask, what temptation there would be to smuggle such an article as sugar for the sake of eight shillings the hundred-weight? He held it to be quite out of the question; and, besides, the temptation already existed to a much greater extent, without the least suspicion of any attempt to substitute foreign sugar for that of Bengal. He understood that all Bengal sugar imported into Bombay must be accompanied by a certificate; and some years ago a ship belonging to the Company was seized by a man-of-war in consequence of some informality in that respect, though afterwards released. Very great advantage would undoubtedly accrue to the presidency of Bombay, and indeed to the whole of Western India, if liberty were given for the exportation of its sugar to England at the lower duty. It would not only encourage the cultivation of sugar, but would also have the effect of extending the cultivation of cotton; so that this country might, in due time, find itself independent of America for that article. If they were ever to become independent of America with reference to cotton-wool, the supply must be drawn from the western side of India. There was ample room for the cultivation of cotton there. All that was wanted was capital, enterprize, and industry, which would speedily follow if due encouragement were given. He had lately heard from Bombay, that nearly 250,000 bales of cotton were now produced on the western side of India, being nearly double the quantity that was raised ten or fifteen years ago. He thought that this was a most important part of the subject—more important, perhaps, than any other consideration—namely, that they should encourage the natives of India to cultivate cotton, in order to render this country independent of America for an article which was indispensable to British manufactures. Bengal produced very good cotton; but, if he were correctly informed, Surat cottons were preferred by our manufacturers to those of Bengal. In conversation with a friend of his, who was perfectly conversant with the subject, he had been informed, that the manufacturers of this country would take as much cotton as India could supply, "only (said he) let it be good cotton." He, therefore, contended, that the liberty to export sugar to England from every part of India ought to be granted, in consequence of which cotton would be more extensively and cheaply imported into this country. He would not call it a boon, but an act of justice, that this facility for the exportation of sugar should be given, by which means, instead of taking on board a cargo of stones (or, as they were facetiously called, *Bombay diamonds*) as ballast, when a cargo of cotton was to be shipped, the dead-weight would consist chiefly of that valuable article, sugar, which would realise a freight of from three to four pounds per ton, yielding an increase of profit to the ship-owner, estimated on an average, at not less than £1,000 or £1,200 on each ship that proceeded from this country to Bombay for a cargo of cotton. Instead of which, they were now obliged to take in a cargo of worthless and expensive stones, by which they were not only deprived of so much freight, but also of an additional means of making returns for imports into India from this country, and thereby injuring not only the shipping, but the manufacturing interests of Great Britain. He confessed, however, he could hardly expect, at the present moment, that Ministers would be able to go quite so far as his hon. friend Mr. Weeding wished, and justly looked for, in behalf of India. They had, for many years, been amused with *sweet words* and promises, that much would be done for India, which he, at one time, thought would never be realized. He was happy, however, to find himself so far mistaken, that a beginning had been made. The Whig

Government had the merit of it, and he hoped the present measure would be followed by others of a more extended and beneficial nature. He regretted the rapidity with which this bill had been carried through Parliament; because it prevented correct information being given as to the effect it would have with reference to Madras and Bombay. He asked, did any one attend the Chancellor of the Exchequer on behalf of those presidencies? He had made inquiry, and he did not learn that a single individual was consulted on the part of Madras or Bombay. As to Bengal, it was considered the most important presidency, and no doubt it was so. It was specially taken care of, but he could not see why the interests of Madras and Bombay should be overlooked. The foreign trade in sugar was of great importance, particularly to Bombay, and must be preserved; but from what he had heard, Madras produced a very considerable quantity of sugar, and was capable of supplying much more; to Madras, therefore, the principle of the bill ought at once to have been applied, even clogged as it was with unnecessary restrictions. He understood that in the West-Indies certain restrictions were imposed for the benefit of the respective colonies. According to those restrictions, sugar was not allowed to be transmitted from one island to another. They all knew, however, that those colonies had their separate governments, laws, and revenues; and he supposed certain regulations were necessary to prevent their interfering with each other. But India was differently situated. India must be considered as one whole and undivided possession—the most valuable possession under the crown; and why, he asked, should they make different laws for different parts of that possession? They might as well make different laws for different portions of the island of Jamaica. He quite agreed in the principle of the petition, and in the propositions which it embraced. He thought that all it prayed for, and much more, should be conceded to the fullest extent, as a matter of right and justice towards India. But, at the present moment, he would be contented that Bengal sugar should continue to be imported into Britain as heretofore, from Madras and Bombay, and at the lower rate of duty. He considered this subject to be of the highest importance, as well to these kingdoms as to India; and he thought that the Court of Directors ought to have been made acquainted with the contents of the bill, and with the precise intention of Ministers, at an earlier period, so as to have enabled them to bring it before the Court of Proprietors. The bill ought not to have been postponed to the eleventh hour, and then urged on so rapidly, that there was not even time to have it printed for the House of Lords; and, unfortunately, in the House of Commons, not one word seems to have been said on the subject which they were that day discussing. The case would have been very different had it been a West-Indian instead of an East-Indian question. He apologised for having detained the court so long, and would conclude with giving his hearty support to the petition. (*Hear, hear !*)

Mr. *Chapman*, M. P., said, he was anxious to address a very few words to the court on this subject. He confessed that he was surprised, nay, he was quite astonished, to find that the provisions of the Act were confined to Bengal. He said this, knowing, as he did, the disadvantage which was experienced when they sent out ships from this country to Bombay for cargoes of cotton. There it was necessary, before the shipment of cotton was made, that a cargo of stones should be taken on board the vessel. Nothing could be more preposterous than this, when it was considered that sugar would afford a most valuable dead-weight. Surely it was a self-evident fact, that nothing could be more beneficial to the commerce of this country, in various ways, than the allowing of sugar to be imported from all the presidencies of India. He conceived that Government had no right to limit and restrict the privilege of exportation, as they had done by this Bill; and he had a hope that they would be induced, by the representations of the Company, to go farther than they had done. The introduction of Bengal sugar from Bombay and Madras ought to be at once permitted. It would answer the purpose of the ship-owners extremely well to carry it, inasmuch as the Company would considerably increase the amount of freight; while, at the same time, it would greatly benefit the natives of India and the manufacturers of this country. He certainly should follow the general impression which appeared to prevail in that Court; and he would second, as far as he could, in the House of Commons, every proposition having for its object the prosperity of India, and the consequent benefit of this country. He would take that course without feeling any hostility to other parties. The West-India interest had been most fairly treated; and he conceived that the Proprietors had a right to express and record their opinion, that the true interests of commerce, in the most extended sense, and without reference to the concerns of any particular body, ought to be carried into effect in every quarter of the globe. (*Hear, hear !*)

Mr. *Fielder* observed, that he came forward upon public grounds, having no local interests, no local prejudices in favour of any one spot in India. He did not look to Bengal, Madras, or Bombay in particular, but to all India as a whole, from one end to the other. He was of opinion that the main question was no other than this, whether the Bill, being limited to Bengal, would give satisfaction throughout all India, to its hundred millions of inhabitants? England only holding India, as it were, not only by a small European force, but by Hindoo opinion, should not we, he inquired, ascertain whether the excluding the presidencies of Madras and Bombay from being benefitted in the growth of the cane, and their ports from the exportation of its produce, would not, by such invidious distinction, create a most dangerous sensation throughout their whole population against the Indian Government. (*Hear !*) This unlooked-for restriction, or rather prohibition, against Madras and Bombay industry, appeared to him any thing but just or sound policy, for he had frequently noted accounts from those two presidencies of there being great distress amongst the natives, arising from want of employment and want of food. Sometimes not less than 35,000 in a single choultry, and 50, 60, and even 70,000 natives collected together in search of labour and of food. This limitation to Bengal no one would contend could give the full relief required by humanity and sound policy at the hands of the India Company. On the contrary, must it not operate against the attainment of that desirable object? (*Hear, hear !*) The true principle of the Government, he apprehended, was not to look to any one spot, but to all India, in order that strict justice be administered throughout the whole country, without distinction of places or individuals. He was, however, pleased to find a beginning; that a Bill had been obtained so far as to extend the benefit to Bengal; and he hoped that Ministers themselves had their doubts whether the Bill went far enough, so as to give entire satisfaction to the Company, and to the natives of India; as he found that the last clause enacted, "that the Act may be altered, &c. during the present session." He really could not conceive why Madras and Bombay should not have the same rights as those given to Bengal, and with that view he had looked through the debates in Parliament for years back, and in no one instance did he find that the Ministers of the day ever held, that the relief sought should be confined to any particular place or people; on the contrary, it was laid down, at least understood, that the boon, as it was called, or rather the *for many years* expected justice, should be equally spread throughout all India. These repeated declarations were never qualified, save that the relief was not then deemed convenient or expedient to be granted—nothing more. To confirm this, he would advert to a minute of conference held between Ministers and the East-India Committee, on the 19th May last, by which it appeared that no restriction, no limitation whatever was even suggested, no particular place named ; on the contrary, it was understood that the benefit should extend throughout the whole of India. (*Hear,hear!*) He fully agreed with the contents of the petition, with the exception, however, of that part relating to importing foreign sugars into Bombay,—with this he entirely dissented ; and he felt surprised, while the India Company was petitioning the British Parliament for the presidencies of Bombay and Madras to have equal benefits with Bengal, that the Company, in the same petition, should require the importation of sugar, the growth of China, Java, and Manilla into Bombay, more particularly when we have sometimes accounts of the many thousands of Hindoos being destitute of employment and of food. The honourable mover, and honourable Baronet the seconder of the petition, appeared to approve of foreign sugars being imported into Bombay in the way of trade, though, as he conceived, such mode must be prejudicial to the grower of the cane of India, and while it was represented our fellow-subjects, the Hindoos, were in want of employment, and frequently of food.—(Cries of *No, no.*)

Sir *C. Forbes.*—I am afraid that my indistinct mode of expression has caused the hon. Proprietor to misunderstand me. I said no such thing.

Mr. *Fielder* wished that part of the petition to which he referred to be read shortly.

The *Chairman* said the petition certainly prayed that the right of exporting foreign sugar from Bombay and Madras should be continued, and to that proposition the honourable Baronet had assented. But the observation of the hon. Baronet by no means warranted the construction which the hon. Proprietor had put upon it. What he said was, not that Java sugars were, or should be, sent to Bombay, but that they never found their way to that or any other presidency, since the portion which was not sent to Holland, was exported to America. The hon. Proprietor was, however, justified in saying that the petition prayed for the preservation of the right which Bombay and Madras now possessed, to import and export foreign sugars.

Mr. *Fielder* proceeded to observe, that the system on which they had acted for the last half century—that of encouraging the importation of foreign sugar—had been ruinous to the Indian trade in that commodity. This was seen by a valuable Report at Calcutta in 1776 ; the valuable Treatise and Reports in 1792 ; Mr. Grant's Memoranda in 1797, and by many other works. In every case the same conclusions were drawn, namely, that the encouragement given to foreign sugars had been ruinous to the sugar trade of British India, which trade it must be admitted had previously been, and would, but for such circumstances, have continued highly beneficial to all India. (*Hear, hear!*) It appeared to him that, by permitting the sugars of Java, Manilla, and China, to compete with those of India, whether for consumption or for the purposes of trade, the sugars of India had for more than threescore years been declining, with the attendant ill consequences to the natives. Every one having the permanent good of India in view, must naturally look with a jealous eye at the introduction of foreign sugar into any one port of India, as it would (as he thought) limit, instead of increasing, the culture of the cane of India. However, for the sake of argument, supposing that the presidencies of Bombay and Madras would not grow the cane to any extent, but was inclined to import foreign sugars, not for their own consumption, but for foreign trade, it could not do otherwise, as it appeared to him, but interfere with the agriculturist of Bengal, inasmuch, that if it was found expedient for Madras and Bombay ships trading up the Persian Gulph, or to other eastern places, to have what is termed a dead weight by way of ballast, in the article of sugar, such ships might, as heretofore, substitute the sugars of Java, Manilla, and China, for the sugars of British India ; thereby, instead of giving employment to the half-starved but patient Hindoo, be encouraging the industry and trade of the Dutch, Chinese, and Spaniard. And he would enquire,what was the conduct of the Government of China, Java, and Manilla, in regard to their own trade, and to the produce of those countries ? Did either of those powers permit foreign produce, particularly sugar, to be imported into their own ports, to the injury of the produce of their own soil ? He believed not. Then he would ask, Why not the India Government pursue the example of Java, Manilla, and China, in taking care of its own people ? (*Hear, hear!*) All agreed that India could grow sufficient sugar, as well for her own use and for her trade in those seas, as for European consumption ; consequently, he considered there could be no reason whatever for allowing foreign sugars to be imported into any part of India. He begged to repeat, that it was owing to the preference given to the trade in sugars belonging to other countries, that the sugars of British India had been thrown into the back-ground. Nothing less, than as the trade of China, Manilla, and Java sugars flourished, so in the same degree the Bengal trade in sugars declined. (*Hear!*) Would it not, he said, be deemed extraordinary for the East-India Company, at the very instant it claimed from the British legislature the right of exporting from the Malabar and Coromandel shores the produce of the cane of India, in whatever part of that country realized, in order to employ and benefit the natives of India, from whom so many millions sterling annually are raised for payments in England, that the same India Company, in the very same petition, should require liberty to import into India the sugars of China, Manilla, and Java, thereby giving employ and benefit to other nations at the expense of the natives of India. (*Hear!*) It had been said, that these foreign sugars were not for India consumption, but for trade up the Persian Gulph, and other places; he would ask in reply, whether the trading in foreign sugars at all would not, as a matter of course lessen the Bombay and Madras demand for sugars, the produce of their own presidencies, or of that of Bengal? (*Hear!*) He really thought, if the India Company stated, as it was bound to do, the wretched situation of the natives of India, their ruined manufactures, produced by British competition, their want of employ in the agricultural districts, added to these their heavy taxation and deprivations, and at the same time urgently called upon the British senate for redress, in order that those natives might be enabled to support their own government, and to meet the views of the English Government in regard to the required annual remittances; the India Company could hardly require leave to keep up the demand for foreign sugars, and thereby to limit the sugars of India. Were the India Company so to do, he thought it would be the greatest anomaly ever experienced in this or in any court. (*Hear!*) He had no doubt that if such part of the petition was expunged, there could be no doubt that the petition would be unanimously adopted, as well by the whole Court of Proprietors, as by the whole Court of Directors. He fully trusted that the Court of Directors, in that case, would use their utmost influence in obtaining the extension of the sugar privilege throughout all India, thereby giving the natives full employment, food, and happiness. (*Hear, hear!*)

Colonel *Sykes* stated, that he was anxious to believe, that the concession of the present sugar bill originated in a dignified and elevated spirit of legislation; that it was not a cold and reluctant acquiescence in the reiterated applications for relief of the Court of Directors and Court of Proprietors, during a course of years: but that there was in operation a philanthrophic and politic desire to apply a stimulus to the agriculture of India, for the purpose of bettering the condition of the farmer, and increasing the revenue; a desire to extend the employment of British shipping, and to facilitate those heavy annual remittances, which were likely to be attended with considerable embarrassments unless the exportable products of India were increased. Considering such to have been the objects in view, he must lament that their operations should be partial; the restricting to Bengal the powers to export sugar, was offering a premium to the agriculture and shipping of that presidency, at the expense of Madras and Bombay. It was not probable the farmers of the two last presidencies would extend their sugar cultivation, in the hope of getting the present bill modified in some future session of Parliament; so long as the bill remained in its present state, so long would the agricultural industry of those presidencies remain stationary, at least as far as the production of sugar was concerned. No doubt the granting a measure of full relief to India was attended with very great difficulty, owing to the jealousy and alarm of strong opposing interests connected with the western world; and the Government was entitled to the gratitude of India for the present boon, such as it was, under the circumstances of the case; but he would endeavour to prove that the bill might have had a much more extensive operation without affording the West-Indians just ground of complaint; he would endeavour to prove that the bill, even in its present state, might be accepted by Madras, and with certain arrangements to insure the continuance of the present carrying trade of Bombay, the bill might be applied to that presidency. In support of these positions, he would found his arguments on numerical data, taken from official sources; and as experience had taught him that it was often unsatisfactory, and even fallacious to make deductions from a comparison of statistical returns of isolated periods, it should be his object to compose averages of periods of several years. With respect to the first point, he would shew that the West-Indies did not supply, and probably never could supply, in their present state, a sufficiency of sugar for the consumption of the United Kingdom. For a septennial period, from 1820 to 1826 inclusive, the average population of the United Kingdom was 21,935,225, and the annual average consumption of sugar was 3,171,151 cwts.; the average consumption per head being 15.7lbs. For the next septennial period, from 1827 to 1833 inclusive, the average population was 22,973,699 souls, and the average consumption of sugar was 3,614,134 cwts., averaging 17.6 lbs. for each person ; the increased consumption in the latter period being 2.1 per cent. This increased consumption might be safely accounted for, by the average price of sugar having diminished eleven and a half per cent. For these deductions a system of averages had been taken, but if the population in the years of the census 1821 and 1831, and the sugar cleared for consumption in those years respectively, had been taken as data, the consumption per head would correspond within some fractions of the consumption resulting from the averages. Supposing the population to have gone on increasing up to the present time, in the same ratio as in the septennial periods before noticed, there are 25,810,913 souls; with the same low standard of consumption as before, they would require 4,009,909 cwts. of sugar ; but the West-Indies supplied, in the year ending 5th Jan. 1836, only 3,524,388 cwts., leaving a deficiency in the annual consumption of 485,521 cwts. ; and for exportation in 1834, of 681,775 cwt. of refined sugar, making a total annual deficiency of 1,167,296 cwts. which the West-Indies cannot supply. This deficiency converted into tons, gives 58,364, the conveyance of which should afford employment to above a hundred ships. He would ask, is the trade of India to be shackled, and its agricultural industry paralyzed ; and are the people of England to be limited in their enjoyment of a necessary of life, to keep up the prices of West-India produce ? Even though the West-Indies could supply the whole quantity required for consumption, our subjects in India have a right to demand to be allowed to compete in the English market, for the supply of *any article*, on terms more favourable to the English public. The West-Indians have no claim to object to the concession. But, even supposing the West-Indies could continue the average annual supply of 3,830,692 cwts. from 1820 to 1839 inclusive, of which there is not any probability, since the emancipation of the slaves,—there would still be a vast deficiency, both for home consumption and for export in the refined state But there is every reason to believe, from the facts before stated, that if the supply of sugar were greater, and the price still further reduced, the average individual consumption, instead of being restricted to less than eight-tenths of an ounce per diem, would increase ten, twenty, or thirty per cent. With respect to the second point, he would proceed to shew, that the import of sugar into Madras was so unimportant, so very trifling compared with the whole consumption, that Madras might at the present moment adopt the bill with all its restrictive clauses, without injury or inconvenience. He then read the tables of imports and exports of sugar, at Madras, from 1830-1 to 1833-4 inclusive.

GENERAL ACCOUNT OF IMPORTS INTO MADRAS BY SEA.

SUGAR.

Years.	Total Quantity.	Total Value.	From Bengal.	From Bombay.	From Malacca, &c.	Mauritius.
	Cwts.	Rs.	Rs.	Rs.	Rs.	Rs.
1829-30	11,815	1,78,705	92,819	40,533	19,373	19,729
1830-31	7,936	1,14,718	19,145	12,459	58,961	4,230
1831-32	7,883	1,20,024	41,991	19,679	40,738	—
1832-33	4,765	66,520	15,158	16,742	30,930	—
1833-34	12,040	1,67,747	1,20,269	33,489	11,265	628
Total	44,439	6,47,714	2,89,392	1,28,902	1,61,287	24,647
Average	8,888	1,29,543	57,878	25,780	32,257	

GENERAL ACCOUNT OF EXPORTS FROM MADRAS BY SEA,

Years.	Total Quantity.	Total Value.	To Bengal.	To Bombay.	To Ceylon.	To New South Wales.	To the United Kingdom.
	Cwts.	Rs.	Rs.	Rs.	Rs.	Rs.	Rs.
1829-30	10,025	1,05,807	—	44,304	9,725	—	47,9.10
1830-31	3,916	49,407	2,803	17,855	1,643	2,850	26,307
1831-32	1,564	16,721	—	4,906	2,824	—	2,696
1832-33	2,445	23,801	—	9,703	5,741	—	7,740
1833-34	1,823	21,965	—	7,252	5,281	6,246	832
Total ...	19,773	2,17,701	2,803	84,020	25,214		18,505
Average	2,954	43,540		16,804	5,043		3,701

They exhibited some curious features: the average annual import amounted only to 8,888 cwts., the half of which came from Bengal, nearly a fourth from Bombay, and the remaining trifle from Malacca, and none from Java. The average annual export amounted to 3,954 cwts. nearly half the trifling import, and it appeared to be sent in minute portions to Bombay, Ceylon, New South Wales, and the United Kingdom; leaving only 493 cwts. to be consumed by the population of the Madras territories. This population amounts to about 13,500,000, and would consume 2,049,125 cwts of sugar, at the rate at which it is consumed in England, which is a low standard; as sweets, to as great an extent as the means of the people allow, form part of the daily food of the natives in India. It is hence shewn, that the imported sugar consumed at Madras does not amount to half a ship load, or about a 415th part of the whole consumption; and yet for this mere trifle the agricultural industry of Madras is to remain under an interdict! There is a good deal of unfounded alarm also, that the supposed present cheapness of sugar in India, will enable exporters at once to drive West-India sugar out of the market; but if the average official value of the annual imports into Madras, of 8,888 cwts., namely 1,29,543 rupees, be just, its cost at Madras of 29 shillings per cwt. would be a sufficient security, while

sugar was selling at 30s. per cwt., without duty, in England. No doubt, at a future period, increased production would diminish the price in Madras, and enable its sugar to enter the English market with greater advantages. He had thus, he trusted, shewn that it was neither necessary nor politic to impose restrictions on Madras with respect to sugar. The application of the principle of the bill to Bombay was certainly attended with some difficulty; Bombay was the depôt for sugar in transit from China, Manilla, the Eastern Islands, and Bengal, to the Persian and Arabian Gulfs, the Indus, Scind and Cutch, &c. Its carrying trade was of the average annual value of twenty-four lakhs of rupees: it would therefore be extremely hazardous to impose upon Bombay restrictions, which would prevent its extensive import trade as a depôt for other parts of the East; but admitting the restrictions to be necessary, which he doubted, unless modified to admit of the continuance of the present import and export trade, he saw no reason whatever why the sugar of Bengal should not be allowed to be imported into Bombay, and re-exported to England. It was the unquestionable growth of India, and the bill was intended for the benefit of India, and the extension of its produce; and yet England refused to allow that produce, unless it were embarked from a solitary spot in all India: to be sure other places might obtain the same right, but clogged with conditions which rendered it valuless. The following are the official tables of the total import of sugar into Bombay; of the total export of sugar from Bombay, not including its subordinates; and of the export of sugar to its subordinates.

IMPORT OF SUGAR INTO BOMBAY.

Years.	Quantity.	Total Value.	From China.	Manilla.	Penang and Eastern Islands.	Bengal.	Malabar and Canara.	Isle of France and Bourbon.	Brazil.
		Rs.	Rs.	Rs.	Rs.	Rs.	Rs.	Rs.	
1829-30 ...	—	36,16,317	26,94,166	—	3,58,894	4,20,055	47,082	96,120	—
1830-31 ...	—	32,39,786	27,08,193	—	3,13,961	1,31,366	20,667	53,852	—
1831-32 ...	—	19,57,071	12,91,820	1,72,610	3,44,090	1,42,432	4,606	9,669	—
1832-33 ...	—	16,71,017	4,14,608	7,37,365	2,30,896	2,70,661	11,198	—	—
1833-34 ...	—	20,62,988	3,98,562	2,40,250	2,80,125	11,34,595	6,940	—	—
Total	—	1,25,47,179	75,07,349	11,50,225	15,27,966	20,99,109	90,493		
Average ...	—	25,09,434	15,01,468	3,83,408	3,08,593	4,19,822	18,098		

EXPORT of SUGAR from BOMBAY.

Years.	Total Quantity.	Total Value.	To United Kingdom.	To Ceylon.	Goa and Demaun.	Malabar and Canara.	Cutch and Scind.	Persian Gulf.	Arabian Gulf.	Coast of Africa.	Bengal.
1829-30 ...	—	Rs. 21,97,527	Rs. 3,36,585	Rs. 17,282	Rs. 28,420	Rs. 65,856	Rs. 4,69,637	Rs. 11,26,615	Rs. 1,14,810	Rs. 14,650	Rs. —
1830-31 ...	—	15,19,549	—	10,595	39,154	42,561	6,01,662	7,03,169	79,596	18,430	20,022
1831-32 ...	—	10,67,864	—	5,535	25,573	50,213	4,52,236	4,29,372	62,115	12,417	—
1832-33 ...	—	8,75,619	1,29,500	3,238	23,997	53,629	4,32,499	1,78,019	44,444	5,859	—
1833-34 ...	—	9,80,835	—	4,910	29,749	63,544	2,85,648	4,62,579	85,607	11,190	2,750
Total	—	66,41,394	—	41,560	1,46,893	2,75,803	22,41,682	28,99,654	3,86,572	62,546	—
Average ...	—	13,28,279	—	8,312	29,378	55,160	4,48,336	5,79,931	77,314	12,509	—

Years.	Total Value.	To Panwell and Konkun.	To Surat.	To Northern Gujerat.	Total Imports.	Total Exports.	Excess of Export over Import.
	Rs.	Rs.	Rs.	Rs.	Rs.	Rs.	Rs.
1829-30 ...	16,60,108	2,59,511	3,07,443	10,93,154	36,16,317	38,57,635	2,41,318
1830-31 ...	19,64,084	3,61,344	2,26,814	13,75,926	32,39,786	34,83,633	2,43,847
1831-32 ...	18,95,013	3,41,256	2,55,930	12,97,827	19,57,071	29,62,877	10,05,806
1832-33 ...	13,09,024	2,47,921	1,94,279	8,66,824	16,71,017	21,84,643	5,13,626
1833-34 ...	14,32,581	3,38,723	2,32,386	8,61,472	20,62,988	24,13,416	3,50,428
Total ...	82,60,810	15,48,755	12,26,852	54,95,203	1,25,47,179	1,49,02,204	23,55,025
Average ...	16,52,162	3,09,751	2,43,370	16,99,040	25,09,434	2,98,04,441	4,71,005

From these tables it appeared, that the annual average value of sugar imported from Bengal was 4,19,822 rupees, and this sugar which could be sent from Bengal to England, could not supply the place of *stones* as dead-weight in homeward-bound ships from Bombay to England, because Bombay allowed sugar from China and Manilla to *rest* in the island on its way to Persia, Arabia, and Scind. He would ask, why the principle of the old act of parliament should have been altered; when India sugar paid 32s. per cwt. duty, all that was demanded was certificates of its growth, of its being *bonâ fide* the production of India; it mattered not what part of India it came from, whether the districts which exported it, also imported sugar from China or elsewhere; it was sufficient that it was the growth of India. If, then, certificates of growth sufficed when the duty was 32s., why should not similar certificates of growth suffice when the duty is 24s. per cwt. ? The bugbear of the presidencies of Madras and Bombay consuming the sugar of China and the Eastern Islands, and sending their own produce to England, might be removed by having bonding warehouses. Lock up foreign sugars the moment they are imported, and only let them out as they are required to be sent to foreign countries: there would then be assurance that the sugars reaching England were the genuine produce of India. He could not see any fair reason why a premium should be held out to one part of India, at the expense of another part; why equal encouragement should not be given to all India, instead of Bengal alone. The present bill repressed the agricultural industry of the farmers of the presidencies of Madras and Bombay, instead of applying a stimulus to it. Bengal had manifested what its territory was capable of, by its surplus sugar for export: he had shewn, that the produce of Madras was nearly equal to its consumption; and he would take upon himself to say, that the production of the territories under Bombay was very great; at least, the production of what was vulgarly called jaggery (the proper name of which was goor or gool) was very great. This was the juice of the sugar-cane, inspissated to the consistence of bread dough, when put into the oven. Indeed, a friend (Col. Miles) had stated, that the half of the revenue of some of the districts in his charge, in Goojrat, was from sugar, and the want of demand only prevented the extension of the cultivation. There could be no doubt the production of sugar could be very considerably increased in India; and it was equally certain, that in proportion as we increased or promoted agriculture there, we increased the means of the people to consume British produce. If the bill only went the length of permitting Bengal sugar being exported from Bombay and Madras, it would do some good; there would be an extended vent for the surplus sugar of Bengal; it would assist the trade between Bengal and the other presidencies; and in homeward-bound ships, it would allow of bags of sugar being used for ballast instead of stones, to the great convenience, and no doubt advantage of the trade of those presidencies, and to the advantage of England also: for the four lakhs of Bengal sugar, which annually pass through Bombay to Persia and Scind, would no doubt find its way to England in preference. Cotton being alien to the present subject, he would barely touch upon it, by stating, what was probably not generally known, that it was brought down the Ghauts to Bombay from the interior of Berar, several hundred miles, on the backs of bullocks, attended with much labour, expense, and inconvenience; that its annual value was very considerable, and that its import from that part of India might be greatly extended. Colonel Sykes concluded by saying, " let us ask, then, for legislation in a more comprehensive spirit; not for a part of India, but the whole; not for particular interests, but for the community at large."

Mr. *Fraser* said he found himself called upon to say a few words on this occasion, as it was one of much importance to the interests with which he had been long particularly connected. The partial character of the Bill under discussion would have been a grievous disappointment to the presidencies of Madras and Bombay, if it were not, as he believed it was, meant to be the prelude to a full and fair equalization of duties throughout the whole of the Company's territories. The declaration of Ministers in the last session of Parliament, left no doubt as to their intentions in this respect. He, therefore, felt thankful to them for their concession to Bengal; and instead of doubting their sincerity as to the future, or embarrassing them with any impatience at this late period of the session, he thought they should leave to them the time for extending to the other presidencies in next session the present substantial mark of their consideration. It appeared to him, however, that the interests of Madras and Bombay had inadvertently been overlooked, inasmuch as they were not allowed by the Bill to ship sugar grown in Bengal, duly bonded and certified as such. This defect, he conceived, only required to be pointed out to be remedied, as the benefit wanted would be of great importance to the minor presidencies, and could not injure any opposing interests : for the permission involves no new principle, no new rival produce which the West-Indians could object to ; no increased importation even from this country, but merely granted to Madras and Bombay, the convenience of a saleable article of dead-weight, for the ships loading there for the mother country, including the interests of the British ship-owner and freighter, by saving them much valuable time; by preserving the health of their crews; avoiding the hazards and charges of insurance, loss of seasons, &c.; the shipping in the case asked being enabled to complete their loading at Madras and Bombay, without the necessity of going to Bengal. Hitherto, the great want at the former ports had been ballast for our homeward ships, and articles utterly worthless, or saleable at a certain and heavy loss, and entire relinquishment of freight, had been resorted to, or, in de-

spair of such ruinous expedients, the ship has gone on to Bengal, or the additional hazards, and charges, and delay, equalled to the loss of one voyage to Europe on an average of three. In short, he would not trespass farther on the time of this court, as the case stood out so clear, and, he should hope, so conclusive, as to carry conviction to the most reluctant parties, to justify his Majesty's Ministers in affording at once the specific relief wanted.

Mr. *Hogg,* M. P., said that he was very unwilling to obtrude himself or his opinions on that court, but he could not resist the opportunity of saying one or two words on the subject of the petition. He must admit that the Bill had been hurried through the Legislature in a manner which did not allow sufficient time for its due consideration ; it appeared to him that it would be much better for that court to act upon some practical ground, than to assert general principles, which were not applicable at present. There could be no doubt that the West-India interests would have a right to complain, if Bengal, or any other portion of India, were allowed to import the sugars of other places for their own consumption, while they exported their own to this country ; but he saw no objection to allowing the sugars of Bengal to be allowed to be placed in bond in the ports of Madras and Bombay, in order to allow them to be used as a dead-weight in making up cargoes for England. This, however, was a very different thing from allowing Madras or Bombay to be exporting countries to England. It was impossible that, with any degree of justice to the West-Indian colonies, Madras or Bombay could be allowed to be at the same time importers of sugar from other countries, and exporters to England. That, however, would not hinder them from receiving sugar in bond from Bengal, and sending it to England ; to that he thought the court should confine themselves at present, rather than to the general principle, on which, for the present, it would be impossible to act.

Mr. *Deans Campbell* having subscribed the requisition for assembling this court, along with several honourable proprietors for whom he entertained a high respect, but from whom he was sorry to find he differed in opinion respecting the measure now under discussion, he must bespeak the indulgence of the court for a short time. It would be in the recollection of the court, that he seconded the motion for petitioning Parliament for the assimilation of the duties on East and West-India produce. He was shortly after honoured by an invitation to accompany the deputations of merchants connected with India, from London and the Outports, to a conference with the Chancellor of the Exchequer on that subject, on the 19th May. At that conference, the discussion was, at the particular desire of all present, opened by his valued and esteemed friend Mr. Larpent, as chairman of the London East-India and China Association; and as there was an hon. proprietor in court who was present on that occasion, he would appeal to him, whether the forcible, clear, and able manner in which Mr. Larpent set forth the claims of India to an *immediate* and *entire* equalization of duties, and the advantages that would result to both countries from such an act of justice, was not calculated to carry conviction to the minds of all who heard him, and to impress every member of the various deputations then present with the highest respect for his talent, and a deep sense of obligation for the service rendered the cause. He would not detain the court by reciting all that was said on that occasion, nor would he trouble them by reading the minute of that conference, as it has already been referred to by an hon. proprietor, and admitted to advocate the general interests of *all India.* He must candidly acknowledge, that having other matters to attend to, and perceiving by what took place at that interview, that the business was in a fair train of satisfactory adjustment, and the conduct of it in the hands of such zealous and able advocates, he did not thereafter pay that attention to the further progress of the negociation which he should, under other circumstances, have considered it his duty to have done. He was not a little surprised and distressed when informed on the day he signed the requisition, that great injustice had been done to Madras and Bombay, in the Sugar Bill which had been submitted to Parliament; and he did not hesitate a moment to sign the requisition for calling a court to take the matter into consideration, which was at that moment presented to him. He immediately, however, began an inquiry as to what had been done in the matter, and after having carefully considered the whole subject, he must confess he had not been able to discover that any injury had been done either to Madras or Bombay. On Saturday, he received a letter from his friend, Mr. Larpent, written in consequence of observing his name to the requisition, and as that letter contains his sentiments on the subject under discussion, and so full and distinct an account of what took place during the progress of the negociation as cannot but satisfy the court that the general principle was throughout maintained, and that no partial measure was ever sought or contemplated, he trusted he might be allowed to read it to the Court.

[The letter was read, see p. 271.]

For the accuracy of what was stated regarding the first conference he could vouch, as he was present; and the high character and great respectability of the writer of the letter, would, without doubt, be considered a sufficient guarantee for the rest; and he appealed to the Court, whether it did not appear that the general interests of all India were maintained throughout the whole proceeding. The petition of this Court prayed, that India might be placed on a footing of equality with the West-Indies, by an assimilation of duties, more particularly in regard to sugar. Now, had the Government inconsiderately granted the prayer of the petitioners, and considering all India as one colony, (in which light the hon. bart. Sir C. Forbes thinks it ought to have been considered,) had prohibited the importation of foreign sugars, in the same manner as is done to those colonies in the West-Indies which enjoy the privilege of importing sugar into this country at the low duties, what, he would ask, would have been the situation of Madras and Bombay? Although sugar is manufactured to some extent in the presidency of Madras, still it has not sufficient for its consumption, and is obliged to import; but Bombay produces little or none, being almost entirely dependant on importation, and would consequently have been subjected to a very serious deprivation, for the sake of a barren privilege, that of exporting an article which it did not possess. But by the statements of the honourable proprietor (Col. Sykes) it appeared, that Bombay carries on a very extensive trade in foreign sugars. That from China alone, it imports annually to the value of upwards of fifteen lacks of rupees, and to the value of ten lacks from other countries, which importations form the bases of a very profitable trade with neighbouring countries, extending to the Gulf of Persia, which are thus supplied with that indispensable article of consumption. What would the honourable proprietors have said had Bombay been deprived of this trade, by being placed on the same footing as Bengal. Had her ships from China, and other Eastern countries, been obliged to return ballasted with stones in place of sugar? Would they have considered the privilege to import Bengal sugar into this country at the low duties, an adequate compensation for what would thereby have been sacrificed? If they did, they would have deceived themselves, for the surplus produce of Bengal is scarcely adequate to the supply of all India, had it been prohibited from importing foreign sugars, so that there would have been in reality no sugar to bring to this country from British India. The system of bonding would have required large establishments, and most particular regulations to prevent fraud and smuggling, more especially in places where the importation of foreign sugar was permitted ; and he appealed to every experienced merchant, whether it would not be attended with great difficuly. When, therefore, the Chancellor of the Exchequer asked, whether the deputation was prepared to say, that Madras and Bombay were in a situation to accept the conditions to be imposed on Bengal, *viz.* the prohibition to import foreign sugar, could they, with any regard to the interests of those presidencies, have answered in the affirmative ? The bill in question, however, was only an annual bill, and if, before it expires, it can be shewn that it inflicts any injury on Madras and Bombay, it would, he had no doubt, be remedied : for the great principle for which they contended was now admitted, *viz.* the assimilation of duties with the West-Indies. Considering the despair so ably and feelingly expressed by the hon. bart. (Sir C. Forbes) at a previous court—a despair founded on a long experience of the hopelessness of expecting to obtain justice for India from any government, whatever their politics—they really had great reason to be satisfied with what had been done by our present liberal government. In his opinion, they were under great obligations, in the first place, to the Honourable Court of Directors, for the readiness with which they took up the matter, and the able support they have given it ; in the next place, to the Deputations ; and particularly the Chairman of the London East-India and China Association, for the indefatigable and persevering efforts, and great commercial knowledge and experience, brought to bear on the subject ; and lastly, to the Government, for the fairness, candour, and liberality with which they entered on the subject. He was therefore of opinion, under all the circumstances of the case, that to disturb what had been done would be unwise ; and he should therefore vote against the petition.

Dr. *Carpue* concurred with the hon. proprietor who had just addressed the Court, in the expression of the thanks which were due to Government, for the desire they had ever anxiously evinced to promote the welfare of India. Indeed, other, and perhaps more important considerations than those of our commercial and political relations with India, ought to make us solicitous to promote its welfare in every way we could. He alluded more particularly to many most important additions to our chirurgical knowledge, which we owed to that country. There was scarcely an important operation in surgery, which we had not derived from India : the operation of lithotomy, cataract, &c. &c. were all derived by us from India : and on the principle that one good turn deserved another, he greatly

rejoiced that his friend Sir Charles Forbes had come forward in the manner he had done, to advocate the interests of India ; he had taken up the cause with great ability, and he trusted that he would continue to advocate it in the same manner.

Mr. *Fielder* wished to know, from the hon. gentleman who recently addressed the Court, whether, at the interview with the Chancellor of the Exchequer which took place on the 19th of May, it was not broadly stated, that the new arrangement with respect to the sugar duties should be for the benefit of all India ; if so, he begged to ask also, why that arrangement had been departed from, and why the advantage was now confined to Bengal alone?

Mr. *Deans Campbell* replied, that when the deputation representing the East-India interests had been asked, on the occasion alluded to, whether Madras and Bombay were in a condition to take on themselves to export sugar, and to do without imports, the deputation replied, that they could not take it on themselves to say, that either of those presidencies could do without imports ; and they added, that with respect to Bombay, it would be highly injurious to prevent such importation ; it would be an injury to Bombay to prevent its continuing an importing country, because it had no sugars of its own.

Colonel *Sykes*, in explanation, begged to assure the hon. proprietor who last addressed the Court, that he was wholly mistaken ; Bombay could not only supply its own consumption, but, by a proper encouragement of its agriculture, it could, in no distant time, be able also to contribute in a considerable degree to the supply of our market at home with its surplus.

Mr. *Weeding* said, that he was present at the conference referred to, but certainly he was no party to the preference given to Bengal over the other presidencies of India. The deputation from the India and China Association, consisting of Mr. Horsley Palmer and Mr. Larpent, were no doubt, he would admit, very intelligent men ; but if on that occasion they said that Madras and Bombay should not be included in the operation of the bill, because they were not able to raise sugar sufficient for themselves, they said that which they had no authority to state from the body whom they represented. Great stress had been laid on the exertions of this Association, as having been the cause of this boon, as it was called, to India. He denied that that was the fact. The discussions in that court, and the petitions to Parliament which had been repeatedly presented on the subject, showed the attention they had previously obtained from his Majesty's Government an admission of the principle, and that the equalization was a question of time only. That time, it seems, had now arrived to develope a partial operation of the principle. He (Mr. Weeding) had a very good opinion of the benefits likely to result from the East-India and China Association, but it was not fair to ascribe to this Association—an institution of embryo growth—the present boon, as it is called, the praise of which should be more justly given to the counsels and the efforts of the East-India Company. It was entirely without foundation, therefore, to ascribe the equalization to the efforts of Mr. Larpent, or of any individual, even if he had been hand and glove with any of his Majesty's ministers. The hon. gentleman (Mr. D. Campbell) had mentioned in the course of his speech, that, though the two gentlemen comprising the deputation had satisfactorily answered the questions of the Chancellor of the Exchequer, he refused, nevertheless, to tell them what he meant to do, which did not speak much in favour of the particular influence. He would now beg to ask the hon. Proprietor (Mr. Campbell), on what authority he had said that Madras and Bombay were intended to be included in the operation of the sugar duties bill? He should like to know on what authority the statement had been made. It was a mistake to suppose that they wanted to export foreign sugars from Bombay to this country; all they wanted for Bombay was, that it should have the power of importing, for the purpose of again exporting to other countries. He presumed, that if any one chose to import sugars for the purpose of exporting them to Holland or any other foreign country, he might do so. It was, he contended, most unjust, most impolitic, to trammel foreign commerce by fiscal regulations. The principle which he sought to extend to Bombay and Madras, was by the bill extended to Bengal. On that ground it was, he thought, that the petition which he proposed would have a good effect, as it would shew that they were equally interested for the prosperity of all parts of India.

Mr. *Hogg* said, it appeared to him that the bill was not well understood, if it was thought that its present application to Madras or Bombay would be a benefit to either place. One effect which such application would have, would be, that the inhabitants of those presidencies would be compelled to eat Bengal sugar, which they did not like, rather than other sugar which they could get cheaper and liked better. It would be impossible that any of our East-Indian presidencies could be at the same time an importing and an exporting country.

Mr. *Fielder* said that what they ought to seek was, not the benefit of the natives

of Siam, or the Manillas, but of the people of our Indian possessions generally.

Mr. *St. George Tucker* thought that honourable proprietors who had addressed the Court on this subject, had been a little too excursive in their observations. He owned that he had not at least expected to hear a dissertation on surgery introduced into the discussion. The question before the Court involved three propositions: the first was, that the surplus sugar of Bengal might be admitted into bond in the other presidencies, and from thence exported to England. The second was, whether the surplus sugar produce of the other presidencies might be transferred in a similar manner. The first proposition he thought might be taken for granted. There could be no doubt that the second proposition involved a principle as good as that of the first; but it would, he thought, be admitted that the other presidencies were not ripe for its application: that they were not in a condition to be exporting countries. The third proposition related to the reservation of the right of foreign commerce to the several presidencies. It appeared to him that his Majesty's ministers could not refuse the first proposition. The question was not that all India should be included. That no doubt would be the case in time, when the several other parts of India were prepared for it; but they should not press the matter too much at present. There would no doubt be *entrepôts* of commerce, with exports to and from the other parts of India; but we ought to wait the proper time, and not anticipate it too soon. He, under these circumstances, would suggest to the honourable proprietor to omit part of the words of the petition to which reference had been made, for at present it would only tend to embarrass the question.

Mr. *Weeding* did not see that there was any difference in point of principle between him and the gentleman who last spoke; but it would be for the Court to consider whether, by the omission of the words alluded to, a risk would not be incurred of creating dissatisfaction among the merchants of Bombay and Madras. For his part, he should be very sorry to deprive those merchants of the foreign trade; he would therefore prefer to retain the words.

Mr. *Fielder* trusted the honourable proprietor would consent to the omission of the words which had been adverted to. The petition would then be adopted unanimously.

The *Chairman* considered it was not expedient at the present moment to mix up with the main question before the Court, the propriety of granting to the minor presidencies the option of exporting their sugar. The great practical object which the Court had now to contend for was, that Bengal sugar might be exported to Bombay and Madras, there to be bonded for re-exportation to this country. This object ought to be kept exclusively in view; and he was rather surprised to find the honourable proprietor, Mr. Weeding, start the other point, after expressing entire satisfaction at the principle recognized in the letter of Sir J. Hobhouse, which was read to the Court in June last. In that letter, the rule was laid down that presidencies importing sugar should not be allowed to export it. That was the principle of the bill; and that seemed at the time to give satisfaction to the honourable proprietor. He (the Chairman) should strongly object to the adoption by that Court of a petition demanding that Bombay and Madras should have the option of exporting sugar, for that might lead to their being placed on the same footing as Bengal, and to their being deprived consequently of the power of importing foreign sugar. Such a result he thought was far from being desirable. Besides, it would be time enough to make application for the concession of this option to Bombay and Madras, whenever it should appear probable that they would grow enough sugar to enable them to export. But at the present moment, the Court should combine their efforts to secure that which it was probable might be obtained; and the justice of conceding which, he begged to inform the proprietors, he had personally impressed on the Chancellor of the Exchequer, viz.—permission to bond Bengal sugar at Bombay and Madras for exportation to England. (*Hear, hear!*) Having not without great difficulty obtained a great good, they ought still to continue in the same judicious course they had hitherto pursued; and while seeking to promote the general happiness of India, it would be wise at the present moment not to ask from the Government more than they were likely to get. The honourable Chairman concluded by moving, in conformity with the opinions he had just expressed, that certain parts of the petition be omitted.

Mr. *St. G. Tucker* said, that the object to which the attention of the Court had been directed by the hon. Chairman, was one of a practical nature; and the question then arose, would it not be better first of all to endeavour to obtain that, and to keep in reserve the other two propositions contained in the petition. If the hon. mover would not object to confine his petition to the one practical object, there could be no doubt that it would be attained; and the concession of the other two would follow in due course of time.

Mr. *Weeding* said, that if the hon. Chairman's amendment was adopted, the effect of the petition would be this: it would set forth the injustice of giving a preference to Bengal, with respect to the export of sugar: but it would pray for one object exclusively, deferring to a subsequent period the demand, that Bombay and Madras should have the right of exporting their sugars. Now he was aware of the value of unanimity in that Court, and he would rather sacrifice any particular judgment of his own on the matter, than cause a division of opinion. He would not therefore oppose the amendment of the hon. Chairman. (*Hear, hear!*)

Sir *R. Campbell* addressed the Court in so low a tone as to be scarcely audible. He was understood to state, that he felt much disappointment at the Government propositions, which fell short of the object which an hon. friend of his said the Government had in view, the promotion of the welfare of the people of India. No encouragement was held out to Madras and Bombay by the bill, to extend the cultivation of sugar. It was said, the bill was an annual one, and that Court would have the opportunity, when the bill came again under consideration, of urging its demands on the Government. But next year a Tory administration might be in existence, and if it acted as Tory administrations had hitherto done, they all knew what they had to expect for India. It was not to be supposed, that so long as the right of Bombay and Madras to export their own sugar remained in suspence, the people of those presidencies would extend the cultivation of that plant, when it was doubtful whether they would be able to find a market for their produce. He looked upon the bill as a measure repressive of industry, and he should have been glad if the hon. proprietor (Mr. Weeding) had not acquiesced in the amendment. He was sorry to find that the hon. Director (Mr. Tucker) was now disposed to adopt the view of the question which had been taken by the Chairman. He believed that they ought, at the present moment, to shew the people of Madras and Bombay, that their interests were not lost sight of.

Mr. *Tucker* stated that he had not changed his opinion in the slightest degree, but he thought it of importance that that court should act in the matter with unanimity. He repeated what he had before stated, that the first proposition in the petition was of a practical and urgent nature. With respect to the second proposition, he contended that the principle was already conceded by the Government. There could not be the smallest doubt that the term "British India," meant the whole of the presidencies; and the principle which had been applied to Bengal, would be carried into practical execution with regard to Bombay and Madras whenever they should be in a situation to export sugar of their own. What was the object of the Government? It was as clear as possible that they wished to protect the West-Indian interest, but also the interest of the British possessions in the East-Indies, by excluding from this country foreign sugar; but fearing that it might be brought in by way of India, they, in the first instance, limited the practical application of the principle they had adopted to one presidency, which they knew to be fully able to export sugar of its own growth. The other presidencies would, as soon as they were in a similar condition, have the same principle applied to them. He, therefore, wished that the court would not attempt to gain more at present than the first object; because the other propositions had commercial considerations connected with them which might cause them to be disputed; and if the court attempted to enforce them, they would be involved in a controversy which, at the present moment, could be productive of no real practical good.

Sir *R. Campbell* said, that the two presidencies which were excluded from the benefit of the bill, having their industry thereby repressed, were not likely to extend the cultivation of the sugar plant; and it was consequently doubtful whether they would ever become exporting countries.

Mr. *Weeding* had not given up his opinion on the subject. He certainly saw objections to the proposed amendment; for it might lead to the impression that the prosperity of Bengal was alone regarded, and that the interests of Bombay and Madras were not attended to. Still, for the sake of unanimity, and because the first part of the petition set forth the right of Bombay and Madras to the same privilege as had been extended to Bengal, he should not oppose the amendment.

Colonel *Sykes* was afraid that the cultivation of sugar would not increase in Bombay and Madras, so long as those presidencies were excluded from the benefit of the bill.

The amended petition was read, as follows:

To the Honourable the Commons of the United Kingdom of Great Britain and Ireland in Parliament assembled,

The humble Petition of the East India Company respectfully sheweth,

That an Act has been passed in the present Session of Parliament for granting certain duties on Sugar imported from the British possessions in the East-Indies into the United Kingdom.

That the said Act, while it declares that " Sugar the growth of any British possession within the limits of the East-India Company's charter into which the importation of foreign Sugar may be by this Act prohibited and imported from thence," shall be subject to a duty of twenty-four shillings per hundred-weight, confines the operation of the Act to the Presidency of Fort William in Bengal, and of the dependencies thereof.

That the Presidencies of Fort St. George and of Bombay, and their dependencies, are excluded from the benefit of the said Act, although they import a considerable quantity of sugar the produce of Bengal and its dependencies.

Your Petitioners feel satisfied that it was the intention of the Legislature to render equal justice to India, and to encourage the industry of its people; but they submit that this justice is denied to them, and their industry is checked, while Madras and Bombay, and the dependencies thereof, are excluded from the beneficial operation of the said Act.

And as it is enacted that the said Act may be altered, amended, or repealed, by any Act to be passed in this present Session of Parliament, your Petitioners entreat your Honourable House to pass a Bill, which may permit Bengal Sugar to be imported into the United Kingdom from Madras and Bombay, as well as from Fort William, at the reduced duty.

Your Petitioners would humbly suggest that such a measure would promote the benefit of the manufacturing, commercial, and shipping interests of Great Britain, as well as the advantage of India. Sugar forms a valuable article of dead weight, and the British merchant, by being allowed to import it from Madras and Bombay at the lower rate of duty, would be enabled to bring the general produce of those Presidencies, especially cotton-wool, more readily and more cheaply for the use of the manufacturers of this country.

At present, the British merchant takes stones as ballast for his ship before he can venture to take on board his cargo of cotton-wool; sugar, if permitted to be brought at the lower rate of duty, (which reduced rate is the same as that levied on West-India sugars), would supply the place of stones, and this would at once tend to advance the interests of the ship-owner, merchant, and manufacturer of Great Britain; encourage the cultivation of the soil of India, enlarge its revenues, and enrich its people.

Your Petitioners, therefore, entreat your Honourable House to grant to Madras and Bombay the privilege which is conceded to Bengal, of exporting to the United Kingdom, at the lower rate of duty, sugar the produce of Bengal and its dependencies.

And your Petitioners shall ever pray.

The petition, as amended by the Chairman was then unanimously adopted, and the court adjourned.

HOME INTELLIGENCE.

IMPERIAL PARLIAMENT.

House of Commons, *July* 14.

Calcutta Petition.—Mr. *Hume* rose to present a petition, which had been printed, and, he trusted, was in the hands of every member. It stated the situation of British India in regard to the effects of the late legislative enactments respecting it. By the late alterations, the protection which British subjects there had hitherto enjoyed, had been in a manner withdrawn—namely, the protection of the Supreme Court; because power was given by the 43d section of the act to the Governor-general in Council to legislate without any interference or advice. The law-makers in India were entirely irresponsible; against their proceedings there was no appeal, save to that house or to the king. No notice was ever given, or required to be given, of any regulations they might think proper to adopt, although they must be implicitly obeyed, and might affect the property, rights, and liberties of the people; it was, therefore, no wonder that they complained of being placed without the pale of the British constitution. The prayer of the petition was, therefore, a reasonable one; it was, that they should be taken under the protection of the British laws, and that they should not be left at the disposal of the Governor-general in Council, that council being composed of five persons, namely, the Governor-general himself, a commissioner-in-chief, two civil officers appointed by them, and another appointed by his majesty. The proceedings of this council were secret; it had no sympathy or communication with the people; it was elevated above their society and a knowledge of the real state of society, with which every law-maker ought to be acquainted. He regretted the rapidity with which the act that conferred this irresponsible power had passed through the house, and he hoped that the house would take an early opportunity to grant the same rights and privileges to the people of India which every Englishman enjoyed, even in the remotest parts of our possessions. The petitioners had complained further, that no provision was made for their education. He regretted that the proposed equalization of the sugar duties was partial in its application, and did not comprehend the whole of the British territories in India, as it ought to do. He complained that the Board of Control had never properly attended to the interest of the people of India, which was

quite apparent, both in the case of the duties on cotton, and other articles of British manufacture. The house, he hoped, would bear in mind that every article of English produce was admitted into India, either free of duty, or at 2½ per cent.; whereas Indian produce was less than from 10 to 30 per cent. Then, again, colonial rum was received in this country at 9 per cent., while Indian rum paid 15; and he would ask, why should Indian tobacco pay more on being imported into England, than tobacco coming from another part of the world? He concluded by moving the following resolutions :—

" 1. That this house will take an early opportunity of considering the allegations made in a petition from the inhabitants of Calcutta, presented in the present session of parliament, against some provisions in the Act passed in the third and fourth years of the reign of his present majesty, and entitled, ' An Act for effecting an arrangement with the East-India Company, and for the better government of his majesty's Indian territories, till the 30th day of April 1834, with a view to a revision of the same, and the redress of such grievances as shall be proved to exist.'

" 2. That the monopolies of salt and opium exercised by the East-India Company within the British dominions in India are incompatible with sound principle, and detrimental to the agricultural and commercial interests of India; and they ought, conformably to the expectations held out by the ministers of the crown, to be abolished as early as the same can be effected, without prejudice to the local revenues of India.

" 3. That the discriminating duties levied within the United Kingdom on various articles, the productions of the British possessions in India, are impolitic and unjust, alike injurious to the producers in India, and to the consumers in the United Kingdom; and that such duties ought, with the least practicable delay, to be reduced to the same amount as those levied on corresponding articles, the produce of his majesty's colonies in the West-Indies.

" 4. That it is just and equitable that the same duties, and no other, should be levied on manufactured articles, the produce of British India imported into the United Kingdom, as are levied on the corresponding articles of British manufactures imported into all British possessions in India."

Sir *J. C. Hobhouse* said, that matters in India were by no means in so desperate a state as might be inferred from the representations of the petitioners, who not only thought proper to make very strong representations, but as it appeared to him were in very great haste to bring these representations under the notice of parliament; they did not wait even nine months to give the provisions of the new charter a fair trial, and this extraordinary haste seemed the less necessary, and the more difficult to be accounted for, when it was recollected that there were no threatenings of hostilities on the part of any foreign power—no symptom of internal disturbance—no complaint on the ground of any alleged mismanagement in the affairs of government. That which appeared to him the principal complaint of the petitioners was, that by the 43d section of the charter a certain quantity of power was taken away from the Supreme Court. It would seem that the petitioners required that the Supreme Court should not only have the power of registering decrees, and carrying them into effect, but should also enjoy concurrent authority with the supreme government. As hon. members would fully recollect, it had been determined by that house that the section to which he referred should be adopted; parliament had determined that the Supreme Court should not possess a concurrent authority with the executive government, and hence the principal amongst the present complaints. That decision had been adopted after much consideration and discussion by parliament, and he certainly should not then occupy their attention by re-arguing such a question. The petitioners demanded an extensive and fundamental change in the new charter, which had not yet had a fair trial. They complained also of the centralization of authority in India, that Madras and Bombay should not have authority concurrent with that of the presidency of Calcutta. This was almost as absurd as another of their complaints, when on the one hand they appeared to contend for the rights of the native, and on the other to complain of that equality of justice of which they appeared to be the warmest advocates. They alleged that the interests of the native, as contradistinguished from those of the European resident in India, were altogether neglected. From the general tenour of the petition he should say, that that complaint came with a very ill grace from those petitioners, even if they had succeeded in proving the grounds on which it rested, but they had not attempted to do any thing of the sort. In the course of the observations with which his hon. friend introduced his resolutions, he made it a sort of charge against the government of that country, that natives did not meet with their fair share of promotion in the public service. To that he should reply that it was unsubstantiated by any evidence; and for his part he felt perfectly satisfied that his noble friend, now at the head of the government of India, would give no just cause for any such complaint, and that if he did he should not do his duty. The next matter of observation to which he should direct attention was, that the natives were said to feel no interest in our religion: on that point he should say that they felt no great interest in our government for the matter of that; but surely the house would agree with him that such a mode of arguing such a question ought not to be sanctioned in parliament. As to recent appointments to offices of large emolument in India, he should content himself with observing that general charges of that nature could hardly be met, and that when specific accusations were brought forward, he should be prepared to afford a full, and, as he trusted, satisfactory explanation.

The resolutions were negatived.

July 15.

Troutback's Case.—Mr. *Warburton* presented a petition from Catherine Robson and Isabella Ainsley, next of kin of Samuel Troutback, late of Madras, merchant, and claimants for his property, now vested in the crown. The circumstances of the case he would state as briefly as possible to the house. In July, 1785, a merchant at Madras, of the name of Samuel Troutback, died at the advanced age of 85, having been a resident merchant in that place for upwards of half a century. After his decease his executors in India remitted the proceeds of his estate to England, and at the first period that he (Mr. Warburton) could obtain an account of what their amount was, namely, in 1815, they amounted to £3,764. 14s. cash, and £139,433. 4s. 4d. 3 per cent. bank annuities. By a will of the deceased, for he left a will, the greater portion of his estate was left to found a new school in the parish of St. John, Wapping. This will was dated July 21, 1780, was proved in the Mayor's Court in Madras, October, 1785, and afterwards in the Prerogative Court of Canterbury, May 31, 1788. In consequence, however, of proceedings which were taken at the instance of the crown in the Court of Chancery, this will was, by a decree of that court in 1794, set aside as being contrary to the provisions of the statute of Mortmain. The proceeds of the estate accordingly remained in the possession of the executors. The crown commenced proceedings against the executors, and by a Chancery decree, in the year 1814, it was decided, that as no next of kin or heir appeared to claim the estate of the testator, his estate, real and personal, should be vested in the crown. Almost immediately after this was done, the house was informed by a copy of a Treasury minute laid before it, in the year 1816, that the stock forming a portion of the testator's estate, had been sold for the purpose of supplying a portion of the deficiency of the civil list, on the 5th of January, 1816. It would appear from this minute, that the proceeds of the testator's estate were regarded as the droits of the crown. He (Mr. Warburton) did not mean to say that they were such, but such they seemed to be considered by those who drew up the minute. It was ordered by the minute that £20,000 of the proceeds should be appropriated for the purchase of land to be annexed to the Royal Palace at Brighton, and the sum of £50,000 additional, was ordered to be appropriated for the payment of furniture for the said palace. It thus appeared that the proceeds of the estate were appropriated, but as the crown remained still responsible to any rightful owners, should they ever appear, it still remained matter for inquiry who the rightful owners were. The petitioners at length appeared as such. Mr. Warburton then entered into a very long detail of the steps taken to obtain the property, which was ineffectual, and concluded by asking for a Committee of Inquiry into the claims of the petitioners.

The *Chancellor of the Exchequer* justified the Treasury in the course it had taken, and contended that the house could not entertain the case after it had been adjudicated upon by the Court of Chancery and a Court of Law.

Motion negatived.

MISCELLANEOUS.

APPOINTMENTS AT THE EAST-INDIA HOUSE.

The public will be gratified to learn, that Horace Hayman Wilson, Esq., Boden Professor of Sanscrit in the University of Oxford, has been appointed Librarian to the East-India Company. The selection of this eminent Oriental scholar is highly honourable to those who have the disposal of the appointment.

The Museum of the East-India Company has been placed under the care of Dr. Horsfield, who will also take charge of the library during the residence of Professor Wilson at Oxford.

Thomas Love Peacock, Esq. has been appointed Examiner of Indian Correspondence, in the place of James Mill, Esq., deceased; and David Hill, Esq., has succeeded to the station of Senior Assistant to the Examiner, vacant by the promotion of Mr. Peacock.

The cessation of the trade of the East-India Company has rendered it unnecessary to fill up the office of Hydrographer, vacant by the death of Capt. Horsburgh. The valuable collection of maps and charts has been placed under the superintendence of Mr. John Walker of the East-India House.

MR. ROYLE.

Mr. James Forbes Royle, author of the "Illustrations of the Botany and Zoology of the Himalayan Mountains," has been elected Professor of Materia Medica, in King's College, London. It is always gratifying to find that individuals like this gentleman, eminent in

the several departments of science, receive these public testimonials to their talents and rewards for their labours.

ENTERTAINMENT TO THE GOVERNOR OF MADRAS.

On the 23d July, the Court of Directors gave a banquet at the Albion Tavern, to Lord Elphinstone, preparatory to his Lordship's departure for Madras.

There were present—Lord Melbourne, the Marquess of Lansdowne, Lord Palmerston, Lord Morpeth, Viscount Howick, Sir J. C. Hobhouse, the Duke of Richmond, the Duke of Sutherland, the Duke of Argyll, the Persian Princes, and other distinguished personages.

The Chairman, Sir R. Carnac, Bart., presided.

The *Chairman* proposed the health of the noble lord who had been appointed to the office of Governor of Fort St. George. That noble lord bore a name which was a guarantee that his administration in India would be beneficial. Among British Statesmen few names deserved more honour in India and this country, than that of Elphinstone. The talents of the noble lord who sat beside him were such as to justify the opinion, that the name he had mentioned would be unsullied by the administration of the noble lord, and that he only required experience and the employment of his talents to be worthy of the honour due to his predecessors. He earnestly wished that the noble lord's appointment may conduce to his own happiness, and to the benefit of the natives of India.

Lord *Elphinstone* briefly returned thanks, and expressed a hope that he should, in the exercise of the important duties he had been called upon to perform, prove himself worthy of the great trust and confidence reposed in him. He most sincerely thanked them for the kindness shown towards him.

The *Chairman* proposed the health of his Majesty's Ministers. He said: "In the administration of the affairs of India we know nothing about those political differences which agitate parties in connection with other affairs of interest relating to matters connected with our own country. We are all confirmed in the opinion that India should be considered neutral ground with respect to party views. Such were the views and principles acted upon by the Right Hon. Bart. in the recommendation he had made to the appointment of the noble lord to the office he was about to fill."

Lord *Melbourne* returned thanks.

One of the Persian Princes was compelled to retire during the dinner through indisposition.

On the 20th July, a Court of Directors

was held at the East-India House, when the usual oaths were administered to the Right Hon. Lord Elphinstone, on being appointed Governor of Fort St. George.

NEW DIRECTOR.

On the 13th July a ballot was taken at the East-India House for the election of a Director, in the room of George Raikes, Esq., who had disqualified. At six o'clock the glasses were closed, and delivered to the scrutineers, who reported the election to have fallen on Francis Warden, Esq.

TRADE WITH PERSIA.

Foreign Office, July 21.

A despatch, of which the following is an extract, has been transmitted to Viscount Palmerston, G.C.B., his Majesty's Principal Secretary of State for Foreign Affairs, by the Right Hon. Henry Ellis, his Majesty's Ambassador Extraordinary at the Court of Persia :—

"Teheran, May 6.

" My Lord,—I have the honour to forward to your Lordship a Persian copy and translation of a Proclamation or Royal Order, issued by his Majesty the Shah, which places the trade of British subjects with Persia on the same footing, with respect to duties, as that of Russian subjects; and, moreover, ensures to British merchants security and protection in the admission and sale of their property.

" I have the honour to be, &c.,

(Signed)　" H. Ellis."

" Whereas the relations of friendship and amity between the powerful and dignified governments of Persia and England are fixed upon the most perfect and firm basis; and whereas it is agreeable to the exalted character of his Majesty that this friendship and amity should daily increase, and that mutual advantage should thence result; therefore, in the present auspicious year, and henceforth, according to this gracious proclamation, we grant liberty and permission to the merchants of the British nation, that having brought their merchandize to the territorial possessions of Persia, they may dispose of the same in perfect security and confidence, and that they shall pay to the officers of government the same public dues upon their goods as are paid by the merchants of the Russian government.

"In the month of Moohurrim, A. H. 1252."

Extract from the third article of the Treaty of Commerce between Russia and Persia :—" It is agreed that goods imported into Persia, or exported from that kingdom by Russian subjects, shall be liable, as heretofore, to a duty of five per cent. levied, once for all, upon their import and export, and shall not be subject afterwards to any other duty.

PLYMOUTH AN EAST-INDIA PORT.

The Lords of the Treasury have allowed to the Port of Plymouth the privilege of importing goods direct from the East-Indies and China.

THE PERSIAN PRINCES.

Their names are Reza Koolee Meerza, Nejeff Koolee Meerza, and Timoor Meerza. They are grandsons of the late Futeh Allee Shah, and children of Hoossein Allee Meerza, late prince-governor of the province of Fars, who was the fourth or fifth son of that monarch. Thus they are first cousins of Mahomed Shah, who at present occupies the throne, and who is the son of Abbas Meerza, late prince royal of Persia. On the death of Futeh Allee Shah, their father, Hoossein Allee Meerza, conceiving his own title to the throne to be as good as that of his nephew, made an attempt to secure it for himself; but being beaten, and driven back to Shirauz he was made prisoner there with several of his family, while the three princes now in question, together with three more of their brothers, cut their way from the gates of that city, escaping to the mountains, and, after a variety of hardships, reached the sanctuary of Meshed Allee, or Nejeff, near Bagdad. From thence they have come to implore the assistance and friendly intervention of the English Government with their cousin, the Shah, in procuring for them pardon, and a restitution of part of their private property. In the meantime they are the guests of the English Government, and are attended on the part of Government by Mr. J. Baillie Fraser, who has himself but lately returned from Persia, and who generally accompanies them in society.—*London Paper, July 25.*

EAST AND WEST INDIA SUGARS.

The following is an extract of a letter from G. G. de H. Larpent, Esq. Chairman of the East-India Association:

" When the East-India and China Association was established, in March last, the question of the East and West India duties was taken up almost immediately by the Committee. A Petition, dated 28th April, was presented to the House of Commons by Mr. Grote, and in conjunction with the deputation from Glasgow, Liverpool, Manchester, Leeds, &c., an interview with the Chancellor of the Exchequer was solicited and obtained on the 19th May. The Chancellor of the Exchequer met us most fairly—he acknowledged that the principle was in our favour, the only point for discussion being the mode and period of its application. On those matters he stated—

1st. That the West Indians had required, and he was prepared to yield to their suggestions, that the British East-India sugars should be accompanied by certificates of growth, to prevent the introduction of foreign under cover of British India sugars;—and,

2dly, That the same prohibition to import foreign sugars, which existed in the British West Indies and the Mauritius, should be extended to those places in India to which the advantage of the import of East India sugars at the low duties should be conceded. In the justice of this stipulation, all the deputation unanimously agreed;—and the only difficulties that remained to be overcome, arose from the apprehension of the West Indians that such a surplus stock of sugar existed in India as would, if the equalization of the duties were immediate, be poured at once into the home market, and seriously reduce the prices of those sugars, and the protection required for the revenue in the matter of the drawbacks.

The Chancellor of the Exchequer left these subjects for the consideration of the deputation, and we were subsequently called upon to give the information he required. This was done on the 4th of June, when we had a very long interview, and produced such a mass of oral and written evidence, as completely established our case, and, as we believed, satisfied the Chancellor of the Exchequer, that the equalization should be immediate. He declined, however, to give us his opinion, being in communication with the West Indians, and he did not do so until he sent for me on the 22d of June, the day on which he brought forward the resolutions in the house. He then declared the intention of Government to propose to Parliament an immediate equalization of duties, and an assimilation of the situations of the East and West-Indies. This assimilation referred obviously to the prohibition to import foreign sugars from those places from whence sugars were to be exported on the low duties; and I certainly understood, that the West-Indians wished the whole of India to be included in the prohibition. But, as it was a question whether, accompanied by this prohibition, the equalization of the duties would be a boon to Bombay and Madras, into which considerable quantities of Siam, China, and Java sugars were imported, it was determined that, as the Sugar Duties Bill was an annual bill, its advantage and its corresponding disadvantage should in the first instance be limited to the Presidency of Fort William, from whence the great mass of the British East-India sugars came, and the bill was so drawn, not, I firmly believe, with the slightest wish to favour Bengal at the expense of Madras or Bombay, but upon the views I have now stated."

RETIREMENTS, &c. FROM THE COMPANY'S SERVICE.

BENGAL ESTABLISHMENT.

Retired in England.—Maj. James Johnstone, of infantry, from 23d May 1836.—Major John Grant, of invalids. — Capt. Francis Crossley, 62d N.L., from 4th Jan. 1836.—Capt. W. W. Rees, of invalids.—Lieut. J. N. O'Halloran, of infantry, from 18th June 1835.—Surg. James Hall, from 9th Feb. 1834.—Assist. Surg. B. C. Sully, M.D., from 31st May 1834.

Resigned.—Capt. H.' Fendall, 20th N.I., from 6th Aug. 1834. — Lieut. George Urquhart, 65th N.I., from 29th Feb. 1836.

MADRAS ESTABLISHMENT.

Retired in England. — Major M. C. Chase, 1st L.C., from 9th Nov. 1835.—Capt. Henry Harkness, 25th N.I., from 27th July 1834.—Capt. Chas. Bradford, 26th N.I., from 11th Jan. 1836.—Capt. W. H. Trollope, 42d N.I., from 8th Feb. 1836.—Capt. Thomas Sharp, 43d N.I., from 1st Feb. 1836.—Capt. Edward Dyer, 46th N.L., from 14th Dec. 1835.—Capt. W. S. Hele, artillery, from 5th Aug. 1835.—Capt. J. T. Webb, invalids.—Lieut. A. E. G. Turnour, 21st N.I., from 7th April 1834.—Surg. Jonathan Sandford, from 15th Sept. 1833.—Assist. Surg. J. H. Heaton (Lord Clive's Fund).

Resigned.—Lieut. Alfred Wilkinson, 33d N.L., from 19th July 1835.—Lieut. Fred. Ensor, 47th N.I., from 23d May 1835.—1st-Lieut. G. W. Harrison, artillery, from 2d Feb. 1836.

BOMBAY ESTABLISHMENT.

Retired in England.—Major J. W. Aitchison, 6th N.L., from 10th Oct. 1833.

Resigned.—Lieut. C. L. J. Du Pre, 1st L.C., from 28th July 1834.

———

HIS MAJESTY'S FORCES IN THE EAST.

PROMOTIONS AND CHANGES.

4th L. Drags. (at Bombay). Capt. E. B. Grant, from 1st Dr. Gu., to be capt. v. Hughes, who exch. (13 May 36).—Randolph Routh to be coronet by purch., v. Cornwall whose app. has not taken place (8 July 36).

13th L. Drags. (at Madras). Capt. Wm. Knox, from 60th F., to be capt., v. Collins, who exch. (10 June 36).—Capt. T. Atkinson, from 7th Dr. Gu., to be capt., v. Crossley who exch. (17 do.).

16th L. Drags. (in Bengal). Lieut. W. A. Rose, from 4th Dr. Gu., to be lieut., v. Clark, who exch. (27th May 36).—Cornet Hon. C. Powys to be lieut. by purch., v. Donnithorne who retires; D. MacKinnon to be cornet by purch., v. Dillon app. to 7th Dr. Gu. (both 1st July); W. S. Mitchell to be cornet by purch., v. Powys (2 do.).—Maj. W. D. Mercer, from 67th F., to be major, v. W. H. Sperling who retires upon h.p. unattached, rec. dif. (8 July) ; Cornet G. Harriott to be lieut. by purch., v. Rose who retires (8 do.).

3d Foot (in Bengal). Capt. R. M'Nabb, from h. p. unattached, to be capt., v. Allan Stewart, who exch. (28 May 36) ; Lieut. R. Jones, from h. p. 58th F., to be lieut., v. M'Nabb (27 ditto) ; Staff Assist. Surg. John Law, to be assist. surg., v. Dyce, app. to 81st F. (27 ditto) ; Ens. h. p. Chamberlain, to be lieut. by purch., v. Jones, who retires ; K. M'Kenzie to be ens. by purch., v. Chamberlain (both 3 June).

6th Foot (at Bombay). Ens. M. Hall to be lieut., v. Walker, dec. (18 March 36) ; C. N. North to be ens., v. Hall (27 May) ; Lieut. Joseph Benyon, from h. p. unattached, to be lieut., v. Kelly, prom. (27 ditto).—Ens. M. Hall to be lieut., v. Latham dec. (7th Jan. 36) ; Ens. A. Barry to be lieut., v. Hall whose prom. on 18th March 36 has not taken place (20th March) ; H. Wheatstone to be ens., v. Barry (17 June).—Ens. H. A. Sullivan to be lieut. by purch., v. Benyon who retires ; and Geo. Cubitt to be ens. by purch., v. Sullivan (both 1 July).

16th Foot (in Bengal). Ens. R. A. Sparkes, from h. p. York Chasseurs, to be ens., v. Brabazon dec. (29 May 36); J. A. Campbell, to be ens. by purch., v. Sparkes who retires (3 June).

20th Foot, (at Bombay). Lieut. Walter Murray, from 55th F., to be lieut., v. Hutchinson, who exch. (9 Jan. 36).—Ens. G. W. Rice to be lieut. by purch., v. Briscoe app. to 2d Dr. Gu.; and B. F. Vernon to be ens. by purch., v. Rice (both 17 June).

31st Foot (in Bengal). Lieut. S. O. Goodwin to be capt., v. Greene, dec.; and Ens. Wm. Maule to be lieut., v. Maule, whose prom. of 29th Dec. 1833, has not taken place; and George Douglas to be ens., v. Thomas (both 20 May 36); Lieut. T. M. Gardiner, from h. p. 17th F., to be lieut., repaying diff. he received, v. Astur, prom. (10 June); Ens. E. S. Mercer to be lieut., by purch., v. Gardiner, who retires (11 ditto); D. Fyffe to be ens. by purch., v. Mercer (11 ditto).

40th Foot (at Bombay). Ens. W. A. Fyers to be lieut. by purch., v. Elton, who retires; and Fred. T. L. G. Russell to be ens. by purch., v. Fyers (both 20 May 36).—Capt. John Kelly, from h. p. unattached, to be capt., v. L. Bulkeley, who exch. (28 do.).

44th Foot (in Bengal). Maj. George Tryon, from h. p. 2d provisional bat. of militia, to be major, v. Gray, prom. (10 June 36); Capt. J. B. Ainsworth to be major by purch., v. Tryon who retires; Lieut. R. B. McCrea to be capt. by purch., v. Ainsworth; Ens. D. T. Grant to be lieut. by purch., v. McCrea; and G. H. Skipton to be ens. by purch., v. Grant (all 11 June).

45th Foot (at Madras). J. G. Smyth to be ens. by purch., v. Priestly app. to 25th F. (4 June.

49th Foot (in Bengal). Serj. Maj. R. Hollis, from 1st Dr. Gu., to be ens., v. Rowen cashiered (1 July 36).— T. P. Gibbons to be ens. by purch., v. Hollis app. to 1st Dr. Gu. (8 do.).

54th Foot (at Madras). Thomas Mostyn to be ens. by purch., v. Hawkshaw who retires (8 July 36).

55th Foot (at Madras). Lieut. Geo. Hutchinson, from 20th F., to be lieut., v. Murray who exch. (9 Jan. 36).—Ens. W. H. L. D. Cuddy to be lieut., v. Hope dec. (27 Nov. 35); Serj.-Maj. T. Gibson, from 33d F., to be ens., v. Cuddy (27 May 36).

57th Foot (at Madras). Ens. W. L. Stewart to be lieut. by purch., v. Armstrong who retires; and H. C. Cardew to be ens. by purch., v. Stewart (both 8 July 36).

58th Foot (in Ceylon). Ens. W. E. Grant to be lieut. by purch., v. Buchanan who retires; R. Denny to be ens. by purch., v. Grant (both 13 May 36).

62d Foot (at Madras). Capt. H. Astler, from h. p. unattached, to be capt., v. C. F. Neynoe, who exch. (21 May 36).—Ens. G. J. Fulton, from 77th F., to be ens., v. Mulock who exch. (3 June).

97th Foot (in Ceylon). S. O. W. Ingram to be ens. by purch., v. Wynne app. to 68th F. (13 May 36).

Ceylon Rifle Regt. H. G. Remmett to be 2d lieut. by purch., v. M'Dougall app. to 79th F. (8 July 36).

Brevet.—Capt. F. C. Irwin, 63d F., to be commandant of troops in Western Australia, with rank of major in the army (28 June 36).—Cadets Richard Strachey and George Macleod, Hon. E. I. Company's service, to have temporary rank of ensign during period of their being placed at Chatham for field instruction in art of sapping and mining.

———

New percussion musket have been issued to infantry regiments for practice experimentally, 16 to each corps; and the 80th regiment has already reported in their favour.

It is reported in the military circles, that the following cavalry regiments are to be made light regiments, like the 4th that are now in India, and sent there to relieve the three regiments that have been there the longest, and those regiments, on their return home, are to be made heavy, in lieu, if wanted, *viz.*—2d Dragoon Guards; 6th do., or Carabineers; 7th Dragoon Guards.

Maj. Gen. Sir George Elder has been appointed to the staff at Madras.

The head-quarters and band of the 28th Foot landed at Sydney on the 20th Jan., and were accompanied to the barracks by the band of the 17th.

The 80th is the next regiment under orders for Sydney, N. S. Wales. They will be forwarded in detachments as soon as the whole of the 28th have been despatched.

The 20th regt. may be expected to arrive from India in the autum of this year.

The 17th regt., from New South Wales, will replace the 2d or Queen's regt. at Poonah, the latter marching to Belgaum.

The 18th Royal Irish are destined for New South Wales. The 4th leave Sydney for India.

———

INDIA SHIPPING.

Arrivals.

JUNE 30. *George the Fourth*, Waugh, from China 2d March; off Plymouth.—JULY 1. *Marquis Camden*, Gribble, from China 2d March; off Plymouth.—*Ann*, Hedges, from China 12th Feb.; off Falmouth.—2. *Eliza Haywood*, Jones, from Singapore 23d Jan., and Cape 18th April; off Holyhead.—*Gabrielle*, Guezenec, from Bengal 10th March; off Plymouth (for Havre)—4. *Robert Quayle*, Bleasdale, from Bombay 3d Nov., Aleppy, and Tutucorin; at Liverpool.—*Sarah*, Whitesides, from China 22d Feb.; and *Lord Saumurez*, Rowe, from Mauritius 25th March; both off Plymouth.—*Alfred*, Tapley, from China 6th Feb.; off Teignmouth.—5. *Tigris*, Stevens, from Ceylon 8th March, and Cape 1st May; off Lymington.—*City of Edinburgh*, Baker, from N. S. Wales 5th March, and Bahia 14th May; off the Wight.—*Isabella*, Ellis, from V. D. Land 21st Feb.; off Torbay.—*Mary Sharp*, Brown, from ditto 9th March; off the Start.—7. *Zenobia*, Owen, from Bengal 6th March, and Cape 11th May; *Britomart*, MacDonald, from V. D. Land 10th March, and Parnambuco 24th May; *Rhoda*, Hurst, from N. S. Wales 6th March; and *Dove*, Haddon, from Algoa Bay, 14th April, and Cape; all off Plymouth.—*John*, Dixon, from V. D. Land 20th Feb., and Bahia 10th May; off Dover.—8. *Coromandel*, Cheeser, from China 3d March; at Deal.—9. *James Colvin*, Maughan, from South Seas; at Deal—11. *Findlater*, Read, from Mauritius 4th March, and Cape 9th April; at Deal.—12. *Cheshire*, Campbell, from Mauritius 23d March. and Cape 29th April; at Liverpool.—*Lady Amherst*, Barnett, from South Seas; at Deal.—13. *Balguerie*, Desse, from China 14th March; at Bordeaux.—14. *Columbia*, Booth, from China 2d Feb.; off Hastings.—21. *Auriga*, Chalmers, from N. S. Wales 14th March; at Deal.—*Louisa Campbell*, Macqueen, from China 17th March; off Margate.—22. *William Metcalfe*, Philipson, from Bombay 25th Feb., and Algoa Bay 25th April; at Deal.—23. *Warrior*, Stone, from N. S. Wales 16th March; at Deal.—*Lady M'Naghten*, Hustwick, from Valparaiso 10th April; at Liverpool.—25. *Reform*, Doble, from Singapore 23d March; off Portsmouth.—*Alexander Johnstone*, M'Larty, from Van Dieman's Land 11th May; at Liverpool.—*Spartan*, Leith, from Siam 20th Feb., and Singapore 12th March; off Cork.—26. *Bombay*, Routh, from China 22d Feb.; off Portland.—27. *William*, Clarke, from N. S. Wales 9th March; off Portsmouth.

Departures.

JUNE 22. *Euphrates*, Hannay, for Bengal; from Liverpool.—*Susannah*, Ridley, for Mauritius *via* Bordeaux; from Deal.—27. *Isabella*, Jones, for Rio and Bombay; from Liverpool.—29. *Bombay Packet*, Garnock, for Bombay; *Hygeia*, Lucy, for Bengal; and *Albion*, Putman, for China; all from Liverpool.—30. *Royal Admiral*, Fotheringham, and *Lady Feversham*, Webster, both from Bombay (with Company's troops); *Lowestoff*, Francis, for Launceston; and *Capricorn*, Smith, for Cape; all from Deal.—JULY 1. *Gipsey*, Bewley, for Bengal; from Liverpool.—*Courier*, Proudfoot, for Cape; from Deal.—2. *Richmond*, Mac Leod, for Bengal; from Liverpool.—*Africane*, Duff, for South Australia; from Deal.—3. *Mary Ann*, Anderson, for St. Helena, Cape, and Ascension; from Deal.—*Sarah*, Buck, for N. S. Wales; from Liverpool.—4. *Barretto Junior*, Saunders, for Madras and Bengal; and *Mountstuart Elphinstone*, Toller, for Bengal; both from Portsmouth.—4. *Diana*, Hawkins, for Bengal; *Annandale*, Hill, for Bombay; and *Annawan*, Rathbone, for China; all from Liverpool.—6. *Java*, Jobling, for Madras and Bengal; and *Glenalvon*, Baird, for Mauritius, via Bordewux; both from Deal.—7. *Copeland*, Crawford, for Bengal (ballast); from Deal.—8. *William*, Dunn, for Algoa Bay and Cape; from Deal.—9. *Volunteer*, Barivise, for Penang and Singapore; from Liverpool.—*Malabar*, Dunlop, for Mauritius; from Greenock.—10. *Gilmore*, Lindsay, for Bombay; from Portsmouth.—13. *Neptune*, Williams, for China; and *Penyard Park*, Middleton, for Mauritius; both from Deal.—14. *Lady Nugent*, Fawcett, for V. D. Land; from Deal.—17. *Atwick*, Mackay, for Hobart Town and Launceston; from Falmouth.—18. *Stirling*, Burnett, for Mauritius; *Albatross*, Westmoreland, for V. D. Land; and *Tally Ho*, Cole, for Cape; all from Deal.—19. *James MacInroy*, Cleland, for Bengal; from Greenock.—20. *Sybilla*, Knowles, for Cape; from Bristol.—22. *Lady Raffles*, Pollock, for Bengal; from Portsmouth.—*Orient*, Scott, for Bombay; and *Sarah and Arsilla*, Gardner, for China; both from Liverpool.—23. *Theodosia*, Coleman, for Bengal; *Herculean*, Huxtable, for Bengal; *Fairy Queene*, Holmes, for Bengal; *John Knox*, Thompson, for Bombay; *Earl Grey*, Adamson, for Singapore and China; *Claudius*, Winsor, for China; *Madora*, Gregg, for Mauritius; and *Thomas Leech*, Coull, for Cape; all from Liverpool.—H. M. S. *Buffalo*, for Vincent's Gulf, South Australia; from Portsmouth.—*Batavia*, Blair, for Batavia; and *Britannia*, Leith, for Cape; both from Deal.—24. *Francis*, Heath, for Madeira and Bombay; from Liverpool.—25. *London*, Wimble, for Bengal; and *Malabar*, Voss, for Bombay; both from Portsmouth.—*Tickler*, White, for Ceylon; from Deal.

PASSENGERS FROM INDIA.

Per George the Fourth, from China: T.C.Smith, Esq.; W. W. Chafy, Esq.; J. J. Nicholson, Esq.—From St. Helena: G. V. Lamb, Esq.; Mrs. Lamb; Mr. Torbutt.

Per Marquis Camden, from China: A. Jardine, Esq.; H. W. Maccaughey, Esq.; Master Wetmore; Master Framjee and servant.—From St. Helena: T. B. Brooke. Esq C. S.; Mrs. Brooke and four children; Captain Brabazon, late master-attendant; Mrs. Brabazon; two Misses Brabazon; two servants.

Per Coromandel, from China: Mrs. Clifton and family; Miss Huffam; Capt. Clifton; P. Maccallum, Esq.

Per Tigris, from Ceylon: Sir Charles Marshall; Lady Marshall; Hon. Robert Boyd; Dr. Forbes, inspector-general of hospitals; John G. Forbes, Esq.; Dr. M'Andrew, H. M. 78th regt.; Lieut. Rothe, H. M. 36th regt.—From the Cape: Sir J. Bryant; Lady Bryant and family; Mr. and Mrs. Merrington.

Per William Metcalfe, from Bombay: Capt. Beek, 9th N. I.; Lieut. Andrews.

Per Cheshire, from Mauritius: Mr. Douglas; Mr. Kemp; Mr. Marot; Mr. Delange; three children.

Per Sarah, from Manilla: The Rev. Frederick Nevering.

Per Zenobia, from Bengal (additional): Lieut. Magrath, H. M. 3d regt.; Misses Turner, Blagrave, Martin, and Dougan; Masters Turner, two Rowcroft, and two Cowie. (Chas. Grant, Esq. was landed at the Cape.)—From the Cape: Major Douglas; Master Douglas.

Per John, from V. D. Land: Capt. and Mrs. Wright and two children; Mr., Mrs., and Miss Burns and servant; Mr. and Mrs. Andrews and two children; Mr. Thorneloe; Mr. Archer; Mr. Hobson.

Per City of Edinburgh, from N. S. Wales: Col. Despard, H. M. 17th regt.; Mrs. Despard and three children; Col. Britton, H. M. 4th regt.; Capt. Clunie, H. M. 17th regt.; Capt. Flusher, H. M. 50th regt.; Dr. Osborn, R. N.; Mrs. Bowen; Mr. Tincombe; Mr. Riley.

Per Auriga, from N. S. Wales: J. B. Montefiore, Esq.; Mrs. Montefiore and family; Dr. M'Fernan; Mr. J. Blow.

Per Warrior, from N. S. Wales: Mr. and Mrs. Brownlow and family; Mr. and Mrs. M'Naghten and family; Mr. and Mrs. Morris and family; Mr. and Mrs. Hill and family; Mr. and Mrs. Ashley; Mr. Isaac Simmons; Mr. Cæsar.

Per Spartan, from Singapore: Rev. J. T. Jones; Mrs. Jones and family.

Per Bombay, from China: James Franklin, Esq.; J. P. Webber, Esq.

Per William, from N. S. Wales: John Malcolm, Esq.; Mrs. Malcolm; Masters John and Wm. Malcolm; Dr. C. F. France, R. N.; Mr. and Mrs. Whyte; Mr. and Mrs. Hall; Mrs. Nixon and child; Mr. and Mrs. Panton and six children; Mr. and Mrs. Hill.

Expected.

Per Java, from Bombay: Capt. Brucks, Indian Navy; Capt. Bankier, R. N.; Mrs. Jeffreys and four children from Mangalore.

PASSENGERS TO INDIA.

Per Malabar, for Bombay: Col. Robertson; Col. Bagnold; Capt. Sir Keith Jackson, H. M. 4th L. Drags., and lady; Dr. Crawford and lady; Mrs. Dunlop and two other ladies; Miss Morse; Miss Dowling; Chas. Sims, Esq.; Capt. Spencer; Mr. Brown.

Per London, for Bengal: Mrs. Lumsden; Mrs. Parsons; Capt. Darby and lady; Mr. Vigernon and family; Mr. Squire, lady, and two other ladies; Miss Carter; Miss Gale; Capt. Robb; Mr. Willis; Mr. Pattison; Mr. Le Page; Mr. Ferguson; Mr. Twisden; two Masters Martindale.

Per Richmond, for Bengal (from Liverpool): Mrs Dunmore; Mrs. M'Leod; Miss Hamilton; J. Sutherland, Esq.; T. Pottinger, Esq.; D. Mackinnon, Esq.; H. Houston, Esq.; J. Macdonald, Esq.; Capt. Dunmore, Bengal army; Lieut. Collins, ditto; Mr. Platt; Mr. Ross; Mr. Reid; Mr. Owens; Mr. C. Sutherland; two servants.

Per Java, for Madras and Bengal: Capt. Burchell, 3d Buffs, in charge of troops; Lieut. Gavin, 16th L. Drags.; Lieut. Macartney, 13th ditto; Lieut. Pierse, 26th F.; Lieut. Gibbs, 16th F.; Ensigns Graves and Cuffe, 45th F.; Ensigns Cumberland and Shelton, 44th F.; Ensigns Burgh, Lawrence, and Langdale, 41st F.; Ens. Mitchell, 49th F.; Ensigns Humphreys and Croker, 39th F.; Ens. Mein, 13th regt.; Ens. Robson, 26th F.; Ensigns Elmhirst, Morgan, and Pirie, 9th F.; Cornet Yule, 16th L. Drags.; Cornet Cathrey, 11th do.; Assist. Surg. Law, 3d Buffs; Assist. Surg. Barnes, 13th regt.; Assist. Surg. Marshall, 39th regt.; also detachments, amounting to 300 men from depôts of Chatham and Maidstone.

Per Duke of Bedford, for Madras and Bengal: Mrs. and Miss Lister; Mrs. and Miss Destiry; Mrs. Anley; Mrs. Hart and family; Miss Shakspeare; two Misses Sinclair; two Misses Johnson; two Misses Brown; Mr. Lister; Rev. Mr. Hammond; Mr. Robinson; Mr. Mackensie; Mr. N. Faudon; Mr. Beattie.

Per Barretto Junior, for Madras and Bengal: Mrs. Davies; Mrs. Rowlandson; Mrs. Becher; Miss Wilkinson; G. Tod, Esq. B. C. S.; Capt. Hallan; Lieut. C. Rowlandson, 46th Madras N.I.; Lieut. D. Birley, 27th do.; Lieut. G. Tyler, 53d B. N. I.; Lieut. J. A. De Balinhard, H. M. service; Lieut. J. Wilkinson, 44th M. N. I.; Ens. H. M. Becher, 50th B. N. I.; Mr. Haslewood; Mr. Wilson; Mr. Fluyd; Mr. Bamfield.

Per Lady Flora, for Madras: The Baroness Kutzleben; Mrs. Cooper; Mrs. Faith; Mrs. Joffie; Mrs. Carthew; Mrs. Scarman; Misses Humfreys, Whannell, Marriot, Home, and three Scarman; Major General Sir George Elder; Capt. Lang; Capt. Carthew; Capt. Ford; Capt. Hill; Capt. Scarman; Capt. Greenville; Lieut. Watts; Lieut. Hamilton; Mr. Lamb; Mr. M'Pherson.

Per Triumph, for Cape and Bombay: Mrs. and Miss Pelly; Mrs. and Miss James; Miss Keay; Mr. Grant; Mr. Russell; Mr. Malcolm; Mr. Eyles.

Per Lord Hungerford, for Bengal: Mrs. Clarke and child; Mr. and Mrs. Palmer; Dr. and Mrs. Duncan; Mr. and Mrs. Russell; Misses Sneyd, Watson, Bacon, and M'Gregor; the Misses Ross; Maj. Campbell; Sir C. Ouchterlony; Mons. Aubin.

Per Windsor, for Bengal: Capt. Somerville; Dr. Colvin; Mr. Bracken; Mr. Sawers; Mr. Ravenshaw; Mr. Darie.

Per Exmouth, *True Briton*, *Royal Admiral*, and *Lady Feversham*, for India: Lieut. Sparke and Ens. Piercy, 2d F.; Lieut. Whitworth, 3d F.; Lieut. Beebee, 6th F.; Lieut. Matthews and Ens. Powell, 17th F.; Capt. Pigott, 26th F.; Lieut.

Stokes and Ens. Wolfe, 89th F.; Ensigns Armstrong and Lee, 40th F.; Lieut. Hill, 41st F.; Ens. Blenkinsopp, 45th F.; Capt. Parr, 54th F.; Lieut. Butler, 55th F.; Ensigns Lynch and Stanley, 57th F.; Ens. Leatham, 63d F.

Per Marquis of Hastings, for Bombay: Mrs. Taylor; Mrs. Langford; Mrs. Griffiths and Master Griffiths; Mrs. Thornton; Misses Taylor, Rose, Tanner, Rawlins, and Skeene; Mr. Langford; Mr. Taylor; Capt. Thornton; Capt. Clarke; Lieut. Atkinson.

Per H. M. S. Buffalo, for South Australia: Capt. Hindmarsh (governor), his family, and 200 male and female emigrants.

LOSS OF SHIPPING.

The *Premier*, Byron, which left Madras 15th February for London, was totally destroyed by fire at Ascension on the 30th May: crew all saved.

The *Hive*, Nutting, from Cork to New South Wales, was lost in Jervis Bay, previous to 15th Dec. last: convicts, guard, and crew saved.

The *Jane and Henry*, Cobern, is totally lost in Torres Straits: crew saved.

BIRTHS, MARRIAGES, AND DEATHS.

BIRTHS.

June 28. At Halket Park, Kilmarnock, the lady of Capt. Carstairs, Bombay N. I., of a daughter.

30. At Camberwell Grove, the lady of Capt. Alexander Nairne, of a son.

July 5. In Portland-place, the lady of James Ruddell Todd, Esq., of a daughter.

6. At Bath, the lady of Robert Brooke, Esq., late of the Bengal civil service, of a son and heir.

7. At Allonby, near Cockermouth, the lady of Capt. J. Steel, of the Bengal army, of a son.

12. The wife of Mr. Villiers Pearce, formerly of the Royal Navy, and late of the post-office department, Sydney, N. S. Wales, of a son.

20. In New Broad-Street, the lady of George Parbury, Esq., of a son.

Lately. At Mitford Lodge, Hants, the lady of Colonel Henry Roberts, C. B., of a son.

MARRIAGES.

May 19. At Weymouth, Dr. J. Horace Freer, of Hackney, late of King-street, Finsbury-square, London, and formerly of Calcutta, to Emily, widow of the late Dr. John Ollive, of Staines, Middlesex, and youngest daughter of the late Thomas Hodson, Esq., of Knapton House, East Riding, county of York.

June 22. At Abbeville (France), Robert William Bertolacci, Esq., officer of the French Royal Studs, second son of the late Anthony Bertolacci, Esq., controller-general of finance, &c. at Ceylon, to Cecilia Cobham, youngest daughter of the late Joseph Martyr, Esq., of Greenwich, Kent.

25. At Edinburgh, Joseph Rampini, Esq., to Eliza, daughter of the late Robert Fulton, Esq., of Calcutta.

27. At Dublin, John Graham, Esq., younger son of the late Lieut. Col. Graham, to Sophia, daughter of the late Capt. G. H. Alley, of the Bengal Native Infantry.

28. At Bath, Lieut. Col. Andrew Campbell, Hon. E. I. Company's artillery, Bombay establishment, retired, and of Avisyard, county of Ayr, to Nicola Anne, daughter of the late Col. Maxwell, of Birdstown, county of Donegal, Ireland.

29. At Paris, Richard Ouseley, Esq., son of Sir William Ouseley, and nephew to the Right Hon. Sir Gore Ouseley, Bart., to Frances Sarah Place, only surviving daughter of the late Wm. Walter Jones, Esq., of Gurrey, Carmarthenshire.

July 2. At Paris, Mr. M. Wilson, to Mary Ann Susannah, daughter of Mr. Henry Kemp, late of the Hon. E. I. Company's marine service.

5. At St. George's Church, Hanover Square, the Rev. George Bingham, of Melcombe Bingham, county of Dorchester, to Frances Byam Blagrave, only daughter of Anthony Blagrave, Esq., formerly of the Hon. E. I. Company's Bengal civil establishment.

12. At Ryde, Isle of Wight, Charles Griffin, Esq., of the Bengal army, to Sophia, only surviving daughter of the late Capt. Steele, of the Royal Marines.

— At Richmond, Surrey, the Rev. George Trevor, S.C.L, of Magdalen Hall, Oxford, chaplain to the forces in Madras, to Elizabeth Louisa, eldest daughter of Christopher P. Garrick, Esq., of Richmond, and of Cleve, in the county of Somerset.

13. At the Cathedral Church of Durham, Viscount Chelsea, eldest son of the Earl of Cadogan, to Mary Sarah, third daughter of the Hon. and Rev. Dr. Wellesley, and niece to the Duke of Wellington and the Marquis Wellesley.

14. At Hitcham, Bucks, Lieut. Col. Home, Madras army, to Harriet, eldest daughter of Duncan Campbell, Esq. of York-place, Barnsbury Park, Islington.

23. At St. Pancras Church, Robert Haycock, Esq. of Shrewsbury, to Susannah Elizabeth, daughter of the late James Hutchinson, Esq., East-India Company's service.

DEATHS.

April 21. On board the *Dorothys*, on her passage to Algoa Bay, Susan M'Donald, wife of the Rev. Robert Niven, missionary to Caffraria.

June 12. At his seat at Bushy, in the 86th year of his age, David Halliburton, Esq., formerly of the Madras Civil Service.

23. At Wandsworth, Robert Rickards, Esq., formerly first in Council at Bombay, afterwards M.P. for Wootton Basset, and latterly Factory Inspector for Lancashire and Yorkshire. Mr. Rickards's literary merits are well known, but he is chiefly distinguished by his long continued public advocacy of a free trade to the East-Indies and with China.

28. At Cheltenham, Lieut. Col. James Lawrie, of the Bengal army.

30. At Barnstaple, Susanna Pegister Richardson, aged 18, eldest daughter of the late Capt. George Richardson, of the Hon. E. I. Company's service.

July 10. Sir Francis Freeling, Bart., Secretary to the General Post Office, in his 73d year.

— At Truro, aged 75, Mr. John Lander, father of the celebrated African travellers.

20. At Stoke Newington, aged 64, Thomas Fisher, Esq., Searcher of the Records to the Hon. East-India Company, in whose service he had been for upwards of 50 years.

Lately. At Corte, in Corsica, M. Paolo Vignale, formerly almoner to the Emperor Napoleon at St. Helena. He was killed by a musket-ball, at the moment of shutting his window. The author, and the cause of this attempt, are equally unknown.

— At Malta, after a few hours' illness, M. Blacque, editor of the *Moniteur Ottoman*.

— At Calais, M. Lalande, the celebrated naturalist.

— At Millburn Tower, near Edinburgh, the Right Hon. Sir R. Liston, Bart., K.G. C.B., lately representative of His Britannic Majesty at Constantinople, in the 94th year of his age.

N.B. *The letters P.C. denote prime cost, or manufacturers' prices ; A. advance (per cent.) on the same ; D. discount (per cent.) on the same ; N.D. no demand.—The bazar maund is equal to 82 ℔. 2 oz. 2 drs., and 100 bazar maunds equal to 110 factory maunds. Goods sold by Sa. Rupees B. mds. produce 5 to 8 per cent. more than when sold by Ct. Rupees F. mds.—The Madras Candy is equal to 500℔. The Surat Candy is equal to 746½ ℔. The Pecul is equal to 133⅓ ℔. The Corge is 20 pieces.*

CALCUTTA, February 11, 1836.

	Rs.A.	Rs. A.		Rs.A.	Rs. A.
Anchors ....Sa.Rs. cwt.	12 8 @	19 0	Iron, Swedish, sq...Sa.Rs. F. md.	5 1 @	5 3
Bottles	100 8 12	— 9 4	——— flat ....do.	5 0 —	5 2
Coals ....B. md.	0 7	— 0 8	——— English, sq. ....do.	2 9 —	2 11
Copper Sheathing, 16-32 ..F. md	34 0	— 34 8	——— flat ....do.	2 7 —	2 9
—— Braziers', ...do.	34 0	— 34 8	—— Bolt ....do.	2 9 —	2 11
—— Thick sheets........do.	—	—	—— Sheet ....do.	5 4 —	5 10
—— Old Gross ....do.	32 4	— 32 8	—— Nails ....cwt.	11 0 —	15 8
—— Bolt ....do.	33 0	— 33 8	—— Hoops...........F. md.	5 2 —	5 5
—— Tile ....do.	31 6	— 32 2	—— Kentledge ....cwt.	1 0 —	1 3
—— Nails, assort.......do.	30 0	— 36 0	Lead, Pig ....F. md.	6 1 —	6 3
—— Peru Slab........Ct.Rs. do.	28 4	— 29 12	—— unstamped........do.	5 13 —	5 15
—— Russia ....Sa.Rs. do.	—	—	Millinery	5 to 25 D.& P.C.	
Copperas ....do.	3 0	— 3 5	Shot, patent ....bag	2 6 —	3 4
Cottons, chintz ....pce.	—	—	Spelter ....Ct.Rs. F. md	6 9 —	6 10
—— Muslins, assort. ....do.	1 5	— 13 0	Stationery	5 to 25 D.& P.C.	
—— Yarn 16 to 170 ....mor.	0 6½	— 0 8½	Steel, English......Ct.Rs. F. md.	5 14 —	6 4
Cutlery, fine	5 to 10A. & P.C.		—— Swedish ....do.	6 8 —	7 0
Glass....................	7A.	— 12A.	Tin Plates ....Sa.Rs. box	14 10 —	15 2
Hardware.................	25 D.	— 50D.	Woollens, Broad cloth, fine ..yd.	5 0 —	9 8
Hosiery, cotton...........	20 to 50A.&P.C.		—— coarse and middling....	1 4 —	4 0
Ditto, silk	20 to 35 D.&P.C		—— Flannel fine	1 0 —	1 12

MADRAS, January 20, 1836.

	Rs.	Rs.		Rs.	Rs.
Bottles 100	12 @	14	Iron Hoops ....candy	18 @	19
Copper, Sheathing ....candy	265	—	—— Nails ....do.	110 —	115
—— Cakes ....do.	—	—	Lead, Pig ....do.	42 —	45
—— Old ....do.	230 —	240	—— Sheet ....do.	38 —	40
—— Nails, assort. ....do.	350 —	370	Millinery	20A. —	25 A.
Cottons, Chintz.........piece	4 —	5	Shot, patent ....bag	3 —	3½
—— Ginghams........do.	2 —	3	Spelter ....candy	40 —	—
—— Longcloth, fine ......do.	9 —	14	Stationery	Overstocked.	
Cutlery, coarse	15A.	20A.	Steel, English..........candy	50 —	55
Glass and Earthenware	10A.	25A.	—— Swedish ....do.	70 —	75
Hardware................	10A.	—	Tin Plates ....box	18 —	19
Hosiery................	25A. —	30A.	Woollens, Broad cloth, fine	10A. —	15A.
Iron, Swedish, ...candy	40 —	50	—— coarse	Wanted	
—— English bar ....do.	18 —	19	—— Flannel, fine	12to14Ans.pr.yd.	
—— Flat and bolt............do.	18 —	19	—— Ditto, coarse ....8to10Ans. do.		

BOMBAY, March 12, 1836.

	Rs.	Rs.		Rs.	Rs.
Anchors ....cwt.	12 @	14	Iron, Swedish ....St. candy	51 @	—
Bottles ....dos.	1.4 —	—	—— English ....do.	23 —	23.8
Coals ....ton	10 —	12	—— Hoops...............cwt.	5.4 —	—
Copper, Sheathing, 16-32 ....cwt.	51 —	—	—— Nails ....do.	12 —	13
—— Thick sheets ....do.	55 —	—	—— Sheet ....do.	5.8 —	—
—— Plate bottoms ....do.	55 —	—	—— Rod for bolts ......St. candy	23 —	24
—— Tile ....do.	44 —	45	—— do. for nails ....do.	28 —	30
Cottons, Chintz, &c., &c.........—			Lead, Pig ....cwt.	10.4 —	—
—— Longcloths...............	—	—	—— Sheet ....do.	10 —	—
—— Muslins	—	—	Millinery	10 D.	—
—— Other goods	—	—	Shot, patent ....cwt.	10 —	12
—— Yarn, Nos. 20 to 100 ....lb .	0.11 —	1.12	Spelter ....do.	7.8 —	—
Cutlery, table............	10A.	—	Stationery	P. C.	—
Glass and Earthenware	10 D. —	20D.	Steel, Swedish ....tub	10 —	—
Hardware...............	P. C.	—	Tin Plates ....box	15.8 —	—
Hosiery, half hose...............	P. C.		Woollens, Broad cloth, fine ..yd.	4 —	7
			—— —— coarse	1.12 —	7
			—— Flannel, fine...............	1.4 —	2

CANTON, March 8, 1836.

	Drs.	Drs.		Drs.	Drs.
Cottons, Chintz, 28 yds..........piece	3 @	4½	Smalts ....pecul	30 @	60
—— Longcloths ....do.	3 —	10	Steel, Swedish ....tub	3.75	—
—— Muslins, 20 yds...........do.	—	—	Woollens, Broad cloth ....yd.	1.30 —	1.40
—— Cambrics, 48 yds ....do.	5 —	9	—— do. ex super ....yd.	2.50 —	2.75
—— Bandannoes ....do.	1.25 —	1.45	Camlets at Lintin ....pce.	28 —	30
—— Yarn, Nos. 16 to 50.........pecul	40 —	46	—— Do. Dutch ....do.	35 —	38
Iron, Bar ....do.	2.25 —		—— Long Ells ....do.	9 —	9½
—— Rod ....do.	3.50 — 3.75		Tin, Straits ....pecul	16 —	—
Lead, Pig ....do.	5.30 —		Tin Plates ....box	7 —	7½

SINGAPORE, March 19, 1836.

		Drs.		Drs.
Anchors	pecul	6	@	7½
Bottles	100	—		—
Copper Nails and Sheathing	pecul	36	—	37
Cottons, Madapollams, 24yd. by 36in.	pcs.	2	—	2¾
—— Imit. Irish 24 34-36	do.	2	—	2¼
—— Longcloths 38 to 40 34-36	do.	4½	—	5
—— ——— do. do. 36fine	do.	5	—	5½
—— ——— do. do. 40-44	do.	4	—	6½
—— ——— do. do. 44-54	do.	5	—	9
—— ——————— 54	do.	—		—
—— Prints, 7-8. *single colours*	do.		—	2½
—— ——— 9-8.	do.	2¼	—	2¾
—— Cambric, 12 yds. by 45 to 50 in.	do.	1¾	—	2¾
—— Jaconet, 20 ...... 40 .. 44	do.	2	—	2¾
—— Lappets, 10 ...... 40 .. 44	do.	1	—	1½
—— Chintz, fancy colours	do.	3	—	5¼

		Drs.		Drs.
Cotton Hkfs. imit. Battick, dble.	doz.	2¼	@	4
—— do. do Pullicat	doz.	1½	—	2
—— Twist, 30 to 40	pecul	55	—	57
Hardware, and coarse Cutlery	scarce & wanted			
Iron, Swedish	pecul	3½	—	3¾
—— English	do.	2⅜	—	2½
—— Nail, rod	do.	3	—	3½
Lead, Pig	do.	5½	—	5¾
—— Sheet	do.	5	—	5½
Shot, patent	bag	—		—
Spelter	pecul	5¾	—	6½
Steel, Swedish	do.	4½	—	4¾
—— English	do.	—		—
Woollens, Long Ells	pcs.	9	—	10
—— Camblets	do.	25	—	30
—— Ladies' cloth	yd.	1	—	2

REMARKS.

Calcutta, March 4, 1836.—The market for Piece Goods is in a healthy condition. The late arrivals from Liverpool and Glasgow found the bazaar bare of several descriptions of light goods, more particularly Lappets, Books, and Mulls, which accordingly met, and would still experience, a ready and profitable sale. Jaconet Muslins, likewise, have had a good demand, and continue to be enquired for, the stock being moderate. The more heavy Cottons, say Shirtings, and Cambrics, are abundant, and less saleable. Of printed Goods, Bengal Stripes, and single coloured Plates, meet with buyers, but recent sales have been effected at rates not generally remunerative. Other description of prints are without enquiry.—The market for Cotton Yarn may be considered in a very uncertain and unsatisfactory state.—The Woollen market offers little subject for remark; the sales for the last two months have certainly been greater, and at better rates than for some time before, but the amount altogether has not been large.—The Copper and Spelter market may be considered in an encouraging state.—English Iron, large imports, and market looking low.—*Exch. Price Current.*

Singapore, March 19, 1836.—During the week our demand for Cotton Piece Goods has been very active, chiefly for the Siam market, and rather extensive sales have been effected.—Woollens: we have no transactions to notice since our last. Camlets and Lady's Cloth are in rather better enquiry at our quotations. The present stock of Long-Ells, which does not exceed 1,200 pieces, will most likely ere long be purchased by the Cochin-Chinese.—Cotton Twist: Grey Mule continues in steady enquiry, and only 150 peculs at market. In coloured Twist we are without any transactions to report; but Turkey and Imperial Red, and Dark Blue, Nos. 36 to 46, will we expect ere long be in good enquiry. The taste for Orange Twist has of late much decreased, and at present the article is unsaleable.—Sales of Bar Iron have been made since our last of 300 peculs at dols. 2¾ per pecul, but an advance is fully anticipated should we be much longer without further importations. Nail Rod Iron of assorted small sizes is at present wanted. Swedish Bar Iron, the market well supplied. Spelter and Pig Lead continue to be much wanted at our quotations. Steel in partial demand.

Penang, Jan. 4, 1836.—Our market continues bare of produce, and much in activity in the demand for Europe manufactures.

Canton, March 1, 1836.—Cotton Piece Goods in good demand. Cotton Yarn still very dull of sale. Long Ells have declined a little in price.—*March* 8. No alteration in the prices of Cotton Piece Goods. Cotton Yarn, no improvement; late importations have been considerable. Woollens, Broad-cloth, dull. Camlets, in demand. Iron Rod has advanced a little in price. Tin Plates are still declining.

Manilla, Jan. 6, 1836.—The market is well supplied with Cotton goods, and overstocked with some descriptions, also with Woollens, and prices are low.—Freights to Europe, nominal.—*March* 4. Exchange on London, 6 months' sight, 4*s.* 7*d.* to 4*s.* 8*d.* per dol., and saleable.

INDIA SECURITIES AND EXCHANGES.

Calcutta, March 4, 1836.

Government Securities.

Buy.] Rs. As.			Rs. As. [Sell.
Prem. 16 0	Six per cent. Remittable	15 6	Prem.
Prem. 0 8	Second 5 per cent.	2 12	
2 12	Third 5 per cent.	2 8	Prem.
Disc. 2 8	Four per cent. Loan	2 10	Disc.

Bank Shares.

Bank of Bengal (10,000) .... Sa. Rs. 5,550 *a* 5,600
Union Bank .. (2,500) .... 600 to 700 prem.

Bank of Bengal Rates.

Discount on private bills .... 7 0 per cent.
Ditto on government and salary bills 4 0 do.
Interest on loans on govt. paper .... 5 0 do.

Rate of Exchange.

On London and Liverpool, six months' sight, to buy, 2*s.* 2*d.*; to sell, 2*s.* 2½*d.* per Sa. Rupee.

Madras, Jan. 20, 1836.

Government Securities.

Remittable Loan, six per cent.—15½ per ct. prem.
Ditto ditto of 18th Aug. 1825, five per cent.—2 prem.—3 disc.
Ditto ditto last five per cent.—2 prem.
Ditto ditto Old four per cent.—4½ disc.
Ditto ditto New four per cent.—4½ disc.

Exchange.

On London, at 6 months,—to buy, 2*s.*; to sell, 1*s.* 11*d.* per Madras Rupee.

Bombay, March 12, 1836.

Exchanges.

Bills on London, at 6 mo. sight, 2*s.* 1½*d.* to 2*s.* 1½*d.* per Rupee.
On Calcutta, at 30 days' sight, 108.4 to 108.8 Bom. Rs. per 100 Sicca Rupees.
On Madras, at 30 days' sight, 102.8 to 103 Bom. Rs. per 100 Madras Rs.

Government Securities.

Remittable Loan, 125 to 125.4 Bom. Rs. per 100 Sa. Rs.
5 per cent. Loan of 1822-23, according to the period of discharge, 109 to 109.4 per ditto.
Ditto of 1825-26, 109 to 111.12 per ditto.
Ditto of 1829-30, 111.12 to 112 per ditto.
4 per cent. Loan of 1832-33, 106.4 to 106.8 per ditto.

Singapore, March 19, 1836.

Exchanges.

On London, 3 to 6 mo. sight, 4*s.* 5½*d.* to 4*s.* 6*d.* per dollar.
On Bengal, gov. bills 206 Sa. Rs. per 100 dollars.

Canton, March 8, 1836.

Exchanges, &c.

On London, 6 mo. sight, 4*s.* 10*d* per Sp. Dol.
E. I. Co's Agents for advances on consignments, 4*s* 9½*d.* sales.
On Bengal. — Private Bills, 212 Sa. Rs. per 100 Sp. Dols.—Company's ditto, 30 days, 210 Sa. Rs.
On Bombay, ditto Bom. Rs. 220 to 222 per ditto.
Sycee Silver at Lintin, 3½ to 4 per cent. prem.

LIST of SHIPS Trading to INDIA and Eastward of the CAPE of GOOD HOPE.

Destination.	Appointed to sail.	Ships' Names.	Ton-nage.	Owners or Consignees.	Captains.	Where loading.	Reference for Freight or Passage.
	1836.						
Bengal	Aug. 1 ..Ports.	Lord Hungerford	734	Charles Farquharson	C. Farquharson	E. I. Docks	Sir C. Cockerill, Bt., & Co.; T. Haviside & Co.
	1 ..do.	Windsor	700	Richard Green	Alex. Henning	E. I. Docks	Thomas Havside & Co.
	3 ..do.	Robert Small	700	Thomas & Wm. Smith	William Fulcher	E. I. Docks	John Pirie & Co.; Small, Colquhoun, & Co., Old Jewry.
	5 ..do.	Svita	700	Thomas & William Smith	John Campbell	E. I. Docks	Walkinshaw & Co.; Lyall, Brothers, & Co.; Pirie & Co.
	5	General Palmer	531	Baring, Brothers, & Co.	John G. Down	Lon. Docks	Baring, Brothers,&Co.; Arnold & Woollett; Robert F. Wade.
	12	Duke of Buccleugh	650	Richard Green	R. F. Martin	E. I. Docks	Thomas Haviside & Co.
	12	Bolton	680	T. B. Oldfield	William Compton	W. I. Docks	Sir C.Cockerill & Co.; Jopp & Scarr; Noel, T. Smith, &Co.
	20	Duke of Northumb.	650	William Langley Pope	William L. Pope	W. I. Docks	Gledstanes & Co.; Thomas Haviside & Co.
	20	Isabella	576	Dunbar and Sons	David Brown	E. I. Docks	Lyall, Brothers, & Co.; John Masson, Lime street-square.
Bengal and China	Sept. 7 ..Ports.	Zenobia	624	John F. Owen	John F. Owen	St.Kt.Dock	Baring, Brothers & Co.; Edmund Reed, Cornhill. [house.
Cape and Bengal	Aug. 6	Antonia Pereira	254	William O. Young	Wm. O. Young	Blackwall	Palmers, Mackillop, & Co.; Capt. Young; Jerus, Coffee-
	5 ..Ports.	Broxbornebury	755	Alfred Chapman	Alfred Chapman	W. I. Docks	Capt. Chapman, Birchin-lane, or Jerusalem Coffee-house.
Madras	Sept. 1	Lady Flora	755	Robert Ford	Robert Ford	W. I. Docks	Crawford, Colvin, & Co.; Tomlin Man, & Co.
	1 ..do.	Mary Ann	540	Gledstanes & Co.	Charles B. Tarbutt	St.Kt.Docks	Gledstanes & Co.; Charles Moss & Co., Mark-lane.
		Alfred	716	John T. E. Flint	Richard Tapley	W. I. Docks	Charles Moss & Co.
Cape and Madras	Aug. 13 ..Ports.	Wellington	540	Gustavus Evans	James Liddell	W. I. Docks	MacGhie, Page, & Smith, Exchange-buildings.
	1	Marq. of Hastings	500	John Clarkson	John Clarkson	W. I. Docks	Capt. Clarkson; Crawford, Colvin, & Co.; Jopp & Scarr.
Bombay	4	Herefordshire	755	Thacker,F&CE.Mangles	H. S. H. Isaacson	E. I. Docks	Thacker & Price; Mangles: Jopp & Scarr; Edm. Read.
	20	Scaleby Castle	1255	James Walkinshaw	Davie Robertson	E. I. Docks	John Pirie & Co.
		John Deniston	350	James Brown	Thomas Mackie	Lon. Docks	Arnold and Wollett; Thomson and Edwards.
Cape and Bombay	Sept. 1 ..Ports.	Triumph	640	Robert & Thomas Green	Thomas Green	W. I. Docks	Robert Green, Birchin-lane; Tomlin and Man.
	6	Carnatic	650	Richard Green	John Brodie	E. I. Docks	John Pirie & Co.
Batavia	20 ..do.	Margaretha	400	Thorntons and West	John Barcham	St.Kt.Docks	John Pirie & Co.
China	15	Emma Eugenia	303	Joseph Somes	David Duchan	St.Kt.Docks	Arnold and Woollett; Edmund Read.
Ceylon	25	Tigris	480	William Tindall	James Stevens	W. I. Docks	L. W. Winkley, Birchin-lane.
Ceylon, Malabar Coast, & Bombay		Cambridge	802	Joseph A. Douglas	Joseph A. Douglas	E. I. Docks	Capt. Douglas, Jerusalem Coffee-house.
Mauritius	6	Atlas	410	Chalmers & Guthrie	Francis Hunt	W. I. Docks	Barclay, Brothers, & Co.; Noel, T. Smith, & Co.
	10	Finlater	239	Francis Read	Francis Read	W. I. Docks	Cookes & Long, Mark-lane.
St. Helena	15	Druad	250	A. Howden	E. P. Godby	Lon. Docks	Edward Luckie, Birchin-lane.
	15	Grace	160	N. Griffiths	Thomas U. Gull	St.Kt.Docks	Cookes & Long.
Algoa Bay	15	Dove	130	John Clarke	T. W. Heddon	St.Kt.Docks	Cookes & Long.
Launceston	1	Ann	340	George Bishop	John Virtue	St.Kt.Docks	George Bishop, New East-India Chambers.
	7	Isabella	250	Robert Brooks	Henry J. Ellis	St.Kt.Docks	Buckles and Co., Mark-lane; Devitt and Moore.
Van Diemen's Land	10	Rhoda	250	Robert Brooks	S. C. Hunt	St.Kt.Docks	Robert Brooks; Buckles & Co.; Devitt & Moore.
	17 ..Conv.S.	Eden	532	Joseph Somes	A. S. Mollison	Portsmouth	Lachlan, Sons, & McLeod.
New South Wales	15	Perseverance	240	James Gunston	R. B. Corkhill	St.Kt.Docks	Hill and Wackerlanth.
	2 ..Sept.10	Ann Lockerby	400	William Lockerby	Thomas Watson	St.Kt.Docks	Buckles & Co.; Devitt & Moore.
Van Diemen's Land and New South Wales	10	Columbia	300	Clint and Co	Henry Thornton	St.Kt.Docks	Bryant & Brothers; Phillipps & Tiplady, George yard.
Cape, V.D.L., and Sydney	Aug. 4 ..Emgr.S.	Royal George	496	John Jacob and Sons	George Richards	St.Kt.Docks	Bryant & Brothers; Phillipps & Tiplady.
South Australia	Aug.10	Fairlie	755	Thomas Ward	Henry Aget	Lon. Docks	John Marshall, Birchin-lane.
		Coromandel	662	Ridgway and Co	William Chesser	St.Kt.Docks	Godwin & Lee.

LONDON PRICE CURRENT, July 26, 1836.

EAST-INDIA AND CHINA PRODUCE.

Article	£.	s.	d.		£.	s.	d.
Coffee, Batavia ......cwt.	2	12	0	@	3	10	0
—— Samarang	2	8	0	—	2	10	0
—— Cheribon	3	0	0	—	3	3	0
—— Sumatra	2	1	0	—	2	8	0
—— Ceylon	2	10	0	—	2	13	0
—— Mocha	2	16	0	—	4	15	0
Cotton, Surat............lb	0	0	5	—	0	0	7¾
—— Madras	0	0	5¼	—	0	0	7¼
—— Bengal	0	0	4¾	—	0	0	6½
—— Bourbon	none				——		
Drugs & for Dyeing.							
Aloes, Epatica......cwt.	9	1	0	—	18	0	0
Anniseeds, Star..........	4	10	0		——		
Borax, Refined..........	3	8	0		——		
—— Unrefined	3	14	0		——		
Camphire, in tub	10	0	0		——		
Cardamoms, Malabar..lb	0	2	11	—	0	3	6
—— Ceylon	0	1	4	—	0	1	6
Cassia Buds ....cwt.	5	0	0	—	5	5	0
—— Lignea	3	7	0	—	3	9	0
Castor Oil ....lb	0	0	5	—	0	0	9½
China Root............cwt.	17	0	0	—	18	0	0
Cubebs..................	2	14	0	—	2	19	0
Dragon's Blood.	10	0	0	—	25	0	0
Gum Ammoniac, drop..	6	0	0	—	8	0	0
—— Arabic	2	15	0	—	4	8	0
—— Assafœtida	1	10	0	—	4	15	0
—— Benjamin, 3d Sort..	3	10	0	—	10	0	0
—— Animi..............	5	0	0	—	8	8	0
—— Gambogium........	5	0	0	—	17	0	0
—— Myrrh		10	0	—	15	0	0
—— Olibanum	6	10	0	—	2	18	0
Kino....................	12	0	0		——		
Lac Lake..............lb	0	4	0		——		
—— Dye..............	0	3	3	—	0	3	9
—— Shell ....cwt.	5	10	0	—	8	8	0
—— Stick	0	2	0	—	0	3	10
Musk, China ....oz.	0	10	0	—	1	5	0
Nux Vomica ....cwt.	0	8	0		0	8	6
Oil, Cassia ....oz.	0	8	0		0	9	0
—— Cinnamon..........	0	4	0	—	0	5	0
—— Cocoa-nut......cwt.	1	14	6	—	1	15	0
—— Cajaputa ....oz.	0	0	4	—	0	0	6
—— Mace	0	0	2	—	0	0	3
—— Nutmegs	0	1	2	—	0	1	5
Opium..................	none				——		
Rhubarb................	0	2	6	—	0	3	6
Sal Ammoniac ......cwt.	3	6	0		3	7	0
Senna ....lb	0	0	3	—	0	1	2
Turmeric, Java ....cwt.	0	12	0	—	0	14	0
—— Bengal	0	16	0	—	0	18	0
—— China..............	1	0	0	—	1	5	0
Galls, in Sorts	none				——		
——, Blue	——				——		
Hides, Buffalo ....lb	0	0	3	—	0	0	4
—— Ox and Cow........	0	0	3	—	0	0	4
Indigo, Blue and Violet....	——			See Sale.	——		
—— Ex. fine Bl. and Violet	——				——		
—— Purple and Violet....	——				——		
—— Fine Violet..........	——				——		
—— Mid. to good Violet ..	——				——		
—— Violet and Copper	——				——		
—— Copper	——				——		
—— Consuming, mid. to fine	——				——		
—— Do. ord. and low	——				——		
—— Do. very low	——				——		
—— Madras, mid. to good	——				——		
—— Oude, good mid. & good	——				——		
Mother-o'-Pearl Shells, China ...cwt.	3	10	0	@	5	0	0
Nankeens............piece	——				——		
Rattans..................100	0	2	9	—	0	6	6
Rice, Bengal White....cwt.	0	13	0	—	0	16	6
—— Patna..............	0	16	6	—	0	17	0
—— Java..............	0	10	6	—	0	13	0
Safflower................	5	1	0	—	9	0	0
Sago....................	0	11	0	—	0	14	6
—— Pearl	0	15	0	—	1	1	0
Saltpetre................	1	8	0	—	1	11	0
Silk, Company's Bengal lb	0	17	6	—	1	7	0
—— Novi	——				——		
—— China Tsatlee........	1	4	0	—	1	8	0
—— Bengal Privilege......	0	15	6	—	1	1	0
—— Taysam..............	1	0	0	—	1	2	0
Spices, Cinnamon..........	0	6	0	—	0	9	6
—— Cloves	0	0	10	—	0	1	1
—— Mace	0	3	6	—	0	7	3
—— Nutmegs	0	4	11	—	0	6	8
—— Ginger ....cwt.	1	18	6	—	3	5	0
—— Pepper, Black......lb	0	0	4¾	—	0	0	5¼
—— —— White	0	1	0	—	0	1	6
Sugar, Bengal ....cwt.	1	18	0	—	2	3	0
—— Siam and China	1	11	0	—	2	0	0
—— Mauritius (duty paid)	3	3	0	—	3	11	6
—— Manilla and Java	1	8	0	—	2	2	0
Tea, Bohea..............lb	——				——		
—— Congou	——				——		
—— Souchong	——				——		
—— Caper	——				——		
—— Campoi	——				——		
—— Twankay	——				——		
—— Pekoe, (Orange, &c.)..	——				——		
—— Hyson Skin	——				——		
—— Hyson..............	——				——		
—— Young Hyson	——				——		
—— Gunpowder, Imperial	——				——		
Tin, Banca............cwt.	6	10	0	—	——		
Tortoiseshell ....lb	1	2	0	—	1	18	0
Vermilion ....lb	0	4	0	—	——		
Wax....................cwt.	7	5	0	—	8	6	0
Wood, Saunders Red ..ton	7	0	0		7	5	0
—— Ebony	16	0	0	—	18	0	0
—— Sapan..............	6	15	0	—	13	0	0

AUSTRALASIAN PRODUCE.

Article	£.	s.	d.		£.	s.	d.
Cedar Wood............foot	0	0	6	—	0	0	7
Oil, Fish................tun	34	10	0	—	35	0	0
Whalebone ....ton	120	0	0		——		
Wool, N. S. Wales, *viz.*							
Best....................lb	0	3	0	—	0	3	3
Inferior	0	1	3	—	0	3	2
—— V. D. Land, *viz.*							
Best......................	0	1	8½	—	0	3	0
Inferior	0	1	0	—	0	1	9

SOUTH AFRICAN PRODUCE.

Article	£.	s.	d.		£.	s.	d.
Aloes ....cwt.	1	10	6	—	1	13	0
Ostrich Feathers, und ....lb	——				——		
Gum Arabic............cwt.	1	5	0	—	1	10	0
Hides, Dry ....lb	0	0	4¾	—	0	0	6½
—— Salted	0	0	3½	—	0	0	5
Oil, Palm ....cwt.	1	18	6	—	1	19	0
Raisins	——				——		
Wax	7	10	0	—	8	0	0
Wine, Cape, Mad., best..pipe	17	0	0	—	19	0	0
—— Do. 2d & 3d quality	14	0	0	—	15	0	0
Wood, Teak............load	9	5	0	—	10	10	0
Wool ....lb.	0	1	6	—	0	2	6

PRICES OF SHARES, July 26, 1836.

	Price.	Dividends.	Capital.	Shares of.	Paid.	Books Shut for Dividends.
DOCKS.	£.	£.	£.	£.	£.	
East-India..............(Stock)....	113	— p. cent.	498,667	—	—	March. Sept.
London ....(Stock)....	58	2½ p. cent.	3,238,000	—	—	June. Dec.
St. Katherine's	91	3 p. cent.	1,352,752	100	—	Jan. July
Ditto Debentures	—	4½ p. cent.	——	—	—	5 April. 5 Oct.
Ditto ditto	102	4 p. cent.	——	—	—	5 April. 5 Oct.
West-India ....(Stock)....	106	5 p. cent.	1,380,000	—	—	June. Dec.
MISCELLANEOUS.						
Australian (Agricultural)............	40	——	10,000	100	26½	——
Bank (Australasian)	57	——	5,000	40	40	——
Van Diemen's Land Company......	13¾	——	10,000	100	17	——
South African Bank................	½	——	——	—	6	——

Wolfe, Brothers, 23, *Change Alley.*

THE LONDON MARKETS, July 26, 1836.

Sugar.—There is a good demand for British Plantation Sugar, principally from the grocers. The stock of West India Sugars is now 26,476 hds. and trs. being 1,906 less than last year. The stock of Mauritius is now 59,432 bags, which is 20,126 less than last year. There has been a steady demand for Mauritius by the grocers at former rates. The demand for Bengal Sugar has been very moderate, owing to the holders refusing to submit to easier prices, and the limited business done has been confined to small parcels taken by the grocers.

Tea.—The fine Teas at the public sales this day, mostly sold briskly at full prices, particularly the Congous, which went off with considerable spirit. Some fine Twankays were taken in at an advance of 2d. The ordinary kinds of Tea are not cheaper, but they went off heavily, and a large portion bought in. Congous, fine, sold at 1s. 10d. to 2s. 5½d; common 1s. 2d. to 1s. 3½d. Hysons, common, 2s. 9d. to 2s. 11d.—The East-India Company have issued their declaration for the sale of Teas in September next. The declaration amounts to 4,000,000lbs., and comprises 500,000lbs. of Bohea, 2,770,000lbs. of Congou, Souchong, and Pekoe; 600,000lbs. of Twankay, and 130,000lbs. of Hyson. In the present declaration there is 100,000lbs. less of Bohea than in the June sale; 100,000lbs. less of Twankay; an increase of 170,000lbs. of Congou, Souchong, &c., and 30,000lbs. more of Hyson. The whole amount of Bohea Teas entered under the treasury minute, for payment of the duty of 1s. 6d. per lb. until the 1st of August next, is above 12,000,000lbs.

Indigo.—The following is Messrs. Patry and Pasteur's report of the result of the July public sales of Indigo, which commenced on the 12th, and closed on the 26th inst.

"The quantity declared for sale was 9,369 chests, which presented the following assortment:—900 chests fine shipping qualities, 2,600 middling to good do., 2,500 fine consumers to middling do., 2,400 ordinary to good consuming qualities, 475 ordinary and very low sorts, 244 Madras, 244 Kurpah, 2 Manilla, and 4 Pondicherry. Previous to the opening, and during the progress of the sales, 103 chests were withdrawn by the proprietors.

"The sale began with spirit at an advance on the April sale of 6d. to 9d., being rather above the previous market prices, the proprietors supporting but at the same time meeting the buyers at these rates: as the sale proceeded, and even as early as the second day, the great competition between the buyers for export drove prices up, and the advance on last sale ranged from 9d. to 1s. for middling good and fine qualities, and 6d. to 9d. for ordinary and consuming sorts. At these rates the sale continued with greater regularity, less difference of opinion, and more general spirit than has been remarked for many years past, and it closed with the same briskness and as high prices as had hitherto been paid.

"The principal feature of this sale, which has been a matter of astonishment to all those connected with the article of Indigo, is, that at a sale of such magnitude, buyers should have been found for nearly the whole quantity, evidently with very little assistance from speculation on the spot; and that prices should have gradually advanced from the beginning to the conclusion of the sale. This result, however, shows that stocks on the Continent, especially Germany and the North, are much reduced, and that the flourishing state of their manufactures, the increased consumption of Indigo, and the very reduced stock in London (from which, excepting France, the whole of Europe draws its supplies) have at last awakened the attention of Foreign consumers, who have, since 1833, allowed their stocks to run unusually low.

"The home trade bought freely, and took full as much as their usual share, say about 1,500 chests. Proprietors bought in about 900 chests, leaving, therefore, 8,400 chests actually disposed of. A great proportion of the Madras in the sale was of the Kurpah kind, and this generally of ordinary quality, it was mostly bought for home consumption at prices fully equal to the relative qualities of Bengal; the dry leaf sort sold very unequally at an advance of 3d. to 9d. on the prices of last sale."

DAILY PRICES OF STOCKS, *from June 25 to July 25*, 1836.

June.	Bank Stock.	3 Pr. Ct. Red.	3 Pr. Ct. Consols.	3½ Pr.Ct. Red.	New 3½ Pr.Cent.	Long Annuities.	India Stock.	Consols for acct.	India Bonds.	Exch. Bills.
25	210	91⅛	Shut.	98¾	Shut.	15¾	Shut.	92⅛ 92¼	1ds. 1p	11 13p
27	210	91 91⅛	—	98¾ 98⅞	—	15 11/16 15¾	—	92⅛ 92¼	1ds. 1p	11 13p
28	209½ 210	91 91⅛	—	98¾ 98⅞	—	15 11/16 15¾	—	92⅛	1p	11 13p
29	209½ 210	91 91⅛	—	98⅞ 99	—	15 11/16 15¾	—	92⅛	1ds. 1p	11 13p
30	—	91⅛ 91⅜	—	99 99¼	—	15 11/16	—	92⅛ 92⅜	1ds. 1p	10 12p
July										
1	210½	91⅝ 91⅞	—	99⅛ 99⅜	—	15¾ 15 13/16	—	92⅝ 92⅞	par 1p	12 14p
2	210¾	91¾ 91⅞	—	99¼ 99½	—	15 13/16 15⅞	—	92¾ 92⅞	1 2p	12 16p
4	211	91⅞ 92	—	99⅜ 99⅝	—	15 13/16 15⅞	—	92⅞ 93	1 3p	14 16p
5	210½ 211	91¾ 91⅞	—	99⅜ 99⅝	—	—	—	92⅞ 93	1 3p	14 17p
6	—	91¾ 91⅞	91⅛ 91¼	99½ 99⅝	99⅜ 99⅝	15⅞	256¾	92¾ 92⅞	1 3p	14 16p
7	211½	91⅝ 91⅞	91⅛ 91¼	99½ 99⅝	99⅜ 99⅝	15 13/16	257¼	92¾ 92⅞	1 3p	13 15p
8	211½	91⅝ 91¾	91 91⅛	99½ 99⅝	99⅛ 99¼	15 11/16	256½ 7	92⅝ 92¾	par 3p	12 14p
9	211½	91¾ 91⅞	91⅛ 91⅜	99½ 99⅝	99½ 99¾	15¾ 15⅞	256½	92⅝ 92¾	2p	12 14p
11	212	91¾ 92½	91¼ 91⅜	99⅜ 99⅝	99⅜ 99¾	15 13/16 15⅞	—	92¼ 92⅞	par 2p	12 14p
12	211½ 212	91⅞ 92	91¼ 91½	99⅝ 99⅞	99½ 99¾	15 13/16 15⅞	257½ 8	92⅞ 93	par 3p	12 15p
13	—	91⅞ 92⅛	91⅜ 91½	99¾ 99⅞	99⅜ 99¾	15 13/16	—	—	—	12 14p
14	212 212½	91¾ 92	91¼ 91½	99⅝ 99⅞	99½ 99¾	15 13/16 15⅞	259½ 0¼	92½ 92⅝	1ds. 1p	10 13p
15	212½ 212¾	91⅞ 92⅛	91⅛ 91⅜	99⅞ 100	99½ 99¾	15 13/16 15⅞	260¼ ½	—	1ds. 2p	8 11p
16	212 212¼	91⅞ 92	91¼ 91½	99¾ 100	99⅝ 99¾	15 13/16 15⅞	260 0¼	91¼ 91⅜	2ds. par	8 10p
18	212¼ 212½	91⅝ 91¾	91⅛ 91¼	99¾ 99⅞	99½ 99⅝	15¾ 15 13/16	258½	91⅛ 91¼	2ds. par	8 10p
19	212 212½	91⅝ 91¾	91⅛ 91¼	99¾ 100	99⅜ 99⅝	—	258 8½	91⅛ 91¼	par	9 11p
20	212¼ 212½	91⅝ 91⅞	91⅛ 91⅜	99⅞ 100	99½ 99⅝	15¾ 15 13/16	259	91¼ 91⅜	1ds. 2p	10 12p
21	212¼ 212½	91¾ 91⅞	91¼ 91⅜	99⅞ 100	99½ 99⅝	15¾ 15 13/16	258½ 9	91¼	par 2p	12 14p
22	212¼	91⅜ 91⅝	90¾ 91¼	99⅝ 99⅞	99⅛ 99⅜	15 11/16 15 13/16	258¾	90⅞ 91⅛	1ds. par	9 11p
23	212¼ 212½	91½	90⅞ 91	99¾	99⅛ 99¼	15 11/16 15 13/16	258¾	91	2ds. par	9 11p
25	212 212½	91⅜ 91½	90⅞ 91	98⅝ 99¾	99⅛ 99¼	15¾ 15 13/16	258¾	90⅞ 91	2ds. par	9 11p

Frederick Barry, Stock and Share Broker, 7, Birchin Lane, Cornhill.

INDEX TO VOL. XX.

PART I.—ORIGINAL AND SELECT PAPERS, &c.

PART II.—ASIATIC AND HOME INTELLIGENCE.

ERRATUM.

Part I. p. 143, l. 7, *for* "THE LATE SHAH OF PERSIA," *read* "FUTTEH ALI THE POET."

LONDON:
Printed by J. L. Cox and Sons, 75, Great Queen Street, Lincoln's-Inn Fields

Lightning Source UK Ltd.
Milton Keynes UK
UKHW051900010219
336488UK00006BA/376/P